STONE
ROAD
PRESS

This is Your Guide to
the National Parks

Come and Explore
Your National Parks

Your Guide to the National Parks, Second Edition
ISBN 978-1-62128-067-5
Library of Congress Control Number (LCCN): 2016909055

Printed in the United States of America
Published by Stone Road Press
Author/Cartographer/Photographer/Designer: Michael Joseph Oswald
Editor: Derek Pankratz

This title is also published in electronic format. Content that appears in print may not be available electronically.

Corrections/Contact

This guidebook has been researched and written with the greatest attention to detail in order to provide you with the most accurate and pertinent information. Unfortunately, travel information—especially pricing—is subject to change and inadvertent errors and omissions do occur. Should you encounter a change, error, or omission while using this guidebook, we'd like to hear about it. (If you found a wonderful place, trail, or activity not mentioned, we'd love to hear about that too.) Please contact us by sending an e-mail to corrections@stoneroadpress.com. Your contributions will help make future editions better than the last.

Find us online at StoneRoadPress.com or follow us on Facebook (facebook.com/thestoneroadpress), Twitter (@stoneroadpress), Instagram (@stoneroadpress), and Flickr (stoneroadpress).

Disclaimer

Your safety is important to us. If any activity is beyond your ability or threatened by forces outside your control, do not attempt it. The maps in this book, although accurate and to scale, are not intended for hiking. Serious hikers should purchase a detailed, waterproof, topographical map. It is also suggested you write or call in advance to confirm information when it matters most.

The primary purpose of this guidebook is to enhance our readers' national park experiences, but the author, editor, and publisher cannot be held responsible for any experiences while traveling.

Cover and Introduction Photo Credits

Front cover: Delicate Arch (Arches)
Introduction Pages: Moose (Rocky Mountain), Halema'uma'u Crater (Hawai'i Volcanoes), a sheep at Homestead Overlook (Badlands), and Mammoth Hot Springs (Yellowstone)
Opposite About the Author: Boyscout Tree (Redwood)
Opposite Contents: Burr Trail Switchbacks (Capitol Reef)
Page 37: Sheep at Conata Basin Overlook (Badlands)
Back Content: Cliff Shelf Trail (Badlands), King's Creek Falls (Lassen Volcanic), a pelican (Dry Tortugas), and an elk along Trail Ridge Road at dusk (Rocky Mountain)
Back Cover: Elk near Rock Cut (Rocky Mountain), Sheep on Highline Trail (Glacier), Moose (Rocky Mountain)

Prairie dog (Theodore Roosevelt)

Acknowledgements

Derek, your red pen makes me want to be a better writer. Unfortunately for you, that hasn't happened yet. Maybe next edition! In all seriousness, I've always admired you and I'm thrilled you're willing to take time out of your busy schedule to help with my mind-numbing work.

Luke, you're one of the all-time great human beings and I hope someone from Google reads this and contacts you (luke@jukes.us) to discuss that $300M idea you're working on! I'd make you an offer, but all I have to give is a rusty old school bus and a couple boxes of books.

To my family, thank you for always being there. These last four years have (oddly enough) been some of the toughest, and I never would have gotten to through them without your unending love and kindness. Mom you're an absolute champ for plowing through all those "What's Nearby" sections. None of this—whatever *this* is—happens without you guys and I'll love you all as long as I'm walking around this green earth.

Pole, Otter, Marty, Sam, Ben, Boy, Box-maker, Mutt, Mike, Erik, Mark, and Duke, I'm not sure where I'd be without your daily doses of levity. Can't say I'm looking forward to growing old(er), but I'm happier knowing we'll be doing it together.

Brad, OstrichFest turned out to be the world's worst good idea. We'll have to try it again sometime. Fortunately it wasn't all a loss. I got to know you better, and you're pretty alright (the highest praise I'll give a lawyer!).

Team Whoa (Patti Jo and Pat), you two are the best. You're probably thinking "why is this guy helping us with our coloring books?" but it's been the other way around. I live a very solitary life, and you've helped simply by letting me be a part of the team. And Patti Jo, I owe you an immense amount of gratitude. All the amazing places discussed in this book serve as my office, but hanging with you at your farm is the place I enjoy most. We're going to find a way to move those coloring books (shameless plug: franciscreekfjords. com)! Special thanks to Powder, Missy Moo Moo, Cali, Stormy, Voss, Daisy, and all the other horses milling about Francis Creek Fjords! Extra treats for everyone!

Morning basketball crew, you guys are heroes for getting up at the crack of dawn to play hoops (and for putting up with my abundance of missed layups).

Book Club, even when I don't read the books, I love sitting down with you for laughter and conversation.

Finally, I'd like to thank everyone else who helped make the first edition a success: Cardinal Publisher's Group, IBPA, National Outdoor Book Awards, ForeWord Reviews, Publisher's Weekly, Dave Estes, On Wisconsin, Manitowoc Public Library, and, of course, the readers. While I may have done most of the work (and the fun stuff touring the parks), I'm not naive enough to think I've done this on my own. It took all of us, and it makes me a little sad knowing these words (and this book) are the best way to show my appreciation. Thank you!

Marmot (Glacier)

Friends of Stone Road Press

FLOW 397

NATIONAL PARKS TRAVELER

THE NATIONAL PARKS

I'd also like to express a bit of gratitude to a few friends I've made because of the career path I chose.

Thanks to the crew at Flow 397 (flow397.com)! You guys are truly inspirational. If I didn't already have national park fever, I certainly would have caught it from you. Your fun-loving and eternally-hopeful attitudes are infectious. Not only do these guys make the coolest clothes around, they give back 3.97% of every purchase to the national parks and public lands! They're always plugging my work, so it's time I returned the favor and tooted my horn for them! Toot! Toot!

Kurt, you were one of the first people I reached out to while trying to figure out how to sell a book. Thank you so much for reviewing my work and sharing your vast amount of national park knowledge. Kurt and his team at National Parks Traveler (nationalparkstraveler.com) are a bunch of busy bees keeping the people up to date on America's national parks. Not only do they cover the nuts and bolts, they take a journalist's approach, raising important questions and sparking discussion about the places all of us love to explore.

Brady and The National Parks (thenationalparksmusic.com) made the soundtrack to my last tour through the parks. I would have been thoroughly satisfied with the incredible tunes, but it turns out they're also the sweetest people ever.

Sorry about the infomercial, but I'm really grateful these people (and the things they're doing) exist. This business stuff leads to a challenging and often lonely life. I find comfort knowing they're out there chasing their dreams, living with intensity and passion, and hustling each and every day, just like me. As is often the case, I only wish there was more I could do to help these good people out.

Glacier Point (Yosemite)

About the Author

You might be wondering "why in the world should I listen to this guy staring at Half Dome?" Allow me to tell you ... while touring the parks I quickly realized most visitors only explore areas accessible by car. Families zip through, stop at the occasional pull-out or parking lot for a quick photo-op, and then continue on their merry way. While most parks cater to motorists, one cannot experience their essence from the comfort of your driver's seat. You must walk among the trees and the mountains. Listen to wildlife all around you. Sit back, close your eyes and immerse yourself in nature. America's 59 national parks are irreplaceable treasures, yet they are our parks, preserved for our enjoyment, and if you want to experience them to their fullest you're going to need a good guide.

That's where I come in. I admit my first trip to a national park was your typical affair. A group of friends drove to the South Rim of the Grand Canyon. We peered in, snapped a few photos, shrugged and returned to our rental car. Did we know adventurous hikers were resting their tired legs at Phantom Ranch nearly 5,000 feet below? No. Did we know how to reach the North Rim? Probably not. The point is, we didn't know much about the Grand Canyon. In all we spent no more than a few

hours in the park. We were your typical park visitors, and each year millions follow in our footsteps.

I've come a long way since those first steps atop the South Rim. I've spent years exploring and photographing the parks. Traveling from park-to-park I learned this was much more than an assignment; it became an awakening. It was a communion with life and land as I learned to immerse myself in nature. (I also learned how to get to the North Rim, and even hiked down to Phantom Ranch to prove to myself people were making regular trips to the canyon floor.) Did I hike all the trails and participate in all of the activities listed in this book? No, but I'm working on it! I have logged thousands of miles hiking, paddling, and pedaling my way across America and through its parks, visiting most of them several times. More importantly, I've exhaustively researched every site in this book, integrating those findings with my unique perspective and with the opinions of hundreds of park patrons and National Park Service employees. These are the footsteps you should follow, and holding this book is the first step to an unforgettable adventure.

Grand Prismatic Spring (Yellowstone)

Contents

Beaver near Moose (Grand Teton)

Plan Your Trip

Park Passes

Most United States National Parks require guests to pay an entrance fee. Entrance fees vary from park-to-park, and rates may be per individual, per vehicle, and a few rates are even charged per day. If you plan on visiting several national parks in a calendar year or visiting the same (fee required) national park several times the America the Beautiful Passes can minimize the damage to your wallet. A pass is not only your ticket to the national parks, it provides access to more than 2,000 federal recreation sites including national monuments (e.g., Devil's Tower), national memorials, national recreation areas, and all other lands managed by the Bureau of Land Management and Bureau of Reclamation.

Annual Pass • $80: This pass is valid for one year, beginning from the date of sale. It is available to the general public and provides access to, and use of, federal recreation sites that charge an entrance fee or standard amenity fee. It does not provide discounted camping or program/tour rates. The pass can be purchased in person or online at store.usgs.gov/pass.

Don't automatically purchase an annual pass if you're planning a multi-park vacation. No entrance fee is charged at the following national parks: Cuyahoga Valley, Mammoth Cave, Great Smoky Mountains, Congaree, Biscayne, Voyageurs, Wind Cave, Hot Springs, Great Basin, Channel Islands, Redwood, North Cascades, Glacier Bay, Wrangell–St. Elias, Kenai Fjords, Lake Clark, Katmai, Gates of the Arctic, Kobuk Valley, U.S. Virgin Islands, and American Samoa.

Senior Pass • $10: This is a lifetime pass for U.S. citizens or permanent residents age 62 and over. The pass provides access to, and use of, federal recreation sites that charge an entrance fee. It also provides a 50% discount on camping fees and certain park programs/tours. The pass can be purchased in person or online at store.usgs.gov/pass (proof of age and citizenship required).

Access Pass • Free: This is a lifetime pass for U.S. citizens or permanent residents with permanent disabilities (documentation required). The pass provides lifetime access to, and use of, federal recreation sites

that charge an entrance or standard amenity fee. It also provides a 50% discount on camping fees and some park programs/tours. It must be obtained in person.

Volunteer Pass • Free: This pass is given to volunteers who accumulate 500 service hours on a cumulative basis. The pass provides access to, and use of, federal recreation sites that charge an entrance fee for a year, beginning from the date of award. The volunteer pass does not provide discounted camping or tour/program rates.

If you plan on visiting one national park several times in a calendar year you may be better off purchasing an individual park annual pass. They range from $15–50 and are typically good for one vehicle for one year from the date of purchase. Even if you think you might return just one more time within a year it is almost always worthwhile to purchase the park annual pass.

Another way to save a few dollars is to visit during National Park Service Free Entrance Days (see NPS.gov for a list of fee-free dates).

What to Pack

If you're like me you probably wait until the night before your vacation to begin packing. You grab everything you might need and throw it in a suitcase or backpack. Anything left behind won't be noticed until you need it on your trip. Avoid these situations by compiling packing lists (for each family member) and packing a few days in advance. Everyone knows to pack the essentials like cell phone charger, money, hygiene products, and clothes, so here are a few suggestions that you may not think of.

For Any Trip

Garbage/Small Resealable Bags: Not only are bags incredibly useful storage devices, you can use them to waterproof your gadgets. I still use a small resealable bag as my wallet. Its combination of transparency, durability, waterproofness, and low-cost-to-quantity ratio cannot be beat.

Duct Tape: I always have a roll of duct tape in my car. It's also a good practice to wrap the base of a water bottle or hiking pole with duct tape for when you venture into the wilderness.

Headlamp: Whether reading in your tent or searching under a car seat for the National Park Pass you just dropped, a headlamp is sure to prove useful. Plus, kids love them.

For the National Parks

Binoculars, clothes that layer (temperature and winds change dramatically based on elevation, location, and time), insect repellent, sunscreen, snacks and water, first-aid kit, journal or sketchpad, a good book, and camera (plus extra batteries).

For Hiking

Backpack, hydration system or water bottle, compass and map (know how to use them), GPS (know how to use it), hiking stick/poles, pocket knife, whistle, and water filter.

For Camping

Camp stove with fuel, rope, clothes pins, flashlight(s), folding chairs, hammock, water jug, tarp, ear plugs, and a deck of cards.

For Biking

Water, spare tube, patch-kit, pump, tire irons, multi-tool, and bike shorts.

For Paddling

Bilge pump, rescue bag, knife, booties, gloves, helmet, and whistle.

Leave No Trace

Remember the national parks are for everyone to enjoy. Whether you're an avid outdoorsman or just passing through, all visitors of the parks should practice these simple Leave No Trace principles.

1. Plan Ahead and Prepare
2. Travel/Camp on Durable Surfaces
3. Dispose of Waste Properly
4. Leave What You Find
5. Minimize Campfire Impacts
6. Respect Wildlife
7. Be Considerate of Other Visitors

Proper waste disposal is commonly referred to as "Pack It In, Pack It Out" or "Leave Only Footprints, Take Only Photographs." Practice these simple and sensible principles and our most remarkable and irreplaceable treasures will remain for the enjoyment of future generations.

Economical Travel

Vacations can be expensive. A trip to a national park is often seen as an affordable adventure, but the costs of lodging, dining, tours, entrance fees, and gas can add up quickly. Some costs are unavoidable; others can be minimized using these practical tips.

Lodging: Park lodges are beautiful but expensive. Discounts are rarely available during peak-season and many lodges book months in advance. Travel during off-season for the best deals on in-park lodging.

More economical lodging is often found beyond park boundaries. Most gateway cities offer everything from chain hotels to B&Bs. A few of the best lodging choices and their standard rates are included in the "What's Nearby" sections of this book. Before making reservations price check your options using online tools like Orbitz or Priceline. It's usually best to make reservations a few weeks in advance. Book too early and you'll pay the standard rate. Book too late and you might pay standard or more depending on availability. If you're making an unplanned stop at a hotel and unable to check pricing with the aforementioned online tools, the best way to receive a discount is to ask for one. Occasionally a hotel will have a room that is not up to their typical standards (e.g., no air conditioning) that they'll offer at a deep discount. If you don't mind the room's defect, the hotel will not mind checking you in. Also consider non-traditional accommodations like AirBnB and CouchSurfing.

Lone wolf (Yellowstone)

Another option is to take the money you would have spent on a hotel room and use it on a tent, sleeping bag, and mat. Camping isn't for everyone, but it's definitely worth a try. You can avoid campground fees (and truly explore the park) by camping in the parks' wilderness areas. Most parks allow backcountry camping with a free permit. By no means do you have to be a seasoned backpacker to enjoy the backcountry. However, you may want to consult with a park ranger to help plan an itinerary suitable for your experience, as well as get a brief overview of backcountry regulations. Most parks require that you set up camp a certain distance from all roads, trails, and water sources and practice Leave No Trace principles.

Walmart provides unexpected savings for travelers with a camper, RV, trailer, or truck. Most stores allow free overnight parking. To take advantage of this courtesy, they ask that you park in the back of the lot and notify a manager that you plan on spending the night (especially if you're the first to set up camp). Walmart's intent is to provide a safe location for weary travelers and truck drivers so they don't endanger other motorists. Do not take advantage of this benefit by getting comfortable and camping out in the parking lot for an extended period of time.

Dining: The best way to avoid dining at expensive restaurants is to pack a cooler. Bringing a loaf of bread, jam, and peanut butter can prevent a few trips to the nearest town for a snack or meal. A list of grocery stores is conveniently located in the "What's Nearby" sections.

Activities: Discounts are more difficult to come by for activities. Asking is a good place to start, especially if you're part of a decent sized group. Outfitters would rather get your business then see you walk out their door. Many outfitters offer "early-bird" discounts or "online only" specials. It's also a good idea to navigate your way around their website looking for coupons or simply search for the "outfitter's name" plus the word "coupon" and see what comes back.

Entrance Fees: These are non-negotiable, but the National Parks Service offers free entrance days. A list of fee free dates is available at nps. gov/findapark/feefreeparks.htm.

If you plan on visiting several federal fee areas in the same year, consider buying an annual pass (page 2).

Gas: Most national parks are vast regions located in extremely remote sections of the U.S. It will take a lot of gas simply to get to the park much less around it. Remember to top off your gas tank before entering. A few parks have gas stations (see park sections), but expect to pay a modest premium for the convenience.

Acadia, Glacier, Rocky Mountain, Bryce Canyon, Zion, Grand Canyon, Pinnacles, Sequoia, Yosemite, and Denali offer free shuttle services during peak tourism season. Take advantage of these shuttles. Not only are they free, they allow you to enjoy the magnificent vistas rather than having to stare at the road.

Camping Regulations
Camping is one of the main attractions. Children and adults alike love the freedom of spending a night under the stars. To do so, campers must adhere to a few basic regulations

Foggy Skyline Drive (Shenandoah)

that help protect park resources and ensure an enjoyable stay for all of the campground's patrons and your fellow park visitors.

1. Camp only in designated sites.
2. Leave something of little value to indicate occupancy (important for vans and RVs).
3. Store all food and cooking equipment in an enclosed vehicle or hard-sided food locker (particularly in parks with healthy bear or raccoon populations).
4. Do not leave fires unattended.
5. Observe campground specific quiet hours and generator hours.
6. Check out on time.
7. Lock valuables in your vehicle and out of sight.

Regulations regarding maximum length of stay, speed limits, gathering wood, and pets change from campground to campground. Specific regulations should be posted at self-check-in stations or handed out when you register for your campsite upon arrival, or they can be found prior to arrival at each park's website.

Road Construction
All of the most popular parks have been adapted to suit the modern motorist. Paved roadways venture across regions once declared impassable by foot. Ingenuity, perseverance, hard work and thousands of miles of concrete and asphalt now allow automobiles to twist and turn along rugged mountain slopes and craggy coastlines through some of the most beautiful scenery you'll find anywhere in the world. Roads were built to increase tourism and accessibility, but they were also carefully designed to retain aesthetic beauty. You won't find a bridge across the Grand Canyon or a parking lot next to Half Dome, but roads lead to stunning viewpoints of these iconic settings.

Park roads require regular maintenance. Repairing roads in these remote and rugged regions can be a difficult task—a task made more challenging since construction and tourism seasons coincide with one another. To get the most of your vacation try to plan around

road construction. Current and upcoming construction plans are typically listed on park websites. If you can't find construction information there, a friendly park ranger is just a phone call away.

Safety
It is important that park visitors follow safety precautions and park regulations to enjoy a safe visit and prevent injuries. In the unlikely event someone is injured, know where to go to receive proper medical treatment. A few parks have medical facilities on-site, but most do not. Carry a cell phone, but do not rely on it; cell coverage is spotty in most parks.

Accidents can still happen, even to the park's most cautious guests. Occasionally an accident results in death. The number one cause of fatalities in the parks might surprise you: it's car accidents. Sure, other drivers are beyond your control, but that doesn't mean you and I should refrain from wearing our seat belts, obeying the rules of the road, and driving attentively and cautiously.

Hazards most often associated with a trip to the national parks take many fewer lives.

Drowning: Visitors should use extreme caution near water. River crossings can be challenging due to uneven footing, moss covered rocks, and slippery logs. One misstep could lead to being swept down river or over a waterfall.

Hypothermia: Rivers and lakes. High elevations. Alaska. These places have one thing in common: they're cold. Extended exposure to any cold environment can lead to hypothermia, the progressive degradation, both physically and mentally, caused by the chilling of the inner core of the human body. To help prevent hypothermia, wear water-resistant clothing or clothing that wicks away moisture. It's also a good idea to pack a sweater, warm hat, and rain gear for any hike.

Dehydration: It's important to stay hydrated. Remember to carry a day pack with ample water and snacks.

Giardia: Giardia is caused by a parasite found in lakes and streams. If consumed it causes persistent, severe diarrhea, abdominal cramps, and nausea. To prevent giardia use an approved filter, boil water, or drink from sources clearly labeled "potable" (e.g., water fountains). Filters should be capable of removing particles as small as one micron.

Falling Trees/Rocks: Parks do their best to proactively close trails that pose a significant threat due to falling rocks or trees, but hikers must always be aware of their surroundings. Also, don't kick or throw rocks off cliffs or ledges. There may be hikers below you.

Wildlife/Bears: Do not approach wildlife. This is particularly true of bears. Know the differences between grizzly and black bears. Grizzlies are blond to nearly black and sometimes have silver-tipped guard hairs. They have a dished-in face and a large hump of heavy muscle above the shoulders. There claws are around 4 inches. Black bears also range from blond to black. They are typically smaller with a straighter face from tip of the nose to ears. They do not have a prominent hump above their shoulders and their claws are about 1.5 inches long. Most bear–human encounters occur when hikers startle or provoke the animal. Visitors often wear bells to scare away bears. I've heard conflicting reports about the bells' effectiveness, but if they make you feel safer you should wear them. The best way to avoid an encounter is to hike with a group and talk as you go. Many hikers carry bear spray, non-lethal deterrent similar to pepper spray.

Firearms: As of February 22, 2010, federal law allows people who can legally possess firearms under applicable federal, state, and local laws, to carry firearms in the national parks.

Where to See Wildlife
Wildlife is transient. The best way to pinpoint your desired animal is to ask a park ranger about current activity and feeding areas. Dawn and dusk are typically prime viewing times for large mammal species.

Respect Wildlife
When you do spot wildlife, remember that these are not tame animals, and should not be approached. Visitors are often injured when they get too close. Stay at least 100 yards away from bears and wolves and 25 yards away from all other animals (like bison, elk, bighorn sheep, moose, deer, and coyotes). Absolutely do not feed wildlife. It harms them and is illegal.

Photography Tips
Modern cameras eliminate most of the difficulty in taking photographs, but a few helpful tips can lead to outstanding results. The best photography is done at dusk and dawn. During these hours light is not too dim and not too bright. Image stabilization has come a long way, but a tripod is useful (especially in low-light).

Know the Rule of Thirds: an image should be imagined as divided into nine equal parts by two equally-spaced horizontal and vertical lines. Place your primary subject along the vertical lines or at any of the four intersections (see below) rather than centering your subject. Use this rule for interesting and well-balanced shots, but don't be afraid to break it from time to time.

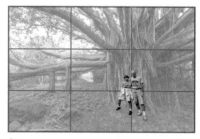

(My mom and dad hiking Pīpīwai Trail at Haleakalā National Park)

Mesquite Flat Sand Dunes (Death Valley)

Social Media

Stone Road Press
TheStoneRoadPress
@StoneRoadPress
@StoneRoadPress

National Park Service
NationalParkService
@NationalParkService
@NationalParkService

National Park Foundation
NationalPark
@GoParks

Acadia
AcadiaNPS
@AcadiaNPS
@AcadiaNPS

Cuyahoga Valley
CuyahogaValleyNPS
@CVNPNPS
@CuyahogaValleyNPS

Shenandoah
ShenandoahNPS
@ShenandoahNPS
@ShenandoahNPS

Mammoth Cave
MammothCaveNPS
@MammothCaveNP

Great Smoky Mountains
GreatSmokyNPS
@GreatSmokyNPS

Congaree
CongareeNP
@CongareeNPS

Biscayne
BiscayneNPS
@BiscayneNPS
@BiscayneNPS

Everglades
EvergladesNPS
@EvergladesNPS
@evergladesNPS

Dry Tortugas
DryTortugasNPS
@DryTortugasNPS

Isle Royale
IsleRoyaleNPS
@IsleRoyaleNPS

Voyageurs
VoyageursNPS
@VoyageursNPS

Badlands
BadlandsNPS
@BadlandsNPS
@BadlandsNPS

Wind Cave
WindCaveNPS
@WindCaveNPS

Theodore Roosevelt
TRooseveltNPS
@TRooseveltNPS

Grand Teton
GrandTetonNPS
@GrandTetonNPS
@GrandTetonNPS

Yellowstone
YellowstoneNPS
YellowstoneNPS
@YellowstoneNPS

Glacier
GlacierNPS
@GlacierNPS
@GlacierNPS

Hot Springs
HotSpringsNPS

Big Bend
BigBendNPS
@BigBendNPS

Guadalupe Mountains
Guadalupe.Mountains
@GuadalupeMtnsNP
@GuadalupeMountainsNPS

Carlsbad Caverns
CavernsNPS
@CavernsNPS

Petrified Forest
PetrifiedForestNPS
@PetrifiedNPS
@petrifiedForestNPS

Saguaro
SaguaroNationalPark
@SaguaroNPS
@SaguaroNationalPark

Rocky Mountain
RockyNPS
@RockyNPS
@RockyNPS

Great Sand Dunes
GreatSandDunesNPP
@GreatSandDunesNPS

Mesa Verde
MesaVerdeNPS

Arches
ArchesNPS
@ArchesNPS
@ArchesNPS

Canyonlands
CanyonlandsNPS
@CanyonlandsNPS
@CanyonlandsNPS

Capitol Reef
CapitolReefNPS
@CapitolReefNPS

Bryce Canyon
BryceCanyonNPS
@BryceCanyonNPS

Zion
ZionNPS
@ZionNPS

Grand Canyon
GrandCanyonNPS
@GrandCanyonNPS
@GrandCanyonNPS

Great Basin
GreatBasinNPS
@GreatBasinNPS

Joshua Tree
JoshuaTreeNPS
@JoshuaTreeNPS
@JoshuaTreeNPS

Channel Islands
ChannelIslandsNPS
@CHISNPS
@ChannelIslandsNPS

Pinnacles
PinnaclesNPS
@PinnaclesNPS

Death Valley
DeathValleyNP
@DeathValleyNPS
@DeathValleyNPS

Sequoia & Kings Canyon
SequoiaKingsNPS
@SequoiaKingsNPS

Yosemite
YosemiteNPS
@YosemiteNPS
@YosemiteNPS

Lassen Volcanic
LassenNPS
@LassenNPS
@LassenNPS

Redwood
RedwoodNPS
@RedwoodNPS
@RedwoodNPS

Crater Lake
CraterLakeNPS
@CraterLakeNPS

Mount Rainier
MountRainierNPS
@MountRainierNPS
@MountRainierNPS

Olympic
OlympicNPS
@OlympicNP
@OlympicNationalPark

North Cascades
NCascadesNPS
@NCascadesNPS
@NCascadesNPS

Glacier Bay
GlacierBayNPS
@GlacierBayNPS

Wrangell–St. Elias
WrangellSt.EliasNPP
@WrangellStENPS
@WrangellStENPS

Denali
DenaliNPS
@DenaliNPS
@DenaliNPS

Kenai Fjords
KenaiFjordsNPS
@KenaiFjordsNPS
@KenaiFjordsNPS

Lake Clark
LakeClarkNPS
@LakeClarkNPS
@LakeClarkNPS

Katmai
KatmaiNPS
@KatmaiNPS
@KatmaiNPS

Gates of the Arctic
GatesOfTheArcticNPS
@GatesArcticNPS
@AlaskaNPS

Kobuk Valley
KotzebueMuseum

Virgin Islands
VirginIslandsNPS

Haleakalā
HaleakalaNPS
@HaleakalaNPS

Hawaiʻi Volcanoes
HawaiiVolcanoesNPS
@Volcanoes_NPS
@HawaiiVolcanoesNPS

American Samoa
NPamericansamoa
@NPamericansamoa

Many parks also have flickr photostreams and youtube channels. Look them up to find high-quality photos and videos.

Highline Trail (Glacier)

Best of the Best

Top 10 Parks

Having trouble deciding which national park to visit? Close your eyes and pick from this short list of the best.

Glacier (page 246): If heaven is here on earth, it's probably Glacier National Park. John Muir called it "the best care-killing scenery in the continent." I agree.

Yosemite (page 514): Yosemite Valley is one of those places you have to see to believe. Throw in sequoia trees, thunderous waterfalls, and some of the best backcountry hiking and you've got an incomparable wonderland.

Zion (page 410): Locals called Zion "Yosemite National Park in color." These colorful sandstone walls are easily accessed thanks to Zion Tunnel (which leads directly into the canyon) and a convenient and easy-to-use shuttle system.

Grand Teton (page 206): The skyline of the Teton Range is as iconic as that of New York City, but it's all natural.

Arches (page 370): Arches is a small park based on Western standards, but boy does it pack some punch. It's home to more than 2,000 sandstone arches, including Delicate Arch, famous from all those Utah license plates.

Mount Rainier (page 566): Such stunning scenery so close to the Seattle metropolitan area makes including Mount Rainier National Park in this list an easy decision.

Yellowstone (page 218): Yellowstone has it all. Gushing geysers, brilliant canyons, alpine lakes, abundant wildlife, and magnificent mountains make a trip here feel like you're visiting several parks at once.

Grand Canyon (page 422): The park is hot and busy during summer, but few guests forget their first sight of this magnificent canyon. Try the North Rim for a less crowded experience.

Crater Lake (page 554): The water of Crater Lake is the deepest, purest blue you'll ever see. The lake is extraordinary all year round, but access is limited in winter.

Acadia (page 38): What once was the premier vacation destination for the wealthy is now a scenic retreat for everyone. Acadia offers extremely diverse activities and geography.

Top 20 Attractions

These are the most beautiful individual landmarks you'll find in the 59 parks. (Listed in order of appearance.)

The Wall • Badlands (page 178): Outside of the Grand Canyon, the Badlands Wall is the most magnificent marvel of eroded rock in the United States.

The Tetons • Grand Teton (page 206): There are so many spots in Jackson Hole where I'd like to sit down and stare up at these three towering giants. It's one of the all-time great skylines.

Grand Canyon of the Yellowstone • Yellowstone (page 218): Golden yellow canyon walls frame Upper and Lower Falls of the Yellowstone River.

Grand Prismatic Spring • Yellowstone (page 218): Uninspiring up close, the concentric circles of oranges, yellows, greens, and blues are mesmerizing from afar (Fairy Falls Trail).

Garden Wall • Glacier (page 246): A steep arête separating the Many Glacier area from Lake McDonald valley.

Big Room • Carlsbad Caverns (page 296): Caves are cool and Carlsbad's Big Room is one of the coolest.

Delicate Arch • Arches (page 370): Delicate Arch joins Crater Lake in the vehicle license plate club. That doesn't mean the site is amazing, but this one is.

Toroweap (Grand Canyon)

Bryce Amphitheater • Bryce Canyon (page 398): This scenery that has a direct connection to your soul. The colorful and eerie hoodoos are unforgettable.

Zion Canyon • Zion (page 410): Zion Narrows, Angel's Landing, and Court of the Patriarchs are a few of the notable landmarks within this beautiful canyon formed by the Virgin River.

Mather Point • Grand Canyon (page 422): The best vista to soak in the size of the canyon carved by the Colorado River.

Toroweap Overlook • Grand Canyon (page 422): Seclusion adds to the scenic views afforded at this overlook towering high above treacherous Lava Falls. It's only accessible via an unpaved road.

The Racetrack • Death Valley (page 490): The Racetrack is the quirkiest entry. Here rocks slowly slide their way across a bone dry playa.

General Sherman • Sequoia (page 502): I never thought a tree would make this list, but stand next to General Sherman and you'll quickly understand why.

Yosemite Valley • Yosemite (page 514): Perhaps the most beautiful valley in the world. Half Dome, El Capitán, and Yosemite Falls (all located in the valley) are worthy of inclusion in this list as separate entries.

Crater Lake • Crater Lake (page 554): This is the one place I'd choose above all others to take a lawn chair, grill, cooler, and a few of my closest friends to sit and enjoy the view.

Mount Rainier • Mount Rainier (page 566): Whether looking down on Mount Rainier from a plane, across Puget Sound from a ferry, or up at it from its base, Mount Rainier is a sight to behold.

Johns Hopkins Inlet • Glacier Bay (page 604): Calving glaciers and abundant sea life make this a hot spot for cruise ships and kayakers.

Denali • Denali (page 620): It's the tallest mountain in North America, and more prominent than Mount Everest. Of course it's on this list.

Brown Bears of Brooks Falls • Katmai (page 642): The scenery here is nice, but its residents are better. Brown bears fish at the falls in July and September.

Haleakalā Summit • Haleakalā (page 674): The summit is more like visiting a distant planet than a park.

More Top Attractions
The parks offer attractions galore, so here are the rest of our personal favorites. (Listed in order of appearance.)

Jordan Pond • Acadia
Cadillac Mountain • Acadia
Carriage Roads • Acadia
Sand Beach • Acadia
Brandywine Falls • Cuyahoga Valley
Frozen Niagara • Mammoth Cave
Mammoth Dome • Mammoth Cave
Cade's Cove • Great Smoky Mtns
Synchronous Fireflies • Smokies & Congaree
Fort Jefferson • Dry Tortugas
Moose • Isle Royale
Ice Roads • Voyageurs
Sheep Mountain Table • Badlands
Boxwork • Wind Cave
Mustangs • Theodore Roosevelt
John Moulton Barn • Grand Teton
Schwabacher Landing • Grand Teton
Jenny Lake • Grand Teton
Old Faithful • Yellowstone
Mammoth Hot Springs • Yellowstone
Norris Geyser Basin • Yellowstone
Great Fountain Geyser • Yellowstone
Hayden Valley • Yellowstone
Lamar Valley • Yellowstone
Grinnell Glacier • Glacier
Hidden Lake • Glacier
Bathhouse Row • Hot Springs
Chisos Mountains • Big Bend
Santa Elena Canyon • Big Bend

Molar Rock and Angel Arch (Canyonlands)

Gypsum Sand Dunes • Guadalupe Mtns
McKittrick Canyon • Guadalupe Mtns
Bat Flight • Carlsbad Caverns
Petrified Logs • Petrified Forest
Saguaro Cactus • Saguaro
Moraine Park • Rocky Mountain
High Dune • Great Sand Dunes
Cedar Point • Black Canyon
Balcony House • Mesa Verde
Long House • Mesa Verde
Landscape Arch • Arches
The Maze • Canyonlands
Horseshoe Canyon • Canyonlands
Grand View Point • Canyonlands
Angel Arch • Canyonlands
Fruita • Capitol Reef
Burr Trail • Capitol Reef
Thor's Hammer • Bryce Canyon
Three Patriarchs • Zion
Hermit's Rest Road • Grand Canyon
Bristlecone Pine Trees • Great Basin
Wheeler Peak • Great Basin
Lehman Cave • Great Basin
Hidden Valley • Joshua Tree
Keys Ranch • Joshua Tree
Anacapa • Channel Islands
High Peaks • Pinnacles

Zabriskie Point • Death Valley
Badwater • Death Valley
Eureka Dunes • Death Valley
Mineral King • Sequoia & Kings Canyon
General Grant • Sequoia & Kings Canyon
Glacier Point • Yosemite
Tenaya Lake • Yosemite
Tuolumne Meadows • Yosemite
Lassen Peak • Lassen Volcanic
Bumpass Hell • Lassen Volcanic
Tall Trees • Redwood
Wizard Island • Crater Lake
Hurricane Ridge • Olympic
Hoh Rain Forest • Olympic
Second Beach • Olympic
Mount Shuksan • North Cascades
Diablo Lake • North Cascades
Cascade Pass • North Cascades
Stehekin • North Cascades
Harding Icefield • Kenai Fjords
Onion Portage • Kobuk Valley
Trunk Bay • Virgin Islands
Salt Pond Bay • Virgin Islands
'Ohe'o Gulch • Haleakalā
Halema'uma'u Crater • Hawaii Volcanoes
Pu'u 'O'o • Hawaii Volcanoes
O'fu Beach • American Samoa

Best Scenic Drives
The parks have become motorists' favorite travel destinations. This book would not be complete without a list of the very best drives they have to offer.

Going-to-the-Sun Road • Glacier (page 253): The best drive in the country is only open from mid-June through mid-September (most years) and cyclists are not permitted during periods of peak motorist traffic.

Denali Park Road • Denali (page 623): Only accessible via shuttle/tour bus from late May through mid-September (most years) with a "Road Lottery" held for individuals in late September.

Rim Drive • Crater Lake (page 556): I absolutely love everything about this lake. In summer you can drive around the caldera filled with the bluest water you'll ever see. In winter the road is closed, but that doesn't stop cross-country skiers and snowshoers from completing the circuit.

Lake Solitude (Grand Teton)

Wawona Road • Yosemite (page 518): Wawona Road makes the list thanks to one of the most memorable views in the world: Tunnel View. It provides the first glimpse of Yosemite Valley.

John D. Rockefeller Jr., Memorial Pkwy • Grand Teton (page 40): It connects two of the American West's greatest treasures: Yellowstone and Grand Teton.

Trail Ridge Road • Rocky Mountain (page 333): This scenic thoroughfare penetrates the Rockies and travels above 11,000 feet elevation for 8 miles. Pullouts along the way provide some of the best mountain vistas and access to trails.

Park Loop Road • Acadia (page 40): 27 miles of pure bliss as it loops around the eastern half of Mount Desert Island with a spur road to Cadillac Mountain, the tallest peak in the park.

US-101 • Redwood (page 549): For my gallons of gas, there are more scenic stretches of the Pacific Coastline along CA-1 and US-101, but the park's towering redwoods add contrast to California's rocky and rugged coast.

Badlands Loop Road • Badlands (page 182): Easily the best scenic detour while traveling across South Dakota on I-90.

Skyline Drive • Shenandoah (page 75): The 105-mile highway is Shenandoah's main attraction.

Best Lodges

Most lodges in the parks were built not just to serve a purpose, but to compliment the environment. These lodging facilities are works of architecture worthy of the landscapes they accent.

El Tovar • Grand Canyon
Ahwahnee (Yosemite Hotel) • Yosemite
Jenny Lake Lodge • Grand Teton
Old Faithful Inn • Yellowstone
Crater Lake Lodge • Crater Lake
Paradise Inn • Mount Rainier
Zion Lodge • Zion
Many Glacier Lodge • Glacier
Glacier Park Lodge • Glacier
Rock Harbor Lodge • Isle Royale
Le Conte Lodge • Great Smoky Mtns

The 20 Best Trails

It's nice to see the parks from the comfort of your vehicle or lodge, but to really explore nature you need to lace up a pair of hiking boots and hit the trails. We provide all our favorites below. (Most of these hikes are considered strenuous.)

Cascade/Paintbrush Canyon (Lake Solitude) • Grand Teton (page 212): One of the most rewarding loop hikes around. It's long, but ambitious hikers can complete the hike to Lake Solitude in a day.

Half Dome • Yosemite (page 527): The climb to the top of Half Dome (aided by cables) is a humbling trek to inspiring views (permit required).

Observation Point • Zion (page 416): Most people prefer Angel's Landing or the Narrows, but this is our favorite hike at Zion. From the conclusion, you get to look down on hikers as they cross the knife-edge ridgeline to Angel's Landing.

Skyline Loop • Mount Rainier (page 572): This truly is paradise. Unfortunately it's often socked in with clouds, and when clouds aren't obscuring Rainier's majesty, crowds fill the trails.

Delicate Arch • Arches (page 374): Delicate Arch is magnificent, but what really makes it "pop" is its presentation. The trail leading to this colorful sandstone arch is designed to perfection.

Grinnell Glacier • Glacier (page 256): Mountains, lakes, and slowly receding glaciers highlight this moderate trek.

Navajo Loop • Bryce Canyon (page 404): Some of the finest artwork Mother Nature has ever sculpted.

Sky Pond • Rocky Mountain (page 333): There's a vertical climb alongside a waterfall (in spring) to reach Glass Lake and Sky Pond.

Highline • Glacier (page 256): The Garden Wall section from Logan Pass to Granite Park Lodge is outstanding. It's a popular hike, but what it lacks in solitude it makes up for in wildlife and expansive mountain views.

Sliding Sands Trail (Haleakala)

Bright Angel • Grand Canyon (page 438): The other route into the canyon. Shade and water are available.

The Narrows • Zion (page 417): There may be better slot canyon hikes in Utah (like nearby Buckskin Gulch), but there isn't a single one more famous than Zion's Narrows. The stretch between its mouth and Orderville Canyon is best.

The Precipice • Acadia (page 45): Steel ladders and rungs aid hikers aiming to reach the summit of Champlain Mountain for classic Acadian views.

High Peaks Loop • Pinnacles (page 485): This adventurous hike is marked by vertical steel ladders and tight squeezes between rocky cliffs. Spotting a California condor can make it unforgettable.

Old Rag • Shenandoah (page 78): Most hikes through Shenandoah begin along Skyline Drive, but not Old Rag. You begin at the park boundary and gradually hike/scramble to the top of Old Rag.

Chimney Tops • Great Smoky Mtns (page 107): Scramble up a rocky escarpment at the end of this hike for outstanding Smoky Mountain views.

Ptarmigan Tunnel • Glacier (page 256): Walk along the Garden Wall, to a pristine lake and then scale a set of switchbacks to a tunnel leading to more premier scenery.

Angel's Landing • Zion (page 416): Hiking to the Landing isn't for everyone. Following the knife-edge ridgeline may stir up a fear of heights you never knew you had.

South Kaibab • Grand Canyon (page 438): One of two routes into the canyon from its South Rim. The views are superb, but there's no water and little shade.

Bristlecone • Great Basin (page 450): Fantastic views of Wheeler Peak are provided from a grove of bristlecone pine, which are some of the oldest living organisms on the planet.

Sentinel Dome • Yosemite (page 526): Much easier than the trek to the top of Half Dome, this (still difficult) hike offers exceptional views.

Sliding Sands • Haleakalā (page 678): This trail transports hikers to an otherworldly landscape inside Haleakalā Crater.

More Hiking Trails

With so many excellent hikes, we decided to add more than 100 extra favorites. They're broken down by difficulty and listed in order of appearance. (Adventure hikes require using ropes, chains, ladders, or guts to traverse somewhat terrifying terrain.)

Easy Hikes

Bar Island • Acadia
Brandywine Falls • Cuyahoga Valley
Blue Hen Falls • Cuyahoga Valley
Towpath Trail • Cuyahoga Valley
River Styx Spring • Mammoth Cave
Clingman's Dome • Great Smoky Mtns
Boardwalk • Congaree
Anhinga • Everglades
Painted Canyon • Theodore Roosevelt
Wind Canyon • Theodore Roosevelt
Jenny Lake Loop • Grand Teton
St. Mary Falls • Glacier
Running Eagle Falls • Glacier
Avalanche Lake • Glacier
Grand Promenade • Hot Springs
Boquillas Canyon • Big Bend
Santa Elena Canyon • Big Bend
McKittrick Canyon • Guadalupe Mtns
Natural Entrance • Carlsbad Caverns
Blue Mesa • Petrified Forest
Freeman Homestead • Saguaro
Emerald Lake • Rocky Mountain
Warner Point • Black Canyon

Smithsonian Hut atop Mount Whitney (Sequoia)

Park Avenue • Arches
Grandview Point • Canyonlands
Mesa Arch • Canyonlands
Bright Angel Point • Grand Canyon
Inspiration Point • Channel Islands
Crescent Meadow • Sequoia & Kings Canyon
Bridalveil Fall • Yosemite
Lower Yosemite Fall • Yosemite
Manzanita Lake • Lassen Volcanic
Discovery Point • Crater Lake
Hall of Mosses • Olympic
Rialto Beach • Olympic
Brooks Falls • Katmai
Ram Head • Virgin Islands
Thurston Lava Tube • Hawai'i Volcanoes

Moderate Hikes
Ledges • Cuyahoga Valley
Hawksbill Summit • Shenandoah
Cedar Sink • Mammoth Cave
Tram Road • Everglades
Mount Ojibway • Isle Royale
Cruiser Lake • Voyageurs
Notch • Badlands
Fairy Falls • Yellowstone
Hidden Lake • Glacier
Iceberg Lake • Glacier
Window • Big Bend
Lost Mine • Big Bend
King Canyon • Saguaro
High Dune • Great Sand Dunes
Confluence Overlook • Canyonlands
Cohab Canyon • Capitol Reef
Rim Overlook • Capitol Reef
Left Fork (Subway) • Zion
Ryan Mountain • Joshua Tree
Dante's Ridge • Death Valley
Mesquite Valley Sand Dunes • Death Valley
Balconies Cave • Pinnacles
Bear Gulch Cave • Pinnacles
Lembert Dome • Yosemite
Gaylor Lakes • Yosemite
Cathedral Lakes • Yosemite
Bumpass Hell • Lassen Volcanic

Tall Trees • Redwood
Ladybird Johnson • Redwood
Boy Scout Tree • Redwood
Watchman Peak • Crater Lake
Spray Park • Mount Rainier
Rainy Lake • North Cascades
Rainbow Loop • North Cascades
Harding Icefield • Kenai Fjords
Mount Healy Overlook • Denali
Pīpīwai • Haleakalā

Strenuous Hikes
Ramsey Cascades • Great Smoky Mtns
Alum Cave • Great Smoky Mountains
Greenstone Ridge • Isle Royale
Amphitheater Lake • Grand Teton
Uncle Tom's • Yellowstone
Sky Rim Loop • Yellowstone
Guadalupe Peak • Guadalupe Mountains
Black Lake • Rocky Mountain
North Kaibab • Grand Canyon
Wheeler Peak • Great Basin
Rae Lakes Loop • Sequoia & Kings Canyon
Franklin Lakes • Sequoia & Kings Canyon
Mist Trail • Yosemite
Lassen Peak • Lassen Volcanic
Mount Scott • Crater Lake
Comet Falls • Mount Rainier
Glacier Basin • Mount Rainier
Burroughs Mountains • Mount Rainier
Cascade Pass • North Cascades
Reef Bay Trail • Virgin Islands
Kīlaeaua Iki • Hawaii Volcanoes
Mount 'Alava • American Samoa

Adventure Hikes
Beehive • Acadia
Acadia Mountain • Acadia
Wilderness Waterway • Everglades
Saddle Pass • Badlands
Longs Peak • Rocky Mountain
Fiery Furnace • Arches
Mount Whitney • Sequoia & Kings Canyon
Mount Rainier • Mount Rainier

Mount Storm King • Olympic
Shi Shi Beach • Olympic
Mauna Loa • Hawaii Volcanoes

Best for Hiking
Try one of these parks if you're looking to put a few miles on your favorite pair of hiking boots.

Yosemite (page 526)
Glacier (page 256)
Sequoia & Kings Canyon (page 510)
Grand Teton (page 212)
North Cascades (page 596)
Rocky Mountain (page 333)
Zion (page 416)
Yellowstone (page 230)
Mount Rainier (page 572)
Acadia (page 45)
Great Smoky Mountains (page 107)
Grand Canyon (page 442)
Denali (page 625)
Isle Royale (page 160)
Haleakalā (page 678)

Best for Backpacking
The best way to commune with these wonderful natural abodes is to strap a pack on your back and enjoy a few days of perfect solitude in the backcountry.

Glacier (page 257)
Yosemite (page 528)
Grand Teton (page 212)
Sequoia & Kings Canyon (page 510)
Isle Royale (page 160)
Rocky Mountain (page 336)
Mount Rainier (page 572)
Denali (page 625)
Lake Clark (page 637)
Canyonlands (page 386)
North Cascades (page 598)
Hawai'i Volcanoes (page 694)
Great Smoky Mountains (page 107)

Yosemite

Intro to Backpacking
Uncertain about hiking with 40+ pounds of gear on your back? Nervous about camping in the untamed wilderness? Try one of these parks. They're like training wheels for beginning backpackers.

Isle Royale (page 160)
Bryce Canyon (page 405)
Wind Cave (page 190)
Redwood (page 552)
Theodore Roosevelt (page 197)
Guadalupe Mountains (page 293)
Mammoth Cave (page 92)
Channel Islands (page 475)

Best for Paddling
Gain a new perspective of these watery wonderlands by floating or boating miles of wide open waterways.

Everglades (page 135)
Voyageurs (page 170)
Glacier Bay (page 610)
Isle Royale (page 162)
Grand Teton (page 214)
Channel Islands (page 473)
Acadia (page 47)
Congaree (page 120)
Big Bend (page 284)

Best for Whitewater
Very few activities get your blood pumping quite like whitewater rafting. These parks offer commercial trips on some of the most turbulent rivers.

Grand Canyon (page 430)
Wrangell–St. Elias (page 619)
Canyonlands (page 387)
Denali (page 627)
Glacier (page 263)

Glacier Bay (page 610)
North Cascades (page 598)
Yellowstone (page 235)
Olympic (page 585)
Black Canyon (page 354)

Best for Biking
Don't forget to bring your bicycle to these national parks.

Death Valley (page 499)
Acadia (page 48)
Denali (page 627)
Zion (page 418)
Everglades (page 136)
Olympic (page 584)
Shenandoah (page 80)
Theodore Roosevelt (page 199)
Glacier (page 262)
Great Smoky Mountains (page 108)
Grand Teton (page 214)
Cuyahoga Valley (page 63)
Saguaro (page 317)
Yellowstone (page 235)

Best for Horseback Riding
Visitors can still wander through these parks on horseback, much like early American explorers did. Each one is horse-/rider-friendly with miles of trails designated for stock, corrals, and commercial outfitters who offer guided trail rides or multi-day pack trips.

Grand Teton (page 214)
Yellowstone (page 235)
Rocky Mountain (page 336)
Bryce Canyon (page 406)
Grand Canyon (mule) (page 432)
Joshua Tree (page 465)
Shenandoah (page 80)
Glacier (page 262)

Great Smoky Mountains (page 108)
Sequoia & Kings Canyon (page 511)
Zion (page 418)
Haleakalā (page 679)
Yosemite (page 529)
Acadia (page 49)

Best for Fishing
Anglers will find plenty of fish here.

Yellowstone (page 236)
Alaska Nat'l Parks (pages 604–663)
Everglades (page 138)
North Cascades (page 598)
Biscayne (page 128)
Great Smoky Mountains (page 108)
Virgin Islands (page 669)
Grand Teton (page 215)
Voyageurs (page 171)
Isle Royale (page 163)
Rocky Mountain (page 336)
Shenandoah (page 80)

Best for Rock Climbing
Rock climbing seems to increase in popularity each year, and many of the best locations in the United States are found among the mountains and cliffs at these national parks.

Yosemite (page 530)
Pinnacles (page 486)
Grand Teton (page 215)
Joshua Tree (page 465)
Zion (page 418)
Black Canyon (page 354)
Acadia (page 47)
Rocky Mountain (page 336)
Sequoia & Kings Canyon (page 511)
Arches (page 376)
Canyonlands (page 387)
Capitol Reef (page 396)

Plenty of creatures beneath the sea at U.S. Virgin Islands

Best for Mountain Climbing

There are mountains and then there are MOUNTAINS. Denali, the tallest peak in North America, is the latter. These parks have outstanding mountain scenery, and climbs range from multi-day treks, requiring specialized equipment, to day-hikes to summits with spectacular vistas.

Denali (page 626)
Mount Rainier (page 574)
Wrangell–St. Elias (page 618)
North Cascades (page 596)
Lake Clark (page 637)
Rocky Mountain (page 333)
Glacier (page 256)
Sequoia & Kings Canyon (page 510)
Yellowstone (page 230)
Olympic (page 586)

Best for Stargazing

One of the national parks' most under-rated activities is stargazing. Many city dwellers aren't able to see the night sky in its natural state, but in the parks, when the sky is clear, the stars twinkle and dance.

Haleakalā (page 679)
Gates of the Arctic (page 648)
Utah National Parks (pages 370–420)
Great Basin (page 452)
Grand Canyon (page 422)
Joshua Tree (page 466)
Big Bend (page 284)
Carlsbad Caverns (page 301)

Best Off-Road Driving

A high-clearance 4WD vehicle allows you to "unlock" seldom visited sites thanks to miles of unpaved (and sometimes impassable) roads at these parks.

Death Valley (page 499)
Canyonlands (page 387)
Capitol Reef (page 394)
Grand Canyon (page 440)
Great Basin (page 450)
Arches (page 370)

Best for SCUBA

The national parks aren't limited to land activities. At these locations you can explore the life, wrecks, and terrain that exist under the sea.

Virgin Islands (page 669)
Isle Royale (page 163)
Dry Tortugas (page 146)
Biscayne (page 128)
Channel Islands (page 475)
American Samoa (page 704)

Best for Beaches

Seldom do you need to pack your swimsuit for a trip to a national park; these are the exceptions.

Virgin Islands (page 668)
American Samoa (page 704)
Dry Tortugas (page 146)
Olympic (page 589)
Haleakalā (page 679)
Acadia (page 49)
Redwood (page 550)
Biscayne (page 128)
Great Sand Dunes (page 346)
Channel Islands (page 475)

Best for Waterfalls

For the soothing sight and sounds of plummeting water pay a visit to one of these parks.

Yosemite (page 514)
Haleakalā (page 674)
Great Smoky Mountains (page 98)
Yellowstone (page 218)
Shenandoah (page 70)
Cuyahoga Valley (page 58)
Olympic (page 578)
Glacier (page 246)
Mount Rainier (page 566)
Rocky Mountain (page 326)
North Cascades (page 592)

Best for Caves

Children love the dark mysterious passages and ornate rock formations found at these national parks.

Carlsbad Caverns (page 299)
Mammoth Cave (page 91)
Wind Cave (page 186)
Great Basin (page 451)
Pinnacles (page 485)
Sequoia & Kings Canyon (page 510)
Hawai'i Volcanoes (page 692)
Channel Islands (page 473)

Best for Culture

Most parks show signs of human occupation spanning the last 10,000 years, only a few have substantial archeological sites.

Mesa Verde (page 356)
Channel Islands (page 468)
Kobuk Valley (page 652)
Shenandoah (page 70)
Badlands (page 178)
Great Smoky Mountains (page 98)
Hawai'i Volcanoes (page 684)
Everglades (page 130)
Theodore Roosevelt (page 194)

Paths are shared at Brooks Camp (Katmai)

Best for Winter
Most visitors flock to the parks in summer when children are out of school and the temperature has warmed, but many are equally inviting during the winter. Some attract visitors thanks to uncommonly warm winters, others offer unique activities like snowmobiling, cross-country skiing, snowboarding, and downhill skiing.

Warm Winters
Death Valley (page 490)
Haleakalā (page 674)
Everglades (page 130)
Hawai'i Volcanoes (page 684)
Joshua Tree (page 460)
Big Bend (page 278)
American Samoa (page 700)
Virgin Islands (page 664)
Saguaro (page 312)

Cold Winters
Yellowstone (page 237)
Yosemite (page 530)
Crater Lake (page 560)
Mount Rainier (page 574)
Sequoia & Kings Canyon (page 511)
Voyageurs (page 171)
Cuyahoga Valley (page 64)

Best for Bird Watching
Birds seem to be everywhere, but these parks are well-known for the diversity and abundance of their flying friends.

Everglades (page 138)
Acadia (page 49)
Dry Tortugas (page 146)
Pinnacles (page 487)
Congaree (page 121)
Haleakalā (page 680)
Big Bend (page 284)

Best for Wildlife
Fishing bears. Migrating caribou. Grazing bison. Feeding whales. This is just a sampling of wildlife on display at these parks.

Katmai (page 646)
Kobuk Valley (page 655)
Yellowstone (page 239)
Everglades (page 138)
Denali (page 628)
Isle Royale (page 164)
Great Smoky Mountains (page 109)
Lake Clark (page 640)
Glacier Bay (page 613)

Best for Photography
If you want to return from your vacation with a postcard-perfect photograph, visit these parks to snap a few pictures.

Yellowstone (page 236)
Yosemite (page 531)
Arches (page 376)
Bryce Canyon (page 398)
Grand Canyon (page 422)
Denali (page 620)
Zion (page 418)

Grand Teton (page 206)
Glacier Bay (page 604)
Canyonlands (page 378)

Best Sunrise Spots
Whether you're in search of that perfect sunrise photograph or a romantic morning with a loved one, you won't regret the early wake-up call to visit these sites.

Haleakalā Summit • Haleakalā
Zabriskie Point • Death Valley
Cadillac Mountain • Acadia
Sunset (Thor's Hammer) • Bryce Canyon
Mesa Arch • Canyonlands
Delicate Arch • Arches
Signal Mountain • Grand Teton
Landscape Arch • Arches
Watchman Overlook • Crater Lake

Best Sunset Spots
Brilliant sunsets are often captured from these picturesque locations.

Cape Royal • Grand Canyon
Hopi Point • Grand Canyon
Shoshone Point • Grand Canyon
Snake River Overlook • Grand Teton
Shi Shi and Rialto Beaches • Olympic
Delicate Arch • Arches
Glacier Point • Yosemite
The Window • Big Bend
Dante's View • Death Valley
Hot Springs • Big Bend

Red Jammers lined up at Logan Pass (Glacier)

Best for Couples

Couples will find these parks exciting, adventurous, and romantic.

Virgin Islands (page 664)
Grand Teton (page 206)
Acadia (page 38)
Hawai'i Volcanoes (page 684)
Haleakalā (page 674)
Mount Rainier (page 566)
Rocky Mountain (page 326)
Glacier (page 246)
Yellowstone (page 218)
Great Smoky Mountains (page 98)

Best for Families

Some parks are more family-friendly than others thanks to easy accessibility, short trails, and guaranteed sights and sounds sure to spark your child's imagination.

Carlsbad Caverns (page 296)
Hawai'i Volcanoes (page 684)
Everglades (page 130)
Great Sand Dunes (page 340)
Yellowstone (page 218)
Sequoia & Kings Canyon (page 502)
Wind Cave (page 186)
Mammoth Cave (page 86)
Pinnacles (page 480)
Cuyahoga Valley (page 58)
Grand Canyon (page 422)
Glacier (page 246)
Grand Teton (page 206)
Theodore Roosevelt (page 194)
Badlands (page 178)
Mount Rainier (page 566)

Best for Day Trips

A few parks are conveniently located near major metropolitan areas, allowing a quick day-trip to hike or sit and relax in these natural wonderlands.

Mount Rainier • Seattle
Olympic • Seattle
Rocky Mountain • Denver
Joshua Tree • Los Angeles
Everglades • Miami
Shenandoah • Washington D.C.
Pinnacles • San Francisco
Congaree • Columbia
Saguaro • Tucson
Cuyahoga Valley • Cleveland/Akron

Best for Train Travel

Railroads played an important role in the establishment of the early national parks, and it is still king at these destinations.

Glacier (page 247)
Grand Canyon (page 437)
Denali (page 621)
Cuyahoga Valley (page 63)

Best Ranger Programs

I highly recommend all ranger programs, but these are a few personal favorites. The price is almost always right, too, as most are free of charge.

Wild Cave Tours (fee) • Mammoth Cave, Wind Cave, and Carlsbad Caverns
Bat Flight Program • Carlsbad Caverns
Sled Dog Demonstration • Denali

Slough Slog • Everglades
Adventure Hikes • Yellowstone
Ranger III (fee) • Isle Royale
Cliff Palace (fee) • Mesa Verde
Balcony House (fee) • Mesa Verde
Guided Canoe Tour • Congaree
Discovery Hikes (fee) • Denali
North Canoe Voyage • Voyageurs

Best Concessioner Tours

Concessioner tours tend to be pricier, but they are an effective and efficient means of touring a national park. These are the best of the concessioner offerings.

Red Jammer Tours • Glacier
Canyon Raft Trip • Grand Canyon
Mule Ride • Grand Canyon
Dive-In Theater • Acadia
Carriage Rides • Acadia
Captain's Cruise • Isle Royale
Snowcoach Tours • Yellowstone
Crater Lake Boat Tour

Most Underrated

Great Smoky Mountains, the most visited park, receives more than 10 million annual visitors. Others are so lightly trafficked people aren't aware they exist. These are a few of the seldom visited and underappreciated national parks.

North Cascades (page 592)
Black Canyon of the Gunnison (page 348)
Great Sand Dunes (page 340)
Capitol Reef (page 390)
Isle Royale (page 154)

The Racetrack (Death Valley)

Worst for Traffic

A trip to a national park is supposed to be a relaxing and rejuvenating experience, allowing you to escape the daily grind. The ideal vacation doesn't include sitting in bumper-to-bumper traffic, but that's the reality at these parks during peak season.

Acadia: July–August
Great Smoky Mtns: Summer & October
Yosemite: May–Sept
Yellowstone: July–August
Rocky Mtn: June–August
Grand Canyon: May–Sept
Zion: April–September
Glacier: July–August
Mount Rainier: July–August

Worst for Bugs

An unusually wet winter or spring can result in bumper crops of black flies and mosquitoes in just about any area, but a few parks are notorious for their pesky insects. Try to avoid these sites during the specified time frame.

Everglades: Summer
Alaska National Parks: June–mid-July
Yosemite: early Summer
Sequoia & Kings Canyon: early Summer
Acadia: mid-May–mid-June
Isle Royale: late June–late July

Backcountry Cabins

Looking to get away from it all without sleeping in a tent? Several parks have backcountry cabins only accessible by foot. Most lack electricity and other luxuries.

Sperry/Granite Park Chalet • Glacier
Phantom Ranch • Grand Canyon
High Sierra Camps • Yosemite and Sequoia & Kings Canyon
Mauna Loa, Puʻuʻulaʻula, & Red Hill • Hawaiʻi Volcanoes
Hōlua, Kapalaua, and Palikū Cabins • Haleakalā
Le Conte Lodge • Great Smoky Mtns
Wrangell–St. Elias
Kenai Fjords
Lake Clark
Katmai
Drakesbad Ranch • Lassen Volcanic

Best Campgrounds

Many of the parks' campgrounds are nondescript accommodations lacking scenic views and privacy. Others are exceptional with stunning vistas, access to great hiking trails, and well-equipped facilities. These are the best of the best.

Squaw Flats • Canyonlands
Wonder Lake • Denali
Jumbo Rocks • Joshua Tree

Hidden Valley • Joshua Tree
Devil's Garden • Arches
Isle au Haut • Acadia
Voyageurs
Jenny Lake • Grand Teton
Cottonwood • Theodore Roosevelt
Cinnamon Bay • Virgin Islands
Many Glacier • Glacier
Pine Springs • Guadalupe Mtns
Isle Royale

Best Oddities

There are weird and unexplainable oddities and events across the country; many exist within the parks.

The Racetrack • Death Valley
Badwater Basin • Death Valley
Ubehebe Crater • Death Valley
Waterpocket Fold • Capitol Reef
Upheaval Dome • Canyonlands
Synchronous Fireflies • Great Smoky Mtns and Congaree
Triple Divide • Glacier

Best Superlatives

The national parks are brimming with superlatives. These are the most impressive.

Denali (page 620): Highest mountain peak in North America, with a summit elevation of 20,320 ft.

Havasu Falls

Badwater Basin • Death Valley (page 490): Lowest point in North America with at 282 feet below sea level.

Mount Whitney • Sequoia (page 502): Highest mountain peak in the contiguous U.S. with an elevation of 14,505 ft.

Mount Rainier (page 566): Rising to 14,410 ft, Mount Rainier is the tallest volcano in the contiguous United States.

Crater Lake (page 554): Deepest lake in the United States with a 1,943-ft maximum depth and average depth of 1,148 ft. It's also the purest lake in North America.

Mammoth Cave (page 86): By far the world's longest known cave system, with more than 405 miles of passageways.

Yosemite Falls • Yosemite (page 514): The tallest waterfall in North America. Sentinel Falls, the second tallest waterfall, is also located in Yosemite National Park.

Kolob Arch • Zion (page 410): The largest free-standing arch in the park system.

Yellowstone (page 218): The largest concentration of geysers in the world.

Wrangell–St. Elias (page 614): Largest unit in the national park system and continent's largest quantity of glaciers.

Harding Icefield • Kenai Fjords (page 630): The largest icefield contained entirely in the United States.

Bristlecone Pines • Great Basin (page 446): Some of the world's oldest living organisms grow here.

General Sherman • Sequoia (page 502): The largest known tree by volume at 52,600 ft^3 (roughly the size of 16 blue whales).

Hyperion • Redwood (page 546): World's tallest known tree at 379.3 ft.

Best Beyond the Parks

Great natural sights and scenes of the United States don't begin and end with the national parks. Here are a few of the non-park wonders mentioned in this guidebook. (NM = National Monument, NME = National Memorial, NRA = National Recreation Area, NVM = National Volcanic Monument, NCA = National Conservation Area, SP = State Parks)

Washington Mall (Lincoln Memorial, Washington Monument, etc. • page 85)
Mt Rushmore NME (page 205)
Custer State Park (page 205)
Jewel Cave NM (page 205)
Devils Tower NM (page 205)
Craters of the Moon NM (page 245)
Lake Ouachita SP (page 277)

White Sands NM (page 323)
Lost Dutchman SP (page 325)
Garden of the Gods (page 368)
Hovenweep NM (page 368)
Dinosaur NM (page 369)
Havasu Falls (page 439)
Dead Horse Point SP (page 457)
Kodachrome Basin SP (page 457)
Grand Staircase–Escalante NM (page 457)
Kanarra Falls (page 458)
Buckskin Gulch (page 458)
The Wave (page 458)
Paria Canyon (page 458)
Cedar Breaks NM (page 458)
Glen Canyon NRA (page 458)
Lake Mead NRA/Hoover Dam (page 459)
Red Rock Canyon NCA (page 459)
Devil's Postpile NM (page 537)
Golden Gate NRA (page 537)
Muir Woods NM (page 537)
Lava Beds NM (page 564)
Oregon Caves NM (page 565)
Mount St. Helens NVM (page 601)
John Day Fossil Beds NM (page 602)
Buck Island Reef NM (page 673)
Molokini (page 683)
Mauna Kea (page 683)
Puʻuhonua o Honaunau Nat'l Hist. Park (page 698)
Green Sand (Papakōlea) Beach/South Point (page 698)
Kekaha Kai SP (page 699)
Waipio Valley (page 699)
ʻAkaka Falls SP (page 699)

Cadillac Mountain sunrise (Acadia)

Did You Know?

Acadia, Maine

It was the first national park established east of the Mississippi River.

It is the 13th smallest and 10th most visited park.

Cadillac Mountain (1,528 feet), the highest point along the North Atlantic Seaboard, sees the first rays of sun in the U.S. from October 7 to March 7.

John D. Rockefeller, Jr. built 57 miles of carriage roads and spent more than $3.5 million developing Mount Desert Island before donating thousands of acres to the park for everyone to enjoy.

Cuyahoga Valley, Ohio

Established in 2000, it is one of the newest national parks.

From the 1830s to the 1860s, Ohio became the third most prosperous state, largely due to success of the Ohio & Erie Canal.

The cities of Boston and Peninsula were centers for ship-building and canal commerce during the booming canal days.

Shenandoah, Virvinia

Established in December of 1935, it became the first national park created from a large, populated expanse of private land.

At 4,051 feet, Hawksbill Mountain is the highest peak in the park. It's more than 10,000 feet lower than the summit of Mount Whitney (located in Sequoia–Kings Canyon National Park), the highest peak in the contiguous United States.

Mammoth Cave, Kentucky

It earned its name from the size of its chambers, not from the prehistoric mammoth.

In 1839, Dr. Croghan purchased Mammoth Cave. He believed its preservative qualities would aid in the recovery of his patients suffering from tuberculosis, which had no known cure at the time.

Great Smoky Mountains, Tennessee/North Carolina

Receiving about 10 million annual visitors, it is the most visited U.S. National Park.

It is the most polluted national park, with about 30 days of poor air quality per year.

It is the first national park in which federal funds were used to buy land.

It has the greatest biodiversity of any region in a temperate climate zone.

At 6,643 feet, Clingman's Dome is the third highest peak east of the Mississippi.

Congaree, South Carolina

This region was called Congaree Swamp National Monument until 2003 (when Congress made it a national park), but it is actually a floodplain. A floodplain is a flat or nearly flat land that experiences periodic flooding. A swamp is a wetland with shallow bodies of water and a number of hammocks, or dry-land protrusions.

Alligator crossing (Everglades)

Everglades, Florida
It was the first park created to protect a threatened ecosystem.

It protects the largest wilderness area east of the Mississippi and is the third largest national park in the contiguous U.S. behind only Yellowstone and Death Valley.

It protects the largest continuous stretch of mangroves in the world and at least 36 threatened or endangered species reside in the park.

Elevation within the park does not surpass eight feet above sea level.

It is the only place in the world where alligators and crocodiles are found side by side.

It is the most significant breeding ground for tropical wading birds in North America.

Isle Royale, Michigan
Lake Superior is the largest of the Great Lakes in surface area (31,820 mi²) and volume (2,900 mi³). It is the largest freshwater lake in the world (by surface area), and the third largest in volume (exceeded only by Lake Baikal in Siberia and Lake Tanganyika in Africa).

Lake Superior accounts for roughly 10% of the world's surface freshwater. Water from all other Great Lakes could fit inside Lake Superior.

Lake Superior holds enough water to cover the 48 contiguous states at a uniform depth of 5 feet.

It is the cleanest Great Lake. Average underwater visibility is 27 feet.

A paddler who stops at Siskiwit Lake's Ryan Island is on the largest island on the largest lake (Siskiwit) on the largest island (Isle Royale) on the largest freshwater lake in the world (Lake Superior).

If you were to walk the entire shoreline of Lake Superior, you would cover 2,726 miles (including islands).

Voyageurs, Minnesota
There are no drive-in campsites at Voyageurs National Park, but there are more than 270 boat accessible sites dispersed across hundreds of miles of shoreline within park boundaries.

This area wasn't popular for just fur-trading, logging, and fishing; during the time of prohibition, it was a haven for bootleggers.

Badlands, South Dakota
It was originally named Teton National Park.

It's one of the world's richest fossil beds. A 35-million-year-old tortoise fossil is one of many big finds.

Wind Cave, South Dakota
It was established in 1903 by President Theodore Roosevelt, one of the leading advocates of the National Park Idea.

It was the first park established to protect a cave.

It was the 8th national park established in the U.S. and today it's the 7th oldest.

With more than 140 miles of explored passages, it is the 6th longest cave in the world. Estimates predict that only 5% of the cave has been discovered.

Old Faithful (Yellowstone)

It is considered to be the densest cave in the world based on volume of passages per area.

Wind Cave is most notable for its calcite formations known as boxwork. It contains 95% of the world's discovered boxwork cave formations, but very few stalactites and stalagmites.

TheodoreRoosevelt, North Dakota

Theodore Roosevelt conserved an estimated 230 million acres of land by establishing 51 Federal Bird Reservations, 4 National Game Reserves, 150 National Forests, 5 National Parks, and 18 National Monuments.

He inspired the creation of the "Teddy" Bear by refusing to shoot a bear tied and beaten by his attendants because it would be unsportsmanlike.

He became the 26th President of the United States after the assassination of President William McKinley.

He remains the youngest person to assume the office of President of the United States.

Theodore Roosevelt survived an attempted assassination while campaigning in Milwaukee, WI as the Bull Moose Party's presidential candidate. The assassin's bullet passed through a 50-page speech and the eyeglasses case he had in his pocket before becoming lodged in his chest. He completed the 90-minute speech before going to the hospital.

He won the Nobel Peace Prize for helping negotiate the end of the Russo–Japanese War.

He served as New York City Police Commissioner, creating drastic reform in one of America's most corrupt police departments.

He was colonel of the "Rough Riders" during the Spanish–American War.

He wrote 35 books and hundreds of articles.

In 1905, he demanded football change their rules to become safer after 18 deaths in the sport that year. From his meeting, the forward pass was installed, a neutral zone where six men needed to be lined up was established, the first down was changed from 5 to 10 yards, and gang tackling and mass formations were banned.

Grand Teton, Wyoming

It is home to the largest wintering elk herd in North America.

No one had settled along the west bank of Snake River until the 1890s when Bill Menor built a ferry at Moose to transport patrons across the river.

Yellowstone, Wyoming/Idaho/Montana

It is the world's first national park.

At more than 2.2 million acres, it is larger than Rhode Island and Delaware combined. Roughly 96% of the land is in Wyoming, another 3% in Montana, and 1% in Idaho. About 80% of the park land is forested.

Yellowstone Lake (131.7 mi²) is one of the largest high-altitude lakes in North America.

There are approximately 290 year-round waterfalls higher than 15 feet, including Lower Falls of the Yellowstone River (308 feet), tallest in the park.

Half of the world's geothermal features, including 300 geysers, are found at Yellowstone.

Steamboat Geyser (Norris Geyser Basin), at more than 400 feet is the tallest geyser in the world, erupting with no noticeable pattern and sometimes years between eruptions.

Old Faithful spouts 3,700 to 8,400 gallons of 204°F water about 100 feet in the air every 60–110 minutes.

Mammoth Hot Springs deposits an estimated two tons of calcium carbonate each day.

Geyser basins are full of interesting color combinations. The blues of Norris are due to silica in suspension in the water. Red-orange colors are often caused by cyanobacteria or iron-oxides and arsenic compounds. Some springs are emerald green in color; this is due to blue refracted light in combination with yellow sulfur lining the pool.

Guadalupe Mountains, Texas
Guadalupe Peak (8,479 feet) is the highest point in Texas. The next three highest peaks are also in the Guadalupe Range.

Carlsbad Caverns, New Mexico
From mid-April until mid-October nearly 400,000 Mexican free-tailed bats call Carlsbad Caverns home.

The park possesses more than 110 caves, and Carlsbad is one of the deepest and most ornate caves ever found.

At more than 138 miles, Lechuguilla Cave is the 7th longest known cave in the world.

Petrified Forest, Arizona
Petrified trees found here have not been alive for at least 225 million years.

Humans have inhabited this area for more than 10,000 years, leaving a wealth of archeological sites in addition to the world class fossil record.

Newspaper Rock features more than 600 petroglyphs. Some are calendars, marking events like the summer solstice.

Rocky Mountain, Colorado
There are more than 60 peaks greater than 12,000 feet (the tallest being Longs Peak at 14,259 ft), 450 miles of streams, and 150 lakes within the park.

Great Sand Dunes, Colorado
The Ladies' PEO (Professional Employer Organization) was the driving force behind the original effort to make Great Sand Dunes a national monument.

Ute, Apache, and other tribes used pine tree bark for food and medicine. Many pealed trees are still living within the park today.

Black Canyon of the Gunnison, Colorado
Black Canyon's Painted Wall is the tallest cliff in Colorado at 2,250 ft.

At 2 billion years old, the canyon's Precambrian rock is some of the oldest on earth.

Mesa Verde, Colorado
It is the first park to celebrate prehistoric culture rather than grand scenery.

There are more than 4,700 archeological sites at Mesa Verde, but only 600 or so are cliff dwellings. Most are mesa top pueblos, farming terraces, towers, reservoirs, and check dams.

With 150 rooms and 75 open areas, Cliff Palace is the largest cliff dwelling in the park (and in North America). It has 21 kivas and could house as many as 100 to 120 Ancestral Puebloans at any one time. Long House also has 150 rooms and Spruce Tree House has 130.

Large structures are not the norm. Roughly 90% of Mesa Verde's cliff dwellings contain fewer than 10 rooms.

Arches, Utah
To be considered an arch, the rock's opening must measure at least three feet (in any direction). There are more than 2,500 arches within the park.

Canyonlands, Utah
Island in the Sky received its name because it sits on a broad and level mesa some 2,000 feet above the Colorado and Green Rivers.

Needles District is named for the pinnacles, featuring red and white layers that dominate the landscape.

Some petroglyphs and pictographs found at Horseshoe Canyon were painted more than 3,000 years ago. They are some of the oldest cultural artifacts in North America.

Capitol Reef, Utah
Fruita is home to roughly 3,000 fruit and nut trees, making it the largest historic orchard in the National Park System.

It was originally called "Wayne Wonderland." The park's original supporters, Ephraim P. Pectol and Joseph S. Hickman named it after Wayne County.

Badwater (Death Valley)

Zion, Utah

In 1918, the director of the National Park Service renamed Mukuntuweap National Park to Zion, making it easier to say and promote.

Red and tan Navajo Sandstone of Zion Canyon has been exposed by the work of the Virgin River, which transports millions of tons of sediment to the Colorado River each year.

The Virgin River drops 50–80 feet per mile, one of the steepest stream gradients in North America.

Grand Canyon, Arizona

Bills to create Grand Canyon National Park were proposed in 1882, 1883, and 1886. Had any one passed it would have been the second national park.

Evidence suggests the Colorado River established its course through the canyon 17 million years ago.

The Colorado River is about 1,450 miles long, of which 277 miles passes through the Grand Canyon.

Great Basin, Nevada

Bristlecone pines live longer (4,000+ years) than any known organism. Their needles alone can live 25–40 years.

Channel Islands, California

Island foxes are extremely small. The average weight of an adult male is 5–6 pounds, roughly the size of a domesticated cat.

Santa Cruz Island's Painted Cave is one of the world's largest and deepest sea caves. It measures 1,215-feet long, 100-feet wide, and has a 160-foot entrance.

Death Valley, California/Nevada

At 282 feet below sea level, Badwater Basin is the lowest place in North America and one of the lowest places in the world. The Dead Sea (1,388 feet) is the lowest.

Pinnacles, California

Over 400 species of bees reside in the park, the greatest diversity per area.

With a 9.5-ft wingspan and weighing up to 25 pounds, the California condor is the largest land bird in North America.

Sequoia & Kings Canyon, California

Sequoia is the second oldest National Park.

The 2,200-year-old giant sequoia named General Sherman is the world's largest tree (by volume). It has a circumference of 103 feet and its trunk weighs 1,385 tons.

General Sherman's estimated volume is 52,600 ft^3, about the same volume as 16 blue whales, the world's largest mammal.

General Sherman's first large branch (which is seven feet in diameter) is 130 feet above the tree's base.

Every year the General Sherman grows enough new wood to make a 60-foot-tall tree of typical proportions.

Giant sequoia seeds are the size of oat flakes.

Hale Tharp, the first settler of European descent, lived in a hollowed-out sequoia.

At 14,494 feet, Mount Whitney is the tallest mountain in the contiguous United States.

Tall Trees Trail (Redwood)

Yosemite, California

On June 10, 1864, Abraham Lincoln signed a bill preserving Yosemite Valley and a grove of sequoias, two sites, thousands of miles away, that he had never seen.

Yosemite Valley's development was designed by Frederick Law Olmsted, the famous designer of New York City's Central Park.

In 1869, a wandering Scottish shepherd, originally raised in Wisconsin, began working at a sawmill in Yosemite Valley. The "unknown nobody" was 31-year-old John Muir.

It took the first tourists 4–5 days to reach Yosemite Valley by carriage, horse, and foot from San Francisco.

Yosemite Falls (2,425 feet) is the tallest waterfall in North America. It is fed mostly by snowmelt, with peak flow usually occurring in late May. It is often dry by August, but begins to flow once more when winter snow arrives in the surrounding mountains.

El Capitán is the largest granite monolith in the world.

Bridalveil Falls, originally named "Pohono," was renamed by James Hutchings for tourism.

Lassen Volcanic, California

Prior to the eruption of Mount St. Helens in 1980, Lassen Peak, the largest plug dome volcano in the world, was the last volcanic explosion in the Cascade Range.

Brokeoff Mountain was once part of a volcano that towered 1,000 feet above Lassen Peak.

Redwood, California

Redwoods are the world's tallest living trees. They can grow to weigh more than 500 tons and taller than the Statue of Liberty (including its base).

Measuring in at 379.1 feet, Hyperion is the tallest tree in the park.

A redwood's trunk can grow up to 22 feet in diameter with bark more than 12 inches thick.

A single coastal redwood tree consumes up to 500 gallons of water each day. Fog can account for up to one third of the water needed for each tree to survive.

Redwoods used to grow all over the northern hemisphere: in Greenland, and much of Europe and Asia.

Crater Lake, Oregon

Crater Lake is the 6th oldest national park.

Crater Lake, a volcanic caldera (not a meteor crater!), was formed when a massive eruption caused Mount Mazama to collapse.

At 1,943 feet, filled almost entirely by rain and snow, it is the deepest Lake in the U.S.

The lake's depth varies about 3 feet seasonally. Incoming flow is balanced by seepage and evaporation.

Grassy Pass (Denali)

Mount Rainier, Washington
Carbon Glacier, located on the mountain's north side, is the lowest (3,500 feet), thickest (700 feet), and largest glacier by volume in the contiguous United States. Emmons Glacier is the largest by area.

North Cascades, Washington
More than half the contiguous United States' glaciers are concentrated in the North Cascades.

Denali, Alaska
In 2005, a dinosaur footprint was found here.

Virgin Islands, U.S. Virgin Islands
Laurence Rockefeller bought 5,000 acres of land on St. Johns (more than half the island) and donated it to the National Park Service.

Haleakalā, Hawai'i
Haleakalā Volcano has been dormant since 1490.

The Kingdom of Hawai'i was annexed as a territory of the United States in 1898, but it didn't become the 50th state until 1959.

Haleakalā and Hawai'i Volcanoes were originally combined as Hawai'i National Park (established in 1916). In 1951 Kīpahulu Valley was added to the park land. Ten years later, it was split into Haleakalā and Hawai'i Volcanoes National Parks.

On a clear day you can see across the channel from the Kīpahulu area to the island of Hawai'i.

Bamboo found along Pīpīwai Trail is one of the park's many non-native plants.

Nēnē, the Hawaiian goose, became extinct at Haleakalā, but they were reintroduced in 1946 with the help of the Boy Scouts.

More endangered species live in Haleakalā than any other national park in the United States.

Hawai'i Volcanoes, Hawai'i
Five volcanoes make up the island of Hawai'i: Kohala, Mauna Kea, Hualalai, Mauna Loa, and Kīlauea.

Kīlauea, the world's most active volcano, has been erupting continuously since 1983.

Lava pouring into the Pacific (2012, Hawai'i Volcanoes)

The current eruption (by volume) of Kīlauea volcano is 250,000–650,000 yards³/day (200,000–500,000 meters³/day). That is enough to resurface a 20-mile-long two lane road (like Chain of Craters Road) every day. Most of Kīlauea's lava is transported by lava tubes to the ocean.

Kīlauea's eruption is the most long-lived in historical times. It's impossible to know when the eruption will stop, but many scientists believe it could last for more than a century.

John Muir and former President Theodore Roosevelt were among the original advocates for Hawai'i Volcanoes National Park.

Stephen Mather and Horace Albright spearheaded the acquisition of the Footprints.

Mauna Loa last erupted in 1984.

The park is home to Anax strenuous, the largest dragonfly in the United States.

Eventually (a long long time from now) the island of Hawai'i will sink beneath the ocean's surface.

Lo'ihi, a future Hawaiian Island, is already being formed 21 miles off the coast of the Big Island by a giant undersea volcano.

It will take Lo'ihi more than 100,000 years to breach the ocean's surface.

Midway Geyser Basin (Yellowstone)

Suggested Trips

I've put together a few suggested trips to help plan your national parks vacation. Trip mileage and duration was estimated based on departure from the nearest major city. Choosing where to spend the night, what to pack, when and where to eat, and whether you obey the speed limit are completely up to you. I've also included a few suggested pit-stops to help break up particularly long stretches spent behind the windshield.

Rocky Mountain High
Parks Visited: Grand Teton (2 nights, page 206), Yellowstone (3 nights, page 218), and Glacier (4 nights, page 246)

Begins/Ends: Jackson, WY
Estimated Driving Distance: 1,200 miles
Estimated Trip Length: 10 days

Road Trip Breakdown
Jackson, WY to Grand Teton: 41 miles, ~1 hour via US-191
Grand Teton to Yellowstone: 55 miles, ~1.5 hours via US-191/ John D. Rockefeller, Jr. Memorial Pkwy
Yellowstone to Glacier: 460 miles, ~9 hours via US-89, I-90, US-287, and US-89.
Glacier to Jackson: 514 miles, ~9 hours via several Montana State Highways, I-90, and I-15

Potential Pit-Stops: Bar T 5 Covered Wagon Cookout (800.772.5386, bart5.com), Museum of the Rockies (406.994.2251, museumoftherock-ies.org), Montana State Capitol, The Montana Historical Society (406.444.2694, mhs.mt.gov), Last Chance Train Tours (406.442.1023, lctours.com), Holter Museum of Art (406.442.6400, holtermuseum.org), Conrad Mansion Museum (406.755.2166, conradmansion.com), Butte Trolley Tour (406.723.3177), Craters of the Moon National Monument (208.527.1335, nps.gov/crmo)

Notes: The parks are open year-round, but Teton Park Road, Yellowstone Park Roads, and Going-to-the-Sun Road all close seasonally.

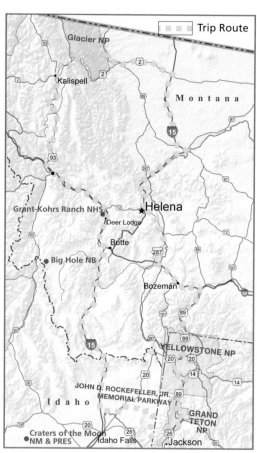

Cascades and Coastland

Parks Visited: North Cascades (2 nights, page 592), Mount Rainier (3 nights, page 566), and Olympic (3 nights, page 578)

Begins/Ends: Seattle, WA
Estimated Driving Distance: 600 miles
Estimated Trip Length: 1 week

Potential Pit-Stops: Mount Vernon, Mount St. Helens National Volcanic Monument (360.449.7800, fs.usda.gov), Harbinger Winery (360.452.4262, harbingerwinery.com)

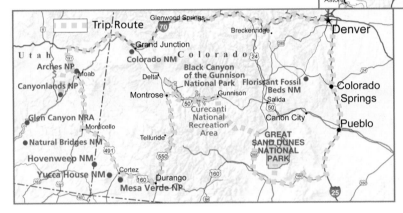

Canyons and Culture

Parks Visited: Great Sand Dunes (2 nights, page 340), Black Canyon of the Gunnison (2 nights, page 348), Mesa Verde (2 nights, page 356), Canyonlands (2 nights, page 378), and Arches (2 nights, page 370)

Begins/Ends: Denver, CO
Estimated Driving Distance: 1,300 miles
Estimated Trip Length: 10 days

Potential Pit-Stops: Florissant Fossil Beds (719.748.3253, nps.gov/flfo), Garden of the Gods (719.634.6666, gardenofgods.com), Maroon Bells, Curecanti NRA (970.641.2337, nps.gov/cure), Museum of the Mountain West (970.240-3400, mountainwestmuseum.com), Durango & Silverton Narrow Gauge Railroad & Museum (888.872.4607, durangotrain.com), Soaring Tree Top Adventures (970.769.2357, soaringcolorado.com), Yucca House NM (970.529.4465, nps.gov/yuho), Hovenweep NM (970.562.4282, nps.gov/hove), Dead Horse Point State Park (435.259.2614, stateparks.utah.gov/parks/dead-horse)

Best of the Midwest

Parks Visited: Isle Royale (3 nights, page 154), and Voyageurs (3 nights, page 166)

Begins/Ends: Minneapolis, MN
Estimated Driving Distance: 850 miles
Estimated Trip Length: 1 week

Potential Pit-Stops: Apostle Islands NL (715.779.3397, nps.gov/apis), Devil's Kettle Waterfall (Judge Magney State Park), Grand Portage NM (218.475.0123, nps.gov/grpo), NA Bear Center (877.365.7879, bear.org), Boundary Waters Canoe Area (canoecountry.com), Dorothy Molter Museum (218.365.4451, rootbeerlady.com), International Wolf Center (wolf.org).

Notes: Isle Royale is only reached by boat or plane. See page 158 for transportation details.

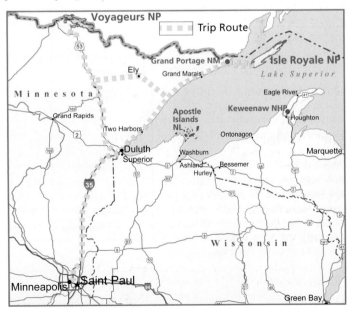

Drive in John Muir's Footsteps

Parks Visited: Yosemite (3 nights, page 514), Sequoia & Kings Canyon (3 nights, page 502)

Begins/Ends: San Francisco, CA
Estimated Distance/Length: 650 miles/1 week

Potential Pit-Stops: Golden Gate NRA (415.561.4700, nps.gov/goga), Alcatraz, John Muir Woods NM (415.388.2595, nps.gov/muwo), Devil's Postpile NM (760.934.2289, nps.gov/depo), Pinnacles National Park (it wasn't one of Muir's favorites, but the newest national park is pretty cool—check out page 480 for details)

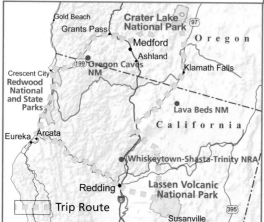

Dormant Volcanoes and Dominant Trees

Parks Visited: Lassen Volcanic (2 nights, page 538), Crater Lake (2 nights, page 554), and Redwood (2 nights, page 546)

Begins/Ends: Redding, CA
Estimated Driving Distance: 700 miles
Estimated Trip Length: 1 week

Potential Pit-Stops: Whiskeytown NRA (530.246.1225, nps.gov/whis), Lava Beds NM (530.667.8113, nps.gov/labe), Oregon Caves NM (541.592.2100, nps.gov/orca), Out 'n' About Treesort (541.592.2208, treehouses.com)

Notes: Crater Lake NP's Rim Drive typically opens completely in July.

Desert Drive

Parks Visited: Saguaro (2 nights, page 312), Guadalupe Mtns (2 nights, page 288), Carlsbad Caverns (2 nights, page 296), Albuquerque (2 nights), Petrified Forest (1 night, page 304)

Begins/Ends: Phoenix, AZ
Distance/Length: 1,400 mi/10 Days

Potential Pit-Stops: The map is covered with national monuments, memorials, and historic sites. In addition to these you'll find Wupatki NM (nps.gov/wupa), Sunset Crater Volcano NM (nps.gov/sucr), and Lava Rider Cave of the Coconino National Forest near Flagstaff.

Orcas (Kenai Fjords)

Exploring the Last Frontier

Parks Visited: Kenai Fjords (2 nights, page 630), Wrangell–St. Elias (3 nights, page 614), and Denali (4 nights, page 620)

Begins/Ends: Anchorage, AK
Estimated Driving Distance: 1,200 miles
Estimated Trip Length: 10 days

Potential Pit-Stops: Anchorage Museum (907.929.9200, anchoragemuseum.org), Alaska Native Heritage Center (800.315.6608, alaskanative.net), Bardy's Trail Rides (907.362.7863, sewardhorses.com)

Notes: All park roads are seasonal. Kenai Fjords offers one road to Exit Glacier. Wrangell–St. Elias has two access roads, but most of the park is undeveloped wilderness. Denali Park Road is only open to tour buses (fee).

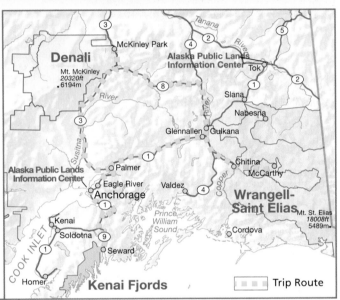

Cruising Canyon Country

Parks Visited: Grand Canyon (3 nights, page 422), Bryce Canyon (2 nights, page 398), Capitol Reef (1 night, page 390), and Zion (3 nights, page 410)

Begins/Ends: Las Vegas, NV
Estimated Driving Distance: 1,100 miles
Estimated Trip Length: 10 days

Potential Pit-Stops: Hoover Dam (702.494.2517), Lake Mead NRA (702.293.8990, nps.gov/lake), Route 66 Museum (866.427.7866, kingmantourism.org), Glen Canyon NRA (928.608.6200, nps.gov/glca), Coral Pink Sand Dunes State Park (435.648.2800, state-parks.utah.gov/parks/coral-pink), Best Friends Animal Sanctuary (435.644.2001, bestfriends.org), Vermillion Cliffs National Monument w/ The Wave and Buckskin Gulch (435.688.3200, blm.gov/az), Grand Staircase Escalante-National Monument (435.644.1200, blm.gov/ut), Cedar Breaks NM (435.586.9451, nps.gov/cebr)

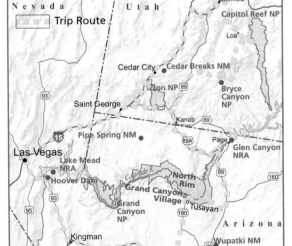

Fort Jefferson on Garden Key (Dry Tortugas)

Badlands are Good Lands

Parks Visited: Wind Cave (2 nights, page 186), Badlands (2 nights, page 178), and Theodore Roosevelt (2 nights, page 194)

Begins/Ends: Rapid City, SD
Estimated Driving Distance: 850 miles
Estimated Trip Length: 1 week

Road Trip Breakdown

Rapid City to Wind Cave: 60 miles, ~1 hour via US-16, US-385, and SD-87
Wind Cave to Badlands: 125 miles, ~2.5 hours via Rapid City and I-90
Badlands to Theodore Roosevelt: 300 miles, ~5.5 hours via Rapid City, US-85, and I-94
Theodore Roosevelt to Rapid City: 240 miles, ~4 hours

Potential Pit-Stops: Mount Rushmore National Memorial (605.574.2523, nps. gov/moru), Jewel Cave National Monument (nps.gov/jeca, 605.673.8300), The Mammoth Site (605.745.6017, mammothsite.com), Motorcycle Hall of Fame (614.856.2222, motorcyclemuseum.org), Reptile Gardens (605.342.5873, reptilegardens.com), Storybook Island (605.342.6357, storybookisland.org), Circle B Chuckwagon (605.574.2129, circle-b-ranch.com), Cosmos Mystery Area (605.343.9802, cosmosmysteryarea.com), Museum of Geology (605.394.2467, museum.sdsmt.edu)

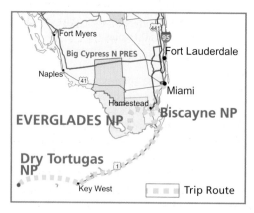

The Scenic Side of South Florida

Parks Visited: Biscayne (1 night, page 124), Everglades (3 nights, page 130), and Dry Tortugas (2 nights, page 142)

Begins/Ends: Miami, FL
Estimated Driving Distance: 450 miles
Estimated Trip Length: 1 week

Potential Pit-Stops: John Pennekamp, Bahia Honda, Curry Hammock, and Long Key State Parks (850. 245.2157, floridastateparks.org)

Notes: Dry Tortugas can only be reached by boat or floatplane and the only overnight accommodations consist of 8 primitive campsites.

Bison crossing the Little Mo (Theodore Roosevelt)

How to Use this Book

About the Guide

The United States has 59 national parks. Each one is uniquely beautiful, brimming with life, adventure, and fun. Activities and attractions differ from park-to-park and season-to-season, and the possibilities are nearly limitless. But most visitors only have a few days to explore these vast expanses of unspoiled wilderness. To make those few days count, plan your trip wisely with the help of a guide who has tested the park's trails and learned its history.

Let this book be *Your Guide to the National Parks of the United States*. The 59 national parks are broken into seven regions: East, North, South, Southwest, West, Alaska, and Remote Islands (see the following page). Within these sections the parks are included in geographical order (not alphabetical), allowing parks that are commonly visited on the same trip to be found adjacent to one another. Each park section includes an introduction, basic logistical information, maps, popular activities, the basics (accessibility, pets, and weather), and a brief vacation planner. You'll also find a collection of popular restaurants, grocery stores, lodging facilities, festivals, and attractions (including commercial outfitters) that are located nearby. All information has been researched and assembled with the greatest attention to detail so that the parks' most interesting facts and exciting activities are right here at your fingertips.

Introductions

"There is nothing more practical than the preservation of beauty, than the preservation of anything that appeals to the higher emotions of mankind."

– Theodore Roosevelt

President Theodore Roosevelt was a practical man who liked big things, so it comes as no surprise that he was one of the most influential individuals in the history of the national parks. Each introduction tells stories about men and women like President Roosevelt and events—both natural and historic—that helped shape the parks as we know them today.

Logistics

Logistical data like contact information, accommodations, operating hours, and entrance fees are listed right up front alongside the introduction. Close by you'll find a "When to Go" section. It includes practical information about peak seasons and closures. Hours of operation for primary visitor facilities may also be detailed here. A "Transportation & Airports" section covers all pertinent information about how to travel to and around each park. Everything you need to know about park shuttles, airports, and Amtrak is found here. Driving directions are typically provided to the park's most popular entrance(s) and are often accompanied with a regional map displaying major highways and interstates. If a park has multiple units or popular developed regions you can expect to find a "Regions" section describing each one. Names, locations, dates, and rates of campgrounds and lodges found within the park are usually listed in an easy to read table. Accommodations beyond park boundaries are discussed in the "What's Nearby" sections of this guidebook.

Maps

Large legible maps are included to aid in planning your trip. Markers help pinpoint trailheads and popular attractions.

The maps in this book are not intended for hiking. You can purchase a high-quality topographical park map at most visitor centers. Suggested Trips (pages 28–32) and What's Nearby maps only show federal highways and interstates. Always use a road map or GPS when traveling.

North

↑

0   100   200 Kilometers
0   100   200 Miles

○ National Park Service unit

North Cascades

Olympic ○

WASHINGTON

Glacier ○

MONTANA

Theodore Roosevelt

Mount Rainier ○

WEST
(pages 460–603)

NORTH
(pages 154–269)

IDAHO

Crater Lake ○

OREGON

Yellowstone ○

Grand Teton ○

Badlands

Wind Cave

Redwood ○

Lassen Volcanic ○

NEVADA

WYOMING

CALIFORNIA

SOUTHWEST
(pages 326–459)

COLORADO

Rocky Mount

ALASKA
(pages 604–663)

Gates of the Arctic

Kobuk Valley ○

Yosemite ○

Great Basin ○

UTAH

Capitol Reef ○

Arches ○

Black Canyon of
the Gunnison

Kings Canyon ○

Zion ○

Canyonlands

Great Sand D

Pinnacles ○

Sequoia ○

Bryce Canyon ○

Denali ○

Death Valley ○

Mesa Verde ○

Grand Canyon ○

Channel Islands ○

Petrified Forest ○

Joshua Tree ○

SOUTH
(pages 270–325)

Wrangell-St. Elias ○

ARIZONA

NEW MEXICO

Lake Clark ○

Saguaro ○

Kenai Fjords

Carlsbad Caverns ○

Katmai ○

Guadalupe Mountains ○

Glacier Bay ○

Big Bend ○

THE REMOTE ISLANDS (pages 664–705)

United States Territories

Haleakala

Virgin Islands

HAWAII

National Park of
American Samoa

VIRGIN ISLANDS

Hawai'i Volcanoes ○

AMERICAN SAMOA

Voyageurs

Isle Royale

NORTH DAKOTA

MINNESOTA

MAINE

Acadia

SOUTH DAKOTA

WISCONSIN

VT.

N.H.

NEW
YORK

MASS.

IOWA

MICHIGAN

CONN.

R.I.

NORTH
(pages 154–269)

NEBRASKA

ILLINOIS

INDIANA

Cuyahoga Valley

OHIO

PENNSYLVANIA

N.J.

tain

KANSAS

MD.

DEL.

WEST
VIRGINIA

Shenandoah

MISSOURI

KENTUCKY

VIRGINIA

Dunes

OKLAHOMA

Mammoth Cave

EAST
(pages 38–153)

ARKANSAS

Great Smoky Mountains

TENNESSEE

NORTH
CAROLINA

SOUTH
CAROLINA

Congaree

Hot Springs

SOUTH
(pages 270–325)

MISSISSIPPI

GEORGIA

ALABAMA

TEXAS

LOUISIANA

North

0   100   200 Kilometers

0   100   200 Miles

National Park Service unit

FLORIDA

Biscayne

Everglades

Dry Tortugas

Activities

The activity most often associated with a trip to one of the national parks is hiking. (Don't forget to pack your hiking shoes.) This guidebook chronicles hiking in great detail. Most park sections include a hiking table with essential trail information like trailhead location, distance, and difficulty. More often than not trailheads are assigned a number corresponding to a marker on the park map at the trailhead location. Hiking is often the main attraction, but there's much more to do. You can do everything from SCUBA diving to flightseeing, mule rides to train excursions, biking to snowmobiling. All the most popular activities are discussed and outfitter information (including pricing) is included whenever applicable. These sections are concluded by a quick discussion about the park's best adult- and child-oriented activities: Ranger and Junior Ranger Programs.

The Basics

Ranger Programs: Ranger Programs vary from park-to-park, but expect a variety of walks, talks, and evening programs to be offered, especially if you're traveling during peak tourism season. Park rangers live in the parks and they are gracious hosts. Take a tour with a ranger to get a taste of their enthusiasm, knowledge, and humor. Most of the programs are free. Ranger program schedules change from week-to-week and year-to-year. For a current schedule of events, check the park's website, free newspaper, or bulletin boards conveniently located at campgrounds, visitor centers, and sometimes along roadways.

For Kids: Kids of all ages are invited to participate in each park's Junior Ranger Program. Activity booklets are typically free. These hard copies allow families to complete the Junior Ranger activities on their own terms. Activities may direct children to places especially interesting to younger visitors, or to other ranger-guided programs. After completing a specified number of activities for the child's age, participants return the booklet to a park ranger and he or she is awarded a patch, badge, and/or certificate. While these activities are designed specifically for kids, your entire family may discover the importance of the park and gain a more intimate connection with these special places.

Flora & Fauna: Information ranges from plants and animals you're likely to encounter to invasive, endangered, and reintroduced species found throughout the park.

Pets: Next up are the animals we bring with us, our pets. In general pets are not allowed on trails, in buildings, or in the backcountry. Bringing your pet with you will greatly limit what you can do during the course of your visit. If you still wish to bring your pet, it must be kept on a leash no more than six feet in length at all times.

Accessibility: The parks are constantly working to increase the accessibility of trails, attractions, and facilities, but many still fail to meet ADA guidelines. If you or someone you are traveling with has any special needs it is best to discuss them with a park employee at least a week before

arriving. We provide a brief overview of accessible facilities and trails.

Weather: A small graph of average temperatures and precipitation provides a quick glimpse of what you can expect weather-wise throughout the year. Weather is difficult to predict, so these averages only provide a baseline for planning. Whether you're departing on a 2-hour hike or a multi-day trek, make a habit of checking the local weather forecast before departing.

Vacation Planner

Vacation planners are provided for the most popular parks, supplying a rough itinerary, quickly hitting the most popular attractions in an efficient manner. With that said, you're doing a disservice to yourself and your family if you only allow a few hours (or a day or two) for a national park excursion. The best advice you can receive is to slow down, take your time, get out of your car and enjoy these magnificent landscapes. Don't be afraid to explore on your own. Venture away from the crowds, off the beaten path. If what they say about "misery loving company" is true, then maybe "happiness loves solitude." In my mind, there's no better place to find solitude than these parks, and it usually only takes a couple miles of hiking to find a little slice of it for yourself.

What's Nearby

This section details the most exciting road-trip pit-stops (many deserve an extended stay) you might be driving by, as well as restaurants, grocery stores, lodging facilities, and festivals outside park boundaries.

Welcome to Your
National Parks

Sun setting over Eagle Lake

Acadia

PO Box 177
Bar Harbor, ME 04609
Phone: (207) 288-3338
Website: nps.gov/acad

Established: February 26, 1919
July 8, 1916 (National Monument)
Size: 47,390 Acres
Annual Visitors: 2.8 Million
Peak Season: July–August
Hiking Trails: 140 Miles
Carriage Trails: 45 Miles

Activities: Hiking, Biking, Rock
Climbing, Fishing, Paddling, and
Whale and Bird Watching

Campgrounds: Blackwoods and
Seawall on Mount Desert Island
and Schoodic Woods on the
Schoodic Peninsula ($30/night),
Duck Harbor on Isle au Haut ($25/
permit, 3-night max)
Backcountry Camping: Not Allowed

Park Hours: All day, every day
Entrance Fee (May–October):
$25/vehicle, $12/individual (foot,
bike, etc.)

The coast of Maine and Mount Desert Island (MDI) has an allure, a gravity that inexplicably draws people away from their big city life and frantic lifestyles. Here time slows down; visitors are given the chance to enjoy the little things that often go unnoticed. Nature is heard. Waves cracking against granite cliffs. A bullfrog's guttural croak. The rat-a-tat-tat of a woodpecker. A choir of singing sparrows. While it can feel like your first time truly experiencing nature, today's tourists are far from the first to enjoy the beauty of Maine's Atlantic Coast. The deep blue lakes, bald granite mountaintops, and surf splashed cliffs of Acadia National Park have been treasured for more than a century.

About 25,000 years ago MDI wasn't even an island. It was continental mainland, occupied by a massive sheet of ice. The ice receded, but not without leaving a number of visible marks. Somes Sound, the only fjord along the U.S. Atlantic Coast, was carved by slow moving glacial ice, and then submerged when it melted. Bubble Rock, a 14-ton glacial erratic, was carried 19 miles from its original resting place to be deposited precariously at the top of South Bubble. As the ice melted, water poured down the slopes of the recently shaved mountaintops; lakebeds were filled, the seas rose, and as the coast drowned in melt water an island was formed.

Long after glaciers covered the coast, the Abenaki people used the island as their seasonal home. A home they called "Pemetic" or "the sloping land." Food was abundant. Fishing and hunting were relatively simple. Shellfish, plants, and berries were easily gathered. For the Abenaki people, life was good along the coast of Maine. It also was an appropriate home for the Abenaki or "People of the Dawn": Cadillac Mountain on MDI, the tallest peak along the U.S. Atlantic Coast, is the first place in the continental U.S. to experience dawn.

In 1604, Samuel de Champlain spotted the barren peak of Cadillac Mountain from his ship. Not noticing the forested hills around it, he declared the island "l'Isle des Monts Déserts" or "the island of the bare mountains." The island may as well have been barren for the next 150 years as nations quarreled over the region. It passed hands several times between Natives, French, English, and Americans, but was never permanently occupied and seldom visited.

Thomas Cole and Frederic Church, painters from the Hudson River School, helped rediscover MDI in the mid-19th century. Their work helped bring the island into the public eye. At first, artists, professors, and other intellectuals known as "rusticators" made the multi-day journey here. These travelers required little in terms of accommodations as they hiked from place-to-place enjoying the area's simple lifestyle and sublime beauty.

Not long after the rusticators exposed MDI's beauty, developers were clamoring to increase access to the island. Direct steamboat service from Boston was offered in the 1860s. A rail line was completed in the 1880s. By this time MDI was the place to be for the East Coast's elite. Some of the wealthiest visitors, known locally as "cottagers," purchased large tracts of land where they built lavish summer homes they ironically referred to as "cottages." A stretch of mansions near Bar Harbor commonly called "Millionaires' Row" burned to the ground during the great fire of 1947. The inferno razed more than 17,000 acres, including 10,000 acres of park land, before blowing into the Atlantic.

Still, development was MDI's main threat, not nature. Residents felt that its scenic beauty needed to be protected. John D. Rockefeller, Jr. and George B. Dorr, both "cottagers" turned conservationists, were two of the park's greatest advocates. Rockefeller built 57 miles of carriage roads, donated thousands of acres of land, and spent $3.5 million on the potential park. Dorr blazed trails, donated land, and became the park's first superintendent. Acadia National Park was eventually created, cobbled together entirely from private donations. It successfully protected some of the area's most rugged shorelines and beautiful landscapes for the enjoyment of the people.

When to Go
Acadia is open all year. The park experiences heavy traffic during July and August. Fall foliage attracts large crowds from September to early October. **Hulls Cove Visitor Center** is closed from November through mid-April. Most of Park Loop Road is closed from December through mid-April.

Blackwoods Campground is open all year. The campground entrance road is closed from December through March; at this time campers must hike in from the entrance on Route 3.

Transportation & Airports
Help reduce traffic congestion, parking, and air pollution by riding the free **Island Explorer Shuttle**. The shuttle runs from late June through mid-October. Eight regularly scheduled routes link hotels, inns, campgrounds, and Bar Harbor Airport with popular park destinations (but not Cadillac Mountain). Maps and timetables are available at the visitor center and on the Island Explorer website (exploreacadia.com).

Bar Harbor Airport (BHB) is 10 miles from Hulls Cove Visitor Center. Bangor International (BGR) is 49 miles away. Portland International (PWM) is about 3 hours away. Logan International (BOS) in Boston is 5–6 hours away.

Regions of Acadia
Acadia National Park is made up of three distinct regions: Mount Desert Island (MDI), Schoodic Peninsula, and Isle au Haut. MDI is the park's centerpiece, where most attractions, lodging, and restaurants are found. The island is broken into eastern (extremely busy) and western (quiet) halves by Somes Sound. Schoodic Peninsula is the only section of the park on the mainland. It's located just east of MDI, across Frenchman Bay. You'll find views similar to those at MDI, but with much smaller crowds. Both MDI and Schoodic Peninsula are accessible by car and have scenic park loop roadways for motorists. Seven smaller islands, including Isle au Haut, are also preserved by the park. None of the smaller islands are accessible by car.

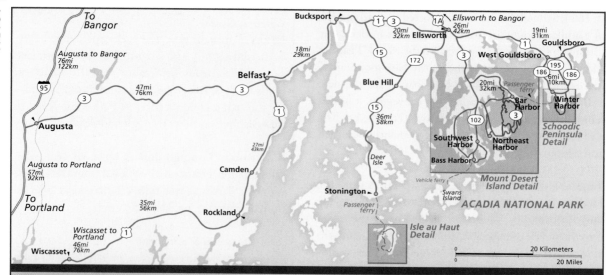

Directions

To arrive at Mount Desert Island from the south, take I-95 north to Augusta, then Route 3 east through Ellsworth and on to Mount Desert Island.

To arrive at Schoodic Peninsula from Ellsworth, take Route 3 south and turn left onto US Hwy 1. Continue east to West Gouldsboro. Go south on Route 186 to Winter Harbor, and then follow signs to the park.

Isle au Haut is inaccessible to automobiles. People may access the island by the Mail Boat from Stonington. To arrive at Stonington from Ellsworth, take Route 172 south to Route 15 and on to Stonington.

Driving

The 27-mile **Park Loop Road** is a must-see for first-time visitors. There are a number of turnouts and parking and picnic areas where you can stop and enjoy the scenery. Parking is also allowed along the road's right-hand side wherever it's one-way. Watch for evidence of the great fire of 1947 as you drive. Thick evergreen forests give way to sun-loving deciduous trees that replaced thousands of acres of pine that perished in flames. One of the most serene Park Loop Road experiences is to drive to Cadillac Mountain's summit early in the morning for sunrise. Grab a blanket, coffee, and a loved one, and then wait atop the barren peak for the first rays of light. If you can resist the temptation to return to your hotel for a nap, the early start allows you to visit popular destinations like Jordan Pond and Otter Cliffs before the afternoon crowds roll in—always a good idea during the summer months. Traffic peaks between 10am and 3pm.

Be sure to plan ahead if you will be arriving in an RV or tall vehicle, as there are four low-clearance bridges (the lowest is 10' 4"). If you'd like to escape Park Loop Road gridlock, drive on over to the Schoodic Peninsula. Here you'll find a 6-mile, one-way loop that takes you along seas that are just as angry and cliffs just as dramatic as those back on MDI.

Small islands, including Isle au Haut, are inaccessible to cars.

If you're visiting during the busy season (late June through mid-October), consider parking your car and hopping aboard the Island Explorer. In 2015, they added an eighth route around Schoodic Peninsula. It runs from the ferry terminal in Winter Harbor, to Schoodic Woods Campground, down to Schoodic Point, up to Prospect Harbor, and back to Winter Harbor. The other seven routes stay on Mount Desert Island, from Bass Harbor to Bar Harbor, and most popular destinations in between (except Cadillac Mountain). For more information about the Island Explorer, check out exploreacadia.com.

Schoodic Peninsula

About one in ten visitors of Acadia National Park make the trip to Schoodic Peninsula. Here you'll find a much more secluded and intimate experience than the park's more popular areas. But fewer visitors mean fewer facilities. There are two restrooms one picnic area, and a campground. Schoodic Woods Campground, located 3 miles southeast of Winter Harbor, offers tent and RV sites from $22 to $40 per night. It is open from late May until Columbus Day. In summer, **Downeast Windjammer Cruises** (207.288.4585, downeastwindjammer.com) operates a passenger ferry that makes the one-hour trip between Bar Harbor and Winter Harbor. **Island Explorer Shuttle** provides transportation to and from the ferry terminals. Should you choose to travel by car, it's a 45-mile drive around Frenchman Bay from Bar Harbor. Once you've arrived at the peninsula, a six-mile, one-way loop road offers stunning views of the dramatic Maine coastline. A narrow gravel road weaves its way up to the highest point on the peninsula, Schoodic Head.

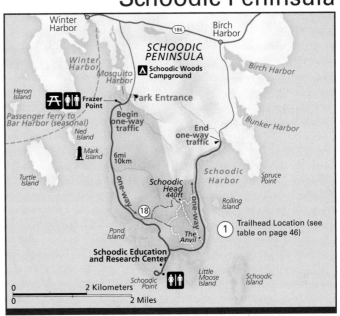

Isle au Haut

Named by Samuel de Champlain in 1604, Isle au Haut or "High Island" is a rugged and relatively remote island five miles south of Stonington. Today, a few thousand day-trippers and some 500 campers travel aboard the **Mail Boat** (207.367.5193, isleauhaut.com) from Stonington each year. About half the island is park land; the rest is owned and occupied by summer residents and a year-round fishing community. Over the years the relationship between residents and visitors has become contentious and a visitor capacity limit has been adopted. Isle au Haut visitors should exit the Mail Boat at Duck Harbor Landing, stay within park boundaries, and camp at one of the five designated sites (each with its own lean-to). Camping costs $25/site with a 3 night maximum stay.

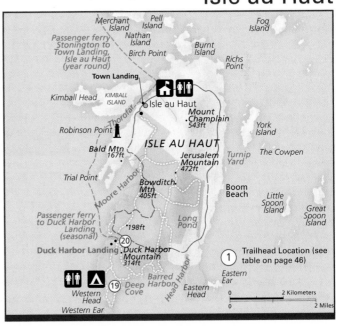

Legend

- Acadia National Park
- Park Loop Rd
- Unpaved road
- Carriage road
- Hiking trail
- Locked gate
- ⛺ Ranger station
- 🏕 Picnic area
- ⛺ Campground
- 🅿 Carriage road access parking
- 🚻 Restrooms
- 🏊 Lifeguarded swimming area (seasonal)
- 🚩 Lighthouse
- 🛥 Boat launch

North ⟲

2 Kilometers
2 Miles

① Trailhead Location (see table on page 46)

Don't Miss Park Loop Road

Hulls Cove Visitor Center

Don't Miss Jordan Pond

Don't Miss Long Pond

Don't Miss Cadillac Mtn

Don't Miss Echo Lake

Don't Miss Carriage Roads

Hancock County-Bar Harbor Airport

Thompson Island Information Center

MOUNT DESERT ISLAND

EASTERN BAY

WESTERN BAY

BLUE HILL BAY

Hadley Point
Sand Point
Salsbury Cove
Parker Point
Hamilton Pond
Lookout Point
Hulls Cove
Bar Island
Witch Hole Pond
Breakneck Ponds
Park HQ
Aunt Betty Pond
Connors Nubble
Cadillac Mountain 1530ft
Dorr Mtn 1270ft
Wild Gardens of Acadia
Nature Center
Sieur de Monts Spring
Abbe Museum
Bubble Pond
North Bubble 872ft
South Bubble 766ft
Jordan Pond Nature Trail
Sargent Mountain 1373ft
Gilmore Peak 1036ft
Parkman Mountain
Bald Peak
Penobscot Mountain 1194ft
Norumbega Mountain
Jordan Pond House
Gatehouse
Wildwood Stables
The Triad
Day Mtn
Blackwood
SEAL HARBOR
Stanley Brook Entrance
Bracy Cove
Bear Island
Ingraham Point
EASTERN WAY
Historical Museum
Islesford
LITTLE CRANBERRY ISLAND
Cranberry Isles
GREAT CRANBERRY ISLAND
The Pool
Seawall
Wonderland
Bass Harbor Head Lighthouse
BASS HARBOR
BERNARD
West Tremont
Goose Cove
Seal Cove
Moose Island
Hardwood Island
Pretty Marsh
Folly Island
BARTLETT ISLAND
Oak Point
High Head
Burnt Point
Squid Island
Green Island
Black Island
Indian Point
Town Hill
ALLEY ISLAND
TINKER ISLAND
Bar Island
Trumpet Island
West Barge
Ship Island East Barge
POND ISLAND
Somesville
Hall Quarry
Echo Lake Beach
Ikes Point
Acadia Mtn 681ft
St. Sauveur Mtn
Valley Cove
Flying Mtn 284ft
Upper Hadlock Pond
Lower Hadlock Pond
Carroll Homestead Interpretive trail
Fernald Point
NORTHEAST HARBOR
SOUTHWEST HARBOR
Manset
GREENING ISLAND
WESTERN WAY
Passenger Ferry (seasonal)
Somes Sound
Bar Island
Somes Pond
Little Round Pond
Round Pond
Long Pond
Echo Lake
Beech Mtn (fire tower)
WESTERN MOUNTAIN
Great Notch
Bernard Mountain 1071ft
Mansell Mtn
Mill Field
Gilley Field
SEAL COVE POND
Hodgdon Pond
Pretty Marsh Harbor
Seal Cove

Roads/labels:
- 3, 102, 198, 233, 102A, 233
- Crooked Road
- Duck Brook Road
- Eagle Lake
- Kebo Mtn 407ft
- Cadillac Mtn Road
- Pretty Marsh Road
- Indian Point Road
- Beech Hill Crossroad
- Beech Hill Road
- Ripple Road
- Long Pond Fire Road
- Seal Cove Road
- Western Mountain Road
- Long Pond Road
- Fernald Pt Rd
- Hio Road
- Tremont Road
- Duck Cove
- Ship Harbor
- Autos only
- Vehicle ferry to Swans Island
- Closed to public
- Carriage roads outside the park closed to bicyclists
- End one-way traffic
- Begin one-way traffic
- Bridge clearance: 12 feet 4 inches
- Start of Park Loop Rd Hulls Cove Entrance
- Cadillac Mtn Entrance
- Vehicle ferry to Bar Island
- 61ft 19m
- 12ft 4m
- Gatehouse

Trailhead numbers: ① ② ④ ⑥ ⑧ ⑩ ⑪ ⑫ ⑬ ⑭ ⑮ ⑯ ⑰

Map labels

STAVE ISLAND

NCHMAN BAY

Road
Burnt Porcupine Island
Yarmouth, Nova Scotia (seasonal)
Sheep Porcupine Island
nd
Jordan Island
Long Porcupine Island

assable at low tide
Passenger ferry to Winter Harbor (seasonal)
IRONBOUND ISLAND
AR BOR
Mountain
Breakwater
Bald Porcupine Island

Adventure Hike
The Precipice

Gardens
adia
Bear Brook
The Tarncap
Beaver Dam Pond
Schooner Head Rd

Sieur de Monts Entrance
Champlain Mountain 1058ft
Precipice Trailhead
Schooner Head
Egg Rock

Entrance Station
Park Loop Road

The Bowl
Overlook
Autos only

The Beehive 520ft
Gorham Mtn
Great Head
Sand Beach
Old Soaker

Thunder Hole
Otter eek
Gorham Mountain Trailhead
Fabbri

Otter Cliff
Otter Cove
Otter Point

oods

ne-way

tle Hunters Beach
ters Head

Don't Miss
Sand Beach

Warning—low bridges!
Four low-clearance bridges on *Park Loop Road* make advance route planning necessary for RVs and tall vehicles. Lowest Clearance is 10 feet 4 inches.

BAKER ISLAND

ATLANTIC OCEAN

LAND

Mount Desert Island (MDI)

To many visitors, Mount Desert Island and Acadia National Park are synonymous. Almost two thirds of the park is on MDI and it is the only destination for most of the 2+ million people who flock to Acadia each year. About half of the island is protected under park ownership. The boundary raggedly weaves its way around private property and the Atlantic seashore. The park and island are nearly split in half by a natural, glacially-carved barrier, Somes Sound. It is the only fjord on the U.S. Atlantic Coast.

Within park boundaries lies an enchanting place where granite cliffs and angry seas, mountaintops and clear blue skies, people and wildlife come together. Eight mountains exceed 1,000 feet. Diminutive in stature compared to their western counterparts, they still find a way to take your breath away. Hiking from sea level to summit is enough to leave even the avid hiker gasping for air. And if that fails to do the trick, the panoramic views afforded from these barren mountaintops definitely will. Should you only go to one mountaintop, make it the Cadillac. Its summit can be reached by car, bike, or foot. Many visitors drive to the summit before the sun rises in order to bask in the first rays of sun as they rise up over the Atlantic Ocean. Don't worry if you aren't a morning person; the views overlooking Bar Harbor, Frenchman Bay, and the Porcupine Islands are spectacular rain or shine, sun or fog, morning until evening. On a clear day you can see Mount Katahdin, Maine's tallest mountain, which stands some 100 miles away. Thrill-seekers unafraid of heights and searching for adventure should scale Champlain Mountain via Precipice Trail. Steel rungs, ladders, and railings aid hikers along the harrowing journey. The Trail is closed during winter, and it closes once more from late spring until early summer when peregrine falcons nest on the precipitous mountain's face.

Twenty-six freshwater lakes and ponds are found on MDI, providing a wide variety of activities. You can swim in the Atlantic at Sand Beach or the much warmer and fresher water of Echo Lake. Long Pond is a great place for a quiet paddle. Jordan Pond offers stunning views of the Bubble Mountains (South and North Bubble). View the bubbles from Jordan Pond House while enjoying one of their famous pastries, a popover.

A trip to Acadia is not complete without touring the 27-mile Park Loop Road, but if you'd like to escape the hum of automobiles go out and explore the carriage roads. These crushed stone paths are enjoyed by bikers, hikers, and horse riders. Be sure to pick up a map at Hulls Cove Visitor Center, just north of Bar Harbor on Route 3, before heading out on the carriage roads.

You'll find the majority of park facilities on MDI, but you won't find any lodging within park boundaries. Bar Harbor, the island's largest city, is the most popular destination for dining, lodging, and shopping. Additional accommodations are available in Northeast Harbor and Southwest Harbor. For a list of the area's popular dining and lodging facilities, please refer to pages 54–55.

Jordan Pond from North Bubble

Acadia Camping (Fees are per night)

Name	Location	Open	Fee	Sites	Notes
Blackwoods*	Route 3, 5 miles south of Bar Harbor	May–October	$30	306	No hookups Showers 0.5-mile away 35-ft max RV Reservations suggested from May–October
		April & November	$15	6 people, 2 tents, 1 car limit per site	
		December–March	Free		
Seawall*	Route 102A, 4 miles south of Southwest Harbor	late May–early Sept	$30 (drive-in)	218	No hookups Showers 0.5-mile away 35-ft max RV Half the sites are sold on a first-come, first-served basis
			$22 (walk-in)	6 people, 2 tents, 1 car limit per site	
Schoodic Woods*	3 miles southeast of Winter Harbor	late May–Columbus Day	$30 (drive-in)	89	32 sites with RV electric and water ($40/night) and 22 sites with electric ($36/night)
			$22 (walk-in)		
Duck Harbor**	Isle au Haut, accessible by mail boat from Stonington, ME	mid-May–mid-October		5 6 people/site	Primitive Camping with lean-to Reservation required
Backcountry Camping		Backcountry camping is prohibited at Acadia National Park			

*Reservations can be made up to six months in advance by calling 877-444-6777 or clicking recreation.gov

**Reservation requests can be made after April 1. Call (207) 288-3338 for a reservation form or visit nps.gov/acad/planyourvisit/upload/iahreserve.pdf

Acadia Lodging

Name	Notes
None Available in Park	See pages 54–55 for accommodations outside the park

Hiking

Acadia National Park has some of the best maintained trails of all the national parks. It's a true day hiker's paradise with more than 140 miles of short, one-way trails. In fact, all of the trails are intended to be day-hikes as backcountry camping is not permitted within park boundaries.

In 1999, Friends of Acadia and the park committed $13 million for trail restoration. That same year Acadia became the first national park whose trails are maintained by a private endowment, Acadia Trails Forever. Their work allows visitors to enjoy the great outdoors without having to worry about getting lost. Trails—many of which were trod by Native Americans or the park's first superintendent, George Dorr—are well marked with cairns (small, pyramid-like rock piles) and blue blazes painted onto trees and rocks.

At least 6,000 years ago—long before cairns were carefully built atop the barren mountaintops and blue blazes were painted on tree trunks—Native Americans forged their own trails across MDI in search of coastal waters where they found nourishment through fishing and gathering shellfish. All that remains of their existence are huge piles of shells and a vast network of well-worn trails. Rumors of a fantastical city of gold drew European sailors to Maine in the mid-1500s. Rusticators arrived in the mid-to-late 1800s to explore the island on foot, taking delight in its earthly wonders. At the turn of the century, the same trails trod by Native Americans, gold-seekers, and rusticators were blazed once more by George B. Dorr, a summer resident and member of the Hancock County Trustees of Public Reservations who worked tirelessly to protect the natural beauty of the area. He set out on these paths, and many of his own, with a new-found purpose: the pursuit of land and monetary donations from wealthy island residents. Today, Dorr is affectionately referred to as the "Father of Acadia National Park." Thanks to the efforts of Dorr and many others, these trails are yours to explore.

While you won't find commemoration to Dorr anywhere along his favorite hiking trails, he is remembered by a mountaintop; **Dorr Mountain** is the third tallest peak in the park. Four trails lead to its

Sand Beach and Beehive from Great Head Trail

Acadia Mountain Trail

Bar Island

Best of Acadia

Adventure Hike: Precipice
Runner-up: Beehive
2nd Runner-up: Penobscot Mountain

Mountain Hike: Acadia Mountain
Runner-up: Cadillac South Ridge
2nd Runner-up: Beech Mountain

Coastal Hike: Great Head
Runner-up: Schoodic Head
2nd Runner-up: Ocean Path

Family Hike: Bar Island
Runner-up: Bubble Rock
2nd Runner-up: Ship Harbor

Acadia Hiking Trails (Distances are roundtrip unless noted otherwise)

Name	Location (# on map)	Length	Difficulty Rating & Notes
Bar Island - ♨	Bar Harbor located at the end of Bridge Street (1)	~1.4 miles	E – A sandbar to Bar Island appears at low tide, be sure to check the tide tables
Great Meadow	Bar Harbor located off Cromwell Harbor Road (1)	2.0 miles	E – A loop trail across private land that connects Bar Harbor to Acadia
Cadillac North Ridge	Park Loop Road, 3.2 miles from the start of Park Loop Road (2)	4.4 miles	M – Views of Bar Harbor • Shorter and steeper than South Ridge Trail
Tarn Trail	Sieur de Monts Spring, Tarn Parking Lot off Route 3 (3)	2.4 miles	M – Hike through woods along Otter Creek and by beaver ponds
Summit Path	Cadillac Mtn Summit Parking Lot (4)	0.3 mile	E – A paved path around the summit
Precipice - ♨	1.75 miles past Sieur de Monts Spring entrance on Park Loop Rd (5)	1.8 miles	S – Iron rungs and ladders • 2.5-mile loop by combining (in order) Precipice, Champlain North Ridge, and Orange & Black Trails • Not for children or those afraid of heights
Bubble Rock - ♨	Bubble Rock Parking Lot, off Park Loop Road (6)	1.0 mile	M – Steep but short hike up South Bubble to a peculiar glacial erratic (big rock)
Ocean Path - ♨	Sand Beach Upper parking lot (7)	4.4 miles	E – Passes Thunder Hole and Otter Cliffs
Great Head	East end of Sand Beach (7)	1.5 miles	M – Loop trail with sea cliff and beach views
Beehive - ♨	Sand Beach Area, across Park Loop Road from Sand Beach parking lot (7)	1.6 miles	S – Iron rungs and ladders • Not for children or those afraid of heights
Jordan Pond - ♨	Jordan Pond Boat Ramp (8)	3.2 miles	M – Loop along the edge of Jordan Pond
Penobscot Mountain	Behind Jordan Pond Gift Shop (8)	~3.7 miles	S – Ascend Jordan Cliff (ladder) Trail or Jordan Pond/Deer Brook Trails and descend Penobscot Mtn Trail
Gorham Mtn	Gorham Mtn Parking Area, 1 mile past Sand Beach on Park Loop Road (9)	1.8 miles	M – Wide open views of the ocean • Connects to The Bowl, Beehive, and Cadillac Cliffs
Cadillac South Ridge	Route 3, about 100 feet south of Blackwoods Campground (10)	7.0 miles	S – Hike to Cadillac from Blackwoods Campground on one of the park's longer trails
Grandgent	Trailhead at Sargent Mtn Summit (11)	1.0 mile	S – Leads to Sargent Mtn's summit
Giant Slide	1.1 mile from the junction of Route 198 and 233 (12)	2.8 miles	S – Fairly challenging trail along Sargent Brook to the summit of Sargent Mtn
Acadia Mtn - ♨	Acadia Mountain Parking Lot, west side of Route 102 (13)	2.5 miles	S – Best views of Somes Sound in the park, return via fire road
Beech Mtn - ♨	Beech Mtn Parking Lot, off Beech Hill Road (14)	1.1 miles	M – Alternate from end of Long Pond Road, ascend West Ridge Trail and return via Valley Trail (~3 miles)
Flying Mtn	Fernald Cove Parking Area, Fernald Point Rd (15)	1.2 miles	M – Explore tide pools at Valley Cove
Wonderland	Seawall Campground, off Route 102A, 0.9 miles from Seawall (16)	1.4 miles	E – Rocky shoreline, cobble beach, and spruce forests
Ship Harbor	Off Rte 102A, 2 miles from Seawall (17)	1.2 miles	E – A good spot for blueberries and birds
Schoodic Head - ♨	Schoodic Peninsula, Blueberry Hill Parking Lot (18)	2.5 miles	M – Combine Alder, Schoodic Head and Anvil Trails for a loop to Schoodic Head
Goat Trail	Isle au Haut, via Western Head Road and Duck Harbor Mountain Trail (19)	2.1 miles (one-way)	M – Rugged and rocky hike with spectacular coastal vistas
Duck Harbor Mountain	Isle au Haut, accessible from Western Head Road (20)	2.4 miles	S – Panoramic views of Isle au Haut • Most strenuous hike on the isle

Mount Desert Island

Difficulty Ratings: E = Easy, M = Moderate, S = Strenuous

summit, including the short and steep **Ladder Trail**. The ascent is aided by three sets of steel ladders and numerous granite steps that were carved and placed in 1893 and restored by the Civilian Conservation Corps (CCC) in the 1930s. The trailhead is found at Sieur de Monts Spring directly behind the Spring House. To complete the 3.3-mile journey to Dorr Mountain summit, take Ladder Trail to Schiff Path (East Face Dorr Trail) and return via South Ridge Dorr Trail and Canon Brook Trail.

There are five more ladder trails. Of these, **Precipice Trail** is the most notorious. The trailhead is 7.3 miles from Hulls Cove Visitor Center on Park Loop Road. It quickly climbs the steep east face of Champlain Mountain. It's recommended that you ascend 0.9 mile along Precipice Trail and return via Champlain Mountain North Ridge Trail and Orange & Black Path, making a 2.5-mile loop. The trail closes from mid-March to mid-August to protect nesting peregrine falcons. During this time you'll often find a park ranger with a telescope conducting Peregrine Watch (page 51) in the Precipice Trail Parking Area. Continuing along Park Loop Road, you will arrive at another popular ladder trail, the **Beehive**. It begins across the road from Sand Beach Parking Area. Follow Beehive Trail 0.8 miles to its summit, and then take Bowl Trail back to Park Loop Road, completing a 1.6-mile loop. **Jordan Cliff Trailhead** is found behind Jordan Pond Gift Shop at Carriage Road junction #15. This hike begins with excellent views of Jordan Pond as you start the 2.2-mile (one-way) ascent to the top of Penobscot Mountain. Take in the 360° panoramic views at the summit before heading back down **Penobscot Mountain Trail**, which loops back to Jordan Pond Gift Shop. The 2.2-mile **Perpendicular (Mansell Mountain) Trail** begins at the south end of Long Pond near Southwest Harbor. The sixth and final ladder trail, 0.5-mile **Beech Cliff Trail**, begins behind the ranger house at Echo Lake Parking Area. Be aware that these are some of the most challenging trails in the park and should not be attempted by small children, anyone afraid of heights, and pets.

Acadia has plenty of trails that appeal to families and people of all ages. **Bar Island** can be reached at low tide by crossing a sand bar right from downtown Bar Harbor. Have your kids try to push a 14-ton boulder over a cliff at the steep but short, 1.0-mile **Bubble Rock Trail**. During a storm or rising tide you may want to head down **Ocean Path** to listen to the waves explode at **Thunder Hole**. (See the hiking table on the opposite page for the location and difficulty of these and many other trails.) Another great destination for casual hiking is the 45 miles of **carriage roads**, which are concentrated around the Jordan Pond Area, but extend as far north as Hulls Cove Visitor Center and south to Route 3 near the Stanley Brook Entrance.

The dense network of short trails and the Island Explorer Shuttle allow Acadia's hikers to be creative with their itineraries. It's easy to avoid out-and-back hikes by combining several trails and utilizing the park shuttle (page 39), which stops at many of the park trailheads.

Rock Climbing

Acadia's mountains may not be big, but they are precipitous. The sheer granite walls offer some of the most unique rock climbing opportunities in the United States. **Otter Cliffs** is the most famous and popular climbing spot. The South Wall of Champlain Mountain, Central Slabs, South Bubble, and Great Head are also great climbing areas. Climbers at Otter Cliffs, Canada Cliffs, and South Wall should sign in at daily use logs, which are available at the climbing areas, park headquarters, visitor center, and campgrounds. With a wide variety of climbing routes Acadia is a wonderful destination for beginners to learn how to rock climb. If you'd like to give it a try, consider contacting one of the outfitters listed on page 56.

Paddling

Acadia National Park has paddling in spades for people of all experience levels. Inexperienced paddlers are sure to enjoy the glacially-carved lakes and ponds or perhaps a guided tour with a local outfitter (page 56). **Eagle Lake**, **Long Pond**, **Jordan Pond**, and **Echo Lake** are a few of the most popular freshwater paddle-spots, with at least one boat launch available at each.

More experienced paddlers can take to the open waters of the Atlantic Ocean where you are free to explore

Bubble Rock

Acadia's islands, inlets, and coves. You can also avoid a ride aboard the **Mail Boat** (207.367.5193, isleauhaut. com) to Isle au Haut by paddling the five miles of water separating it from Stonington, ME.

Paddling allows visitors to see the park from a different perspective and gain a new appreciation for this scenic land. It's also an excellent way to view the park's wildlife. Enjoy the tranquility of these majestic waters but remember to use caution, especially when paddling alone. Cold water, swift currents, erratic weather, and dense fog can make paddling at Acadia challenging. Check the weather and tide tables before heading out on the water. If you plan to explore any of Acadia's remote smaller islands, be sure to discuss your itinerary with a local park ranger, because birds may be nesting on the shorelines.

Boat Tours
Baker Island Cruise explores the island's unique natural and cultural history with the help of a park ranger. Call (207) 288-2386 for reservations and info.

Dive-In Theater Boat Cruise searches for underwater life. Passengers scour the surface of Frenchman Bay for seals, porpoises, and seabirds, while a diver hunts for marine life on the ocean floor. Occasionally the diver returns with live specimens for a real hands-on experience. For more information call (207) 288-3483 or click divered.com. For tickets call (800) 979-3370.

Frenchman Bay Cruise takes you aboard a 151-foot, four-mast schooner, where you'll search for wildlife as a ranger narrates the tour. For more information call (207) 288-4585 or click downeastwindjammer.com.

Discover Acadia's past aboard the **Islesford Historical Cruise** by visiting Little Cranberry Island's Islesford Historical Museum. For more information call (207) 276-5352 or click barharborcruises.com.

Bass Harbor Cruises (207.244.5785, bassharbor-cruises.com) offers a variety of wildlife and historical cruises. Or sail aboard the oldest working friendship sloop with **Downeast Friendship Sloop Charters** (207.266.5210, sailacadia.com). You can also go on a whale or puffin watch with **Bar Harbor Whale Watching** (207.288.2386, barharborwhales.com).

Reservations are recommended for all cruises. Schedules and fees vary. All tours are seasonal.

Biking
Eastern MDI's **carriage roads** are your best bet for a relaxing bike ride at Acadia National Park. The 45-mile network of broken-stone roads extends all the way from Hulls Cove Visitor Center to Seal Harbor and includes 17 carefully-crafted stone-faced bridges. Some of the most scenic stretches skirt Jordan Pond and Eagle Lake. The 8-mile roundtrip ride to Day Mountain is one of the circuits beginning from Jordan Pond Gatehouse and is the only summit that can be reached via carriage path. No matter where you go, be sure to carry a map of the carriage roads (available at Hulls Cove Visitor Center or the park's website), because you'll encounter several junctions even on short rides. Also note that the 12 miles of carriage roads south of Jordan Pond are on private property and off-limits to cyclists. However, horses and walkers are allowed to wander along these roadways.

The quieter western side of Mount Desert Island has two gravel roads for biking. **Seal Cove Road** (4 miles) connects Southwest Harbor and Seal Cove. **Hio Road** (2.5 miles) connects Seawall Campground with Highway 102 at Bass Harbor Marsh.

The 27-mile **Park Loop Road** offers scenic and hilly terrain for road cyclists. If you feel like challenging yourself, take the 3.5-mile **Mountain Loop Road** to the summit of **Cadillac Mountain**. It's seriously tough pedaling going up, but the return trip downhill is a breeze (make sure your brakes work well). Due to Park Loop Road's steep grades, tight turns, and abundance of tourist traffic during the summer months, it's best to pedal here in the off-season. For less congested biking try the loop around Schoodic Peninsula's scenic coastline or Route 102/102A on the western side of MDI. Bike rental is available in Bar Harbor and Southwest Harbor. See page 56 for contact information.

Biking at Isle au Haut is not encouraged. You are not allowed to bike on any hiking trails and there is no single track within the park.

Carriage Tours

Wildwood Stables (877.276.3622) offers carriage tours along the park's 45 miles of crushed stone paths. They offer a Tea & Popover Ride (2 hours, $20/adult), Day Mountain Sightseeing Tour (1 hour, $20/adult), Day Mountain Summit Tour (2 hours, $26/adult), and a tour of Mr. Rockefeller's Bridges (2 hours, $26/adult). Children receive discounted rates at about half the cost of an adult. Private carriage charters are also available.

Swimming

On hot summer days many of Acadia's guests migrate to the beaches. **Sand Beach** and **Echo Lake Beach** are staffed with a lifeguard during the summer. The 55°F water found at Sand Beach might be refreshing to some, but it's downright frigid to others. The freshwater of Echo Lake is considerably warmer, especially near the end of summer. For more secluded swimming head to the park's western side where you can paddle yourself to swimming holes in **Seal Cove**, and **Round** and **Hodgdon Ponds**. **Lake Wood**, on the north end of the island, has a small beach with automobile access.

Swimming is prohibited at all lakes used for drinking water. These include Upper and Lower Hadlock Ponds, Bubble and Jordan Ponds, Eagle Lake, and the southern half of Long Pond.

Fishing

To fish any of the freshwater lakes in Acadia you'll need a freshwater fishing license. Maine residents 16 and older and non-residents 12 and older require a license. Licenses are available at Walmart in Ellsworth and Paradis True Value in Bar Harbor. Freshwater fishing season is generally from April until September. Trout, salmon, perch, and bass are commonly caught in freshwater lakes and ponds.

A license is not required for salt water fishing. **Sargent Drive** (Somes Sound) and **Frazer Point** (Schoodic Peninsula) are two salt water fishing areas within the park. Mackerel typically run from mid-July to September at these locations.

Be sure to respect private property and follow all boating and fishing regulations.

Bird Watching

Acadia is one of the premier bird-watching areas in the United States. More than 300 bird species have been identified on MDI and the surrounding waters.

After being reintroduced in the 1980s, **peregrine falcons** have become one of the main flying attractions. They have been nesting on the cliffs of **Champlain Mountain** since 1991. If you'd like to observe these magnificent birds, join a park ranger or volunteer for **Peregrine Watch**. The program takes place at Precipice Trail Parking Area and is offered most days from mid-May through mid-August, weather permitting. Another popular nesting location is **Beech Cliffs** above Echo Lake.

Birds are everywhere, but a few locations are better than others. **Sieur de Monts Springs** is an excellent choice if you're looking to spot cedar waxwings, pileated woodpeckers, and the minuscule ruby-throated hummingbird. **Beaver Brook** and **Beaver Dam Pond** are popular habitats for herons, ducks, and bald eagles.

Birdwatchers will definitely want to walk around the **Otter Cliffs** area. Here you might find any number of seabirds, including double breasted cormorant, black guillemot, and northern gannet. **Schoodic Peninsula**,

Bass Harbor Head Lighthouse

Wonderland, Ship Harbor, and Seawall provide bird enthusiasts with promising chances of seeing a wide variety of seabirds. Songbirds serenade cyclists, carriage riders, and hikers along the many miles of carriage roads.

Cadillac Mountain's wide open summit provides an excellent vantage point to see bald eagles and peregrine falcons as they patrol the sky high above the park's granite peaks. In fact, bird watching is so good here the park has a Hawk Watch station at Cadillac's summit from mid-August until mid-October. Park rangers aid visitors in spotting raptors as they make their winter migration from Maine and Canada to warmer locales further south.

Birdwatchers on a trip to Acadia will not want to forget their binoculars and bird book. Also, be sure to stop at Hulls Cove Visitor Center to get the latest information on migratory birds, peregrine falcons, and ranger-led bird watch programs.

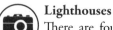 **Lighthouses**
There are four lighthouses in the vicinity of MDI. Of these, Bass Harbor Head Lighthouse is the easiest to access. It marks the entrance into Blue Hill Bay and is located at the end of Route 102A on the western half of MDI near Bass Harbor. Egg Rock Lighthouse is located at the mouth of Frenchman Bay.

It can be seen from Park Loop Road. Baker Island is the oldest lighthouse in the area. It's located seven miles from MDI, and can be accessed by kayak or boat. Bear Island Lighthouse is closed to the public, but it can be viewed on boat cruises departing from Northeast Harbor.

Winter Activities
Winter activities at Acadia are hit or miss. The park averages about five feet of snow each year, but rain is just as likely during the winter months. January and February are the most reliable months for winter weather. When there is snow, Acadia becomes a winter wonderland with plenty to do.

Two short sections of Park Loop Road remain open during winter for motorists. Blackwoods Campground remains open, but campers must walk from the campground entrance road on Route 3 to the campsites. Snowmobiles are allowed on Park Loop Road and most fire roads. However, the maximum speed is 35 mph on Park Loop Road, and 25 mph on all unpaved roads. Snowmobilers must follow all state snowmobile laws. Dog sleds may be pulled by no more than four dogs. Ice fishing is popular on the many lakes and ponds. Snowshoe, cross-country ski, and ice skate rentals are available in Bar Harbor.

Visitor Centers
Hulls Cove Visitor Center • (207) 288-3338
On Route 3 just south of Hulls Cove
Open: mid-April–October
Hours: 8am–4:30pm (July–August, 8am–6pm)
A long staircase leads up to the Visitor Center, but there is alternate parking for people with disabilities if you follow a short road at the south end of the main parking area.

Thompson Island Information Center
On Route 3 at the head of MDI
Open: mid-May–mid-September

Park Headquarters
On Route 233 near Eagle Lake
Open: All Year, M–F (except federal holidays and weekends from mid-April–October)
Serves as the park's visitor center during winter

Ranger Programs

Be sure to check with a park ranger or at the visitor center to see a current schedule of ranger-led programs. You'll find a wide variety of regularly scheduled educational walks, bike rides, and even a photography tour. Most of the programs are free of charge. The knowledge and enthusiasm exhibited by the park rangers makes activities, from hiking to stargazing, more exciting and interesting. If you have an extra hour or two and aren't exactly sure what to do, you cannot go wrong by joining a ranger program.

For Kids

Kids of all ages can become **Junior Rangers** from mid-May through mid-October. Acadia also offers numerous children's programs exploring the park's ecology, geography, and history. Families also enjoy playing at Sand Beach (page 49), picking blueberries, hiking (page 45), or taking a boat tour (page 48).

Flora & Fauna

Many of Acadia's picturesque attractions are named for their occupants: Seal Harbor, Beaver Pond, Eagle Lake, and Otter Cliffs. All of these creatures reside in the park (although "otter" areas were named for the river dwelling variety, not the playful sea otters). Fortunate visitors might spot moose, black bear, red fox, porcupine, deer, whale, sea urchin, starfish, or lobster while exploring the park. Black flies and mosquitoes are two pests that you'd rather not encounter on vacation, but if you plan on traveling between May and June, chances are you'll be greeted by these winged nuisances, so pack your bug repellent.

Over 1,100 plant species live in Acadia, and 25 of these are state-listed rare plants. Walking about the park you're sure to notice a wide variety of trees, wildflowers, ferns, shrubs, mosses, lichens, and freshwater plants. The favorite plant of many visitors is the wild blueberry bush. Maine is the country's number one producer of wild blueberries, and these delectable snacks can be found all over MDI. They are typically ripe for the picking in late summer.

Pets

Pets are permitted in the park, but must be kept on a leash no more than six feet in length at all times, and are

Echo Lake Beach from Beech Cliffs

not allowed on swimming beaches, in public buildings, on ladder trails, and at Isle au Haut.

Accessibility

The Visitor Center, some restrooms, carriage paths, and Island Explorer Shuttle are wheelchair accessible. The Wild Gardens of Acadia paths, Wonderland Trail, Ship Harbor Trail, and Jordan Pond Trails are accessible to wheelchair users, but may require some assistance. Wildwood Stables (page 49) operates two wheelchair-accessible carriages. If you have accessibility questions, please call the park information center at (207) 288-3338, ext. 0.

Weather

Acadia's weather is extremely unpredictable and can change without warning any day of the year, so come prepared for all conditions. Rainfall is common in every month. MDI is often shrouded in fog during the summer months. Daytime summer highs can range from 45°F to 90°F. Below is a graph of the area's average temperatures and precipitation.

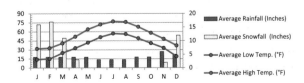

Sand Beach from Beehive Trail

Vacation Planner

The average visitor spends three-and-a-half days at Acadia. So, here's a 3-day itinerary to help get you started. Nearby dining, grocery stores, lodging, festivals, and attractions are listed on pages 54–57.

Day 1: You'll want to begin your Acadian adventure at **Hulls Cove Visitor Center**. It's the best place to introduce yourself to the park and rangers will be on duty, ready and willing to answer your questions. Before you leave, grab a park brochure, check the schedule of ranger programs watch the 15-minute video, and browse the exhibits until your curiosities have been satisfied. Next, begin driving **Park Loop Road**. Be sure to stop at **Sand Beach Parking Area**. Adventurous souls in your group should head across Park Loop Road to hike up **Beehive Ladder Trail**. The rest can play at the beach or hike **Great Head Trail**. When everyone has returned, it's time to get back in your car to continue along Park Loop Road to **Jordan Pond House**, which has been serving tourists for more than a century. This is a great place to enjoy lunch or a snack, like one of their famous popovers. At the very least take in the views of Jordan Pond where Two Bubbles stand guard at the pond's far end. These bubbles are your next destination. As you're driving to the **Bubble Rock Parking Area**, look up at the east face of South Bubble. You'll notice a large boulder (Bubble Rock) precariously positioned as if it could roll down the mountain slope with the slightest nudge. Check it out by hiking up the 1-mile trail to the top of South Bubble. You don't have to race up the trail, Bubble Rock isn't going anywhere. To prove it, give it a

push and see if it will budge. After you've had your fun, hike to the top of North Bubble for outstanding views of Jordan Pond or return to the car and complete the circuit around Park Loop Road. You may want to end your first day in Acadia with an evening boat tour of Frenchman Bay (page 48).

Day 2: Catch a morning photography or bird-watching tour if the schedule of ranger programs aligns with yours. Then drive over to MDI's quiet western side. If the weather cooperates, rent a kayak from **National Park Canoe & Kayak** (207.244.5854, nationalpark-canoerental.com, reservations may be required). The outfitter is conveniently located on **Long Pond**, so there's no need to transport heavy gear in order to enjoy a casual paddle in a pristine wilderness area. Return your kayak(s) and once you've lost your sea legs, hike to the top of nearby **Acadia Mountain**. It's one of the best hikes in the park, and the views are sublime. Relaxing at **Echo Lake Beach** is a nice alternative for anyone not interested in a somewhat strenuous hike. Whenever you feel like eating you can find plenty of good restaurants in Southwest Harbor. It's also a quality place to pit-stop before continuing south on Route 102 to the end of Route 102A, where you'll find **Bass Harbor Head Lighthouse**. This is one of the best locations to watch the sun set on another glorious day in Acadia.

Day 3: Make today count by waking up early enough to see the sunrise from **Cadillac Mountain**. Bring a thermos of hot chocolate or coffee and a blanket along, because early Acadian mornings can be chilly and the barren mountaintop is unprotected from the wind. Dragging yourself out of bed will be completely justified as the first rays of light peek out from beyond the Atlantic Ocean. An early morning also means you'll have more time to enjoy your final day of vacation. Perhaps you have some unfinished shopping to complete in downtown Bar Harbor or you'd like to hike **Precipice Trail**. If you have the time, you might even want to leave MDI in favor of Acadia's **Schoodic Peninsula**. Should you choose to make the 45-minute drive back to Maine's mainland, you'll find the effort worthwhile. The same majestic coastlines are here, but without the crowds. **Frazer Head** is a great place to picnic and you can drive up to **Schoodic Head**, the peninsula's highest point.

Thunder Hole

Dining

Bar Harbor

Jordan Pond House • (207) 276-3316
Next to Jordan Pond, Park Loop Rd
acadiajordanpondhouse.com • Popovers: $5

Lompoc Café & Brew Pub
36 Rodick St • (207) 288-9392 • Entrée: $10–16
lompoccafe.com • *Bocce Ball & Live Entertainment*

Jordan's Restaurant • (207) 288-3586
80 Cottage St • Entrée: $7–14

McKay's Public House • (207) 288-2002
231 Main St
mckayspublichouse.com • Entrée: $17–25

The Thirsty Whale • (207) 288-9335
40 Cottage St
thirstywhaletavern.com • Entrée: $9–16

Havana • (207) 288-2822
318 Main St • Entrée: $22–29
havanamaine.com

2 Cats • (207) 288-2808
130 Cottage St • *Best Breakfast in town!*
2catsbarharbor.com

Rupununi American Bar and Grill
119 Main St • (207) 288-2886
rupununi.com • Entrée: $16–29

Fathom Restaurant • (207) 288-9664
6 Summer St
fathombarharbor.com • Entrée: $19–32

Jeannie's Breakfast House • (207) 288-4166
15 Cottage St
jeanniesbreakfast.com • Entrée: ~$10

Galyn's • (207) 288-9706
17 Main St
galynsbarharbor.com • Entrée: $13–54

Rosalie's Pizza • (207) 288-5666
46 Cottage St
rosaliespizza.com • Pizza: $7–25

West Street Café • (207) 288-5242
76 West St
weststreetcafe.com • Entrée: $13–30

Mache Bistro • (207) 288-0447
321 Main St
machebistro.com • Entrée: $13–32

Geddy's Pub • (207) 288-5077
19 Main St
geddys.com • Entrée: $10–27

Poor Boy's Gourmet • (207) 288-4148
300 Main St
poorboysgourmet.com • Entrée: $12–35

Café This Way • (207) 288-4483
14 Mount Desert St
cafethisway.com • Entrée: $18–29

Side Street Café • (207) 801-2591
49 Rodick St
sidestreetbarharbor.com • Entrée: $9–23

Leary's Landing Irish Pub • (207) 801-2599
2 Mount Desert St
learyslanding.com • Entrée: $11–15

Mama Di Matteo's • (207) 288-3666
34 Kennebec Place
mamadimatteos.com • Entrée: $12–25

Michelle's Fine Dining • (207) 288-0038
194 Main St
ivymanor.com • Entrée: $24–54

China Joy • (207) 288-8666
195 Main St • Entrée: $7–17

Bar Harbor Blues Café • (207) 288-2600
16 Mount Desert St
barharborbluescafe.com • Entrée: ~$9

Randonnee Café • (207) 288-9592
37 Cottage St • Entrée: $5–7

Jack Russell's Steak House & Brewery
102 Eden St • (207) 288-5214
jackrussellssteakhouse.com • Entrée: $13–34

The Reading Room • (207) 288-3351
7 Newport Dr
barharborinn.com • Entrée: $29–41

MDI's Quiet Side

Red Sky • (207) 244-0476
14 Clark Point Rd, Southwest Harbor
redskyrestaurant.com • Entrée: $22–31

Fiddlers' Green • (207) 244-9416
411 Main St, Southwest Harbor
fiddlersgreenrestaurant.com • Entrée: $16–38

Little Notch Bread Café • (207) 244-3357
340 Main St, Southwest Harbor • Entrée: $6–18

Eat-A-Pita & Café 2 • (207) 244-4344
326 Main St, Southwest Harbor

Sips • (207) 244-4550 • sipsmdi.com
4 Clark Point Rd, Southwest Harbor

Quietside Café & Ice Cream Shop
360 Main St, Southwest Harbor • (207) 244-9444

Beal's Lobster Pier • (207) 244-3202
182 Clark Point Rd, Southwest Harbor
bealslobster.com • Lobster: Market Price

Chow Maine Ciao Maine • (207) 669-4142
19 Clark Point Rd, Southwest Harbor
chow-maine.com • Entrée: $8–28

Breakfast At Grumpy's • (207) 244-1082
11 Apple Ln, Southwest Harbor • Entrée: ~$10

XYZ Restaurant • (207) 244-5221
80 Seawall Rd, Southwest Harbor
xyzmaine.com • Entrée: $26

Xanthus Restaurant • (207) 244-5036
22 Claremont Rd, Southwest Harbor
theclaremonthotel.com • Entrée: ~$24–30

Thurston's Lobster Pound
9 Thurston Rd, Bernard • (207) 244-7600
thurstonslobster.com • Lobster: Market Price

Schoodic Peninsula

Chase's Restaurant • (207) 963-7171
193 Main St, Winter Harbor

Fisherman's Inn • (207) 963-5585
7 Newman St, Winter Harbor
fishermansinnmaine.com

Downeast Deli • (207) 963-2700
ME-186, Prospect Harbor, ME 04693

Grocery Stores

Hannaford Supermarkets • (207) 288-5680
86 Cottage St, Bar Harbor

Sawyer's Market • (207) 244-3315
344 Main St, Southwest Harbor

Pine Tree Market • (207) 276-3335
121 Main St, Northeast Harbor

Walmart Supercenter • (207) 667-6780
461 High St, Ellsworth

Lodging

Bar Harbor

Bar Harbor Inn • (207) 288-3351
7 Newport Dr
barharborinn.com • Rates: $105–399/night

Harborside Hotel, Spa & Marina
55 West St • (207) 288-5033
theharborsidehotel.com • Rates: $229–949

Bar Harbor Hotel-Bluenose Inn
90 Eden St • (207) 288-3348
barharborhotel.com • Rates: $125–449

Castlemaine Inn • (207) 288-4563
39 Holland Ave
castlemaineinn.com • Rates: $119–269

Bar Harbor Manor • (207) 288-3829
47 Holland Ave
barharbormanor.com • Rates: $99–209

Mira Monte Inn • (207) 288-4263
69 Mount Desert St
miramonte.com • Rates: $141–305

Highbrook Motel • (207) 288-3591
94 Eden St
highbrookmotel.com • Rates: $89–175

Bar Harbor Grand Hotel • (207) 288-5226
269 Main St • barharborgrand.com • $165–225

Balance Rock Inn • (207) 288-2610
21 Albert Meadow
balancerockinn.com • Rates: $185–555

Acadia Inn • (207) 288-3500
98 Eden St
acadiainn.com • Rates: $189–209

Acadia Hotel • (207) 288-5721
20 Mt Desert St
acadiahotel.com • Rates: $99–299

Primrose Inn B&B • (207) 288-4031
73 Mt Desert St
primroseinn.com • Rates: $152–280

Bar Harbor Motel • (207) 288-3453
100 Eden St
barharbormotel.com • Rates: $89–245

Edenbrook Motel • (207) 288-4975
96 Eden St
edenbrookmotelbh.com • Rates: $90–120

Quimby House Inn • (207) 288-5811
109 Cottage St
quimbyhouse.com • Rates: $89–220

Black Friar Inn • (207) 288-5091
10 Summer St
blackfriarinn.com • Rates: $100–195

Moseley Cottage • (207) 288-5548
12 Atlantic Ave
moseleycottage.net • Rates: $165–295

Cleftstone Manor • (207) 288-8086
92 Eden St
cleftstone.com • Rates: $139–269

Maples Inn • (207) 288-3443
16 Roberts Ave
maplesinn.com • Rates: $129–219

Anne's White Columns Inn • (207) 288-5357
57 Mt Desert St
anneswhitecolumns.com • Rates: $129–209

Aysgarth Station • (207) 288-9655
20 Roberts Ave
aysgarth.com • Rates: $120–170

Canterbury Cottage • (207) 288-2112
12 Roberts Ave
canterburycottage.com • Rates: $145–165

Bar Harbor Regency • (207) 288-9723
123 Eden St
barharborregency.com • Rates: $144–381

Primrose Place • (207) 288-3771
51 Holland Ave
aurorainn.com • Rates: $115–175

The Bayview • (207) 288-5861
111 Eden St
thebayviewbarharbor.com • Rates: $270–330

Seacroft Inn • (207) 288-4669
18 Albert Meadows
seacroftinn.com • Rates: $109–149

Anchorage Motel • (207) 288-3959
51 Mount Desert St
anchoragebarharbor.com • Rates: $89–169

Holbrook House • (207) 288-4970
74 Mount Desert St
holbrookhouse.com • Rates: $109–269

High Seas Motel • (207) 288-5836
339 ME-3
highseasmotel.com • Rates: $50–135

Inn At Bay Ledge • (207) 288-4204
150 Sand Point Rd
innatbayledge.info • Rates: $175–350

Emery's On the Shore • (207) 288-3432
181 Sand Point Rd
emeryscottages.com • Weekly: $570–1,275

Bass Cottage Inn • (207) 288-1234
14 The Field
basscottage.com • Rates: $220–420

Hearthside Inn • (207) 288-4533
7 High St
hearthsideinn.com • Rates: $135–230

Ullikana In the Field • (207) 288-9552
16 The Field
ullikana.com • Rates: $205–385

Atlantean Cottage B&B • (207) 288-5703
11 Atlantic Ave
atlanteancottage.com • Rates: $200–295

Chiltern Inn • (207) 288-3371
11 Cromwell Harbor Rd
chilterninnbarharbor.com • Rates: $199–399

MDI's Quiet Side
Asticou Inn • (207) 276-3344
15 Peabody Dr, Northeast Harbor
asticou.com • Rates: $155–380

Colonels Suites • (207) 288-4775
143 Main St, Northeast Harbor
colonelssuites.com • Rates: $139–229

Harborside Inn • (207) 276-3272
48 Harborside Rd, Northeast Harbor
harboursideinn.com • Rates: $160–275

Clark Point Inn B&B • (207) 244-9828
109 Clark Point Rd, Southwest Harbor
clarkpointinn.com • Rates: $129–239

The Kingsleigh B&B • (207) 244-5302
373 Main St, Southwest Harbor
kingsleighinn.com • Rates: $170–315

Café Dry Dock & Inn • (207) 244-5842
357 Main St, Southwest Harbor
cafedrydockinn.com • Rates: $110–200

Lindenwood Inn • (207) 244-5335
118 Clark Point Rd, Southwest Harbor
lindenwoodinn.com • Rates: $169–349

The Inn at Southwest • (207) 244-3835
371 Main St, Southwest Harbor
innatsouthwest.com • Rates: $120–215

Cranberry Hill Inn • (207) 244-5007
60 Clark Point Rd, Southwest Harbor
cranberryhillinn.com • Rates: $145–200

The Claremont Hotel • (207) 244-5036
22 Claremont Rd, Southwest Harbor
theclaremonthotel.com • Rates: $150–342

Harbor Ridge • (207) 244-7000
39 Freeman Ridge Rd, Southwest Harbor
harborridge.com • Rates: $150–250

Schoodic Peninsula
Acadia's Oceanside Meadows Inn
Rt 195 Prospect Harbor Rd • (207) 963-5557
oceaninn.com • Rates: $179–219

Black Duck Inn • (207) 963-2689
36 Crowley Island Rd, Corea
blackduck.com • Rates: $140–200

Bluff House • (207) 963-7805
57 Bluff House Rd, Gouldsboro
bluffinn.com • Rates: $85–120

Many chain restaurants and hotels can be found nearby in Ellsworth, ME (~22 miles/40 minutes northwest of Acadia NP).

Festivals
Bar Harbor
Birding Festival • June
acadiabirdingfestival.com

Fourth of July • pancake breakfast, parade, lobster bake, lobster races, and fireworks

Strawberry Festival • July

Bar Harbor Music Festival • July
barharbormusicfestival.org

Native American Festival • July

Acadia Outdoor Concert • July

Bar Harbor Jazz Festival • August

Bar Harbor Fine Arts Festival • August

Acadia Night Sky Festival • September
acadianightskyfestival.com

Garlic Festival • September • nostrano.com

Early Bird PJ Sale and Bed Races • November

MDI's Quiet Side
Open Garden Day • July
Northeast Harbor • gcmdgardenday.com

MDI Marathon • October
Northeast Harbor • mdimarathon.org

Flamingo Festival • July • Southwest Harbor

Oktoberfest • October
Southwest Harbor • acadiaoktoberfest.com

Beyond MDI
Windjammer Days Festival • June
Boothbay Harbor • boothbayharbor.com

Old Port Festival • June
Portland • portlandmaine.com

Blistered Fingers Bluegrass Festival • June
Litchfield • blisteredfingers.com

Legacy of the Arts Festival • June
Trenton • legacyartsfestival.com

Yarmouth Clam Festival • July
Yarmouth • clamfestival.com

Bates Dance Festival • July
Lewiston • batesdancefestival.org

Bowdoin Int'l Music Festival • July
Brunswick • bowdoinfestival.org

North Atlantic Blues Festival • July
Rockland • northatlanticbluesfestival.com

Maine International Film Festival • July
Waterville • miff.org

Maine Lobster Festival • August
Rockland • mainelobsterfestival.com

Machias Blueberry Festival • August
Machias • machiasblueberry.com

Great Falls Balloon Festival • August
Lewiston • greatfallsballoonfestival.com

American Folk Festival • August
Bangor, ME • americanfolkfestival.com

Camden Int'l Film Festival • September
Camden • camdenfilmfest.orgAttractions

Attractions
In the Park
Wildwood Stables • (877) 276-3622
Park Loop Road, half mile south of Jordan Pond
Open: mid-June–early October • $20–26

Isleford Historical Museum • Cranberry Island
Open: Seasonal • Admission: Free (transport fee)

Abbe Museum
Sieur de Monts Spring • abbemuseum.org
Open: Seasonal • Admission: $3

Wild Gardens of Acadia • Sieur de Monts Spring
Open: All Year • Admission: Free

Near the Park
Bar Harbor Bicycle • (207) 288-3886
141 Cottage Street, Bar Harbor
barharborbike.com • Open: March–December

Acadia Bike • (207) 288-5000 • acadiabike.com
48 Cottage Street, Bar Harbor • Open: All Year

Southwest Cycle • (207) 244-5856
370 Main Street, Southwest Harbor
southwestcycle.com • Open: April–January

National Park Canoe & Kayak Rental
Pretty Marsh Road, Rte 102, Mount Desert
Open: May–October • (207) 244-5854
nationalparkcanoerental.com

Maine State Kayak • (877) 481-9500
254 Main Street, Southwest Harbor
mainestatekayak.com • Open: May–September

National Park Sea Kayak Tours
39 Cottage Street, Bar Harbor
Open: Memorial Day–October
acadiakayak.com • (800) 347-0940

Acadia Outfitters • (207) 288-8118
106 Cottage Street, Bar Harbor
acadiaoutfitters.com • Open: June–mid-October

Aquaterra Adventures • (877) 386-4124
1 West Street, Bar Harbor
aquaterra-adventures.com • Open: May–September

Coastal Kayaking Tours • (800) 526-8615
48 Cottage Street, Bar Harbor
acadiafun.com • Open: All Year

Atlantic Climbing School • (207) 288-2521 •
67 Main Street, Bar Harbor
Rock Climbing: $105/person (half-day, 2 People)
acadiaclimbing.com • Open: Seasonal

Acadia Mountain Guides • (207) 288-8186 •
228 Main Street, Bar Harbor
Rock Climbing: $99/person (half-day, 2 People)
acadiamountainguides.com • Open: Seasonal '

Cadillac Mountain Sports • (207) 288-2521 •
67 Main Street, Bar Harbor
cadillacsports.com • Open: All Year

Acadia Nat'l Park Tours • (207) 288-0300
Bus tour of the park and Bar Harbor
53 Main St, Bar Harbor
acadiatours.com • Open: Seasonal • $30/adult

Lulu Lobster Boat • (207) 963-2341
55 West St, Bar Harbor • Open: Seasonal
lululobsterboat.com • $35/adult

Oli's Trolley • (207) 288-9899
Trolley tour of the park and MDI
1 Harbor Ln, Bar Harbor • Open: Seasonal
acadiaislandtours.com • $18–32/adult

Scenic Flights of Acadia • (207) 667-6527
Bar Harbor Rd, Trenton • Open: All Year
scenicflightsofacadia.com • Tours: $49–209

Acadia Air Tours • (207) 288-0703
1 West St, Bar Harbor • Open: All Year
acadiaairtours.com • Tours: $149–399

Pirate's Cove Miniature Golf • (207) 288-2133
368 ME-3, Bar Harbor
piratescove.net/location/7
Open: Seasonal • $8.95/adult

Kebo Valley Golf Club • (207) 288-3000
136 Eagle Lake Rd, Bar Harbor
kebovalleyclub.com

Ben&Bill's Chocolate Emporium
66 Main St, Bar Harbor • (207) 288-3281
benandbills.com • Seasonal

Criterion Theatre • (207) 288-0829
35 Cottage St, Bar Harbor • Open: All Year
criteriontheatre.org • Tickets: $8/adult

Real Pizza Cinerama • (207) 288-3811
33 Kennebec Pl, Bar Harbor • Open: All Year
reelpizza.net • Tickets: $6/Seat

ImprovAcadia • (207) 288-2503
15 Cottage St, 2nd Floor, Bar Harbor
improvacadia.com
Open: Seasonal • Tickets: $18/adult

Acadia Repertory Theater • (207) 244-7260
1154 Main St, Mount Desert • Open: Seasonal
acadiarep.com • Tickets: $23/adult

Bar Harbor Oceanarium • (207) 288-5005
1351 ME-3, Bar Harbor •Open: Seasonal
theoceanarium.com

Abbe Downtown Museum • (207) 288-3519
Explores Maine's Native American Heritage
24 Mount Desert St, Bar Harbor
abbemuseum.org
Open: All Year • Admission: $8/adult

Bar Harbor Historical Society • (207) 288-0000
33 Ledgelawn Ave, Bar Harbor • Open: Seasonal
barharborhistorical.org• Admission: Free

Atlantic Brewing Co • (207) 288-2337
15 Knox Rd, Bar Harbor • Open: Seasonal
atlanticbrewing.com • Admission: Free

Seal Cove Auto Museum • (207) 244-9242
1414 Tremont Rd, Seal Cove
Open: Seasonal • Admission: $6/adult

Wendell Gilley Museum • (207) 244-7555
4 Herrick Rd, Southwest Harbor
wendellgilleymuseum.org
Open: Seasonal • Admission: $5/adult

Big Chicken Barn • (207) 667-7308
Antiques and paper collectibles
1768 Bucksport Rd, Ellsworth
bigchickenbarn.com

Beyond the Park
Burnham Tavern Museum
Site of American Revolution's first naval battle
14 Colonial Way, Machias • Seasonal
burnhamtavern.com

Seashore Trolley Museum • (207) 967-2800
World's largest electric rail museum
195 Log Cabin Rd, Kennebunkport
trolleymuseum.org
Open: Seasonal • Admission: $10/adult

Desert of Maine • (207) 865-6962
96 Desert Rd, Freeport • desertofmaine.com
Open: Seasonal • Admission: $12.50/adult

L.L. Bean Flagship Store • (877) 755-2326
95 Maine St, Freeport

Camden Hills State Park • (207) 256-3109
280 Belfast Rd, Camden, ME 04843

Maine Coastal Islands NWR • (207) 546-2124
9 Water St, Rockland

Baxter State Park • (207) 723-5140
*Mt Katahdin, the northern terminus of the
Appalachian Trail, is this park's centerpiece*
64 Balsam Dr, Millinocket
baxterstateparkauthority.com

Northern Outdoors Adventure Resort
Old Canada Rd National Scenic Byway, 1771
US Route 201, The Forks
northernoutdoors.com • (207) 663-4466
Seasonal • $69+/Paddler

North Country Rivers • (207) 672-4814
36 Main St, Bingham
northcountryrivers.com
Open: Seasonal • Rafting: $59+/Paddler

Victoria Mansion • (207) 772-4841
109 Danforth St, Portland
victoriamansion.org
Open: All Year • Admission: $15/adult

Portland Museum of Art • (207) 775-6148
Seven Congress Square, Portland
portlandmuseum.org
Open: All Year • Admission: $15/adult

Allagash Brewing • (207) 878-5385
50 Industrial Way, Portland • allagash.com
Open: All Year • Admission: Free

Children's Museum & Theatre of Maine
142 Free St, Portland
kitetails.org • (207) 828-1234
Open: All Year • Admission: $10/person

Portland Observatory • (207) 774-5561
138 Congress St, Portland
portlandlandmarks.org
Open: Seasonal

Pineapple Ketch • (207) 468-7262
95 Ocean Ave, Kennebunkport
pineappleketch.com • *Sailing excursions*
Open: Seasonal • Sailing: $45/person

Franciscan Monastery • (207) 967-2011
28 Beach Ave, Kennebunk • framon.net
Open: All Year • Admission: Free

Salem Witchhouse • (978) 744-8815
Home of Judge Corwin's witch trials
310½ Essex St, Salem, MA
salemweb.com/witchhouse
Open: Seasonal • Admission: $10.25/adult

Hammond's Castle • (978) 283-2080
An eccentric inventor's castle
80 Hesperus Ave, Gloucester, MA
hammondcastle.org
Open: Seasonal • Admission: $10/adult

Paper House • (972) 546-2629
House built in 1922 out of newspapers
52 Pigeon Hill St, Rockport, MA
paperhouserockport.com
Open: Seasonal • Admission: $2/adult

Boston Science Museum • (617) 723-2500
1 Science Park Driveway, Boston • mos.org
Open: All Year • Admission: $25/adult

Museum of Fine Arts • (617) 267-9300
465 Huntington Ave, Boston
mfa.org • Admission: $25/adult

USS Constitution Museum • (617) 426-1812
Building 22, Charlestown Navy Yard, Boston
ussconstitutionmuseum.org
Open: All Year • Tour: Donation Suggested

JFK Presidential Library and Museum
Columbia Point, Boston • (617) 514-1600
jfklibrary.org
Open: All Year • Admission: $12/adult

Fenway Park • (617) 226-6666
4 Yawkey Way, Boston • redsox.com
Open: All Year • Tour: $18/adult

Samuel Adams Brewery • (617) 368-5080
30 Germania St, Boston • samueladams.com
Open: All Year • Tour: Donation Suggested

Harpoon Brewery • (617) 456-2322
306 Northern Ave, Boston • harpoonbrewery.com
Open: All Year • Tour: $5

Skinny House
4-story narrow (10.4 feet) house built out of spite
44 Hull St, Boston, MA

Great Boston Molasses Flood Plaque
*In 1919, 2-million gallons of molasses flooded these
streets • The molasses was clocked at ~35 mph*
529 Commercial St, Boston, MA

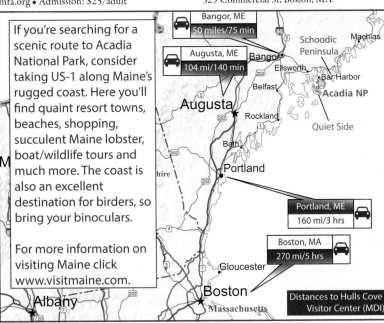

If you're searching for a scenic route to Acadia National Park, consider taking US-1 along Maine's rugged coast. Here you'll find quaint resort towns, beaches, shopping, succulent Maine lobster, boat/wildlife tours and much more. The coast is also an excellent destination for birders, so bring your binoculars.

For more information on visiting Maine click www.visitmaine.com.

Bangor, ME — 50 miles/75 min
Augusta, ME — 104 mi/140 min
Portland, ME — 160 mi/3 hrs
Boston, MA — 270 mi/5 hrs

Distances to Hulls Cove Visitor Center (MDI)

Cuyahoga Valley

A heron fishing near Beaver Marsh

15610 Vaughn Road
Brecksville, OH 44141
(330) 657-2752
Website: nps.gov/cuva

Established: October 11, 2000
Size: 33,000 Acres
Annual Visitors: 2.2 Million
Peak Season: Summer
Hiking Trails: 186 Miles

Activities: Hiking, Biking, Train
Rides, Picnicking, Golf, Horseback
Riding, Fishing, Paddling, Bird
Watching, Cross-Country Skiing,
Snowshoeing, Downhill Skiing,
Sledding, Concerts, Theater, Art
Exhibits, Museums, and Festivals

Campgrounds: No Car Camping
5 Primitive Sites are available at
Stanford House for long distance
bikers/hikers on Towpath Trail

Park Hours: All day, every day
(some areas close at dusk)
Cuyahoga Valley Scenic Railroad
offers train excursions year-round
Entrance Fee: None

Northeastern Ohio might not be a place you expect to find a national park. Towering mountains and gaping gorges are nowhere to be found. But the national parks are all about surprises, and considering its location deep in the middle of the rust belt, Cuyahoga Valley might be the greatest surprise of them all. Miles of undeveloped land are nestled between the sprawling cities of Akron and Cleveland. The valley's geographic beauty may not be as grand or majestic as the natural wonders of the West, but it's an area rich in history and culture. Now a recreational respite, this area has endured decades of development, trade, industry, and pollution before a few thoughtful conservationists began to push for a new era of preservation and protection. The Cuyahoga Valley's history is far from typical of most national parks, but its present is the same: the area has been restored and protected for the enjoyment of the people.

As the Cuyahoga River twists and turns for 22 miles through the center of the park it lives up to its name, meaning "crooked" in the Iroquois language. The same Native Americans who named the river used it as a trade route for thousands of years. By 1795 the river formed the northern boundary between Indian Territory and the United States.

Imaginary boundaries were drawn and erased. Treaties written then ignored. It wasn't long until Ohio became the hub of American industrialization. In 1827, the Ohio & Erie Canal was completed, connecting the Great Lakes region with the Gulf of Mexico via the Mississippi, Ohio, and Cuyahoga Rivers. The route dramatically improved shipping of goods and people to the Great Plains States. Companies like BF Goodrich and Standard Oil prospered, while the Cuyahoga River perished.

The region's rapid development, booming industry, alarming population growth, and inadequate infrastructure spawned a river filled with sewage and industrial waste. So saturated with oils, gases, and chemicals, it was infamously referred to as "the river that burned," catching fire at least thirteen times between 1868 and 1969. A fire in 1969 was short in duration, lasting only 24 minutes, but huge in environmental impact, prompting Time Magazine to write that the water "oozes rather than flows" and that a person "does not drown but decays." The pointed article helped galvanize an environmental movement, which spurred the passing of water quality legislation. State and federal environmental agencies and Earth Day were established thanks to the "river that burned" and the activism it inspired. President Gerald Ford signed a bill creating Cuyahoga Valley National Recreation Area in 1974, and in 2000 Congress changed its designation to a national park. Decades of treatment and restoration efforts have improved water quality. Wildlife has returned. But it's far from the pristine waterway it once was. Boating and swimming are still not recommended and fish caught in these waters are not to be eaten.

The Cuyahoga Valley has been used for recreational purposes since the late 19th century. Recreation began with modest boat trips and carriage rides. Eventually, railroads led to obsolescence of the Ohio & Erie Canal, but the path used by horses and mules to tow seafaring vessels is still used today by hikers and bikers. Twenty miles of the 101-mile Towpath Trail passes through Cuyahoga Valley and it is one of the park's most popular destinations. The railway also serves as a tourist attraction. Cuyahoga Valley Scenic Railroad travels from Canton to Akron and on to Cleveland, making seven stops within the park. Themed excursions, including everything from beer tasting to book reading, are offered throughout the year. The park's urban location lends itself to some atypical attractions like golf courses, a music center and theater, and a ski resort. You can also explore several original and re-created heritage sites where employees in time-period wardrobe serve as your guides.

Cuyahoga Valley's unique combination of nature, history, development, destruction, and restoration has formed a park that is as much a walk through history as it is a walk in the wild. If you take the time to experience some of the park's time period presentations and ranger-led excursions you are sure to have an entertaining, educational, and memorable experience.

Blue Hen Falls

When to Go
Cuyahoga Valley is open all year. Weekends are busy, especially during summer. Spring wildflowers and fall foliage tend to attract larger-than-usual crowds. Winter visitation is moderate.

Boston Store Visitor Center is open all year, daily from 10am–4:30pm, with extended hours in spring and summer.

Canal Exploration Center is open daily from 10am–4:30pm in summer and from 10am–4pm, Wednesday–Sunday in spring; 10am–4:30pm, Wednesday–Sunday in September and October; and 10am–4:30pm, Saturdays and Sundays from November until February.

Frazee House, located at 7733 Canal Road in Valley View, about 3 miles south of Rockside Road, was closed for stabilization at the time of publication.

Hunt House has the following hours:
Spring: Saturdays and Sundays, 10am–4pm
Summer: Daily, 10am–4pm
Fall: Saturdays and Sundays, 10am–4pm
Winter: Closed

Winter Sports Center at Kendall Lake opens in December if at least four inches of snow is present. Call (330) 657-2752 for current snowfall depth.

Stanford Campsites (6093 Stanford Road, Peninsula • 330.657.2909, ext. 119)
Thru-hikers and bikers only • Reservation required
Open late May–Oct • $20/day

Transportation & Airports

Cuyahoga Valley National Park is located in an urban area. Many roads provide access to the park. Greyhound (800.231.2222, greyhound.com) has a bus station in downtown Cleveland and Akron. Amtrak (800.872.7245 or amtrak.com) serves Cleveland.

Cuyahoga Valley Scenic Railroad (800.468.4070, cvsr.com) travels from Canton–Akron–Cleveland, making seven stops within park boundaries.

The closest airports are Cleveland Hopkins International Airport (CLE) and Akron–Canton Regional Airport (CAK).

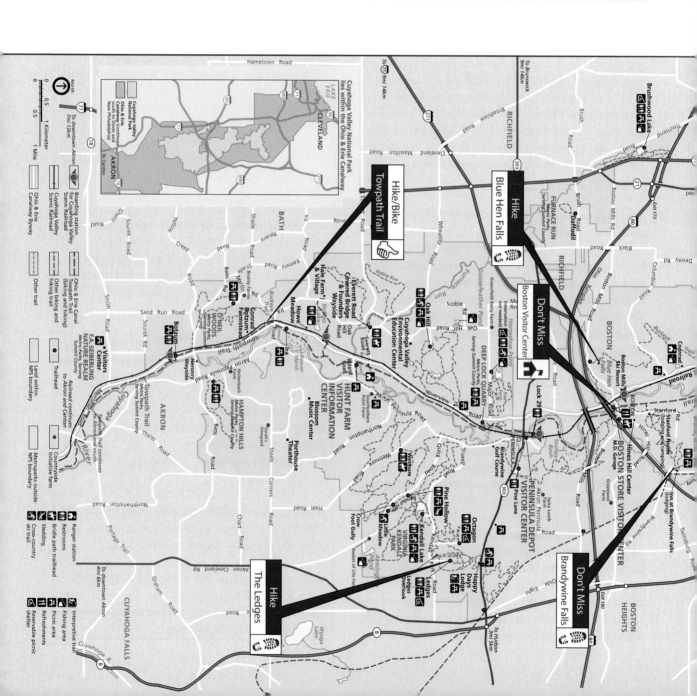

Directions

Canal Visitor Center (7104 Canal Road, Valley View) is approximately 11 miles from downtown Cleveland. Traveling by car from the north, take I-77 south to exit 157 for OH-21/Granger Road/Brecksville Road toward OH-17. Merge onto OH-21/Brecksville Rd. Turn left at Rockside Road. Turn right at Canal Road. The visitor center will be on your right

Boston Store Visitor Center (1550 Boston Mills Road, Peninsula) is approximately 18 miles from downtown Akron. Traveling by car from the south, take OH-8 north. Turn left at E Hines Road and continue on to Boston Mills Road. The visitor center will be on your left.

Brandywine Falls

Best of Cuyahoga Valley

Waterfall Hike: Brandywine Falls
Runner-up: Blue Hen Falls
2nd Runner-up: Buttermilk Falls

Leaf-Peeping Hike: The Ledges
Runner-up: Tinkers Creek Gorge

Family Fun: Ride the Railroad
Runner-up: Bike Ohio & Erie Towpath
2nd Runner-up: Hike to Ice Box Cave

Hiking

Many city dwellers search out sites of natural beauty to escape the stress and frenetic pace of an urban lifestyle. Cuyahoga Valley provides such a location for the people of Akron and Cleveland. With 186 miles of hiking trails it's a great place to clear your mind and enjoy some fresh air.

Cuyahoga Valley was used for recreation as early as the late 1800s, but the region wasn't developed as a park until the early 1900s. In 1929, Hayward Kendall, a Cleveland coal baron, willed 430 acres around Ritchie Ledges to the state of Ohio with the lone stipulation that the "property should be perpetually used for park purposes." His generous donation created Virginia Kendall Park, named in honor of Hayward's mother. Here you'll find one of the park's premier hikes, **Ledges Trail**. Its trailhead is located at Ledges Parking Area just off Kendall Park Road, which becomes Truxell Road. This moderate 2.2-mile hike leads to dramatic eroded sandstone formations known as The Ledges.

Haskell Run Trail is located near The Ledges. Parking is available at Happy Days Lodge Parking Area on the north side of Route 303. The trailhead for this easy 0.5-mile hike is in the southeast corner of the parking lot directly adjacent to the lodge.

Haskell Run and Ledges Trail intersect the short spur to **Ice Box Cave**. It's not exactly a cave, but kids still enjoy the trek to a cool, moist, 50-foot deep slit in solid rock. To pick up the trail from Haskell Run, simply take a short connector trail up a hill and to the left after crossing the first wooden bridge. Wooden steps make the climb easier, and the connector trail intersects Ledges Trail. Turn left along the base of Ritchie Ledges and continue about 0.4-mile to the cave. An excursion to Ice Box Cave adds about 1 mile to the total hiking distance of either The Ledges or Haskell Run trails. It may not be a cave, but it still can be cold and dark in the Ice Box, so remember to pack a jacket and flashlight. (Note: Ice Box Cave was taped off during our last visit to prevent the spread of white-nose syndrome.)

There are more than 70 waterfalls in Cuyahoga Valley. The most popular is 60-foot **Brandywine Falls**, which you can view from an overlook near Inn at Brandywine Falls, or trek 1.25 miles through Brandywine Gorge to get a firsthand look. This moderate hike begins at Brandywine Falls Parking Area on Stanford Mills Road, west of Brandywine Road in Boston Heights. The trail to Brandywine Falls and its overlook are two of the most popular park destinations. You can expect a bit of company, but the views and hike are well worth it.

Blue Hen is next on the pecking order of popular waterfalls. Compared to Brandywine Falls, Blue Hen is merely a trickle, but the small amount of water cascading over rock has considerable appeal. Three narrow ribbons of water fall over a wide, rocky face before cascading into a shallow pool. The 1.2-mile trail is easy to moderate, and its trailhead is located in Boston, on Boston Mills Road, one mile west of Riverview Road. The trailhead parking area is quite small, but overflow parking has been added on the south side of the road. A viewing area offers excellent views of the falls. A bit of scrambling will get you to the waterfall's base. The slightly more impressive 20-foot **Buttermilk Falls** is less than 1-mile downstream from Blue Hen. This trail was recently added and is a more rugged trek.

Tinkers Creek Gorge is a National Natural Landmark in the northeast corner of the park, and holds the Great Falls of Tinkers Creek in Viaduct Park and **Bridal Veil Falls**. Bridal Veil Falls Trailhead is located on Gorge Parkway, 1.4 miles northwest of Egbert Road and about 1 mile east of Overlook Lane in Bedford Reservation. It's an easy 0.25-mile hike to the falls.

Chippewa Creek Trail begins at Brecksville Nature Center parking lot on Chippewa Creek Drive, about 0.5-mile south of State Route 82. This scenic 2.5-mile loop follows both sides of Chippewa Creek. Note that the creek may be impassable during periods of high water. For a moderate to difficult hike, try the Old Carriage Trail between Jaite and Boston. This 5.25-mile trip starts at Red Lock Trailhead located on Highland Road, 0.5-mile east of Riverview and Vaughn Roads.

The 1,300-mile **Buckeye Trail** circles the state of Ohio and runs for 30 miles through Cuyahoga Valley, briefly joining Towpath Trail in the park's southern half. It is well maintained by the Buckeye Trail Association and can be accessed from eight locations within the park. Stretches vary from easy to difficult and anywhere from 1.5 to 7 miles between access points. **Towpath Trail** is another great hiking choice. The segment north of Ira Road Trailhead (see map on page 60) is particularly nice.

Biking
There are four major bicycle trails in the Cuyahoga Valley. Most renowned of these is the **Ohio & Erie Towpath Trail**. This 101-mile crushed stone path follows the historic Ohio & Erie Canal Route, and 20 of its most scenic miles span the length of the park. Along the way you'll find picnic areas, restrooms, and train depots. Thanks to the **Cuyahoga Valley Scenic Valley Railroad** you can have an incredibly unique biking experience. Bike from depot to depot and then take the train back to where you started. With the railroad's **Bike Aboard!** Program cyclists and their bikes ride the train for the reasonable price of $3/person.

You'll also find more than 70 miles of paved bike paths in the park. **Summit County Bike & Hike Trail** follows the park's border for nearly 17 miles. Just between Brecksville and Bedford Metroparks you'll find over 60 miles of paved trails.

If you need to rent a bike or pick up last minute parts there are a few shops in the area (see page 68).

Scenic Railroad
One of the most unique and entertaining experiences in the valley is taking a ride aboard the **Cuyahoga Valley Scenic Railroad (CVSR)**. Owned by the National Parks Service (NPS), it's one of the oldest, longest, and most scenic tourist excursions the NPS offers. The hard part isn't deciding whether or not to ride the CVSR; it's choosing which excursion to take.

Most common is National Park Scenic Excursion ($18–28), which provides visitors a relaxing, enjoyable trip to see the wildlife and scenery of Cuyahoga Valley. You'll also find beer and wine tasting excursions or breakfast, brunch or lunch trips. There are night rides ($10/person), Murder Mysteries ($50/person), and a special program titled "Royalty on the Rails" ($35/person), featuring appearances from your children's favorite characters: Cinderella, Snow White, the Little Mermaid, et al. (Passengers are encouraged to dress up in costume for Royalty on Rails.) In winter, The Polar Express is offered, when children are welcome to wear pajamas aboard the train while *The Polar Express* is read out loud.

Be sure to call CVSR or click cvsr.com to view all seasonal excursions. It's common for National Park rangers to narrate train rides. Passengers will find their knowledge and spirit to be both enlightening and entertaining. Depth and variety of excursions make CVSR an attraction that appeals to just about everyone.

Horseback Riding
Exploring the park on horseback provides an interesting perspective of the park's landscapes and wildlife, and there are 86 miles of signed and designated horse trails at Cuyahoga Valley. However, horse rental and guide services are not available within the park, so visitors keen on riding must trailer their own

horses in. Station Road parking lot, close to Brecksville Reservation, has large pull-through parking spots allowing easy parking and access. Here you'll find several miles of trails around Brecksville Stables Area. Be sure to inquire about trail closures, difficulty, and access before heading out for a ride.

Golf

There are four privately owned and operated golf courses within the park. See page 68 for their locations and rates.

Water Activities

Current restoration efforts are improving water quality of the Cuyahoga River, but high pollutant levels are frequently recorded, especially after heavy rainfalls. While it is navigable, **paddling** isn't recommended and there are no paddle-sport outfitters in the area. Swimming is prohibited.

Fishing, however, is permitted. More than 65 species of fish are found in the park. Catch-and-release fishing is encouraged, and eating fish from the river is not recommended. Motorboats are prohibited within the park, and lakes are occasionally closed for resource management. A fishing license is required in accordance with Ohio regulations. Kendall Lake, Indigo Lake, Brushwood Lake, Conrad Farm Pond, Goosefeather Pond, and Arrington Pond are recommended fishing locations.

Bird Watching

Cuyahoga Valley is an ideal location for bird watching. The park's varied landscapes provide habitat for more than 248 species. After an extended absence due to excessive pollution, blue herons and bald eagles are once again nesting here. Herons are often seen in February as they scavenge for materials to build or repair their nests. Hundreds of nests have been found perched high above the Cuyahoga River at sites north of Route 82 and just south of Bath Road. From February until July you can see herons at either **Bath Road heronry** (from a pullout along Bath Road) or **Pinery Narrows heronry** (from Towpath Trail, 0.5-mile north of Station Road Bridge). Nesting bald eagles can also be found in this area. They returned in 2006 after an absence of more than 70 years.

Beaver Marsh is a great place to spot wood ducks and other waterfowl during their migrations in March and November. Solitary vireos, winter wrens, hermit thrushes, and black-throated warblers frequent the moist hemlocks near Ritchie Ledges in late spring. Red-breasted nuthatches and golden-crowned kinglets call **Horseshoe Pond** their home from late October through early March. Grassland around the former coliseum site (near the intersection of I-80 and I-271 on W. Streetsboro Rd/OH-303) is now habitat for eastern meadowlark, bobolink, savannah sparrow, grasshopper sparrow, and Henslow's sparrow. These species can be seen during their summer breeding season, and it is asked that you stay on the edge of the grassland from April to August because many of these birds nest on the ground.

Winter Activities

There are nearly as many ways to enjoy Cuyahoga Valley National Park in winter as there are in summer. **Winter Sports Center** at Kendall Lake Shelter (located in Peninsula at 1000 Truxell Road, two miles west of Akron Cleveland Road) offers **cross-country skiing** and **snowshoeing**. The Winter Sports Center is open daily (when snow depth is greater than four inches), Dec 26–31; Sat & Sun, Jan 2–Feb 28; Martin Luther King Day, and President's Day, 10am–4pm. Call (330) 657-2752 to confirm.

Snowshoe rental is available at **Boston Store Visitor Center** (open daily from 10am–4:30pm except Christmas and New Year's Day) when snow depth is four inches or greater. Snowshoes cost $5 per pair per day. A popular winter hike is The Ledges where you may be able to see spectacular icicle formations.

Cross-country ski rental is available at the **Winter Sports Center** ($15/day, $7.50/half-day) when snow depth is six inches or greater. Ski instruction is also available with advanced registration (330.657.2752). Towpath Trail is straight, flat, and popular among cross-country skiers.

Ice fishing is permitted at lakes and ponds. **Sledding** is available at Kendall Hills on Quick Road, with parking at Pine Hallow (5465 Quick Road, Peninsula) or Little Meadow (5249 Quick Road, Peninsula) Parking Areas.

Brandywine Ski Resort offers **downhill skiing** and **snowboarding** (daily), and **polar blast tubing** (Thursday–Sunday). See page 68 for location and rates.

Ranger Programs

If the land is the park's body, then the rangers are its soul. Joining a ranger-led excursion is one of the best ways to enhance your visit. You have myriad choices, ranging from bird watching to monarch butterfly monitoring, alien invasions (invasive plant and animal species) to surveying a cemetery, and stargazing to bat watching. Check the park's schedule online or at a visitor center, and then let the rangers make your visit a little more memorable.

For Kids

Kids (ages 7–12) can take part in the park's **Junior Ranger Program** and children (ages 4–6) can participate in the **Junior Ranger, Jr. Program**. These programs are typically offered during the summer. The park also offers multi-day camps and ranger-led hikes throughout summer. Check seasonal park schedules online or at a visitor center for an up-to-date listing of all the great programs geared for children. Hiking to Blue Hen Falls or Ice Box Cave (page 62), or riding the rails (page 63) are excellent family activities.

Flora & Fauna

More than 900 plant species thrive in Cuyahoga Valley. Spring, when wildflowers are in bloom, and fall, when deciduous trees are shedding their leaves, are the most popular seasons to view the valley's plant life. Wildflowers are most abundant in moist areas near creeks and streams, far from trees whose leaves block the sun's light. You may encounter these flowers: spring beauty, yellow trout lily, toothwort, hepatica, bloodroot, dwarf ginseng, Virginia bluebells, spring cress, purple cress, rue anemone, foam flower, twin leaf, bishop's cap, squirrel corn, violets, jack-in-the-pulpit, and many species of trillium. The grasses, trees, and wildflowers play an important role in making this a special place, so appreciate them, or at the very least, don't step on or pick any flowers.

Just as the park serves as a retreat for weary city-dwellers, it is a refuge for a variety of wildlife. For the most part mammals consist of small critters like squirrels,

The Ledges

chipmunks, and mice. But you'll also find white-tailed deer, raccoons, and woodchucks scurrying about. You may not see beavers, but you will see their handiwork in the form of felled trees and dammed streams. If you're lucky you may catch a glimpse of a coyote or river otter. These species naturally returned to the park in recent years. Also residing here are dozens of species of reptiles, amphibians, insects, and birds.

Pets

Pets must be kept on a leash no more than six feet in length at all times. Only service animals are allowed in park buildings and on the train.

Accessibility

Canal and Boston Store Visitor Centers, as well as Hunt Farm Visitor Information Center, Frazee House, Happy Days Lodge, and Towpath Trail are accessible to wheelchair users. Contact the park or CVSR (page 63) with specific questions, comments, and concerns.

Bridalveil Falls

Weather

Weather at Cuyahoga Valley is typical of the Midwest. Winters are cold and often snowy. The Cleveland area averages 61 inches of snowfall, but annual accumulation varies greatly from year-to-year. Average annual precipitation is 35 inches, with 20 inches accumulating between the months of April and September. Summers are typically hot and humid with unpredictable thunderstorms. Most guests travel to the park in summer, but fall might be the ideal time to visit, when cool, crisp, clear days and colorful foliage make the valley particularly inviting.

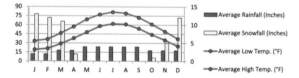

Vacation Planner

Most visitors travel to the park on a summer weekend when many ranger programs are offered and the majority of park attractions are open for business. The following two day itinerary will help you plan your Cuyahoga Valley vacation. Please note that camping is not available in the park and **Inn at Brandywine Falls** (page 68) provides the only lodging. Nearby dining, grocery stores, lodging, festivals, and attractions are listed on pages 68–69.

Day 1: Begin your trip at **Canal Visitor Center**. It's a renovated 1820's Canal House where you can watch a short video on the park, view exhibits, and have your questions answered. Exhibits explore the history of the Ohio & Erie Canal. You can even witness a demonstration of how a lock works at Lock 38, the last operational lock in the park. Remember to browse the list of ranger-led activities, and plan around any excursions you want to take part in. From here it's a short drive to **Tinker's Creek Gorge** (page 63). Decide for yourself whether you walk the trails or take in the beautiful vistas from overlooks along Tinkers Creek Road, then return to **Ohio & Erie Canal Scenic Byway** and head south along the length of the park. Along the way you'll pass **Frazee House** (stop if you're interested in early 19th-century architecture). Continue south to Boston Mills Road, where you'll want to head west to **Blue Hen Falls** parking area (page 62). Stretch your legs on this short but rewarding hike. Before calling it a day in the Cuyahoga Valley, stop at **Brandywine Falls** (page 62), the crown jewel of the park. It's an excellent place to picnic or watch the sunset.

Day 2: Start your day by driving to Kendall Park Road. Stop at **Ledges** for a late morning hike. Then return to Riverview Road, continuing south to Ira. Here you'll explore **Towpath Trail** on foot (or bike). As you walk through **Beaver Marsh**, imagine horses and mules pulling boats through the canal. Nearby is a reconstructed version of the 1870s **Everett Road Covered Bridge**. Ohio led the nation in covered bridge construction when they were in fashion. Everett Road Covered Bridge is one of more than 2,000 covered bridges in the state, but it is important enough to the community and the park that it was rebuilt after a flood destroyed it in 1975. **Hale Farm and Village** is located nearby. You could easily spend an entire day at this site where you are transported to the 1860s. Watch spinning, weaving, pottery-making, blacksmithing, candle-making, glass-blowing, basket-making, and other aspects of 19th-century farm-life in Cuyahoga Valley.

With everything Cuyahoga Valley has to offer, two days isn't nearly enough time to experience it all. Be sure to come back and ride the **Cuyahoga Valley Scenic Railroad** (page 63), take in a concert at **Blossom Music Center** (summer home of the Cleveland Orchestra) or a play at **Porthouse Theater** (page 68).

Dining

Winking Lizard • (330) 467-1002
1615 Main St, Peninsula
winkinglizard.com • Entrée: $8–23

Fisher's Café • (330) 657-2651
1607 Main St, Peninsula
fisherscafe.com • Entrée: $8–19

The Wine Mill • (234) 571-2594
4964 Akron Cleveland Rd, Peninsula
thewinemill.com

Aladdin's Eatery • (216) 642-7550
6901 Rockside Rd, Independence
aladdinseatery.com

Lockkeepers • (216) 524-9404
8001 Rockside Rd, Valley View
lockkeepers.com • Entrée: $15–39

Austin's Wood Fire Grille • (440) 546-1003
8121 Chippewa Rd, Brecksville
austinsrestaurants.com • Entrée: $11–45

Vaccaro's Trattoria • (330) 666-6158
1000 Ghent Rd, Akron
vactrat.com • Entrée: $8–37

George's Donuts • (330) 963-9902
7995 Darrow Rd # 6, Twinsburg

Downtown 140 • (330) 655-2940
140 N Main St, Hudson
downtown140.com • Entrée: $28–40

Flip Side • (330) 655-3547
49 Village Way, Hudson
flipsideburger.com

3 Palms Pizzeria • (330) 342-4545
60 Village Way, Hudso
3palmspizzeria.com

Yours Truly Restaurant • (330) 656-2900
36 S Main St, Hudson
ytr.com • Entrée: $9–13

Carrie Cerino's Ristorante • (440) 237-3434
8922 Ridge Rd, North Royalton
carriecerinos.com • Entrée: $9–29

Creekside Restaurant and Bar • (440) 546-0555
8803 Brecksville Rd, Brecksville
creeksiderestaurant.com • Entrée: $9–23

Courtyard Café • (440) 526-9292
7600 Chippewa Rd, Brecksville
courtyardbrecksville.com • Entrée: $9–23

Tinkers Creek Road Tavern • (216) 642-3900
14000 Tinkers Creek Rd, Walton Hills
tinkerstavern.com

Pulp Juice & Smoothie Bar • (330) 467-0022
746 E Aurora Rd # 11, Macedonia
pulpjuiceandsmoothie.com

Grocery Stores

Heinen's Fine Foods • (440) 740-0535
8383 Chippewa Rd, Brecksville

Sam's Club • (440) 232-2582
23300 Broadway Ave, Oakwood Village

Walmart Supercenter • (216) 587-0110
22209 Rockside Rd, Bedford

Lodging

Inn At Brandywine Falls • (330) 467-1812
8230 Brandywine Rd, Northfield
innatbrandywinefalls.com • $149–499/night

Shady Oaks Farm B&B • (330) 468-2909
241 West Highland Road, Northfield
shadyoaksfarmbnb.com • $150–350/night

Jeremiah B King Guest House • (330) 650-0199
272 N Main St, Hudson
kingguesthouse.com • $125–175/night

The Cobbler Shop B&B • (800) 287-1547
121 E Second St, Zoar • $125–150/night

Hilton Garden Inn • (330) 405-4488
8971 Wilcox Dr, Twinsburg • $159–193/night

Many chain restaurants and hotels can be found nearby in Macedonia and Richfield.

Festivals

Riverfront Irish Festival • June
Falls River Square • Cuyahoga Falls
riverfrontirishfest.org

Avon Heritage Duct Tape Festival • June
Veteran's Mem. Park, 37001 Detroit Rd, Avon
ducttapefestival.com

Italian American Festival • July • (330) 699-9911
Cuyahoga Falls • festaitalianacf.com

Pro Football Hall of Fame Festival • July
2121 George Halas Dr NW, Canton
profootballhoffestival.com • (330) 456-7253

Akron Arts Expo • July • (330) 375-2835
Hardesty Park, Akron • akronartsexpo.org

National Hamburger Festival • August
Lock 3 Park, 200 S Main St, Akron
hamburgerfestival.com • (716) 565-4141

Twins Day Festival • August • Twinsburg
World's largest gathering of twins • twinsdays.org

Yankee Peddler Festival • September
Clay's Park Resort, Canal Fulton
yankeepeddlerfestival.com

Norton Cider Festival • September
Columbia Woods Park, Norton
nortonciderfestival.com • (330) 825-8866

IngenuityFest • September
Voinovich Park, Cleveland
ingenuitycleveland.com

Oktoberfest • September
Riverfront Centre, Riverfront Parkway,
Cuyahoga Falls• oktoberfestcfo.com

Barberton Mum Fest • September
Lake Anna Park & Gazebo, Barberton
cityofbarberton.com/govt/MumFest

Hale Farm Harvest Festival • October
Hale Farm and Village • (330) 666-3711
2686 Oak Hill Rd, Bath

Covered Bridge Festival • October
Covered Bridge Capital of the World: Ashtabula
coveredbridgefestival.org

Attractions
In the Park

Cuyahoga Valley Railroad • (800) 468-4070
1630 West Mill St, Peninsula
cvsr.com • Adult: $18–28, Child: $13–23

Blossom Music Center • (330) 920-8040
1145 W Steels Corners Rd, Cuyahoga Falls

Hale Farm & Village • (330) 666-3711
2686 Oak Hill Rd, Bath
wrhs.org

Cuyahoga Valley Historical Museum
1775 Main St, Peninsula • (330) 657-2892
peninsulalibrary.org

Brecksville Nature Center • (440) 526-1012
9000 Chippewa Creek Dr, Cleveland
clevelandmetroparks.com

Porthouse Theatre Co • (330) 672-3884
3143 O'Neil Rd, Cuyahoga Falls

Astorhurst Country Club • (440) 439-3636
7000 Dunham Road, Cleveland
golfastorhurst.com
Rates: $14–15.50/9-holes, $17.50–23/18-holes

Brandywine Golf Course • (330) 657-2525
5555 Akron Peninsula Road, Peninsula
golfbrandywine.com
Rates: $11–15/9-holes, $18–29/18-holes

Shawnee Hills Golf Course • (440) 232-7184
18753 Egbert Road, Bedford
clemetparks.com
Rates: $15–19/9-holes, $26–32/18-holes

Sleepy Hollow Golf Course • (440) 526-4285
9445 Brecksville Road, Cleveland
clemetparks.com
Rates: $8–25/9-holes, $31–39/18-holes

Boston Mills & Brandywine Ski Resort
1146 W Highland Road, Sagamore Hills
bmbw.com • (800) 875-4241
Lift Ticket: $28–43 (Adult), $28–38 Junior,
$10 (Child & Senior) • Rental: $30 (Adult &
Senior), $25 (Junior & Child) • Helmet: $10 •
Lessons: $25 (Group)

Near the Park

Century Cycles • (330) 657-2209
1621 Main St, Peninsula • centurycycles.com
Bike Rental: $9/hour, Tag-a-long: $4.50/hour

Blimp City Bike & Hike • (330) 836-6600
1720 Merriman Road, Akron
blimpcitybikeandhike.com
Bike Rental: $9/hour

Ernie's Bicycle Shop • (330) 832-5111
135 Lake Ave NW, Massillon
erniesbikeshop.com • Bike Rental: $5–10/hour

Falls Wheel & Wrench Bike Shop
2445 State Road, Cuyahoga Falls
fallswheelandwrench.com • (330) 928-0533

Geauga Lake's Wildwater Kingdom
1100 Squires Rd, Aurora • (330) 562-8303
wildwaterfun.com • Admission: $35/adult

Regal Cinemas Hudson Cinema 10
5339 Darrow Rd, Hudson • (330) 655-7722
regmovies.com • Tickets: $9.50/adult

Cinemark At Macedonia • (330) 908-1005
8161 Macedonia Commons Blvd, Macedonia
cinemark.com • Tickets: $9.50/adult

Fun 'n' Stuff • (330) 467-0820
661 Highland Rd E, Macedonia
fun-n-stuff.com

North Woods Bowling Lanes • (330) 467-7925
10435 Valley View Rd, Macedonia
northwoodslanes.com

Dittrick Museum of Medical History
11000 Euclid Ave, Cleveland
case.edu • Admission: Free • (216) 368-3648

Cleveland Museum of Art • (216) 421-7340
11150 E Blvd, Cleveland
clevelandart.org • Admission: Free

USS Cod • (216) 566-8770
1201 N Marginal Rd, Cleveland
usscod.org • Admission: $10/adult

A Christmas Story House • (216) 298-4919
Original house from the movie: A Christmas Story
3159 W 11th St, Cleveland
achristmasstoryhouse.com • Admission: $10/adult

West Side Market • (216) 664-3387
Ste C9, 1979 W 25th St, Cleveland
westsidemarket.org

Cleveland Browns Stadium • (440) 891-5001
100 Alfred Lerner Way, Cleveland
clevelandbrowns.com • Tours: $5/person

Progressive Field • (216) 420-4487
Home of the Cleveland Indians
2401 Ontario St, Cleveland
cleveland.indians.mlb.com • Tours: $10/adult

Quicken Loans Arena • (216) 420-2000
Home of the Cleveland Cavaliers
1 Center Court, Cleveland • theqarena.com

Lake View Cemetery • (216) 421-2665
12316 Euclid Ave, Cleveland
lakeviewcemetery.com

Great Lakes Science Center • (216) 574-6262
601 Erieside Ave, Cleveland
glsc.org • Admission: $15/adult

Cleveland Metroparks Zoo • (216) 661-6500
3900 Wildlife Way, Cleveland
clevelandmetroparks.com/zoo • $13.25/adult

Rock and Roll Hall of Fame and Museum
1100 E 9th St, Cleveland • (216) 781-7625
rockhall.com • Admission: $23.50/adult

Old Arcade • (216) 696-1408
401 Euclid Ave # 155, Cleveland
theclevelandarcade.com

Akron Zoological Park • (330) 375-2550
500 Edgewood Ave, Akron
akronzoo.org • Admission: $12/adult

McKinley Presidential Library & Museum
800 McKinley Monument Drive NW, Canton
mckinleymuseum.org • (330) 455-7043 • $9/adult

Canton Classic Car Museum • (330) 455-3603
123 6th St SW, Canton
cantonclassiccar.org • Admission: $7.50/adult

Pro Football Hall of Fame • (330) 456-8207
2121 George Halas Dr NW, Canton
profootballhof.com • Admission: $24/adult

Canton Palace Theatre • (330) 454-8172
605 Market Ave N, Canton
cantonpalacetheatre.org

Beyond the Park

Kelleys Island Ferry • (419) 798-9763
See Kelly's Island's Glacial Grooves
510 W Main St, Lakeside Marblehead
kelleysislandferry.com

Warther Museum • (330) 343-7513
331 Karl Ave, Dover • *Incredible wood carvings*
warthers.com • Admission: $13/adult

Henry Ford Museum • (313) 982-6001
Home of Edison's Last Breath
20900 Oakwood Blvd, Dearborn, MI
thehenryford.org • Admission: $21/adult

Cedar Point/Soak City Amusent Parks
1 Cedar Point Dr, Sandusky • (419) 627-2350
cedarpoint.com • Admission: $65/adult

Kalahari Waterpark Resort • (419) 433-4958
7000 Kalahari Dr, Sandusky
kalahariresorts.com • Admission: $59/adult

The Merry-Go-Round Museum • (419) 626-6111
301 Jackson St, Sandusky • Admission: $6/adult
merrygoroundmuseum.org

Ghostly Manor Thrill Center • (419) 626-4467
Ghostly Manor ($11), 4D Theater ($7), Skateworld
3319 Milan Rd, Sandusky • ghostlymanor.com

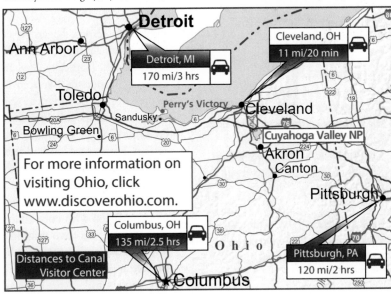

Detroit

Ann Arbor

Detroit, MI
170 mi/3 hrs

Cleveland, OH
11 mi/20 min

Toledo

Perry's Victory

Sandusky

Cleveland

Bowling Green

Cuyahoga Valley NP

Akron
Canton

For more information on
visiting Ohio, click
www.discoverohio.com.

Pittsburgh

Ohio

Columbus, OH
135 mi/2.5 hrs

Pittsburgh, PA
120 mi/2 hrs

Distances to Canal
Visitor Center

Columbus

The rocky path to Old Rag

Shenandoah

3655 US Highway 211 East
Luray, VA 22835
Phone: (540) 999-3500
Website: nps.gov/shen

Established: December 26, 1935
Size: 199,000 Acres
Annual Visitors: 1.3 Million
Peak Season: October
Hiking Trails: 516 Miles
Horse Trails: 201 Miles
Driving: 105-Mile Skyline Drive

Activities: Hiking, Rapidan Camp Tours, Backpacking, Biking, Rock Climbing, Horseback Riding, Bird Watching, and Fishing

Campgrounds ($15–17/night): Big Meadows, Mathews Arm, Loft Mountain, Lewis Mountain
Lodging ($87–285/night): Big Meadows Lodge, Skyland Resort, Lewis Mountain

Park Hours: All day, every day
Entrance Fee: $20/vehicle, $10/individual (foot, bike, etc.)

Shenandoah National Park is centered on a long narrow stretch of the Blue Ridge Mountains. Forested mountaintops give way to the Shenandoah River Valley to the west and the gentle hills of the Virginia Piedmont to the east. The 105-mile Skyline Drive bisects the park as it follows the mountains' crest. Located just 75 miles from the nation's capital, it may come as no surprise that the park's creation had as much to do with politics and personalities as with natural forces.

Long before it received federal government protection, the Shenandoah region served many purposes to many people. Native Americans hunted and gathered for survival. Loggers and miners tapped the land for its resources. Union and Confederate soldiers shed blood deep in the Shenandoah Valley.

Eventually resorts began to crop up high atop the mountains, and for the past century Skyland Resort has served as recreational hub of Shenandoah. Ironically, Skyland never intended to be a company specializing in tourism. Between 1854 and 1866, a large tract of land within present park boundaries exchanged hands between numerous mining companies on speculation of substantial copper and iron deposits. Miners Lode Copper Company found the land to be commercially unsuccessful. However, George Freeman Pollock, son of one of the primary shareholders, convinced his father the land had value as a resort. On October 1, 1889, Pollock's father and Stephen M. Allen formed the Blue Ridge Stonyman Park Preserve. Guests paid $9.50 per week to sleep in tents outfitted with cots, chairs, washstands, and pitchers. An idea far more prosperous than mining ever was, but not enough to cover debt owed on the land's initial purchase. Stonyman Preserve had to be put up for sale at public auction to satisfy the mortgage. George Freeman Pollock, jobless and unsure of his future, was allowed to buy the Blue Ridge land on credit. He renamed it Skyland Resort, but his attempts at business fared much like his father's. He found himself in continuous debt, never actually gaining title to the land. Pollock may not have been much of a businessman, but he was a successful marketer. He threw elaborate balls, costume parties, jousts, musicals, pageants, and bonfires. His other skill was pandering to Washington's politicians. He became one of the most influential local advocates for the construction of Skyline Drive and the formation of a national park, but at the time of the park's establishment in 1935, Pollock had $67,107 in outstanding liens against a property appraised at less than $30,000.

Growth and success of national parks in the west sparked Congress to commission the Southern Appalachian Committee to perform a thorough and wide-ranging survey of prospective locations in the east. The committee's survey proposed that land of present day Mammoth Cave, Shenandoah, and the Great Smoky Mountains met the ideals of a U.S. National Park, and on February 25, 1924, Congress authorized establishment of Shenandoah National Park. Authorization was easy, but procuring land for the park proved challenging. More than 1,000 privately owned tracts had to be turned over to federal ownership, a drastic change compared to western parks where most land was already federally owned. The state of Virginia responded by acquiring 1,088 tracts of land through condemnation and eminent domain, then donating all of it to the federal government. Some 465 mountain residents moved or were forced to move, but a few were allowed to live out their lives within the park. The last life-long resident, Annie Bradley Shenk, passed away in 1979 at the age of 92.

By the time the park was established, development was well underway thanks to the effort of George Freeman Pollock and President Roosevelt's New Deal. Forty miles of Skyline Drive were already completed. Ten CCC camps, housing as many as 1,000 workers, were set-up. The CCC built trails and facilities around Skyland and Skyline Drive, which would become the primary attractions of a successful park that presently receives more than one million annual visitors.

When to Go
Shenandoah National Park is open all year, but the majority of visitors arrive in October for colorful displays of fall foliage. If you plan on visiting during this time, it is advised you arrive early, preferably on a weekday. Skyline Drive, the only public road through the park, closes occasionally for inclement weather. Several park facilities operate seasonally.

It's a good idea to begin your trip at one of its **visitor centers**: Dickey Ridge or Harry F. Byrd, Sr. Both locations offer exhibits, an information desk, a bookstore, and an orientation film. You'll also find restrooms, first aid, and backcountry permits. The best resource the visitor centers offer is their staff of friendly park rangers. They lead guests on ranger programs and are available to answer questions.

Transportation & Airports
Shenandoah National Park was designed with motorists in mind. Four entrances provide access to 105-mile scenic Skyline Drive.

The closest airports are Washington Dulles International (IAD) (56 miles east of Front Royal) and Reagan International (DCA) (70 miles east of Front Royal). Closer to the park you'll find two smaller airports: Shenandoah Valley Regional Airport (SHD) (27 miles west of Swift Run Gap), and Charlottesville–Albemarle (CHO) (31 miles east of Rockfish Gap).

Directions
The park has four entrances: Front Royal, via I-66 and Route 340; Thornton Gap, via Route 211; Swift Run Gap, via Route 33; and Rockfish Gap, via I-64 and Route 250.

Pittsburgh, PA to North Entrance (~190 miles): Travel east on I-76 to exit 161. Take I-70 East to US-522 South. Continue on US-522 to Route 37 South to I-81. Take I-81 South to I-66 East. Take I-66 to Front Royal, and then follow park signs to the park's entrance.

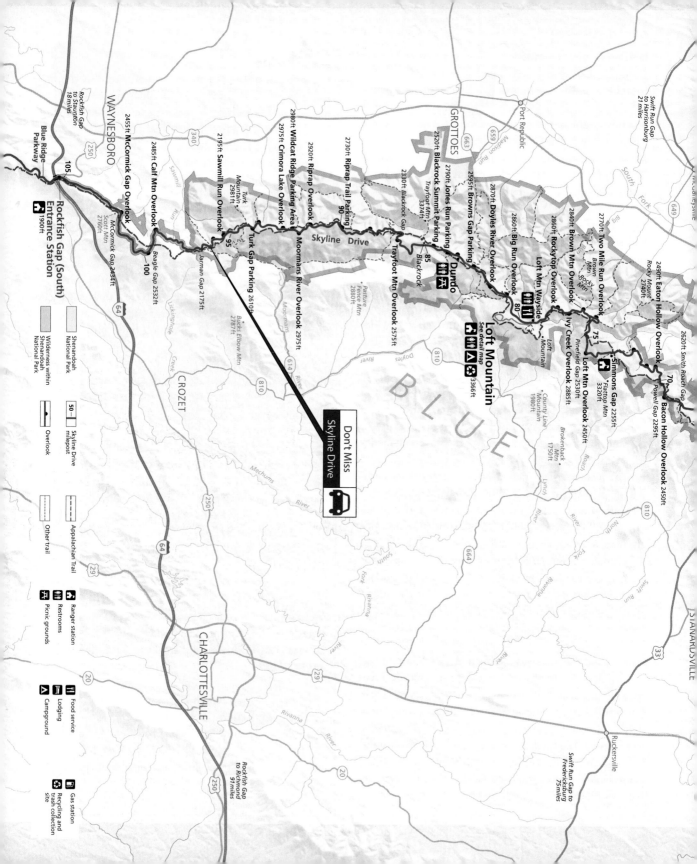

WAYNESBORO

GROTTOES

Port Republic

Madison Run

Brown Run

South Fork

Piedmont

Swift Run Gap
to Harrisonburg
21 miles

Rockfish Gap
to Staunton
18 miles

Blue Ridge
Parkway

105

**Rockfish Gap (South)
Entrance Station**
1900ft

2455ft **McCormick Gap Overlook**

McCormick Gap 2435ft

Scott Mtn
2760ft

2485ft **Calf Mtn Overlook**

Beagle Gap 2532ft

100

2195ft **Sawmill Run Overlook**

Jarman Gap 2175ft

Turk
Mountain
2981ft

95

2980ft **Wildcat Ridge Parking Area**

2975ft **Crimora Lake Overlook**

2920ft **Riprap Overlook**

Moormans River Overlook 2975ft

Turk Gap Parking 2610ft

Skyline   Drive

Black Elbow Mtn
2787ft

Buck's
Elbow Mtn
2880ft

Pasture
Fence Mtn
2880ft

2730ft **Riprap Trail Parking**
90

2330ft **Blackrock Gap**

Trayfoot Mtn Overlook 2575ft

85

Blackrock

2520ft **Blackrock Summit Parking**

2790ft **Jones Run Parking**

Trayfoot Mtn
3374ft

2595ft **Browns Gap Parking**

Dundo 🏕 ⛺

2870ft **Doyles River Overlook**

2860ft **Big Run Overlook**

Doyles River

Loft Mountain
See detail map
🏕 🚻 🏕 ⚠️ ⛺
3366ft

2490ft **Rockytop Overlook**

Loft Mtn Wayside
🚻 🍴

80

Loft
Mountain

2840ft **Brown Mtn Overlook**

Brown
Mtn

Rocky
Mtn

2770ft **Two Mile Run Overlook**

Ivy Creek Overlook 2885ft

Pinefield Gap 2530ft

75

County Line
Mountain
1980ft

Brokenback
Mtn
1750ft

Loft Mtn Overlook 2530ft

2450ft

Flattop Mtn
3320ft

2255ft **Simmons Gap** ⛺

Powell Gap 2295ft

70

Bacon Hollow Overlook 2450ft

2490ft **Eaton Hollow Overlook**
Rocky Mount
2740ft

2620ft **Smith Roach Gap**

B L U E

Lynch River

Mechums   River

Rivanna River

South   Fork   Rivanna   River

North Fork

CROZET

CHARLOTTESVILLE

STANARDSVILLE

RUCKERSVILLE

Swift Run Gap
to Fredericksburg
75 miles

Rockfish Gap
to Richmond
91 miles

Don't Miss

Skyline Drive

🚗

Shenandoah
National Park

Wilderness within
Shenandoah
National Park

50 — Skyline Drive
milepost

Overlook

Appalachian Trail

Other trail

🏕 Ranger station

🚻 Restrooms

🏕 Picnic grounds

🍴 Food service

🏨 Lodging

⚠️ Campground

⛽ Gas station

♻️ Recycling and
trash collection
site

New Market
*Thornton Gap
to Harrisonburg
42 miles*

M A S S A N U T T E N

M O U N T A I N

211

211

340

340

BUS
340

STANLEY

SHENANDOAH

ELKTON

LURAY

Park
Headquarters

Hike
Limberlost Trail

Pass Mountain Overlook 2460ft

2085ft

30

231

522

Shenandoah River

340

33

Shenandoah River

65

60

55

50

45

40

35

R I D G E

Byrd Visitor Center
3535ft **Big Meadows**
See detail map

Skyland
3680ft Highest point on drive
See detail map

**Swift Run Gap
Entrance Station**
2710ft
2365ft

Swift Run Overlook
Hightop Mountain Parking 2637ft
Hightop Mountain 3587ft

3125ft The Oaks Overlook
South River Overlook
2950ft
South River
Saddleback Mountain 3375ft

3235ft The Point Overlook
3295ft Bearfence Mtn Parking

Piney Mountain 1975ft
Green Mountain 2149ft
Huckleberry Mountain 2158ft
Grindstone Mountain 2850ft

Naked Creek
Dry Run
Elk Run

3323ft Milam Gap Parking
3230ft Naked Creek Overlook
Lewis Mountain
See detail map
Bearfence Mountain 3441ft

Lewis Mountain 3325ft
Bush Mountain 3235ft
Booten Gap 3527ft
Hazeltop 3812ft

Tanners Ridge

3250ft Naked Creek Overlook
3070ft Fishers Gap Overlook
3140ft Franklin Cliffs Overlook
3150ft Spitler Knoll Overlook

Dark Hollow Falls Parking 3490ft
Tanners Ridge Overlook 3465ft
Upper Hawksbill Parking 3630ft
405ft Hawksbill *Highest peak in park*
3365ft Hawksbill Gap Parking
3550ft Timber Hollow Overlook
3560ft Crescent Rock Overlook
3710ft Betty's Rock

Old Rag Overlook
3710ft
Whiteoak Canyon Parking 3510ft
Limberlost Parking
Thorofare Mtn Overlook 3595ft
Pinnacle Peak 3401ft
Hemlock Springs Overlook 3380ft
Hughes River Gap 3100ft
3215ft Little Stony Man Parking
4011ft Stony Man
3100ft Stony Man Overlook
Pinnacles
Pinnacles Overlook 3350ft
Pinnacles Overlook 3320ft
Jewell Hollow Overlook 3320ft

Rapidan Camp

Ranger Tour
Rapidan Camp

Hike
Dark Hollow Falls

Adventure Hike
Old Rag

Old Rag Mtn 3268ft

Hazel Mtn Overlook 2770ft
Meadow Spring Parking 2510ft
Tunnel Parking Overlook 2840ft
Hazel Mtn 2860ft
Tunnel clearance 12'8"
Mary's Rock
2300ft

STANARDSVILLE

South River

230

662

Rapidan River

Fork Mountain

Bluff Mountain
Jones Mountain

Kirtley Mountain 2593ft

Doubletop Mountain

WOLFTOWN

MADISON

29

230

670

Syria

600

643

670

600

231

Banco

601

707

600

Robinson River

Hughes River

BANCO

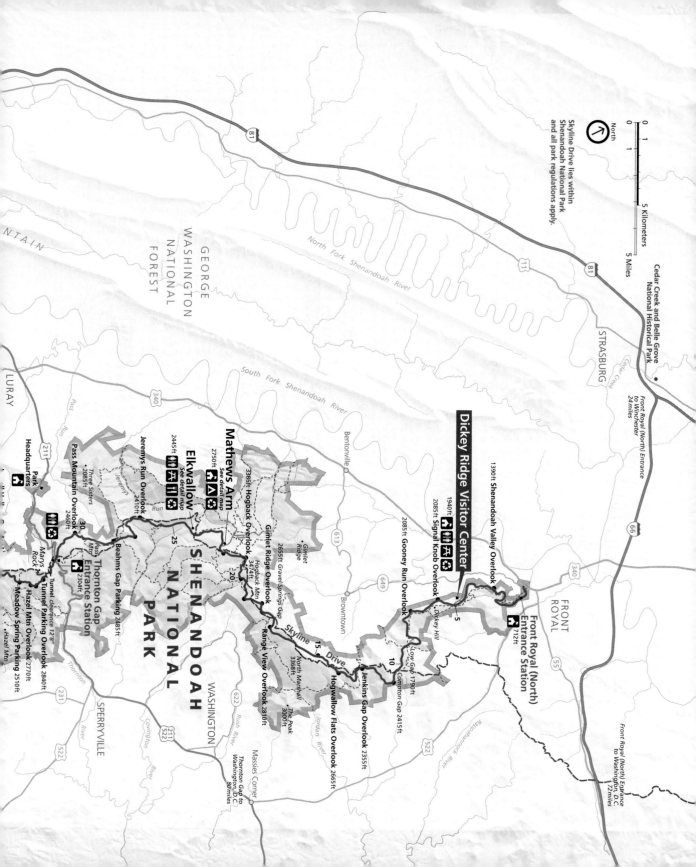

North

Skyline Drive lies within
Shenandoah National Park
and all park regulations apply.

0   1   5 Kilometers
0   1   5 Miles

Cedar Creek and Belle Grove
National Historical Park

STRASBURG

North Fork Shenandoah River

Cedar Creek

81

111

66

55

340

522

Front Royal (North) Entrance
to Winchester
24 miles

Front Royal (North) Entrance
to Washington, D.C.
72 miles

FRONT
ROYAL

Front Royal (North)
Entrance Station
712ft

1390ft Shenandoah Valley Overlook

1940ft
2085ft Signal Knob Overlook

Dickey Ridge Visitor Center

2085ft Gooney Run Overlook

Dickey Hill

5

Low Gap 1790ft

Compton Gap 2415ft

10

Jenkins Gap Overlook 2355ft

Hogwallow Flats Overlook 2665ft

The Peak
3000ft

North Marshall
3368ft

15

Range View Overlook 2810ft

Skyline Drive

Bentonville

Browntown

Massies Corner

613

649

522

Rappahannock River

Jordan River

Rush River

Thornton Gap to
Washington, D.C.
80 miles

622

211
522

SPERRYVILLE

231

Thornton River

Covington River

WASHINGTON

SHENANDOAH
NATIONAL
PARK

Gravel Springs Gap
2666ft

Gimlet Ridge Overlook
Hogback Mtn
3474ft

Gimlet
Ridge

3386ft Hogback Overlook

Mathews Arm
See detail map

2750ft

Elkwallow
See detail map

2445ft

Jeremys Run Overlook
2410ft

Jeremys Run

Three Sisters
2085ft

Pass Mountain Overlook 2460ft

30

Pass Mtr

Beahms Gap Parking 2485ft

25

20

**Thornton Gap
Entrance Station**
2304ft

Tunnel clearance 12'8"

Tunnel Parking Overlook 2840ft

Marys
Rock

Hazel Mtn Overlook 2770ft

Meadow Spring Parking 2510ft

Hazel Mtn.

Park
Headquarters

211

LURAY

340

South Fork Shenandoah River

Pass Run

GEORGE
WASHINGTON
NATIONAL
FOREST

N T A I N

Washington, D.C. to North Entrance (~70 miles): Travel west on I-66 to Front Royal. Exit onto Route 34. From here, signs will direct you to the park's entrance.

Washington, D.C. to Thornton Gap Entrance (~81 miles): Travel west on I-66 to exit 43A. Take US-29 South to Warrenton. Take US-211 West into the park.

Richmond, VA to South Entrance (~90 miles): Travel west on I-64 to exit 99. From here, signs will direct you to the park's entrance.

Richmond, VA to Swift Run Gap Entrance (~95 miles): Travel west on I-64 to Charlottesville. Take the exit to US-29 North. Turn left onto US-33 West into the park.

Skyline Drive

Skyline Drive is a National Scenic Byway that runs 105 miles from north to south spanning the entire length of the park. Milepost markers, located on the west side of the road, make locating the park's facilities and services on Skyline Drive a snap. They're also an important tool for using this guidebook as the location of park trailheads, campgrounds, and lodgings are all defined by their milepost. When travelling this scenic drive, be sure to follow the 35 mph speed limit. Typical to mountain driving, you'll find steep hills, sharp turns, and frequent stops (75 overlooks). Be aware of **Mary's Rock Tunnel** (Mile 32)—RVs, horse trailers, and other vehicles taller than 12' 8" will have to detour around it.

In 1931, crews broke ground on Skyline Drive. Political posturing and the Great Depression slowed the pace of the project. The stretch from Rockfish Gap to Front Royal wasn't completed until 1939 at a total cost near $5 million or $50,000 per mile. Contractors built the highway, but it would not have been completed without the CCC's help. They graded the slope on either side of the roadway, and built many of the guardrails and guard walls. Other sections of road were built simply to see if it was possible. Legend holds that the 670-foot Mary's Rock Tunnel was designed to settle a challenge between the Bureau of Public Roads and National Park Landscape Architects. After completion, facilities were needed to accommodate guests. In western parks infrastructure was developed independently by powerful railways. Shenandoah didn't have the luxury of a railroad's deep pockets. In 1937, with no plan and few ideas, Congress turned to a concessioner, Virginia Sky-Line Company (now Aramark). Sky-Line dictated much of the park's direction and development from 1937 to 1942.

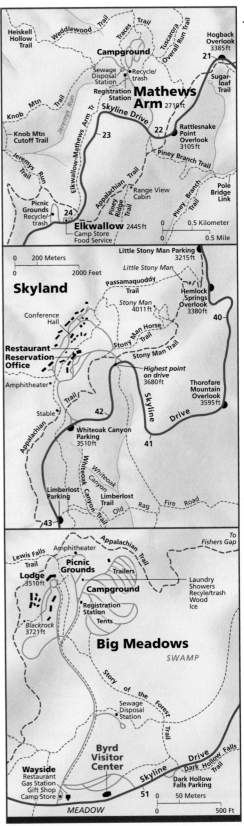

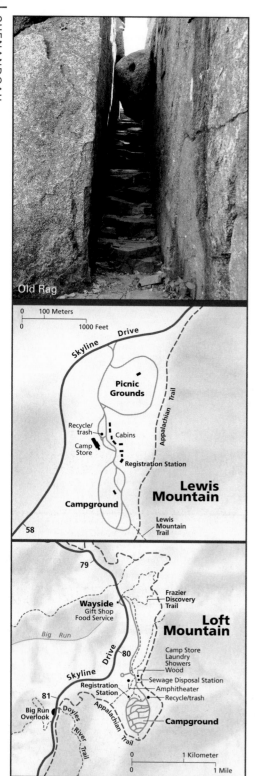

Old Rag

Lewis Mountain

Loft Mountain

There are two **visitor centers**: Dickey Ridge (Mile 4.6) and Harry F. Byrd (Mile 51). Both close from November until March. Loft Mountain Information Center (Mile 19.5) is open on weekends and holidays, mid-May until October.

You'll also find a number of **picnic grounds** along Skyline Drive. Elkwallow (Mile 24.1), Pinnacles (Mile 36.7), South River (Mile 62.8) and Dundo (Mile 83.7) Picnic Grounds are open all year. Dickey Ridge (Mile 4.6), Big Meadows (Mile 51.2) and Lewis Mountain (Mile 57.6) are open from May until November.

Food, gifts, and camping supplies can be found at three **waysides** along Skyline Drive. Elkwallow (Mile 24.1) and Loft Mountain (Mile 79.5) are open from mid-April until early November. Big Meadows, the only place to get gas in the park (pay at the pump is available), is open from mid-March until late November.

Dining is available at Elkwallow Wayside (Mile 24.1), Skyland (Mile 41.7 and 42.5), Big Meadows Wayside and Big Meadows Lodge (Mile 51.2), and Loft Mountain Wayside (Mile 79.5). All establishments are operated by the park's concessioner, Delaware North (goshenandoah.com). Each restaurant offers traditional sit-down dining as well as quick meals to take with you. Operating hours and menus can be found at their website.

Rustic **lodging** can be found at Big Meadows Lodge, Skyland Resort, and Lewis Mountain Cabins. For details refer to the table below.

Four **Campgrounds** are located at Mathews Arm (Mile 22.1), Big Meadows (Mile 51.2), Lewis Mountain (Mile 57.5), and Loft Mountain (Mile 79.5). Reservations can be made at (877) 444-6777 or recreation.gov. Mathews Arm, Big Meadows, and Loft Mountain campgrounds have pull-through sites that accommodate RVs. No sites have hookups.

Backcountry camping is allowed with a free permit, which can be obtained at any of the visitor contact stations during regular business hours.

Additional camping and lodging details are provided on the following page. We highly recommend spending the night in the park at one of the lodges or campgrounds and maybe spending one night east of the park at a bed and breakfast (page 83) to be closer to the trailhead for Old Rag.

Dark Hollow Falls

Shenandoah Lodging (Fees are per night)

Name	Open	Fee	Location & Notes
Big Meadows Lodge	mid-May–November	$123–199	Mile 51.2 • 25 rooms in the main lodge as well as 72 additional rooms in rustic cabins
Skyland Resort	April–November	$116–272	Mile 41.7 • 179 guest rooms, rustic cabins, modern suites
Lewis Mtn Cabins	April–November	$130	Mile 57.6 • Furnished cabins with private baths and grills

Call (877) 847-1919 or click goshenandoah.com for reservations and additional information

Shenandoah Camping (Fees are per night)

Name	Location	Open	Fee	Sites	Notes
Mathews Arm*	Mile 22.1	mid-May–October	$15	179	No Showers, No Laundry
Big Meadows*	Mile 51.2	late March–Nov	$20	217	Showers, Laundry, and Store
Lewis Mountain	Mile 57.5	mid-April–October	$15	31	Showers, Laundry, and Store
Loft Mountain*	Mile 79.5	mid-May–October	$15	45 Tent/167 RV	Showers, Laundry, and Store

*Reservations can be made up to six months in advance by calling (877) 444-6777 or clicking recreation.gov
Each campground is near a section of the Appalachian Trail, and has at least one accessible site. No campgrounds have hookups for water, electricity, or sewage. Mathews Arm, Big Meadows, and Loft Mountain have dump stations and sites that will accommodate large RVs. About 80% of the sites at Mathews Arm and Loft Mountain are first-come, first-served.

Backcountry	A free permit is required. Backcountry planning information and application form are available at any visitor center, the park website, or call (540) 999-3500.
Group	Available at Big Meadows and Loft Mountain. Reserve at recreation.gov or (877) 444-6777.

Best of Shenandoah

Mountain Hike: Old Rag
    Runner-up: Bearfence Mountain

Waterfall Hike: Cedar Run/Whiteoak
    Runner-up: Rose River Falls
    2nd Runner-up: Dark Hollow Falls

Family Hike: Fox Hollow Nature Trail
    Runner-up: Stony Man Nature Trail

Historic Hike: Mill Prong (Rapidan Camp)
    Runner-up: Hickerson Hollow

Picnic Locations: Big Meadows
    Runner-up: Pinnacles
    2nd Runner-up: South River

Activities: Drive Skyline Drive
    Runner-up: Horseback Riding

Presidents in the Park

Before the region became a national park, it provided recreation, refuge, and a backdrop to promote political agendas for several U.S. Presidents.

In the summer of 1929, Herbert Hoover, the 31st President, bought Rapidan Camp. At the time, it was a 164-acre parcel on the eastern slope of the Blue Ridge Mountains. Hoover envisioned using the camp as a place of rest and recreation for himself and his wife during difficult times. Unfortunately, difficult times were the norm during his term. The stock market crashed in October of 1929, less than eight months after inauguration. The remainder of his first and only term was spent combatting the Great Depression that ensued.

But life at Rapidan Camp wasn't all trials and tribulations. Friends, family, and politicians were frequently entertained there during Hoover's presidency. Charles Lindbergh, Mrs. Thomas A. Edison, the Edsel Fords, and British Prime Minister Ramsay MacDonald all show up in the cabin's guest registry. Being just a 3-hour drive from Washington, Rapidan Camp was used as a meeting place for Hoover and his cabinet members and department heads. It was a fully functional Summer White House;

an airplane dropped off mail and telephones were conveniently located in the President's Cabin.

In 1932, the Hoovers donated Rapidan Camp to the Commonwealth of Virginia for use as a Presidential summer retreat. It officially became part of Shenandoah National Park in 1935. Jimmy Carter was the last sitting President to visit the camp, but the "Brown House" or President's Cabin and the Prime Minister's Cabin still stand today. These structures have been restored to their original appearance and are open to the public only during ranger-led tours.

Franklin D. Roosevelt, the 32nd President, used the region as part of a highly visible public relations effort to buoy the negative psychological impact of the Great Depression. He visited a CCC camp in 1933, and three years later he returned to officially dedicate the park.

Hiking & Backpacking

Leave Skyline Drive in favor of Shenandoah's wilder side. Yes, some of the views from the road are postcard-perfect, especially in October, but you won't see a single waterfall and wildlife sightings are limited to deer, squirrels, and birds. To witness the depth of history and nature Shenandoah has to offer one must lace up a pair of hiking shoes and ramble a few miles beyond the road.

There are 516 miles of trails here, ranging from short strolls through open meadows to steep, rocky scrambles atop exposed mountains. All trails are marked with colored blazes. White is for the **Appalachian Trail**; roughly 101 miles of the 2,184-mile trail run parallel to Skyline Drive through the park. Blue indicates park hiking trails and yellow marks trails designated for horse use, which are also open to hikers. Most of the trailheads are located at parking areas along Skyline Drive. A few, like that of immensely popular **Old Rag Trail**, are located near the park boundary. Old Rag is a long (5.6 miles roundtrip) and challenging scramble to the summit of Old Rag Mountain (3,268 feet). The shortest route begins near Nethers on Route 600 which terminates at the park's eastern boundary. Old Rag can also be reached from the park's interior via Old Rag Fire Road, but it's longer (15+ miles roundtrip) and less scenic.

Hawksbill Mountain Summit

Shenandoah Hiking Trails (Distances are roundtrip)

Skyline Drive

Name	Location	Length	Difficulty Rating & Notes
Fox Hollow Nature	Mile 4.6	2.0 miles	E – Leads to Fox Home Site • Cemetery and old farm fence remnants are visible (can be shortened to 1.2 miles)
Dickey Ridge	Mile 4.6	2.7 miles	E – Hike along a small stream through overgrown fields
Snead Farm	Mile 4.6	1.4 miles	E – Gravel fire road leads hikers to an old farm and orchard
Hickerson Hollow	Mile 9.2	2.2 miles	E – A horse trail leads into an old mountain resident's hollow
Compton Peak	Mile 10.4	2.4 miles	M – Fairly steep and rocky hike to scenic views
Little Devil Stairs	Mile 19.4	7.7 miles	S – Follow Keyser Run Fire Road to Little Devil Stairs
Overall Run Falls	Mile 21.1	6.5 miles	S – Hike to the tallest waterfall in the park (93-ft tall)
Traces Nature	Mile 22.2	1.7 miles	E – Trail through a mature oak forest and old homesteads
Mary's Rock (Meadow Spring)	Mile 32.7	2.8 miles	M – Outstanding views of the Panorama area
Little Stony Man Cliffs	Mile 39.1	0.9 mile	E – Excellent views along this extremely short hike
Stony Man Nature - ⚲	Mile 41.7	1.6 miles	E – Easy climb to the park's second highest point (4,011 ft)
Cedar Run/ Whiteoak Circuit - ⚲	Mile 42.6	8.2 miles	S – One of the most strenuous hikes in the park • From Hawksbill Gap, take Cedar Run–Link–Whiteoak–Whiteoak Fire Road–Horse Trail • Multiple waterfalls and cascades
Limberlost	Mile 43	1.3 miles	E – Winding trail through hemlock forests, old homesteads, wetlands, and over Whiteoak Canyon Run
Crescent Rock	Mile 45.6	3.3 miles	E – Leads hikers to a grove of Limberlost hemlock
Hawksbill Mtn Summit - ⚲	Mile 46.7	2.1 miles	M – Park's tallest peak (4,051 ft) • You can also find a 1.7-mile (roundtrip) and 2.9-mile circuit to Hawksbill at Mile 45.6
Rose River Falls	Mile 49.4	4.0 miles	M – See as many as four cascades after a heavy rain
Dark Hollow Falls	Mile 50.7	1.4 miles	M – Shortest waterfall hike in the park
Lewis Falls	Mile 51.4	2.0 miles/ 3.3 miles	M – Out-and-back from Skyline Drive to the 81-ft falls • 3.3-mile circuit begins from Big Meadows Amphitheater
Mill Prong - ⚲	Mile 52.8	4.0 miles	M – Roundtrip hike to Hoover's Rapidan Camp
Bearfence Mountain - ⚲	Mile 56.4	0.8 mile	M – Short scramble over rocks to broad panoramic views
South River Falls	Mile 62.8	2.6 miles	M – Third tallest waterfall in the park (83-ft tall)
Deadening Nature	Mile 79.4	1.3 miles	E – Leads to a spectacular overlook atop Loft Mountain
Doyles River Falls	Mile 81.1	3.2 miles	S – Rigorous hike to the 28-ft upper falls and 63-ft lower falls
Jones Run Falls	Mile 84.1	3.4 miles	M – A nice casual hike to 42-foot cascade
Blackrock Summit	Mile 84.8	0.8 mile	E – Short hike to rock outcroppings and beautiful views
Old Rag - ⚲	Near Nethers on Route 600	5.6 miles	S – Challenging and popular hike/scramble • Parking area is at the park's eastern boundary, not Skyline Drive • Start on Ridge Tr and return via Saddle Tr (7.2 miles)

Difficulty Ratings: E = Easy, M = Moderate, S = Strenuous

Old Rag isn't for everyone, but there are trails to satisfy hikers of all interests and abilities along Skyline Drive. The shortest and most popular waterfall hike is **Dark Hollow Falls Trail**. Thomas Jefferson once admired this 70-ft falls. **Limberlost Trail** is fully accessible to wheelchair users and is an excellent hike in June when mountain laurel is in bloom. Hiking on **Fox and Hickerson Hollow Trails** allows hikers with an active imagination to travel to the times of early mountain residents who lived in the hollows for more than 100 years before being moved off their land for the creation of the park. Remnants of their presence still stand to this day. Simple mountain folk weren't the only occupants of these hills. **Rapidan Camp** served as the Summer White House for President Herbert Hoover. **Mill Prong Trail** leads to the historic structure (only open and accessible during ranger programs).

Backpackers have more than 500 miles of trails and 190,000 acres of wilderness at their disposal. A free permit is required for all overnight stays in the backcountry. Permits are available by mail, phone (540.999.3500, fill out online application before calling), or in person.

Biking

The twists, turns, and hills of **Skyline Drive** are a welcome challenge to road cyclists visiting Shenandoah National Park. Bikes are permitted on all paved surfaces within the park, but Skyline Drive, in particular, experiences heavy motorist traffic during the summer and October. Most park rangers won't recommend biking along Skyline Drive because it's fairly narrow and busy, but if you start your ride early enough (before 10am) traffic shouldn't be much of a problem. However, at this time cyclists should be prepared for poor visibility. Early morning fog is common, and you'll encounter darkness any time of year at the 600-foot-long Mary's Rock Tunnel (Mile 32). Bikes are prohibited on unpaved roads, grass, and trails. No mountain bike trails exist within the park. If you'd like to join a group on a multi-day bicycle adventure, a few companies offer guided tours. See page 84 for details.

Rock Climbing

It's no Yosemite (page 514), but **Little Stony Man** Cliffs is a great place for beginners to learn the basics of climbing and rappelling. From April to early September visitors can take part in an **introductory rock climbing course** offered by Shenandoah Mountain Guides (877.847.1919, goshenandoah. com). Classes generally start at 9am and depart from Skyland Resort. Advance reservation is required.

Horseback Riding

Horses are allowed on 201 miles of trails. To help visitors with their own horse(s), you can find a Trail Ride Planning Guide at the park website. You'll also find a list of parking areas suitable for horse trailers with an estimate of available parking based on the season. Be aware that the park's lodges and campgrounds do not accommodate horses and they are not allowed to sleep in their trailer. Bringing your own horse gives riders the freedom to explore deeper into Shenandoah's wilderness. However, these freedoms require more responsibility. You should travel with a map, ride trails that are suitable to your ability, and check the extended weather forecast before heading out.

Skyland Stables (877.847.1919, goshenandoah.com) offers guided horse rides. An hour-long ride costs $50 per person, while a 2.5-hour ride costs $90. Pony rides are available for children 5 and under (as long as their feet reach the stirrups and they wear a helmet). The stable is open from early April until late November, and the long ride is only given on Saturdays. Skyland Stables is located near Skyland Resort (Mile 41.7). All riders must be at least 4'10" and weigh less than 250 pounds.

Fishing

Some 70 streams begin in the Blue Ridge Mountains and flow into the valleys surrounding the park. These streams are inhabited by a variety of species, with eastern brook trout among the most popular game fish. When fishing in the park, anglers must adhere to Virginia fishing regulations. All Virginia residents 16 years and older and non-residents 12 years and older are required to have a Virginia state fishing license. A 5-day non-resident license can be purchased at **Big Meadows Wayside** or from local sporting goods stores outside park boundaries. If you're looking for sound fishing advice or to hire a guide, check out the local outfitters listed on page 84.

Bird Watching

About 95% of Shenandoah National Park is forested and 40% of the total area is designated wilderness, providing an excellent habitat for birds. More than 200 species of resident and transient birds use the park. Nearly half of the species breed here, but only thirty make the park their year-round home. Local species include tufted titmice, red-tailed hawk, Carolina chickadee, wild turkey, barred owl, and downy woodpecker.

Exotic species also call the park home. In the summer of 2000 the park resumed its **Peregrine Falcon Restoration Program**. It has been a success and today visitors may spot these beautiful raptors soaring high above the Blue Ridge Mountains. Cerulean warbler and scarlet tanager also reside in the park, but are seldom seen. The Cerulean warbler, once common in the lower Mississippi valley, has declined in numbers due to loss of habitat. The park hosts a healthy population of scarlet tanagers, but most bird watchers wouldn't know it. These feathered friends spend most of their time high above the ground in the upper canopy of trees.

Winter Activities

Shenandoah is more or less neglected during the winter months. All campgrounds, lodging, and waysides are closed. Skyline Drive occasionally closes during inclement weather. Big Meadows averages more than thirty inches of snow each year. Still, many hardy **hikers** enter the park to view a completely different environment. Ground covered in snow. Trees without leaves. Waterfalls turned to ice. Bears holed up for winter. Facilities may be closed, but there's still 196,000 acres of land open for **backcountry camping**.

Ranger Programs

The best way to truly see the park is under the thoughtful guidance of a park ranger. They are happy to share with you knowledge of bears, raptors, and other wildlife and plant life on a series of walks, talks, and evening programs. You can learn about the history of Skyland Resort on a tour of Historic Massanutten Lodge, hike the Appalachian Trail, or stroll through CCC-era structures as Shenandoah rangers shower you with entertaining and educational anecdotes that have been passed down through generations of park stewards. Be sure to stop in at a visitor center for a current schedule of all of the programs.

For Kids

Children (ages 7–12) have the opportunity to become a **Shenandoah National Park Junior Ranger**. Kids (ages 13 and older) will enjoy the entire set of Ranger Explorer Guides. Activity booklets can be picked up in the park or are available for print at the park website.

Ranger-led tours and talks are another family favorite. In fact, attending a ranger program may be the spark your child needs to ignite interest in the Junior Ranger Program. The personalities of the rangers are so infectious they may even inspire your child to one day don the iconic "Smoky the Bear" hat that has become the symbol of the illustrious park rangers. If they like the hats, but don't want the job that comes with it, you can also pick one up at a nearby visitor center.

Flora & Fauna

Shenandoah's forests are classified as "oak-hickory," but many other trees take root within the park. Pine, maple, birch, basswood, blackgum, tulip poplar, chestnut, and a few stands of hemlock can all be found here. Mountain laurel, which blooms in June, can be found along Skyline Drive. It is a native species, but these shrubs were planted by the CCC in the 1930s. Variation in latitude and elevation help create astounding diversity. More than 1,000 species of ferns, grasses, lichens, mosses, fungi and wildflowers exist in the park.

The creation of Shenandoah National Park helped reestablish the area as a refuge for wildlife. In the 1700s, early European settlers noted the region's abundance and diversity of animals. By the late 1800s, American bison, elk, beaver, and river otter were extirpated. Many overhunted species have now returned or been reintroduced. Shenandoah is home to one of the densest populations of black bears in the United States. Somewhere between 300 and 500 bears reside here. In all there are more than 50 species of mammals in the park. White-tail deer and gray squirrels are often seen along the roadway, while bobcats, black bears, moles, and shrews are more elusive. Ten species of toads and frogs and fourteen species of salamanders or newts live here. Twenty-five species of reptiles have found refuge in Shenandoah including eighteen snakes, five turtles, three skinks, and one lizard. Viewing and photographing wildlife is a popular activity, but please help keep wildlife wild. Be sure to stay a safe distance from animals and never feed or provoke them.

Pets

Pets are allowed in the park, but must be kept on a leash no more than six feet in length at all times. They are allowed on the following trails: Limberlost, Old Rag, and Dark Hollow Falls. Only service animals are permitted in park buildings.

Accessibility

Sites accessible to wheelchair users are available at all picnic areas and campgrounds. Most facilities and restrooms are accessible with assistance. Lewis Mountain, Skyland Resort, and Big Meadows Lodge offer wheelchair-accessible lodging. Many ranger programs are accessible, including a van tour to Rapidan Camp. Limberlost Trail is fully accessible.

Weather

Come prepared for all kinds of weather. Storms are common throughout the year, but peak in September. Snow can fall any day from October to April, but is most common in January and February. Roads are often slippery with ice in winter and foggy in spring. The mountains in Shenandoah are usually 10°F cooler than the valley.

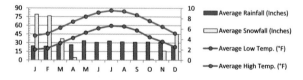

Vacation Planner

Shenandoah is a popular weekend getaway for citizens of nearby communities and Washington, D.C. The park can become excessively busy along **Skyline Drive**, but peace and quiet is only a few miles away along a tranquil hiking trail. Most trails and overlooks feature similar views and scenery, but a few are better than others. This two-day vacation planner is provided to help you choose what to do on your Shenandoah National Park

vacation. The hike to **Old Rag** (page 78) is highly recommended, but not included in the planner because its trailhead is not located along Skyline Drive and it requires considerable scrambling. Joining a **ranger program** (page 81) is also encouraged. First-time visitors should stop at one of the park's two visitor centers. **Dickey Ridge Visitor Center** (Mile 4.7) is conveniently located near the park's north entrance. If entering the park from the south, you won't reach a visitor center (**Harry F. Byrd**) until Mile 51.2. Regardless which one you stop at, a short orientation video, exhibits, a bookstore, information desk, backcountry permits, and park rangers will be at your disposal to help introduce yourself to the park. This template assumes you are entering from the north entrance (Front Royal). **Camping** and **lodging** are available within the park (page 77). Nearby dining, grocery stores, lodging, festivals, and attractions are listed on pages 83–85.

Day 1: After stopping at **Dickey Ridge Visitor Center**, catch a glimpse of what Virginia mountain life was like by hiking the short **Fox Hollow Trail**. The trailhead is located just across the road from the visitor center. After the hike, return to Skyline Drive and head south about 30 miles to **Mary's Rock Tunnel** (Mile 32). Here you'll hike to the top of Mary's Rock, which provides outstanding views of the Virginia piedmont and Thornton Gap Entrance Station. Two trails lead to the top of Mary's Rock. The trail north of the tunnel is shorter and easier than the one on the south side. This is a good place to settle in for the night. There are plenty of lodging accommodations outside the park in Luray and Sperryville, or continue along Skyline Drive a few miles further south to Skyland or Big Meadows (stop at **Stony Man Overlook** along the way).

Day 2: On your second day in the park, sign up for a **guided trail ride** (page 80) or spend the day on a **rock climbing adventure** (page 80, advance reservation required). If not, take one of the park's longer and more scenic hikes, like **Cedar Run/Whiteoak Circuit**. **Bearfence Mountain** is a short yet challenging climb, providing breathtaking views that should not be missed before exiting the park.

Dining

Spelunker's • (540) 631-0300
116 South St, Front Royal
spelunkerscustard.com • Entrée: $4–7

The Wine and Duck Restaurant • (540) 636-1000
117 E Main St, Front Royal

Melting Pot Pizza • (540) 636-6146
138 W 14th St, Front Royal
meltingpotpizza.com • Entrée: $6–20

L'Dees Pancake House • (540) 635-3791
522 E Main St, Front Royal
ldeespancakehouse.com

Lucky Star Lounge • (540) 635-5297
205 A E Main St, Front Royal
manta.com • Entrée: $12

Apartment 2g • (540) 636-9293
206 S Royal Ave, Front Royal
jsgourmet.com • Entrée: $50 (5-course)

Mamma Mia Pizza Pasta & Subs • (540) 652-6062
701 S 3rd St, Shenandoah
mammamiarestaurant.net • Entrée: $8–19

Ciro's Pizza • (540) 778-1112
558 W Main St, Stanley

Hawksbill Diner • (540) 778-2006
1388 E Main St, Stanley

Prince Michel Vineyard and Winery
154 Winery Ln, Leon
princemichel.com • (540) 547-9720

West Main Market • (540) 743-1125
123 W Main St, Lura • westmainmarket.com

Triple Crown BBQ • (540) 743-5311
1079 US-211, Luray

Gathering Grounds • (540) 743-1121
24 E Main St, Luray • ggrounds.com

Thunderbird Café • (540) 289-5094
42 Island Ford Rd, McGaheysville
thethunderbirdcafe.com • Entrée: $9–13

Hank's Smokehouse • (540) 289-7667
49 Bloomer Springs Rd, McGaheysville
hankssmokehouse.com • Entrée: $11–20

Log Cabin Barbecue • (540) 289-9400
11672 Spotswood Tr, Elkton
logcabinbarbecue.com • Entrée: $8–22

Ciro's Italian Eatery • (540) 298-1205
101 Downey Knolls Dr, Elkton
cirositalianeatery.com

Pig-N-Steak • (540) 948-3130
313 Washington St, Madison
pigandsteak.com • Entrée: $11–13

Giovanna's Italian Eatery • (540) 948-5454
2679 S Seminole Tr, Madison

Thornton River Grille • (540) 987-8790
3710 Sperryville Pike, Sperryville
thorntonrivergrille.com • Entrée: $12–34

Rudy's Pizza • (540) 987-9494
3710 Sperryville Pike, Sperryville

Griffin Tavern • (540) 675-3227
659 Zachary Taylor Hwy, Flint Hill
griffintavern.com • Entrée: $11–24

Scotto's Italian Restaurant & Pizzeria
1412 W Broad St, Waynesboro
scottos.net • (540) 942-8715 • Entrée: $10–18

Gavid's Steak House • (540) 949-6353
1501 W Broad St, Waynesboro

Massaki Japanese Steakhouse • (540) 886-9191
1027 Richmond Ave, Staunton
massakisteakhouse.com

Mi Rancho • (540) 941-5980
408 E Main St, Waynesboro

Weasie's Kitchen • (540) 943-0500
130 E Broad St, Waynesboro

Tailgate Grill • (540) 941-8451
1106 W Broad St, Waynesboro

Blue Mountain Brewery • (540) 456-8020
9519 Critzers Shop Rd, Afton
bluemountainbrewery.com • Entrée: $10–21

Crozet Pizza • (434) 823-2132
5794 3 Notch'd Rd, Crozet
crozetpizza.net • Entrée: $11–23

Tea House • (434) 823-2868
325 Four Leaf Ln, # 6, Charlottesville

Grocery Stores

Whole Foods Market • (434) 973-4900
300 Shoppers World Court, Charlottesville

Walmart • (434) 973-1412
975 Hilton Heights Rd, Charlottesville

Food Lion • (540) 942-2992
990 Hopeman Parkway, Waynesboro

Food Lion • (540) 298-9455
14811 Spotswood Tr, Elkton

Food Lion • (540) 249-0665
83 Augusta Ave, Grottoes

Food Lion • (540) 778-2081
558 W Main St # A, Stanley

Walmart Supercenter • (540) 743-4111
1036 US-211 West, Luray

Food Lion • (540) 743-4502
1400 US-211 West, Luray

Food Lion • (540) 622-2704
260 Remount Rd, Front Royal

Lodging

Woodward House • (800) 635-7011
413 S Royal Ave, Front Royal
acountryhome.com • Rates: $110–225/night

Killahevlin B&B • (540) 636-7335
1401 N Royal Dr, Front Royal • Rates: $155–285

Cool Harbor Motel • (540) 635-2191
141 W 15th St, Front Royal
coolharbormotel.com • Rates: $85–89

Lackawanna B&B • (540) 636-7945
236 Riverside Dr, Front Royal
lackawannabb.com • Rates: $154–184

Middleton Inn • (540) 675-2020
176 Main St, Washington
middletoninn.com • Rates: $325–575

Gay Street Inn • (540) 316-9220
160 Gay St, Washington
gaystreetinn.com • Rates: $199–269

White Moose Inn • (540) 675-3207
291 Main St, Washington
whitemooseinn.com • Rates: $275+

Inn At Little Washington • (540) 675-3800
309 Middle St, Washington
theinnatlittlewashington.com • Rates: $655–3,450

Foster Harris House B&B • (540) 675-3757
189 Main St, Washington
fosterharris.com • Rates: $239–369

Fairlea Farm B&B • (540) 675-3679
636 Mount Salem Ave, Washington
fairleafarm.com • Rates: $155–205

Bear Bluff • (503) 383-9336
551 River Valley Rd, Rileyville
shenandoahcabinrentals.com • Rates: $215–245

Hopkins Ordinary B&B • (540) 987-3383
47 Main St, Sperryville
hopkinsordinary.com • Rates: $139–319

Cave Hill Farm B&B • (540) 289-7441
9875 Cave Hill Rd, McGaheysville
cavehillfarmbandb.com • Rates: $129–159

Massanutten • (540) 289-9441
1822 Resort Dr, McGaheysville
massresort.com • Rates: $150

Once Upon A Mountain • (540) 743-1724
974 Cross Mountain Rd, Luray

Old Massanutten Lodge B&B • (540) 269-8800
3448 Caverns Dr, Keezletown
oldmassanuttenlodge.com • Rates: $140–170

Shadow Mountain Escape • (540) 843-0584
1132 Jewell Hollow Rd, Luray
shadowmountainescape.com • Rates: $175–225

South Court Inn B&B • (888) 749-8055
160 S Court St, Luray
southcourtinn.com • Rates: $150–225

Yogi Bear's Jellystone Camp • (540) 743-4002
2250 US-211 E, Luray
campluray.com • Rates: $38–109

Graves Mountain Lodge • (540) 923-4231
Rt. 670, Syria • gravesmountain.com • Rates: $90–135

Sharp Rock Vineyards and B&B • (540) 987-8020
5 Sharp Rock Rd, Sperryville
sharprockvineyards.com • Rates: $200–240

Piney Hill B&B • (540) 860-8470
1048 Piney Hill Rd, Luray
pineyhillbandb.com • Rates: $160–195

Mimslyn Inn • (540) 743-5105
401 W Main St, Luray
mimslyninn.com • Rates: $175–250

Inn of the Shenandoah • (540) 300-9777
138 E Main St, Luray • innoftheshenandoah.com

Mayne View B&B • (540) 244-7588
439 Mechanic St, Luray
mayneview.com • Rates: $129–175

White Fence B&B • (540) 778-1390
275 Chapel Rd, Stanley
whitefencebb.com • Rates: $175

Dulaney Hollow Old Rag Mountain
VA-231, Madison • (540) 923-4470

Shenandoah Hill KOA • (540) 948-4186
110 Campground Ln, Madison
shenandoahhills.com

Inn at Sugar Hollow Farm • (434) 823-7086
6051 Sugar Hollow Rd, Crozet
sugarhollow.com • Rates: $169–319

Montfair Resort Farm • (434) 823-5202
2500 Bezaleel Dr, Crozet
montfairresortfarm.com • Rates: $159–240

Iris Inn B&B • (540) 943-1991
191 Chinquapin Dr, Waynesboro
irisinn.com • Rates: $219–339

Residence Inn • (540) 943-7426
44 Windigrove Dr, Waynesboro
marriott.com • Rates: $179

Tree Streets Inn • (540) 949-4484
421 Walnut Ave, Waynesboro
treestreetsinn.com • Rates: $115–150

Belle Hearth B&B • (540) 943-1910
320 S Wayne Ave, Waynesboro
bellehearth.com • Rates: $105–160

Many chain restaurants and hotels can be found nearby in Harrisonburg, Luray, Waynesboro, and Front Royal.

Festivals
Near the Park
Virginia Wine Expo • February
300+ locally-grown award-winning wines
vawineshowcase.org • Richmond

Chocolate Lovers Festival • February
A variety of chocolate-related activities
chocolatefestival.net • Fairfax

Highland Maple Festival • March
50+ year tradition explores maple syrup-making
highlandcounty.org/maple • Monterey

Virginia Festival of the Book • March
vabook.org • Charlottesville

Historic Garden Week • April
Dubbed "America's Largest Open House"
vagardenweek.org • Statewide

Virginia Wine & Craft Festival • May
Wine, food, crafts, and live entertainment
wineandcraftfestival.com • Front Royal

Hot Air Balloon Rally • 4th of July
Music, balloon rides, classic car show, and more
sunriserotarylexva.org • Lexington

Old Fiddlers Convention • August
World's oldest and largest fiddlers' convention
oldfiddlersconvention.com • Galax

Smith Mtn Lake Wine Festival • September
visitsmithmountainlake.com • Moneta

Apple Butter Festival • September
goshenandoah.com • Skyland Resort

Richmond Folk Festival • October
richmondfolkfestival.org • Richmond

International Gold Cup • October
Horse steeplechase races
vagoldcup.com • The Plains

Fall Foliage Art Show • October
SVACart.com • Waynesboro

Apple Harvest Festival • October
gravesmountain.com • Syria

Taste of Culpeper • October
culpeperdowntown.com • Culpeper

Harvest & Leaf Peep Festival • October
ducardvineyards.com • Madison

Virginia Film Festival • November
virginiafilmfestival.org • Charlottesville

Washington DC
Int'l Wine & Food Festival • February
wineandfooddc.com

National Cherry Blossom Festival • March/April
One of the best times to visit Washington DC
nationalcherryblossomfestival.org

Filmfest DC • April
filmfestdc.org • (202) 274-5782

National Capitol Barbecue Battle • June
bbqdc.com • (202) 488-6990

Capitol Jazz Fest • June
capitaljazz.com • (301) 780-9300

Capitol Pride • June
capitalpride.org • (202) 719-5304

Festa Italiana • June
festaitalianadc.com • (202) 923-7845

DC Jazz Festival • June
dcjazzfest.org

Smithsonian Folklife Festival • June/July
festival.si.edu • (202) 633-6440

Adams Morgan Days Festival • September
DC's longest running street festival
adamsmorgandayfestival.com

National Book Festival • September
loc.gov/bookfest • (888) 714-4696

Turkish Festival • September/October
turkishfestival.org • (888) 282-3236

Attractions
Near the Park
Carolina Tailwinds, Inc. • (888) 251-3206
carolinatailwinds.com • Bike Tours: $1,625–1,950

Women Tours, Inc. • (800) 247-1444
womantours.com • Bike Tours: $1,990+

Shenandoah Mountain Guides • (877) 847-1919
goshenandoah.com

Skyland Stables • (877) 847-1919
goshenandoah.com
Trail Rides: $50 (1 hour), $90 (2.5 hours)

Murray's Fly Shop • (540) 984-4212
murraysflyshop.com • 1–2 People $425 (full-day)

Page Valley Fly Fishing • (540) 743-7952
pagevalleyflyfishing.com • 2 People $200 (half-day)

Appalachian Outdoors Adventure • (540) 743-7400
18 E Main St, Luray • aoaluray.com

Shenandoah River Outfitters • (800) 622-6632
6502 S Page Valley Rd, Luray
shenandoahriver.com • Rafting: $36–90

Luray Zoo • (540) 743-4113
1087 US-211, West Luray
lurayzoo.com • Admission: $10/adult

Shenandoah Caverns • (540) 477-3115
261 Caverns Rd, Quicksburg
shenandoahcaverns.com • Admission: $24/adult

Luray Caverns • (540) 743-6551
101 Cave Hill Rd, Luray
luraycaverns.com • Admission: $26/adult

Page Twin Theatre • (540) 743-4444
33 E Main St, Luray

Luray Lanes • (540) 743-3535
52 W Main St, Luray

George Washington NF • Roanoke

Edith J. Carrier Arboretum and Botanical Gardens
MSC 3705, 780 University Blvd, Harrisonburg
• (540) 568-3194

Virginia Quilt Museum • (540) 433-3818
301 S Main St, Harrisonburg
vaquiltmuseum.org • Admission: $7/adult

Regal Cinemas Stadium 14 • (844) 462-7342
381 University Blvd, Harrisonburg
regmovies.com

New Market Walking Tours • (540) 740-3747
9317 N Congress St, New Market • virginia.org

Civil War Museum • (540) 832-2944
400 S Main St, Gordonsville
hgiexchange.org • Admission: $10/adult

Page County Heritage Museums • (540) 743-6698
223 Hamburg Rd, Luray

Massanutten Ski Resort • (540) 289-4954
Waterpark, golf, snow sports, and spa
1822 Resort Dr, McGaheysville
massresort.com

Bryce Resort • (540) 856-2124
Golf, Zip Line, Bungee, and Snow Sports
1982 Fairway Dr, Mt Jackson
bryceresort.com

Caverns Country Club • (540) 743-7111
910 TC Northcott Blvd, Luray
luraycaverns.com • 18 Holes: $30–40

Woodstone Meadows Golf Course • (540) 289-4919
1822 Resort Dr, McGaheysville

Packsaddle Ridge Golf Club • (540) 269-8188
3067 Pack Saddle Tr, Keezletown
packsaddle.net • 18 Holes: $30–40

Hull's Drive In • (540) 463-2621
2367 N Lee Hwy, Lexington
hullsdrivein.com

Cows-N-Corn • (540) 439-4806
Fall • Corn Maze, Haunted Hayride
5225 Catlett Road, Midland
cows-n-corn.com

Jefferson National Forest • (540) 291-2188
27 Ranger Ln, Natural Bridge

Foamhenge • (540) 464-2253
A scale foam version of the UK's Stonehenge
Hwy 11 South, Natural Bridge

Virginia Safari Park • (540) 291-3205
229 Safari Ln, Natural Bridge
virginiasafaripark.com

Dinosaur Land • (540) 869-2222
3848 Stonewall Jackson Hwy, White Post
dinosaurland.com

Washington DC

Library of Congress • (202) 707-5000
loc.gov • Tours Available

The Pentagon • (703) 697-1776
Reservations req'd (available 8–90 days in advance)
1400 Defense Pentagon • pentagontours.osd.mil

Arlington National Cemetery • (877) 907-8585
arlingtoncemetery.org

City Segway Tours • (877) 734-8687
citysegwaytours.com • Tours: $65–85

Bike and Roll • (202) 842-2453
bikeandrolldc.com • Tours: $40–75

DC by Foot • (202) 370-1830
freetoursbyfoot.com • Free (Private Tours for fee)

DC Metro Food Tours • (202) 683-8847
dcmetrofoodtours.com • Tours: $55–65

Lincoln Memorial • (202) 426-6895
The entire National Mall is great!
2 Lincoln Memorial Cir NW

National Shrine of the Immaculate Conception
400 Michigan Ave NE • (202) 526-8300
nationalshrine.com • Free Tours

Newseum • (202) 292-6100
555 Pennsylvania Ave
newseum.org • Admission: $22.95/adult

Washington Monument • (202) 426-6841
nps.gov/wamo • Free Admission (ticket Req'd)

Washington National Cathedral • (202) 537-6200
Massachusetts Ave NW & Wisconsin Ave NW
cathedral.org

Walk of the Town • (240) 672-6306
walkofthetowndc.com • Free

Old Town Trolley Tours • (202) 600-2524
trolleytours.com • Tour: $32/adult

National Gallery of Art Sculpture Garden
6th and Constitutional Ave • (202) 737-4215
nga.gov • Free

Korean War Veterans Memorial • (202) 426-6841
10 Daniel French Dr Southwest

National Air and Space Museum • (202) 633-1000
600 Independence Ave SW
airandspace.si.edu • Free

U.S. Holocaust Memorial Museum
100 Raoul Wallenberg Place SW
ushmm.org • Free • (202) 488-0400

Smithsonian National Museum of Natural History
1000 Constitution Ave Northwest
mnh.si.edu • Free • (202) 633-1000

Smithsonian American Art Museum
F Street Northwest
americanart.si.edu • Free • (202) 633-7970

Smithsonian National Zoo • (202) 633-4888
3001 Connecticut Ave
nationalzoo.si.edu • Free

National Portrait Gallery • (202) 633-8300
8th St NW & F St NW
npg.si.edu • Free

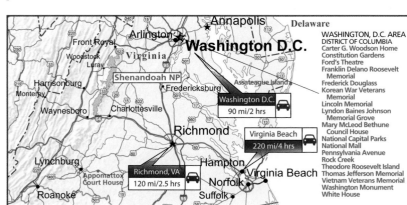

WASHINGTON, D.C. AREA
DISTRICT OF COLUMBIA
Carter G. Woodson Home
Constitution Gardens
Ford's Theatre
Franklin Delano Roosevelt
 Memorial
Frederick Douglass
Korean War Veterans
 Memorial
Lincoln Memorial
Lyndon Baines Johnson
 Memorial Grove
Mary McLeod Bethune
 Council House
National Capital Parks
National Mall
Pennsylvania Avenue
Rock Creek
Theodore Roosevelt Island
Thomas Jefferson Memorial
Vietnam Veterans Memorial
Washington Monument
White House

World War II Memorial
MARYLAND
Antietam
Catoctin Mountain
Chesapeake and Ohio Canal
 (also D.C., W.Va.)
Clara Barton
Fort Washington
Greenbelt
Monocacy
Piscataway
Potomac Heritage Trail
 (also Pa., Va., D.C.)
Thomas Stone
VIRGINIA
Arlington House,
 The Robert E. Lee Memorial
George Washington Birthplace
George Washington Memorial
 Parkway (also Md.)
Manassas
Prince William Forest
Wolf Trap

WASHINGTON, D.C. AREA
PROFESSIONAL SPORTS TEAMS:

DC United (MLS)
Washington Redskins (NFL)
Washington Nationals (MLB)
Washington Wizards (NBA)
Washington Mystics (WNBA)
Washington Capitals (NHL)

For more informa-
tion on visiting
Virginia, click
www.virginia.org

Driving Distances to
Byrd Visitor Center

Washington D.C.
90 mi/2 hrs

Virginia Beach
220 mi/4 hrs

Richmond, VA
120 mi/2.5 hrs

A park ranger leading the Historic Tour

Mammoth Cave

1 Mammoth Cave Parkway
Mammoth Cave, KY 42259
Phone: (270) 758-2180
Website: nps.gov/maca

Established: July 1, 1941
Size: 52,830 Acres
Annual Visitors: 570,000
Peak Season: Summer & Weekends
Total Cave Length: 405+ Miles
Public Cave Trails: ~14 Miles
Hiking Trails: 80 Miles

Activities: Cave Tours ($5–55),
Backpacking, Hiking, Paddling,
Biking, Horseback Riding, Fishing

Campgrounds ($12–25/night):
Mammoth Cave, Houchin's Ferry
and Maple Grove Campgrounds
Lodging: Mammoth Cave Hotel

Park Hours: All day, every day
Cave Tours available daily from
8am–5pm (extended hours during
summer and holidays, closed
December 25)
Entrance Fee: None

At more than 400 miles in length, Mammoth Cave is the longest cave system in the world, and the competition isn't close. Mammoth earns its name by being nearly twice as long as its next closest rival, Sistema Sac Actum in Mexico. And several new miles of passages are discovered each year, leaving geologists to believe there could be as many as 600 additional miles of cave yet to be discovered.

The first known cave exploration took place some 4,000 years ago. Native Americans mined the cave's upper levels for more than two millennia. They sought gypsum, selenite, and mirabilite, among other minerals. Proof of their presence was left in the form of ancient artifacts: cane torches, gourd bowls, cloth, a handful of petroglyphs, and even their remains. Constant temperature, humidity, and salty soil make a cave a particularly good environment for preserving human remains. Several "mummies" were buried in an organized fashion. Others, like the remains of a primitive man pinned beneath a rock, tell stories about the lives and times of these ancient people. Decades of exploration have uncovered thousands of artifacts but few answers about the purpose of minerals sought by these early residents. Perhaps a greater mystery is why—after 2,000 years—they left Mammoth Cave and never returned.

Mammoth Cave was rediscovered by John Houchins near the turn of the 19th century. Legend states Houchins shot and wounded a black bear near the cave's entrance. The injured animal led its hunter to the cave, and the rest, as they say, is history.

In 1812, after 2,000 years of anonymity, the cave's underground passageways were once again being mined. The War of 1812 was brewing, and the British successfully cut-off America's gunpowder supplies in the east. Fortunately for the American Army, Mammoth Cave had large deposits of calcium nitrate, which through a simple process could be converted into gunpowder. This cave and its minerals ended up playing a pivotal role in a war hundreds of miles away.

As a result Mammoth Cave received considerable publicity, and by 1816 visitors were showing up to tour the mysterious labyrinth. But local citizens had other uses in mind. An enthusiastic clergyman used the cave as a church, and a doctor from Louisville purchased it for use as a tuberculosis treatment center. These ventures failed, but cave tours were an undeniable success—so successful that they have been conducted without interruption, through the Civil War to the present day. Slaves led many of the tours. Stephen Bishop, a slave with quick wit, good humor, and a curious spirit, was one of the best and most passionate guides. He became the first to map the cave system and cross Bottomless Pit. Along the way, he discovered and named many of the cave's features, including Gorin's Dome and 192-ft-tall Mammoth Dome. Work continued by Max Kämper, a German geologist and mapmaker who set out to create a comprehensive map of the cave in 1908. Guided by Ed Bishop, great-nephew of Stephen, Kämper discovered Kämper Hall, Elizabeth's Dome, and Violet City. Together, they mapped and surveyed all of the passages known at the time.

By 1920, tens of thousands of tourists visited Mammoth Cave each year, causing locals to seek out their piece of the tourism pie. George Morrison, a wealthy oilman, found what he called the "New Entrance to Mammoth Cave." He "found" it with the help of drills and explosives. Floyd Collins, pioneer and explorer, was determined to find a lucrative new cave. While exploring Sand Cave, a rock wedged his ankle, leaving him trapped near the cave's entrance. After 17 days of failed rescue attempts Collins died of exposure. The event created a "carnival atmosphere" rife with dozens of journalists and sensational stories, which sparked the movement to make Mammoth Cave a national park. When this idea came to fruition in 1941, only 40 miles of passageways had been surveyed. Since then, several cave networks have been connected, creating the largest such area in the world, of which about fourteen miles of passages are available for tours.

River Styx Spring Trail

When to Go
Mammoth Cave National Park is open all year. The weather underground is nearly a constant 54°F. The park is busiest in summer and on holiday weekends. During this time reservations are recommended for cave tours (especially for Wild Cave, River Styx, and Intro to Caving Tours). Tours are given daily throughout the year, except on Christmas Day. Fewer tours are offered during the park's off-season.

Transportation & Airports
Mammoth Cave Railroad Bike and Hike Trail connects Mammoth Cave Hotel to Park City. There are no bridges across Green River within the park, but it can be crossed with the aid of a free ferry. Green River Ferry operates year-round from 6am–9:55pm. Houchin's Ferry operates March–November from 10:15am–9:55pm.

The nearest large commercial airports are Louisville International (SDF) and Nashville International (BNA). Both are approximately 90 miles from the park. Bowling Green-Warren County Regional (BWG) is a smaller airport located 35 miles southwest of the park.

Directions
Arriving from the north: Take I-65 South to Exit 53 (Cave City). Turn Right onto KY-70. Follow KY-70/255 as it becomes Mammoth Cave Parkway. Mammoth Cave Parkway leads directly to the Visitor Center.

Arriving from the south: Take I-65 North to Exit 48 (Park City). Turn left onto KY-255. Follow KY-255 until it becomes Park City Road, which leads into the park. Turn left where Park City Road joins Mammoth Cave Parkway and follow it to the Visitor Center.

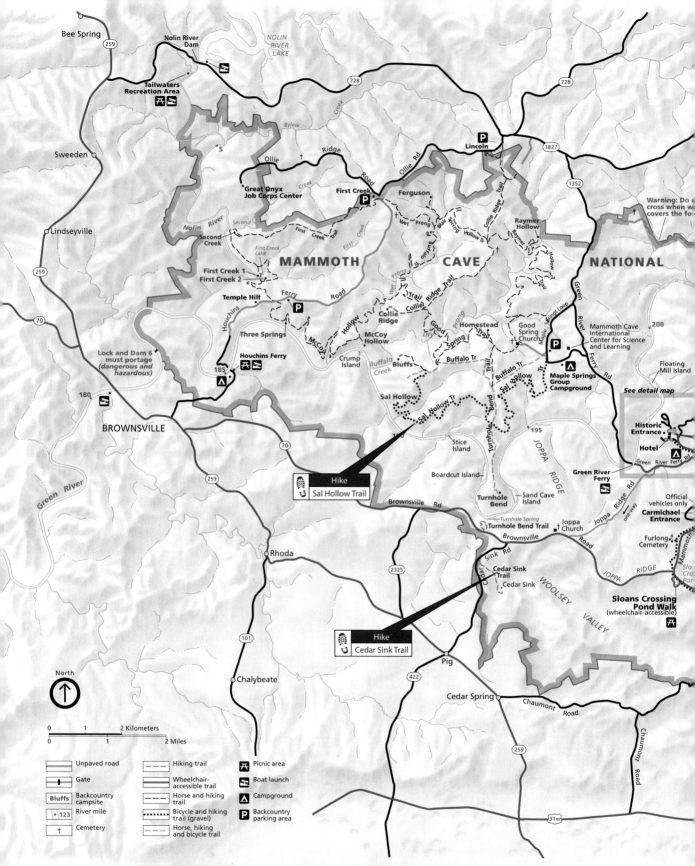

Bee Spring

259

Nolin River Dam

NOLIN RIVER LAKE

Tailwaters Recreation Area

728

728

Lincoln P

1827

Sweeden

Ollie Ridge Road

Creek

Bylew

5

Ollie Rd

Ferguson

1352

Great Onyx Job Corps Center

First Creek P

Wet Prong

Blair Spring Hollow Tr

Collie Ridge Trail

Raymer Hollow

Warning: Do cross when covers the fo

Lindseyville

Nolin River

Second Creek

First Creek Trail

MAMMOTH

CAVE

NATIONAL

Raymer Hollow Trail

259

First Creek Lake

First Creek 1
First Creek 2

Temple Hill

Ferry

P

Three Springs

McCoy

Houchins

Collie Ridge

McCoy Hollow

Good Spring

Homestead Trail

Good Spring Church

Maple Springs Loop

Green River Ferry Rd

Mammoth Cave International Center for Science and Learning

200

Lock and Dam 6 must portage (dangerous and hazardous)

70

Crump Island

Buffalo Creek

Bluffs

Buffalo Tr

Floating Mill Island

Houchins Ferry

185

Sal Hollow

Buffalo Tr

Maple Springs Group Campground

See detail map

180

BROWNSVILLE

Sal Hollow Tr

Sal Hollow Tr

Turnhole Bend

Sal Hollow Tr

Historic Entrance

Hotel

Green River Ferry

Hike
Sal Hollow Trail

190

Stice Island

195

JOPPA RIDGE

Green River Ferry

Official vehicles only

Green River

70

Boardcut Island

Turnhole Bend

Sand Cave Island

Carmichael Entrance

Furlong Cemetery

259

Brownsville Rd

Turnhole Spring

Turnhole Bend Trail

Joppa Church

Joppa Ridge Rd

one-way

Rhoda

Brownsville

Road

JOPPA RIDGE

Sloans Crossing

2325

Cedar Sink Rd

Cedar Sink Trail

Cedar Sink

WOOLSEY VALLEY

Sloans Crossing Pond Walk (wheelchair-accessible)

101

Hike
Cedar Sink Trail

Chalybeate

Pig

422

Cedar Spring

Chaumont Road

259

Chaumont Road

31w

North

↑

| 0 | 1 | 2 Kilometers |
| 0 | 1 | 2 Miles |

	Unpaved road		Hiking trail	⚲	Picnic area
	Gate		Wheelchair-accessible trail		Boat launch
Bluffs	Backcountry campsite		Horse and hiking trail	▲	Campground
• 123	River mile		Bicycle and hiking trail (gravel)	P	Backcountry parking area
✝	Cemetery		Horse, hiking and bicycle trail		

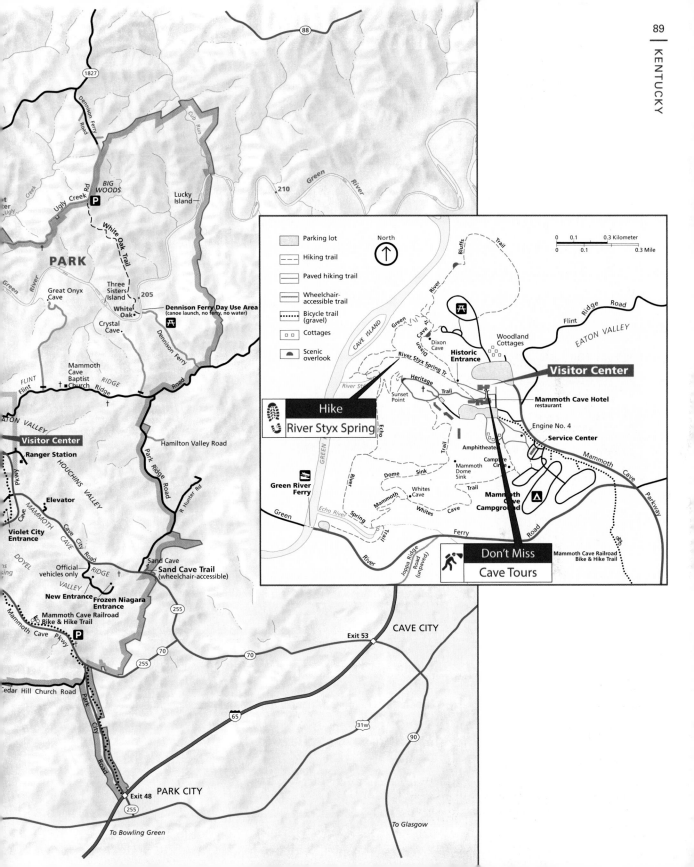

88

1827

Dennison Ferry Road

Cub Run

BIG
WOODS

P

Ugly Creek

Creek

White Oak Trail

Green River

210

Lucky
Island

PARK

Great Onyx
Cave

Three
Sisters
Island

205

White
Oak

Crystal
Cave

Dennison Ferry Day Use Area
(canoe launch, no ferry, no water)

Dennison Ferry Road

Green River

Mammoth
Cave
Baptist
Church

FLINT
Flint

RIDGE
Ridge

Hamilton Valley Road

Park Ridge Road

EATON VALLEY

Visitor Center

Ranger Station

HOUCHINS VALLEY

R Hunter Rd

Elevator

Cave City Road

Violet City
Entrance

DOYEL

MAMMOTH CAVE PKWY

Official
vehicles only

RIDGE

VALLEY

Sand Cave

Sand Cave Trail
(wheelchair-accessible)

New Entrance

Frozen Niagara
Entrance

Mammoth Cave Railroad
Bike & Hike Trail

Mammoth Cave Pkwy

P

255

70

255

70

255

65

Cedar Hill Church Road

Park City Road

Exit 53

CAVE CITY

31w

90

PARK CITY

Exit 48

255

To Bowling Green

To Glasgow

Map legend:

Parking lot

North ↑

Hiking trail

Paved hiking trail

Wheelchair-accessible trail

Bicycle trail (gravel)

Cottages

Scenic overlook

0   0.1   0.3 Kilometer
0   0.1   0.3 Mile

Bluffs Trail

Green River

CAVE ISLAND

Cave Run

Dixon Cave

Woodland Cottages

Flint Ridge Road

EATON VALLEY

River Styx Spring Tr

Historic Entrance

Visitor Center

River Styx

Heritage

Sunset Point

Trail

Mammoth Cave Hotel
restaurant

Engine No. 4

Service Center

Hike
River Styx Spring

GREEN RIVER

Echo River Trail

Amphitheater

Campsite
Circle

Mammoth Dome Sink

Mammoth
Cave
Campground

Green River Ferry

Dome Sink

Whites
Cave

Mammoth Trail

Whites Cave Trail

Mammoth Cave Road

Green River

Echo River Spring

Ferry

Joppa Ridge Road
(unpaved)

Don't Miss
Cave Tours

Mammoth Cave Railroad
Bike & Hike Trail

Signatures written with candles on the cave's walls

Mammoth Cave Camping (Fees are per night)

Name	Location	Open	Fee	Sites	Notes
Mammoth Cave*	0.25 mile from the Visitor Center	All Year	$20 $25	105 4 Group	Showers at Service Center (March–Nov)
Houchin's Ferry	15 miles from the Visitor Center	All Year	$12	12	Water and Pit Toilets No RVs, No Showers
Maple Springs*	6 miles from Visitor Center	All Year	$25–35	7 3 Group	Water and Pit Toilets No RVs, No Showers
Backcountry	A free permit, available at the visitor center, is required to camp at any of the twelve backcountry sites.				
Group	Available at Mammoth Cave (4 sites) and Maple Springs (3 sites) Campgrounds.				

Mammoth Cave Lodging (Fees are per night)

Name	Open	Fee	Location & Notes
Mammoth Cave Hotel	All Year	$66–125	Next to the Visitor Center • Variety of rooms and cottages

Mammoth Cave Tours

Name	Fee	Duration	Notes
Mammoth Passage	$7 (Adult)/ $5 (Youth)	1.25 hours	Easy tour delving into the cave's cultural and natural history
Frozen Niagara	$13/8	1.25 hours	Short trek suitable for all ages
Discovery - ♿	$5/3.50	0.5 hour	Self-guiding tour of the Rotunda
Historic*	$14/9	2 hours	Learn about the cave's 19th- and early 20th-century visitors
Domes and Dripstones*	$15/10	2 hours	Domes, pits, and dripstone formations
Grand Avenue*	$26/19	4 hours	Strenuous tour providing idea of the cave system's size
Cleaveland Avenue*	$16/10	2.5 hours	See various gypsum formations, follows Grand Avenue route
Gothic Avenue*	$12/9	2 hours	Portions of Star Chamber, Historic, and Violet City Lantern tours
Violet City Lantern* - ♿	$18/13	3 hours	Strenuous trip lit only by lanterns
Great Onyx Lantern*	$18/13	2.25 hours	Explore dripstone gypsum and helicitite formations by lantern
River Styx* - ♿	$15/10	2.5 hours	View a few underground waterways
Star Chamber*	$14/10	2.25 hours	Visit site of the Tuberculosis Hospital
Focus on Frozen Niagara*	$13/9	1.75 hours	Photo-friendly tour of cave's most famous formations
Trog*	n/a/$16	2.75 hours	Kids-only trip of rarely used passages
Intro to Caving*	$26/20	3.5 hours	Hiking boots required, chest/hip measurement less than 42"
Wild Cave* - ♿	$55	6 hours	Hiking boots , less than 42" chest/hip, and 16+ years old required

Youth is 6–12 years of age. Golden Age, Golden Access, and America the Beautiful Senior and Access Passes receive a 50% discount from the listed adult tour prices. River Styx, Focus on Frozen Niagara, and Trog are only offered in summer.

*Campground and tour reservations can be made in advance by calling (877) 444-6777 or clicking recreation.gov

Cave Tours

Tours began in 1816 and have continued to the present day without interruption. All of the original tours entered the cave's **Historic Entrance**. Native Americans from some 4,000 years ago, wealthy easterners under the guidance of a slave named Stephen Bishop, and patients hoping an extended stay underground at Dr. Croghan's Tuberculosis Hospital would cure what ailed them, all have at least one thing in common. They walked through the Historic Entrance and into the mystery and darkness of Mammoth Cave. Today, it is reserved for tourists. Tours such as **Gothic Avenue**, **Historic**, **Discovery**, **Star Chamber**, **Violet City Lantern**, **River Styx**, and **Trog** all begin here. Park rangers guide visitors through the passages, slowly satisfying guests' curiosities while regaling them with stories of the cave's incredible history and geology. More than two-thirds of the park's guests take a cave tour.

Images of caves usually begin with dripping stalactites hanging from the ceiling; stubby, rounded stalagmites protruding from the floor; and a collection of otherworldly rock formations, but most of Mammoth Cave is drab and undecorated. Its plainness is caused by a hard, thick layer of sandstone just above the passageways. This cap prevents water, the key component of cave feature formation, from seeping in. However, there are a few locations, like **Frozen Niagara**, where the sandstone cap rock has dissolved, allowing water to seep through the cave's limestone strata. In these sections, formations were slowly created by water combined with carbon dioxide, which is able to dissolve limestone. These solutes precipitate and over time—tens of thousands of years—accumulation of precipitates leads to cave formations. The most noteworthy of which can be seen on these tours: **Frozen Niagara**, **Focus on Frozen Niagara** (for photographers), **Domes and Dripstones**, **Grand Avenue**, and **Snowball**.

Kentucky Cave Shrimp are the park's most notable occupants. These eyeless, albino shrimp were discovered by Stephen Bishop, and it was later determined that they live exclusively in the water of the cave's lower levels. While no tours explore these regions, you can walk the banks of River Styx, the Dead Sea, and Lake Lethe on the **River Styx Tour**.

While exploring the cave take note of the names of each room. Many names come from their shape or appearance, but others are derived from the cave's unique history. Names of owners, explorers, and visitors are all found among the passages and rooms. **Booth's Amphitheater** is named for Edwin Booth, who recited Hamlet's famous soliloquy in that room. Edwin is overshadowed by his infamous brother, John Wilkes Booth, who assassinated President Lincoln. **Ole Bule Concert Hall** is named for the famous violinist. John Muir, conservationist, writer, and national park advocate, visited in September of 1867, but he was just an "unknown nobody" walking to Florida at the time.

Tours come in all lengths and difficulties. **Frozen Niagara** is the easiest, and it is suitable for visitors who require the aid of a cane or walker. **Wild Cave** is the most strenuous. It's a real spelunking adventure. Participants spend much of the six hour tour crawling on hands and knees as they squeeze through tight spaces. All Wild Cave participants must be at least 16 years old, meet certain size requirements (to fit through openings), and wear high-top, lace-up hiking boots. An adult must accompany visitors under age 18. Cameras are not allowed, because there isn't any opportunity to use them. It is recommended that you wear gym shorts and a t-shirt under coveralls (provided). You will get dirty, but coin-operated **showers** are available at the service center on Mammoth Cave Parkway.

All tours except Passage and Discovery can be reserved at least one day in advance by calling (877) 444-6777 or clicking recreation.gov.

Note: White-nose syndrome, a bat-killing fungal disease spreading through the eastern United States, is present in Mammoth Cave. Do not wear any clothing or carry any objects with you that have been in another cave or mine since 2005 to help prevent spread of this disease that has already resulted in the death of millions of bats. Likewise, whatever clothing and objects go into Mammoth Cave with you should not enter any other cave or mine. Be prepared to clean your shoes at the white-nose station after completing your tour. (It only takes a minute or two.) White-nose syndrome is not known to be harmful to humans.

Best of Mammoth Cave

Adventure Cave Tours: Wild Cave
    Runner-up: Intro to Caving

Family Cave Tour: Violet City Lantern
    Runner-up: River Styx
    2nd Runner-up: Discovery

Family Hike: Cedar Sink Trail
    Runner-up: Green River Bluffs Trail

World's Longest Caves

1. Mammoth Cave (USA, 405 Miles)
2. Sistema Sac Actum (Mexico, 208 Miles)
3. Jewel Cave (USA, 180 Miles)
4. Sistema Ox Bel Ha (Mexico, 160 Miles)
5. Optymistychna (Ukraine, 147 Miles)
6. Wind Cave (USA, 143 Miles)
7. Lechuguilla Cave (USA, 138 Miles)
8. Clearwater Cave (Malaysia, 129 Miles)
9. Fisher Ridge (USA, 125 Miles)

How did the cave form?

Mammoth Cave's limestone was laid down 325 million years ago by an ancient sea that covered the central U.S. The sea disappeared and a river proceeded to deposit a sandstone and shale cap on top of the limestone. Erosional forces began to slowly wear away the sandstone. About 10 million years ago cracks and holes formed, exposing the limestone and allowing rainwater to work its way underground. Sinking streams began to hollow out the cave, and underground rivers formed.

Erosional forces played a part in the cave's formation, but they were not responsible for carving the passageways. The cave was created and continues to grow because limestone is soluble in groundwater under the right conditions. Water combined with carbon dioxide forms a weak carbonic acid able to dissolve limestone. Limestone that previously inhabited Mammoth's subterranean passages was dissolved and carried away in solution by rainwater.

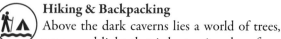

Hiking & Backpacking

Above the dark caverns lies a world of trees, water, and light that is best enjoyed on foot. On a busy day several thousand visitors explore the park's underground world, but few of them experience what's right out in the open, just waiting to be hiked. Above ground are signs of the caves beneath your feet. Trails skirt alongside rivers that disappear into the earth via sinkholes.

There are 23 miles of hiking trails south of the Green River. Most of these begin at or near the visitor center or Mammoth Cave Campground. If you don't plan on taking a cave tour that enters through the Historic Entrance be sure to hike **River Styx Spring Trail**. This 0.6-mile trail leads past the Historic Entrance, which is worth a quick look. The trail continues on to the site where River Styx exits Mammoth Cave. Eventually it leads to the banks of the Green River before looping back to the visitor center. If you care to extend River Styx Spring Trail, continue north along the 1.1-mile **Green River Bluffs Trail**. From this stretch you'll see Cave Island protruding from the Green River. Continue past the island to a scenic overlook. The trail concludes at the visitor center picnic area. Just south of the visitor center is **Heritage Trail**. This 0.3-mile trek loops around "Old Guides Cemetery," where tour guides like Stephen Bishop are buried. It terminates at sunset point, and then loops back to the visitor center. The 2.2-mile **Echo River Trail** and 2.0-mile Mammoth Dome Sink Trail connect to Heritage Trail Loop. **Cedar Sink Trail** is another good hiking opportunity. Its trailhead is located on Cedar Sink Road just south of Brownsville Road.

More than 55 miles of backcountry trails are found north of the Green River. To reach them you must cross the river—using Green River Ferry—to Maple Springs Group Campground, which serves as a hub for many hiking trails. This is the best area of the park to escape overcrowding that may occur near the visitor center. Even during peak season you may feel like you're the only person around (which might be true). The 8.1-mile **Sal Hollow Trail** and 2.8-mile **Buffalo Trail** are two of the most beautiful and secluded hikes. This region also provides excellent backpacking opportunities thanks to 12 campsites sprinkled throughout the backcountry.

Horseback Riding

The entire network of trails north of Green River is open to horse use. Overnight accommodations are available for horseback riders at **Maple Springs Group Campground**; sites 1–4 are designed specifically to accommodate horses. Day-use riders can park trailers at Lincoln Trailhead, across the road from Maple Springs Campground bulletin board at Maple Springs Trailhead, and 0.25-mile north of Maple Springs Campground at Good Springs Church. Be sure to follow all rules specific to visitors with horses. Double J Stables (270.286.8167, doublejstables.com) and Jesse James Riding Stables (270.773.2560) offer **guided trail rides**. Double J even **rents horses**.

Biking

Mammoth Cave Railroad Bike and Hike Trail is popular among pedalers. It follows the route used by early visitors arriving at Mammoth Cave from Park City by rail and stagecoach. You can also bike on 101 miles of roadway found in the park. During the off-season, the 10-mile circuit leaving the visitor center via **Flint Ridge Road** to **Park Ridge Road** to Cave City Road is a pleasant pedal with easy to moderate climbs. Bicycles are prohibited on hiking trails south of Green River and around the visitor center. Mountain biking is allowed on some trails north of the Green River including **Big Hollow Trail** (recommended). Stop in at the visitor center for mountain bike trail information and maps.

Paddling

Paddling is another great way to enjoy Mammoth Cave's above ground attractions. At normal water levels **Green and Nolin Rivers** provide a casual float for paddlers of any experience level. Green River meanders through the park for 25 miles, with boat landings at Dennison Ferry, Green River Ferry, and Houchin's Ferry. Be aware that there is an unmarked lock and dam past Houchin's Ferry just a short distance beyond the park boundary. For a nice paddle launch your canoe or kayak on Nolin River just below Nolin River Dam at Tailwaters Recreation Area. Paddle downstream to the confluence of Nolin and Green Rivers. When you reach Green River paddle upstream a short distance to the take-out at Houchin's Ferry.

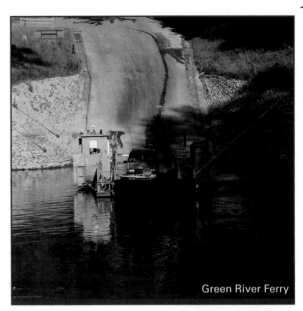
Green River Ferry

To rent a canoe or hire a guide, contact Big Buffalo Crossing (270.774.7883, bigbuffalocrossing.com), Green River Canoeing (270.773.5712, mammothcave-canoe.com), Kentucky River Runners (270.776.2876, kyriverrunners.com), or Mammoth Cave Canoes & Kayak (270.773.3366, mammothcavecanoe-k.com).

Fishing

A state fishing license is not required for fishing in **Green and Nolin Rivers** as long as you are within park boundaries. Bass, crappie, bluegill, muskellunge, and catfish are commonly caught in these waters.

Live bait other than worms is prohibited at Sloan's Crossing Pond and First Creek Lake. Minnows and worms are allowed for river fishing. Fish size and quantity restrictions follow Kentucky Department of Fish & Wildlife regulations.

Ranger Programs

In addition to all of the ranger-led cave tours, Mammoth Cave offers ranger-led walks, campfires, evening programs, and auditorium programs. If you have some time to burn during your visit, look no further than the ranger programs. All of the activities (outside of the cave tours) are free of charge and exceptionally entertaining. A schedule of these events is available at the visitor center or park website.

The Natural Entrance

For Kids
Mammoth Cave offers a few kid-centric tours and programs. Trog (page 91) is a kid-only (ages 8–12) cave tour. Introduction to Caving is open to children 10 and up, as well as their parents. Refer to the activity schedules for all ranger-led programs (available online or at the visitor center).

Kids can also participate in the park's **Junior Ranger Program**. Grab a free Junior Ranger booklet at the Visitor Center Information Desk, and then complete enough activities to receive a Junior Ranger badge and certificate.

Flora & Fauna
More than 1,300 species of flowering plants grow within park boundaries. This extreme biodiversity is due to being situated in a transitional zone between cooler climates to the north and sub-tropical climates to the south. In spring, meadows erupt in a colorful display of wildflowers. Between February and March, more than 60 species of herbaceous wildflowers bloom to the delight of hikers. During this time the park hosts an annual wildflower day, with programs focusing on flowers, ecology, and conservation held throughout the day by park rangers and volunteers. Please refer to the park's website for event details.

The park also protects a few swaths of grassland similar to what once covered 3 to 5 million acres of neighboring land before it was settled and developed. You'll find several species of grasses including the western dwarf dandelion, which is common in western prairie states, but can only be found in Kentucky at Mammoth Cave National Park.

About 45 species of mammals inhabit this park. You'll probably see white-tailed deer and squirrels, while bobcats, coyotes, foxes, raccoons, skunks, beaver, and mink are seldom spotted. Wild turkeys, bald eagles, and blue herons are just a few bird species that provide some pretty decent bird watching. Several species of bat reside in the cave. It also supports a wide variety of creepy-crawly insects, crustaceans, and fish. About 130 animal species are regular inhabitants of the cave system.

Pets
Pets must be kept on a leash no more than six feet in length at all times. All pets, except service animals, are prohibited in the cave. Mammoth Cave Hotel allows them in Woodland Cottages, but they are not allowed in any other facilities. The hotel also operates a kennel for visitors with pets.

Accessibility
While the park offers wheelchair-accessible camping, picnicking, lodging, trails, dining, and visitor center facilities, its main attraction—the cave—is not accessible to individuals in wheelchairs.

Weather
The weather above ground is moderate. Wet springs, hot summers, dry falls, and cold winters are the norm. While the weather above ground is difficult to predict, weather in the cave is easily anticipated. Subterranean temperatures only fluctuate a degree or two from the 54°F average. Cave temperature doesn't stabilize until you're a fair distance from its entrance.

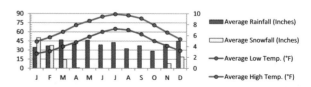

Vacation Planner

Vacations are almost always too short, and for that reason, most visitors race into the park, take a quick tour, and head on to their next destination. A lot can be missed in these whirlwind visits. This simple 2-day itinerary helps maximize your valuable time. First, a few basics on cave tours and park facilities need to be covered. When considering which cave tour to take, be honest about your size, fitness level, and any phobias you might have. Park rangers will measure guests to make sure you will fit through tight spaces encountered on **Wild Cave** and **Introduction to Caving Tours**. Don't be afraid to split up if your group can't settle on a "one-size-fits-all" tour. Most tours can be reserved in advance. Making reservations is always a good idea, but it's imperative for **Wild Cave**, **Intro to Caving**, **River Styx**, and **Violet City Lantern Tours** (page 91). If the tour you want is full, you can check for cancellations 30 minutes prior to departure; you might get lucky. The park offers several **campgrounds** (page 90) for overnight visitors, but only one **hotel** (page 90). Nearby dining, grocery stores, lodging, festivals, and attractions are listed on pages 96–97.

Day 1: Every trip to Mammoth Cave should begin at the **visitor center**. This is where you can grab brochures, receive answers to all the questions you conjured while cooped up in the car, and view a current schedule of cave tours and ranger programs. It's basically the main hub for all park activities, and more importantly the location where cave tour tickets are purchased (if you haven't made advance reservations) and tour groups meet before heading beneath the surface. Do not forget to check the schedule of above-ground ranger-led activities, and take note of any that interest you. For example, a campfire program is a fantastic way to spend the evening. For a proper introduction to Mammoth Cave hike **River Styx Spring Trail** and take the **Discovery Tour**. Try to catch a **Campfire Talk**; if not, get some rest because a big day of spelunking awaits you tomorrow.

Day 2: If you like crawling through tight passages in complete darkness, sign up for the **Wild Cave Tour** (reservations recommended). To us, every knee-bruising, pants-ripping, belly-crawling, head-bumping (you

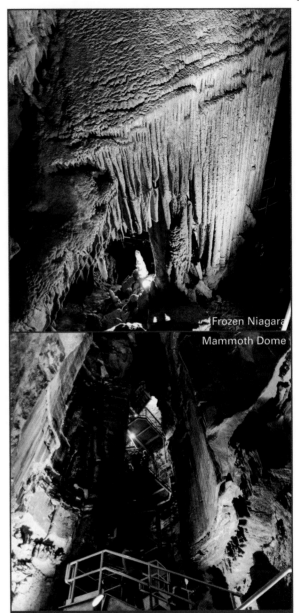

Frozen Niagara
Mammoth Dome

wear a helmet) minute is worth the trouble. However, it's definitely not for everyone. You spend six hours in cramped, damp darkness, but what makes this and the rest of the Mammoth Cave tours so memorable are the park rangers' spellbinding stories. Non-Wild Cavers in your group should consider taking **Domes and Dripstones**, **Violet City Lantern**, or **River Styx Tour**. If they'd rather stay above ground, **Sal Hollow Trail** is the place to be.

Dining
In the Park
Mammoth Cave Hotel • (877) 386-4383
27 Entrance Rd, Mammoth Cave
mammothcavehotel.com

Near the Park
Porky Pig Diner • (270) 597-2422
125 Park Boundary Rd, Smiths Grove

Watermill Restaurant • (270) 773-3186
803 Mammoth Cave Rd, Cave City

El Mazatlan • (270) 773-7448
105 Gardner Ln, Cave City
el-mazatlan.com • Entrée: $8–19

Sahara Steak House • (270) 773-345
413 E Happy Valley St, Cave City

Laura's Hilltop Restaurant • (270) 597-9945
1409 KY-259 N, Brownsville

Mis Amigos Mexican Grill • (270) 597-9105
600 KY-259, Brownsville

Pizza Paradise • (270) 597-2224
1457 KY-259 N, Brownsville

Red Roof BBQ • (270) 286-0121
898 Moutardier Rd, Leitchfield

TurtleLini's Pizza and Pasta • (270) 786-8686
103 S Dixie St, Horse Cave
turtlelinis.com • Pizza: $5–17

Big Moose's BBQ Smokehouse • (270) 261-5002
525 W Main St, Glasgow

Los Mariachis • (270) 651-3229
802 Happy Valley Rd, Glasgow

Gale 'n' Dale's • (270) 651-2489
405 Happy Valley Rd, Glasgow

Grocery Stores
Save-A-Lot • (270) 773-2402
9584 Happy Valley Rd, Cave City

Walmart Supercenter • (270) 678-1003
2345 Happy Valley Rd, Glasgow

Save-A-Lot • (270) 597-2171
1445 Ky Hwy 259 N, Brownsville

Food Lion • (270) 651-1718
214 South L Rogers Wells Blvd, Glasgow

Lodging
In the Park
Mammoth Cave Hotel • (877) 386-4383
27 Entrance Rd, Mammoth Cave
mammothcavehotel.com • Rates: $66–125

Near the Park
Bryce Inn • (270) 563-5141
592 S Main St, Smiths Grove
bryceinn.com

Victorian House B&B • (270) 563-9403
110 N Main St, Smiths Grove

Wayfarer • (270) 773-3366
1240 Old Mammoth Cave Rd, Cave City

Rock Cabin Camping • (270) 773-4740
5091 Mammoth Cave Rd, Cave City
rockcabincamping.com

Wigwam Village • (270) 773-3381
601 N Dixie Hwy, Cave City
wigwamvillage.com • Rates: $45–75

Cave Country RV Campground • (270) 773-4678
216 Gaunce Dr, Cave City
cavecountryrv.com • Rates: $39–41

Diamond Caverns Resort • (270) 749-2891
660 Doyle Rd, Cave City

Jellystone Park Camp Resort • (270) 773-3840
1002 Mammoth Cave Rd, Cave City
jellystonemammothcave.com • Rates: $29–277

Park View Motel • (270) 773-3463
3906 Mammoth Cave Rd, Cave City

Park Mammoth Resort • (270) 749-4101
22850 Louisville Rd, Park City
parkmammothresort.us

Horse Cave KOA • (270) 786-2819
489 Flint Ridge Rd, Horse Cave

Serenity Hill B&B • (270) 597-9647
3600 Mammoth Cave Rd, Brownsville
serenityhillbedandbreakfast.com • Rates: $100–170

Four Seasons Country Inn B&B • (270) 678-1000
4107 Scottsville Rd, Glasgow
fourseasonscountryinn.com • Rates: $79–130

Hall Place • (270) 651-3176
313 S Green St, Glasgow

Many chain restaurants and hotels can be found nearby in Cave City, Park City, Glasgow, and Bowling Green.

Festivals
Hillbilly Days • April
hillbillydays.com • Pikeville, KY

Kentucky Derby Festival • May
kdf.org • Louisville, KY

International Bar-B-Q Festival • May
bbqfest.com • Owensboro, KY

Great American Brass Band Festival • June
gabbf.com • Danville, KY

CMA Music Festival • June
Largest country music party in the world
cmaworld.com • Nashville, TN

Jane Austen Festival • July
jasnalouisville.com • Louisville, KY

International Newgrass Festival • August
newgrassfestival.com • Bowling Green, KY

Horse Cave Heritage Festival • September
horsecaveheritagefestival.com • Horse Cave, KY

International Festival • September
BGInternationalFest.com • Bowling Green

National Jug Band Jubilee • September
jugbandjubilee.com • Louisville, KY

Kentucky Bourbon Festival • September
kybourbonfestival.com • Bardstown, KY

World Chicken Festival • September
Dedicated to the first KFC and its history
chickenfestival.com • London, KY

Jerusalem Ridge Festival • September/October
Real bluegrass from its birthplace
jerusalemridgefestival.org • Rosine, KY

St James Court Art Show • September/October
stjamescourtartshow.com • Louisville, KY

Festival of Trains • December
historicrailpark.com • Bowling Green, KY

Attractions
Near the Park
Double J Stables & Campgrounds • (270) 286-8167
542 Lincoln School Road, Mammoth Cave
doublejstables.com
Trail Rides: $20/hr, $25/1.5 hrs, $30/2 hrs

Jesse James Riding Stables • (270) 773-2560
3057 Mammoth Cave Rd, Cave City

Big Buffalo Crossing • (270) 774-7883
100 River Road, Munfordville
bigbuffalocrossing.com
Paddle/Float Trips: $30–50 (half-day), $40–60 (full-day), $80–85/canoe (overnight)

Green River Canoeing • (270) 773-5712
3057 Mammoth Cave Road, Cave City
mammothcavecanoe.com
Paddle Trips: $50–60 (half-day), $65 (full-day), $65–75/canoe (overnight)

Kentucky River Runners • (270) 776-2876
kyriverrunners.com
Paddle Trips: $75–85 (full-day)

Mammoth Cave Canoes & Kayak • (270) 773-3366
1240 Old Mammoth Cave Road, Cave City
mammothcavecanoe-k.com
Paddle Trips: $50 (half-day), $65 (full-day), $85/canoe (overnight)

Onyx Cave • (270) 773-3530
101 Huckleberry Knob Rd, Cave City
visitonyxcave.com

Hidden River Cave • (270) 786-1466
119 E Main St, Horse Cave
hiddenrivercave.com • Tours: $15–50

Historic Diamond Caverns • (270) 749-2233
1900 Mammoth Cave Parkway, Park City
diamondcaverns.com • Tour: $17/adult

Kentucky Down Under • (270) 786-2635
Kangeroos to didgeridoos, a little Australia in KY
3700 L and N Turnpike Rd, Horse Cave
kdu.com • Admission: $22/adult

Mammoth Cave Wildlife Museum • (270) 773-2255
409 E Happy Valley St, Cave City
Admission: $8/adult
mammothcavewildlifemuseum.com

Dinosaur World • (270) 773-4345
711 Mammoth Cave Rd, Cave City
dinoworld.net • Admission: $13/adult

Highlander Bowl • (270) 651-9020
110 Park Ave, Glasgow

Beyond the Park
Skyline Drive-in Theatre • (270) 932-2800
5600 Hodgenville Rd, Greensburg
skylinedrivein.com • Tickets: $7/adult

Lost River Cave • (270) 393-0077
2818 Nashville Rd, Bowling Green
lostrivercave.com • Admission: $17/adult

Regal Cinemas • (270) 782-9047
2625 Scottsville Rd, Bowling Green

National Corvette Museum • (270) 781-7973
350 Corvette Dr, Bowling Green
corvettemuseum.org • Admission: $10/adult

Shaker Village of Pleasant Hill • (800) 734-5611
3501 Lexington Rd, Harrodsburg
shakervillageky.org • Admission: $10/adult

Heaven Hill Bourbon • (502) 337-1000
1311 Gilkey Run Rd, Bardstown
bourbonheritagecenter.com • Tours: $10–20

Abraham Lincoln Birthplace • (502) 549-3741
7120 Bardstown Rd, Hodgenville
nps.gov/abli • Admission: Free

Louisville Historic Tours • (502) 718-2764
1340 S 4th St, Louisville
louisvillehistorictours.com • Tours: $15

City Taste Tours • (502) 457-8686
332 W Broadway, Louisville
citytastetours.com • Tours: $59–89

Thomas Edison House • (502) 585-5247
729 E Washington St, Louisville
edisonhouse.org • Admission: $5/adult

Frazier Int'l History Museum • (502) 753-5663
829 W Main St, Louisville
fraziermuseum.org • Admission: $12/adult

Waverly Hills Sanatorium • (502) 933-2142
Paralee Ln, Louisville
therealwaverlyhills.com • Tours: $25–100

Louisville Slugger Museum • (888) 775-8443
800 W Main St, Louisville
sluggermuseum.com • Admission: $14/adult

Muhammad Ali Center • (502) 584-9254
144 N 6th St, Louisville
alicenter.org • Admission: $9/adult

Speed Art Museum • (502) 634-2700
2035 S 3rd St, Louisville
speedmuseum.org • Admission: $12/adult

Kentucky Derby Museum • (502) 637-1111
704 Central Ave, Louisville
derbymuseum.org • Admission: $15/adult

Churchill Downs • (502) 636-4400
700 Central Ave, Louisville
churchilldowns.com

Louisville Zoo • (502) 459-2181
1100 Trevilian Way, Louisville
louisvillezoo.org • Admission: $16.25/adult

KentuckyShow! • (502) 560-7128
501 W Main St, Louisville
kentuckyshow.com • Tickets: $8

Louisville Equestrian Center • (502) 477-0830
6720 Mt Washington Rd, Taylorsville
louisvilleequestriancenter.com

NashTrash Tours • (615) 226-7300
1038 Rosa L Parks Blvd, Nashville, TN
nashtrash.com • Tours: $36/adult

Ryman Auditorium • (615) 889-3060
116 5th Ave N, Nashville, TN
ryman.com • Tours: $20–30

Tennessee State Museum • (615) 741-2692
505 Deaderick St, Nashville, TN
tnmuseum.org • Admission: Free

Chaffin's Barn Dinner Theatre • (615) 646-9977
8204 TN-100, Nashville, TN
dinnertheatre.com • Tickets: $30–50

Hatch Showprint • (615) 256-2805
Oldest letterpress poster print shop in the U.S.
224 5th Ave S, Nashville, TN

Buffalo Trace Distillery • (502) 696-5926
113 Great Buffalo Tr, Frankfort
buffalotrace.com • Tour: Free

Mary Todd Lincoln House • (859) 233-9999
578 West Main St, Lexington
mtlhouse.org • Admission: $10/adult

Kentucky Horse Park • (859) 233-4303
4089 Iron Works Pkwy, Lexington
kyhorsepark.com • Admission: $12–20/adult

Keeneland • (859) 254-3412
4201 Versailles Rd, Lexington
keeneland.com • Horse races & Tours Available

Alltech's Lexington Brewing • (859) 225-8095
401 Cross St, Lexington
kentuckyale.com • Tour: $8.50

For more information on visiting Kentucky, click www.kentuckytourism.com.

Louisville, KY
100 mi/1.75 hrs

Lexington, KY
140 mi/2.5 hrs

Bowling Green, KY
30 mi/45 min

Nashville, TN
95 mi/1.5 hrs

Distances to the Visitor Center

Mingus Mill

Great Smoky Mountains

107 Park Headquarters Road
Gatlinburg, TN 37738
Phone: (865) 436-1200
Website: nps.gov/grsm

Established: June 15, 1934
Size: 521,621 Acres
Annual Visitors: 10.7 Million
Peak Season: Summer & October
Hiking Trails: 850 Miles
Horse Trails: 550 Miles

Activities: Driving, Hiking,
Backpacking, Paddling, Biking,
Horseback Riding, and Fishing
Synchronous Fireflies: Elkmont
(usually in the middle of June)

Campgrounds ($14–23/night):
Abrams Creek, Balsam Mountain,
Big Creek, Cades Cove (All Year),
Cataloochee, Cosby, Deep Creek,
Elkmont, Look Rock, Smokemont
Backcountry Camping: Permitted
Lodging: Le Conte Lodge ($140
per person per night, hike-in only)

Park Hours: All day, every day
Entrance Fee: None

The location and geography of Great Smoky Mountains National Park (GRSM) have led to two incredible phenomena: mass tourism and unparalleled biodiversity. The park straddles the Smoky Mountains on the Tennessee–North Carolina border, less than a day's drive from one-third of the entire U.S. population—and on a busy day it might feel like they are all visiting at the same time. It's not true, but the park's 10.7 million annual visitors is still impressive. That's more than double the next closest national park's annual total. Another 11 million people pass through each year for non-recreational purposes. These staggering numbers lead to frequent bouts of bumper-to-bumper traffic and occasional gridlock, making the park feel constrictive and small even though it is one of the largest protected areas in the country.

This region sought protection under the formation of a national park to spare trees covering the mountains' slopes from logging and paper companies bent on stripping the land bare. Both sides got what they wanted. Many trees were clear-cut, but others were saved by a park, and eventually the region was designated an International Biosphere Reserve and a UNESCO World Heritage Site due to its biodiversity. GRSM is home to the greatest diversity of plant, animal, and insect life of any region in a temperate climate zone. A fact largely due to abundant annual precipitation (as much as 85 inches in some locations) and varied elevation (ranging from 876 feet at the mouth of Abrams Creek to 6,643 feet at the summit of Clingman's Dome). A hiker travelling from these two extremes experiences the same flora and fauna diversity as hiking all 2,184 miles from Georgia to Maine along the Appalachian Trail. That same hiker passes one of the largest blocks of deciduous old-growth forest in North America, home to 100 species of trees, more than any other U.S. National Park.

For centuries Cherokee Indians have lived among these trees, hunting and gathering what they needed to survive. Mining claims and the

Indian Removal Act forced them to Oklahoma on what came to be known as the "Trail of Tears." A few small American settlements sprang up, but substantial amounts of gold were never found. As the East continued to develop, industry's eye focused on the area's most abundant natural resource, its trees. By the mid-1920s, 300,000 acres had been clear-cut by logging and paper companies. Dramatic changes caused by reckless logging inspired Horace Kephart, author and park supporter, to ask the question "Shall the Smoky Mountains be made a national park or a desert?"

A question demanding an immediate answer. In 1926, President Calvin Coolidge signed a bill authorizing the formation of Great Smoky Mountains National Park, with the provision that no federal funds would be used to procure land. It was a serious hurdle to overcome. Parks in the West were formed mostly from land already owned by the federal government. Here on the East Coast, some 6,600 tracts of land needed to be purchased from more than 1,000 private landowners and a handful of logging and paper companies for a total price of $10 million. People from all walks of life banded together, donating every penny they could spare. Overwhelming public support prompted Tennessee and North Carolina to promise $3 million for the potential park, bringing the total to $5 million—still only half the required sum.

Thankfully, a philanthropist with deep pockets came to the park's aid. John D. Rockefeller, Jr., son of the wealthiest man in America, ultimately donated the entire $5 million balance. He made just one request. That a plaque honoring his mother be placed within the park (Rockefeller Memorial at Newfound Gap).

Despite this promising turn, the stock market crash in 1929 resulted in North Carolina and Tennessee being unable to honor their pledges to the new park. During these troubling times, Franklin D. Roosevelt intervened, allocating $1.5 million of federal funds to complete the land purchase. This marked the first time the U.S. government spent its own money to buy land for a national park. Effort, time, and money from small communities to wealthy philanthropists and governments helped create what is now the most popular national park in the United States.

Alum Cave Trail

When to Go
The park is almost perfect in summer and fall. "Almost" is the operative word. The problem is that this perfection is nobody's secret. A typical weekend summer day draws more than 60,000 visitors. Unless bumper-to-bumper traffic is your idea of a good time, you may want to schedule your vacation around the two peak seasons: mid-June to mid-August, and the month of October. During these times, visitation is so heavy even park officials advise trying to visit during the "off-season." Should you choose to ignore the park's advice, you can still enjoy its attractions. Start touring early (before 10am), as most visitors explore the park between 10am and 6pm. When the masses are out-and-about, you'll want to avoid popular destinations like Cades Cove Loop and Newfound Gap. But the best way to escape the crowds is to park your car and hike some of the park's 850 miles of trails. Relatively speaking, very few visitors explore the park on foot.

The park is open all year. **Sugarlands**, **Cades Cove**, **Oconaluftee** and **Sevierville Visitor Centers**, and **Gatlinburg Welcome Center** are open every day except Christmas. **Townsend Visitor Center** is open every day except Thanksgiving and Christmas. **Cades Cove** and **Smokemont** are the only year-round **campgrounds**. Note that a few of Cades Cove Loop's historic structures are seasonal.

Transportation & Airports
Public transportation does not provide service to the park from any major city in the area. Gatlinburg offers a trolley service (Tan Route, $2 fare) to the park between June and October.

Asheville Regional Airport (AVL) is 55 miles east of the park's Cherokee Entrance. McGhee Tyson Airport (TYS), just south of Knoxville in Alcoa, TN is 50 miles west of the Gatlinburg Entrance.

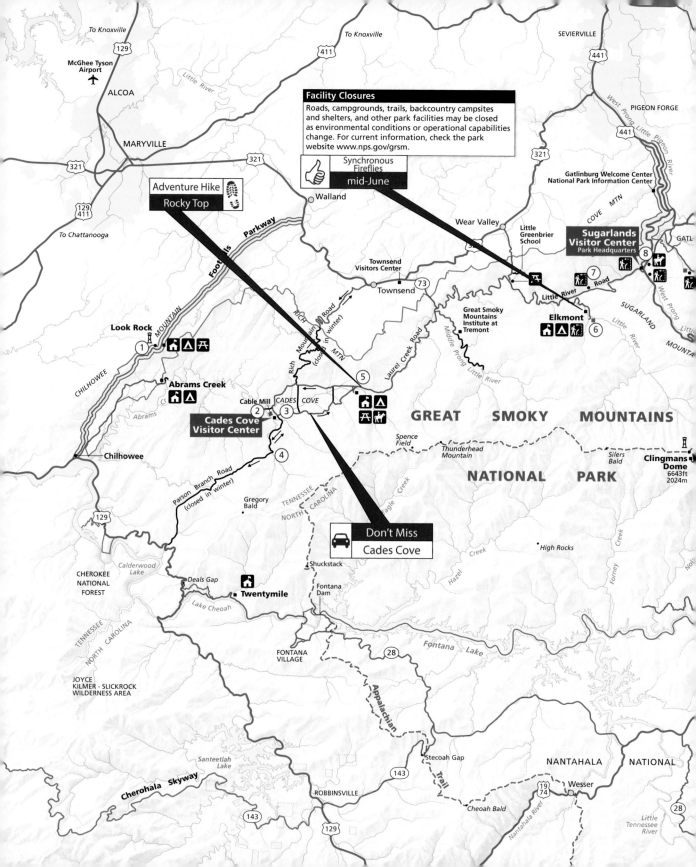

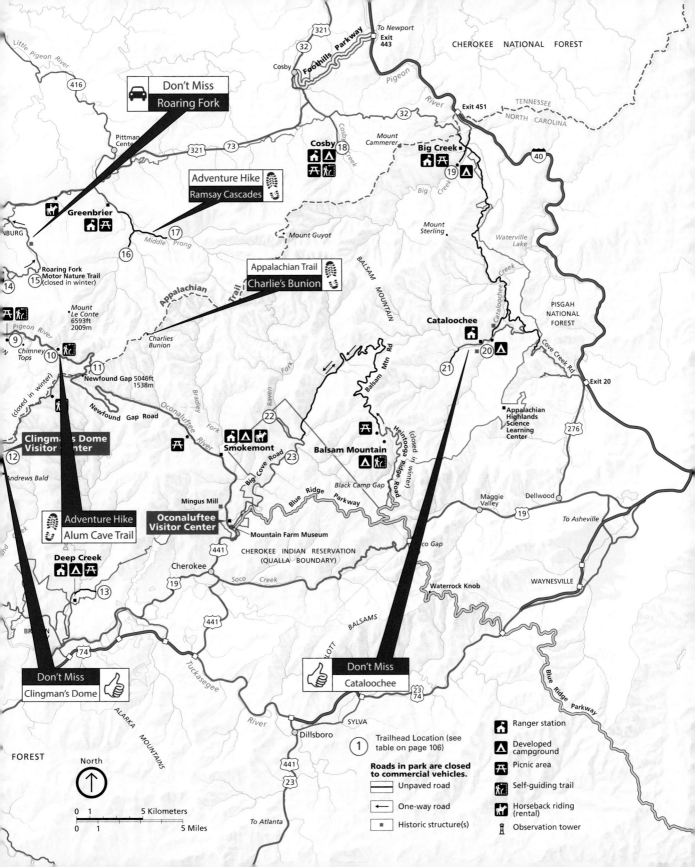

Don't Miss
Roaring Fork

Adventure Hike
Ramsay Cascades

Appalachian Trail
Charlie's Bunion

Clingmans Dome Visitor Center

Adventure Hike
Alum Cave Trail

Oconaluftee Visitor Center

Deep Creek

Don't Miss
Clingman's Dome

Don't Miss
Cataloochee

321
32
Foothills Parkway
Cosby
To Newport
Exit 443
CHEROKEE NATIONAL FOREST

32
Exit 451
TENNESSEE
NORTH CAROLINA

Pigeon River

416
Little Pigeon River

Pittman Center

321
73

Cosby
18

Mount Cammerer

Big Creek
19
40

Cosby Creek
Big Creek

Mount Sterling

Waterville Lake

Greenbrier

NBURG

Middle Prong

17

16

Mount Guyot

BALSAM MOUNTAIN

Cataloochee
20
21

Caldwell Creek

PISGAH NATIONAL FOREST

Cove Creek Rd

Exit 20

276

14
15
Roaring Fork Motor Nature Trail (closed in winter)

Appalachian Trail

Mount Le Conte 6593ft 2009m

9
Pigeon River

10
Chimney Tops

Charlies Bunion

11
Newfound Gap 5046ft 1538m

Newfound Gap Road

Oconaluftee River

Bradley Fork

Raven Fork

Appalachian Highlands Science Learning Center

Balsam Mtn Rd

22

Balsam Mountain

Heintooga Ridge Road (closed in winter)

12
Andrews Bald

(closed in winter)

Smokemont
23

Big Cove Road

Black Camp Gap

Blue Ridge Parkway

Maggie Valley
Dellwood

19
To Asheville

Mingus Mill

Mountain Farm Museum

441

CHEROKEE INDIAN RESERVATION (QUALLA BOUNDARY)

13
Deep Creek

Cherokee

19

Soco Creek

Soco Gap

Waterrock Knob

WAYNESVILLE

BROWN

ALARKA MOUNTAINS

FOREST

441

74
Tuckasegee River

BALSAMS

PLOTT

23
74

Dillsboro
SYLVA

441

23

To Atlanta

North

0   1   5 Kilometers
0   1   5 Miles

1 Trailhead Location (see table on page 106)

Roads in park are closed to commercial vehicles.

☐ Unpaved road
← One-way road
■ Historic structure(s)

🏠 Ranger station
△ Developed campground
⊼ Picnic area
Self-guiding trail
Horseback riding (rental)
Observation tower

Directions

There are three main entrances.

Gatlinburg, TN Entrance: From I-40, take Exit 407 (Sevierville) to TN-66 S. Continue straight onto US-441 S at the Sevierville intersection. US-441 leads directly into the park.

Townsend, TN Entrance: From the north via I-40 in Knoxville, take Exit 386B to US-129 S to Alcoa/Maryville. At Maryville, proceed on US-321/TN-73 E through Townsend. Continue on TN-73 into the park.

From the south via I-75, take Exit 376 to I-140 E towards Oak Ridge/Maryville. Merge onto I-140 E via Exit 376B toward Maryville. Turn onto US-129 S (Alcoa Highway) at Exit 11A and head toward Alcoa. Turn onto TN-35 and follow it to US-321 N. Follow US-321 N/TN-73 E through Townsend and continue on TN-73 into the park.

Cherokee, NC Entrance: From the north via I-40, take Exit 27 to US-74 W toward Waynesville. Turn onto US-19 headed to Cherokee. Turn onto US-441 N at Cherokee and follow it into the park.

From the south, follow US-441/US-23 N. At Dillsboro, merge onto US-74 W/US-441 N. Merge onto US-441 at Exit 74. Continue on US-441 into the park.

These are the main entrances to the park, but there are several ancillary entrances leading to sites and facilities that are more remote and less crowded. Balsam

Mountain, Abrams Creek, Big Creek, and Cataloochee are great first-come, first-served campgrounds where visitors can enjoy a more relaxed and quaint experience at Great Smoky Mountains National Park.

Driving

Great Smoky Mountains is a motorists' park. Indeed, the idea of a park in the Smoky Mountains drew much of its support from the people's demands for a highway between Knoxville, TN and Asheville, NC. Today, more than 384 miles of drivable roads, most of them paved, provide unprecedented access to the Smokies' interior. **Cades Cove Loop Road** is the park's most popular destination, and **Roaring Fork Motor Nature Trail** isn't far behind. Both of these routes allow visitors to see wildlife and nature from the comfort of their vehicle.

The perimeter of **Cades Cove** is traced by an 11-mile, one-way loop road, beginning and ending at the eastern terminus of **Laurel Creek Road**. If you'd like to conclude your driving tour of Cades Cove prematurely (maybe because of excessive traffic), you can exit the loop via two seasonal, steep, winding, unpaved roads: **Rich Mountain Road** and **Parson Branch Road**. If traffic is manageable you'll want to stick around, because the loop provides some of the best opportunities to spot white-tailed deer and black bear. You'll also find the largest open-air museum in the Smoky Mountains, where pioneer homesteads, barns, churches, and mills have been restored to their 19th-century appearances. While many of these structures are removed from the road, all of them are well-marked and easily accessible.

The loop starts where Smoky Mountain settlement began. First stop is also the first cabin built in the Smokies, **John Oliver Place**. Next you'll find **Primitive Baptist Church**, which was established in 1827, but the congregation worshipped in a small log structure until 1887 when the larger white frame church (seen at this stop) was erected. A small cemetery where many of the early settlers are buried is located nearby. Religion was the cause of many disagreements in the Cove. In 1839, expelled members of Primitive Baptist Church formed **Missionary Baptist Church** (site 7). (Once the Civil

War began, the church was forced to close its doors because the congregation was mostly Union sympathizers, but Confederate support also ran deep among the cove's 700 citizens.) Continuing along the loop is a short spur road to **Abrams Falls Trailhead** and **Elijah Oliver Place**. A 0.5-mile hike leads to the homestead of another Oliver family. It's 5 miles (roundtrip) to 20-foot Abrams Falls. **John Cable Mill** and **Cades Cove Visitor Center** are located near the loop's midway point. Rangers, gifts, and restrooms make this one of the more popular stops, but you shouldn't leave without browsing the time-period exhibits on display. The only original building left behind is the mill where early settlers ground corn. All others were brought here by the National Park Service to aid in their demonstrations of early farm life (schedules are available at the visitor center). Energy and attitudes permitting, there are a few more sites to see on the second half of the loop. You'll pass **Henry Whitehead Place**, **Cades Cove Nature Trail**, **Dan Lawson Place**, and **Carter Shields Cabin** before you've come full circle.

Roaring Fork Nature Trail is a 6-mile one-way road that begins and ends in Gatlinburg. The road's 10 mph speed limit is testament to the amount of twists, turns, and traffic you'll encounter. Along the way you'll pass several restored homes and buildings and **Rainbow Falls Trailhead**. Rainbow Falls is best seen on a sunny day after a heavy rain, when the trail lives up to its name and the **Place of a Thousand Drips** will be dripping. Rain or shine, the hike is pleasant any time of year.

Newfound Gap and **Clingman's Dome Roads** are must-sees. **Balsam Mountain** and **Heintooga Ridge Roads** around **Balsam Mountain**, and **Cove Creek Road** to the **Cataloochee Valley** are great places to avoid summer and fall crowds while enjoying similar majestic views of the Smoky Mountains.

Great Smoky Mountains Lodging

Name	Open	Fee	Location & Notes
Le Conte Lodge (Hike-in only)	March–November	$140/person per night	Shortest hike is 5.5 miles up Alum Cave Trail • Meals are included • 2 and 3 bedroom cabins are available

Call (865) 429-5704 or click leconte-lodge.com for reservations and additional information.

Great Smoky Mountains Camping (Fees are per night)

Name	Location	Open	Fee	Sites	Notes
Abrams Creek	West side, NE of Chilhowee	mid-March–October	$14	16	RVs up to 12'
Balsam Mtn	Heintooga Ridge Rd, SE corner	mid-May–mid-October	$14	46	RVs up to 30'
Big Creek	NE corner, take Exit 451 (I-40)	mid-March–October	$14	12	Tent-only
Cades Cove*	Entrance of Cades Cove Loop	All Year	$17–20	159	RVs up to 40'
Cataloochee	East side off Cove Creek Road	mid-March–October	$20	27	RVs up to 31', Reservations are required
Cosby*	NE corner, just south of TN-73	mid-March–October	$14	157	RVs up to 25'
Deep Creek	North of Bryson City	April–October	$17	92	RVs up to 26'
Elkmont*	Near Sugarlands Visitor Center	mid-March–November	$17–23	220	RVs up to 32'
Look Rock	West side off Foothills Pkwy	mid-May–October	$14	68	No size limit
Smokemont*	Near Oconaluftee Visitor Center	All Year	$17–20	142	RVs up to 40'

*Reservations for mid-May through October can be made in advance at 877-444-6777 or recreation.gov
There are no showers or electrical or water hookups in the park. Shower facilities are available in nearby communities. Inquire about the nearest facilities upon check-in. Group sites are available at Big Creek, Cades Cove, Cataloochee, Cosby, Deep Creek, Elkmont, and Smokemont (15–30 people/site, $26–65/night, reservations required)

Backcountry	A free permit (apply online) is required for all backcountry camping. Permits must be picked up in person at one of the Visitor Centers, Ranger Stations, or Campground Offices. You must stay at a designated campsite or shelter. All shelters and many campsites require advance reservation. For more information and trip planning help call the Backcountry Information Office at (865) 436-1297.

Original Settlers

Uncertainty exists as to when Cherokee Indians settled in the Smokies, but Hernando de Soto passed through numerous Cherokee villages during his exploration of the southern Appalachian Mountains in 1540. Cherokee people called this region "Tsiyahi" or "place of the river otter," and they referred to the mountains as being "shaconage" or "blue, like smoke." Life in the mountains may have been simple, but their culture was advanced. They established permanent villages, cultivated crops, had a sophisticated political system, and women were given an equal voice among tribal members. Marriage was only allowed between different clans and children took the clan of their mother. Each village had a seven-sided council house where tribal meetings took place, one side for each of the seven Cherokee Clans: Bird, Paint, Deer, Wolf, Blue, Long Hair, and Wild Potato. Each tribe selected a Peace Chief who ruled during peaceful times, and a War Chief who ruled during times of war—an ancient system of checks and balances.

Unfortunately, no balance was found between Native American and American interests. By 1820 many Cherokee had adopted an American way of life, purchasing store-bought goods and running plantations. But even with their refined lifestyle, the prospect of gold and President Andrew Jackson's political leanings doomed their chances of retaining land they inhabited for centuries. The Indian Removal Act, signed into law by President Jackson in 1830, and Treaty of New Echota led to the forced removal of Cherokee people. More than 14,000 Cherokee were escorted by the U.S. Army out of Southern Appalachia in 1838. Battling despair, disease, and bitter cold, only 10,000 survived the six-month journey to Oklahoma. The National Park Service protects a physical Trail of Tears today, but the actual "Trail" is far more figurative in nature. It refers to the forcible relocation and movement of Native Americans, which opened up more land for settlement and commercialization. About 400 Cherokee, known as the Oconaluftee, were allowed to continue living on land in the Great Smoky Mountains owned by a sympathetic white man, William Holland Thomas. Thomas, who was adopted by Cherokee Indians as a boy, repaid their kindness by serving as their attorney and advisor. Other Cherokee, without their own defender, were left to fend for themselves as refugees in the mountains. Tsali, one of the refugees, was a Cherokee hero who urged his people to fight against the Americans. He surrendered and was executed, but his ultimate sacrifice allowed the remaining Cherokee to live among the Oconaluftee. Today, some 11,000 Cherokee Indians still reside here within the Qualla Boundary.

By 1850, 685 American settlers populated Cades Cove. For the most part they lived self-sufficiently, farming the fertile land once used by the Cherokee. Families lived in simple log homes about 18'-by-20' (360 square feet) where an entire family consisting of grandparents, parents, and five to twelve children would sleep under one roof. Children attended school for three to five years, with each "year" lasting about three months and costing $1 a month per child.

Much like the fate of the Cherokee Indians, sadness and turmoil would find the American settlers of the Smoky Mountains. When the Civil War began in 1861, settlements, even families, were torn apart by conflicting loyalties. No slaves had ever worked the land of Cades Cove, yet young men fought for both the Union and the Confederacy. In one particularly sad story, Russell Gregory, a father and Union sympathizer, was murdered by Confederate rebels after his son pointed out their home. Today, Russell is remembered by a tombstone, which reads "Russell Gregory murdered by North Carolina rebels." His son was eventually buried next to him in Cades Cove's Primitive Baptist Church Cemetery.

Once again, families were forced to leave the Smoky Mountains in the 1930s. Many residents had become dependent of logging companies who were clear-cutting the area's trees at a frantic rate. About half of the 1,000 families living in the mountains opposed creation of a national park to protect their jobs and homes. The park won out. Families were forced to move, but not without a fight. They took their battle all the way to the Supreme Court where they won and were awarded a life-time lease on their land. One family remains in the park to this day, and 78 historic structures preserve Southern Appalachian heritage.

The inspiring landscapes of GRSM—once home to Indians and settlers alike, including significant historic and cultural landmarks as well as the Cherokee Indian Reservation (Qualla Boundary)—are now visited by millions of tourists.

The final scramble at Chimney Tops

Great Smoky Mountains Hiking Trails (Distances are roundtrip)

Name	Location (# on map)	Length	Difficulty Rating & Notes
Look Rock	Near Look Rock Camp (1)	0.5 mile	E – Similar views to Clingman's Dome, fewer visitors
Abram's Falls	Cades Cove Loop, past Stop #10 (2)	5.0 miles	M – Flat, popular, well-maintained trail leading to a 20-foot waterfall
Cades Cove Nature Trail	About 1 mile past Cades Cove Visitor Center (3)	2.0 miles	E – Great family hike • Brochures explain the area's cultural and historical significance
Gregory Bald	Cades Cove, Parson Branch Road (4)	11.3 miles	S – Bald named for Russell Gregory who was murdered by Confederate troops
Rich Mountain	Cades Cove (5)	8.5 miles	S – Excellent views of Cades Cove and wildlife
Rocky Top - ♨	Cades Cove Campground, Anthony Creek Trailhead (5)	13.9 miles	S – Hike to Spence Field then continue along the Appalachian Trail to Rocky Top (inspiration for the University of Tennessee's fight song)
Cucumber Gap	Elkmont / Little River (6)	5.6 miles	E – Wildflowers in spring and a 20-foot waterfall
Laurel Falls - ♨	Laurel Falls (7)	2.6 miles	E – One of the park's most popular destinations
Sugarlands Valley Nature Trail	Sugarlands Visitor Center (8)	0.5 mile	E – Self-guiding nature trail that is accessible to individuals in wheelchairs
Chimney Tops - ♨	Newfound Gap Road (9)	4.0 miles	S – Most popular hike, final scramble to summit
Alum Cave - ♨	Alum Cave Bluffs (10)	4.6 miles	S – Views to the west from Cliff Top and to the east from Myrtle Point • 11 miles to Mount Le Conte
Charlie's Bunion	Newfound Gap (11)	8.1 miles	M – Follows the Appalachian Trail to a rock outcropping named for Charlie Conner's bunion
Clingman's Dome - ♨	Clingman's Dome (12)	0.5 mile	E – Short but steep hike to an observation tower atop the highest peak in the Smoky Mountains
Andrews Bald	Clingman's Dome (12)	3.5 miles	M – Highly rewarding, relatively short hike
Indian Creek	End of Deep Creek Rd (13)	1.6 miles	E – Toms Branch Falls and Indian Creek Falls
Rainbow Falls	Rainbow Falls (14)	5.4 miles	M – 80-foot falls produces rainbows when sunny
Bullhead	Just off Cherokee Orchard Loop Rd (14)	14.4 miles	S – Least traveled route to Mount Le Conte
Grotto Falls	Roaring Fork Motor Nature Trail Stop #5 (15)	2.8 miles	M – Pass old growth hemlock forest to a 25-foot high falls that you hike above and below
Porter's Creek	Greenbrier Entrance (16)	4.0 miles	M – Spring wildflowers, old-growth forest and waterfalls • Spur trail (1 mile) to cantilevered barn
Ramsay Cascades - ♨	Greenbrier Entrance (17)	8.0 miles	S – Tallest waterfall in the park at 100 feet
Hen Wallow Falls	Cosby Picnic Area (18)	4.4 miles	M – Hike to a narrow 90-foot high waterfall
Mt Cammerer	Cosby, Lower Gap Trailhead (18)	12.0 miles	S – Great hike to panoramic views and a fire tower built by the CCC in the 1930s
Mouse Creek Falls - ♨	Big Creek Trail, Waterville Road, Exit 451 from I-40 (19)	4.0 miles	M – Follows an old railroad grade, there's a great swimming hole (Midnight Hole) at 1.4 miles
Boogerman Loop	Cataloochee Camp (20)	7.4 miles	M – Great hike in a less popular portion of the park
Little Cataloochee - ♨	Just west of Cataloochee Campground (20)	6.0 miles	M – Hike through remnants of Little Cataloochee Cove where 1,200 people used to live
Woody Place	End of Cataloochee Rd (21)	2.0 miles	E – Follow the Rough Fork Trail to an 1880s home
Smokemont Loop	Smokemont Camp (22)	6.5 miles	M – The journey begins on the Bradley Fork Trail
Mingo Falls - ♨	Qualla Boundary (23)	0.4 mile	M – Spectacular 120-foot waterfall (outside the park)

Difficulty Ratings: E = Easy, M = Moderate, S = Strenuous

Hiking & Backpacking

There are 850 miles of hiking trails, including 70 miles of the **Appalachian Trail**, at GRSM. Many of which either start at or lead to 10 frontcountry campgrounds, dozens of backcountry campsites, or 15 backcountry shelters. Whether it's a multi-day trek along the Appalachian Trail, a short jaunt through historic settlements; a knee-jarring, mountain-climbing workout to a 6,000 foot summit; or a casual creek-side stroll to a cascading waterfall, the Smokies have it all. Here are a few of the park's best trails to help you choose where to hike.

Spring brings about some of the most colorful wildflower displays on the East Coast. Creekside trails are ideal locations to see wildflowers due to cool moist air and wet ground. **Oconaluftee River Trail** (begins at Oconaluftee Visitor Center), **Deep Creek Trail** (begins at the end of Deep Creek Road), **Kanati Fork Trail** (begins just north of Kephart Prong footbridge on Newfound Gap Road), **Little River Trail** (begins just before Elkmont Campground Entrance), **Middle Prong Trail** (begins at the end of Tremont Road), and **Porters Creek Trail** (begins at Greenbrier Entrance) are all excellent spring wildflower hikes.

The park's waterfalls are popular hiking destinations all year. Spring snowmelt causes streams and waterfalls to swell, but trails are often muddy and busy. Crowds subside from late fall to early spring, and trees have shed their leaves opening up new views. **Cataract Falls** is a short hike departing from Sugarlands Visitor Center. The paved path to **Laurel Falls** is one of the easiest and most popular waterfall hikes in the park. The route to **Grotto and Abrams Falls** are a little more challenging, but nothing to intimidate the average hiker. Then there's **Ramsay Cascades**, the tallest waterfall in the park, and quite possibly its most strenuous day-hike. There's plenty of beautiful scenery along the way, and most of the hike is a gradual climb, before a little scrambling is optional near the cascades.

Summer is a great time to hike to one of the park's sun-soaked, wind-swept balds or 6,000-foot summits. To reach a summit you must inevitably head uphill, but not all of these trails are difficult. **Clingman's Dome**

Best of The Smokies

Adventure Hike: Chimney Tops
Runner-up: Rocky Top
2nd Runner-up: Mt Cammerer

Waterfall Hike: Ramsay Cascades
Runner-up: Rainbow Falls

Family Hike: Clingman's Dome
Runner-up: Cades Cove Nature Trail
2nd Runner-up: Laurel Falls

Scenic Drive: Cades Cove
Runner-up: Roaring Fork Motor Trail

Trail (0.5 mile) leads to the park's highest point, but it's also one of the easiest summit hikes. One of the most difficult trails is the 14.4-mile **Bullhead Trail** to Mount Le Conte. It's sure to make you sweat as you gain 3,993 feet in elevation along the way. **Rocky Top** is another strenuous trail, but it rewards hardy hikers with the best views in the park. With a pinch of planning you can take one of four trails to the top of **Mount Le Conte** (the park's third highest peak) and spend a relaxing night at **Le Conte Lodge** (leconte-lodge.com). **Alum Cave Trail** is short, steep, and strenuous, but it provides some of the most majestic scenery anywhere in the park. **Trillium Gap and Boulevard Trails** are longer, more gradual hikes to the summit. **Bullhead Trail** is both long and difficult. No matter which route you choose it's going to be a challenge, but your effort will be rewarded with a night at Le Conte Lodge, a Smoky Mountain paradise. **Chimney Tops** is one of our favorite adventures, as it ends with a rocky scramble that will test your fear of heights.

For easy hikes look no further than the old homesteaders' villages. **Woody Place, Cades Cove Nature, Porter's Creek**, and **Little Cataloochee Trails** are relatively flat hikes that allow visitors to reimagine life in the Smokies during the 1800s.

Backpackers are required to obtain a free permit (available online) and stay at designated campsites and shelters while camping in the backcountry. To plan your backpacking trip visit the park's website or call the Backcountry Information Office (865.436.1297).

Biking

Bicycles are allowed on most of the roads within the park, but that doesn't mean you should bike them. **Cades Cove Loop Road**—the one recommended location—is narrow, bumpy, and packed with motorists, but it gets better during scheduled motor-free periods. During these times cyclists are free to enjoy the sights and sounds of the Cove, without having to navigate through throngs of traffic stopping and starting whenever they like. If you miss out on these designated times, try to pedal the loop early in the day (before 10am). Bicycles can be rented ($7.50/hour) from Cades Cove Campground Store (865.448.9034, cadescovetrading.com) near Cades Cove Campground, which is open from summer through fall.

Clingman's Dome Road is a good challenge for cyclists, but this climb should also be reserved for an early morning or during the brief window when the steep road is closed to motorists but free of snow in early spring.

Bikes are prohibited on all park trails except Gatlinburg, Oconaluftee River, and Lower Deep Creek Trails.

Paddling

Mountain lakes and streams provide water activities ranging from leisurely flatwater paddling to adrenaline-pumping whitewater runs. Paddling offers an unobtrusive, peaceful, and less stressful way to view wildlife and fall colors. **Fontana and Calderwood Lakes** are the most popular locations for flatwater. Both of these lakes skirt the park's southeastern boundary. Fontana Lake has a handful of marinas between Bryson City and Fontana Dam where you can launch your boat. At Calderwood Lake, a 5-mile dammed section of the Little Tennessee River, you'll find a boat ramp near Cheoah Dam. It's an ideal location for an out-and-back paddle.

Steep mountain slopes and an abundance of rain and snow make for some of the East Coast's best whitewater paddling. Smoky Mountain Kayaking (865.705.8678, smokymountainkayaking.com), River Rat Tubing (865.448.8888, smokymtnriverrat.com), and Smoky Mountain Rafting (800.771.7238, smokymountainrafting.com) offer whitewater raft, kayak, and tubing

trips. Turn to page 114 for a complete list of water trip outfitters in Tennessee and North Carolina.

Fishing

Fishing is allowed in all of the park's 2,900 miles of streams. Depending on which state you are in, a valid Tennessee or North Carolina fishing license is required. Trout (brook, brown, and rainbow) and smallmouth bass have a seven inch minimum and possession limit of five. Fishing is permitted year-round and there are several outfitters that can help you catch your limit (see page 114).

Horseback Riding

Nearly 550 of the park's 850 miles of hiking trails are open to horses. Five drive-in horse campgrounds are open from April until mid-November: Anthony Creek (near Cades Cove Campground), Big Creek, Cataloochee, Round Bottom (near Oconaluftee Visitor Center), and Tow String (near Oconaluftee Visitor Center). Guests without their own horses can take a ride at **Cades Cove Riding Stables** (865.448.9009, cadescovestables.com), **Smokemont Riding Stables** (828.497.2373, smokemontriding-stable.com), or **Smoky Mountain Riding Stable** (865.436.5634, smokymountainridingstables.com).

Ranger Programs

Attending a ranger program should be a mandatory requirement at all national parks. Be sure to browse a current schedule of ranger-led activities online or at a visitor center, and pick out which program(s) you'll attend. GRSM offers Cable Mill Demonstrations and hayrides in Cades Cove, but there are many other hikes, lunches, talks, and campfires held throughout the park where rangers impart their wisdom and humor on those willing to listen. One ranger program even invites visitors to learn to play the hog fiddle. Seasonal programs like Autumn Arrives and **The Smokies Synchronous Fireflies** (mid-June) are so unique and enjoyable you may want to specifically plan your trip around them.

For Kids

The park offers ranger-led programs for children from spring to fall (check online or in person at a visitor center for a current schedule of events). Children between the ages of 5 and 12 have the opportunity to become a **Junior Ranger**. Junior Ranger Activity Booklets can be purchased for $2.50 at any visitor centers or at Elkmont and Cades Cove Campgrounds. Complete the booklet, and then return to a visitor center to receive a junior ranger badge. The junior ranger program runs all year long.

Flora & Fauna

Incomparable biodiversity resulted in the park's designation as a **UNESCO World Heritage Site and International Biosphere Reserve**. GRSM is home to more than 1,600 species of flowering plants, which helped inspire its billing as "the Wildflower National Park." Wildflowers bloom year-round, but spring is the ultimate time to view an abundance of colorful blossoms. The week-long **Spring Wildflower Pilgrimage Festival** celebrates these living decorations and features programs and guided walks that explore the park's amazing biodiversity. You can help save the wildflowers by staying on hiking trails when exploring the backcountry. It is illegal to pick wildflowers. Beyond flowers, you'll find more than 100 native tree species and over 100 native shrub species. There are more tree species here than any other U.S. National Park, and more species than in all of Northern Europe.

More than 200 species of birds, 50 native species of fish, 80 types of reptiles and amphibians, and 66 species of mammals are protected in GRSM. Spotting wildlife is often easiest in winter after trees have shed their leaves. During the remainder of the year, open areas like Chataloochee and Cades Cove are great spots for wildlife viewing. White-tailed deer, wild turkey, squirrels, and bats are your most probable sightings, but don't count out seeing the symbol of the park, the black bear. GRSM provides the largest protected bear habitat in the East, and it's home to approximately 1,500 bears. The park's 30 species of salamander are enough to earn the title of **"Salamander Capital of the World."** However, the most unique wildlife display comes from one of its smallest occupants, the **Smoky Mountain Synchronous Fireflies**. The name sounds like a circus act—a description not far from reality— but these tiny insects aren't performing for you; their flashing light patterns are part of a mating display. It's

special because the individual fireflies are able to synchronize their light patterns. Such a spectacle is only known to occur in a few other place in the world, like Congaree National Park (page 122). These phosphorescent flies perform nightly for a two-week period around the middle of June (dates change from year to year). To see the show you must camp at Elkmont or take a $1 round-trip trolley ride from Sugarlands Visitor Center. (Personal vehicles are not permitted.) Visitors should follow a few simple rules so you do not disrupt the fireflies or other guests. Cover your flashlight with red or blue cellophane. Only use your flashlight (pointed toward the ground) when walking to your viewing spot. Stay on the trail at all times, do not catch fireflies, and pack out your garbage.

Pets

Pets are allowed in the park, but must be kept on a leash no more than six feet in length at all times. They are not allowed on hiking trails with the exception of Gatlinburg Trail and Oconaluftee River Trail.

Accessibility

Temporary Parking Permits are available at Sugarlands and Oconaluftee Visitor Centers for visitors with disabilities. Elkmont, Smokemont, and Cades Cove have campsites accessible to wheelchair users. Much of the park is accessible by car, but almost all trails are rugged and inaccessible. Cades Cove Complex and Amphiteater, Oconaluftee Mountain Farm Museum, and Sugarlands Valley Nature Trail are fully accessible.

Weather

Visitors can receive current park weather forecasts by calling (865) 436-1200 ext. 630. The area's temperate climate makes the park a pleasant place to visit just about any time of year. However, high elevation areas receive considerable precipitation (85" annually). Lower elevations average 55" of precipitation each year. September and October are the driest months.

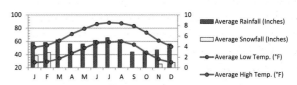

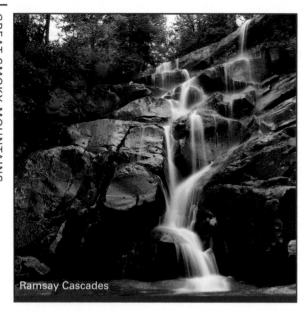
Ramsay Cascades

Vacation Planner

The park is big. The roads are busy. There's a lot to see and visitors typically have a limited amount of time. This is the predicament faced by GRSM visitors. Here's a full 3-day itinerary to use as a blueprint for planning your Smoky Mountains vacation. Try to fit at least one ranger program into your schedule. If you plan on traveling in June, check the park's website to see if **fireflies** are lighting the night sky at Elkmont (page 108). **Camping** and **lodging** (hike-in only) are available within the park (page 103). Gatlinburg, Sevierville, and Pigeon Forge are three of the largest tourist traps you'll ever find. Pick one, and plan a full day just to have a look around. Where to stay and eat is up to you, but a fairly thorough list including some of the area's finer dining, grocery stores, lodging, festivals, and attractions can be found on pages 112–115.

Day 1: Enter via Gatlinburg, TN and continue directly to **Sugarlands Visitor Center**. Browse the exhibits, watch a short film, and ask rangers any questions you've come up with. Once you've introduced yourselves to the park, head back to your car and backtrack to Gatlinburg. Catch **Roaring Fork Motor Nature Trail**. Follow the 10 mph speed limit, and if you've already had too much windshield time for the day, get out and hike to **Rainbow Falls** (5.4 miles). Time permitting continue east on TN-73 to Greenbrier Entrance. Work

up a hunger by completing the strenuous 8-mile trek to **Ramsay Cascades**. If you don't have the time or energy for a difficult hike, no problem, continue driving east around the park's perimeter to Cosby and/or Cataloochee. Both regions offer excellent scenery.

Day 2: Staying on the TN side, return to Sugarlands, but this time follow Little River Road west to Laurel Creek Road all the way to **Cades Cove**. Try to arrive early, because this is the most visited destination in the park, and traffic begins to pile up around 10 am. Cades Cove is popular because there's a little something for everyone here. History buffs will be intrigued by old settlement homesteads, mills, and churches. Nature lovers can hike to **Abrams Falls** or take the 13.9-mile trek to **Rocky Top**. Activity lovers can **ride horses** (page 108), **rent bicycles** (page 108), enjoy a **carriage ride**, or even sit on a bale of hay while a park ranger tells stories about early settler life in the cove. It's conceivable to spend the entire day here. If you plan on camping in summer, hopefully you have reservations at Cades Cove or Elkmont Campgrounds, otherwise you may want to exit the park via Parson Branch Road (unpaved) and check out Abrams Creek and Look Rock campgrounds for availability.

Day 3: There's no better way of spending a night in the Smokies than hiking to **Le Conte Lodge**. Once again pass Sugarlands Visitor Center, but continue on Newfound Gap Road. Take note of Alum Cave Trail Parking Area; you'll be returning here later. Drive to **Clingman's Dome Road** and follow it to its end where you will hike the short trail to a scenic overlook. This is the highest peak in the Smokies. Next you'll hike to the third tallest peak. Return to **Alum Cave Trail** Parking Area and hike 5.5 miles (one-way) to spend the night at **Le Conte Lodge** (reservations required), where you'll be served a hearty dinner with wine. It's a perfect spot to enjoy all the grandeur the Smokies have to offer. Breakfast will be served in the morning before you have to hike back down to the parking area. Once you've returned to your car, continue along Newfound Gap Road and stop at **Newfound Gap** to read the plaque placed here in memory of Laura Rockefeller before exiting the park. If the lodge isn't your thing, hike to **Laurel Falls** (a park favorite) or **Chimney Tops** (strenuous).

Elk at Cataloochee

A Cades Cove Carriage Ride

Dining

West Side/Tennessee

Smoky Mtn Brewery • (865) 288-5500
1004 Parkway, # 501, Gatlinburg
smoky-mtn-brewery.com • Entrée: $8–25

Park Grill • (865) 436-2300
1110 Parkway, Gatlinburg
parkgrillgatlinburg.com • Entrée: $12–35

Best Italian Café & Pizzeria • (865) 430-4090
968 Parkway, # 9, Gatlinburg
englandfoodgroup.com • Entrée: $13–22

Pancake Pantry • (865) 436-4724
628 Parkway, Gatlinburg
pancakepantry.com

Bennett's Pitt Bar B Que • (865) 436-2400
714 River Rd, Gatlinburg
bennetts-bbq.com

Cherokee Grill • (865) 436-4287
1002 Parkway, Gatlinburg
cherokeegrill.com • Entrée: $13–30

Wild Plum • (865) 436-3808
555 Buckhorn Rd, Gatlinburg

Mountain Lodge Restaurant • (865) 436-2547
913 E Parkway, Gatlinburg

Log Cabin Pancake House • (865) 436-7894
327 Historic Nature Tr, Gatlinburg
logcabinpancakehouse.com

Donut Friar • (865) 436-7306
634 Parkway, # 15, Gatlinburg

The Peddler Steakhouse • (865) 436-5794
820 River Rd, Gatlinburg
peddlergatlinburg.com • Entrée: $23–40

Calhoun's Restaurant • (865) 436-4100
1004 Parkway, # 101, Gatlinburg
calhouns.com • Entrée: $8–22

Mountain Edge Grill • (865) 436-0013
631 Parkway, # B4, Gatlinburg
mtnedge.com • Entrée: $8–13

Cheese Cupboard & Hofbrauhaus • (865) 436-9511
634 Parkway, # 14, Gatlinburg

Coffee & Company • (865) 430-3650
634 E Parkway, Gatlinburg

Gondolier Italian Restaurant • (865) 428-8050
964 Dolly Parton Pkwy, Sevierville
gondolierpizza.com

Applewood Farmhouse • (865) 428-1222
220 Apple Valley Rd, Sevierville
applewoodrestaurant.com

Red Rooster Pancake House • (865) 428-3322
3215 Parkway, Pigeon Forge

Kinkaku Japanese Steakhouse • (865) 774-7598
3152 Parkway, # 1, Pigeon Forge
pigeonforgejapanese.com

Little Tokyo Japanese Restaurant • (865) 908-0555
2430 Teaster Ln, # 212, Pigeon Forge

Huck Finn's Catfish • (865) 429-3353
3330 Parkway, Pigeon Forge
huckfinnsrestaurant.com

Old Mill Restaurant • (865) 429-3463
175 Old Mill Ave, Pigeon Forge
old-mill.com

East Side/North Carolina

Jimmy Mac's Restaurant • (828) 488-4700
121 Main St, Bryson City

Cork & Bean • (828) 488-1934
24 Everett St, Bryson City
theeveretthotel.com

Filling Station Deli Sub Shop • (828) 488-1919
145 Everett St, Bryson City
thefillingstationdeli.com • Entrée: $4–7

Everett Street Diner • (828) 488-0123
126 Everett St, Bryson City

Nabers Drive In • (828) 488-2877
1245 Main St, Bryson City

Bar-B-Que Wagon • (828) 488-9521
610 Main St, Bryson City

Mountain Perks Espresso Bar • (828) 488-9561
9 Depot St, Bryson City • mtnperks.com

Sweet Onion • (828) 456-5559
39 Miller St, Waynesville
sweetonionrestaurant.com • Entrée: $13–27

Bogart's Restaurant • (828) 452-1313
303 S Main St, Waynesville
bogartswaynesville.com • Entrée: $15–23

Clyde's Restaurant • (828) 456-9135
2107 South Main St, Waynesville

Bocelli's Italian Eatery • (828) 456-4900
319 N Haywood St, Waynesville
bocellisitalianeatery.com • Entrée: $14–20

Tap Room • (828) 456-3551
176 Country Club Dr, Waynesville
thewaynesvilleinn.com • Entrée: $9–25

Fat Buddies Ribs & BBQ • (828) 456-6368
193 Waynesville Plz, Waynesville
fatbuddiesribsandbbq.com • Entrée: $12–22

Sagebrush Steakhouse • (828) 452-5822
895 Russ Ave, Waynesville
sagebrushsteakhouse.com • Entrée: $11–22

Guadalupe Café • (828) 586-9877
606 W Main St, Sylva • guadalupecafe.com

Snappy's Italian Pizzeria • (828) 926-6126
2769 Soco Rd, Maggie Valley
snappysitalian.net • Entrée: $13–21

Joey's Pancake House • (828) 926-0212
4309 Soco Rd, Maggie Valley
joeyspancake.com

Cataloochee Ranch • (828) 926-1401
119 Ranch Dr, Maggie Valley
cataloocheeranch.com

Country Vittles Restaurant • (828) 926-1820
3589 Soco Rd, Maggie Valley

Legends Sports Grill • (828) 926-9464
3865 Soco Rd, Maggie Valley
legendssportsgrill.org

Grocery Stores
Food City • (865) 430-3116
1219 E Parkway, Gatlinburg

Kroger • (865) 429-0874
220 Wears Valley Rd, Pigeon Forge

Walmart Supercenter • (865) 429-0029
1414 Parkway, Sevierville

Townsend IGA • (865) 448-3010
7945 E Lamar Alexander Pkwy, Townsend

Walmart Supercenter • (828) 456-4828
135 Town Center Loop, Waynesville

Lodging
In the Park
Le Conte Lodge • (865) 429-5704
On top of Mount Le Conte, hike-in only, no electricity, shared bathroom
Reservations: 250 Apple Valley Rd, Sevierville
leconte-lodge.com • Rates: $140/adult

West Side/Tennessee
Lodge At Buckberry Creek • (865) 430-8030
961 Campbell Lead Rd, Gatlinburg
buckberrylodge.com • Rates: $180–460

Jack Huff's Hotel • (800) 322-1817
204 Cherokee Orchard Rd, Gatlinburg
jackhuffs.com • Rates: $56–150

Mountain Laurel Chalets • (865) 436-5277
440 Ski Mountain Rd, Gatlinburg
mtnlaurelchalets.com • Rates: $99+

Riverhouse Motor Lodge • (865) 436-7821
610 River Rd, Gatlinburg
riverhousemotels.com • Rates: $67–183

Riverhouse at the Park • (865) 436-2070
205 Ski Mountain Rd, Gatlinburg
riverhousemotels.com • Rates: $47–174

Deer Ridge Resort • (865) 436-2325
3710 Weber Rd, Gatlinburg
deerridge.com • Rates: $107–417

Brookside Resort • (865) 436-5611
463 E Parkway, Gatlinburg
brooksideresort.com • Rates: $72–148

Laurel Springs Lodge B&B • (888) 430-9211
204 Hill St, Gatlinburg
laurelspringslodge.com • Rates: $135–169

The Foxtrot B&B • (888) 436-3033
1520 Garrett Ln, Gatlinburg
thefoxtrot.com • Rates: $190–230

Buckhorn Inn • (865) 436-4668
2140 Tudor Mtn Rd, Gatlinburg
buckhorninn.com • Rates: $125–320

Four Sisters Inn • (865) 430-8411
425 Stuart Ln, Gatlinburg
Rates: $180–575

Cabins For You • (800) 684-7865
436 East Parkway, Gatlinburg
cabinsforyou.com • Rates: $126+

Hippensteal's Mtn View Inn • (865) 436-5761
4201 Tatem Marr Way, Sevierville
hippensteal.com • Rates: $194

Mountain Aire Inn • (865) 453-5576
1008 Parkway, Sevierville

Berry Springs Lodge • (865) 908-7935
2149 Seaton Springs Rd, Sevierville
berrysprings.com • Rates: $205–265

Blue Mtn Mist Country Inn • (865) 428-2335
1811 Pullen Rd, Sevierville
bluemountainmist.com • Rates: $180–460

Timber Tops • (865) 429-0831
1440 Upper Middle Creek Rd, Sevierville
yourcabin.com • Rates: $95–450

Little Valley Mtn Resort • (800) 581-7225
2229 Little Valley Rd, Sevierville
littlevalleymountainresort.com • Rates: $149+

Quail Ridge Inn B&B • (865) 436-8287
2765 King Hollow Rd, Sevierville
quailridgebandb.com • Rates: $139–149

Inn At Christmas Place • (865) 868-0525
119 Christmas Tree Ln, Pigeon Forge
innatchristmasplace.com • Rates: $124–309

Park Tower Inn • (865) 453-8605
201 Sharon Dr, Pigeon Forge
parktowerinn.com • Rates: $55–120

Music Road Inn • (800) 429-7700
303 Henderson Chapel Rd, Pigeon Forge
musicroadresort.com • Rates: $140–178

Riverstone Resort • (866) 908-0990
212 Dollywood Ln, Pigeon Forge
riverstoneresort.com • Rates: $144–514

Dancing Bear Lodge • (800) 369-0111
137 Apple Valley Way, Townsend
dancingbearlodge.com • Rates: $155–265

Pioneer Cabins • (865) 448-6100
288 Boat Gunnel Rd, Townsend
pioneercabins.com

Riverstone Lodge • (865) 448-6677
8511 TN-73, Townsend
riverstonelodge.com

Highland Manor Inn • (800) 213-9462
7766 E Larmar Alexander Pkwy, Townsend
highlandmanor.com • Rates: $70–130

Creekwalk Inn • (423) 487-4000
166 Midddle Creek Rd, Cosby
whisperwoodretreat.com • Rates: $249–289

East Side/North Carolina
Lake View Lodge • (800) 742-6492
171 Lakeview Lodge Dr, Bryson City

Windover Inn B&B • (866) 452-4411
40 Old Hickory St, Waynesville
windoverinn.com • Rates: $130–199

Folkestone Inn B&B • (828) 488-2730
101 Folkestone Rd, Bryson City
folkestoneinn.com • Rates: $119–159

Inn at Iris Meadows • (828) 456-3877
304 Love Ln, Waynesville
irismeadows.com • Rates: $225–300

Oak Hill B&B • (828) 456-7037
224 Love Ln, Waynesville
oakhillonlovelane.com • Rates: $160–235

Brookside Mtn Mist B&B • (828) 452-6880
142 Country Club Dr, Waynesville
brooksidemountainmistbb.com • Rates: $139–199

Yellow House • (828) 452-0991
89 Oakview Dr, Waynesville
theyellowhouse.com • Rates: $165–265

Andon-Reid Inn B&B • (828) 452-3089
92 Daisy Ave, Waynesville
andonreidinn.com • Rates: $145–215

Alamo Motel • (828) 926-8750
1485 Soco Rd, Maggie Valley
alamomotel.com • Rates: $49–139

Many chain restaurants and hotels can be found nearby in Sevierville, Gatlinburg, Pigeon Forge, TN; and Waynesville and Asheville, NC.

Festivals
Mountain Quiltfest • March • Pigeon Forge

Winter Carnival of Magic • March
wintercarnivalofmagic.com • Pigeon Forge

Blue Ridge Food & Wine Festival • April • Blowing Rock, NC

Spring Wildflower Pilgrimage • April/May
springwildflowerpilgrimage.org • GRSM

The Biltmore Festival of Flowers • March/May
biltmore.com • Asheville, NC

TroutFest • May
troutfest.org • Townsend, TN

Scottish Festival & Games • May
smokymountaingames.com • Maryville, TN

Bloomin' BBQ and Bluegrass Festival • May
bloominbbq.com • Sevierville, TN

Riverbend Festival • June
riverbendfestival.com • Chattanooga, TN

Secret City Festival • June
secretcityfestival.com • Oak Ridge, TN

Bonnaroo Music & Arts Festival • June
One of the premier music festivals in the U.S.
bonnaroo.com • Manchester, TN

Great American Summer Festival • June/August
dollywood.com • Dollywood (Pigeon Forge)

Midnight 4th of July Parade • July
eventsgatlinburg.com • Gatlinburg, TN

Tomato Festival • July • Rutledge, TN
graingercountytomatofestival.com

Grandfather Mtn Scottish Highland Games • July
gmhg.org • Linville, NC

Folkmoot USA • July • folkmootusa.org
Waynesville and Maggie Valley, NC

Cherokee Bluegrass Festival • August
adamsbluegrass.com • Cherokee, NC

Smoky Mountain Folk Festival
Lake Junaluska, NC • August/September
smokymountainfolkfestival.com

Moonlight Race • August • Maggie Valley, NC

Southern Sauce Festival • September
southernsaucecclt.com • Charlotte, NC

Smoky Mtn Harvest Festival • Sept/Oct •
Gatlinburg

Dumplin Valley Bluegrass Festival • September
dumplinvalleybluegrass.com • Kodak, TN

Davy Crockett Days • October
townofrutherford.org • Rutherford, TN

Lake Eden Arts Festival • May/Oct
theleaf.com • Black Mountain, NC

Woolly Worm Festival • October
woollyworm.com • Banner Elk, NC

National Storytelling Festival • October
storytellingcenter.net • Jonesborough, TN

Winterfest • November–February
Gatlinburg • Pigeon Forge • Sevierville
smokymountainwinterfest.com

Attractions
In the Park
Cades Cove Riding Stables • (865) 448-9009
Ranger-led hayrides and carriage rides are available
10018 Campground Drive, Townsend
cadescovestables.com • Trail Rides: $30/hr
Open: mid-March–November (9am–4:30pm)

Smokemont Riding Stables • (828) 497-2373
1–4 hour rides, waterfall ride, and wagon rides available, riders must be at least 5 years old and weigh no more than 225 pounds
135 Smokemont Riding Stables Rd, Cherokee
smokemontridingstable.com • Trail Rides: $30/hr
Open: late March–October (9am–5pm)

Smoky Mountain Riding Stables • (865) 436-5634
1729 E Parkway, Gatlinburg
smokymountainridingstables.com
Open: mid-March–November
Trail Rides: $25/45 min, $45/1.5 hrs

West Side/Tennessee
Smoky Mountain Kayaking • (865) 705-8678
3002 Shadowbrook Drive, Maryville
smokymountainkayaking.com
Kayaking: $40/person (4 hrs, guided flatwater)

River Rat Tubing • (865) 448-8888
205 Wears Valley Road, Townsend
smokymtnriverrat.com
Tubing: $13/person, Kayaking: $15/person

Smoky Mountain Outdoors • (800) 771-7238
3299 Hartford Rd, Hartford
smokymountainrafting.com • Rafting: $29–35

Rafting In the Smokies • (800) 776-7238
813 E Parkway, Gatlinburg
raftinginthesmokies.com

Smoky Mountain Gillies • 865-964-6403
smokymountaingillies.com
Fishing: 1 Person $200 (half-day)/$300 (full-day)

The Smoky Mtn Angler • (865)436-8746
smokymountainangler.com
Fishing: 1 Person $175 (half-day)/$250 (full-day)

Fly Fishing the Smokies • (828) 488-7665
flyfishingthesmokies.net
Fishing: 1 Person $150 (half-day)/$200 (full-day)

CLIMB Works Canopy • (865) 325-8116
155 Branam Hollow Rd, Gatlinburg
climbworks.com • Rock Climbing: $89/adult

A Walk In the Woods • (865) 436-8283
4413 E Scenic Dr, Gatlinburg
awalkinthewoods.com • Tours: $31+

Ripley's Aquarium • (865) 436-5096
88 River Rd, Gatlinburg
ripleys.com/gatlinburg • Admission: $19+/adult

Sweet Fanny Adams Theatre • (865) 436-4039
461 Parkway, Gatlinburg
sweetfannyadams.com • Tickets: $35–39

Ole Smoky Distillery • (865) 436-6995
903 Parkway, # 129, Gatlinburg

Space Needle • (865) 436-4629
115 Historic Nature Tr, Gatlinburg
gatlinburgspaceneedle.com • Tickets: $9.50/adult

Fannie Farkle's Amusement • (865) 436-4057
656 Parkway, Gatlinburg
fanniefarkles.com

Ripley's Old Macdonald's Mini Golf
800 Parkway, Gatlinburg
ripleys.com • (865) 436-5096

Foxfire Mtn Adventures • (865) 446-5149
3757 Thomas Lane, Sevierville
foxfiremountain.com

Five Oaks Riding Stables • (877) 741-8070
1630 Parkway, Sevierville
fiveoaksridingstables.com

Walden Creek Stables • (865) 429-0411
2709 Waldens Creek Rd, Sevierville
waldencreekstables.com • Rates: $30–90

Wahoo Zip Lines • (865) 366-1111
605 Stoctton Dr, Sevierville
wahooziplines.com • Rates: $89

Adventure Park at Five Oaks • (865) 453-8644
1620 Parkway, Sevierville
adventureparkatfiveoaks.com • Zipline: $60

Rainforest Adventures • (865) 428-4091
109 Nascar Dr, Sevierville
rfadventures.com • Admission: $13/adult

Forbidden Caverns • (865) 453-5972
455 Blowing Cave Rd, Sevierville
forbiddencavern.com • Tours: $14+

Parrot Mtn and Gardens • (865) 774-1749
1471 McCarter Hollow Rd, Sevierville
parrotmountainandgardens.com • $17/adult

Hillside Winery • (865) 908-8482
229 Collier Dr, Sevierville
hillsidewine.com

Smoky Mtn Llama Treks • (423) 487-0600
640Padgett Mill Rd, Cosby • Trail Rides: $45+
smokymountainllamatreks.com

Scenic Helicopter Tours • (865) 453-6342
1949 Winfield Pkwy, Sevierville
scenichelicoptertours.com • Tours: $30–1,300

Smoky Mtn Zipline • (865) 429-9004
509 Mill Creek Rd, Pigeon Forge
smokymountainziplines.com • $79+

Bluff Mtn Adventures • (865) 428-7711
2186 Parkway, Pigeon Forge
bluffmountainadventures.com • $48+

Wonder Works • (865) 868-1800
100 Music Rd, Pigeon Forge
wonderworksonline.com • Admission: $25/adult

Dixie Stampede Dinner & Show • (877) 782-6733
3849 Parkway, Pigeon Forge
dixiestampede.com • Tickets: $50/adult

Miracle Theater • (800) 768-1170
2046 Parkway, Pigeon Forge
miracletheater.com • Tickets: $45/adult

Comedy Barn Theater • (865) 428-5222
2775 Parkway, Pigeon Forge
comedybarn.com • Tickets: $30/adult

Dollywood • (800) 365-5996
2700 Dollywood Parks Blvd, Pigeon Forge
dollywood.com • Admission: $65/adult

Smith Family Theater • (865) 774-7777
2330 Parkway, Pigeon Forge
smithfamilytheater.com • Tickets: $40/adult

Adventure Raceway • (865) 428-2971
2945 Parkway, Pigeon Forge
adventureraceway.com • Go-Karts: $6

The Forge Cinemas • (865) 774-6602
2530 Parkway, #7, Pigeon Forge
theforgecinemas.com

Grand Majestic Theater • (865) 774-7777
2330 Parkway, Pigeon Forge
thegrandmajestic.com

Parkway Drive-In Theatre • (865) 379-7884
2909 E Lamar Alexander Pkwy, Maryville
bluemoontheatres.com • Tickets: $7/adult

East Side/North Carolina

Nantahala National Forest • (828) 524-6441
90 Sloan Rd, Franklin • *Dry Falls (above)*

Nantahala Outdoor Center • (828) 785-4835
13077 US-19 W, Bryson City
noc.com • Rafting: $29+/adult

Endless River Adventures • (828) 488-6199
14157 US-19 W, Bryson City
endlessriveradventures.com • Rafting: $39+

Adventurous Fast Rivers Rafting • (828) 488-2386
14690 US-19 W, Bryson City
nantaharafting.com • Rafting: $29+

Wildwater • (866) 319-8870
wildwaterrafting.com • Rafting: $46+

Deep Creek Tube Center • (828) 488-6055
1090 West Deep Creek Rd, Bryson City
deepcreekcamping.com • Rental: $5/Tube

Nantahala Gorge Canopy Tours • (866) 319-8870
10345 US-19 W, Bryson City • Zipline: $89
adventureamericaziplinecanopytours.com

Smoky Mtn Jet boats • (888) 900-9091
22 Needmore Rd, Bryson City
needmore.com • Boat Rides: $32+/adult

Great Smoky Mtns Railroad • (828) 586-8811
45 Mitchell St, Bryson City
gsmr.com • Tickets: $51–94/adult

Tweetsie Railroad • (828) 264-9061
300 Tweetsie Railroad Ln, Blowing Rock
tweetsie.com • Admission: $44/adult

Docs Rocks Gem Mine • (828) 264-4499
129 Mystery Hill Ln, Blowing Rock
docsrocks.net • Buckets: $12–55

Pisgah National Forest • (828) 257-4200
NC-80 and Blue Ridge Pkwy, Burnsville

Beyond the Park

Tennessee Theatre • (865) 684-1200
604 South Gay St, Knoxville
tennesseetheatre.com • Tickets: Vary

Regal Cinemas Riviera Stadium 8 • (844) 462-7342
510 South Gay St, Knoxville, TN
regmovies.com

Ijams Nature Center • (865) 577-4717
2915 Island Home Ave, Knoxville, TN
ijams.org • Admission: Free

Minister's Treehouse • The World's Biggest
Treehouse • Beehive Lane, Crossville, TN

Tennessee Aquarium • (423) 265-0695
1 Broad St, Chattanooga, TN
tnaqua.org • Admission: $30/adult

Raccoon Mtn Caverns • (423) 821-9403
319 West Hills Dr, Chattanooga, TN
raccoonmountain.com • Tours: $15+

Lake Winnepesaukah Amusement Park
1730 Lakeview Dr, Rossville, GA
lakewinnie.com • (706) 866-5681 • $18

Blue Ridge Parkway • (828) 298-0398
199 Hemphill Knob Rd, Asheville, NC
nps.gov/blri

Ghost Hunters of Asheville • (828) 779-4868
1 Battery Park Ave, Asheville, NC
ghosthuntersofasheville.com • Tours: $20/adult

Biltmore Estate • (800) 411-3812
1 Lodge St, Asheville, NC
biltmore.com • Tickets: $59/adult

Thomas Wolfe Memorial • (828) 253-8304
52 N Market St, Asheville, NC
wolfememorial.com • Admission: $5/adult

Billy Graham Library • (704) 401-3200
4330 Westmont Dr, Charlotte, NC
billygrahamlibrary.org • Admission: Free

U.S. National Whitewater Center
5000 Whitewater Center PKWY, Charlotte, NC
usnwc.org • Multiple Activities

NASCAR Hall of Fame • (704) 654-4400
400 E MLK Blvd, Charlotte, NC
nascarhall.com • Admission: $20/adult

Hendrick Motorsports • (877) 467-4890
4400 Papa Joe Hendrick Blvd, Charlotte, NC
hendrickmotorsports.com

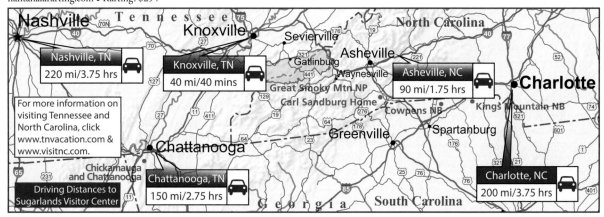

Nashville, TN — 220 mi/3.75 hrs
Knoxville, TN — 40 mi/40 mins
Asheville, NC — 90 mi/1.75 hrs
Chattanooga, TN — 150 mi/2.75 hrs
Charlotte, NC — 200 mi/3.75 hrs

For more information on visiting Tennessee and North Carolina, click www.tnvacation.com & www.visitnc.com.

Driving Distances to Sugarlands Visitor Center

Congaree

Paddling to Wise Lake

100 National Park Road
Hopkins, SC 29061
Phone: (803) 776-4396
Website: nps.gov/cong

Established: November 10, 2003
Size: 24,000 Acres
Annual Visitors: 87,000
Peak Season: Spring & Fall

Activities: Hiking, Paddling, Bird
Watching, Fishing, Ranger Tours
(reservations required for Owl
Prowl and Guided Canoe Tour)

Campgrounds: Longleaf
Campground* ($10/night) and
Bluff Campground* ($5/night)
Backcountry Camping: Permitted
with a free permit (available at
Longleaf Campground only)

Park Hours: All day, every day
Visitor Center Hours: 9am–5pm,
Tuesday–Saturday
Entrance Fee: None

*Reservations required. Call (877)
444-6777 or click recreation.gov

Congaree is akin to a rarely visited, scaled down combination of Redwood and Everglades National Parks. It protects the largest contiguous expanse of old growth bottomland hardwood forest left in the United States. You'll never confuse the towering bald cypress and loblolly pine for their West Coast rivals, the redwood and giant sequoia, but they are massive by East Coast standards. Several national and state champion trees reside within the park's boundary. Congaree's canopy averages an impressive 130 feet, making it as tall as any temperate deciduous forest in the world. When navigable, Cedar Creek provides a narrow, maze-like waterway reminiscent of the Everglade's "River of Grass" (minus the grass and throw in some moss). Trees and waterways provide habitat for a multitude of plants and animals. In fact, the park was recognized as an International Biosphere Reserve in 1983, and was designated a Globally Important Bird Area in 2001. A floodplain forest draped with Spanish moss, and the natural tranquility and wildness, give the illusion of traveling back in time to a primeval forest. These waterways and trees have helped shape the history of not only a park, but the entire region. Water protected and nourished trees. Trees attracted conservationists. And now this unique environment is protected and preserved for future generations to enjoy.

Hernando de Soto was first to detail an encounter with Congaree Indians in 1540. His exploration continued north through Appalachia, but natives stayed, living along what is now named the Congaree River. Around the turn of the 18th century, Congaree Indians were decimated by smallpox brought by European explorers. By 1715, the tribe consisted of 22 men and 70 women and children. Today they are gone but not forgotten; a river and park bear the name of the area's original inhabitants.

Frequent flooding rapidly renewed the soil's nutrients, enabling trees to thrive and reach record heights. Surprisingly, floods weren't beneficial to area farmers. Decades were spent trying to coax crops from the nutrient-rich land, but standing water stifled most agricultural activities. Farmers moved out of the floodplain, and Santee River Cypress Logging Company moved in. They purchased an exceptional tract of hardwood along the Congaree River in 1905, but regular flooding proved to be as troublesome to loggers as it was to farmers. Heavy logging equipment couldn't be moved across the wet and muddy earth. They could only access trees along the waterways where another problem arose—actually they sank, many of these trees were too green to float. Some remain to this day in the places they fell along the riverbank. After ten years of logging, the floodplain was left relatively unscathed. In 1969, high timber prices and advancements in logging equipment brought attention back to the uncut lumber of the Congaree River. This time floodwaters wouldn't be enough to save the trees. Thankfully, the Sierra Club stepped in. Their grassroots campaign to save the trees culminated in establishment of Congaree Swamp National Monument in 1976. Incorrectly labeled a swamp, the area does not contain standing water throughout most of the year, so it's actually a floodplain. Regardless, new legislation protected this land, its trees, and its waterways from future human exploitation.

Nothing could protect the monument from Hurricane Hugo. In 1989 winds whipped through the forests, toppling many champion trees and permanently changing the park's landscape. But with tragedy came new life and diversity. Sunlight could once again penetrate the canopy. Nature ran its course, and new growth sprang up across the floodplain. Downed trees became habitat for plants and animals. Land unsuitable for farming and logging proved to be suitable for life. A flourishing ecosystem for bobcat, white-tailed deer, river otter, snakes and insects, fungi and ferns, is on display at Congaree National Park.

Trees big enough to hug

When to Go
Congaree National Park is open all year. **Harry Hampton Visitor Center** is open from 9am to 5pm, Tuesday through Saturday. Note that the visitor center is closed Sundays, Mondays, and all national holidays. **Synchronous fireflies**, thought to only exist at in the Smokies (page 109) and Southeast Asia, perform in late May/early June.

Congaree rarely receives larger crowds than it can accommodate, but if you intend on joining a park ranger on a free Owl Prowl, canoe trip, or hike, it's a good idea to call the park at (803) 776-4396 or reservation information is available at the park website. Part of the reason why the park's visitation rate is so low is the fact that its least hospitable time is summer when most families go on vacation. Summers are hot, humid, and buggy. The best time to visit is between fall and spring when there are fewer bugs and temperatures are moderate. Congaree is a floodplain, not a swamp, and flooding is most common in late winter/early spring. Cedar Creek can be impossible to navigate during periods of high and low water. If you plan on paddling, it's a good idea to call the park for current water conditions before you depart.

Transportation & Airports
Public transportation does not provide service to or around the park. The closest airports are Columbia Metropolitan (CAE), Charlotte Douglas International (CLT), and Charleston International (CHS), 24, 96, and 100 miles away, respectively.

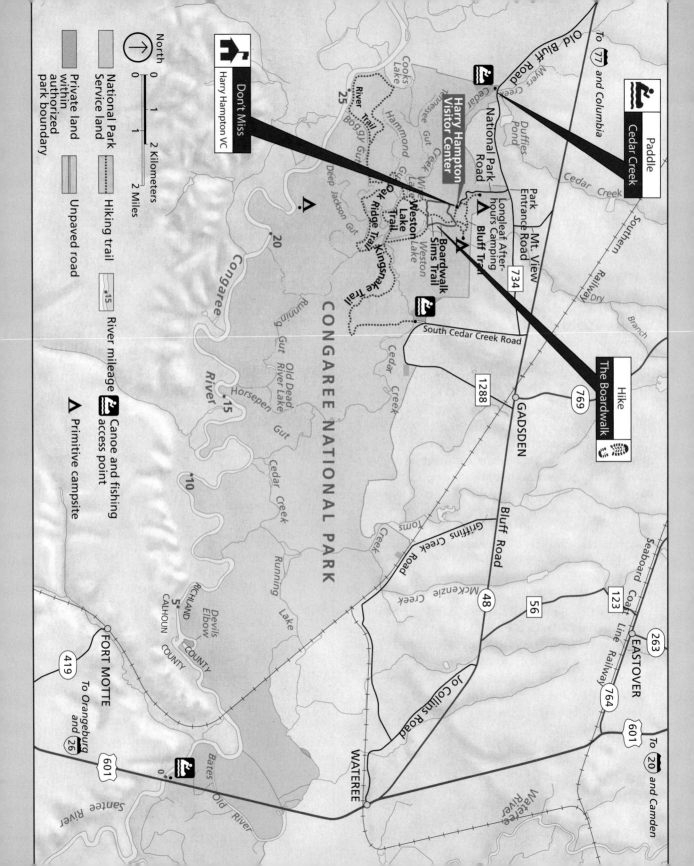

Camping

The park has three camping options: Longleaf Campground, Bluff Campground, and backcountry camping. **Longleaf Campground** is located on the east side of National Park Road, near the park gate. All ten sites are walk-in, not more than 50 yards from the parking area. Chemical toilets are nearby, and drinking water is available from a spigot outside the visitor center when it's open. Tent sites cost $10 per night, while group sites are $20 per night. **Bluff Campground** has six designated walk-in sites for $5 per night, located about one mile from the visitor center parking area. Restrooms and water are not available. Reservations are required to camp in the frontcountry at Longleaf and Bluff campgrounds. Make reservations by calling (877) 444-6777 or clicking recreation.gov. Camping is tent-only. RV and/or car camping is not permitted. **Backcountry camping** is allowed with a free backcountry permit (available at Longleaf Campground only) as long as you are at least 200 feet from trails and 500 feet from buildings and The Boardwalk.

Hiking

The park is small and wet, allowing just 20 miles of hiking trails. An ambitious hiker with an early start can easily hike Congaree's entire trail network in a single day. All of the trails except the Boardwalk are well-marked with colored blazes leading you through primeval forests and wetland.

The Boardwalk is the only trail most visitors hike. It's an elevated, wheelchair-accessible walkway. Self-guided brochures for this 2.4-mile circuit through old-growth forest to Weston Lake are available at the visitor center. The forest drips with Spanish moss and cypress knees protrude from the earth, creating a setting worthy of a mystical fairy tale. (Knees are part of the bald cypress root system and they have been measured up to six feet tall.) The Boardwalk is elevated, but sections can become inaccessible during periods of flooding.

Bluff Trail is a 1.7-mile hike, marked by blue blazes, providing access to The Boardwalk and campground. Along the way you'll pass through a young plantation of loblolly pines.

Be sure to check the visitor center's Mosquito Meter

Best of Congaree

Hikes: The Boardwalk
  Runner-up: Weston Lake Loop
  2nd Runner-up: River Trail

Ranger Programs: Owl Prowl
  Runner-up: Guided Canoe Tour
  2nd Runner-up: Big Tree Hike

Directions

Congaree National Park is located 20 miles southeast of Columbia, SC.

From Columbia/Spartanburg (~20 miles): Take I-26 E (toward Charleston) to Exit 116. Turn onto I-77 N toward Charlotte (left exit). After about five miles, take Exit 5. Turn off onto SC-48 E (Bluff Road), following the brown and white Congaree National Park signs. Continue southeast toward Gadsden for approximately 14 miles before turning right onto Mt. View Road. Turn right onto Old Bluff Road. Turn left at the large park entrance sign and proceed to Harry Hampton Visitor Center and park.

From Charleston (~115 miles): Take I-26 W (toward Spartanburg) to Exit 116. Turn onto I-77 N toward Charlotte, taking exit 5. Follow the directions above for Columbia/Spartanburg (from Exit 5) to reach the park.

From Charlotte (~110 miles): Take I-77 S to Exit 5. Follow the directions above for Columbia/Spartanburg (from Exit 5) to reach the park.

The 4.4-mile **Weston Lake Loop** is marked by yellow blazes. This trail continues from Weston Lake to the northern shore of Cedar Creek. It skirts the creek for a short distance through old growth forest before returning to the visitor center.

Oak Ridge Trail is a 6.6-mile hike, marked by red blazes, that loops around the southern shoreline of Cedar Creek before joining River Trail and returning to the visitor center.

River Trail is 10 miles long and marked by white blazes. As the name suggests, this trail reaches the shores of the Congaree River. Along the way you'll be able to see successional stages of forest life, since much of the forest along the river was logged prior to the park's establishment.

The 11.7-mile **Kingsnake Trail** is marked by orange blazes and connects South Cedar Creek Road Canoe Landing to the visitor center. It's an excellent choice for bird watching or spotting wildlife as you pass through a large cypress–tupelo slough.

Paddling

Paddling is an excellent way to explore the park and to view its record holding trees. You are welcome to bring your own canoe or kayak to explore **Cedar Creek** or the **Congaree River**, but a better alternative is to join a park ranger on one of the free canoe trips that depart regularly (check online for an up-to-date schedule). The park provides everything you need: canoes, life jackets, and paddles. Children must be at least six years old to attend. Reservations are required, and can be made through the park's website. Always check the weather before leaving, because trips are cancelled if it's 45°F or below, the water level on Cedar Creek is 10 feet or above, or wind speed is 30 mph or greater.

Two landings on Cedar Creek within the park, and another landing on the Congaree River outside the park, allow paddlers to create a variety of trips. Cedar Creek slowly meanders through Congaree's old-growth forest, making it perfect for an out-and-back paddle. Start at **Cedar Creek Landing**, just east of the park entrance at the end of South Cedar Creek Road. Pick your pleasure,

upstream or downstream, and then paddle until your heart's content (half content, actually) before turning around. Even though the current is slow, remember paddling upstream will be more difficult and take more time than paddling downstream. Plan appropriately.

By putting in at **Bannister's Bridge**, west of the park entrance on Old Bluff Road, paddlers can float along Cedar Creek as it winds through swaths of bald cypress. The trail is fairly well marked, but there's always a chance you paddle into a dead end or two, especially when the water level is high. Near the half-way point you can take a narrow passage to **Wise Lake**, which was a channel of the Congaree River some 10,000 years ago before the river altered course to its current location nearly 2.5 miles away. It is located on the right-hand side of Cedar Creek, shortly after you pass beneath a small hiking bridge. Note that it may be inaccessible at low water levels. The entire trip is roughly 7 miles (4–6 hours) to the take-out at **Cedar Creek Landing**. You will need to arrange transportation between put-in and take-out.

A 20-mile trip from **Cedar Creek Landing** to the **601 Bridge** is perfect for tireless or overnight paddlers. (If you plan on spending the night, be sure to stop at the visitor center for a camping permit.) Cedar Creek eventually joins the **Congaree River**, but the paddle trail takes a safer detour following **Mazyck's Cut** to the Congaree. Beyond the junction with Mazyck's Cut, Cedar Creek is unmarked and uncleared, so we highly recommend paddlers follow the trail. Three trail markers and a wooden sign point paddlers in the appropriate direction. Once you've reached the Congaree, you've got another 13 miles to the 601 bridge take-out. Once again, you'll have to arrange transport.

If that isn't enough, paddlers can take on the **Congaree River Blue Trail**. It's a 50-mile adventure beginning in Columbia, the capital of South Carolina, and continuing downstream to Congaree National Park.

Fishing

Fishing is permitted anywhere in the park except Weston Lake. A valid South Carolina State Fishing License is required, and all state laws and limits apply. To help prevent introduction of non-native species, live bait, such as minnows, amphibians, and fish eggs, are prohibited. When trying to reach your desired fishing location, please use access roads rather than The Boardwalk.

Congaree's fish are almost as varied as the species of trees lining the shores. Largemouth bass, striped bass, perch, and crappie are a few of the commonly caught game fish. Prehistoric fish like garfish, mudfish, and shortnose sturgeon can also be found lurking beneath the surface of the murky water. Congaree River has a healthy population of white perch, white bass, catfish, carp, and suckers.

Biking

Bicycles are allowed in the park but all trails, including The Boardwalk, are closed to cyclists. That leaves the 1.5-mile **National Park Road** as the lone stretch of pavement for bikers. A few roads surrounding the park offer decent, flat pedaling, but it's not really worth the effort of bringing a bike to Congaree.

Bird Watching

Remember to pack your binoculars. Congaree is a park for birds and bird watchers, with more than 170 species spotted here. This includes eight species of woodpeckers: red-bellied, red-cockaded, red-headed, pileated, downy, hairy, yellow-bellied sapsucker, and yellow shafted flicker. Even the legendary ivory-billed woodpecker is believed to reside among the old-growth forest.

Owls are one of the most popular residents. More than 20 years ago a park ranger decided to lead a night-time **"Owl Prowl."** It was a hit then, and still is today. If you'd like to go on the prowl for owls, make sure you plan ahead, because reservations are required (reservations can be made online, check the park website).

Flora & Fauna

The park's skyline is dominated by many of the eastern United States' tallest trees. About 20 trees hold state or national records for size. The largest is a 169-foot-tall, 17-foot-diameter loblolly pine. More than 98% of park land is designated wilderness covered with 75 species of trees, including: cherrybark oak, paw, water

oak, bald cypress, tupelo, American holly, laurel oak, and ironwood. The Congaree River flows through the park for 23 miles, with a miniscule elevation change of 20 feet. The elevation difference, no matter how slight, affects vegetation growth. You'll find that loblolly pines grow on higher ground, while bald cypress and tupelo thrive in low areas of standing water. And the park isn't all about trees. There are 22 distinct plant communities filled with fungi, ferns, flowers, and shrubs that flourish beneath the park's dense canopy.

Most animals found in the park are commonly described with words like creepy, crawly, or nocturnal. For the most part insects aren't bothersome until the middle of summer, when mosquitoes rule the wetlands. Four poisonous snake species inhabit the park. These include coral snake, copperhead, canebrake rattler, and cottonmouth. Snakes are fairly common, so use caution when near rocks, holes, downed trees, or other spots where a snake might be hiding. Bobcats, raccoons, opossums, and owls are most active at night. In the morning and evening you may see white-tailed deer, squirrels, or river otter. You might be tempted to stare at the ground searching for poisonous snakes, but look up from time to time. The park is loaded with interesting moths, butterflies, and birds. A good spotting can be the fondest memory of a trip to Congaree.

Ranger Programs

A little bit of planning is required for a few of the park's ranger programs: Big Tree Hike, Guided Canoe Tour, and Owl Prowl require reservations which can be made online (see the park website). If you miss out on one of these programs, don't worry, there are additional regularly scheduled, ranger-led hikes, chats, lectures, and campfires that are all free of charge and do not require a reservation. A current schedule of events can be found at the park's website.

For Kids

Congaree's **Junior Ranger Program** gives kids of all ages the opportunity to receive a badge for completing a free activity booklet (available at the visitor center). The booklet takes approximately three hours to complete. These activities help engage children in their surroundings while exploring the park. It's also filled with

A green anole

facts that both children and adults will find fun and exciting. If workbooks aren't your kid's style, a short introductory film plays regularly at the visitor center.

Pets

Pets are allowed in the park, but must be kept on a leash no more than six feet in length at all times. Pets, except service animals, are not permitted in park buildings.

Accessibility

The park's two most popular attractions, Harry Hampton Visitor Center and The Boardwalk, are completely accessible to individuals in wheelchairs. Some Ranger Programs like Congaree Campfire Chronicles are accessible.

Weather

Summers are hot and humid. Memorial Day and Thanksgiving are the two busiest days due to comfortable weather during spring and fall. Winters are mild. On average the park floods ten times each year. Most flooding occurs in winter.

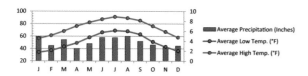

Vacation Planner

For all intents and purposes Congaree is for day-trippers. It only has sixteen designated campsites and there are no lodging facilities in or around the park. Day-

trips are often spontaneous, but you should do a bit of advance planning for a trip to Congaree. Joining an **Owl Prowl** or **Canoe Tour** requires advance reservations (page 121). They're popular and highly recommended. Paddlers should anticipate the stretch of water from **Bannister's Bridge** to **Cedar Creek Landing** to take at least a half-day, and **Cedar Creek** to the **Congaree** is a full day. **Synchronous fireflies** perform in the park during a two week period around late May/early June. They also perform at Great Smoky Mountain National Park (page 109), a location with a friendlier population of mosquitoes. If you're looking for a place to sleep or eat, your best bet is Columbia (20 miles to the north). Nearby dining, grocery stores, lodging, festivals, and attractions are listed on page 123.

Day 1: Begin your trip at **Harry Hampton Visitor Center**. Here you'll find an exhibit area, a small gift shop, and a short introductory film. Park rangers are available to answer your questions. If you failed to reserve a spot for a **Canoe Tour**, **Big Tree Hike**, or **Owl Prowl**, you should definitely browse the day's schedule of events. If you can't find anything that meets your interests or schedule, head outdoors and walk **The Boardwalk** (self-guiding brochures are available at the visitor center). Notice the bald cypress knees piercing the ground. They are actually part of the tree's root system, making them exceedingly difficult to topple even though they're planted in wet soil. If you have time and energy, continue along **Weston Lake Trail** or **Kingsnake Trail**. Be sure to arrive back at the visitor center in time for any ranger programs you may have selected.

Dining
Big T Bar-B-Q • (803) 353-0488
2520 Congaree Rd, Gadsden

Eric's San Jose Mexican Rest. • (803) 783-6650
6118 Garners Ferry Rd, Columbia
ericssanjose.com • Entrée: $9–14

Blue Marlin • (803) 799-3838
1200 Lincoln St, Columbia
bluemarlincolumbia.com

Motor Supply Co Bistro • (803) 256-6687
920 Gervais St, Columbia
motorsupplycobistro.com • Entrée: $21+

Julia's German Stammtisch • (803) 738-0630
4341 Fort Jackson Blvd, Columbia
julias.vpweb.com • Entrée: $15–19

Za's Brick Oven Pizza • (803) 771-7334
2930 Devine St, # E, Columbia
zasbrickovenpizza.com • Entrée: $7–13

Blue Cactus Café • (803) 929-0782
2002 Greene St, # H, Columbia

Saluda's Restaurant • (803) 799-9500
751 Saluda Ave, Columbia
saludas.com • Entrée: $21–39

Grocery Stores
Piggly Wiggly • (803) 874-1212
615 Harry C Raysor Dr, St Matthews

Food Lion • (803) 695-9757
9013 Garners Ferry Rd, Hopkins

Walmart Supercenter • (803) 783-1277
7520 Garners Ferry Rd, Columbia

Publix • (803) 806-8839
2800 Rosewood Drive, Columbia

Lodging
The Inn at USC • (803) 779-7779
1619 Pendleton Street, Columbia
innatusc.com • Rates: $109

The Inn At Claussen's • (803) 765-0440
2003 Greene St, Columbia
theinnatclaussens.com • Rates: $100

TownePlace Suites • (803) 695-0062
250 East Exchange Blvd, Columbia

Candlewood Suites • (803) 727-1299
921 Atlas Road, Columbia • Rates: ~$75

Chestnut Cottage B&B • (803) 256-1718
1718 Hampton St, Columbia
chesnutcottage.com • Rates: $159–229

Southern Lodge • (803) 531-7333
3616 Saint Matthews Rd, Orangeburg

*Many chain restaurants and hotels can be found
nearby in Columbia and Orangeburg.*

Festivals
Spoleto USA • May/June
spoletousa.org • Charleston, SC

Greek Festival • September
columbiasgreekfestival.com • Columbia, SC

South Carolina State Fair • October
scstatefair.org • Columbia, SC

Chitlin Strut • November
chitlinstrut.com • Salley, SC

Nearby Attractions
Poinsett State Park • (803) 494-8177
6660 Poinsett Park Rd, Wedgefield

House Museum Tours • (803) 252-7742
1616 Blanding St, Columbia
historiccolumbia.org • Admission: $8/adult

Riverbanks Zoo • (803) 779-8717
500 Wildlife Parkway, Columbia
riverbanks.org • Admission: $14/adult

SC State Museum • (803) 898-4921
301 Gervais Street, Columbia, SC 29201
scmuseum.org • Admission: $9

Columbia Museum of Art • (803) 799-2810
1515 Main St, Columbia
columbiamuseum.org • Admission: $12/adult

Edventure Children's Museum • (803) 779-3100
211 Gervais St, Columbia
edventure.org • Admission: $11.50

Nickelodeon Movie Theater • (803) 254-3433
937 Main Street, Columbia
nickelodeon.org • Tickets: ~$10

AMC Theatres - Dutch Square 14 • (888) 262-4386
421-80 Bush River Rd, Columbia

The Comedy House • (803) 798-9898
2768 Decker Blvd, Columbia
comedyhouse.us

Marionette Theatre • (803) 252-7366
401 Laurel St, Columbia
cmtpuppet.org • Tickets: ~$6

Morris Museum of Art • 706-724-7501
1 Tenth St, Augusta, GA
themorris.org • Admission: $5/adult

Museum of History • (706) 722-8454
560 Reynolds Street, Augusta, GA
augustamuseum.org • Admission: $4/adult

Country Club • (706) 364-1862
Suite F, 2834 Washington Rd, Augusta, GA
augustacountry.com • *Dance Lessons & Shows*

Spiritline Harbor Tours • (843) 722-2628
360 Concord St, # 201, Charleston
spiritlinecruises.com • Tours: $20+

Original Charleston Walks • (843) 408-0010
charlestonwalks.com

Culinary Tours • (843) 722-8687
40 North Market St, Charleston
culinarytoursofcharleston.com • $60

Classic Carriage Works • (843) 853-3747
10 Guignard Street, Charleston
classiccarriage.com • Rates: $25

SC Aquarium • (843) 577-3474
100 Aquarium Wharf, Charleston
scaquarium.org • Admission: $25/adult

Charleston Museum • (843) 722-2996
360 Meeting Street, Charleston
charlestonmuseum.org • Admission: $12

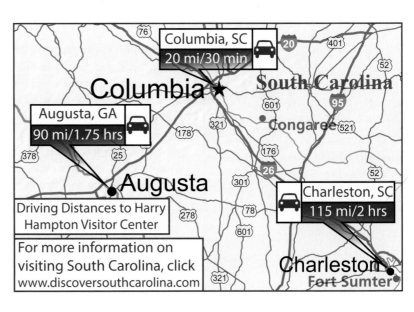

Driving Distances to Harry Hampton Visitor Center

For more information on visiting South Carolina, click www.discoversouthcarolina.com

Snorkeling Biscayne

Biscayne

Dante Fascell Visitor Center
9700 SW 328 Street
Homestead, FL 33033
Phone: (305) 230-1114
Website: nps.gov/bisc

Established: June 28, 1980
Size: 172,971 Acres
Annual Visitors: 508,000
Peak Season: Winter and Spring

Hiking Trails (8.25 total miles)
Convoy Point • 0.25 mile
Elliott Key • 0.75 mile, self-guided
Elliott Key • 7 miles, self-guided
Adams Key • 0.25 mile, self-guided

Activities: SCUBA, Snorkeling,
Paddling, and Bird Watching

Campgrounds: Boca Chita Key
and Elliott Key (primitive camping)
Camping Fee: $25/night
Backcountry Camping: Prohibited
Lodging: None within Park

Park Hours: All day, every day
(water) • Day-use only (Adams Key)
Entrance Fee: None

In the 1960s, Biscayne Bay's mangrove forests were declared "a form of wasteland" by well-to-do businessmen, who saw roads, bridges, buildings, and an oil refinery as the only way to revitalize an otherwise useless wilderness. Thankfully, a swell of opposition rose up from the public. Politicians, actors, writers, and environmentalists banded together to help preserve the longest undeveloped shoreline on Florida's east coast. Today, 40 small emerald isles and their mangrove shorelines remain untethered to civilization by roads thanks to the creation of Biscayne National Park. But there's more here than unaltered islands and forests. More than 95% of the park is water, and beneath its surface lies an underwater wilderness completely unique among United States National Parks. A vast array of wildlife—along with thousands of weary urban dwellers—seeks refuge and respite here. Not a single one of these visitors would consider this priceless landscape a "form of wasteland."

Israel Jones was among the first to enjoy the seclusion and wilderness of Biscayne. He moved to Florida in 1892, searching for work. After nine years as caretaker to the Walter S. Davies Grant, handyman at the Peacock Inn, and foreman of a pineapple farm, he chose to work for himself. With his savings, he purchased two islands on the southern edge of Caesar Creek. Two years later he moved his family to Old Rhodes Key, where he started a business, raised a family, and left a legacy. Israel cleared gumbo-limbo, palmetto, and mahogany trees to reveal a coral limestone base suitable for farming key limes and pineapples. Weathering several years of indebtedness, he eventually became one of the largest producers of pineapples and limes on the east coast of Florida. Reinvesting his profits into real estate, he purchased Totten Key for $1 an acre. The property, all 212 acres, later sold for $250,000. Good, lucky, or both, Israel had proven himself to be a keen businessman who understood the value of an education. He hired a live-in teacher for his sons, and helped create the Negro Industrial School in Jacksonville. His children used their education to follow in their father's footsteps. Arthur and Lancelot Jones continued to farm limes after the death of their parents. They also began guiding visitors on fishing excursions. Lancelot's fishing expertise was well known in the area and he was often hired to guide wealthy visitors of the Cocolobo Club on Adams Key. During the 1940s and 50s Lancelot served as fishing guide to the likes of Herbert Hoover, Lyndon B. Johnson, Richard Nixon, and other well-known politicians.

Other prominent people wanted to use the region for more than its fish. Daniel Ludwig, a billionaire developer, announced plans for an industrial seaport called Seadade in 1962. Development included an oil refinery and dredging a 40-foot wide channel through Biscayne Bay. Fill from the dredging project would be used to form new islands, which would eventually connect North Key Largo to Key Biscayne by a series of roads and bridges. The project drew considerable support thanks to the prospect of new jobs and increased property value. But it also had opponents. Herbert W. Hoover, vacuum cleaner magnate and childhood visitor to the area, led legislators on dramatic blimp rides over the proposed development. As the park movement gained momentum, Seadade supporters razed a 6-lane "spite highway" the entire 7-mile length of Elliott Key. Today, Elliott Key Boulevard follows Spite Highway, and it is the only significant hiking trail in the park. In 1968 Congress, led by Representative Dante Fascell (the visitor center's namesake), passed a bill to protect "a rare combination of terrestrial, marine, and amphibious life in a tropical setting of great natural beauty." On October 18, 1968, President Lyndon Johnson, who decades earlier had gone fishing with Lancelot Jones, signed a bill creating Biscayne National Monument. Lancelot Jones sold his property to the National Parks Service in 1970 and was granted the right to live out his life in his family home.

When to Go
95% of the park is water, and it is open 24 hours a day. Adams Key (accessible by boat) is a day-use area only. Winter is the most pleasant time to visit. In summer, visitors must brave mosquitoes, high temperatures and humidity, frequent thunderstorms, and the occasional hurricane.

Convoy Point, where you'll find the park's headquarters and visitor center, is open daily from 7am–5:30pm. **Dante Fascell Visitor Center** is open daily from 9am–5pm during winter (November through April) and from 10am–5pm for the rest of the year. If you'd like to join an Island Boat Tour, check the park's website for a current schedule of events. Tours are typically offered on weekends.

Transportation & Airports
Most visitors reach the park's islands by private boat, but you can also arrange a guided tour (page 128).

Miami International (MIA) is the closest large commercial airport (about 35 miles away).

Directions
Most visitors enter the park by private boat, but Convoy Point serves as hub for all land activities.

From Miami to Convoy Point (37 miles): Take FL-821 South (Partial Toll Road) to Exit 6 for SW 137th Ave toward Speedway Blvd (Toll Road). Keep left at the fork, following signs to Air Reserve Station/Job Cargs Canter. Turn left at SW 137th Ave. Turn left at SW 328th St/N Canal Drive, which leads to the park entrance and visitor center.

You can also take US-1 South to SW 137th Ave. Turn left onto 137th Ave. Turn right onto SW 328th St/N Canal Drive, which leads to the park entrance and visitor center.

From Everglades National Park/Flamingo Area (56 miles): Follow the Main Park Rd east to Ingraham Hwy. Continue on Ingraham Hwy until Tower Rd. Turn left on Tower Rd. After about 2 miles, turn right onto SW 344th St. Continue onto W Palm Dr, which will turn into SW 138th Ct and then Speedway Blvd, and finally SW 137th Ave. Turn right at SW 328th St/N Canal Dr, which leads to the park entrance and visitor center.

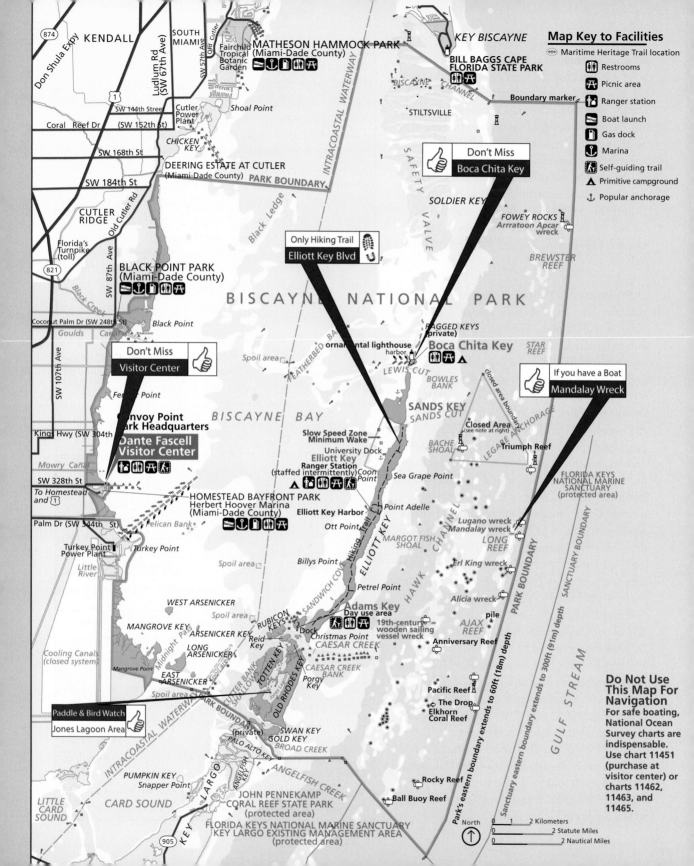

Map Key to Facilities

- Maritime Heritage Trail location
- Restrooms
- Picnic area
- Ranger station
- Boat launch
- Gas dock
- Marina
- Self-guiding trail
- Primitive campground
- Popular anchorage

KENDALL

874

Don Shula Expy

Ludlum Rd (SW 67th Ave)

SW 57th Ave

SOUTH MIAMI

Fairchild Tropical Botanic Garden

MATHESON HAMMOCK PARK (Miami-Dade County)

US 1

SW 144th Street

Coral Reef Dr (SW 152th St)

Cutler Power Plant

Shoal Point

SW 168th St

CHICKEN KEY

SW 184th St

DEERING ESTATE AT CUTLER (Miami-Dade County)

PARK BOUNDARY

CUTLER RIDGE

Florida's Turnpike (toll)

821

SW 87th Ave

Black Ledge

Black Creek

BLACK POINT PARK (Miami-Dade County)

Coconut Palm Dr (SW 248th St)

Black Point

Goulds Canal

Breakwater

SW 107th Ave

Ferril Point

Kings Hwy (SW 304th

Mowry Canal

SW 328th St

To Homestead and 1

Palm Dr (SW 344th St)

Pelican Bank

Turkey Point Power Plant

Little River

Turkey Point

WEST ARSENICKER

Spoil area

MANGROVE KEY

ARSENICKER KEY

Mangrove Key

LONG ARSENICKER

Cooling Canals (closed system)

Mangrove Point

EAST ARSENICKER

Spoil area

LITTLE CARD SOUND

CARD SOUND

PUMPKIN KEY

Snapper Point

905

KEY LARGO

INTRACOASTAL WATERWAY

PARK BOUNDARY

JOHN PENNEKAMP CORAL REEF STATE PARK (protected area)

FLORIDA KEYS NATIONAL MARINE SANCTUARY KEY LARGO EXISTING MANAGEMENT AREA (protected area)

KEY BISCAYNE

BILL BAGGS CAPE FLORIDA STATE PARK

BISCAYNE CHANNEL

STILTSVILLE

Boundary marker

SAFETY VALVE

SOLDIER KEY

FOWEY ROCKS

Arrratoon Apcar wreck

BREWSTER REEF

Don't Miss | Boca Chita Key 👍

Only Hiking Trail | Elliott Key Blvd 👣

BISCAYNE NATIONAL PARK

RAGGED KEYS (private)

ornamental lighthouse

harbor

Boca Chita Key

STAR REEF

LEWIS CUT

BOWLES BANK

SANDS KEY

SANDS CUT

Closed Area (see note at right)

closed area boundary

If you have a Boat | Mandalay Wreck 👍

Don't Miss | Visitor Center 👍

FEATHERBED BANK

Spoil area

BISCAYNE BAY

Convoy Point Park Headquarters

Dante Fascell Visitor Center

Slow Speed Zone Minimum Wake

University Dock

Elliott Key Ranger Station (staffed intermittently)

Coon Point

BACHE SHOAL

LEGARE ANCHORAGE

Triumph Reef

FLORIDA KEYS NATIONAL MARINE SANCTUARY (protected area)

HOMESTEAD BAYFRONT PARK Herbert Hoover Marina (Miami-Dade County)

Sea Grape Point

Elliott Key Harbor

Point Adelle

Ott Point

ELLIOTT KEY

MARGOT FISH SHOAL

HAWK CHANNEL

Lugano wreck
Mandalay wreck

LONG REEF

Sandwich Cove Hiking Trail

Billys Point

Erl King wreck

Petrel Point

Alicia wreck

Paddle & Bird Watch | Jones Lagoon Area 👍

RUBICON KEYS

Dock

Adams Key
Day use area

19th-century wooden sailing vessel wreck

pile

AJAX REEF

PARK BOUNDARY

SANCTUARY BOUNDARY

Reid Key

Christmas Point

CAESAR CREEK

Anniversary Reef

Pacific Reef

TOTTEN KEY

CAESAR CREEK BANK

OLD RHODES KEY

Porgy Key

The Drop
Elkhorn Coral Reef

GULF STREAM

INTRACOASTAL WATERWAY

PARK BOUNDARY

SWAN KEY

GOLD KEY

PALO ALTO KEY

BROAD CREEK

ANGELFISH KEY

ANGELFISH CREEK

(private)

Rocky Reef

Ball Buoy Reef

Park's eastern boundary extends to 60ft (18m) depth

Sanctuary eastern boundary extends to 300ft (91m) depth

Do Not Use This Map For Navigation
For safe boating, National Ocean Survey charts are indispensable. Use chart 11451 (purchase at visitor center) or charts 11462, 11463, and 11465.

North

0   1   2 Kilometers
0   2 Statute Miles
0   2 Nautical Miles

Indians & Pirates

Long before developers envisioned the Florida Keys connected from Miami to Key West and the Joneses were living on Old Rhodes Island, the area was inhabited by Tequesta Indians. Little evidence of their existence remains, but scientists believe many archeological sites are hidden beneath the floor of Biscayne Bay. It is also presumed the bay was a vast savannah prior to the last Ice Age, where Indians hunted mastodons and woolly mammoths.

In the more recent past, Native Americans fished and hunted sea turtles, sharks, sailfish, stingrays, and other sea mammals like manatee and porpoise. By the time Ponce de León sailed across Biscayne Bay in 1513, the Tequesta were using hollowed-out canoes, making pottery, and hunting with bows and arrows. The tribe prospered. Sea life was abundant. Not having to tend crops of corn for sustenance allowed considerable free time to focus on religion and art. As elsewhere, the arrival of Europeans marked the beginning of their end. By 1763, smallpox and measles, coupled with raids by other Indian tribes and the Spanish, had wiped out the entire Tequesta tribe.

Spanish explorers left the Americas with boatloads of riches, riches that would spark an era of violence and greed. Nations of the world began patrolling the seas waiting to loot Spanish ships, and pirate activity was common near what is now Biscayne National Park. One of the most famous pirates was Black Caesar, whom Caesar Creek is now named for. Black Caesar was an 18th-century African pirate who had evaded numerous slave traders before a hurricane left him shipwrecked along the Florida reefs. Eventually he was able to recruit a crew, and together they attacked ships on the open sea. They frequently avoided capture by running into Caesar Creek and other narrow inlets between Elliott and Old Rhodes Key. Legend claims they would hide their boat by sinking it in shallow water. Once the patrol boat passed, they would pump out the water, raising the boat. Another legend states Black Caesar buried 26 bars of solid gold on Elliott Key, a treasure that remains hidden to this day. His work led to a pirate promotion, when he left the waters of Biscayne Bay to join Blackbeard in raiding American ships sailing across the mid-Atlantic.

Stiltsville

In 1933, at the tail end of prohibition, "Crawfish" Eddie Walker decided to build a shack on stilts above the shallow waters of Biscayne Bay just south of Cape Florida. He was the first to build a home in this strategic location, one mile off shore where gambling was legal. Eddie's idea caught on. In 1940, the Quarterback Club was built near Crawfish Eddie's, and it became the place to be in Miami. Illicit activities were common, forcing police to make regular raids. During Stiltsville's heyday, as many as 27 structures rose out of the waters of Biscayne Bay. Hurricanes made for relatively short-lived establishments, and in 1992 Hurricane Andrew wiped out all but seven buildings.

Today, access to these buildings is by permission only. Those wishing to tour Stiltsville should contact the Stiltsville Trust Group (stiltsvilletrust.org). If you aren't curious enough to take a tour, the history and sheer existence of these precariously perched domiciles is at least worth a photograph.

Camping

Boca Chita and Elliott Campgrounds are open all year. Sites fill early on a first-come, first-served basis, especially between December and April. Camping costs $25/night, which includes docking a boat. Group sites are available for $30/night. Payment should be made upon arrival at the kiosks available near the harbor. Camping fees are waived from May through September each year. You must bring your own food and water to the islands. RV camping is not available, and the islands can only be reached by boat. The previous park concessioner went out of business, so to reach the campgrounds, you'll have to provide your own transportation or hire a charter (page 152).

Boca Chita Key is the most popular island in the park. Here you'll find 39 designated waterfront sites. Toilets are available but drinking water, showers, and sinks are not.

Elliott Key, the park's largest island, has 40 waterfront and forested sites. Restrooms with sinks and cold water **showers** are available. Drinking water is also available, but the system occasionally goes down.

Boat Tours

Check the calendar of events at the park website for boat tours providing an opportunity to explore Boca Chita Key. Tours depart from Dante Fascell Visitor Center on select Fridays, Saturdays, and Sundays. Tickets cost $29 per adult and $19 per child (ages 5–12). Children 4 and under are free. Reservations are recommended and can be made by calling the **Florida National Parks Association** at (786) 335-3644 or by stopping in at the visitor center's bookstore. In addition, Island Dreamer Sailing (561.281.2689, biscaynenationalparksailing.com) offers **full day sailing adventures** departing Dante Fascell Visitor Center.

SCUBA & Snorkel

More than 50 shipwrecks and a significant portion of the **third largest barrier reef in the world** make Biscayne National Park one of the best SCUBA and snorkel destinations in the United States.

Wreck-diving was first made popular by treasure hunters who inhabited Elliott Key. Today, a **Maritime Heritage Trail** connects six of the park's wrecks. Mooring buoys, maps, and site cards aid divers and snorkelers on their exploration of each site. All sites except the *Mandalay* are best suited for SCUBA divers. Ranger-guided snorkel trips to selected sites on the trail are offered (additional details available at the park's website and visitor center).

Paddling

Paddling is a great way to explore the mangrove shorelines and shallow flats surrounding **Jones Lagoon**, where you might see sharks, rays, upside-down jellies, and wading birds. Visitors with their own boats can launch for free from the visitor center. Overnight parking is available for anyone planning on camping at either of the park's primitive campgrounds (page 127), but you must obtain a free permit (available at the visitor center) prior to departure. Elliott Key is approximately seven miles from shore. Do not attempt to cross the bay during periods of inclement weather or adverse water conditions.

Fishing

Biscayne Bay's fishing is nearly as good today as it was when Lancelot Jones guided future presidents to local hotspots. For the most part, fishing and harvesting is regulated by state law. All anglers 16 and older require a Florida State Saltwater Fishing License to fish in Biscayne National Park, and they must follow regulations pertaining to size, season, limit, and method. Outfitters (page 152) offer fishing excursions in Biscayne Bay, where you can expect to catch bonefish, tarpon, and permit.

Bird Watching

More than 170 species of birds have been recorded within the park. **Convoy Point** and **Black Point** are two of the better mainland birding locations, but to really experience the multitude of sea birds visitors must hit the water. **Jones Lagoon**, just south of Caesar Creek, is the park's premier birding location. Here you're sure to spot cormorants, brown pelicans, and anhinga.

Ranger Programs

Ranger-led activities are available at several locations within the park, with most programs offered during the park's busy season (Christmas Day–April). Visit the park's website to check out a current schedule of events before arriving at the park.

For Kids

Kids will enjoy boat tours, snorkel trips, and paddling, but there are also several attractions geared especially for children. On the second Sunday of each month, from December to April, the park holds a **Family Fun Fest**. It's a free program at Dante Fascell Visitor Center that highlights the region's diverse resources using five hands-on activity booths. Participants receive a "passport" that is punched each time they complete a station. Anyone who completes all five stations receives a special prize.

Children can also participate in the park's **Junior Ranger Program**. An activity booklet can be downloaded from the park website or hard copies are available free of charge at Dante Fascell Visitor Center. The program is jointly administered between Big Cypress National Preserve, Biscayne National Park, and Everglades National Park. Complete the activities for Biscayne National Park to earn a badge. If you complete the entire book you will earn a South Florida National Parks Junior Ranger Patch.

Flora & Fauna

Hundreds of species of plants can be found here. Most obvious are the mangrove forests lining the shores, a cornerstone of the entire ecosystem. Birds, manatees, and crocodiles visit these masses of twisted roots and branches with great frequency. Smaller fish seek protection from larger predators among the half-sunken mangrove roots where trapped leaves provide nourishment for a variety of sea-life. If you go on a SCUBA, snorkel, or boat tour, it's likely that you'll see beds of sea grass. These underwater pastures are all-you-can-eat, self-service buffets for sea turtles and manatees, and a nursery for small fishes and invertebrates. The park's islands and mainland contain numerous cacti, ferns, trees, shrubs, and wildflowers. Many appear on lists of threatened and endangered species while others are non-native, exotic plants introduced by humans. Non-native species pose a serious threat to native plants as they compete for the same limited supply of water and nutrients.

The majority of wildlife at Biscayne National Park is hidden beneath the sea. Underwater inhabitants include 512 species of fish, a handful of crustaceans like crabs and lobsters, dolphins, manatees, a few species of whale, and several mollusks like squid, snails, and oysters. Lucky snorkelers or SCUBA divers may spot a graceful sea turtle. Green, loggerhead, leatherback, and hawksbill turtles, all endangered species, can be found here. The American crocodile is another endangered species that finds refuge among the park's mangrove islands. Harvest, harassment, harm, or any other interference with these species is strictly prohibited.

Rare creatures also live above the water. Schaus' swallowtail butterfly, for example, are estimated at fewer than 70 adults remaining in the world, and they are only found on North Key Largo and a few small Keys in Biscayne National Park. That said, most animals living above sea level fall under the category of pests. Mosquitoes are common year-round, but are particularly pesky during summer. Raccoons inhabit the islands and are frequently found rummaging through visitors' coolers and picnic baskets. Travel with animal-proof coolers and do not sleep with food in your tent.

Pets

Pets are only allowed in the developed areas of Elliott Key and Convoy Point. They must be kept on a leash no more than six feet in length at all times. Pets, except service animals, are prohibited from all other areas of the park.

Accessibility

More than 95% of the park is covered by water, so accessibility is directly dependent on your transportation (usually a boat). Dante Fascell Visitor Center and Jetty Trail are fully accessible to wheelchair users. Boca Chita Key is the only island within the park that has sidewalks.

Weather

When visiting Biscayne National Park be especially observant of the weather. A subtropical climate provides abundant sunshine all year long, but thunderstorms with massive amounts of lightning are common, and hurricanes batter the land occasionally. Winters are generally dry and mild, with an average high temperature of 68°F in January. Summers are often hot and humid with an average high temperature of 82°F in July. Scattered thunderstorms are most common in summer. Hurricane season lasts from June to November. Biscayne Bay is relatively well protected, but if skies grow dark or the wind begins to pick up, boaters should head for shore rather than get caught in a thunderstorm.

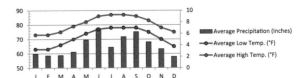

Vacation Planner

To get the most out of a trip to Biscayne National Park you need to be prepared. Whether it's joining a **boat tour** (page 128) or just checking the park's website for a current schedule of events, every little bit you do beforehand will increase your chances of an enjoyable experience. **Paddling** is great but you'll need to bring your own watercraft, and then you're free to paddle across the bay to the northern Florida Keys. Most visitors arrive via private boat, but it's not a requirement. Nearby dining, grocery stores, lodging, festivals, and attractions are listed on pages 149–153.

Morning dew

Everglades

40001 State Road 9336
Homestead, FL 33034
Phone: (305) 242-7700
Website: nps.gov/ever

Established: December 6, 1947
Size: 1,509,000 Acres
Annual Visitors: 1.1 Million
Peak Season: December–April
Hiking Trails: 50+ Miles
Wilderness Waterway: 99 Miles

Activities: Paddling, Hiking,
Biking, Fishing, Bird Watching,
Ranger Programs, Boat Tours

Campgrounds: Long Pine Key
(first-come, first-served) and
Flamingo (reservations accepted)
Camping Fee: $20/night
Backcountry Camping: Permitted
at Designated Sites with a
Backcountry Permit ($15 plus $2
per night)
Lodging: None

Park Hours: All day, every day
Entrance Fee: $20/vehicle,
$8/individual (foot, bike, etc.)

Wherever you look the circle of life is on display in the Everglades. From alligator holes to mangrove coasts, lofty pine to dwarf cypress forests, grassy waterways to man-made canals, life flourishes and flounders, thrives and perishes, dies and is reborn. When Americans began to develop South Florida in the late 19th century, humans threw this circle of life into a tailspin. It's not too late to recover, but our actions will ultimately destroy or preserve this irreplaceable wilderness.

Whether you're looking at the Everglades from above, atop the 45-foot high observation deck at Shark Valley, or from the seat of a kayak in a maze of waterways, one thing you're sure to notice is its size. At 1,509,000 acres, it's the largest wilderness area east of the Mississippi River. Hidden among its immensity are small pockets of life that are even more incredible.

Alligators reside at the top of the food chain for good reason. Their vise-like jaws and razor sharp teeth make a fearsome predator. Alligators burrow in mud creating small pools of water. When the dry season sets in, water levels decrease so much that alligator holes are often the only available source of freshwater, providing an important habitat for fish and amphibians trying to survive from one year to the next. Mammals congregate at these gator holes, drinking water and feeding on smaller prey. Meanwhile, alligators lay motionless, waiting to attack as they feed. Eventually, the region floods again, and fish and amphibians, survivors of life in a gator hole, are free to repopulate the fresh water prairies.

Quantity, quality, and type of water shape the plant and animal life of the Everglades' ecosystems. Cypress trees adapted to survive in areas frequently covered with standing fresh water. These hearty conifers are surrounded by woody, conical protrusions called "knees" that provide oxygen to the roots below. Dwarf cypresses reside in areas with less water and poorer soil. Spanish moss, orchids, and ferns grow from the trees' branches and trunks. Along the salt water coast you'll find jungle-like mangrove forests. The park protects the largest continuous system of mangroves in the world. These plants have also acclimated to extreme conditions. They acquired a high tolerance for salt water, winds, tides, temperatures, and muddy soils. Mangroves also serve as the first line of defense against hurricanes. Sturdy roots and dense branches are capable of absorbing and deflecting flood water, helping prevent coastal erosion. They also act as a nursery and food depot for marine and bird species.

Sadly, human actions are altering many of the area's natural life cycles. Nearly all of the park land's pine forests were logged. Dade County was once covered with more than 186,000 acres of pine rockland forest. Today, only 20,000 acres remain. Florida panthers have been ravaged by loss of habitat, poor water quality, and hunting. Now, perhaps ten exist in the park. In the early 1900s, alligators, birds, frogs, and fish were hunted on a massive scale. Since the 1930s, the number of nesting wading birds in the southern Everglades has declined by 93% from 265,000 to 18,500. Most were killed for their plumes, commonly used to decorate women's hats. Today, the greatest threat the Everglades faces is depletion and diversion of water. Man-made dikes, levees, and canals have been constructed to bring water to South Florida's urban areas, cutting off the region's water supply. A park brochure offers a sad and honest description of the state of the Everglades' water: "Freshwater flowing into the park is engineered. With the help of pumps, floodgates, and retention ponds along the park's boundary, Everglades is presently on life support, alive but diminished." Come to the Everglades. Witness the abundance of life still struggling to survive. See for yourself if condos, strip malls, and roadways are worth destroying one of the world's most magnificent natural wonders. It's not too late to save the Everglades. Changing its course is up to us. All we need to do is act now, before it really is too late.

When to Go
Everglades National Park is open all year, but some tours, attractions, and hours of operation are seasonal. Southern Florida experiences two seasons. Most guests visit the Everglades during the dry season (December–April). It's typically comfortable with fewer bugs, thunderstorms, and hurricanes. The wet season (March–November) is hot and humid, with thick swarms of mosquitoes. Thunderstorms are common and hurricanes may pass through the area. Hurricane season spans from June to November. Needless to say, you do not want to be camping when hurricane force winds rip through the Everglades. Very few visitors come to the park during the wet season. All three of South Florida's National Parks are best visited during winter.

Ernest F. Coe Visitor Center Entrance and Gulf Coast Entrance are open 24 hours per day. Shark Valley Entrance is open daily from 8:30am–6pm. Chekika Entrance is closed indefinitely due to insufficient resources.

Transportation & Airports
Transportation is not available to or around Everglades National Park.

Miami International Airport (MIA) is about 40 miles northeast of Ernest F. Coe Visitor Center. On the Gulf Coast, Southwest Florida International Airport (RSW), located in Fort Myers, is about 80 miles northwest of Everglades City. The smaller Naples Municipal Airport (APF) is just 35 miles northwest of Everglades City.

Directions
Everglades has five visitor centers and four park entrances that are frequented by motorists.

Main Entrance/Ernest F. Coe Visitor Center/Flamingo Visitor Center (from Miami): Take Florida Turnpike/Route 821 (Toll Road) south until it ends and merges with US-1 at Florida City. Turn right at the first traffic light. Follow the signs to the park.

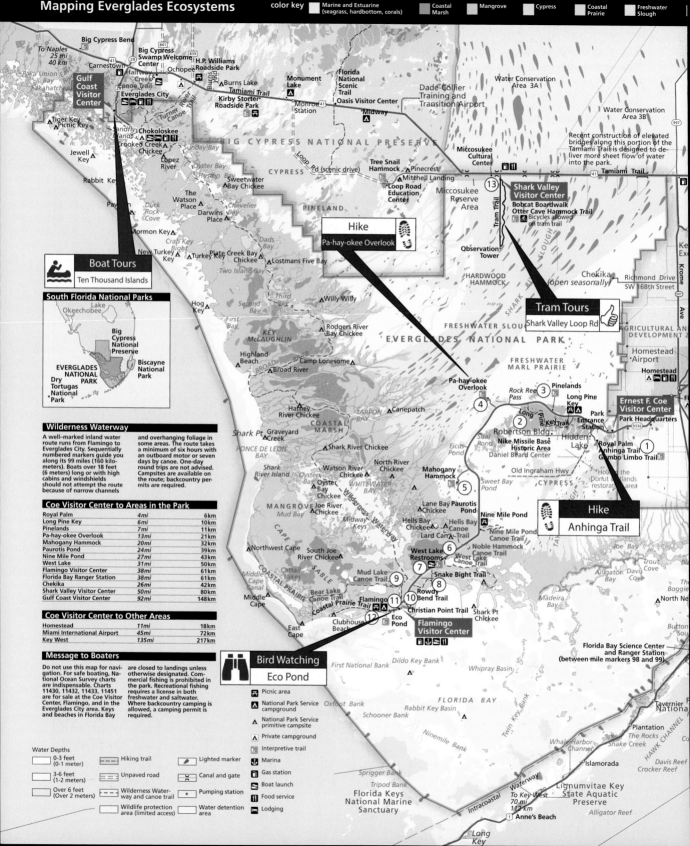

Freshwater Marl Prairie / Hardwood Hammock

Trailhead Location (see table on page 137)

North

0 1   5   10 Kilometers
0 1   5   10 Miles

If arriving from the Florida Keys, turn left on Palm Drive in Florida City and follow signs to the park.

Ernest F. Coe Visitor Center is on your right just before the park entrance station. Flamingo is another 38 miles southwest of the entrance station. Visitors should allow an hour to drive from the Main Entrance Station to Flamingo.

Shark Valley Visitor Center (from US-41/Tamiami Trail): US-41 crosses the Florida peninsula from east to west, providing access to Shark Valley and its visitor center. Follow US-41 (~40 miles from downtown Miami and 75 miles from Naples). Shark Valley Loop Road is south of US-41. The visitor center and Tram Tour departure point are a short distance from the highway.

Gulf Coast Visitor Center (from I-75): Gulf Coast Visitor Center is located on the very western edge of the park, 5 miles south of US-41 (Tamiami Trail). From I-75 (Toll Road), take exit 80 to merge onto FL-29 S. Follow FL-29 for 20 miles to Everglades City and follow signs to the park.

Regions
Everglades is an expansive wilderness, much of which is completely inaccessible to automobiles. There are four entrances dispersed along the park's perimeter. Main Entrance (located along the eastern boundary) and Shark Valley Entrance are the most popular entry points due to a variety of attractions and proximity to Miami. A short description of each region is provided below.

Main Entrance/Ernest F. Coe/Flamingo: The main entrance is your number one choice for hiking, biking, and paddling trails. Flamingo is situated at the end of Main Park Road, 38 miles southwest of the entrance. Flamingo marks the terminus of the 99-mile Wilderness Waterway. It's also a spot where boat tours and canoe and kayak rentals are offered. Both of the park's campgrounds, numerous hiking/biking/paddling trails, and three picnic areas are found between the Main Park Entrance and Flamingo.

Shark Valley: Shark Valley is popular for its 15-mile paved loop road. Visitors are no longer allowed to drive the loop, but you are encouraged to bike or walk as much as time and attitudes allow. The only vehicles permitted on the loop are open-sided trams (fee) that transport visitors to and from an observation tower at the loop's half-way point. This is arguably the best location to see vast sawgrass prairies that have become synonymous with the Everglades. Shark Valley also provides excellent opportunities for alligator viewing and bird watching. Nearby you'll find several non-park affiliated attractions, including air-boat tours and alligator farms (page 152).

Gulf Coast: This region is the gateway to Ten Thousand Islands and the northwestern end of the Wilderness Waterway. Boat tours and kayak rentals are available for those wishing to explore the maze of mangrove islands. There are no hiking trails. A visitor center provides backcountry permits, brochures, exhibits, and an introductory film.

The river of grass

People

"There are no other Everglades in the world. They are, they have always been, one of the unique regions of the earth; remote, never wholly known. Nothing anywhere else is like them." – Marjory Stoneman Douglas

In 1904, Napoleon Bonaparte Broward ran his campaign for governor of Florida on a platform of draining South Florida, to create "The Empire of the Everglades." Broward won, ordered drainage to commence, and faced staunch opposition. Frank Stoneman, publisher of the *Miami Herald*, was one of his most stalwart opponents. The governor took note and turned to childish pranks, refusing to validate an election for Circuit Court Judge won by Stoneman. In 1915, Frank's daughter, Marjory, moved to Florida, joining *The Herald* as a society columnist. By 1923 she had become a freelance writer and joined the Everglades Tropical National Park Committee. Later she would become the most powerful public voice supporting the Everglades.

Ernest F. Coe, a land developer turned conservationist, moved to South Florida in 1925 when he was 60 years old. He spent his next 25 years leading the Everglades Tropical National Park Committee, earning him the title of "father of the Everglades." He drew up plans for a park that included more than two million acres, including Key Largo and Big Cypress. Driven by Coe's passion and Senator Spessard Holland's politicking, a smaller park was finally authorized in 1934, with the stipulation that no federal funds be allocated for at least five years.

Thanks to Coe's tireless work procuring funds and the Florida legislature's commitment to raise $2 million to purchase private land, the park was formally established in December 1947. That same year, Marjory Stoneman Douglas published *The Everglades: River of Grass* after spending five years studying the land and water. Her

work helped convince public opinion of the Everglades' value as a treasured river rather than a worthless swamp. Douglas lived to be 108 years old and worked to restore the Everglades until the end. Today, many of the regions originally in Ernest F. Coe's vision of Everglades National Park have been protected. They include Big Cypress National Preserve, Biscayne National Park, John Pennekamp Coral Reef State Park, Ten Thousand Islands National Wildlife Reserve, and Florida Keys National Marine Sanctuary. Parks exist, but they still face many of the threats Douglas and Coe fought against.

Restoration

More than 50% of the original Everglades have already been destroyed by development and changes in water flow. Everglades National Park protects half of what remains, but without immediate intervention the entire area will soon dry up and become devoid of life. The region used to be one of the most uniquely balanced ecosystems in the world, where all forms of life adapted to the rise and fall of water flowing into the 'Glades from Lake Okeechobee and the Kissimmee River. The same year the park was established, Congress authorized creation of the Central and South Florida Flood Control Project. More than 1,000 miles of canals and flood control structures were built to divert excess water to the Gulf, the Atlantic, and Florida Bay. Once completed, the Everglades was completely cut-off from its natural water supplies. By the 1960s, the park was visibly suffering.

In response, the federal government (which had effectively starved the region of water for more than a decade) approved legislation set to improve the health of the Everglades. In 1989, President H. W. Bush signed the Everglades National Park Protection and Expansion Act. It closed the park to air boats, directed the Department of the Army to restore water to the area, and put an additional 100,000 acres of land under park control. The Comprehensive Everglades Restoration Plan was passed in 2000. It promised $10.5 billion to restore, preserve, and protect the Everglades, but none of the assigned projects have been completed. Clearly, there's more to be done. Please, donate your time and/or money to help restore the park, or write a letter to your representatives. We must act now, before it's too late and there's nothing left to save.

Camping

Long Pine Key Campground ($20/night) is located seven miles from the main entrance. It's open seasonally from November until May. The camp has 108 sites for tents and RVs and one group site. Restrooms, **showers**, water, grills, picnic tables, and a dump station are available. There's a small pond for fishing, an amphitheater, and several hiking trails in the area. Hookups are not available. All sites (except the group site) are first-come, first-served basis.

Flamingo Campground ($20/night, $30/night with electric hookups) is located at the end of Main Park Road. It has 234 drive-in sites (55 with a view of the water, 41 with electric hookups). Restrooms, cold water **showers**, grills, picnic tables, dump stations, and an amphitheater are available. Full hookups are not. Hiking, paddling, and salt water fishing are popular activities. Reservations are accepted from mid-November through mid-April at recreation.gov or (877) 444-6777. During this time half the sites are available on a first-come, first-served basis.

Backcountry camping is available at several designated sites throughout the park. A permit is required and must be obtained in person at the main entrance station (for Ernest Coe and Old Ingraham sites) and Flamingo or Gulf Coast Visitor Centers (for all other sites). Permits cost $15 plus $2 per person per night from mid-November through mid-April and are free (but still required) for the rest of the year.

Paddling

The essence of the Everglades is found among its grassy waterways. To get there you must paddle. Day-trips or multi-day adventures? You'll find some of the best in the world. Whitewater? Look somewhere else. There's little to no current; it's all paddling here. These creeks and rivers flow into Florida Bay at the blistering speed of 0.25-mile per day. At that rate, it would take more than a year to float the 99-mile Wilderness Waterway. Low water levels can impede your paddling goals. If you plan on departing between late February and March, discuss your itinerary with a park ranger to assure your desired route is completely navigable. Also be prepared for strong winds and tides.

Flamingo has the most paddling variety. **Nine Mile Pond** is a great place to spot birds and alligators. Access to the 5.2-mile trail is just off Main Park Road at Nine Mile Pond Picnic/Parking Area. A little further south is **Noble Hammock Canoe Trail**. This 2-mile loop requires good maneuvering skills (or a small kayak) to navigate a maze of mangrove-lined creeks and ponds. Opposite this launch site is **Hells Bay Canoe Trail** (5.5 miles, one-way), another extremely narrow trail through dense mangroves. Hells Bay is an excellent location to test yourself for the Wilderness Waterway. One campsite and two chickees (permit required) are found along the way. Anyone looking down on this trail from above would wonder how this maze of mangroves is navigated. It's actually quite easy thanks to more than 160 poles marking the way. Continuing along Main Park Road is **West Lake Trail** (7.7 miles, one-way), which leads to Alligator Creek backcountry campsite. Next up is **Mud Lake Loop**, a 7-mile trail with excellent birding opportunities (requires a short portage between Bear Lake and Buttonwood Canal). You can also venture out into **Florida Bay** for more wide open paddling. **Kayak and canoe rentals** are available at Flamingo and Gulf Coast Visitor Centers. Shurr Adventure Kayaking (877.455.2925, shurradventures.net) in Everglades City offers **guided paddle trips**.

Wilderness Waterway

The Wilderness Waterway is a 99-mile trail connecting Flamingo and Everglades City. The best time to paddle is between December and April. It takes at least eight days to complete. Do not consider this to be the sort of adventure that you can complete on a whim. You must plan ahead. There are many routes and dozens of campsites along the way. The park's website provides a trip planning guide to make sure you are properly prepared. Park rangers at Flamingo and Gulf Coast Visitor Centers are also happy to help plan your trip. Backcountry permits are required and must be obtained in person at Flamingo or Gulf Coast Visitor Centers. Permits cost $15 plus $2 per night per person. They are only available up to one day prior to your departure date. You'll be in the backcountry, but solitude can still be difficult to find. Remember that motorboats are allowed in most wilderness areas, and some campsites have capacity for as many as 60 campers.

Anhinga Trail

Best of Everglades

Hike: Anhinga Trail
Runner-up: Bobcat Boardwalk

Ranger Program: Slough Slog
Runner-up: Anhinga Amble

Paddle: Ten Thousand Islands Area
Runner-up: Whitewater Bay

Bird Watching: Eco Pond
Runner-up: Christian Point Loop

Hiking

The best way to explore the park may be by boat, but that doesn't mean great hiking trails don't exist in the Everglades. Most trailheads are found along Main Park Road between Ernest Coe Visitor Center and Flamingo. **Anhinga Trail** is an absolute must hike. It's a short and easy stroll that begins at Royal Palm Visitor Center and immediately immerses hikers into the park's amazingly unique biodiversity. It's highly likely you'll see alligators along this 0.8-mile loop.

If toothy, prehistoric-looking creatures aren't your cup of tea, try **Mahogany Hammock Trail**. It's a 0.5-mile boardwalk located 20 miles from the Main Park Entrance. Trees are the main attraction here, including the largest living mahogany tree in the United States. **West Lake Trail** (31 miles from the Main Park Entrance) is a short boardwalk through mangroves. Visitors will also find good hiking opportunities at Long Pine Key and Flamingo Campgrounds. Hiking is more enjoyable if you see a little wildlife (at a safe distance), so always discuss your intentions with a park ranger to learn the best hiking locations to see animals during your visit. A more complete list of the park's hiking trails is provided on the following page.

Biking

If you're looking for grueling mountain climbs, this isn't the place for you. The park's maximum elevation is 8 feet above sea level, and no, that is not a typo. What you will find are flat paved roads and a handful of dirt hiking trails that allow bicycles. The 15-mile **Shark Valley Loop** is the most popular biking destination. Taking a bike to the 45-foot observation tower is a great alternative to the tram tour. **Bike rental** is available at Shark Valley Tram Tours (350.221.8455, sharkvalleytramtours.com) for $9/hour.

Snake Bight, **Rowdy Bend**, **Bear Lake**, and **Guy Bradley Trails**, near Flamingo, permit bicycles. **Long Pine Key** and **Old Ingraham Highway** are two trails near Long Pine Key Campground where bikes are permitted. Use caution when biking on trails to avoid hikers who share these paths.

Main Park Road is a longer option for early-risers. During peak-season, traffic begins to pick up around 10am and die down around 5pm.

Boat Tours

Boat tours are available courtesy of concessioners at **Flamingo** (239.695.3101, evergladesnationalparkboattoursflamingo.com) and **Gulf Coast** (239.695.2591, evergladesnationalparkboattoursgulfcoast.com), located within the area's respective visitor center. Flamingo's tour leads guests through the Buttonwood Canal where they explore **Whitewater Bay** backcountry. Stop in at Flamingo Marina to purchase tickets or make reservations. On the opposite end of the park visitors can enjoy a tour of **Ten Thousand Islands**. While sailing the seas, you may see all sorts of wildlife, including bottle-nosed dolphins, manatees, ospreys, and pelicans. As you pass the sea of islands (far fewer than 10,000) imagine a time when Calusa Indians paddled from island to island and fished these waterways. It has been hundreds of years since they inhabited the area, but archaeological evidence remains to this day, including mountains of shells left on small tree islands. **Boat and bike rentals** are also available at both locations.

Everglades Hiking Trails (Distances are roundtrip unless noted otherwise)

	Name	Location (# on map)	Length	Difficulty Rating & Notes
Long Pine Key	Anhinga - 🐾	Royal Palm Visitor Center (1)	0.8 mile	E – If you only hike one trail in the park, this is the one • Great opportunities to spot wildlife • Ranger-led hikes available per schedule
	Gumbo-Limbo - 🐾	Royal Palm Visitor Center (1)	0.4 mile	E – Self-guiding trail leading to a hardwood hammock in the middle of a sea of sawgrass
	Old Ingraham Highway	Royal Palm Visitor Center (1)	11.0 miles (one-way)	S– Provides access to two backcountry campsites • Bikes allowed
	Long Pine Key	Begins west of Long Pine Key Camp/Ends at Pine Glades Lake along Main Park Road (2)	7.0 miles (one-way)	M – Running parallel to Main Park Road you travel from the campground to Pine Glades Lake • Bikes allowed
	Pineland	About 7 miles from the Main Park Entrance (3)	0.5 mile	E – A short loop through a forest of pines, palmettos, and wildflowers
	Pa-hay-okee Overlook - 🐾	About 13 miles from the Main Park Entrance (4)	0.25 mile	E – A great hike to a bird's eye view of the vast "river of grass"
	Mahogany Hammock - 🐾	About 20 miles from the Main Park Entrance (5)	0.5 mile	E – A short self-guiding trail leading to Mahogany Hammock where the largest living mahogany tree in the U.S. resides
Flamingo	West Lake - 🐾	About 7 miles north of Flamingo on Main Park Road (6)	0.5 mile	E – Self-guiding boardwalk trail passing through mangroves to the edge of West Lake
	Snake Bight	About 4 miles north of Flamingo on Main Park Road (7)	1.8 miles (one-way)	E –Tropical hardwood hammock, another excellent birding location • Bikes allowed
	Rowdy Bend	About 3 miles north of Flamingo on Main Park Road (8)	2.6 miles (one-way)	E – Connects Snake Bight Trail • Bikes allowed
	Bear Lake	About 2 miles north of Flamingo on Main Park Road (9)	1.6 miles (one-way)	E –Trail ends at Bear Lake after meandering through a hardwood hammock mixed with a variety of mangroves
	Christian Point	About 1 mile north of Flamingo on Main Park Road (10)	1.6 miles (one-way)	E – Excellent location for bird watching
	Eco Pond	Flamingo (11)	0.5 mile	E – A small fresh water pond often frequented by wading birds, song birds, and alligators
	Guy Bradley	Flamingo (11)	1.0 mile (one-way)	E – Connects the visitor center and the amphitheater along the shore of Florida Bay
	Bayshore Loop	Flamingo (11)	2.0 miles	E –Trail along Florida Bay providing good opportunities for spotting butterflies and birds
	Coastal Prairie	At the back of Flamingo Campground's Loop C (12)	6.0 miles (one-way)	E – An old settlement road leading to Clubhouse Beach and a backcountry campsite
Shark Valley	Bobcat Boardwalk	Behind Shark Valley Visitor Center (13)	0.3 mile	E – Short, self-guiding trail passes through a sawgrass slough and hardwood forest
	Otter Cave Hammock	Behind Shark Valley Visitor Center (13)	1.0 mile	E – Limestone trail passes through a tropical hardwood forest • Often flooded in summer
	Tram Road - 🐾	Shark Loop Road (13)	15.0 miles	M – Paved road leads to a 45-foot-tall observation tower • May spot alligators, egrets, and snail kites • Bikes allowed

Difficulty Ratings: E = Easy, M = Moderate, S = Strenuous

Ranger tour along Long Pine Key Nature Trail

An osprey near Flamingo

Fishing

More than one-third of the park is covered by navigable water, creating ample fishing opportunities. Whether it's fresh or salt water you're fishing in, a Florida State Fishing License is required for anyone 16 and older. A few of the fish that are frequently caught within the park include: snapper, sea trout, bass, and bluegill. It is possible to fish from the shoreline, but good locations are extremely limited. There are countless fishing spots for those with a boat. Before heading out on the water, be sure to know the state fishing regulations and catch limits. No boat? No problem. A number of fishing guides provide service from Everglades City for guests looking to spend a few hours out on the water. A few fishing charters are listed on page 152.

Ranger Programs

Most programs begin at one of the park's visitor centers. Guests are able to enjoy a variety of programs from canoe trips to starlight walks at Ernest F. Coe and Flamingo Visitor Centers. Gulf Coast Visitor Center offers canoe trips, walks, and talks. Guests are invited to join an "Anhinga Amble" or "Glades Glimpses," which depart from the Royal Palm benches (three miles from the main entrance). Shark Bites Program offers hands on learning at Shark Valley. Note that you'll need to

bring your own watercraft or rent one for ranger-led canoe trips. A current schedule of ranger programs can be found at the park website. You can also call or stop in at a visitor center.

Ernest F. Coe Visitor Center (305.242.7700) and **Flamingo Visitor Center** (239.695.2945) are accessed via the main entrance near Homestead and are open from 8am–5pm and 8am–4:30pm, respectively during peak tourism season (mid-November through mid-April). **Shark Valley Visitor Center** (305.221.8776) is open daily from 8:30am–5pm. **Gulf Coast Visitor Center** (239.695.3311) is open from 8am–4:30pm. All visitor centers hold slightly shorter hours during the off-season.

For Kids

Kids get a kick out of seeing alligators. The best chance to see these reptilian friends is at Shark Valley Loop Road, Anhinga Trail, or outside the park along Tamiami Trail (US-41). Children ages 12 and older will love the ranger-led Slough Slog. Slough sloggers must bring water, sturdy close-toed, lace up shoes, and long pants. The program is limited to 15 participants. To sign up or receive additional information, visit Ernest F. Coe Visitor Center or call (305) 242-7700.

Children are encouraged to participate in the **Junior Ranger Program**. Junior Ranger booklets are available at the park website or visitor centers. Complete the activities for Everglades National Park to earn a park badge. The program is jointly administered by Big Cypress National Preserve, Biscayne National Park, and Everglades National Park. Completing the entire book will earn you a South Florida National Parks Junior Ranger Patch.

Flora & Fauna

Visitors constantly pass from one ecosystem to the next while exploring the Everglades. Each has its own unique plant and animal life. (See the map on page 132 for a pictorial view of the park's ecosystems.) A multitude of trees, lichens, ferns, fungi, and wildflowers combine to total more than 1,000 species of documented plants. Sawgrass marshes cover the heart of the park. These marshes are the largest of their kind in the world and the reason it is known as "the river of grass." The region is uncommonly flat, yet "high" ground plays an important role in its biodiversity. Slash pines and palmetto trees occupy the elevated regions, while other trees have adapted to grow in marshy areas. Hardwood hammocks of mahogany, gumbo-limbo, and cocoa palm trees are able to grow within the marsh in places where limestone is situated slightly above sea level. Trees capable of surviving in standing water are also found here. Cypress trees manage to live in fresh water, while mangroves have become resilient to the extreme and salty conditions along the coast.

The Everglades is the most important breeding ground for tropical wading birds in North America. Sixteen species inhabit the park. Most common is the white ibis, but you may also encounter wood storks, great blue herons, green-backed herons, and roseate spoonbills. Birds of prey, such as ospreys, short-tailed hawks, bald eagles, red-tailed hawks and snail kites also soar high above the "river of grass." In all more than 350 species of birds have been identified within the park, making it a favorite destination among the bird-watching community.

For others, it's alligators that steal the show. Alligators only reside in the park's fresh water. Anhinga Trail and Shark Valley are two of the best locations to spot a gator. The lower the water level, the farther north you have to go to find these freshwater reptiles. Others aren't welcome, like the invasive Burmese python, which has decimated the small animal population in recent years.

There are more than 50 other species of reptiles inhabiting the park, including the endangered or threatened American crocodile, green sea turtle, and eastern indigo. With so many flying and swimming attractions, the park's 40 species of mammals often go unnoticed. The Florida panther is rarely seen because of its stealthy travel and diminished numbers (maybe 10 left in the park) due to habitat loss. Other popular mammals include white-tailed deer, river otter, cottontail, and manatee.

A world of life exists beneath the water's surface. Nearly 300 species of fresh and salt water fish swim in the park's waters. You won't find any sweeping mountain panoramas here, but you'll definitely find some of the world's most diverse and interesting wildlife.

Pets

Pets must be kept on a leash no more than six feet in length at all times and are only permitted on public roadways, roadside campgrounds and picnic areas, maintained grounds surrounding public facilities and residential areas, and aboard boats.

Accessibility

All five visitor centers are accessible to individuals in wheelchairs. Several hiking trails have a paved or boardwalk surface allowing wheelchair accessibility. They include: Anhinga Trail, Gumbo Limbo Trail, Pineland Trail, Pa-hay-okee Overlook, Mahogany Hammock Trail, West Lake Trail, and Bobcat Hammock. Long Pine Key and Flamingo Campgrounds have accessible campsites, restrooms, and parking. Only one backcountry campsite is accessible to individuals with mobility impairments, Pearl Bay Chickees, located about four hours (by canoe) from Main Park Road. The site features handrails, a canoe dock, and an accessible chemical toilet. Many of the ranger-led programs are fully accessible. Check the park website or newspaper for details. Boat and Shark Valley Tram Tours (350.221.8455, sharkvalleytramtours.com) are accessible.

Weather

The Everglades enjoy the same subtropical climate as the rest of southern Florida. Summers are hot and humid with frequent thunderstorms. Hurricane season stretches from June to November. Thunderstorms and hurricanes are bad news, but mosquitoes are a constant nuisance in summer when they reign over the park. If you plan on traveling to the Everglades between May and November pack plenty of bug spray. Most visitors choose to visit between December and April, when temperatures are comfortable and regular winds keep the bugs at bay. This time frame also features the widest variety of attractions and longest hours of operation.

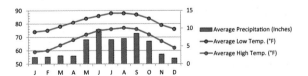

Immature white ibis along Anhinga Trail

Gator viewing from Shark Valley's observation tower

Vacation Planner

Everglades National Park has three main regions (page 133): Main Entrance to Flamingo, Shark Valley, and Gulf Coast. It's conceivable that you could visit all three in a single day, but to do so would require an awful lot of driving (300+ miles beginning and ending in Miami). It's better to take your time, enjoy the sites, and enjoy a region one day at a time. Feel free to treat each day as an individual trip, since none of the regions are connected by roadways. Lodging and dining facilities are not available inside the park. Nearby dining, grocery stores, lodging, festivals, and attractions are listed on pages 149–153.

Day 1: A trip to the Everglades should begin at **Ernest F. Coe Visitor Center**. Quickly introduce yourself to the park by browsing exhibits and watching a short film. Don't forget to check the schedule of ranger-led activities. You may even want to make advance reservations (305.242.7700) for a **Slough Slog**, which is exceptional. If not, don't worry, as all the ranger programs are enjoyable. Note the time and location of any interesting programs, and head into the park.

Immediately stop at Royal Palm to hike **Anhinga Trail**. It's the best hiking trail. Take your time searching for wildlife before returning to your car and Main Park Road. If you plan on camping at Long Pine Key, now is the time to secure a site. You don't have to set up camp right away, but at least register and leave something of little value in your site. If you packed a cooler and are planning an extended hike/bike/paddle, you may want to set up camp right away since there's a good chance you won't return until evening. Continue southwest on the park road. **Pa-hay-okee** is worth a stop, especially if you don't plan on visiting Shark Valley (Day 2). Next is Mahogany Hammock. If you like trees, pull over and have a look. Return to your car and drive to **Flamingo**. This stretch of road (and Flamingo) is home to some of the park's best hiking, biking, and paddling. You won't have time to do them all, but **West Lake Trail** is recommended for hiking, **Hell's Bay Trail** for paddling, and **Snake Bight/Rowdy Bend Trail** for biking. You'll also find a nice campground at Flamingo.

Day 2: If you spent the night in Flamingo, wake up early to watch for wildlife. **Eco and Mrazek Ponds** are good locations to watch for birds. If you camped at Long Pine Key, you've got another opportunity to catch one of the rangers' **Glades Glimpses**, **Anhinga Ambles**, or **Slough Slogs**. You have plenty of time to spare, because today you're just heading to Shark Valley. While driving, decide whether you want to take bicycles (available for rent at Shark Valley) or the **Tram Tour** along 15-mile Shark Valley Loop Road to an observation deck. The Tram Tour (305.221.8455, sharkvalleytramtours.com) takes 2 hours and costs $24/person. Biking at a casual pace requires a similar amount of time. You may want to allow even more time, because you'll be mesmerized by the amount of wildlife you'll see along the way. Exploring Shark Valley is at the top of the list when it comes to "must-do" activities at Everglades.

Day 3: Complete your adventure by traveling to **Gulf Coast Visitor Center** at the park's western edge. This area is popular as a terminus for the 99-mile **Wilderness Waterway**, **boat tours**, and **paddling**. If you aren't interested in any of these things, you may want to skip this region altogether, or head further up the coast to **Marco Island** to sit on the beach.

Nine Mile Pond

Pelicans will greet you at Garden Key

YANKEE FREEDOM III
KEY WEST, FLORIDA

Dry Tortugas

Dry Tortugas Park Headquarters is
at Everglades National Park
40001 State Road 9336
Homestead, FL 33034
Phone: (305) 242-7700
Write the Park at:
PO Box 6208; Key West, FL 33041
Website: nps.gov/drto

Established: October 26, 1992
January 4, 1935 (Nat'l Monument)
Size: 64,700 Acres
Annual Visitors: 70,000
Peak Season: April–May

Activities: Snorkeling, SCUBA,
Bird Watching, Paddling, Fishing

Campgrounds: There are 10
primitive campsites on Garden Key
Camping Fee: $15/night
Overflow camping and one group
site are also available.
Lodging: None

Park Hours: All Year
Entrance Fee: $10/person (16 &
older)

The collection of United States national parks is best defined by its awe-inspiring vistas, gaping canyons, rugged mountains, and spouting geysers. Natural wonders whose images proved America was as beautiful as it was prosperous. Among this collection hides an aberration of sorts. Just 70 miles southwest of Key West is a park centered on a military fort. Fort Jefferson is a man-made military relic, whose massive brick structure serves as centerpiece of the Dry Tortugas. Many visitors are attracted to the area's military past, but there's also a unique world of natural wonders to be enjoyed above and below the sea. Seven low-lying keys and their surrounding waters provide sanctuary for an array of bird and marine life. Beneath the water is a snorkeler's playground filled with colorful corals, corroding shipwrecks, and casual sea turtles.

Now endangered, the region's once dense population of sea turtles provided inspiration for the archipelago's name. In 1513, Juan Ponce de León claimed to have caught some 160 turtles in the waters surrounding the islands, declaring them "las Tortugas (The Turtles)." Years later the word "Dry" was added to warn mariners of the island's lack of fresh water. As American prosperity increased, the 75-mile wide strait between the Gulf of Mexico and Atlantic Ocean became a busy shipping route as massive amounts of cotton, meat, livestock, coffee, tobacco, and other merchandise were shipped from the Gulf Coast. Something was needed to suppress piracy and protect the trade route.

Fort Jefferson was the solution. Construction began in 1847, and after 16 million bricks and 30 years of intermittent work, the fortress remained unfinished. Even in its incomplete state it was the most sophisticated coastal fortress from Maine to California and the largest masonry structure in the western hemisphere. Its design called for 420 heavy-guns and 2,000 soldiers. The fort served as a prison for deserters of the Union Army during the Civil War. In 1888, the Army turned the fortress over to the Marine Hospital Service to be used as a quarantine station. In 1908, President Theodore Roosevelt observed the area's importance as a refuge for birds and created Tortugas Keys Reservation.

Nearly a quarter of a century later, the area's recreational usefulness was recognized when President Franklin D. Roosevelt established Fort Jefferson National Monument in 1935, and in 1992 it was designated as a national park. Fort Jefferson, although in need of maintenance, is still standing guard over the gulf. Life is teeming beneath the sea. Thousands of migratory birds flock to the islands, including about 100,000 sooty terns that nest here between February and September. In fact, more sooty terns visit the park each year than tourists, making Dry Tortugas an excellent choice for a relaxing vacation in a tropical paradise with a military past.

Fort Jefferson
In the early 19th century, the U.S. was in search of an ideal location for a fort to protect the profitable Gulf Coast–Atlantic Ocean trade route. Dry Tortugas was just the place, but when U.S. Navy Commodore David Porter visited these remote keys in 1825, he declared them completely unsuitable. He called the islands specks of land without a trace of fresh water among a sea of blue, and probably not even stable enough to build the fort they desired.

Four years later, Commodore John Rodgers revisited the Dry Tortugas. He believed it to be the perfect location. In 1847, after 17 years of engineering studies and bureaucratic delays construction of Fort Jefferson began. The fort, named for the third president, was to be the scourge of the seas, equipped with 420 heavy-guns and a fleet of warships capable of running down ships wise enough to remain beyond firing range. It took a huge workforce to build such an immense structure, including blacksmiths, machinists, carpenters, and masons. Even the resident prisoners and slaves helped build the behemoth. By 1860, more than $250,000 (~$10 million today) had been spent on a fort that wasn't half completed. During the Civil War an influx of prisoners,

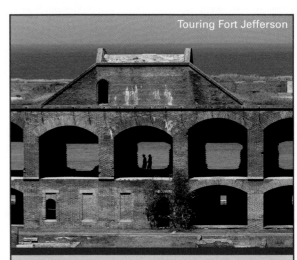
Touring Fort Jefferson

When to Go
The park is open all year. April and May are considered the best months to visit due to calm seas, few thunderstorms, and comfortable temperatures. Fort Jefferson and Loggerhead Key are open daily from dawn until dusk. Bush Key is closed seasonally from mid-January through mid-October during the sooty tern nesting season. East Key, Middle Key, Hospital Key, and Long Key are closed for nesting wildlife. **Florida Keys Eco Discovery Center** is open Tuesday through Saturday from 9am–4pm. Garden Key Visitor Center is open daily from 8:30am–4:30pm.

Directions & Transportation
The park is 70 miles southwest of Key West. It can only be reached by sea plane or boat. Dry Tortugas National Park Ferry (800.634.0939, drytortugas.com) provides water transportation and Key West Seaplane Adventures (305.293.9300, keywestseaplanecharters.com) provides air transportation.

Dry Tortugas National Park Ferry • (800) 634-0939 Key West Ferry Terminal, 100 Grinnell St drytortugas.com • Rates: $175 (adult)/$125 (child 4–16) (Includes Park Entrance)

Key West Seaplane Adventures • (305) 293-9300 3471 South Roosevelt Blvd; Key West, FL 33040 keywestseaplanecharters.com • Adults: $317 (half-day)/$555 (full-day), Children (3–12): $253/$444

TORTUGAS ECOLOGICAL RESERVE
TORTUGAS NORTH

Y "I"
Fl Y 4s
24°43′32″N
82°52′00″W

W "A"
24°43′32″N
82°51′00″W   Y "J"

Y "H"
Fl Y 2.5s
24°43′00″N
82°54′00″W

NORTHWEST CHANNEL

Y "G"

PARK BOUNDARY

RESEARCH NATURAL AREA BOUNDARY

Y "F"

Texas Rock

Northkey Harb

DRY TORTUGAS NATIONAL P

Brilliant

Y "E"
Fl Y 6s
24°39′00″N
82°58′00″W

Middle Key
(closed to public)

Ea
(cl

"7"

Middle
Ground

Hospital Key
(closed to public)

"4"

Loggerhead Key
Fl W 20s 167ft 24M

White Shoal

Windjammer wreck

Loggerhead Reef

"3"   "4"

Fort Jefferson
on Garden Key
(see inset below right)

R "2"
Fl R 4s

DRY
TORTUGAS

SOUTHEAST CHANNEL

G "1"

Research Natural Area Boundary

Y "D"

RESEARCH NATURAL AREA BOUNDARY

W "C"
24°36′00″N
82°58′00″W

W "B"
24°36′00″N
82°51′00″W   Y "P"

"1"

SOUTHWEST

"6"

Fe
on

"2"

PARK BOUNDARY

Y "Q"

"2BK"

FLORIDA KEYS
NATIONAL MARINE
SANCTUARY

"3BK"   "4

Brick wreck   Bird K
GOOD   Bird
SNORKELING   ancho

24°34′00″N
82°58′00″W
Y "C"
Fl Y 4s

Y "B"   Y "A"
Fl Y 2.5s
24°34′00″N
82°54′00″W

This map is an orientation aid for
visitors to Dry Tortugas National Park.
It should not be used in place of
National Ocean Survey chart 11438,
which is indispensable for safe
boating on these waters.

Bird Key
Bank

Symbol	Description	Symbol	Description	Symbol	Description	Buoy characteristics	Light characteristics
▲	Red daymark	▫	White daymark	⌀	Buoy	⌀ Light	⊕ Sunken wreck	R Red	Fl Flashing

Red daymark   White daymark   Buoy   Light   Sunken wreck   Buoy characteristics   Light characteristics
Green daymark   Daybeacon   Lighted buoy   Lighthouse   Rock
R Red   Fl Flashing
G Green   W White
Y Yellow   R Red
s Period (in seconds)   Y Yellow
s Period (in seconds)

mostly Union deserters, caused the fort's population to peak at more than 1,500, and new prisoners were immediately put to work.

In 1865, the fort welcomed its most famous prisoner, Dr. Samuel Mudd, who was convicted of conspiracy in the assassination of President Abraham Lincoln. It is believed he set, splinted, and bandaged John Wilkes Booth's broken leg shortly after Booth shot the President at Ford's Theater. Not long after his arrival, the prison's doctor died during an outbreak of yellow fever. Mudd temporarily took over the position. Soldiers, feeling indebted to Mudd, petitioned the president on his behalf, and four years after he arrived, Mudd was pardoned by President Andrew Johnson.

By 1888, the usefulness of Fort Jefferson was waning and damage caused by the corrosive tropical environment and frequent hurricanes created high maintenance costs. The Army decided to turn the fort over to the Marine Hospital Service. They used it as a quarantine station up until the 1930s when it was officially handed over to the National Park Service, which possesses it today. The fort was never completed and never fired upon, but this long-since obsolete maritime base is an interesting piece of American military history set in a tropical paradise.

Camping

There are 10 primitive campsites on **Garden Key**. Sites are available on a first-come, first-served basis for $15 per night, payable at a self-service pay station (but the ferry only brings over a limited number of campers, so make reservations early with them). If the primitive sites are full, an overflow camping area is available. One group site is available for groups of 10–40 campers by reservation (call 305.242.7700). Campers must bring all food and water required for the duration of their stay. Composting toilets are available in the campground. Wood fires are prohibited.

Hiking

Besides underwater, the only real place to explore Dry Tortugas is **Fort Jefferson** itself. Here you'll find a self-guided tour that takes visitors through the history of the 50-foot tall, three-story, heavily armored fort. Visitors can also walk along the park's 0.6-mile-long seawall and moat, where you may be able to spot various sea creatures.

Paddling

Paddling allows observant visitors to keep an eye on what's happening above and below the water. Crystal clear waters provide a window to life beneath the sea. When you aren't watching the creatures stirring below your boat, look along the horizon for migratory birds. **Bush and Long Keys** are the closest islands to Fort Jefferson and where you are most likely to find nesting birds. **Loggerhead**, the largest key of the Dry Tortugas, is three miles away. It's perfect for swimming and snorkeling and never busy, since visitation is limited to daylight hours. To get to Loggerhead Key you must pass deep open water with a swift current. (Inexperienced paddlers should not head out into open water.) No matter where you paddle, a **boating permit** is required. If you plan on paddling to Loggerhead Key, it must be listed on your permit. Permits are free and may be obtained on arrival from a park staff member. **Shark and Coral Special Protection Zones** are closed to paddling. You should ask where these areas are in order to avoid them. Ferries will transport your kayak(s) to Dry Tortugas, but they have limited space. It is a good idea to confirm space requirements prior to arrival.

SCUBA Diving

Dry Tortugas National Park is located at the far western end of the Florida Keys. These islands are not tethered to the mainland by roads and bridges, so SCUBA divers must arrive by private boat or charter.

Beneath the water divers will find the **Caribbean's largest and healthiest reef system**. One of the highlights is **Sherwood Forest**, featuring a canopy of mushroom-shaped formations. More than 400 species of fish reside here; of them, hammerhead sharks, barracuda, and Goliath grouper are frequently seen. Dolphins and turtles are also common to the area. Sea Clusive (305.744.9928, seaclusive.com), Spree Expeditions (281.970.0534, researchvesselspree.com), and Getaway Adventures (239.466.0466, ultimategetaway.net) are permitted to conduct dives within the park.

Snorkeling

More than 99% of the park is water, so you really have to get in or under the water to experience it. Dry Tortugas just might be the best snorkeling the Florida Keys have to offer. The water is clean, clear, and warm. A boat or seaplane trip is required to reach them, but once you're there, the reef is yours to explore whenever you want. A designated snorkel area is available on **Garden Key**, southwest of Fort Jefferson along its outer wall. You can walk right into the water from the designated swimming area. The area features chest-deep water, turtle grass, and coral. Coral reefs make up a very small fraction of the underwater environment, but they provide habitat for more than 25% of the area's fish population. *Yankee Freedom* has snorkel sets for their passengers, but one opinionated snorkeler said several masks didn't seal well, so you may want to bring your own snorkel gear (or at least the mask).

Fishing

Due to excessive commercial fishing new regulations prohibit fishing in about half of the park's waters. The ban was required to help repopulate a once thriving fish community. Good fishing is still possible in and around Dry Tortugas, and the scenery and climate is a serious bonus. Calm water makes spring and summer the preferred seasons for fishing. Grouper and snapper are commonly caught. Fishing excursions are available from several Key West area charters, which are conveniently listed on page 152.

Boat Tours

Yankee Freedom (800.634.0939, drytortugas. com) provides boat service to Dry Tortugas National Park from Key West Ferry Terminal on Grinnell Street. Tickets cost $175 per adult and $125 per child (ages 4–16). The park fee is included in these prices, so if you have a National Parks Pass, present it at the ticket booth for a refund. The trip takes approximately 2.5 hours each way and check-in begins at 7am for 8am departure. Breakfast and lunch are served aboard the boat. They have limited space available to transport personal kayaks. Snorkel gear is provided. Knowledgeable guides provide tours of Fort Jefferson. Snorkelers and swimmers will be able to rinse off with freshwater on board the boat. Complimentary soft drinks, water, and tea are available throughout the day.

Bird Watching

Nearly 300 bird species have been identified within park boundaries. Most notable are tropical and migratory species that delight bird watchers when they pit-stop in the Dry Tortugas. Only 7 species nest here regularly; most commonly seen are brown and black noddies, magnificent frigatebirds, and masked and brown boobies. Spring is prime time for bird watching. Between May and September 100,000 sooty terns nest on Bush Key. Bush Key is visible from Garden Key and Fort Jefferson, but don't leave your binoculars at home.

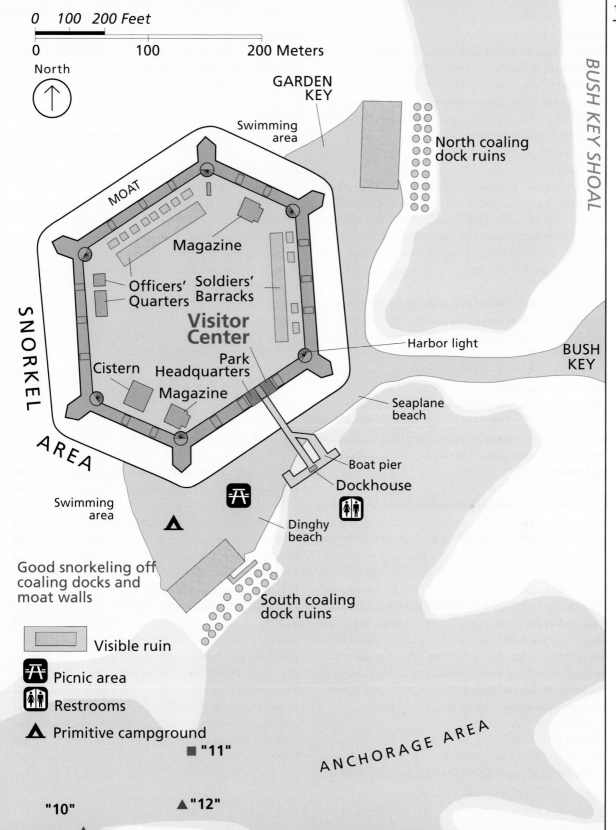

0 100 200 Feet

0 100 200 Meters

North

BUSH KEY SHOAL

GARDEN KEY

Swimming area

North coaling dock ruins

MOAT

Magazine

Officers' Quarters

Soldiers' Barracks

Visitor Center

Harbor light

BUSH KEY

Cistern

Park Headquarters

Seaplane beach

Magazine

SNORKEL AREA

Swimming area

Boat pier

Dockhouse

Dinghy beach

Good snorkeling off coaling docks and moat walls

South coaling dock ruins

Visible ruin

Picnic area

Restrooms

Primitive campground

■ "11"

ANCHORAGE AREA

"10"

▲ "12"

▲

Ranger Programs

Check online or with a park ranger upon arrival to see what ranger-led activities are taking place the day you visit. Several rangers live on the island, and they provide intermittent tours. Guests who reach the island via the *Yankee Freedom* (page 146) typically receive a 45-minute guided tour of the fort.

For Kids

Dry Tortugas is a great park for kids. Children of all ages love the water, the beach, the wildlife, and they might even love Fort Jefferson. If the fort's history isn't holding their attention, they will at least have fun climbing the spiral staircases, gazing into the moat, and pretending to fire 19th century cannons.

Children can also become **Junior Rangers**. A free workbook is available online, at the visitor center, or aboard the *Yankee Freedom*. Complete it to earn a park badge. The program is recommended for children ages 8–13.

Flora & Fauna

The park's vegetation is fairly limited. You'll find a variety of palms and succulents, but several islands are nothing more than sand, almost completely devoid of life. Sea grasses and other marine plant life can be found underwater.

Nearly 300 species of birds have been identified in the park, but only 7 species nest here regularly. The park protects the most active turtle nesting site in the Florida Keys. Hawksbill, loggerhead, and green sea turtles are commonly seen swimming in the park's waters. Each year female sea turtles climb onto sandy beaches of Middle and East Keys to lay their eggs before retreating back to the sea. You'll also find an amazing variety of coral, fish, and other marine life underwater. Sea fans, anemones, lobster, and sponges are often found on the sea floor. Coral reef inhabitants may include numerous colorful reef fish and their predators: amberjacks, groupers, wahoos, tarpon, sharks, and barracudas.

Pets

Pets are permitted on Garden Key but are not allowed inside Fort Jefferson. They must be kept on a leash no more than six feet in length.

Accessibility

The dock, campground, visitor center, bottom level of Fort Jefferson, and tour boats are accessible to individuals in wheelchairs.

Weather

Dry Tortugas National Park experiences three seasons. December to March is the winter season when you can expect windy weather and angry seas. The tropical storm season spans from June to November. It is marked by hot and humid days with occasional thunderstorms. Hurricane activity is not unheard of during this time. Finally, there's tourist season, which includes April and May. This period provides nearly perfect weather for a tropical vacation. Due to the highly erratic nature of the area's weather, visitors should check an extended weather forecast the day before you intend to leave for vacation.

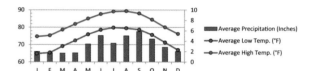

Vacation Planner

The length of your Dry Tortugas Vacation depends on how you arrive and if you're going to camp. Taking the *Yankee Freedom* (page 146) affords guests right around 4 hours of free time on **Garden Key**, and schedules are somewhat predetermined. While you can do your own thing, most guests take a tour of **Fort Jefferson** with the boat operator. Then you have lunch aboard the boat, and are left with a small amount of free time to **swim** or **snorkel**. If you arrive by seaplane you can choose whether you want to spend 4 or 8 hours basking in the tropical setting. For most visitors four hours is more than enough to tour Fort Jefferson, swim, paddle (if you brought along your kayak), and relax in the South Florida sun. If you'd like more time, bring your tent with you and **camp** (page 145) at one of 10 primitive sites on the island. South Florida's best restaurants, grocery stores, lodging, festivals, and attractions are listed on pages 149–153.

Dining

East of the Everglades
Casita Tejas • (305) 248-8224
27 N Krome Ave, Homestead
casitatejas.com

Mario's Latin Café • (305) 247-2470
1090 N Homestead Blvd, Homestead

La Quebradita Taqueria • (305) 245-4586
702 N Krome Ave, Homestead

Sams Kitchen • (305) 246-2990
1320 N Krome Ave, Homestead

Mamma Mia • (305) 248-3133
538 Washington Ave, Homestead

Royal Palm Grill & Deli • (305) 246-5701
806 N Krome Ave, Homestead

Nikko Japanese Restaurant • (305) 242-8772
827 N Homestead Blvd, Homestead

China Yan • (305) 245-8822
2846 NE 8th St, Homestead

Shiver's BBQ • (305) 248-2272
28001 S Dixie Hwy, Homestead
shiversbbq.com

Portofino Coal Fired Pizza • (786) 243-4000
Ste 112, 650 NE 22 Ter, Homestead
portofinocoalfiredpizza.com • Pizza: $12+

Bangkok Cuisine • (305) 248-6611
45 N Homestead Rd, Homestead
bangkokcuisinemiami.com • Entrée: $15–19

Black Point Ocean Grill • (305) 258-3918
24775 SW 87th Ave, Homestead

Sonny's Real Pit Bar-B-Q • (305) 245-8585
33505 S Dixie Hwy, Homestead
sonnysbbq.com

Rosita's Restaurant • (305) 246-3114
199 W Palm Dr, Florida City

West of the Everglades
Joanie's Blue Crab Café • (239) 695-2682
39395 Tamiami Tr E, Ochopee
joaniesbluecrabcafe.com • Entrée: $12–25

City Seafood • (239) 695-4700
709 Begonia St, Everglades
cityseafood1.com • Entrée: $9–15

Camellia Street Grill • (239) 695-2003
208 Camellia St, Everglades

Little Bar Restaurant • (239) 394-5663
205 Harbor Pl, Goodland
littlebarrestaurant.com

Da Vinci Ristorante Italiano • (239) 389-1888
599 S Collier Blvd, # 113, Marco Island
ristorantedavinci.com • Entrée: $12–38

Cocomo's Grill • (239) 394-3600
945 N Collier Blvd, Marco Island
cocomosgrill.com • Entrée: $14–35

Island Pizza • (239) 642-5662
910 N Collier Blvd, Marco Island
marcoislandpizza.com

Dolphin Tiki Bar & Café • (239) 394-4048
2 Anglers Cove, Marco Island

Hoot's Breakfast & Lunch • (239) 394-4644
563 E Elkcam Circle, Marco Island
hootsbreakfastandlunch.com • $8–16

Island Café • (239) 394-7578
918 N Collier Blvd, Marco Island
theislandcafe.com • Entrée: $19–37

Café de Marco • (239) 394-6262
244 Palm St, Marco Island
cafedemarco.com

Davide Italian Café & Deli • (239) 393-2233
688 Bald Eagle Dr, Marco Island
davideitaliancafe.com • Pizza: $16+

Italian Deli • (239) 394-9493
247 N Collier Blvd # 104, Marco Island

The Florida Keys
Sundowner • (305) 451-4502
103900 Overseas Hwy, Key Largo
sundownerskeylargo.com • Entrée: $18–32

The Buzzards Roost • (305) 453-3746
21 Garden Cove Dr, Key Largo
buzzardsroostkeylargo.com • Entrée: $18–36

Mrs. Mac's Kitchen • (305) 451-3722
99336 Overseas Hwy, Key Largo
mrsmacskitchen.com • Entrée: $14–36

Snappers Restaurant • (305) 852-5956
139 Seaside Ave, Key Largo
snapperskeylargo.com

New York Style Pizza • (305) 451-1461
100600 Overseas Hwy, Key Largo

Marlin's Restaurant • (305) 451-2454
102770 Overseas Hwy, Key Largo

Num-Thai & Sushi Bar • (305) 451-5955
103200 Overseas Hwy, # 3, Key Largo

Eco Eats • (305) 451-3902
99607 Overseas Hwy, Key Largo

Harriette's Restaurant • (305) 852-8689
95710 Overseas Hwy, Key Largo

Vallarta Mexican Seafood • (305) 451-4083
86701 Overseas Hwy, Key Largo

Old Tavernier • (305) 852-6012
90311 Old Highway, Tavernier
oldtavernier.com • Entrée: $17–37

Pierre's • (305) 664-3225
81600 Overseas Hwy, Islamorada
moradabay.com • Entrée: $17–39

Marker 88 Restaurant • (305) 852-9315
88000 Overseas Hwy, Islamorada
marker88.info

Midway Café • (305) 664-2622
80499 Overseas Hwy, Islamorada

Made 2 Order Café • (305) 852-3251
90691 Old Highway, Tavernier
made2orderonline.com • Entrée: $9–20

Sparky's Landing • (305) 289-7445
Key Colony Beach
sparkyslanding.com • Entrée: $14–34

Barracuda Grill • (305) 743-3314
4290 Overseas Hwy, Marathon

The Hurricane • (305) 743-2220
4650 Overseas Hwy, Marathon
hurricaneblues.com • Entrée: $11–18

Fish Tales Market & Eatery • (305) 743-9196
11711 Overseas Hwy, Marathon
floridalobster.com • Sandwich: $5–13

Butterfly Café • (305) 289-7177
2600 Overseas Hwy, Marathon

Stuffed Pig • (305) 743-4059
3520 Overseas Hwy, Marathon
thestuffedpig.com

Frank's Grill • (305) 289-7772
11400 Overseas Hwy, Marathon
franksgrillmarathon.com

Stout's Restaurant • (305) 743-6437
8349 Overseas Hwy, Marathon

Herbie's Restaurant • (305) 743-6373
6350 Overseas Hwy, Marathon

Keys Fisheries Market • (305) 743-4353
3502 Gulfview Ave, Marathon
keysfisheries.com • Entrée: $11–30

Boondock's Grille & Drafthouse • (305) 872-4094
27205 Overseas Hwy, Summerland Key

Square Grouper • (305) 745-8880
22658 Overseas Hwy, Summerland Key
squaregrouperbarandgrill.com • Entrée: $12–32

Wharf Waterside • (305) 745-3322
25163 Overseas Hwy, Summerland Key
wharfbarandgrill.com • Entrée: $10–20

The Dining Room • (305) 872-2551
28500 Overseas Hwy, Little Torch Key

Blue Heaven • (305) 296-8666
729 Thomas St, Key West
blueheavenkw.com

Hurricane Hole • (305) 294-0200
5130 US-1, Key West
hurricaneholekeywest.com • Entrée: $8–22

HogFish Bar & Grille • (305) 293-4041
6810 Front St, Stock Island
hogfishbar.com • Entrée: $9–26

Camille's Restaurant • (305) 296-4811
1202 Simonton St, Key West
camilleskeywest.com • Entrée: $17–26

Thai Life Floating • (305) 296-9907
1801 N Roosevelt Blvd, Key West
thailifekeywest.com

El Siboney Restaurant • (305) 296-4184
900 Catherine St, Key West
elsiboneyrestaurant.com • Sandwich: $3–8

Better Than Sex • (305) 296-8102
906 Simonton, Key West

La Trattoria • (305) 296-1075
524 Duval St, Key West
latrattoria.us • Entrée: $14–40

Shanna Key Irish Pub & Grill • (305) 295-8880
1900 Flagler Ave, Key West
shannakeyirishpub.com

Azur Restaurant • (305) 292-2987
425 Grinnell St, Key West
azurkeywest.com • Entrée: $30–34

Sarabeth's Kitchen • (305) 293-8181
530 Simonton St, Key West • sarabeth.com

Santiago's Bodega • (305) 296-7691
207 Petronia St, Key West
santiagosbodega.com • Tapas: $7–12

B O's Fish Wagon • (305) 294-9272
801 Caroline St, Key West • bosfishwagon.com

Date & Thyme • (305) 296-7766
829 Fleming St, Key West

Sandy's Café • (305) 295-0159
1026 White St, Key West

Kennedy Café • (305) 809-9000
924 Kennedy Dr, # A, Key West

Flaming Buoy Filet • (305) 295-7970
1100 Packer St, Key West

Pepe's Café • (305) 294-7192
806 Caroline St, Key West • pepeskeywest.com

Thai Island • (305) 296-9198
711 Eisenhower Dr, Key West
thaiislandrestaurant.com • Entrée: $15–23

The Café • (305) 296-5515
509 Southard St, Key West • thecafekw.com

Caroline's • (305) 294-7511
310 Duval St, Key West

Grocery Stores
East of the Everglades
Whole Foods Market • (305) 969-5800
11701 South Dixie Hwy, Pinecrest

Costco • (305) 964-4227
13450 SW 120th St, Kendall

Publix Super Market • (305) 242-0954
3060 NE 41st Ter, Homestead

Winn-Dixie • (305) 246-3998
30346 Old Dixie Hwy, Homestead

Walmart Supercenter • (305) 242-4447
33501 S Dixie Hwy, Florida City

West of the Everglades
Whole Foods Market • (239) 552-5100
9101 Strada Pl, Naples

Publix Super Market • (239) 732-7216
4860 Davis Blvd, Naples

Walmart Supercenter • (239) 254-8310
5420 Juliet Blvd, Naples

Costco • (239) 596-6404
6275 Naples Blvd, Naples

Winn-Dixie • (239) 455-5244
4849 Golden Gate Pkwy, Naples

The Florida Keys
Winn-Dixie • (305) 451-0328
105300 Overseas Hwy, Key Largo

Publix Super Market • (305) 451-0808
101437 Overseas Hwy, Key Largo

Winn-Dixie • (305) 852-5904
91200 Overseas Hwy, # 14, Tavernier

Winn-Dixie • (305) 743-3636
5585 Overseas Hwy, Marathon

Publix Super Market • (305) 289-2920
5407 Overseas Hwy, Marathon

Winn-Dixie • (305) 872-4124
251 Key Deer Blvd, Big Pine Key

Publix Super Market • (305) 296-2225
3316 N Roosevelt Blvd, Key West

Winn-Dixie • (305) 294-0491
2778 N Roosevelt Blvd, Key West

Albertsons • (305) 292-2013
1112 Key Plz, Key West

Lodging
East of the Everglades
Floridian Inn • (305) 247-7020
990 N Homestead Blvd, Homestead
floridianhotel.com • Rates: $109–129/night

Everglades Int'l Hostel • (305) 248-1122
20 SW 2nd Ave, Florida City
evergladeshostel.com • Rates: $28–75

Florida City RV Park • (305) 248-7889
601 NW 3rd Ave, Florida City

Everglades Motel • (305) 247-4117
605 S Krome Ave, Homestead

The Inn of Homestead • (305) 248-2121
1020 N Homestead Blvd, Homestead
theinn.ofhomestead.com

West of the Everglades
Ivey House B&B • (239) 695-3299
107 Camelia St, Everglades
iveyhouse.com • Rates: $89–179

Everglades City Motel • (239) 695-4224
310 Collier Ave, Everglades
evergladescitymotel.com

River Wilderness Waterfront Villas
210 Collier Ave, Everglades
river-wilderness.com • (239) 695-4499

The Captain's Table Lodge & Villas
102 E Broadway St, Everglades • (239) 695-4211
captainstablehotel.com

Everglades Rod and Gun Club Hotel
200 Riverside Dr, Everglades • (239) 695-2101
evergladesrodandgun.com

Marco Beach Ocean Resort • (239) 393-1400
480 S Collier Blvd, Marco Island
marcoresort.com • Rates: $674+

Olde Marco Island Inn & Suites
100 Palm St, Marco Island • (239) 394-3131
oldemarcoinn.com • Rates: $197+

The Boat House Motel • (239) 642-2400
1180 Edington Pl, Marco Island
theboathousemotel.com

Beach Club of Marco • (239) 394-9951
901 S Collier Blvd, Marco Island
beachclubvacationrentals.com • Rates: $180+

Surf Club • (239) 642-5800
540 S Collier Blvd, Marco Island
surfclub.hgvc.com

Lakeside Inn • (239) 394-1161
155 1st Ave, Marco Island
marcoislandlakeside.com

The Florida Keys
Rock Reef Resort • (305) 852-2401
97850 Overseas Hwy, Key Largo
rockreefresort.com • Rates: $150+

Dove Creek Lodge • (305) 852-6200
147 Seaside Ave, Key Largo
dovecreeklodge.com • Rates: $209+

Kona Kai Resort • (305) 852-7200
97802 Overseas Hwy, Key Largo
konakairesort.com • Rates: $219–439

Azul Del Mar • (305) 451-0337
104300 Overseas Hwy, Key Largo
azulkeylargo.com • Rates: $199+

Largo Resort • (305) 451-0424
101740 Overseas Hwy, Key Largo
largolodge.com

Island Bay Resort • (305) 852-4087
92530 Overseas Hwy, Tavernier
islandbayresort.com • Rates: $189–309

Coconut Palm Inn • (305) 852-3017
198 Harborview Dr, Tavernier
coconutpalminn.com • Rates: $186+

The Moorings Village • (305) 664-4708
123 Beach Rd, Islamorada
themooringsvillage.com

Coral Bay Resort • (305) 664-5568
75690 Overseas Hwy, Islamorada
coralbayresort.com • Rates: $129–325

Pines and Palms Resort • (305) 664-4343
80401 Old Hwy, Islamorada
pinesandpalms.com

Tranquility Bay • (305) 289-0888
2600 Overseas Hwy, Marathon
tranquilitybay.com • Rates: $300+

Cocoplum Beach and Tennis Club
109 Coco Plum Dr, Marathon • (305) 743-0240
cocoplum.com • Rates: $150–450

Bay View Inn • (305) 289-1525
3 North Conch Ave, Marathon
bayviewinn.com • Rates: $139–229

Coral Lagoon • (305) 289-1323
12399 Overseas Hwy, # 1, Marathon
corallagoonresort.com • Rates: $279+

Sea Scape Resort • (305) 743-6212
1075 75th St Ocean E, Marathon
seascapemotelandmarina.com • Rates: $200+

Anchor Inn Motel • (305) 743-2213
7931 Overseas Hwy, Marathon
anchorinnkeys.com

Deer Run B&B • (305) 872-2015
1997 Long Beach Dr, Big Pine Key
deerrunfloridabb.com

Parmer's Resort • (305) 872-2157
565 Barry Ave, Summerland Key
parmersresort.com

Royal Palm RV Park • (305) 872-9856
163 Cunningham Ln, Big Pine Key
royalpalmrvpark.homestead.com • Rates: $45

White Ibis Inn • (954) 304-8667
125 Colson Dr, Cudjoe Key
whiteibisinn.com

Pier House Resort and Spa • (305) 296-4600
1 Duval St, Key West
pierhouse.com • Rates: $300+

Southernmost Hotel • (305) 296-6577
1319 Duval St, Key West
southernmostresorts.com • Rates: $185+

The Southernmost House • (877) 296-3141
508 South St, Key West
southernmosthouse.com • Rates: $269+

Ocean Key Resort & Spa • (305) 296-7701
0 Duval St, Key West
oceankey.com • Rates: $419+

Key West Harbor Inn • (305) 296-2978
219 Elizabeth St, Key West
keywestharborinn.com • Rates: $205–375

Almond Tree Inn • (305) 296-5415
512 Truman Ave, Key West
almondtreeinn.com

Marrero's Guest Mansion • (305) 294-6977
410 Fleming St, Key West
marreros.com • Rates: $120–310

Duval Inn • (877) 418-6900
511 Angela St, Key West
duvalinn.com • Rates: $145–309

Mermaid & The Alligator B&B
729 Truman Ave, Key West • (800) 773-1894
kwmermaid.com • Rates: $198–368

Eden House • (305) 296-6868
1015 Fleming St, Key West
edenhouse.com

Orchid Key Inn • (305) 296-9915
1004 Duval St, Key West
orchidkey.com

Paradise Inn • (305) 293-8007
819 Simonton St, Key West
theparadiseinn.com

Tropical Inn • (305) 294-9977
812 Duval St, Key West
tropicalinn.com • Rates: 310–565

The Gardens Hotel • (305) 294-2661
526 Angela St, Key West
gardenshotel.com • Rates: $199–844

Seascape, An Inn • (305) 296-7776
420 Olivia St, Key West
seascapetropicalinn.com • Rates: $239–425

Santa Maria Suites Resort • (305) 296-5678
1401 Simonton St, Key West
santamariasuites.com • Rates: $459+

Coco Plum Inn • (305) 295-2955
615 Whitehead St, Key West
cocopluminn.com • Rates: $179–389

The Grand B&B • (888) 947-2630
1116 Grinnell St, Key West
thegrandguesthouse.com • Rates: $187–316

Alexander Palms Court • (305) 296-6413
715 South St, Key West • alexanderpalms.com

Café Marquesa • (305) 292-1244
600 Fleming St, Key West • marquesa.com

Speakeasy Inn Guesthouse • (305) 296-2680
1117 Duval St, Key West
speakeasyinn.com • Rates: $172+

Parrot Key Resort • (305) 809-2200
2801 N Roosevelt Blvd, Key West
parrotkeyresort.com • Rates: $273+

Knowles House B&B • (305) 296-8132
1004 Eaton St, Key West
knowleshouse.com • Rates: $159–299

Casa 325 Guest House • (305) 292-0011
325 Duval St, Key West
casa325.com • Rates: $155–405

Key West B&B • (305) 296-7274
415 William St, Key West
keywestbandb.com • Rates: $89–250

Many chain restaurants and hotels can be found nearby in Miami, Homestead, Naples, Key Largo, Islamorada, and Key West.

Festivals

Art Deco Weekend Festival •January
Miami Beach, FL • miamiandbeaches.com

Florida Renaissance Festival • February/March
ren-fest.com • Miami

South Beach Wine&Food Festival • February
sobewineandfoodfest.com • South Beach

Big "O" Birding Festival • March
bigobirdingfestival.com • LaBelle

Sunfest • April/May
sunfest.com • West Palm Beach, FL

Underwater Music Festival • July
31020 Overseas Hwy, Big Pine Key, FL

Hemingway Days • July
sloppyjoes.com/lookalikes.htm • Key West

Bon Festival • October
morikami.org • Delray Beach, FL

International Film Festival • October
fliff.com/events/asp • Fort Lauderdale

Biketoberfest • October
biketoberfest.org • Daytona Beach, FL

American Sandsculpting Festival • November
fmbsandsculpting.com • Fort Myers

Winterfest • December • Fort Lauderdale, FL
winterfestparade.com

Attractions

Miami/South Beach

Oleta River State Park • (305) 919-1844
3400 NE 163rd St, Miami
floridastateparks.org • Fee: $6/vehicle

Kestrel Outfitters • (561) 271-6006
flatsfishingmiami.com • Fishing: 1–2 People
$500 (half-day)/$650 (full-day)

Biscayne Fishing Guide • (786) 412-4859
biscaynefishingguide.com • Fishing: 1–2 People $375 (half-day)/$450 (full-day)

Miami Culinary Tours • (786) 942-8856
1000 5th St, Ste 200, Miami Beach
miamiculinarytours.com • Tours: $59

Miami Food Tours • (786) 361-0991
111 Lincoln Rd, Miami Beach
miamifoodtours.com • Tours: $53–60

Miami Tour Company • (305) 260-6855
1521 Alton Rd, Miami Beach
miamitourcompany.com • Boat/Bus Tours

Miami Jet Ski Rental • (305) 457-1619
401 Biscayne Blvd, #31, Miami
miamijetskirental.com

Santa's Enchanted Forest • (305) 559-9689
7900 40th St, Miami
santasenchantedforest.com

Holocaust Memorial • (305) 538-1663
1933 Meridian Ave, Miami • Admission: Free
holocaustmemorialmiamibeach.org

Vizcaya Museum & Gardens • (305) 250-9133
3251 S Miami Ave, Miami
vizcayamuseum.org • Admission: $18/adult

Zoo Miami • (305) 251-0400
12400 SW 152nd St, Miami
zoomiami.org • Admission: $20/adult

East of the Everglades

Gator Park • Airboat Tours • (305) 559-2255
24050 SW 8th St, Miami
gatorpark.com • Airboat: $24/adult

Everglades Safari Park • (305) 226-6923
26700 SW 8th St, Miami
evergladessafaripark.com • Airboat: $25/adult

Everglades Alligator Farm • (305) 247-2628
40351 SW 192nd Ave, Florida City
everglades.com • Show + Airboat: $20/adult

Shallow Tails Guide Service • (786) 390-9069
shallowtails.com • Fishing: 1–2 People $450 (half-day)/$650 (full-day)

Shark Valley Tram Tours • (305) 221-8455
Shark Valley Loop Road, Miami
sharkvalleytramtours.com • Tram Tour: $24/adult • Bike Rental: $9/hr

Miami Gliders • (786) 243-7640
Bldg 10, 28790 SW 217th Ave, Homestead
miamigliders.com • Glider Rides: $99+

Coral Castle • (305) 248-6345
28655 S Dixie Hwy, Miami
coralcastle.com • Admission: $15/adult

R F Orchids • (305) 245-4570
28100 SW 182nd Ave, Homestead
rforchids.com

Flagship Cinemas • (305) 248-7001
2250 NE 8th St, Homestead
flagshipcinemas.com • Tickets: $9.25

West of the Everglades

Shurr Adventures Kayaking • (877) 455-2925
shurradventures.net • Paddle: $89 (2 hrs)

Everglades City Go Fish • (239) 695-0687
gofishguides.com • Fishing: 1 Person $350 (half-day)/$550 (full-day)

Captain Derrick Daffin • (239) 695-3513 •
fishingintheeverglades.com

Hook N Line Charters • (239) 253-9926
hooknlinecharters.com • Fishing: 1–3 People $400 (half-day)/$600 (full-day)

Everglades Absolute Fishing Charters
evergladesabsolutefishing.com • (239) 695-2608 •
Fishing: 1–2 People $400 (half-day)/$600 (full-day)

Capt Becky Campbell Fishing Charters
evergladesfishingcharters.com • (239) 695-2029 •
Fishing: 1–2 People $450 (half-day)/$650 (full-day)

Steve Cox Guide Service • (561) 371-2087
fish-everglades.com • Fishing: 1–2 People $350 (half-day)/$550 (full-day)

Everglades City Fishing Charters • (239) 253-9926
evergladescityfishingcharters.com • Fishing:
1–3 People $400 (half-day)/$600 (full-day)

Corkscrew Swamp Audubon • (239) 348-9151
375 Sanctuary Rd, Naples

Big Cypress National Preserve • (239) 695-4758
33100 Tamiami Trl E, Ochopee

Skunk Ape Research HQ • (239) 695-2275
40904 Tamiami Tr E, Ochopee • skunkape.info

Island Hoppers • (239) 777-4046
2005 Mainsail Dr, Naples
ravenair.net • Tours: $159+

Naples Pier
25 12th St, Naples

Delnor-Wiggins Pass State Park • (239) 597-6196
11135 Gulfshore Dr, Naples
floridastateparks.org • Fee: $6/vehicle

Marco Movies • (239) 642-1111
599 S Collier Blvd, #103, Marco Island
marcomovies.com

The Florida Keys

Adventure Watersport Charters • (305) 453-6070 • adventurewatersportcharters.com

Dream Catcher Charters • (888) 362-3474
dreamcatchercharters.com

Lethal Weapon • (305) 774-8225
lethalweaponcharters.com

Andy Griffiths Charters • (305) 296-2639
fishandy.com

Eddie Griffiths Charters • (305) 587-3437
fishcapteddie.com

Compass Rose Charters • (305) 395-3479
fishnkw.com

Charter Boat Triple Time • (305) 296-8210
fishtripletime.com

Sterling Capt Everglades Tours • (305) 853-5161
100 Buttonwood Ave, Key Largo

John Pennekamp Coral Reef State Park
Snorkel/SCUBA destination with Christ of the Abyss (an 8.5-ft Jesus statue in 25-ft of water)
102601 US-1, Key Largo
pennekamppark.com • (305) 451-6300

Sea Dwellers Dive Center • (800) 451-3640
99850 Overseas Hwy, Key Largo
seadwellers.com • Charters: $80+

Caribbean Watersports • (305) 852-4707
97000 Overseas Hwy, Key Largo
caribbeanwatersports.com

Key Largo Parasail • (877) 904-8865
103900 Overseas Hwy, Key Largo
keylargoparasail.com • Parasail: $65+

Skydive Key West • (305) 745-4386
MM 17 Overseas Hwy, Sugarloaf Key
skydivekeywest.com • Sky Dive: $265

Wild Bird Center • (305) 852-4486
92080 Overseas Hwy, Tavernier
keepthemflying.org

Dolphin Plus Bayside • (305) 451-4060
101900 Overseas Hwy, Key Largo
dolphinsplus.com • Rates: $135+

Dolphins Plus Oceanside • (305) 451-1993
31 Corrine Pl, Key Largo
dolphinsplus.com • Rates: $135+

Sea Horse Charters • (305) 664-5020
83413 Overseas Hwy, Islamorada
floridakeysfishing-charters.com • $700+

Robbie's • (305) 664-8070
77522 B Overseas Hwy, Islamorada
robbies.com • Party Boat Fishing & More

Bud N' Mary's Marina • (800) 742-7945
79851 Overseas Hwy, Islamorada
budnmarys.com • Fishing: $750 (half-day)

Skins and Fins Charters • (305) 393-0363
84001 Overseas Hwy, Islamorada
skinsandfinscharters.com • Call for Rates

Catch Em' All Florida Keys Charter Fishing
13205 Overseas Hwy, Marathon
catch-em-all.com • (888) 882-7766

History of Diving Museum • (305) 664-9737
82990 Overseas Hwy, Islamorada
divingmuseum.org • Admission: $12/adult

Theater of the Sea • (305) 664-2431
84721 Overseas Hwy, Islamorada
theaterofthesea.com • Admission: $32

Paradise Yoga • (305) 517-9642
81927 Overseas Hwy, Islamorada
paradiseyoga.com

Bahia Honda State Park • (305) 872-3210
36850 Overseas Hwy, Big Pine Key
bahiahondapark.com • Fee: $8/vehicle

Curry Hammock State Park
Marathon • (305) 289-2690
floridastateparks.org • Fee: $5/vehicle

Turtle Hospital • (305) 743-2552
2396 Overseas Hwy, Marathon
turtlehospital.org

Captain Hook's Marina & Dive Center
11833 Overseas Hwy, Marathon
captainhooks.com • (305) 743-2444

Marathon Cinema • (305) 743-0288
5101 Overseas Hwy, Marathon

Long Key State Park • (305) 664-4815
67400 Overseas Hwy, Long Key
floridastateparks.org • Fee: $5/vehicle

Ernest Hemingway Home & Museum
907 Whitehead St, Key West • (305) 294-1575
hemingwayhome.com • $13/adult

Captain Conch Charter • (305) 293-7993
1801 N Roosevelt Blvd, Key West
keywestcaptconch.com • Call for Rates

Key West Butterfly and Nature Conservatory
1316 Duval St, Key West
keywestbutterfly.com • (305) 296-2988

Harry S Truman Little White House
111 Front St, Key West • (305) 294-9911
trumanlittlewhitehouse.com • $16/adult

Fort Zachary Taylor Historic State Park
Key West • (305) 292-6713

Mel Fisher Maritime Heritage Museum
200 Greene St, Key West • (305) 294-2633
melfisher.org • Admission: $15/adult

Key West Shipwreck Historeum Museum
1 Whitehead St, Key West • (305) 292-8990
keywestshipwreck.com • $15/adult

Key West Aquarium • (305) 296-2051
1 Whitehead St, Key West
keywestaquarium.com • $15/adult

Wild about Dolphins • (305) 294-5026
6000 Peninsular Ave, Key West
wildaboutdolphins.com

Eco-Discovery Center • (305) 809-4750
35 E Quay Rd, Key West
floridakeys.noaa.gov • Admission: Free

Yoga on the Beach • (305) 296-7352
100 Southard St, Key West

Tropic Cinema • (305) 295-9493
416 Eaton St, Key West

Regal Cinemas • (305) 294-0000
3338 N Roosevelt Blvd, Key West

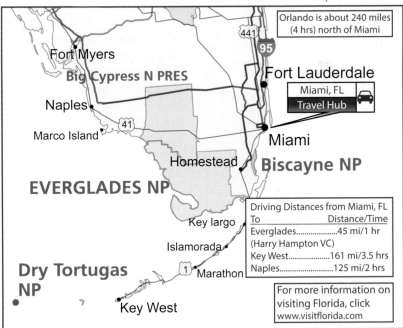

Orlando is about 240 miles (4 hrs) north of Miami

Miami, FL Travel Hub

Driving Distances from Miami, FL
To .... Distance/Time
Everglades .... 45 mi/1 hr
(Harry Hampton VC)
Key West .... 161 mi/3.5 hrs
Naples .... 125 mi/2 hrs

For more information on visiting Florida, click www.visitflorida.com

A moose near Lookout Louise

Isle Royale

800 East Lakeshore Drive
Houghton, MI 49931
Phone: (906) 482-0984
Website: nps.gov/isro

Established: April 3, 1940
Size: 571,790 Acres
Annual Visitors: 19,000
Peak Season: July–August
Hiking Trails: 165 Miles

Activities: Hiking, Camping,
Backpacking, Paddling, Fishing,
Boat Tours, and SCUBA Diving

Campgrounds: 36 Campgrounds
accessible by boat and trail*
Camping Fee: Free
Reservations: None
Lodging: Rock Harbor Lodge
(Rooms and Cottages available)
Rates: $231–256/night

Open: mid-April–October
Entrance Fee: $4/person per day

*A permit is required for all
overnight stays in the park.

Isle Royale, born of fire, sculpted by glaciers, nearly drowned in water, is a wilderness wonderland left mostly unaltered by man's creations. Millions of years ago this archipelago of about 400 islands was formed by what scientists believe to have been the world's largest lava flow. An amount of lava so immense the earth's surface sunk under its weight, forming the Superior basin. As the basin formed, Isle Royale began to rise and tilt. Today, effects of this ancient geologic activity can still be seen in Isle Royale's ridgelines. Northwest ridges are generally steep and rugged, because the lagging edge ripped away from the crust. The leading edge (southeast slope) is more gradual, as it faces the point of compression.

About 10,000 years ago, the last glacier to reach Lake Superior receded. As it scraped the island's ridgelines, pulverizing rock, a thin layer of soil was left behind. As the glacier melted, Isle Royale appeared and water poured into Lake Superior. Wind and water brought plant life to the island. Birds and insects arrived. Moose and caribou swam 15 miles from Canada's shoreline. Unseasonably cold winters allow wolves to reach the island by crossing a frozen sheet of ice.

The trip to these remote islands, while not nearly as difficult as it was for plants and animals, is still challenging for humans. Isle Royale remains untethered to the mainland, completely inaccessible to motorists. The only way to reach the park is by boat or seaplane. Diehard backpackers and paddlers make the trip across Lake Superior to immerse themselves in something increasingly scarce: undeveloped wilderness.

Long before tourists stepped foot on the island, Indians were exploring its ridges and shorelines. Thousands of shallow pits indicate they were mining copper here more than 4,000 years ago. They continued to mine for some 1,500 years, but no one knows why. Benjamin Franklin was well aware of the mineral's value. Some historians believe Franklin insisted the Treaty of Paris draw the border between a newly formed United States and England's Canada north of Isle Royale because of its copper. By the 1920s, lumber and mining companies—having exhausted nearly all the dollarable resources of Michigan's mainland—eyed the island's trees and minerals. Albert Stoll, a journalist for the Detroit News, wanted to preserve what commercial interests sought to exploit. Inspired by Stoll's passion and enthusiasm, *The Detroit News* backed his interest and launched a decade-long campaign to protect the region as a national park. In 1931 the federal government acted upon their pleas. President Herbert Hoover signed into law a bill creating Isle Royale National Park, provided no federal funds were used to acquire land. Timing couldn't have been worse as the economy was reeling during the Great Depression and money was hard to appropriate. President Franklin D. Roosevelt ignored the federal mandate and steered funds from the New Deal to buy land for the park, preserving one of the most majestic and undeveloped regions of the contiguous United States.

Lodging & Camping
Rock Harbor Lodge (906.337.4993, rockharborlodge.com) provides the park's only (non-camping) overnight accommodations. It is located on Rock Harbor, near the northeast tip of Isle Royale. The location is hard to beat, but the accommodations are basic and it's fairly expensive. For the nightly rate ($231) a visitor could purchase a tent, sleeping bag, and mat to be used exploring the **36 backcountry campsites** littered across the 45-mile long, 9-mile wide Isle Royale and a few smaller islands. Camping is free and sites are assigned on a first-come, first-served basis. Visitation is relatively modest and sites are almost always available, but those closest to the docks usually the first to fill. A free permit is required for all camping trips. Permits are obtained at a visitor center or aboard the *Ranger III*. All visitors 12 and older must pay a $4 per person per day user fee. If you plan on arriving via the *Ranger III,* the fee is collected during the reservation process. All other guests should pay in advance at Pay.gov. Annual, Senior, or Access Passes do not cover the user fee.

When to Go
Isle Royale National Park is one of the few parks in the contiguous United States that closes during winter (November until mid-April). August is the best time of year to make a trip to the island. Weather is typically warm, pests like black flies and mosquitoes are beginning to diminish, and blueberries are often ripe for the picking. Park facilities hold regular operating hours during peak season (July–August).

Rock Harbor and Windigo Visitor Centers are open from 8am–6pm every day in July and August. Hours are reduced in May, June, and September. Please call (906) 482-0984 for a current schedule.

Houghton Visitor Center is open from 8am–6pm, Monday–Saturday, from June through mid-September and from 8am–4pm, Monday–Friday, for the rest of the year. It's closed for all federal holidays in fall and winter.

Transportation & Airports
Most visitors reach Isle Royale by ferry from one of three locations: Houghton, Michigan; Copper Harbor, Michigan; or Grand Portage, Minnesota. If you have a choice, take the *Ranger III* out of Houghton. It's the longest trip (6 hours, one-way), but also the least expensive and most enjoyable. As an added convenience, you'll be able to obtain a backcountry permit while aboard the *Ranger III*, rather than having to stop at the visitor center when you arrive. Additional information is provided in the table on page 158.

The closest airport to Grand Portage, MN is Thunder Bay International (YQT) in Ontario, Canada. It is approximately 40 miles northeast of Grand Portage. Houghton County Memorial (CMX) is located in Houghton, MI, about 40 miles southwest of Copper Harbor.

Ferry Terminal Information:
Grand Portage Transportation Line • (218) 475-0024
402 Upper Road, Grand Portage, MN 55605
isleroyaleboats.com

Isle Royale Ferry Services • (906) 289-4437
14 Waterfront Landing, Copper Harbor, MI 49918
isleroyale.com

Isle Royale National Park • (906) 482-0984
800 East Lakeshore Drive, Houghton, MI 49931
Reservation form is available at the park website.

Directions
Vehicles are not allowed on Isle Royale, but parking is available at all departure locations (for a nominal fee).

To Grand Portage, MN (145 miles from Duluth):
From the south, follow MN-61 northeast along the coast of Lake Superior. Turn right onto Stevens Road to enter

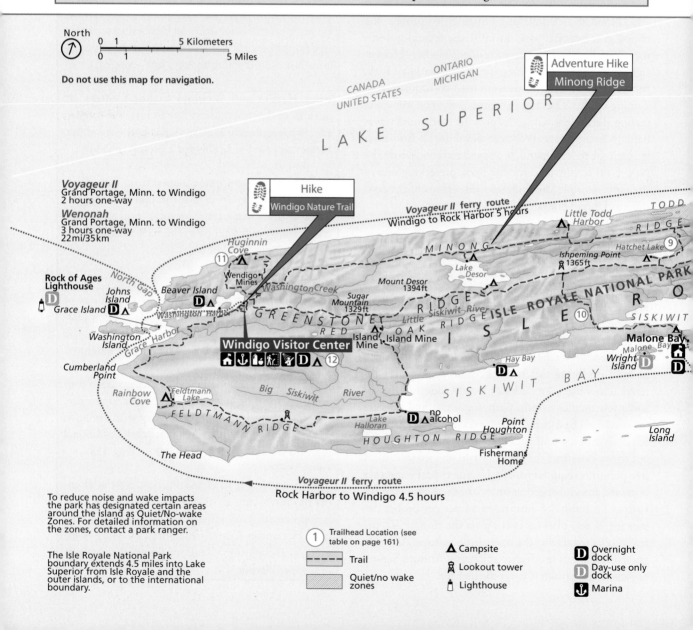

North

0   1   5 Kilometers
0   1   5 Miles

Do not use this map for navigation.

Adventure Hike
Minong Ridge

CANADA
UNITED STATES

ONTARIO
MICHIGAN

LAKE SUPERIOR

Voyageur II
Grand Portage, Minn. to Windigo
2 hours one-way
Wenonah
Grand Portage, Minn. to Windigo
3 hours one-way
22mi/35km

Hike
Windigo Nature Trail

Voyageur II ferry route
Windigo to Rock Harbor 5 hours

Little Todd Harbor

TODD RIDGE

MINONG

Huginnin Cove

Lake Desor

Ishpeming Point
1365ft

Hatchet Lake

9

Rock of Ages Lighthouse

Johns Island

Grace Island

Beaver Island

Wendigo Mines

Washington Creek

RIDGE

Mount Desor
1394ft

Sugar Mountain
1329ft

Little Siskiwit River

OAK RIDGE

ISLE ROYALE NATIONAL PARK

10

SISKIWIT

North Gap

Washington Harbor

GREENSTONE

RED

Island Mine

Island Mine

Malone Bay

Malone Bay

Wright Island

Washington Island

Grace Harbor

Cumberland Point

Rainbow Cove

Feldtmann Lake

Big Siskiwit River

SISKIWIT BAY

Hay Bay

FELDTMANN RIDGE

Lake Halloran

no alcohol

HOUGHTON RIDGE

Point Houghton

Long Island

The Head

Fishermans Home

Voyageur II ferry route
Rock Harbor to Windigo 4.5 hours

To reduce noise and wake impacts the park has designated certain areas around the island as Quiet/No-wake Zones. For detailed information on the zones, contact a park ranger.

The Isle Royale National Park boundary extends 4.5 miles into Lake Superior from Isle Royale and the outer islands, or to the international boundary.

1   Trailhead Location (see table on page 161)

– – –   Trail

Quiet/no wake zones

▲ Campsite

Lookout tower

Lighthouse

D Overnight dock

D Day-use only dock

Marina

Grand Portage. Follow County Road 73/Store Road to the right. Turn left on Mile Creek Road. Turn right onto Bay Road. After a little more than one mile, turn right onto Upper Road, which leads to the ferry terminal.

From Thunder Bay, travel southwest on MN-61. Turn left onto County Rd 73/Store Road to head into Grand Portage, which leads to Mile Creek Road. Follow the previous directions from this point.

To Houghton/Copper Harbor (215/261 miles from Green Bay, WI): US-41 passes Isle Royale Visitor Center in Houghton. To arrive at the visitor center, turn right onto Franklin Street just after US-41 becomes one-way. Continue onto Lakeshore Drive and the visitor center. US-41 continues north to Copper Harbor. In Copper Harbor take the first left onto 5th St to reach the ferry terminal.

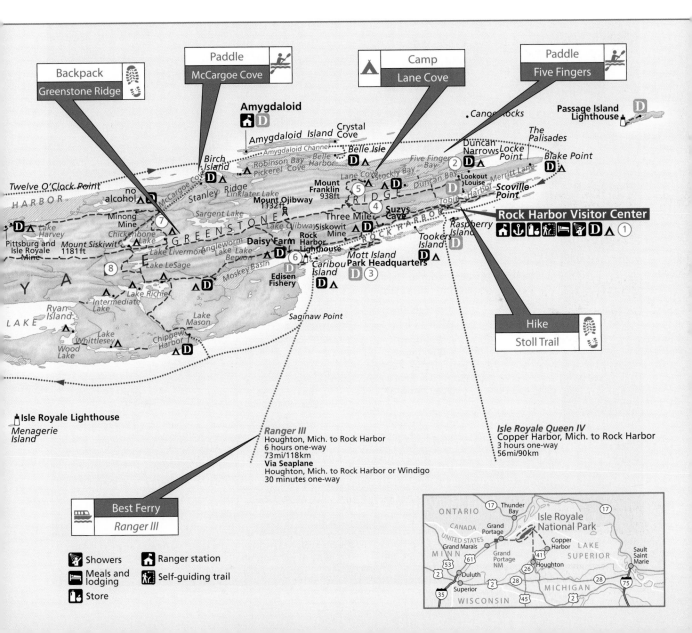

The *Ranger III*

Isle Royale Transportation Services

	Ranger III	Isle Royale Queen IV	Voyageur II	Sea Hunter	Seaplane
Operator	National Park	Private	Private	Private	Private
Departs	Hougton, MI	Copper Harbor, MI	Grand Portage, MN		Houghton, MI
Duration	6 hours	3 hours	2 hours	1.5 hours	1 hour
Open	June–Sept	May–Sept	May–Sept	June–Sept	May–Sept
Schedule	9am*	8am (Copper Harbor) 2:45pm (Rock Harbor)	7:30am	8:30am (Grand Portage) 2pm (Windigo)	Ever 2 hours starting at 8am
Adults	$53 (low) $63 (high)	$62 (low) $68 (high)	$71	$67	$310 (roundtrip)
Children	$23	$31 (low) $34 (high)	$49	$37	Free (under 2)
Kayak	$22	$25	$40	$40	N/A
Phone	(906) 482-0984	(906) 289-4437	(651) 653-5872 (winter) (218) 475-0024 (summer)		(906) 483-4991
Website	nps.gov/isro	isleroyale.com	grand-isle-royale.com		royaleairservice.com

Rates (one-way)

Trips to Isle Royale are not made every day of the week. Check the operator's website or call to confirm departure schedules. Fares and duration are for one-way trips except where stated otherwise. Operators consider children to be 11 and under. The *Ranger III* offers free rides to kids (age 6 and under). Reservations require full payment.
*Departs at 9am from Houghton on Tuesdays and Fridays and from Rock Harbor on Wednesdays and Saturdays.

Isle Royale Lodging (Fees are per night)

Name	Open	Fee	Location & Notes
Rock Harbor Lodge	May–September	$231–256 (Room) $248 (Cottage)	Rock Harbor •The lower rate is for non-peak season (May–July 4) • Dining and boat rental is available on-site

Call (906) 337-4993 in summer or (866) 644-2003 in winter or click rockharborlodge.com to make reservations.

Isle Royale Camping

Campground	Max Nigths	Tent Sites	Shelters	Group Sites	Fire Pit	Boat Access
Merritt Lane	3	1	1	0	No	Yes
Duncan Narrows	3	1	2	0	Yes	Yes
Rock Harbor	1	11	9	3	No	Yes
Tookers Island	3	0	2	0	No	Yes
Duncan Bay	3	1	2	0	Yes	Yes
Lane Cove - 🛶	3	5	0	0	No	Yes
Belle Isle	5	1	6	0	Yes	Yes
Three Mile	1	4	8	3	No	Yes
Caribou Island	3	1	2	0	No	Yes
Daisy Farm - 🛶	3	6	16	3	No	Yes
Pickerel Cove	2	1	0	0	No	Yes
Birch Island	3	1	1	0	No	Yes
Moskey Basin - 🛶	3	2	6	2	No	Yes
Chippewa Harbor - 🛶	3	2	4	1	Yes	Yes
McCargoe Cove - 🛶	3	3	6	3	Yes	Yes
Chickenbone East	2	3	0	1	No	Yes
Chickenbone West	2	6	0	3	No	Yes
Lake Richie Canoe	2	3	0	0	No	Yes
Lake Whittlesey	2	3	0	0	No	Yes
Lake Richie	2	4	0	2	No	Yes
Intermediate Lake	2	3	0	0	No	Yes
Wood Lake	2	3	0	0	No	Yes
Todd Harbor	3	5	1	3	Yes	Yes
Malone Bay - 🛶	3	0	5	2	Yes	Yes
Hatchet Lake	2	5	0	3	No	No
Little Todd	2	4	0	0	Yes	Yes
Desor North	2	3	0	0	No	No
Desor South	2	7	0	3	No	No
Hay Bay	3	1	0	0	No	Yes
Siskiwit Bay - 🛶	3	4	2	3	Yes	Yes
Island Mine	3	4	0	2	Yes	No
Huginnin Cove	3	5	0	0	No	No
Washington Creek (Windigo)	3	5	10	4	No	Yes
Beaver Island	3	0	3	0	No	Yes
Feldtmann Lake	2	5	0	2	No	No
Grace Island	3	0	2	0	No	Yes

Hiking

More than 99% of the park is designated wilderness, making Isle Royale and its 165-mile network of trails one of the best hiking regions in the Midwest. Most trails are hidden in the backcountry, far from landing docks, only trafficked by backpackers and overnight paddlers. But there are some extremely rewarding short hikes around Windigo and Rock Harbor where most visitors arrive. **Windigo Nature Walk** is a great first hike and introduction to the island. Trail guides for the 1.2-mile walk are available at the visitor center. Another pleasant hike near Windigo is the 3.6-mile (roundtrip) trek along **Feldtmann Lake Trail** to Grace Creek Overlook. The rest of Feldtmann Lake/Island Mine Trail is seldom hiked, but the first 1.8 miles is a popular destination for day-hikers seeking views of Grace Harbor from this majestic overlook. Adventurous day-hikers may want to try taking **Minong Ridge Trail** to Minong Ridge Overlook. After hiking up and down over rocky and rugged terrain for 3 miles (one-way) you'll be rewarded with spectacular vistas of Canada's shoreline.

Rock Harbor is precariously positioned on a thin slice of land between Tobin Harbor and Lake Superior. There's more water than land, but you can still find several good hiking trails in the area. **Stoll Memorial Trail** is just northeast of the dock. It recognizes the time and energy Albert Stoll, a *Detroit News* journalist, spent in his effort to protect the region. About 2 miles of it are self-guided. In all, it's nearly 5 miles to the trail's terminus at Scoville Point and back. You'll pass craggy cliffs, harbor views, and remnants of ancient mines along the way. Heading southwest from Rock Harbor are **Tobin Harbor and Rock Harbor Trails**. They run parallel to one another, weaving from shoreline to thick forests as they follow alongside the bodies of water that share their names. Regardless of which trail you choose, you'll have the opportunity to take a short spur trail to **Suzy's Cave**. It's more of an eroded arch than a cave, but still worth a quick peek. Both of these trails are among the park's busiest. Rock Harbor is usually the busier of the two because it serves as a direct route to Three Mile and Daisy Farm Campgrounds. Hikers like to beeline to these locations in order to secure a shelter for the night. Raspberry Island, only accessible by boat, has a short interpretive trail to Rock Harbor Lighthouse near Edisen Fishery.

Backpacking

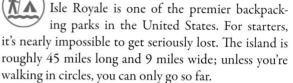

Isle Royale is one of the premier backpacking parks in the United States. For starters, it's nearly impossible to get seriously lost. The island is roughly 45 miles long and 9 miles wide; unless you're walking in circles, you can only go so far.

Greenstone Ridge, commonly referred to as "The Greenstone," follows the spine of the island and is the most notable long-distance hiking trail at Isle Royale. There aren't any campsites located directly on its 42-mile length, but several short spur trails lead to more secluded camping locations. It is reasonable to cover the entire length of the trail from Lookout Louise to Windigo in 3 days, camping at Chickenbone Lake and Lake Desor. However, plan a longer trip allowing more time to explore the many bays and lakes, and to wait out bad weather (if needed).

Running parallel to The Greenstone is **Minong Ridge Trail**. It covers 26 miles of wild and rugged terrain, and is much more difficult to traverse than its well-maintained counterpart. The challenge, abundance of wildlife, and lack of hikers attract backpackers to Minong, but these adventurous souls are few and far between. You have a better chance of spotting moose than another hiker. Just don't get lost while looking for wildlife; pay close attention to the cairns lining the barren ridgelines. Also, watch where you step because the terrain is rugged and the trail is undeveloped, lacking bridges and walkways that are integrated into most of Isle Royale's other trails. Minong Trail is best hiked from east to west (McCargoe Cove to Windigo). *Voyageur II* makes scheduled stops at McCargoe Cove. You can also hike in or take a water-taxi.

You must stay at established campsites (previous page) unless off-trail arrangements are made in advance while obtaining your backcountry permit. Permits are required for all overnight stays at campgrounds, off-trail (only recommended for experienced backpackers) sites, docks, or at anchor, and can be obtained aboard the *Ranger III* (page 158) or upon arrival at Rock Harbor or Windigo Visitor Centers.

Snowshoe hare near Moskey Basin

Isle Royale Hiking Trails (Distances are one-way unless loop)

Name	Location (# on map)	Length	Difficulty Rating & Notes
Tobin Harbor	Near Rock Harbor Seaplane Dock (1)	3.0 miles	E – Alternative to Rock Harbor Trail
Stoll - 🐾	Northeast corner of Rock Harbor (1)	4.2 miles	E – Two loops cross back and forth from the shorelines of Lake Superior and Tobin Harbor to Scoville Point
Suzy's Cave	Southwest of Rock Harbor's Dock (1)	3.8 miles	E – Take Rock Harbor Trail to the spur trail to Suzy's Cave • Loop back to Rock Harbor via Tobin Harbor Trail
Rock Harbor and Lake Ritchie	Southwest of Rock Harbor's Dock (1)	12.9 miles	M – Combine Rock Harbor and Lake Ritchie Trails to hike past busy camps at Three Mile and Daisy Farm to more remote locations near the center of the island
Lookout Louise	Northeast terminus of Greenstone Ridge (2)	1.0 mile	S – Seldom visited corner of the park, outstanding views overlooking Duncan Bay
Greenstone Ridge - 🐾	Spans from Windigo to Lookout Louise (2, 5)	42.2 miles	M – Best known trail on Isle Royale
Mott Island Circuit	Mott Island Seaplane Dock (3)	2.6 miles	E – Short, seldom-hiked loop trail accessible by boat
Mount Franklin	0.2 miles west of Three Mile Camp (4)	2.0 miles	M – Hike between Rock Harbor and Greenstone Ridge to a dramatic view of the Island's north side
Lane Cove	Continues north from Mount Franklin (5)	2.4 miles	S – Great first destination for hikers leaving Rock Harbor
Daisy Farm and Mount Ojibway	Daisy Farm Campground (6)	5.1 miles	M – Loop trail starting and ending at Daisy Farm • Passes Mount Ojibway Tower on Greenstone Ridge
East Chickenbone	0.5 miles from McCargoe Cove (7)	1.6 miles	E – Connects McCargoe Cove and Greenstone Ridge Trail
Minong Ridge - 🐾	Spans from Windigo to McCargoe Cove (7, 11)	26.0 miles	S – Wilder, less maintained and less traveled alternative to The Greenstone • Excellent chances of seeing moose
Indian Portage and Lake Mason	Spans the island's width from McCargoe Cove to Chippewa Harbor (8)	10.6 miles	M – Isolated trail accessible by The Greenstone and Rock Harbor Trail or by boat at McCargoe Cove and Chippewa Harbor • South section is lightly traveled
Hatchet Lake	Greenstone and Minong Connector (9)	2.6 miles	M – Short connecting trail between ridgelines
Ishpeming	Malone Bay Camp to Ishpeming Point (10)	7.0 miles	S – Steady climb to the park's second highest point
Huginnin Cove	Near Washington Creek Campground (11)	9.4 miles	M – Loop trail passes ridges, wetlands, and a mine
Windigo Nature Walk	Up the hill past Windigo Visitor Center (12)	1.2 miles	E – Self-guided nature trail through hardwood forest
Feldtmann Lake/ Ridge and Island Mine	Near the main dock at Windigo (12)	23.5 miles	M – A loop that leads to Grace Creek Overlook, Feldtmann Lake, Siskiwit Bay, Island Mine, and 3 campgrounds, before returning on Greenstone Ridge

Difficulty Ratings: E = Easy, M = Moderate, S = Strenuous

Best of Isle Royale

Transportation Service: *Ranger III* (out of Houghton, MI; operated by the NPS)

Campsite (near Rock Harbor): Lane Cove
  Runner-up: McCargoe Cove
  2nd Runner-up: Moskey Basin
  3rd Runner-up: Chippewa Harbor

Campsite (near Windigo): Huginnin Cove
  Runner-up: Little Todd
  2nd Runner-up: Siskiwit Bay

Hike (near Rock Harbor): Stoll Trail
  Runner-up: Suzy's Cave

Hike (near Windigo): Feldtmann Lake
  Runner-up: Windigo Nature Walk

Paddle Destination: Todd Harbor
  Runner-up: Five Finger Bay

Paddling

Experienced paddlers will find some amazing open water paddling opportunities at Isle Royale. Bringing your kayak or canoe with you unlocks a multitude of campsites, coves, and bays that cannot be reached on foot. You can explore the island's inland lakes, but you better have sturdy shoulders or a kayak cart. Portages can be as long as two miles, covering steep and rugged terrain. However, the rewards are always worth the effort. After putting a mile or two of dirt path behind you, you'll be left to enjoy the tranquil side of the island from the seat of your watercraft. One of the more rigorous routes beginning at Rock Harbor takes paddlers southwest past **Rock Harbor Lighthouse** into **Moskey Basin**. From Moskey Basin dock, it's a two-mile (mostly flat) portage to **Lake Ritchie** (a popular paddle site). Four more portages take you from **Lake LeSage** to **Lake Livermore** to **Chickenbone Lake** and finally to **McCargoe Cove**, crossing the width of the island to its northern shoreline. **Five Fingers** is another great destination for paddlers departing Rock Harbor. Remember weather and waves can change in an instant. *Voyageur II* offers paddler and boat transportation (fee) to several locations.

Rock Harbor Marina (rockharborlodge.com) has canoes and kayaks available for rent. Canoes cost $23 (half-day) and $40 (full-day), while kayaks cost $33 (half-day) and $58 (full-day). They also offer a **Kayak Ecotour** (woodswaterecotours.com), departing from Houghton aboard the *Ranger III*. It costs $1,629 for an individual and $2,995 for a couple. The price includes all meals, 4 nights lodging at Rock Harbor Lodge, sea kayak gear, and guide.

Boat Tours

A unique and easy way to explore the park's coastline and harder to reach sections is to hop aboard the *M.V. Sandy* on a sightseeing tour. All tours depart from Rock Harbor dock. A list of available tours with a short description and rates is provided below. Children are considered to be 11 years of age and younger.

Passage Island • ($38/adult, $19/child)
This tour stops at Passage Island Lighthouse, which was built in 1881. You'll be required to hike about 2 miles and traverse several steep inclines on this 4.5-hour journey.

Hidden Lake/Lookout Louise • ($38/adult, $19/child)
If your goal is to hike the entire Greenstone Ridge Trail you may want to take this shuttle/tour to Lookout Louise, the trail's northeast endpoint. The section of Greenstone Ridge between Lookout Louise and Mount Franklin is one of the most scenic stretches, but its location beyond Rock Harbor causes it to be skipped by most visitors. Roundtrip takes 3.5 hours.

Captain's Cruise • ($38/adult, $19/child)
You'll pass Rock Harbor Lighthouse as the Captain of the *M.V. Sandy* guides passengers to scenic locations like Middle Island Passage and Lorelei Lane during this 3.5-hour scenic cruise.

Northside Cruise • ($45.50/adult, $22.75/child)
This tour heads to the opposite side of the island, stopping at McCargoe Cove where passengers tour a late 19th-century copper mine. From here you'll have the option to climb back aboard the *M.V. Sandy* for the return trip or hike 15 miles back to Rock Harbor. It's a 6.5-hour adventure, so remember to pack a lunch and plenty of water.

Edisen Fishery/Rock Harbor Lighthouse • ($38/adult, $19/child)
Tour a lighthouse and historic commercial fishery on this 4-hour trip.

Raspberry Island/Sunset Cruise • ($38/adult, $19/child)
Passengers walk about Raspberry Island before cruising around Scoville and Blake Points as the sun sets.

The *M.V. Sandy* is also available for use as a one-way water bus to Hidden Lake ($16/passenger, no child discount), McCargoe Cove ($26), or Daisy Farm ($18). They'll drop you off or pick you up from any spot on the island (weather permitting). You can make reservations for water taxi service at Rock Harbor Marina. Rates are based on number of passengers and mileage. There is a maximum of six people with backpacks or four people and two canoes per trip.

1–5 miles: $58 for 1–2 People ($4/additional person)
6–10 miles: $117 for 1–2 People ($6/additional person)
11–15 miles: $166 for 1–2 People ($8/additional person)
16–20 miles: $231 for 1–2 People ($10/additional person)
21–15 miles: $326 for 1–2 People ($12/additional person)

Boats can be rented from Rock Harbor Marina.
14' & 16' Aluminum Boat: $23 (half-day), $40 (full-day)
15hp Engine: $39 (half-day), $65 (full-day)

SCUBA Diving

Isle Royale's rugged landscape is enough to include it with the United States' great natural landmarks, but there's a completely different world to be explored beneath the frigid waters of Lake Superior. The park boundary extends 4.5 miles from the islands' shorelines. **More than 25 ships have run aground or wrecked** on the surrounding reefs, and most are relatively well-maintained due to the cool, clean, fresh water. Mooring buoys are available at nine wrecks, including the 183-foot SS America, the park's most popular wreck. This passenger and package steamer ran aground in the North Gap of Washington Harbor, and its bow is visible from above water (its bow sits just two feet below the surface, while its stern is some 80 feet deep). Visitors arriving at Windigo aboard the ferry from Grand Portage, MN will stop to view the massive steamer without having to jump into Lake Superior's water, which ranges from 34–55°F.

Even though it's some of the best wreck diving anywhere, only a few hundred visitors experience this underwater world each year. Divers must be experienced and prepared for the lake's cold water and potentially tight confines of its many shipwrecks. No facilities are available to fill air tanks within the park. All divers must register at one of the visitor centers before diving. Superior Trips (763.785.9516, superiortrips.com), SCUBA Center (612.925.4818, scubacenter.com), Isle Royale Charters (855.348.3472, isleroyalecharters.com) and Blackdog Diving (507.236.2280, mn-blackdogdiving.com) are available back on the mainland to take you on an **ultimate Isle Royale underwater adventure.**

Fishing

Isle Royale's lake trout populations are the most productive and genetically diverse in all of Lake Superior. Waters within park boundaries provide excellent opportunities for catching both trout and salmon. Interior lakes offer habitat for a healthy population of walleye and northern pike. Anglers (17 and older) must have a Michigan State Fishing License if you plan to fish inland lakes or streams. A license is not required to fish Lake Superior. **Rock Harbor Lodge** (906.337.4993, rockharborlodge.com) provides fishing charter services for island visitors. Charter costs $394 for four anglers for four hours and $729 for four anglers for eight hours.

Ranger Programs
In addition to the *M.V. Sandy* Boat Tours (page 162) from Rock Harbor Marina and the ranger narrated boat ride to Isle Royale aboard the *Ranger III* (page 158), there are many ranger-led programs offered at the park's Windigo and Rock Harbor locations.

It's amazing how much more enjoyable a park ranger can make a simple walk along the shorelines. If you have the chance to join one of these activities, do it! The program schedule is subject to change, so check online or at the visitor center for a current listing.

Following the boardwalk to Richie Lake

For Kids

Most children will like the boat ride across Lake Superior (unless the water is rough). You'll also find activities specifically designed for children once you arrive at Rock Harbor or Windigo. The park's **Junior Ranger Program** is designed for children ages 6–12, but kids of all ages are welcome to participate. Complete the free activity booklet (takes 1–2 days) with the help of parents and the park rangers to receive a unique certificate and badge. Rangers also provide engaging interactive programs. All guests will find the ranger programs enjoyable.

Flora & Fauna

Compared to the rest of the contiguous U.S., Isle Royale is extremely isolated. It's so isolated only a few mammal species reside here. You'll find more than 40 mammals on the surrounding mainland, but only 18 inhabit the park. Species like caribou and coyote have disappeared. Others, like **moose and wolves**, have found a way to reach the island within the last century. It's widely believed that moose, excellent swimmers among the animal kingdom, swam to the island, motivated by the scent of abundant vegetation. Wolves arrived a few decades later when an exceptionally cold winter left the passage between Ontario, Canada and Isle Royale frozen solid. The presence of moose and their natural predator, wolves, in a closed environment such as Isle Royale creates an ideal setting to study predator-prey

relationship. Scientists have studied the park's wolves and moose since 1958. You can even lend a hand by joining a research expedition ($450 for 9 days). Find out more at isleroyalewolf.org. (Note that during our last visit in 2015, only two wolves remained, but we heard one at night while camping at McCargoe Cove.) In addition to these larger mammals, snowshoe hare, beaver, red fox, red squirrel, at least 40 species of fish, and a handful of amphibians and reptiles reside in the park. Pests are also abundant. **Mosquitoes, black flies, and gnats are worst in June and July.**

The island is primarily forested with a mixture of boreal and northern hardwoods. Spruce, fir, pine, birch, aspen, maple, and ash are commonly found. Blueberries and thimbleberries grow wild on open ridge tops. They typically ripen between late July and August, providing a tasty snack while hiking about the island.

Pets

Pets are not allowed within the park. However, special conditions do apply to guide dogs. Please contact the park (906.482.0984) for additional information.

Accessibility

All transportation services and Rock Harbor Lodge are accessible with assistance to individuals in wheelchairs. Trails are narrow and rugged with limited access.

Weather

The park's weather is moderated by Lake Superior. Its massive body of water has an average temperature of 45°F, cooling summer highs and warming winter lows. Ambient temperature seldom reaches 80°F on the islands. Dense fog and thunder storms are common during spring and summer. Paddlers should be prepared to head to shore if the wind changes abruptly. Lake Superior's rough waters have received notoriety, thanks largely to the *Edmund Fitzgerald* and Gordon Lightfoot, but weather rarely delays or postpones a departure to or from the island.

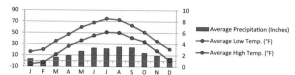

Vacation Planners

Remote location and a contingent of moderately-obsessed regulars help give Isle Royale an average stay of 3.5 days. A day-trip is conceivable from Grand Portage or Copper Harbor, but you'll spend more than $100 to ride a ferry for 4–6 hours, which leaves you with just a few hours to enjoy the scenery. For the real Isle Royale experience, the wild side is where you need to go. To get there you'll need at least three days. It's possible to hike from Rock Harbor to Windigo in 3 days, but for this exercise it's more prudent to create a separate 3-day itinerary for visitors of Rock Harbor and visitors of Windigo. Dining, grocery stores, lodging, festivals, and attractions on the mainland are listed on pages 175–177.

Vacation Planner (Rock Harbor)

A sample 3-day itinerary for guests arriving at **Rock Harbor** is provided below. **This is a backpacking trip.** A tent is required for camping at Lane Cove. Shelters are available at Daisy Farm.

Day 1: If you don't plan on arriving aboard *Ranger III*, pop in the visitor center to get a backcountry permit (let the ranger know you would like to camp at Lane Cove and Daisy Farm). Today, you'll hike 7.4 miles to **Lane Cove.** Begin by heading west on **Tobin Harbor Trail** (a flat, easy stroll). (You can also take Rock Harbor Trail, which is rocky and more tedious, but also quite beautiful.) Making a quick stop at **Suzy's Cave** is up to you; It's closer to Rock Harbor Trail (your return route). What you're looking for is **Mount Franklin Trail.** Take it north to Greenstone Ridge, where the trail intersects Greenstone and Lane Cove Trails. Mount Franklin, a short distance west along The Greenstone is a nice place to pause for a snack, drink, or photo. Otherwise, Lane Cove, where you'll spend the night, is 2.4 miles from the intersection.

Day 2: There's no need to rush today, you're only going to hike seven miles. The route backtracks along **Lane Cove Trail,** to **Mount Franklin** and **Mount Ojibway Overlook** via **The Greenstone.** From Mount Ojibway Overlook it's 5.1 miles along **Daisy Farm Trail** to **Daisy Farm** (often busy). Listen to your surroundings and you may stumble upon a moose grazing in a pond.

Moose antler found along The Greenstone

Day 3: Return to **Rock Harbor** (either to camp for the night, to catch the *Ranger III* back to Houghton, or to catch the *Royale Queen IV* back to Copper Harbor). The last leg is 7.2 miles along **Rock Harbor Trail.** You should have plenty of time to check out **Suzy's Cave** (accessed via a short spur trail), catch a ranger program, hike **Stoll Trail,** take a **shower** (coin operated), or sit back and relax.

Vacation Planner (Windigo)

A sample 3-day itinerary beginning at **Windigo** is provided below. A tent is required for Feldtmann Lake and Island Mine Camps. Siskiwit Bay has two shelters.

Day 1: First stop in at the **visitor center** to get a backcountry permit (let the ranger know you would like to camp at Feldtmann Lake and Siskiwit Bay). You'll probably want to start hiking right away, because it's 8.8 miles along **Feldtmann Lake/Ridge Trail** to camp.

Day 2: Hike 10.5 miles from Feldtmann Lake Camp to **Siskiwit Bay Camp** via **Feldtmann Ridge Trail.** Along the way you'll skirt the shores of Siskiwit Bay. If you want to continue hiking, it's another 4.4 miles to Island Mine Camp, but this site is one of the least desirable camping destinations on the island.

Day 3: To return to **Windigo** (11.0 miles from Siskiwit Bay) you'll take **Indian Mine Trail** to **The Greenstone,** which leads back to Windigo where you can catch your ferry or spend another night close to the docks. You'll probably want to take advantage of the coin-operated **showers** too.

Northern Lights

Voyageurs

360 Highway 11 East
International Falls, MN 56649
Phone: (218) 283-6600
Website: nps.gov/voya

Established: April 8, 1975
Size: 218,054 Acres
Annual Visitors: 240,000
Peak Season: Summer

Activities: Paddling, Boating, Fishing, Hiking, Camping, and Winter Activities

Drive-in Campgrounds: None
Backcountry Campsites*: 270+
Access: Boat Only
Camping Fee: $16–35/night + $10 Reservation Fee
Lodging: Kettle Falls Hotel
Access: Boat or Seaplane
Rates: $60–80/night (room), $180–340/night (villa, 3 day min)

Park Hours: All day, every day
Entrance Fee: None

*A permit is required for all overnight stays in the park.

It is appropriate that Minnesota, the land of 10,000 lakes, is home to a national park made mostly of islands and lakes. It's a park where travel is by boat, not car. Visitors carry a paddle in their hands rather than a walking stick. After a long day's journey adventurers rest their tired arms and blistered hands by a campfire, rather than their sore feet.

One other thing about this place that feels like Minnesota: the winters are numbingly cold. Freezing temperatures can make the region feel downright unbearable, but it's far from uninhabitable. In fact, people have lived here since glacial waters of Lake Agassiz receded some 10,000 years ago. Cree, Monsoni, and Assiniboin tribes were living here in the late 17th century. In 1688, these tribes were the first Native American contacts of French–Canadian explorer Jacques de Noyon. He and his band of voyageurs, known for their strength and endurance, were in search of beaver pelts. Fur trade was the leading industry in the New World, and animal populations in the east were approaching extinction due to overhunting. Trappers like de Noyon were continually pushing west seeking new animal populations to harvest. By the mid-18th century, Ojibwa Indians took up residence in the Rainy Lake area, supplying fur traders with food, furs, and canoes in exchange for manufactured goods.

Over the course of the next century rapid development stressed the United States' resources. By the 1880s, a logging frenzy had reached Minnesota's U.S.–Canada border and the present-day site of Voyageurs National Park. Forests were clear-cut as quickly as humanly possible, with logs rafted down the rivers to increase efficiency. Hoist Bay was named for the act of hoisting floating logs from the waters of Namakan Lake, where they were loaded onto a train.

While loggers were clear-cutting trees, miners were blasting through rock hoping for gold. Several gold mines, most notable being Little American Mine, were constructed beginning in the 1880s. Rainy Lake City, a town bustling with miners and their families, sprang up overnight. By 1898 gold mines went bust, and in 1901 Rainy Lake City was a ghost town.

The next enterprise to take the region by storm was commercial fishing, especially for caviar, eggs of lake sturgeon. Without refrigeration there was no way to transport their catch. Fishing fizzled and gave way to bootlegging during the era of Prohibition. The maze of waterways along the United States–Canada border proved to be a perfect location for boaters to smuggle alcohol.

Today's industry is tourism. As early as 1891, legislation had been written to protect the area now known as Voyageurs National Park, but the request fell on deaf ears. Trees were harvested. Minerals were mined. Dams were constructed at International Falls, Kettle Falls, and Squirrel Falls. Commercial interests scarred the scenic landscapes, and Ernest Oberholtzer stood in opposition. He championed the park idea and was one of eight founding members of the Wilderness Society. He used his position to lobby Washington to create a national park of the region he explored as a child by canoe. It took decades, but in 1975—when Oberholtzer was 90 years old—the park was finally established.

Voyageurs is a place changed by human enterprises, but nature itself is a powerful agent of change. In summer boats glide across the water as loons float on its surface. Bald eagles soar above the lakes and trees. Quietly, leaves turn yellow, brown, and orange. Rain turns to snow. Water becomes ice. Year-to-year, day-to-day, the park is in a constant state of flux. But one thing remains the same: visitors find peace and solace out on the water. They are at home in the wilderness, much like the voyageurs and Ernest Oberholtzer were before them.

When to Go
The park is open all year, but its weather and landscapes are dramatically different from summer to winter. In summer, most visitors explore the region by houseboat, canoe, or kayak. In winter, snowmobilers race across the frozen lakes while cross-country skiers and snowshoers make use of snow-covered hiking trails. **Rainy Lake** (218.286.5258), **Kabetogama** (218.875.2111), and **Ash River** (218.374.3221) **Visitor Centers** are open daily from 9am–5pm from late May until late September. Kabetogama and Ash River are closed the rest of the year, while Rainy Lake remains open but with shorter hours.

Transportation & Airports
Most of the park, including all campsites and Kettle Falls Hotel, is only accessible by boat or seaplane. Public transportation does not reach this remote location. The closest airport is Falls International (INL) in International Falls, MN, located about 25 miles northwest of Kabetogama. Taxis and rental cars are available at the airport.

Directions
The park is best explored by boat, but all three of the park's visitor centers can be reached by car.

To Rainy Lake Visitor Center (13 miles from International Falls): Take MN-11 east out of International Falls. The visitor center is located along MN-11.

Ash River and Kabetogama Lake Visitor Centers are accessed via US-53.

To Ash River Visitor Center (145 miles from Duluth): Take US-53 North about 131 miles. Turn right at Ash River Trail/Ness Road. Continue for 8 miles before turning left onto Mead Wood Road, which leads directly to the visitor center.

To Kabetogama Lake Visitor Center (140 miles from Duluth): Take US-53 N about 134 miles. Turn right onto Gamma Road/Salmi Road. After 1.3 miles, turn right onto Gappa Road. Keep left at the fork, and then turn right into the visitor center parking lot.

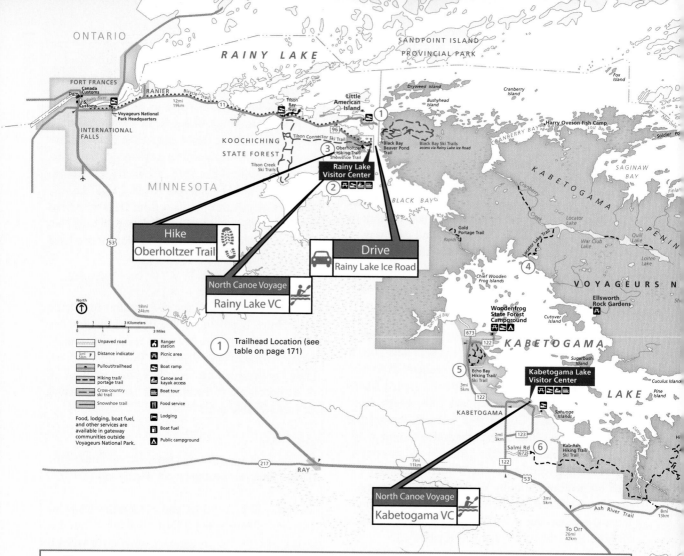

Camping & Lodging

Camping is a fantastic way to see the stars and hear the wildlife of Minnesota's northwoods. **More than 270 campsites** dot the shorelines of Voyageurs National Park. Not a single one is accessible by car (except during winter, via Rainy Lake Ice Road). With 655 miles of shoreline, that's roughly one campsite every other mile.

A permit is required for all overnight stays (including houseboats) in the park. Permits can be reserved in advance at (877) 444-6777 or recreation.gov. No matter what time of year you'd like to visit, you will have to pay a $10 reservation fee. During high season (mid-May until mid-September) you'll also have to pay an amenity fee ranging from $16 per night for a small campsite with no tent pad to $35 per night for a group campsite. There are four group sites and four handicap accessible sites. Once you've made your reservations, you must print your permit and bring it with you, placing it inside the site's waterproof box. You can make same-day reservations at self-help kiosks at any of the visitor centers for that night only. Any additional nights must be reserved through (877) 444-6777 or recreation.gov.

The only lodging within park boundaries is at **Kettle Falls Hotel** (218.240-1724, kettlefallshotel.com), which has been in operation since 1918. Just like the rest of the park it's only accessible by boat or plane.

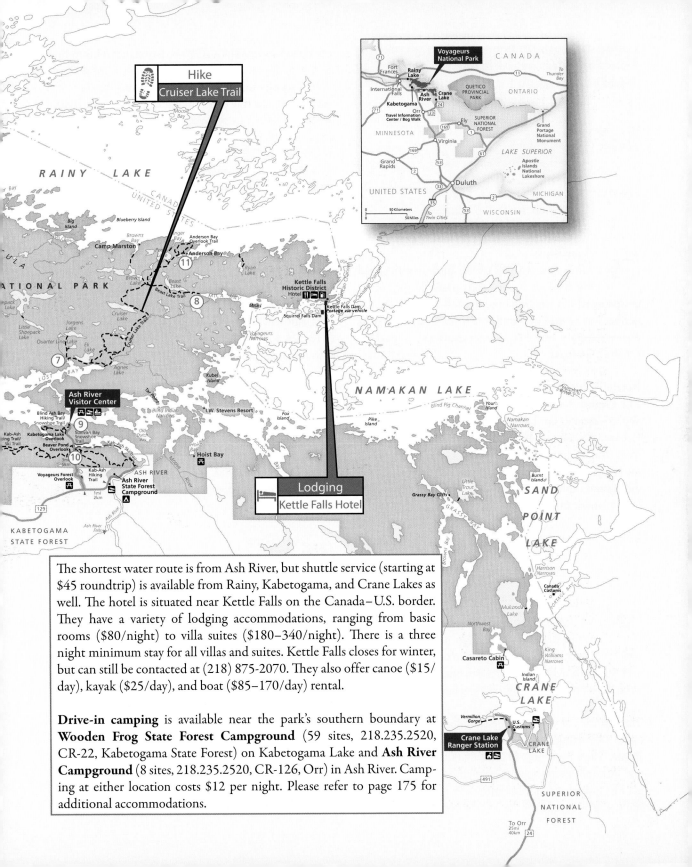

Hike
Cruiser Lake Trail

Lodging
Kettle Falls Hotel

Voyageurs National Park

The shortest water route is from Ash River, but shuttle service (starting at $45 roundtrip) is available from Rainy, Kabetogama, and Crane Lakes as well. The hotel is situated near Kettle Falls on the Canada–U.S. border. They have a variety of lodging accommodations, ranging from basic rooms ($80/night) to villa suites ($180–340/night). There is a three night minimum stay for all villas and suites. Kettle Falls closes for winter, but can still be contacted at (218) 875-2070. They also offer canoe ($15/day), kayak ($25/day), and boat ($85–170/day) rental.

Drive-in camping is available near the park's southern boundary at **Wooden Frog State Forest Campground** (59 sites, 218.235.2520, CR-22, Kabetogama State Forest) on Kabetogama Lake and **Ash River Campground** (8 sites, 218.235.2520, CR-126, Orr) in Ash River. Camping at either location costs $12 per night. Please refer to page 175 for additional accommodations.

Best of Voyageurs

Paddle Destination: Kabetogama Peninsula
Runner-up: Kettle Falls Hotel
2nd Runner-up: Cranberry Bay

Hike: Cruiser Lake System
Runner-up: Oberholtzer Trail

Activity: North Canoe Voyage
Runner-up: Kettle Falls Cruise

Boat Tours

More than a third of the park is water, and much of its beauty and mystique cannot be grasped without heading out to sea. Boat tours are the perfect way to explore Voyageurs if you don't have your own watercraft, but they can get expensive (especially for large families).

Kettle Falls Cruise (6.5 hours, $45/adult, $25/child) and **Grand Tour** (2.5 hours, $30/adult, $15/child) depart from Rainy Lake Visitor Center. **Kettle Falls Cruise** (5.5 hours, $40/adult, $20/child) also departs from Kabetogama Lake Visitor Center. Kettle Falls tours spend two hours at the historic Kettle Falls Hotel, dining and exploring the dam area. Grand Tour stops at Little American Island.

Reservations can be made in person at each respective visitor center or until midnight the night before the tour at 877.444.6777 or recreation.gov.

Paddling

Voyageurs is an anomaly among national parks in that there are only 8 miles of paved roadways within its boundaries. If you're going to really get out there and explore the region, you'll have to head out on the open water, by canoe, kayak, motorboat, or houseboat.

The majority of water exploration occurs in four main lakes: **Kabetogama**, **Namakan**, **Rainy**, and **Sand Point**. More than 500 islands, 84,000 acres of water, and infinitely many boating possibilities make it easy to get lost in a maze of forests and water. If your intent is a multi-day or even a half-day trip, be sure to travel with a

good map and compass (GPS is optional, just know how to use it). If you don't have your own boat, think about taking a **water taxi** to Kabetogama Peninsula where you can hike to any one of 17 inland lake campsites. **Rental boats** ($12/day) are provided by the park for your enjoyment at 6 of these sites. Like the campsites, boats can be reserved at (877) 444-6777 or recreation.gov. You can also rent boats at many of the nearby resorts or **Kettle Falls Hotel** (page 168), or a **marina** like Handberg's (218.993.2214, handbergs.com) near Crane Lake.

Check at a visitor center for a current schedule of ranger-led activities (page 172). **Free guided canoe trips** are offered regularly. One trip takes visitors back in time by traveling aboard a 26-foot **North Canoe** similar to those used by original voyageurs. You can also find full-service outfitters like Border Guide Service (218.324.2430, borderguideservice.com) to take you into the backcountry.

If you believe the strength and endurance of the voyageurs is in you, consider navigating around **Kabetogama Peninsula**. This 75-mile voyage requires two short portages, one at Gold Portage, a rapid between Kabetogama and Rainy Lake, and another at Kettle Falls Dam. Other than that, it's all wide open flat water as you trace the jagged shoreline for seven days (on average).

Hiking

Voyageurs is dominated by water, making its hiking trails more afterthought than main attraction. Even so, you'll find some great opportunities within the park and a boat isn't needed to reach all of them. **Oberholtzer Trail** begins near Rainy Lake Visitor Center before passing through forests and wetlands. The first 0.25-mile is wheelchair accessible and you'll find two overlooks along its 1.7-mile length.

Not surprisingly, most trailheads are only accessible by boat. **Cruiser Lake Trail System**, a 9.5-mile network, is the best way to explore Kabetogama Peninsula by foot. It leads to several inland lakes as the path crosses from Kabetogama Lake to Rainy Lake. It's also a great trail for backpackers. Campsites are available at Little Shoepack, Jorgens, Quarter Line, Elk, Agnes, Cruiser, Beast, Brown, and Oslo Lakes—many of which have boats available for rent ($12/day • reserve at 877.444.6777 or recreation. gov). **Black Bay Beaver Pond**, near the northwest point of Kabetogama Peninsula, provides a fairly short hike through pine forest to an active beaver pond.

Fishing

Voyageurs is home to some of the best fishing in the Midwest. Walleye, northern pike, muskellunge, panfish, yellow perch, and bass are commonly caught. Visitors with their own boat can launch at any of ten boat ramps lining the southern shorelines of the park's lakes. If you don't have your own boat or would like access to a **knowledgeable guide**, consider contacting Border Country Outfitters (218.324.0668, bcoaonline.com) on Rainy Lake or Northern Limits Guiding (320.266.4514, northernlimitsguiding.com) or Granger Guide Service (218.875.3062, fishingkabetogama.com) on Kabetogama Lake and Ash River.

Winter Activities

In winter, canoes and hiking boots are retired in favor of **cross-country skis** and **snowshoes**. **Black Bay and Echo Bay Trails** are two popular destinations for cross-country skiing. **Tilson Connector Trail**, accessible from Rainy Lake Visitor Center, is a 10-mile network of well-groomed trails. **Kab-Ash Trail** from Kabetogama Lake to Ash River is a long ungroomed trail for experienced skiers. Trail maps and conditions are available at the park website. Park personnel maintain three tracked snowshoe trails: Blind Ash Bay, Sullivan Bay, and Oberholtzer. Rainy Lake Visitor Center has snowshoes and cross-country skis they'll lend out on a first-come, first-served basis for free. You may want to call the visitor center at (218) 286-5258 for sizing and availability.

Ice fishing is also popular. Winter anglers must come prepared for northern Minnesota's brand of cold. Temperatures are frequently below zero, snow drifts and the wind whips, leaving even the hardiest of fishermen dreading the thought of exiting their warm fishing shanties. Dave's Guide Service (218.993.2453, davesguideservice.biz) and Woody's Fairly Reliable Guide Service (218.286.5001, fairlyreliable.com) will take you out in winter and show you how ice fishing is done. A complete list of **Voyageurs National Park outfitters** is available in the park's newspaper, *The Rendesvous*.

Voyageurs Hiking Trails (Distances are roundtrip unless noted otherwise)

Name	Location (# on map)	Access	Length	Difficulty Rating & Notes
Little American Island	Rainy Lake (1)	Boat	0.25 mile	E – Self-guided loop exploring Minnesota's late 19th-century gold rush
Black Bay Beaver Pond	Across Black Bay north of Rainy Lake Visitor Center (2)	Boat	1.2 miles	E – Visits an active beaver pond
Oberholtzer	Rainy Lake Visitor Center (3)	Land/Car	1.7 miles	E – Hikes to two scenic overlooks
Locator Lake	Across Kabetogama Lake North of the Visitor Center (4)	Boat	4.0 miles	S – A hilly out-and-back that passes through forests and wetlands
Echo Bay	Off County Rd 122, 3 miles from Kabetogama Lake Visitor Center (5)	Land/Car	2.5 miles	E – Excellent bird-watching trail • Good site for cross-country skiing
Kab-Ash	Connects Kabetogama Lake and Ash River Visitor Centers (6)	Land/Car	28.0 miles	S – Four separate trailheads are located along the trail (one-way & loops)
Cruiser Lake - ♨	Rainy or Kabetogama Lake (7)	Boat	9.5 miles	S – Crosses Kabetogama Peninsula (1-way)
Beast Lake	Namakan Lake (8)	Boat	2.5 miles	M – Steep climbs at the beginning and end to reach ridgeline (1-way)
Blind Ash	Kabetogama Lake Overlook (9)	Land/Car	2.8 miles	M – A pleasant wooded loop
Sullivan Bay	Ash River Visitor Center (10)	Land/Car	1.5 miles	E – Tracked snowshoe trail in winter
Anderson Bay	East end of Rainy Lake just past Kempton Channel (11)	Boat	1.8 miles	M – This short loop rewards hikers with a cliff top view of Rainy Lake

Difficulty Ratings: E = Easy, M = Moderate, S = Strenuous

One of the more controversial winter activities is **snowmobiling**. Critics contend their noise and air pollution are ruining the pristine environment, but snowmobilers are still allowed on **frozen lake surfaces** and **Chain of Lakes Scenic Trail**. In all, there are 110 miles of staked and groomed trails to explore the vast expanses of snow, ice, and forests.

Snowmobilers aren't the only motorized vehicles driving on ice, as the magic of wintertime turns a paddler's paradise into a motorist's retreat. Any automobile can drive straight down the boat ramp near Rainy Lake Visitor Center and keep going for seven miles to the mouth of Cranberry Bay. **Rainy Lake Ice Road** is open to cars and trucks weighing less than 7,000 pounds. Islands usually only accessible by boat can be viewed from the warmth of your car. Winter also provides the only opportunity for **drive-up camping**. You are allowed to park and camp along the ice road if you can endure the cold. An overnight permit (reserve at 877.444.6777 or recreation.gov) is required for winter camping. Even without spending the night, driving an ice road is a unique national park experience. A trip that becomes even more memorable if you're lucky enough to spot a lone gray wolf crossing the ice surface, or more likely, a pack of fishing shanties where ice fishermen escape the harsh Minnesotan winter.

You'll also find a **sledding hill** at Sphunge Island. It can be accessed by taking Kabetogama–Ash River Ice Road from Kabetogama Visitor Center and turning left onto **Sphunge Island Loop**. There are two hills (one for older children and adults, the other for young children), picnic tables, and a fire ring.

Ranger Programs

In addition to boat tours (page 170), the park offers numerous free ranger-led activities. Visitors can explore the history of the voyageurs, for whom the park is named, on the free **North Canoe Voyage** that departs from both Rainy Lake (218.286.5258) and Kabetogama Lake (218.875.2111) Visitor Centers. Paddling is required. Minimum age is 5. All tours are weather dependent. Advance reservations are recommended. They are available beginning in late May by calling the respective visitor center.

Campfire programs are held frequently and special speakers discuss topics suitable to their expertise. A list of scheduled activities is provided in the current issue of *The Rendezvous* (available at any visitor center), but it's a better idea to view the park's online calendar. If you don't have a boat and no ranger programs or boat tours are offered, the activities here are limited to a few short hiking trails.

For Kids

Voyageurs has more activities geared to children than the average park. For starters, children of all ages can dress up in traditional voyageurs' clothing at any of the park's visitor centers. To feel like a modern day voyageur, sign up for the free ranger-led North Canoe Voyage. **Children's tables** are available at each visitor center, filled with kid-friendly activities like coloring and stamping. Children also have the opportunity to become **Junior Rangers** by completing a free activity booklet (available online or at any of the visitor centers). Upon completion, children are rewarded with a certificate and badge. Six **Discovery Packs** are also available at the visitor centers. They help families explore the park's geology, wildlife, and history through an assortment of educational materials. Packs are loaned out, free of charge, for an hour or an entire day. They must be checked out by an adult with a valid driver's license.

Flora & Fauna

Wildlife has attracted visitors to Voyageurs since the first European explorers arrived in 1688. In summer, bear, deer, Canadian lynx, and moose are roaming about. But, you're more likely to see some of the 240 species of birds. Two of the most frequently spotted and popular species are the common loon and bald eagle. In winter you may see tracks of snowshoe hare or gray wolf.

The park is dominated by water, but you can find forests, marshes, and peatlands. Spruce, fir, pine, aspen, and birch are common trees.

Pets

Pets are not allowed on trails or in the backcountry. They are allowed in developed areas like visitor centers, picnic areas, and boat ramps, but must be on a leash no longer than six feet in length at all times.

Accessibility

The park's visitor centers, Kettle Falls Hotel, the first 0.25-mile of Oberholtzer Trail, four campsites, and most boat tours are wheelchair accessible. Most of the park is reached by boat, making accessibility dependent on your individual method of transport (private or commercial). If you plan on hiring the services of an outfitter, discuss any potential accessibility requirements with them prior to arrival.

Weather

International Falls, the closest city to Voyageurs National Park, holds the title for coldest city in the Lower 48. This standard should give you a pretty good idea what the weather is going to be like. Summers are short and comfortable with average highs reaching the upper 70s°F in July and August. Winters tend to be long and cold. Temperatures below 0°F are common and average January highs are in the teens.

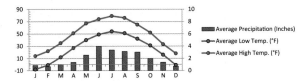

Average Precipitation (Inches)
Average Low Temp. (°F)
Average High Temp. (°F)

Vacation Planner

Not sure what to do? Where to paddle? Whether or not you should even visit Voyageurs? Here's a 3-day itinerary to jump-start your Voyageurs vacation planning. It assumes you have your own kayak(s) or canoe(s). If you don't have a boat, make sure you visit when boat tours (page 170) and ranger programs (page 172) are offered. Nearby dining, grocery stores, lodging, festivals, and attractions are listed on pages 175–177.

Day 1: Ash River Visitor Center is a great place to introduce yourself to the region. You can ask park rangers questions, watch a short film, browse updated exhibits, and find information on upcoming **ranger programs** and **Boat Tours** (available in the current issue of *The Rendezvous*). Schedule permitting, the **North Canoe Voyage** (page 172) is highly recommended. Make advance reservations in person at Kabetogama Lake Visitor Center or by calling (218) 875-2111. The North Canoe Voyage Program is also offered at Rainy Lake Visitor Center (call 218.286.5258 for reservations).

Don't worry if you can't fit it into your schedule, because you're going to be spending two nights in the wilderness camping on Kabetogama Peninsula. It also means you're going to need an **overnight camping permit** (reserve in advance at recreation.gov or 877.444.6777). Try to reserve sites B6 on **Elk Lake** and K34 on **Sugarbush Island**. (There are many sites along the shore of Kabetogama Lake and in the backcountry of Kabetogama Peninsula, so don't worry if these sites aren't available. However, you will have to come up with an alternate itinerary.) You'll want to make sure you have enough time to paddle 4 miles and set up camp (1–2 hours). If time permits, hike the short **Blind Ash Bay Trail**. It begins near the visitor center at Kabetogama Lake Overlook. From here you'll be able to see Sugarbush Island, where you'll camp the following night. With your permit secured and second night's camping location scouted, prep your gear for launch at Ash River boat ramp. Begin paddling north to **Round Bear Island**. You can paddle around either side of the island, but heading to the east requires a short and easy portage. After passing the island, head to your right into **Lost Bay**. Near the back of the bay you'll find a short portage leading to **Elk Lake** and your campsite.

Day 2: Today all you have to get done is an 8-mile paddle to **Sugarbush Island**, so you'll have some free time. Fortunately, nearby **Cruiser Lake Trail System** is one of the best places to burn a little time. Once you're finished hiking, make the portage back into **Lost Bay** and follow the northern shore of Kabetogama Lake all the way to **Nashata Point**. Paddle around to the island's southern shore where you'll camp for the night.

Day 3: Back to **Ash River Visitor Center** you go. It's about an 8-mile paddle (depending on what path you take). If you're lucky, you may return in time to catch a ranger program and the ranger might suggest a new paddle route for your next visit to Voyageurs.

As your map-reading and navigational skills progress, think about venturing farther from the visitor centers into Rainy Lake and even Canadian waters.

Before the North Canoe Voyage

Dining

Michigan's Upper Peninsula

Harbor Haus Restaurant • (906) 289-4502
Dining with a German/Austrian flavor
77 Brockway Ave, Copper Harbor
harborhaus.com

Slim's Café • (906) 337-3212
Well-known for their Sunday turkey dinner
8 Mohawk St, Mohawk

Michigan House Café & Brew Pub
300 6th St, Calumet • (906) 337-1910
michiganhousecafe.com • Entrée: $11–28

Lindell's Chocolate Shoppe • (906) 296-8083
300 Calumet St, Lake Linden

Kaleva Café • (906) 482-6001
234 Quincy St, Hancock
mykaleva.com • Breakfast: $5–10

Ambassador Restaurant • (906) 482-5054
126 Shelden Ave, Houghton
theambassadorhoughton.com • Entrée: $8–20

Mine Shaft • (906) 482-1230
Bowling, go-carts, arcade, and food
915 Razorback Dr, Houghton
mineshaftfun.com • Entrée: $10–20

Library Restaurant Bar Brew • (906) 487-5882
62 Isle Royale St, Houghton • librarybrewpub.com

Suomi Home Bakery & Restaurant
54 Huron St, Houghton • (906) 482-3220

Joey's Seafood & Grill • (906) 483-0500
304 Shelden Ave, Houghton
joeys-grill.com • Entrée: $11–26

Four Seasons Tea Room • (906) 482-3233
606 Shelden Ave, Houghton
fourseasonstearoom.com

Pilgrim River Steakhouse • (906) 482-8595
47409 US-41, Houghton
pilgrimriversteakhouse.com

J J's Wok N Grill • (906) 483-4868
200 Pearl St, # 6, Houghton

Northern Minnesota

Sven & Ole's • (218) 387-1713
9 W Wisconsin St, Grand Marais
svenandoles.com • Specialty Pizza: $15–21

Crooked Spoon Café • (218) 387-2779
17 W Wisconsin St, Grand Marais
crookedspooncafe.com • Entrée: $20–26

Angry Trout Café • (218) 387-1265
408 W MN-61, Grand Marais • angrytroutcafe.com

My Sister's Place • (218) 387-1915
410 E MN-61, Grand Marais
mysistersplacerestaurant.com

Gun Flint Tavern • (218) 387-1563
111 W Wisconsin St, Grand Marais
gunflinttavern.com

Blue Water Café • (218) 387-1597
20 Wisconsin St, Grand Marais
bluewatercafe.com

World's Best Donuts • (218) 387-1345
Title is not much of an exaggeration
10 E Wisconsin St, Grand Marais
worldsbestdonutsmn.com

Sydney's Frozen Custard • (218) 387-2632
14 S Broadway, Grand Marais

Fitger's Brewhouse Brewery and Grille
Elk burgers, custom brews, and live music
600 E Superior St, Duluth
fitgersbrewhouse.com • (218) 279-2739

Pickwick Restaurant • (218) 623-7425
508 E Superior St, Duluth
pickwickduluth.com • Entrée: $19–41

Pizza Luce • (218) 727-7400
11 E Superior St, Duluth
pizzaluce.com • Specialty Pizza: $14–20

Hanabi • (218) 464-4412
110 N 1st Ave W, Duluth
hanabimn.com • Entrée: $12–24

Sir Benedict's Tavern On The Lake
805 E Superior St, Duluth • (218) 728-1192
sirbens.com • Sandwiches: $8–11

Sammy's Pizza & Restaurant • (218) 727-8551
103 W 1st Ave, Duluth • mysammys.com

Bait N' Bite • (218) 875-2281
9634 Gamma Rd, Kabetogama

Lure Me In • (218) 875-2100
9602 Gamma Rd, Kabetogama

Almost Lindys Swill & Grill • (218) 286-3364
3003 County Road 20, International Falls
almostlindys.com • Entrée: $10–25

Coffee Landing Café • (218) 373-2233
444 3rd St, International Falls

Chocolate Moose Restaurant • (218) 283-8888
2501 2nd Ave. W, International Falls
chocolatemooserestaurant.com • Entrée: $14–23

Giovanni's • (218) 283-2600
301 3rd Ave, International Falls
giosifalls.com • Pasta: $10–15

Grocery Stores

Michigan's Upper Peninsula

Gas Lite General Store • (906) 289-4652
39 Gratiot St, Copper Harbor

Mohawk Superette • (906) 337-2102
158 Stanton Ave, Mohawk

Louie's Super Foods • (906) 337-2311
340 4th St, Calumet

SuperValu • (906) 296-3221
5400 Bridge St, Lake Linden

Econofoods • (906) 487-9675
1000 W Sharon Ave, Houghton

Walmart Supercenter • (906) 482-0639
995 Razorback Dr, Houghton

Festival Foods • (906) 482-7500
47401 M-26, Houghton

Northern Minnesota

Super One • (218) 283-8440
1313 3rd St, International Falls

SuperValu • (218) 283-4475
1907 Valley Pine Circle, International Falls

Lodging

Michigan's Upper Peninsula

Mariner North • (906) 289-4637
245 Gratiot St, Copper Harbor
manorth.com • Rates: $109–149

Minnetonka Resort • (906) 289-4449
560 Gratiot St, Copper Harbor
minnetonkaresort.com • Rates: $70+

Bella Vista Motel • (906) 289-4213
180 6th St, Copper Harbor
bellavistamotel.com • Rates: $75–92

Lake Fanny Hooe Resort & Camp
505 2nd St, Copper Harbor
fannyhooe.com • (906) 289-4451
Rates: Motel/cottage/chalet ($100–130),
campsites ($32–44)

Shoreline Resort • (906) 289-4441
122 Front St, Eagle Harbor

Eagle Lodge • (906) 289-4294
13051 M-26 Lakeshore Dr, Eagle Harbor

Laurium Manor Inn • (906) 337-2549
320 Tamarack St, Laurium
laurium.info • Rates: $99–200

Eagle River Inn • (906) 337-0666
5033 Front St, Eagle River
eagleriverinn.com • Rates: $90+

Keweenaw Mountain Lodge • (906) 289-4403
14252 US-41, Mohawk
atthelodge.com • Rates: $125–199

Sunset Bay Resort & Campground
2701 Sunset Bay Beach Rd, Allouez
sunset-bay.com • (906) 337-2494
Cabins ($140), RV ($30–35) and Tent ($25) sites

White House Motel • (906) 337-3010
3606 US-41, Mohawk
whitehousemotel.com • Rates: $55–66

Mt Bohemia • (906) 289-4105
6532 Lac La Belle Rd, Mohawk
mtbohemia.com • Rates: $65–80

Big Bay Point Lighthouse B&B • (906) 345-9957
You actually sleep inside the lighthouse
3 Lighthouse Rd, Big Bay
bigbaylighthouse.com • Rates: $144+

Vic's Cabins • (906) 337-8427
58696 US-41, Calumet
vicscabins.com • Rates: $50–65

Magnuson Hotel Franklin Square Inn
820 Shelden Ave, Houghton • (866) 9041309
magnusonhotels.com • Rates: $108+

Sheridan on the Lake B&B • (906) 482-7079
47026 Sheridan Place, Houghton
sheridanonthelake.com • Rates: $119–149

City of Houghton RV Park • (906) 482-8745
1100 W Lakeshore Dr, Houghton

Northern Minnesota
Grand Portage Lodge • (218) 475-2401
70 Casino Dr, Grand Portage
grandportage.com • Rates: $95+

Ryden's • (218) 475-2330 • rydensstore.net
9301 Ryden Rd, Grand Portage

Sweetgrass Cove Guesthouse • (218) 475-2421
6880 E MN-61, Grand Portage
sweetgrasscove.com • Rates: $169

Best Western Plus • (218) 387-2240
104 1st Ave E, Grand Marais

MacArthur House B&B • (218) 387-1840
520 W 2nd St, Grand Marais
macarthurhouse.net • Rates: $114+

Gunflint Motel • (218) 387-1454
101 5th Ave W, Grand Marais
gunflintmotel.com • Rates: $59–99

Golden Eagle Lodge & Nordic Ski Center
468 Clearwater Rd, Grand Marais
golden-eagle.com • (218) 388-2203

East Bay Suites • (800) 414-2807
21 Wisconsin St, Grand Marais
eastbaysuites.com • Rates: $136+

Naniboujou Lodge & Restaurant
20 Naniboujou Tr, Grand Marais • (218) 387-2688
naniboujou.com • Rates: $74+

The Inn on Lake Superior • (218) 726-1111
350 Canal Park Dr, Duluth
innonlakesuperior.com • Rates: $174+

Fitger's Inn • (888) 348-4377
600 E Superior St, Duluth
fitgers.com • Rates: $149+

A G Thomson House B&B
2617 E 3rd St, Duluth • (218) 724-3464
thomsonhouse.biz • Rates: $169+

Kettle Falls Hotel • (218) 875-2070
Only in-park (Voyageurs) lodging, boat/plane access
12977 Chippewa Trail, Kabetogama
kettlefallshotel.com • Rates: $80–340

Harmony Beach Resort • (218) 875-2811
10002 Gappa Rd, Lake Kabetogama
harmonybeachresort.com • Rates: $125+

Northern Lights Resort • (218) 875-2591
10176 Bay Club Dr, Lake Kabetogama
nlro.com • Rates: $555/week

Voyageur Park Lodge • (218) 875-2131
10436 Waltz Rd, Kabetogama
voyageurparklodge.com • Rates: $157+

Arrowhead Lodge • (218) 875-2141
10473 Waltz Rd, Kabetogama
arrowheadlodgeresort.com • Rates: $35/person

Trails End Resort • (218) 993-2257
6310 Crane Lake Rd • trails-end-resort.com
Cabins ($125+), rooms ($85), or camp ($40–50)

Ash-Ka-Nam Resort • (218) 374-3181
10209 Ash River Tr, Orr
ashkanamresortandlodge.com • Rates: $100+

Voyageurs Landing Resort • (218) 993-2401
7510 Gold Coast Rd, Crane Lake
voyageurslanding.com • Rates: $75+

Scott's Peaceful Valley Resort • (218) 993-2330
7559 Gold Coast Rd, Crane Lake
scottspeacefulvalley.com • Rates: $130+

Voyageur Motel • (218) 283-9424
1210 3rd Ave, International Falls
voyageurmotel.net

Tee Pee Motel • (218) 283-8494
1501 2nd Ave W, International Falls

Sha Sha Resort • (218) 286-3241
1664 MN-11 E, International Falls
shashaonrainylake.com • Cabins: $240+

Thunderbird Lodge • (218) 286-3151
2170 County Rd 139, International Falls
thunderbirdrainylake.com • Rates: $89+

Home Town Café Motel & RV Park
112 Main St, Littlefork • (218) 278-4788

Arnold's Campground & RV Park
2031 2nd Ave, International Falls • (218) 285-9100
arnoldsfishing.com • Camping: $20–30

*Many chain restaurants and hotels can be found
in Houghton, MI; International Falls, MN; and
Duluth, MN.*

Festivals
Michigan's Upper Peninsula
Winter Carnival • February
Houghton • mtu.edu/carnival

Great Bear Chase • March
Cross-Country ski marathon
Calumet • greatbearchase.com

Porcupine Mtns Music Fest • August
Ontonagon • porkiesfestival.org

Marquette Blues Festival • September
Marquette • marquetteareabluessociety.org

Northern Minnesota
Icebox Days • January
International Falls • internationalfallsmn.us

Voyageurs Classic Sled Dog Race • January
Northome • voyageursclassic.com

Doheny Curling Bonspiel • January
Eveleth • (218) 744-1302

Homegrown Music Festival • May
Duluth • duluthhomegrown.org

Dylan Fest • May
Duluth • bobdylanway.com

Pulling for Peace "International Tug-of-War"
International Falls • peacepull.org • July

Moondance Jam • July
Walker • moondancejam.com

Bayfront Blues • August
Duluth • bayfrontblues.com

Attractions
Michigan's Upper Peninsula
Keweenaw Adventure • (906) 289-4303
Sea kayaking, bike tours, and canoe rentals
155 Gratiot St, Copper Harbor
keweenawadventure.com

Copper Harbor Lighthouse • (906) 289-4966
Provides a short (1.5 hours) Lighthouse Boat Tour
14447 M-26, Copper Harbor Marina
copperharborlighthousetours.com • Tours: $17/adult

Delaware Copper Mine Tours • (906) 289-4688
7804 Delaware Mine Rd, Mohawk
delawarecopperminetours.com

🦆**McLain State Park** • (906) 482-0278
Really nice park with Lake Superior views
18350 M-203, Hancock
michigan.gov/dnr • Camping: $28

Hancock Rec. Area • (906) 482-7413
Fishing, swimming, volleyball, and horseshoes
Portage Lake (M-203), Hancock
cityofhancock.com • Camping: $14–22

Quincy Mine Tours • (906) 482-3101
49750 US-41, Hancock
quincymine.com • Admission: $20/adult

🦆**Mount Bohemia** • (906) 289-4105
Possibly the best ski resort east of the Mississippi
6532 Lac Labelle Rd, Mohawk
mtbohemia.com • Lift Ticket: $59

Mont Ripley Ski Area • (906) 487-2340
49051 N Ski Hill, Hancock
sportsrec.mtu.edu • Lift Ticket: $30+

Michigan Tech Nordic Ski Trails and Forest
22 miles of trails for biking, hiking, skiing
Sharon Ave, Houghton
sportsrec.mtu.edu • Pass: $10

🦆**Keweenaw Brewing Co** • (906) 482-5596
408 Shelden Ave, Houghton • kbc.beer

Rogers Cinema 5 • (906) 482-3470
47420 Highway 26, Houghton

Orpheum Theater • (906) 482-5100
426 Quincy St, Hancock

Pictured Rocks National Lakeshore
Munising • (906) 387-3700
nps.gov/piro • Boat Tour: $38/adult

Island Resort & Casino • (906) 466-2941
US 399 Hwy 2, Harris
islandresortandcasino.com

Northern Minnesota
Grand Portage National Monument
170 Mile Creek Rd, Grand Portage
nps.gov/grpo • (218) 475-0123

Grand Portage Casino • (218) 475-2401
72 Casino Dr, Grand Portage

Great Lakes Aquarium • (218) 740-3474
353 Harbor Dr, Duluth
glaquarium.org • Admission: $16.50/adult

Lake Superior Railroad Museum
506 W Michigan St, Duluth • (218) 727-8025
lsrm.org • Admission: $12/adult

Vista Fleet • (218) 722-6218
323 Harbor Dr, Duluth
vistafleet.com • Rates: $16+

Lake Superior Maritime Center
600 S Lake Ave, Duluth • (218) 720-5260
lsmma.com • Admission: Free

Glensheen Historic Estate • (218) 726-8910
3300 London Rd, Duluth
glensheen.wp.d.umn.edu • Admission: $15+/adult

Edgewater Resort & Waterpark
2400 London Rd, Duluth • (800) 777-7925
duluthwaterpark.com

Spirit Mountain Recreation • (218) 628-2891
9500 Spirit Mountain Pl, Duluth
spiritmt.com • Lift Tickets: $29+

🦆**Lake Superior Zoo** • (218) 730-4500
7210 Fremont St, Duluth
lszooduluth.org • Admission: $10/adult

Marcus Duluth Cinema • (218) 729-0335
300 Harbor Dr, Duluth

Ebels Voyageur Houseboats • (888) 883-2357
10326 Ash River Tr, Orr
ebels.com • Rates: $325+/day

Northernaire Houseboats • (218) 286-5221
2690 County Rd 94, International Falls
northernairehouseboats.com • Rates: $285+/day

Comet Theater • (218) 666-5814
102 S River St, Cook
comettheater.com • Tickets: $8/adult

Cine 1 & 2 • (218) 283-3063
1319 3rd Street, International Falls
cine5theatre.com

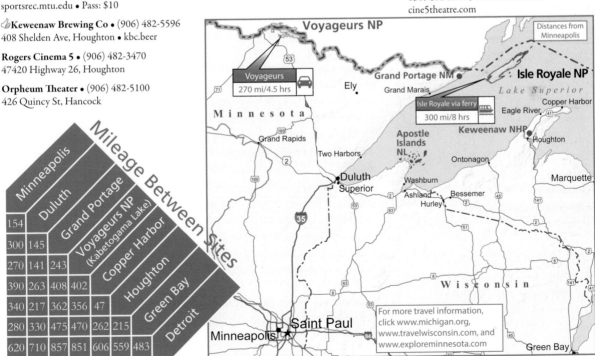

Mileage Between Sites

	Minneapolis	Duluth	Grand Portage	Voyageurs NP (Kabetogama Lake)	Copper Harbor	Houghton	Green Bay
Duluth	154						
Grand Portage	300	145					
Voyageurs NP (Kabetogama Lake)	270	141	243				
Copper Harbor	390	263	408	402			
Houghton	340	217	362	356	47		
Green Bay	280	330	475	470	262	215	
Detroit	620	710	857	851	606	559	483

Distances from Minneapolis

Voyageurs — 270 mi/4.5 hrs
Isle Royale via ferry — 300 mi/8 hrs

For more travel information, click www.michigan.org, www.travelwisconsin.com, and www.exploreminnesota.com

Sheep in the Badlands near Hay Butte Overlook

Badlands

25216 Ben Reifel Road
Interior, SD 57750
Phone: (605) 433-5361
Website: nps.gov/badl

Established: November 10, 1978
Size: 244,000 Acres
Annual Visitors: 900,000
Peak Season: Summer

Activities: Camping, Hiking,
Driving, Biking, Stargazing, Fossil
Hunting, and Horseback Riding

Campgrounds: Cedar Pass Camp
($22–37/night), Sage Creek Camp
(primitive, free)
Backcountry Camping: Permitted
(free, no permit required)
Lodging: Cedar Pass Lodge
Open: mid-April–mid-October
Rates: $176/night

Park Hours: All day, every day
Entrance Fee: $15/vehicle,
$7/individual (foot, bike, etc.)

The Badlands is a swath of semi-arid land bisected by a 60-mile rock wall with steep pinnacles and spires that used to be a daunting site to Indians, fur trappers, and homesteaders. Lack of water, scorching sun, arctic winters, and bone-chilling north winds make the mixed-grass prairies and colorful rock formations of western South Dakota uncommonly hostile. Lakota Sioux and French fur trappers felt the same way. Lakota called it "mako sica." To trappers, it was "les mauvaises terres à traverser." Two languages, one translation: "bad lands." Spanish explorers were even less complimentary. They referred to the rugged buttes, dusty siltstones, and gaping gullies as "tierra baldía" or "waste land." But as they say, one man's trash is another man's treasure.

For more than 150 years, the Badlands have been treasured by archaeologists and paleontologists. Buried in layers of shale, sandstone, volcanic ash, and siltstone are millions of years of history. Ancient fossils, some 35 million years old, retell the story of a shallow sea that once covered the region. Geologic forces caused the sea to drain. Subtropical forests began to grow and rivers and streams deposited layers of debris. Ash from volcanic eruptions in the West was carried by the wind, adding to the geologic stratification. Within it you'll find fossils of small saber-toothed cats, hornless rhinos, three-toed horses, ancient camels, squid, and turtles. As water and wind wear away the earth's surface new fossils are exposed. Each discovery is another page turned in the history of the Badlands, a story scientists are eager to read. Today, the park's White River area is widely regarded as one of the richest mammal fossil beds in the world.

Erosion and deposition have also played a part in this extreme topography. Intense rains and piercing winds have worn away layers of loose, fine-grained rock. Steep slopes funnel water and sediment to the valley floor rapidly and efficiently. Vegetation capable of slowing these erosional forces is unable to grow in the semi-arid climate and jagged rock formations. It's the perfect storm of climatic and geologic conditions, resulting in an inch of rock eroding each year. It will continue for centuries until the "Badlands Wall" is nothing at all.

A perfectly flat plain may have been all homesteaders were expecting. Drawn to the Badlands by promises of free land and prospect of gold in the Black Hills, easterners began gobbling up lots of land, 160 acres at a time. An abundance of land didn't make up for the harsh conditions. Much like the lives of Lakota Indians and French fur trappers before them, it was a struggle to survive and nearly impossible to coax enough crops out of the ground to support a family. But they tried; cattle replaced bison and wheat fields displaced grasslands. They tended to the land as best they could, but the land never gave back, and only the hardiest homesteaders hung on to life in the Badlands.

Homesteaders and other 19th-century developments left their mark on South Dakota's prairies. Today only one in every 50 prairie areas remain, and Badlands protects the largest prairie in the National Park System. Inexplicably, the prairie is teeming with life. Bison and pronghorn graze. Prairie dogs scurry about their burrows. Sure-footed bighorn sheep traverse the rocky slopes. Swift fox and black-footed ferret (once thought to be extinct) have been reintroduced by biologists. Where humans failed to survive a healthy prairie ecosystem has flourished, showing the land might not be so bad after all.

Lodging

Cedar Pass Lodge (877.386.4383, cedarpass-lodge.com, $176/night) provides the only lodging, gift store, and restaurant in the park. It is located near Ben Reifel Visitor Center on Badlands Loop Road. Before its first incarnation burned down in the 1930s, Cedar Pass Lodge was a dance hall where bands like "Hotsy Totsy Boys" and "Honolulu Fruit Gum Orchestra" were conducted by a bandleader named Lawrence Welk.

Saddle Pass Trail

When to Go

The park is open all year, but extreme weather conditions can cause uncomfortable or difficult touring. Summer high temperatures can exceed 110°F. Winter lows may dip below -40°F. **Ben Reifel Visitor Center**, located on Badlands Loop Road (Hwy 240), is open every day except Thanksgiving, Christmas, and New Year's. It is typically open from 8am to 5pm, but hours are extended in summer and shortened in winter. **Cedar Pass Lodge**, near the visitor center, is the only in-park lodging and is open in summer. On South Dakota Hwy 27, about 20 miles south of the town of Scenic, you'll find White River Visitor Center. It's open seasonally (June to mid-September) from 10am to 4pm.

Transportation & Airports

Public transportation does not serve the park. The closest airport is Rapid City Regional (RAP), located 67 miles west of the park on Hwy 44. Car rental is available at the airport.

Directions

Badlands National Park is located in southwestern South Dakota just south of Interstate 90.

Arriving on I-90 from the east, take Exit 131 (Interior) and follow park signs to the Northeast Entrance. From the west, take Exit 110 (Wall) and follow signs leading to the park's Pinnacles Entrance. Highway 44 (from Rapid City) provides a more scenic alternate route. Take Hwy 44 east to Interior. Continue on Hwy 377, which leads directly to the park's Interior Entrance.

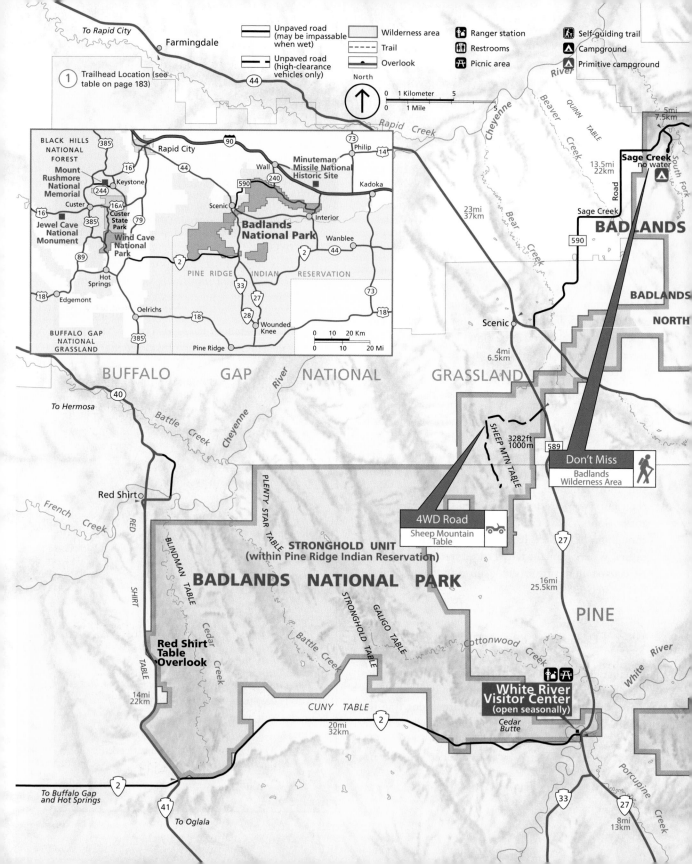

Legend (top of map):

Unpaved road (may be impassable when wet)

Unpaved road (high-clearance vehicles only)

Wilderness area

Trail

Overlook

Ranger station

Restrooms

Picnic area

Self-guiding trail

Campground

Primitive campground

(1) Trailhead Location (see table on page 183)

North

0   1 Kilometer   5

0   1 Mile

To Rapid City

Farmingdale

44

Inset map:

BLACK HILLS NATIONAL FOREST

Mount Rushmore National Memorial

385

16

Rapid City

90

Keystone

244

16A

Custer

Custer State Park

Jewel Cave National Monument

79

Wind Cave National Park

385

16

89

Hot Springs

18

Edgemont

Oelrichs

18

385

BUFFALO GAP NATIONAL GRASSLAND

Pine Ridge

2

33

27

28

Wounded Knee

PINE RIDGE INDIAN RESERVATION

Wall

240

590

Scenic

Badlands National Park

Interior

Minuteman Missile National Historic Site

Philip

14

Kadoka

Wanblee

44

2

73

18

0   10   20 Km
0   10   20 Mi

Rapid Creek

Cheyenne River

Beaver Creek

QUINN TABLE

River

Philip

14

5mi 7.5km

Sage Creek
no water

13.5mi 22km

Road

South Fork

Sage Creek

BADLANDS

590

23mi 37km

Bear Creek

BADLANDS

NORTH

Scenic

4mi 6.5km

SHEEP MTN TABLE

3282ft 1000m

589

Don't Miss
Badlands Wilderness Area

4WD Road
Sheep Mountain Table

27

16mi 25.5km

BUFFALO   GAP   NATIONAL   GRASSLAND

To Hermosa

40

Battle Creek

Cheyenne River

Red Shirt

French Creek

RED SHIRT TABLE

PLENTY STAR TABLE

BLINDMAN TABLE

Cedar Creek

STRONGHOLD UNIT
(within Pine Ridge Indian Reservation)

BADLANDS   NATIONAL   PARK

Battle Creek

STRONGHOLD TABLE

GALIGO TABLE

Cottonwood Creek

PINE

White River

Red Shirt Table Overlook

14mi 22km

CUNY TABLE

20mi 32km

2

White River Visitor Center
(open seasonally)

Cedar Butte

33

27

8mi 13km

Porcupine Creek

To Buffalo Gap and Hot Springs

2

41

To Oglala

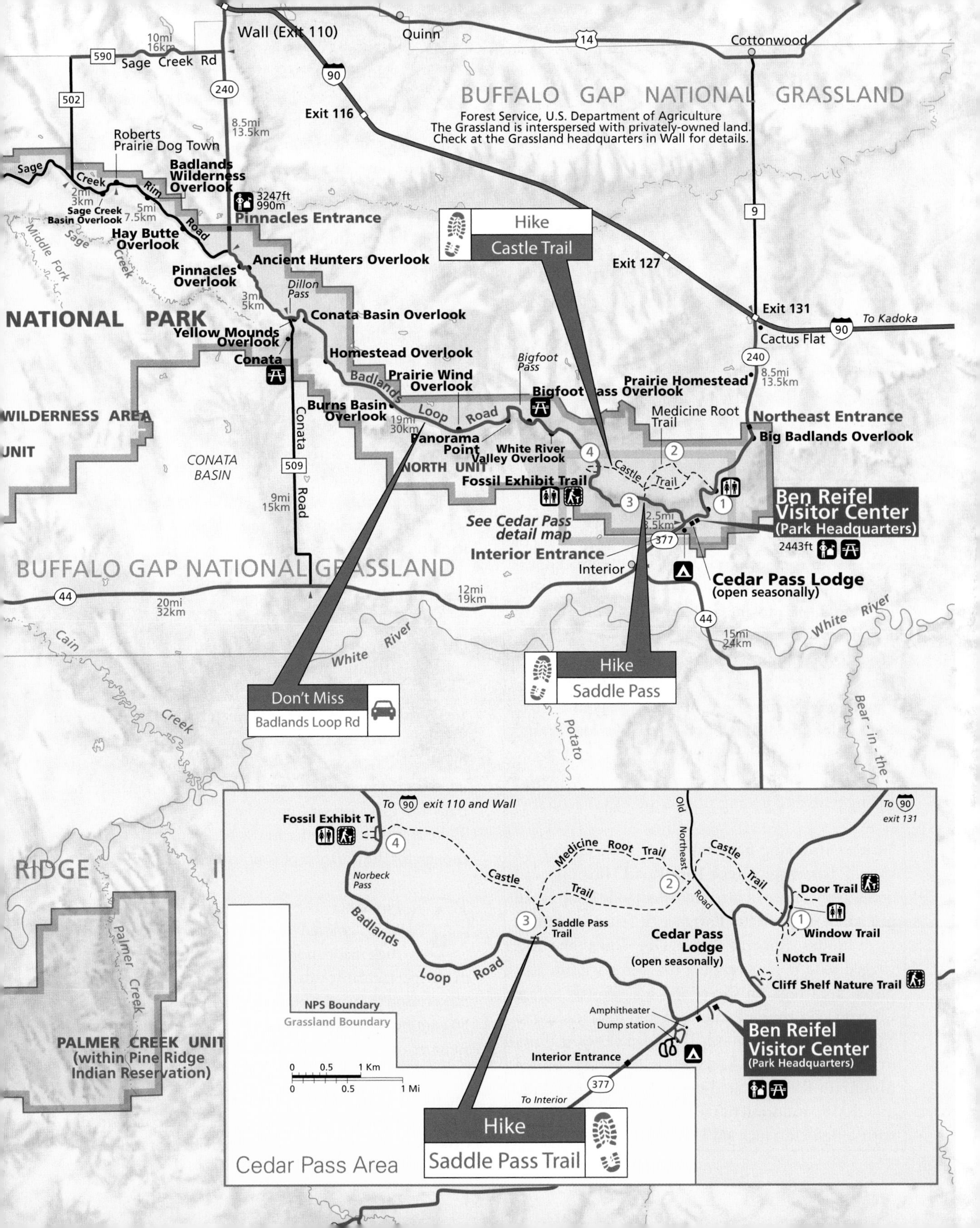

Wall (Exit 110)
Quinn
Cottonwood
590
Sage Creek Rd
10mi 16km
502
240
90
14
BUFFALO GAP NATIONAL GRASSLAND
Forest Service, U.S. Department of Agriculture
The Grassland is interspersed with privately-owned land.
Check at the Grassland headquarters in Wall for details.
Exit 116
8.5mi 13.5km
Roberts Prairie Dog Town
Badlands Wilderness Overlook
3247ft 990m
Pinnacles Entrance
Sage Creek Rim Road
2mi 3km
Sage Creek Basin Overlook
5mi 7.5km
Hay Butte Overlook
Middle Fork Sage Creek
Ancient Hunters Overlook
Pinnacles Overlook
Dillon Pass
3mi 5km
NATIONAL PARK
Conata Basin Overlook
Yellow Mounds Overlook
Conata
Homestead Overlook
Badlands Loop Road
Prairie Wind Overlook
Bigfoot Pass
Bigfoot Pass Overlook
Burns Basin Overlook
19mi 30km
Panorama Point
White River Valley Overlook
WILDERNESS AREA
UNIT
CONATA BASIN
Conata Road
509
NORTH UNIT
Fossil Exhibit Trail
9mi 15km
Hike
Castle Trail
Exit 127
Exit 131
To Kadoka
Cactus Flat
9
8.5mi 13.5km
Prairie Homestead Overlook
Medicine Root Trail
Northeast Entrance
Big Badlands Overlook
Castle Trail
Ben Reifel Visitor Center (Park Headquarters)
2443ft
See Cedar Pass detail map
2.5mi 3.5km
377
Interior Entrance
Interior
Cedar Pass Lodge (open seasonally)
BUFFALO GAP NATIONAL GRASSLAND
44
20mi 32km
12mi 19km
15mi 24km
White River
Cain Creek
Hike
Saddle Pass
Don't Miss
Badlands Loop Rd
Potato Creek
Bear-in-the-Lodge Creek
RIDGE
Palmer Creek
PALMER CREEK UNIT (within Pine Ridge Indian Reservation)
To 90 exit 110 and Wall
Fossil Exhibit Tr
Norbeck Pass
Medicine Root Trail
Castle Trail
Old Northeast Road
Castle Trail
To 90 exit 131
Door Trail
Window Trail
Notch Trail
Cliff Shelf Nature Trail
Saddle Pass Trail
Badlands Loop Road
Cedar Pass Lodge (open seasonally)
NPS Boundary
Grassland Boundary
Amphitheater
Dump station
Interior Entrance
Ben Reifel Visitor Center (Park Headquarters)
0 0.5 1 Km
0 0.5 1 Mi
377
To Interior
Hike
Saddle Pass Trail
Cedar Pass Area

Sheep Mountain Table

Driving

A park was authorized here in 1929 with the stipulation that South Dakota had to construct a road through its most significant rock formations. **Badlands Loop Road** was built and Badlands National Monument was established in 1939. For your gallon of gas, Badlands is one of the best scenic detours you'll find in the country. While driving along I-90, you can take Hwy 240 for a 42-mile scenic detour through the Badlands between Exits 110 and 131. From the interstate it's not obvious that one of the most amazing natural wonders in the world is a few miles to the south. Once you reach the Pinnacles or Northeast Entrance, eroded stone formations appear out of nowhere and Hwy 240 becomes Badlands Loop Road. It provides access to 11 overlooks, Ben Reifel Visitor Center, Cedar Pass Lodge and Campground, and trailheads for the park's most popular hikes. Door, Window, Notch, Cliff Shelf Nature, and Fossil Exhibit Trails are pleasant short hikes found along Badlands Loop Road. Visitors should allow at least 60 minutes to drive the 42-mile loop, but it wouldn't be difficult to spend an entire day hiking trails and poking around the visitor center.

Visitors searching for a more primitive experience should drive **Sage Creek Rim Road**. This unpaved and washboard road intersects Badlands Loop Road just south of Pinnacles Entrance. It features a bunch of overlooks, Robert's Prairie Dog Town, and this rugged road is your best bet for seeing wildlife like bison, deer, bighorn sheep, and fox. Shortly before the road exits the park, there is a spur road leading to Sage Creek Campground. The Road closes at times in winter and after heavy rains in spring. **Sheep Mountain Road**, located four miles south of Scenic on CR-589 is unreal, but it's only passable when dry with a high-clearance 4WD vehicle.

Camping

Badlands National Park has two maintained drive-in campgrounds, both are open year-round. Backcountry camping is also allowed. **The park does not have showers.** Open campfires are not permitted due to the flammable nature of prairie grass.

Cedar Pass Campground: Cedar Pass is the only developed campground. It is located near Ben Reifel Visitor Center. All 96 sites have covered picnic tables and exceptional views of Badlands Wall. Cold running water and flush toilets are available nearby. There is a dump station ($1.00 per use). Sites cost $22 per night or $37 per night with hookups. They can be reserved at (605) 433-5460 or cedarpasslodge.com.

Sage Creek Primitive Campground: Sage Creek is accessed via the unpaved, deep-rutted Sage Creek Rim Road. The campground is free on a first-come, first-served basis. Water is not available. Pit toilets and picnic tables are located nearby.

Backcountry Camping: Camping in the park's backcountry is allowed and does not require an overnight permit. However, backpackers should contact a staff member at Ben Reifel Visitor Center or Pinnacles Entrance Station before setting out on an overnight trip. Backcountry users are also advised to register at Medicine/Castle Trail Loop, Saddle Pass Trailhead, Conata Picnic Area, Sage Creek Basin Overlook, or Sage Creek Campground before departing. Set up your campsite at least 0.5-mile from roads and trails and make sure it cannot be seen from the roadway. There is little to no water in the backcountry, so carry in enough for the duration of your trip.

Fossils

Multi-colored layers of fragile sedimentary rock made more than spectacular scenery, they made spectacular fossils. Prehistoric fossils are extremely rare around the world, but in Badlands they are common. So common, a visitor occasionally stumbles upon one. In summer of 2010, a seven-year-old girl from Atlanta discovered a museum-quality skull of a small saber-toothed cat. Should you unearth the next amazing fossil, leave it where it is and notify a ranger. It is illegal to collect fossils, flowers, rocks, and animals from federal property.

If you don't spark the next big dig, you can still learn all about paleontology, fossils, and the park's ancient history by viewing exhibits and replicas at **Ben Reifel Visitor Center** and **Fossil Exhibit Trail**. Fossil Exhibit is the last hiking trail on Badlands Loop Road if you entered via Northeast Entrance, or the first trail from Pinnacles Entrance. It is educational in nature, but expect your kids to be playing on the Badlands formations rather than learning about extinct animals found within the rock's layers. Regardless, this trail is a great stop for families.

Hiking

If the temperature is 110°F or you've arrived in the middle of a "gully washers," not leaving your car is understandable. If not, get out and meet the Badlands face-to-face. Hiking through passes in the wall along deep canyons and towering pinnacles is a perfect way to commune with this unique landscape. On a comfortable day you may be tempted to take a long, casual hike on **Castle Trail**. A few miles south of Northeast Entrance is Door/Window Trail Parking Area where three excellent trails (**Door, Window, and Notch**) begin. Each one is less than a mile roundtrip, supplying its own perspective of Badlands Wall and the erosional forces responsible for it. Short on time, sure-footed guests in search of fantastic views should drive no further than **Saddle Pass Trailhead**. It's a 0.25-mile climb up and into the Badlands. Please refer to the hiking table below for a complete list of trails. You are allowed to explore beyond designated trails, but be aware of hidden canyons and cracks in the floor. Off-trail hikers must have exceptional map reading skills, as similar looking landscapes make route finding difficult.

Biking

Biking is not a very common activity. For starters, bicycles are not permitted on any of the park's hiking trails. They are only allowed on paved and unpaved roadways. **Badlands Loop Road** can be a challenging and scenic bike ride when motorists aren't racing back and forth at 45 mph. The road is narrow and filled with twists, turns, and climbs. It's best to pedal early in the morning or closer to evening when fewer vehicles are out and about. **Sage Creek Rim Road** is an option for mountain bikers, but this rutted roadway is not the most posterior-friendly biking surface. Another reason to skip Sage Creek Rim Road is **Sheep Mountain Road**. Located about 4 miles south of the tiny town of Scenic, it's an excellent mountain biking destination. The road follows Sheep Mountain Table for 7 miles (one-way). Biking the Badlands may sound uninviting, but you may want to seriously consider toting your two-wheelers for other trails located nearby. George S. Mickelson Trail in Deadwood and Centennial Trail in Sturgis are excellent pedaling alternatives for the adrenaline junky.

Stargazing

Stargazing is one of the most underrated activities in any location far from big city lights that tend to drown out nightscapes. At Badlands you

Badlands Hiking Trails (Distances are roundtrip)

Name	Location (# on map)	Length	Difficulty Rating & Notes
Door - 🥾	Badlands Loop Road (1)	0.75 mile	E – Self-guided trail accesses other side of Badlands Wall
Window	Badlands Loop Road (1)	0.25 mile	E – Peek the Badlands from an eroded "window"
Notch - 🥾	Badlands Loop Road (1)	1.5 miles	M – Views of White River Valley, must climb a wooden ladder or scramble up a gully
Cliff Shelf	Badlands Loop Road (1)	0.5 mile	M – Short loop follows a boardwalk and climbs stairs
Castle - 🥾	Badlands Loop Road (1, 4)	10.0 miles	M – Passes mostly level terrain and Badlands formations, connects Fossil Exhibit and Door/Window Parking Areas
Medicine Root	Spur from Castle Trail (2)	4.0 miles	M – Detour through a mixed-grass prairie
Saddle Pass - 🥾	Badlands Loop Road (3)	0.25 mile	M – Short, steep climb straight up the Badlands Wall
Fossil Exhibit	Badlands Loop Road (4)	0.25 mile	E – View replicas of fossils that were unearthed here
Difficulty Ratings: E = Easy, M = Moderate, S = Strenuous			

can admire otherworldly rock formations by day, and gaze into another world at night. Enjoy an evening stargazing program with a park ranger or simply sit outside your tent, staring up at the stars.

Horseback Riding

Horseback Riding is allowed anywhere in the park except on marked trails, roads, highways, and developed areas. You must trailer in your own horses, as guided rides are not offered. A portion of Sage Creek Campground is designated for horse use, and there is a watering hole 0.5-mile southwest of camp.

Ranger Programs

From June to mid-September Badlands' rangers give walks, talks, and presentations. You can find a weekly listing of ranger-led activities on white bulletin boards along Badlands Loop Road, at visitor centers (call or stop-in), or at the park's website. If you're enchanted by the spires and buttes of Badlands Wall, you may want to join a ranger on "Geology Walk." Confused about why fossils of ancient sea creatures were found in the middle of this prairie land? "Fossil Talk" is the ranger program for you. Curious about more recent life on the prairie, including today's wildlife? Hop aboard a "Prairie Walk." In addition to these activities the park offers a Night Sky Program, a Junior Ranger Program, and a "ranger's choice" Evening Program. Most programs take place at Cedar Pass Campground's Amphitheater.

For Kids

Fossils and kids are almost always a winning combination, so Fossil Exhibit Trail and Ben Reifel Visitor Center are two good destinations for families. Everyone's favorite fossils, dinosaurs, have yet to be unearthed here, but many other prehistoric beasts have been found fossilized in Badlands' soft rock layers. The elephant-sized titanothere and the ancient scavenger archaeotherium (nicknamed the "big pig" even though it's not genetically related to pigs) lived in the area millions of years ago. A three-toed horse, an ancient camel, a small sabretooth cat, and several other mammals and sea creatures have also been found. As the ground continues to erode, new fossils are exposed and discovered by paleontologists and visitors. The White River Area is one of the world's most productive fossil beds.

If your children are more interested in animals that are still scurrying about, stop at **Robert's Prairie Dog Town** on Sage Creek Rim Road. These little critters are sure to draw a few giggles as they pop in and out of their burrows, barking among their friends.

Kids also have the opportunity to become a **Junior Ranger**. Your child can join this exclusive club one of two ways: by completing the free junior ranger activity book (available online or at Ben Reifel Visitor Center) or by attending an official Junior Ranger Program during summer. Check online or at a visitor center for an up-to-date schedule of events. When completed, return the booklet to the visitor center, where your child will be awarded an official Badlands National Park Junior Ranger badge.

Flora & Fauna

There was a time when prairie sprawled across more than a third of North America. These areas were too wet to be deserts and too dry to support trees. Today, most are gone, but the largest remaining prairie protected by the National Park System is located at Badlands. Nearly 50% of the park is mixed-grass prairie, a combination of short and tall grass. The other half is Badlands rock formations with small areas of woodlands, wetlands, and shrublands mixed in. More than 400 species of plants survive in this dry and rocky environment. Of these, nearly 60 are grasses.

Semi-arid land also provides habitat for a surprising diversity of wildlife: 55 mammal species, 120 bird species, and 19 species of reptiles and amphibians. Park biologists have determined these prairies can sustain nearly 800 bison, far fewer than the original herds that numbered more than one million but a healthy population by today's standards. Bighorn sheep, swift fox, pronghorn, mule deer, coyotes, and prairie dogs also reside here. Among Badlands' animals, **black-footed ferrets** have the most remarkable story. These nocturnal critters—once thought to be extinct—were accidentally rediscovered in Wyoming. About 12 ferrets were taken into captivity, and search for suitable habitats began. Badlands was selected because its prairie dog population (black-footed ferrets' primary food source) was healthy and free of diseases. Today, park biologists monitor the ferret population. They are reproducing naturally and in an apparent state of self-sustainability.

The seldom-visited **Badlands Wilderness Area**, accessed via Sage Rim Road (unpaved), is by far the best location to view wildlife.

Pets

Pets are permitted in the park, but must be kept on a leash no more than six feet in length at all times. They are allowed in developed areas like campgrounds. Pets, with the exception of service animals, are not allowed on hiking trails, in public buildings, or in the backcountry.

Accessibility

Ben Reifel and White River Visitor Centers are accessible to wheelchair users. Cedar Pass Campground has two fully-accessible sites. Cedar Pass Lodge is fully accessible. Fossil Exhibit and Windows Trails as well as the first section of Door and Cliff Shelf Trails have accessible boardwalks. Ranger programs held at Cedar Pass Campground Amphitheater are accessible, but ranger-led walks and hikes generally are not, due to rugged terrain.

Weather

The Badlands received its name due to relatively inhospitable living conditions. Lack of water and extreme weather made even the hardiest homesteaders pack up and move elsewhere. Things haven't changed much. The region is semiarid, receiving an average of 16 inches of rain each year, but it's known for brief, intense rainfalls, commonly called "gully-washers." The driest months are from November to January, when it can be bitterly cold. The wettest months are May and June, at which time trails are often muddy and unhikeable. Average high temperatures in July and August reach the low 90s°F but it's not uncommon to crack 100°F. January is the coldest month with average highs around freezing.

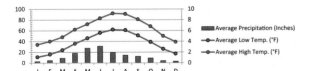

Vacation Planner

The average Badlands trip lasts a little more than 5 hours, just long enough to drive through, hike a trail or two, and make a quick stop at the visitor center. Try to spend at least one night, allowing time to join a **ranger program** (page 184) and see the **stars** (page 183). If you're driving a high-clearance 4WD vehicle, you won't regret checking out **Sheep Mountain Road**, four miles south of Scenic on CR-589. **Cedar Pass Lodge** (page 179) and **two campgrounds** (page 182) are located within the park. Nearby dining, grocery stores, lodging, festivals, and attractions are listed on pages 203–205.

Day 1: Arrive at **Northeast Entrance**, stopping at **Door/Window Trail Parking Area** to get a closer look at Badlands Wall. Hike any or all three of the trails that begin here (Door, Window, and Notch). Together they shouldn't take more than 2–3 hours. Next stop is **Ben Reifel Visitor Center**, where you can watch a short film and browse exhibits. If you haven't already checked the program schedule online or on the white bulletin boards lining Badlands Loop Road, take a look at the visitor center. **Ranger programs** are always a recommended activity. The visitor center also has a nice picnic area, making it a good spot to stop and have lunch. A few hours before sunset return to Door/Window Parking Area. This time head to the west side of the road and hike **Castle Trail** to Saddle Pass then return to the parking area via **Medicine Root Trail**. Notice as the sun gets closer to the horizon the rock's colors become more vibrant and distinct. Castle Trail is also a good destination for a day hike. It connects to **Fossil Exhibit Trail**, where any individuals and children uninterested in a long hike can be waiting to pick up one-way hikers. It's roughly 10 miles from Door/Window Parking Area to Fossil Exhibit Trail.

Day 2: Complete the rest of **Badlands Loop Road**. If anyone missed the view from Saddle Pass, stop to hike the 0.25-mile **Saddle Pass Trail**. Although short, it is definitely not for the timid. Continue west, stopping at overlooks whenever the scenery strikes you, and drive down **Sage Creek Rim Road**. This is where most of the Badlands' wildlife hangs out (particularly in the evening). Here you'll have an excellent chance of seeing bison, prairie dogs, and pronghorn before you leave.

Boxwork seen on the Fairgrounds Tour

Wind Cave

26611 US Highway 385
Hot Springs, South Dakota 57747
Phone: (605) 745-4600
Website: nps.gov/wica

Established: January 9, 1903
Size: 28,295 Acres
Annual Visitors: 610,000
Peak Season: Summer

Activities: Hiking, Scenic Driving, Biking, and Horseback Riding

<u>Cave Tours</u>
Open: All Year
Fee: $10–30
Duration: 1–4 hours

Campgrounds: Elk Mountain
Fee: $18/night ($9/night in winter)
Backcountry Camping: Permitted*
Lodging: None

Park Hours: All day, every day
Entrance Fee: None

*Backcountry camping is restricted to the northwest corner of the park and requires a free permit

Long before European fur traders and eastern miners arrived, Lakota Sioux considered the area now known as Wind Cave National Park sacred. They spoke of a "hole that breathes cool air" and left tipi rings near the cave's only natural entrance. Indian legend describes this opening as the site where bison first emerged to roam the prairies. While evidence bison originated from the cave is scant, scientists know, with some certainty, why the cave is so "windy." It's all about air pressure. Air flows into the abyss when pressure outside the cave is greater than pressure inside. However, when pressure is greater inside the cave, gusts of air blow out of its natural opening.

One summer day, a strong wind blowing out of this opening knocked a hat from the top of Tom Bingham's head. Tom and his brother, Jesse, re-discovered the cave in 1881. And so the story goes. While displaying their find to a few locals, Tom leaned over the small chasm only to have a gust of wind blow off his hat, ultimately falling into the cavern below. Tom and Jesse were first to rediscover the cave, but they weren't willing to be first to enter the unknown world below. That honor was left for Charlie Crary, a local miner, who entered Wind Cave with a small lantern and a ball of twine to trace his path. Shortly after this discovery, South Dakota Mining Company took an interest in the cave. The company hired J. D. McDonald to lay claim to a homestead directly above the cave and begin examining its passages for gold. His 16-year-old son, Alvin, did most of the exploring. Much to the mining company's dismay he wasn't seeking gold. Alvin charted new passages for the simple pleasure of witnessing and exploring a place never seen before by human eyes.

Things turned contentious in 1899. J. D. McDonald and a partner en-tered a dispute over land ownership with South Dakota Mining Com-pany. The Department of Interior ruled that no one was entitled to the land, as it was not being used properly for mining nor did it comply with the terms of the Homestead Act. Two years later, 1,000 acres surrounding the cave became federal property and tours were given for free by Elmer McDonald (another son of J. D.). On January 9, 1903, legislation passed creating Wind Cave, the eighth national park of the United States and first created to protect a cave, ensuring visitors could satisfy their own curiosities exploring the mysteries of the unknown just like Alvin McDonald did.

Very few visitors explore the rolling grasslands and ponderosa pine forests above this subterranean labyrinth. These landscapes and the wildlife living here are worthy of federal protection by themselves. Lakota called this region "Pahá Sápa" or "Black Hills," a name earned by the cover of trees that look black compared to a sea of grass surrounding them. By the time the park was established in 1903, bison, elk, and pronghorn were no longer found here. Park employees attempted reintroduction programs to restore the habitat to its original state. Today, Wind Cave National Park is home to one of four free-roaming, genetically pure bison herds on publicly owned lands. Pronghorn are seen in the prairies and elk can be heard bugling in the backcountry.

Whether your curiosity takes you to the backcountry or underground passages, you'll begin to realize why Lakota Sioux considered this area sacred. It's the same indescribable gravitational force that drew Alvin McDonald deeper and deeper into the cave.

Camping

For the reasonable price of $18 per night visitors can camp at **Elk Mountain Campground**, located near the park's western boundary, one mile north of the visitor center. All sites are available on a first-come, first-served basis, but the camp rarely fills to capacity. Pull-through sites are available for RVs. Hookups, dump stations, and **showers are not available**. Restrooms with cold water are located nearby. Water is turned off from late fall through early spring. During this time vault toilets are available and the camping fee is reduced to $9/night. Campfire wood is available near the camp's entrance. No cost is associated with wood, but donations are accepted. Group camping is available by reservation only. Reservations can be made by calling (605) 745-4600.

Prairie Dog town along NPS 5

When to Go
The park is open all year. **Wind Cave Visitor Center** is open daily from 8am to 4:30pm, with extended hours in summer. It closes on Thanksgiving, Christmas, and New Year's Day. Cave tours are offered daily at the visitor center.

Transportation & Airports
Public transportation does not serve the park. The closest airport is Rapid City Regional (RAP), located about 60 miles to the northeast.

Directions
Wind Cave is located at the southern tip of South Dakota's Black Hills. It is 6 miles north of Hot Springs, SD and 1.5 hours (driving) from Rapid City, SD. Several routes are available if traveling from the north (two are listed below).

Via US-385/US-16 (60 miles): The longest and fastest route provides opportunity for a short detour to **Mount Rushmore**. Follow US-16 W for 40 miles. Turn right at Custer St/Mt. Rushmore Rd. Continue for 0.5 mile before turning left at US-385 S, which leads into the park.

Via SD-79/SD-87 (55 miles): Take SD-79 S from Rapid City. Turn right at SD-36W and continue onto US-16 Alt W. Turn left to follow SD-87 S, which leads into the park.

Driving
You don't have to hit the trails to get a good view of prairie dog towns, bison, and undulating hills. The park is extremely accessible to motorists. Pullouts along **US-385** and **SD-87** provide outstanding views of underappreciated scenery. Obey the speed limits and watch for wildlife. In the past 20 years more than 80 bison have been hit by motorists, and you don't want an ornery bison on your hands, do you?

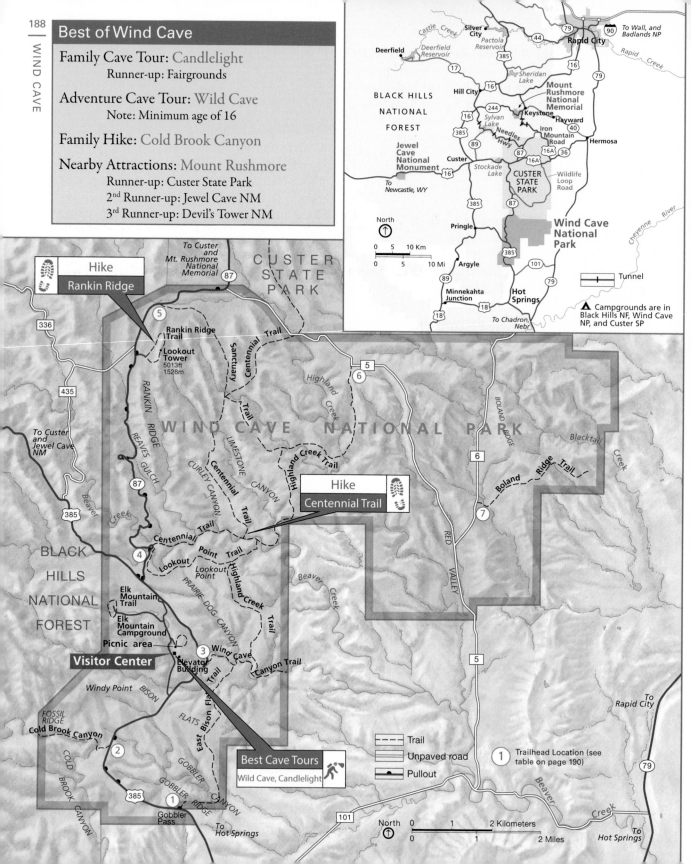

Best of Wind Cave

Family Cave Tour: Candlelight
Runner-up: Fairgrounds

Adventure Cave Tour: Wild Cave
Note: Minimum age of 16

Family Hike: Cold Brook Canyon

Nearby Attractions: Mount Rushmore
Runner-up: Custer State Park
2nd Runner-up: Jewel Cave NM
3rd Runner-up: Devil's Tower NM

North

0   5   10 Km
0   5   10 Mi

Tunnel

△ Campgrounds are in
Black Hills NF, Wind Cave
NP, and Custer SP

To Wall, and
Badlands NP

Rapid City
Silver City
Deerfield
Deerfield Reservoir
Pactola Reservoir
Castle Creek
Rapid Creek
BLACK HILLS NATIONAL FOREST
Hill City
Sheridan Lake
Mount Rushmore National Memorial
Keystone
Hayward
Sylvan Lake
Needles Hwy
Iron Mountain Road
Hermosa
Jewel Cave National Monument
Custer
Stockade Lake
CUSTER STATE PARK
Wildlife Loop Road
To Newcastle, WY
Wind Cave National Park
Pringle
Cheyenne River
Argyle
Minnekahta Junction
Hot Springs
To Chadron, Nebr.

Hike
Rankin Ridge

To Custer and
Mt. Rushmore
National Memorial

CUSTER STATE PARK

Rankin Ridge Trail
Lookout Tower
5013ft
1528m

Sanctuary Trail
Centennial Trail
Highland Creek

RANKIN RIDGE
REAVES GULCH
LIMESTONE CANYON
CURLEY CANYON
Centennial Trail
Highland Creek Trail

To Custer and
Jewel Cave NM

BLACK HILLS NATIONAL FOREST

WIND CAVE NATIONAL PARK

Hike
Centennial Trail

Centennial Trail
Lookout Point Trail
Lookout Point
Highland Creek Trail

Beaver Creek

BOLAND RIDGE
Boland Ridge Trail
Blacktail Creek
RED VALLEY

Elk Mountain Trail
Elk Mountain Campground
Picnic area

Visitor Center

PRAIRIE DOG CANYON

Windy Point

Wind Cave
Canyon Trail
Elevator Building

BISON FLATS

FOSSIL RIDGE
Cold Brook Canyon

COLD BROOK CANYON

EAST BISON FLATS Trail

GOBBLER CANYON
GOBBLER RIDGE

Best Cave Tours
Wild Cave, Candlelight

To Rapid City

Gobbler Pass
To Hot Springs

To Hot Springs

Beaver Creek

To Hot Springs

Trail
Unpaved road
Pullout

① Trailhead Location (see
table on page 190)

North

0   1   2 Kilometers
0   1   2 Miles

Wind Cave Tours

Name	Fee (Adult/Youth)	Duration	Notes
Garden of Eden	$10 / 5	1 hour	Least strenuous tour visits small samples of boxwork, popcorn, and flowstone (page 190) • Enter/exit by elevator
Natural Entrance	$12 / 6	1.25 hours	A quick hike to the natural entrance before entering via a man-made entrance • Exit by elevator • 300 stairs
Fairgrounds - 🖐	$12 / 6	1.5 hours	Explore boxwork, popcorn, and frostwork in two levels of the cave • Enter and exit by elevator • 450 stairs
Candlelight* - 🖐	$12 / 6	2 hours	Harken back to the original cave tours by Alvin McDonald • Each visitor carries a candle bucket • Minimum age of 8
Wild Cave* - 🖐	$30 / Not Permitted	4 hours	Cavers get dirty as you crawl, squeeze, and climb through sections of the cave very few visit • Minimum age of 16

Youth is 6–16 years of age. Senior or Golfen Age/Access Pass holders pay youth rates.
*Tours are limited to groups of 10. Reservations can be made up to one month in advance by calling (605) 745-4600 (reservations are required for Wild Cave Tour). Tours are only available from mid-June to early September. Long pants, long-sleeved shirts, and sturdy boots are required apparel for the Wild Cave Tour. Gloves are recommended. Tickets are sold at the visitor center. All tours except Wild Cave and Candlelight Tours are sold on a first-come, first-served basis. The cave is a constant 53°F all year, so dress accordingly. Sandals are not recommended footwear.

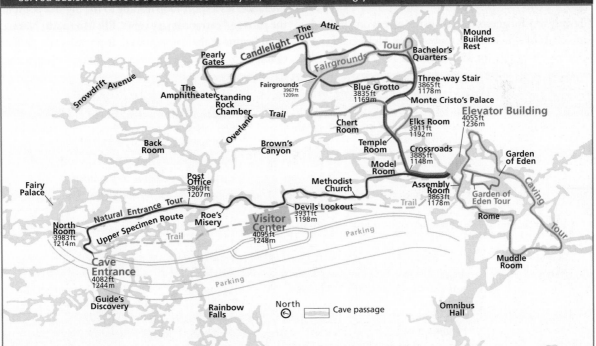

Cave Tours

In 1891, Alvin McDonald, self-proclaimed "permanent guide" of Wind Cave, began a systematic exploration of the cave's passageways. The young man first entered the cave when he was 16 years old with a candle and a ball of twine to trace his path back to the surface. For the next three years he spent several hours per day mapping passages, inspecting chasms, and exploring the unknown. In March of 1891 alone he registered 134 hours in the cave over the course of 34 trips. By the end of that year he had surveyed several miles of passages and had written in his diary..."have given up the idea of finding the end of Wind Cave." Sadly, Alvin died at the age of 20 while in Chicago with his father showing cave specimens. His body was returned to the place he loved so much, buried near the cave's natural entrance where a bronze plaque marks his grave. His diary is on display at the visitor center. In all, Alvin McDonald explored 8 to 10 miles of the cave, naming many of its rooms and passages. Alvin gave up on finding the cave's end, but modern explorers have not. Today, it measures 143 miles in length, the 6th longest cave in the world, and experts believe that only 5 percent of the entire network has been discovered. Each year, about four new miles are mapped out, with no end in sight.

The only way for guests to explore the cave is on a guided tour, many of which follow routes Alvin McDonald and Katie Stable (guide for 11 years until 1902) pioneered more than a century ago. If you'd like to share a similar experience, take the **Candlelight Tour**. A park ranger leads groups of no more than 10 through an unlit section of the cave. The candle bucket you hold in your hand provides the only light. It's an excellent tour and one of two that allow reservations (strongly recommended). **Wild Cave Tour** requires reservations. It's a blast for adventurous individuals who have a little spelunker inside (and who are not the least bit claustrophobic or afraid of getting dirty). The trip lasts four hours. Much of the time will be spent on your hands and knees or in other precarious positions as you traverse sections of the cave few visitors get the chance to see. Tour schedules are subject to change. Please call (605) 745-4600 to make reservations or confirm tour times.

Hiking & Backpacking

Hiking is one of the most underrated and underutilized activities. These badlands are a transitional region, highlighted by the convergence of western ponderosa pine forests and eastern mixed-grass prairies. Three self-guided nature trails (featuring interpretive signs along the way or brochures at the trailhead) help you learn about the park's ecology. **Rankin Ridge Nature Trail** is located on SD-87 near the North Entrance. It's a short loop leading to the highest point in the park and extraordinary views. **Elk Mountain Nature Trail** begins at the campground. It provides the perfect example of overlapping pine and prairie ecosystems.

Wind Cave Hiking Trails (Distances are roundtrip)

Name	Location (# on map)	Length	Difficulty Rating & Notes
East Bison Flats	Gobbler Pass near the south entrance (1)	7.4 miles	M – Traverses rolling prairies then joins Wind Cave Canyon 0.5 mile from its trailhead
Cold Brook Canyon	US-385 (2)	2.8 miles	E – Passes a prairie dog town, ends at boundary fence
Wind Cave Canyon	US-385 (3)	3.6 miles	E – Great trail for bird watching
Highland Creek - ♿	US-385 (3) and NPS 5 (6)	17.2 miles	S – Begins off Wind Cave Canyon Trail and continues to NPS 5, crosses prairies and pine forests
Lookout Point	Centennial Trailhead (4)	4.4 miles	M – Views of 1999 wildfire and vast prairies before ending at Beaver Creek
Centennial	SD-87 (4)	12.0 miles	M – A 6-mile sampling of the 111-mile Centennial Trail through the Black Hills that ends at Bear Butte
Sanctuary	Near the north entrance (5)	7.2 miles	M – Cross rolling hills before intersecting Centennial Trail, which continues to Highland Creek Trail
Boland Ridge	NPS 6 (7)	5.4 miles	S – Guaranteed excellent views • May see elk
Difficulty Ratings: E = Easy, M = Moderate, S = Strenuous			

Prairie Vista Nature Trail begins near the visitor center, and then loops around a quiet prairie grassland. All three of these trails are about one mile long.

The remaining trails are longer out-and-back treks, but a nice scenic loop (< 5 miles) can be formed by connecting a few trails together. Begin on **Lookout Point Trail**, and follow a short stretch of **Highland Creek Trail** to **Centennial Trail**. From the intersection, take Centennial Trail west, along Beaver Creek, back to Lookout Point/Centennial Trailhead where you started. The park's northwest corner is open to backcountry camping. **Backpackers** can extend this smaller loop by making a figure 8. Hike in on **Lookout Point Trail**, but continue east on **Highland Creek Trail**. Return via **Centennial Trail**, but this time use **Sanctuary Trail** as the connector.

Cold Brook Canyon Trail

Biking

All paved roadways are open to cyclists. If there's heavy traffic moving about the park, you may want to stick to pedaling **US-385**, because it has wider shoulders. **SD-87** is winding and narrow, but it can be fun (and challenging) to bike up to **Rankin Ridge**, the highest point in the park at 5,013 feet. The other two roads, **NPS-5** and **NPS-6**, pass through rolling grasslands. As a whole, Wind Cave is small and very manageable by way of bicycle. Bikes are not permitted on hiking trails or in the backcountry.

Horseback Riding

An alternative method of transportation is to travel by horse. The entire park, except for hiking trails, near water sources, on roadways, and in campground and picnic areas, is open to horseback riding. All visitors must obtain a free permit from the visitor center prior to riding. Currently no outfitters provide guided horse rides within the park.

Ranger Programs

The park's most notable tours are those that occur in the cave's passageways, but you'll also find quality ranger programs above the surface. Prairie hikes (2 hours long) are offered daily during the summer beginning at 9am and departing from the visitor center. Occasionally, the park offers evening hikes to a nearby prairie dog town. You arrive at dusk, because the goal is to spot the endangered (and nocturnal) black-footed ferret. Remember to bring a flashlight. Evening hikes depart from Elk Mountain Campground Amphitheater. Interested visitors should call or stop by the visitor center (605.745.4600) for more details. Additionally, campfire programs and Ranger Talks are offered throughout summer. For a complete schedule, check online or in the latest issue of the park's free publication, *Passages*.

For Kids

Wind Cave is one of the best national parks for children. Below the surface lies the 6th longest cave network in the world. Children can poke around these dimly lit passageways on any one of the park's **guided cave tours** (page 190). If confined dark spaces aren't for you, there's just as much to do back on the surface. A relatively small area and healthy animal populations make Wind Cave a great place to view wildlife. Sometimes you see them up-close and personal without even trying. Bison can be found lumbering alongside (or on) the paved roadways. Children up to age 12 may participate in the **Junior Ranger Program**. Free activity booklets are available online or at the visitor center. Once completed, return to the visitor center to receive a certificate and badge.

Elk near Rankin Ridge

Bison

Flora & Fauna

Today, Wind Cave is one of the best national parks for animal watching and its small size makes wildlife viewing easy and fairly predictable. This wasn't the case in 1903 when it was established. At the time bison, pronghorn, bear, and elk were all extirpated from the region. In 1913, 14 bison were donated to the park by the New York Zoological Society. **Black-footed ferret**, a predator of prairie dogs, was reintroduced in 2007. The reintroduction program has been successful and now you can attend evening programs, where visitors—armed with a flashlight—try to spot these mink-like critters. Sometimes a brigade of bison forms a road-block holding up traffic. Even though they are the largest terrestrial animal in North America, a motivated bison can reach speeds up to 40 mph. On the other end of the size spectrum, prairie dogs scurry from burrow to burrow squawking all the while.

Ponderosa pine forests, common to North America's western regions, occur in great abundance. Prairies, covering more than half the park, erupt in a sea of color from late spring to summer when wildflowers are in bloom.

Pets

When in the park, pets must be kept on a leash no more than six feet in length. They are prohibited from public buildings, the backcountry, and all hiking trails (except Elk Mountain and Prairie Vista Nature Trails). Pets are allowed at Elk Mountain Campground.

Accessibility

The cave and visitor center are accessible to wheelchair users. A special cave tour is offered for visitors with special needs if you call ahead (605.745.4600). Elk Mountain Campground has two accessible campsites.

Weather

Situated at the southern tip of South Dakota's Badlands, Wind Cave enjoys a much warmer and drier climate than the northern hills. January is the coldest month, with average high temperatures around 37°F. Average annual snowfall is 30 inches, fairly evenly distributed from December through March. May and June are the wettest months of the year, receiving roughly 3 inches of rain per month. The hottest month of the year is August when highs average 88°F. However, warm afternoons can quickly turn into brisk evenings with strong winds blowing from the north.

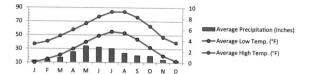
Average Precipitation (Inches)
— Average Low Temp. (°F)
— Average High Temp. (°F)

Vacation Planner

Wind Cave's primary attractions can all be seen in an action-packed, fun-filled day, but a longer visit gives you the opportunity to take another cave tour or explore the backcountry. Try to visit the park during summer so you can enjoy its two best cave tours: **Wild Cave and Candlelight Tours** (reservations can be made up to one month in advance and are required for Wild Cave). Nearby dining, grocery stores, lodging, festivals, and attractions are listed on pages 203–205. (Note: the park hopes to open **Sanson/Casey Ranch** in 2016.)

Day 1: Note that your day is going to be scheduled around a cave tour. If you did not make reservations for the **Candlelight or Wild Cave Tour**, head directly to the visitor center to check availability. If they're booked, **Fairgrounds Tour** (page 190) is a more than passable substitute. Before, after, and in between cave tours hike **Prairie Vista Nature Trail**, (begins near the visitor center), and **Rankin Ridge Nature Trail** (begins near the North Entrance). Stopping at a **prairie dog town** is another good idea.

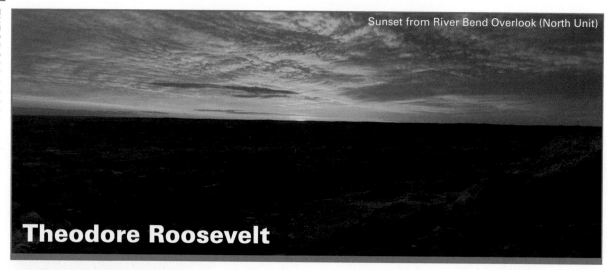

Sunset from River Bend Overlook (North Unit)

Theodore Roosevelt

PO Box 7, Medora, ND 58645
Phone: (701) 623-4466
Website: nps.gov/thro

Established: November 10, 1978
Size: 70,447 Acres
Annual Visitors: 580,000
Peak Season: Summer

Activities: Hiking, Paddling,
Camping, Scenic Driving, Horseback
Riding, Biking, Fishing, Cross-
Country Skiing, and Snowshoeing

Campgrounds: Cottonwood and
Roundup Horse Campground (South
Unit) and Juniper (North Unit)
Fee: $14/night (peak season)
$7/night (off-season)
Backcountry Camping: Permitted*
Lodging: None

Park Hours: All day, every day
Entrance Fee: $20/vehicle,
$10/individual (foot, bike, etc.)

*A free permit is required for
backcountry camping and multi-
day horseback trips in the park

Cliffs, gullies, and badlands formations of Theodore Roosevelt National Park are as rugged and relentless as its namesake. September of 1883, Theodore Roosevelt arrived in the town of Little Missouri a bespectacled, affluent New York City kid. Time spent in the Dakota badlands influenced him so deeply he later wrote, "I would not have been President if it had not been for my experiences in North Dakota." Roosevelt came to "bag a buffalo," but he would do much more than hunt. Romanced by the West's lawless lifestyle and potential for economic success, Roosevelt bought into the booming cattle industry, purchasing Maltese Cross Ranch for $14,000. The one-and-a-half story cabin with wooden floors and separate rooms was, to locals, a "mansion." Today, it is preserved at the park's South Unit.

Roosevelt returned to New York, where tragedy struck on February 14, 1884. Just hours apart, Theodore's mother and wife passed away. Stricken by grief, all Roosevelt could write in his diary was a large "X" and one sentence: "The light has gone out in my life." Searching for solace, he returned to Maltese Cross Ranch. However, the ranch's location on a busy carriage road near the train station lacked the sort of solitude he desired for thought and reflection, prompting him to establish Elkhorn Ranch.

Roosevelt's days as a ranchman were short-lived. Nearly 60 percent of his cattle froze or starved to death during the winter of 1886–87. (His livestock's fate was better than most; nearly 80 percent of the area's cattle died that year.) Within two years, the small meat-packing town of Medora turned into a ghost town. Roosevelt closed Elkhorn Ranch, and in 1898 sold his remaining cattle interests. Today, Elkhorn Ranch is a part of the park. The structures' materials have been scavenged, leaving nothing more than sections of foundation. Interpretive panels provide insight into Roosevelt's domain that once stood proudly above the banks of the Little Missouri.

Roosevelt may have left Elkhorn Ranch as a failure in cattle business, but he returned to New York a hardened ranchman with newfound appreciation of wilderness and the strenuous life of a frontiersman, which helped him ascend to the presidency. He is often referred to as America's "Conservationist President," earning this title by preserving and protecting an estimated 230 million acres of land of ecological and scenic value.

Through efforts of the National Park Service, visitors can experience North Dakota's badlands just as Theodore Roosevelt did (except while driving in cars rather than riding on horseback). Bison (or buffalo), pronghorn, and elk have been reintroduced after being overhunted. Artifacts from Roosevelt's time are on display, including rifles and ranch clothing. Period pieces and several of Roosevelt's personal effects, including a traveling trunk, remain in Maltese Cross Cabin, which can be toured with a park ranger. For all he has done for future generations of America and the welfare of the nation's irreplaceable resources, it is fitting the land that helped mold such an extraordinary man now bears his name.

Camping

Cottonwood (76 sites) and **Juniper** (50 sites) are the primary campgrounds in the South and North Units, respectively. Half Cottonwood's sites can be reserved at (877) 444-6777 or recreation.gov. The rest are available on a first-come, first-served basis. Both campgrounds have pull-through sites for RVs, but hookups are not available. Restrooms, water, grills, and picnic tables are located nearby. The camping fee is $14/night. It is reduced to $7/night during the off-season (October–mid-May). Each campground has a group campsite that accommodates a minimum of 6 campers. **Roundup Group Horse Campground** is intended for horseback riders. It may also be used by groups of 7–20 campers. Fees for a group site are $40/night. All group sites must be reserved at (877) 444-6777 or recreation.gov.

Backcountry camping is allowed with a free permit available at North or South Unit Visitor Center.

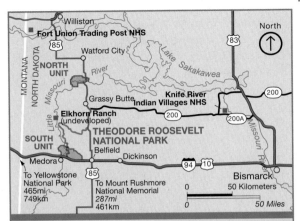

When to Go

The park is open all year. In winter, portions of the South Unit's Scenic Loop Drive and the North Unit's Scenic Road may be closed due to snow and ice. **South Unit Visitor Center** is open daily from 8am–4:30pm (closed on Thanksgiving, Christmas, and New Year's Day). **Painted Canyon Visitor Center** is open from April to mid-November from 8:30am–4:30pm. **North Unit Visitor Center** is open daily from April to mid-November and from Friday to Sunday for the rest of the year from 9am–5:30pm. **Cottonwood and Juniper Campgrounds** are open all year, but with limited services from October to mid-May. May and June are typically the best months to see wildflowers and to paddle the Little Missouri River.

Transportation & Airports

Public transportation does not serve the park. There are small regional airports at Williston and Dickinson. Bismarck Municipal Airport (BIS) is 136 miles east of the South Unit on I-94.

Directions

The park consists of three separate units, all of which are in western North Dakota, north of I-94.

To the South Unit: South Unit's entrance is in the old meat-packing town of Medora. Medora can be reached by taking Exits 24 or 27 from I-94. South Unit Visitor Center and Maltese Cross Cabin are located on the west side of East River Road near the entrance. The Montana–North Dakota State Line is 26 miles west of Medora and Bismarck is 134 miles to the east.

To Painted Canyon Visitor Center: Painted Canyon Visitor Center is located just off I-94 at Exit 32, 7 miles east of Medora. The visitor center, overlook and Painted Canyon hiking trail are all found at the dead end on the north side of the interstate.

To the North Unit: North Unit's entrance is just off US-85, 69 miles north of the South Unit. Head east on I-94 to Exit 43. Take US-85 North to the park's entrance and North Unit Visitor Center.

To the Elkhorn Ranch Unit: From I-94, take Exit 10. Turn right onto County Road 11 and continue for 8.8 miles. Turn right onto Westerheim Road and follow it for 6.5 miles. Turn left on Bell Lake Road. Continue for 11.7 miles. Turn right onto FH 2 towards the USFS Elkhorn Campground. Continue for 3 miles (past the campground) to Elkhorn Ranch Unit Parking Area. (High-clearance vehicle recommended.)

Driving

Driving is the most popular activity. South Unit visitors circle the park via 36-mile **Scenic Loop Drive**, stopping at pullouts to read interpretive signs and soak in the views. It begins just beyond East River Road and provides access to many of the South Unit's hiking trails and overlooks. Drive slowly to spot bison, pronghorn, elk, and wild horses. Residents you can't miss are playful prairie dogs who scurry about their little prairie dog towns.

The North Unit offers a 14-mile (one-way) **Scenic Drive** ending at Oxbow Overlook, where you'll find outstanding panoramic views. As you make your way, watch for wildlife. Mule deer are frequently seen crossing the upper grasslands. Witness the power of erosion at Cannonball Concretions Pullout. Eye the main agent of erosion, the Little Missouri River, from River Bend and Oxbow Overlooks.

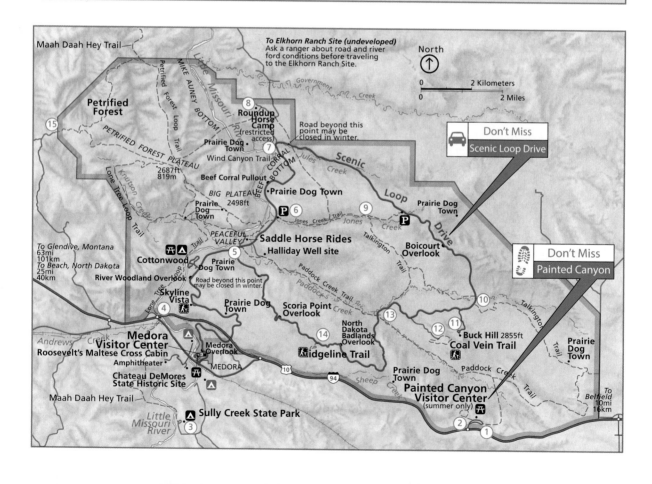

Hiking

A multitude of hiking opportunities exists at both the North and South Unit of Theodore Roosevelt National Park. Whether by horse or foot, all visitors should leave the roadways and explore a few miles of trails that provide a closer look at eroded badlands, bustling prairie dog towns, steep canyons, colorful rock layers, and lush bottomlands. These are the landscapes that helped transform Theodore Roosevelt into the United States' "Conservationist President."

Most of the **South Unit's hiking trails** are accessed via Scenic Loop Drive. Jones Creek, Lower Talkington, and Paddock Creek Trails bisect the loop drive as they follow (usually) dry creek beds. If you arrive after a heavy thunderstorm or recent snow melt check trail conditions prior to hiking, as the creeks occasionally run, causing trails to be muddy or impassable. At times you may have to cross running water.

Paddock and Talkington Trails continue east past Scenic Loop Drive all the way to the park's eastern boundary. The boundary is difficult to miss because you'll encounter a 7-foot fence meant to keep bison and wild horses in and grazing cattle out.

You'll find the **3rd largest Petrified Forest in the U.S.** in the northwest corner of the South Unit. To have a look, take the 10.4-mile **Petrified Loop Trail**, accessed by taking exit 23 on I-94 and heading north along Forest

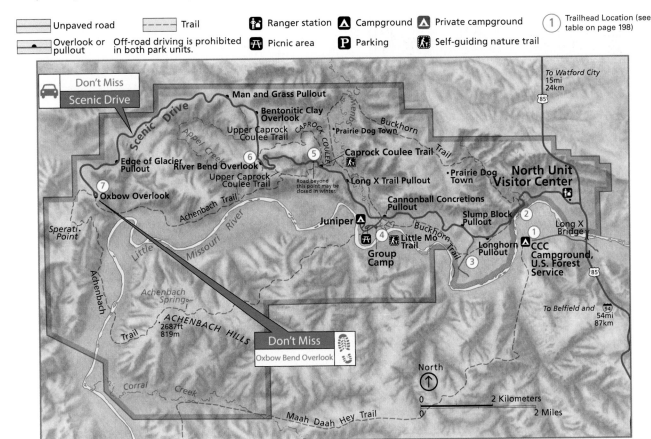

Service Road 730. Turn left at a "Petrified Forest" sign to follow Road 730. Continue until you reach 730-2. Turn right at another "Petrified Forest" sign and take an immediate left. Veer left at the next Y-intersection to the parking area. The trail begins at the lift gate in the fence. Pack plenty of water if you intend to hike the entire loop. Otherwise we recommend doing a shorter out-and-back following the loop to the north, where you'll find the best (and most abundant) petrified wood specimens.

North Unit's Buckhorn Trail is great for seeing bison, prairie dogs, and deer. It's fairly long (11.0 miles) but can be completed in a day. If you really want to push day-hiking to the limits, try **Achenbach Trail**. Check with park rangers about Little Missouri River crossing conditions (2 crossings required) before you begin. Hiking the trail after a heavy rain is not advised. Wear sturdy shoes when hiking, because the park's clay surfaces become slippery when wet.

Theodore Roosevelt Hiking Trails (Distances are one-way unless loop)

	Name	Location (# on map)	Length	Difficulty Rating & Notes
South Unit	Painted Canyon	Painted Canyon Visitor Center (1)	2.1 miles	M – Extremely steep descent into the canyon • Ends at Upper Paddock Creek Trail
	Painted Canyon Nature Trail - ⚲	Painted Canyon Visitor Center (2)	0.9 mile	M – Short loop descends into the canyon
	Lone Tree Loop	I-94 Ramp (4)	12.8 miles	S – Joins Maah Daah Hey Trail from Medora into the park before diverging for a 6.3-mile loop
	Lower Paddock Creek	Scenic Loop Drive (5)	3.6 miles	M – Passes a prairie dog town and crosses the creek numerous times
	Jones Creek	Scenic Loop Drive (6)	3.5 miles	M – Follows Jones Creek, crossing it twice, creek can be muddy and wet (especially in spring)
	Wind Canyon Loop	Scenic Loop Drive (7)	0.4 mile	E – Short climb to an overlook of the Little Missouri River and a wind sculpted canyon
	Petrified Forest Loop - ⚲	Roundup Horse Camp (8) West Park Boundary (15)	16.0 miles 10.4 miles	S – Immediately crosses the Little Missouri River M – Remote Trailhead, but easier hiking
	Lower Talkington	Multiple locations (9, 10, 13)	4.1 miles	M – Follows a creek that is usually dry
	Upper Talkington	Scenic Loop Drive (10)	3.8 miles	M – Continues east from Lower Talkington • Ends at the park's eastern boundary
	Buck Hill	Buck Hill (11)	0.1 mile	E – Note differences in vegetation between drier south-facing slopes and wetter north-facing slopes
	Coal Vein Loop	Coal Vein (unpaved) (12)	0.8 mile	E – Visible after-effects of a fire that burned here from 1951 to 1977 when a coal seam caught fire
	Upper Paddock Creek	Scenic Loop Drive (13)	6.5 miles	M – Intersects Painted Canyon and Upper Talkington Trails before ending at the eastern boundary
	Ridgeline Nature	Scenic Loop Drive (14)	0.6 mile	M – Steep climb to a self-guided loop
North Unit	Buckhorn Loop	Multiple locations (2, 3, 4)	11.4 miles	S – Loops around the park's northeastern section
	Little Mo	Juniper Campground (4)	1.1 miles	E – Paved (inner) and unpaved (outer) loops
	Achenbach Loop - ⚲	Multiple locations (4, 5, 7)	18.0 miles	S – Crosses the river twice
	Caprock Coulee Nature Trail	Scenic Drive, 1.5 miles west of Juniper Camp (5)	0.8 mile	M – This is the trail's self-guided portion, where you'll learn what a "coulee" is
	Upper Caprock Coulee Loop - ⚲	River Bend Overlook (6)	4.3 miles	M – A continuation of Caprock Coulee's self-guided portion that loops back to the trailhead
	Sperati - ⚲	Oxbow Overlook (7)	1.5 miles	M – Short portion of Achenbach Trail
	Maah Daah Hey	South Unit (3) North Unit (1)	96.0 miles	S – Hikers and horses can take this trail that connects South and North Units

Difficulty Ratings: E = Easy, M = Moderate, S = Strenuous

Horseback Riding

You can explore North Dakota's badlands by horse just like Theodore Roosevelt did more than 100 years ago. All hiking trails, except developed nature trails, are open to stock. The South Unit is better suited for horse riders thanks to a larger network of trails and Roundup Group Horse Campground. Unless you're using Roundup Horse Camp (page 195), multi-day trips require horse riders to camp in the backcountry. Permits are required and can be obtained at the North or South Unit Visitor Center. Another option is to board your horse(s) and camp at Cottonwood or Juniper Campgrounds (page 195). **Boarding stables** are available at Eagle Ridge Lodge (866.863.2453, eagleridgelodge.com) near the South Unit and at Lone Butte Ranch (701.863.6864, lonebutteranch.com) near the North Unit. The CCC Campground near the North Unit's entrance also allows horses.

Peaceful Valley Ranch, located near the beginning of South Unit's Scenic Loop Drive, was one of the United States' first "dude" ranches. They used to offer guided tours and horse boarding, but they were closed for business at time of publication.

Paddling

Just as Maah Daah Hey Trail connects South and North Units for hikers, the **Little Missouri River** connects the two for paddlers. A trip from Medora (South Unit) to Long X Bridge (North Unit) on US-85 is 110 miles. The journey takes a week and requires considerable planning, as you are traversing relatively uncivilized terrain where cell phones rarely work and drinkable water is not readily available (without treatment). The river is not navigable all year round. Water levels must be raised by heavy rains or snowmelt. May and June are the best months to paddle, as temperatures are comfortable and the water is usually navigable after spring thaw. It's a trip that you won't soon forget. The route is filled with spectacular scenery and wildlife viewing opportunities abound. There are no designated campsites along the way, but camping is allowed on National Forest land. Camping is prohibited on adjacent private property. You will have to portage around the wildlife fence crossing the river at park boundaries.

Biking

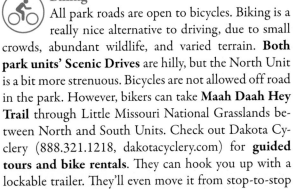

All park roads are open to bicycles. Biking is a really nice alternative to driving, due to small crowds, abundant wildlife, and varied terrain. **Both park units' Scenic Drives** are hilly, but the North Unit is a bit more strenuous. Bicycles are not allowed off road in the park. However, bikers can take **Maah Daah Hey Trail** through Little Missouri National Grasslands between North and South Units. Check out Dakota Cyclery (888.321.1218, dakotacyclery.com) for **guided tours and bike rentals**. They can hook you up with a lockable trailer. They'll even move it from stop-to-stop so you don't have to carry heavy gear. Altogether this is some of the best pedaling you'll find in the Dakotas.

Fishing

It's not a very popular activity, but blue gills and catfish can be caught in the Little Missouri River. North Dakota state law and license requirements apply.

Winter Activities

What the Little Missouri River is good for is **cross-country skiing**. Frozen water creates a flat, well-defined surface to explore on skis during winter (which can extend from October to April). Park Roads are also used for skiing. With 30 inches of annual snowfall, snowshoeing is possible, but snow tends to blow and drift.

Ranger Programs

Park rangers provide guided walks, talks, and campfire programs from mid-June to early September. A current schedule of activities is available online or at a visitor center. A typical talk or walk exposes visitors to a ranger's perspective regarding the life and land you are about to explore. South Unit visitors have the opportunity **to tour Roosevelt's Maltese Cross Cabin** (available daily in summer).

For Kids

Theodore Roosevelt National Park is a wonderful place for children to see wildlife and appreciate nature. The park offers **Family Fun Packs**, which help explore these amazing surroundings. The packs contain field guides, binoculars, hand lenses, and suggested activities. Check

Bison at Beef Bottom Corral (South Unit) scratching itself on a prairie dog's hovel

one out for a day at either North or South Unit Visitor Center. Children (ages 6 and up) are invited to become **Junior Rangers**. Pick up a free Junior Ranger Activity Booklet from either visitor center, complete the activities, and return to a visitor center to receive a certificate and an official Junior Ranger Badge. During summer, Junior Ranger Family Fun Days are offered about once a month. For more information or to inquire about registering your Junior Ranger, call South Unit Visitor Center at (701) 623-4466.

Flora & Fauna

Badlands are known for their inhospitable conditions, but a visit to Theodore Roosevelt National Park reveals a world of great plant and animal diversity. More than 400 species of plants are found in the park. Prairies burst with life when wildflowers bloom in spring. They also help sustain healthy populations of large grazing mammals.

Bison, wild horses, elk, pronghorn, mule deer, and white-tailed deer all reside in the wide-open prairies. The North Unit keeps a small herd of longhorn steers as a living history exhibit. Stop at a prairie dog town and you'll hear the occupants barking from the stoop of their burrows. This region wasn't always as rich in wildlife as it is today. Westward expansion led to severe overhunting. Several species were eliminated from North Dakota only to be reintroduced by the National Park Service. Bison were restored at the South Unit in 1956 and the North Unit in 1962. Elk were next to return to the South Unit in 1985 and bighorn sheep eventually followed at the North Unit. Through the

park's conservation efforts the land and wildlife are much like they were when a wealthy easterner named Theodore Roosevelt arrived in September of 1883.

Pets

Pets are permitted in the park, but must be kept on a leash no more than six feet in length at all times. They are not allowed in park buildings, on trails, or in the backcountry.

Accessibility

The park's visitor centers and Maltese Cross Cabin are wheelchair accessible. Accessible sites and restrooms are available at Cottonwood and Juniper Campgrounds. A few shorter trails like Skyline Vista Overlook and Boicourt Overlook in the South Unit and Little Mo Nature Trail in the North Unit are wheelchair accessible.

Weather

The three park units share fairly similar climates. Summers are hot with average highs in the 70s and 80s°F. Winters are cold with average lows in the single digits. It's fairly dry, receiving only about 15 inches of precipitation each year, but thunderstorms in summer and blizzards in winter can occur with little to no warning.

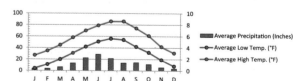

Average Precipitation (Inches)
Average Low Temp. (°F)
Average High Temp. (°F)

Vacation Planner

Each park unit has its own distinct features and attractions. The road to **Elkhorn Ranch** is rough (and sometimes impassable) and its structures are gone, but the scenery is nice and interpretive signs with Roosevelt's words describe the land as he saw it. **Painted Canyon Visitor Center/Overlook** is well worth a stop (especially during early morning/late evening); take Exit 32 off I-94 to have a look at Painted Canyon's colorful broken hills. While these areas are nice, this vacation planner will spend one day each at the park's South and North Units. Nearby dining, grocery stores, lodging, festivals, and attractions are listed on pages 203–205.

Day 1 (South Unit): Begin at the **visitor center**. You'll find relics from Roosevelt's time, a short video, and information on ranger programs. If you'd like to see what an 1880's North Dakotan mansion looked like, check out **Roosevelt's Maltese Cross Cabin** just behind the visitor center. You must be accompanied by a park ranger, but tours are given regularly and often upon request. First (and often the only) thing visitors do upon arriving at the South Unit is drive the 36-mile **Scenic Loop Drive**. You should too. Driving clockwise, make the following stops: Beef Bottom Corral, Wind Canyon Trail, Boicourt Overlook, Buck Hill, and Scoria Point Overlook. Bison like to hang out at Beef Bottom. Wind Canyon Overlook provides a bird's eye view of Little Missouri River as it ambles northward. Boicourt Overlook provides fantastic views of badlands formations. It's fairly common to spot a number of the park's 100-plus wild horses between this stop and Buck Hill, so keep your eyes open. Squeeze in a stop or two at **prairie dog towns**; they're hilariously chatty. We also recommend completing the 1.5-hour, out-and-back trek on **Lower Paddock Creek Trail. Petrified Forest Loop** is better, but you have to drive out of the park to reach its remote trailhead located at the South Unit's northwestern boundary. Completing the entire 10.4 miles requires plenty of water and a bit of planning. We suggest walking past the return leg of the loop, that you may or may not notice approaching from the right (south). Following the loop in a clockwise direction you'll come to some really great petrified wood specimens within the first mile or two, which makes for an easier out-and-back (and you can go as far as you want).

A prairie dog watches a mustang at Beef Bottom Corral (South Unit)

Caprock Coulee Trail (North Unit)

Prairie dogs are everywhere!

Day 1 (North Unit): North Unit Visitor Center is conveniently located at the park's entrance. Stop in, look around, inquire about ranger programs, watch the park's short introductory film, and head back to the 14-mile **Scenic Drive**. Cannonball Concretions Pullout is an easy stop to witness stone oddities created by erosional forces. Continuing along, stop at River Bend Overlook. Here you'll find a shelter built by the CCC in the 1930s where outstanding views of a gentle bend in the Little Missouri are available. Continue northwest on Scenic Drive. You'll pass through a perfect example of grassland that once covered nearly a third of the United States. The drive ends at Oxbow Overlook where you can hike 1.5 miles (roundtrip) to **Sperati Point**. If you want more, return to Juniper Campground to hike the 11.4-mile (4–7 hours) **Buckhorn Trail**. It provides a tour of the park's finest prairie dog towns and passes through sagebrush flats and badlands. Opt for **Little Mo** (short for Missouri) **Trail** if you're short on time.

Petrified Forest Loop (South Unit)

Dining

Near Badlands & Wind Cave

Red Rock Restaurant • (605) 279-2388
506 Glenn St, Wall

Mocha Moose • (605) 279-2023
511 Main St, Wall • Ice Cream

Elkton House Restaurant • (605) 279-2152
203 South Blvd, Wall

Firehouse Brewing Co • (605) 348-1915
610 Main St, Rapid City
firehousebrewing.com • Entrée: $13–26

Katmandu Bistro • (605) 343-5070
727 Main St, Rapid City
katmandubistro.com • Entrée: $10–30

Delmonico Grill • (605) 791-1664
609 Main St, Rapid City
delmonicogrill.com • Entrée: $24–39

Golden Phoenix • (605) 348-4195
2421 W Main St, Rapid City

Philly Ted's Cheesesteak & Subs
1415 N Lacrosse St, Rapid City • (605) 348-6113

Colonial House Restaurant • (605) 342-4640
2315 Mt Rushmore Rd, Rapid City
colonialhousernb.com • Entrée: $11–22

Tally's Silver Spoon • (605) 342-7621
530 6th St, Rapid City
tallyssilverspoon.com • Entrée: $10–33

Minervas Restaurant & Bar • (605) 394-9505
2211 N Lacrosse St, Rapid City
minervas.net • Entrée: $10–32

Piesano's Pacchia • (605) 341-6941
3618 Canyon Lake Dr, # 121, Rapid City
piesanospacchia.com • Pizza: $12–24

Sanford's Grub & Pub • (605) 721-1463
306 7th St, Rapid City

Hitchrail Restaurant & Saloon
421 Northern St, Pringle • (605) 673-2697

Dale's Family Restaurant • (605) 745-3028
745 Battle Mountain Ave, Hot Springs

China Buffet • (605) 745-4126
333 N River St, Hot Springs

Wooly's Western Grill • (605) 745-6414
1648 US Hwy 18, Hot Springs • woolys.com

Dakota Cowboy Restaurant • (605) 673-4613
216 W Mt Rushmore Rd, Custer

Sage Creek Grille • (605) 673-2424
611 Mt Rushmore Rd, Custer

Baker's Bakery & Café • (605) 673-2253
541 Mt Rushmore Rd, Custer
bakersbakery.com • Breakfast: $5–9

Pizza Works • (605) 673-2020
429 Mt Rushmore Rd, Custer
pizzaworkscuster.com • Pizza: $6–28

Purple Pie Place • (605) 673-4070
19 Mt Rushmore Rd, Custer
purplepieplace.com

Near Theodore Roosevelt

Cowboy Café • (701) 623-4343
215 4th St, Medora

Bully Café • (701) 623-5854
316 Pacific Ave, Medora

Elkhorn Café • (701) 623-2239
314 Pacific Ave, Medora

Boots Bar & Grill • (701) 623-2668
300 Pacific Ave, Medora

Trapper's Kettle • (701) 575-8585
803 US-85 N, Belfield
trapperskettle.com

J D's BBQ • (701) 483-2277
789 State Ave, Dickinson

Brickhouse Grille • (701) 483-9900
2 W Villard St, Dickinson
brickhousegrilleonline.com

Twist Drive-In • (701) 842-3595
404 2nd Ave SW, Watford City

Outlaws Bar Grill • (701) 842-6859
120 S Main St, Watford City
outlawsbarngrill.com • Entrée: $13–26

Little Missouri Grille • (701) 444-6315
601 2nd Ave SW, Watford City

Tokyo Japanese Steakhouse • (701) 842-3885
105 9th Ave SE, Watford City

Grocery Stores

Near Badlands & Wind Cave

Badland's Grocery • (605) 433-5445
101 Main St, Interior

Wall Food Center • (605) 279-2331
103 W South Blvd, Wall

Safeway • (605) 342-8455
730 Mtn View Rd, Rapid City

Safeway • (605) 348-5125
2120 Mt Rushmore Rd, Rapid City

Walmart Supercenter • (605) 342-9444
1200 N Lacrosse St, Rapid City

Lynn's Dakotamart • (605) 745-3203
505 S 6th St, Hot Springs

Sonny's Super Foods • (605) 745-5979
801 Jensen Hwy, Hot Springs

Robb's Inc Grocery • (605) 745-4557
144 S Chicago St, Hot Springs

Custer County Market • (605) 673-2247
444 Mt Rushmore Rd, Custer

Near Theodore Roosevelt

Ferris Store • (701) 623-4447
251 Main St, Medora

Beach Food Center • (701) 872-4364
181 Central Ave N, Beach

Walmart Supercenter • (701) 225-8504
2456 3rd Ave W, Dickinson

Walmart Supercenter • (701) 572-8550
4001 2nd Ave W, Williston

Lodging

Near Badlands & Wind Cave

Cedar Pass Lodge • (605) 433-5460
Only lodging in Badlands National Park
20681 Hwy 240, Interior
cedarpasslodge.com • Rates: $176/night

Circle View Guest Ranch • (605) 433-5582
20055 E SD-44, Interior
circleviewranch.com • Rates: $95–150

Frontier Cabins • (605) 279-2619
1101 S Glenn St, Wall
frontiercabins.net • Rates: $64–150

Sunshine Inn • (605) 279-2178
608 Main St, Wall
sunshineinnatwallsd.com • Rates: $65–190

Sleepy Hollow Campground
118 4th Ave W, Wall • (605) 279-2100
sleepyhollowsd.com • Rates: $20–34

Triangle Ranch B&B • (605) 859-2122
Lodge, motel, RV sites, cabins, trail rides, archery, volleyball, and fishing available
23950 Recluse Rd, Philip
triangleranchbb.com

Badlands/White River KOA
20720 SD-44, Interior • (605) 433-5337

Historic Log Cabin Motel • (605) 745-5166
1246 Sherman St, Hot Springs
historiclogcabins.com • Rates: $64+

Lake Park Campground • (800) 644-2267
Lodge, cottage, RV, and camping available
2850 Chapel Ln, Rapid City
lakeparkcampground.com

Rapid City KOA • (605) 348-2111
3010 E SD-44, Rapid City

Mystery Mtn Resort • (605) 342-5368
13752 S US-16, Rapid City
blackhillsresorts.com • Rates: $74–279

Peregrine Pointe B&B • (605) 388-8378
23451 Peregrine Pt, Rapid City
peregrinebb.com • Rates: $120–220

Red Rock River Resort • (605) 745-4400
603 N River St, Hot Springs
redrockriverresort.com • Rates: $85+

FlatIron Hist. Sandstone Inn
745 N River St, Hot Springs • (877)548-2822
flatiron.bz • Rates: $49–179

A Dakota Dream B&B • (605) 517-2292
12350 Moss Lake, Custer

Bavarian Inn Motel • (605) 673-2802
855 N 5th St, Custer
bavarianinnsd.com • Rates: $91+

White House Resort • (605) 666-4917
115 Swanzey St, Keystone

President's View Mt Rushmore
106 US-16A, Keystone • (605) 666-4212

Powder House Lodge • (605) 666-4646
24125 US-16A, Keystone
powderhouselodge.com

Alpine Inn • (605) 574-2749
133 Main St, Hill City
alpineinnhillcity.com • Rates: $75+

Mount Rushmore KOA • (605) 574-2525
12620 SD-244, Hill City
palmergulch.com • *Lodge/Cabins/Camp*

Rafter J Bar Ranch • (605) 574-2527
12325 Rafter J-Bar Rd, Hill City
rafterj.com • Rates: $68+

Horse Thief Campground & Resort
24391 SD-87 S, Hill City • (605) 574-2668
horsethief.com • Rates: $19+

Heartland Campground • (605) 255-5460
24743 S SD-79, Hermosa
heartlandcampground.com • Rates: $20+

Near Theodore Roosevelt
Rough Riders Hotel • (701) 623-4444
301 3rd Ave, Medora
medora.com • Rates: $199

Diamond Bar B&B • (701) 623-4913
14996 27th St SW, Medora

Eagle Ridge Lodge • (701) 623-2216
14937 Dutchmans Rd SW, Medora
eagleridgelodge.com

McKenzie Inn • (701) 444-3980
132 3rd St SW, Watford City
mckenzieinn.com

Roosevelt Inn & Suites • (701) 842-3686
600 2nd Ave SW, Watford City
rooseveltinn.com • Rates: $109+

El Rancho Motor Hotel • (701) 572-6321
1623 2nd Ave West, Williston
elranchomotel.net

Tobacco Gardens Resort • (701) 842-4199
4781 Hwy 1806 W, Watford City
tobaccogardens.com

Coyote Charlie's RV Park • (701) 842-2868
1612 11th Ave SE, Watford City

Cherry Creek RV Park • (701) 842-2626
1008 4 Ave, Watford City

Many chain restaurants and hotels can be found along I-90 (SD) and I-94 (ND).

Festivals
Near Badlands & Wind Cave
Black Hills Stock Show & Rodeo
January • Rapid City • blackhillsstockchow.com

Mt Rushmore Independence Day • July
Mount Rushmore • mtrushmore.org

Sturgis Motorcycle Rally • August
Sturgis • sturgismotorcyclerally.com

Buffalo Roundup & Arts Festival
September • Custer State Park

Mickelson Trail Trek • September
Black Hills • mickelsontrail.com

Black Hills Pow Wow • October
Rapid City • blackhillspowwow.com

Near Theodore Roosevelt
Antique Classic Car Show • June
Medora • medora.com

Roughrider Days • June
Dickinson • roughriderdaysfair.com

Mountain Roundup Rodeo • July
Killdeer • killdeer.com

Roughrider 4WD Rendezvous • May
Watford City • (701) 774-3914

Ukrainian Festival • July
Dickinson • (701) 483-1486

Northern Plains Ethnic Festival • August
Dickinson • visitdickinson.com

Attractions
Near Badlands & Wind Cave
Wall Drug Store • (605) 279-2175
510 Main St, Wall • walldrug.com

1880 Town • (605) 344-2236
I-90, Exit 170
1880town.com • Admission: $12/adult

Minute Man Missile NHP • (605) 433-5552
24545 Cottonwood Rd, Philip • nps.gov/mima

Pirates Cove Adventure Golf • (605) 343-8540
1500 N Lacrosse St, Rapid City

Gray Line Tours • (605) 342-4461
1600 E St Patrick St, Rapid City
blackhillsgrayline.com • Tours: $80+

Circle B Ranch • (605) 574-2129
Gun fights, trail rides, and chuckwagon jamboree
22735 US-385, Rapid City
circle-b-ranch.com

Museum of Geology • (605) 394-2467
501 E Saint Joseph St, Rapid City
museum.sdsmt.edu • Free

Flags & Wheels Indoor Racing
405 12th St, Rapid City • (605) 341-2186
flagsandwheels.com • Rates: $5+

Chapel In the Hills • (605) 342-8281
3788 Chapel Ln, Rapid City
chapel-in-the-hills.org • Free

Bear Country USA • (605) 343-2290
13820 S US-16, Rapid City
bearcountryusa.com • Admission: $16/adult

Storybook Island • (605) 342-6357
1301 Sheridan Lake Rd, Rapid City
storybookisland.org • Admission: $Free

Cosmos Mystery Area • (605) 343-9802
24040 Cosmos Rd, Rapid City
cosmosmysteryarea.com • Tours: $11/adult

The Journey Museum • (605) 394-6923
222 New York St, Rapid City
journeymuseum.org • Tours: $10/adult

Black Hills Maze • (605) 343-5439
6400 S US-16, Rapid City
blackhillsmaze.com • Maze: $10

Old MacDonald's Farm • (605) 737-4815
23691 Busted 5 Court, Rapid City
oldmacdonaldsfarmrc.com • Admission: $13

Reptile Gardens • (605) 342-5873
8955 S US-16, Rapid City
reptilegardens.com • Admission: $13–17/adult

Watiki Indoor Water Park • (866) 928-4543
1314 N Elk Vale Rd, Rapid City
watikiwaterpark.com • Admission: $14/adult

Mostly Chocolates • (605) 341-2264
1919 Mt Rushmore Rd, # 1, Rapid City
bhchocolates.com

Carmike Cinema 10 • (605) 341-5888
230 Knollwood Dr, Rapid City

Elks Theatre • (605) 343-7888
512 6th St, Rapid City, SD 57701

South Dakota Air and Space Museum • Free
2890 Rushmore Drive, Ellsworth AFB, Rapid City
sdairandspacemuseum.com • (605) 385-5189

Big Thunder Gold Mine • (605) 666-4847
604 Blair Street, Keystone
bigthundermine.com • Tours: $10/adult

Mt Rushmore Nat'l Mem. • (605) 574-2523
13000 SD-244, #81, Keystone
nps.gov/moru • Parking: $11/vehicle

Rushmore Cave • (605) 255-4384
13622 Hwy 40, Keystone

Crazy Horse Memorial • (605) 673-4681
12151 Ave of the Chiefs, Crazy Horse
crazyhorsememorial.org • Admission: $28/car

Ponderosa Trail Rides • (940) 222-1978
24105 Highway 16A, Keystone
ponderosatrailrides.com • Trail Rides: $35/hr

Rockin R Rides • (605) 673-2999
24853 Village Ave, Custer
rockingrtrailrides.com • Rates: $37 (1 hr)

Custer State Park • (605) 255-4515
Great park featuring Sylvan Lake (above)
13329 US-16A, Custer • gfp.sd.gov

Golden Circle Tours • (605) 673-4349
12021 US Hwy 16, Custer
goldencircletours.com

Jewel Cave NM • (605) 673-8300
11149 US-16, Custer
nps.gov/jeca • Cave Tours: $4–31/adult

Black Hills Playhouse • (605) 255-4141
24834 S Playhouse Rd, Rapid City
blackhillsplayhouse.com • Tickets: $34/adult

Black Hills Balloons • (605) 673-2520 • Custer
blackhillsballoons.com • Rides: $295/adult

The Mammoth Site • (605) 745-6017
1800 US-18 Bypass, Hot Springs
mammothsite.org • Admission: $11/adult

Pioneer Museum • (605) 745-5147
300 N Chicago St, Hot Springs
pioneer-museum.com • Admission: $6/adult

Black Hills Putt 4 Fun • (605) 745-7888
640 S 6th St, Hot Springs

Hot Springs Theatre • (605) 745-4169
241 N River St, Hot Springs

Black Hills Wild Horse Sanctuary
12165 Highland Rd, Hot Springs • (605) 745-5955
wildmustangs.com • $150 (3 hr bus tour)

1880 Train • (605) 574-2222
222 Railroad Ave, Hill City
1880train.com • Rates: $28/adult

Sylvan Rocks Climbing School
Discover Climbing Adventure: $82 (3–4 hours)
301 Main St, Hill City
sylvanrocks.com • (605) 484-7585

Rabbit Bike Rental • (605) 574-4302
175 Walnut Ave, Hill City
rabbitbike.com • Rental: $25–45/4 hrs

Stables at Palmer Gulch • (605) 574-3412
12620 SD Highway 244, Hill City
ridesouthdakota.com • Trail Rides: $39–47

Devil's Tower NM • (307) 467-5283
US Highway 14, Devils Tower, WY
nps.gov/deto • Entrance Fee: $10/car

Near Theodore Roosevelt
Cowboy Hall of Fame • (701) 623-2000
250 Main St, Medora • northdakotacowboy.com

Medora Musical • (800) 663-6721
Burning Hills Amphitheater
medora.com • Tickets: $39/adult

Chateau de Mores • (701) 623-4355
3448 Chateau Road, Medora
history.nd.gov • Admission: $10/adult

Medora Riding Stables • (800) 633-6721

Cedar Canyon Spa • (701) 623-1772
350 3rd Ave, Medora
cedarcanyonspa.com • Massage: $45 (30 min)

Lewis & Clark Trail Museum • (701) 828-3595
102 Indiana Ave E, Alexander

							Mileage Between Sites	
Pierre	Badlands NP (Visitor Center)	Rapid City	Mt Rushmore Nat'l Mem.	Jewel Cave NM	Wind Cave NP (Visitor Center)	Deadwood	Sturgis	Bismarck	Theodore Roosevelt NP (South Unit)
124								
173	84							
195	106	23						
229	138	57	37					
220	123	53	34	45				
187	122	42	49	76	78			
174	109	29	51	85	75	14		
210	318	325	348	399	372	319	297	
318	319	239	262	298	286	219	211	134

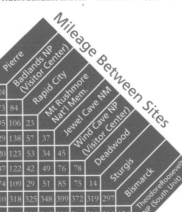

For more travel information,
click www.ndtourism.com and
www.travelsd.com

Lake Solitude

Grand Teton

PO Drawer 170
Moose, WY 83012
Phone: (307) 739-3300
Website: nps.gov/grte

Established: February 26, 1929
Size: 309,995 Acres
Annual Visitors: 3.1 Million
Peak Season: July–August
Hiking Trails: ~230 Miles

Activities: Hiking, Backpacking, Biking, Horseback Riding, Paddling, Rock Climbing, Fishing, and Winter Activities

Campgrounds: Colter Bay, Headwaters, Gros Ventre, Jenny Lake, Lizard Creek, and Signal Mountain
Camping Fee: $22–70/night
Backcountry Camping: Permitted*

Park Hours: All day, every day
Entrance Fee: $30/vehicle, $15/individual (foot, bike, etc.)

*Permit (fee) and approved bear-resistant food canister required

"If you have ever stood at Jenny Lake and looked across to Cascade Canyon weaving its sinuous way toward the summit of the Tetons, you will know the joy of being in a sacred place, designed by God to be protected forever."

– Horace Albright

Thanks to the tireless efforts of Horace Albright and deep pockets of John D. Rockefeller, Jr., Grand Teton National Park now preserves one of America's iconic landmarks, allowing future generations to stand at Jenny Lake, looking across to Cascade Canyon and Grand Teton, but creating the park was no easy task. The Teton's remarkable, if not sacred, appearance was indisputable, however not all residents believed it should be protected.

Native Americans camped along Jackson Lake while hunting game more than 11,000 years ago. In the 17th century, French fur trappers named the range's three tallest peaks "Les Trois Tetons" or "The Three Nipples." Would you expect anything less from rugged frontiersmen removed from society (and women) for long periods? By the 18th and 19th centuries, trappers had thoroughly explored the Three Tetons, and the valley below had become fur trapper David Jackson's favorite place to "hole-up." Today this valley is known as Jackson Hole, named after David in 1829. In the late 19th century, homesteaders began trickling into the Hole. Only the hardiest—or most stubborn—were able to endure unforgiving winters, living off crops grown during the brief summer. That very same Jackson Hole brand of stubbornness would greet Horace Albright head on in the 1920s, when he made it his mission to preserve the Tetons under protection of the recently created National Park Service.

Albright's pet project took shape while serving as Super-intendent of Yellowstone, where he had the opportunity to escort congressmen, dignitaries, and two Presidents to the southern expanses of Yellowstone. From Yellowstone, the Tetons could be seen looming in the background. It wasn't until 1926 that Albright met a man with the re-sources and ambition to make his dream a reality. John D. Rockefeller, Jr. and his wife toured the Tetons with Al-bright and then invited him to New York to discuss his project. Rockefeller, convinced of the park idea, formed Snake River Land Company of Salt Lake City and began buying up properties surrounding the Tetons under the guise of a cattle ranch. Subterfuge was required because a vast majority of ranchers were anti-park. Bull-headed and stubborn, they refused to cede rights to the land.

In 1929, Congress redesignated national forest land consisting of the Teton Range and six glacial lakes at its base to form a small Grand Teton National Park. Rock-efeller tried to donate his properties, only to have it re-fused. Undeterred, he continued to purchase land, ac-quiring an additional 35,000 acres for $1.4 million. In 1943, more than a decade later, he became increasingly frustrated that donating his land was more difficult than acquiring it. He wrote a letter to President Frank-lin D. Roosevelt suggesting he would sell the land if the government would not accept it. That same year Presi-dent Roosevelt invoked the Antiquities Act to create Jackson Hole National Monument. It placed 221,610 acres of land east of Grand Teton National Park under Park Service control, but once again failed to include Rockefeller's holdings.

Many locals were outraged by use of executive order, and in protest they drove 500 cattle across the monu-ment. The dispute wasn't settled until 1950. After WWII the economy in Jackson Hole improved largely due to tourism to the new National Monument. Anti-park sentiment began to wane and finally the monu-ment, park, and Rockefeller's properties were merged to form today's Grand Teton National Park. To this day the Rockefellers' conservation efforts have continued. In 2001, Laurance Rockefeller, son of John D. Rock-efeller, Jr., donated the family's JY Ranch, which is now open to the public as Laurance S. Rockefeller Preserve (just as his father would have wanted it).

Moose near Moose

Amphitheater Lake

When to Go

Grand Teton National Park is open all year. **Craig Thomas Discovery & Visitor Center** is open daily from March through October. All established camp-grounds close in winter, but camping is still avail-able at Colter Bay Visitor Center Parking Lot ($5/ night). The park is incredibly crowded during July and August. At this time campgrounds fill up before noon, parking lots are often full, and hiking trails and roads become congested. You can still find isola-tion and solitude by hiking into the backcountry, or travel during September and October when the park is less crowded and weather remains pleasant.

Transportation & Airports

Grand Teton Lodge Co. (800.628.9988, gtlc.com) provides transportation around Jackson Hole, and narrated bus tours. **Alltrans** (800.443.6133, all-transparkshuttle.com) offers daily service between Jackson and the park for $15 per person per day (un-limited rides) from late May until late September.

Jackson Hole Airport (JAC) is located inside the park. Car rental is available on-site. The nearest large airport is Salt Lake City International (SLC), more than 300 miles to the south.

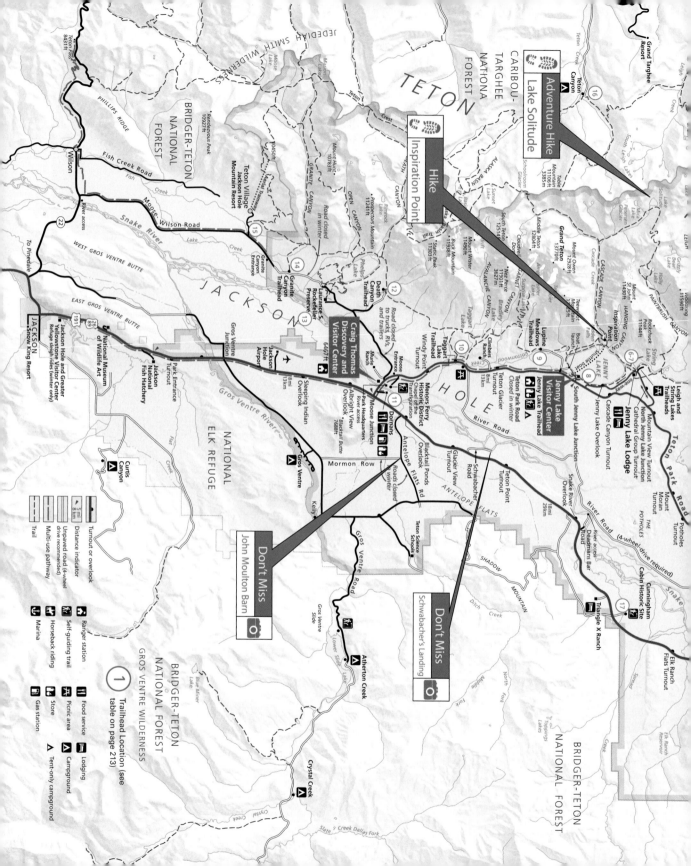

Adventure Hike
Lake Solitude

Hike
Inspiration Point

Don't Miss
John Moulton Barn

Don't Miss
Schwabacher's Landing

TETON

JACKSON HOLE

CARIBOU-TARGHEE NATIONAL FOREST

BRIDGER-TETON NATIONAL FOREST

NATIONAL ELK REFUGE

GROS VENTRE WILDERNESS

BRIDGER-TETON NATIONAL FOREST

JEDEDIAH SMITH WILDERNESS

Grand Targhee Resort

Teton Pass 8431ft

Wilson

To Pinedale

Jackson

Jackson Snow King Resort

National Museum of Wildlife Art

Jackson National Fish Hatchery

Jackson Hole and Greater Yellowstone Visitor Center

Phillips Ridge

Rendezvous Peak 10927ft

Teton Village Jackson Hole Mountain Resort

Fish Creek Road

Moose-Wilson Road

West Gros Ventre Butte

East Gros Ventre Butte

Snake River

River access

Refuge sleigh rides (winter only)

Granite Canyon Entrance

Granite Canyon Trailhead

Laurance S. Rockefeller Preserve

Death Canyon Trailhead

Craig Thomas Discovery and Visitor Center

Park Entrance

Jackson Hole Airport

Moose Entrance

Moose Junction

Menors Ferry Historic District Chapel of the Transfiguration

Dornan's

Park Headquarters

Albright View Overlook

Sleeping Indian Overlook

Windy Point Turnout

Blacktail Butte 7688ft

Blacktail Ponds Overlook

Mormon Row

Gros Ventre

Kelly

Curtis Canyon

Gros Ventre River

Gros Ventre Road

Atherton Creek

Gros Ventre Slide

Lower Slide Lake

Blue Miner Lake

Crystal Creek

Crystal Creek

Slate Creek Dallas Fork

Prospectors Mountain 11241ft

Mount Hunt 10783ft

Open Canyon

Granite Canyon

Buck Mountain 11938ft

Static Peak 11303ft

Avalanche Canyon

Nez Perce 11901ft

South Teton 12514ft

Cloudveil Dome

Middle Teton 12804ft

Grand Teton 13770ft

Mount Owen 12928ft

Teewinot Mountain 12325ft

Mount St. John 11430ft

Rockchuck Peak 11144ft

Mount Moran 12605ft

Table Mountain 11106ft 3385m

Teton Canyon

Moose

Taggart Lake

Bradley Lake

Jenny Lake

String Lake

Leigh Lake

Jackson Lake

Phelps Lake

Lupine Meadows Trailhead

Teton Glacier Turnout

Taggart Lake Trailhead

Climbers Ranch

Jenny Lake Visitor Center

Jenny Lake Trailhead

Jenny Lake Lodge

South Jenny Lake Junction

Cascade Canyon Turnout

Jenny Lake Overlook

Cathedral Group Turnout

North Jenny Lake Junction

Mountain View Turnout

Leigh and String Lakes Trailheads

Inspiration Point

Cascade Canyon

Hanging Canyon

Paintbrush Canyon

Teton Park Road

Snake River

River Road (4-wheel drive required)

The Potholes

Potholes Turnout

Mount Moran Turnout

Teton Point Turnout

Glacier View Turnout

Schwabacher Road

Antelope Flats Road

Antelope Flats

Teton Science Schools

Shadow Mountain

Ditch Creek

North Fork

Middle Fork

Snake River Overlook

Deadmans Bar Road

Cunningham Cabin Historic Site

Triangle X Ranch

Elk Ranch Flats Turnout

Elk Ranch Reservoir

Spread Creek

Cottonwood

Legend / Symbols

Trail

Multi-use pathway

Unpaved road (4-wheel drive recommended)

Distance indicator

.5 mi .8 km

5 mi 8 km

Turnout or overlook

Ranger station

Self-guiding trail

Horseback riding

Marina

Food service

Picnic area

Store

Lodging

Campground

Gas station

Tent-only campground

① Trailhead Location (see table on page 213)

6467ft

8 mi 13km

8 mi 13km

18 mi 29km

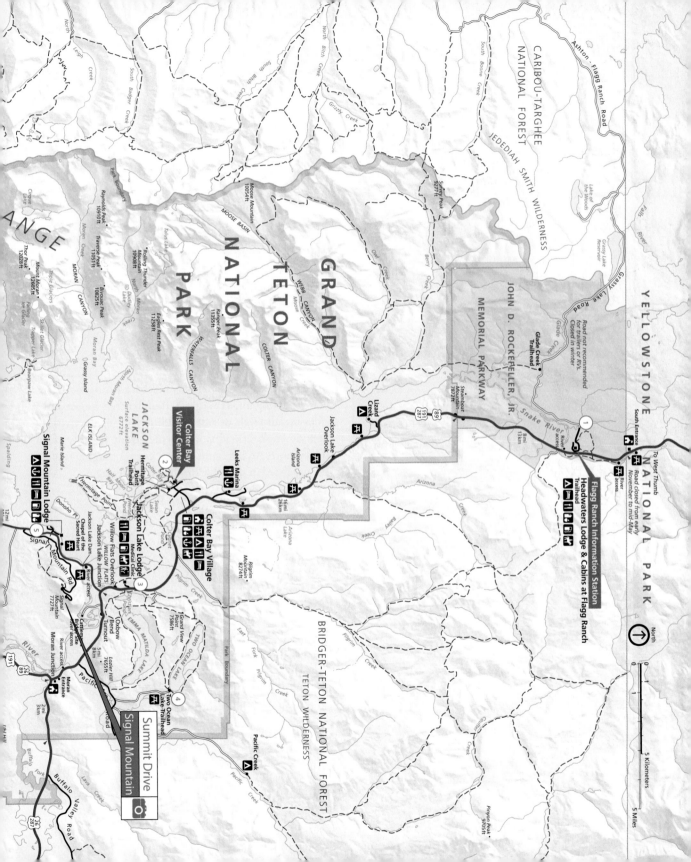

CARIBOU-TARGHEE
NATIONAL FOREST

Ashton - Flagg Ranch Road

Grassy Lake Reservoir

Lake of the Woods

Survey Peak 9277ft

JEDEDIAH SMITH WILDERNESS

YELLOWSTONE

South Entrance

To West Thumb

NATIONAL PARK

North

Leigh Creek

North Badger Creek

South Badger Creek

North Bitch Creek

South Boone Creek

Grizzly Creek

Berry Creek

Owl Creek

Grassy Lake Road

Glade Creek Trailhead

JOHN D. ROCKEFELLER, JR.

MEMORIAL PARKWAY

Road not recommended for trailers or RVs. Closed in winter.

Glade Creek

Falls River

Grassy Lake Road

South Entrance 8mi 13km

River access

River access

ANGE

Cirque Lake

Reynolds Peak 10910ft

Traverse Peak 11051ft

Bivouac Peak 10825ft

Rolling Thunder Mountain 10908ft

Moose Mountain 10054ft

MOOSE BASIN

Thor Peak 12028ft

Mount Moran 12605ft

Skillet Glacier Falling Ice Glacier Triple Glaciers

MORAN CANYON

Eagles Rest Peak 11258ft

Ranger Peak 11355ft

WEBB CANYON

Moose Creek

COLTER CANYON

WATERFALLS CANYON

GRAND TETON NATIONAL PARK

Snake River

191 287

89

Lizard Creek

Steamboat Mountain 7872ft

Headwaters Lodge & Cabins at Flagg Ranch

Flagg Ranch Information Station

BRIDGER-TETON NATIONAL FOREST

North Moran Bay

Moran Bay

Grassy Island

Bearpaw Lake Trapper Lake

Leigh Lake

Dudley Lake

North Moran Creek

Marie Island

ELK ISLAND

JACKSON LAKE Surface elevation 6772ft

Hermitage Point Trailhead

Colter Bay Visitor Center

Half Moon Bay

Donoho Pt.

Hermitage Point

Jackson Lake Lodge

Colter Bay Village

Jackson Lake Overlook

Arizona Island

Leeks Marina

16mi 26km

Jackson Lake Junction

Willow Flats Overlook

WILLOW FLATS

Chapel of the Sacred Heart

Medical Clinic

Arizona Creek

Arizona Lake

Bailey Creek

Pilgrim Mountain 8274ft

Signal Mountain Lodge

Signal Mountain Road

12mi

Spalding Bay

Jackson Lake Dam

River access

Signal Mountain 7727ft

Cottonwood Creek river access

Oxbow Bend Turnout

EMMA MATILDA LAKE

TWO OCEAN LAKE

Grand View Point 7586ft

Lozier Hill 7655ft

Two Ocean Lake Trailhead

Pacific Creek

Pilgrim Creek

Park Boundary

East Fork Pilgrim Creek

Pilgrim Creek

TETON WILDERNESS

Moran Junction

191 26 89

Moran Entrance

Buffalo Fork

Lava Creek

Buffalo Valley Road

Pacific Creek Road

2mi 3km

191 26 287

Summit Drive

Signal Mountain

North

0 5 Kilometers

0 5 Miles

Pinyon Peak 9705ft

Directions

The Teton Range forms an impassable wall to the west, making the park accessible to motorists from the north, south, and east.

From the North: Most visitors arrive by car from Yellowstone National Park's South Entrance (~6 miles away) via John D. Rockefeller, Jr. Memorial Parkway. It's one of the most scenic highways in the United States.

From the South: From Jackson, WY (~4 miles) take US-26/US-89/US-191 north, which leads directly to the south entrance station and Craig Thomas Discovery & Visitor Center.

From the East: US-26/287 enters from the east at Moran where it intersects US-26/89/191, at Moran Entrance Station.

Driving

There are miles upon miles of roadways with strategically placed pullouts and picnic areas allowing motorists to enjoy the park's magnificence through their windshield. Beginning at the north end you'll encounter **John D. Rockefeller, Jr. Memorial Parkway** (NPS Unit connecting Grand Teton and Yellowstone). After entering the park, you'll skirt around Jackson Lake until **Teton Park Road** veers west of the Snake River and US-89/US-191/US-287 continues along its eastern shore. Teton Park Road follows the base of the Teton Range to Moose Junction. In between are side-trips up **Signal Mountain Road** and one-way **Jenny Lake Scenic Drive**. As you approach Moose Junction you'll come across **Moose–Wilson Road**, which leads to fantastic hiking trails and Laurence S. Rockefeller Preserve. Views from US-26/US-89/US-191 on the east side of Snake River are equally amazing. We recommend exploring **Schwabacher's Landing** or catching the sunset from **Snake River Overlook** (site of a well-known Ansel Adams photograph). If you'd rather let someone else do the driving, **Alltrans** (800.443.6133, jacksonholealltrans.com) offers full-day bus tours for $124/adult and $82/child (ages 8–12).

Lodging

The unique, and often contentious, history of Grand Teton's creation has allowed a variety of commercial interests to be tucked away within park boundaries. From **Dornan's Spur Ranch** at the park's southern reaches to **Headwaters Lodge & Resort** (at Flagg Ranch) near the northern boundary, you can find lodging accommodations that suit your itinerary, if not your budget. **Jenny Lake Lodge** has earned the title of "most expensive lodging in the National Park System." Warranted or not, rates aren't steep enough to prevent guests, drawn to the lodge's incomparable combination of fine dining and majestic scenery, from returning annually. Note that selecting Jenny Lake Lodge's Signature Stay Package includes a 5-course dinner, gourmet breakfast, horseback riding, and use of cruiser style bicycles. On the other end of the spectrum, **American Alpine Club Climber's Ranch** caters to rock climbers. Not only is it affordable, it's extremely accessible, merely three miles south of Jenny Lake and four miles north of Park Headquarters. If it's a horseback riding vacation you're looking for, **Triangle X Ranch** offers horses and rides for all levels of rider. Additional ranch activities include cookouts, square dancing, trout fishing, and much more. All of Grand Teton's in-park lodging facilities are listed in the table on the opposite page.

Camping

Don't let prohibitive lodging rates keep you from spending the night in the park. There are several reasonably priced, well-maintained, and extremely popular campgrounds. Most campsites are available on a first-come, first-served basis. **Jenny Lake and Signal Mountain Campgrounds** are the most popular, typically filling to capacity before 10am in summer. You should plan on arriving before 9am. Reservations are only available at **Headwaters Campground at Flagg Ranch** (307.543.2861, gtlc.com) and **Colter Bay RV Park** (800.628.9988, gltc.com). The only in-park, public **showers** and **laundry** are available at Colter Bay. A few free primitive campgrounds are dispersed throughout the park, like those located along unpaved Grassy Lake Road near Flagg Ranch Information Station. Additional campground details are provided on the opposite page. Note that opening dates are weather dependent.

Sunset from Mormon Row

Grand Teton Lodging (Fees are per night)

Name	Open	Fee	Notes
Dornan's Spur Ranch (307.733.2522, dornans.com)	All Year	$195–225	Dining, grocery, deli, gasoline, and equipment rental available
AAC Climber's Ranch - ♿ (307.733.7271, americanalpineclub.org)	mid-June–mid-Sept	$16–25	Lower rate is for AAC members
Jenny Lake Lodge - ♿ (307.543.3100, gtlc.com)	mid-May–mid-Oct	$485+	Dining, horseback riding, cruiser bicycles available to guests
Signal Mountain Lodge (307.543.2831, signalmountainlodge.com)	May–mid-Oct	$185–245	Dining, float trips, guided fishing excursions available
Jackson Lake Lodge - ♿ (307.543.3100, gtlc.com)	late May–early Oct	$299–359	Restaurants, adventure outfitters, and park tours
Triangle X Ranch (307.733.2183, trianglex.com)	mid-May–Oct late Dec–mid-March	$1,850+/person per week	Lodging, meals, horseback riding, and activities included
Colter Bay Cabins (307.543.3100, gtlc.com)	late May–late Sept	$65–249	Semi-private (shared bathroom) and private cabins are available
Headwaters Lodge & Resort (307.543.3100, gtlc.com)	mid-May–late Sept	$205–359	Adventure outfitter and national park tour services available

Grand Teton Camping (Fees are per night)

Name	Location	Open	Fee	Sites	Notes
Gros Ventre (gltc.com)	11.5 miles SE of Moose	early May–early Oct	$25 (tent) $51 (RV)	300+	Sites along Gros Ventre River rarely fill
Jenny Lake - ♿ (gltc.com)	8 miles N of Moose	early May–Late Sept	$25	49	Tents only, 10 walk-in sites available
Signal Mountain - ♿ (signalmountainlodge.com)	9 miles N of Jenny Lake	early May–mid-Oct	$22 (tent) $45 (RV)	86	24 RV hookup sites available
Colter Bay Village (gltc.com)	US-89, 25 miles north of Moose	mid-May–late Sept	$25 (tent) $50 (RV)	335	Walk-in sites available ($11/night)
Colter Bay RV Park (gltc.com)	Colter Bay Village	late May–late Sept	$58–68	112	Full hookups available
Lizard Creek - ♿ (signalmountainlodge.com)	32 miles N of Moose	mid-June–early Sept	$22	60	$5/night for hikers or bikers w/o a car
Headwaters at Flagg Ranch (gltc.com)	Just south of Yellowstone NP	early June–late-Sept	$35 (tent) $70 (RV)	175	Full hookups available
Backcountry Camping	Permitted at designated sites and regions of the park with a permit obtained in person from Craig Thomas Discovery & Visitor Center, Jenny Lake Ranger Station, or Colter Bay Visitor Center ($25) or online at recreation.gov ($35). Approved bear canisters must be used.				
Group Camping	Camping for groups of 10–100 people are available at Colter Bay and Gros Venture Campgrounds. Reservations are required and may be made through the Grand Teton Lodge Company (307.543.3100, gltc.com)				
Winter Camping	In winter, guests may camp in the parking lot near Colter Bay Visitor Center ($5/night)				

Hiking

Spectacular views of the Teton Range and amazing hiking trails are everywhere. More than 230 miles of trails cross the flats of Jackson Hole, wind through picturesque canyons into the Teton Range, and weave their way to majestic mountaintops. Jenny Lake's postcard-perfect backdrops set the stage for a few of the park's most popular hiking trails. A few of which should not be skipped: **Jenny Lake Loop, Hidden Falls Trail, and Cascade Canyon Trail.** (Extreme beauty also makes them three of the most heavily trafficked trails.) If you'd like to enjoy all of these sites while limiting the wear and tear on your favorite set of hiking boots, shorten these trails by taking a **shuttle boat** (307.734.9227, jennylakeboating.com) across Jenny Lake to the mouth of Cascade Canyon. The shuttle departs near Jenny Lake Visitor Center from mid-May through September. This shortcut—sparing your feet four miles of hiking—costs $15 (roundtrip) per adult and $8 for children. (Subtract four miles from Hidden Falls/Inspiration Point hikes, if you take the boat.) Still, with an early start, an ambitious hiker can complete the loop through Cascade Canyon (past Inspiration Point and Hidden Falls) to **Lake Solitude** and back to String Lake Trailhead via Paintbrush Canyon in a day without taking the boat.

Many of the park's features have been named accurately. For example, there's no finer place to search your mind and soul for encouragement than Inspiration Point. Others are not so accurate; you'll almost always have company hiking to Lake Solitude, and the trails through Paintbrush and Cascade Canyons continue to increase in popularity. We aren't talking shoulder-to-shoulder traffic here, but you're going to run into similarly adventurous hikers along the way.

If it's solitude you crave, you'll have to get away from the tourism hubs centered on Jenny and Jackson Lakes. **Emma Matilda Lake and Two Ocean Lake Trails** can be combined to make a large 13.2-mile loop around the lakes. To see what the area looked like in the early 20th century when hardy homesteaders were moving in, hike around **Menor's Ferry Historic District** or take the **Cunningham Cabin Loop.** Or drive down to **Death Canyon Trailhead** on Moose–Wilson Road.

Backpacking

Many hikes listed on page 213 can be combined into multi-day backpacking loops, which are ideal treks. Loops eliminate repeating scenery, arranging a shuttle service, or using multiple cars. From String Lake Trailhead (Trailhead # 7 on page 208) backpackers can combine **Cascade Canyon and Paintbrush Canyon Trails** to make a 19.2-mile loop to **Lake Solitude**. If you're a little wary of being in the backcountry alone this is a good option as it's quite busy in summer. The loop passes Hidden Falls, Inspiration Point, Lake Solitude, and Holly Lake. Alternatively, from Granite Canyon Parking Area (Trailhead # 14 on page 208) backpackers can hike a 19.3-mile loop, the Granite Canyon and Open Canyon Circuit via Valley Trail. Hikers looking to add a few more miles should continue past the junction on Open Canyon Trail to Marion Lake. And **Teton Crest Trail** is one of the classic backpacking routes.

There are more than 230 miles of hiking trails here and many more extend beyond park boundaries. The wilderness is to be explored, but it must also be respected. **Permits** are required for all overnight stays in the backcountry. Walk-in permits are available at Jenny Lake Ranger Station, and Craig Thomas and Colter Bay Visitor Centers for $25. Reservations are accepted for one-third of the park's designated backcountry sites (and all group sites), and can be made at recreation.gov for a one-time $35 reservation fee. Even if you reserve your permit, you still must pick it up at Craig Thomas or Colter Bay Visitor Center, or Jenny Lake Ranger Station. Any permit involving camping in Garnet Canyon, climbing, or mountaineering must be picked up at Jenny Lake Ranger Station. If you aren't going to use a permit, cancel it so someone else can use it.

Always travel with a good topographic map. Try to be as realistic as possible about how many miles you can cover in a day. Be sure to consider the ability of every member of your group and the weight of your pack. Snow cover can persist in the high country well into summer; prospective hikers must carry (and know how to use) an ice axe if they wish to pass these regions. It's also bear country. Food must be stored in approved, portable bear-proof canisters. Canisters are available to check out from ranger stations and visitor centers.

Grand Teton Hiking Trails (Distances are roundtrip)

Name	Location (# on map)	Length	Difficulty Rating & Notes
Polecat Creek Loop	Flagg Ranch (1)	2.5 miles	E – Short, flat hike above a marsh
Flagg Canyon	Flagg Ranch (1)	4.0 miles	E – Out-and-back along Snake River
Lakeshore	Colter Bay (2)	2.0 miles	E – Views of Teton Range across Jackson Lake
Heron Pond & Swan Lake	Colter Bay (2)	3.0 miles	E – Hike to two ponds through bird habitat
Hermitage Point	Colter Bay (2)	9.7 miles	M – Long but easy hike to Jackson Lake shore
Lunch Tree Hill	Jackson Lake Lodge (3)	0.5 mile	E – Self-guiding trail overlooking Willow Flats
Christian Pond Loop	Jackson Lake Lodge (3)	3.3 miles	E – Nice loop to Teton views and pond
Two Ocean Lake	Two Ocean Lake (4)	6.4 miles	M – Trail loops around Two Ocean Lake
Emma Matilda Lake	Two Ocean Lake (4)	10.7 miles	M – Trail loops around Emma Matilda Lake
Signal Mountain	Signal Mountain (5)	6.8 miles	M – Hike to motorist-friendly summit
Leigh Lake - ♨	Leigh Lake (6)	1.8 miles	E – Hike along String and Leigh Lake's shores
Bearpaw Lake - ♨	Leigh Lake (6)	8.0 miles	M – Views of Mount Moran and alpine lakes
Holly Lake	Leigh Lake (6)	13.0 miles	S – Through Paintbrush Canyon to lake
String Lake	String Lake (7)	3.7 miles	E – Trail loops around the lake
Paintbrush–Cascade Loop/Lake Solitude - ♨	String Lake (7)	19.2 miles	S – Phenomenal but difficult circuit to Lake Solitude (spur trails to Inspiration Point and Hidden Falls)
Jenny Lake Loop - ♨	Jenny Lake (8)	7.1 miles	E – Trail follows the park's second largest lake
Hidden Falls - ♨	Jenny Lake (8)	5.2 miles	M – Hike around Jenny Lake to 200-ft cascade
Inspiration Point - ♨	Jenny Lake (8)	6.0 miles	S – Past Hidden Falls overlooks Jenny Lake
Forks of Cascade Canyon	Jenny Lake (8)	13.6 miles	S – Excellent mountain views (popular)
South Fork Cascade	Jenny Lake (8)	24.8 miles	S – Leads to Schoolroom Glacier
Amphitheater Lake - ♨	Lupine Meadows (9)	10.1 miles	S – Difficult but incredible hike to glacial lakes
Garnet Canyon	Lupine Meadows (9)	8.4 miles	S – Hike through a Teton Range Canyon
Taggart Lake	Taggart Lake (10)	3.0 miles	E – Hike across sagebrush flats
Taggart Lake–Beaver Creek	Taggart Lake (10)	3.9 miles	M – To Taggart Lake, returns via Beaver Creek
Taggart Lake–Bradley Lake	Taggart Lake (10)	5.9 miles	M – Very nice loop to two glacial lakes
Menors Ferry District - ♨	Menors Ferry (11)	0.3 mile	E – Homesteaders lived here in 1894
Phelps Lake Overlook	Death Canyon (12)	2.0 miles	M – Climbs to an overlook of Phelps Lake
Phelps Lake	Death Canyon (12)	4.2 miles	S – Proceeds past overlook to Phelps Lake
Death Canyon–Static Peak	Death Canyon (12)	7.9 miles	S – To Phelps Lake and back to Death Canyon
Static Peak Divide	Death Canyon (12)	16.3 miles	S – A series of switchbacks leads to high ridge
Lake Creek–Woodland	Rockefeller Preserve (13)	3.1 miles	E – Loop leads to north shore of Phelps Lake
Aspen–Boulder Ridge	Rockefeller Preserve (13)	5.8 miles	M – Loop Reaches the shore of Phelps Lake
Phelps Lake Loop	Rockefeller Preserve (13)	6.6 miles	M – Travels around Phelps Lake
Granite Canyon	Top of the Tram (15)	12.3 miles	M – Downhill from mountaintop to village
Marion Lake	Top of the Tram (15)	11.8 miles	S – Follows Granite Creek to a pristine lake
Table Mountain	Teton Canyon (16)	12.0 miles	S – Great views of Grand Teton
Cabin Loop	Cunningham Cabin (17)	0.8 mile	E – Preserved historic homestead

Difficulty Ratings: E = Easy, M = Moderate, S = Strenuous

Boating & Floating

Grand Teton National Park provides an incredible array of water adventures. **Float trips** down the winding Snake River are a peaceful way to enjoy mountain vistas and view wildlife. The standard 10-mile trip is offered by many of the park's lodging facilities: Grand Teton Lodge Company (307.543.3100, gtlc.com, $69/adult, $46/child), Signal Mountain Lodge (307.543.2831, signalmtnlodge.com, $72/$47), Triangle X Ranch (307.733.5500, trianglex.com, $70), and Lost Creek Ranch (included in lodging rate). Barker–Ewing Float Trips (800.448.4202, barker-ewing.com, $70/$58) and Solitude Float Trips (307.733.2871, grand-teton-scenic-floats.com, $75/$55) are also authorized park outfitters. These trips cover 10 of the most picturesque miles of water you'll ever see in your life. Grand Teton looms in the background for the entire three-hour journey. Trips are generally available from mid-May until late September. O.A.R.S. (800.346.6277, oars.com) provides an alternative to the float trip with their 2–3 day **kayak adventures** ($359–569) or a half-day paddle for $79.

With your own kayak, canoe, or raft, you can take the float trip route. All you have to do is launch at Deadman's Bar Road and land near Moose Junction/Menor's Ferry. This stretch of water is not especially technical or treacherous and current is generally gentle as you wind your way across Jackson Hole. You may encounter bars, eddies, and the occasional downed tree, but it's rarely splashy. In order to float the river you must obtain a **non-motorized boat permit** ($10/season) and an Aquatic Invasive Species decal ($5 WY residents, $15 non-residents). Motorized boats also require permits ($40/season).

If you don't have your own boat or you'd rather leave it at home, **canoe or kayak rental** is available from Jenny Lake Boating (307.734.9227, jennylakeboating.com), Grand Teton Lodge Company (307.543.3100, gtlc.com), and Signal Mountain Lodge (307.543.2831, signalmtnlodge.com). Rentals are available for use at Jenny or Jackson Lake on a first-come, first-served basis for $18–22 per hour. Jackson Lake Marina also provides **fishing boats** ($42/hour), pontoon boats ($95/hour), and deck cruisers ($129/hour) for rent. Grand Teton Lodging Company also offers **scenic cruises** of Jackson Lake that are exceptional. They'll even feed you breakfast, lunch, or dinner along the way. Cruises depart daily from late May through mid-September and cost anywhere from $31–65 per adult.

Biking

Biking is permitted on all park roadways. Pedaling is relatively easy because most roads cross the flat expanse of Jackson Hole rather than working their way into the mountains, rewarding cyclists with beautiful mountain landscapes without all the heavy cranking associated with arduous climbs. Roads are often crowded (especially in summer), but early morning or late evening and off-season rides can be splendid. In 2009, a **Multi-Use Pathway** (non-motorized transport only) was completed between Dornan's Spur Ranch and South Jenny Lake. Teton Park Road is recommended for **road cyclists**, and the 52-mile unpaved Grassy Lake Road is a hot-spot for **mountain bikers** (but it's not single track). Adventure Sports (307.733.3307, dornans.com) at Dornan's Spur Ranch provides **bike rental** for $15 (hour), $34 (half-day), or $40 (24 hours).

Horseback Riding

Dude ranches are alive-and-well at Grand Teton. In fact, business is so good ranches are often booked to capacity months in advance. These ranches are hardly inexpensive, but horse enthusiasts seeking "all-you-can-ride" accommodations will not find a better destination in the National Park System. Triangle X Ranch (307.733.2183, trianglex.com) offers an all-inclusive modern western adventure for $1,850 per person per week. Lost Creek Ranch & Spa (307.733.3435, lostcreek.com) offers an all-inclusive package for $13,400 for as many as 4 people per week. Each additional person costs another $800 per week. (Alcohol, babysitting, fishing trips, skeet shooting, and other activities cost extra.) A more affordable alternative for the horse enthusiast is to take a **trail or wagon ride** provided by Grand Teton Lodge Company (307.543.3100, gtlc.com) at Colter Bay Village, Jackson Lake Lodge or Headwaters Lodge & Resort, which costs $40–78 (1–2 hours). Pony Rides ($5) are also available at Jackson Lake Lodge. Horseback riding is also available at **Jenny Lake Lodge**, but only to their guests.

Rock Climbing

Grand Teton has plenty of granite to go around. It's one of the premier rock climbing parks, drawing climbers from all around the world. Everyone from beginners to experts will find routes suitable to their ability level. Check the park's climbing and backcountry website at tetonclimbing.blogspot.com for additional information, routes, and conditions. Information can also be obtained at Jenny Lake Ranger Station in person or on the phone by calling (307) 739-3343 in summer and (307) 739-3309 in winter. Exum Mountain Guides (307.733.2297, exumguides.com) and Jackson Hole Mountain Guides (307.733.4979, jhmg.com) offer **guided rock climbing classes** for $170 and $185 per person (group pricing must reach minimum # of people). They'll also take you out for day climbs or summit adventures matched to your ability level.

Fishing

Grand Teton's 50 miles of the 1,056-mile-long Snake River and more than 100 alpine lakes provide ample opportunity for anglers searching for the catch of the day. Fishermen must follow Wyoming regulations and licensing requirements. Most park lodges sell fishing licenses. Grand Teton Lodge Company (Jackson Lake, $95/hour • Snake River, $555 full-day), Triangle X Ranch (Snake River, $545 full-day, $425 half-day), and Signal Mountain Lodge (Jackson Lake, $99/hour, $295 half-day) all offer **guided fishing tours**. Snake River Angler (307.733.3699, snakeriverangler.com) and Jack Dennis Fly Fishing Trips (307.690.0910, jackdennisfishingtrips.com) offer full-day trips for $575 and $550 respectively.

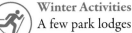

Winter Activities

A few park lodges remain open during winter and visitors can **camp** on Colter Bay Visitor Center's parking area. It's quite the contrast from summer when lodges are filled to capacity and parking spots are hard to come by. Cars and visitors may be few and far between but activities are everywhere. The best way to explore the park in winter is with the aid of a set of cross-country skis or snowshoes. Moose–Wilson, Signal Mountain, and Teton Park roads close in winter, providing a proper surface for **skiers** and **snowshoers**. Phelps Lake Overlook, Jenny Lake Trail, Taggart Lake/

Beaver Creek Loop, Swan Lake–Heron Pond Loop, and Polecat Creek Loop listed in the hiking table on page 213 are popular ski/snowshoe trails. If you don't want to explore the Tetons on your own, you can join a park ranger for a **guided snowshoe trek**. Trips usually take place from late December to mid-March and they depart from Craig Thomas Discovery & Visitor Center. Each year, reservations can be made starting on December 1 by calling (307) 739-3399. These excursions are free, but a donation of $5 per adult and $2 per child is suggested.

Some areas of the park allow **snowmobiling**. It is a highly controversial activity due to the associated noise and air pollution. Interested parties should contact a visitor center for current information. **Backcountry skiing and snowboarding** are allowed within the park, and many of the park's lakes are open for **ice fishing**.

Ranger Programs

It may seem like it costs a fortune to experience the Tetons. But the best way to discover them is free: with a park ranger on one of their guided programs that are equally enjoyable for children and adults. From June until early September you'll find a wide variety of programs offered in and around the park's Visitor Centers and Laurance S. Rockefeller Preserve (see the table on the following page for a list of all Grand Teton's visitor centers, where they are, and when they're open).

Activities range from a 30-minute talk about the park's biology to a 3-hour ramble on a trail. There are also campfire programs, a boat cruise, museum tours, and all sorts of walks and talks. The hike to Hidden Falls from Jenny Lake can be enhanced by joining a ranger on a first-come, first-served basis for the first 25 hikers. They take Jenny Lake Boat Shuttle (307.734.9227, jennylakeboating.com) to shorten the hike, so show up prepared with your shuttle token ($15 round-trip/$9 one-way for adults, $8/$6 for children ages 2–11). There are dozens of additional programs listed in the park's newspaper, *Grand Teton Guide* (available online or at any visitor center). So, for your trip to the Tetons think about skipping the expensive commercial experiences and join a ranger on your exploration of this natural wonderland.

For Kids

Children like the Tetons. They'll enjoy just about everything: floating Snake River, paddling Jenny Lake, watching wildlife, joining a park ranger on a guided tour, and much more. In addition to child-oriented ranger activities, the park offers a **Junior Ranger Program**. Children of all ages may participate in this unique program that explores the wonders of Grand Teton and its environs. Upon completion of the Junior Ranger Activity Booklet (available online or at a visitor center), return to a visitor center so your child can be christened as the park's newest Junior Naturalist and receive a badge.

Flora & Fauna

More than 1,000 species of vascular plants inhabit Grand Teton National Park, including 900 flowering species. The park's forests are mostly coniferous, with whitebark pine, limber pine, subalpine fir, and Englemann spruce capable of surviving at elevations up to 10,000 feet. Lodgepole pine, Douglas fir, and blue spruce are found closer to the valley floor where the soil is deep enough to support tree growth. A smaller sampling of deciduous trees resides along rivers and lakeshores.

Seeing the park's wildlife in its natural environment is just as enthralling as a brilliant Teton sunset. Moose, bear, and elk are the most popular residents, but there are 61 mammals inhabiting the park. Bison, pronghorn, and mule deer are often seen grazing along the road side. Motorists should pass with caution as these animals have become indifferent to traffic. Car accidents kill more than 100 large mammals each year at Grand Teton.

Pets

Pets are permitted in the park, but must be kept on a leash no more than six feet in length at all times. They are prohibited from all hiking trails, visitor centers, other public buildings, and the backcountry. Pets are allowed at campgrounds, picnic areas, and parking lots.

Accessibility

All visitor centers are accessible to individuals who require the use of a wheelchair. All in-park lodging facilities have accessible rooms. The Multi-use Pathway, which runs parallel to Teton Park Road, and South Jenny Lake Trail are easily accessible paved trails. Colter Bay, Jackson Lake Dam, Laurance S. Rockefeller Preserve, Menor's Ferry Historic District, and String Lake are other areas of the park suggested for wheelchairs users. Most of the ranger programs are accessible.

Weather

Most visitors arrive between May and September. Long intimidating winters keep tourists away. Snowfall

Grand Teton Visitor and Information Centers

Name	Location	Open	Notes
Craig Thomas Discovery & Visitor Center (307.739.3399)	In Moose, 0.5-mile west of Moose Junction on Teton Park Road	March–October Daily from 9am–5pm Extended hours in summer	Primary Visitor Center, boat and backcountry permits available
Jenny Lake Visitor Center (307.739.3392)	On Teton Park Road, 8 miles north of Moose Junction	late May–September Daily from 8am–5pm Extended hours in summer	Boat permits available
Jenny Lake Ranger Station (307.739.3343)	On Teton Park Road, 8 miles north of Moose Junction	June–early September Daily from 8am–5pm	Rock climbing info and backcountry permits available
Colter Bay Visitor Center & Indian Arts Museum (307.739.3594)	On Highway 89/191/287, 0.5-mile west of Colter Bay Junction	May–mid-October Daily from 8am–5pm Extended hours in summer	Boat and backcountry permits available, museum tours
Flagg Ranch Information Station (307.543.2372)	On Highway 89/191/287, 16 miles north of Colter Bay	early June–early Sept Daily from 9am–4pm	Info on John D. Rockefeller, Jr. Memorial Parkway
Laurence S. Rockefeller Preserve Center (307.739.3654)	On Moose-Wilson Road, 4 miles south of Moose	June–late September Daily from 9am–5pm	Interactive exhibits, sales and permits are not available

averages more than 170 inches per year, most of which falls between November and March, but snow and frost are possible during any month. Jackson Hole has a semi-arid climate, receiving about 20 inches of precipitation annually, fairly evenly distributed throughout the year. Even the warmest months are cool at night near the Tetons. July and August have an average low temperature right around 40°F. That's a stark contrast to average highs, which are about 80°F. No matter what time of year, it's best to wear multiple layers of clothing while exploring the park. Temperatures change with wind, elevation, and time of day, and afternoon thunderstorms are common.

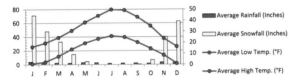

Vacation Planner

Grand Teton is an excellent alternative to its busy neighbor to the north, Yellowstone National Park (page 218). If you're headed to Yellowstone and only planning a day at Grand Teton, you may want to re-calibrate your schedule, allowing more time with the Tetons. Three days is enough to experience its main attractions. A little more time and you can head into the **backcountry** (page 212), take a **fishing excursion** (page 215), or attend a slew of **ranger programs** (page 215). Nearby dining, grocery stores, lodging, festivals, and attractions are listed on pages 242–245.

Day 1: First stop: **Craig Thomas Discovery & Visitor Center**. The recently renovated facility has excellent exhibits and it's the perfect place to receive a proper introduction to the park. Don't forget to pick up a newspaper, *Grand Teton Guide*. It will tell you when and where to go for ranger programs (plus loads of other useful information). Once you've had a thorough look around, return to Moose Junction and turn left onto US-26/US-89/US-191. Drive the entire length through Moran Junction all the way to **Colter Bay Village**. Grand Teton looms to the west all the while. Pull over whenever it strikes your fancy. **Glacier View Turnout** and **Snake River Overlook** are two of the best pit-stops. Spend the night in (or near) Colter Bay. If you have an hour to spare, walk along **Lakeshore Path**. It's an excellent trail to wander about

at dusk as the sun is ducking behind the Teton Range. If you don't feel like hiking, check the newspaper to see if you can catch an evening program at the campground. Better yet, do both.

Day 2: Wake-up before the sun and backtrack to Jackson Lake Junction where you'll turn right onto Teton Park Road. After a few miles, take a left onto **Signal Mountain Road**. Drive to the summit (large vehicles and trailers should not attempt) to watch the **sunrise**. Sitting atop Signal Mountain while the first rays of sunlight illuminate the Tetons is often worth the effort of packing up on a crisp and cool morning. (Photographers may want to skip Signal Mountain and head over to **Mormon Row** east of Moose Junction, via Antelope Flats Road, to photograph John Moulton Barn. It's probably the most photographed barn in the world, but the weathered barn with Grand Teton standing behind it is a site to behold. **Schwabacher Landing** is another extremely popular destination among photographers.) The early morning yields another bonus. You'll have a decent shot at securing a site at **Jenny Lake Campground** (page 210). (No guarantees though, it's extremely difficult to predict day-to-day camping volume.) You'll also have enough time to reach **Hidden Falls** and **Inspiration Point** (continue to **Lake Solitude** if you feel up to it and don't mind spending the entire day on foot). These Jenny Lake Area trails are often busy by 10am. To avoid the masses, consider taking the challenging 10.2-mile hike to **Amphitheater Lake** instead, which departs from Lupine Meadows Trailhead. If you suspect a stunning sunset is on the horizon, drive back to **Snake River Overlook** on US 26/US-89/US-191. For sunsets, this spot cannot be beat.

Day 3: End your vacation in style by exploring the park by horse on a **trail ride** (page 214), by raft on a **float trip** of the Snake River (page 214), or on one of Grand Teton Lodge Company's **boat cruises** of Jackson Lake (page 214). If you've exceeded your budget or find yourself uninterested in horses or boats, check the newspaper once more to see what **ranger programs** are offered today. If all else fails, take Moose-Wilson Road (near Moose Junction) to **Laurance S. Rockefeller Preserve**. Browse the exhibits and then hike 6.6 miles around **Phelps Lake Loop**.

Yellowstone

Avalanche Peak

PO Box 168
Yellowstone Nat'l Park, WY 82190
Phone: (307) 344-7381
Website: nps.gov/yell

Established: March 1, 1872
Size: 2,221,766 Acres
Annual Visitors: 4.1 Million
Peak Season: July–August
Hiking Trails: 900+ Miles

Activities: Hiking, Biking, Fishing, Photography, Horseback Riding, Boating, Wildlife Viewing, Scenic Driving, and Winter Activities

Facilities: 12 Campgrounds, 9 Lodges, 10 Visitor Centers
Camping Fee: $15–47.50/night
Backcountry Camping: Permitted*

Park Hours: All day, every day

Entrance Fee: $30/vehicle, $15/individual (foot, bike, etc.)

*Must obtain a permit no more than 48 hours prior to departure

Long after Americans reached the Pacific Ocean, explorers, fur trappers, and frontiersmen began filling in blank spots left on maps between the East and West Coasts. In the 1850s—before Wyoming became a state—one of these unmapped regions was reported as a rugged wilderness of boiling mud, steaming rivers, and petrified birds. Such reports were promptly disregarded as myth in the East, colorful yarns spun by colorful men, and publishers curtly responded "We do not print fiction." Still, these landscapes captured the curiosity of several expedition parties. In 1871, the U.S. government deployed the Hayden Geological Survey to uncover the truth. Ferdinand V. Hayden, painter Thomas Moran, and photographer William Henry Jackson were sent to assess what really existed. Less than one year later, President Ulysses S. Grant signed the Act of Dedication, effectively making Yellowstone the world's first National Park. This large tract of land in northwestern Wyoming Territory, barely extending into Montana and Idaho Territories, was set aside, preserved for the enjoyment of the people. Much like the area's first explorers, today's visitors come across steaming rivers, towering waterfalls dropping into deep canyons, bubbling mud-pots, hot spring terraces, and boiling water gushing from the earth. Sights so amazing they inspire the same disbelief of 19th-century publishers and politicians. Yet it is real. Guests can see it. Touch it. Smell it. It is Yellowstone.

The first people known to have explored the land known today as Yellowstone were Native Americans. Discovery of obsidian arrowheads dating back 11,000 years suggests they used this land as a hunting ground shortly after glaciers from the last great ice age receded. By the time of the Lewis and Clark Expedition in 1805, trappers had already named the river "Roche Jaune" or "Rock Yellow River," referring to yellow sandstones found along its banks. (It is a common misconception that the river was named for yellow coloring caused by rhyolite lava seen at the Grand Canyon of the Yellowstone.) In 1806, John Colter left Lewis and Clark's Expedition to work for the Missouri Fur Company, exploring the regions comprising present-day Yellowstone and Grand Teton National Parks. He is believed to be the first white man to see Yellowstone Lake, at least one geyser, and the Teton Range. While Lewis and Clark would have believed Colter's accounts, many jokingly referred to the land of boiling mudpots and steaming rivers as "Colter's Hell."

Few explorers ventured into Colter's Hell until 1871, when Hayden's Geological Survey explored the region. During the expedition, a party member suggested the area should be set aside as a national park. Hayden agreed and became the most enthusiastic and devoted advocate of this newly conceived park idea. His report declared the land unsuitable for farming because of its high elevation. Mining was impossible because of its volcanic origins. These findings combined with images and paintings collected during the expedition were enough to convince Congress to withdraw this region from public auction. On March 1, 1872, President Grant signed a law creating Yellowstone National Park, the first of its kind anywhere in the world.

N. P. Langford became the park's first superintendent (allowing him to sign his name "National Park Langford"). It was not a glamorous position. He was denied salary, funding, and staff. Without resources to protect the park, it was vulnerable to poachers, vandals, and others seeking to raid its resources. Philetus Norris was appointed as Yellowstone's second superintendent, and first to receive a salary. Although meager, he received enough funding to begin construction on a system of roads and to hire Henry Yount as gamekeeper. Yount is widely regarded as the first park ranger, but he resigned when it was obvious the job of preventing poaching and vandalism was far too great a task for one man.

Protecting the park would only become more difficult as tourism increased. Completion of the Northern Pacific Railroad line to Livingston, MT and the park's northern entrance had dramatic results. Visitation increased from 300 in 1872 to more than 5,000 in

When to Go

Yellowstone is open all year, but more than half of the park's four million annual visitors arrive between July and August. Visiting in September or October is a nice alternative. It's less crowded, wildlife is still active, and the weather is comfortable. About 120,000 people visit the park each winter to see an enchanting wonderland created by the combination of snow and geothermal features. **Mammoth Campground** is open all year. Year-round lodging is available at Old Faithful and Mammoth Hot Springs. North and Northeast Entrance provide the only year-round access to wheeled vehicles. All other entrances close, allowing roads to be groomed for the winter season. The road between North and Northeast Entrances and the road from Mammoth Hot Springs to the parking area at Upper Terraces are the only roads plowed for wheeled vehicles during winter. All interior roads can only be accessed by over-snow vehicles in winter. The open/close dates for over-snow vehicle roads is subject to change based on the amount of snowfall. Park entrances are closed once again in late March or early April to clear roads for the upcoming summer season.

Transportation & Airports

Public transportation is available to several gateway cities near Yellowstone. Visitors can reach West Yellowstone aboard a bus/shuttle from Salt Lake City (208.656.8824, saltlakeexpress.com) and airports at Bozeman, MT; Idaho Falls, ID; and Jackson Hole, WY. Commercial transportation to the park is also available from Cody and Jackson, WY (406.640.0631, yellowstoneroadrunner.com). At this time, the park does not provide a public shuttle to explore its 142-mile Grand Loop Road.

Yellowstone Regional (COD) in Cody, WY is close to the East (27 miles) and Northeast Entrances (76 miles). Jackson Hole Airport (JAC), located in Grand Teton National Park is about 50 miles from the Southern Entrance. Gallatin Field (BZN) just outside Bozeman, MT, is about 90 miles from the North Entrance. Billings' Logan International (BIL) is 67 miles from the Northeast Entrance. Idaho Falls

Regional (IDA) is about 110 miles from the West Entrance. Between June and early September, Yellowstone Airport, (WYS) located in West Yellowstone, MT, is serviced from Salt Lake City International Airport (SCL) in Utah.

Directions

Yellowstone is huge. It's larger than the states of Delaware and Rhode Island combined. Five roads lead into the park: one from each side, and another from the northeast corner. Current road conditions are available by calling (307) 344-2117. Below you'll find short descriptions of traveling directions to each entrance from the nearest major city.

North Entrance (40 miles from Livingston, MT): From I-90, take Exit 333 near Livingston, MT for US-89 S toward City Center/Yellowstone National Park. Turn onto US-89 S. Drive about 52 miles through Gardiner, MT, under Roosevelt Arch, and into the park's North Entrance.

West Entrance (108 miles from Idaho Falls, ID): From Idaho Falls (I-15), take US-20 E more than 100 miles to West Yellowstone, MT. Turn left at US-191 S/US-20 E/US-287 S/Yellowstone Ave, which leads across the Montana–Wyoming border and into the park.

South Entrance (57 miles from Jackson, WY): You'll take one of the most scenic highways in the United States, US-191 N/US-287 N/US-89 N/John D. Rockefeller, Jr. Parkway, about 38 miles north through Grand Teton National Park to South Entrance.

East Entrance (52 miles from Cody, WY): Take US-14 W/US-16 W/US-20 W/Sheridan Avenue (following signs to Yellowstone) about 25 miles west to the park entrance. (This route is gorgeous, too.)

Northeast Entrance (81 miles from Cody, WY): Take WY-120/Depot Road north about 16 miles. Turn left at Chief Joseph Hwy/WY-296, which turns into Crandall Road then Dead Indian Hill Road, and finally Sunlight Basin Road before it

1883. The railroad sought to develop the area's prime locations with help from an amiable superintendent named Rufus Hatch. Under Hatch's leadership, trash was discarded in streams and fumaroles, tourists were charged exorbitant amounts, animals were killed for food, trees were chopped for construction, and coal was mined from park land. America's first and only national park was being exploited by visitors, developers, poachers, and its stewards. Many sympathetic Americans believed Hatch was destroying the park. To prove this point, Civil War hero General Phillip Sheridan invited President Chester A. Arthur to join him on a Yellowstone camping trip. The first Presidential visit led to legislation appropriating $40,000 for the park, regulating Hatch's development, and allowing the Secretary of the Interior to summon troops to prevent vandalism and hunting.

To protect the country's last free-roaming bison herd, General Sheridan and Troop M of the 1st United States Cavalry, summoned by order of the Secretary of the Interior, rode to the rescue. Their temporary residence lasted 32 years, during which they built structures, enforced regulations, oversaw construction of Roosevelt Arch, and created many of the management principles adopted by the National Park Service when it assumed control in 1918. More than half a century after its establishment, the park idea was beginning to take shape. It was a long and arduous journey to form a park that is truly "for the Benefit and Enjoyment of the People," as Roosevelt Arch states, but this too has become as real as the yarn-spinners' tales of bubbling mud, towering geysers, and golden canyons.

Geysers & Hot Springs

The park is centered on top **Yellowstone Caldera**, the largest supervolcano on the continent, measuring 45-by-30 miles. It is considered an active volcano, but there have only been three eruptions in the last 2 million years. The last one, 640,000 years ago, was 1,000 times larger than Mt St. Helens' eruption in 1980. Although few and far between, volcanic activity helped shape the region and its caldera. The Yellowstone hotspot, consisting of the heat source (earth's core), plume, and magma chamber, have endowed the region with **more than 10,000 geothermal features, including 300 geysers.**

Thermal features and one-to-three thousand tiny annual earthquakes (all virtually undetectable by people) are proof of present-day volcanic activity.

Now that you're scared silly, remember, scientists are constantly monitoring these activities, and it is very unlikely an eruption will occur in the next thousand or even 10,000 years. So, scratch "witness a cataclysmic volcanic eruption" off your "Yellowstone To-Do List." It's just not going to happen. However, you'll definitely want to visit the ever-changing geyser basins.

Mammoth Hot Springs is located in the northwest corner just beyond the caldera boundary. A road leads through the upper terrace, but there's also a self-guiding boardwalk that winds its way through the terraced pools and travertine formations.

Traveling south on Grand Loop Road from Mammoth you'll encounter **Norris Geyser Basin**. Its unique acidic (opposed to alkaline) waters allow different classes of bacterial thermophiles to live here. Thermophiles create the different color patterns you see in and around the basin's water. Norris is home to several geysers. Among them is **Steamboat**, the world's tallest active geyser. Its eruptions hurl super-heated water more than 300 feet into the air, but they occur irregularly, often separated by more than a year. **Echinus Geyser** is also on the unpredictable side, but it may erupt multiple times per day. There's no guarantee that you'll see a geyser erupt like at Old Faithful, but Norris Geyser Basin and its self-guiding boardwalk is a "must-do" activity. There's just something about Norris that feels more unique and ethereal than other basins. Its baby blue pools surrounded by white rocks are inviting and comforting, even as steam ominously billows out of vents lining the boardwalk.

Continuing on Grand Loop Road between Norris and Madison, is **Monument Geyser Basin**. Contrary to the name there are no active geysers here. Its monuments are rocky spires containing silica (glass) that have also been discovered on the floor of Yellowstone Lake. Scientists believe these spires formed thousands of years ago when the area was submerged by a glacially dammed lake. Reach this

intersects with US-212 W/Beartooth Hwy (closed seasonally). Turn left onto Beartooth Hwy to Cooke City, MT and Northeast Entrance.

Developed Areas
Yellowstone has eight main developed areas centered on the park's most breathtaking natural attractions. Each area is located on or near Grand Loop Road (GLR). GLR forms a giant figure-8 connecting all five entrances. See pages 228–229 for detailed maps of most developed areas.

Mammoth Hot Springs: Located just 5 miles from the North Entrance, you'll find spectacular terraces formed of travertine (calcium carbonate—the main ingredient in heartburn relief tablets). Lodging, dining, gas, campground, post office, shopping, visitor center, and medical station are available.

Tower–Roosevelt: Located at the NE corner of GLR, you'll find Petrified Tree, Specimen Ridge, Tower Fall, and some of the best hiking trails. Lodging, camping, store, and gas are available.

Canyon Village: Located near GLR's center, this is one of the most popular regions, including Grand Canyon of the Yellowstone. Gas, lodging, dining, store, visitor center, and showers are available.

Norris: Situated opposite Canyon Village at the center of GLR is Norris, the oldest and hottest thermal area, and home to Steamboat, the world's tallest geyser. A campground and Museum of the National Park Ranger are available.

Madison: Located southwest of Norris, where Madison and Firehole Rivers converge. Thermal features, a popular 75–80°F swimming hole just below Firehole Falls, campground, and information station are available nearby.

Old Faithful: Old Faithful—the most iconic feature of the park—is located at the southwest corner of GLR. Nearby you'll find Midway Geyser Basin, home to the most colorful feature, Grand Prismatic Spring.

Just about everything you can imaging is available at Old Faithful Village (except a campground).

West Thumb & Grant Village: Located at the southern end of GLR, West Thumb of Yellowstone Lake offers a geyser basin near the shoreline. Campground, store, lodging, showers, gas, and visitor center are available.

Fishing Bridge & Lake Village: Located at the north end of Yellowstone Lake, Fishing Bridge is a popular place to watch cutthroat trout, but fishing is banned. An RV park, gas, store, and dining are available at fishing bridge. You will find lodging, dining, camping, medical station, store, and a ranger station at Lake Village.

Driving

Driving Yellowstone is all about 142-mile **Grand Loop Road** that makes a giant "figure-eight" in the center of the park. Much of this loop was planned during the park's early days when it was still under U.S. military administration. All five park entrances lead to the loop. The top half takes visitors to locations such as Mammoth Hot Springs, Petrified Tree, Tower Fall, Norris Geyser Basin, and Sheepeater Cliff. Lamar Valley is located along Northeast Entrance Road, which is an immensely popular hiking and wildlife viewing area. The lower half passes Grand Canyon of the Yellowstone, Hayden Valley, Fishing Bridge, West Thumb Geyser Basin, Upper Geyser Basin (Old Faithful), Midway Geyser Basin (Grand Prismatic Spring), and Lower Geyser Basin. Motorists cross the Continental Divide twice between West Thumb and Old Faithful. South Entrance Road leads to Lewis Lake (popular for paddling), coming from the ultra-scenic **John D. Rockefeller, Jr. Memorial Parkway** and Grand Teton National Park (page 206). One of the biggest mistakes Yellowstone visitors can make is to believe they can drive Grand Loop Road in one day. Plan to spend a minimum of three days. In summer, the roadway can be extremely busy. Start touring early, and don't forget to pull completely off the road when you stop to view wildlife. Finally, drive safely and have fun.

basin by taking a steep 1-mile trail beginning just south of **Artists' Paint Pots**. The Paint Pots are two bubbling mudpots.

Between Madison and Old Faithful you'll find, in order, **Lower, Midway, and Upper Geyser Basins.** Lower Geyser Basin has a much lower concentration of geothermal features and it's highlight is **Fountain Paint Pots** and **Great Fountain Geyser** (an extremely popular sunset photo destination). You'll find a self-guiding trail explaining the four types of geothermal features: geysers, hot springs, fumaroles, and mud pots. Mud pots are hot springs containing boiling mud rather than water. **Midway Geyser Basin** is small in size, but its geothermal features are large and colorful. Midway is home to **Grand Prismatic Spring**, the largest hot spring in Yellowstone (370-ft wide, 121-ft deep). From up-close its beauty is obscured by its size. The best vantage point is from a nearby hill situated along **Fairy Falls Trail** (page 233). Of all the geothermal features to see, the sight of Grand Prismatic Spring from Fairy Falls Trail (although you aren't supposed to climb the hill) is the most likely to leave you breathless. **Excelsior Geyser**, which pours hot water into the Firehole River, is another noteworthy site.

Upper Geyser Basin boasts **Old Faithful** and the highest concentration of geothermal features in the park. If you want to see a geyser erupt, this is the spot. Old Faithful pumps 200+°F water 100–185 feet in the air once every 60–110 minutes. Prediction times are posted at most buildings in the area. **Observation Point** (accessed by a short but steep 1-mile trail) is a more peaceful position to watch the eruption. **Castle Geyser** also erupts regularly, approximately once every 13 hours.

East of Old Faithful is **West Thumb Geyser Basin**. Thermal features extend from the shoreline to beneath the surface of Yellowstone Lake, providing some outstanding views along the lakeshore.

All major geothermal areas are listed above, but many others are scattered throughout the park. **Mud Volcano** and **Sulfur Cauldron** are located near Hayden Valley. **Gibbon, Heart Lake, Lone Star, and Shoshone Geyser Basins** are all found in the backcountry.

Bison jam near Hayden Valley

GALLATIN

West Yellowstone to Bozeman
90 mi
145 km

West Yellowstone to Big Sky
48 mi
77 km

GALLATIN

NATIONAL FOREST

Gardiner to Livingston
52 mi
84 km
Gardiner to Bozeman
84 mi
135 km

Old Yellowstone Trail

ABSA

Jardine

no water

Gardiner

(89)

Roosevelt Arch

North Entrance
5314 ft
1620 m

Road between Gardiner and
Cooke City is open all year

Yellowstone

5 mi
8 km

9

Mount Everts
7841 ft
2390 m

Forces of the
Northern Range

one-way

8

Hot Springs
Mammoth Hot Springs

LEE
METCALF
WILDERNESS

(31)

(30)

Gallatin River

Specimen Creek

Electric Peak
10969 ft
3343 m

Sportsman
Lake

Mammoth Hot Springs
Albright Visitor Center

Mammoth Hot Springs Terraces
Park Headquarters

6

5

7

Blacktail
Pond

Undine
Falls

Phantom
Lake

Blacktail Plateau

Blacktail
Falls

(11)

Wraith
Falls

BLACKTAIL DEER
PLATEAU

GALLATIN

NATIONAL

FOREST

(191)

Fan Creek

Little Quadrant
Mountain
9885 ft
3013 m

31 mi
50 km

Gardners Hole

Gardner River

Road closed from
early November
to mid-April

Bunsen
Peak
8564 ft
2610 m

Golden
Gate

4

Swan
Lake

Gardner River

Prospect Peak
9525 ft
2903 m

WASHBURN

RANGE

West Yellowstone to
Earthquake Lake
Visitor Center
28 mi
45 km

(287)

(191)

Hebgen
Lake

(287)

Hebgen Lake

Grayling Creek

Gneiss Creek

Quadrant
Mountain
9944 ft
3031 m

Panther Creek

Indian Creek

3

Sheepeater Cliff

Willow Park

21 mi
34 km

Indian Creek

Antler
Peak
10023 ft
3055 m

Winter Creek

Dome Mountain
9894 ft
3016 m

Mount Holmes
10336 ft
3150 m

Grizzly
Lake

Straight Creek

Beaver
Lake

1

Obsidian Cliff
7383 ft
2250 m

2

Lava Creek

Road betwee
and Canyon
mid-Octobe

Road betw
and Canyo
mid-Octobe

Don't Miss
Norris Geyser Basin

MADISON

MONTANA
WYOMING

VALLEY

Roaring Mountain

Twin
Lakes

Nymph
Lake

Gibbon River

Observation Pe
9397 ft
2864 m

Grebe
Lake

Wolf
Lake

Cascade
Lake

(23)

Ice Lake

Museum of the
National Park Ranger

Norris
7526 ft 2311 m
Museum and
Information Station

NORRIS GEYSER BASIN
Steamboat Geyser

27

12 mi
19 km

(26)

Otter Creek

West Yellowstone to Ashton
60 mi
97 km

(20)

West
Yellowstone

West Entrance
6667 ft
2032 m

Two
Ribbons

West Yellowstone Visitor
Information Center

Madison River

14 mi
23 km

Road closed from
early November
to mid-April

29

Gibbon River

Monument
Geyser Basin

Beryl Spring

Artists
Paintpots

28

14 mi
23 km

Gibbon Falls
84 ft
26 m

Virginia
Cascade

Wildlife
Hayden Valley

Madison
6806 ft 2074 m
Information Station

Mount Haynes
8235 ft
2510 m

National Park
Mountain
7500 ft
2286 m

Firehole Falls

Firehole Canyon Drive

Firehole R.

Nez Perce Creek

YELLOWSTONE

HAYDEN

CENTRAL PLATEAU

Mary
Lake

Fountain Flat Drive

32

Fairy Creek

33

LOWER GEYSER BASIN
Fountain Paint Pot
Firehole Lake Drive
Great Fountain Geyser

Goose

Beach
Lake

Br

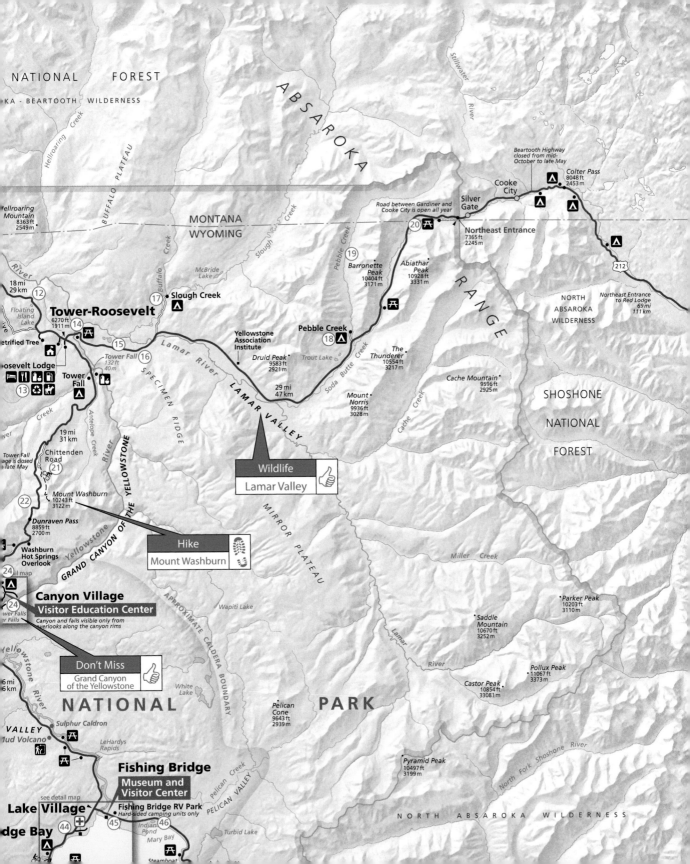

NATIONAL FOREST
KA - BEARTOOTH WILDERNESS

ABSAROKA

Stillwater

River

Hellroaring Creek

Beartooth Highway
closed from mid-
October to late May

Colter Pass
8048 ft
2453 m

Cooke City

Silver
Gate

MONTANA
WYOMING

Road between Gardiner and
Cooke City is open all year

Northeast Entrance
7365 ft
2245 m

RANGE

212

NORTH
ABSAROKA
WILDERNESS

Northeast Entrance
to Red Lodge
69 mi
111 km

20

Buffalo Creek

McBride
Lake

Slough Creek

19

Barronette
Peak
10404 ft
3171 m

Abiathar
Peak
10928 ft
3331 m

Hellroaring
Mountain
8363 ft
2549 m

BUFFALO PLATEAU

River

18 mi
29 km

12

Floating
Island
Lake

Tower-Roosevelt
6270 ft
1911 m

17

14

Slough Creek

15

Tower Fall
132 ft
40 m

16

Yellowstone
Association
Institute

Pebble Creek

18

The
Thunderer
10554 ft
3217 m

Cache Mountain
9596 ft
2925 m

SHOSHONE

NATIONAL

FOREST

Petrified Tree

osevelt Lodge

13

Tower
Fall

Druid Peak
9583 ft
2921 m

Trout Lake

Mount
Norris
9936 ft
3028 m

LAMAR RIVER

Lamar River

29 mi
47 km

LAMAR VALLEY

SPECIMEN RIDGE

Soda Butte Creek

Cache Creek

Pebble Creek

Tower Fall
age is closed
e late May

Chittenden
Road

19 mi
31 km

21

Antelope Creek

River

GRAND CANYON OF THE YELLOWSTONE

Mount Washburn
10243 ft
3122 m

22

Dunraven Pass
8859 ft
2700 m

Washburn
Hot Springs
Overlook

Wildlife
Lamar Valley 👍

MIRROR PLATEAU

Hike
Mount Washburn 👣

Miller Creek

Parker Peak
10203 ft
3110 m

Saddle
Mountain
10670 ft
3252 m

24

l map

Canyon Village
Visitor Education Center
Canyon and falls visible only from
overlooks along the canyon rims

24

Wapiti Lake

APPROXIMATE CALDERA BOUNDARY

Lamar

River

Pollux Peak
11067 ft
3373 m

wer Falls
r Falls

Yellowstone River

Don't Miss
Grand Canyon
of the Yellowstone 👍

White
Lake

NATIONAL

PARK

Pelican
Cone
9643 ft
2939 m

Castor Peak
10854 ft
33081 m

VALLEY
lud Volcano

Sulphur Caldron

LeHardys
Rapids

Pyramid Peak
10497 ft
3199 m

North Fork Shoshone River

Fishing Bridge
**Museum and
Visitor Center**

Pelican Creek

PELICAN VALLEY

NORTH   ABSAROKA   WILDERNESS

see detail map

Lake Village

dge Bay

44

45

46

Fishing Bridge RV Park
Hard-sided camping units only

Indian
Pond

Mary Bay

Turbid Lake

Steamboat

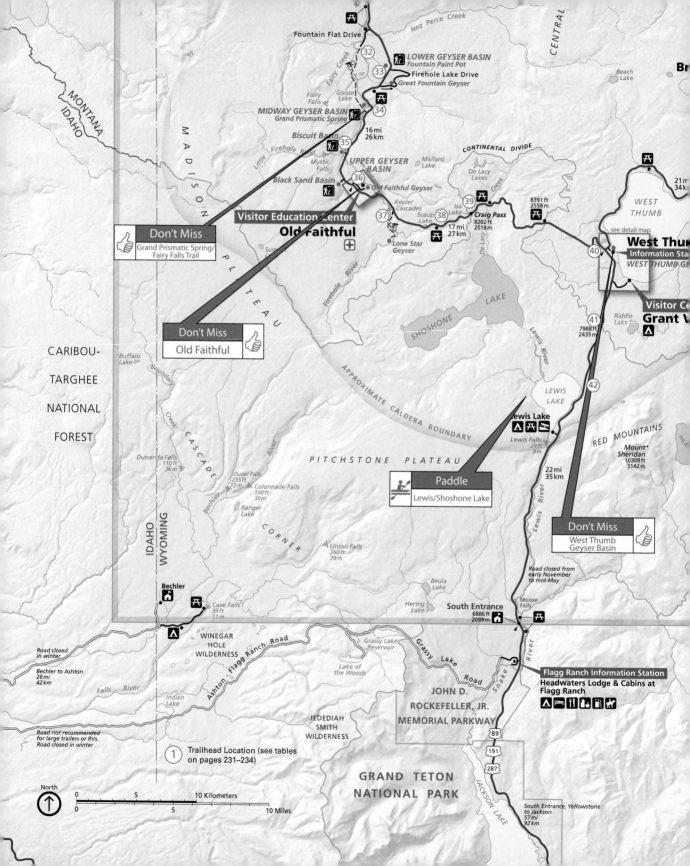

Fountain Flat Drive

Nez Perce Creek

CENTRAL

Beach
Lake

Br

MONTANA
IDAHO

32

33

LOWER GEYSER BASIN
Fountain Paint Pot

Firehole Lake Drive
Great Fountain Geyser

Fairy Creek

34

16 mi
26 km

Fairy
Falls

Goose
Lake

MIDWAY GEYSER BASIN
Grand Prismatic Spring

CONTINENTAL DIVIDE

21 m
34 k

WEST
THUMB

Biscuit Basin

Firehole River

35

Mallard
Lake

De Lacy
Lakes

8391 ft
2558 m

Little

Mystic
Falls

**UPPER GEYSER
BASIN**

Creek

Black Sand Basin

36

Old Faithful Geyser

39

see detail map

West Thu
Information Sta
WEST THUMB GE

Kepler
Cascades

Isa
Lake

Craig Pass
8262 ft
2518 m

40

**Visitor Education Center
Old Faithful** ✚

37

Scaup
Lake

38

17 mi
27 km

De Lacy

MADISON PLATEAU

Don't Miss 👍
Grand Prismatic Spring/
Fairy Falls Trail

Lone Star
Geyser

SHOSHONE
LAKE

**Visitor Ce
Grant V**

41

7988 ft
2435 m

Riddle
Lake

Don't Miss 👍
Old Faithful

Firehole River

CARIBOU-

TARGHEE

NATIONAL

FOREST

Buffalo
Lake

Boundary

Creek

APPROXIMATE CALDERA BOUNDARY

Lewis River

42

LEWIS
LAKE

RED MOUNTAINS

Mount
Sheridan
10308 ft
3142 m

CASCADE

River

Dunanda Falls
110 ft
36 m

PITCHSTONE PLATEAU

Ouzel Falls
235 ft
72 m

Colonnade Falls
100 ft
30 m

Ranger
Lake

Paddle 🛶
Lewis/Shoshone Lake

Lewis Lake
Lewis Falls
29 ft
9 m

22 mi
35 km

IDAHO
WYOMING

CORNER

Union Falls
260 ft
79 m

Beula
Lake

Don't Miss 👍
West Thumb
Geyser Basin

Road closed from
early November
to mid-May

Hering
Lake

Moose
Falls

Bechler

Cave Falls
35 ft
11 m

WINEGAR
HOLE
WILDERNESS

Grassy
Lake
Reservoir

South Entrance
6886 ft
2099 m

Road closed
in winter

Ashton-Flagg Ranch Road

Lake of
the Woods

Snake River

Flagg Ranch Information Station
**Headwaters Lodge & Cabins at
Flagg Ranch**

Bechler to Ashton
26 mi
42 km

Falls River

Indian
Lake

JEDEDIAH
SMITH
WILDERNESS

JOHN D.
ROCKEFELLER, JR.
MEMORIAL PARKWAY

Grassy Lake Road

Road not recommended
for large trailers or RVs.
Road closed in winter

89

191

① Trailhead Location (see tables
on pages 231–234)

287

**GRAND TETON
NATIONAL PARK**

JACKSON LAKE

North

0   5   10 Kilometers

0   5   10 Miles

South Entrance, Yellowstone
to Jackson
57 mi
92 km

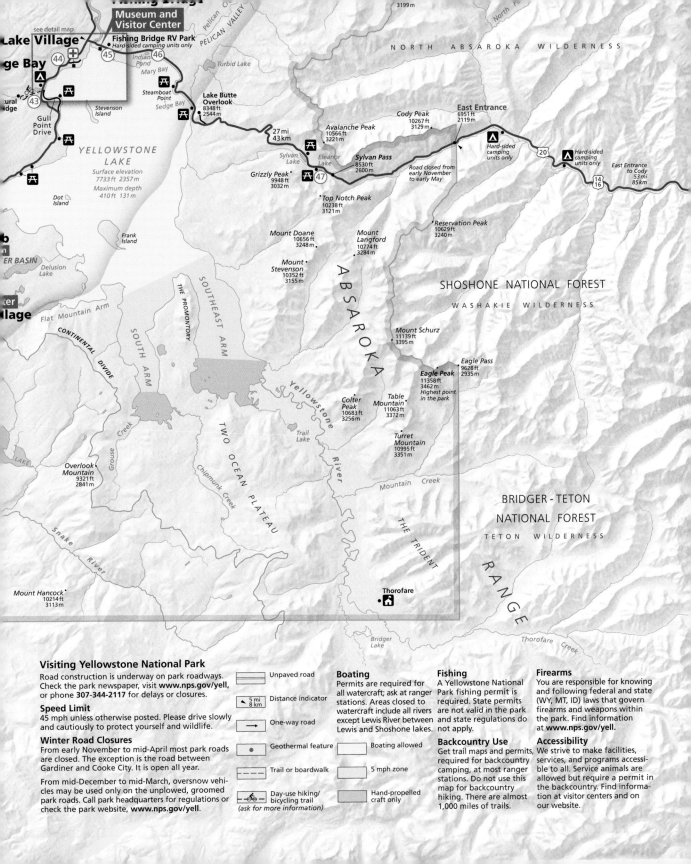

Visiting Yellowstone National Park

Road construction is underway on park roadways. Check the park newspaper, visit www.nps.gov/yell, or phone 307-344-2117 for delays or closures.

Speed Limit

45 mph unless otherwise posted. Please drive slowly and cautiously to protect yourself and wildlife.

Winter Road Closures

From early November to mid-April most park roads are closed. The exception is the road between Gardiner and Cooke City. It is open all year.

From mid-December to mid-March, oversnow vehicles may be used only on the unplowed, groomed park roads. Call park headquarters for regulations or check the park website, www.nps.gov/yell.

Unpaved road
Distance indicator
One-way road
Geothermal feature
Trail or boardwalk
Day-use hiking/ bicycling trail (ask for more information)

Boating

Permits are required for all watercraft; ask at ranger stations. Areas closed to watercraft include all rivers except Lewis River between Lewis and Shoshone lakes.

Boating allowed
5 mph zone
Hand-propelled craft only

Fishing

A Yellowstone National Park fishing permit is required. State permits are not valid in the park and state regulations do not apply.

Backcountry Use

Get trail maps and permits, required for backcountry camping, at most ranger stations. Do not use this map for backcountry hiking. There are almost 1,000 miles of trails.

Firearms

You are responsible for knowing and following federal and state (WY, MT, ID) laws that govern firearms and weapons within the park. Find information at www.nps.gov/yell.

Accessibility

We strive to make facilities, services, and programs accessible to all. Service animals are allowed but require a permit in the backcountry. Find information at visitor centers and on our website.

Yellowstone Camping (Fees are per night)

Name	Location	Open	Fee	Sites	Notes
Bridge Bay*	Bridge Bay	late May–early Sept	$23.50	431	Dump station
Canyon*	Canyon Village	late May–mid-Sept	$27	273	Shower and laundry
Fishing Bridge RV*	Fishing Bridge	early May–mid-Sept	$47.50	>325	Hookups, sewer, shower and laundry
Grant Village*	Grant Village	mid-June–mid-Sept	$27	430	Dump station, shower and laundry
Madison*	Madison	late April–mid-Oct	$22.50	278	Dump station, no hookups
Indian Creek	Near Sheepeater Cliff	mid-June–mid-Sept	$15	70	No generators or hook-ups, vault toilets
Lewis Lake - 🛶	South Entrance Road	mid-June–early Nov	$15	85	Very few pull-through sites
Mammoth	Mammoth	All Year	$20	85	Only year-round camp
Norris	Norris	late May–late Sept	$20	>111	Few RV-friendly sites
Pebble Creek - 🛶	Northeast Entrance	mid-June–late Sept	$15	27	Few RV-friendly sites
Slough Creek - 🛶	Northeast Entrance	mid-June–early Oct	$15	23	2.5-mile dirt access road (popular)
Tower Fall	Tower/Roosevelt	late May–late Sept	$15	31	Best for tents/small RVs

*Run by Xanterra Parks & Resorts and available for reservation (866.439.7375, yellowstonenationalparklodges.com) All other campgrounds are operated by the National Park Service and available on a first-come, first-served basis

Backcountry	Backcountry campsites are available for advance reservation ($25/trip fee). Permits ($3/person per night) must be obtained in person not more than 48 hours in advance from Canyon, Grant Village, and Mammoth Visitor Centers; Bechler, Bridge Bay, Old Faithful, and South Entrance Ranger Stations; Tower Backcountry Office, or West Yellowstone Information Center between June and August. See page 229 and 231 for more backcountry camping information.
Group Camping	Available at Madison, Grant, and Bridge Bay Campgrounds for large organized groups with a group leader ($131–255/night). Reservations are required. Call (307) 344-7311 or (866) 439-7375.
Winter Camping	Mammoth Campground is open and backcountry camping is available with a permit

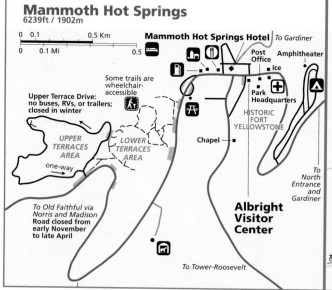

Mammoth Hot Springs
6239ft / 1902m

Fishing Bridge, Lake Village and Bridge Bay
7784ft / 2373m

Camping

Yellowstone has 12 established campgrounds providing more than 2,000 campsites. That's a lot of campsites, but as many as 50,000 visitors enter the park on a single day in July or August. This influx of guests causes congested roads, shoulder-to-shoulder hiking, and full campgrounds. Yellowstone does not offer overflow camping areas, but there are a fair amount of campgrounds and RV parks outside the park.

Campgrounds fill up from time-to-time (particularly in July and August), but try not to feel pressured into making reservations before you arrive. In fact, the best way to visit Yellowstone is to have a bit of flexibility in your travel arrangements. With all the amazing scenery, wildlife, and tourists, it's inevitable that you end up deviating from your pre-planned itinerary. When these instances occur, it's nice to have flexible overnight arrangements, allowing you to sleep nearby rather than forcing a potentially long drive (possibly at night) to the next destination or reserved accommodations. Reservations are recommended if you plan on traveling in July and August, as most campgrounds fill by noon.

You also don't want to get caught scrambling around the park (and beyond), searching for a campsite or else you'll spend all day in your car, driving great distances, rather than seeing Yellowstone.

Pebble Creek, Slough Creek, and Tower Fall are primitive campgrounds with vault toilets. Their small size and stunning environment cause them to fill early. A camper who secures a site at one of these locations is also more likely to spend a few extra nights, exacerbating the shortage problem.

Most campgrounds have a couple pull-through campsites, but very few can accommodate RVs longer than 30 feet. It is recommended that visitors with large RVs make reservations at **Fishing Bridge RV Park**. This campground is for hard-sided vehicles only. Tents and tent-trailers are prohibited.

Backcountry camping is also popular. A backcountry user permit is required for any overnight stay in the backcountry. Permits can be reserved ($25 fee), but they must be obtained in person at one of the locations

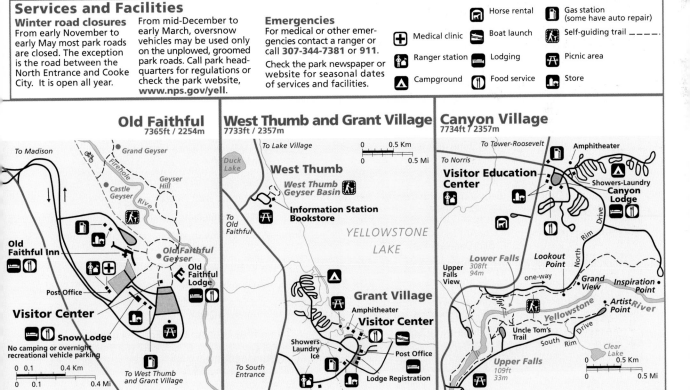

Services and Facilities

Winter road closures
From early November to early May most park roads are closed. The exception is the road between the North Entrance and Cooke City. It is open all year.

From mid-December to early March, oversnow vehicles may be used only on the unplowed, groomed park roads. Call park headquarters for regulations or check the park website, **www.nps.gov/yell**.

Emergencies
For medical or other emergencies contact a ranger or call **307-344-7381** or **911**.

Check the park newspaper or website for seasonal dates of services and facilities.

Horse rental   Gas station (some have auto repair)

Medical clinic   Boat launch   Self-guiding trail _ _ _ _ .

Ranger station   Lodging   Picnic area

Campground   Food service   Store

Old Faithful
7365ft / 2254m

West Thumb and Grant Village
7733ft / 2357m

Canyon Village
7734ft / 2357m

listed in the camping table on page 228. Pick up your permit at the location closest to where your trip begins so you can receive up-to-date information regarding trail conditions and wildlife activity. Most backcountry campsites have a maximum stay of three days. Permits cost $3 per person per night for backpackers and boaters and $5 per person per night for stock parties (horses/mules/llamas).

All campers should be aware that Yellowstone is bear country. Do not keep food in your tent, keep a clean camp, and store food in air-tight containers (bear canisters for backpackers).

Lodging

Yellowstone's lodging facilities are attractions themselves, worthy of standing side-by-side with the most wonderful natural architecture the United States has to offer. Many visitors find **Old Faithful Inn** more impressive than the eponymous geyser visible from many of the rooms. It's priced reasonably, with rooms starting at $115/night. Stopping in to admire the architecture is free. Other lodgings are equally rustic and more secluded. If it's a true Wild West experience you seek, **Roosevelt Lodge** is where you'll find it. The Lodge's Roughrider Cabins—the park's most economical lodging—are suitable for 2–4 adults and cost just $84/night. Inspired by President Theodore Roosevelt, who frequented the park, they provide no-frills lodging

with few furnishings, no bathroom, and heat supplied by a wood burning stove. Mammoth Hot Springs and Old Faithful Snow Lodge are the only **winter accommodations** (note that Mammoth Hot Springs will be closed for the 2016/2017 and 2017/2018 winters to undergo renovations). All accommodations are non-smoking, and televisions, radios, air conditioning, and internet are not available at most facilities.

Hiking

More than 900 miles of trails makes selecting the right one challenging. To begin whittling down your hiking options, consider which regions you plan on visiting. Trails have been sorted geographically into six distinct regions. Many trails close seasonally due to poor conditions or increases in bear activity. It's a good idea to stop in at a visitor center prior to hiking to inquire about trail conditions and wildlife activity. Boardwalks connect the most interesting geothermal features (page 220). Dirt-packed, tree-covered, gloriously natural hiking trails lead far away from traffic-filled roads and bustling facilities.

Don't pass on some of the longer hikes. The first few miles of long trails can be just as rewarding as their entirety. For instance, **Specimen Ridge Trail** is seldom used even though it provides exceptional wildlife viewing opportunities, petrified tree specimens, and Grand Canyon of the Yellowstone vistas in the first couple

Yellowstone Lodging (Fees are per night)

Name	Open	Fee	Notes
Canyon Lodge - ♨	early June–late Sept	$122–499	Canyon Village's Dunraven Lodge is widely regarded as the best lodging in the park
Grant Village	late May–early Oct	$168–211	Overlooks Yellowstone Lake
Lake Lodge Cabins	early June–early Oct	$85–204	Cozy cabins with cafeteria style dining
Lake Yellowstone	mid-May–early Oct	$157–690	Basic rooms to a Presidential Suite
Mammoth Hot Springs	late April–mid-Oct mid-Dec–late Feb	$98–499	Motel-style rooms with shared restrooms to suites with cable TV
Old Faithful Lodge	mid-May–early Oct	$88–146	Simple accommodations
Old Faithful Inn	early May–early Oct	$115–572	Most requested lodging in the park
Old Faithful Snow Lodge - ♨	late April–late Oct mid-Dec–late Feb	$114–315	Stays true to park style design • Only accessible in winter via snow transportation
Roosevelt Lodge	mid-June–early Sept	$84–142	Primitive Lodging based on 2–4 people

For reservations call Xanterra Parks and Resorts at (866) 439-7375 or click yellowstonenationalparklodges.com
Rates are per night, for up to 2 adults and do not include tax and utility fee

miles. (Note: Pick up an area trail map at Tower/Roosevelt Ranger Station first, as there are a few trail junctions along the way.) Don't confuse this trail with the park's other Specimen Ridge Trail, which we call Fossil Forest in the hiking table on page 232. Fossil Forest is short, steep, unmarked, and unmaintained. **Forces of the Northern Range** (not listed) is a popular self-guiding trail that explains how volcanoes, glaciers, and fire shaped the land. Its trailhead is located 8 miles east of Mammoth Hot Springs on Mammoth–Tower Road.

Canyon, one of the busiest areas, is often filled with motorists. You can avoid the commotion by taking one of the trails listed on page 232. All short trails around Upper and Lower Falls have been omitted from the table; you can't miss them as you drive along the north and south sides of the canyon. **Uncle Tom's Trail**, is a must-hike (even though it's quite strenuous). It descends 500 feet via a series of paved inclines and more than 300 steps to an up close look at Lower Falls. **Brink of Lower Falls** and **Brink of Upper Falls** are also worth a visit.

It's hard to appreciate the size of Yellowstone Lake from its shores. View this massive alpine lake from shore-to-shore by driving to **Lake Butte** (East Entrance Road) or hiking to **Lake Overlook**, where on a clear day you can see clear across Yellowstone Lake to the Teton Range. You'll also have a bird's eye view of West Thumb, a smaller caldera created by volcanic eruption some 100,000 years ago that has since filled with water. If you're looking to challenge yourself, try the 2-mile, 2,100-ft-nearly-vertical climb to the top of **Avalanche Peak**. It's a real thigh burner!

Backpacking
There are more than 900 miles of trails and 300 designated backcountry campsites at Yellowstone. Backpackers planning on spending the night in the backcountry must obtain a **Backcountry Use Permit** ($3 per person per night). Only with special permission are you allowed to camp beyond designated sites. Advance reservations are accepted in person or by mail for a one-time $25 non-refundable permit fee.

Mammoth Area Hiking Trails (Distances are roundtrip unless noted otherwise)

Name	Location (# on map)	Length	Difficulty Rating & Notes
Grizzly Lake	1 mile south of Beaver Lake Picnic Area on Mammoth–Norris Road (1)	4.0 miles	E – Hike into a valley and to Grizzly Lake • Trail continues, joining Mt Holmes Trail
Mount Holmes	3 miles south of Indian Creek Camp (2)	20.0 miles	S – Hike to 10,336-ft summit of Mount Holmes
Bighorn Pass	Indian Creek Campground (3)	16.0 miles	S – Through grizzly country to 9,022-ft pass
Bunsen Peak	Mammoth–Norris Road (4, 6 alt.)	4.2 miles	M – Fairly easy summit to panoramic views
Osprey Falls	Mammoth–Norris Road (4, 6 alt.)	8.0 miles	M – Alt. Sheepeater Canyon to 150-ft falls
Electric Peak	4 miles south of Mammoth on Mammoth–Norris Road (5)	18.0 miles	S – Take Snow Pass/Sportsman Lake Trail to a 3.1-mile spur trail that leads to the summit
Beaver Ponds Loop	Just north of Liberty Cap (6)	5.0 miles	M – Nice loop through meadows and aspen
Sepulcher Mtn	Between Liberty Cap and the stone house next to Mammoth Terraces (6)	11.0 miles	S – Follows Beaver Ponds Trail to Sepulcher Mt Trail junction and to the 9,652-ft summit
Lava Creek - ♨	Across from Lava Creek Picnic Area on Mammoth–Tower Rd (7, 11)	3.5 miles (one-way)	M – Pass 60-ft Undine Falls, follow Gardner River, cross a bridge to Mammoth Camp
Boiling River - ♨	Parking Area near 45th parallel sign north of Mammoth Hot Springs (8)	1.0 mile	E – Short hike to a swimming area where hot spring water and Gardner River meet
Rescue Creek	7 miles east of Mammoth on Mammoth-Tower Road (9, 11)	8.0 miles (one-way)	M – Ends 1 mile south of NE Entrance
Black Canyon of the Yellowstone - ♨	Hellroaring Trailhead 3.5 miles west of Tower Junction (10, 11, 12)	18.5 miles (one-way)	M – Long day or 2-day hike from Hellroaring Trailhead to Gardiner, MT
Blacktail Creek/ Yellowstone River	7 miles east of Mammoth on Mammoth–Tower Road (11, 12)	12.0 miles (one-way)	M – Crosses a river, joins Yellowstone River Trail, and ends in Gardiner, MT

Difficulty Ratings: E = Easy, M = Moderate, S = Strenuous

Can you imagine hiking in winter? Bison can. Here they are breaking a trail near Tower Junction

Tower Hiking Trails (Distances are roundtrip unless noted otherwise)

Name	Location (# on map)	Length	Difficulty Rating & Notes
Hellroaring -	3.5 miles west of Tower Junction (12)	4.0 miles	S – Definitely one of the best hikes
Lost Lake	Behind Roosevelt Lodge (13)	4.0 miles	M – Loop trail skirts Lost Lake, reaches Petrified Tree before returning to the lodge
Yellowstone River Picnic Area -	1.25 miles northeast of Tower Junction on Northeast Entrance Road (14)	3.7 miles	M – Follows rim of Yellowstone Canyon • May spot peregrine falcons and osprey
Garnet Hill	50 yards north of Tower Junction on Northeast Entrance Road (14)	7.5 miles	M – Follows an old dirt coach road, then Elk Creek to intersection with Hellroaring Trail
Specimen Ridge	2.5 miles east of Tower Junction on Northeast Entrance Road (15)	17.5 miles (one-way)	S – Follow the ridgeline and rock cairns past Grand Canyon of the Yellowstone
Fossil Forest	4 miles east of Tower Junction on Northeast Entrance Road (16)	3–4 miles	M – Lightly traveled, unmaintained, unmarked trail leads to several petrified samples
Petrified Trees	5.3 miles east of Roosevelt Junction (16)	3.0 miles	S – Climbs 1,200 feet rapidly to nice petrified trees
Slough Creek	On dirt road toward Slough Creek Camp where the road bears left (17)	2.0/4.5 mi. (one-way)	M – Follows an old wagon trail • Distances are to the first two meadows •Trail continues beyond
Pebble Creek	Near Pebble Creek Bridge (18) and Warm Creek (20) on NE Entrance Road	12.0 miles (one-way)	M – Do a portion of this trail between Pebble Creek Camp and Warm Creek Trailhead
Bliss Pass	Pebble Creek Trail intersects Bliss Pass at mile 6.6 (19)	20.6 miles (one-way)	S – Connects Slough Creek and Pebble Creek Trails over Bliss Pass
Mt Washburn -	Chittenden (21) or Dunraven Pass (22) Parking Areas	2.5/3.0 mi. (one-way)	S – Out-and-back or arrange a shuttle between the two parking areas • Bicycles permitted

Canyon Hiking Trails (Distances are roundtrip unless noted otherwise)

Name	Location (# on map)	Length	Difficulty Rating & Notes
Cascade Lake	0.3 mile south of Cascade Lake Picnic Area (23)	5.0 miles	E –Two trails lead to Cascade Lake •This is the prettier of the two
Observation Peak	Cascade Lake Trailhead (23)	9.6 miles	S – Climbs 1,400 feet in 3 miles
Seven Mile Hole	Glacial Boulder Pullout near Inspiration Point (24)	10.0 miles	S – Follow Glacial Boulder Trail, only trail leading into Grand Canyon of the Yellowstone
Point Sublime	Artist Point Overlook (25)	2.5 miles	E – Follow South Rim Trail to this point
Grebe Lake	3.5 miles west of Canyon Junction (26)	6.2 miles	M – Follows an old fire road

Difficulty Ratings: E = Easy, M = Moderate, S = Strenuous

Old Faithful

Old Faithful–Norris Hiking Trails (Distances are roundtrip unless noted otherwise)

	Name	Location (# on map)	Length	Difficulty Rating & Notes
Norris	Artists' Paint Pot	4.5 miles south of Norris Junction (28)	1.0 mile	E – Peculiar geothermal features
Norris	Solfatara Creek	Norris Campground (27)	6.5 miles	M – One-way trail along creek
Norris	Monument Valley	5 miles south of Norris Junction (28)	2.0 miles	M – Tough, views of Gibbon Canyon
Norris	Purple Mountain	0.25-mile north of Madison Junction, near Madison Camp (29)	6.0 miles	M – Not the most picturesque mountain, convenient for campers
Old Faithful	Fairy Falls - 👍	End of Fountain Flat Drive (32) Fairy Falls Trailhead (34)	7.0/5.0 miles	E – Shorter from Fairy Falls Trailhead with views of Grand Prismatic Spring
Old Faithful	Sentinel Meadows	End of Fountain Flat Drive (32)	3.0 miles	M – Skirts along Firehole River
Old Faithful	Mallard Creek	3.8 miles north of Old Faithful Junction toward Madison (34)	9.2 miles	S – Alternate route to Mallard Lake across hilly terrain and burned forest
Old Faithful	Mystic Falls	Back of Biscuit Basin Boardwalk (35)	2.4 miles	M – 70-ft falls of the Firehole River
Old Faithful	Observation Pt - 👍	Behind Old Faithful (36)	1.6 mile	M – Better spot to view Old Faithful than the bleachers
Old Faithful	Mallard Lake - 👍	South of Old Faithful Lodge Cabins (36)	6.8 miles	M – Can return via Mallard Creek to complete a 12-mile loop
Old Faithful	Howard Eaton	Across Grand Loop Road from Old Faithful Ranger Station (36)	5.8 miles	M – Out-and-back traverses spruce forests down to Lone Star Geyser
Old Faithful	Lone Star Geyser - 👍	Near Kepler Cascades Parking Area (37)	4.8 miles	M – Partially paved along Firehole River
Old Faithful	Divide	6.8 miles south of Old Faithful Junction (38)	3.4 miles	M – Views of Shoshone Lake en route to the Continental Divide
Other	High Lake Loop	Access via Specimen Creek Trail at Milepost 26 of US-191 (30)	23.0 miles	S – Multi-day hike to two alpine loops through mountain country
Other	Sky Rim Loop - 👍	Access via Dailey Creek Trail at Milepost 31 of US-191 (31)	18.0 miles	S – Steep, rocky, exposed trail with superb mountain scenery and wildlife

Difficulty Ratings: E = Easy, M = Moderate, S = Strenuous

Fires are only allowed in established fire rings, and dead and down wood may be used as firewood. Trailheads have a trail registration box, so record your itinerary on the registration sheet before departing for your trek. This information aids rangers if you or your party becomes lost and a search is required. Orange metal tags on trees and posts mark established trails. Very few of Yellowstone's rivers and streams have bridges. Seal important items in plastic bags, and use a long sturdy stick when attempting to ford a river. If a waterway looks impassable, you probably shouldn't attempt to cross it. Water is cold and swift (especially after it rains). Much of the park's backcountry is unprotected and experiences severe winds. Carry a tent suitable for windy conditions. Finally, Yellowstone is grizzly bear country. Keep your camp clean, and sleep at least 100 yards up wind from where you cook. For additional information and a permit reservation form, check out the *Backcountry Trip Planner* available at the park website.

First-time backpackers should start with one of the shorter trails listed in the hiking tables beginning on page 231 (maps with locations of all backcountry campsites and trailheads are available in the *Backcountry Trip Planner*). A good place for your first backcountry trip is **Yellowstone River/Hellroaring Creek Area**. Multiple trailheads access the area and designated campsites are frequent, rarely more than 0.5-mile apart. No matter where you go, discuss your plans with a ranger prior to filling out your reservation form.

The **Thorofare Area** is a fantastic spot for backpackers. Try starting at Nine Mile Trailhead, located nine miles east of Fishing Bridge on East Entrance Road. From here, the trail leads 34 miles to Bridger Lake, just past Thorofare Ranger Station (presently holding the distinction of "most remote location in the Lower 48" by being 20 miles from the nearest road of any kind). **Shoshone Lake Area** is another popular backpacking destination. Sites along the lake's shoreline are occupied almost every night in summer. Several land trails lead to the lake, but it's also accessible to paddlers via Lewis Lake and Lewis River Channel. Xanterra (307.242.3893, yellowstonenationalparklodges.com) also offers backcountry boat shuttle service to some of the more remote locations along Yellowstone Lake.

Yellowstone Lake Hiking Trails (Distances are roundtrip unless noted otherwise)

	Name	Location (# on map)	Length	Difficulty Rating & Notes
Fishing Bridge/Lake Village	Shoshone Lake	8.8 mi W of West Thumb Junction (39)	5.8 miles	E – The park's largest backcountry lake
	Lake Overlook	West Thumb Geyser Parking Lot (40)	1.5 miles	M – High view of Yellowstone's West Thumb
	Duck Lake	West Thumb Geyser Parking Lot (40)	1.0 mile	E – Views of Duck and Yellowstone Lake
	Riddle Lake	3 miles south of Grant Village intersection (41)	4.8 miles	E – Trail crosses the Continental Divide to a pretty little lake
	Lewis River Channel/ Dogshead Loop	5 miles south of Grant Village intersection (42)	10.8 miles	S – 7-mile out-and-back through rugged terrain with a 4-mile loop at the end
	Heart Lake - 🏕	5.4 miles south of Grant Village (42)	15.0 miles	S – Day-hike to the lake and return
	Mt Sheridan Lookout	Intersects Heart Lake Trail (42)	6.0 miles	S – Leads to a fire lookout station
West Thumb/Grant Village	Natural Bridge	Bridge Bay Marina Parking Lot (43)	2.5 miles	E – Convenient for campers at Bridge Bay
	Elephant Back Mtn	South of Fishing Bridge Junction (44)	3.5 miles	M – Views of massive Yellowstone Lake
	Howard Eaton	East side of Fishing Bridge (45)	7.0 miles	M – Ends at LeHardy's Rapids
	Pelican Creek	West end of Pelican Cr Bridge (46)	0.6 mile	E – Traverses several different habitats
	Storm Point - 🏕	Indian Pond Pullout (46)	2.3 miles	E – Views Indian Pond & Yellowstone Lake
	Pelican Valley	End of a gravel road across from Indian Pond (46)	6.2 miles	M – Prime grizzly habitat above Pelican Valley and into the park's backcountry
	Avalanche Peak	Pullout at west end of Eleanor Lake toward East Entrance (47)	4.2 miles	S – 2,100-ft climb in just 2 miles to view some of the park's tallest peaks

Difficulty Ratings: E = Easy, M = Moderate, S = Strenuous

Boating

Whether you plan on exploring Yellowstone's waters in a motorized boat, kayak, canoe, or even a float tube, you must obtain a **permit** before hitting the water. They are available in person at South Entrance, Lewis Lake Campground, Grant Village Backcountry Office, and Bridge Bay Ranger Station. Float tube-only permits are available at Mammoth, Canyon, and Old Faithful backcountry offices, Northeast Entrance, and Bechler Ranger Station. Permits are $20/$10 (annual/7-day) for motorized boats and $10/$5 for non-motorized watercrafts. Grand Teton boating permits are honored, but owners still need to register their watercraft in Yellowstone and obtain a validation sticker. To help protect wildlife, all types of watercraft are prohibited from streams and rivers with the exception of the channel between **Lewis and Shoshone Lakes** where non-motorized boats are allowed.

Motorized boats are permitted on most of Yellowstone Lake and Lewis Lake. Boat launches are located at Lewis Lake and Bridge Bay Marina. Xanterra has motorized boats ($50/hour) and rowboats ($10/hour) for rent at Bridge Bay Marina. **Boat rentals** are available from mid-June to early September on a first-come, first-served basis. The rental office opens at 8am.

Horseback Riding

Xanterra (307.344.7311, yellowstonenationalparklodges.com) offers 1-hour ($45) and 2-hour ($68) **trail rides** departing from Roosevelt Lodge and Cabins, and Canyon Lodge and Cabins. A favorite activity from Roosevelt Lodge is the 1–2 hour ($79–88) trail ride to a **western style cookout**. Both are interpretive rides featuring knowledgeable guides who educate riders on the park's history and geography. Minimum age is 8 years old. Riders ages 8–11 must be accompanied by an adult. Minimum height is 4-ft. Maximum weight is 240 pounds. Helmets are available upon request. You can also join an outfitter (page 244) on a multi-day backcountry llama, mule, or horse excursion.

Guided Bus/Van Tours

Xanterra (307.344.7311, yellowstonenationalparklodges.com) offers bus/van tours like "Lamar Valley Wildlife Excursion" ($44–70/adult),

---

Best of Yellowstone

Attraction: Grand Canyon of the Yellowstone
Runner-up: Grand Prismatic Spring
2nd Runner-up: Norris Geyser Basin
3rd Runner-up: Boiling River
4th Runner-up: Yellowstone Lake

Activity: Yellowstone Association Programs
Runner-up: Western Cookout & Trail Ride
2nd Runner-up: Snowcoach Tours

Wildlife Viewing: Lamar Valley
Runner-up: Hayden Valley

Short Hike: Mount Washburn Trail
Runner-up: Uncle Tom's Trail

Backpack: Black Canyon of the Yellowstone
Runner-up: Sky Rim Loop

"Twilight on the Firehole" ($34), "Firehole Basin Adventure" ($50/adult), a tour of the lower half of Grand Loop Road; "Evening Wildlife Encounters" ($61), a great opportunity to spot bear and bison; "Geyser Gazers" ($26), 1.5 hours in the Fire Hole where steam billows from the earth; "Wake up to Wildlife" ($83); the extremely popular 10.5-hour "Yellowstone in a Day" ($105–111); and the classic Yellowstone Tour, "Circle of Fire" ($75). Tours are half-price for children ages 3–11, and children 2 years and under are free. Don't see anything you like? Xanterra can help you plan a **custom guided bus/van tour** ($800–1,500+/passenger for 8 hours). **The Yellowstone Association** (406.848.2400, yellowstoneassociation.org) offers once-in-a-lifetime tours exploring the parks wilderness and wildlife with an Institute naturalist guide.

Biking

Bicycles are allowed on all park roads and a few trails, but strictly prohibited from backcountry trails and boardwalks. Two gravel roads are ideal for **mountain bikes**: Old Gardiner Road, which connects Mammoth Hot Springs and Gardiner, and Blacktail Plateau Drive, which runs parallel to a short section of Grand Loop Road (GLR) between Tower and Mammoth. These roads are one-way for motorists,

Grand Prismatic Spring

but cyclists may travel in either direction. These roads are also a good alternative to the busy GLR.

To explore some of the park's 300 miles of paved roadways, you'll want to pedal early or late in the day or between mid-May and mid-April when the winter snowmobiling season has ended and roads remain closed to motorized vehicles in order to prepare for the upcoming tourist season. During this time, cyclists are free to pedal between West Entrance (West Yellowstone) and Mammoth Hot Springs (weather permitting). If you're thinking about it, make sure you come prepared. It will be cold, and all of the park's services and facilities will be closed. Dress in layers and stock up on supplies in Gardiner or West Yellowstone before you arrive. To pedal when the weather is more pleasant, try going early in the morning or later in the evening during the busy tourist season. Occasionally, bicycle clubs hold evening **full moon rides**. The moon may be bright, but not bright enough. You'll need front and rear lights. Still, pedaling GLR at night is not the best idea.

The simplest pedaling excursions are found at **bicycle approved trails**. Bunsen Peak Road (6 miles) near Mammoth, Riverside Trail (1.4 miles) near the West Entrance, Fountain Freight Road (5.5 miles) and Lone Star Geyser Road (2 miles) near Old Faithful, and Mount Washburn (3 miles) from Chittenden Road to its summit near Tower are open to bicycles. Xanterra has **bike rentals** ($8/hour, $25/4-hour, $35/24-hour) at Old Faithful Snow Lodge. Touring cyclists receive discounted rates at campgrounds with biker/hiker campsites.

Swimming
There are two popular swimming holes. One spot is located on **Gardner River**, two miles north of Mammoth on North Entrance Road at a spot known as **Boiling River**. The other is a pool below **Firehole Falls** near Madison Junction. Swimming in Yellowstone Lake is not advised because water temperature rarely exceeds 60°F.

Fishing
Fishing has been a popular activity since the park was established. Before dipping your line in the water in hope of catching the renowned **Yellowstone cutthroat**, you'll have to obtain a **permit** for all anglers 16 and older. 3-day ($18), 7-day ($25), and season ($40) permits are available. Children under 15 may fish without one if they are under direct supervision of an adult with a permit or they may obtain a free permit that must be signed by a responsible adult. Permits are available at all ranger stations, visitor centers, and Yellowstone Park General Stores. Yellowstone fishing regulations, seasons, and recommendations are lengthy and complicated. Anglers should visit the park website or discuss their plans with a park ranger prior to fishing. Popular locations for watching trout like **LeHardy's Rapids** (June only) and **Fishing Bridge** prohibit fishing. A list of **guides and outfitters** along with rates is provided on page 243. Xanterra provides charter fishing on Yellowstone Lake for $180 (2 hours). Private fishing outfitters are listed on page 243.

Photography
What better way to remember Yellowstone than a collection of your very own professional-quality photographs. Whether you're taking images with a point-and-shoot or high-end DSLR, a Yellowstone photo tour is sure to send you home with jaw-dropping images you can't wait to decorate your home with. While the scenery does most of the work, an experienced photo tour guide can teach subtle tips and techniques that will make your vacation shots pop. Xanterra offers a 5-hour **Picture Perfect Photo Safari** aboard a historic yellow bus (page 235). Tours depart from Old Faithful Inn and Yellowstone Hotel, and require a minimum of two paying customers. They are generally available from late May until late September.

Skiing the hoodoos near Mammoth Hot Springs

They meet at the hotel between 5:45am and 6:30am to take advantage of the soft morning light. Rates are $30 per adult. Several outfitters are permitted to conduct photography tours and classes within the park. Refer to page 243 for a list of outfitters, complete with contact information and rates.

Winter Activities
Even though you lose the unbridled freedom to cruise its **open roads** in your car, Yellowstone is more incredible in winter. North Entrance Road, Northeast Entrance Road and Mammoth–Tower Road of the Grand Loop are the only roads open to wheeled vehicles during winter. Cars are left behind in favor of snowmobiles and snowcoaches. All **snowmobile parties** must be accompanied by a professional guide employed by a licensed concessioner (page 243).

Xanterra offers an array of **snowcoach tours** from Mammoth and Old Faithful between late December and early March. Rates listed below are for adults. Children (ages 3–11) cost about half the adult rate. Mammoth to Old Faithful ($117) and Tour of the Grand Canyon ($141.50) are two of the basic trips. From Mammoth you can take tours of Norris Geyser Basin ($85) and Wake Up to Wildlife ($66.50). The following tours depart from Old Faithful: Firehole Basin Adventure ($64.50); Steam, Stars, and Soundscapes ($51.50); Lone Star Excursion ($58), Across the Great Divide ($71), Madison Wildlife Excursion ($93), Grand Canyon ($234.50), and Winter Photo Safari ($264).

A few of the parks most popular hiking trails are groomed for **skiers** during winter. Xanterra offers a weekend **cross-country skier shuttle** from Mammoth for $27 (each way). You'll even find **guided ski tours** at Grand Canyon of the Yellowstone ($194/adult) and snowshoe tours at both Grand Canyon ($194) and Old Faithful ($30). Snowshoe and ski rental, as well as **ski repair and instruction** is available at Bear Den Ski Shop at Old Faithful Snow Lodge and at Mammoth Hot Spring's Terrace Grill.

Ranger Programs

Yellowstone is brash and exuberant. Water drops hundreds of feet before passing through a beautiful yellow canyon. Water and mud boil vigorously. Bison and bear lumber along roadways. Geysers send columns of water shooting into the air. And then there's the smell. Many of the geothermal features are accompanied with a sulfuric smell, similar to rotten eggs. Yellowstone gets in your face and your nose. It's screaming for attention. And the best way to immerse all of your senses is on a ranger-led activity.

Rangers entertain guests with talks, walks, adventure hikes, and evening programs all year long. Programs take place in all areas. To find out exactly what, when, and where they are, pick up a park newspaper from a visitor center or entrance station. It is also available for download at the park website.

Almost all programs are free of charge. One exception is **Yellowstone Lake Scenic Cruise**, which requires a fee and advance reservation. Xanterra Parks & Resorts operates the tour, while a park ranger narrates. It costs $17 for adults and $10 for children (ages 2–11). For reservations call (307) 344-7311 or stop by the Bridge Bay Marina.

Talks, walks, and evening programs are all great, but the **Adventure Hikes** are where it's at. If your schedule permits, join a ranger on at least one of the following: Hayden Valley Venture, Gem of the Rockies, or Fairy Falls Frolic. You will not regret it. Tours are limited to 15 people. You must sign up in person, in advance, at a specific visitor center. Refer to the park newspaper for details. Most Adventure Hikes are available from mid-June through August. The selection is reduced for fall, but programs are still available at all major areas. In winter only evening programs, afternoon talks, and snowshoe walks are available.

Since there are dozens of programs, all of which are incredibly rewarding, it's a good practice to take your favorite (or what you think will be your favorite) Yellowstone attraction and join a ranger-led activity for that feature. Ultimately you can't go wrong. You can close your eyes and point to the list of activities in the newspaper if you'd like.

Park rangers can even help plan your vacation before you arrive through a series of free videos and podcasts available at the park website and iTunes, respectively.

Yellowstone Visitor and Information Centers

Name & Phone	Open	Notes
Albright Visitor Center (Mammoth) (307) 344-2263	Daily, All Year, 9am–5pm extended hours in summer	Museum of people in the park from Native Americans to NPS Rangers, Thomas Moran Gallery, and Theater
West Yellowstone Info Center (307) 344-2876	mid-April–early November	Information for West Entrance users, located at West Yellowstone Chamber of Commerce
Old Faithful Visitor Center (307) 344-2751	mid-April–early November mid-December–mid-March	Newest facility features exhibits on hydrothermal features and other geologic phenomena
Canyon Visitor Education Center (307) 344-2550	mid-April–early November	Explores the geology of Yellowstone, including its volcanoes, geysers, hot springs, and geologic history
Fishing Bridge Visitor Center (307) 344-2450	late May–mid-October	Explores the park's wildlife • Backcountry office and bookstore are available
Grant Visitor Center (307) 344-2650	late May–mid-October	Named for President Ulysses S. Grant, it explores the role of fire at Yellowstone
Madison Information Station (307) 344-2876	late May–mid-October	Information and Yellowstone Association bookstore
Museum of Park Rangers (Norris) (307) 344-7353	May–late September	Short movie and exhibits about Park Rangers
Norris Geyser Basin Museum (307) 344-2812	May–mid-October	Explores the park's unique geothermal geology
West Thumb Info Station (307) 344-2650	May–mid-October	Information and Yellowstone Association bookstore

For Kids

Yellowstone provides several online and in-park activities designed specifically for kids. **Online activities** include things like an Animal Alphabet Book or an Antler/Horn Match Game. It's educational fun for all ages that can help build excitement for your Yellowstone vacation.

Once you've arrived, children (ages 4 and up) have the opportunity to become a **Yellowstone National Park Junior Ranger**. The program introduces kids to the wonders of Yellowstone and their role in preserving these treasures for future generations. Children must complete a 12-page activity booklet to become a Junior Ranger. The booklet is available at any visitor center for the reasonable price of $3. Once your child completes the activities, attends a ranger-led program , and hikes a park trail, he/she will receive a Junior Ranger Badge, marking admission into the Yellowstone Junior Ranger Club. You may need to check out one of the Junior Ranger Snowpacks to become a Junior Ranger during winter. Snowshoes may also be required. Packs and snowshoes are available at Mammoth and Old Faithful Visitor Centers.

Flora & Fauna

Yellowstone is more zoo than park. There are over 1,350 plant species and 67 species of mammals. It is home to the **highest density of mammals in the contiguous United States**, making Yellowstone one of the absolute best locations to view wildlife.

Bison, grizzly bears, and wolves are the stars. You may see Yellowstone cutthroat trout, elk, moose, coyote, and bighorn sheep. Lynx, mountain lion, and bobcat also reside here, but it's highly unlikely you'll cross their paths. There are two easily accessible areas for wildlife viewing: Hayden Valley, located between Canyon and Lake Villages, and Lamar Valley, located along Northeast Entrance Road just east of Tower. Lamar Valley is one of your best bets to spot a wolf. Be careful when viewing wildlife. You should stay at least 25 yards away from all mammals, and 100 yards away from predatory species like bears and wolves.

The landscape is covered with forests (80% of area), grasslands (15%), and water (5%). Forests are dominated by lodgepole pines, but much of the plant life is still recovering from a forest fire that burned more than one-third of the park in 1988.

Pets

Pets are allowed in the park, but must be kept on a leash no more than six feet in length at all times. They are prohibited from trails, the backcountry, and all hydrothermal basins. They can go where your car can go and they may be walked no more than 100 feet from a road or parking area. Visitors with pets must be careful. There's a possibility pets could become prey for bear, coyote, wolf, owl, or other predators commonly found in the park.

Accessibility

Wheelchair-accessible lodging is available in all areas of the park. Most campgrounds have at least one wheelchair-accessible campsite. Old Faithful, Canyon, Grant, and Albright (Mammoth) Visitor Centers are fully accessible. A wheelchair-accessible fishing ramp and platform are available on Madison River at Mt Haynes Overlook (3.5 miles west of Madison Junction). Many of the walkways and self-guiding trails have at least one wheelchair-accessible walkway. Wheelchairs are available for rent at medical clinics.

Weather

Yellowstone has a typical mountain climate: cold long winters and short hot summers. Average highs in summer max out around 80°F, and average winter lows hover around 10°F. Snow is common from fall to spring, with an annual average accumulation of 72 inches. It's not a secret that the best months to visit (weather-wise) are July and August. The weather is great, but crowds can be unbearable. June and September are nice alternatives.

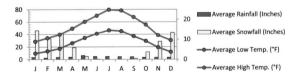

Grand Canyon of the Yellowstone from Artist Point

Vacation Planner

Planning a Yellowstone vacation is a daunting task. Camping or lodging? What regions to visit? Are Xanterra's activities worth the money? What's the best section of **Grand Loop Road**? The first three questions are personal preferences. The last one, well, that's easy too. Drive all 142-miles. To drive the loop and see its main attractions, **plan on spending at least three FULL days at Yellowstone**. Browse the park's newspaper for a current listing of **ranger programs** (page 238). Find time to attend at least one ranger-led tour during your visit. A rough outline for three perfect days in the park is provided below. The planner assumes you will arrive at South Entrance via John D. Rockefeller Jr., Memorial Parkway and Grand Teton National Park (page 206). Nearby dining, grocery stores, lodging, festivals, and attractions are listed on pages 242–245.

Day 1: Entering South Entrance, you'll pass Lewis and Shoshone Lakes, the park's best destination for paddling. Paddlers should stop and enjoy the morning from the seat of your kayak; everyone else should continue north toward **Grant Village**. Stop at **West Thumb Geyser Basin**, which provides a sampling of geothermal features and a great location to appreciate the sheer size of Yellowstone Lake. Its most notable features are Fishing Cone, a small geyser where a fisherman famously caught and boiled a fish when it fell off his hook into the roiling water (fishing is prohibited), and Abyss Pool. Walk the basin's boardwalk (1–2 hours). If you're still looking for a hike, the 2-mile **Lake Overlook Trail**, which departs from West Thumb

Geyser Basin Parking Area is a great choice. Return to Grand Loop Road following the shoreline of Yellowstone Lake to the northeast. If it's June when trout are running, stop at **Fishing Bridge**. Your next stop is **Hayden Valley**. Watch for bison grazing the grasslands and search for grizzlies along the shores of Yellowstone River. Allow at least an hour in the valley before continuing on to **Canyon** (a good place to spend your first night). Spend the evening exploring **Grand Canyon of the Yellowstone** and its surroundings. Take South Rim Drive to Artist Point and North Rim Drive to Grand View and Inspiration Point. Uncle Tom's Trail is a bit of a challenge but well worth the effort. Allow a minimum of 2–3 hours at Canyon Village. Visit Grand Canyon of the Yellowstone in late evening or early morning for the best photos (morning is better).

Day 2: If yesterday's stop at Hayden Valley didn't produce the kind of wildlife viewing you were imagining, join the 2-hour-long **"Wildlife Watching in Hayden Valley"** program that usually meets at 7am (confirm time in your park newspaper or at a visitor center) or backtrack and have another look around on your own. If your photographs of Grand Canyon of the Yellowstone failed to meet your expectations, catch the early rays of sun as they illuminate yellow rock and plummeting waters of Upper and Lower Falls. Once you're ready to return to Grand Loop Road take the middle of the figure-eight from Canyon to Norris. Stop at **Norris Geyser Basin**. If you're pressed for time, quickly hike around Porcelain Basin, located just north of the museum. If there's no rush spend 1–2 hours wandering about the extensive boardwalk. Next, drive north to **Mammoth Hot Springs**. Roaring Mountain and Sheepeater Cliff are excellent stops in between. The travertine terraces of Mammoth Hot Springs are nice and Albright Visitor Center is fantastic, but this is the one destination you should consider skipping if you're running behind schedule. Upper Terrace is slightly better than Lower Terrace. Now drive east to **Tower–Roosevelt**. With enough time, money, and love of horses, take a 1- or 2-hour **horseback ride** to a delicious steak dinner. The Western Dinner Cookout/ Trail Ride (page 235) is wonderful. Regular trail rides are offered for those not wanting a hearty meal. The last cookout checks-in at Roosevelt Lodge at 1:45pm. Work off the extra weight you just put on by hiking **Specimen Ridge Trail**, located in **Lamar Valley**. This fantastic wildlife viewing area is situated along Northeast Entrance Road, where you're all but guaranteed to see free-roaming buffalo. Specimen Ridge is an excellent hike that leads into the mountains to views of Grand Canyon of the Yellowstone and good chances of spotting wildlife. You'll also come across ancient petrified trees. Speaking of petrified trees, as you're driving Grand Loop, you'll see signs for "Petrified Tree." It's a quick stop, but skipping it in favor of **Tower Falls** or taking another hike is a recommended alternative.

Day 3: Start your morning out right with a waterfall and a hike. To reach **Tower Fall** return to Grand Loop Road and turn left at Tower–Roosevelt Junction toward Canyon Village. You can't miss the parking area. Check out the falls then drive south to **Mount Washburn**. Two trails lead to its 10,243-ft summit, and on clear days you can see all the way to the Teton Range. From Dunraven Pass the trail is 3.1 miles with an elevation gain near 1,400 feet. The route from Chittenden Parking Area is shorter but steeper, gaining about 1,500 feet in 2.5 miles. Driving south on Grand Loop Road, Chittenden Parking Area is before Dunraven Pass Parking Area. Regardless which route you hike, it's beautiful and the trek will take roughly 3–4 hours to complete. This is one of the most popular trails, so expect it to be busy, particularly during summer. Once you've completed the hike, return to your car to complete Grand Loop Road. Travel past Canyon Village, Norris, and Madison, stopping at **Midway Geyser Basin**. Monument Geyser Basin, Gibbon Falls, and Madison are decent areas to stop, but hardly essential. Stop if you have time, but allot at least 4 hours to explore Lower, Midway, and Upper Geyser Basins. For stunning views of Grand Prismatic Spring, stop at **Fairy Falls Trailhead** and scramble up the nearby hill (there may be no hiking signs). It's nice from the boardwalk, but its color and beauty is often obscured by the size of this somewhat psychedelic hot spring. Finish your trip by stopping at Upper Geyser Basin to see the park's most iconic feature, **Old Faithful**. Hike to Observation Point, where the geyser will salute you with one of its reliable eruptions. Looking for a great sunset photo? Backtrack to Firehole Lake Drive and stop at Great Fountain Geyser.

Pronghorn at Lamar Valley

Lost in the Park

In 1870, Truman C. Everts joined an expedition exploring present-day Yellowstone. At Yellowstone Lake, Everts wandered away from the group. After being lost for two days, his horse ran away. Left with little more than the clothes on his back, Everts began walking aimlessly. A month passed without success from the expedition's search attempts; they decided to complete their work and return East to confirm the existence of "Colter's Hell" and spread word of the unfortunate predicament of their companion.

Everts's situation worsened when he broke through brittle ground while crossing a geyser basin, scalding his hip. Next, he managed to start a fire with an opera glass, only to severely burn his hands. Consuming only elk thistle, he withered away to skin and bones. A full 37 days after his separation, a man, no more than 50 pounds, was spotted crawling along a hillside. Incoherent but alive, Everts was able to make a full recovery and later pen the book *Thirty-Seven Days in Peril*. His adventure created considerable publicity for Yellowstone and helped create the world's first national park. He was even given the opportunity to be its first superintendent. (Not surprisingly, he declined.) Today, the legend lives on. Elk thistle is called Everts' Thistle and a 7,831-ft peak in northwestern Wyoming is named Mount Everts.

Don't expect to be rewarded for getting lost. It's a huge inconvenience, not only to you, but to park staff. Be prepared. Carry a compass and quality map. GPS users should know how to use it and carry extra batteries. Plan your route, stay on marked trails, and keep track of your group at all times.

Dining

West Yellowstone Area

Ernie's Bakery & Deli • (406) 646-9467
406 US-20, West Yellowstone
erniesbakery.com • Sandwiches: $8–18

Pete's Rocky Mtn Pizza Co • (406) 646-7820
112 N Canyon St, West Yellowstone

Beartooth Barbecue • (406) 646-0227
111 N Canyon St, West Yellowstone

Buckaroo Bills Ice Cream • (406) 646-7901
24 N Canyon St, West Yellowstone

Bar N Ranch • (406) 646-0300
890 Buttermilk Creek Rd, West Yellowstone
bar-n-ranch.com • Entrée: $16–39

Arrowleaf Ice Cream • (406) 646-9776
27 N Canyon St, West Yellowstone

Madison Crossing Lounge • (406) 646-7621
121 Madison Ave, West Yellowstone
madisoncrossinglounge.com • Entrée: $19–26

Running Bear Pancake House • (406) 646-7703
538 Madison Ave, West Yellowstone

Wild West Pizzeria • (406) 646-4400
14 Madison Ave, West Yellowstone
wildwestpizza.com

Woodside Bakery • (406) 646-7779
17 Madison Ave, West Yellowstone

North Entrance/Gardiner

K Bar & Café • (406) 848-9995
202 W Main St, Gardiner

Outlaws Pizza • (406) 848-7733
906 Scott St, Gardiner

East of the Parks

Miners Saloon • (406) 838-2214
208 Main St, Cooke City

Beartooth Café • (406) 838-2475
14 Main St, Cooke City
beartoothcafe.com • Entrée: $13–30

Red Lodge Café & Lounge • (406) 446-1619
16 S Broadway Ave, Red Lodge

Adriano's Italian Restaurant • (307) 527-7320
1244 Sheridan Ave, Cody

Wyoming's Rib & Chop House
1367 Sheridan Ave, Cody • (307) 527-7731
ribandchophouse.com • Entrée: $12–35

Proud Cut Saloon • (307) 527-6905
1227 Sheridan Ave, Cody

Sunset House Restaurant • (307) 587-2257
1651 8th St, Cody • sunsethousecody.com

Peter's Café & Bakery • (307) 527-5040
1219 Sheridan Ave, Cody

Jackson/Grand Teton Area

Rendezvous Bistro • (307) 739-1100
380 S US-89, Jackson
rendezvousbistro.net • Entrée: $16–30

Pearl Street Bagels • (307) 739-1218
145 West Pearl Ave, Jackson

Moo's Gourmet Ice Cream • (307) 733-1998
110 Center St, Jackson

Blue Lion Restaurant • (307) 733-3912
160 N Millward St, Jackson
bluelionrestaurant.com • Entrée: $18–45

Wild Sage Restaurant • (307) 733-2000
175 N Jackson St, #2, Jackson
rustyparrot.com • Entrée: $31–58

The Bird in Jackson • (307) 732-2473
4125 S Pub Pl, Jackson
thebirdinjackson.com • Burgers: $7–16

Bar T Five • (307) 733-5386
812 Cache Creek Dr, Jackson
bart5.com • Covered Wagon Cookout: $45

Stiegler's Restaurant • (307) 733-1071
3535 Moose Wilson Rd, Wilson
stieglersrestaurant.com • Entrée: $13–48

Million Dollar Cowboy Steakhouse
25 N Cache Dr, Jackson • (307) 733-4790
milliondollarcowboybar.com • Entrée: $23–42

Snake River Grill • (307) 733-0557
84 E Broadway, Jackson
snakerivergrill.com • Entrée: $22–56

The Bunnery Bakery • (307) 734-5474
130 N Cache Dr, Jackson
bunnery.com • Breakfast: $6–12

Sweetwater Restaurant • (307) 733-3553
855 King St, Jackson
sweetwaterjackson.com • Entrée: $19–30

Teton Thai Plate • (307) 733-2654
135 N Cache Dr, Jackson
tetonthaiplate.com • Curry/Rice Dishes: $14–18

Trio An American Bistro • (307) 734-8038
45 S Glenwood St, Jackson
triobistro.com • Entrée: $18–34

Merry Piglets Mexican Café • (307) 733-2966
160 N Cache Dr, Jackson
merrypiglets.com • Tex-Mex: $9–24

The Kitchen • (307) 734-1633
155 N Glenwood St, Jackson
kitchenjacksonhole.com

e.leaven Food Co • (307) 733-5600
175 Center St, Jackson
eleavenfood.com • Breakfast: $6–11

Snake River Brew Co. • (307) 739-2337
265 S Millward St, Jackson
snakeriverbrewing.com

Grocery Stores

West Yellowstone Area

Food Roundup Supermarket • (406) 646-7501
107 Dunraven St, West Yellowstone

North Entrance/Gardiner

North Entrance Shopping Center
701 Scott St, Gardiner • (406) 848-7524

Emigrant General Store • (406) 333-4434
3 Murphy Ln, Emigrant

Albertsons-Sav-on • (406) 222-1177
2120 Park St S, Livingston

East of the Parks

Albertsons-Osco • (307) 527-7007
1825 17th St, Cody

Walmart Supercenter • (307) 527-4673
321 Yellowstone Ave, Cody

Jackson/Grand Teton Area

Albertsons-Sav-on • (307) 733-5950
105 Buffalo Way, Jackson

Lodging

West Yellowstone Area

Firehole Ranch • (406) 646-7294
11500 Hebgen Lake Rd, West Yellowstone
fireholeranch.com • Rates: $850/couple/night

Yellowstone Inn • (406) 646-7633
601 US-20, West Yellowstone • yellowstoneinn.net

One Horse Motel • (406) 646-7677
216 N Dunraven St, West Yellowstone
onehorsemotel.com • Rates: $79+

Brandin' Iron Inn • (406) 646-9411
201 Canyon St, West Yellowstone
vacationyellowstone.com • Rates: $139+

Alpine Motel • (406) 646-7544
120 Madison Ave, West Yellowstone
alpinemotelwestyellowstone.com • Rates: $95+

Lazy G Motel • (406) 646-7586
123 N Hayden St, West Yellowstone
lazygmotel.com • Rates: $89+

Three Bear Lodge • (800) 646-7353
217 Yellowstone Ave, West Yellowstone
threebearlodge.com

Madison Arm Resort • (406) 646-9328
5475 Madison Arm Rd, Hebgen Lake, MT
madisonarmresort.com • *Tent & RV sites available*

North Entrance/Gardiner

Yellowstone River Motel • (406) 848-7303
14 E Park St, Gardiner
yellowstonerivermotel.com • Rates: $82–132

Rodeway Inn & Suites • (406) 848-7520
109 Hellroaring, Gardiner • Rates: $220/night

Hillcrest Cottages • (406) 848-7353
400 Scott St, Gardiner
hillcrestcottages.com • Rates: $92–170

Gardiner Guest House B&B • (406) 848-9414
112 Main St, Gardiner
gardinerguesthouse.com • Rates: $90–145

Headwaters of the Yellowstone B&B
9 Olson Ln, Gardiner • (406) 848-7073
headwatersbandb.com • Rates: $125+

Yellowstone Basin Inn • (406) 848-7080
4 Maiden Basin Dr, Gardiner
yellowstonebasininn.com • Rates: $205–390

Mtn Sky Guest Ranch • (406) 333-4911
480 Big Creek Rd, Emigrant
mtnsky.com • Rates: $4,060+/week

Hawley Mtn Guest Ranch • (406) 932-5791
4188 Main Boulder Rd, McLeod, MT
hawleymountain.com • Rates: $2,086+/person/week

Lone Mountain Guest Ranch
750 Lone Mtn Ranch Rd, Big Sky, MT
lonemountainranch.com • (406) 995-4644

Elkhorn Ranch • (406) 995-4291
33133 Gallatin Rd, Gallatin Gateway, MT
elkhornranchmontana.com • $2,465/rider/week

Covered Wagon Ranch • (406) 995-4237
34035 Gallatin Rd, Gallatin Gateway, MT
coveredwagonranch.com • Rates: $1,100+/3 nights

East of the Parks
Log Cabin Café & B&B • (800) 863-0807
106 US-212 W, Silver Gate, MT
thelogcabincafe.com • Rates: $99+

Elk Horn Lodge • (406) 838-2332
103 Main St, Cooke City
elkhornlodgemt.com

Seven D Ranch • (307) 587-9885
907 Spruce Dr, Cody
7dranch.com • Rates: $1,680+/person/week

Crossed Sabres Ranch • (307) 587-3750
829 N Fork Hwy, Cody
crossedsabresranch.com • Rates: $125+

Pahaska Tepee Resort • (307) 527-7701
183 N Fork Hwy, # 1, Cody
pahaska.com • Rates: $130+

Jackson/Grand Teton Area
Pony Express Motel • (307) 733-3835
1075 W Broadway, Jackson
ponyexpressmotel.com • Rates: $67+

Flat Creek Ranch • (307) 733-0603
Upper Flat Creek Rd, Jackson
flatcreekranch.com • Rates: $950/cabin/night

The Wort Hotel • (307) 733-2190
50 N Glenwood St, Jackson
preferredboutique.com • Rates: $409+

Jackson Hole Lodge • (307) 733-2992
420 W Broadway, Jackson
jacksonholelodge.com • Rates: $215+

Amangani Resort • (307) 734-7333
1535 N E Butte Rd, Jackson
amanresorts.com • Rates: $1,401+

Rusty Parrot Lodge • (307) 733-2000
175 N Jackson St, Jackson
rustyparrot.com • Rates: $225+

Homewood Suites • (307) 739-0808
260 Millward St, Jackson • Rates: $174+

Miller Park Lodge • (307) 733-4858
155 N Jackson, Jackson
millerparklodge.net • Rates: $189+

Anglers Inn • (307) 733-3682 • Rates: $120+
265 N Millward, Jackson • anglersinn.net

Cowboy Village Resort • (307) 733-3121
120 Flat Creek Dr, Jackson

Elk Country Inn • (307) 733-2364
480 W Pearl St, Jackson

Rustic Inn/Creekside Resort & Spa
475 N Cache, Jackson • (800) 323-9279
rusticinnatjh.com • Rates: $318+

Four Seasons • (307) 732-5000
7680 Granite Loop Rd, Teton Village
fourseasons.com • Rates: $719+

Heart Six Ranch • (307) 543-2477
16985 Buffalo Valley Rd, Moran
heartsix.com • Rates: $105+

Bitterroot Ranch • (800) 545-0019
1480 E. Fork Rd, Dubois
bitterrootranch.com • $2,400/person/week

Many chain restaurants and hotels can be found in Livingston, MT, Cody, WY, and Jackson, WY.

Festivals
Buffalo Bill Birthday Ball • February
Cody, WY • codykc.org/ball.html

Snowmobile Expo • March
West Yellowstone • snowmobileexpo.com

Elkfest/Antler Sale • May
Jackson, WY • jacksonholechamber.com

Custer's Last Stand/Little Bighorn Days
June • Hardin, MT • custerlaststand.org

Grand Teton Music Festival • June/July
Jackson Hole Ski Resort • gtmf.org

Red Ants Pants Festival • July
redantspantsmusicfestival.com

Montana Folk Festival • July
Butte, MT • montanafolkfestival.com

Cody Stampede • June–August
Cody, WY • codystampederodeo.com

An Ri Ra Montana Irish Festival
August • Butte, MT • mtgaelic.org

Sweet Pea Festival • August
Bozeman • sweetpeafestival.org

Crow Fair and Rodeo • August
Crow Agency, MT

Running of the Sheep 'Sheep Drive'
September • Reed Point, MT • (406) 326-2315

Yellowstone Ski Festival • November
West Yellowstone • skirunbikemt.com

Attractions
West Yellowstone Area
Pinecone Playhouse • (406) 640-1019
121 Madison Ave, West Yellowstone
pineconeplayhouse.com

Yellowstone IMAX Theatre • (406) 646-4100
101 S Canyon St, West Yellowstone
yellowstonegiantscreen.com • Tickets: $9/adult

Bears Den Cinema • (406) 646-7777
15 N Electric St, West Yellowstone

Grizzly & Wolf Discovery Center • (800) 257-2570
201 South Canyon, West Yellowstone
grizzlydiscoveryctr.org • Admission: $11.50/adult

Trout Hunter • (208) 558-9900
trouthunt.com • Fishing: $550+ (full-day)

Arrick's Fly Shop • (406) 646-7290
37 Canyon St, West Yellowstone
arricks.com • Fishing: $495+ (full-day)

Henry's Fork Anglers • (208) 558-7525
henrysforkanglers.com • Fishing: $550+ (full-day)

Madison River Outfitters • (406) 646-9644
madisonriveroutfitters.com • Fishing: $495 (full-day)

Yellowstone Mtn Guides • (406) 646-7230
yellowstone-guides.com

Yellowstone Expeditions • (406) 646-9333
Snowcoach, cross-country ski, & snowshoe tours
yellowstoneexpeditions.com

Yellowstone Alpen Guides • (406) 646-9591
yellowstoneguides.com

*⚲***Diamond P Ranch** • (406) 646-7246
2865 Targhee Pass Hwy, West Yellowstone
thediamondpranch.com • Trail Ride: $68 (half-day)

Backcountry Adventures • (406) 646-9317
Snowmobile rental & tours ($209+), Snowcoach
backcountry-adventures.com

SeeYellowstone • (800) 221-1151
seeyellowstone.com • *Snowcoach Tours*

Yellowstone Vacations • (800) 426-7669
yellowstonevacations.com • *Year-round tours*

Yellowstone Adventures • (406) 646-7735
Snowmobile rental & tours ($189+)
yellowstoneadventures.com

Sun Valley Trekking • (208) 788-1966
Hiking, climbing, mtn biking, snowshoe, and ski tours
svtrek.com

North Entrance/Gardiner
*⚲***Wild West Rafting** • (406) 848-2252
Whitewater, float trips, trail rides, and kayaking
906 Scott St, Gardiner
wildwestrafting.com • Rafting: $55 (half-day)

*⚲***Flying Pig Rafting** • (406) 848-7510
Whitewater, trail rides, and Yellowstone Tours
511 Scott St, Gardiner
flyingpigrafting.com • Rafting: $42 (half-day)

*⚲***Montana Whitewater Rafting**
Whitewater, kayak, trail rides, fly fishing, and ziplining
603 Scott St, Gardiner • (406) 763-4465
montanawhitewater.com • Rafting: $42 (half-day)

*⚲***Yellowstone Association** • (406) 848-2400
Tours, seminars, and field courses available
308 W Park St, Gardiner
yellowstoneassociation.org

Yellowstone Rough Riders • (406) 223-3924
Horse rides ($105+), pack trips ($390/day/person), and fishing trips ($200+/person)
yellowstoneroughriders.com

Hell's A Roarin' Outfitters • (406) 848-7578
hellsaroarinoutfitters.com

Big Wild Adventures • (406) 848-7000
Backpacking & Canoe Trips ($1,900–2,400)
bigwildadventures.com

Slough Creek Outfitters • (406) 222-7455
sloughcreekoutfitters.com • Rates: $400 (full-day)

Black Mountain Outfitters • (406) 222-7455
blackmountainoutfitters.com • $200/person/day

Black Otter Guide Services • (406) 333-4362
blackotterguideservice.com • $250+/person/day

Safari Yellowstone • (406) 222-8557
Livingston, MT • *Available winter & summer*
safariyellowstone.com • Rates: $150+

Wilderness Photo Expeditions
tmurphywild.com • (406) 222-2302

Karst Stage • (406) 556-3500
511 N Wallace Ave, Bozeman
karststage.com • *Tours & shuttle*

Rockin' HK Outfitters • (406) 333-4505
116 Chicory Rd, Livingston
rockinhk.com • *3–10 day trips available*

Anderson's Yellowstone Angler • (406) 222-7130
yellowstoneangler.com • Fishing: $500 (full-day)

Hatch Finders Flyshop • (406) 222-0989
113 W Park St, #3, Livingston • hatchfinders.com

Empire Twin Theatre • (406) 222-0111
106 N 2nd St, Livingston

Headwaters Guide Services • (406) 763-4761
headwatersguideservice.com • $450 (full-day)

*⚲***Sunrise Pack Station** • (406) 579-9642
202 Custer Ave, Belgrade • sunrisepackstation.com

Yellowstone Safari Company • (406) 586-1155
All sorts of safaris, available winter and summer
yellowstonesafari.com

Medicine Lake Outfitters • (406) 388-4938
Pack trips, trail rides, and fishing available
packtrips.com

Off the Beaten Path • (800) 445-2995
offthebeatenpath.com • $2,595+ (6 days)

Llama Trips in Yellowstone • (406) 539-3522
Bozeman, MT • yellowstonellamatrips.com

Custer National Forest • (406) 657-6200
10 E Babcock Ave, Bozeman

The Club at Spanish Peaks • (406) 993-5400
Skiing, horseback rides, mountain biking, + more
181 Clubhouse Fork, Big Sky
findyourbigsky.com

Jake's Horses • (406) 995-4630
200 Beaver Creek Rd, Gallatin
jakeshorses.com • Rates: $275+/person/day

*⚲***Big Sky Resort** • (800) 548-4486
Skiing, sleigh rides, Yellowstone tours, + more
50 Big Sky Resort Rd, Big Sky
bigskyresort.com

East of the Parks
Beartooth Plateau Outfitters • (406) 445-2293
beartoothoutfitters.com • $250+/person/day

Skyline Guide Services • (406) 838-2380
Fishing, trail rides, hunting, and snowmobiling
flyfishyellowstone.com

Ron Dube's Wilderness Adv • (307) 527-7815

Sheep Mesa Outfitters • (307) 587-4305
sheepmesaoutfitters.com • $350/person/day

*⚲***K Bar Z Ranch & Outfitter**
3477 Crandall Rd, Cody • (307) 587-4410
kbarzguestranch.com

Grub Steak Expeditions • (307) 527-6316
tourtoyellowstone.com • Rates: $550 (full-day)

Boulder Basin Outfitters • (307) 587-3404
boulderbasinoutfitters.com

The Cody Cattle Co. • (307) 272-5770
1910 Demaris Dr, Cody
thecodycattlecompany.com • Tickets: $30/adult

*⚲***Buffalo Bill Hist. Center** • (307) 587-4771
720 Sheridan Ave, Cody
centerofthewest.org • Admission: $18/adult

Jackson/Grand Teton Area
Teton Mountain Bike Tours • (307) 733-0712
545 N Cache St, Jackson
tetonmtbike.com • Tours: $70 (half-day)

Rendezvous River Sports • (307) 733-2471
945 W Broadway, Jackson
jacksonholekayak.com

World Cast Anglers • (307) 733-6934
worldcastanglers.com • Rates: $555 (full-day)

Jackson Hole Kayak School • (307) 733-2471
Lessons, tours, and rentals available
945 W Broadway, Jackson
jacksonholekayak.com

Wilderness Trails • (307) 733-5171
Horseback trips or big game hunts
wildernesstrailsinc.com

Granite Hot Springs • (307)690-6353
Granite Creek Rd, Jackson

Snow King Resort • (307) 733-5200
400 E Snow King Ave, Jackson
snowking.com • Lift Ticket: $47/adult

Jackson Hole Historical Society & Museum
225 N Cache St, Jackson • (307) 733-2414
jacksonholehistory.org • Admission: $5

National Elk Refuge • (307) 733-9212
675 E Broadway, Jackson • fws.gov

Mill Iron Ranch • (307) 733-6390
3495 E Horse Creek Rd, Jackson
millironranch.net

Jackson Hole Llamas
jacksonholellamatrekking.com • Rides: $850+

BrushBuck Guide Services • (370) 200-2352
Jackson • brushbucktours.com

Grand Teton Tours • (307) 413-5488
Jackson, WY • grandtetontours.com

Jackson Hole Wildlife Safaris • (307) 690-6402
jacksonholewildlifesafaris.com

Scenic Safaris • (307) 734-8898
scenic-safaris.com • *Winter Tours*

Teton Science Schools • (307) 733-2623
tetonscience.org • *Winter Tours*

Shurr Adventures • (239) 300-3004
shurradventuresyellowstone.com • Eco-tours

Lewis & Clark River Expeditions
Whitewater & float trips available
lewisandclarkriverrafting.com • (800) 824-5375

Teton Theatre • (307) 733-4939
120 N Cache, Jackson

Jackson Hole Playhouse • (307) 733-6994
145 W Deloney Ave, Jackson
jacksonplayhouse.com

Jackson Hole Cinema • (307) 733-4939
295 W Pearl St, Jackson
jacksonholecinemas.com • Tickets: $9.75/adult

Jackson Hole Rafting & Whitewater
650 W Broadway, Jackson
jhww.com • (307) 733-1007

Wilderness Ventures • (307) 733-2122
Multi-day hiking expeditions
wildernessventures.com

Buffalo Roam Tours • (307) 413-0954
buffaloroamtours.com

AJ De Rosa's Wooden Boat Tours • (307)733-3061
woodboattours.com • Rates: $875

Teton Troutfitters • (307) 733-5362
tetontroutfitters.com

Westbank Anglers • (307) 733-6483
westbank.com • Fishing: $535 (full-day)

Yellowstone Outfitters • (307) 543-2418
Trail and wagon rides, and hunting
23590 Buffalo Valley Rd, Moran
yellowstoneoutfitters.com

Dry Ridge Outfitters • (208) 351-1796
dryridge.com • Pack Trips: $235/person/day

Craters of the Moon Nat'l Monument
US-26, Arco, ID • (208) 527-1300
nps.gov/crmo • Entrance Fee: $10/vehicle

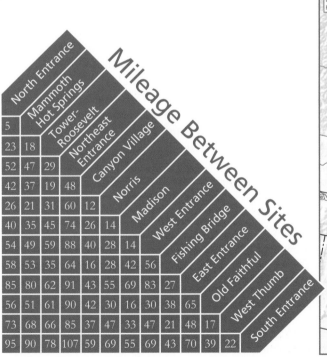

Mileage Between Sites

North Entrance	Mammoth Hot Springs	Tower-Roosevelt	Northeast Entrance	Canyon Village	Norris	Madison	West Entrance	Fishing Bridge	East Entrance	Old Faithful	West Thumb	South Entrance
5												
23	18											
52	47	29										
42	37	19	48									
26	21	31	60	12								
40	35	45	74	26	14							
54	49	59	88	40	28	14						
58	53	35	64	16	28	42	56					
85	80	62	91	43	56	69	83	27				
56	51	61	90	42	30	16	30	38	65			
73	68	66	85	37	47	33	47	21	48	17		
95	90	78	107	59	69	55	69	43	70	39	22	

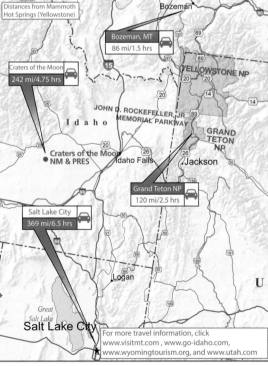

Distances from Mammoth Hot Springs (Yellowstone)

Bozeman, MT
86 mi/1.5 hrs

Craters of the Moon
242 mi/4.75 hrs

Grand Teton NP
120 mi/2.5 hrs

Salt Lake City
369 mi/6.5 hrs

For more travel information, click
www.visitmt.com , www.go-idaho.com,
www.wyomingtourism.org, and www.utah.com

Grinnell Glacier Overlook (Highline Trail)

Glacier

PO Box 128
West Glacier, MT 59936
Phone: (406) 888-7800
Website: nps.gov/glac

Established: May 11, 1910
Size: 1,013,594 Acres
Annual Visitors: 2.3 Million
Peak Season: July–August
Hiking Trails: 745 Miles

Activities: Hiking, Biking, Fishing, Horseback Riding, Boating, Bus and Boat Tours, Photography, Skiing and Snowshoeing

13 Established Campgrounds
Camping Fee: $10–23/night
Backcountry Camping: Permitted*
6 Park Lodges and Hotels
Rates: $70–229/night

Park Hours: All day, every day
Entrance Fee: $25/vehicle, $12/individual (foot, bike, etc.)

*A $7 per person per night Backcountry Permit is required

George Bird Grinnell came to northwestern Montana on a hunting expedition; he found a land so beautiful and majestic he named it "the Crown of the Continent." More than 100 glaciers capped the mountains' rugged peaks. Turquoise lakes dotted the high country. Green forests spread out as far as his eye could see. It was a land completely unspoiled by human hands. Grinnell returned again and again. He was drawn by the prominence of the mountains, purity of the lakes, and peacefulness of his surroundings. These Rocky Mountain landscapes inspired him to spend the better part of two decades working to protect this special area as a national park.

Grinnell found an unlikely ally in the Great Northern Railway. Following the blueprint created by Southern Pacific Railroad at Yosemite National Park, the Great Northern hoped to stimulate passenger service by promoting scenic wonders like Glacier. In 1891, rail crossed the Continental Divide at Marias Pass, just south of the present-day park boundary. That same year, George Bird Grinnell wrote in his journal that the land surrounding St. Mary Lake should be a national park. The Great Northern couldn't agree more. They knew it would be much easier to deal with the federal government rather than negotiating with hundreds of private land owners.

In 1897 land was set aside as the Lewis and Clark Forest Preserve, largely due to lobbying by Grinnell and the railway. Grinnell continued to pursue the idea of a national park, and his efforts proved successful on May 11, 1910, when President William Howard Taft signed legislation establishing Glacier, the nation's tenth National Park.

The Great Northern Railway had gotten their wish too, receiving sole rights to develop the area. Glacier Park Lodge and Many Glacier Hotel were erected. Chalets were built in the backcountry at Sperry, Granite Park, Cut Bank, and Gunsight Lake. Blackfeet Indians, who once hunted the Rockies' western slopes and performed ceremonies on the shores of St. Mary Lake, sold more than 800,000 acres of their land to the U.S. government for $1.5 million. Not long after tribal members were camped in tipis atop McAlpin Hotel in New York City as a publicity stunt for the railroad. They rode the subway and visited the Brooklyn Bridge. They danced at the annual Travel and Vacation Show. Everywhere they went, people referred to them as "the Indians of Glacier National Park." Blackfeet were at the park too, standing in traditional clothing, waiting to greet visitors. This advertising campaign was yet another attempt by the Great Northern Railway to get Americans to "See America First."

The campaign worked. Upper-middle class Americans were flocking to these wonders of the western frontier. Tourists arrived by train and were catered to by the railway's subsidiary companies. George Bird Grinnell believed tourism ruined Yellowstone and Glacier. Stephen Mather, the first director of the National Park Service, understood that tourism was the only thing that could save them. The parks needed to be made dollarable or the government would give in to constant pressures of commercial interests like mining, logging, and oil. Mather envisioned park roads as spectacular feats of engineering, an attraction in and of themselves. At Glacier, the goal was to build a road through the center of the park, across the Continental Divide, and Mather approved construction of a much more expensive route carved into the face of Garden Wall.

Dedicated on July 15, 1933, Going-to-the-Sun Road still serves as the park's main attraction. It crosses the crown of the continent, providing access for millions of guests to the awe-inspiring alpine lakes, knife-edge ridgelines, and craggy mountaintops George Bird Grinnell so admired. It connects lodges originally established by the Great Northern Railway, the very same places where today's visitors spend a night or two after exploring Glacier National Park and taking the time to "See America First."

Running Eagle Falls

When to Go

Glacier is open all year, but long winters cause road and facility closures from fall through spring. Most roads and facilities are open from late May to early September, but Going-to-the-Sun Road (GTSR) first opens for public use around mid-June and it usually stays open until October. Exact dates vary from year-to-year. In 2011, GTSR didn't open fully until July 12. Most park visitors arrive in July and August when the weather is best and GTSR is open. Cross-country skiers and snowshoers frequent the park from December to April.

Airports & Amtrak

The nearest airport is Glacier Park International (GPI), located near Kalispell, 30 miles from the West Entrance. Great Falls International (GTF) is the closest airport to the eastern boundary (about 140 miles from East Glacier Village). Spokane International (GEG), 280 miles to the west, is the closest large airport. Car rental is available at each airport.

Amtrak (800.872.7245 or amtrak.com) serves East Glacier, West Glacier, and Whitefish. One-way fare from Chicago costs about $200. Glacier Park Inc. (406.892.2525, glacierparkinc.com), operates shuttles on the east side ($15–75, one-way). Glacier National Park Lodges (855.733.4522, glaciernational-parklodges.com) provides shuttle service from West Glacier Train Station to Apgar ($5–10, one-way).

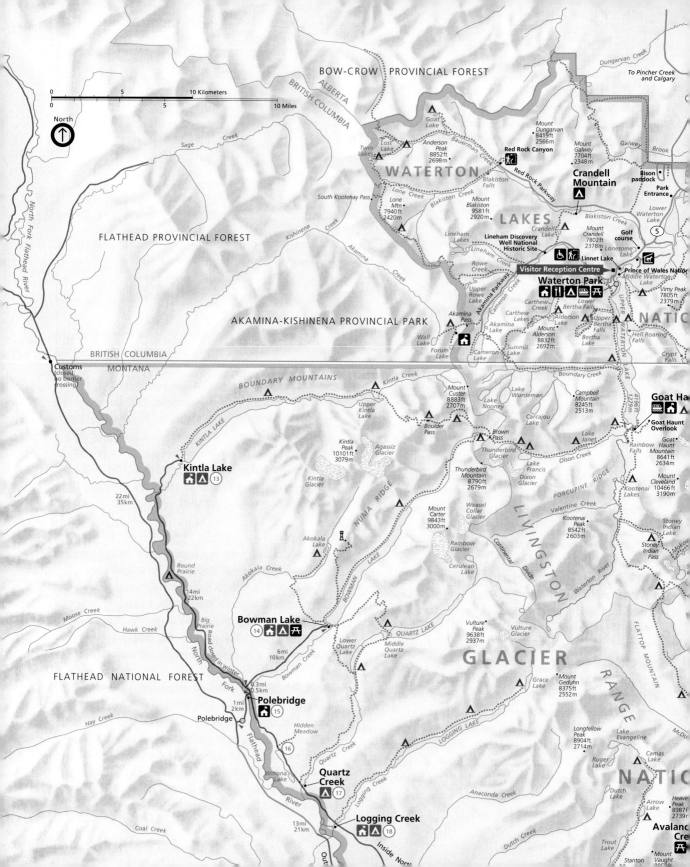

BOW-CROW PROVINCIAL FOREST

To Pincher Creek
and Calgary

BRITISH COLUMBIA

ALBERTA

Dungarvan Creek

Galwey Brook

0 5 10 Kilometers
0 5 10 Miles

North

Sage Creek

Goat Lake

Mount Dungarvan 8419ft 2566m

Red Rock Canyon

Mount Galwey 7704ft 2348m

Bison paddock

Park Entrance

WATERTON

Lost Lake

Twin Lakes

Anderson Peak 8852ft 2698m

Blakiston Falls

Red Rock Parkway

Crandell Mountain

FLATHEAD PROVINCIAL FOREST

South Kootenay Pass

Lone Creek

Lone Mtn 7940ft 2420m

Blakiston Creek

Mount Blakiston 9581ft 2920m

LAKES

Crandell Lake

Blakiston Creek

Kishinena Creek

Akamina Creek

Lineham Lakes

Lineham Creek

Lineham Discovery Well National Historic Site

Mount Crandell 7802ft 2378m

Golf course

5

Rowe Creek

Visitor Reception Centre

Linnet Lake

Lonesome Lake

Prince of Wales Nation

Lower Waterton Lake

Waterton Park

Middle Waterton Lake

Upper Rowe Lake

Akamina Parkway

Cameron Creek

Carthew Creek

Lower Bertha Falls

Vimy Peak 7805ft 2379m

AKAMINA-KISHINENA PROVINCIAL PARK

Akamina Pass

Carthew Lakes

Alderson Lake

Upper Bertha Falls

NATI

Wall Lake

Forum Lake

Akamina Lake

Mount Alderson 8832m 2692m

Summit Lake

Bertha Lake

Hell Roaring Falls

Cameron Lake

Crypt Falls

Customs (closed; no border crossing)

BRITISH COLUMBIA

MONTANA

BOUNDARY MOUNTAINS

Kintla Creek

Boundary Creek

UPPER WATERTON LAKE

Mount Custer 8883ft 2707m

Lake Wurdeman

Campbell Mountain 8245ft 2513m

4196ft 1713m

Goat Ha

Goat Haunt Overlook

North Fork Flathead River

Upper Kintla Lake

Lake Nooney

Carcajou Lake

Boulder Pass

Brown Pass

Lake Janet

Goat Haunt Mountain 8641ft 2634m

Rainbow Falls

KINTLA LAKE

Kintla Peak 10101ft 3079m

Agassiz Glacier

Thunderbird Glacier

Brown Lake

Thunderbird Mountain 8790ft 2679m

Lake Francis

Dixon Glacier

Olson Creek

Mount Cleveland 10466ft 3190m

Kootenai Lakes

Kintla Lake

13

Kintla Glacier

NUMA RIDGE

Akokala Lake

Mount Carter 9843ft 3000m

Weasel Collar Glacier

PORCUPINE RIDGE

Valentine Creek

Kootenai Peak 8542ft 2603m

Stoney Indian Lake

22mi 35km

LIVINGSTON

Stoney Indian Pass

Akokala Creek

Rainbow Glacier

Continental Divide

Waterton River

Round Prairie

BOWMAN LAKE

Cerulean Lake

14mi 22km

Moose Creek

Hawk Creek

Big Prairie

Road closed in winter

Bowman Lake

14

6mi 10km

QUARTZ LAKE

GLACIER

Vulture Peak 9638ft 2937m

Vulture Glacier

RANGE

FLATTOP MOUNTAIN

FLATHEAD NATIONAL FOREST

North Fork

Lower Quartz Lake

Middle Quartz Lake

Grace Lake

Mount Geduhn 8375ft 2552m

0.3mi 0.5km

Polebridge

15

1mi 2km

Polebridge

Hidden Meadow

16

Quartz Creek

LOGGING LAKE

Longfellow Peak 8904ft 2714m

Lake Evangeline

Camas Lake

Lake McDo

NATIO

Flathead River

Winona Lake

Quartz Creek

17

Quartz Creek

Ruger Lake

Dutch Lake

Arrow Lake

Avalanch Cre

Heave Peak 8987ft 2739m

13mi 21km

Logging Creek

18

Logging Creek

Inside North

Anaconda Creek

Dutch Creek

Trout Lake

Stanton

Mount Vaught

Coal Creek

Hay Creek

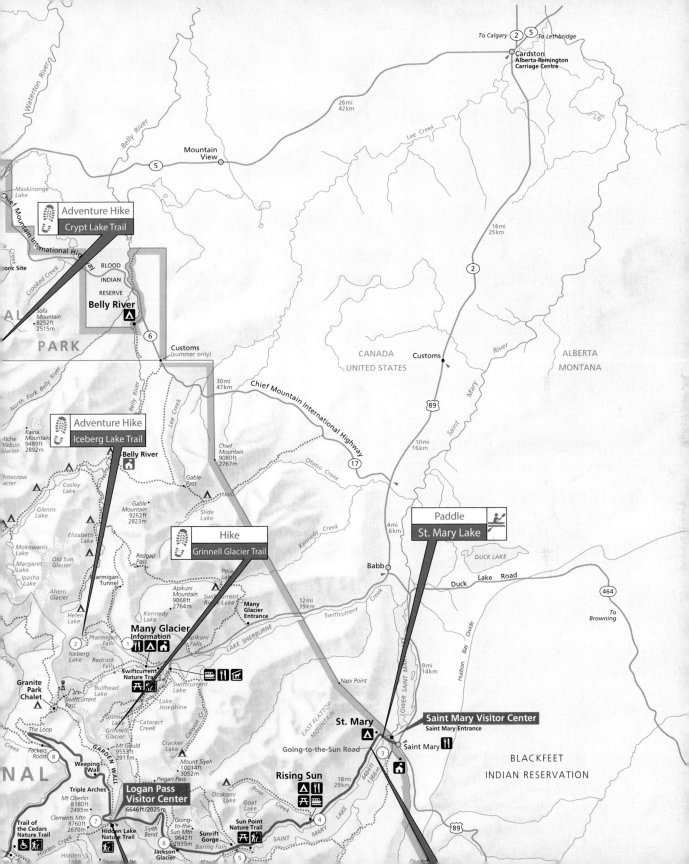

Adventure Hike
Crypt Lake Trail

Belly River

Adventure Hike
Iceberg Lake Trail

Hike
Grinnell Glacier Trail

Paddle
St. Mary Lake

To Calgary — To Lethbridge

Cardston
Alberta-Remington
Carriage Centre

Mountain View

26mi
42km

16mi
25km

Waterton River

Belly River

Lee Creek

BLOOD

INDIAN

RESERVE

Maskinonge
Lake

Chief Mountain International Highway

Historic Site

Sofa
Mountain
8252ft
2515m

Crooked Creek

AL

PARK

North Fork Belly River

Customs
(summer only)

30mi
47km

Chief Mountain International Highway

CANADA
UNITED STATES

Customs

ALBERTA
MONTANA

Kaina
Mountain
9489ft
2892m

Miche
Wabun
Glacier

Belly River

Gable
Pass

Chief Mountain
9080ft
2767m

Otatso Creek

Saint Mary River

River

89

10mi
16km

Whitecrow
Glacier

Cosley
Lake

Gable
Mountain
9262ft
2823m

Slide
Lake

17

Glenns
Lake

Elizabeth
Lake

Gable
Lake

Kennedy Creek

4mi
6km

DUCK LAKE

Mokowanis
Lake

Old Sun
Glacier

Redgap
Pass

Poia
Lake

Babb

Duck   Lake   Road

464

Margaret
Lake

Ipasha
Lake

Ptarmigan
Tunnel

Apikuni
Mountain
9068ft
2764m

Swiftcurrent Ridge Lake

Many Glacier
Entrance

12mi
19km

To
Browning

Ahern
Glacier

Helen
Lake

Kennedy
Lake

Apikuni
Falls

LAKE SHERBURNE

Swiftcurrent   Creek

2

Ptarmigan
Falls

Many Glacier
Information

1

9mi
14km

Iceberg
Lake

Redrock
Falls

Swiftcurrent
Nature Trail

Hudson   Bay   Divide

Granite
Park
Chalet

Bullhead
Lake

Swiftcurrent
Lake

Swiftcurrent
Pass

Lake
Josephine

Napi Point

LOWER SAINT MARY

Saint Mary Visitor Center

Saint Mary Entrance

The Loop

Grinnell
Lake

Cataract
Creek

Cracker
Lake

Mt Gould
9553ft
2911m

Canyon Cr

EAST FLATTOP MOUNTAIN

St. Mary

4484ft
1366m

Packers
Roost

8

GARDEN   WALL

Mount Siyeh
10014ft
3052m

Piegan Pass

Going-to-the-Sun Road

Saint Mary

Weeping
Wall

Cracker
Lake

Rising Sun

18mi
29km

SAINT   MARY   LAKE

BLACKFEET

INDIAN RESERVATION

Triple Arches

Mt Oberlin
8180ft
2493m

Logan Pass Visitor Center
6646ft/2025m

Clements Mtn
8760ft
2670m

7

Going-to-the-Sun Mtn
9642ft
2939m

Otokomi
Lake

Goat Lake

Rose   Creek

Sunrift
Gorge

4

Sun Point
Nature Trail

89

Trail of
the Cedars
Nature Trail

Hidden Lake
Nature Trail

6

Siyeh Bend

Going-to-the-Sun Rd

SAINT

Baring Falls

Hidden Lake

Jackson
Glacier

Piegan Mtn

5

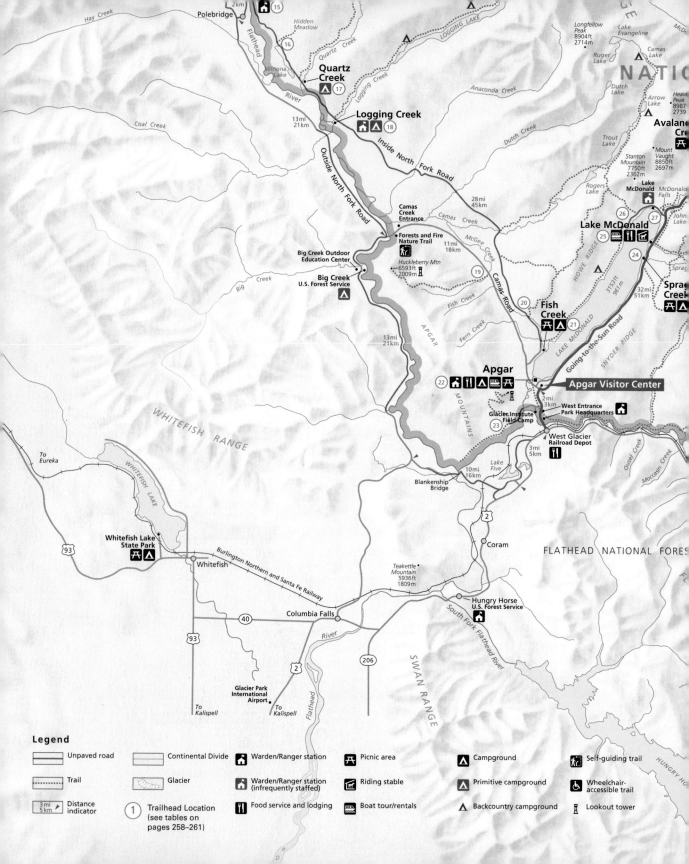

Polebridge

2km

15

Hay Creek

Hidden
Meadow

16

Longfellow
Peak
8904ft
2714m

Lake
Evangeline

Camas
Lake

NATIO

Quartz
Creek

17

Winona
Lake

Quartz Creek

Logging Creek

Coal Creek

13mi
21km

Logging Creek

18

Inside North Fork Road

LOGGING LAKE

Anaconda Creek

Dutch Creek

Dutch
Lake

Arrow
Lake

Heave
Peak
8987
2739

Ruger
Lake

Avalan
Cr

Trout
Lake

Mount
Vaught
8850ft
2697m

Camas
Creek
Entrance

Camas Creek

McGee Creek

Stanton
Mountain
7750ft
2362m

Lake
McDonald

McDonald
Falls

Forests and Fire
Nature Trail

Rogers
Lake

Lake McDonald

25   26   27

Big Creek Outdoor
Education Center

Huckleberry Mtn
6593ft
2009m

11mi
18km

19

HOWE RIDGE

3153ft
961m

24

John
Lake

Big Creek
U.S. Forest Service

Big
Creek

Fish Creek

20

Fish
Creek

21

32mi
51km

Sprac
Creek

Outside North Fork Road

Flathead River

APGAR

Fern Creek

Going-to-the-Sun Road

LAKE McDONALD

SNYDER RIDGE

Sprag

13mi
21km

22

Apgar

Apgar Visitor Center

MOUNTAINS

23

Glacier Institute
Field Camp

2mi
3km

West Entrance
Park Headquarters

West Glacier
Railroad Depot

3mi
5km

Ousel Creek

WHITEFISH   RANGE

To
Eureka

WHITEFISH LAKE

Lake
Five

10mi
16km

Blankenship
Bridge

2

Moccasin Creek

Whitefish Lake
State Park

93

Whitefish

Burlington Northern and Santa Fe Railway

Coram

FLATHEAD NATIONAL FORES

40

93

Columbia Falls

2

Flathead
River

Teakettle
Mountain
5936ft
1809m

SWAN RANGE

South Fork Flathead River

Hungry Horse
U.S. Forest Service

FL

HUNGRY HO

206

Glacier Park
International
Airport

To
Kalispell

To
Kalispell

Legend

Unpaved road	Continental Divide	Warden/Ranger station	Picnic area	Campground	Self-guiding trail
Trail	Glacier	Warden/Ranger station (infrequently staffed)	Riding stable	Primitive campground	Wheelchair-accessible trail
3 mi / 5 km Distance indicator	1 Trailhead Location (see tables on pages 258–261)	Food service and lodging	Boat tour/rentals	Backcountry campground	Lookout tower

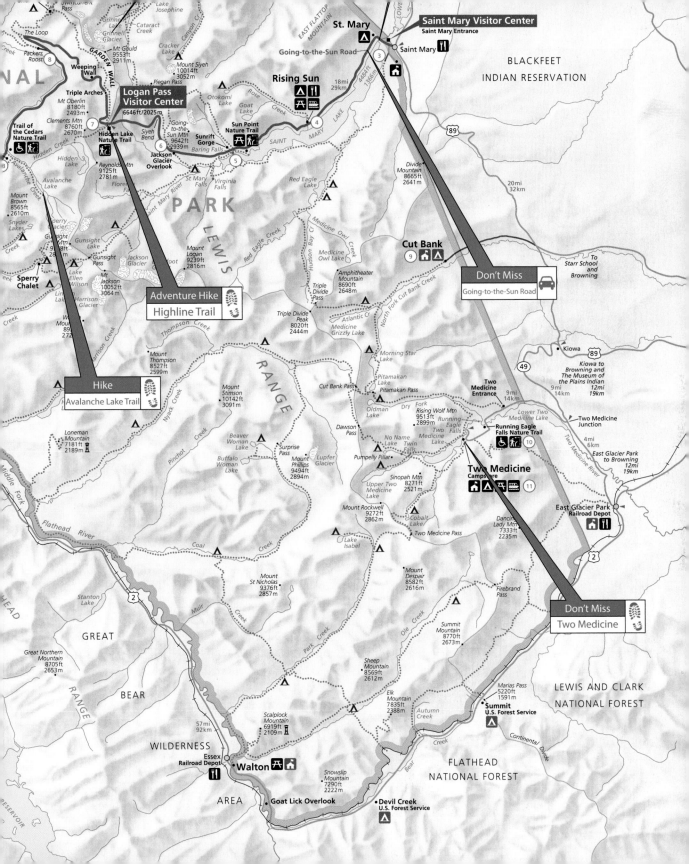

Bowman Lake

Directions

Glacier has four main entrances. Many Glacier and Two Medicine are isolated, road-accessible regions along the park's eastern boundary. St. Mary and West Entrance near Apgar serve as the east and west ends, respectively, of the ever-popular Going-to-the-Sun Road.

To Many Glacier: From Browning (45 miles), take US-89 N/W from Browning to Many Glacier Road. Turn left onto Many Glacier Road, which leads into the park. The alternative (5 miles shorter, but a bit longer) is to take Duck Lake Road north and then west to US-89, and turn right onto US-89 N.

To St. Mary (East End of Going-to-the-Sun Road): From Great Falls (160 miles), take US-89 N to Going-to-the-Sun Road (Glacier Route 1). You can also arrive from the east via US-2. From US-2, head north on US-89 at Browning.

To Two Medicine (East): From Browning (20 miles), continue west on US-2. Turn right at MT-49 N/Looking Glass Hill. Turn left at 2 Medicine Road and follow it into the park.

To West Glacier (West End of Going-to-the-Sun Road): From Kalispell (33 miles), take US-2 E about 13 miles. Turn right at MT-40 E/US-2 E. Continue for 19 miles before turning left onto Going-to-the-Sun Road (Glacier Route 1).

Shuttle Services

To help reduce pollution and congestion, the park provides free shuttle service along Going-to-the-Sun Road from late June/early July through early September. Shuttles make several stops in between Apgar Transit Center (west) and St. Mary Visitor Center (east). They depart every 15–30 minutes. They're extremely convenient, especially considering parking at stops like Logan Pass fill by 9am on busy days. But shuttles fill up too, and you can find yourself waiting a shuttle or two before getting a ride. Glacier Park Express (406.253.9192) operates a shuttle between Whitefish and Apgar Transit Station.

Waterton–Glacier International Peace Park

On June 18, 1932, **Waterton Lakes National Park** in Canada united with Glacier National Park to form the world's first International Peace Park. The parks retain well-defined borders and independent staffs, but they cooperate in wildlife management, scientific research, and some visitor services (like the ranger-led **International Peace Park Hike**, page 264). Waterton Lakes' activities are not covered in this guide, but the hike to **Crypt Lake** is worth a quick mention. It is one of the best hikes in the world, but not one to be attempted by individuals scared of heights or confined spaces. A short boat ride ($24/adult, $12/Child) leads to the trailhead, where you'll hike past running streams and sparkling waterfalls before a steel ladder climbs to a short tunnel. Next, you traverse a narrow, completely exposed cliff-edge with the aid of a cable. Continuing,

Many Glacier

you end at a perfect cirque nestled on the Canada–U.S. border. Remember to leave Crypt Lake with enough time to catch the return ferry (hikers have been left behind). Also remember to **bring your passport**. You'll need it to pass through the customs station where you drive in and out of Canada.

Regions

Many Glacier: Revered as the most beautiful area of Glacier National Park, Many Glacier is as close to the park's backcountry as you can get in a car. (But please leave your car behind for a while, the hiking here is first-rate.)

Goat Haunt: Goat Haunt is in the park's backcountry. You can hike in, or arrive by boat from Waterton Lakes National Park in Canada (ID required if arriving by boat and hiking south into Glacier National Park).

Inside North Fork Road from South to North: Logging Creek, Quartz Creek, Polebridge, Bowman Lake, and Kintla Lake are relatively uncrowded thanks to access via unpaved (rough and narrow) North Fork Road. While it's much less congested than Going-to-the-Sun Road it isn't much less stressful.

Two Medicine: Original train depot before Going-to-the-Sun Road (GTSR) was constructed. Today, it's a somewhat off-the-beaten-path destination with outstanding hiking and camping.

Cut Bank: More remote region as access is via an unpaved road. Cut Bank Creek Trail is outstanding.

Along GTSR (from East to West)

St. Mary: The park's eastern gateway is heavily trafficked and for good reason: vistas along St. Mary Lake are some of the most spectacular, not only in the park, but in the world.

Logan Pass: Extremely popular, but Logan Pass is THE one must-stop destination along GTSR.

Lake McDonald: This area, boasting the largest lake in the park, bustles with activity all summer long. Lodging, dining, boat and horse tours are all available here.

Apgar: The park's western gateway is Apgar. Here you'll find lodging, dining, camping, boat tours, and a visitor center.

Driving

Going-to-the-Sun Road (GTSR) exists because of the foresight of Stephen Mather, the National Park Service's first Director, who chose to construct a more expensive, less obtrusive route across the divide. This route unlocks many of the most spectacular landscapes to motorists. Whether it's in your own car, a Red Jammer (page 262), or the park's free shuttle, do not skip touring GTSR. A word of warning about taking your own car: parking areas (Logan Pass in particular) do fill up. During peak season Logan Pass parking area fills by 9am. Consider taking the free shuttle. **Inside North Fork Road**, which nearly parallels the park's western boundary from Fish Creek to Kintla Lake (portions of it are sometimes closed), provides solitude but at a price: this gravel road is narrow and bumpy.

Glacier Lodging (Fees are per night)

Name	Open	Fee	Location & Notes
Glacier Park Lodge	mid-June–late Sept	$159–499	East Glacier • Golf, spa, and dining are available
St. Mary Lodge	mid-June–late Sept	$99–385	St. Mary • Just outside the park's east entrance
Apgar Village Lodge	mid-May–late Sept	$109–319	Apgar • Located inside the park at Apgar Village
West Glacier Motel	late May–mid-Sept	$99–189	West Glacier • Just outside the park's west entrance
Motel Lake McDonald	mid-June–mid-Sept	$149	Lake McDonald • Inside park, 10 miles from west entrance
Grouse Mountain Lodge	All Year	$114–194	Whitefish • 30 miles from Apgar Visitor Center
Prince of Wales Hotel	early June–mid-Sept	$184–233	Waterton Lakes National Park (Canada) • Unreal setting
For reservations contact Glacier Park Inc. at (406) 892-2525 or glacierparkinc.com			
Lake McDonald Lodge	late May–late Sept	$105–339	SW region of park on Going-to-the-Sun Road • Cabins available, dining on-site • Swiss chalet-style design
Many Glacier Hotel - ♨	mid-June–mid-Sept	$191–400	Many Glacier • Dining and boat tours on-site
Rising Sun Motor Inn	mid-June–mid-Sept	$152–165	Going-to-the-Sun Road, 5.5 miles from St. Mary • Centralized location with Two Dog Flats Grill
Swiftcurrent Motor Inn	mid-June–mid-Sept	$95-165	Many Glacier Area • Rooms are in three separate buildings, some rooms have a shared bathroom
Village Inn at Apgar	late May–mid-Sept	$159–276	Apgar • All rooms are rustic yet comfortable
For reservations contact Glacier National Parks Lodges (Xanterra) at (855) 733-4522 or glaciernationalparklodges.com			

Glacier Camping (Fees are per night)

Name	Location	Open	Fee	Sites	Notes
St. Mary* - ♨	GTSR	early June–mid-Sept	$23	148	Up to 35-ft parking space • F, DS, PC, HB
Rising Sun	GTSR	mid-June–mid-Sept	$20	84	Up to 25-ft parking space • F, DS, PC, HB
Avalanche	GTSR	mid-June–mid-Sept	$20	87	Up to 26-ft parking space • F, HB
Sprague Creek	GTSR	early May–mid-Sept	$20	25	No towed units, Up to 21-ft parking space • F, HB
Apgar - ♨	Apgar Village	early May –mid-Oct	$20	194	Up to 40-ft parking space • F, DS, PC, HB
Two Medicine	East Side	mid-April–late Sept	$20	100	Up to 35-ft parking space • F, DS, PC, HB
Cut Bank	East Side	early May–late Sept	$10	14	Dirt road, primitive camping, no potable H_2O
Many Glacier - ♨	East Side	late May–late Sept	$20	109	Up to 35-ft parking space • F, DS, PC, HB
Fish Creek* - ♨	West Side	early June–early Sept	$23	178	Up to 35-ft parking space • F, DS, PC, HB
Logging Creek	West Side	early July–late Sept	$10	7	Dirt road, primitive camping, no potable H_2O
Quartz Creek	West Side	early July–late Oct	$10	7	Dirt road, primitive camping, no potable H_2O
Bowman Lake	West Side	late May–mid-Sept	$15	48	Dirt road, large units not recommended • PC
Kintla Lake - ♨	West Side	early May–mid-Sept	$15	13	Dirt road, large units not recommended • PC

	*Campsites can be reserved, June through Labor Day, by calling (877) 444-6777 or clicking recreation.gov F = Flush Toilets, DS = Dump Station, PC = Primitive Camping (after the open dates), HB = Hike/Bike Sites ($5–8/night)
Backcountry	A Backcountry User Permit is required for all overnight camping in the backcountry. Trips between June 15 and September 30 may be reserved for a $30 reservation fee, plus a $10 processing fee. Advance reservations must be made online via Pay.gov. Permits may be obtained from the following locations: Apgar Backcountry Permit Center, St. Mary Visitor Center, Many Glacier Ranger Station, Two Medicine Ranger Station, Polebridge Ranger Station, and Waterton Lakes National Park Visitor Reception Center.
Group Camping	Available at Apgar*, Many Glacier, St. Mary, and Two Medicine ($53 plus $5 per person after first 9 campers)
Winter Camping	Available at St. Mary and Apgar from December 1–March 31

Lodging

Glacier has several in-park accommodations available for summer visitors. All properties are operated by **Glacier Park Inc** (406.892.2525, glacierparkinc.com) and **Xanterra** (855.733.4522, glaciernationalparklodges.com). **Glacier Park Lodge** and **Many Glacier Hotel** are original structures built by the Great Northern Railway in the early 1900s, a few years after the park was established. John Lewis established Lewis Glacier Hotel in 1913-1914. He envisioned Glacier as "America's Switzerland," and used traditional Swiss chalet-style architecture. In 1930 it was bought by Great Northern Railway and renamed **Lake McDonald Lodge**. Today, the park's lodges are as popular as ever. Reservations are recommended. Most fill to capacity during their brief tourist season. It is expensive to spend a night in America's Switzerland. You're paying for location, and there's no better way to visit the park than sleeping within its boundaries.

Camping

Drive-in campgrounds are located along Going-to-the-Sun Road and the park's east and west boundaries. Many Glacier, a highly recommended camping destination, is a popular campground in a spectacular setting on the eastern side. St. Mary, Fish Creek, and Many Glacier are the only campgrounds that allow reservations (up to six months in advance). Make reservations at (877) 444-6777 or recreation.gov. Note that half of Many Glacier's sites are still available on a first-come, first-served basis. All other campgrounds are listed in the table on the opposite page.

Two hike-in chalets located in the backcountry allow visitors to access the heart of the park, miles from roads and automobiles, without sacrificing a bed and warm meal. Granite Park Chalet (graniteparkchalet.com, $105/night) is located just west of the Continental Divide, a few miles north of Going-to-the-Sun Road. It can be accessed via Highline, Loop, Swiftcurrent, and Fifty Mountain/Waterton Lake Trails. A kitchen with stove is available for guests to cook their own meals (carried in or chosen from the chalet's menu of freeze-dried foods). Sperry Chalet (sperrychalet.com, $220/night per person) sits on a ledge overlooking Lake McDonald. Guests are served dinner and breakfast at

Ptarmigan Lake

Glacier's Glaciers

In 1850 there were 150 glaciers in the park. Today, there are 25, all of which are shrinking in size. The climate is changing, and the glaciers are receding. If current climate patterns persist, scientists predict no glaciers will remain by the year 2030.

specified times, and are given a trail lunch. Sperry Trail starts at Lake McDonald Lodge's parking lot and heads southeast to the chalet. Horse trips (page 262) from the park's concessioner are also available from Lake McDonald Horse Barn to Sperry Chalet. An alternative hiking route is Gunsight Pass Trail (more scenic, but longer). All visitors must pack out what is packed in. If you only intend on staying at a chalet, a Backcountry User Permit is not required. These chalets provide a unique opportunity to explore hiking trails that few guests take the time to enjoy. The alternative for exploring the park's backcountry is to stay at one of the designated backcountry campsites located along more than 700 miles of trails.

Best of Glacier

Attraction: Going-to-the-Sun Road
    Runner-up: Logan Pass
    2nd Runner-up: Many Glacier
    3rd Runner-up: St. Mary Lake

Activity: Red Bus Tours
    Runner-up: Flathead River Rafting

Short Hike: Avalanche Lake
    Runner-up: Hidden Lake/Overlook

Moderate Hike: Highline Trail
    Runner-up: Grinnell Glacier
    2nd Runner-up: Ptarmigan Tunnel
    3rd Runner-up: Siyeh Pass

Area to Backpack: Goat Haunt
    Runner-up: Two Medicine

Hiking

Glacier is the ultimate hiking destination. More than 700 miles of trails crisscross one million acres of mountainous terrain, providing access to an unparalleled collection of blue-green alpine lakes, knife-edge arêtes, rugged and prominent mountains, and textbook examples of glacial geology. A hiker could spend a month here and still be left in awe of the rocky pinnacles reaching toward the sky.

Every area has its gems, but one region stands out. **Many Glacier** is without a doubt the best of the best. The second you pass through the entrance you feel like you've driven into a postcard and it only gets better from here. The prominence and jagged nature of these mountains is overwhelming. Here you'll find three of the best treks: Grinnell Glacier, Iceberg Lake, and Ptarmigan Tunnel Trails. Each can be completed in 3–5 hours, but pack a lunch and make a day of it. **Grinnell Glacier Trail** allows hikers to view (and step foot on) one of the park's endangered species: glaciers. It begins near Many Glacier Hotel and once you reach the shores of Lake Josephine, you are showered with spectacular mountain views as the snow-melt pours from their steep slopes. Just beyond the lake is a viewpoint/picnic area, where you can continue on to the glacier and Upper Grinnell

Lake. Glacier Park Boat Co. (glacierparkboats.com) offers guided tours of Grinnell Lake and Grinnell Glacier for $26/adult and $13/child (ages 4–12). The tour includes boat rides across Swiftcurrent Lake and Lake Josephine. Reservations require three days advance notice due to limited seating. Walk-up reservations are allowed up to 3 days in advance if there's availability.

Iceberg Lake Trail begins at Iceberg/Ptarmigan Trailhead, and continues to Ptarmigan Falls before passing through a field of beargrass, along a babbling creek, and up into the high-country. Left in the shadows of Mount Wilbur and the Continental Divide, Iceberg Lake receives little sunlight. The result is massive icebergs floating about the perfect glacial cirque (sometimes into August). **Ptarmigan Tunnel Trail** shares the same trailhead and is an equally stunning trek.

Highline Trail begins at Logan Pass (Going-to-the-Sun Road) and follows Garden Wall along the Continental Divide. This hike is outstanding, especially the short but thigh-burning ascent to Grinnell Glacier Overlook. (You'll know the junction when you see it. The trail goes up, up, and up to a notch in Garden Wall.) The only drawback for some visitors is that Highline follows the road for a considerable distance, which means you can get similar views from your car seat. We'll take the trail any day! After the spur to Grinnell Glacier Overlook, you continue on to Granite Park Chalet (which can also be reached via Swiftcurrent Pass from Many Glacier—another great hike!), and you can return to Going-to-the-Sun Road via The Loop (free shuttle back to Logan Pass required).

Even though Grinnell Glacier, Iceberg Lake, Ptarmigan Tunnel, and Highline Trails are fairly long day hikes, don't anticipate much solitude. These are four of the park's most beautiful and popular adventures.

The following pages provide additional hiking information broken down by region. Listed mileages are roundtrip. Trails at Glacier are more difficult than those found at most parks. Expect a strenuous trail to traverse several steep climbs with the potential for switchbacks; even moderate trails may encounter more than 1,000 feet in elevation change. Remember you're in grizzly country. Hike in groups, and know what to do should you encounter an aggressive bear. Any trailhead followed by a (Shuttle Stop) means it is on or near the park's shuttle route that follows Going-to-the-Sun Road (page 253).

Cut Bank is the place for you, if you are looking for seclusion and solitude. Located in the southeast corner, it is seldom visited. Even though it doesn't attract swarms of tourists like Going-to-the-Sun Road, there's plenty of majestic mountain scenery (if you're willing to hike). Triple Divide Pass is one of the more unique hiking destinations. Depending on where a drop of water lands within a one-square-foot area of Triple Divide Peak, that droplet could end up in Hudson Bay, the Gulf of Mexico, or the Pacific Ocean. The views along the way to the peak are equally amazing.

North Fork is located along the park's western boundary, north of Going-to-the-Sun Road. It's a nice, relatively secluded area with a variety of easy and mostly flat hikes exploring the western foothills. Goat Haunt is located in the backcountry at the south end of Upper Waterton Lake near the U.S.–Canada Border. It's a popular stop for backpackers, but can also be reached as a day hike from Canada's Waterton Lakes National Park. Here, an out-and-back trek to Goat Haunt is possible thanks to Waterton Shoreline Cruise's (403.859.2362, watertoncruise.com) boat rides back to Waterton. One-way fare is $24/adults, $12/youth (ages 13–17), and $9/child (ages 4–12). Boats typically run from June until September.

The **Lake McDonald** Area has a fairly dense collection of easy-to-moderate hiking trails. Apgar Lookout Trail provides expansive panoramas. And Sperry Trailhead, located on Going-to-the-Sun Road, serves as an access point to the region's most beautiful hikes, including the 6.4-mile (one-way) trail to Sperry Chalet (page 255), where you can spend a night in the wilderness and enjoy a warm dinner and breakfast before returning to civilization.

Backpacking
The one sure-fire way to escape the sea of summer tourists along Going-to-the-Sun Road is to strap a pack to your back, and head into the wilderness (more than 95% of the park's area).

That's not to say backpacking isn't popular here. It is. All backpackers must camp in designated sites with an overnight **backcountry use permit**. Permits cost $7 per person per night. Half the sites can be reserved for a $40 fee ($30 of which is refundable if your request isn't successful) through pay.gov. (Fax, phone, or in-person applications are no longer accepted.) Reservations are highly recommended, especially for any site within a day's hike of a primary trailhead. Permits must be obtained in person no sooner than one day before your trip's departure. You cannot request a backcountry permit without planning your route. Along the park's trails there are more than 60 backcountry campgrounds and 200+ campsites. Choose a route with every member of the group in mind. If it's your first time camping in the backcountry think about staying near Going-to-the-Sun Road or one of the park's developed areas. If your plans change and you can no longer use your permit, please call (406) 888-7800 to cancel your trip. You won't receive a refund, but karma will be in your favor as your site will become available to another visitor.

All **campgrounds** have tent sites, pit toilets, food hanging or storage devices, and food preparation areas. Set up camp and prepare and store food where you're supposed to. Fires are only allowed in designated fire pits, and are not available at all camps. For the most part, all that is expected of you is simple courtesy toward your surroundings and fellow backpackers.

Very few incidents occur, but backpackers must be well aware of the inherent dangers. To some, the danger is part of the allure; to others, it's a reason to stay away. Weather, wildlife, and accidents are all unpredictable forces of nature that can cause serious problems in the backcountry. Check the extended weather forecast before your trip. Travel with a group and carry a first-aid kit, a good topographic map, and a compass (most importantly, know how to use them). Treat your water (boil or filter). Know how to react should you encounter a bear or mountain lion. In reality these dangers are nothing to be afraid of. While there are no guarantees, with a little bit of knowledge and ample preparation you can nearly assure yourself a safe once-in-a-lifetime experience in a one-of-a-kind environment. Every first-time, multi-day expeditions should be planned carefully, well in advance (no exceptions!).

St. Mary Lake

Many Glacier, St. Mary, and Logan Pass Hiking Trails (Distances are roundtrip)

Name	Location (# on map)	Length	Difficulty Rating & Notes
Apikuni Falls	1.1 miles east of Many Glacier Hotel (1)	2.0 miles	E – Viewpoint of water falling from a hanging valley
Grinnell Lake - ♨	Grinnell Glacier TH or Many Glacier Hotel (2) With boat ride from Many Glacier Hotel	6.8 miles 1.8 miles	E – Hike in and out, or take shortcut via boat trip
Redrock Falls	Swiftcurrent Trailhead (2)	3.6 miles	E – Short leisurely hike
Ptarmigan Falls	Iceberg Ptarmigan Trailhead (2)	5.2 miles	E – Falls on Iceberg Lake route
Swiftcurrent Nature	Grinnell Glacier TH or Many Glacier Hotel (2)	5.0 miles	E – Short and flat path
Cracker Lake	South end of Many Glacier Hotel Parking Area (2)	12.2 miles	M – Follows horse trail
Grinnell Glacier Viewpoint - ♨	Grinnell Glacier TH or Many Glacier Hotel (2) With boat ride from Many Glacier Hotel	11.0 miles 7.6 miles	M – Definitely one of the best hikes in the park
Iceberg Lake - ♨	Iceberg Ptarmigan Trailhead (2)	9.6 miles	M – Another day hiker's favorite
Ptarmigan Lake - ♨	Iceberg Ptarmigan Trailhead (2)	8.6 miles	M – Veers from Iceberg Lake Trail to Ptarmigan Lake
Piegan Pass	South end of Many Glacier Hotel Parking Area (2) Piegan Pass TH (Siyeh Bend Shuttle Stop) (6)	16.6 miles 9.0 miles	M – Less popular east side of the Garden Wall
Granite Park Chalet	Swiftcurrent Trailhead at Many Glacier (2) Cross GTSR at Logan Pass (Shuttle Stop) (7) Loop Trailhead on Going-to-the-Sun Road (8)	15.0 miles 15.2 miles 8.0 miles	S – Tedious Swiftcurrent Pass S – The amazing Highline Trail M – Shortest route via the Loop
Ptarmigan Tunnel - ♨	Iceberg Ptarmigan Trailhead (2)	10.4 miles	S – Connects Many Glacier and Belly River Areas
Swiftcurrent Pass - ♨	Swiftcurrent Trailhead (2)	13.2 miles	S – Leads to Granite Park Chalet
St. Mary Falls - ♨	St. Mary Falls Trailhead (Shuttle Stop) (3) With boat ride from Rising Sun	2.2 miles 3.0 miles	E – Very popular trail with multiple access options
Virginia Falls - ♨	St. Mary Falls Trailhead (Shuttle Stop) (3) With boat ride from Rising Sun	3.0 miles 4.4 miles	E – Switchbacks from St. Mary Falls lead to Virginia Falls
Beaver Pond Loop	1913 Ranger Station Parking Area (3)	6.0 miles	E – Popular short, flat loop trail
Red Eagle Lake	1913 Ranger Station Parking Area (3)	15.2 miles	E – Easy hike, but long
Otokomi Lake	Next to Rising Sun Campstore (4)	10.4 miles	M – Meadows lead to scenic lake
Baring Falls	Sunrift Gorge Pullout (Shuttle Stop) (5)	2.0 miles	E – Short descent to falls
Sun Point Nature	Sun Point Parking Area (Shuttle Stop) (5)	1.6 miles	E – Skirts along St. Mary Lake
Sunrift Gorge	Sunrift Gorge Pullout (Shuttle Stop) (5)	400 feet	E – Very short, easily accessible
Siyeh Pass - ♨	Sunrift Gorge Pullout (Shuttle Stop) (5) Piegan Pass TH (Siyeh Bend Shuttle Stop) (6)	11.2 miles 9.4 miles	S – High elevation hike through varied ecosystems
Gunsight Pass - ♨	Gunsight Pass Trailhead (Shuttle Stop) (6)	18.4 miles	S – More difficult (and more beautiful) route to Sperry Chalet
Hidden Lake / Overlook - ♨	Logan Pass Visitor Center (Shuttle Stop) (7)	7.0/3.0 mi	M – One of the best
Highline Trail - ♨	Cross GTSR at Logan Pass (Shuttle Stop) (7)	15.2–40+ miles	S – Follows Continental Divide to U.S.–Canada Border

Difficulty Ratings: E = Easy, M = Moderate, S = Strenuous

Hidden Lake

Cut Bank and Two Medicine Hiking Trails (Distances are roundtrip)

Name	Location (# on map)	Length	Difficulty Rating & Notes
Atlantic Falls	Cut Bank Trailhead (9)	8.0 miles	E – Waterfall seen en route to Pitamakan Pass
Medicine Grizzly Lake	Cut Bank Trailhead (9)	12.0 miles	M – Spur trail from Triple Divide Trail
Triple Divide Pass	Cut Bank Trailhead (9)	14.4 miles	S – From here water flows west, south, and north
Running Eagle Fall - ♿	Running Eagle Falls TH (10)	0.6 mile	E – A short wheelchair-accessible trail
Apistoki Falls	0.25-mile east of Two Medicine Ranger Station (11)	1.2 miles	E – Short and easy waterfall hike
Scenic Point	0.25-mile east of Two Medicine Ranger Station (11)	6.2 miles	S – Short climb to a wonderful viewpoint
Aster Park/Falls - ♿	South Shore Trailhead (11)	3.8 miles	E – Views of Two Medicine Lake
Rockwell Falls	South Shore Trailhead (11)	6.8 miles	M – Follow South Shore Trail to Cobalt Lake
Cobalt Lake - ♿	South Shore Trailhead (11)	11.4 miles	M – Last two miles to the lake are steep
Twin Falls - ♿	North Shore Trailhead (11) Using concession boat	7.6 miles 1.8 mile	E – A short spur trail from Upper Two Medicine Lake Trail leads to Twin Falls
Upper Two Medicine Lake	North Shore Trailhead (11) Using concession boat	10.0 miles 4.4 miles	E – After Twin Falls the trail continues to Upper Two Medicine Lake
No Name Lake	North Shore Trailhead (11)	10.0 miles	M – Pretty lake north of Upper Two Medicine
Dawson Pass - ♿	North Shore Trailhead (11)	13.4 miles	S – Combine with Pitamakan Pass for 18.8-mi loop
Pitamakan Pass	North Shore Trailhead (11)	13.8 miles	S – Follows Cut Bank Creek to two lakes
Oldman Lake	North Shore Trailhead (11)	11.4 miles	S – Follows Dry Fork to lake near Pitamakan Pass

Difficulty Ratings: E = Easy, M = Moderate, S = Strenuous

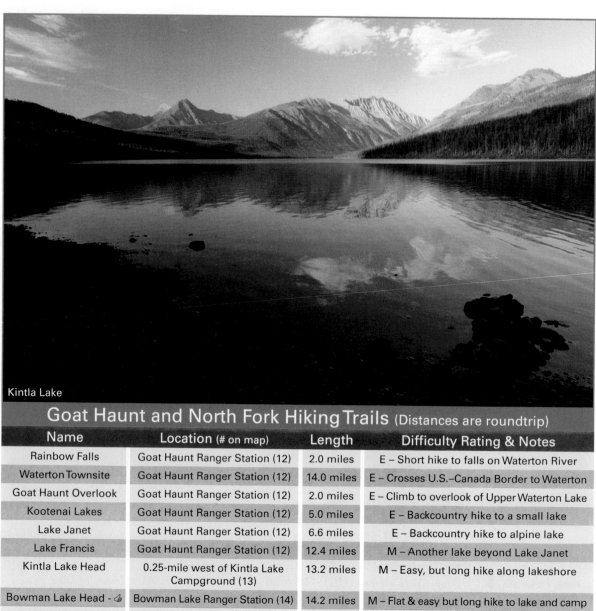

Kintla Lake

Goat Haunt and North Fork Hiking Trails (Distances are roundtrip)

Name	Location (# on map)	Length	Difficulty Rating & Notes
Rainbow Falls	Goat Haunt Ranger Station (12)	2.0 miles	E – Short hike to falls on Waterton River
Waterton Townsite	Goat Haunt Ranger Station (12)	14.0 miles	E – Crosses U.S.–Canada Border to Waterton
Goat Haunt Overlook	Goat Haunt Ranger Station (12)	2.0 miles	E – Climb to overlook of Upper Waterton Lake
Kootenai Lakes	Goat Haunt Ranger Station (12)	5.0 miles	E – Backcountry hike to a small lake
Lake Janet	Goat Haunt Ranger Station (12)	6.6 miles	E – Backcountry hike to alpine lake
Lake Francis	Goat Haunt Ranger Station (12)	12.4 miles	M – Another lake beyond Lake Janet
Kintla Lake Head	0.25-mile west of Kintla Lake Campground (13)	13.2 miles	M – Easy, but long hike along lakeshore
Bowman Lake Head - 🐾	Bowman Lake Ranger Station (14)	14.2 miles	M – Flat & easy but long hike to lake and camp
Akokala Lake	Bowman Lake Ranger Station (14)	11.6 miles	M – Crosses Akokala Creek to small lake
Numa Lookout	Bowman Lake Ranger Station (14)	14.4 miles	M – Views across Bowman Lake
Quartz Lake - 🐾	Bowman Lake Picnic Area (14)	12.0 miles	M – Most scenic of the three Quartz Lakes
Lower Quartz Lake	Bowman Lake Picnic Area (14) North of Quartz Creek Camp (17)	6.0 miles 13.8 miles	M – Combine with Quartz Lake Trail for a strenuous (but exceptional) 12+ mile loop
Covey Meadow	Polebridge Ranger Station (15)	3.0 miles	E – Short and easy loop through meadow
Hidden Meadow	3 miles south of Polebridge Ranger Station (16)	2.4 miles	E – Short and flat hike through nice meadow
Logging Lake	Logging Creek Ranger Station (18)	9.0 miles	E – This trail is popular among fishermen

Difficulty Ratings: E = Easy, M = Moderate, S = Strenuous

Avalanche Lake

Lake McDonald Hiking Trails (Distances are roundtrip)

Name	Location (# on map)	Length	Difficulty Rating & Notes
Huckleberry Lookout	Huckleberry Mt Trailhead on Camas Road (19)	12.0 miles	S – Look for a huckleberry snack
Howe Lake	Howe Lake TH on Inside North Fork Road (20)	4.0 miles	E – Continues past lake to ridge
Rocky Point	0.2 miles north of Fish Creek Campground (21)	2.2 miles	E – Overlook of Lake McDonald
Fish Creek to Apgar Hiking Path	Near McDonald Creek Bridge (Shuttle Stop) (21, 22)	2.4 miles	E – Short and flat connector between Fish Creek and Apgar
Lake McDonald West Shore	Lakeshore at Fish Creek Campground (21) 2.8 miles west on North Lake McDonald Rd (26)	14.0 miles	E – A mostly level and easily accessible trail around the lake
McDonald Creek Bike Path	Asphalt path 50 yards south of Apgar Visitor Center (Shuttle Stop) (22)	3.0 miles	E – Connects Apgar and West Glacier
Apgar Lookout - ♨	At the end of Glacier Institute Road, about 2.0 miles from Going-to-the-Sun Road (23)	6.6 miles	M – Hike up switchbacks to a view of several 10,000-ft peaks
Lincoln Lake - ♨	Lincoln Lake (24)	16.0 miles	M – Secluded/Beaver Chief Falls
Fish Lake	Sperry Trailhead (Shuttle Stop) (25)	5.8 miles	M – Just south of Sperry Trail
Mt Brown Lookout	Sperry Trailhead (Shuttle Stop) (25)	10.6 miles	S – Steep, but spectacular
Sperry Chalet - ♨	Sperry Trailhead (Shuttle Stop) (25)	12.8 miles	S – Shortest route to the chalet
Snyder Lake	Sperry Trailhead (Shuttle Stop) (25)	8.8 miles	S – Breaks north of Sperry Trail
Trout Lake	Trout Lake Trailhead (26)	8.4 miles	M – Popular horse trail
Johns Lake Loop	Johns Lake Trailhead (27)	6.0 miles	E – Short loop off GTSR
Trail of Cedars	Avalanche Picnic Area (Shuttle Stop) (28)	1.4 miles	E – Wheelchair-accessible loop
Avalanche Lake - ♨	Avalanche Gorge Bridge on Trail of the Cedars (28)	4.0 miles	E – Extremely popular hike

Difficulty Ratings: E = Easy, M = Moderate, S = Strenuous

Biking

Biking **Going-to-the-Sun Road (GTSR)** is becoming more popular each year. Cross-country pedalers often choose Logan Pass as their destination to cross the Continental Divide because of its breathtaking scenery. However, it typically first opens in mid-June, depending on the amount of spring snow. But have an alternate route in mind, because in 2011 GTSR did not open completely until July 12.

Once it opens, it is almost immediately flooded with motorists. Traffic is heaviest between 10am and 3pm, and GTSR is closed to bike use from 11am to 4pm (mid-June until Labor Day). This closure affects the road from Apgar turn-off to Sprague Creek Campground and eastbound from Logan Creek to Logan Pass. This means you'll have to squeeze in your heart-pumping, leg-burning ride in the morning or evening.

Winds can be extremely strong, especially on the park's eastern side. Portions of GTSR can be under construction, and often unpaved, so use extreme caution when approaching blind corners and steep downhill stretches. The road is narrow and cyclists must pull to the shoulder if four or more vehicles stack behind you. Several campgrounds (page 255) along GTSR have reduced fee campsites for cyclists traveling without a vehicle. Bike rental is not available in the park.

Horseback Riding

Guided trail rides are available at Many Glacier, Lake McDonald, and Apgar. Swan Mountain Outfitters (877.888.5557, swanmountain-outfitters.com) is the park's trail ride concessioner. Stables are typically open from late April until late October. Rides come in a variety of lengths for reasonable prices: 1-hour ($45), 2-hour ($70), half-day ($177), and full-day ($255).

Red Jammer & Bus Tours

Red Jammers are 17-passenger convertible touring sedans, forming the oldest fleet of passenger carrying vehicles. Operating since the late 1930s, these antique autos have earned the name "red jammers," because of the gear jamming that occurred while scaling the steep grades of Going-to-the-Sun Road. Do not let their antique status deter you from the tour. The entire fleet was rebuilt to run on propane, and they've been going strong ever since.

If you only have a day, a red jammer tour is the most relaxing, informative, and comprehensive way to experience the park. A variety of tours are offered departing from various lodging facilities. The most inclusive is Big Sky Circle Tour. It departs from Glacier Park Lodge ($92/adult, $46/Child), Many Glacier Hotel ($90/45), Swiftcurrent Motor Inn ($90/45), St. Mary Lodge ($70/35), and Rising Sun Motor Inn ($60/30). In 8.5 hours you'll loop around the southern boundary following US-2, crossing the Continental Divide at Marias Pass, and then you'll return through the heart of the park via all 50 miles of Going-to-the-Sun Road, crossing the divide once more at Logan Pass. Individual tours of Going-to-the-Sun Road, Waterton Lakes National Park (Canada), and the park's other entrances are also available. Eastern Alpine Tour is the least expensive offering. This 2.5-hour-long tour departs Rising Sun Motor Inn, and costs $32/adult and $16/Child. It's also available from St. Mary Lodge, St. Mary KOA, Many Glacier Hotel, and Swiftcurrent Motor Inn, but is longer and more expensive from these locations. All tours typically run from mid-June until mid-September. For a complete listing of departure locations, rates, and dates, click glaciernationalparklodges.com or call (855) 733-4522.

Sun Tours (800.786.9220, glaciersuntours.com) offers park tours aboard 25-passenger, large windowed, air-conditioned coaches. Trips departing East Glacier or Browning are 7.5 hours and cost $75/adult, $25/Child (5 – 12 years old), and children under 5 are free. A four hour tour costs $40/adult and $20/Child.

Boat Tours

Not to be outdone by the "Red Jammers," many of the wooden tour boats have been in operation since before the Great Depression. From these historic boats you can sit back and enjoy some of the most majestic alpine scenery found anywhere in the world (without having to trudge up a steep mountain trail). Boat tours are available at Lake McDonald Lodge (Lake McDonald), Many Glacier Hotel (Swiftcurrent

Lake), Rising Sun Motor Inn (St. Mary Lake), and Two Medicine (Two Medicine Lake). Cruises range from 45 minutes to 1.5 hours, and cost between $13 and $26 per adult and $6.50 and $13 per child. Tours typically operate from mid-June until Labor Day. For a complete listing of tour descriptions, rates, and dates, call (406) 257-2426 or click glacierparkboats.com.

Fishing

Fishing is allowed, but strict regulations are enforced to preserve the park's native fish populations. A few areas experience fishing closures to aid in repopulating certain species. River and stream fishing season is from the third Saturday in May through November 30. Lake fishing is open all year. Cutthroat trout are subject to catch and release, except at a few designated areas. A fishing license is not required, but park regulations must be followed. Stop at a visitor center to obtain a copy of current regulations and to be briefed on fishing closures. Glacier Park Inc., offers full-day and half-day **fishing excursions** starting at $400 for two anglers. For more information call (406) 892-2525 or click their website at glacierparkinc.com.

Boating & Rafting

Hundreds of streams originate and flow from these mountains. Triple Divide Peak, just west of Cut Bank, is essentially the apex of the continent. Within one square-foot, water from the peak can become part of the Columbia, Mississippi, and Saskatchewan River systems. Respectively, these rivers flow into the Pacific Ocean, Gulf of Mexico, and Hudson Bay. Altogether there are more than 700 lakes here, but only 131 are named. Lake McDonald is the largest at 9.4 miles long and 1.5 miles wide. It's also the deepest at 464 feet. The lakes are popular spots for boating and paddling. **Motorized watercraft** (except jet-skis) are permitted on Lake McDonald, Waterton, Sherburne, St. Mary, Bowman, and Two Medicine Lakes. Bowman and Two Medicine Lakes are limited to boats with motors not exceeding ten horsepower. A **free launch permit** is required and all boats must be inspected for invasive species. Between Memorial Day and Labor Day, permits can be obtained at Park Headquarters in West Glacier, St. Mary Visitor Center, and Two Medicine and Many Glacier Ranger Stations. Motorboats,

Black bear near Huckleberry Mountain

rowboats, canoes, and kayaks are available for rent at Many Glacier, Lake McDonald Lodge, Apgar, and Two Medicine Lake. **Rentals** are provided by Glacier Boat Co. (406.257.2426, glacierparkboats.com).

Several **rafting companies** (page 268) offer inflatable kayak trips on the Middle and North Forks of Flathead River. North Fork forms the park's western boundary while Middle Fork is just outside the park.

Winter Activities

In winter, Going-to-the-Sun Road is buried beneath several feet of snow, but trails remain open to intrepid **snowshoers** and **cross-country skiers**. If you plan on visiting in winter, it's a good idea to check with a park ranger about weather and snow conditions before heading out. Information is available at Apgar Information Center on weekends, and Park headquarters (near West Glacier) and Hudson Bay District Office (near St. Mary) on weekdays. Ranger stations are open intermittently depending on staffing. Ski trails are available at Apgar (West Glacier), Lake McDonald, North Fork, St. Mary, Two Medicine, and Marias Pass. Most routes are unmarked, so plan ahead and carry a map. Be sure to sign the trail registry before heading out. **Backcountry camping** is allowed (with a free permit) during winter, but it should only be attempted by experienced, well-equipped parties. **Ice fishing** is allowed within park boundaries.

Visitor Centers

Glacier has three visitor centers. All three are situated along Going-to-the-Sun Road: one on each end, and another in the middle. **St. Mary Visitor Center** is located at the scenic byway's eastern end. It's open daily, May through late September, from 8am–5pm. Hours are extended to 8am–6pm from late June to late August. **Logan Pass Visitor Center** is located on the Continental Divide. It's opening date depends on the amount of spring snow, but it usually opens by mid-June. Hours are typically 9:30am–4:30pm, but extend to 7am–9pm from late June through Labor Day. **Apgar Visitor Center** is located on the western end of GTSR. It's open daily from mid-May until mid-October from 9am–4:30pm, with extended hours from 8am–6pm from mid-June until Labor Day. **Ranger stations** at Many Glacier and Two Medicine are open from late May until mid-September, 7am–5pm.

Glacier Institute (406.755.1211, glacierinstitute.org) provides educational adventures for children and adults.

Ranger Programs

Intimidated by the vast network of trails? Unsure what activities are worth the money? Scared of bears? Join a Ranger Program. They're structured, free (unless a boat trip is required), and safe. Grab a copy of the park's newspaper, *The Glacier Visitor Guide*, for a complete listing of ranger-led activities.

Thanks to the park's partnership with Canada's Waterton Lakes National Park, you can take part in the unique **International Peace Park Hike** with rangers from both parks. The journey begins at Waterton (Canada) and from there you hike across the U.S.–Canada border to Goat Haunt. The trip back to Waterton is an easy one. All you have to do is hop aboard a boat (fee) and enjoy the ride as you travel the length of Waterton Lake. Remember your passport. You won't need it to cross the backcountry border, but it is required at all roadway customs stations found along the U.S.–Canada border. Each hike is limited to 35 people. Registration is required. Reservations are only accepted for the next scheduled hike in person or over the phone at Waterton (403.859.5133) or St. Mary Visitor Center (604.732.7750).

Many Glacier is a great area for ranger programs. The best hikes are made even better by joining a ranger to Grinnell Glacier or Iceberg Lake (page 256). The trip to Grinnell Glacier includes a short boat trip for a moderate fee ($26, one-way).

Two Medicine area offers programs less frequently than sites like Many Glacier or Logan Pass, but they are no less spectacular. Full-day hikes to Cobalt Lake, Dawson Pass, and Fireband Pass are a few of the highlighted programs. At St. Mary, the "History in the Making" program is great for families. In just three hours you'll explore the park's past, present, and future. You'll even get to write a letter that will be placed in a time capsule. At Logan Pass you can join a ranger on a Highline Trail Hike (page 256) to Granite Park Chalet or skirt Garden Wall to Haystack Butte. An assortment of walks, talks, and evening programs are available at Lake McDonald Valley. In short, you can't go wrong wherever you go. In summer, you'll find engaging ranger programs in any developed area.

For Kids

For children, whether it's the rugged magnificence of the Rocky Mountains, coming face-to-face with a mountain goat, or catching a glimpse of a grizzly bear as it runs away, Glacier National Park is often a spell-binding place. To help introduce them to these experiences and other natural wonders, a **Junior Ranger Program** is offered for children 5 and older. To become a Junior Ranger, children are asked to complete five activities from the free Junior Ranger booklet (available online or at any visitor center), and to attend a Ranger-led Program. Children receive an official Junior Ranger badge and certificate upon completion.

Flora & Fauna

Grizzly bears are constantly on the minds of visitors. You might be afraid of them. Are you intrigued by them? Maybe, you want to cuddle with a grizzly (not recommended). A healthy population of some 700 grizzlies roams the northern continental divide area. For the most part bears are shy and skittish, just like the rest of the animal kingdom (only bigger and furrier). But some can be extremely dangerous, especially if you startle one or find yourself between a mother and her cub. Still, bears have only been responsible for a handful of deaths, nowhere near the quantity of the park's number one killer (drowning).

You may see a bear on your visit to Glacier, but it's more likely you return home having seen mountain goats, bighorn sheep, and deer. Glacier protects a remarkably intact ecosystem. Nearly all of its known plant and animal species still exist. Woodland caribou and bison are the only missing mammals. Gray wolf naturally returned to the area in the 1980s. Canadian lynx, wolverine, moose, elk, coyote, and mountain lion also call glacier home. More than 270 species of birds visit or reside here as well.

About 1,000 species of plants exist at Glacier. Wildflowers can be seen during every season except winter. Beargrass is commonly found between June and July. Trees are dominated by conifers, but deciduous cottonwoods and aspens can be found in the lower elevations.

Pets

Pets are allowed in the park, but must be kept on a leash no more than six feet in length at all times. They are only allowed in drive-in campgrounds, along park roads open to motor vehicles, and in picnic areas. Pets are prohibited from all hiking trails and the backcountry.

Accessibility

Apgar and St. Mary Visitor Centers are wheelchair accessible. A few of the park's interpretive programs are accessible; these programs are highlighted in the park's ranger-led activities newspaper available throughout the park. Trail of the Cedars and Running Eagle Falls Nature Trail are accessible.

Weather

Visitors should come prepared for all weather conditions. The temperature difference from low altitude to high altitude is usually about 15°F. Most rain falls in the park's western valleys. The eastern slopes are normally sunny and windy. Summer highs can reach 90°F, but overnight lows can drop into the 20s°F. Snow is possible any month of the year. In August of 2005, eight inches of snow fell in a single night, forcing hundreds of backpackers out of the backcountry. Winter snowpack

averages 16 feet. It closes Going-to-the-Sun Road for most of the year. The scenic byway is usually completely open by mid-June.

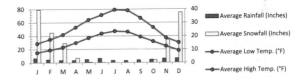

Vacation Planner

To hikers, backpackers, and admirers of natural beauty, Glacier invokes feelings of pure bliss. Enter this majestic land and you'll want to stay forever. Sadly, visitors come and go, taking with them only memories and photographs. It's incredibly difficult to get enough of Glacier. There are dozens of sites where you'd like to pull out a lawn chair, kick-up your feet and enjoy the views. But, this is unrealistic. Busy work schedules and busier lifestyles limit most guests' time to no more than a few days. **If you only have a day**, drive Going-to-the-Sun Road, stopping at Logan Pass to hike Hidden Lake Trail. Three days allows enough time to visit the most beautiful developed areas, but it's hardly enough time to get into the **backcountry** (page 257) or explore **Waterton Lakes National Park** (page 252). Below is a sample three day itinerary. It visits the most popular areas and attractions. This isn't to say that **Cut Bank** and **Two Medicine**, along the park's eastern boundary, aren't worth a visit. (Two Medicine certainly is!) Nor that hiking to **Goat Haunt** isn't a good idea. It covers the most popular and arguably the most beautiful destinations. As is the case with any national park vacation, squeeze in **ranger programs** whenever you can. Nearby dining, grocery stores, lodging, festivals, and attractions are listed on pages 267–269.

Day 1: Begin your trip at **Many Glacier** and plan on arriving early. You'll have to if you haven't reserved a campsite and want to secure one. An early arrival also allows sufficient time to hike a couple of this area's wonderful trails (a must for all hiking enthusiasts). Two in particular should be at the top of your wish list. **Ptarmigan Tunnel** (once you reach Ptarmigan Lake, you may not feel like hiking the switchback up to the tunnel, but do it—it's worth it) and **Grinnell Glacier Trails** are essential hikes. An ambitious hiker can complete both

Wild Goose Island Overlook

trails in a day (more than 20 miles of hiking). Grinnell Glacier Trail can be shortened by 3.4 miles (roundtrip) by boarding a boat operated by Glacier Parks Boat Co. (406.257.2426, glacierparkboats.com). A one-way ticket costs $26/adult and $13/Child. Those of you who enjoy hiking at a more leisurely pace or sitting and enjoying a picnic should choose one or the other. It's extremely easy to fill free time at Many Glacier. You can complete the short hike to **Apikuni Falls** or rest your feet in the waters of **Swiftcurrent Lake**. Schedule permitting, spend the evening with a park ranger at the campground or Many Glacier Hotel.

Day 2: Tired of hiking? If you answered "yes" spend today on a **Red Jammer Tour** (page 262). **International Peace Park Tour** (valid passport required) departs from Many Glacier Hotel, but other locations are available on the park's east side.

Red Jammer Tours aren't for everyone. Although unique, educational and altogether enjoyable, they are expensive and can take all day. An alternative is to head over to **St. Mary Lake Visitor Center**. Take the shuttle to **Logan Pass** (drive yourself if you plan on camping). Here you'll find **Highline and Hidden Lake Trails**. Underline it. Circle it. Star it. Highlight it. Do whatever you have to do to remind yourself to stop here. Start with Hidden Lake, because Highline is much longer and more grueling (if you do the entire loop and trudge up to **Grinnell Glacier Overlook**, which you should). Highline follows the Continental

Divide and Garden Wall and GTSR for much of its length, so you're passing a lot of the same mountain landscapes you see from the road. Still, the cliffs are precipitous, the scenery is mesmerizing, and the trail is relatively easy. To experience the backcountry without sleeping in a tent consider reserving a night at **Granite Park Chalet** (page 255), which can be accessed via Highline Trail (among others). You may also want to stop in at the chalet for a cold refreshing beverage while out on a day hike.

Day 3: If you went with the Red Jammer yesterday, hike Hidden Lake and/or Highline Trails today. Otherwise, get an early start and take the shuttle (or car, if you must) to **Avalanche Lake** for a 4-mile hike to waterfalls and an alpine lake. It's a popular destination, so the earlier the better. If, through some sort of Glacier Park miracle your legs are fresh and ready for another 12-mile hike, climb back aboard the shuttle and exit at Sperry Trailhead. Hike to **Sperry Chalet** for an incredible view of Lake McDonald. If you were interested in spending the night at Granite Park Chalet but it was booked, give Sperry a try. There'd be no better way to end a trip in this magical place. Those hiking out-and-back to Sperry Chalet should make sure you return in time to catch the last shuttle).

Non-hikers should skip Sperry Trail and exit the shuttle at Lake McDonald Lodge, where you can wander the shores, reflecting upon your vacation as the mountains reflect in the shimmering water.

Dining

East of Glacier National Park

Park Café • (406) 732-5566
3147 US-89, Browning • parkcafe.us

The 50's Diner • (406) 338-2749
101 4th Ave, Browning

The Nation's Burger Station • (406) 338-2422
205 Central Ave, Browning
nationsburgerstation.com

Junction Café • (406) 338-2386
330 W Central Ave, Browning

Serranos Mexican Rest. • (406) 226-9392
29 Dawson Ave, East Glacier Park

Luna's Restaurant • (406) 226-4433
1112 US-49, East Glacier Park

Firebrand Food & Ale • (406) 226-9374
20629 US-2, East Glacier Park

Two Medicine Grill • (406) 226-9227
314 US-2, East Glacier Park

Brownie's Hostel & Bakery • (406) 727-4448
1020 MT-49, East Glacier Park
brownieshostel.com

Cattle Baron • (406) 732-4033
3 Babb St, Babb

Two Sisters Café • (406) 732-5535
3600 US-89, Babb • twosistersofmontana.com

Leaning Tree Café • (406) 338-5322
MT-464, Blackfeet

West of Glacier National Park

Eddie's Café & Ice Cream • (406) 888-5361
1 Fish Creek Campground, Apgar
eddiescafegifts.com

Northern Lights Saloon & Café • (406) 888-9963
255 Polebridge Loop, Polebridge

Glacier Grill & Pizza • (406) 387-4223
10126 E US-2, Coram

Elkhorn Grill • (406) 387-4030
105 Hungry Horse Blvd, Hungry Horse

The Huckleberry Patch • (800) 527-7340
8868 US-2 E, Hungry Horse
huckleberrypatch.com • *pie, fudge, & gifts*

Montana Coffee Traders • (406) 892-7696
30 9th St W, Columbia Falls
coffeetraders.com • *coffee, tea, & gifts*

Nite Owl Restaurant • (406) 892-3131
522 9th St W, Columbia Falls
niteowlbackroom.com

Three Forks Grille • (406) 892-2900
729 Nucleus Ave, Columbia Falls
threeforksgrille.com • Entrée: $16–25

Buffalo Café • (406) 862-2833
514 3rd St, Whitefish

Café Kandahar • (406) 862-6247
3824 Big Mtn Rd, Whitefish
cafekandahar.com

Tupelo Grille • (406) 862-6136
15 Central Ave, Whitefish
tupelogrille.com • Entrée: $16–39

Wasabi Sushi Bar • (406) 863-9283
419 2nd St E, Whitefish
wasabimt.com

Ciao Mambo • (406) 863-9600
234 2nd St E, Whitefish
ciaomambo.com

Great Northern Bar & Grill • (406) 862-2816
27 Central Ave, Whitefish
greatnorthernbar.com • Sandwiches: $6–11

Sweet Peaks Ice Cream • (406) 863-9973
419 3rd St, Whitefish
sweetpeaksicecream.com

MacKenzie River Pizza • (406) 862-6601
9 Central Ave, Whitefish
mackenzieriverpizza.com

McGarry's Roadhouse • (406) 862-6223
510 Wisconsin Ave, Whitefish
mcgarrysroadhouse.com • Entrée: $13–38

Ed & Mully's Restaurant • (406) 862-1980
3905 Big Mtn Rd, Whitefish

Pescado Blanco • (406) 862-3290
235 1st St, Whitefish
pescadoblanco.com • Dinners: $11–22

Bulldog Saloon • (406) 862-5636
144 Central Ave, Whitefish

Piggyback Barbeque • (406) 863-9895
102 Wisconsin Ave, Whitefish
piggybackbbq.com • Sandwiches: $9–15

Quickee Sandwich Shop • (406) 862-9866
250 E Second St, Whitefish

Whitefish Lake Restaurant • (406) 862-5285
1200 US-93 N, Whitefish
whitefishlakerestaurant.com • Entrée: $24–48

Red Caboose Café • (406) 863-4563
103 Central Ave, Whitefish
redcaboosecafe.com • Sandwiches: $7–10

LouLa's • (406) 862-5614
300 2nd St E, # B, Whitefish

Moose's Saloon • (406) 755-2337
173 N Main St, Kalispell • moosessaloon.com

Heaven's Peak Restaurant • (406) 387-4754
US-2, Kalispell

Grocery Stores

East of Glacier National Park

Glacier Park Trading Co • (406) 226-9227
316 US-2, East Glacier Park

Albertsons • (406) 873-5035
501 W Main, Cut Bank

West of Glacier National Park

Super 1 Foods • (406) 892-9996
2100 9th St W, Columbia Falls

Safeway • (406) 862-3006
6580 US-93, Whitefish

Walmart Supercenter • (406) 257-7535
170 Hutton Ranch Rd, Kalispell

Lodging

East of Glacier National Park

Mountain Pine Motel • (406) 226-4403
909 US-49, East Glacier Park
mtnpine.com • Rates: $86–195/night

Travelers Rest Lodge • (406) 226-9143
20987 US-2 E, East Glacier Park
travelersrestlodge.net • Rates: $129–159

East Glacier Motel • (406) 226-5593
1107 US-49, East Glacier Park • Rates: $71+

Bison Creek Ranch • (406) 226-4482
20722 US-2 W, East Glacier Park
bisoncreekranch.com • Rates: $84–114

St Mary-Glacier Park KOA • (406) 732-4122
106 W Shore Dr, St. Mary

Izaak Walton Inn • (406) 888-5700
290 Izaak Walton Inn Rd, Essex
izaakwaltoninn.com • Rates: $129–299

Glacier Haven Inn • (406) 888-5720
14305 US-2 E, Essex • glacierhaveninn.com

St Mary Lodge & Resort • (406) 732-4431
US-89 and GTSR, Saint Mary
stmarylodgeandresort.com • Rates: $99–385

Duck Lake Lodge • (406) 338-5770
3215 Duck Lake Rd, Babb
ducklakelodge.com

West of Glacier National Park

Belton Chalet and Lodge • (406) 888-5000
12575 US-2 E, West Glacier
beltonchalet.com • Rates: $115–335

Glacier Highland Motel • (406) 888-5427
US-2 E, West Glacier • glacierhighland.com

Glacier Guides Lodge • (406) 387-5555
120 Highline Blvd, West Glacier
glacierguides.com • Rates: $168–224

Vista Motel • (406) 888-5311
12340 US-2 E, West Glacier
glaciervistamotel.com • Rates: $115–165

Great Northern Resort • (800) 735-7897
12127 US-E, West Glacier
greatnorthernresort.com • Chalets: $315–345

The Great Bear Inn • (406) 250-4577
5672 Blankenship Rd, West Glacier
thegreatbearinn.com • Cabins: $345–385

Moccasin Lodge • (406) 888-5545
US-2 E , West Glacier

Glacier Wilderness Resort • (406) 888-5664
163 US-2 E, West Glacier
glacierwildernessresort.com • Cabins: $250–295

San-Suz-Ed Trailer Park • (406) 387-5280
11505 US-2 E, West Glacier
sansuzedrvpark.com • Rates: $34–95

Glaciers' Mountain Resort • (406) 387-5712
1385 Old Hwy 2, Coram, Montana 59913

Mini Golden Inns Motel • (406) 387-4313
8955 US-2 E, Hungry Horse, MT 59919
hungryhorselodging.com • Rates: $118–136

Historic Tamarack Lodge & Cabins
9549 US-2 E, Hungry Horse • (406) 387-4420
historictamaracklodge.com • Rates: $100–192

Meadow Lake Resort • (406) 892-8700
100 Saint Andrews Dr, Columbia Falls
meadowlake.com

Evergreen Motel • (406) 387-5365
10159 US-2, Coram
evergreenmotelglacier.com • Rates: $65–95

Smoky Bear Ranch B&B • (800) 555-3806
4761 Smokey Bear Ln, Columbia Falls
smokybear.com • Rates: $150–610

Moss Mountain Inn • (406) 387-4605
4655 N Fork Rd, Columbia Falls
mossmountaininn.com • Rates: $180–195

Glacier Chalet • (406) 250-6546
5010 Blankenship Rd, Columbia Falls

Bad Rock B&B • (406) 892-2829
480 Bad Rock Dr, Columbia Falls
badrock.com • Rates: $179–229

Garden Wall Inn • (888) 530-1700
504 Spokane Ave, Whitefish
gardenwallinn.com • Rates: $155–365

North Forty Resort • (406) 862-7740
3765 Mt Hwy 40 W, Columbia Falls
northfortyresort.com • Cabins: $199–269

Lodge At Whitefish Lake • (406) 863-4000
1380 Wisconsin Ave, Whitefish
lodgeatwhitefishlake.com • Rates: $272–442

Julie's Country Manor • (406) 270-4595
1065 K M Ranch Rd, Whitefish
juliescountrymanor.com • Rates: $175–275

Chalet Motel • (406) 862-5581
6430 US-93 S, Whitefish

Bailey's Bed 'N Bale • (406) 270-1603
475 Timber Doodle Ln, Whitefish
montanabednbale.com

Duck Inn Lodge • (406) 862-3825
1305 Columbia Ave, Whitefish
duckinn.com • Rates: $94–250

Cheap Sleep Motel • (406) 862-5515
6400 US-93 S, Whitefish
cheapsleepmotel.com • Rates: $110–120

Hidden Moose Lodge • (406) 862-6516
1735 East Lakeshore Dr, Whitefish
hiddenmooselodge.com • Rates: $99–189

Good Medicine Lodge • (406) 862-5488
537 Wisconsin Ave, Whitefish
goodmedicinelodge.com • Rates: $130–315

Bay Point On the Lake • (406) 420-3003
300 Bay Point Dr, Whitefish
baypoint.org

Festivals

Winterfest • January
Seeley Lake • seeleylakechamber.com

Whitefish Winter Carnival • February
Whitefish • whitefishwintercarnival.com

Race to the Sky Sled Dog Race • February
Helena • racetothesky.org

International Wildlife Film Festival • April
Missoula • wildlifefilms.org

Lewis & Clark Festival • June
Great Falls • lewisandclarkfoundation.org

North American Indian Days • July
Browning • blackfeetnation.com

Libby Nordicfest • September
Libby • libbynordicfest.org

Arts in the Park • July
Kalispell • hockadaymuseum.org

Montana Quilt Show • August
Eureka • eurekaquiltshow.com

Glacier Jazz Stampede • October
Kalispell • glacierjazzstampede.com

Coeur d'Alene Resort Holiday Light Show
November–December • coeurdalene.org

Attractions

East of Glacier National Park
Glacier Peaks Casino • (406) 338-2274
416 W Central Ave, Browning
glacierpeakscasino.com

Museum of the Plains Indian • (406) 338-2230
US-89 & US-2, South Browning

Blackfeet Outfitters • (406) 450-8420
Fishing and hunting trips, RV sites available
#10, Hwy 17, Babb • blackfeetoutfitters.com

Rocky Mtn Elk Foundation • (800) 225-5355
5705 Grant Creek Rd, Missoula • rmef.org

Waterton Lakes Nat'l Park • (888) 773-8888
Alberta 5, Alberta T0K2M0, Canada
pc.gc.ca • Entrance Fee: $8/adult

Discovery Ski • (406) 563-2184
180 Discovery Basin Rd, Anaconda
skidiscovery.com • Lift Ticket: $42/adult

Giant Springs State Park • (406) 444-3750
Great Falls

C M Russell Museum • (406) 727-8787
400 13th St N, Great Falls
cmrussell.org • Admission: $9/adult

The Lewis and Clark Interpretive Center
4201 Giant Springs Rd, # 2, Great Falls
fs.usda.gov • (406) 727-8733

Montana State Capitol • 406-444-4789
1301 E 6th Ave, Helena
visit-the-capitol.mt.gov • Tours: Free

Montana Hist. Society • (406) 444-2694
225 N Roberts, Helena
mhs.mt.gov • Admission: $5/adult

Cathedral of Saint Helena • (406) 442-5825
530 N Ewing St, Helena
sthelenas.org • Tours Available

Last Chance Ranch • (406) 442-2884
Wagon ride dinners, lodging, and music
2884 Grizzly Gulch Dr, Helena
lastchanceranch.biz

Mount Helena Park • Helena, MT

Holter Museum of Art • (406) 442-6400
12 East Lawrence St, Helena
holtermuseum.org

Great Northern Carousel • (406) 457-5353
989 Carousel Way, Helena • gncarousel.com

West of Glacier National Park
Great Northern Whitewater • (406) 387-5340
Lodging, rafting, fishing, and kayaking
greatnorthernresort.com

Wild River Adventures • (406) 387-9453
Rafting, trail rides, and fishing • riverwild.com

Glacier Outdoor Center • (800) 235-6781
Lodging, rafting, and fishing
12400 US-2 E, West Glacier • glacierraftco.com

Glacier Guides & Raft • (800) 521-7238
Lodging, hiking, fishing, and rafting
11970 US-2 E, West Glacier • glacierguides.com

Glacier Heli-Tours • (406) 387-4141
Explore the park from above for stunning aerial imagery like the shot of Kennedy Lake above
12205 US-2 E, West Glacier

Kruger Helicop-Tours • (406) 387-4565
11892 US-2 E, West Glacier

Swan Mountain Outfitters
Guided hunting, fishing and pack trips, and horseback and wagon rides
Apgar Corral, Coram • (406) 888-5010
swanmountainoutfitters.com

Amazing Fun Center • (406) 387-5902
Maze, bumper cars, go-carts, and mini-golf
10265 US-2 E, Coram
amazingfuncenter.com

Rocky Mountain Nature Co • (406) 387-4079
111 Hungry Horse Blvd, Hungry Horse
rockymountainnatureco.com

Meadow Lake Golf Course • (406) 892-2111
100 Saint Andrews Dr, Columbia Falls
meadowlakegolf.com • Rates: $68/18 holes

Glacier View Golf Course • (406) 888-5471
640 River Bend Dr, Columbia Falls
glacierviewgolf.com • Rates: $32/18 holes

House of Mystery • (406) 892-1210
7800 US-2 E, Columbia Falls
montanavortex.com • Admission: $10/adult

Big Sky Waterpark • (406) 892-5025
7211 US-2 E, Columbia Falls
bigskywp.com • Admission: $27/adult

Glacier Lanes & Casino • (406) 892-5858
307 Nucleus Ave, Columbia Falls

Great Northern Llama Co
600 Blackmer Ln, Columbia Falls
gnllama.com • (406) 755-9044

J & L RV Rentals • (406) 892-7666
5410 US-2 W, Columbia Falls
jandlsnowmobile.com • *Tours & Rental*

Glacier Park Boat • (406) 257-2426
Boat tours, rentals, and guided hikes
glacierparkboats.com

Winter Wonderland Sports • (406) 881-2525
162 Bell St, Olney • winterwonderlandsports.com

Flathead National Forest • (406) 758-5200
650 Wolfpack Way, Kalispell • fs.usda.gov

Conrad Mansion • (406) 755-2166
330 Woodland Ave, Kalispell
conradmansion.com • Tours: $8–15/adult

Signature Theatres • (406) 752-7804
185 Hutton Ranch Rd, Kalispell

Best Bet Casino • (406) 862-2949
6588 US-93 S, Whitefish

Dog Sled Adventures • (406) 881-2275
8400 US-93 N, Whitefish
dogsledadventuresmontana.com

Glacier Cyclery & Nordic • (406) 862-6446
326 2nd St E, Whitefish
glaciercyclery.com • *Rentals available*

Winter Woods Dog Sled Tours • (406) 862-7232
242 Lupfer Ave, Whitefish

Whitefish Theatre Co • (406) 862-5371
1 Central Ave, Whitefish
whitefishtheatreco.org

Mountain Cinema • (406) 862-3130
6475 US-93 S, Whitefish

Whitefish Mtn Resort • (877) 754-3474
3910 Big Mtn Rd, Whitefish
skiwhitefish.com • Lift Ticket: $73/adult

Bar W Guest Ranch • (406) 863-9099
2875 US-93 W, Whitefish
thebarw.com • *Excellent dude ranch*

Black Star Brewery • (406) 863-1000
2 Central Ave, Whitefish
greatnorthernbrewing.com • Summer Tours

Daly Mansion • (406) 363-6004
251 Eastside Hwy, Hamilton
dalymansion.org • Tours: $9/adult

St Ignatius Mission • (406) 745-2768
300 Beartrack Ave, St. Ignatius
stignatiusmt.com

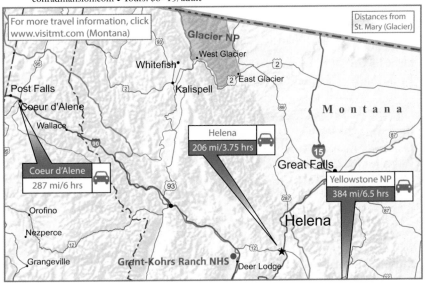

For more travel information, click www.visitmt.com (Montana)

Distances from St. Mary (Glacier)

Glacier NP
West Glacier
Whitefish
East Glacier
Kalispell
Post Falls
Coeur d'Alene
Wallace
Montana
Helena
206 mi/3.75 hrs
Great Falls
Coeur d'Alene
287 mi/6 hrs
Yellowstone NP
384 mi/6.5 hrs
Orofino
Helena
Nezperce
Grant-Kohrs Ranch NHS
Deer Lodge
Grangeville

Grand Promenade and Quapaw Bathhouse

Hot Springs

101 Reserve Street
Hot Springs, AR 71901
Phone: (501) 620-6715
Website: nps.gov/hosp

Established: March 4, 1921
Size: 5,550 Acres
Annual Visitors: 1.4 Million
Peak Season: Late Fall
Hiking Trails: 26 Miles

Activities: Baths, Massages, Other Spa Treatments, Hiking, and Museum Tours

Campgrounds: Gulpha Gorge ($10/night, $30/night with hookups)
Backcountry Camping: None

Operational Bathhouses (Bath Rate):
Buckstaff Baths ($33)
Quapaw Baths & Spa ($40)
Park Visitor Center & Museum occupies historic Fordyce Bathhouse

Park Hours: All day, every day (except Bathhouses and Visitor Center)
Entrance Fee: None

Tree-covered mountains, natural hot springs, and ridgeline hiking trails are common ingredients for a national park. Hot Springs possesses these traits, but it's far from your typical park. Mountains crest at 1,400 feet. Mineral hot springs' rich water is collected, monitored, and managed via a complex plumbing system. Trails connect the area's mountains, but the entire network measures just 26 miles, a day of hiking for an industrious individual. So, what attracted Native Americans to this very spot for thousands of years? The answer is hidden underground. In a gap between Hot Springs Mountain and West Mountain, rainwater seeps into the earth at a rate of one foot per year. After some 4,400 years, water has traveled a mile below the surface where it achieves a high temperature, naturally heated by rock under immense pressure. Pressure builds and what took several millennia to flow down now takes one year to return to the surface. Water flowing from the springs today fell as rain when ancient Egyptians were building the pyramids.

The first European to see the springs arrived after an epic journey of his own. It is believed Native Americans led Hernando de Soto to the place they called "Valley of the Vapors" in 1541, after the famed Spanish explorer had sailed half-way around the world. More than a century later, Father Jacques Marquette and Louis Jolliet explored the area and claimed its land for France. Ownership exchanged hands between French and Spanish several times before becoming American territory in 1803 as part of the Louisiana Purchase. Less than one year after the acquisition, President Thomas Jefferson sent a scientific team led by Dr. George Hunter and William Dunbar to explore the region known to them as "the hot springs of Washita." Here they discovered a log cabin and several small huts of canvas and wood, built by visitors who believed in the water's healing properties.

The first baths were nothing more than excavated rock, spanned by wooden planks where bathers sat and soaked their feet in 150°F water. A true log bathhouse wasn't built until 1830. In 1832, prompted by 12 years of requests by Arkansas Territory, President Andrew Jackson signed a law giving the hot springs federal protection as a reservation. This act makes Hot Springs the oldest unit in the national park system, 40 years older than Yellowstone, the world's first national park.

During the early days of government operation, hot springs' water was declared federal property and was subsequently sold to bathhouses. Even with having to pay for their water, the baths of Hot Springs proved profitable and by the late 19th century, facilities on Bathhouse Row rivaled the finest establishments found anywhere in Europe. Opulent structures and rejuvenating waters attracted sports heroes, politicians, and mobsters. From the late 1800s to mid-1900s, Hot Springs became known for organized crime such as gambling, prostitution, and bootlegging. Some of the nation's most infamous gangsters moved in. Al Capone, Frank Costello, and Bugs Moran are just a few who sought refuge at Hot Springs—the original Sin City.

Stephen T. Mather, first director of the National Park Service, remained unfazed by the area's corruption. He was actually quite enthusiastic about the hot springs, largely due to his affinity for rubdowns. Shortly thereafter Mather ordered construction of a new, free bathhouse and persuaded Congress to redesignate the reservation as Hot Springs National Park in 1921. Business on Bathhouse Row waxed and waned over the years. Only one bathhouse has remained in continuous operation, and just two are open today.

Hot Springs is an anomaly among its fellow parks whose calling cards are indescribable natural beauty. It's the smallest national park, formed around a natural resource that's used commercially. And that's exactly what's refreshing about Hot Springs—it's different. Oh, and the baths are nice too.

When to Go
Hot Springs National Park is open all year. If you're passing nearby, it can provide a nice break from the road for a couple hours. Just be warned that summers are often uncomfortably hot and humid. Late fall, when leaves are changing color, is the best time to visit.

Transportation & Airports
Greyhound has a bus station in Hot Springs (1001 Central Ave, Suite D), which is just one mile south of the park on Central Ave. For more information contact Greyhound by calling (800) 231-2222 or clicking greyhound.com.

Hot Springs Memorial Field is located just 4 miles from the park. Little Rock National Airport is located 55 miles to the east, in Little Rock.

Directions
Hot Springs National Park Visitor Center is located at Fordyce Bathhouse (369 Central Ave). Hot Springs is easily accessed via US-70 from the east and west. Visitors arriving from the west should take Exit 70B on US-70 into Hot Springs and follow the signs to the park. From the east, take US-70 to US-70 Business W/E Grand Ave. Turn right onto Spring St. Continue onto Reserve St, then turn right onto Central Ave, which leads to the visitor center.

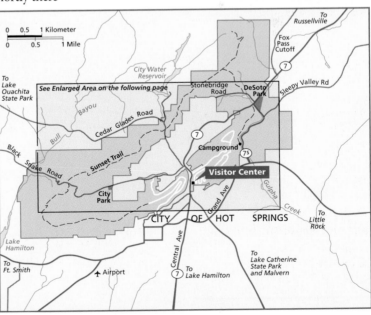

Camping & Lodging

Gulpha Gorge (305 Gorge Road), located off US-70B on the east side of Hot Springs, is the park's only campground. All sites are available on a first-come, first-served basis. Restrooms are located nearby. Showers are not available. Camping fees are $10/night for a standard site and $30/night for a site with electrical, water, and sewer hookups. Sites are not pull-through. There are no park/concessioner operated lodgings within park boundaries, but several options exist in the surrounding Hot Springs area (see page 277 for additional lodging information).

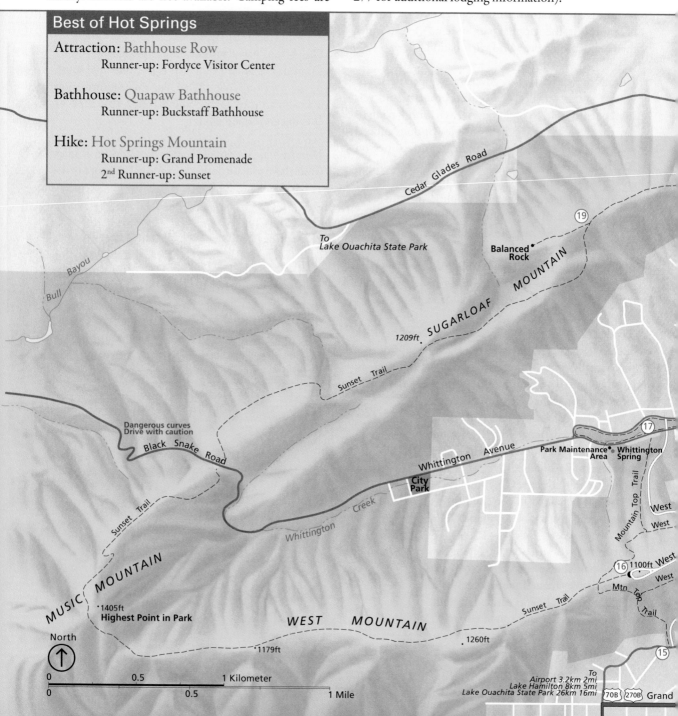

Best of Hot Springs

Attraction: Bathhouse Row
Runner-up: Fordyce Visitor Center

Bathhouse: Quapaw Bathhouse
Runner-up: Buckstaff Bathhouse

Hike: Hot Springs Mountain
Runner-up: Grand Promenade
2nd Runner-up: Sunset

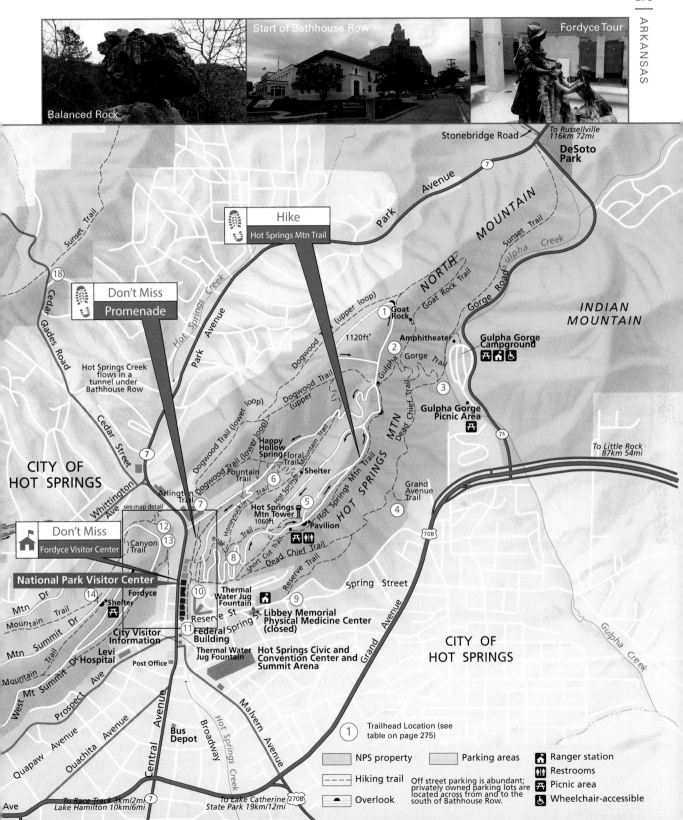

Balanced Rock

Start of Bathhouse Row

Fordyce Tour

Stonebridge Road

To Russellville
116km 72mi

DeSoto
Park

7

Park   Avenue

NORTH   MOUNTAIN

Gulpha   Creek

Sunset   Trail

INDIAN
MOUNTAIN

Hike
Hot Springs Mtn Trail

(upper loop)

1 Goat
Rock

Goat Rock Trail

Gorge Road

Gulpha Gorge
Campground

Don't Miss
Promenade

18

Sunset Trail

Cedar Glades Road

Hot Springs Creek

1120ft

2

Amphitheater

Gorge   Trail

3

Gulpha Gorge
Picnic Area

75

Park   Avenue

Dogwood

Dogwood Trail
(upper

Gulpha

Dead Chief Trail

To Little Rock
87km 54mi

Hot Springs Creek
flows in a
tunnel under
Bathhouse Row

Cedar   Street

7

Dogwood Trail (lower loop)

Dogwood Trail (lower loop)

Happy
Hollow
Spring

Floral
Trail

Mountain Trail

Shelter

HOT   SPRINGS   MTN

Grand
Avenue
Trail

**CITY OF
HOT SPRINGS**

Arlington
Trail

7

Fountain
Trail

6

5

Hot Springs Mtn Trail

Honeysuckle   Trail

Hot Springs
Mtn Tower
1060ft

Pavilion

4

70B

Don't Miss
Fordyce Visitor Center

12

Canyon
Trail

13

Peak   Trail

8

Short Cut Trail

Dead Chief Trail

Reserve Trail

National Park Visitor Center

14

Fordyce

Mtn
Dr

Shelter

10

Thermal
Water Jug
Fountain

9

Spring   Street

Grand   Avenue

**CITY OF
HOT SPRINGS**

Mountain   Trail

Mtn Summit Dr

City Visitor
Information

11

Reserve   St

Libbey Memorial
Physical Medicine Center
(closed)

Gulpha   Creek

Levi
Hospital

Federal
Building

Thermal Water
Jug Fountain

Hot Springs Civic and
Convention Center and
Summit Arena

West Mt Summit Dr

Mountain Summit

Prospect   Ave

Post Office

Quapaw   Avenue

Ouachita   Avenue

Central   Avenue

Broadway

Bus
Depot

Hot Springs Creek

Malvern   Avenue

Ave

To Race Track 3km/2mi
Lake Hamilton 10km/6mi

7

To Lake Catherine 19km/12mi
State Park

270B

1 Trailhead Location (see
table on page 275)

◻ NPS property
◻ Parking areas

- - - Hiking trail
◼ Overlook

Off street parking is abundant;
privately owned parking lots are
located across from and to the
south of Bathhouse Row.

♦ Ranger station
♦ Restrooms
♦ Picnic area
♦ Wheelchair-accessible

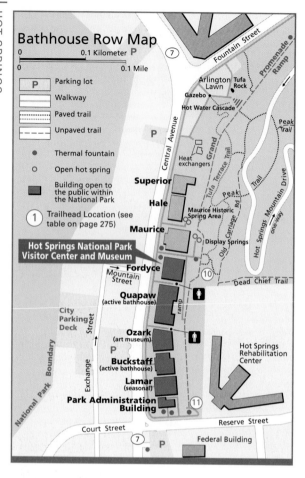

Bathhouse Row Map

0   0.1 Kilometer   P

0   0.1 Mile

P   Parking lot

    Walkway

    Paved trail

    Unpaved trail

●   Thermal fountain

○   Open hot spring

▮   Building open to the public within the National Park

①   Trailhead Location (see table on page 275)

Hot Springs National Park Visitor Center and Museum

Fountain Street

Promenade Ramp

Arlington Lawn   Tufa Rock

Gazebo

Hot Water Cascade

Peak Trail

Central Avenue

Grand

Heat exchangers

Tufa Terrace Trail

Peak Rd. Trail

Hot Springs Mountain Drive one-way

Maurice Historic Spring Area

Old Carriage Rd.

Display Springs

Dead Chief Trail

Superior

Hale

Maurice

Fordyce

Mountain Street

Quapaw (active bathhouse)

ramp

Ozark (art museum)

Buckstaff (active bathhouse)

Lamar (seasonal)

Park Administration Building

City Parking Deck

Exchange Street

National Park Boundary

Court Street

Reserve Street

Federal Building

Hot Springs Rehabilitation Center

7

⑩

⑪

7

visitation. Penicillin and other modern medicines were being prescribed rather than frequent baths in mineral rich water.

In its prime, The Fordyce was the most elegant of all the bathhouses, and today it serves as the park's visitor center and museum. Buckstaff Baths still provides traditional treatment and is the only bathhouse in continuous operation since being established in 1912. Quapaw Baths & Spas recently reopened as a modern spa. It is the first bathhouse to open under the park's new lease program. Like the Quapaw, old bathhouses are being restored by the park for lease. Lamar Bathhouse is a seasonal office and bookstore. Ozark Bathhouse hosts events and community programs. And Superior Bathhouse (superiorbathhouse.com) is now home to a craft brewery.

Buckstaff Baths • (501) 623-2308 • buckstaffbaths.com
Open: March–November • Monday–Saturday,
8am–11:45am & 1:30pm–3pm; Closed Sundays
December–February • Monday–Friday, 7am–11:45am
& 1:30pm–3pm; Saturday, 8am–11:45am
Closed: New Year's Day, Christmas Day, Easter Sunday, July 4, and Thanksgiving Day
Rates: Bath: $33 • Bath/Loofa/Massage: $71
Facials, manicures, and pedicures are available

Quapaw Baths • (501) 609-9822 • quapawbaths.com
Open: Monday, Wednesday, Thursday, Friday, and
Saturday, 10am–6pm; Sunday, 10am–3pm
Rates: Private Bath: $40 (Single)/$45 (Couple) •
Swedish Massage: $50 (25 minutes)/$80 (50 minutes)
• Hot Stone: $95 (50 minutes) • Thermal Pool: $20
Facials, aroma baths, body polishes are available

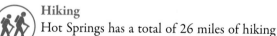

Hiking
Hot Springs has a total of 26 miles of hiking trails. **Sunset Trail** (10+ miles) circles the mountains surrounding Hot Springs, passing the highest point in the park, Music Mountain (1,405 ft). It traverses the park's most remote areas, providing good opportunities to see white-tailed deer and wild turkeys, but it's often broken into smaller sections. The most scenic stretch is the 2.8 miles following Sugarloaf Mountain's ridge. It's located in the northwest corner

Bathhouse Row

The first bathhouses were nothing more than small canvas and lumber structures situated on openings cut into rock. But by the late 19th century, Hot Springs' bathhouses could go toe-to-toe with the best Europe had to offer. Health seekers, wealthy and indigent alike, sought Hot Springs Mountain's rejuvenating waters. Doctors prescribed a strict bathing regimen for all sorts of ailments including rheumatism, paralysis, syphilis, gout, and bunions. Hot Springs reemerged as a popular destination in the 1920s when it was brought into the fold of national parks, and when construction began on a free government bathhouse in 1922. Each successive bathhouse was more extravagant than the last. During Hot Springs' heydays in the mid-1940s as many as 24 bathhouses were open for business at one time. They gave more than one million baths in a single year. In time, medical advancements led to a severe decrease in and can be accessed via Cedar Glades Road or Black Snake Road. Here you'll also find a short spur to **Balanced Rock**, a large novaculite boulder precariously positioned atop another sloped boulder. The remainder of park trails (see below) are less than 2 miles in length, forming very manageable networks on Hot Springs, North, and West Mountains. The brick path known as Grand Promenade is the one trail you shouldn't skip.

Ranger Programs
Outdoor tours of Bathhouse Row are offered periodically during summer. **Tours of Fordyce Bathhouse** are offered daily (staff permitting). Fordyce Bathhouse is the park's visitor center, but it was also the most highly regarded bathhouse on Bathhouse Row during the early 1900s. You'll find a variety of modern and time period bathhouse exhibits inside. The visitor center is open daily from 9am to 5pm, except New Year's Day, Thanksgiving, and Christmas.

For Kids
Free **Junior Ranger** activity booklets are available online and at Hot Springs Visitor Center. Children can earn a Junior Ranger patch by completing part of the booklet or by participating in four activities at a special park event such as nature walks and summer programs.

Hot Springs Hiking Trails (Distances are one-way unless loop)

	Name	Location (# on map)	Length	Difficulty Rating & Notes
Hot Springs & North Mountains	Upper Dogwood	North Mountain Overlook (1)	1.0 mile	M – Ends at Hot Springs Mountain Trail
	Goat Rock	Gulpha Gorge Camp (1, 2)	1.1 miles	M – Up North Mountain to Goat Rock
	Gulpha Gorge	Camp Amphitheater (3)	0.8 mile	S – Intersects Goat Rock and Hot Springs Mtn
	Dead Chief	Camp/Bathhouse Row (3, 10)	1.4 miles	M – Combine with Gulpha Gorge to hike from the campground to Bathhouse Row
	Grand Avenue	Spur Trail (4)	0.2 mile	E – Spur from Dead Chief to Grand Ave
	Hot Springs Mtn - ♿	Hot Springs Mtn Tower (5)	1.7 miles	M – One of the better hiking trails
	Carriage Road	Hot Springs Mtn Tower (5)	0.1 mile	E – Old Carriage Road from Army–Navy Hospital to the summit of Hot Springs Mtn
	Peak	Hot Springs Mtn Tower (5, 10)	0.6 mile	M – Steep climb from Tufa Terrace to Mtn Tower
	Floral	Connector Trail (6)	0.4 mile	M – Connects Dogwood and Honeysuckle
	Fountain	Honeysuckle Trail (6)	528 feet	M – Short and steep trail with concrete steps
	Honeysuckle	Connector Trail (6, 8)	0.5 mile	M – Connects Peak, Fountain, and Floral Trails
	Arlington	Arlington Hotel (7)	0.1 mile	E – Continues to Lower Dogwood Trail
	Lower Dogwood	Arlington Hotel (7)	0.7 mile	M – Steep gravel trail that climbs North Mtn
	Shortcut	Hot Springs Mtn Picnic Area (8)	0.2 mile	M – Connects Dead Chief and Picnic Area
	Reserve	Dead Chief Trail (9)	0.3 mile	M – Shortcut to Gulpha Gorge Campground
	Tufa Terrace	Near Grand Promenade (10)	0.2 mile	E - Pass calcium carbonate (tufa) deposits
	Grand Promenade - ♿	Reserve Street (11)	0.5 mile	E – Brick path through historic Hot Springs
West & Sugarloaf Mtn	Canyon	West Mountain (12)	0.7 mile	M – Once an old carriage road to Bathhouse Row
	Oak	Mountain Street (13)	1.0 mile	M – Intersects Canyon Trail (13)
	West Mountain	West Mtn Summit Drive (14)	1.2 mile	M –Trail loops around the road
	Mountain Top	Whittington/Prospect Ave (15, 17)	1.5 mile	M – Crosses West Mountain and Sunset Trails
	Sunset	West Mtn Summit Drive/ Cedar Glades Rd (16, 18)	10+ miles	M – Passes Ricks Pond and varied terrain along the park's longest trail
	Whittington	Whittington Park (17)	1.2 miles	E – Loop trail with unmaintained jogging path
	Balanced Rock Spur	Spur Trail (19)	0.2 mile	E – Spur from Sunset, leading to a balanced rock
	Fordyce Peak Spur	Spur Trail (off map)	1.5 miles	M – Spur from Sunset Trail to Fordyce Peak

Difficulty Ratings: E = Easy, M = Moderate, S = Strenuous

Display spring along Bathhouse Row

Flora & Fauna

Hot Springs is the smallest national park, and unlike most, it is set in an urban environment. A portion of the Ouachita Mountain Range, including Hot Spring Mountain, is protected by the park. Here you'll find bats, rodents, and other small mammals typical of the region. When exploring the area near the bathhouses, you'll probably only encounter squirrels and a few of the park's 100+ species of native birds. In more remote regions northwest of Bathhouse Row, you may encounter wild turkeys, deer, opossum, gray fox, coyote, or nine-banded armadillo. Forested mountain slopes are dominated by oak and hickory. Pines cover the southern slope. In all, there are more than 300 acres of old growth forests consisting of shortleaf pine, blackjack oak, and white oak; many of the trees are over 130 years old, and a few exceed 200 years of age.

Pets

Pets are allowed on trails and in the campground, but must be kept on a leash no more than six feet in length at all times. Pets, with the exception of service animals, are not allowed in the visitor center or other park buildings.

Accessibility

The visitor center is wheelchair accessible and has a wheelchair available for loan. There is one wheelchair-accessible campsite at Gulpha Gorge Campground.

Weather

Arkansas summers are what visitors need to be prepared for. They are extremely hot and humid. Standing in the Arkansas heat can feel an awful lot like a steaming hot bath. Average high temperatures in July and August reach the mid-90s°F. Fall and spring are mild. Winter is comfortable with average highs in the 50s°F and lows around freezing.

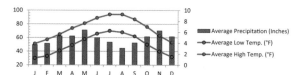

Vacation Planner

Hot Springs isn't the sort of park you should drive several hours out of your way to visit. But, if you're passing nearby and have been in the driver's seat too long, it's a good place to get out and stretch a few kinks out of your back (or grab a beer at Superior Bathhouse). Just like the olden days, a **Hot Springs' bath** (page 274) might be just what the doctor ordered. If you do visit the park, it's pretty easy to knock out the main attractions in a couple hours. There is one developed **campground** (page 272) within park boundaries, but no lodging facilities. Nearby dining, grocery stores, lodging, festivals, and attractions are listed on page 277.

Day 1: Begin at the **visitor center**, located on Bathhouse Row in Fordyce Bathhouse. Here you'll find a museum offering several historical exhibits, and a short introductory film is played upon request. You may have the chance to join a park ranger on a tour of the building. It's highly recommended, so tag along if you can. Once you're finished at the visitor center, head back outside to take a look around Bathhouse Row. Stop in for a bath or massage if that's your sort of thing. Regardless of your bathing proclivities, head behind the Row to walk the **Promenade**. Continue east into the park's modest network of trails and hike to the tower on top of **Hot Springs Mountain** (you can also drive here). For $7/adult and $4/child, you can go to its top for some of the best views of Hot Springs. (The tower is not operated by the National Park Service and is best on a clear day. Also note that there's an overlook on Hot Springs Mountain Drive with similar views.)

Dining

Café 1217 • (501) 318-1094
1217 Malvern Ave, # B, Hot Springs
cafe1217.net • Entrée: $7–9

Rolandos Restaurante • (501) 318-6054
210 Central Ave, Hot Springs
rolandosrestaurante.com

Pancake Shop • (501) 624-5720
216 Central Ave, Hot Springs
pancakeshop.com

McClard's Bar-B-Q • (501) 623-9665
505 Albert Pike Rd, Hot Springs • mcclards.com

Bleu Monkey Grill • (501) 520-4800
4263 Central Ave, Hot Springs
bleumonkeygrill.com • Entrée: $11–22

Taco Mama • (501) 624-6262
1209 Malvern Ave, Hot Springs
tacomama.net

Colonial Pancake & Waffle House
111 Central Ave, Hot Springs • (501) 624-9273

Grocery Stores

Walmart Supercenter • (501) 624-2498
1601 Albert Pike Blvd, Hot Springs

Kroger • (501) 623-3340
215 Airport Rd, Hot Springs

Lodging

Arlington Resort Hotel & Spa • (501) 623-7771
*Sleep in the suites that housed Al Capone, Ronald
Reagan, Bill Clinton, or Smarty Jones*
239 Central Ave, Hot Springs
arlingtonhotel.com • Rates: $99–395

Wildwood 1884 B&B • (501) 624-4267
808 Park Ave, Hot Springs
wildwood1884.com • Rates: $139–199

Alpine Inn • (501) 624-9164
741 Park Ave, Hot Springs
alpineinnhotsprings.com • Rates: $65–95

1890 Williams House Inn • (501) 624-4275
420 Quapaw Ave, Hot Springs
1890williamshouse.com • Rates: $169–239

Spring Street Inn • (501) 318-1958
522 Spring St, Hot Springs
springstreetinn.net • Rates: $75–219

Hilltop Manor B&B • (501) 625-7829
2009 Park Ave, Hot Springs
hilltopmanorhotsprings.com • Rates: $170–400

Prospect Place B&B • (501) 772-5050
472 Prospect Ave, Hot Springs
prospectplacebnb.com

Dogwood Manor B&B • (501) 609-0100
906 Malvern Ave, Hot Springs
dogwoodmanorbnb.com • Rates: $99–169

Lookout Point Lakeside Inn • (501) 525-6155
104 Lookout Circle, Hot Springs
lookoutpointinn.com • Rates: $222–412

*Many chain restaurants and hotels can be found
in or nearby Little Rock and Hot Springs.*

Festivals

Riverfest • June
Little Rock • riverfestarkansas.com

Cardboard Boat Races • July
Haber Springs • heber-springs.com

Rodeo of the Ozarks • July
Springdale • rodeooftheozarks.org

Watermelon Festival • August
Hope • hopemelonfest.com

Documentary Film Festival • October
Hot Springs • hsdfi.org

Attractions

Crater of Diamonds State Park • (870) 285-3113
209 State Park Rd, Murfreesboro
craterofdiamondsstatepark.com • Fee: $8/adult

National Park Duck Tours • (501) 321-2911
418 Central Ave, Hot Springs • rideaduck.com

Tussaud Josephine Wax Museum
250 Central Ave, Hot Springs • (501) 623-5836
hotspringswaxmuseum.com

Hot Springs Haunted Tours • (501) 339-3751
430 Central Ave, Hot Springs
hotspringshauntedtours.com • Tickets: $15/adult

Gangster Museum of America
510 Central Ave, Hot Springs • (501) 318-1717
tgmoa.com • Admission: $15/adult

Hot Springs National Park Aquarium
209 Central Ave, Hot Springs • (501) 624-3474

Museum of Contemporary Art
425 Central Ave, Hot Springs • (501) 609-9966
museumofcontemporaryart.com • Admission: $5

Central City 10 Cinemas • (501) 623-1615
909 Higdon Ferry Rd, Hot Springs

Tiny Town Trains • (501) 624-4742
374 Whittington Ave, Hot Springs
tinytowntrains.com • Admission: $5

Arkansas Alligator Farm • (501) 623-6172
847 Whittington Ave, Hot Springs
arkansasalligatorfarm.com • Admission: $9

Pirate's Cove Adventure Golf • (501) 525-9311
4612 Central Ave, Hot Springs

Lake Catherine State Park • (501) 844-4176
1200 Catherine Park Rd, Hot Springs
arkansasstateparks.com

Oaklawn Racing & Gaming • (501) 623-4411
2705 Central Ave, Hot Springs • oaklawn.com

Ritz Theatre • (501) 332-2451
213 S Main St, Malvern • theritzmalvern.com

Lake Ouachita State Park • (501) 767-9366
5451 Mtn Pine Rd, Mtn Pine
arkansasstateparks.com

Little Rock Central HS • (501) 374-1957
2120 Daisy Bates Dr, Little Rock
nps.gov/chsc • Free Admission

Clinton Presidential Library • (501) 374-4242
1200 President Clinton Ave, Little Rock
clintonlibrary.gov • Admission: $10/adult

Heifer Village • (501) 907-8800
1 World Avenue, Little Rock • heifer.org

Arkansas State Capitol • (501) 682-5080
500 Woodlane St, Little Rock

Graceland • (901) 332-3322
3734 Elvis Presley Blvd, Memphis, TN
graceland.com • Tours: $39–80/adult

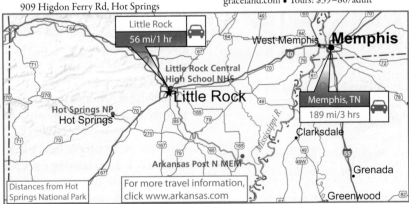

Distances from Hot Springs National Park

For more travel information, click www.arkansas.com

Santa Elena Canyon

Big Bend

PO Box 129
Big Bend National Park, TX 79834
Phone: (432) 477-2251
Website: nps.gov/bibe

Established: June 12, 1944
Size: 801,163 Acres
Annual Visitors: 380,000
Peak Season: March–April
Hiking Trails: 150+ Miles

Activities: Hiking, Bird Watching, Backpacking, Paddling/Floating, Stargazing, and Mountain Biking

Campgrounds: Cottonwood and Chisos Basin
Camping Fee: $14/night
RV Park: Rio Grande Village
RV Fee: $33/night plus $3/person
Backcountry Camping: Permitted*

Park Hours: All day, every day
Entrance Fee: $25/vehicle, $12/individual (foot, bike, etc.)

*A Backcountry Use Permit ($12) is required for overnight stays

"I wish you would take a map of the State showing the counties, put your pencil point on the Rio Grande, just where the Brewster and Presidio County line hit that stream; then draw a line due East and at a distance of sixty miles it will again strike the River. My dream is to make the area south of this line into a park and I shall live to see it done."

– Everett Townsend, 1933

Congress authorized the park in 1935, but it wasn't until 1944 that Everett Townsend's dream came true. Since its establishment, Big Bend has had its fair share of admirers, including geologists, paleontologists, botanists, and bird watchers. But it is seldom visited by the average national park-goer. Taking a look at a county map of Texas like Townsend did, you begin to understand why only the most dedicated visitors reach this scenic wilderness in the southwest corner of Texas. It isn't close to anything, unless you count the United States–Mexico border. Then there's the stigma associated with desert; it's known for being a barren wasteland, not the diverse wonderlands national parks have been made out to be. But the park's faithful continue to return time and time again. They drive dirt roads, hike dusty trails, and run the Rio Grande in canoes and rafts. To them the steep limestone canyons, mountain vistas, and desert wilderness of Big Bend are every bit as wondrous as the western parks. It's just that Big Bend isn't as vibrant. You can't truly understand its size and desolation by looking at a 4" x 6" glossy image. But those willing to make the long journey, understand exactly what Townsend was dreaming about.

Over the years, people have freely crossed the Rio Grande, observing this area's beauty, hunting its wildlife, and seasonally farming its land. Ancient Native American artifacts date back some 9,000 years. In the 16th and 17th centuries, Spanish explorers passed through current park land, crossing the Rio Grande in search of gold, silver, and fertile soil. In the 19th century, Comanche Indians blazed a path across the desert into Mexico where they carried out raids. Today, when visitors enter at Persimmon Gap, they are following a section of the same Comanche Trail. In the early 1900s Mexican settlers lived on both sides of the river. Some tried to eke out a life farming an arid land, while others worked as ranchers.

After a mining settlement was established at Boquillas in 1898, more attention was given to the United States–Mexico border. Mounted inspectors began to patrol the boundary. Everett Ewing Townsend was one of them. He grew up on a ranch, eventually joining Company E Frontier Battalion of the Texas Rangers. While stationed at Big Bend as a U.S. Marshall, Townsend "saw God" and realized the "awesomeness of the region" while tracking a pack of stolen mules through the Chisos Mountains. His mountaintop epiphany inspired a new hobby: lobbying politicians to protect the region as a park. Unsuccessful as a lobbyist, he decided to join the ranks of politicians. Elected to the state legislature after 18 years as a ranchman, his new role allowed time to co-author legislation creating Texas Canyons State Park.

Townsend was also instrumental in establishing a CCC camp at Chisos Basin. Many of the area's trails and facilities were constructed by the CCC in the 1930s. Living during the Great Depression was a struggle for everyone, but it was incredibly difficult at Big Bend. There was no electricity, they had few reliable water sources, roads were not paved, and the nearest telephone was 100 miles away. But the CCC managed, completing much of the present-day infrastructure, setting the stage for establishment of Big Bend National Park in 1944. Townsend was eventually appointed as its first commissioner. Today, he's remembered as the "Father of Big Bend" and forever recognized thanks to Townsend Point (7,580 ft), the second highest peak in the Chisos Mountains and site of his epiphany. Many of today's guests share the same fervor as Everett Townsend. They travel great distances to reach a barren, but uniquely beautiful region. Beauty only witnessed by those willing to make the trip to Rio Grande's Big Bend.

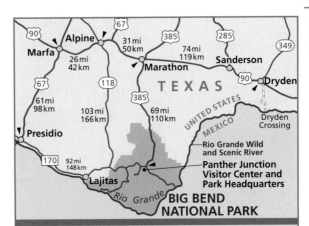

When to Go
The park is open all year, but most visitors come to Big Bend between October and April when weather is comfortable. Although remote, things do get pretty busy around holidays and spring break (late March/early April). Summer can be unbearable, with high temperatures frequently surpassing the century mark. Thunderstorms, overcast skies, and high elevations can make for a more enjoyable climate than you might expect, but it's still very, very hot in summer.

Transportation & Airports
Public transportation does not serve Big Bend due to its extreme isolation. However, Amtrak (800.872.7245, amtrak.com) and Greyhound (800.231.2222, greyhound.com) provide service to Alpine, TX (100 miles from park headquarters). Car rental is available in Alpine.

The closest airports are Midland International (MAF) in Midland, TX (223 miles from the park) and El Paso International (ELP) in El Paso, TX (315 miles from the park). Car rental is available at each destination.

Directions
Big Bend is located in southwestern Texas on the U.S.–Mexico border. Arriving from the east via I-10, the park is 125 miles south from Fort Stockton on US-385. Arriving from the west via I-10, the park is 197 miles south from Van Horn via US-90 and US-385. Due to the area's remote nature, be sure to have plenty of food, and water (although there is a gas station near Panther Junction).

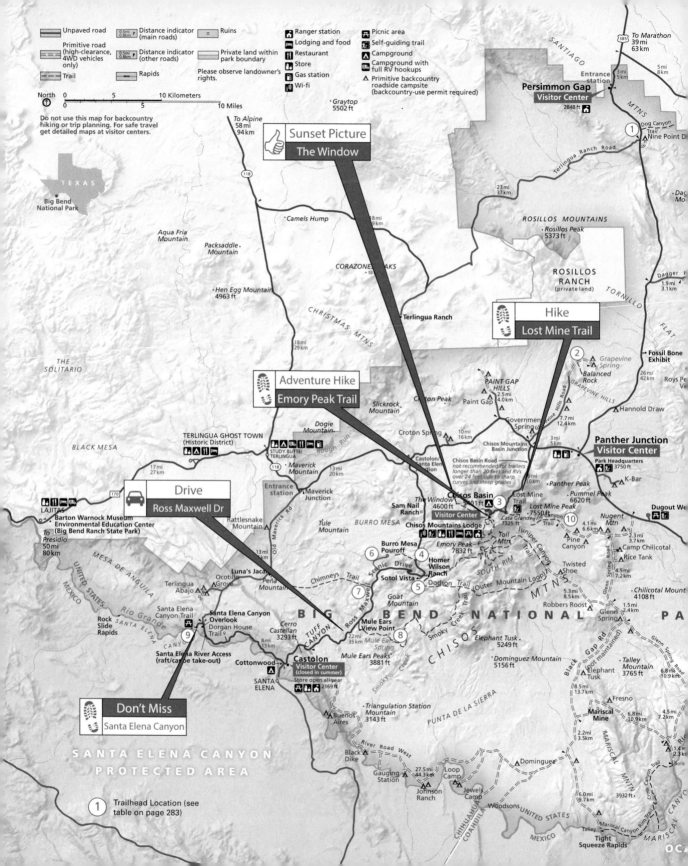

Map Legend

Unpaved road
Primitive road (high-clearance, 4WD vehicles only)
Trail

Distance indicator (main roads) 0.5mi / 0.8km
Distance indicator (other roads) 0.5mi / 0.8km
Rapids

Ruins
Private land within park boundary. Please observe landowner's rights.

Ranger station
Lodging and food
Restaurant
Store
Gas station
Wi-fi

Picnic area
Self-guiding trail
Campground
Campground with full RV hookups
Primitive backcountry roadside campsite (backcountry-use permit required)

North
0 — 5 — 10 Kilometers
0 — 5 — 10 Miles

Do not use this map for backcountry hiking or trip planning. For safe travel get detailed maps at visitor centers.

TEXAS
Big Bend National Park

Sunset Picture
The Window

Hike
Lost Mine Trail

Adventure Hike
Emory Peak Trail

Drive
Ross Maxwell Dr

Don't Miss
Santa Elena Canyon

Graytop 5502 ft

To Alpine 58 mi / 94 km

To Marathon 39 mi / 63 km

Persimmon Gap
Visitor Center
2848 ft

Dog Canyon
Nine Point D

Entrance station 3 mi / 5 km
5 mi / 8 km

SANTIAGO MTNS

Camels Hump

Aqua Fria Mountain

Packsaddle Mountain

Hen Egg Mountain 4963 ft

CORAZONE PEAKS

Terlingua Ranch

ROSILLOS MOUNTAINS
Rosillos Peak 5373 ft

ROSILLOS RANCH (private land)

TORNILLO FLAT

Dagger F
1.9 mi / 3.1 km

Terlingua Ranch Road
23 mi / 37 km

THE SOLITARIO

CHRISTMAS MTNS
8 mi / 9 km
18 mi / 29 km

Grapevine Spring
Balanced Rock
2
Fossil Bone Exhibit
26 mi / 42 km
Roys P Vi

GRAPEVINE HILLS

Slickrock Mountain

Dogie Mountain

Croton Peak

PAINT GAP HILLS 2.5 mi / 4.0 km
Paint Gap

Government Springs
7.7 mi / 12.4 km

Hannold Draw

Dugout We

TERLINGUA GHOST TOWN (Historic District)

STUDY BUTTE/ TERLINGUA

BLACK MESA

Croton Spring
10 mi / 16 km

Chisos Mountains Basin Junction
3 mi / 5 km

Panther Junction
Visitor Center
Park Headquarters 3750 ft

Panther Peak
K-Bar

Maverick Mountain

Maverick Junction

13 mi / 20 km

Castolon/ Santa Elena Junction

Chisos Basin Road not recommended for trailers longer than 20 feet and RVs over 24 feet due to sharp curves and steep grades
5 mi / 10 km

LAJITAS
Barton Warnock Museum Environmental Education Center (Big Bend Ranch State Park)
17 mi / 27 km

To Presidio 50 mi / 80 km

Entrance station

Rattlesnake Mountain

Sam Nail Ranch

The Window 4600 ft
Chisos Basin 5401 ft
3
Visitor Center
Chisos Mountains Lodge

Lost Mine Trail
Lost Mine Peak 7550 ft
10

Casa Grande 7325 ft

Pummel Peak 6620 ft

Pine Canyon
4.1 mi / 6.6 km

Nugent Mtn

2.3 mi / 3.7 km
Camp Chilicotal
Rice Tank

Tule Mountain

BURRO MESA

Emory Peak 7832 ft

Toll Mtn

Homer Wilson Ranch
4

Burro Mesa Pouroff
6

Sotol Vista
5

Ocotillo Grove

Luna's Jacal

Pena Mountain

13 mi / 20 km

Chimneys Trail

Dodson Trail

Outer Mountain Loop

SOUTH RIM

Twisted Shoe
4.5 mi / 7.2 km
Chilicotal Mount 4108 ft
Robbers Roost
1.5 mi / 2.4 km
Glenn Spring

MESA DE ANGUILLA

UNITED STATES
MEXICO

Rio Grande

Rock Slide Rapids

Terlingua Abajo

Santa Elena Canyon Trail

Santa Elena Canyon Overlook
Dorgan House

Cerro Castellan 3293 ft

Goat Mountain

Mule Ears View Point
8

Mule Ears Spring

Mule Ears Peaks 3881 ft

CHISOS MTNS

BIG BEND NATIONAL PARK

Elephant Tusk 5249 ft

Dominguez Mountain 5156 ft

Talley Mountain 3765 ft
6.8 mi / 10.9 km

Black Gap Rd (not maintained)

Glenn Spring Road

Elephant Tusk
8.5 mi / 13.7 km

Fresno

Mariscal Mine
6.8 mi / 10.9 km
4.5 mi / 7.2 km

22 mi / 35 km

7

TUFF CANYON

Santa Elena River Access (raft/canoe take-out)
9

Castolon
Visitor Center (closed in summer)
Store open all year
2169 ft

SANTA ELENA

Cottonwood

Buenos Aires

Triangulation Station Mountain 3143 ft

PUNTA DE LA SIERRA

Smoky Creek

River Road West

Black Dike

Gauging Station

27.5 mi / 44.3 km

Loop Camp

Johnson Ranch

Jewels Camp

Dominguez

Woodsons

UNITED STATES
MEXICO

CHIHUAHUA
COAHUILA

Talley

Tight Squeeze Rapids

MARISCAL MTN

2.2 mi / 3.5 km

6.0 mi / 9.7 km
3932 ft

Mariscal Canyon Rim Trail

Cross Canyon Trail

1.4 mi / 2.3 km

Solis

6.8 mi / 10.9 km

MARISCAL CANYO

SANTA ELENA CANYON PROTECTED AREA

1
Trailhead Location (see table on page 283)

OCA

Hike
Boquillas Canyon Trail

Soak
Hot Springs

A coyote crossing the desert

Visitor Centers

Big Bend has five visitor centers. **Panther Junction Visitor Center** (432.477.2251), located at the intersection of US-385 and TX-118, is open year-round, daily from 8am–5pm, with reduced hours on Christmas Day. **Chisos Basin Visitor Center** is located near Chisos Mountain Lodge. It's also open year-round and operates from 8:30am–4pm. Hours are reduced on Christmas, and it closes from noon until 1pm for lunch every day. **Persimmon Gap Visitor Center**, located where US-385 enters the park, is open year-round from 9am to 4pm. It is the ideal location for a brief orientation before hiking or driving into the backcountry or floating the Rio Grande. **Rio Grande Village** and **Castolon** are the easternmost and westernmost visitor centers, respectively. Both locations are only open during the busy season (November–April). Rio Grande Village is open from 8:30am–4pm. Castolon is open from 10am–4pm, but closed for lunch. Backcountry camping and river use permits, and spigots to fill personal water containers are available at all visitor centers.

Driving

A considerable amount of Big Bend can be explored without leaving your vehicle, thanks to roughly 100 miles of paved roadways suitable for the average motorist. The most scenic stretch is 30-mile **Ross Maxwell Scenic Drive**, which leads to Santa Elena Canyon and Castolon. You'll also find a network of dirt roads; some are improved to the point standard 2WD vehicles traveling at low speeds can pass. Others can only be accessed by high-clearance vehicles. **River Road** loosely follows the Rio Grande and is one of the best off-road drives. Sections of dirt roads may require 4WD and an experienced off-road driver. Always check current road conditions at a visitor center before traveling on them. Gas is available near Panther Junction.

Lodging

Chisos Mountains Lodge (877.386.4383, chisosmountainslodge.com), located high in the Chisos Mountains near the park's center, is the only in-park lodging. If you aren't into camping, it is the only option within a 50 mile radius. Rooms cost $137–144/night. Cottages are available for $159/night. A restaurant is located on-site.

Camping

Big Bend has three established campgrounds. **Cottonwood Campground** is located on Ross Maxwell Scenic Drive near Castolon Historic District and the Mexico–U.S. border. It has 24 sites, pit toilets, and potable water. **Chisos Basin Campground** has 60 sites, running water, and flush toilets. Between November 15 and April 15, 26 of these sites are available for reservation (877.444.6777, recreation.gov). **Rio Grande Village Campground** has 100 sites (43 can be reserved from November 15–April 15), flush toilets, and running water. All campsites listed above are available year-round for $14/night. Rio Grande Village has a 25-site RV Park. It's open year-round, and sites cost $33/night (plus $3/person). These are the only sites with full hookups. Call the RV Park's concessioner at (877) 386-4383 or (432) 477-2293 to make reservations. Rio Grande Village is also the only location with **showers** and **laundry**. Each campground has at least one group site designed to accommodate more than 9 campers. Group sites must be reserved in advance at (877) 444-6777 or recreation.gov.

Backcountry Camping

More than 70 primitive campsites line the park's unpaved backcountry roads. They provide secluded camping with drive-up convenience. There are also a number of designated primitive campsites along hiking trails in the Chisos Mountains. A $12 **backcountry use permit** must be obtained at any visitor center during regular hours of operation in order to spend a night in the backcountry. Backpacking outside the Chisos Mountains requires a zone camping permit. Backpacking is good, but you're somewhat limited since you have to carry ample water with you for most trips. You're also subject to huge differences in temperature between day and night.

Hiking

The Chisos Mountains provide the densest network of trails, allowing visitors to choose between short, flat hikes and long overnight backpacking trips. The 10.5-mile roundtrip hike to the park's highest point, **Emory Peak** (7,832 feet), is a challenging trek. Hikers who complete the journey, which ends with a short completely exposed (and kind of frightening) scramble to the top, are rewarded with sweeping desert panoramas. **South Rim Trail** is longer and just as rewarding. It can be done as a loop by taking **Pinnacles and Laguna Meadows Trails**. All three begin at Chisos Basin Trailhead, located near the Lodge, Basin Store, and visitor center. A really nice shorter hike in the Chisos Mountains is **Lost Mine Trail**. This 4.8-mile trail leads to a promontory overlooking Pine and Juniper Canyons. It's the park's most popular hike. And for good reason, views at the conclusion are exceptional. Trail guides are available at the trailhead for $1.

There are a lot of great locations at Big Bend to watch the sunset. **Rio Grande Village Nature Trail** and **Sotol Vista Overlook** on Ross Maxwell Scenic Drive come to mind. The most noteworthy are viewpoints along **Window View Trail**, also located at Chisos Basin, where you can watch the sun melt into the earth through the V-shaped window carved into the Chisos Mountains by Oak Creek. During the daytime you can hike **Window Trail** across slickrock and into Oak Creek Canyon all the way to the rocky window. When running, you'll cross Oak Creek a few times along the way.

Most visitors explore the Chisos Mountains by foot, but that doesn't mean it's the only place in the park worth hiking. **Santa Elena Canyon and Boquillas Canyon Trails** are located along the Rio Grande on opposite ends of the park. They provide beautiful canyon views, and are as short as the canyons are impressive. If you only have enough time to drive to one, head west and hike Santa Elena Canyon Trail. It's more spectacular. **Grapevine Hills**, leading to a balanced rock, is another good hike (the rock is best scene/photographed in the morning). Somewhat of a novelty (and often crowded), you can hike to Hot Springs accessed via a short trail at the end of Hot Springs Road (also accessible via Hot Springs Canyon Trail).

The Chisos Mountains

Big Bend Hiking Trails (Distances are roundtrip)

	Name	Location (# on map)	Length	Difficulty Rating & Notes
East	Rio Grande Village Nature Trail	Rio Grande Village Camp, Site #18 (12)	0.8 mile	E – Self-guiding trail with great bird-watching opportunities and nice scenery
	Hot Springs Canyon	Daniel's Ranch (12)	6.0 miles	M – Follows the river to the Hot Springs
	Ore Terminal - ⚲	Boquillas Canyon Road (13)	8.0 miles	M – Follows an old tramway that carried ore from Mexican mines
	Marufo Vega	Boquillas Canyon Road (13)	14.0 miles	S – Long loop through mountains to the Rio Grande's banks
	Boquillas Canyon - ⚲	End of Boquillas Canyon Road (14)	1.4 miles	M – Up and down and into the canyon until the canyon's walls close in on the river
North	Dog Canyon & Devil's Den - ⚲	3.5 miles south of Persimmon Gap on the main park road (1)	4.0 miles 5.6 miles	M – After 1.5 miles you head into a wash and meet a junction • A left turn leads to Dog Canyon, a right to Devil's Den
Chisos Mtns	Window View	Near Basin Store (3)	0.3 mile	E – Hike to watch the sunset through "the window"
	Lost Mine - ⚲	Mile 5 of Basin Rd (3)	4.8 miles	M – Steep, popular self-guiding hike
	Window - ⚲	Basin Camp (3)	5.6 miles	M – Awkward scramble across slickrock
	Emory Peak - ⚲	Near Basin Store (3)	10.5 miles	S – Park's highest point and best panoramic views
	South Rim - ⚲	Near Basin Store (3)	12–14.5 miles	S – Extremely long day hike or backpack, taking advantage of campsites along the way
West	Ward Spring	Ross Maxwell Drive (RMD) mile 5.5 (4)	3.6 miles	E – Seldom used trail to volcanic dike and spring
	Red Rocks Canyon (Also Blue Creek)	Homer Wilson Ranch Overlook (5)	3.0 miles	M – Colorful rocks and an old cabin (Trail continues beyond into the Chisos Mountains)
	Upper Burro Mesa Pour-off	RMD mile 6 (6)	3.8 miles	M – Through a wash and two canyons • Requires a bit of scrambling, gorge's floor is mostly sandy
	Chimneys	RMD mile 13 (7)	4.8 miles	M – Long and flat with desert and rock formations
	Mule Ears Spring	RMD mile 15 (8)	3.8 miles	M – Nice views through foothills of the Chisos Mtns
	Santa Elena Canyon - ⚲	End of RMD (9)	1.7 miles	E – Cross Terlingua Creek into the canyon
Backcountry	Grapevine Hills - ⚲	7 miles down Grapevine Hills Rd (2)	2.2 miles	M – Kids' favorite to balanced rock, mostly flat until you must climb into the nearby boulders
	Mariscal Canyon Rim	River Rd/Talley Rd (4)	6.6 miles	M – Great views, requires a high-clearance vehicle
	Pine Canyon	Pine Canyon Rd (10)	4.0 miles	M – The trail leads to a waterfall (after rain), high-clearance vehicle required
	Ernst Tinaja	Old Ore Rd (11)	1.4 miles	High-clearance vehicle required

Difficulty Ratings: E = Easy, M = Moderate, S = Strenuous

Best of Big Bend

Activity: Paddle/Float the Rio Grande
Runner-up: Stargazing

Family Hike: Santa Elena Canyon
Runner-up: Grapevine Hills

Adventure Hike: Emory Peak
Runner-up: Lost Mine

Stargazing

As one of the most isolated national parks, Big Bend is also one of the best locations for stargazing. Far away from busy streets and city lights, stars twinkle and shimmer across the perfectly dark night sky. A night spent here can provide an especially inspiring experience for city-folk accustomed to lights and smog that obscure the stars above. Occasionally, the park offers a **"Starlight, Starbright"** ranger-led evening program providing a more scientific look at things that go twinkle in the night. If you'd rather view the stars on your own, consider spending a night in the backcountry (page 282). Many sites are available for backpackers and motorists (a few require high-clearance and 4WD).

Biking

Cyclists are allowed on all 301 miles of roads. Traffic is typically sparse, but cyclists should use extreme caution as roads, especially Chisos Basin, are steep and winding with narrow shoulders. **Chisos Basin Road** is also the most scenic and strenuous stretch of pavement. Pedal the 10 miles between Panther Junction and Chisos Basin for a nice ride. En route you'll encounter 15% grades, gaining 1,650 feet of elevation before reaching its end. Turn around and enjoy the cruise back to Panther Junction. If you can arrange a shuttle, biking between **Panther Junction** and **Rio Grande Village** is an easy 20-mile ride, most of which is downhill.

Dirt roads are suitable for **mountain bikers. Old Maverick Road** is easiest from north to south and its southern end reaches picturesque Santa Elena Canyon. An out-and-back of Old Maverick Road is 26 miles from Maverick Junction and takes about 3–4 hours. You can make a 48-mile loop by combining Old Maverick Road and Ross Maxwell Drive. Mountain bikers will not find single track. Bikes are not allowed off road or on trails. However, 50 miles of the area's best **single track** are located nearby in Lajitas. See page 322 for a list of outfitters who provide rentals and tours.

Floating & Rafting

For 118 miles the **Rio Grande** serves double duty as Big Bend's southern boundary and natural border between the U.S. and Mexico. Many visitors find a float through Santa Elena Canyon to be the most dramatic way to view Big Bend. Picture yourself winding through 1,500-ft cliffs for 13 miles and it's easy to understand why. Then there's Rock Slide, the canyon's largest rapid, which becomes Class IV whitewater under the right conditions. This section of the Rio Grande is easily accessed with a put-in outside the park at Lajitas and take-out inside the park at Santa Elena Canyon Trail.

If you have your own boat but uninterested in shuttling between put-in and take-out, launch at Santa Elena Canyon Trail and paddle up river for two miles to Fern Canyon before turning around (only possible at low water levels and you may have to walk your kayak through some shallow rapids to the canyon's mouth). Within the park, you'll find **two established campgrounds and 11 designated campsites** along the Rio Grande. To use these sites, you must first obtain a **Backcountry Use Permit** ($12, page 282) from a visitor center. If Big Bend isn't big enough for you, **Rio Grande Wild and Scenic River** extends downstream beyond the park boundary an additional 127 miles.

Big Bend River Tours (800.545.4240, bigbendrivertours.com), Desert Sports (888.989.6900, desertsportstx.com), and Far Flung Outdoor Center (800.839.7238, bigbendfarflung.com) provide **shuttles, equipment, and guided trips.**

Bird Watching

Big Bend possesses a unique location where bird species converge from three distinct geographical regions: eastern U.S., western U.S., and Mexico. It's also located along a major avian migratory route. This combination yields more than 450 documented species of birds, more than any other national park.

Balanced Rock (Grapevine Hills Trail)

Birds are somewhat like humans, residing where they can find food, water, and safe habitat. That makes camping areas like **Cottonwood**, **Chisos Basin**, and **Rio Grande Village** a few of the best birding destinations. However, not all birds follow the vacation patterns of humans. One of the most prized species, the Colima warbler, visits Big Bend during the summer after wintering in Mexico. Fortunately, they're usually spotted in the higher elevations of the Chisos Mountains, where you'll also find a bit of relief from summer's heat. Peregrine falcons, Montezuma quail, flammulated owls, and Lucifer hummingbirds are a few other highly sought after species found in the Chisos Mountains and along the Rio Grande.

Ranger Programs

Park rangers can help satisfy all of your Big Bend curiosities through a series of regularly scheduled interpretive programs. Activities range from walks to talks, campfire programs to stargazing. Whatever you choose you're sure to come away with a better understanding of Big Bend's natural and cultural history. Check the park website or current issue of *The Big Bend Paisano* for an up-to-date schedule of activities. If you're interested in a specific program but can't fit it into your specific vacation plans, you can request a personal guided ranger tour. Private tours are provided for a minimum of four hours at $40/hour.

For Kids

Big Bend's **Junior Ranger Program** is for kids of all ages. Children learn about the park's history and geology as they explore its geography. To participate, pick up a Junior Ranger Activity Booklet at one of the visitor centers or download it from the park website. Upon completion, they will be awarded a certificate and a Junior Ranger patch. Kids also love playing in the sand (there used to be more) at Boquillas Canyon or hiking Grapevine Hills Trail to Balanced Rock.

Flora & Fauna

Big Bend appears to be a lifeless wasteland. It's actually one of the most ecologically diverse areas in the country. There are two major flowering periods: spring and late summer. Flower blooms are dependent on seasonal rain; without enough, the spring bloom is postponed for another year. The summer monsoon is far more dependable. More than 1,200 species of plants, including 60 cactus species, inhabit steep mountain sides, dry desert lands, and relatively lush river floodplains. The park is also home to 11 species of amphibians, 56 species of reptiles, 40 species of fish, 75 species of mammals, 450 species of birds, and 3,600 species of insects. That's more birds, bats, and cacti than all other national parks. Mountain lions, black bear, pig-like javelinas, and coyotes are a few of the big mammals spotted each year.

Pets

As a rule of thumb, pets can only go where your car can. That includes parking areas, roadways, and drive-in campgrounds. They must be kept on a leash no more than six feet in length at all times. Pets are prohibited from all hiking trails and public buildings. Boarding is another possibility. Kennels are available in Alpine, TX at the Veterinary Clinic (432.837.3888) and Small Animal Clinic (432.837.5416).

Final scramble to Emory Peak

Accessibility

All visitor centers are wheelchair accessible. Both Chisos Basin and Rio Grande Village Campgrounds have a fully-accessible campsite. Chisos Mountains Lodge has wheelchair-accessible rooms. Dugout Wells and Persimmon Gap Picnic Areas are fully accessible. Panther Path, Window View Trail, and Rio Grande Village Nature Trail Boardwalk are short, flat, relatively smooth wheelchair-friendly trails. The park's amphitheaters and auditorium, where ranger programs are held, are wheelchair accessible. Check at a visitor center or online for a complete listing of accessible ranger programs.

Weather

Hot! That's really the only way to describe the weather at Big Bend. In winter, average high temperatures reach the 80s°F, but evening lows can drop below freezing. Most guests visit between fall and spring when temperatures are comfortable and humidity is low. During summer, temperatures max out above 110°F. What little rain the park receives usually falls between June and October. A high degree of temperature variance is also found here. Temperature in the high Chisos Mountains is typically 20°F cooler than that along the Rio Grande.

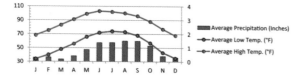

Average Precipitation (Inches)
Average Low Temp. (°F)
Average High Temp. (°F)

Vacation Planner

Big Bend isn't well known among national park enthusiasts. It's hundreds of miles from the nearest big city, interstate, and major airport, nestled deep in southwestern Texas, where it brushes up against Mexico and the Rio Grande. Simply put, it's inconvenient and left to be enjoyed by only its most dedicated fans. If you make the arduous journey, plan on spending a couple of days. **Lodging** and **camping** (page 282) are available at the park. A 2-day itinerary is provided to help plan your Big Bend vacation. Nearby dining, grocery stores, lodging, festivals, and attractions are listed on pages 320–325.

Day 1: First thing you're going to want to do is stop at a visitor center. (**Panther Junction** is generally your best choice.) Browse exhibits. Ask questions. If you're thinking about driving on the park's primitive roads, inquire about current road conditions and accessibility. Be sure to check the schedule of ranger programs for the duration of your stay. For now, let's skip the road to Chisos Mountains, and continue west to **Ross Maxwell Scenic Drive**. Drive to Santa Elena Canyon, stopping along the way wherever you feel the urge to take a closer look. (Sotol Vista Overlook and Mule Ears Viewpoint are nice. Tuff Canyon is kind of cool.) At **Santa Elena**, hike the canyon trail and return to the road. If you have extra time before settling in, hike **Chimneys Trail** or **Grapevine Hills**. Better yet, join a ranger program before you sleep under Big Bend's starry sky.

Day 2: Spend today in the **Chisos Mountains**. Choose between hiking **Emory Peak** or **South Rim Trails**. Better yet, hike both. You can scramble to Emory Peak, and then return to the South Rim before looping back to the trailhead. (Both of these hikes are strenuous and the final 25-ft scramble to the summit of Emory Peak isn't for everyone.) **Lost Mine Trail** is less strenuous and less scary. It's also a good challenge and features some of the best vistas in the park. After your hike (time permitting), travel to the canyon on the other end of the park, **Boquillas Canyon**. This trail will be somewhat underwhelming having already explored Santa Elena Canyon, but children enjoy playing in the sand (which used to be larger dunes).

Santa Elena Canyon

The moon, sand dunes, and Guadalupe Peak

Guadalupe Mountains

400 Pine Canyon Road
Salt Flat, TX 79847
Phone: (915) 828-3251
Website: nps.gov/gumo

Established: September 30, 1972
Size: 86,416 Acres
Annual Visitors: 170,000
Peak Season: March and October
Hiking Trails: 85 Miles

Activities: Hiking, Bird Watching,
Horseback Riding, and Stargazing

Campgrounds: Pine Springs
(South) and Dog Canyon (North)
Camping Fee: $8/night
Backcountry Camping: Permitted*
Lodging: None

Park Hours: All day, every day
Day-use Areas: McKittrick
Canyon, Williams Ranch**, and
Salt Basin Dunes
Entrance Fee: $5/person

*A free Backcountry Use Permit is
required for all overnight stays
**High-clearance 4WD required

Set on the Texas–New Mexico state line, the Guadalupe Mountains are too remote, rugged, and dry to be hospitable. They're also too prominent and mysterious to be ignored. Native Americans and Spaniards brought attention to the area with elaborate stories of gold hidden deep in the mountains. The mountains had stories of their own. Mysteries about the region's underwater past were revealed rock by rock, fossil by fossil. Today, guests visit the park and create their own stories while hiking and camping in these hills of hidden gold and buried fossils.

Also hidden in the mountains is proof of more than 10,000 years of human habitation. The earliest of which were hunter–gatherers who followed game and collected edible vegetation. The only remnants of their existence are projectile points, baskets, pottery, and rock art. Spaniards passed through in the 16th century. They didn't establish settlements, but they left their mark by introducing horses to the Mescalero Apache. Horses proved to be an invaluable asset to the Apache as they tried to protect their land.

In 1858, Pinery Station was constructed near Pine Springs for the Butterfield Overland Mail. Apache considered this development and America's westward expansion an invasion. They retaliated by carrying out raids of nearby settlements and mail stagecoaches. After the Civil War, a new transportation route allowed homesteaders and miners to encroach further on Apache land. This new surge of settlers forced Mescalero Apache to take refuge in the Guadalupe Mountains, which served as their last stronghold. Here they hunted elk, mule deer, and bighorn sheep; they harvested agave (mescal), sotol, and beargrass. Eventually, Lt. H.B. Cushing and a troop of Buffalo Soldiers were ordered to stop the raids on settlements and mail coaches. The small brigade marched into the mountains, destroying two Apache camps. By the 1880s, surviving Mescalero Apache were driven onto reservations.

Many new settlers from the East took up ranching. But most found the land to be rugged and inhospitable. Frijole Ranch, built by the Rader Brothers in 1876, was the first permanent home built in the area. For much of the 20th century, Frijole Ranch remained the area's only major building, serving as community center and regional post office. Today, it has been restored as a museum of local ranching history.

The area's history changed when Wallace Pratt came to the Guadalupe Mountains. Pratt, a petroleum geologist for Humble Oil and Refining Company, visited McKittrick Canyon and fell in love with the lush oasis. He purchased nearly 6,000 acres surrounding the only year-round water source and built two homes: Ship-On-The-Desert near the canyon's mouth, and Pratt Cabin at the confluence of north and south McKittrick Canyons. Pratt and his family enjoyed the summer retreat for two decades before deciding to donate it to the federal government. His donation became the heart of Guadalupe Mountains National Park.

Since Pratt's time in McKittrick Canyon other geologists have been busy studying exposed reefs found in the mountains. The reefs help paint a picture of the area's past, when Texas and New Mexico were covered by a shallow, tropical sea. Algae, sponges, and other aquatic organisms formed a giant reef that looped around the present day Guadalupe, Apache, and Glass Mountains. A visitor walking into McKittrick Canyon today is entering El Capitán Reef from its seaward side.

An evaporated sea. A sanctuary for Apache. A summer retreat. These are the stories of the Guadalupe Mountains' past. Today's story is about a park. A park for the enjoyment of the people. A park that protects the past and ensures the future. A park for each and every one of us.

When to Go
Guadalupe Mountains is open all year, with just two brief periods when the park approaches "busy" status. In March and April, college kids on spring break hit the trails to go backpacking. During this time, parking areas and campgrounds fill early. You may find yourself having to park at Pine Springs Visitor Center to access Pine Springs Trailhead. In October, leaf-peepers flock to McKittrick Canyon to see its colorful foliage. Spring and fall are the most pleasant times of year to visit.

Pine Springs Visitor Center is open daily (except Christmas Day) from 8am–4:30pm. Frijole Ranch is open as staffing allows, from 8am–4:30pm. McKittrick Canyon, Williams Ranch, and Salt Basin Dunes are **day-use areas**. McKittrick Canyon's gate is open daily from 8am–4:30pm (Nov–March), and 8am–6pm the rest of the year. To access Williams Ranch (high-clearance 4WD required), you must obtain a gate key from Pine Springs Visitor Center. Salt Basin Dunes is open from sunrise until 30 minutes after sunset. Dog Canyon (505.981.2418) is open all year, with a small ranger station (open intermittently).

Transportation & Airports
Public transportation is not available to or around the park. The closest major airports are Midland International (MAF) in Midland, TX (219 miles from the park) and El Paso International (ELP) in El Paso, TX (102 miles from the park). Cavern City Air Terminal (CNM) in Carlsbad, NM (66 miles from the park) offers passenger service between Albuquerque International Sunport (ABQ) and Carlsbad, NM. Car rental is available at each destination.

Directions
Guadalupe Mountains National Park is located in West Texas on US-62/180 between Carlsbad, NM (near Carlsbad Caverns National Park, page 296) and El Paso, TX. Dog Canyon is located on the park's north side near the Texas–New Mexico state border. It's about a 120-mile drive from Pine Springs Visitor Center. NM-137 leads directly to Dog Canyon Entrance, Campground, and Ranger Station.

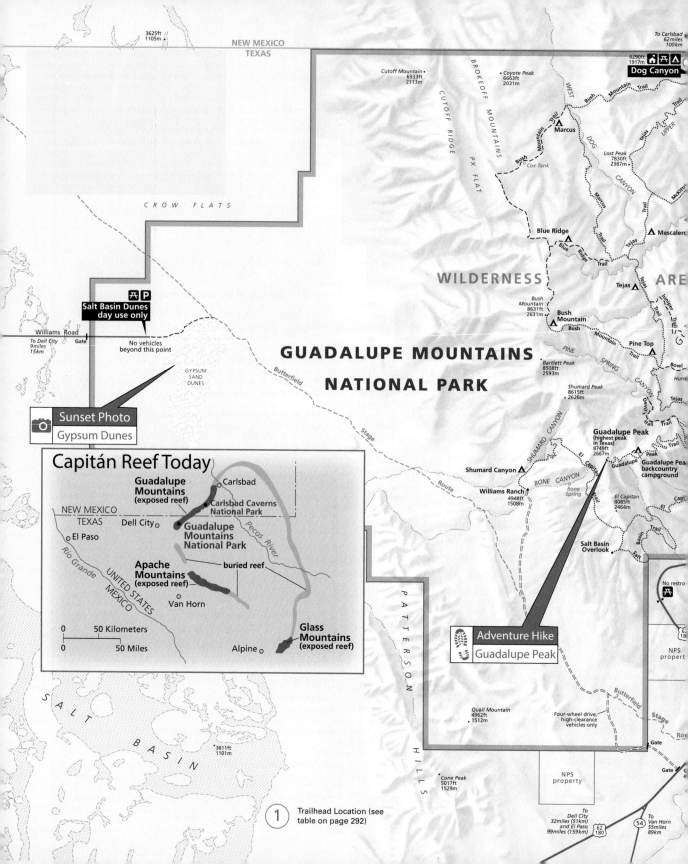

3625ft
1105m

NEW MEXICO
TEXAS

To Carlsbad
62 miles
100km

6290ft
1917m
Dog Canyon

Cutoff Mountain •
6933ft
2113m

• Coyote Peak
6663ft
2031m

BROKEOFF MOUNTAINS

WEST

Bush Mountain Trail

Marcus

CUTOFF RIDGE

PX FLAT

Cox Tank

Bush

DOG

Lost Peak
7830ft
2387m

Marcus

CANYON

Tejas Trail

UPPER

McKittr

C R O W   F L A T S

Blue Ridge ▲

Blue Ridge Trail

Mescalero ▲

WILDERNESS

Tejas Trail

Tejas ▲

A R E

Juniper Trail

⚇P
**Salt Basin Dunes
day use only**

Williams Road

Bush Mountain
8631ft
2631m

Bush Mountain ⚇

Bush Mountain Trail

Pine Top ▲

To Dell City
9miles
15km

Gate

No vehicles
beyond this point

GYPSUM SAND
DUNES

Butterfield

PINE SPRING

Bartlett Peak
8508ft
2593m

Pine Spring

Bowl

Hun

📷 **Sunset Photo**
Gypsum Dunes

Stage

Shumard Peak
8615ft
• 2626m

Tejas Trail

Devils Hall Trail

SHUMARD CANYON

GUADALUPE MOUNTAINS

NATIONAL PARK

Capitán Reef Today

**Guadalupe
Mountains**
(exposed reef)

○ Carlsbad

● Carlsbad Caverns
National Park

Guadalupe Peak
(highest peak
in Texas)
8749ft
2667m ▲

Guadalupe Peak
backcountry
campground

NEW MEXICO
TEXAS

Dell City ○

**Guadalupe
Mountains
National Park**

Route

Shumard Canyon ▲

BONE CANYON

Williams Ranch
4948ft
1508m

Bone
Spring

El Capitan
Trail

El Capitan
8085ft
2464m

Capi

El Paso ○

**Apache
Mountains**
(exposed reef)

buried reef

Pecos River

Guadalupe

No restro

Rio Grande

UNITED STATES
MEXICO

Van Horn •

Salt Basin
Overlook

Salt Basin Trail

⚇

0   50 Kilometers

0   50 Miles

Alpine ○

**Glass
Mountains**
(exposed reef)

P A T T E R S O N

👣 **Adventure Hike**
Guadalupe Peak

6.
18

NPS
propert

S A L T

B A S I N

3611ft
1101m

H I L L S

Quail Mountain
4962ft
• 1512m

Four-wheel drive,
high-clearance
vehicles only

Butterfield

Stage

Ro

Gate

Gate

NPS
property

• Cone Peak
5017ft
1529m

NPS
property

To
Dell City
32miles (51km)
and El Paso
99miles (159km)

62
180

To
Van Horn
55miles
89km

54

① Trailhead Location (see
table on page 292)

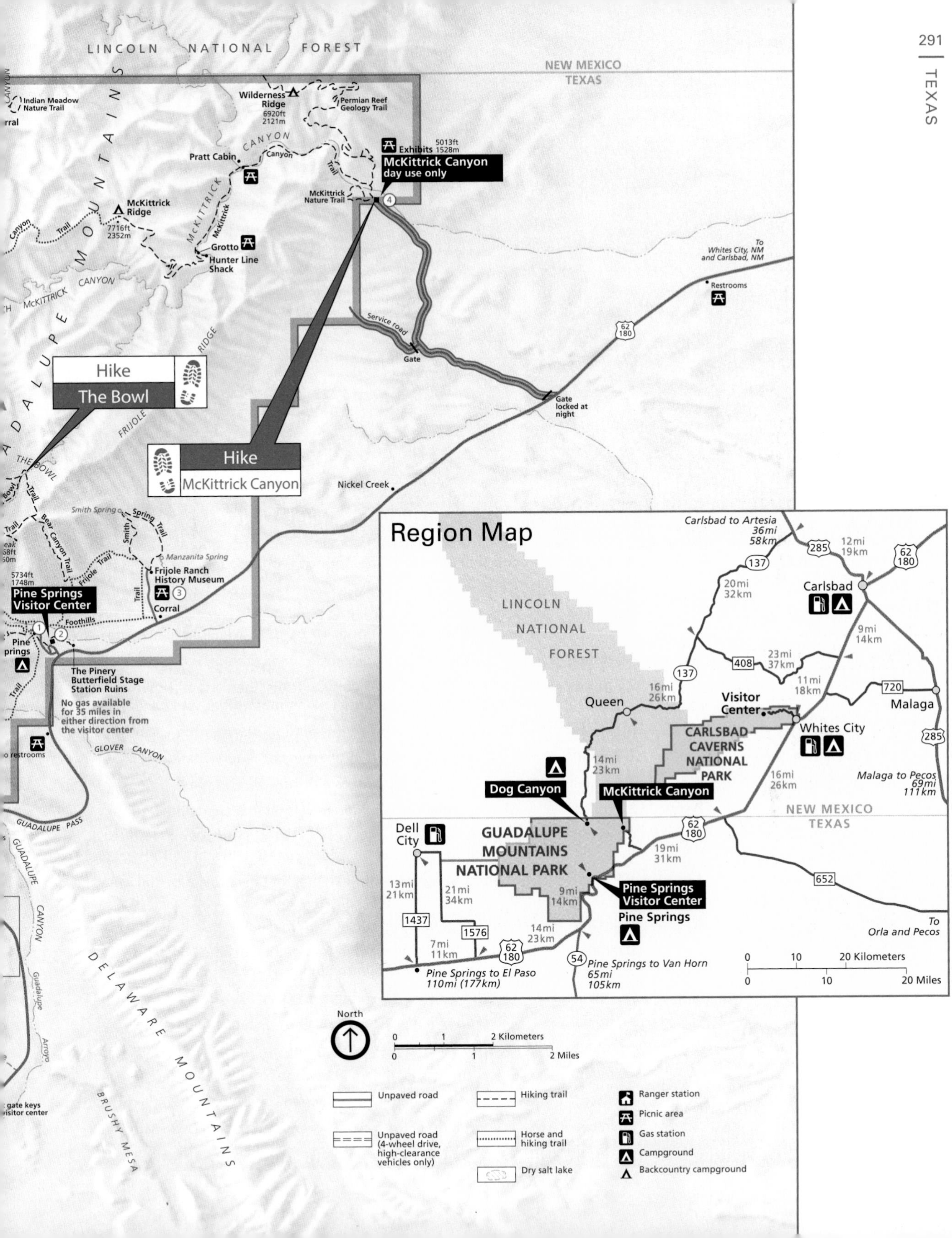

LINCOLN NATIONAL FOREST

NEW MEXICO
TEXAS

Indian Meadow
Nature Trail

Wilderness
Ridge
6920ft
2121m

Permian Reef
Geology Trail

Pratt Cabin

Canyon

Exhibits 5013ft
1528m

McKittrick Canyon
day use only

McKittrick
Ridge
7716ft
2352m

McKittrick
Nature Trail

Grotto

Hunter Line
Shack

Service road

Gate

To
Whites City, NM
and Carlsbad, NM

Restrooms

62
180

Gate
locked at
night

Hike
The Bowl

Hike
McKittrick Canyon

Nickel Creek

Smith Spring

Spring Trail

Manzanita Spring

Frijole Ranch
History Museum

5734ft
1748m

Pine Springs
Visitor Center

Corral

Foothills

Pine
prings

The Pinery
Butterfield Stage
Station Ruins

No gas available
for 35 miles in
either direction from
the visitor center

GLOVER CANYON

o restrooms

GUADALUPE PASS

GUADALUPE
CANYON

DELAWARE MOUNTAINS

BRUSHY MESA

gate keys
visitor center

Region Map

Carlsbad to Artesia
36mi
58km

285

12mi
19km

62
180

137

20mi
32km

Carlsbad

LINCOLN

NATIONAL

FOREST

137

408

23mi
37km

9mi
14km

16mi
26km

11mi
18km

720

Queen

Visitor
Center

Malaga

CARLSBAD
CAVERNS
NATIONAL
PARK

Whites City

14mi
23km

16mi
26km

Malaga to Pecos
69mi
111km

Dog Canyon

McKittrick Canyon

NEW MEXICO
TEXAS

Dell
City

GUADALUPE
MOUNTAINS
NATIONAL
PARK

62
180

19mi
31km

652

Pine Springs
Visitor Center

Pine Springs

13mi
21km

21mi
34km

9mi
14km

1437

7mi
11km

1576

62
180

14mi
23km

54

Pine Springs to Van Horn
65mi
105km

To
Orla and Pecos

Pine Springs to El Paso
110mi (177km)

0   10   20 Kilometers
0   10   20 Miles

North

0   1   2 Kilometers
0   1   2 Miles

	Unpaved road		Hiking trail		Ranger station
	Unpaved road (4-wheel drive, high-clearance vehicles only)		Horse and hiking trail		Picnic area
			Dry salt lake		Gas station
					Campground
					Backcountry campground

Guadalupe Peak

The Grotto (McKittrick Canyon Trail)

Guadalupe Mtns Hiking Trails (Distances are roundtrip unless noted otherwise)

Name	Location (# on map)	Length	Difficulty Rating & Notes
Frijole/Foothills	1, 3	3.7 miles	E – Loop trail between Pine Springs Campground and Frijole Ranch
Devil's Hall - ♨	1	4.2 miles	M – Follow Pine Springs Canyon to a staircase and Devil's Hall
El Capitán/Salt Basin Overlooks	1	11.3 miles	M – A flat hike to the base of El Capitán and an overlook •Trail can be extended an additional 4.7 miles to Williams Ranch site
Guadalupe Peak - ♨	1	8.5 miles	S – Pass El Capitán and exposed cliffs to Texas's highest peak
The Bowl - ♨	1	9.1 miles	S – Follow Frijole and Bear Canyon Trails, then left on Bowl Trail to a beautiful coniferous forest along high ridges and canyons
Tejas	1, 5	11.7 miles	S – One-way distance from Pine Springs to Dog Canyon
The Pinery	2	0.8 mile	E – Paved path to the ruins of Pinery Station
Manzanita Spring	3	0.4 mile	E – Paved path to a desert watering hole
Smith Spring	3	2.3 miles	M – Potential for wildlife viewing at this shady little oasis
McKittrick Canyon - ♨	4	4.8 miles	M – Follow the park's only year-round stream to Pratt Lodge (4.8 miles), continue on to the Grotto, Hunter Cabin, and McKittrick Ridge
McKittrick Canyon Nature Trail	4	0.9 mile	M – Self-guiding trail with exhibits that help describe the area's geology and ecology
Permian Reef - ♨	4	8.4 miles	S – Geology guides for this trail are available at the visitor center
Indian Meadow Nature Loop	5	0.6 mile	E – Nearly level trail • A free trail guide educates hikers on the natural and cultural history of the meadow
Marcus Overlook	5	4.6 miles	M – Dramatic views down into West Dog Canyon via Bush Mtn Tr
Lost Peak	5	6.4 miles	S – Follows Tejas Trail for a short distance to Lost Peak
Bush Mountain	5	12.0 miles	S – One-way distance from Dog Canyon to The Bowl/Tejas Trails
Juniper	N/A	2.0 miles	M – A short connector trail between The Bowl and Tejas Trails
Bear Canyon	N/A	1.0 mile	M – A short connector trail between The Bowl and Frijole Trails
Blue Ridge	N/A	1.5 miles	M – A short connector trail between Marcus and Bush Mtn Trails

Difficulty Ratings: E = Easy, M = Moderate, S = Strenuous

Camping

The park has two established campgrounds. **Pine Springs**, located just off US-62/180 near Pine Springs Visitor Center, has 20 tent sites, 20 RV sites (50-ft maximum length), a stock corral site, and two group sites. **Dog Canyon** is located on the less visited north side of the park. It has 9 tent sites, 4 RV sites, a stock corral site, and one group site. Both campgrounds have potable water, flush toilets and sinks. They do not have showers, hookups, or dump stations. Fires are not permitted. Campsites are available on a first-come, first-served basis for $8/night. Group campsites must be reserved up to 60 days in advance by calling (915) 828-3251 ext. 2124 between 8am and 4:30pm. They accommodate 10–20 people and cost $3 per person per night.

Hiking

Guadalupe Mountains is a great place to introduce yourself to hiking or backpacking. The park is extremely manageable. Hikers can easily trek from Pine Springs (south end) to Dog Canyon (north end) in a day. Campgrounds are abundant and seldom occupied. Best of all, it's very difficult to get lost. Just as the park's southern sentinel, El Capitán, marked the way for homesteaders, Native Americans, and mail coaches, the mountains rising out of the Chihuahuan Desert form an extremely well-defined natural boundary to the east, south, and west. If you've been itching to give backpacking a shot or test your day-hiking limits but are intimidated by the size and wildlife of places like Rocky Mountain or Glacier National Parks, give the Guadalupe Mountains a shot. The main precaution is to carry enough water with you, as there are no reliable water sources in the backcountry. You also must be prepared for the elements. It can get really hot and windy, and many of the trails are completely exposed. Evenings in the mountains are often chilly.

If you're only doing one hike, it should be the 8.5-mile out-and-back to **Guadalupe Peak**, the highest point in Texas. At just 8,749 feet, not everything is bigger in Texas; this would be a molehill in Colorado. However, it's a strenuous hike, gaining more than 3,000 feet in elevation. The trail begins at Pine Springs Campground's RV loop. Make it past the first 1.5 miles and you'll have no trouble completing the hike. This stretch is the steepest section of trail with switchbacks leading up the side of the mountain. Along the way you can sneak a peak of El Capitán from above. Later in the journey, you'll pass Guadalupe Peak Campground and horse-hitching posts before reaching the monument marking its summit.

McKittrick Canyon and Devil's Hall Trails are nice any time of year, but they're particularly popular between late October and early November when big-tooth maple trees lining the canyons turn shades of yellow, orange, and red. **McKittrick Canyon Trail**, located in the park's northeast corner, is often called the best hike in Texas, but be aware that it is a day-use area. A gated entrance opens at 8am and closes at 4:30pm in winter and 6pm in summer. The trail is 4.8 miles (roundtrip) to Pratt Cabin or 6.8 miles to the Grotto (well worth the additional 2 miles). **Devil's Hall** is accessed from Pine Springs Campground's RV loop, which is open 24/7. It is highlighted by a natural rock stairway (Hiker's Staircase) leading into a narrow canyon called Devil's Hall.

Backpacking

Ten backcountry campgrounds (free permit required) are spread out along 85 miles of hiking trails. The closest campground to Pine Springs is found at Guadalupe Peak, just 3.1 miles from Pine Springs Trailhead and parking area. It offers 5 secluded campsites. Pine Top, located on Bush Mountain Trail near the Bowl, is another easy one night backpacking trip. It consists of 8 campsites, and is just 6.2 miles from Pine Springs, providing some of the park's best sunset views. Tejas, Mescalero, McKittrick Ridge, Blue Ridge, Marcus, and Wilderness Ridge are other remote campgrounds in Guadalupe's high country. The only low elevation campground is found on the park's west side at Shumard Canyon, 9.2 miles from Pine Springs Trailhead. There are no reliable water sources in the backcountry, so carry in all the water you'll need.

Stargazing

One of the best ways to enjoy the peaceful calm of a night in the Guadalupe Mountains is to look up. On a cloudless night, whether you're lying in your tent or enjoying campfire conversation, look to the sky to see the galaxy's immensity. From down here looking up, even Guadalupe Mountain, the highest peak in Texas, looks small. Stargazing is best from one of the many backcountry campsites, but the stars twinkle and shine above Pine Springs and Dog Canyon Campgrounds (page 293) as well.

Horseback Riding

More than 50 miles of hiking trails are open to horseback riding. If you want to explore the region on horseback, you'll have to trailer your own stock in; there are no outfitters nearby. Horse corrals are available at Dog Canyon (575.981.2418) and Frijole Ranch (915.828.3251 ext. 2124). Call between 8am and 4:30pm to make a reservation. You are required to camp near your stock at the corrals and a camping fee is charged.

Trails open to stock are denoted on the park map with a dotted line. Easy trails include Foothills Trail, Williams Ranch Road, and Frijole Trail. Experienced riders and animals will want to try Bush Mountain or Tejas Trails, beginning at Dog Canyon. Even though riding is limited to day trips only, visitors with stock must obtain a **free backcountry permit** from Pine Springs Visitor Center or Dog Canyon Ranger Station.

Bird Watching

Birding is another popular activity at Guadalupe Mountains. The best and most easily accessible locations for birders are **Smith Spring Trail**, near **Frijole Ranch**, and **McKittrick Canyon Trail**. These destinations reward guests with sightings of greater roadrunners, northern mockingbirds, and western scrub jays. McKittrick Canyon protects more than 40 species of nesting birds, including ash-throated flycatchers and Cassin's kingbirds in spring and summer. If you'd like to mix a little hiking with your birding, try the 8.5-mile roundtrip hike to the **Bowl**. The trail leads through a relict forest of ponderosa pine and Douglas fir, where you'll have a chance of seeing mountain chickadees, pygmy, white-breasted nuthatches, dark-eyed juncos, hairy woodpeckers, band-tailed pigeons, and red crossbills. If you make the trek in the fall, watch for Townsend's warblers. To see the birds of the high country without having to hike long trails with steep grades, drive around the park to **Dog Canyon** (elevation 6,290 ft).

Ranger Programs

Ranger programs are not offered throughout the year. Typically, programs are held in March, throughout summer, and from late October to early November. These are the best times of year to visit, and ranger programs provide the best activity. Programs vary and depend on staffing, so it is a good idea to check online or at Pine Springs Visitor Center for a current schedule of activities when you arrive.

For Kids

Guadalupe Mountains is a great place for kids' imaginations to run wild. The wealth of fossils has inspired a new **Junior Paleontologist Program**. If your kids are aspiring fossil hunters, stop in at the visitor center for more information or go online to find an activity booklet.

There's also a **Junior Ranger Program** for children. You can find the activity booklet online or at Pine Springs Visitor Center. Complete three activities and your child will earn a certificate and badge. Complete 6 to receive a certificate, badge, and patch. You can substitute hiking a trail, attending a ranger program, or visiting the stage ruins in place of a workbook activity.

Flora & Fauna

The most interesting flora and fauna in the Guadalupe Mountains have been dead for hundreds of millions of years. Ancient calcareous sponges, algae, and other sea organisms were growing on a 400-mile-long horseshoe-shaped reef within an ancient sea once covering much of Texas and New Mexico. After the sea evaporated, the reef was buried in eroded sediment deposited by streams and rivers. Entombed for millions of years, the reef returned to the surface when uplift raised it more than 2 miles. Today, scientists consider the exposed reef at Guadalupe Mountains and nearby Apache and Glass Mountains as one of the finest examples of ancient marine fossil reef on earth.

Still, not all creatures are fossils. Black bear, elk, mountain lions, and over 1,000 species of plants live here.

Pets

Pets are allowed in the park, but must be kept on a leash no more than six feet in length at all times. They are allowed in developed areas (campgrounds, roadways, and parking lots) but are not allowed inside buildings or on hiking trails (with the exception of Pinery Trail).

Accessibility

Pine Springs Visitor Center, Frijole Ranch Museum, and McKittrick Canyon Contact Station are all accessible to individuals in wheelchairs. Pinery Trail and Manzanita Spring Trail (page 292) are paved, mostly flat, and accessible with assistance.

Weather

Weather can change just as abruptly as the Guadalupe range rises out of the Chihuahuan Desert. Summers are hot, but are more comfortable than expected thanks to frequent thunderstorms and high elevation. Evenings in the mountains are cool any time of year. Temperatures are typically pleasant from fall through spring, but snow storms and freezing rain may occur in winter. The most common annoyance from winter to spring is gusting wind.

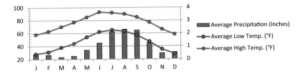

Vacation Planner

Most of Guadalupe Mountains' main attractions can be visited in a day, but a **backpacking expedition** (page 293) is an excellent multi-day adventure (although you'll be limited by the amount of water you can carry). Many visitors aren't even aware of **Dog Canyon**, located on the park's northern boundary near the Texas–New Mexico border. It is worth the side trip, but it will take some gas (120 miles) and time (at least 2 hours) to get there. It's also possible to hike to Dog Canyon via **Tejas or Bush Mountain Trails**. This can be an intimate experience, allowing you and your companions the opportunity to commune with nature undisturbed by sights and sounds of civilization. If you're short on time like most people, here's how to spend a single day at Guadalupe Mountains. Always view a current schedule

Devil's Hall

of **ranger programs**. Join them whenever and wherever you can. Nearby dining, grocery stores, lodging, festivals, and attractions are listed on pages 320–325.

Day 1: Arrive at **McKittrick Canyon** around 8am when the gates open. Shadows cast by riparian woodlands will dance across the canyon floor as the sun rises out of the east. Hike **McKittrick Canyon Trail**. With each step the canyon becomes lusher and greener. It's 6.8 miles roundtrip to the **Grotto** (great picnic spot). Geologists or those interested in geology should scrap the hike up McKittrick Canyon in favor of the 8.4-mile **Permian Reef Trail** (strenuous). Return to US-62/180 and head south/east to **Pine Springs Visitor Center**. Quickly browse the exhibits and slide show. Drive over to Pine Springs Trailhead, located in the campground's RV loop. Individuals looking for a leisurely stroll should take **Devil's Hall Trail**. Those of you interested in a strenuous hike should take the 8.4-mile path to **Guadalupe Peak**. If you want to spend the night and see the stars, think about backpacking to Guadalupe Peak backcountry campground. It's just one mile from the peak and a great place for solitude. The highway pullout just west of the park on US-62/180 is a great place to view El Capitán in the evening.

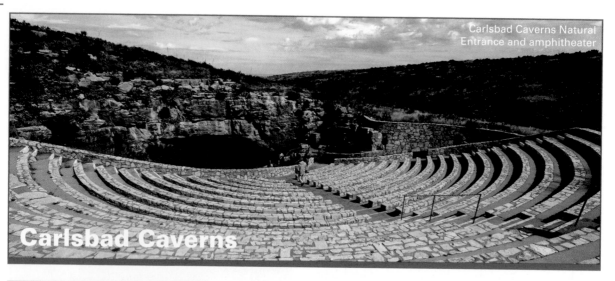

Carlsbad Caverns Natural Entrance and amphitheater

Carlsbad Caverns

3225 National Parks Highway
Carlsbad, NM 88220
Phone: (575) 785-2232
Website: nps.gov/cave

Established: May 14, 1930
Size: 46,766 Acres
Annual Visitors: 450,000
Peak Season: Holiday Weekends
Hiking Trails: 50+ Miles
Self-Guided Cave Trails: 2.5 Miles

Activities: Cave Tours, Hiking,
Stargazing, and Scenic Driving

Campgrounds & Lodging: None
Backcountry Camping: Permitted
in certain areas with a free
Backcountry Use Permit

Park Hours: All day, every day
(Except Thanksgiving, Christmas,
and New Year's Day)
Entrance Fee: $10/person
Free for Children 15 and under
Audio Guide Fee: $5
Cave Tours: $7–$20 (Reservations
recommended)
Cave Tour Duration: 1.5–5.5 hours

Beneath the Guadalupe Mountains lies a magnificent world, a maze of passages and chambers decorated with indescribable rock formations. Soda straws and stalactites pierce the ceiling. Stalagmites rise from the ground. Draperies adorn the sloped walls where water dripped. Clusters of popcorn-like protrusions cover the chambers. Fragile helictites defy gravity as they twist and turn in every direction. At Carlsbad Caverns, Mother Nature, like an eccentric collector, has filled rooms upon rooms with thousands of formations. Every last bit of cave real estate is plastered, ceiling-to-floor, with what is considered the world's most wondrous collection of cave formations.

An ancient reef, visible in areas of Guadalupe Mountains National Park (page 288), made cave formation possible. Some 250 million years ago, the area was covered by a shallow, tropical sea. Changes in climate caused it to evaporate and calcite to precipitate from the water. Uplift raised the mountains and reef nearly two miles, creating many cracks and faults. This newly formed grade and openings allowed rainwater to flow through the limestone substrate. As rainwater seeped through the rock, pressurized hydrogen sulfide-rich water migrated upward from huge reservoirs of oil and gas. Mixing, they formed a sulfuric acid capable of dissolving limestone at a rapid rate. As limestone dissolved from the bottom up, cracks and faults widened, forming large chambers and passages we walk through today. Creation began nearly one million years ago and continues today, one drop of water at a time. As rainwater seeps through the layers of earth above the cave, it absorbs carbon dioxide from the air and soil forming a weak acid. This weak acid is able to dissolve a small amount of limestone and absorb it as calcite. Once the water droplet emerges in the cave, carbon dioxide is released into the air and dissolved calcite precipitates from water. Each droplet deposits its miniscule mineral load. Over hundreds of thousands of years, enough deposits are made to create the otherworldly features you see today while touring Carlsbad Caverns.

Carlsbad truly is one of the sights you need to see to believe. Indeed, the folks in Washington, D.C. didn't believe reports of the elaborate caves until 1923 when the Department of the Interior sent Robert Holley and a photographer paid the cave a visit. Holley described the cave as work of the Divine Creator, invoking "deep conflicting emotions of fear and awe." One year later, President Calvin Coolidge used the power of the Antiquities Act to establish Carlsbad Cave National Monument. In 1928, additional land was added to the monument, and two years later Congress established Carlsbad Caverns National Park, protecting one of America's most unique natural treasures for future generations.

Carlsbad Caverns

Ancient artifacts indicate the area around Carlsbad Caverns has been inhabited for nearly 10,000 years, but very little is known about these early people. Native Americans entered Carlsbad more than 1,000 years ago, but it's unlikely they used the cave for anything more than shelter. They left behind drawings, including an ancient petroglyph near the natural entrance. Exploration of the cave didn't occur until the 1800s, when settlers were drawn to a mysterious cloud (of bats) rising out of the desert each summer night.

It's disputable whether Jim White was first to discover the cave, but after he entered in 1898 as a 16-year-old boy he would become its primary explorer. During his expeditions he named many of the rooms: Big Room (the seventh largest cave chamber in the world), New Mexico Room, King's Palace, Queen's Chamber, Papoose Room, and Green Lake Room. He also named features like Totem Pole, Witch's Finger, Giant Dome, Bottomless Pit, Fairyland, Iceberg Rock, Temple of the Sun, and Rock of the Ages. White offered to take locals on tours, but few

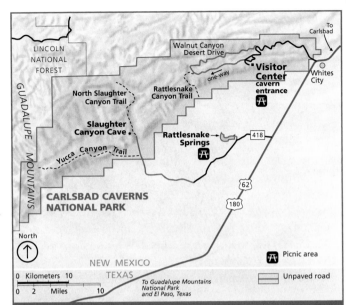

When to Go

Carlsbad Caverns is open every day of the year except Thanksgiving, Christmas, and New Year's Day. Between Memorial Day weekend and Labor Day weekend the **visitor center** is open from 8am–7pm, and the last cavern entry is at 3:30pm via the natural entrance, and 5pm via elevator. For the rest of the year, the visitor center is open from 8am–5pm, the last entry at the natural entrance is 2pm, and the last elevator entry is at 3:30pm.

Unless you like crowds, you'll want to avoid visiting the park on summer holiday weekends. If you are interested in a specific tour, be sure to make advance reservations. Kings Palace and Left Hand Tunnel are the only tours offered daily. Wild Caving tours are only offered on specific days of the week. Dress in layers, because the cave's temperature remains relatively constant throughout the year. The cave is hotter the deeper you go, but temperatures are always cool, ranging from the 50s–60s°F.

Transportation & Airports

Public transportation does not serve Carlsbad Caverns. Greyhound (800.231.2222, greyhound.com) has a bus station in Carlsbad (24 miles from the park's visitor center). Cavern City Air Terminal (CNM) in Carlsbad (23 miles from the visitor center) offers passenger service to and from Albuquerque International Sunport (ABQ). El Paso International (ELP), in El Paso, TX, is a nice alternative (144 miles from the visitor center). Car rental is available at each destination.

Bat flight

Directions

Carlsbad Caverns has one entrance road, NM-7, which runs west from US-62/180 at Whites City. It is 16 miles southwest of Carlsbad, NM and 151 miles northeast of El Paso, TX.

If you're looking to take Slaughter Canyon Cave (tour required) or to hike Yucca or Slaughter Canyon Trails, take US-62/180 south from Carlsbad/Whites City. Head west on County Road 418. From here, follow the signs to the cave parking area and trailheads.

Driving

You can't drive through the cave, but most vehicles can observe the Chihuahuan Desert by driving the 9.5-mile **Walnut Canyon Desert Drive** (also called **Desert Loop Road**). This narrow and twisting one-way gravel loop is not recommended for trailers or RVs, but your typical 2WD vehicle should be able to navigate this seldom traveled road just fine. It also provides access to a few hiking trails.

accepted. One day he crossed paths with a man who was more interested in a different kind of deposit: bat guano. Bat's natural waste is a high quality fertilizer, and as you can imagine, the cave's millions of bats produce an awful lot. Drop by drop, guano piles up kind of like formation of stalagmites, just messier and faster. Jim White started mining guano, bringing each payload out the natural entrance in a bucket via a 170-foot ascent. They even lifted burros in and out to aid production. Guano was packed in gunny-sacks and shipped to citrus groves of California. Unfortunately for them, this industry wasn't very profitable. Companies formed and folded, but Jim White never left.

In 1915, the first photographs of the cave were taken by Ray V. Davis. After seeing pictures of its brilliant formations, individuals who had turned down Jim White's tour offerings were now clamoring to enter. The first tourists made the 170-foot descent via the old "guano bucket." In 1924, members of the National Geographic Society joined White on an extensive exploration of the caverns, bringing along with them even more publicity. The following year a staircase was built, setting the stage for the present-day era of tourism at Carlsbad Caverns. Today, you can enter the cave by descending stairs into the natural entrance or an elevator will drop you off in the Big Room, where you are free to explore the well-lit passages.

Carlsbad Caverns Cave Tours

Tour (Group Size, Age Limit, Offered)	Fee (Adult/Youth)	Length	Notes
King's Palace (Capacity: 55, Age Limit: 4, daily, all year) - 👍	$8/4	1.5 hours	Classic 1-mile tour through several rooms named by Jim White
Left Hand Tunnel (15, 6, daily, late May through mid-August)	$7/3.50	2 hours	Easiest adventure tour • Uneven and slippery surface, lit by NPS-provided lanterns
Lower Cave (12, 12, Mondays, Thursdays & Fridays, June through mid-August) - 👍	$20/10	3 hours	Guests must descend down a 10-ft flowstone using knotted rope • Bring (3) AA batteries and wear hiking boots
Slaughter Canyon Cave (25, 8, Tuesdays & Saturdays, June through mid-August) - 👍	$15/7.50	5.5 hours	Strenuous tour through undeveloped cave • Bring (3) AA batteries, wear hiking boots and long pants
Hall of the White Giant (8, 12, Wednesdays, June through mid-August) - 👍	$20/10	4 hours	Crawling, squeezing, and sliding through narrow openings •You will get dirty • Bring (3) AA batteries and wear hiking boots
Spider Cave (8, 12, Sundays, June through mid-August) - 👍	$20/10	4 hours	Wild caving experience • Bring (3) AA batteries and wear hiking boots

Youth is 4–15 years of age. Senior Access Pass holders pay youth rates. All tours can be reserved in advance at (877) 446-6777 or recreation.gov. Reservations are highly recommended for all tours. Pick up tickets at the visitor center.

Other Caves

Caves are the last terrestrial frontier. They're full of mystery and the unknown, and most have yet to be mapped completely. Bones of Ice Age mammals, such as jaguars, camels, and giant sloths have been found near or in these caves. There are more than 300 caves in the Guadalupe Mountains, about 110 within park boundaries.

Lechuguilla Cave (whose location has not been disclosed by the National Park Service to protect its environment from tourists and spelunkers) has been the caving community's focus since its discovery in 1986. It has already surpassed Carlsbad in depth, size, and variety of cave formations, many of which have never been seen anywhere else in the world. Lechuguilla is more than 138 miles long, the 7th longest cave known to exist in the world and the deepest in the country. Carlsbad Caverns big open rooms feel gigantic, but when all its known passageways are measured, they total just over 30 miles in length, more than 100 fewer than Lechuguilla. It has also replaced Carlsbad Caverns as the world's most beautiful cave. This is just the tip of the iceberg of noteworthy facts about Lechuguilla. Scientists even found microbes capable of producing cancer-destroying enzymes. The cave is restricted to exploratory and scientific groups. However, you can explore Lechuguilla from your living room by watching the fourth episode ("Caves") of the hit BBC documentary series *Planet Earth*.

If you'd like to explore caves other than Carlsbad, a few are open to the public. Park rangers lead general tours of **Slaughter Canyon Cave** and wild tours (think crawling, sliding, and getting dirty) of **Spider Cave**. Additionally, there are more vertical and horizontal caves open to experienced cavers with the proper skills and equipment. These caves can only be accessed with a permit. To schedule a trip, interested parties must download and complete an application (available at the park website). Reservations are made on a first-come, first served basis. All caves open to private parties are of natural significance and should not be treated carelessly. Defacing or causing irreparable damage to any cave will result in its closure. A list of open backcountry caves can be found in the park's backcountry caving brochure (available online).

Crystal Spring Dome, the largest active stalagmite in Carlsbad Caverns

Cave Tours

Carlsbad displays some of the most elaborate cave formations in the world. A little more than 3 miles of paved and lit trails weave through rooms and past fragile features. After paying the entrance fee, you are free to explore two self-guided trails: The Natural Entrance Tour and The Big Room Tour. Audio guides are available for $5. **The Natural Entrance Tour** begins exactly where you would expect, the Natural Entrance. It's 1.25 miles and 800 feet down to the Big Room. Along the way you'll pass Bat Cave, Witch's Finger, and many other features. Once you've reached the Big Room, you can take the elevator back to the surface or continue on the **Big Room self-guiding tour** (also accessible via the elevator from the visitor center). You'll find features named Lion's Tail, Hall of Giants, Bottomless Pit, and Rock of Ages while perusing the Big Room. The 1.25-mile tour is paved and mostly level. Sturdy shoes are recommended for the Natural Entrance Tour, and you should be in decent physical shape without any respiratory problems. Ranger-led Cave Tours are highly recommended. Spider Cave and Hall of the White Giant are **"Wild Caving"** options for the adventurous. **King's Palace Tour** is a popular, easy walk past ornate formations like helictites, draperies, columns, and soda straws. Rangers also give guests a taste of pure darkness during a "blackout." For a less developed cave experience sign up for **Slaughter Canyon Cave Tour**, where you'll see eerie formations like the Klansman.

King's Palace Tour

Bat Flight Program

Tourists aren't the only mammals flocking to Carlsbad Caverns in summer. From mid-April to mid-October, the Bat Cave is home to hundreds of thousands of Mexican free-tailed bats. They leave the safety of the cave at dusk to gorge on insects, returning just before dawn. Evening Bat Programs are offered (weather permitting) when the bats are in residence. Guests fill the amphitheater near the Natural Entrance while a ranger discusses these winged friends. Just as the talk is winding down, a swarm of bats begins their mass exodus to fly about the Chihuahuan Desert in search of food. The exit flight can last anywhere from 20 minutes to 2 hours. Programs are offered beginning in mid-May and they usually start 30–60 minutes before sunset. For the exact time, check at the visitor center or call (575) 785-3012. Cameras (including cell phone cameras) and camcorders may not be used during the Bat Flight Program.

You're going to want a little **bat background information** before you meet Carlsbad's bats face-to-face. First, there's nothing to be afraid of. Bats are not dangerous. In fact, they're amazing little creatures, being the only mammal capable of flight. They also help control the insect population. Carlsbad's Mexican free-tailed bats eat about three tons of insects each night. A single bat can eat as much as half its body weight in a single meal. One of their favorite appetizers is one of our least favorite pests: the mosquito. It has been estimated

that Carlsbad's Mexican free-tailed bat population once counted in the millions, not hundreds of thousands like today. No one knows exactly what caused this dramatic decline, but use of pesticides like DDT and loss of habitat for their prey are likely causes.

Bats that occupy the cave today still live the same interesting bat-life. Days are spent hanging from the ceiling. About 250 and 300 bats huddle together in one square-foot of ceiling space. Nights are spent searching for food. Their reentry at dawn is nearly as impressive as the exit. Bats at Carlsbad are considered a maternity colony, because females seek the cave's safe-haven to give birth. In June, females typically bear just one pup. It is born hairless and clings to the mother or ceiling after birth. The pup remains on the ceiling for 4–5 weeks before its first flight. After summer the pups are mature enough to retreat to warmer climates in Mexico or Central America for winter with the rest of Carlsbad's bat population.

Hiking & Backpacking

The world above Carlsbad Caverns often goes unnoticed by visitors. There are 50+ miles of hiking trails, providing the perfect place to escape the cave-exploring crowds.

Chihuahuan Desert Nature Trail is located at the base of the hill in front of the visitor center's main entrance. It's a paved 0.5-mile loop around historic guano-mining ruins. The trail closes at dawn and dusk when Mexican free-tailed bats (page 300) are occupying the cave.

Adjacent to the park entrance is a dirt road suitable for hiking. This 3.7-mile (one-way) road follows the original path used by miners and burros to haul bat guano in the early 1900s. It ends at Whites City Campground, just beyond the park boundary.

The rest of the trails fan out into the Chihuahuan Desert where water is unavailable and shade is uncommon. Trails are marked by sporadic rock cairns, so hike with a good topographic map and plenty of water.

Juniper Ridge Trail is located on Walnut Canyon Desert Drive (also known as Desert Loop Road/DLR), about one mile past interpretive marker #15. It's a 3.5-mile (one-way) ridgeline hike ending at a canyon overlook.

Rattlesnake Canyon Trail begins on DLR, two miles from the visitor center at interpretive marker #9. This 3-mile (one-way) path descends into a deep canyon and past ruins of a 1930's homesteader's cabin. You can also make a 6-mile loop following Upper Rattlesnake Canyon to Guadalupe Ridge Road (GRR) from this trailhead. The loop returns to DLR and Rattlesnake Canyon Trailhead by following GRR to the east. The 12-mile GRR can also be hiked in its entirety. You are allowed to leave your vehicle at the gate where GRR intersects DLR.

There's a trailhead at Slaughter Canyon Parking Area (page 298). **Slaughter Canyon Trail** leads to Slaughter Canyon Cave and continues 5.3 more miles (one-way), where it intersects Guadalupe Ridge Road. It's a large canyon with several branches; a good map and map reading skills are essential.

Yucca Canyon Trail branches off from the road to Slaughter Canyon at the park boundary. Here you'll find a dirt road heading west, which can only be accessed by high-clearance 4WD vehicles. The 7.7-mile (one-way) trail climbs up a canyon to a ridgeline. **Backpackers** may camp west of Rattlesnake Canyon Trailhead off of DLR and south of Guadalupe Ridge Trail to the park boundary. A free Backcountry Use Permit (available at the visitor center) is required.

Stargazing

Carlsbad Caverns hosts several "Star Parties." Like most national parks, Carlsbad is far removed from city lights, making it an ideal location to gaze up at the stars. During these "parties," rangers guide you across the galaxy. Telescopes are available for use (weather permitting), and it's free. Arrive early, so your car's headlights don't drown out the stars. Check the park website's calendar for details.

Ranger Programs

Ranger programs consist of **Cave Tours** (page 298) and **Bat Flight Programs**. Bat Flight Programs are occasionally cancelled due to weather, so it's a good idea to check at the visitor center or online. Note that cameras (including cellphones) and camcorders are not allowed at the Bat Flight Program.

For Kids

Children are drawn to caves like they're to mud puddles. Something about these mysterious underground passages and rock formations lights the wick of a child's imagination. If you have a child (12+ years old) who loves crawling through tight spaces and getting dirty, you may want to send him/her on the **Spider Cave Tour** (page 298). A less adventurous way to enjoy the park with your child is to take part in the **Junior Ranger Program**. Free activity booklets are available online or at the visitor center. Complete its activities to become an official Carlsbad Caverns Junior Ranger.

Flora & Fauna

The most notable inhabitant is the Mexican (or Brazilian) free-tailed bat, but there are other living things in the desert.

The park reports 67 species of mammals (17 bats), 357 species of birds, 55 species of reptiles and amphibians, 5 species of fish, at least 600 species of insects, and more than 900 species of vascular plants. Black bear, mountain lion, elk, pronghorn, bighorn sheep, and javelina are a few of the seldom-seen larger mammals.

Sharing a mountain range with Guadalupe Mountains National Park (page 294), a particularly good birding destination, you'll find many similar species here. But

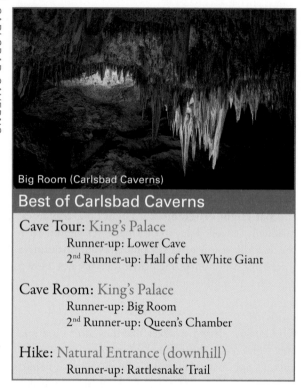

Big Room (Carlsbad Caverns)

Best of Carlsbad Caverns

Cave Tour: King's Palace
  Runner-up: Lower Cave
  2nd Runner-up: Hall of the White Giant

Cave Room: King's Palace
  Runner-up: Big Room
  2nd Runner-up: Queen's Chamber

Hike: Natural Entrance (downhill)
  Runner-up: Rattlesnake Trail

the best birding locations are also some of the most difficult sites to reach. The southwest corner of the park, several miles into Yucca Canyon Trail, hosts a few stands of coniferous forest; this is a great place for birding, but is only accessible to experienced backpackers with 4WD vehicles.

Pets

Pets are permitted, but if you want to tour the cave, hike a trail, or attend a Bat Flight Program, it's best to leave them at home. They are not permitted in caves, on hiking trails, or at Bat Flight Programs. Pets are not to be left unattended in vehicles (citations are issued on days when ambient air temperatures are 70°F or higher). If you still choose to bring your pet along with you, it can be boarded at the park's kennel for a small fee.

Accessibility

The visitor center, book store, theater, gift shop, restaurant, and amphitheater (site of Bat Flight Programs) are accessible to wheelchair users. Inside the cave, the Big Room is accessible with assistance. There's also a 1-mile nature trail beginning at the visitor center that is accessible.

Weather

Temperature inside Carlsbad Caverns' Big Room is a cool 56°F all year long. It's chilly and damp in the cave, with humidity levels usually close to 100%. As the cave's passages go deeper, average temperature increases due to heat rising from the earth's core. Climate on the surface is semi-arid, typical to the Chihuahuan Desert. The park receives an average of 15 inches of precipitation each year. Summers are hot. Winters are mild, but snowstorms can occur. No matter when you visit, you'll want to dress in layers to account for differences in temperature in-and-out of the cave.

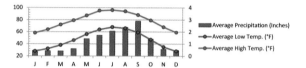

Vacation Planner

A visit to Carlsbad Caverns should be planned out in advance. Once you know when you're going, figure out how long you'd like to stay and reserve your **cave tours** (page 299) right away (especially tours that are not offered daily). Unless you plan on doing multiple cave tours, a single day should provide ample time. Spending a night or two in Carlsbad allows you to take another cave tour, hike a few trails or join a **Bat Flight Program** (page 300) or **Star Party** (page 301). On the other hand, if you're passing through and only have a couple hours, take the self-guiding Big Room Tour (page 299). If you can squeeze in a ranger tour, go for it. Also remember that **Guadalupe Mountains National Park** (page 288) is right around the corner.

King's Palace Tour visits the cave's most famous formations and a ranger will regale you with stories of the cave's history and geology. **Left Hand and Lower Cave Tours** visit more remote sections of Carlsbad Caverns. They are a bit more strenuous, but very doable as long as you're in decent physical condition. If you like your caves undeveloped but don't want to crawl through tight passages, you should tour **Slaughter Canyon Cave**. The most extreme tours are **Hall of the White Giant and Spider Cave**. Nearby dining, grocery stores, lodging, festivals, and attractions are listed on pages 320–325.

The Klansman (Slaughter Canyon Cave Tour)

Blue Mesa

Petrified Forest

PO Box 2217
Petrified Forest, AZ 86028
Phone: (928) 524-6228
Website: nps.gov/pefo

Established: December 9, 1962
Size: 100,000+ Acres
Annual Visitors: 800,000
Peak Season: Summer
Hiking Trails: 7 Miles

Activities: Hiking, Biking, and
Horseback Riding

Campgrounds: None
Lodging: None
Backcountry Camping: Permitted
in the Wilderness Area with a free
permit (available at visitor center)

Park Hours: See "When to Go"
**Visitor Center and Museum
Hours:** 8am–5pm (late Oct to late
Feb), 7am–7pm (early May to early
Sept), 7am–6pm (the rest of the
year)
Entrance Fee: $10/vehicle,
$5/individual (foot, bike, etc.)

Forests of fallen trees made of stone. Ruins and petroglyphs of ancient
civilizations. Fossils of prehistoric plants and animals. Pastel colored
badlands. Wilderness. Peace. Solitude. Silence. All of these are found
at Petrified Forest, located just a short distance from the whir of traffic
along Interstate 40. Nearby communities like Holbrook are sleepy ex-
railway towns or ghost towns like Adamana. Oddly enough, signs of the
past outnumber signs of the present. This rich history of life exists in a
place that is anything but lively. Most desert animals are small rodents,
amphibians, and reptiles, many of which only emerge during the summer nights, long after tourists have left the park. Plants are primarily
grasses, cacti, and wildflowers that have managed to adapt to life with
little water and arid soil.

Trees, some as tall as 200 feet, thrived in what was a humid and subtropical climate 225 million years ago. They were washed away by ancient rivers and streams, and then buried by silt, soil, and volcanic ash—
conditions ripe for fossilization. Many plants and animals were cast in
stone, preserved for millions of years, and today they help tell the story
of prehistoric life in the Painted Desert. The story is still incomplete,
but scientists believe present-day park land was once situated near the
equator. Large crocodile-like reptiles and oversized salamanders coex-
isted with early dinosaurs. Visitors can view fossils of these creatures
and ancient plants at Painted Desert Visitor Center and Rainbow Forest Museum.

Fossils are not the only signs of life revealed through rocks. Ancient
cultures, from 650 to 2,000 years ago, drew thousands of petroglyphs.
There are more than 600 petroglyphs at Newspaper Rock alone. It's difficult to determine what these symbols mean; descendants of ancient

Hopi, Zuni, and Navajo cultures only recognize some of them. As always, scientists are full of hypotheses regarding their meaning. Ideas ranging from trail markers to family stories to fertility charms abound. It's likely most held some spiritual significance, others more practical, like the petroglyphs near Puerco Pueblo that form a sundial signaling the summer solstice.

People have lived in the region for more than 10,000 years, but most evidence of inhabitation is from the same cultures that left us ancient petroglyphs. Tools, pottery, and village ruins from Puebloan cultures have been found at more than 600 archeological sites. They originally lived in single family huts built over a dugout section of earth. Around the turn of the 13th century, climatic changes caused families to group together near reliable sources of water where they built large pueblos capable of housing as many as 200 people in about 100, 1-story rooms. The rooms were constructed without doors or windows around an open plaza. They entered using a ladder. Puerco Pueblo, located along the main park road, is home to some of the most well-preserved ruins.

Modern civilization saw value in the Painted Desert as a tourist destination. Rail was laid through the present park boundary and soon the railroad began promoting America's scenic wonders hoping to boost passenger service. Arizona's Painted Desert and Petrified Forest were near the top of the list of wonders. Tourists could take a train to Adamana, book a hotel room, and walk among the petrified trees of what was known at the time as Chalcedony Forest. Trains dropped off tourists and loaded petrified wood to be taken back East. One man even proposed to crush petrified logs turning them into an abrasive grit. John Muir, already the driving force behind creation of Yosemite National Park, conducted the first scientific excavation in Petrified Forest. What he saw was destruction of a unique resource that was clearly exhaustible. To protect the region, he enlisted service of friend and fellow conservationist, President Theodore Roosevelt. Roosevelt promptly created Petrified Forest National Monument by executive order. Fifty-six years later it was made a national park.

Newspaper Rock

Painted Desert Inn

When to Go
Petrified Forest is open every day of the year. However, it's not your typical 24/7 national park. It opens at 7am from mid-February until October, and at 8am from November until mid-February. The park road closes around dusk via an automated gate at the Painted Desert (north) Entrance. **Painted Desert Visitor Center** and **Rainbow Forest Museum** are open most days from 7am–6pm. Hours extend to 7pm from early April to mid-September. In winter (late October–late February), hours are reduced to 8am–5pm. **Painted Desert Inn National Historic Landmark** is open every day from 9am–5pm. It's hot in summer, cool in winter, and comfortable in between. Summer thunderstorms can bring dangerous lightning and frightening thunder, but an ideal time to visit is after a storm; when sedimentary rocks of the Painted Desert are wet, their colors appear brighter and more pronounced in the soft morning or evening light. April and May are typically the best months to see wildflowers.

Transportation & Airports
Public transportation is not available to or around Petrified Forest. The closest major airports are Albuquerque International Sunport (ABQ) in Albuquerque, NM (228 miles east of the park) and Sky Harbor International Airport (PHX) in Phoenix, AZ (213 miles southwest of the park). Pulliam Airport (FLG) in Flagstaff, AZ is 135 miles to the west.

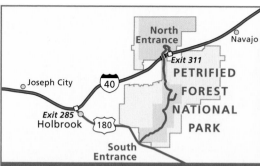

Directions

Petrified Forest is located in northeastern Arizona, straddling Interstate 40 between Albuquerque, NM and Flagstaff, AZ. Visitors arriving via I-40 from the east should take Exit 311. It leads directly to the park and Painted Desert Visitor Center, where you'll find an automated gate (know the park hours). From here, begin by touring the park north of I-40 before crossing the interstate and exiting near Rainbow Forest Museum. Those traveling from the west will want to take Exit 285 into Holbrook. Drive 19 miles south on US-180 to the south entrance near Rainbow Forest Museum.

Visitor Centers & Museums

Painted Desert Visitor Center is located near I-40's Exit 311. Here you'll find a short orientation film, several exhibits, a bookstore, and restrooms. A restaurant, gas station, gift shop, and convenience store are available adjacent to the visitor center. **Painted Desert Inn** is located at Kachina Point just north of the visitor center. It used to be a rest stop for travelers on historic Route 66, but now the Inn is a museum. Two miles north of the south entrance is **Rainbow Forest Museum**. Here you'll find fossil exhibits, a short film, snack bar, and restrooms.

Driving

If you don't have enough time for any of the other park activities, the 28-mile **Park Road** and **Blue Mesa Loop** are worth the detour from I-40. They offer overlooks, picnic areas, and access to hiking trails. Expect it to take a solid two hours to drive through the park.

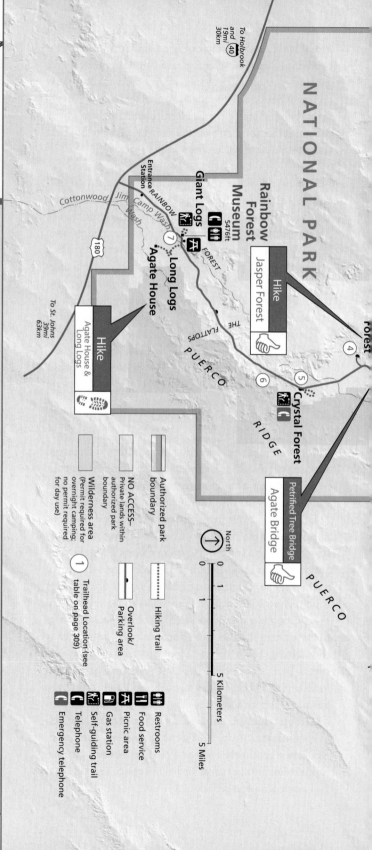

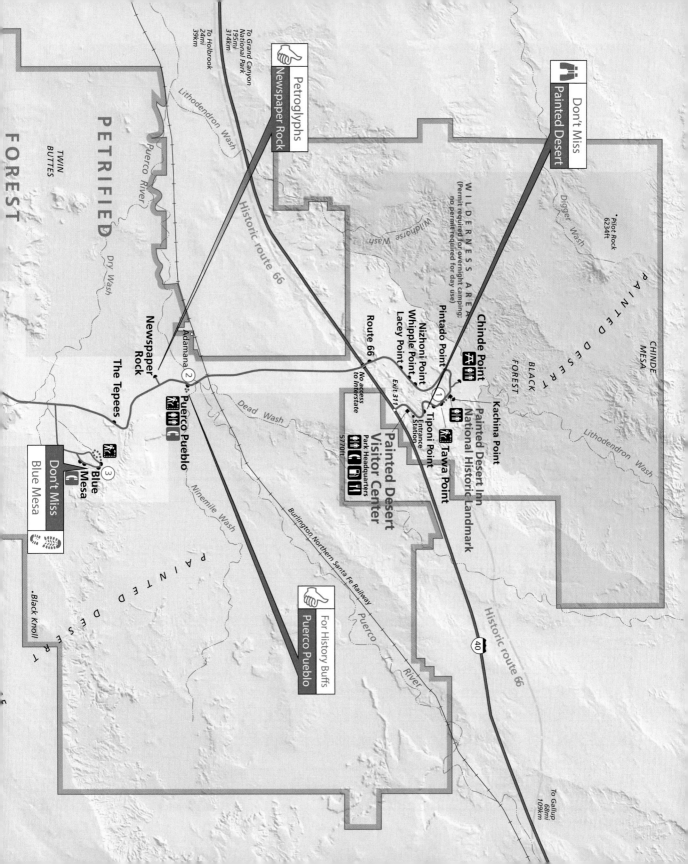

Petroglyphs
Newspaper Rock

Don't Miss
Painted Desert

To Grand Canyon
National Park
195mi
314km

To Holbrook
24mi
39km

Lithodendron Wash

PETRIFIED

Puerco River

TWIN
BUTTES

FOREST

Dry Wash

Historic route 66

PAINTED DESERT

Digger Wash

• Pilot Rock
6234ft

CHINDE
MESA

Lithodendron Wash

WILDERNESS AREA
(Permit required for overnight camping;
no permit required for day use)

Wildhorse Wash

BLACK
FOREST

Chinde Point

Kachina Point

Pintado Point

Nizhoni Point
Whipple Point
Lacey Point

Route 66

Exit 311

No access
to Interstate

Painted Desert Inn
National Historic Landmark

Tiponi Point

Entrance
Station

Tawa Point

5770ft

Painted Desert
Visitor Center

Park Headquarters

Newspaper
Rock

Adamana

②

Puerco Pueblo

The Tepees

Dead Wash

Don't Miss
Blue Mesa

Blue
Mesa

③

Ninemile Wash

Burlington Northern Santa Fe Railway

Puerco River

P A I N T E D   D E S E R T

• Black Knoll

40

Historic route 66

To Gallup
68mi
109km

For History Buffs
Puerco Pueblo

Jasper Forest

Recipe For: *Petrified Wood*   Ready In: *Millions of years*

Ingredients: *Trees (as many as you desire), sediment that includes volcanic ash*

1. Take your trees and bury them in sediment (A nice layer of sediment with volcanic ash will help slow down the natural decomposition process by cutting off the amount of oxygen that reaches them)

2. Pour large amounts of water onto the sediment (Water dissolves silica from the volcanic ash - The solution of silica in water slowly replaces the wood's original tissues)

3. Let sit for a few million years (Over time silica crystalizes to quartz - Colors develop based on mineral content, like manganese, carbon, iron, cobalt, and chromium, that were in your original sediment)

4. Remove sediment and observe your tree(s) made of stone

Camping & Lodging

There are **no designated campgrounds or lodgings** within the park. Lodging is available nearby (page 321). **Backcountry camping** is allowed within Petrified Forest National Wilderness Area. Backpackers must obtain a **free backcountry permit** from the visitor center during normal operating hours. Permits are not available in advance, and must be obtained at least one hour before the park closes. You are required to hike at least one mile from the two designated parking spots (Painted Desert Inn or Tawa Point) before camping.

Hiking & Backpacking

Petrified Forest isn't renowned for its spectacular hikes. It features seven maintained trails, all of which are less than 3 miles long. Still, they provide access to some of the finer petrified rock specimens, badlands formations, and archaeological sites. **Long Logs** and **Giant Logs Trails** are pretty self-explanatory; you're going to see some petrified wood. Giant Logs leads to "Old Faithful," a petrified tree nearly ten feet in diameter. If you're interested in the

area's ancient history, take **Puerco Pueblo Trail**. It leads to a hundred room village that was built and occupied between 1250 and 1400 AD. Agate House Trail leads to a more modern habitation. About 700 years ago this structure was built using materials on hand: mud and petrified wood. It begins at the same trailhead as Long Logs Trail. You can combine the two to make a 2.6-mile semi-loop. Our favorite hike in the park is **Blue Mesa Trail**, located off Blue Mesa Road. It's a short loop that descends from the mesa to deposits of petrified wood and spectacular views of badlands infused with bluish bentonite. The park has recently added a few "Off the Beaten Path" adventures that are more like suggested routes than maintained hiking paths. They explore some of more interesting areas like Jasper Forest and Blue Mesa. Then there's Devil's Playground, which requires a permit (three available per week on a first-come, first-served basis) and driving along a treacherous access road. You are also free to hike (and camp) in the park's wilderness area. Fifty-thousand acres of undeveloped desert. No trails. No water. Little shade. If you choose to blaze your own path, come prepared with a map, compass, and plenty of water.

Petrified Forest Hiking Trails (Distances are roundtrip)

Name	Location (# on map)	Length	Difficulty Rating & Notes
Painted Desert Rim - ♿	Tawa and Kachina Points (1)	1.0 mile	E – Follows the picturesque rim
Onyx Bridge*	Painted Desert Inn (1)	4.0 miles	M – Hiking in wilderness area, no trails
Puerco Pueblo	Puerco Pueblo Parking Area (2)	0.3 mile	E – Visits ruins of an ancient people
Blue Mesa - ♿	Blue Mesa sunshelter (3)	1.0 mile	M – Loop trail through wood and blue badlands
Billings Gap Overlook*	Blue Mesa Loop Road (3)	3.0 miles	M – Follow the edge of Blue Mesa
Blue Forest*	Blue Mesa Loop (3)	3.0 miles	M – Connects Blue Mesa Trail to the Main Park Rd
Red Basin/Clam Beds*	Blue Mesa Road (3)	8.5 miles	M – GPS recommended, the park's guide provides waypoints
Jasper Forest* - ♿	Jasper Forest Parking Area (4)	2.5 miles	M – Follows an old 1930s road into the forest
First Forest Point*	Jasper Forest Parking Area (4)	2.1 miles	M – More petrified wood at Jasper Forest
Crystal Forest	Crystal Forest (5)	0.8 mile	E – Crystals hide in a few petrified logs
Martha's Butte*	Dry Wash Bridge (mile 22) (6)	2.0 miles	M – Many petroglyphs on rocks at the butte
Long Logs - ♿	Rainbow Forest Museum (7)	1.6 miles	E – Loop trail to a large concentration of wood
Agate House	Rainbow Forest Museum (7)	2.0 miles	E – Visit a rehabilitated 700-year-old pueblo
Giant Logs	Rainbow Forest Museum (7)	0.4 mile	E – Large logs including "Old Faithful"
Devil's Playground*	Directions to access road provided with permit (call park at 928.524.6228 x 236 for status)		
Wilderness Hiking	Painted Desert Inn or Tawa Point (1)	50% of the park is designated wilderness. No trails. Permit required for overnight stays. Bring map and water.	

*These are suggested routes, not maintained trails and should only be attempted with a map and/or GPS

Difficulty Ratings: E = Easy, M = Moderate, S = Strenuous

Best of Petrified Forest

Attraction: Painted Desert
　　Runner-up: Rainbow Forest
　　2 Runner-up: Blue Mesa

Activity: Drive Main Park Road
　　Runner-up: Backpack in the Wilderness

Cultural Sites: Agate House
　　Runner-up: Newspaper Rock

Overlook: Chinde Point
　　Runner-up: Kachina Point

Family Hike: Blue Mesa
　　Runner-up: Painted Desert Rim

Horseback Riding

Bring your own horse(s) to explore Painted Desert's colorful badlands. However, riders and their stock are restricted to the wilderness area (northern half). It can be accessed via Wilderness Access Trail near Kachina Point, on the northwest side of Painted Desert Inn, two miles north of the visitor center. You and your horse are permitted to camp overnight north of Lithodendron Wash with an overnight use permit (available at the visitor center). Water is not available in the backcountry, which makes a multi-day trip with stock extremely challenging.

Biking

Motorists rule the road, but cyclists can also enjoy the scenic vistas afforded by the 28-mile park road and 3.5-mile Blue Mesa Loop. These roads are relatively straight, flat, and narrow. It's best to pedal as early in the morning or as late in the evening as operating hours allow. Summer is often hot, windy, and a poor time to pedal the roads. Cyclists are not allowed off road and may not use paved walking trails. Always be aware of motorists.

Ranger Programs

The area's interesting and sometimes unexplainable geology and history stirs all sorts of questions. And park rangers are always nearby, ready and willing to answer them for you. "Where's the restroom?" They'll point you to it. "How'd the trees turn to stone?" They'll explain it to you. You are also invited to join their ranger programs. Rangers enlighten and entertain guests on tours of Painted Desert Inn, talks about the Triassic Period, and walks at Puerco Pueblo. For a current schedule of programs and events visit the park website, call (928) 524-6228, or stop in at Painted Desert Visitor Center upon arrival. The park also holds a multitude of special events and cultural demonstrations throughout the year.

For Kids

Children of all ages are invited to participate in the **Junior Ranger Program**. The program encourages you and your children to learn about fossils and human history while exploring the park. To become a Junior Ranger you must first pick up a free activity booklet from Painted Desert Visitor Center, Painted Desert Inn, or Rainbow Forest Museum. A free download is also available at the park website. Complete the activities during your visit to receive a badge or patch and be anointed the newest Junior Ranger at Petrified Forest National Park.

Flora & Fauna

The park is home to more than 200 species of birds. Pronghorn, coyote, and bobcats endure the unforgiving desert climate along with dozens of other mammals, reptiles, and amphibians. This desolate terrain is dominated by grasses, but at least 400 species of plants survive here. However, the most fascinating plants and animals are those that lived here 225 million years ago. Their existence is recorded in rock of the Chinle Formation, one of the richest Late Triassic fossil-plant deposits in the world. More than 200 plant and animal fossils have been discovered including crocodile-like phytosaurs, large salamanders named Buettneria, and a few early dinosaurs.

Pets

Petrified Forest is one of few parks where pets won't limit your activities. Pets must be kept on a leash no more than six feet in length at all times, but they are allowed on all developed trails (except Wilderness Access Trail). They are not allowed in buildings, but are welcome in picnic and parking areas, and along roadways.

Accessibility

All facilities, including visitor centers, museums, restrooms, and picnic areas, are accessible (assistance may be necessary) to wheelchair users. Park trails are not.

Weather

Weather is as peculiar as the Painted Desert, petrified wood, and ancient petroglyphs. A high-altitude desert with predominantly clear nights creates extreme cooling between day and night, often as much as 40°F. This effect makes for cool summer evenings and hot afternoons. Summer highs are in the mid-to-high 90s°F. Evening lows dip into the mid-60s°F. Summers can also be windy and wet. Most rain falls during the monsoon season (July and August). Summer dust devils are common. During winter, snow can fall any day, October through March, but it rarely lasts through the afternoon. Enjoy the rain and snow because moisture on the badlands can really make the Painted Desert's colors pop on a sunny day.

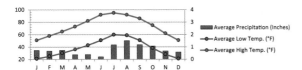

Vacation Planner

In 2010, Congress approved funds for park expansion. Today, the park is 50% larger than it was in 2004, and these new additions are beginning to be developed. With or without the extra land, the park is still quite manageable. Most **hiking trails** are less than 3 miles long, the **main park road** is only 28 miles, there are no outfitter-run activities like trail rides or rafting trips, which allows all the major sites to be seen in a single day. Actually, it's fairly difficult to spend the night. This is one of the few parks that close (to prevent theft of petrified wood). There are no campgrounds or lodging facilities within park boundaries. The only way to stay overnight is to **backpack** in Painted Desert Wilderness Area (free permit required). With that said, you should try to visit the park at one end of its operating hours, because Painted Desert is most beautiful at dusk and dawn. Nearby dining, grocery stores, lodging, festivals, and attractions are listed on pages 320–325.

Painted Desert

Agate House

Day 1: Begin at **Painted Desert Visitor Center**. Browse the exhibits and bookstore. Watch a 20-minute introductory film. Inquire about ranger programs. Once you're finished, head back to your car and begin driving the 28-mile road. You start at its most beautiful stretch through the Painted Desert. Depending on time, interests, and attitudes, stop at overlooks along the way. **Chinde Point** and **Kachina Point** are two of the best. Fans of museums or Route 66 should pit-stop at **Painted Desert Inn National Historic Landmark**, which has been renovated to house a bookstore and museum (no lodging available). Back on the road you'll pass an exhibit commemorating Route 66 just before crossing I-40, where you head into the park's southern half. Stop at **Puerco Pueblo**. You may be able to join a ranger-led tour of these ancient ruins. Stopping at **Newspaper Rock** isn't mandatory, but it provides views of petroglyphs (from a distance). Stop at the **Tepees** and **Blue Mesa**. If you love petrified wood, stop at **Agate Bridge**, **Crystal Forest**, and **Giant Logs**. If you like it, hike **Long Logs Trail** (and **Agate House**) and stop at **Rainbow Forest Museum**. Just don't like petrified wood so much that you take a little home (unless it's from the gift shop); theft will get you a hefty fine.

Gila woodpecker in a saguaro

Saguaro

3693 South Old Spanish Trail
Tucson, AZ 85730
Rincon Mountain: (520) 733-5153
Tucson Mountain: (520) 733-5158
Website: nps.gov/sagu

Established: October 14, 1994
Size: 91,440 Acres
Annual Visitors: 750,000
Peak Season: November–March
Hiking Trails: 150+ Miles

Activities: Hiking, Biking, Birding, and Horseback Riding

Campgrounds/Lodging: None
Backcountry Camping: Permitted*

Park Hours:
7am–Sunset (Rincon Mountain)
Sunrise–Sunset (Tucson Mountain)
Entrance Fee: $10/vehicle,
$5/individual (foot, bike, etc.)

*Only in Rincon Mountain District at designated sites with a backcountry permit ($8/night) • The closest backcountry campsite is a 5.9-mile hike

In 1933, University of Arizona president Homer Shantz urged President Hoover to protect saguaro forests surrounding the Rincon Mountains. Several generations of saguaro had already been affected by grazing cattle, as their small hooves and immense weight compacted the ground until saguaro seeds, no bigger than a pinhead, could not penetrate the earth's surface and take root. President Hoover agreed that the "monarch of the Sonoran Desert" needed to be preserved, invoking the Antiquities Act and establishing Saguaro National Monument. Cattle no longer grazed saguaro forests, but soon another mammal was getting too close for comfort. Tucson had once been a sleepy little town, 15 miles away from the present-day park land. Today, Tucson is a bustling city, sprawling-to-and-around the park's boundaries. Humans introduced invasive plant species that need water, the desert's most valuable commodity, to survive. Vandalism and poaching increased. Cacti were stolen for landscaping projects. By 1994, Congress continued trying to protect this unique natural resource by adding the Tucson Mountain District, expanding both regions, and establishing Saguaro National Park.

As conservationists try to protect the saguaro, cacti do their best to protect and provide for Sonoran Desert wildlife. To birds, the mighty saguaros are multi-tower condominiums that are constantly expanding. Gila woodpeckers and gilded flickers drill out one-room accommodations in the saguaros' trunk and large branches. Often they make several holes, rejecting one after another before finding a suitable home and settling down to raise a family. Other birds waste no time to begin squatting in vacant units. Elf owls, screech owls, purple martins, American kestrel, Lucy's warblers, cactus wrens, kingbirds, even honeybees seek the saguaro's protection. Not only does living within these monstrous succulents provide protection from predators, it shields them from hot summer days and cool winter nights. In summer the inner column of a saguaro is 20°F cooler than the ambient temperature. In winter, it's 20°F warmer. Outside, red-tailed and Harris hawks build nests in the crooks of the saguaro's arms. These are the condominium's suites, custom-built with beautiful 360-degree views of the surrounding mountains.

Fruit of the saguaro is just as useful as its woody frame. For centuries the Tohono O'odham people harvested fruit to make syrup, jam, and wine; it was also dried and eaten like a fig. It is so important, they marked their new year as the beginning of the saguaro fruit harvest. The fruit are also important to creatures that creep and fly in the cool of the night. In June and July when it ripens, foragers like javelina, coyote, fox, harvester ants, birds, and small rodents feast on its succulent flesh.

The saguaro itself is a masterpiece of adaptation to an unforgiving environment. It's built on a wooden framework sturdy enough to support its weight, which can exceed 16,000 pounds. Its skin is pleated, allowing the cactus to expand as its roots sop up surrounding water. Inside is spongy flesh made of a gelatin-like substance capable of absorbing large amounts of water to survive months of drought. A waxy coating covers its skin, slowing the perspiration of water, and thorny spines protrude from it, deterring animals while providing shade. Most importantly, the needles serve as the succulent's power plant, performing the vital function of photosynthesis.

Saguaro cactus. "Monarch of the Sonoran Desert." Icon of the southwest. Not only does it enhance the desert's scenic value, it is an ecological keystone species, one that plays an integral role in maintaining the structure of its ecological community. A decline in saguaro population would not only diminish the area's scenic value and cause devastation to a unique and iconic species, it would cripple a lively community trying to beat the odds by surviving in the desert. The same odds the saguaro has managed to endure for centuries.

When to Go

Rincon Mountain District (East) is open every day of the year from 7am until sunset. Tucson Mountain District (West) is open daily from sunrise to sunset. **Visitor centers** are open daily from 9am to 5pm with the exception of Christmas Day. Most visitors come to the park between November and March when the weather is comfortable. Park land can erupt with colorful wildflowers after a wet winter. Saguaros bloom at night during the month of May and into June. Not all winters are wet. Call the park to verify wildflower blooms before arriving.

Transportation & Airports

Public transportation is not available to or around either unit. Tucson International Airport (TUS) is located along the southern outskirts of Tucson, AZ, less than 20 miles from each unit.

Directions

Saguaro National Park consists of two separate districts, one east and one west of Tucson, AZ.

Rincon Mountain District/East Unit (3693 S Old Spanish Trail): From I-10, take Exit 275 (Houghton Rd). Head north on Houghton Rd for about 8 miles. Turn right at E Escalante Rd. Continue east for 2 miles before turning left onto Old Spanish Rd, which leads into the park.

Tucson Mountain District/West Unit (2700 N Kinney Road): Heading southeast on I-10 toward Tucson, take Exit 242 (Avra Valley Rd). Head west on Avra Valley Rd about 5 miles. Turn left at N Sandario Rd and continue south for 9 miles. Turn left at N Kinney Rd, which leads into the park. (Consider returning to Tucson via Gates Pass Road; it's extremely scenic drive with saguaro, pullouts, hiking trails, etc.)

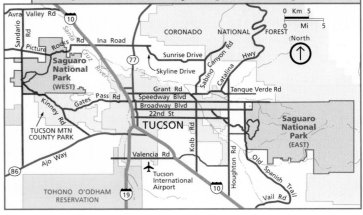

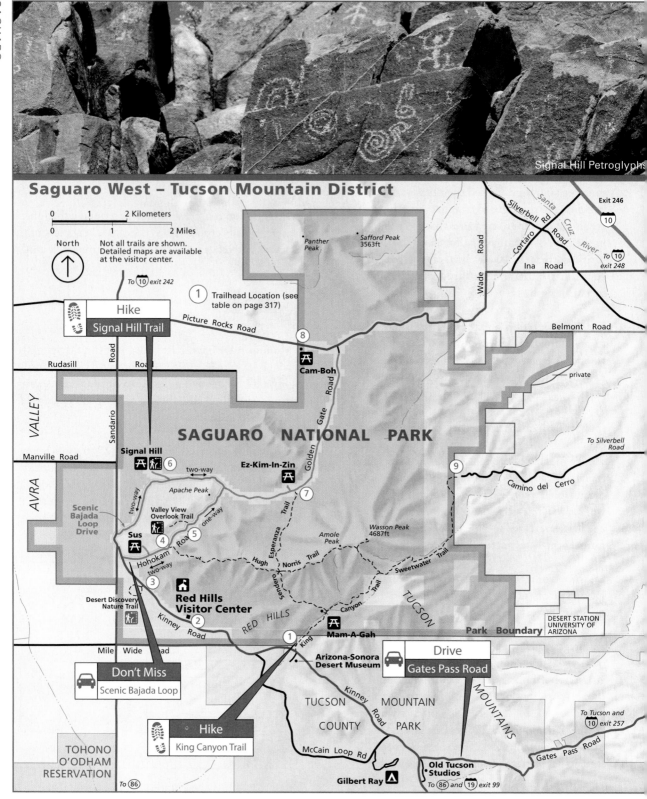

Signal Hill Petroglyphs

Saguaro West – Tucson Mountain District

0   1   2 Kilometers
0   1   2 Miles

North

Not all trails are shown.
Detailed maps are available
at the visitor center.

To (10) exit 242

① Trailhead Location (see table on page 317)

Hike
Signal Hill Trail

Picture Rocks Road

⑧

Cam-Boh

Rudasill   Road

Wade Road

Belmont Road

Exit 246
(10)

Silverbell Rd

Santa Cruz River

Cortaro Road

Ina   Road

To (10) exit 248

private

VALLEY

Sandario   Road

Manville Road

SAGUARO   NATIONAL   PARK

Panther Peak

Safford Peak
3563ft

Golden Gate Road

To Silverbell Road

AVRA

Signal Hill ⑥
two-way

two-way

Apache Peak

Ez-Kim-In-Zin

⑦

⑨

Camino del Cerro

Scenic
Bajada
Loop
Drive

Valley View
Overlook Trail
one-way

Sus ④ ⑤
Road

Hohokam Road
two-way

③

Esperanza Trail

Hugh

Norris Trail

Amole Peak

Wasson Peak
4687ft

Sweetwater Trail

TUCSON

Desert Discovery
Nature Trail

Red Hills
Visitor Center

Sendero

Canyon Trail

RED   HILLS

Park   Boundary

DESERT STATION
UNIVERSITY OF
ARIZONA

Kinney   Road

②

Mam-A-Gah

① King

Drive
Gates Pass Road

Mile   Wide   Road

Don't Miss
Scenic Bajada Loop

Arizona-Sonora
Desert Museum

Kinney Road

TUCSON   MOUNTAIN
COUNTY   PARK

MOUNTAINS

To Tucson and
(10) exit 257

Hike
King Canyon Trail

McCain Loop Rd

Gates Pass Road

TOHONO
O'ODHAM
RESERVATION

To (86)

Gilbert Ray

Old Tucson
Studios

To (86) and (19) exit 99

Regions

Two park regions are separated by Tucson. **Tucson Mountain District** is west of the city. This small mountain range is made of volcanic rock and its highest point is Wasson Peak (4,687 ft). **Rincon Mountain District** is on the east side of Tucson. It's about twice the size and elevation of its western counterpart. Rincon is another relatively small mountain range made of volcanic rock that has been heavily eroded over the years. Its highest peak is Mica Mountain (8,666 ft). Each region has a visitor center, picnic areas, a scenic loop drive, and miles of hiking trails.

Visitor Centers & Museums

Red Hills Visitor Center is located in the western unit, on Kinney Road near the south entrance. Here you'll find exhibits, a bookstore, and brochures and maps that help introduce you to the area. Two films, "A Home in the Desert" (15 minutes) and "Sentinel in the Desert" (53 minutes) are shown daily. Also located on Kinney Road near the park boundary is the popular zoo/garden/museum, **Arizona–Sonora Desert Museum** (page 324). East Unit's **Rincon Mountain Visitor Center** has exhibits, a bookstore, brochures, and maps. It also shows the same videos as West Unit's Visitor Center. The most useful resource found at either visitor center is their friendly staff. Park rangers are ready to answer your questions and provide activity suggestions based on how much time you have to explore the unit.

Driving

Each unit has a well-maintained scenic drive. These stretches of road have become their primary attractions. In the west, you'll find 5-mile **Bajada Loop Drive**. It's a graded unpaved road (suitable for any vehicle) that passes through dense saguaro forest. In the east, motorists circle around 8-mile **Cactus Forest Drive**, a one-way, paved road that passes through a well preserved desert ecosystem. Cyclists, runners, and walkers flock to Cactus Forest Drive early in the day, before the road opens and things heat up. Both roads provide access to the most popular trailheads, picnic areas, and desert vistas.

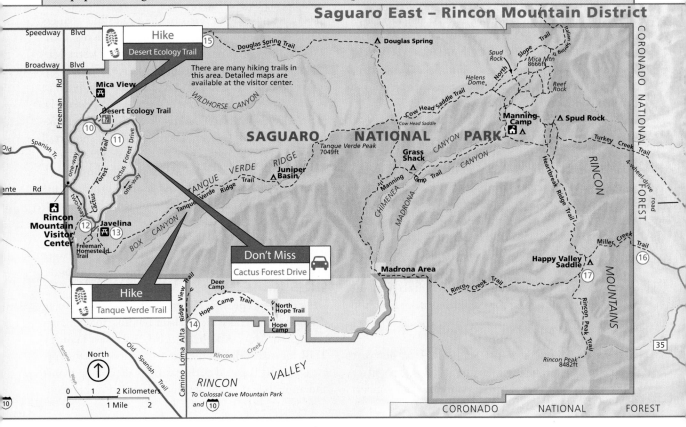

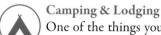

Camping & Lodging

One of the things you can't do in the park is spend the night. There are **no drive-in campgrounds** or lodging facilities within its boundaries. See page 321 for a list of nearby lodging and campground alternatives. **Backpackers** are the exception. They are allowed to camp in Rincon Mountain Wilderness Area at one of six designated backcountry campgrounds scattered throughout the mountains. The closest camp is a 5.9-mile hike along Douglas Spring Trail. Its trailhead is located on Speedway Blvd. Backpackers must obtain a **backcountry permit** ($8 per person per night) from Rincon Mountain Visitor Center.

Saguaro Cactus

Saguaro is an icon of the American southwest and giant of the Sonoran Desert. Almost human-like, the saguaro stands tall, towering above the arid and rocky ground, arms extended in a welcoming manner. These are the redwoods of the desert, offering protection and provisions for a wealth of life in a seemingly inhospitable landscape. Their roots fan out from the trunk as far as it is tall, sopping up water with a voracious thirst. In a single rainfall, a saguaro may soak up as much as 200 gallons of water, enough to last an entire year. They can live to be more than 150 years old, 50 feet tall, and weigh up to 8 tons. That makes the saguaro not only the largest cactus in the United States, but the largest living organism in the Sonoran Desert.

In contrast, its life begins as a tiny black seed, no bigger than the head of a pin. Each year a single saguaro produces tens of thousands of seeds, which fall to the desert floor and try to take root in one of the hottest and driest regions on the continent. Hungry birds and rodents snack on these miniscule morsels. Even with an abundance of seeds, the chances of a saguaro reaching adulthood is on par with being struck by lightning. Chances increase beneath trees like palo verde and mesquite, where they find shade from the summer heat, insulation from the winter cold, and safe harbor from the constant threat of hungry animals.

Seeds that take root grow ever so slowly. After one year a saguaro may measure one-quarter inch, one foot after 15 years, and after 30 years of life in the desert, a saguaro

finally begins to flower and produce fruit. There can be as many as 100 flowers on a single cactus, each blooming at sunset. They are pollinated in the night by white-winged doves, long-nosed bats, honeybees, and moths. By the following afternoon the flower has wilted in the direct rays of desert sun. Flowers turn to fruit and by June they have ripened. Each fruit contains as many as 2,000 seeds that fall to the desert floor in hope of becoming a "Sentinel of the Sonoran Desert."

Hiking & Backpacking

Even desert can appeal to the avid hiker. You'll find trails ranging from short and flat paved loops to long-distance, rugged paths along steep, barren mountain slopes. Most of Tucson Mountain District's trails are short and relatively easy. **Desert Discovery Trail**, located just off Kinney Road, south of Bajada Loop Drive, is a popular short loop. It has several exhibits discussing the region's native plants and animals. If you'd like to hike to the west unit's tallest point, Wasson Peak, you have a couple choices. The easiest route is to take **Sendero Esperanza Trail** (located on Golden Gate Road) to its intersection with Hugh Norris Trail. Head east on Hugh Norris to the peak. This route is about 4.1 miles (one-way). Alternatively, **King Canyon Trail**, located near Arizona–Sonora Desert Museum, is slightly shorter but more strenuous. It's a 3.5-mile (one-way) hike to the peak, beginning with a nice gradual ascent before a series of switchbacks lead to the intersection with Hugh Norris Trail. **Signal Hill Picnic Area**, just off Golden Gate Road, has a short trail that wanders past more than 200 ancient petroglyphs. The meaning behind these images scratched onto rock is left to your interpretation. As you walk through the desert, imagine what stories these ancient scribes wanted to tell their descendants.

Rincon Mountain District contains a much larger network of trails and **six backcountry campgrounds**. Several short and easy trails begin along Cactus Forest Drive. **Cactus Forest Trail** runs north–south, bisecting the loop drive. This is an excellent flat hike to see saguaro cactus up close. Another nice hike is **Desert Ecology Trail**, located at the southernmost point of Cactus Forest Drive. This paved path has signs describing plants and animals you might see during your visit. North of

Cactus Forest Drive is a fairly complex maze-like network of trails. Combining several short trails allows a multitude of loop routes through the foothills. You can also explore the park's wilderness area. It is most easily accessed via **Tanque Verde** or **Douglas Spring Trails**, but it's also accessible from the east via **Middle Creek Trail** through Coronado National Forest.

The Sonoran Desert provides ample terrain for exploration, but it doesn't offer shade or water. Pace yourself and drink plenty of water. If you plan on doing extensive hiking, ask for a detailed hiking map at the visitor center. They should be available free of charge.

Biking

Cyclists are limited to the park's roadways. Off-road and on-trail riding is not permitted. **Road cyclists** enjoy riding through saguaro forests surrounding the East Unit's 8-mile Cactus Forest Drive. It's twisty, hilly, narrow, and can become congested during peak tourism season (November–March). The lone opportunity for **mountain bike trail riding** is a 2.5-mile stretch of Cactus Forest Trail that bisects Cactus Forest Drive. It's not a trail, but mountain bikers can also pedal the West Unit's Bajada Loop Drive. It's a 5-mile loop road that traverses a small portion of Tucson Mountain's lower elevations.

Horseback Riding

Horses, mules, and donkeys are allowed on more than 100 miles of trails, so don't be startled if you come face-to-face with a donkey while hiking through the desert. Horse riders and their stock are also permitted to camp at designated backcountry campgrounds (with a permit from Rincon Mountain Visitor Center). If you'd like to experience the true southwest but don't have your own stock, Cocoraque Ranch (520.682.8594, cocoraque.com) operates near the West Unit and Pantano Riding Stables (520.298.8980) operates near the East Unit.

Saguaro Hiking Trails (Distances are roundtrip unless noted otherwise)

	Name	Location (# on map)	Length	Difficulty Rating & Notes
Tucson Mountain District	King Canyon -	Across from Arizona–Sonora Desert Museum (1)	7.0 miles	M/S – Trek up switchbacks to Wasson Peak (Tucson Mountain's highest peak)
	Cactus Garden -	Red Hills Visitor Center (2)	300 feet	E – Self-guiding introduction to plants
	Desert Discovery	Kinney Road (3)	0.5 mile	E – Self-guiding loop
	Hugh Norris	Bajada Loop Drive (4)	9.8 miles	S – Long hike to Wasson Peak
	Valley View Overlook -	Bajada Loop Drive (5)	0.8 mile	E/M – Cross two washes, ascend a ridge
	Signal Hill -	Signal Hill Picnic Area (6)	0.5 mile	E – Passes numerous petroglyphs
	Cactus Wren	Signal Hill Picnic Area (6)	3.0 miles	E – Flat, through washes to Sandario Road
	Sendero Esperanza	Golden Gate Road (7)	6.4 miles	M – Cross Hugh Norris and King Canyon Trails
	Cam-Boh	Pictured Rocks Road (8)	5.4 miles	M – Leads to a small network of trails
	Sweetwater	End of Camino del Cerro Rd (9)	6.8 miles	M – Leads to the top of Wasson Peak
Rincon Mountain District	Desert Ecology -	Cactus Forest Drive (10)	0.25 mile	E – Paved trail, explores plant and animal life
	Cactus Forest	Cactus Forest Drive (11)	5.2 miles	E – Flat, open to hikers, bikers, and horse riders
	Freeman Homestead -	Cactus Forest Drive (12)	1.0 mile	E – Self-guiding, large saguaro, old home
	Tanque Verde -	Javelina Picnic Area (13)	18.0 miles	S – 6.9 miles to Juniper Basin Camp, continues to Tanque Verde Peak and Cow Head Saddle
	Hope Camp	Comino Loma Alta (14)	5.6 miles	M – Used by horse riders • Provides views of Tanque Verde Ridge and Rincon Peak
	Ridge View	Comino Loma Alta (14)	1.6 miles	M – Leads to views of rocky side canyons
	Douglas Spring	Speedway Blvd (15)	16+ miles	M – 5.9 miles to Douglas Spring Camp
	Miller Creek	North Happy Valley Rd (16)	4.4 miles	M – Not accessed at main park area
	Rincon Peak -	Spur Trail (17)	3.3 miles	S – Via Heartbreak Ridge/Miller Creek (1-way)

Difficulty Ratings: E = Easy, M = Moderate, S = Strenuous

Beauty and the desert

Ranger Programs

Many visitors have a difficult time appreciating the desert, so attending a ranger program is a good way to absorb a bit of knowledge and enthusiasm for this desolate region. Ranger-led walks, talks, and interpretive programs (offered November–March) explore the park's history, geology, and ecology, ranging from morning bird-watching tours to evening stargazing. Visitors should check online or at a visitor center for a current schedule of events.

For Kids

Children (ages 5–12) are welcome to participate in the **Junior Ranger Program**. Complete an activity booklet (free at either visitor center) aided by the contents of a **Discovery Pack** to receive a ranger badge. Discovery Packs are available for check-out at either visitor center with an adult's valid driver's license or picture ID. Children (ages 6–11) can sign up for a 3-day **Junior Ranger Camp** that is held in June. It costs $25 per child and applications are available at the park website. Call (520) 733–5153 for additional information. (They also offer a "Not So Junior Ranger Program" for everyone else.)

Flora & Fauna

Saguaros aren't the only show in town. More than 25 species of cacti are found here. Less famous succulents include hedgehog, cholla, and prickly pear. Be careful not to be pricked by a cholla cactus. Its barbed needles are difficult to remove and extremely painful. In lower elevations of the West Unit, you can find animals like desert tortoise and coyote. There's also plenty of creosote bush, the most common North American desert plant. East Unit's higher elevations provide habitat for larger animals. Black bear, white-tailed deer, and Mexican spotted owl live among Douglas fir and ponderosa pine that grow on the high mountain slopes. Bird watchers appreciate more than 200 species of birds that live in or visit the region. One of the most sought after birds is the elf owl. It's often seen roosting in small saguaro cavities drilled out by gila woodpeckers or gilded flickers. High mountains also provide an opportunity to see birds not commonly found on the desert floor, like red-faced warbler and golden eagle.

Pets

Pets are limited to the park's roadways and picnic areas, and must be kept on a leash no more than six feet in length at all times.

Accessibility

Both visitor centers are accessible to individuals in wheelchairs. Desert Ecology Trail in Rincon Mountain District and Desert Discovery Trail in Tucson Mountain District are accessible. All other trails are inaccessible. A few ranger-led programs are accessible.

Weather

There are a few reasons why so many Americans retire in Arizona. Mild winters is one of them. Winter average high temperatures are about 65°F before dropping into the 40s°F at night. Summers are hot and dry. Daytime highs commonly exceed 100°F in the shade. Summer visitors must remember to pack your sunglasses, plenty of water, and sunscreen.

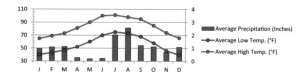

Valley View (Tucson Mountain District)

Vacation Planner

Even with two park units separated by Tucson, you don't need a lot of time to tour Saguaro. **Hiking trails** and **roads** are short and easily accessible. Plus, You won't find any lodging or camping facilities within the park. You could spend a few nights **backpacking** through the Rincon Mountains, but those types of visitors are few and far between. Always check a schedule of **ranger-led programs** in advance and join whenever possible. Nearby dining, grocery stores, lodging, festivals, and attractions are listed on pages 320–325.

Day 1: Begin at **Tucson Mountain District**, stopping first at **Red Hills Visitor Center**. If you haven't already, get the day's schedule of ranger-led activities (check for the East Unit while you're at it). Do not skip a ranger program if one is occurring during your visit. Getting back to business, drive **Scenic Bajada Loop**. It's a short drive on a gravel road. Take your time and enjoy the views of saguaro forests. Here, saguaros are far denser than at the East Unit. Along the way, stop at Signal Hill Picnic Area to hike its **Petroglyph Trail**. (**Valley View Overlook Trail** is another good one.) On your way out, stop at **Arizona–Sonora Desert Museum** or hike **King Canyon Trail**. (If you're arriving early in the morning, we suggest taking **Gates Pass Road**, which is incredibly scenic and covered in saguaro. If you think you'll be exiting the west district late, leave via Gates Pass Road.)

Best of Saguaro

Hike (West District): King Canyon
    Runner-up: Valley View Overlook

Hike (East District): Freeman Homestead
    Runner-up: Rincon Peak (Strenuous)
    2nd Runner-up: Tanque Verde (Strenuous)

Activity: Bike Cactus Forest Drive
    Runner-up: Arizona–Sonora Desert Museum

Drive across Tucson to **Rincon Mountain District**. Stop in at its visitor center if you skipped the West Unit's, or maybe you want to catch the park video or confirm the activity schedule. If you're out of questions and have seen both park videos, leave the visitor center and head out onto **Cactus Forest Drive**. It's a paved loop providing access to **Cactus Forest Trail** at two points (and many other trailheads and viewpoints). Cactus Forest is a nice, easy, and flat trail that explores saguaro forests. You'll find **Desert Ecology Self-Guiding Trail** on the northern end of Cactus Forest Drive. Hike it if you're interested in the park's desert ecology, but our favorite short hike is **Freeman Homestead Trail**. On a comfortable day you may want to continue hiking. **Tanque Verde Trail** begins at Javelina Picnic Area and climbs steeply into the mountains, where you'll find outstanding views and slightly cooler temperatures.

Dining

Big Bend Area

La Kiva • (432) 371-2250
FM-170 at Terlingua Creek, Terlingua
la-kiva.com • Entrée: $10–20

Star Light Theatre • (432) 371-2326
631 Ivey Rd, Terlingua • starlighttheatre.com

Tivo's Restaurant • (432) 371-2133
TX-118, Terlingua

Long Draw Pizza • (432) 371-2608
Farm to Market 170, Terlingua

Chili Pepper Café • (432) 371-2233
100 TX-118, Terlingua

Guadalupe Mts/Carlsbad Area

Spanish Angels Café • (915) 964-2208
103 Main St, Dell City, TX

The Lucky Bull • (575) 725-5444
220 W Fox St, Carlsbad, NM

Carlsbad Caverns Restaurant • (575) 785-2281
727 Carlsbad Cavern Hwy, Carlsbad, NM

Happy's • (575) 887-8489
4103 National Parks Hwy, Carlsbad, NM

Rojas Mexican Grill • (575) 885-2146
2704 San Jose Blvd, Carlsbad, NM

Danny's Place • (575) 885-8739
902 S Canal St, Carlsbad, NM

Pizza Inn • (575) 887-5049
3005 National Parks Hwy, Carlsbad, NM
pizzainn.com • Pizza: $10+

No Whiner Diner • (575) 234-2815
1801 S Canal St, Carlsbad, NM
nowhinerdiner.com

Pecos River Café • (575) 887-8882
409 S Canal St, Carlsbad, NM

Blue House Bakery • (575) 628-0555
609 N Canyon St, Carlsbad, NM

Red Chimney Pit Bar-B-Q • (575) 885-8744
817 N Canal St, Carlsbad, NM
redchimneybbq.com

Blake's Lotaburger • (575) 885-0152
1230 W Pierce St, Carlsbad, NM
lotaburger.com

Becky's Drive In • (575) 885-3262
901 W Church St, Carlsbad, NM

Sno to Go • (575) 885-0477
1713 S Canal St, Carlsbad, NM

Kaleidoscoops Ice Cream • (575) 887-1931
425 N Canal St, Carlsbad, NM • kalscoops.com

Dari-Lea Drive In • (575) 885-3976
2216 W Lea St, Carlsbad, NM

Church Street Grill • (575) 885-3074
301 W Church St, Carlsbad, NM
churchstreetgrill.com

Petrified Forest Area

Joe & Aggie's Café • (928) 524-6540
Served as inspiration for the Pixar movie Cars
120 W Hopi Dr, Holbrook • joeandaggiescafe.com

Butterfield Stage Co Steak House
609 W Hopi Dr, Holbrook • (928) 524-3447

Bear Café • (928) 524-1884
2600 Navajo Blvd, Holbrook

Hopi Travel Plaza Café • (928) 524-7820
1851 AZ-77, Holbrook

El Rancho Restaurant & Motel • (928) 524-3332
867 Navajo Blvd, Holbrook

Mesa Italiana Restaurant • (928) 524-6696
2318 Navajo Blvd, Holbrook

Romo's Restaurant • (928) 524-2153
121 W Hopi Dr, Holbrook

Mandarin Beauty Chinese • (928) 524-3663
2218 Navajo Blvd, Holbrook
mandarinbeautyrestaurant.com

Bubba Big Pig Bar BQ • (928) 524-1581
1002 W Hopi Dr, Holbrook

El Rinconcito Mexicano • (928) 524-3167
1150 W Hopi Dr, Holbrook

Saguaro Area

Mama's Famous Pizza • (520) 751-4600
50 S Houghton Rd, # 190, Tucson
mamasfamous.com • Pizza: $13–29

Vivace • (520) 795-7221
6440 N Campbell Ave, Tucson
vivacetucson.com • Entrée: $18–47

Guiseppe's • (520) 505-4187
6060 N Oracle Rd, Tucson
guiseppesristorante.com • Entrée: $10–23

Viro's Real Italian Bakery • (520) 885-4045
8301 E 22nd St, Tucson
virosbakery.com • Entrée: $10–16

Dolce Vita • (520) 298-3700
7895 E Broadway Blvd, # 9, Tucson

Kenney D's Chicago Style • (520) 722-8900
8060 E 22nd St, # 100, Tucson

Papa Locos Tacos and Burgers • (520) 663-3333
8201 S Rita Rd, Tucson • papalocos.com

Baggin's Gourmet • (520) 290-9383
7233 E Speedway Blvd, Tucson
bagginsgourmet.com • Sandwiches: $7–9

Epic Café • (520) 624-6844
745 N 4th Ave, Tucson • epic-cafe.com

Ba-Dar Chinese • (520) 296-8888
7321 E Broadway Blvd, Tucson
ba-dar.com • Chinese: $9–15

HUB Restaurant & Ice Creamery
266 E Congress St, Tucson • (520) 207-8201
hubdowntown.com • Entrée: $14–22

Zona 78 • (520) 296-7878
7301 E Tanque Verde Rd, Tucson
zona78.com • Entrée: $11–19

Little Anthony's Diner • (520) 296-0456
7010 E Broadway Blvd, Tucson
littleanthonysdiner.com

The Good Egg • (520) 885-4838
7189 E Speedway Blvd, Tucson
thegoodeggaz.com • Breakfast: $8–12

Poco & Mom's Restaurant • (520) 325-7044
1060 South Kolb Rd, Tucson
pocoandmoms.com

Ha Long Bay • (520) 571-1338
7245 E Tanque Verde, Tucson
halongbaymenu.com • Vietnamese: $9–14

Beyond Bread • (520) 747-7477
6260 E Speedway Blvd, Tucson
beyondbread.com • Sandwiches: $7–12

Neo of Melaka • (520) 747-7811
6133 E Broadway Blvd, Tucson
neotucson.com • Entrée: $13–29

Dakota Café • (520) 298-7188
6541 E Tanque Verde Rd, # 7, Tucson
dakotatucson.com • Entrée: $10–24

Blue Willow Restaurant • (520) 327-7577
2616 N Campbell Ave, Tucson
bluewillowtucson.com • Entrée: $11–19

Café Poca Cosa • (520) 622-6400
110 E Pennington St, Tucson
cafepocacosatucson.com

Mi Nidito • (520) 622-5081
1813 S 4th Ave, Tucson
minidito.net • Entrée: $7–12

El Guero Canelo • (520) 882-8977
2480 N Oracle Rd, Tucson • elguerocanelo.com

Old Town Artisans Galleries • (520) 623-6024
201 N Court Ave, Tucson
oldtownartisans.com • Entrée: $9–14

Mama Louisa's • (520) 790-4702
2041 S Craycroft Rd, Tucson • mamalouisas.com

Cup Café • (520) 798-1618
311 E Congress St, Tucson
hotelcongress.com • Entrée: $15–20

Taqueria Pico De Gallo • (520) 623-8775
2618 S 6th Ave, # A, Tucson

Nimbus Brewing Co • (520) 745-9175
3850 E 44th St, Tucson
nimbusbeer.com • Entrée: $9–17

Barrio Brewing Co • (520) 791-2739
800 E 16th St, Tucson • barriobrewing.com

Pastiche Modern Eatery • (520) 325-3333
3025 N Campbell Ave, Tucson
pasticheme.com

Frost Gelato • (520) 797-0188
7131 N Oracle Rd, # 101, Tucson
frostgelato.com • Gelato: $3–5

Frost Gelato • (520) 886-0354
7301 E Tanque Verde Rd, # 191, Tucson
frostgelato.com • Gelato: $3–5

Frost Gelato • (520) 615-9490
2905 E Skyline Dr, Tucson
frostgelato.com • Gelato: $3–5

Grocery Stores
Big Bend Area
Study Butte Store • (432) 371-2231
TX-118, Study Butte

Terlingua Springs Market • (432) 371-2332
FM-170, Terlingua

Walmart • (432) 336-3389
2610 W Dickinson Blvd, Fort Stockton

Guadalupe Mts/Carlsbad Area
Walmart Supercenter • (575) 885-0727
2401 S Canal St, Carlsbad, NM

Albertsons • (575) 885-2161
808 N Canal St, Carlsbad, NM

Petrified Forest Area
Safeway • (928) 524-3313
702 W Hopi Dr, Holbrook

Walmart Supercenter • (928) 289-4641
700 Mikes Pike St, Winslow

Saguaro Area
Safeway • (520) 206-9047
1940 E Broadway Blvd, Tucson

Albertson-Osco • (520) 751-7699
9595 E Broadway Blvd, Tucson

Fry's • (520) 721-8575
9401 E 22nd St, Tucson

Walmart • (520) 751-1882
7150 E Speedway Blvd, Tucson

Walmart Supercenter • (520) 573-3777
1650 W Valencia, Tucson

Lodging
Big Bend Area
Chisos Mountains Lodge • (877) 386-4383
Chisos Area, Big Bend National Park
chisosmountainslodge.com • Rates: $137–144

Big Bend Motor Inn • (432) 371-2218
100 Main St, Terlingua

Oasis Hotel & RV • (432) 371-2218
TX-118, Terlingua

Ten Bits Ranch • (432) 371-3110
6000 N County Rd, Terlingua
tenbitsranch.com • Rates: $159–199

BJ's RV Park • (432) 371-2259
FM-170, Terlingua • bjrvpark.com • Rates: $28

El Dorado Hotel • (432) 371-2111
100 Ghostown Rd, Terlingua

La Posada Milagro • (432) 371-3044
100 Milagro Rd, Terlingua
laposadamilagro.net • Rates: $1185–210

Lajitas Golf Resort & Spa • (432) 424-5100
HC 70 Box 400, Lajitas
lajitasgolfresort.com • Rates: $175+

Chisos Mining Company Motel
23280 FM-170, Terlingua • (432) 371-2254

Terlingua Ranch Lodge • (432) 371-2416
16000 Terlingua Ranch Rd, Terlingua
terlinguaranch.com

Las Ruinas Camping Hostel • (432) 371-2219
Terlingua Ghost Town Rd, Terlingua

Wildhorse Station • (432) 371-2526
53071 TX-118, Terlingua

Guadalupe Mts/Carlsbad Area
Trinity Hotel • (575) 234-9891
201 S Canal St, Carlsbad, NM
thetrinityhotel.com • Rates: $189+

White's City Resort • (575) 785-2294
12 Yellowstone Dr, NM

Carlsbad Inn • (575) 887-1171
2019 S Canal St, Carlsbad, NM

Stage Coach Inn • (575) 887-1148
1819 S Canal St, Carlsbad, NM

Caverns Motel • (575) 887-6522
844 S Canal St, Carlsbad, NM

Economy Inn • (575) 885-4914
1621 S Canal St, Carlsbad, NM

Parkview Motel • (575) 885-3117
401 E Greene St, Carlsbad, NM

Carlsbad RV Park • (575) 885-6333
4301 National Parks Hwy, Carlsbad, NM
carlsbadrvpark.com

Windmill RV Park • (575) 887-1387
3624 National Parks Hwy, Carlsbad, NM

KOA • (575) 457-2000
2 Manthei Rd, Carlsbad, NM

Petrified Forest Area
Wigwam Motel • (928) 524-3048
811 W Hopi Dr, Holbrook

Globetrotter Lodge • (928) 297-0158
902 W Hopi Dr, Holbrook
hotelsholbrookaz.com • Rates: $75–93

Travelodge • (928) 524-6815
2418 E Navajo Blvd, Holbrook

La Posada Hotel • (928) 289-4366
303 E 2nd St, Winslow
laposada.org • Rates: $119–169

Heritage Inn B&B • (928) 536-3322
161 N Main St, Snowflake
heritage-inn.net • Rates: $105+

KOA Kampground • (928) 524-6689
102 Hermosa Dr, Holbrook

Saguaro Area
Canyon Ranch • (800) 742-9000
All-inclusive multi-day packages available
8600 E Rockcliff Rd, Tucson
canyonranchdestinations.com

Arizona Inn • (800) 933-1093
2200 E Elm St, Tucson
arizonainn.com • Rates: $219+

Lodge on the Desert • (520) 320-2000
306 N Alvernon Way, Tucson
lodgeonthedesert.com • Rates: $129–179

Mira Vista Resort • (520) 744-2355
7501 N Wade Rd, Tucson
miravistaresort.com • Rates: $170–280

Cat Mountain Lodge • (520) 578-6085
2720 S Kinney Rd, Tucson
catmountainlodge.com • Rates: $109–179

White Stallion Ranch • (520) 297-0252
9251 W Twin Peaks Rd, Tucson
whitestallion.com • Rates: $167–275

Starr Pass Golf Suites • (520) 670-0500
3645 W Starr Pass Blvd, Tucson
shellhospitality.com • Rates: $129+

Loews Ventana Canyon Resort • (520) 299-2020
7000 N Resort Dr, Tucson
loewshotels.com • Rates: $199+

The Big Blue House • (520) 891-1827
144 E University Blvd, Tucson
144university.com • Rates: $120–180

Royal Elizabeth B&B • (877) 670-9022
204 S Scott Ave, Tucson
royalelizabeth.com • Rates: $169–229

Roadrunner Hostel • (520) 628-4709
346 E 12th St, Tucson
roadrunnerhostelinn.com • Rates: $22–45

Westward Look Resort • (800) 722-2500
245 E Ina Rd, Tucson
westwardlook.com • Rates: $211–415

Sonoran Suites Of Tucson • (480) 607-6665
7990 E Snyder Rd, Tucson • sonoransuites.com

Adobe Rose Inn • (520) 369-4417
940 N Olsen Ave, Tucson
aroseinn.com • Rates: $90–230

Azure Gate B&B • (520) 749-8157
9351 E Morrill Way, Tucson
azuregate.com • Rates: $140–195

Cactus Cove B&B • (520) 760-7730
10066 E Kleindale Rd, Tucson
cactuscove.com • Rates: $245–345

Desert Dove B&B • (520) 722-6879
11707 E Old Spanish Tr, Tucson
desertdovebb.com • Rates: $130–145

Desert Trails B&B • (520) 885-7295
12851 E Speedway Blvd, Tucson
deserttrails.com • Rates: $90–175

SunCatcher Inn • (520) 444-3077
105 N Avenida Javalina, Tucson
suncatchertucson.com

Casitas at Smokey Springs • (520) 870-8778
1451 N Smokey Springs Rd, Tucson
casitas.com • Rates: $135–209

Hacienda Del Desierto B&B • (520) 298-1764
11770 E Rambling Tr, Tucson
tucson-bed-breakfast.com • Rates: $129–289

Jeremiah Inn B&B • (520) 749-3072
10921 E Snyder Rd, Tucson
jeremiahinn.com • Rates: $110–240

Inn at Civano • (520) 296-5428
10448 E 7 Generations Way, Tucson
innatcivano.com • Rates: $79–179

Casa Tierra Adobe B&B • (520) 578-3058
11155 W Calle Pima, Tucson
casatierratucson.com • Rates: $135–195

Rincon Country E RV Resort • (520) 886-8431
8989 E Escalante Rd, Tucson
rinconcountry.com • Rates: $49+

Far Horizons Tucson Village RV • (520) 296-1234
555 N Pantano Rd, Tucson
tucsonvillage.com • Rates: $41+

Desert Trails RV Park • (520) 883-8340
3551 S San Joaquin Rd, Tucson
deserttrailsrvpark.com • Rates: $29+

*Many chain restaurants and hotels can be found
nearby in El Paso, TX; Carlsbad, NM; Albuquerque, NM; Flagstaff, AZ; Phoenix, AZ; and
Tucson AZ; as well as along Interstates 10, 25,
40, and 17.*

Festivals
Big Bend Area
Int'l Chili Championship • November
Terilingua • abowlofred.com

Guadalupe Mts/Carlsbad Area
UFO Festival • July
Roswell, NM • ufofestivalroswell.com

New Mexico State Fair • September
Albuquerque, NM • exponm.com/state-fair/

Hatch Valley Chile Festival • September
Hatch Valley, NM • hatchchilefest.com

International Balloon Fiesta • October
Albuquerque, NM • balloonfiesta.com

Festival of the Cranes • November
Socorro, NM • friendsofthebosque.org/crane

Petrified Forest Area
Nature and Birding Festival • April
Cottonwood, AZ • birdyverde.org

Navajo Nation Fair • August/September
Window Rock, AZ • navajonationfair.com

Saguaro Area
World Championship Hoop Dance Contest
February • Phoenix, AZ • heard.org

Arabian Horse Show • February
Scottsdale, AZ • scottsdaleshow.com

Cowgirl Up! • March
Wickenburg, AZ

SalsaFest • September
Safford, AZ • SalsaTrail.com

1000 The Great Stair Climb • October
Bisbee, AZ • bisbee1000.org

All Souls Procession • November
Tucson, AZ • allsoulsprocession.org

Attractions
Big Bend Area
Big Bend River Tours • (800) 545-4240
River, hiking, & backroad tours • *Rental & Shuttle*
23331 FM-170, Terlingua
bigbendrivertours.com • Raft: $75 (half-day)

Far Flung Outdoor Center • (432) 371-2634
River, Jeep, & ATV Tours • *Rental & Shuttle*
23310 FM-170, Terlingua
bigbendfarflung.com • Raft: $79 (half-day)

Desert Sports • (888) 989-6900
Bike, Hike, River & Combo Tours • *Rental & Shuttle*
22937 FM-170, Terlingua
desertsportstx.com • Raft: $225 (full-day)

Big Bend Stables • (800) 887-4331
1-hr to half-day trail rides, must be at least 6 years old
TX-118, Terlingua
lajitasstables.com • Trail Rides: $65 (2 hr)

Lajitas Stables • (800) 887-4331
21315 FM-170, Redford
lajitasstables.com • Trail Rides: $75 (2 hr)

Big Bend Ranch State Park • (432) 358-4444
1900 S Saucedo, Presidio
tpwd.texas.gov • Entrance Fee: $3–5/person

Railroad Blues • (432) 837-3103
504 W Holland Ave, Alpine
railroadblues.com • Live Music

Guadalupe Mts/Carlsbad Area
Franklin Mtns State Park • (915) 566-6441
1331 McKelligon Canyon Rd, El Paso, TX
tpwd.texas.gov • Entrance Fee: $5/person

Wyler Aerial Tramway • (915) 566-6622
1700 McKinley, El Paso, TX
tpwd.texas.gov • Tickets: $8/person

El Paso Zoo • (915) 212-0966
4001 E Paisano Dr, El Paso, TX
elpasozoo.org • Admission: $12/adult

El Paso Museum of Art • (915) 212-0300
1 Arts Festival Plz, El Paso, TX
elpasoartmuseum.org • Free

Living Desert State Park • (575) 887-5516
1504 Miehls Dr, Carlsbad, NM
emnrd.state.nm.us • Entrance Fee: $5/vehicle

Sitting Bull Falls (Lincoln National Forest)
Sitting Bull Falls Rd, Carlsbad, NM

Carlsbad Community Theatre • (575) 887-3157
National Parks Hwy, Carlsbad, NM
cctinfo.com

Cavern City Cinemas • (575) 885-4126
401 W Fiesta Dr, Carlsbad, NM

Mall Cinema • (575) 885-0777
2322 W Pierce St, Carlsbad, NM

Cal's Cactus Lanes • (575) 887-1933
1609 S Canal St, Carlsbad, NM

Brantley Lake State Park • (575) 457-2384
33 E Brantley Lake Rd, Carlsbad, NM
emnrd.state.nm.us • Entrance Fee: $5/vehicle

Riverbend Hot Springs • (575) 894-7625
NM's only hot springs spa • on Rio Grande
100 Austin St, Truth or Consequences, NM
riverbendhotsprings.com

Geronimo Springs Museum • (575) 894-6600
211 Main St, Truth or Consequences, NM
geronimospringsmuseum.com • $6/adult

Bitter Lake Nat'l Wildlife Refuge • Chaves, NM
fws.gov/refuge/bitter_lake

Bottomless Lakes State Park • (575) 624-6058
545 A Bottomless lakes Rd, Roswell, NM
emnrd.state.nm.us • Entrance Fee: $5/vehicle

Roswell Museum and Art Center • (575) 624-6744
100 W 11th St, Roswell, NM
roswellmuseum.org • Free

Alien Zone • (575) 627-6982
216 N Main St, Roswell, NM
alienzoneroswellnm.com

Spring River Zoo • (575) 624-6760
1306 E College Blvd, Roswell, NM

International UFO Museum • (800) 822-3545
114 N Main St, Roswell, NM
roswellufomuseum.com • Admission: $5/adult

Beyond Petrified Forest

Turquoise Museum • (505) 247-8650
2107 Central Ave NW, Albuquerque, NM
turquoisemuseum.com • Admission: $12/adult

The Box Performance Space • (505) 404-1578
Improv classes, camps, and shows ($10/Ticket)
114 Gold Ave SW, Albuquerque, NM
theboxabq.com

Hinkle Family Fun Center • (505) 299-3100
Bumper cars/boats, go-carts, mini-golf, and more
12931 Indian School Rd NE, Albuquerque, NM
hinklefamilyfuncenter.com

Rattlesnake Museum • (505) 242-6569
202 San Felipe St NW, Albuquerque, NM
rattlesnakes.com • Admission: $5/adult

Nat'l Museum of Nuclear Science & History
Learn about the atomic age • (505) 245-2137
601 Eubank Blvd SE, Albuquerque, NM
nuclearmuseum.org • Admission: $12/adult

Unser Racing Museum • (505) 341-1776
1776 Montano Rd NW, Los Ranchos, NM
unserracingmuseum.com • Admission: $10/adult

ABQ BioPark - Zoo • (505) 768-2000
903 10th St SW, Albuquerque, NM
cabq.gov • Admission: $12.50/adult

ABQ BioPark - Botanic Garden & Aquarium
2601 Central Ave NW, Albuquerque, NM
cabq.gov • $12.50/adult (includes zoo)

Albuquerque Museum • (505) 243-7255
2000 Mtn Rd NW, Albuquerque, NM
albuquerquemuseum.org • Admission: $4/adult

Nat'l Hispanic Cultural Center • (505) 246-2261
1701 4th St SW, # 211, Albuquerque, NM
nhccnm.org • Admission: $3/adult

Sandia Peak Ski Area • (505) 242-9052
10 Tramway Rd NE, Albuquerque, NM
sandiapeak.com • Tram: $20/adult

The Spy House • (505) 842-0223
This B&B holds a monthly murder mystery event
209 High St. NE, Albuquerque, NM
albuquerquebedandbreakfasts.com

Explora • (505) 224-8300
1701 Mtn Rd NW, Albuquerque, NM

New Mexico Museum of Natural History & Science • (505) 841-2800
1801 Mtn Rd NW, Albuquerque, NM
nmnaturalhistory.org • Admission: $7/adult

Indian Pueblo Cultural Center • (505) 843-7270
2401 12th St NW, Albuquerque • indianpueblo.org

Rainbow Ryders • (505) 823-1111
5601 Eagle Rock Ave NE, Albuquerque, NM
rainbowryders.com • Balloon Ride: $179+

ABQ Int'l Balloon Museum • (505) 768-6020
9201 Balloon Museum Dr NE, Albuquerque, NM
balloonmuseum.com • Admission: $4/adult

White Sands Nat'l Mon • (575) 479-6124
PO Box 1086, Holloman AFB, NM
nps.gov/whsa • Entrance Fee: $5/person

Trinity Site near White Sands NM
Site of the first atomic bomb explosion in the northern section of White Sands Missile Range
Open twice per year (view link below for next scheduled open house) • Free
wsmr.army.mil/PAO/Trinity

Gila Cliff Dwellings NM • (575) 536-9461
HC 68 Box 100, Silver City, NM
nps.gov/gicl • Entrance Fee: $10/family/day

El Malpais NM • (505) 876-2783
1900 E Santa Fe Ave, Grants, NM
nps.gov/elma • Free

Bandelier NM • (505) 672-3861 ext. 517
15 Entrance Rd, Los Alamos, NM
nps.gov/band • Entrance Fee: $20/vehicle

Petroglyph NM • (505) 899-0205
6001 Unser Blvd, NW, Albuquerque, NM
nps.gov/petr • Entrance Fee: $1–2/vehicle

⚘Flagstaff Area National Monuments
6400 N US-89, Flagstaff, AZ

Walnut Canyon NM • (928) 526-3367
nps.gov/waca • Entrance Fee: $8/person

Wupatki NM • (928) 679-2365
nps.gov/wupa • Entrance Fee: $10/person

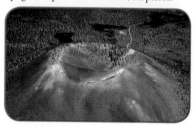

Sunset Crater Volcano NM • (928) 526-0502
nps.gov/sucr • Entrance Fee: $10/person

⚘Lowell Observatory • (928) 774-3358
1400 W Mars Hill Rd, Flagstaff, AZ
lowell.edu • Admission: $12/adult

Eliphante
A sculptural home created by a local artist
Cornville AZ • eliphante.org

Saguaro Area
⚘AZ-Sonora Desert Museum • (520) 883-2702
2021 N Kinney Rd, Tucson
desertmuseum.org • Admission: $20.50/adult

Cocoraque Ranch • (520) 682-8594
*Working Cattle Ranch offers cattle drives, trail/
hay rides, and rodeos • Saguaro West*
3199 Reservation Rd, Marana
cocoraque.com

Pantano Riding Stables • (520) 298-8980
Offers regular trail rides at Saguaro East
4450 S Houghton Rd, Tucson
canyon-country.com/tucson/html/pantano.html
Rates: Dinner Ride • $60/person (2.5 hours),
Sunset Ride • $55/person (1.5 hours), Trail
Rides • 0.5-hr ($30/person), 1-hr ($35), 1.5-hr
($45), and 2-hr ($60)

⚘Houston's Horseback Riding • (520) 298-7450
Trail rides ($120) into Saguaro NP w/ BBQ
12801 E Speedway Blvd, Tucson
tucsonhorsebackriding.com

Foolish Pleasure Hot Air Balloon Rides
(520) 578-0610 • 4920 W Ina Rd, Tucson
foolishpleasureaz.com • Rates: $230+

Marana Skydiving Center • (520) 682-4441
11700 W Avra Valley Rd, Marana
skydivemarana.com

Quarry Pines Golf Club At Marana
8480 N Continental Links Dr, Tucson
playthepines.com • (520) 744-7443

Crooked Tree Golf Course • (520) 744-3366
9101 N Thornydale Rd, Tucson
crookedtreegc.net

Tohono Chul Park • (520) 742-6455
7366 N Paseo del Norte, Tucson
tohonochulpark.org • Admission: $10/adult

Arizona Historical Society • (520) 628-5774
949 East 2nd Street, Tucson
arizonahistoricalsociety.org • Admission: $8/adult

⚘Kitt Peak Visitor Center • (520) 318-8726
Hwy 386, Sells • noao.edu • Tours: $9.75/adult

Mission San Xavier del Bac • (520) 294-2624
*A National Historic Landmark, this Catholic
mission was constructed in 1791 making it the
oldest intact European structure in Arizona. Museum and gift shop on-site.*
1950 W San Xavier Rd, Tucson
sanxaviermission.org

Int'l Wildlife Museum • (520) 629-0100
4800 W Gates Pass Rd, Tucson
thewildlifemuseum.org • Admission: $9/adult

Flandrau Science Center & Planetarium
1601 E University Blvd, Tucson
flandrau.org • (520) 621-4516
Admission: $14/adult

Pima Air & Space Museum • (520) 574-0462
6000 E Valencia Rd, Tucson
pimaair.org • Admission: $15.50/adult

Tucson Museum Of Art • (520) 624-2333
140 N Main Ave, Tucson
tucsonmuseumofart.org • Admission: $12/adult

Center for Creative Photography
1030 N Olive Rd, Tucson • (520) 621-7968
creativephotography.org • Free

⚘The Mini-Time Machine • (520) 881-0606
A Museum of Miniatures
4455 E Camp Lowell Dr, Tucson
theminitimemachine.org • Admission: $7/adult

Reid Park Zoo • (520) 791-4022
960 S Randolph Way, Tucson
reidparkzoo.org • Admission: $9/adult

Breakers Water Park • (520) 682-2530
8555 W Tangerine Rd, Marana
breakerswaterpark.com • Admission: $24/adult

Bedroxx Bowling • (520) 744-7655
4385 W Ina Rd, Tucson • bedroxx.com

The Flycatcher • (520) 207-9251
340 E 6th St, Tucson
flycatchertucson.com • Live Music

⚘Carnival of Illusion • (520) 615-5299
Doubletree Hotel, 306 N Alvernon Way, Tucson
carnivalofillusion.com • Tickets: $35+

Casino Del Sol • (855) 765-7829
5655 W Valencia Rd, Tucson • casinodelsol.com

Broadway In Tucson • (520) 903-2929
100 N Stone Ave, # 905, Tucson
broadwayintucson.com

⚘Gaslight Theatre • (520) 886-9428
Offers a variety of off-beat and lighthearted shows
7010 E Broadway Blvd, Tucson
thegaslighttheatre.com

Borderlands Theatre • (520) 882-8607
40 W Broadway Blvd, Tucson
borderlandstheater.org

Harkins Theatres • (520) 579-0500
5755 W Arizona Pavilions Dr, Tucson

Fox Tucson Theatre • (520) 547-3040
17 W Congress St, Tucson • foxtucson.com

AMC Loews Theatres/Foothills 15
7401 N La Cholla Blvd, Tucson • (507) 742-5050

Century Park 20 Theatre • (520) 745-2321
5870 E Broadway Blvd, Tucson

Loft Cinema • (520) 795-7777
3233 E Speedway Blvd, Tucson • loftcinema.com

Colossal Cave Mtn Park • (520) 647-7275
16721 E Old Spanish Trail, Vail
colossalcave.com • Cave Tours: $16+

Kartchner Caverns State Park • (520) 586-4100
2980 S Hwy 90, Benson
azstateparks.com • Cave Tours: $23/adult

⚘Sabino Canyon • (520) 749-2861
5900 N Sabino Canyon Rd, Catalina Foothills
sabinocanyon.com • Tours available

Biosphere 2 • (520) 838-6200
Unique research, outreach, and learning center
32540 S Biosphere Rd, Oracle
biosphere2.org • Admission: $20/adult

Organ Pipe Cactus National Monument
(520) 387-6849 • *Dangerous due to drug runners*
10 Organ Pipe Dr, Ajo
nps.gov/orpi • Entrance Fee: $12/vehicle

⚘Hot Air Expeditions • (480) 502-6999
704W Deer Valley Rd, Phoenix
hotairexpeditions.com

Octane Raceway • (602) 302-7223
9119 Talking Stick Way, Scottsdale
octaneraceway.com

✍Camelback Mountain
Some of the best hiking in Phoenix (strenuous)
McDonald Dr, Phoenix

✍Lost Dutchman State Park • (480) 982-4485
6109 N Apache Tr, Apache Junction
azstateparks.com • Entrance Fee: $7/vehicle

Open Road Tours • (602) 997-6474
Tours (departing Phoenix) to Grand Canyon,
Antelope Canyon, Sedona • openroadtours.com

Musical Instrument Museum • (480) 478-6000
4725 E Mayo Blvd, Phoenix
mim.org • Admission: $20/adult

✍Children's Museum • (602) 253-0501
215 N 7th St, Phoenix
childrensmuseumofphoenix.org • $11

Desert Botanical Gardens • (480) 941-1225
1201 N Galvin Parkway, Phoenix
dbg.org • Admission: $22/adult

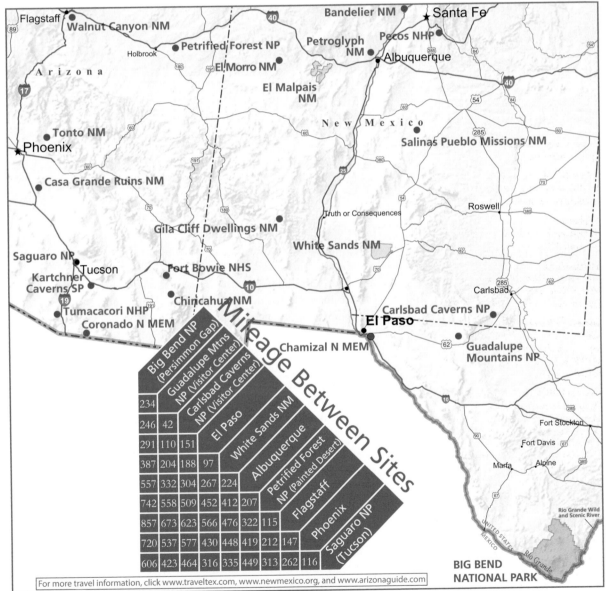

Mileage Between Sites

	Big Bend NP (Persimmon Gap)	Guadalupe Mtns NP (Visitor Center)	Carlsbad Caverns NP (Visitor Center)	El Paso	White Sands NM	Albuquerque	Petrified Forest NP (Painted Desert)	Flagstaff	Phoenix	Saguaro NP (Tucson)
Guadalupe Mtns NP	234									
Carlsbad Caverns NP	246	42								
El Paso	291	110	151							
White Sands NM	387	204	188	97						
Albuquerque	557	332	304	267	224					
Petrified Forest NP	742	558	509	452	412	207				
Flagstaff	857	673	623	566	476	322	115			
Phoenix	720	537	577	430	448	419	212	147		
Saguaro NP (Tucson)	606	423	464	316	335	449	313	262	116	

For more travel information, click www.traveltex.com, www.newmexico.org, and www.arizonaguide.com

Elk near Rock Cut

Rocky Mountain

1000 US Highway 36
Estes Park, CO 80517
Phone: (970) 586-1206
Website: nps.gov/romo

Established: January 26, 1915
Size: 265,828 Acres
Annual Visitors: 4.2 Million
Peak Season: June–August
Hiking Trails: 355 Miles

Activities: Hiking, Backpacking, Driving, Camping, Fishing, Rock Climbing, and Horseback Riding

Campgrounds: 571 total sites at Aspenglen, Glacier Basin, Longs Peak, Moraine Park, and Timber Creek Campgrounds
Fee: $26/night, $18/night (during off-season without water)
Backcountry Camping: Permitted with a Backcountry Use Permit
Lodging: None

Park Hours: All day, every day
Entrance Fee: $30/vehicle, $15/individual (foot, bike, etc.)

Romancing the American West inevitably leads to visions of the Rocky Mountains. They form a natural barrier, stretching 2,700 miles from New Mexico to northern British Columbia. Often referred to as the backbone of the continent, they could just as easily be viewed as the continent's lifeline. The Rockies are the main artery providing land with its most valuable resource: water. Snow collects in the rugged peaks. When it melts, water falls from the steep slopes, pooling into hundreds of alpine lakes, and streams become rivers, carving valleys as they drain into the oceans. These lakes and rivers supply water for one quarter of the United States, eventually coursing across the continent to the Pacific, Arctic, and Atlantic Oceans. In north-central Colorado, just a 2-hour drive from Denver, there's a collection of snowy peaks, meandering streams, and pristine lakes that epitomize the most grandiose Rocky Mountain images you can conjure.

The Rockies are as imposing as they are vast. Native Americans rarely ventured beyond the foothills. Some 6,000 years ago, Ute Indians, also known as Mountain People, were scattered throughout much of modern-day Utah and Colorado (primarily around the Grand Lake area), hunting elk and gathering plants. On the other side of the Continental Divide, Arapaho and Cheyenne lived on the plains, occasionally visiting the present-day Estes Park region to hunt. Natives dominated the area until the late 1700s. Both tribes were separated by a seemingly impenetrable barrier. A barrier they chose not to cross because food was bountiful and everything they needed was available right where they were.

Things changed following the Louisiana Purchase in 1803. Natives were moved to reservations and Americans moved in, but the Rockies failed to draw the public's attention until the gold rush of

1858. Boom towns of Denver, Boulder, and Golden were established, but mining was never very successful. Prospectors made at least one substantial discovery: the allure of the Rockies. Gold-seeking never panned out for Joel Estes either. He found a particularly beautiful location in a valley at the foot of the mountains where he hunted with his son to supply Denver's meat markets and subsidize his meager prospecting income. By 1860 he built cabins for farming and meat production, the humble beginnings of Estes Park.

In 1886, a 16 year-old boy named Enos Mills moved to Estes Park of his own accord. Enos sought what prospectors found by accident, the Rockies and life in the wilderness. In 1889 he met John Muir on a camping trip in California. Muir inspired the young man to study nature and practice conservation. Mills listened and turned his attention back to the Rockies, spending countless hours in the mountains and climbing Longs Peak more than 250 times. He established Longs Peak Inn where guests could attend trail school and be educated on the area's natural wonders. He wrote books and articles on the area's scenic value. The more time spent in the mountains, the more convinced he became that the region should preserved for the enjoyment of the people. He needed to act because the buzz of sawmills' blades and sight of grazing cattle were closing in on his cherished landscapes.

In 1907, President Theodore Roosevelt appointed Mills to be a lecturer for the National Forest Service, an opportunity used to spread his ideas about conservation and to tell others about his beloved Rocky Mountains. Unlike parks before it, Rocky Mountain did not have a major railway lobbying its cause. Nevertheless, Mills remained dedicated to the idea of a park. He found allies in conservation groups like the Colorado Mountain Club. Denver Chamber of Commerce was convinced of the merits of a national park, too. Momentum was building, and in 1915 Congress approved legislation drafted by James Grafton Rogers, and President Woodrow Wilson signed it, creating Rocky Mountain National Park.

A Trail Ridge Road Sunset

When to Go
The park is open year-round. Beaver Meadows and Kawuneeche Visitor Centers are open every day of the year except Thanksgiving and Christmas. Typical hours are from 8am until 5pm, with shorter hours in winter and extended hours in summer. **Fall River, Alpine, and Moraine Park Visitor Centers** close during winter (see page 337 for details).

More than half the park's four million visitors arrive between June and August. If you think Yellowstone is busy in summer, consider the fact Rocky Mountain receives just as many annual visitors but is one-eighth Yellowstone's size. September is a popular time of year, when leaves begin to change color and elk can be heard bugling. To escape the crowds, visit in May or October. The downside is that **Trail Ridge Road** usually first opens in late May and closes for the season around the middle of October. Many high elevation trails can be impassable to hikers without special equipment until well into June and again in October. **Bear Lake Road** is open year-round. The park is always busy in summer, but it's such a popular weekend destination that traveling early in the week often yields significantly smaller crowds. Weekends in Estes Park are usually marred with bumper-to-bumper traffic, approaching complete gridlock.

Transportation & Airports
Public transportation does not provide service to the park. A **free shuttle** runs on Bear Lake Road between Beaver Meadows Visitor Center and Bear Lake Trailhead. There are three separate shuttle routes. Two routes connect Bear Lake Road's trailheads with Moraine Park and Glacier Basin Campgrounds. The third route ferries visitors between Estes Park Visitor Center and Beaver Meadows Visitor Center. Use the shuttles to help reduce traffic congestion. The closest airport is Denver International (DEN), about 80 miles southeast of Beaver Meadows Visitor Center.

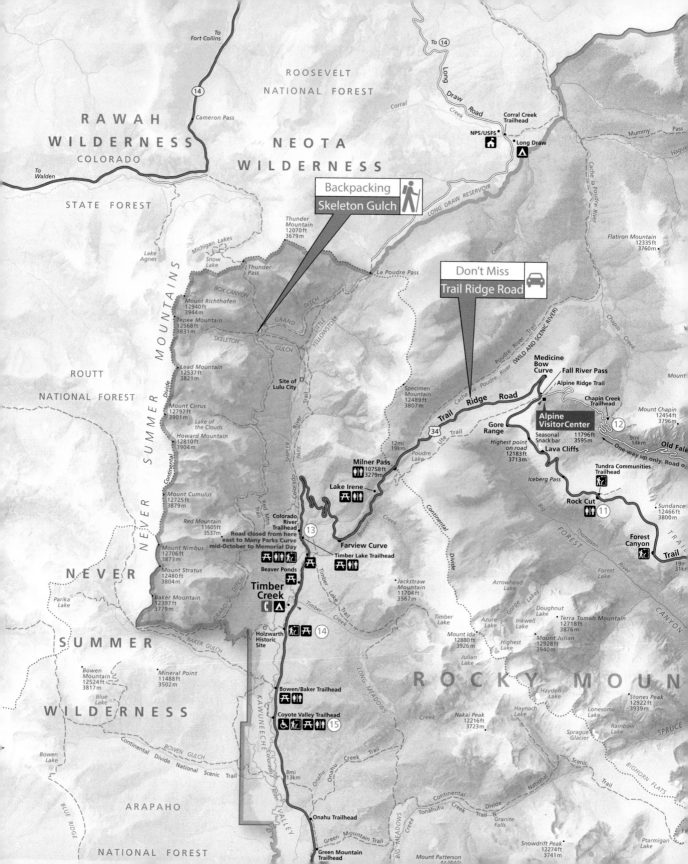

To Fort Collins

To (14)

ROOSEVELT
NATIONAL FOREST

To Walden

R A W A H
W I L D E R N E S S
COLORADO

Cameron Pass

N E O T A
W I L D E R N E S S

Corral Creek
Trailhead

NPS/USFS

Long Draw

STATE FOREST

Mummy Pass

Hague Creek

Backpacking
Skeleton Gulch

Flatiron Mountain
12335ft
3760m

Thunder Mountain
12070ft
3679m

Lake Agnes

Snow Lake

Michigan Lakes

Thunder Pass

La Poudre Pass

LONG DRAW RESERVOIR

Cache la Poudre River

BOX CANYON

Mount Richthofen
12940ft
3944m

Tepee Mountain
12568ft
3831m

SKELETON

GRAND DITCH

LITTLE YELLOWSTONE

Don't Miss
Trail Ridge Road

Medicine Bow Curve

Fall River Pass

Chapin Creek

ROUTT

NATIONAL FOREST

Lead Mountain
12537ft
3821m

Site of Lulu City

GULCH

Poudre River Trail (WILD AND SCENIC RIVER)

Alpine Ridge Trail

Chapin Creek Trailhead

Mount Chapin
12454ft
3796m

Mount Cirrus
12797ft
3901m

Lake of the Clouds

River Trail

Specimen Mountain
12489ft
3807m

Cache la Poudre River

Trail

Ridge

Road

Alpine Visitor Center
11796ft
3595m

(12)

Mount

Howard Mountain
12810ft
3904m

SHIPLER PARK

Ute Trail

34

Gore Range

Seasonal Snackbar

Highest point on road
12183ft
3713m

Lava Cliffs

One-way up only. Road o

9mi
14km

Old Fal

Mount Cumulus
12725ft
3879m

Red Mtn Trail

12mi
19km

Milner Pass
10758ft
3279m

Poudre Lake

Continental

Iceberg Pass

Tundra Communities Trailhead

Rock Cut

(11)

Sundance
12466ft
3800m

Red Mountain
11605ft
3537m

Lake Irene

Continental Divide

Big

FOREST

Thompson River

Mount Nimbus
12706ft
3873m

Road closed from here east to Many Parks Curve mid-October to Memorial Day

Colorado River Trailhead

(13)

Farview Curve

Timber Lake Trailhead

Forest Canyon

Trail

19mi
31km

N E V E R

Mount Stratus
12480ft
3804m

Beaver Ponds

(14)

Jackstraw Mountain
11704ft
3567m

Arrowhead Lake

Forest Lake

Parika Lake

Baker Mountain
12397ft
3779m

GRAND DITCH

BAKER GULCH

Timber Creek

Timber Lake Trail

Timber Lake

Azure Lake

Gorge Lakes

Doughnut Lake

Terra Tomah Mountain
12718ft
3876m

Mount Julian
12928ft
3940m

S U M M E R

Holzwarth Historic Site

Mount Ida
12880ft
3926m

Highest Lake

Inkwell Lake

W I L D E R N E S S

Bowen Mountain
12524ft
3817m

Mineral Point
11488ft
3502m

Blue Lake

Bowen/Baker Trailhead

KAWUNEECHE

Long Meadows

R O C K Y   M O U N

Julian Lake

Hayden Lake

Stones Peak
12922ft
3939m

Coyote Valley Trailhead

(15)

Colorado River Trail

Nakai Peak
12216ft
3723m

Haynach Lake

Lonesome Lake

Sprague Glacier

Rainbow Lake

BIGHORN FLATS

Bowen Lake

Continental Divide National Scenic Trail

BOWEN GULCH

VALLEY

8mi
13km

Onahu Creek Trail

Creek Trail

Big Meadows

Continental Divide

Tonahutu Creek Trail

National

SPRUCE

A R A P A H O

BLUE RIDGE

Onahu Trailhead

Colorado River Trail

Green Mountain Trail

Granite Falls

Scenic Trail

Snowdrift Peak
12274ft
3741m

Ptarmigan Lake

N A T I O N A L   F O R E S T

Green Mountain Trailhead

Mount Patterson

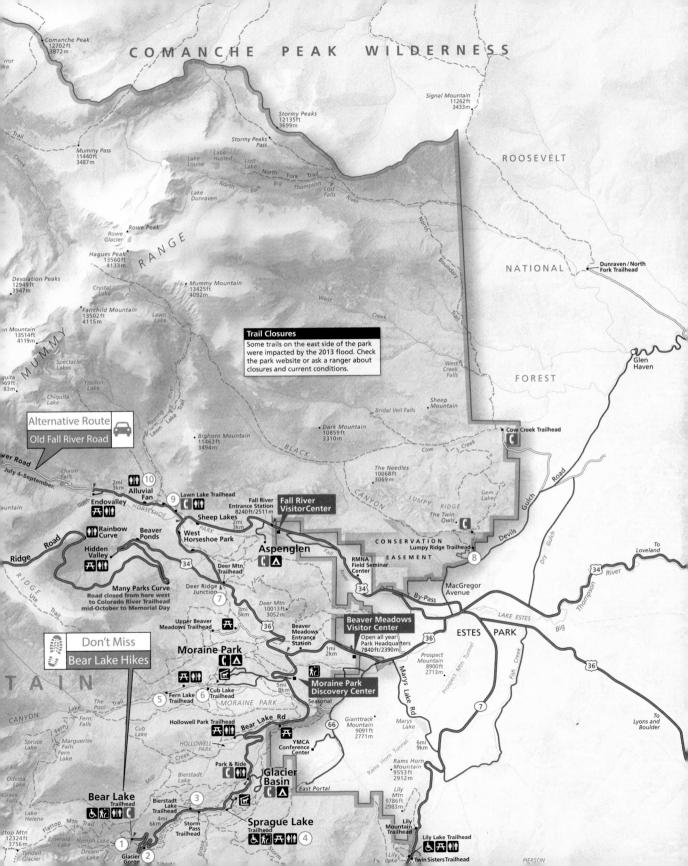

ARAPAHO   NATIONAL   P

BLUE RIDGE

NATIONAL FOREST

Onahu Trailhead

Green Mountain Trail

Green Mountain
Trailhead

Snowdrift Peak
12274ft
3741m

Ptarmigan
Lake

Mount Patterson
11424ft
3482m

Green Mtn
10313ft
3143m

34

491

Bench
Lake

492

Harbison
Meadows

Cascade
Falls

Pettingell
Lake

8720ft/2658m
Open all year

Grand
Lake Entrance
Station

Kawuneeche
Visitor Center

491

Summerland
Park

Lake
Nokoni

Tonahutu Spur
Trail

49

Tonahutu/
North Inlet
Trailheads

Ptarmigan Mountain
12324ft
3756m

GRAND
LAKE

16

Alva B. Adams Tunnel
(water diversion structure)

Lake
Nanita

Apiatan Mountain
10319ft
3145m

GRAND LAKE
8367ft
2550m

17

East Inlet
Trailhead

Andrews Peak
12565ft
3830m

East Shore
Trailhead

West Portal

Adams Falls

East

Supply Creek

Colorado River

Lookout
tower

Shadow
Mtn Trail

Shadow Mountain
10155ft
3095m

East Inlet

East Falls

Lone
Pine
Lake

Mount Craig
12007ft
3660m

Lake
Verna

SHADOW
MOUNTAIN
LAKE

Pine Beach

Mount Bryant
11034ft
3363m

PARADISE PARK

Shadow
Mountain

Shadow
Mountain
Dam

Green
Ridge

Continental

Divide

National

Scenic

Trail

Columbine Creek

Mount Adams
12121ft
3694m

Cutthroat Bay
(group campground)

GREEN RIDGE

Mount Acoma
10508ft
3203m

Adams
Lake

Stillwater

Watanga Mountain
12375ft
3772m

ARAPAHO NATIONAL RECREATION AREA

Twin Peaks
11957ft
3644m

TABLE MOUNTAIN

Sunset Point

Granby
Dam

LAKE GRANBY

Knight

Ridge

Trail

Roaring

Fork

INDIAN

Willow
Creek
Reservoir

Willow Creek

Rainbow Bay

Quinette Point

Pump
Canal

Willow Creek

Rainbow
Bay

Colorado River

Arapaho Bay-Roaring Fork Loop
Knight Ridge Trailhead

34

Arapaho

Bay

Arapaho Bay-Moraine Loop

Arapaho Bay-Big Rock Loop

ARAPAHO

NATIONAL FOREST

Strawberry
Lake

North

To
Granby and 40

Monarch
Lake

Continental Divide
National Scenic Trail

North

0   1   2   3 Kilometers

0   1   2   3 Miles

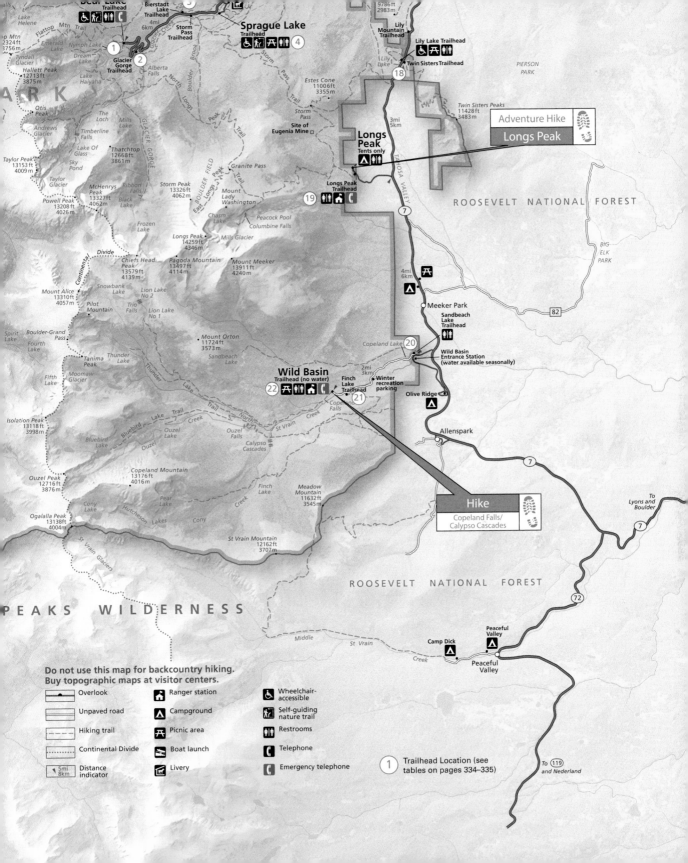

Lake Helene
Flattop Mtn
Emerald Lake
op Mtn 2324ft 3756m
Tyndall Glacier
Hallett Peak 12713ft 3875m
Otis Peak
Andrews Glacier
Taylor Peak 13153ft 4009m
Taylor Glacier
Powell Peak 13208ft 4026m
McHenrys Peak 13327ft 4062m
Isolation Peak 13118ft 3998m
Ouzel Peak 12716ft 3876m
Ogalalla Peak 13138ft 4004m

Nymph Lake
Dream Lake
Lake Haiyaha
The Loch
Lake Of Glass
Sky Pond
Timberline Falls
Mills Lake
Thatchtop 12668ft 3861m
Ribbon Falls
Black Lake
Frozen Lake
Storm Peak 13326ft 4062m
Mount Lady Washington
Chasm Lake
Longs Peak 14259ft 4346m
Mills Glacier
Peacock Pool
Columbine Falls

Bear Lake Trailhead 🚶🚻🅿️📞
Bierstadt Lake Trailhead 🏞️
Sprague Lake ♿🚻🏕️🚻 ④
Storm Pass Trailhead
① ② Glacier Gorge Trailhead

Bear Lake Trailhead 4mi 6km

P A R K

Lily Mountain Trailhead
9786ft 2983m
Lily Lake Trailhead ♿🚻🚻
Twin Sisters Trailhead
⑱

PIERSON PARK

Twin Sisters Peaks 11428ft 3483m

Estes Cone 11006ft 3355m
Storm Pass
Site of Eugenia Mine ☐

Granite Pass

Longs Peak Tents only 🏕️🚻

Longs Peak Trailhead ⑲ 🚻🏠📞

3mi 5km

┌─────────────────────────────┐
│ Adventure Hike   👣 │
│ **Longs Peak**   👣 │
└─────────────────────────────┘

R O O S E V E L T   N A T I O N A L   F O R E S T

⑦

Chiefs Head Peak 13579ft 4139m
Pagoda Mountain 13497ft 4114m
Mount Meeker 13911ft 4240m

Mount Orton 11724ft 3573m

Divide
Continental Divide
Snowbank Lake
Mount Alice 13310ft 4057m
Pilot Mountain
Lion Lake No 2
Trio Falls
Lion Lake No 1

Spirit Lake
Fourth Lake
Boulder-Grand Pass
Tanima Peak
Thunder Lake
Moomaw Glacier
Fifth Lake

Bluebird Lake
Bluebird
Ouzel Lake
Ouzel
Lake
Ouzel Falls
Calypso Cascades
St Vrain Creek
Sandbeach Lake

Thunder Lake Trail
North

Copeland Mountain 13176m 4016m
Pear Lake
Finch Lake
Cony Lake
Cony Lakes
Hutcheson Lakes
Sr Vrain Glaciers
Cony Creek
Finch Creek

Meadow Mountain 11632ft 3545m

St Vrain Mountain 12162ft 3707m

4mi 6km 🏞️
🏕️
Meeker Park
Sandbeach Lake Trailhead 🚻🚻

Copeland Lake ⑳
Wild Basin Entrance Station (water available seasonally)

Wild Basin Trailhead (no water) ㉒ 🏞️🚻🏠📞
Finch Lake Trailhead ㉑
Winter recreation parking
2mi 3km

Copeland Falls

Olive Ridge 🏕️

Allenspark

⑦

82

BIG ELK PARK

┌─────────────────────────────┐
│ **Hike**   👣 │
│ Copeland Falls/ Calypso Cascades │
└─────────────────────────────┘

⑦
To Lyons and Boulder

R O O S E V E L T   N A T I O N A L   F O R E S T

72

Middle St Vrain
Camp Dick 🏕️
Peaceful Valley 🏕️
Peaceful Valley
St Vrain Creek

P E A K S   W I L D E R N E S S

To **119** and Nederland

Do not use this map for backcountry hiking.
Buy topographic maps at visitor centers.

🔲 Overlook	🏠 Ranger station	♿ Wheelchair-accessible
Unpaved road	🏕️ Campground	🚶 Self-guiding nature trail
Hiking trail	🏞️ Picnic area	🚻 Restrooms
Continental Divide	🛶 Boat launch	📞 Telephone
5mi 8km Distance indicator	🖼️ Livery	📞 Emergency telephone

① Trailhead Location (see tables on pages 334–335)

Directions

The park straddles the Continental Divide about 80 miles north of Denver. Trail Ridge Road (US-34), the highest continuous paved road in the United States, crosses the imposing mountain range.

From Denver (64 miles): Take I-25 N toward Fort Collins. Exit onto CO-66. Turn left onto CO-66/Co Rd 30. It becomes US-36/CO-66. Continue through Estes Park, and follow signs to the park.

From the West/I-70 Exit 232 (62 miles): Traveling east on I-70, take exit 157 for CO-131 N toward Wolcott/Steamboat Springs. Turn left at CO-131 N/Bellyache Ridge Rd, and then another left onto CO-131 N/US-6 W. After crossing the Colorado River you'll come to a T-intersection, turn right onto County Rd 1/Trough Rd. Continue on County Rd 1 until it meets CO-9 N. Turn left and drive into Kremmling. As soon as you enter the small city, turn right onto Tyler Ave. After less than half a mile, turn right again onto US-40 E/Park Ave. US-40 follows the Colorado River to Granby. Before entering Granby, turn left onto US-34/Trail Ridge Road, which leads to Grand Lake/East Entrance.

Camping

If you want to spend a night in the park, you're going to have to stay at a campground. There are five drive-in campgrounds. **Aspenglen, Moraine Park, and Glacier Basin Campgrounds** are located near Estes Park. Glacier Basin has lost much of its appeal because most trees were removed due to damage caused by the pine beetle. **Longs Peak Campground** is located south of Estes Park, just off CO-7. It features tent-only sites available on a first-come, first-served basis. It's also a good location to use as a base camp for those attempting to day hike to the summit of Longs Peak (14,259 ft), the highest point in the park. On the west side you'll find **Timber Creek Campground**. It has relatively little seclusion and shade (also because of the pine beetle), but it's the only frontcountry camping option this side of the Continental Divide. Campgrounds often fill during the summer months. To guarantee a site, make a reservation at Aspenglen, Glacier Basin, or Moraine Park (up to six months in advance) at (877) 444-6777 or recreation.gov.

Backpackers have more than 250 backcountry sites to choose from. They are distributed fairly evenly between the western and eastern halves of the park. Backcountry camping requires a permit (page 336).

Rocky Mountain Camping (Fees are per night)

Name	Location	Open	Fee	Sites	Notes
Aspenglen*	Near Fall River Entrance on US-34 (Trail Ridge Rd)	late May–late Sept	$26	53	30-ft max RV length, Near visitor center
Glacier Basin*	Bear Lake Road, 6 miles south of Beaver Meadows	late May–early Sept	$26	150	35-ft max RV Length, Summer shuttle stop
Longs Peak	CO-7, 11 miles south of Beaver Meadows VC	late May–early Nov	$26	26	Tents Only, Access to Longs Peak Trailhead
Moraine Park*	Bear Lake Road, above Moraine Park	All Year	$26	244	40-ft max RV length, Summer shuttle stop
Timber Creek	US-34, 10 miles north of Grand Lake	late May–early Nov	$26	98	30-ft max RV length, Only west-side option

*Campsites can be reserved up to six months in advance by calling (877) 444-6777 or clicking recreation.gov. Water is only available during the summer months. Rates are reduced to $18/night when the water is off. Cold running water and restrooms with flush toilets are available when the water is on. Otherwise vault toilets are available. All campsites have fire rings. Ice is sold at all campgrounds except Timber Creek and Longs Peak. Dump Stations are available at Glacier Basin, Moraine Park, and Timber Creek. No campgrounds have showers or hookups.

Backcountry	267 sites are available with a backcountry/wilderness permit. A limited number of permits can be obtained at Beaver Meadows Visitor Center's Backcountry Office or Kawuneeche Visitor Center. Online (Pay.gov) reservations ($26 fee, May–Oct) are available. See page 336 for details.
Group	Sites available for groups of 9–40 people at Glacier Basin in summer. In winter, sites are available at Moraine Park. Cost is $4 per person per night.

Hiking

No trip to the Rocky Mountains is complete without taking a little hike. Unfortunately, this also means you're sure to run into plenty of hikers. Parking areas may fill up by eight in the morning. **Bear Lake Hiker's Shuttle** is often packed tight with like-minded individuals. But Bear Lake's incomparable beauty, vast collection of rugged lakes, meadows brimming with spring wildflowers, and majestic mountains make it easy to endure the crowds and congestion. The area is best explored by foot and all of the most popular trailheads are located along **Bear Lake Road**. Shuttles may be cramped at times, but you should use them or get an early start. They're far better than circling the parking lots until a spot opens up. Shuttles also allow easy hiking from one trailhead to another (as long as it's on the shuttle route). See page 334 for more Bear Lake area trails. There's no denying the splendor of Dream and Emerald Lakes, but Sky Pond (a bit of scrambling required) and Black Lake are our favorite trails in this area. Remember, the further you hike, the more seclusion (and beauty) you will find. A nice, fairly-long (roughly 10 miles) trek begins at Cub Lake Trailhead. Hike to Cub Lake and continue on to The Pool, Fern Falls, and Odessa Lake, before returning to the shores of Bear Lake.

Alluvial Fan Trail, near the beginning of Old Fall River Road, is a short (and somewhat precarious) climb to dramatic views. **Wild Basin** is located in the park's southeastern corner. The short hikes to Copeland Falls and Calypso Cascades are fantastic. If you're feeling energetic, you can continue on to three alpine lakes that lie close to the Continental Divide. The Keyhole Route to **Longs Peak** is another hike that requires plenty of energy. It's a 4,000-ft climb to the 14,259-ft summit and park's tallest peak. It begins at Longs Peak Trailhead off CO-7. From there it's 8 miles up, with the last 1.5 miles to the summit being the most difficult. You follow bullseyes marked on the rocks. It's no easy feat; hikers have lost their lives attempting it. Elevation change and distance from start to summit is similar to hiking out of the Grand Canyon and right back in. The trail is often impassable (without special equipment) until mid-July, so inquire about conditions at a visitor center before attempting it.

Baby moose in the Never Summer Mountains

Bighorn sheep near Rock Cut

Driving

Driving through the park is all about **Trail Ridge Road**. This high-altitude thoroughfare unlocks the mountain range's rugged interior to motorists. Completed in 1932, the 48-mile road connects Estes Park and Grand Lake. Its grade never exceeds 7% even though it boasts an 8-mile continuous stretch above 11,000 feet elevation. Whether you enter from the east or west you are sure to notice drastic changes in the ecosystem. First you'll pass through forests of aspen and ponderosa pine. As you climb more than 4,000 feet, you cross the tree line and emerge on top of barren mountains covered with fragile alpine tundra. Overlooks and trailheads are dispersed along the scenic byway. From east to west, Many Parks Curve, Forest Canyon, and Rock Cut are pit-stops that should not be skipped. If you'd like to enjoy the Rockies at a slower pace (15 mph), take the one-way, gravel **Old Fall River Road** (usually closed until late June/early July) from Endovalley to Alpine Visitor Center. Note that Old Fall River and Trail Ridge roads are closed for most of the year. Check online or call (970) 586-1222 for current road status.

Most hiking is done on the busier eastern side, but some excellent hiking opportunities can be found along Trail Ridge Road and the park's west side. **Ute Trail** begins on Trail Ridge Road between Rainbow Curve and Forest Canyon. It extends 6.1 miles, descending 3,000 feet through amazing backcountry to Upper Beaver Meadows. It's recommended that you arrange a shuttle and hike one-way to Beaver Meadows. (To make things confusing, Ute Trail also runs from Alpine Visitor Center to Milner Pass. The first quarter-mile or so near Alpine Visitor Center is an exceptional sunset photography spot.) **Tundra Communities and Alpine Ridge Trails**, located on Trail Ridge Road, are worth a quick stop. They are short hikes (about 1 mile each) with outstanding scenery. If you came to Rocky Mountains searching for solitude, choose any of the hiking trails at **East Inlet Trailhead** located near Grand Lake. You probably won't be alone, but it won't be anything like the hustle and bustle of Bear Lake. Scenery here is nearly as inspiring, and the gentle western slopes make for easier hiking.

Rocky Mountain Hiking Trails (Distances are roundtrip)

	Name	Location (# on map)	Length	Difficulty Rating & Notes
South End of Bear Lake Road	Bear Lake Nature	Bear Lake (1)	0.5 mile	E – Self-guiding nature trail
	Nymph, Dream, and Emerald Lakes - ⚲	Bear Lake (1)	1.0/2.2/3.6 miles	E – These three lakes are some of the most well-known and popular attractions in the park
	Lake Haiyaha	Bear Lake (1)	4.2 miles	M – Proof that even the lakes are rocky
	Flattop Mountain	Bear Lake (1)	8.8 miles	S – Hike to the mountain shouldering Hallet Peak
	Hallet Peak - ⚲	Bear Lake (1)	10.0 miles	S – Hike to the peak towering above Dream Lake
	Bierstadt Lake	Bierstadt Lake (3) Bear Lake (1)	2.8 miles 3.2 miles	E – Pleasant trail to alpine lake • Hike from Bear Lake to Bierstadt and use the shuttle to return
	Odessa Lake - ⚲	Bear Lake (1) Fern Lake (5)	8.2 miles 9.8 miles	M – Mountain-lined lake • 8.5-mile trek from Bear Lake Trailhead to Fern Lake Trailhead
	Alberta Falls	Glacier Gorge (2) Bear Lake (1)	1.6 miles 1.8 miles	E – Nice warm-up to venture deeper into the Rockies • Extremely enjoyable all year round
	Mills Lake	Glacier Gorge (2)	5.6 miles	M – One of the park's most beautiful lakes
	The Loch	Glacier Gorge (2)	6.0 miles	M – Beyond Alberta Falls, but before Timberline Falls
	Timberline Falls	Glacier Gorge (2)	8.0 miles	M – Can continue on to Lake of Glass and Sky Pond
	Sky Pond - ⚲	Glacier Gorge (2)	9.8 miles	S – Gorgeous! Scrambling at Timberline Falls
	Black Lake - ⚲	Glacier Gorge (2)	10.0 miles	S – Exceptional continuation beyond Mills Lake
	Sprague Lake - ⚲	Sprague Lake (4)	0.5 mile	E – Self-guiding (great sunset location)
North of Glacier Basin	The Pool	Fern Lake (5)	3.4 miles	E – Pretty hike along a stream
	Fern Falls	Fern Lake (5)	5.0 miles	M – Hike through Arch Rocks to a nice falls
	Fern Lake	Fern Lake (5)	7.6 miles	M – Continues past Fern Falls to the lake
	Cub Lake	Cub Lake (6)	4.6 miles	M – Can loop with Fern Lake Trail
	Moraine Park	Moraine Park (6)	0.8 mile	E – Self-guiding nature loop
	Deer Mountain - ⚲	Deer Mountain (7)	6.0 miles	M – 10,000-ft summit, 360-degree views
	Gem Lake	Lumpy Ridge (8)	3.2 miles	M – Pass rocky terrain to a little lake
	Ypsilon Lake	Lawn Lake (9)	9.0 miles	S – Another popular mountain-lined lake
	Lawn Lake	Lawn Lake (9)	12.4 miles	S – Pristine lake in the Mummy Range
	Alluvial Fan - ⚲	Endovalley Rd (10)	0.4 mile	M – Waterfall and rocks, kids have fun here
	Tundra Communities - ⚲	Rock Cut (11)	1.0 mile	E – Paved trail across the tundra that leads to Toll Memorial (in honor of the first superintendent)
	Ypsilon Mountain	Chapin Creek (12)	7.0 miles	S – Cross Chapin and Chiquita Peaks to Ypsilon

Difficulty Ratings: E = Easy, M = Moderate, S = Strenuous

Sky Pond

Rocky Mountain Hiking Trails (Distances are roundtrip)

	Name	Location (# on map)	Length	Difficulty Rating & Notes
West Rocky Mountain	Lulu City	Colorado River (13)	7.4 miles	M – Flat, old mining town, cross-country skiing
	Timber Lake	Timber Lake (13)	9.6 miles	S – Pass through dense forests to alpine lake
	Holzwarth Hist. Site	Trail Ridge Road (14)	1.0 mile	E – Gravel path to an old dude ranch
	Coyote Valley	Coyote Valley (15)	1.0 mile	E – Moose and elk are often spotted here
	Adams Falls - ⚓	East Inlet (16)	0.6 mile	E – Popular walk near Grand Lake
	Lone Pine Lake	East Inlet (16)	11.0 miles	M – First lake along East Inlet Trail
	Lake Verna	East Inlet (16)	13.8 miles	M – Pass a small falls to a wooded alpine lake
	Spirit Lake	East Inlet (16)	15.6 miles	S – Continues past Lone Pine Lake and Lake Verna
	Cascade Falls	North Inlet (17)	6.8 miles	E – Hike through lodgepole pine to the falls
	Lake Nokoni	North Inlet (17)	19.8 miles	M – Long, seldom visited trail
	Lake Nanita	North Inlet (17)	22.0 miles	S – Long and peaceful, good for backpackers
Southeast Rocky Mountain	Lily Lake - ⚓	Lily Lake (18)	0.7 mile	E – Level gravel path to a pretty mountain lake
	Twin Sisters	Twin Sisters (18)	7.4 miles	S – Summit hike with superb views of Longs Peak
	Eugenia Mine	Longs Peak (19)	2.8 miles	E – Hike to prospecting remnants from the 1800s
	Estes Cone - ⚓	Longs Peak (19) / Storm Pass (3)	6.6 miles / 7.4 miles	M – Excellent views, ends with a sketchy scramble / S – More than 2,000-ft elevation gain
	Chasm Lake - ⚓	Longs Peak (19)	8.4 miles	S – Alpine lake lying in the shadow of Longs Peak
	Longs Peak - ⚓	Longs Peak (19)	16.0 miles	S – Extremely strenuous! 4,000-ft elevation gain
	Sandbeach Lake	Sandbeach Lake (20)	8.4 miles	S – 2,000-ft elevation gain, sand beach and wildlife
	Finch Lake	Finch Lake (21)	9.0 miles	S – Can loop back via Calypso Cascades
	Pear Lake	Finch Lake (21)	13.0 miles	S – Continues past Finch Lake
	Copeland Falls - ⚓	Wild Basin (22)	0.6 mile	E – First site en route to Calypso Cascades/Ouzel Falls
	Calypso Cascades - ⚓	Wild Basin (22)	3.6 miles	E – Excellent riverside scenery
	Ouzel Falls	Wild Basin (22)	5.4 miles	M – Continue past Calypso Cascades to Falls
	Bluebird Lake	Wild Basin (22)	12.0 miles	M – Long day hike or camp in the backcountry
	Thunder Lake	Wild Basin (22)	13.6 miles	S – Passes through a wildflower meadow (spring)
	Lion Lake No. 1	Wild Basin (22)	14.0 miles	S – Follows Thunder Lake Trail for much of the way

Difficulty Ratings: E = Easy, M = Moderate, S = Strenuous

Backpacking

Want to enjoy a summer trip to the Rockies and evade the crowds and congestion? The most reliable solution is to pack up your gear and head into the backcountry. All day-hiking areas (pages 334–335) offer great backpacking opportunities. There are also more remote locations for experienced backpackers. The park's northeastern limits can be explored from **Dunraven/North Fork Trailhead**, which begins in Roosevelt National Forest off unpaved Dunraven Glade Road. From here, hike about 10 miles into the Rockies' Mummy Range to Lost Lake. This remote location can also be reached from **Cow Creek Trailhead** within McGraw Ranch at the end of an unpaved road north of Estes Park off Devil's Gulch Road. From Cow Creek Trailhead take North Boundary Trail to North Fork Trail to Lost Lake. Bridal Veil Falls is another popular destination from Cow Creek trailhead. The 20-ft falls is reached via a short spur from Cow Creek Trail. It is 3 miles (one-way) from the trailhead. Cow Creek Trail continues deeper into the Rockies. It follows Black Canyon all the way to Lawn and Crystal Lakes. Those looking to explore the northwestern corner should begin at **Corral Creek Trailhead**. It's also located in Roosevelt National Forest, along unpaved Long Draw Road. From here you can hike Poudre River Trail for 10.5 miles to Trail Ridge Road. It is lightly traveled with two campsites along the way. **Skeleton Gulch**, accessed from Colorado River Trail, is a moderately popular backpacking area with mountain vistas all around as you hike along the river valley, but few make the steep climb to Skeleton Gulch, where you'll find peace in the form of one lone campsite.

After you've mapped out your backpacking route on a good topographical map (essential to any backpacking adventure), it's time to get a **backcountry/wilderness permit**. The number of permits issued is limited, so you may want to make a reservation. Reservation requests are accepted online through Pay.gov and there's a $26 (non-refundable, non-exchangeable) fee per permit reservation for travel between May and October. (You are also allowed to make reservations in person at Beaver Meadows Backcountry Wilderness Office.) Reservation requests must be made at least three days before your desired departure date. For the rest of the year, you can make backcountry reservations by phone (970.586.1242) or in person at Beaver Meadows Backcountry Wilderness Office. If you are unable to use your permit, please notify the park so your sites will be released for other campers.

Horseback Riding

Horses are allowed on approximately 260 of the 355 miles of hiking trails. Before Old Fall River Road and Trail Ridge Road were constructed, riding on horseback through the park was the way of life. Adventurous souls galloped through meadows and climbed steep summits aboard their sure-footed steeds. Horseback riding through the Rockies remains just as gratifying and practical as it was before automobiles arrived on the scene. Horse owners can trailer in stock to explore the trails and enjoy backcountry camping (permit required), but most visitors join a group of riders on a **trail ride** provided by one of the park's approved outfitters. Rides range from 1–9 hours, starting at $40/rider. Multi-day trips are also available. Check out SK Horses (970.586.5890, skyhorses.com) and Sombrero Ranch (970.586.4577, sombrero.com) for details.

Fishing

Fishing is a popular activity even though many of the alpine lakes and streams are too high to support reproducing populations of fish. But there are many fine locations to catch brown, brook, rainbow, and cutthroat trout. All anglers 16 years of age and older require a Colorado fishing license. You can only use one rod and reel with artificial bait. A number of rules and regulations regarding open and closed waters, catch and release, and possession limits are enforced. If you don't receive current information regarding rules and regulations when you purchase your fishing license, be sure to stop at a visitor center to discuss your plans with a friendly park ranger. The **best guides** in the area are Sasquatch Fly Fishing (970.586.3341, sasquatchflyfishing.com), Estes Angler (800.586.2110, estesangler.com), or Kirk's Fly Shop (970.577.0790, kirksflyshop.com). All three are based out of Estes Park.

Rock Climbing

Boulder and Denver have earned their distinction as extreme sports hubs. Rock climbing is one of their specialties, and there are few better playgrounds for rock climbers than Rocky Mountain National Park. It is one of the area's premier climbing locations, offering everything from highly technical routes to basic scrambling. If you're interested in exploring the vertical side of the Rockies, check out the park's approved **rock climbing outfitter**, Colorado Mountain School (800.836.4008, coloradomountainschool. com), who offers a variety of group excursions (rates are based on size and length of tour).

Winter Activities

Winter is when you'll find tranquility along the roadways and hiking trails in summer. Often it feels like you're the only visitor in this vast expanse of untamed wilderness. Most winter guests explore hiking trails with **cross-country skis** or **snowshoes**. Bear Lake Area remains the most popular destination even when it's blanketed in snow. Several trails, like Bierstadt Lake and Chasm Falls, are marked for winter use. A winter play area is maintained at Hidden Valley, located at the end of a short access road off Trail Ridge Road (US-34) just past Beaver Ponds Pullout. It is the only site in the park that permits **sledding**. Bring your own

equipment or rent from one of the outdoor **equipment outfitters** in Estes Park, like The Warming House (790 Moraine Ave, 970.586.9426, warminghouse.com). On the west side of the park, you can rent gear from Never Summer Mountain Products in Grand Lake (919 Grand Ave, 970.627.3642, neversummermtn. com). It's a good idea to call (970) 586-1206 for snow information before visiting Hidden Valley, Estes Park, or any other low elevation area on the park's east side. This region receives very little precipitation because of its location just east of the Continental Divide. Winds are typically strong, resulting in patchy snow cover and drifting. It's also mostly steep and rugged terrain, not suitable for beginner cross-country skiers.

The **west side** of the park (not accessible via Trail Ridge Road in winter) is more reliable. It receives more precipitation, less wind, and features gentler slopes. Many of the west side's hiking trails remain open for hiking, snowshoeing, and cross-country skiing. Whether you visit the west or east side, it is always a good idea to stop in at a visitor center before entering the park. You'll receive up-to-date trail information, and may have the opportunity to join a ranger-led **ski or snowshoe tour**.

Rocky Mountain Visitor and Information Centers

Name	Open	Hours	Location & Notes
Beaver Meadows Visitor Center (closed Thanksgiving and Christmas)	late October–late April late April–mid-June mid-June–late Aug late Aug–early Sept early Sept–late Oct	8am–4:30pm 8am–5pm 8am–9pm 8am–7pm 8am–5pm	Located on US-36, 3 miles west of Estes Park. Designed by Frank Lloyd Wright's School of Architecture. Watch a short introductory film, browse or purchase books and gifts, reserve backcountry campsites, or use the restrooms.
Fall River Visitor Center	late March–mid-Oct, daily • 9am–5pm late-Nov–early Jan, weekends; the Friday after Thankgsiving, and the week after Christmas • 9am–4pm		Located on US-34, 5 miles west of Estes Park. It has a bookstore, exhibits, and restrooms.
Moraine Park Visitor Center	late April–mid-June mid-June–early Sept early Sept–early Oct	9am–4:30pm 9am–5pm 9am–4:30pm	Located on Bear Lake Road, 1.5 miles from Beaver Meadows Entrance. A nature trail, exhibits, restrooms, and museum are open to visitors.
Alpine Visitor Center	late May–mid-June mid-June–early Sept early Sept–early Oct	10:30am–4:30pm 9am–5pm 10:30am–4:30pm	Located at Trail Ridge Rd/Old Fall River Rd Intersection. Ranger programs, exhibits, bookstore, gift store, snacks, and restrooms are available.
Kawuneeche Visitor Center	late Sept–late April late April–mid-June mid-June–early Sept early Sept–late Sept (closed Christmas)	8am–4:30pm 8am–5pm 8am–6pm 8am–4:30pm	Located one mile north of Grand Lake on US-34 at the park's entrance. You can watch a short introductory film (upon request); browse books, merchandise, and exhibits; use the restrooms, and reserve backcountry sites.
Sheeps Lake Information Station	mid-May–mid-August	9am–4pm	Located in Horseshoe Park, on US-34 just beyond Fall River Entrance.

Ranger Programs

Do not skip the park's ranger programs. A huge variety of walks, talks, and evening programs are offered regularly during summer. In winter, you can join a ranger on a snowshoe or cross-country ski tour (reservations required and you must provide your own equipment—see rental details in the Winter Activities section). Rangers are here to educate you on all sorts of subjects, including elk, lightning, geology, wildflowers, and much more. Some programs are geared toward children, bird watchers, stargazers, and hikers. They're all free and fantastic. It's not a crazy idea to plan your entire vacation around ranger activities.

Maybe you've never thought much about beavers. What do they do? How do they survive? Why do they build dams? Everyone seems to know that they have an amazing set of choppers, but few people understand how they change their environment. Learn all about it at Amazing Beavers, a one-hour talk that takes place at Sprague Lake Picnic Area, offered every day in summer except Sundays. Dozens of other programs are offered during summer. You can find a complete list of scheduled events at the park website or in its newspaper (you'll receive a copy at the entrance), or stop in at a visitor center and ask "what's happening?"

For Kids

Children (12 and under) are welcome to participate in the **Junior Ranger Program**. Pick up a free activity booklet at any visitor center. Complete it and show your work to a park ranger to receive an official Junior Ranger Badge.

Flora & Fauna

The Rockies' wildlife and wildflowers are attractions worth visiting on their own. More than one-quarter of the park is alpine tundra, a seemingly barren and lifeless place for most of the year, but after the snow melts and sun thaws its frozen crust, wildflowers begin to grow. In early July, fields of flowers bloom, painting tundra in bright colors that accent the magnificence of the park's mountains standing tall in the background. 66 mammals reside here. Most popular are big and furry or small and mischievous. Elk can be seen (or heard bugling) in places like Moraine Park, where they graze around dawn and dusk. Moose are often spotted in

Kawuneeche Valley. Mountain lions and black bears (no grizzlies) live here, but are seldom seen. Industrious pikas live in the alpine tundra.

Pets

Pets are allowed in the park, but they are prohibited from all hiking trails and the backcountry. As a rule of thumb pets are permitted wherever your car can go. This includes roadsides, parking areas, picnic areas, and drive-in campgrounds. Pets must be kept on a leash no more than six feet in length at all times.

Accessibility

All visitor centers are fully accessible with the exception of Beaver Meadows Visitor Center/Park Headquarters which is accessible with assistance. Glacier Basin, Moraine Park, and Timber Creek Campgrounds have accessible campsites. Most hiking trails are steep, rugged, and inaccessible to wheelchair users. The exceptions are Coyote Valley, Sprague Lake, Lily Lake, and Bear Lake Trails. They are all well-maintained, heavily trafficked, relatively flat, and accessible with assistance.

Weather

Rocky Mountain has two distinct climate patterns created and separated by the Continental Divide. The eastern region is dry and windy. The wetter, western half receives about 20 inches of precipitation annually, about six inches more than the eastern side. Both regions experience long frigid winters. Areas of high elevation can experience snowfall well into July. Expect a wide variation between day and nighttime temperatures. Summers are hot with temperatures frequenting the 70s and 80s°F. Temperatures drop into the 40s°F at night.

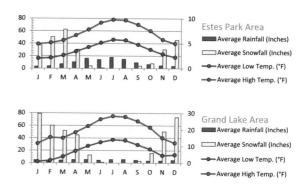

Vacation Planner

What to do while visiting the Rockies varies greatly depending on when you plan on travelling. If you arrive between fall and spring, forget about driving across the Continental Divide via **Old Fall River Road** or **Trail Ridge Road**. They will be closed. **Bear Lake Road** is open all year, but **free hiker's shuttles** only run during summer. The planner below assumes a summer vacation and begins at **Wild Basin** in the park's southeast corner, but it's simple enough to reverse the itinerary, begin at **Grand Lake** and stop at **Kawuneeche Visitor Center** first. Other than **campgrounds** (page 332) there are no lodging facilities within park boundaries, but there are hundreds of options in surrounding communities. Nearby dining, grocery stores, lodging, festivals, and attractions are listed on pages 364–369.

Day 1: Begin by driving up CO-7 to **Wild Basin**. From **Wild Basin Trailhead**, hike to **Copeland Falls** and continue to **Calypso Cascades**. If wildflowers are in bloom and you're enjoying the scenery, continue on to **Ouzel Falls** and **Bluebird Lake**. It's 3.6 miles (roundtrip) to Calypso Cascades and 12 miles (roundtrip) to Bluebird Lake. Allow at least 2 and 6 hours, respectively. Return to CO-7 and head north to **Longs Peak**. Hiking these trails isn't for everyone. The 6.6-mile (roundtrip) hike to Estes Cone is pretty cool. It's not extremely difficult, but after a fairly-long stretch at a moderate grade, the trail becomes steep and faint, with a short (and dangerous) scramble to the summit. If you want to summit Longs Peak (conditions permitting), spend the night at Longs Peak Campground (tent-only) and start before sunrise. If it's peak-season (especially a weekend), and you'll be passing the Longs Peak area in the afternoon, just keep driving. The main parking area and overflow along the side of the road fills up early, as most people attempting Longs arrive well before the sun rises. So, continue along CO-7 to **Beaver Meadows Visitor Center**. Unless you feel compelled to visit Estes Park (extremely busy in summer), bypass it via Mary's Lake Road. Have a look around, get a current schedule of the park's ranger programs, and see if you can catch an evening program before settling into your accommodations for the night or, if you're feeling energized, head into the park and hike a trail or watch the **sunset** from Rock Cut or Ute Trail (the Ute Trail near Alpine Visitor Center).

Day 2: Start at **Bear Lake Trailhead**. Drive in or park at Beaver Meadows and take the park shuttle (recommended). The trek to **Emerald Lake** is a good place to begin, but you can't go wrong with any of these trails. (**Sky Pond** is a great choice for a bit of an adventure. You have to free climb up a chute to Lake of Glass before finally trekking back to Sky Pond. You'll need to be able to lift your own body weight for the scramble.) Hike until you've had enough and return to your car to drive the park's number one attraction: **Trail Ridge Road**. Consider taking **Old Fall River Road** as an alternative (you will return via Trail Ridge Road). It is slower (15 mph speed limit), less crowded, and more stressful (switchbacks and gravel), but it's amazing. Stop at **Alpine Visitor Center** to hike **Alpine Trail** and join a ranger program if possible. From here, continue west on Trail Ridge Road to **Coyote Valley Trailhead**. This is a good location to see moose at dusk. If you'd rather test your luck on a good sunset, there are many great places to watch the sun slip behind the Rockies along Trail Ridge Road, like Rock Cut.

Day 3: Assuming you spent the night on the west side, work your way back across the Rockies on **Trail Ridge Road**. Stop at **Rock Cut** to hike **Tundra Communities Trail**. Anyone looking for a good morning hike can be dropped off at **Ute Trail** (between Rainbow Curve and Forest Canyon) that connects Trail Ridge Road with Upper Beaver Meadows Trailhead. (Following this trail can be challenging.) Let them hike one-way, just remember to pick them up on your way out after stopping at Forest Canyon, Rainbow Curve, and Many Parks Curve. If you didn't stop at **Alluvial Fan** on your way to Old Fall River Road, stop for one last Rocky Mountain hike. It's short and interesting, particularly popular with kids who enjoy climbing the rocks.

Great Sand Dunes

Hiking the dunes

11999 Highway 150
Mosca, CO 81146
Phone: (719) 378-6300
Website: nps.gov/grsa

Established: September 13, 2004
(National Monument in 1932)
Size: 84,670 Acres
Annual Visitors: 300,000
Peak Season: Summer
Hiking Trails: 50+ Miles

Activities: Hiking, Backpacking,
Camping, Fishing, Sandboarding,
Sledding, and Horseback Riding

Campgrounds: Piñon Flats
Fee: $20/night
Backcountry Camping: Permitted*
Lodging: None (See page 344 for
nearby lodging facilities)

Park Hours: All day, every day
Entrance Fee: $15/vehicle,
$10/motorcycle

*Must obtain a free Backcountry
Use Permit from the visitor center

Would you guess the tallest dunes in North America are located in Colorado? They are! The Great Sand Dunes sprawl across San Luis Valley, an arid plain between the San Juan and Sangre de Cristo Mountains. This massive sand box began forming millions of years ago and the region has been inhabited for at least the last 11,000 years. Nomadic hunter–gatherers were initially drawn here by herds of mammoth and bison. Thousands of years later Ute and Jicarilla Apache lived and hunted in the San Luis Valley. Ute called the dunes "sowapopheuveha" or "the land that moves back and forth." Jicarilla Apache called them "sei-anyedi" or "it goes up and down." In 1807, an American soldier, Zebulon Pike regarded the dunes in a similar fashion, describing them as a "sea in a storm." He first encountered the dunes on the Pike Expedition, sent to explore land acquired in the Louisiana Purchase.

Wind drives the rise and fall of waves in a storm, and is also the impetus of these dunes' creation. Crests of sand—sinuous ridgelines—rise up from the plains, crossing arid land at the foot of the Sangre de Cristo Mountains. It's a bizarre sight that immediately begs the question: How were the Great Sand Dunes formed? To understand the formation of the dunes, one must first understand the formation of the mountains. Uplift, caused by collision of two tectonic plates, forced the Sangre de Cristo Mountains to rise from the earth. Their sister range 65 miles west of the dune field, the San Juan Mountains, formed when a massive volcano erupted millions of years ago. Many scientists regard that event as the largest explosive volcanic eruption in the history of earth, with a resulting deposit 5,000 times larger than that of Mount St. Helen's. The two mountain ranges surround a vast plain, roughly the size of Connecticut, known today as San Luis Valley.

This valley used to be covered by an immense lake, which served as a collection site for massive amounts of sediment eroded away from the mountains. Climate change caused the lake to recede, a process that may have been expedited when the valley's southern end wore away, forming Rio Grande Gorge, which allowed water to drain directly into the river. Left behind was a giant sheet of sand.

A huge supply of sand was completely exposed to the forces of Mother Nature. Predominant southwesterly winds went to work. This indomitable force pushed sand across the valley to the Sangre de Cristo Mountains where it funneled into Mosca, Medano, and Music Passes. Storm winds blowing from the northeast took sand pinned against the mountain's slopes and pushed it back toward the valley's floor, causing dunes to grow vertically. Sand blown into the mountains is slowly collected and returned to the dune field by Sand and Medano Creeks.

After hundreds of millennia, the opposing winds seem to have found satisfaction in their grainy masterpiece. Beneath the top layer of loose sand is a wet and cool sandy base, resilient to the forces of nature. These dunes may look like they're rising and falling like a "sea in a storm," but they're actually quite stable, having been roughly the same size and shape for more than 100 years.

A tourist's journey to Great Sand Dunes is nearly as laborious as the sand's. The park is well off the beaten path, far removed from major interstates and metropolitan areas. Like other national parks the greatest architecture here was created by the hands of Mother Nature. Through water and wind she's sculpted a sea of sand that is easily one of the best kept secrets among the entire collection of national parks. Pack up your family and come to the dunes to surf (and sled) the seas of sand and explore this natural phenomenon that has been enchanting and mystifying everyone who's passed its sandy foot for hundreds of years.

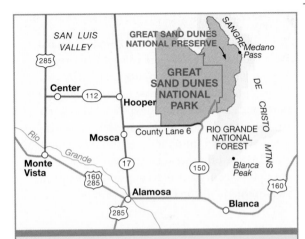

When to Go
Great Sand Dunes is open all year. The **visitor center** is open every day, with the exception of Thanksgiving, Christmas, New Year's Day, and Martin Luther King Jr. Day. Spring through fall, the visitor center's operating hours are from 9am–4:30pm. Summer hours are 8:30am–6pm. Even though summer sun brings the majority of visitors, spring and fall are typically the most pleasant seasons to visit. Dunes can be unbearably hot on a summer afternoon (you may want to wear shoes).

Transportation & Airports
Public transportation does not go to or around the park. There is a small airport in Alamosa, CO, but you are better off flying into Denver International (DEN), 250 miles to the north, or Albuquerque International Sunport (ABQ), 230 miles to the south. Car rental is available at each destination.

Directions
Great Sand Dunes has been described as the quietest park in the contiguous U.S. That title gives you an idea of how removed this scenic wonder is from the rest of civilization. Most visitors arrive from the north via I-25. Heading south on I-25, take Exit 52 for US-160. Turn right onto US-160. After 57 miles, turn right at CO-150 N. Continue for 13 miles and turn left onto Lane 6. After 6 miles turn right at Medano Road, which leads into the park.

Regions

The official name is **Great Sand Dunes National Park and Preserve**. The park comprises the dunes and arid flatlands surrounding them. The preserve is the slice of Sangre de Cristo Mountains north and east of the dune field. Park land was expanded after scientists determined the important role water played in creation of the sand dunes. Regulations differ between the two regions; for example you can hunt and camp at non-designated locations in the preserve, but not in the park.

Visitor Center

The **visitor center** (719.378.6395) is where you'll want to introduce yourself to Great Sand Dunes. You'll find interactive exhibits, a short film, bookstore, and restrooms. It's also the main hub for visitor information and the ever-popular ranger programs. Even if your children are eager to play in the sand, stop quickly to browse through the facility and its exhibits, and obtain a current schedule of ranger programs before exploring the park.

Driving

CO-150 enters the park along the eastern edge of San Luis Valley. Entering from the south, the Sangre de Cristo Mountains rise high above you to the east and North America's largest sand dunes come into view to the north. From the scenic byway these undulating sand hills appear to be a sand replica of the sky-scraping mountains whose foot they sit at. You'll get a closer look as the paved roadway closes in on the dunes, eventually terminating at Piñon Flats Campground. Guests with a high-clearance 4WD vehicle can continue along the foot of the mountains and then deep into them on **Medano Pass Primitive Road**. It actually crosses the mountains at Medano Pass and exits the park on County Road 559, which leads to CO-69. Before attempting to drive Medano Pass, stop in at the visitor center (or call them) to assure that it's not closed due to snow or high water levels (there are several creek crossings).

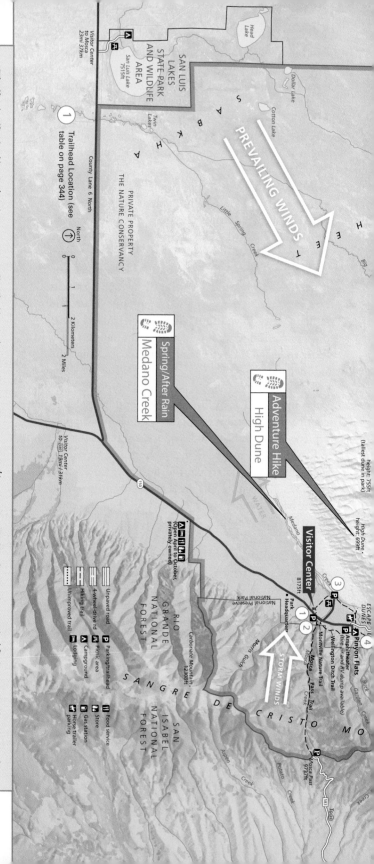

BACA
NATIONAL
WILDLIFE
REFUGE
Ask a ranger for
access information

SAN LUIS VALLEY

SAND

GREAT SAND DUNES
NATIONAL PARK

DUNEFIELD

STAR DUNE
COMPLEX

Indian
Spring

Sand   Creek

Creek

WATER

Sand Ramp Trail

Cold   Creek

Little   Medano   Creek

8600ft

National
Preserve
National Park

Castle Creek

Sand Pit

Hike
Dunes Overlook

Medano Pass Primitive Road
4-wheel drive beyond this point

Point of
No Return

5

Medano   Pass   Primitive   Road

Sand   Ramp   Trail

STORM WINDS

STORM WINDS

GREAT SAND DUNES
NATIONAL PRESERVE

Road closed in winter

Many primitive campsites
along road in this area.
High-clearance 4WD only.

Pinyon Flats
campground to
Medano Pass
12mi / 19km

Castle   Creek

Sawmill Canyon

Horse Canyon

Mount Zwischen
1200ft

NTAINS

May   Creek

North

Medano   Creek

Sand   Creek

Short   Creek

Pole   Creek

Alpine   Creek

Sand   Creek

Saw   Creek

Little Sand Creek

RIO GRANDE
NATIONAL
FOREST

Cottonwood   Creek

Crestone Peak
14294ft

Music Mountain
13355ft

Cleveland Peak
13414ft

Deadman
Lakes

Tijeras Peak
13604ft

Upper
Sand Creek
Lake
11745ft

Lower
Sand Creek Lake
11475ft

Little Sand
Creek Lakes

SANGRE   DE   CRISTO   MOUNTAINS

Milwaukee Peak
13522ft

Marble Mountain
13268ft

Music Pass
11380ft

Snowslide Mountain
11664ft

Blueberry Peak
12015ft

Mount Herard
13297ft

Medano Lake
11518ft

Adventure Hike
Mount Herard

Medano   Creek

Hudson   Creek

North   Creek

Middle   Creek

Cottonwood   Creek

Medano Pass
9982ft

To 69

SAN ISABEL
NATIONAL
FOREST

Crystal Falls Creek

Grape   Creek

Music   Pass   Creek

Grape   Creek

To 69

Liberty Gate
(backcountry access)

Liberty Road

PRIVATE PROPERTY

Deadman   Creek

Camino Del Rey

Camino Baca Grande

Camino Del Rey

Wagon Wheel Road

Camino Real

7

6

165

165

165

Camping & Lodging

Piñon Flats, located one mile north of the visitor center, is the only drive-in campground. It has two, 44-site loops. Campsites at Loop 1 are available on a first-come, first-served basis. Campsites at Loop 2 can be reserved from May until September by calling (877) 444-6777 or clicking recreation.gov. All sites are $20/night and just a half-mile from the sand dunes via Campground Trail. Restrooms with flush toilets and sinks are available, but there are no showers. Not all sites can accommodate RVs or camping trailers over 35 feet. There are no hookups. Three group sites (15–40 people) are available from April through October by reservation only. Group sites cost $3 per person per night with a minimum of $65/night for a 15–30 person site, and $80 for a 20–40 person site. Visitors with a high-clearance 4WD vehicle can access **campsites along Medano Pass Primitive Road** in the national preserve region (road conditions permitting). Camping here is limited to the designated first-come, first-served campsites. Those looking to explore the **backcountry** by foot may camp at one of seven designated sites along Sand Ramp Trail. You can also camp off-trail in the dunes or national preserve. Backpackers must obtain a free backcountry use permit from the visitor center before departing. There are no lodging facilities within park boundaries, but a few options exist in nearby communities (page 366), including **Great Sand Dunes Lodge** (719.378.2900, gsdlodge.com), situated just outside the park's entrance.

Hiking

Great Sand Dunes is one of the National Park Service's pleasant surprises. It's easy to feel like you've been whisked away to some far away desert as you hike across the sandy ridgelines.

At 750 feet, **Star Dune** is the tallest dune in the park. It's a difficult 3.8-mile (one-way) trudge through loose sand to the summit. Views from this sandy peak are phenomenal, but the return trip is where the fun begins. Forget about retracing your original footprints back to Medano Creek in favor of bounding down the sandy slopes. As the sand gives way beneath your feet, you gain a small sense of what it must feel like to walk on the moon. Note: Should you leave the ridgelines you will be forced to scale several dunes (a real thigh-burning experience). The hike to Star Dune begins at Dunes

Great Sand Dunes Hiking Trails (Distances are roundtrip)

	Name	Location (# on map)	Length	Difficulty Rating & Notes
Medano Rd - Piñon Flats	Carbonate Peak	Visitor Center (1)	8.0 miles	S – Unmaintained trail to 12,308-ft summit
	Montville	Montville Parking Lot (2)	0.5 mile	E – Short nature trail with abundant shade
	Wellington Ditch	Montville Parking Lot (2)	2.0 miles	E – Connects visitor center and campground
	Mosca Pass	Montville Parking Lot (2)	7.0 miles	M – Forested hike, not great for dune viewing
	High Dune - 🥾	Dunes Parking Lot (3)	2.5 miles	M – Trudge up 650-ft dune for nice views
	Star Dune - 🥾	Dunes Parking Lot (3)	7.6 miles	S – Hike to the tallest dune in the park
	Dunes Overlook - 🥾	Sand Ramp/Campground (Loop 2) (4)	2.3 miles	M – Good views of the dunes for a short hike
	Sand Ramp	Sand Ramp/Campground (Loop 2) (4)	22.0 miles	E – Backpackers access designated sites and remote dunes, can start at Point of No Return
	Sand Pit	Point of No Return (5)	1.4 miles	E – Can drive here with high-clearance 4WD
	Castle Creek	Point of No Return (5)	3.0 miles	E – Continue from Sand Pit to picnic area
Primitive Rd	Medano Lake	Medano Lake (6)	7.4 miles	S – 4WD required • 1,900-ft elevation gain
	Mount Herard	Medano Lake (6)	10.4 miles	S – Arduous journey to 13,297-ft summit
	Music Pass	Upper Lot (4WD req'd) (7) / Lower Lot (7)	2.0 miles / 7.4 miles	S – Located in the park's northeastern corner, this trail provides access to Sand Creek Lakes
	Sand Creek Lakes	Music Pass (7)	8–23 miles	S – 3 lakes, 3 trails, Lower Sand Creek is closest

Difficulty Ratings: E = Easy, M = Moderate, S = Strenuous

Medano Lake

Lower Sand Creek Lake

Parking Lot, off CO-150/Medano Road. If you want to keep the sand out of your shoes, hike along **Medano Creek** or to **Escape Dunes** (0.75 miles, one-way) just north of the parking area. The trail to Escape Dunes follows a portion of the 0.5-mile (one-way) **Campground Trail**, which connects Dunes Parking Area with Piñon Flats Campground. Another short and easy hike is **Montville Nature Trail**. This 0.5-mile loop begins on top of the hill just north of the visitor center at Montville/Mosca Pass Trailhead.

After playing in the sandbox, empty your shoes, lace them back up, and hike into the mountains. The 3.5-mile (one-way) **Mosca Pass Trail** is the most accessible mountain hike, beginning at the same trailhead as Montville Nature Trail, but it doesn't offer any substantial views of the dunefield. To really get into the mountains you'll need a high-clearance 4WD vehicle to traverse Medano Pass Primitive Road. Near Medano Pass, at the end of a short spur road, you'll find **Medano Lake Trailhead** and a small parking area. From here you can hike 3.5 miles (one-way) to Medano Lake, where you are free to continue an additional 1.7 miles to the top of looming **Mount Herard** (a spectacular viewpoint). If you don't have a 4WD vehicle but still want a panoramic view of the dunes, take the 2-mile (roundtrip) trail from Loop 2 of Piñon Flats Campground to **Dunes Overlook**. It's nestled in the foothills of the Sangre de Cristo Mountains, and can be accessed via a short spur trail from **Sand Ramp Trail**. (You can also hike back to the overlook's spur trail by beginning at **Point of No Return Trailhead**.)

Backpacking

On-trail backpacking adventures are fairly limited without a 4WD vehicle. The only lengthy hike from the paved park road is **Sand Ramp Trail**, beginning at the north end of Piñon Flats Campground's second loop. From here you can hike 11 miles between the dunes and Sangre de Cristo Mountains. At the trail's end you can follow Sand Creek into the mountains. It's about 10 miles from Sand Ramp Trail to Upper Sand Creek Lake with optional spur trails to Milwaukee Peak, Lower Sand Creek Lake, and Little Sand Creek Lake. You must return the way you came or park a second vehicle at Music Pass Trailhead (4WD required). (Note that you'll be following an unmaintained section of trail from Sand Ramp to Sand Creek.) Once you're in the mountains (the preserve region), you are free to camp off-trail wherever you choose.

The best (and most unique) place to backpack is in the dunes. You're welcome to camp anywhere in the dunefield outside of the day use area. There are no marked trails, simply hike at least 1.5 miles into the dunes and pick a spot. It's easiest to follow the ridgelines, but you'll probably want to camp in a depression. It's imperative that you check the weather before departing. Blowing sand is a nuisance, and lightning is a serious threat. You can also camp at any one of seven designated sites along Sand Ramp Trail. They offer better protection from the elements. All overnight trips in the backcountry require a **free backcountry permit** available at the visitor center. Permits must be obtained in person and they cannot be reserved in advance.

Avocet fledglings

Elk crossing in front of the dunes

Sand Activities

To locals, a trip to Great Sand Dunes is like going to the beach. Pack a cooler, umbrella, beach ball, and towel, and you're ready for some fun in the sun. When **Medano Creek** is running you can even play in water and surf one-foot waves when backed up water bursts through dams of sand. Don't forget your bucket and shovel; this is one of the few parks where you can build a sand castle. It's also a popular location to write messages. Vandalism in the parks has been an endemic problem, but writing your name (or a message to outer space) in the dune's sand is encouraged. Wind will eventually wipe the slate clean. You can also **sandboard, sled, or ski** down these sandy slopes. It's best to use boards and sleds designed for use in the sand. **Rentals** are available at Kristi Mountain Sports (719.589.9759, kristimountain-sports.com, $18/day) in Alamosa and at the Oasis Store (719.378.2222, greatdunes.com, $20/day), located just outside the park. Boards and sleds are not rented in winter. Frozen sand can wreck them.

Horseback Riding

Horseback riders are welcome in all of the national preserve and most of the national park. If you have your own horse and you'd like to explore Great Sand Dunes, check the park website or call the visitor center at (719) 378-6395 for information on where to park your trailer, closed areas, camping, regulations, etc. Visitors who lack their own animals but would still like to ride the mountains or valley currently have one option: **Zapata Ranch** (719.378.2356, zranch.com), located in Mosca on CO-150, 6 miles from the visitor center. They provide all-inclusive ranch vacations for serious adventurers seeking a true western experience. Guests learn all about horsemanship at a working ranch. Adult rates range from $1,380/person for three nights to $2,530 for a week.

Ranger Programs

Great Sand Dunes is a peculiar place. To gain a better understanding of the area, join one of its many interpretive programs. These walks and talks give you a better understanding of the region's history, geology, and ecology. They also discuss how in the world all this sand got here (but you'll already know that from reading the introduction). Be sure to stop in at the visitor center to see what programs will be offered during your visit to the park. Large groups can arrange a free tour by calling the park at (719) 378-6395. No programs are scheduled in winter.

For Kids

To kids, Great Sand Dunes is one giant sandbox. Kids of all ages love to play in the sand, bound down the dunes, and splash in Medano Creek during spring and early summer snowmelt. In between playing, children of all ages are welcome to participate in the park's **Junior Ranger Program**. To become a Junior Ranger and receive an official badge, your child must complete an activity booklet (available at the visitor center).

Flora & Fauna

Billions of grains of sand (most of which you will believe made their way into your car) may lead a person to believe that this is a desert region inhabited by cacti and reptiles adapted to life in an arid environment. This couldn't be farther from the truth; Great Sand Dunes has some of the most diverse plant and animal life of the national parks. In lower elevations you may see pronghorn, bison, badgers, mule deer, elk, or the occasional beaver. Mountain slopes are home to yellow-bellied marmots, pikas, bighorn sheep, black bears, and a small population of mountain lions.

There are also more than 200 species of birds, a healthy variety of reptiles, insects, and amphibians, and a few varieties of fish.

Hundreds of species of plants live in the park. Most thrive in the area's wetlands or foothills, but a few species—such as Indian ricegrass and scrufpea—are capable of surviving in the dunes themselves.

Pets

Pets are not allowed in the backcountry, but are permitted in the main day-use areas as long as they are kept on a leash no more than six feet in length.

Accessibility

Rolling hills of sand don't make for the most accessible park. However, there is a wheelchair-accessible viewing platform at Dunes Parking Lot. Wheelchair users hoping to get closer to the dunes can check out one of two sand wheelchairs available at the visitor center. They are designed specifically for sand travel thanks to large, inflatable wheels that do not sink into sand, allowing guests to maneuver about the dunes with assistance. To reserve a sand wheelchair, call the visitor center at (719) 378-6395. The visitor center is fully accessible. Campsites suitable for wheelchair users are available at Piñon Flats and in the backcountry at Sawmill Canyon.

Weather

Temperatures in the summer average between 70 and 90°F, but the sand can get as hot as 150°F on a sunny day. Wear shoes in the dunes to protect your feet from these blazing temperatures. Like most high mountain climates, the temperature changes 30–40°F from afternoon highs to overnight lows. Spring and fall are mild. Winter is cold with significant snowfall. Visitors should be prepared for strong winds and scattered thunderstorms any time of year.

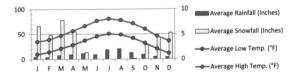

Average Rainfall (Inches)
Average Snowfall (Inches)
Average Low Temp. (°F)
Average High Temp. (°F)

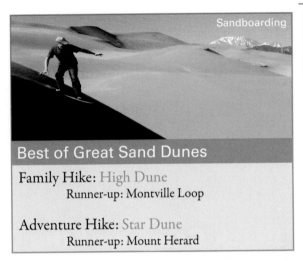

Sandboarding

Best of Great Sand Dunes

Family Hike: High Dune
Runner-up: Montville Loop

Adventure Hike: Star Dune
Runner-up: Mount Herard

Vacation Planner

Visitors can easily spend a week hiking through the dunes and Sangre de Cristo Mountains, but if you only want to dip your toes in sand and take a quick hike through the mountains, you can do so in a day with time to spare. You definitely should **consider renting a sled** (page 346). Last time we were here, we overheard a young child say, "Dad, this was awesome! Thanks for planning a great trip." Now it's your turn to plan a great trip to the tallest dunes in North America. The only in-park overnight accommodation is **Piñon Flats Campground** (page 344). Nearby dining, grocery stores, lodging, festivals, and attractions are listed on pages 364–369.

Day 1: Begin your trip at the **visitor center**. You'll want to check out its exhibits, watch the introductory film, and get a current schedule of ranger programs. If you have enough time, join a ranger program or two. Just north of the visitor center is the short and easy **Montville Nature Trail**. It's a nice 0.5-mile hike through a wooded area with panoramic views of the dunes, but without the crowds you'll find at **Dunes Parking Area** and along Medano Creek. Next, join the crowds at Dunes Parking Area to explore the dunes (no marked trails) or sit by Medano Creek (if it's running) and enjoy the spectacle. Most hikers follow the dune's ridgelines. If you're looking for a bit of non-sand-based-hiking and a more exclusive site, consider driving Medano Pass Primitive Road to Point of No Return (accessible to 2WD vehicles), and hike down to **Sand Pit**.

Cedar Point

Black Canyon of the Gunnison

102 Elk Creek
Gunnison, CO 81230
Phone: (970) 641-2337
Website: nps.gov/blca

Established: October 21, 1999
March 2, 1933 (National Monument)
Size: 30,750 Acres
Annual Visitors: 209,000
Peak Season: Summer

Activities: Hiking, Backpacking,
Kayaking, Rock Climbing, Biking,
Horseback Riding, Snowshoeing,
and Cross-country Skiing

Camping: South Rim Camp*
Fee: $16/night or $22 w/ hookups
North Rim Campground (seasonal)
Fee: $16/night
Backcountry Camping: Permitted
with a free Backcountry Use Permit
Lodging: None
Park Hours: All day, every day
Entrance Fee: $15/vehicle,
$7/individual (foot, bike, etc.)

*Reserve at recreation.gov or (877)
444-6777

Western Colorado's Black Canyon of the Gunnison has been a source of frustration, irrigation, and recreation for more than a century. Its 2,200 foot walls of gray gneiss and schist rise precipitously from the raucous waters of the Gunnison River; walls so deep and narrow sunlight only penetrates their depths at midday, leaving the canyon constantly enveloped in its own shadow. It's an ominous setting, accentuated by the angry river carving through the canyon's floor at a rate of one inch every 100 years. When the river is running, it tears through the canyon with reckless abandon, dropping 34 feet every mile. The Gunnison River loses more elevation in 48 miles than the Mississippi River does in more than 2,000. This is the Black Canyon of the Gunnison. Impassable to explorers. Incorrigible to settlers. Incredible to recreational visitors.

Fur traders and Utes undoubtedly witnessed the Black Canyon, but none were foolish enough to call such a foreboding location home. An expedition led by Captain John W. Gunnison in 1849 and the Hayden Expedition (of 1871), both declared the canyon impassable. Only a railway company, driven by the almighty dollar, had the courage to attempt passage and settlement in the midst of these mighty walls. In 1881, the Denver and Rio Grande Railroad successfully reached the small town of Gunnison from Denver. They proceeded to punch their way through the canyon, building what would be called the "Scenic Line of the World." Construction cost $165,000 per mile in 1882. The last mile of track took an entire year to construct, but they persevered through the deaths of several immigrant laborers to successfully push on to Salt Lake City. For nearly a decade it served as the main route for transcontinental travel, but the combination of a new route through Glenwood Springs and the canyon's frequent bouts of inclement weather and rock slides led to a decrease in popularity of the "Scenic Line of the World." It was finally abandoned in 1955.

By the 1890s, settlers of Uncompahgre Valley began to take a serious look at the Gunnison River as a source of water for irrigation. It required new expeditions into the Black Canyon to analyze the feasibility of blasting a diversion tunnel through its walls of rock and in 1901 Abraham Lincoln Fellows, a hydrologist and Yale graduate, attempted to hike, swim, and float on a rubber mattress through the canyon. Accompanied by William Torrence, together they were the first to run the canyon, covering a distance of 33 miles in 9 days. They also declared that irrigation was possible. Construction followed thanks to funding from Theodore Roosevelt's National Reclamation Act of 1902, and a 5.8-mile, 11-foot-by-12-foot diversion tunnel was built, providing much needed water to an arid farm valley.

In 1916, Emery Kolb, a noted oarsman who owned a photography studio on the rim of the Grand Canyon with his brother, attempted the first recreational trip through the Black Canyon. Years of paddling the Colorado River had left him wanting more and he set his sights on something wilder: the Gunnison. It took five attempts, several boats, canoes, and supplies, but he eventually completed the journey to Delta Bridge.

Today, a park protects the deepest and most spectacular 12 miles of the 48-mile-long canyon. A campground and visitor center sit where a railway town once thrived. Water still pours through a diversion tunnel. And thousands of visitors come to the Black Canyon of the Gunnison each year in pursuit of adventure just like Emery Kolb.

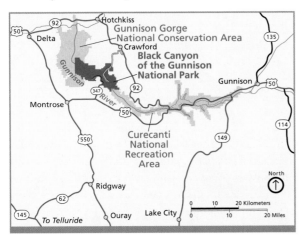

When to Go
The South Rim is open every day of the year, but South Rim Road beyond Gunnison Point closes in winter (typically mid-November until April). East Portal Road, a steep roadway down to the canyon floor, is typically closed from mid-November until mid-April. **South Rim Visitor Center** is open every day except Thanksgiving, Christmas, and New Year's Day. Hours are 8:30am until 4pm for fall, winter, and spring, but are extended to 8am until 6pm in summer. The North Rim is typically closed from late November until mid-April. Black Canyon is busy in summer, but not wildly so like Rocky Mountain NP.

Transportation & Airports
Public transportation does not provide service to or around the park. Greyhound (800.231.2222, greyhound.com) has a bus station in Montrose (15 miles from the visitor center) and Grand Junction (76 miles). Amtrak (800.872.7245, amtrak.com) provides train service to Grand Junction. The closest regional airports are Montrose Regional (MTJ), 18 miles away; Gunnison-Crested Butte Regional (GUC), 62 miles to the east; and Grand Junction Regional (GJT), 82 miles northwest of the park's visitor center. Denver International (DEN) is 335 miles to the east along I-70. Car rental is available at each destination.

Directions
South Rim Visitor Center is 76 miles from Grand Junction (I-70, Exit 37). Take US-50 south through Montrose. Turn left at CO-347 N. Continue for roughly 5 miles before making a slight right onto South Rim Road, which leads into the park. A mere 1,100 feet separates the North and South Rims at spots (canyon walls are as narrow as 40 feet at the floor), but you will not find a bridge connecting the two. Visitors must make an 80+ mile drive to reach one rim from the other. From the south rim, return to US-50, and turn either way at the intersection of US-50 and CO-347. Heading east is about 7 miles longer, but more scenic. Regardless of which way you head on US-50 drive until you reach CO-92. Follow CO-92 to Black Canyon Road, which leads to the North Rim.

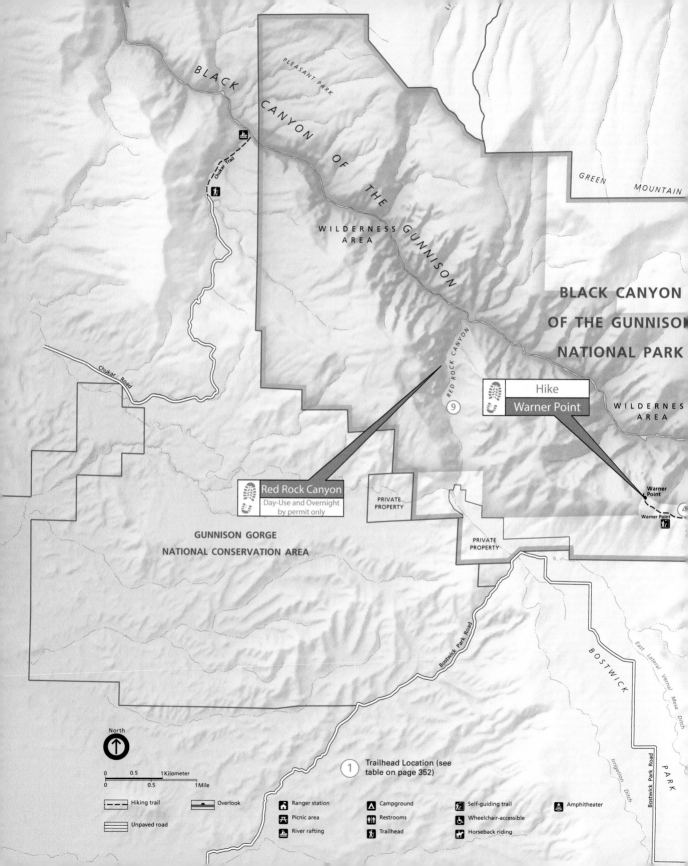

BLACK CANYON OF THE GUNNISON

PLEASANT PARK

WILDERNESS AREA

BLACK CANYON
OF THE GUNNISON
NATIONAL PARK

GREEN MOUNTAIN

Chukar Trail

Chukar Road

RED ROCK CANYON

(9)

WILDERNESS AREA

Hike
Warner Point

Red Rock Canyon
Day-Use and Overnight
by permit only

PRIVATE
PROPERTY

Warner
Point

Warner Point

GUNNISON GORGE
NATIONAL CONSERVATION AREA

PRIVATE
PROPERTY

Bostwick Park Road

BOSTWICK

PARK

East Lateral Vernal Mesa Ditch

Irrigation Ditch

Bostwick Park Road

North

0   0.5   1 Kilometer
0   0.5   1 Mile

1   Trailhead Location (see
    table on page 352)

--- Hiking trail   Overlook

    Unpaved road

🏛 Ranger station   ⛺ Campground   🚶 Self-guiding trail   🎭 Amphitheater

🏕 Picnic area   🚻 Restrooms   ♿ Wheelchair-accessible

🚣 River rafting   🥾 Trailhead   🐎 Horseback riding

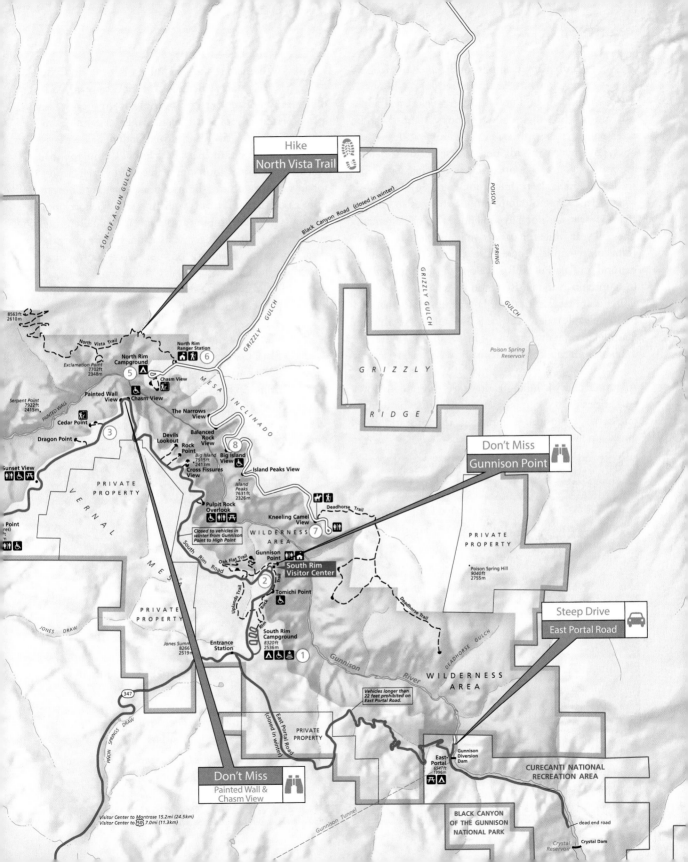

Hike
North Vista Trail

Don't Miss
Gunnison Point

Steep Drive
East Portal Road

Don't Miss
Painted Wall & Chasm View

SON-OF-A-GUN GULCH

POISON   SPRING   GULCH

Black Canyon Road (closed in winter)

GRIZZLY GULCH

GRIZZLY   GULCH

Poison Spring
Reservoir

G R I Z Z L Y

R I D G E

8563 ft
2610 m

North Vista Trail

Exclamation Point
7702 ft
2348 m

North Rim Ranger Station

North Rim
Campground   ⑥

⑤

Chasm View

M E S A   I N C L I N A D O

Serpent Point
7922 ft
2415 m

Painted Wall
View

Chasm View

The Narrows
View

Cedar Point

③

Dragon Point

Devils
Lookout

Rock
Point

Balanced
Rock View

Big Island
7915 ft
2413 m

⑧

Big Island
View

Cross Fissures
View

Island Peaks View

Island
Peaks
7631 ft
2326 m

Sunset View

PRIVATE

V E R N A L

Pulpit Rock
Overlook

Kneeling Camel
View

Deadhorse   Trail

Point

P R I V A T E

P R O P E R T Y

Poison Spring Hill
9040 ft
2755 m

WILDERNESS
AREA

⑦

M E S A

PRIVATE

PROPERTY

Closed to vehicles in
winter from Gunnison
Point to High Point

Oak Flat Trail

Gunnison
Point

South Rim
Visitor Center

②

Uplands Trail

Tomichi Point

Rim

Rock

South Rim
Campground
8320 ft
2536 m

①

JONES DRAW

Jones Summit
8266 ft
2519 m

Entrance
Station

Deadhorse   Trail

DEADHORSE   GULCH

Gunnison   River

W I L D E R N E S S

A R E A

347

PINON SPRINGS DRAW

East Portal Road
(closed in winter)

PRIVATE
PROPERTY

Vehicles longer than
22 feet prohibited on
East Portal Road.

East-
Portal
6547 ft
1996 m

Gunnison
Diversion
Dam

CURECANTI NATIONAL
RECREATION AREA

Visitor Center to Montrose 15.2mi (24.5km)
Visitor Center to 50 7.0mi (11.3km)

Gunnison Tunnel

BLACK CANYON
OF THE GUNNISON
NATIONAL PARK

dead end road

Crystal
Reservoir

Crystal Dam

Camping

South Rim Campground has a total of 88 campsites broken into three loops. Loops A and C are $16/night. Loop B sites have electrical hookups and cost $22/night. Sites at Loops A and B can be reserved by calling (877) 444-6777 or clicking recreation.gov (there is an additional $3 reservation fee). Sites at loop C are available on a first-come, first-served basis. Each loop has its own restroom with sinks and flush toilets. There are no dump stations and vehicles longer than 35 feet are not recommended. Loop A remains open all year while the other two loops close for winter (November–April). There's also a small **15-site campground** on **East Portal Road** along the Gunnison River in Curecanti National Recreation Area (nps.gov/cure). Water is available from mid-May to mid-September and there are vault toilets. The fee is $16/night. **North Rim Campground** is open from spring to fall. All 13 sites are available on a first-come, first-served basis for $16/night.

All **inner canyon** hiking routes (see the table below) end at designated camping areas with anywhere from one to six campsites. Camping in these locations requires a free permit (see the next section).

Wilderness Permit

Whether you're planning on exploring the backcountry (including the inner canyon), paddling the Gunnison, or climbing the canyon's sheer walls, a free permit is required. Obtain yours at South Rim Visitor Center, North Rim Ranger Station, or East Portal Registration Board (near East Portal Campground). A self-registration station is available nearby each facility for anyone arriving after hours. Speak with a park ranger prior to departure if this is your first time backpacking, kayaking, or rock climbing at Black Canyon. Discussing your itinerary with a ranger helps assure you are properly prepared and experienced for your selected adventure. This is a very unforgiving place. Canyon walls are steep, the river is wild, but a safe and enjoyable adventure can be had with proper preparation.

Hiking & Backpacking

Black Canyon is too often a drive-in and drive-out attraction. Visitors should spend some time hiking the rim-top trails, if not a few days going off-trail into the wilderness or inner canyon. A number of short and easy hikes are located along South and North Rim Roads. **Rim Rock Trail** begins at South Rim Campground and

Black Canyon of the Gunnison Hiking Trails (Distances are roundtrip)

	Name	Location (# on map)	Length	Difficulty Rating & Notes
South Rim	Rim Rock	Campground Loop C (1)	1.0 mile	M – Self-guiding trail following the rim
	Uplands	Rim Rock Trail (1)	1.0 mile	M – Combine with Rim Rock to make a 2-mile loop
	Oak Flat Loop	Near the Visitor Center (2)	2.0 miles	S – Unmarked overlooks and narrow passages
	Cedar Point	Cedar Point (3)	0.7 mile	E – Self-guiding, views of Painted Wall
	Warner Point- ⚲	High Point (4)	1.5 miles	M –Trail guides available at High Point
North Rim	Chasm View	In Campground Loop (5)	0.3 mile	M – Short trail with views of Painted Wall
	North Vista - ⚲	North Rim Ranger Station (6)	3.0 miles / 7.0 miles	M – Route to Exclamation Point / S – Continue to Green Mountain and 360° views
	Deadhorse	Kneeling Camel View (7)	5.0 miles	E/M – Follows old service road, East Portal views
Inner Canyon	Tomichi Route	Rim Rock Trail Post #13 (1)	2.0 miles	S – Steepest South Rim route with loose rock
	Gunnison Route	Near the Visitor Center (2)	2.0 miles	S – South Rim • Good first-timers route, still steep
	Warner Route	Warner Point Nature Trail, just past post #13 (4)	5.5 miles	S – Out-and-back will take a full (and exhausting) day • Camp at 1 of 5 sites at the canyon floor
	S.O.B. Draw	North Rim Ranger Station (6)	3.5 miles	S – Easiest of the 3 North Rim inner canyon hikes
	Slide Draw	Kneeling Camel View (7)	2.0 miles	S – North Rim • Extremely steep and dangerous
	Long Draw	Balanced Rock Overlook (8)	2.0 miles	S – North Rim • Access to a very narrow area
	Red Rock Canyon	East Parking Area (9)	6.8 miles	M – Permit Required, lottery application system

Difficulty Ratings: E = Easy, M = Moderate, S = Strenuous

Warner Point

follows the rim north to Tomichi Point, Gunnison Point, and the Visitor Center. From the Visitor Center you can continue hiking on **Oak Flat Loop**, which provides spectacular views of the canyon as you descend slightly below the rim. After looping back to the visitor center it's possible to return to the campground via **Uplands Trail**, which veers away from the canyon on the opposite side of South Rim Road. There are a series of overlooks accessible by short hikes in between the Visitor Center and High Point. **Pulpit Rock** provides a nice long view of the Gunnison River as it rambles beneath the canyon walls. **Chasm, Painted Wall, and Cedar Point Viewpoints** are exceptional. At Chasm View you're standing above the river's steepest grade, where turbulent water drops some 240 feet over a 2-mile stretch. Painted Wall View gives onlookers the opportunity to photograph Colorado's tallest cliff, standing nearly twice the height of the Empire State Building. Its name comes from pink veins of igneous pegmatite rock that interrupt the layers of gneiss and schist.

South Rim Road ends at High Point and **Warner Point Nature Trail**. Mark Warner was a driving force behind the park's establishment, and this trail provides an opportunity to view the area's ecology, history, and geology through his eyes thanks to printed handouts (available at High Point and the Visitor Center). Along the way, you'll notice markers corresponding to sections of the handout. The hike is well worth the effort, with amazing views looking back into the vertical canyon walls along with the Gunnison River. **The North Rim** provides longer trails with similar canyon views. Hiking to Exclamation Point via **North Vista Trail** is particularly nice. This trek begins at North Rim Ranger Station.

Hikers in good physical condition can descend into the canyon via one of **seven inner canyon routes**. They are unmaintained, unmarked, steep, and littered with loose rocks. Poison ivy is practically unavoidable (wear long pants). So why hike into the canyon when you can drive there via East Portal Road? The thrill? Perhaps. The exercise? Maybe. Having such magnificent scenery to yourself is also appealing. Where each route hits the canyon floor you'll find at least one campsite. **Gunnison Route** (South Rim) and **S.O.B. Route** (North Rim) are respectively the easiest routes on either side of the rim, but are still extremely strenuous and challenging. An 80-foot chain is anchored to the canyon wall to aid hikers attempting the Gunnison Route. Don't throw rocks from the rim, there may be hikers on their way into the canyon below.

Red Rock Canyon Route is only available to 8 visitors per day through a reservation lottery system (visit the park website for reservation request forms). This trail is popular with fisherman and hikers because it is significantly less steep than other routes into the gorge. Restrictions are enforced to prevent overuse and because a portion of the trail crosses private land. It is only open from late May until early October and is accessed via Bostwick Park Road, located in the park's southwest corner.

If you plan on hiking the inner canyon or exploring off-trail wilderness areas, regardless of whether it's day-use or overnight, you must obtain a **free wilderness permit** (see opposite page). Permits are an essential tool to help monitor backcountry use and aid in identifying potential emergencies.

Pulpit Rock

Black Canyon is not a place for beginners. Even the most experienced climbers will find the aid of a climbing guide helpful when making a first attempt at Black Canyon's cliffs. The most popular climbing area is north and south Chasm View. Climbing is popular from mid-April to early June, and then from mid-September through early November. All rock climbers must obtain a **wilderness use permit** (page 352).

Other Activities

Less popular activities include horseback riding, winter sports, and biking. Visitors with their own horse(s) can ride North Rim's Deadhorse Trail. Cyclists are permitted on all paved roadways. In winter, snowshoers and cross-country skiers enjoy the section of South Rim Road beyond Gunnison Point, which closes until spring.

Ranger Programs

Black Canyon provides free ranger-guided activities in summer and winter. You might meet a ranger at one of the scenic overlooks to discuss topics ranging from how the canyon was formed to what birds of prey nest within its walls. They also offer short walks at East Portal or along one of the nature trails. Evening programs are administered at South Rim Visitor Center and South Rim Campground's Amphitheater. Stargazing programs are held periodically throughout summer. Only a few programs are held in winter when staffing allows. At the adjacent **Curecanti National Recreation Area** (nps.gov/cure) visitors can take a **boat tour** into the Black Canyon of the Gunnison ($24/adult, $12/child, call (970) 641-2337, ext. 205 for reservations and additional information). Tours are available every day except Tuesdays, Memorial Day weekend through Labor Day. Reservations are required.

For Kids

Children love peering into the depths of Black Canyon (just don't let them throw rocks into the abyss, there could be unsuspecting hikers, climbers, or paddlers below the rim). Kids are invited to become **Black Canyon of the Gunnison National Park Junior Rangers**. To do so, complete the free activity booklet (available at the South Rim Visitor Center). Once completed, your child will be sworn into the club and receive a badge.

Kayaking

Three upstream dams have tamed the Gunnison River dramatically, but the 18-mile stretch within park boundaries can still be extremely dangerous at times. At high water levels, several sections are unrunnable and the remainder of the corridor rates as class III–V rapids. The Gunnison should only be run by expert kayakers, and even then it should be run with individuals who are familiar with the water, its drops, and its hydraulics. All boaters must obtain a **wilderness use permit** (page 352).

Rock Climbing

Hard rock walls rising vertically out of the canyon floor more than 2,000 feet are sure to attract a few rock climbers. Experienced climbers love the challenge of Black Canyon's multi-pitch traditional routes. The Park Service knows about more than 145 climbs, but very few are used with any regularity. This is largely due to extreme difficulty accessing routes and challenging nature of the routes themselves.

Flora & Fauna

It's likely you'll spot a few mule deer on your visit to the Black Canyon. Black bear have become a regular inhabitant, so be sure to use the bear-proof storage lockers for all food and scented products. Canyons aren't as prohibitive to birds as they are to humans. Peregrine falcons nest on canyon walls, occasionally forcing rock-climbing routes to close. Many different species of plants live here. Serviceberry and Gambel oak are common along the rim, while cottonwood, box elder, and Douglas fir grow in the shade of the canyon. Perhaps the most prevalent and annoying plant is poison ivy. Guests must watch diligently for the three-leafed plant when hiking the inner canyon (wear long pants).

Pets

Pets are permitted in several areas, but must be kept on a leash no more than six feet in length at all times. They are allowed on roads, in campgrounds, at overlooks, and on Rim Rock Trail, Cedar Point Nature Trail, and North Rim Chasm View Nature Trail. Do not leave your pet unattended anywhere in the park (including your car).

Accessibility

South Rim Visitor Center, all restrooms, Tomichi Point, Chasm View, and Sunset View are fully accessible to wheelchair users. South Rim Campground has two accessible campsites. The restrooms at North Rim Ranger Station and Balanced Rock Overlook are accessible.

Weather

Black Canyon of the Gunnison experiences extreme variation in temperature from day-to-night, day-to-day, and canyon rim-to-floor. During summer average highs reach the 80s°F and lows dip into the 40s°F overnight. Average lows in December and January fall below zero, while highs are usually in the mid-20s°F. The canyon floor is typically 8°F warmer than its rim, even with the canyon's vertical walls preventing sunlight from penetrating its depths except around midday.

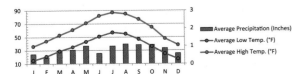

Best of Black Canyon

Hike: Warner Point (South Rim)
    Runner-up: North Vista (North Rim)

Hike (Inner Canyon): Red Rock Canyon
    (Permit Required)

Overlook: Cedar Point (South)
    Runner-up: Painted Wall View (South)
    2nd Runner-up: Gunnison Point (South)
    3rd Runner-up: Chasm View (North)
    4th Runner-up: Pulpit Rock (South)

Vacation Planner

Black Canyon of the Gunnison's **South Rim Road** makes viewing the most popular attractions in a single day possible, while visiting both the South and North Rims in a single day is a race against time. There isn't a bridge between the two rims, so you have to make an 80+ mile trip (about 2 hours) from one rim to the other. Most people only stop at the South Rim. Provided below is a one-day itinerary for a typical Black Canyon vacation. Each rim of the canyon has a campground, but you'll have to look outside the park for lodging and dining facilities (pages 364–369).

Day 1: Begin your trip to the **South Rim** by looking through the canyon from its floor. Take **East Portal Road**, which is extremely steep (16% grade) with tight corners. It supplies tremendous views and you can see how most of the canyon is shrouded in shadows. The canyon floor is also an excellent location to have a picnic. Have a look around and return to the rim to stop at the visitor center. Browse the exhibits, watch the short film, and check out the schedule of ranger-guided interpretive programs. If you have the opportunity to join a guided walk or talk, do so. If not, start exploring the canyon from above by hiking **Oak Flat Trail**. (Note: The view from **Gunnison Point** is nearly the same without 2 miles of hiking.) Return to your car and continue along South Rim Road. Make the following stops: **Pulpit Rock**, **Chasm View**, **Painted Wall View**, and **Cedar Point** (similar to Painted Wall). The road terminates at High Point, where you should hike the 2.75-mile trail to **Warner Point**. Exit the park by retracing your route along South Rim Road.

Mesa Verde

Cliff Palace

PO Box 8
Mesa Verde, CO 81330
Phone: (970) 529-4465
Website: nps.gov/meve

Established: June 29, 1906
Size: 52,122 Acres
Annual Visitors: 550,000
Peak Season: Summer

Ranger-Guided Tours and Fees
Cliff Palace: $4/person
Cliff Palace (Twilight): $20/person
Balcony House: $4/person
Long House: $4/person
Mug House: $25/person

Camping: Morefield Campground
Fee: $30/night, $40/night (w/
hookups)
Backcountry Camping: Prohibited
Lodging: Far View Lodge
Rates: $91–186/night

Park Hours: All day, every day
Entrance Fee: $15 (peak), $10
(off-season) per vehicle; $8 (peak),
$5 (off-season) per individual (foot,
bike, etc.)

Let's say you arrive at Mesa Verde completely unaware of the area's history and culture. A quick drive across the mesa and you would be left scratching your head, wondering where the majestic scenery went. Mesa Verde's deep gorges and tall mesas have a bit of scenic appeal, but it pales in comparison to other southwestern parks. But what it lacks in natural beauty it redeems in cultural significance. When the park was established in 1906, it became the first tract of land set aside to protect a prehistoric culture and its ruins, pottery, tools, and other ancient artifacts.

Somewhere around 750 AD, Puebloans were living in modest pit-houses on top of the mesa, clustered together forming small villages. They found sustenance farming and hunting. Judging by the circular underground chambers, called kivas, religion was important and rituals and ceremonies were performed regularly. By the late 12th century, they began building homes in alcoves beneath the rim of the mesa. These cliff dwellings became larger and more numerous.

Scientists and volunteers are attempting to piece together the history of Ancestral Puebloan People by scouring thousands of archeological sites. To date, there are more than 4,700 archeological sites within the park; roughly 600 are cliff dwellings. About 90 percent of the cliff dwellings contain fewer than 10 rooms, but a few are enormous. Cliff Palace, the largest and most famous dwelling, contains 150 rooms. Long House and Spruce Tree House exceed 100 rooms, and Balcony House has more than 40. These sites have attracted archeologists and vandals, pothunters and politicians, tourists and explorers.

John Moss, a local prospector, is the first person in recorded history to have seen the ruins. In 1874, he led a photographer through Mancos Canyon along the base of Mesa Verde. Resulting photos inspired geologists to visit the site in 1875, and more than a decade later Richard Wetherill and his brothers began the first serious excavations. They spent the next 15 months exploring over 100 dwellings. Frederick H. Chapin, a noted mountaineer, photographer, and author, aided the excavation. Later, he wrote an article and book on the area's geologic and cultural significance. In 1889 and once again in 1890, Benjamin Wetherill wrote to the Smithsonian, warning that the area would be plundered by looters and tourists if it was not protected as a national park. He also requested that he and his brothers be placed in the employ of the government to carry out careful excavation of the ruins even though they were not legitimate archeologists.

The requests went unanswered, and the following year the Wetherills hosted Gustaf Nordenskiöld of the Academy of Sciences in Sweden. Using scientific methods and meticulous data collection, he began a thorough excavation of many ruins including Cliff Palace. Incensed locals charged Nordenskiöld with "devastating the ruins" and held him on $1,000 bond when he tried to transport some 600 artifacts, including a mummified corpse, on the Denver and Rio Grande Railroad. He was released because no laws existed to prevent treasure hunting. The artifacts were shipped to Sweden and today they reside in the National Museum in Helsinki, Finland. Upon his return home, he examined the artifacts and published a book titled *The Cliff Dwellers of the Mesa Verde*.

At this time, pothunters and vandals were becoming a serious problem. Dynamite was used to blow holes in walls to let light in or to scare away rattlesnakes. Colorado Cliff Dwelling Association (CCDA) picked up the mantle of advocating a national park. But when Virginia Donaghe McClurg, head of the CCDA, expressed her opinion that it should be a "woman's park," Lucy Peabody left the association and continued to search for support on her own. Finally in 1906, President Theodore Roosevelt signed a bill creating Mesa Verde National Park, protecting an area of unique history and culture for future generations.

When to Go
Mesa Verde is open all year, but some of its more notable attractions are closed during the off-season (November–March). The popular Cliff Palace Tour is only available from late May to late September. Balcony House Tours are offered between mid-April and late October. Wetherill Mesa Road is open from 8am until sunset, May through mid-October, but all sites (including the cliff dwellings, Long House and Step House) are only accessible from late May until early September.

If you visit during the off-season, you'll be limited to exploring the visitor center, Chapin Mesa Archeological Museum, Spruce Tree House (at time of publication Spruce Tree House was closed due to safety concerns), Mesa Top Loop sites, Far View sites, and the park's overlooks. Morefield Campground, public showers, laundry, gas services, and Far View Lodge also close in winter. Summers can be busy, but the park increases its tour offerings to accommodate increased traffic. During summer, visitors can also investigate the quieter side, Wetherill Mesa. Motorists can drive as far as Step House. (Vehicles longer than 25 feet and bicycles are not permitted on Wetherill Mesa Road.) From there, the 5-mile Long House Loop is open to hiking and bicycle riding.

Transportation & Airports
Public transportation does not provide service to or around the park. Greyhound (800.231.2222, greyhound.com) has a bus station 35 miles from the park entrance in Durango, CO, but a rental car is needed to reach the park. There are small regional airports nearby at Cortez, CO (10 miles to park entrance); Durango, CO (35 miles); and Farmington, NM (70 miles). Albuquerque International Sunport (ABQ) is located 250 miles to the southeast. Car rental is available at each destination.

Directions
Mesa Verde is located in the remote southwestern corner of Colorado. It is accessed via the Mesa Verde National Park Exit from US-160. The park entrance is 35 miles west of Durango, CO and 12 miles east of Cortez, CO. Chapin Mesa, where you'll find many of the main attractions, is located 22 miles south of the park entrance and visitor center (stop at the visitor center first!).

Regions

Mesa Verde is essentially broken into two distinct regions: Chapin Mesa and Wetherill Mesa. **Chapin Mesa** reaches all the way down to the park's southern boundary. This is where you'll find the most recognizable cliff dwellings and Chapin Mesa Museum. A one-way loop road circles around the Museum, providing plenty of parking and access to **Spruce Tree House** (self-guiding from spring to fall, free guided tours in winter, closed at time of publication due to safety concerns). Continuing south beyond the museum and Spruce Tree House is Mesa Top Loop. Several stops provide a tour of Ancestral Puebloan pit-houses and overlooks with views of their cliff dwellings. East of Mesa Top Loop is Cliff Palace Loop. Along this loop are parking areas for **Cliff Palace** and **Balcony House**. Both of these cliff dwellings are only accessible from spring to fall on ranger-guided tours with a ticket ($4/person • available at the visitor center—stop at the visitor center before entering the park!).

Wetherill Mesa runs parallel to Chapin Mesa, just to its west. This quiet side of Mesa Verde is open from late May to early September. Wetherill Mesa Road begins near Far View Visitor Lodge and winds its way to a collection of archeological sites in the park's southwest corner. **Long House**, the park's second largest cliff dwelling, is available for tour with a ticket ($4/person). Visitors are free to explore **Step House**, pit-houses, and nature trails on their own. Long House Loop is open to walkers and bicyclists.

Visitor Center & Museum

In December 2012, the park opened its new visitor center located near the park entrance. Make this your first stop, as it's the only place you can get tickets to tour Cliff Palace, Balcony House, or Long House. The **visitor center** is generally open from 8:30am–4:30pm, but hours are extended from 7:30am–7pm from late May through early September. **Chapin Mesa Archeological Museum** is open all year with hours from 9am–4:30pm that extend to 8am–6:30pm from early April until mid-October. The museum features a wealth of exhibits on Ancestral Puebloan life and numerous artifacts that were found at the park's archeological sites, and a 25-minute introductory film is shown every half-hour. The museum and visitor center close for Thanksgiving, Christmas, and New Year's Day.

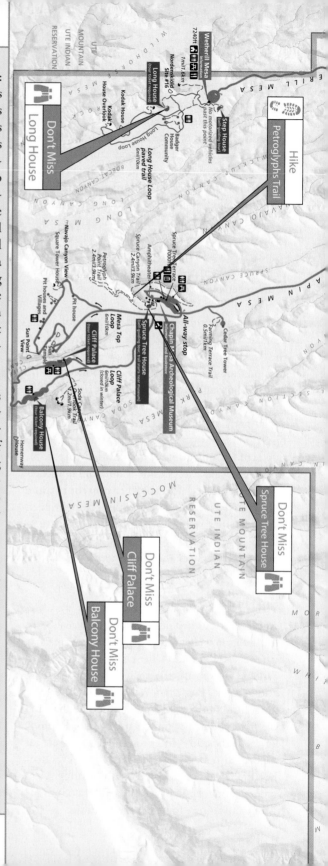

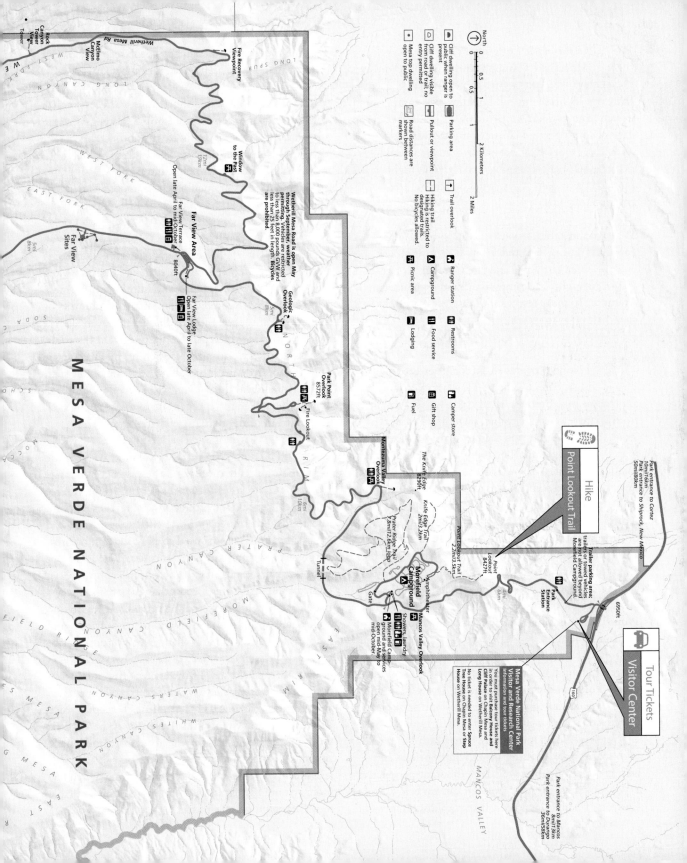

Camping & Lodging

Morefield Campground has 267 campsites available on a first-come, first-served basis. There are 15 sites with full hookups. The campground is open from mid-May until early October. A free dump station, coin-operated **showers** and **laundry**, a general store, and gas are available nearby (only from mid-May to early October). Camping fees are: $30/night (standard site) and $40/night (with hookups). The campground rarely fills.

More comfortable accommodations are available at **Far View Lodge**, located 15 miles into the park. It's open between late April and late October. Rooms cost $91–186/night. The campground and lodge are run by Aramark. To make reservations call (800) 449-2288 or click visitmesaverde.com.

Hiking

Hiking provides an excellent retreat from the busy cliff dwellings. However, you are only allowed to hike on designated trails. Several originate from Morefield Campground, including **Prater Ridge Trail**, located just beyond the campground gate. It follows Prater Ridge, and then loops around the ridgetop totaling 7.8 miles. There is a short bisecting trail, allowing hikers to complete just the 3.6-mile north loop or 2.4-mile south loop. The easy 2-mile, out-and-back **Knife Edge Trail** departs from the campground's northwest corner and follows an old road that served as the main entrance beginning in 1914. Today, it provides hikers with excellent views of Montezuma Valley and a great vantage point for watching the sunset. Another excellent hike for watching the sunset is 2.2-mile **Point Lookout Trail**. It begins at the very north end of the campground.

There are four trails at Chapin Mesa. To hike **Petroglyph Point and Spruce Canyon Trails** (2.4 miles each), you must register at the museum or trailhead (gated, contact a ranger if closed). These trails are steep and for sure-footed individuals. Petroglyph Point leads to the park's only accessible petroglyphs. Spruce Canyon isn't as interesting, but provides a different perspective as you look up at the mesa from the canyon below. **Soda Canyon** (1.2 miles) is an easy hike with distant views of Balcony House (and a telescope at the second lookout, where you can peep on people touring Balcony House).

Wetherill Mesa has three short trails, each less than 3 miles roundtrip. **Step House Loop Trail** begins at the information kiosk. It leads to pit-houses and a cliff dwelling. **Nordenskiöld Site #16** leads to a cliff dwelling overlook. **Badger House Community Trail** passes through 600 years of pueblo development. Trail guides are available for all three of these hikes.

Cliff Dwellings

About 1,400 years ago Ancestral Puebloans inhabited the region that has become Mesa Verde National Park, farming and hunting on the mesa tops. Over time they moved from small communities of pit-houses on top the mesa to cliff dwellings in alcoves beneath its rim. Much can be inferred from the tools, basketry, pottery, and ruins left behind by this ancient culture, but little is certain about why they built such large structures in the canyon walls or why they abandoned them in the late 1200s. Were they seeking protection from conflict? From wildfires? From weather?

Of the 4,700 archeological sites found at Mesa Verde about 600 are cliff dwellings. These structures range from one-room houses to massive 150-room villages (like Cliff Palace). They could only be reached by hand and foot holds carved into the cliff wall. Several had kivas, ceremonial rooms used to pray for rain or prosperous hunting and farming. Ancestral Puebloans put a lot of time and effort into their homes, but they occupied these structures for less than 100 years. Success may have helped lead to their demise. Overpopulation could have stripped the farmland of its nutrients and land of its game. Climatic changes or political squabbles may have played their parts, too. Your guess is as good as anyone else's. Tour the ancient ruins and wonder to yourself why they abandoned these homes with such fantastic views. **All cliff dwellings (except Spruce Tree House and Step House) are not to be entered without the accompaniment of a uniformed park ranger.** Today, the park offers guided tours of Cliff Palace, Balcony House and Long House, along with a few more remote backcountry destinations (only available to small groups on select dates).

Guided Tours

A visit to Mesa Verde is not complete without touring one (or all three) of the large cliff dwellings (**Cliff Palace, Balcony House, and Long House**). It's the best $4 you can spend in all of the parks. Tickets must be purchased at the visitor center, located near the park entrance. You'll also find a few unique ranger-led cliff dwelling tours that can be reserved at recreation.gov. Please refer to the table below for a complete listing. Rangers also lead a 4.5-hour **Wetherill Mesa Bike and Hike Adventure**, where you bike 5 miles and hike 4. Tours can be reserved at recreation.gov for $18/adult. (Bring your own bike.)

Winter Activities

Winter activities at Mesa Verde are different than those found during the rest of the year. Park rangers-led guests on tours of **Spruce Tree House**, but the rest of the cliff dwellings are closed until spring. You can still view many of the dwellings from a distance at overlooks. **Cliff Palace Loop Road** is not plowed during winter, making it an excellent location for cross-country skiing, snowshoeing, and winter hiking. **Mesa Top Loop Road** provides views of Cliff Palace and is open in winter. Before hiking, snowshoeing, or cross-country skiing in the park, you should discuss your plans with a ranger to receive information regarding current trail conditions. You might have to register to hike in specific areas. Overnight stays are not permitted during winter and all sites are off-limits after sunset.

Ranger Programs

In addition to ranger-guided cliff dwelling tours, the park provides ranger-accompanied walks through Far View Sites and evening programs at Morefield Campground and Far View Lodge. Programs are offered daily from late May through early September, free of charge. To get the exact time of a particular program, visit the park website or look inside the free newspaper you'll receive at the entrance when you arrive.

Mesa Verde Cliff Dwelling Tours (Fees are per person)

Name	Dates	Duration	Fee	Notes
Cliff Palace - ♿	late May–late Sept	1 hour	$4	Begins at Cliff Palace Parking Area
Balcony House - ♿	mid-April–late Oct	1 hour	$4	Begins at Balcony House Parking Area
Spruce Tree House - ♿	All Year	N/A	Self-Guiding and guided	Access near Chapin Mesa Museum • Free guided tours are offered in winter
Long House - ♿	mid-May–mid-Oct	1.5 hours	$4	Tour begins at Wetherill Mesa Info Kiosk
Step House	mid-May–mid-Oct	N/A	Self-Guiding	Access near Wetherill Mesa Info Kiosk
Tours listed above are provided by the National Park Service. Tickets must be purchased in advance at the visitor center (located before the park entrance). Visitors must climb ladders and/or stairs at each site.				
700 Years (Motor Coach Tour)	late April–mid-Oct	4 hours	$46 (Adult) $33 (Child)	Guided tour of mesatop sites and Cliff Palace (stairs and ladder required)
Far View Explorer (Motor Coach Tour)	late April–mid-Oct	4.5 hours	$38 (Adult) $20 (Child)	Explores Far View Sites and Chapin Mesa Museum Area (easy walking tour)
Tours listed above are offered by Aramark (800.449.2288, visitmesaverde.com). Tickets may be purchased at the visitor center, Far View Lodge, Far View Terrace, Morefield Campground Store, and online at visitmesaverde.com.				
Balcony House (Sunrise)	Select Dates	1.5 hours	$15	Bring a flashlight, dress for early morning temperatures, and enjoy the sunrise
Mug House	Select Dates	2 hours	$25	Strenuous 3-mile trip on unpaved terrain
Oak Tree House	Select Dates	2 hours	$25	Moderate 1-mile trip along narrow trail
Spring House	Select Dates	8 hours	$40	Strenuous 8-mile trek to unexcavated site
Yucca House	Select Dates	2 hours	$5	Easy half-mile walk to Ancestral Puebloan site
Tours listed above are special backcountry hikes offered periodically in summer by the National Park Service. Tickets must be purchased in advance at (877) 444-6777 or recreation.gov. Do not bring sugary snacks or drinks.				

Spruce Tree House

For Kids

In all likelihood your child will find the history and ruins of Ancestral Puebloans to be captivating. If not, engage your child in this unique environment by picking up a free **Junior Ranger** activity booklet at the visitor center or Chapin Mesa Museum. The award for a completed booklet is a Mesa Verde Junior Ranger badge. (Booklets are also available at the park's website.)

Flora & Fauna

Mesa Verde was preserved for its historic culture, but its present inhabitants are nearly as interesting. About 74 species of mammals, 200 species of birds, 16 species of reptiles, and a handful of species of fish and amphibians have been documented in the park. You have a good chance of seeing animals like coyote, mule deer, spotted bat, and spotted owl.

Over 640 species of plants exist here. Cottonwood, willow, and buffaloberry survive on the banks of Mancos River and near seep springs. Over the past decade, a number of wildfires have cut the size of the park's piñon-juniper forests in half. Several extremely old and champion-sized trees survived, with one Utah juniper's trunk measuring 52 inches in diameter, a record for the state of Colorado. Another is dated at more than 1,300 years old. In the lower elevations you'll find sagebrushes. Higher up you'll find mostly shrubs, but Gambel oak and Douglas fir grow along the north rim in sheltered areas. Plants like Cliff Palace milkvetch, Schmoll's milkvetch, Mesa Verde wandering aletes, and Mesa Verde stickseed do not exist anywhere else in the world.

Pets

Pets are allowed in the park, but are not permitted on trails, in archeological sites, or in buildings (with the exception of service animals). They are permitted along roadways, in parking lots, and at the campground, but must be kept on a leash no more than six feet in length at all times. You may not leave your pet unattended or tied to any object within the park.

Accessibility

Mesa Verde is a tricky place for individuals with limited mobility. Its cliff dwellings are built into alcoves below the rim of the mesa. Visitors must descend tall ladders or stairs carved into the steep cliff wall to access Cliff Palace and Balcony House. Many other sites are accessible with assistance. The park's scenic overlooks, Far View Visitor Center, Chapin Mesa Museum, Far View Sites, and Spruce Tree House are all potential destinations. Step House and Badger House Community are accessible with assistance. Long House is not accessible. Morefield Campground has a few accessible campsites.

Weather

Weather at Mesa Verde is quite comfortable year-round. On average, every other day is clear and cloudless regardless of the month. An occasional snowstorm passes through in winter, but average high temperatures in January are above 40°F and average lows are around 20°F. In the middle of summer high temperatures can reach into the 90s°F. You may sweat during the day, but don't worry about it being too hot to sleep. Temperatures usually fall into the 50s°F during summer evenings.

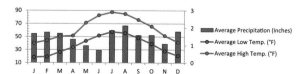

Square Tower House

Long House

Far View Sites

Best of Mesa Verde

Guided Tour: Cliff Palace
Runner-up: Balcony House

Hike: Petroglyph Point

Vacation Planner

Ranger-led tours provide the only access to **Mesa Verde's best attractions**: Cliff Palace, Balcony House, and Long House (page 361). If you intend on touring any of these destinations you must buy tickets at the **visitor center** (located near the entrance). Plan at least 2 hours to drive in and out of the park, and an additional 2 hours to tour one of the major cliff dwellings, but note that there's plenty to see atop the mesa even if you don't tour one of the cliff dwellings. Gas is available near Morefield Campground from mid-May to mid-October. The one-day trip itinerary provided below suggests activities to supplement your ranger-guided tours. Spend the night in the park at **Morefield Campground** or **Far View Lodge** (page 360). Food is available at Far View Lodge and Chapin Mesa. Nearby dining, grocery stores, lodging, festivals, and attractions are listed on pages 364–369.

Day 1: If you're at **Chapin Mesa** with a little bit of time to burn before or after a cliff dwelling tour, hike **Petroglyph Point Trail** (registration required). On your way to the trailhead be sure to stop at **Spruce Tree House** (closed at time of publication), the best maintained cliff dwelling in the park. Petroglyph Point Trail is steep, rocky, and somewhat strenuous. If you'd like a flatter alternative, go to **Soda Canyon Overlook Trail**. It's mostly flat and relatively easy, providing excellent views of **Balcony House** from across the canyon. If the crowds are putting a damper on your family vacation, head over to **Wetherill Mesa** (open late May to early September). Even if you don't tour **Long House** (the second largest cave dwelling behind Cliff Palace), there's a lot to see. You can walk or bike to a series of archeological sites. Once you've had your fill of Ancestral Puebloans' living quarters, start heading back to the park entrance on main park road. If you have spare time, especially around dusk, take a quick hike along **Point Lookout Trail** located near Morefield Campground, which is a great spot for sunsets).

Dining

Rocky Mountain Area
Other Side Restaurant • (970) 586-2171
900 Moraine Ave, Estes Park
theothersideofestes.com • Entrée: $13–25

Twin Owls Steakhouse • (970) 586-9344
800 MacGregor Ave, Estes Park
twinowls.net • Entrée: $22–39

Rock Inn • (970) 586-4116
1675 CO-66, Estes Park
rockinnestes.com • Entrée: $10–33

Mama Rose's Homemade Italian
338 E Elkhorn Ave, Estes Park
mamarosesrestaurant.com • (970) 586-3330

Dunraven Inn • (970) 586-6409
2470 CO-66, Estes Park
dunraveninn.com • Entrée: $15–34

Claire's on the Park • (970) 586-9564
225 Park Ln, Estes Park
clairesonthepark.net

Smokin' Dave's BBQ • (970) 283-3361
820 Moraine Ave, Estes Park
smokindavesq.com

Estes Park Brewery • (970) 586-5421
470 Prospect Village Dr, Estes Park
epbrewery.com • Entrée: $9–28

Ed's Cantina • (970) 586-2919
390 E Elkhorn Ave, Estes Park
edscantina.com • Burgers: $9+

Penelope's Old Time Burgers • (970) 586-2277
229 W Elkhorn Ave, Estes Park

Molly B Restaurant • (970) 586-2766
200 Moraine Ave, Estes Park
estesparkmollyb.com • Entrée: $13–18

The Egg and I • (970) 586-1173
393 E Elkhorn Ave, Estes Park
theeggandirestaurants.com

Thai Kitchen • (970) 577-7112
401 S Saint Vrain Ave, Estes Park
thaikitchenestespark.com

Chicago's Best • (970) 586-4796
112 W Elkhorn Ave, Estes Park
chicagosbestep.com

Village Pizza • (970) 586-6031
633 Big Thompson Ave, Estes Park
villagepizzaestespark.com

Bob & Tony's Pizza • (970) 586-2044
124 W Elkhorn Ave, Estes Park

Poppy's Pizza & Grill • (970) 586-8282
342 E Elkhorn Ave, Estes Park
poppyspizzaandgrill.com • Pizza: $5+

Casa Grande • (970) 577-0799
220 E Elkhorn Ave, Estes Park
casagrandemexicana.com

Sweet Basilico Café • (970) 586-3899
Prospect Village Dr, Estes Park
sweetbasilico.com • Entrée: $12–21

Nepal Café • (970) 577-7035
184 E Elkhorn Ave, Estes Park

Mountain Home Café • (970) 586-6624
457 E Wonder View Ave, Estes Park
mountainhomecafe.com

Coffee on the Rocks • (970) 586-5181
510 Moraine Ave, Estes Park

Donut Haus • (970) 586-2988
342 Moraine Ave, Estes Park
donuthaus-estespark.com

Shakes Alive • (970) 577-7007
513 Big Thompson Ave, Estes Park
shakesalive.com

Laura's Fudge Shop • (970) 586-4004
129 E Elkhorn Ave, Estes Park

O–A Bistro • (970) 627-5080
928 Grand Ave, Grand Lake
o-abistro.com • Entrée: $16–25

Sagebrush BBQ & Grill • (970) 627-1404
1101 Grand Ave, Grand Lake
sagebrushbbq.com • Entrée: $10–15

Backstreet Steakhouse • (970) 627-8144
604 Marina Dr, Grand Lake
davenhavenlodge.com • Entrée: $18–29

Sly Fox • (970) 627-3922
1415 County Rd 48, Grand Lake

Grand Pizza • (970) 627-8390
1131 Grand Ave, Grand Lake • grand-pizza.com

Blue Water Bakery • (970) 627-5416
928 Grand Ave, Grand Lake
bluewaterbakery.com

Cy's Deli • (970) 627-3354
717 Grand Ave, Grand Lake • cysdeli.com

Great Sand Dunes Area
Desert Sage Restaurant • (719) 256-4402
242 Baca Townhouse, Crestone

Painted Sky Café & Bakery • (719) 256-4202
121 E Galena Ave, Crestone

Bliss Café • (719) 256-6400
187 W Silver Ave, Crestone

True Grits Steakhouse • (719) 589-9954
100 Santa Fe Ave, Alamosa

San Luis Valley Brewing • (719) 587-2337
631 Main St, Alamosa • slvbrewco.com

Cavillo's Mexican Restaurant
400 Main St, Alamosa • (719) 587-5500

Bistro Rialto • (719) 589 -3039
716 Main St, Alamosa • bistrorialto.com

San Luis Valley Pizza • (719) 589-4749
2069 1st St, Alamosa • slvpizza.com

Milagros Coffeehouse • (719) 589-9299
529 Main St, Alamosa

San Marcos Mexican Restaurant
402 Main St, Blanca • (719) 379-5290

Old West Café • (719) 379-2448
403 Miranda Ave, Fort Garland

All-Gon Pizza • (719) 379-2222
319 Beaubien Ave, Fort Garland
allgonrestaurant.com

Black Canyon Area
Simmer Food & Wine • (970) 252-1152
320 E Main St, Montrose

Red Barn Restaurant • (970) 249-9202
1413 E Main St, Montrose • redbarnmontrose.com

Stone House • (970) 240-8899
1415 Hawk Parkway, Montrose
stonehousemontrose.com

Camp Robber Restaurant • (970) 240-1590
1515 Ogden Rd, Montrose
camprobber.com • Entrée: $12–24

Starvin Arvins • (970) 249-7787
1320 S Townsend Ave, Montrose

Pahgre's • (970) 249-6442
1541 Oxbow Dr, #1800, Montrose
pahgres.com • Sandwich: $8

Guru's Restaurant • (970) 252-8777
Indian and Himalayan food
448 S Main St, Montrose
gurunepal.com

Daily Bread • (970) 249-8444
346 E Main St, Montrose

Mesa Verde Area
Pepperhead • (970) 565-3303
44 W Main St, Cortez
pepperheadcortez.com • Burrito: $8

Shiloh Steak House • (970) 565-6560
5 Veach St, Cortez

Main Street Brewery • (970) 564-9112
21 E Main St, Cortez
mainstreetbrewerycortez.com

Jack & Janelle's Country Kitchen
801 E Main St, Cortez • (970) 565-2572

Pippo's Diner • (970) 565-6039
100 W Main St, Cortez

Stonefish Sushi & More • (970) 565-9244
16 W Main St, Cortez

Silver Bean • (970) 946-4404
410 1/2 W Main St, Cortez

Once Upon A Sandwich • (970) 565-8292
9 W Main St, Cortez

Ocean Pearl • (970) 565-3888
300 E Main St, Cortez

Hunan Chinese Restaurant • (970) 565-0919
2561 E Main St, Cortez

Fiesta Mexicana • (970) 565-4267
430 Hwy 145, Cortez

Nero's • (970) 565-7366
303 W Main St, Cortez • neroscortez.com

Absolute Bakery & Café • (970) 533-1200
110 S Main, Mancos • absolutebakery.com

Spruce Tree Coffeehouse • (970) 565-6789
318 E Main St, Cortez

Destination Grill • (970) 565-6789
2121 E Main St, Cortez

Home Slice Pizza • (970) 259-5551
441 E College Dr, Durango
homeslicedelivers.com • Pizza: $13.50+

Grocery Stores
Rocky Mountain Area
Safeway • (970) 586-4447
451 E Wonder View Ave, Estes Park

Country Market • (970) 586-2702
900 Moraine Ave, Estes Park

Circle 3 Foods • (970) 627-3210
701 Grand Ave, Grand Lake

Mountain Food Market • (970) 627-3470
400 Grand Ave, Grand Lake

Great Sand Dunes Area
Fort Market • (719) 379-3482
330 Miranda St, Fort Garland

Crestone General Store • (719) 256-4887
200 S Cottonwood, Crestone

Westcliffe Supermarket • (719) 783-0550
50 Main St, Westcliffe

Walmart Supercenter • (719) 589-9071
3333 Clark St, Alamosa

Safeway • (719) 587-3075
1301 Main St, Alamosa

Black Canyon Area
Safeway • (970) 249-1160
1329 S Townsend Ave, Montrose

Walmart Supercenter • (970) 249-7544
16750 S Townsend Ave, Montrose

Mesa Verde Area
Walmart Supercenter • (970) 565-6138
1835 E Main St, Cortez

Safeway • (970) 564-9590
1580 E Main St, Cortez

Lodging
Rocky Mountain Area
The Stanley Hotel • (970) 577-4000
Portions of The Shining *and* Dumb and Dumber
were filmed here • *Tours available*
333 Wonder View Ave, Estes Park
stanleyhotel.com • Rates: $219+/night

Inn On Fall River • (970) 586-4118
1660 Fall River Rd, Estes Park
innonfallriver.com • Rates: $139+

Saddle & Surrey Motel • (970) 586-3326
1341 S Saint Vrain Ave, Estes Park
saddleandsurrey.com

The Haber Motel • (970) 449-1660
397 E Elkhorn Ave, Estes Park
thehabermotel.com

Stonebrook Resort • (970) 586-4629
1710 Fall River Rd, Estes Park
stonebrookresort.com • Rates: $135+

Deer Crest Resort • (970) 586-2324
1200 Fall River Rd, Estes Park
deercrestresort.com

Kokopelli Inn • (970) 586-4420
6777 US-36, Estes Park
kokopelliinn.net • Rates: $129+

Taharaa Mountain Lodge • (970) 577-0098
3110 S Saint Vrain Ave, Estes Park
taharaa.com • Rates: $209+

Pine Haven Resort • (800) 586-3184
1580 Fall River Rd, Estes Park
estesparkcabins.com • Rates: $482+

McGregor Mountain Lodge • (970) 586-3457
2815 Fall River Rd, Estes Park
mcgregormountainlodge.com • Rates: $155+

Boulder Brook on Fall River • (970) 586-0910
1900 Fall River Rd, Estes Park
boulderbrook.com • Rates: $210+

Dripping Springs Resort • (970) 586-3406
Off US-34, Big Thompson Canyon Rd, 37
Dripping Springs Ln, Estes Park
drippingsprings.com • Rates: $175+

Colorado Cottages • (970) 586-4637
1241 High Dr, Estes Park
colocottages.com • Rates: $100+

Sunnyside Knoll Resort • (970) 586-5759
1675 Fall River Rd, Estes Park
rockymtnresorts.com • Rates: $89+

Solitude Cabins • (970) 577-7777
1885 Sketch Box Ln, # 7, Estes Park
solitudecabins.com • Rates: $299+

Discovery Lodge • (970) 586-3336
800 Big Thompson Ave, Estes Park
estesdiscoverylodge.com • Rates: $129+

Silver Moon Inn • (970) 586-6006
175 Spruce Dr, Estes Park
silvermooninn.com • Rates: $180+

Alpine Trail Ridge Inn • (970) 586-4585
927 Moraine Ave, Estes Park

Black Canyon Inn • (970) 586-8113
800 MacGregor Ave, Estes Park
blackcanyoninn.com • Rates: $150+

Della Terra Mountain Chateau • (970) 586-2501
3501 Fall River Rd, Estes Park
dellaterramountainchateau.com • Rates: $215+

Fawn Valley Inn • (970) 586-2388
2760 Fall River Rd, Estes Park
rockymtnresorts.com • $79+

Rustic Acre • (970) 586-0374
650 S St Vrain Ave, Estes Park
rusticacre.com • Rates: $175+

River Song A B&B • (970) 586-4666
1766 Lower Broadview Rd, Estes Park
romanticriversong.com • Rates: $199+

Hotel Estes • (970) 586-3382
1240 Big Thompson Rd, Estes Park
Hotelestes.com • Rates: $145+

Brynwood On the River • (970) 586-3475
710 Moraine Ave, Estes Park
brynwood.com • Rates: $135+

River Spruce • (970) 586-4543 • Rates: $155+
2334 CO-66, Estes Park • riverspruce.com

Gilded Meadows B&B • (970) 586-2124
861 Big Horn Dr, Estes Park
gildedpinemeadows.com • Rates: $120+

River Stone Resorts • (970) 586-4005
2120 Fall River Rd, Estes Park
riverstoneresorts.com • Rates: $229+

Peak To Peak Lodge • (970) 586-4451
760 S St Vrain Ave, Estes Park
peaktopeaklodge.com • Rates: $86+

Anniversary Inn B&B • (970) 586-6200
1060 Marys Lake Rd, Estes Park
estesinn.com • Rates: $170+

Streamside On Fall River • (970) 586-6464
1260 Fall River Rd, Estes Park
streamsideonfallriver.com • Rates: $125+

Elkhorn Lodge & Guest Ranch • (970) 586-4416
600 W Elkhorn Ave, Estes Park

Amberwood • (970) 586-4385
1889 Fall River Rd, Estes Park
amberwoodestespark.com • Rates: $130+

Estes Park Condos • (970) 577-0068
1400 David Dr, Estes Park
estescondos.com • Rates: $200+

Woodlands On Fall River • (970) 586-0404
1888 Fall River Rd, Estes Park
woodlandsestes.com • Rates: $197+

Estes Park KOA • (970) 586-2888
2051 Big Thompson Ave, Estes Park

Meeker Park Lodge • (303) 747-2266
11733 CO-7, Allenspark
meekerparklodge.com • Rates: $85+

Wild Basin Lodge • (303) 747-2274
1130 CR-84 W, Allenspark
wildbasinlodge.com

Grand Mountain Rentals • (970) 627-1131
1028 Grand Ave, Grand Lake
grandmountainrentals.com • Rates: $150+

Gateway Inn • (970) 627-2400
200 W Portal Rd, Grand Lake
gatewayinn.com • Rates: $149+

Rapids Lodge • (970) 627-3707
210 Rapids Ln, Grand Lake
rapidslodge.com • Rates: $95+

Spirit Lake Lodge • (970) 627-3344
Snowmobile rental available on-site
829 Grand Ave, Grand Lake
spiritlakelodge.com • Rates: $175+

Grand Escape Cottages • (970) 627-3410
1204 Grand Ave, Grand Lake
grandescapecottages.com • Rates: $139+

The Terrace Inn • (970) 627-3000
813 Grand Ave, Grand Lake
grandlaketerraceinn.com • Rates: $100+

Grand Lake Lodge • (970) 627-3967
15500 US-34, Grand Lake
grandlakelodge.com • Rates: $150+

Winding River Resort • (970) 627-3215
Horse boarding & rides, snowmobile & ATV
rental, animal farm, and sleigh rides are available
1447 CR-491, Grand Lake
windingriverresort.com • Rates: $110+

Mountain Lakes Lodge • (970) 627-8448
10480 US-34, Grand Lake
grandlakelodging.net • Rates: $99+

Black Bear Lodge • (970) 627-3654
12255 US-34, Grand Lake • blackbeargrandlake.com

Grand Lake Treehouse • (888) 214-6845
1901 W Portal Rd, Grand Lake
grandlaketreehouse.com • Rates: $350

Great Sand Dunes Area

Great Sand Dunes Lodge • (719) 378-2900
7900 CO-150, Mosca
gsdlodge.com • Rates: $100+

Zapata Ranch • (719) 378-2356
5305 CO-150, Mosca
zranch.org • $1,380 for 3 nights (all-inclusive)

Great Sand Dunes Oasis • (719) 378-2222
Sand sled rentals available at store
7800 CO-150, Mosca
greatdunes.com • RV: $38/night, Cabins: $55

KOA Alamosa • (719) 589-9757
6900 Juniper Ln, Alamosa

Enchanted Forest • (719) 256-5768
3459 Enchanted Way, Crestone
enchantedforestcrestone.net • Rates: $65+

Coll House B&B • (719) 256-4475
1019 Moonlight Way, Crestone
collhouse.com • Rates: $115+

Sangre De Cristo Inn • (719) 256-4975
116 S Alder, Crestone

Sand Dunes Swimming RV • (719) 378-2807
1991 CR-63, Hooper
sanddunespool.com • Rates: $30+

Grape Creek RV Park • (719) 783-2588
56491 CO-69, Westcliffe
grapecreekrv.net • Rates: $44+

Ute Creek Campground • (719) 379-3238
071 5th Ave, Fort Garland

Black Canyon Area

Black Canyon Motel • (970) 249-3495
1605 E Main St, Montrose
blackcanyonmotel.com • Rates: $50+

Canyon Creek B&B • (970) 249-2886
820 Main St, Montrose
canyoncreekbedandbreakfast.com • Rates: $135

Kings Riverbend RV & Cabins
65120 Old Chipeta Tr, Montrose
kingsriverbend.com • (970) 249-8235

Cedar Creek RV Park • (970) 249-3884
126 Rose Ln, Montrose
cedarcreekrv.com • Rates: $40.50+

Last Frontier Lodge • (970) 921-5150
40300 D Ln, Crawford
lastfrontierlodge.com

Stone House Inn • (970) 921-5683
270 CO-92, Crawford

French Country Inn B&B • (970) 921-7111
38400 French Field Way, Crawford
frenchcountryinnbb.com

Mesa Verde Area

Tomahawk Lodge • (970) 565-8521
728 S Broadway, Cortez

Flagstone Meadows • (970) 533-9838
38080 Rd K.4, Mancos
flagstonemeadows.com • Rates: $115+

Aneth Lodge-Budget Six • (970) 565-3453
645 E Main St, Cortez

Sundance Bear Lodge • (970) 533-1504
11555 Road 39, Mancos • sundancebear.com

Enchanted Mesa Motel • (970) 533-7729
862 W Grand Ave, Mancos
enchantedmesamotel.com

Abode at Willowtail Springs • (800) 698-0603
10451 Rd 39, Mancos
willowtailsprings.com • Rates: $259+

La Mesa RV Park • (970) 565-0997
2380 E Main St, Cortez
lamesarvpark.com • Rates: $41

A&A Mesa Verde RV • (970) 565-3517
34979 US-160, Mancos

Mesa Verde RV Resort • (800) 776-7421
35303 US-160, Mancos
mesaverdervresort.com • Rates: 35+

KOA Kampgrounds • (970) 565-9301
27432 E US-160, Cortez

Many chain restaurants and hotels can be found
in Estes Park, Alamosa, Montrose, Cortez, Durango, and along Interstates 25 and 70.

Festivals

National Western Stock Show • January
Denver • nationalwestern.com

Winter Carnival • February
Steamboat Springs • steamboat-chamber.com

Crane Festival • March
Monte Vista • mvcranefest.org

Santa Fe Trail Festival • June
Trinidad • santafetrailscenicandhistoricbyway.org

Bluegrass Festival • June
Telluride • bluegrass.com

Cowboys' Roundup Days • July
Steamboat Springs • steamboat-chamber.com

Arts Festival • July
Cherry Creek • cherrycreekartsfestival.org

Colorado State Fair • August
Pueblo • coloradostatefair.com

Festival of the Arts • August
Crested Butte • crestedbutteartfestival.com

Rocky Mountain Irish Festival • July
Littleton • coloradoirishfestival.org

A Taste of Colorado • September
Denver • atasteofcolorado.com

Colorado Mountain Winefest • September
Palisade • coloradowineexperience.com

Long Peak Scottish Irish Highland Festival
September • Estes Park • scotfest.com

Great American Beer Festival • October
Denver • greatamericanbeerfestival.com

Attractions

Rocky Mountain Area
SK Horses • (970) 586-5890
1-to-4 hour ($40–85) trail rides offered
Estes Park (multiple locations) • skhorses.com

Sombrero Ranch
*Trail, breakfast, steak dinner, sleigh, and wagon
rides available • horse drives too!*
Estes Park (multiple locations) • sombrero.com

YMCA of the Rockies • (970) 586-3341
*Trail rides from 1-hour ($40) to all-day ($170),
hay ($20) and pony ($15) rides also available*
2515 Tunnel Rd, Estes Park • jacksonstables.com

Colorado Mountain School • (970) 586-5758
Intro Rock Climb ($195) and many other courses
341 Moraine Ave, Estes Park
coloradomountainschool.com

Apex Ex • (303) 731-6160
160 Woodstock Dr, Estes Park
apexex.com • *hiking/climbing guides*

Grand Adventures • (970) 726-9247
Snowmobile tours and rentals ($105 • 2 hrs)
304 W Portal Rd, Grand Lake
grandadventures.com

Estes Park Aerial Tramway • (970) 586-3675
420 E Riverside Dr, Estes Park
estestram.com • Tickets: $12/adult

Estes Park Ride-A-Kart • (970) 586-6495
2250 Big Thompson Ave, Estes Park
rideakart.com • Go-Karts: $7.50

MacGregor Ranch Museum • (970) 586-3749
180 MacGregor Ln, Estes Park
macgregorranch.org

Estes Park Museum • (970) 586-6256
200 4th St, Estes Park
estesparkmuseumfriends.org • Free

Stanley Steamcar Museum • (800) 976-1377
333 Wonderview Ave, Estes Park
stanleysteamcarmuseum.com

Tiny Town Miniature Golf • (970) 586-6333
840 Moraine Ave, Estes Park

Affinity Massage • (970) 586-3401
312 E Elkhorn, Estes Park
affinitymassageandwellness.com

Riverspointe Spa • (970) 577-6841
121 Wiest Dr, Estes Park
riverspointespa.com

Elements of Touch Spa • (970) 586-6597
477 Pine River Ln, Estes Park
elementsoftouchestespark.com

Snowy Peaks Winery • (970) 586-2099
292 Moraine Ave, Estes Park
snowypeakswinery.com

Park Theater • (970) 586-8904
130 Moraine Ave, Estes Park
historicparktheatre.com • Tickets: $9/adult

Rocky Mountain Repertory Theatre
800 Grand Ave, Grand Lake
rockymountainrep.com • (970) 627-3421

Great Sand Dunes Area

🤚**Zapata Falls**
*From Great Sand Dunes Visitor Center, drive
south about 8 miles, turn left (east) onto a
gravel road, and continue about 3.5 miles to
the trailhead. The hike is 0.5 miles and requires that you cross a creek and scramble up
slippery rocks to the 25-ft falls.*

Baca National Wildlife Refuge (NWR)
Crestone • fws.gov/refuge/baca

Alamosa NWR • (719) 589-4021
9383 El Rancho Ln, Alamosa
fws.gov/refuge/alamosa

San Luis Lakes State Park • (719) 378-2020
16399 Lane 6 N, Mosca

Francisco Fort Museum • (719) 742-5501
306 S Main St, La Veta
franciscofort.org

Rio Grande Scenic Railroad
610 State St, Alamosa • (877) 726-7245
coloradotrain.com • Tickets: $99+

UFO Watchtower • (719) 378-2296
2502 County Road 61, Center
ufowatchtower.com • Admission: $2

Alligator Farm • (719) 378-2612
9162 CR 9 N, Mosca
coloradogators.com • Admission: $15/adult

ABC Pro Bowl • (719) 589-2240
204 Victoria Ave, Alamosa

Joyful Journey Hot Springs Spa
28640 County Rd 58EE, Moffat
joyfuljourneyhotsprings.com • (719) 256-4328

Sky Hi 6 Theatres • (719) 589-4471
7089 US-160, Alamosa

Francisco Theater • (719) 695-0687
127 Francisco, La Veta

Grandote Peaks Golf Course
5540 CO-12, La Veta • (719) 742-3390
grandotepeaks.com • 9 holes: $35+

Black Canyon Area
Crawford State Park • (970) 921-5721
40468 CO-92, Crawford
cpw.state.co.us • Entrance Fee: $7/vehicle

Curecanti National Rec Area
102 Elk Creek, Gunnison • (970) 641-2337
nps.gov/cure

Museum of the Mountain West
68169 Miami Rd, Montrose • (970) 240-3400
museumofthemountainwest.org • $10/adult

Ute Indian Museum • (970) 249-3098
17253 Chipeta Rd, Montrose

Bridges Golf Course • (970) 252-1119
2500 Bridges Ave, Montrose
montrosebridges.com • 9 holes: $50 (w/ cart)

San Juan Cinema • (970) 252-9096
1869 E Main St, Montrose
montrosemovies.com • Tickets: $9/adult

Star Drive-In Theatre • (970) 249-6170
600 Miami St, Montrose
stardrivein.com • Tickets: $8/adult

Magic Circle Theatre • (970) 249-7838
420 S 12th St, Montrose
magiccircleplayers.com

Tru Vu Drive In Theatre • (970) 874-9556
1001 CO-92, Delta

Mesa Verde Area

☝**Hovenweep National Monument**
McElmo Route, Cortez • (970) 562-4282
nps.gov/hove • Free

Canyons of the Ancients National Monument
27501 CO-184, Dolores
Admission: $3/adult • (970) 882-5600
blm.gov/co/st/en/nm/canm.html

☝**Canyon Trails Ranch •** (970) 565-1499
13987 Road G, Cortez • canyontrailsranch.com

☝**Cortez Cultural Center •** (970) 565-1151
25 North Market St, Cortez
cortezculturalcenter.org

☝**Crow Canyon Archaeological Center**
23390 Road K, Cortez
crowcanyon.org • (970) 565-8975

Conquistador Golf Course • (970) 565-9208
2018 N Dolores Rd, Cortez • fourcornersgolf.com

Lakeside Lanes • (970) 564-1450
410 Lakeside Dr, Cortez

Fiesta Theatre • (970) 565-9003
23 W Main St, Cortez

Southwest Adventure Guides
Rock, ice, alpine, ski, avalanche, and backpack trips
1111 Camino del Rio, Durango
mtnguide.net • (800) 642-5389

Kling Mountain Guides • (970) 259-1708
Rock, ice, alpine, ski, avalanche, and backpack trips
1205 Camino Del Rio, Durango
klingmountainguides.com

☝**Mild to Wild Rafting •** (970) 247-4789
Rafting, Jeep, kayak, and train tours
50 Animas View Dr, Durango
mild2wildrafting.com

Durango & Silverton Train • (888) 872-4607
479 Main Ave, Durango
durangotrain.com • Rates: $95.23+/adult

Beyond the Parks

Colorado State Capitol • (303) 866-2604
200 E Colfax Ave, Denver
colorado.gov • Free Tours

United States Mint • (303) 405-4761
320 W Colfax Ave, Denver
usmint.gov • Tours: Reservation required

Denver Museum Of Nature & Science
2001 Colorado Blvd, Denver
dmns.org • (303) 370-6000 • $14.95/adult

☝**Denver Zoo •** (720) 337-1400
2300 Steele St, Denver
denverzoo.org • Admission: $13/adult

Denver Botanic Gardens • (720) 865-3501
1007 York St, Denver
botanicgardens.org • Admission: $14/adult

Kirkland Museum of Fine & Decorative Art
1311 Pearl St, Denver • (303) 832-8576
kirklandmuseum.org • Admission: $8/adult

☝**Denver Art Museum •** (720) 865-5000
100 W 14th Ave Parkway, Denver
denverartmuseum.org • Admission: $13/adult

The Denver Center for Performing Arts
1101 13th St, Denver
denvercenter.org • (303) 893-4100

Mayan Theatre • (303) 744-6799
110 Broadway, Denver

Observatory Park • (303) 871-5172
2930 E Warren Ave, Denver

Mile-Hi Skydiving Center • (303) 759-3493
229 Airport Rd, # 34G, Longmont
mile-hi-skydiving.com

☝**Mount Evans Road •** (303) 567-3000
Idaho Springs • *Highest paved road in America*
mountevans.com • Entrance Fee: $10/vehicle

Clear Creek Rafting • (303) 567-1000
350 Whitewater Rd, Idaho Springs
clearcreekrafting.com • Trips: $47+

Bob Culp Climbing School • (720) 724-3079
10 S 32nd St, Boulder
bobculp.com • Rates: $100+/person

☝**Colorado Wilderness Rides And Guides •**
(720) 242-9828 & (970) 480-7780
4865 Darwin Court, Boulder, CO 80301 &
2625 Marys Lake Rd, Estes Park
coloradowildernessridesandguides.com

☝**Garden of the Gods •** (719) 634-6666
*Wild sandstone formations, like those pictured
above with Pike's Peak in the background*
1805 N 30th St, Colorado Springs
gardenofgods.com • Free

☝**Pike's Peak/Pike National Forest**
*Another 14,000-ft mountain you drive up! To
drive the 19-mile Pike's Peak Highway (Cascade,
CO), you'll have to pay $12/adult, $5/child, or
$40/carload (5 people max). It's busy (try to go
on a weekday) and cold (pack a jacket), but the
views are incredible. The road has many switchbacks and is not for the faint of heart. You can also
take the Cog Railway (below) or hike (overnight)
via Barr Trail.*
s.usda.gov/psicc

Pikes Peak Cog Railway • (719) 685-5401
515 Ruxton Ave, Manitou Springs
cograilway.com • Rates: $38/adult

Colorado Climbing Company • (719) 209-6649
Half-day ($70+) to multi-day climbing trips
Colorado Springs • coclimbing.com

☝**Cheyenne Mountain Zoo •** (719) 633-9925
You get to feed giraffes here!
4250 Cheyenne Mtn Zoo Rd, Colorado Springs
cmzoo.org • Admission: $17.25/adult

☝**Lost Paddle Rafting •** (719) 275-7507
1420 Royal Gorge Blvd, Cañon City
lostpaddlerafting.com • Trips: $42+

Royal Gorge Bridge and Park • (888) 333-5597
4218 County Rd, 3A, Cañon City
royalgorgebridge.com • Rates: $20/adult

Royal Gorge Route Railroad • (719) 276-4000
330 Royal Gorge Blvd, Cañon City
royalgorgeroute.com • Rates: $44+/adult

Bishop's Castle • (719) 485-3040
Man-made castle • May not be suitable for children
12705 CO-165, Rye

Rocky Mountain Outdoor Center
14825 US-285, Salida • (800) 255-5784
rmoc.com • *multi-sport outfitter*

Cano's Castle
Castle built of scrap metal, beer cans, and hub caps
Between 10th and 11th on State St, Antonito

Breckenridge Ski Resort • (800) 789-7669
1599 Ski Hill Rd, Breckenridge
breckenridge.com • Life Ticket: $132/adult

Performance Tours Rafting • (970) 453-0661
351 County Rd 500, Breckenridge
performancetours.com • Trips: $60+

Nova Guides • (719) 486-2656
Snowmobile tours ($260+) and rental
7088 US-24, Red Cliff • novaguides.com

American Adventure Expeditions
12844 US-24/285, Buena Vista • (719) 766-8628
americanadventure.com • Trips: $45+

Buffalo Joe's Whitewater • (866) 283-3563
801 Front Loop, Buena Vista
buffalojoe.com • Trips: $60+

Dvorak's Kayak & Rafting
Kayak, rafting, fishing, and photography
17921 US-285, Nathrop
dvorakexpeditions.com • (719) 539-6851

Aspen Ski Mountain • (970) 923-1227
601 E Dean St, Aspen
aspensnowmass.com • Lift Ticket: $149+/adult

Aspen Expeditions • (970) 925-7625
Backcountry, avalanche, and ice climbing trips
133 Prospector Rd, Ste 4115, Aspen Highlands
aspenexpeditions.com

Doc Holliday's Grave
Cemetery accessible by a short trail
Linwood Cemetery, 12th St, Glenwood Springs

Maroon Bells/White River National Forest
One of the most photographed spots in Colorado. Located just 10 miles from Aspen via Maroon Creek Road, this is an incredibly popular area. Parking is limited, but bus tours ($8/adult, $6/child) run throughout the day in summer (typically beginning mid-June). Note that you must take the bus from 8am–5pm. During this time, buses depart Rubey Park in Aspen every 20 minutes. You can drive if you're camping at Silver Bar, Silver Bell, or Silver Queen Campground.
900 Grand Ave, Glenwood Springs
fs.usda.gov/whiteriver • Fee: $10/vehicle

Winter Park Resort • (970) 726-5514
85 Parsenn Rd, Winter Park
winterparkresort.com • Lift ticket: $89/adult

Steamboat Ski & Resort • (877) 783-2628
2305 Mt Werner Ci, Steamboat Springs
steamboat.com

Dinosaur National Monument
4545 E US-40, Dinosaur • (970) 374-3000
nps.gov/dino • Entrance Fee: $20/vehicle

Chicks Climbing • (970) 626-4424
163 County Rd, 12 A, Ridgway
chickswithpicks.net • *Ice & Rock Clinics*

Skyward Mountaineering • (970) 325-3305
Ice & rock climbing, and backcountry trips based out of Ridgway • skywardmountaineering.com

Crested Butte Mountain Guides
Offers a multitude of backcountry adventures based out of Crested Butte
crestedbutteguides.com • (970) 349-5430

Colorado National Monument
1750 Rimrock Dr, Fruita • (970) 858-3617
nps.gov/colm • Entrance Fee: $10/vehicle

San Juan Mountain Guides • (800) 642-5389
Ice, rock, ski, and mountain courses based out of Ouray • mtnguide.net

Telluride Outside • (970) 728-3895
Fishing, 4WD, raft, MTB, and photo tours
121 W Colorado Ave, Telluride
tellurideoutside.com

Telluride • (970) 728-6900
565 Mountain Village Blvd, Telluride
tellurideskiresort.com

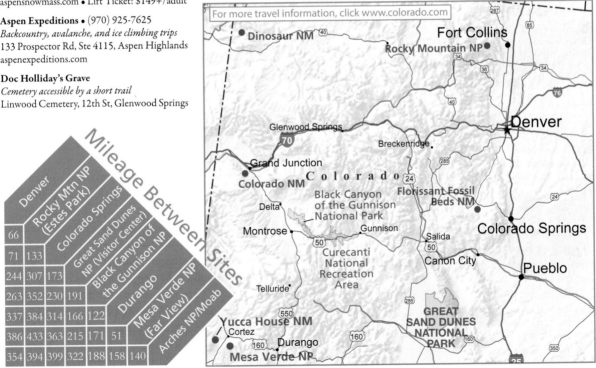

Mileage Between Sites						
Denver						
66	Rocky Mtn NP (Estes Park)					
71	133	Colorado Springs				
244	307	173	Great Sand Dunes NP (Visitor Center)			
263	352	230	191	Black Canyon of the Gunnison NP		
337	384	314	166	122	Durango	
386	433	363	215	171	51	Mesa Verde NP (Far View)
354	394	399	322	188	158	140	Arches NP/Moab

For more travel information, click www.colorado.com

Dinosaur NM
Fort Collins
Rocky Mountain NP
Denver
Glenwood Springs
Breckenridge
Grand Junction
Colorado NM
C o l o r a d o
Black Canyon of the Gunnison National Park
Florissant Fossil Beds NM
Delta
Montrose
Gunnison
Salida
Colorado Springs
Canon City
Curecanti National Recreation Area
Pueblo
Telluride
Yucca House NM
Cortez
Durango
GREAT SAND DUNES NATIONAL PARK
Mesa Verde NP

Delicate Arch

Arches

PO Box 907
Moab, UT 84532
Phone: (435) 719-2299
Website: nps.gov/arch

Established: November 12, 1971
April 12, 1929 (National Monument)
Size: 76,519 Acres
Annual Visitors: 1.4 Million
Peak Season: Spring & Fall

Activities: Hiking, Backpacking,
Rock Climbing, Biking, and
Photography

Campgrounds: Devil's Garden*
Fee: $25/night
Backcountry Camping: Permitted
with a free Backcountry Use Permit
Lodging: None

Park Hours: All day, every day
Entrance Fee: $25/vehicle,
$10/individual (foot, bike, etc.)

*Reserve at recreation.gov or (877)
444-6777 from March through
October

The only arches you see on a typical family vacation are golden, raised high above the ground, advertising the ubiquitous fast-food chain. But in southeast Utah, high atop the Colorado Plateau, is a collection of more than 2,000 natural sandstone arches, colored striking shades of pink, orange, and red. Standing tall, they frame the surrounding mountains. These natural advertisements are just as good at capturing the attention of passersby, but they have nothing to sell. In fact, all they do is give. They give inspiration to the many guests who come to admire Mother Nature's patient handiwork.

Patient is a gross understatement; these fragile features began forming more than 300 million years ago. First a massive sea covering the region evaporated, depositing a salt bed thousands of feet thick in some places. During the Uncompahgre Uplift, rivers and streams buried the salt beds with debris and sediment. Desert conditions of the early Jurassic period allowed a layer of Navajo sandstone to be covered by a layer of Entrada sandstone (the substrate of most arches). But before sandstone could be sculpted by wind, water and ice, it was buried by another 5,000 feet of sediment. The weight of material caused lower salt beds to heat up and liquefy. Layers of rock became unstable. Faulting occurred and plumes of less dense liquefied salt penetrated the upper layers of rock forming salt domes. Domes provided a curve to sections of sandstone. Years of erosion wore away the surface sediment, eventually exposing the underlying sandstone. Water seeped into cracks in its surface, gradually enlarging them until walls of sandstone called fins were left, isolated from one another. As wind and water continued to work on these fins, the salt bed layer wore away faster than sandstone. Water collected in joints and fissures, freezes and expands, causing chunks of rock to flake and crumble. Many fins collapsed into piles of rubble. Others formed magnificent arches that continue to be sculpted by wind, water, and ice. These too will concede to erosion and gravity. Since 1970, 43 arches have collapsed within the park.

The first inhabitants weren't all that interested in seeing sandstone arches. More than 10,000 years ago, nomadic people came to the region hunting and gathering. Until 700 years ago, Fremont People and Ancestral Puebloans lived here, growing crops of maize, beans, and squash. Just as they picked up and moved south, Paiute and Ute Indians moved in. Spanish missionaries encountered natives in the late 1700s while searching for a route between Santa Fe and Los Angeles. In 1855, European Americans settled in the region. Mormons established Elk Mountain Mission, but difficult farming and disputes with Native Americans led them to abandon their settlements. By the 1880s, ranchers, farmers, and prospectors were trickling into the area. John Wesley Wolfe, a Civil War veteran, was among them. He built a small ranch along Salt Wash with his son in 1898, which is still preserved in its original location near present-day Delicate Arch Trailhead.

It wasn't until 1911 that locals began to understand the recreational value of the area. Loren "Bish" Taylor, a local newspaperman, and John "Doc" Williams, Moab's first doctor, frequented the area, marveling at these sandstone formations. Bish wrote about the natural wonders just north of Moab, and eventually, publicity grew to the point that Denver and Rio Grande Western Railroad and the federal government took notice. Both parties were impressed, and in 1929 President Hoover signed legislation creating Arches National Monument. In 1971, Congress redesignated it as a national park. It's an eroded landscape protected from man, but not from nature, and the landscapes are constantly changing. Changes unnoticed by the average visitor: visitors drawn to and inspired by grand natural landmarks millions of years in the making.

Park Avenue

When to Go
Arches is open all day every day, but the temperate weather of spring and fall attracts most visitors. The **visitor center** is open every day except Christmas. Its operating hours are 7:30am to 6pm from April through October. Hours are shortened to 9am to 4pm from November through March. Arches is one of the most spectacularly unique parks. If you'd like to return home with stunning images, plan on waking up before the sun rises or remaining in the park until sunset at least a time or two.

Transportation & Airports
Public transportation does not provide service to or around the park. The closest large commercial airport is Salt Lake City International (SLC), located 237 miles to the northwest. There are three regional airports nearby. Canyonlands Field (CNY) is 14 miles to the north. Grand Junction Regional (GJT) is 114 miles to the northeast. Green River Municipal (RVR) is 55 miles to the northwest.

Directions
Arches is located in southeastern Utah, just 28 miles south of I-70, between Green River, UT and Grand Junction, CO. To reach the park from I-70, take Exit 182 for US-191 toward Crescent Jct/Moab. Continue south on US-191 for approximately 27 miles, where you will see the visitor center to the east and signs for the entrance.

Visitors arriving from the southwest (Mesa Verde National Park • page 356) should take US-160 west. At Cortez, turn right onto US-491 North/North Broadway. Continue for 60 miles before turning right at US-191. Drive another 60 miles and you will pass through Moab to the park entrance and visitor center. You will also pass the entrance to Newspaper Rock/Canyonlands' Needles District (page 378) and Wilson Arch (all worthy pit-stops).

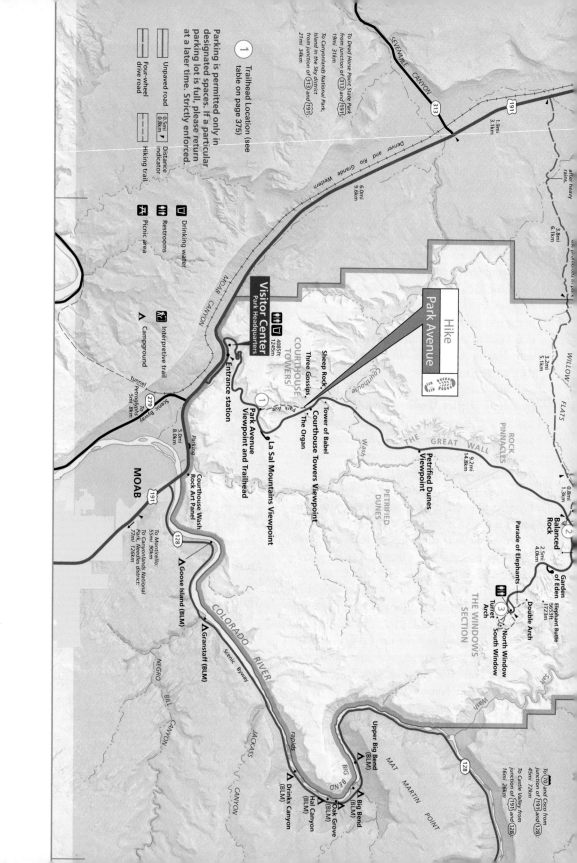

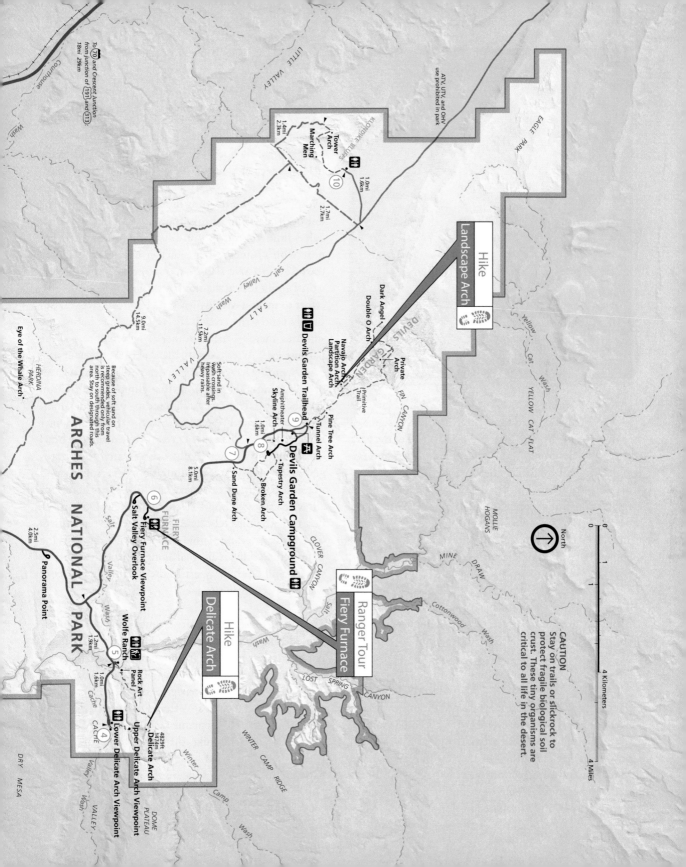

ARCHES NATIONAL PARK

Hike
Landscape Arch

Hike
Delicate Arch

Ranger Tour
Fiery Furnace

CAUTION
Stay on trails or slickrock to
protect fragile biological soil
crust. These tiny organisms are
critical to all life in the desert.

North

0
1 Kilometers
4

0
1 Miles
4

To 70 and Crescent junction
from junction of 191 and 313
18mi 29km

ATV, UTV, and OHV
use prohibited in park

LITTLE VALLEY

KLONDIKE BLUFFS

EAGLE PARK

Tower
Arch
1.4mi
2.3km

Marching
Men

1.0mi
1.6km

10

1.7mi
2.7km

YELLOW CAT WASH

Courthouse Wash

Eye of the Whale Arch

HERDINA PARK

9.0mi
14.5km

Dark Angel
Double O Arch

Navajo Arch
Partition Arch
Landscape Arch

Private
Arch

Primitive
Trail

DEVILS GARDEN

FIN CANYON

7.2mi
11.5km

Devils Garden Trailhead

Pine Tree Arch
Tunnel Arch

Amphitheater
Skyline Arch

9

8

1.0mi
1.6km

Devils Garden Campground

Tapestry Arch

Broken Arch

YELLOW CAT FLAT

MOLLIE HOGANS

Because of soft sand on
steep grades, vehicular travel
is recommended only from
north to south through this
area. Stay on designated roads.

SALT VALLEY

Soft sand in
wash crossings.
Impassable after
heavy rains.

7

5.0mi
8.1km

Sand Dune Arch

CLOVER CANYON

MINE DRAW

2.5mi
4.0km

Panorama Point

ARCHES NATIONAL PARK

Salt Valley Wash

6

Fiery Furnace Viewpoint
Salt Valley Overlook

FIERY FURNACE

Fiery Furnace

Cottonwood Wash

1.2mi
1.9km

Wolfe Ranch

5

Rock Art
Panel

1.0mi
1.6km

CACHE

Lower Delicate Arch Viewpoint

4

Upper Delicate Arch Viewpoint

Delicate Arch
4829ft
1471m

LOST SPRING CANYON

WINTER CAMP RIDGE

DOME PLATEAU

DRY MESA

Cache Valley Wash

Winter Camp Wash

Skyline Arch

Double O Arch

Camping

Devil's Garden is Arches' only designated campground. It's located at the end of the park road, 18 miles from the entrance. Flush toilets and potable water are available. There are no showers or laundry. The camp has 50 sites, all of which are available for reservation from March through October. Sites must be reserved (877.444.6777, recreation.gov) between 4 and 180 days in advance. They are available on a first-come, first-served basis for the remainder of the year. Rates are $25 per night.

Two group sites are available for groups of 11 or more people. They must be reserved (877.444.6777, recreation.gov) at a cost of $75–250 depending on the size of your group, plus a $9 reservation fee.

All sites are typically reserved in advance during the reservation period, so make your reservations early. You need to reserve sites the moment they become available for popular holidays like Easter, Memorial Day, and Labor Day. Fortunately, there are several **Bureau of Land Management campgrounds** nearby (page 455). **Backpackers** are also welcome to camp in the backcountry with a **free permit** (available at the visitor center). (Note:

Devil's Garden is scheduled to be closed between March and October 2017 due to road construction.)

Hiking

Seeing **Delicate Arch** on Utah license plates gives an idea of its beauty, but a little paint on metal hardly does it justice. To truly appreciate the magnificence of Utah's natural icon you need to hike to its base. Pose with it. Marvel its rocky delicateness. Even without the arch providing the crescendo, this would be one of the park's must-hike trails. It's a moderately difficult 3-mile (roundtrip) fun-filled adventure. You begin near Wolf's Ranch, where you'll cross a small wash and traverse a massive slab of unmarked slickrock. Don't worry about losing the trail, it would take considerable effort to make a wrong turn. And on most days you can simply follow the crowd. (Even if you start before the sun rises, there's usually another early-bird or two in the parking lot.) After crossing the slickrock, the trail narrows, winding its way along an exposed ledge to the rim of a large natural bowl. Your first glimpse over the rim and there it is, Delicate Arch standing proud, an anomaly that wind and water have yet to wear away. Don't expect to enjoy this experience on your own. The bowl is usually busy. Hikers pose with the arch for photographs, or simply stare in admiration. A person in good physical condition can make the hike in an hour, but allow at least two hours to enjoy the view. Dusk is the best time to visit Delicate Arch. As the sun sets it gives off a brilliant orange glow. Also, be aware that parking is limited. Parking is allowed alongside the road, just be sure to pull all the way off to the side. Bring plenty of water (especially in summer).

The other "must-do" activity is embarking on a ranger-guided hike through the **Fiery Furnace**. As its name implies, it gets hot here in summer. Individuals are required to carry at least one quart of water in a backpack (to free your hands to navigate sandstone obstacles). Tours of Fiery Furnace are offered twice each day from April through early September. It's a 3-hour (2-mile), moderately-difficult hike through a sandstone maze, where a fair amount of scrambling is required. Participants must be able to squeeze through narrow spaces, pull themselves over rocks, and climb reasonably steep rock faces. Good hiking shoes are required. The tour costs $16 per adult and $8 per child (ages 5–12). It is extremely popular and space is rarely available the day of the hike. Reservations can be made in advance by calling (877) 444-6777 or clicking recreation.gov. Visitors can explore Fiery Furnace on their own by obtaining a permit ($6/adult, $3/child) from the visitor center. Permits cannot be reserved or held over the phone. They must be obtained in person at the visitor center. Everyone in your group will be required to watch a short orientation video.

If it's your first time in the Fiery Furnace, the park suggests you join one of the ranger-guided tours (without an experienced guide you're likely to miss most of the highlights). There are several good hiking alternatives for those unable to secure a spot on a Fiery Furnace Tour. **Devil's Garden** (7.2 miles including all spur trails to rock formations) is the park's longest maintained trail. The loop passes Landscape Arch, Partition Arch, Navajo Arch, Double O Arch, Dark Angel, and Private Arch. Note that it's a primitive trail beyond Landscape Arch (the longest arch in the park). It's well maintained, but a bit of scrambling is required. If you're unsure about completing the loop, check out the first ascent past Landscape Arch. It's a pretty good example of the type of obstacles you'll have to traverse. Good hiking shoes are recommended. Additional trails begin at the campground and in the Windows Area. See the table below for a complete list.

Backpacking

Don't let the park's small size fool you. You can only get a few miles away from paved roads and developed areas, but there's more than enough land to escape the crowds and find that perfect location for a night under the stars. There are no designated trails or campsites in the backcountry, and there are no reliable sources of water.

The park's small size and abundance of unique rock formations may lead you to believe that navigating the wilderness will be a snap. Do not make this assumption. In reality, the terrain is repetitive, with miles and miles of sandstone decorated with shrubs and the occasional tumbling tumbleweed, so bring a good map and know how to use it. Seasoned hikers may be able to navigate their way through the park's backcountry by the 2,000+ arches, but even many of them are indistinguishable to the untrained eye. Any overnight stay in the backcountry requires a **free permit** (available at the visitor center).

Arches Hiking Trails (Distances are roundtrip unless noted otherwise)

Name	Location (# on map)	Length	Difficulty Rating & Notes
Park Avenue	Park Avenue Parking Area (1)	1.0 mile	M – From viewpoint to Courthouse Towers (1-way)
Balanced Rock	Balanced Rock Parking Area (2)	0.3 mile	E – Short walk around the base of balanced rock
Double Arch	Double Arch Parking Area (3)	0.5 mile	E – Short walk to a wonderful arch
The Windows	The Windows Parking Area (3)	1.0 mile	E – Views through two windows and Turret Arch
Delicate Arch Viewpoint	Delicate Arch Viewpoint (4)	300 feet	E – Cannot reach the base of Delicate Arch, bring binoculars, the arch is off in the distance
Delicate Arch	Wolf Ranch Parking Area (5)	3.0 miles	M – Adventurous hike to Delicate Arch bowl/base
Fiery Furnace	Fiery Furnace Parking Area (6)	Varies	S – Ranger-guided tour (fee, reservations)
Sand Dune Arch	Sand Dune Arch Parking Area (7)	0.3 mile	E – Also accessible from campground
Broken Arch	Sand Dune Arch Parking Area (7)	1.3 miles	E – Also accessible from campground
Skyline Arch	Skyline Arch Parking Area (8)	0.4 mile	E – Short but rocky hike across grassland
Landscape Arch	Devil's Garden Trailhead (9)	1.6 miles	E – Largest arch in the park • 306-ft base-to-base
Double O Arch	Devil's Garden Trailhead (9)	4.2 miles	S – Continue beyond Landscape Arch
Devil's Garden	Devil's Garden Trailhead (9)	7.2 miles	S – The complete Devil's Garden Trail and all its spurs
Tower Arch	Klondike Bluffs Parking Area, via Salt Valley Road (10)	3.4 miles	S – Remote area of the park accessed via Salt Valley Road or 4WD road • Moderately strenuous

Difficulty Ratings: E = Easy, M = Moderate, S = Strenuous

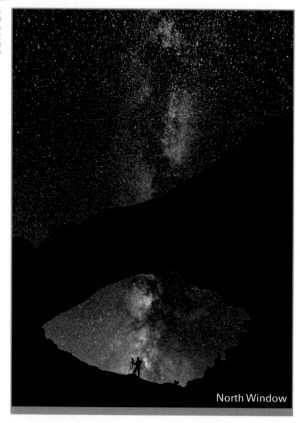

North Window

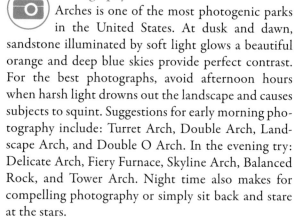

Photography

Arches is one of the most photogenic parks in the United States. At dusk and dawn, sandstone illuminated by soft light glows a beautiful orange and deep blue skies provide perfect contrast. For the best photographs, avoid afternoon hours when harsh light drowns out the landscape and causes subjects to squint. Suggestions for early morning photography include: Turret Arch, Double Arch, Landscape Arch, and Double O Arch. In the evening try: Delicate Arch, Fiery Furnace, Skyline Arch, Balanced Rock, and Tower Arch. Night time also makes for compelling photography or simply sit back and stare at the stars.

Ranger Programs

Fiery Furnace Walks (page 374) are the crown jewel of Arches' ranger-led programs, but additional interpretive programs and activities are offered throughout the summer. Find a current schedule of events at the visitor center or online.

For Kids

Arches is a family favorite. Most trails are short and relatively easy (even the hike to Delicate Arch is kid-friendly), and the arches are pretty cool, too. Children are invited to take part in the **Junior Ranger Program**. It helps encourage children to explore the park in an educational yet entertaining manner. Activity booklets are available for free online or at the visitor center. Your child will be rewarded with a badge and signed certificate for completing five or more exercises.

Flora & Fauna

At first sight, Utah's high desert isn't exactly teeming with life. It's very uncommon to see large mammals grazing. Trees are few and far apart. Upon closer inspection, you may spot a skittish lizard between the cracks in a rock or a bird flying high above the desert monuments. Astute visitors will notice cacti, yuccas, and mosses built to withstand long periods of drought. Spacing between shrubs depends on the amount of seasonal rain. Most diversity is due to the Colorado River, which flows along the park's southeastern boundary. Here, and along Courthouse Wash, you'll find cottonwoods and willows.

Biking

Driving the roadways, viewing the scenery from overlooks and observation points, and taking an occasional short hike, are satisfying activities, but there's much more to do at Arches. Cyclists are allowed on all park roads. The main park road is suitable (but often busy) for road cyclists. There isn't any singletrack, but Salt Valley and Willow Springs Roads are ideal for mountain biking. If it's singletrack you desire, well, you're in the right place. Moab is Mecca to mountain bikers.

Rock Climbing

Rock Climbing is another popular activity. Climbers are encouraged to register, either online or at the self-registration kiosk outside the visitor center. There are many rules and regulations, but these are the big ones: Groups are limited to five or less. Climbers must be free or clean aid climbing. Do not physically alter the rock. White chalk is prohibited. Guided rock climbing is prohibited.

Pets

Pets are permitted at overlooks, pullouts, paved road-ways, parking lots, and developed campgrounds, but must be kept on a leash no more than six feet in length at all times. They are prohibited from all hiking trails and the backcountry. Pets can be boarded at Karen's Canine Campground (435.259.7922) or Moab Vet Clinic (435.259.8710).

Accessibility

Most of Arches is inaccessible to wheelchair users, but the visitor center, Park Avenue and Delicate Arch Viewpoints, and all restrooms are accessible. Devil's Garden Campground has one accessible campsite.

Weather

Arches is located in southeast Utah's high desert. The climate is extremely dry, receiving less than 10 inches of precipitation each year on average. Summers are hot, winters are cold, and the seasons in between are comfortable. Another characteristic of the high desert is extreme weather variation. A single day's temperature can vary more than 40°F. Summer highs often reach into the 100s°F, but evenings are almost always comfortable with average lows in the 60s°F. During winter, average highs are in the 40s°F with lows averaging around 25°F. Spring and fall tend to be the most popular seasons, when average daytime highs range from the 60s–80s°F.

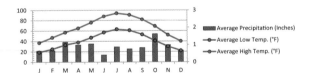

Vacation Planner

Arches is relatively small and can be extremely busy during spring break and Memorial Day and Labor Day weekends. From March through October, **campers** must reserve a site at **Devil's Garden**. Without reservations, you'll have to camp outside the park at nearby Bureau of Land Management (BLM) campgrounds (page 455). Small size also makes for a very manageable day-trip. Provided below is a one-day itinerary to jump-start your Arches vacation planning. Nearby dining, grocery stores, lodging, festivals, and attractions are listed on pages 454–459.

Fiery Furnace

Day 1: Begin your trip at the **visitor center. Fiery Furnace Tours** (page 374) are highly recommended. They are offered twice daily from April through early September, but each tour is limited to just 15 guests. If you didn't make reservations already, ask if any space is available. Browse the exhibits and bookstore, and then return to your car. Stop at **Park Avenue** and at least go to the viewpoint. If you arrange a pick-up at Courthouse Towers, you can take a very casual downhill walk from here (or do it as an out-and-back). Continue driving along the main park road. View **Balanced Rock** on your right, and bypass Windows for now. If you have about 2 hours, stop at Wolf Ranch to hike to **Delicate Arch**. Its base can only be reached via the hiking trail, and this is a really fun trek. The arch is particularly beautiful near dusk or dawn, so plan accordingly. You can also view the arch from Delicate Arch Viewpoint, but it's so far off in the distance it's hardly worth it. Return to the main park road and head north. Drive all the way to **Devil's Garden Trailhead** at the road's end. Hike to **Landscape Arch** (complete the loop if time and attitudes permit, and you're up for a bit of an adventure). If you haven't seen too many arches already, stop at **The Windows** before exiting. It's another great sunset spot.

Grand View Point Overlook

Canyonlands

2282 SW Resource Blvd
Moab, UT 84532
Phone: (435) 719-2313
Website: nps.gov/cany

Established: September 12, 1964
Size: 337,598 Acres
Annual Visitors: 634,000
Peak Season: Spring and Fall
Hiking Trails: 200+ Miles

Activities: Hiking, Backpacking*, Stargazing, Paddling*, Horseback Riding*, Biking, and Rock Climbing

Campgrounds: Willow Flat (Island in the Sky) and Squaw Flat (Needles)
Fee: $15–20/night
Backcountry Camping: Permitted*

Park Hours: All day, every day
Entrance Fee: $25/vehicle, $10/individual (foot, bike, etc.)

*Must obtain a Backcountry Use Permit (fee). Any activity spending a night in the backcountry requires a permit.

Canyonlands, as its name implies, is an intricate landscape of canyons carved into the Colorado Plateau. Years of erosion have revealed colorful layers of rock and formed buttes and mesas rising high above the Colorado and Green Rivers. Their water continues to carry sediment from the canyon walls and floor all the way to the Pacific Ocean. Controversial conservationist and author, Edward Abbey, described the region best when he wrote it's "the most weird wonderful, magical place on earth—there is nothing else like it anywhere."

He's absolutely right. Proof lies in the geologic history recorded in layers of rock, and stories passed down over the course of 10,000 years of human inhabitance. Geology meets history at places like Horseshoe Canyon, where pictographs and petroglyphs are etched into the canyon's walls. These are places that weren't explored or studied until miners in search of uranium fanned out across the labyrinthine canyons.

Scientists believe at one time the Colorado Plateau region was completely flat and near sea level before layers of sedimentary rock were deposited. Millions of years ago a series of geologic events, including uplifts and volcanic activity, caused the area to rise more than 5,000 feet, on average, above sea level. This increase in elevation set the stage for the Colorado and Green Rivers to cut their way through soft sedimentary rock, revealing its geologic history in the process. Look closely at the rocks when you visit. Notice the horizontal bands of rock in the spires and canyon walls. Red and white layers seem to alternate as you move up the geologic column. Red is created from iron-rich deposits carried here by rivers from nearby mountains. White layers are mostly sand left behind from a shallow sea that covered the region millions of years ago. The park's Upheaval Dome is an anomaly in the geologic order.

It's impossible to be sure what caused this crater-like formation, and scientists continue to debate its origin. Some believe it was formed by a meteorite, while others contend a giant salt-bubble, known as a salt dome, is responsible for the abnormality.

Humans have lived in the region for more than 10,000 years. Artifacts recovered in Horseshoe Canyon date back as early as 9000–7000 BC, when mammoths still roamed the American Southwest. Pictographs and petroglyphs are also present in the canyon and most notably at its Great Gallery. Ancestral Puebloans and Fremont People left mud dwellings similar in style but much smaller in size than those found at Mesa Verde National Park (page 356). It is believed that large populations of Ancestral Puebloans moved into this area around 1200 AD from Mesa Verde, planting maize, beans, and squash, and raising turkeys and dogs.

Paiute and Ute Indians moved in during the tail end of the Ancestral Puebloans' presence. Neither culture did much exploration of the canyons. They simply used the land to hunt game and gather plants. European Americans arrived in the early 1800s. To fur trappers and missionaries the canyons were nothing more than an impediment to collecting pelts and reaching the West Coast. By the 1880s local ranchers used the land as winter pasture. Cowboy camps, like the one visible at Cave Spring Trail in Needles, were established to help safeguard their livestock.

After WWII, the uranium boom hit southeast Utah. Prospectors filed claims all over present-day Canyonlands and nearly 1,000 miles of roads were built thanks to incentives offered by the Atomic Energy Commission. Very little uranium was found, but this new form of exploitation caused concern for Bates Wilson, Superintendent of Arches National Monument. He passionately advocated the creation of a national park, leading jeep tours through the area hoping to gain allies. Fatefully, Secretary of the Interior Stewart Udall joined a tour after peering into the canyons while flying above the Colorado Plateau. He lobbied for the park, and in 1964 legislation was passed and signed by President Lyndon B. Johnson.

Buck Canyon Overlook

When to Go
Canyonlands National Park is open every day of the year. **Island in the Sky Visitor Center** is open daily, spring through fall. It's closed Thanksgiving, Christmas, and late December through early March. **Needles Visitor Center** is open daily, early March through November. It's closed Thanksgiving, and late November through early March. **Hans Flat Ranger Station**, located in the Maze District, is open daily, all year. See page 387 for complete operating hours. Summers are hot and dry, winters are cold and snow poses a serious problem for hikers and drivers. Spring and fall bring temperate weather and the majority of visitors.

Transportation & Airports
Public transportation does not provide service to or around the park. Salt Lake City International (SLC) is the closest large commercial airport. Grand Junction Regional (GJT), Green River Municipal (RVR), and Canyonlands Field (CNY) are nearby regional airports.

Directions
More than 94% of Canyonlands' visitors enter either Needles or Island in the Sky Districts. Access roads to these districts are located off US-191. Island in the Sky is reached via UT-313, 20 miles south of I-70 and 6.5 miles north of the entrance to Arches National Park (page 370). Needles District is accessed via UT-212, which is 50 miles south of UT-313. From US-191 it is roughly 40 miles to the end of the park road at Needles and Island in the Sky.

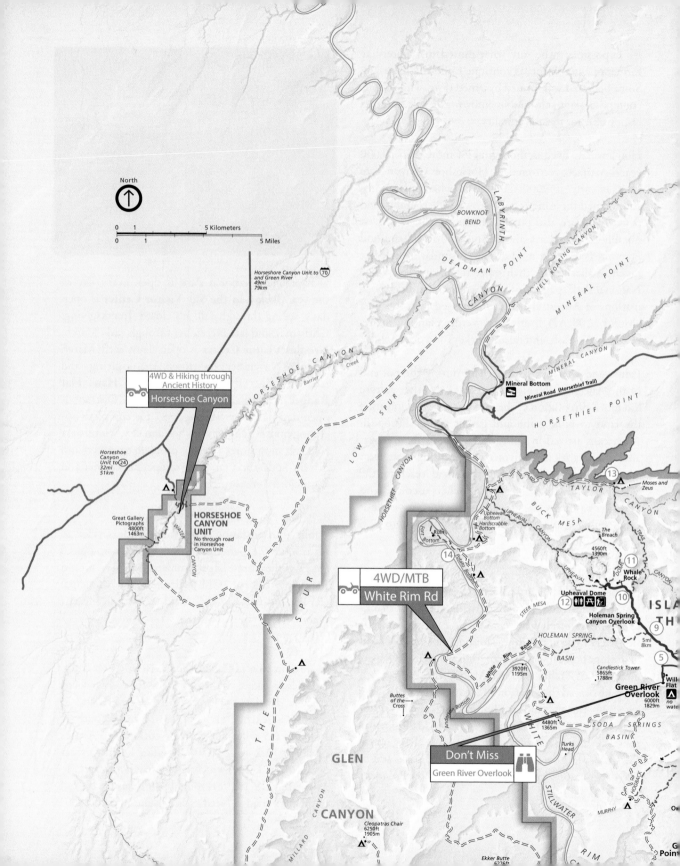

North

0 1   5 Kilometers

0 1   5 Miles

Horseshoe Canyon Unit to (70)
and Green River
49mi
79km

4WD & Hiking through Ancient History
Horseshoe Canyon

Horseshoe Canyon Unit to (24)
32mi
51km

Great Gallery
Pictographs
4800ft
1463m

HORSESHOE CANYON UNIT
No through road in Horseshoe Canyon Unit

WATER CANYON

HORSESHOE CANYON

Barrier Creek

LOW SPUR

HORSETHIEF CANYON

Mineral Bottom
Mineral Road (Horsethief Trail)

DEADMAN CANYON

BOWKNOT BEND

LABYRINTH

HELL ROARING CANYON

MINERAL POINT

MINERAL CANYON

HORSETHIEF POINT

(13)
Moses and Zeus

TAYLOR CANYON

BUCK MESA

Upheaval Bottom
Hardscrabble Bottom

Fort Bottom
Ruin

The Breach
4560ft
1390m

DOME CANYON

(14)

Potato Bottom

STEER MESA

UPHEAVAL CANYON

Whale Rock

(11)

4WD/MTB
White Rim Rd

Upheaval Dome
(12)

(10)

Holeman Spring Canyon Overlook

(9)

ISLAND THE

HOLEMAN SPRING BASIN

5mi
8km

(5)

THE SPUR

White Rim Road

3920ft
1195m

Candlestick Tower
5865ft
1788m

Green River Overlook
6000ft
1829m

Willow Flat
no water

Anderson Bottom

Buttes of the Cross

WHITE

4480ft
1365m

SODA SPRINGS BASIN

Don't Miss
Green River Overlook

GLEN

Turks Head

MURPHY

STILLWATER CANYON

HOGBACK

CANYON

CANYON

Cleopatras Chair
6250ft
1905m

MILLARD

RIM

Ekker Butte

G Point

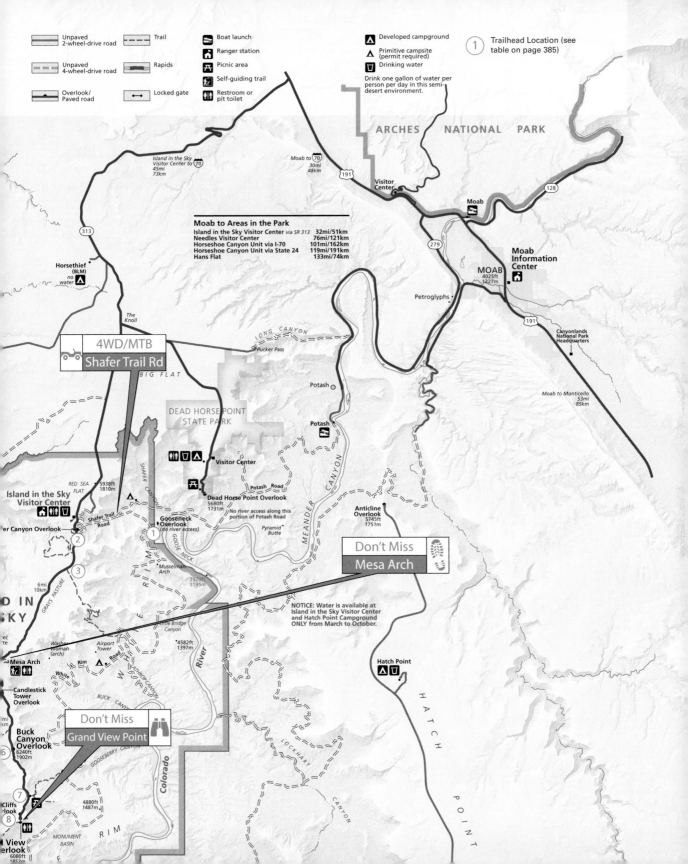

Legend

- Unpaved 2-wheel-drive road
- Unpaved 4-wheel-drive road
- Overlook/Paved road
- Trail
- Rapids
- Locked gate
- Boat launch
- Ranger station
- Picnic area
- Self-guiding trail
- Restroom or pit toilet
- Developed campground
- Primitive campsite (permit required)
- Drinking water

Drink one gallon of water per person per day in this semi-desert environment.

(1) Trailhead Location (see table on page 385)

ARCHES NATIONAL PARK

Island in the Sky Visitor Center to 70 45mi 73km

Moab to 70 30mi 48km

Visitor Center

Moab

Moab Information Center

MOAB 4025ft 1227m

Petroglyphs

Canyonlands National Park Headquarters

Moab to Monticello 53mi 85km

Moab to Areas in the Park
Island in the Sky Visitor Center *via SR 313* 32mi/51km
Needles Visitor Center 76mi/121km
Horseshoe Canyon Unit via I-70 101mi/162km
Horseshoe Canyon Unit via State 24 119mi/191km
Hans Flat 133mi/74km

Horsethief (BLM) no water

The Knoll

LONG CANYON

Pucker Pass

BIG FLAT

4WD/MTB
Shafer Trail Rd

DEAD HORSE POINT STATE PARK

Potash

Potash

Visitor Center

RED SEA FLAT

5938ft 1810m

Island in the Sky Visitor Center

Shafer Trail Road

er Canyon Overlook

Dead Horse Point Overlook 5680ft 1731m

Potash Road

No river access along this portion of Potash Road

Gooseneck Overlook (no river access)

Pyramid Butte

MEANDER CANYON

Anticline Overlook 5745ft 1751m

GOOSE NECK

Musselman Arch

3920ft 1195m

Don't Miss
Mesa Arch

NOTICE: Water is available at Island in the Sky Visitor Center and Hatch Point Campground ONLY from March to October.

GRAYS PASTURE

6mi 10km

Little Bridge Canyon

4582ft 1397m

Washer Woman (arch)

Airport Tower

Rim

White

BUCK CANYON

River

Colorado

LATHROP CANYON Road

Mesa Arch

Candlestick Tower Overlook

Hatch Point

Buck Canyon Overlook 6240ft 1902m

GOOSEBERRY CANYON

HATCH POINT

Don't Miss
Grand View Point

LOCKHART CANYON

4880ft 1487m

Cliffs look

View Overlook 6080ft 1853m

MONUMENT BASIN

RIM

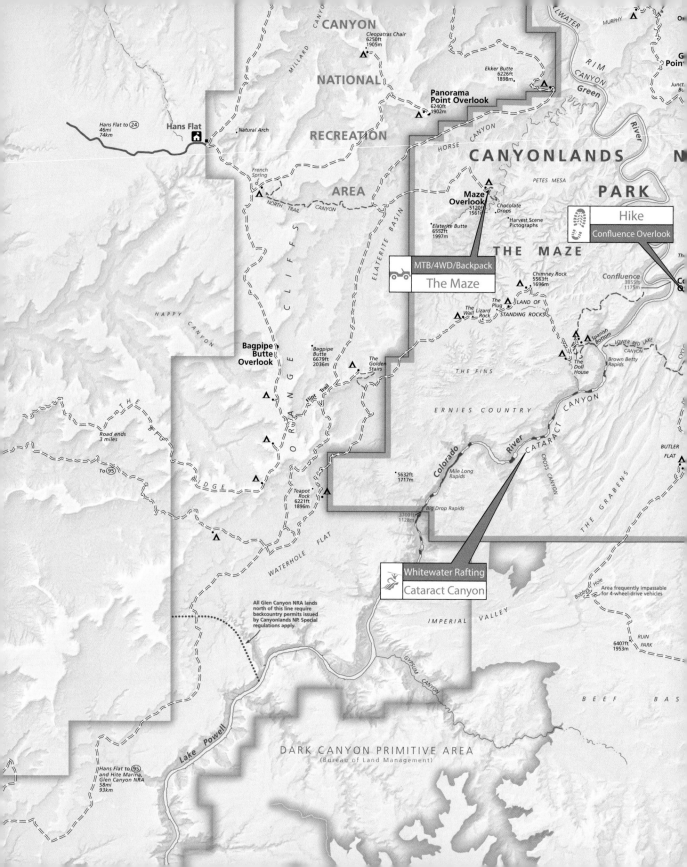

CANYON

NATIONAL

RECREATION

AREA

Cleopatras Chair
6250ft
1905m

Ekker Butte
6226ft
1898m

Green
River

Panorama
Point Overlook
6240ft
1902m

Hans Flat to (24)
46mi
74km

Hans Flat

Natural Arch

French
Spring

NORTH TRAIL CANYON

MILLARD CANYON

HORSE CANYON

PETES MESA

CANYONLANDS

PARK

Maze
Overlook
5120ft
1561m

Chocolate
Drops

Harvest Scene
Pictographs

THE MAZE

ELATERITE BASIN

Elaterite Butte
6552ft
1997m

Hike
Confluence Overlook

MTB/4WD/Backpack
The Maze

Chimney Rock
5563ft
1696m

Confluence
3855ft
1175m

The
Plug

LAND OF
STANDING ROCKS

The Wall
Lizard
Rock

HAPPY CANYON

Bagpipe
Butte
Overlook

Bagpipe
Butte
6679ft
2036m

The
Golden
Stairs

THE FINS

Spanish
Bottom

LOWER RED LAKE
CANYON

Brown Betty
Rapids

The Doll House

THE ORANGE CLIFFS

Flint Trail

ERNIES COUNTRY

CATARACT CANYON

CROSS CANYON

BUTLER
FLAT

Road ends
3 miles

Colorado

River

THE GRABENS

To (95)

THE ... RIDGE

5632ft
1717m

Mile Long
Rapids

Teapot
Rock
6221ft
1896m

3700ft
1128m

Big Drop Rapids

Whitewater Rafting
Cataract Canyon

WATERHOLE FLAT

IMPERIAL VALLEY

Bobby
Hole

Area frequently impassable
for 4-wheel-drive vehicles

RUIN
PARK

6407ft
1953m

BEEF BAS

All Glen Canyon NRA lands
north of this line require
backcountry permits issued
by Canyonlands NP. Special
regulations apply.

GYPSUM CANYON

DARK CANYON PRIMITIVE AREA
(Bureau of Land Management)

Lake Powell

Hans Flat to (95)
and Hite Marina,
Glen Canyon NRA
58mi
93km

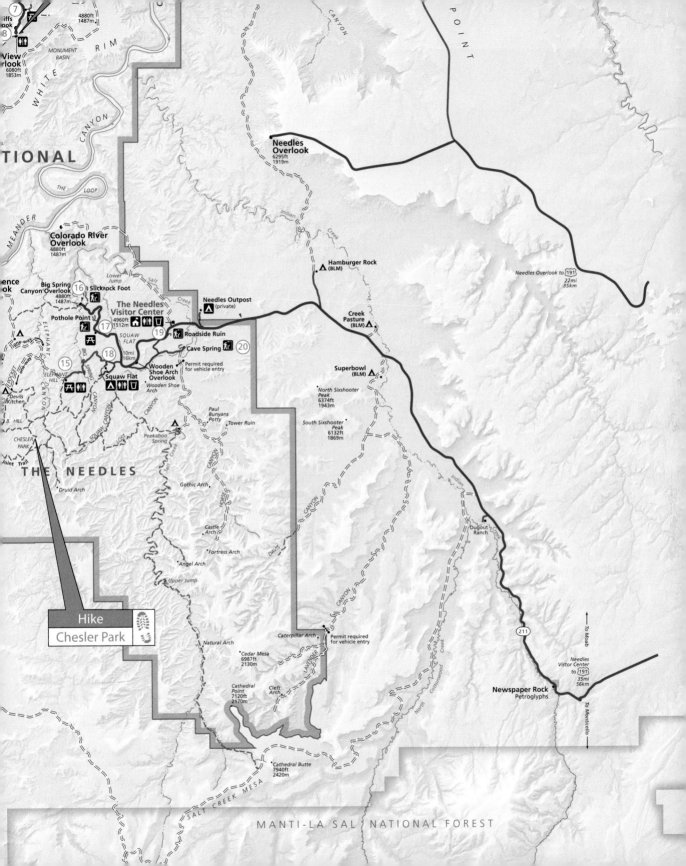

Whale Rock

Regions

Horseshoe Canyon: Located west of Island in the Sky, detached from the main park area, Horseshoe Canyon is accessed via a 4WD road from the Maze District. It preserves some of the oldest dwellings, pictographs, and murals found in America; some date back more than 3,000 years.

Island in the Sky: Located between the Green and Colorado Rivers, north of their confluence, it is accessed by UT-313, situated just south of Dead Horse Point State Park (also worth visiting). Along the access road you'll find overlooks and short nature trails, providing dramatic vistas of the surrounding terrain more than 1,000 feet below the island. It is the most visited park district, receiving nearly 60% of all visitors, and the only region frequented by rock climbers. White Rim Road is unpaved and a favorite destination for mountain bikers and motorists with a high-clearance 4WD vehicle. A visitor center and campground (Willow Flat) are available.

Needles: Located just east of the Colorado River, this region is named for its red and white sandstone spires that dominate the landscape. It's the second most popular region of the park, receiving about 35% of all visitors. You'll find exceptional hiking, a visitor center and campground (Squaw Flat) here.

The Maze: Located west of the Green and Colorado Rivers, it's the most remote and inaccessible region, and one of the most remote areas of the contiguous United States. Roughly 3% of park visitors venture into the Maze, which is accessed via an unpaved road suitable to 2WD vehicles. The road becomes more rugged at the park boundary where it can only be traversed by 4WD vehicles, mountain bikes, or foot. Hans Flat Ranger Station is located at the boundary.

Camping

Canyonlands has two established campgrounds: **Willow Flat** at Island in the Sky and **Squaw Flat** at Needles. Willow Flat has 12 sites available on a first-come, first-served basis. Water is not available and the maximum RV length is 28 feet. Fees are $15 per night. Squaw Flat has 26 sites available on a first-come, first-served basis. Water is available. Fees are $20 per night. Group sites are available at Needles for $70–225/night, depending on group size. Both campgrounds fill to capacity almost every day from late March through June and again from early September to mid-October. Nearby camping locations include Arches National Park (page 374) and Bureau of Land Management (BLM) campgrounds in and around Moab (page 455). **Backpackers** are allowed to camp in the park's backcountry with a **free permit**.

Hiking

Looking at Island in the Sky's labyrinth of eroded canyons from above may lead you to believe it is utterly impassable. Water found its way across this arid plateau as it carved these canyons, as did park employees, ranchers, prospectors, and ancient inhabitants who spent decades blazing paths across a seemingly impenetrable landscape. Many of their trails are still used today. The park's most popular trails are well maintained, marked by cairns, and have signposts at intersections. The trails are good, but no reliable water sources exist, so be sure to pack enough for the duration of your hike. One of the most popular trails at Island in the Sky is the easy 0.5-mile loop to **Mesa Arch**. Its views warrant the popularity. The arch frames distant canyons for unsurpassed photo opportunities (especially at sunrise). A great place to hike into a canyon is **Syncline Loop** (8.3 miles). This strenuous trail is short enough to complete in a day, but you can also turn it into an overnighter thanks to a few spur trails. Note that it's also the site of most park rescues, so come prepared with plenty of water, a map, and flashlight. Hike in a clockwise direction to maximize afternoon shade.

Needles District, located on the opposite side of the Colorado River, has equally exciting hiking opportunities. **Confluence Overlook Trail** is quite nice. This 10-mile (roundtrip) trek leads in and out of Big Spring

Canyonlands Hiking Trails (Distances are roundtrip)

Name	Location (# on map)	Length	Difficulty Rating & Notes
Gooseneck Overlook	NE corner on White Rim Rd (1)	0.6 mile	E – Views of the Colorado River
Neck Spring	Main Park Road (MPR) (2)	5.8 miles	M – Explores old ranch and springs (loop)
Lathrop	MPR • South of Neck Spring (3)	13.6 miles 21.6 miles	S – To White Rim Road S – To Colorado River (2,000 ft elevation)
Mesa Arch - 👣	MPR • North of Willow Flat (4)	0.5 mile	E – Popular self-guiding trail (loop)
Aztec Butte	MPR • North of Willow Flat (5)	2.0 miles	M – Ancestral Puebloan granaries
Murphy Point Overlook	MPR • Between Buck Canyon and Candlestick Tower Overlooks (6)	3.6 miles	E – Popular trail with continuous views
Murphy Loop	MPR • Between Buck Canyon and Candlestick Tower Overlooks (6)	10.8 miles	S – Steep trail descends from the mesa rim (1,400-ft elevation loss)
Gooseberry	MPR • White Rim Overlook (7)	5.4 miles	S – Shortest route to White Rim Road
White Rim Overlook	MPR • North of Grand View (8)	1.8 miles	E – One of the best views from the island
Grand View Point - 👣	South end of MPR (8)	2.0 miles	E – Amazing panoramic views
Wilhite	MPR • West of Willow Flat (9)	12.2 miles	S – Slot canyon leads to White Rim Road
Alcove Spring	MPR • Before Upheaval Dome (10)	11.2 miles	S – Provides views of Taylor Canyon
Whale Rock	MPR • Near Upheaval Dome (11)	1.0 mile	M – Handrails aid crossing steep slickrock
Upheaval Dome	MPR • Upheaval Dome (12)	1.8 miles	M – Popular hike to two overlooks
Syncline Loop - 👣	MPR • Upheaval Dome (12)	8.3 miles	S – Optional 3- and 7-mile spur trails, great for 1-night backpack (loop)
Moses and Zeus	Alcove Spring/White Rim Rd (13)	1.0 mile	E – Views of Taylor Canyon, climbing routes
Fort Bottom Ruin	NW Corner off White Rim Rd (14)	3.0 miles	M – An ancient tower ruin
Chesler Park View - 👣	Elephant Trailhead (15)	6.0 miles	S – Grassland lined with spires (popular)
Chesler Park Loop	Elephant Trailhead (15)	11.0 miles	S – Continues past viewpoint (semi-loop)
Druid Arch	Elephant Trailhead (15)	11.0 miles	S – Scrambling and a ladder, good hike
Slickrock	South of Big Canyon Spring (16)	2.4 miles	E – Self-guiding trail with 360-degree views
Confluence Overlook - 👣	Big Spring Canyon Trailhead (16)	10.0 miles	S – Not the most exciting trail in the park (flat and open), but cool conclusion
Pothole Point	Pothole Point (17)	0.6 mile	E – Views of Needles, follow cairns
Squaw Canyon	Squaw Flat Loop A (18)	7.5 miles	S – Connects with Big Spring Canyon (loop)
Elephant Canyon	Squaw Flat Loop A (18)	10.8 miles	S – Option for several spurs (semi-loop)
Lost Canyon - 👣	Squaw Flat Loop A (18)	8.7 miles	S – Scrambling and solitude (semi-loop)
Peekaboo	Squaw Flat Loop A (18)	10.0 miles	S – Arch, pictograph, and (2) ladders
Roadside Ruin	Just past visitor center (19)	0.3 mile	E – Old ancestral Puebloan granary
Cave Spring	Near Horse Canyon Road (20)	0.6 mile	E – Historic cowboy camp, (2) ladders

Island in the Sky (rows Gooseneck Overlook through Fort Bottom Ruin)

Needles (rows Chesler Park View through Cave Spring)

The Maze District: There are no designated trails and no reliable water sources. Come prepared.

Horseshoe Canyon District: There is a 7.5-mile roundtrip hiking trail through the canyon (ancient pictographs).

Difficulty Ratings: E = Easy, M = Moderate, S = Strenuous

Canyon, across Elephant Canyon, before joining a 4WD road. Much of the scenery looks similar and it is possible to lose your way, so look closely for cairns marking the trail. The 4WD road leads to a parking area with a vault toilet. From here you make the final push to the point where sheer canyon walls and the waters of the Green and Colorado Rivers that carved them converge. The hike to **Chesler Park** is another exceptional journey, and ambitious hikers can continue beyond Chesler Park Viewpoint along a sandy trail to **Druid Arch** or loop around the park via Joint Trail (a narrow rocky passage). The final ascent to Druid Arch is quite strenuous, and you're required to climb a ladder. The hike to Chesler Park is great and not that difficult, although you'll encounter all kinds of uneven terrain and you'll have to watch the trail carefully, spotting cairns as you go.

If you prefer things that are a little more extreme, you'll enjoy the **Maze district**, where the average visitor spends three days poking around the extensive network of canyons. A 25-foot length of rope is useful (if not essential) to raise and lower your pack, and a good topographical map is indispensable in the Maze, where side canyons can be difficult to identify and getting lost is easy (as the name implies).

Backcountry & Day-Use Permits

Several activities require a backcountry permit. **River permits** can be reserved up to four months in advance and no later than two days prior to your trip start date at canypermits.nps.gov. You can also submit your application in person at any visitor center or by mail (download the application from the park website). Flat water and Cataract Canyon permits cost $30 plus $20 per person. They are valid for groups up to 40 people.

Overnight backcountry permits are issued online at canypermits.nps.gov up to four months in advance and no later than two days prior to your trip start date from their respective district visitor centers. Reservations can also be made by mail (download the application from the park website). Reservations are recommended for White Rim Road trips, Needles Backpacking trips, and Needles Group Camping during peak season. All

backcountry permits require a $30 fee per permit. Each permit is good for 7 people at Island in the Sky and Needles Districts and 5 people at the Maze. 4WD and Mountain Bike Permits cost $30 and are good for up to 15 people and 3 vehicles at Island in the Sky, 10 people and 3 vehicles at Needles, and 9 people and 3 vehicles at the Maze. **Day-use permits** are required for all vehicles (including motorcycles and bicycles) on White Rim Road, Elephant Hill, Lavender Canyon, and Salt Creek/Horse Canyon roads. They can be obtained up to 24 hours before your trip at canypermits.nps.gov or in person at the road's respective visitor center. Day-use permits are free.

Backpacking

Overnight backpacking at Canyonlands is limited to camping zones and designated sites, like those found around many of the 4WD roads. **All overnight stays in the backcountry require a permit**. A limited number of permits are available and demand often exceeds supply during spring and fall, so plan your itinerary in advance and reserve one. The next hurdle is to assure you'll have plenty of water for the length of your trip, because most water sources are unreliable. Inquire about potential water sources when you arrive at the park. **The Maze** is enjoyed, almost exclusively, by backpackers. Trails at Island in the Sky and Needles can be taken more casually or combined to make a suitable backpacking route. **Chesler Park** is a popular backpacking area in Needles, but **Salt Creek Trail** (25+ miles) to **Angel Arch** and **Molar Rock** is another option. With careful planning, considering the ability of all members of your party, you're sure to have a rewarding experience in a magical place.

Biking

Located at the doorstep of Moab, the epicenter of mountain biking, it shouldn't come as a surprise that Canyonlands is a popular destination for pedalers. The 100-mile **White Rim Road** circling Island in the Sky is the primary biking destination. **The Maze** offers more secluded biking opportunities. All overnight bike trips require a permit. Several outfitters (page 457) provide **guided mountain bike tours** of Canyonlands.

Rafting & Paddling

In 1869, Major John Wesley Powell became the first to officially explore Canyonlands. He traveled from Green River, WY all the way through the Grand Canyon. Much like Powell, today's visitors are inspired by the scenery and invigorated by the water's power as they float the **Green River** or raft the 14-mile stretch of Class III–IV rapids of Cataract Canyon just beyond the confluence of the Green and Colorado Rivers. All public launches are located outside the park and private parties require a permit. Several **outfitters** (page 457) provide everything from day-trips to week-long whitewater adventures.

4WD Roads

A 4WD vehicle unlocks vast portions of Canyonlands that few visitors get to see. It allows you to go backpacking without putting in the work. Your gear (including plenty of water) is in your trunk, and the only things strained are the muscles of your brake foot—and maybe your nerves as you slowly make your way up and down narrow switchbacks that ascend and descend precipitous cliffs.

Island in the Sky's **White Rim Road** is a popular destination. Plan for this 100-mile journey to take two-to-three days in a 4WD vehicle, and three-to-four days on a mountain bike. **Shafer Rim Trail** near Island in the Sky's Entrance is a great (more like terrifying) 4WD alternative route to and from Moab. Routes like **Elephant Hill** (Needles) and the road to the **Land of Standing Rocks** (Maze) are extremely technical. A **backcountry permit** (fee) is required to camp at designated sites along the way, and several roads require a day-use permit (free).

Inquire about road conditions before attempting. Fill up with gas in Moab. There are no services in the park. Rental vehicles are often restricted to paved roads, so look closely at your agreement or ask about it before driving off the lot. Drive carefully; a tow can exceed $1,000.

Rock Climbing

Sandstone isn't the best for rock climbing, but climbers regularly come to Island in the Sky to test their skills against its towers and spires. If you're interested in climbing Canyonlands visit the park website for a list of regulations. A permit (fee) is only required if you intend on spending the night in the backcountry.

Horseback Riding

Horses and other saddle stock are permitted on all backcountry roads. A backcountry permit (fee) is required for all stock-use, and all feed and manure must be packed out. Finding reliable water sources is a significant problem for hikers, and it is even more critical for horseback riders. Discuss where you might find water with a park ranger before departing, especially for overnight trips.

Stargazing

Just because it's dark at night doesn't mean there's nothing to see. Canyonlands' distinction as one of the most remote regions in the contiguous United States has its perks, one being extremely dark skies. Don't forget to look up on a cloudless night. The stargazing is phenomenal.

Visitor Centers

Each district (except Horseshoe Canyon) has a visitor center or ranger station. **Island in the Sky Visitor Center** is open daily, 8am to 5pm from early March through late December. Hours are extended to 6pm during peak season from late April until fall. It's closed on Thanksgiving, Christmas, and from late December through early March. **Needles Visitor Center** is open daily, 8:30am to 4pm from early March through late November. Hours are extended to 8am to 5pm from early April until fall. It's closed on Thanksgiving, and from late November through early March. Both visitor centers feature exhibits, book and map sales, audio-visual programs, restrooms, and backcountry permits. **Hans Flat Ranger Station**, located at the Maze entry point, is open daily from 8am to 4:30pm.

Ranger Programs

Park rangers provide various interpretive programs from April to late October. Evening programs are frequently given at each of the campgrounds' amphitheaters. During the daytime, rangers give short talks on unique features or lead guests along a popular trail. Ranger programs are highly recommended. Attend one (or more) if you have the chance.

Shafer Trail

Mesa Arch

Green River Overlook

Best of Canyonlands

Attraction: Green River Overlook
    Runner-up: Mesa Arch
    2nd Runner-up: The Maze

Activity: Raft Cataract Canyon
    Runner-up: Bike/Drive White Rim Road
    2nd Runner-up: Drive Shafer Trail (4WD)

Hike (Island in the Sky): Grand View Point
    Runner-up: Mesa Arch
    2nd Runner-up: Syncline Loop

Hike (Needles): Chesler Park
    Runner-up: Lost Canyon
    2nd Runner-up: Confluence Overlook

For Kids

Kids are welcome to participate in Canyonlands' **Junior Ranger Program**. Free booklets are available online or at either visitor center. Complete five or more activities to receive an official junior ranger badge. Even if you don't participate in the Junior Ranger Program, children are sure to enjoy the contrasting views of canyons and cliffs that are easily accessible along park roads. And if you have a high-clearance 4WD vehicle and the spirit of adventure, your children are sure to love a little off-roading!

Flora & Fauna

The ecology of Canyonlands is similar to Arches National Park. See page 376 for a brief description of the area's plants and animals.

Pets

Pets are allowed in Canyonlands' developed campgrounds and along its roadways. They are not permitted on hiking trails or the backcountry (including unpaved roads). Pets must be kept on a leash no more than six feet in length at all times. If you'd like to bring yours on vacation and fully experience Canyonlands, you will want to board your pet at Karen's Canine Campground (435.259.7922) or Moab Vet Clinic (435.259.8710).

Accessibility

Needles and Island in the Sky Visitor Centers and restrooms are accessible to individuals in wheelchairs. Buck Canyon, Green River and Grand View Point Overlooks, and Willow Flat Campground are accessible at Island in the Sky. Squaw Flat Campground and Wooden Shoe Overlook are accessible at Needles.

Weather

Canyonlands nearly borders Arches National Park (page 377). Both parks are situated on the Colorado Plateau in southeast Utah's high desert. See page 377 for weather information.

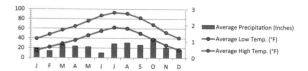

False Kiva

Vacation Planner

Visitors can spend a week **paddling** the Colorado River (page 387) or days exploring the Maze's canyons, but most drive into Island in the Sky and/or Needles. Provided below is a one-day itinerary for each. If you intend on **camping** (page 384) in spring or fall be sure to arrive early, as campgrounds often fill before noon. Nearby dining, grocery stores, lodging, festivals, and attractions are listed on pages 454–459. Visitors to the Maze, Horseshoe Canyon, or the park's backcountry should plan their trips well in advance with a high-quality topographic map. Restock supplies and top-off your gas tank before entering any district. You won't find gas stations or convenience stores within park boundaries.

Day 1: Island in the Sky: Begin your trip at the **visitor center** located near the entrance. Check out a current schedule of ranger programs and browse the exhibits. Time permitting, join a ranger program. Return to the park road, stopping next at **Mesa Arch**. Hike the 0.5-mile loop, which is a very popular destination among photographers (especially at sunrise). If you plan on camping, consider returning to Mesa Arch in the morning. Back on the main park road you'll come to a Y-intersection. Head south all the way to **Grand View Point Overlook** and hike the 2-mile trail located nearby. Return to the Y-intersection, but this time turn left to complete the last leg of the Y. Pull into Willow Flat Campground area and check out **Green River**

Overlook. Once you've finished soaking in the views drive to **Upheaval Dome**, located at the end of the road. Geology buffs will be especially interested in this oddity, but it's a spectacle everyone should enjoy. Another favorite photo-stop is **False Kiva**. It's accessed via an unmarked trail. The proper way to do this hike is to receive trail access information from a park ranger as it's a Class II archeological site and restrictions/access may change depending on use. It's a moderately strenuous hike, requiring a pretty steep up-and-down scramble to the alcove/kiva.

Day 1: Needles: Before entering Canyonlands, make a quick stop at **Newspaper Rock** to view some well-preserved petroglyphs. Return to your car, enter the park, and stop at the **visitor center** to browse its exhibits. **Roadside Ruins**, located near the visitor center, is a short trail to a small Ancestral Puebloan dwelling. If you're pressed for time, skip the ruins and follow the park road north stopping at **Pothole Point** and **Slickrock Foot Nature Trail**. Those looking to venture deeper into the backcountry should drive the narrow but manageable (for any 2WD car most of the time) Elephant Hill Access Road to Elephant Hill trailhead. From here, hike to **Chesler Park Viewpoint**, or, if your legs are fresh and you have the time, continue to loop around the park via **Joint Trail**. It's a great hike and not too difficult as long as you're in reasonably good shape and an above average cairn spotter/trail finder.

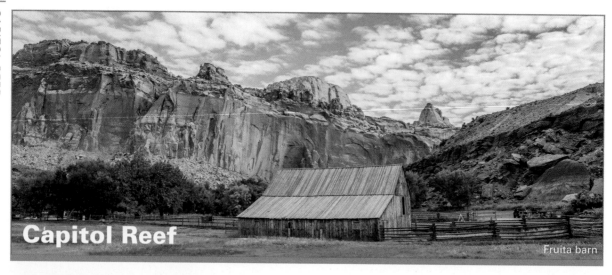
Fruita barn

Capitol Reef

HC 70 Box 15
Torrey, UT 84775
Phone: (435) 425-3791 ext. 111
Website: nps.gov/care

Established: December 18, 1971
August 2, 1937 (National Monument)
Size: 241,904 Acres
Annual Visitors: 940,000
Peak Season: Spring & Fall

Activities: Hiking, Backpacking,
Camping, Fruit Picking,
Backcountry Roads, Rock
Climbing, Biking, and Horseback
Riding

Campgrounds: Fruita Campground
Fee: $20/night
Primitive Campgrounds: Cedar
Mesa and Cathedral Valley (free)
Backcountry Camping: Permitted
with a free Backcountry Use Permit
Lodging: None

Park Hours: All day, every day

Entrance Fee: $10/vehicle,
$7/individual (foot, bike, etc.)

The name "Capitol Reef" hints that this region was once a growing, living underwater organism. However, the park's reef refers to sinuous canyons, colorful monoliths, obtrusive buttes, and giant white domes of Navajo sandstone that form the Waterpocket Fold, a 75-million-year-old warp in the earth's crust running the entire length of the park. These features make a nearly impassable rugged landscape, exactly what locals called a "reef." Today, the Waterpocket Fold defines Capitol Reef National Park, but scientists are still trying to understand its origin. No doubt the twisting of two layers of crust into S-shaped folds required exceptional force. As luck would have it, about the time the fold was created two continental plates were colliding with one another. A collision so forceful a great uplift occurred, raising the Rocky Mountains and potentially wrenching land nearly 400 miles away. From the ground you hardly notice the violence and scars at the earth's surface. From the air, it's dramatic. To view it from above without leaving the ground, stop at the visitor center where a scaled version of the park is on display.

Early inhabitants were oblivious to the area's unique geology. With only a few perennial sources of water to choose from, the Fremont People settled along the Fremont River's shores. They farmed and hunted for more than two centuries, only to abandon their granaries and dwellings in the 13th century. At the same time, Ancestral Puebloans were evacuating the region of present day Mesa Verde (page 356) and Canyonlands (page 378) National Parks. Scientists believe they all left because of significant change in climate, resulting in extended drought. Decades later, Paiute and Ute Indians entered the region, discovering abandoned Fremont granaries, they called moki huts (homes of a tiny people or moki).

It wasn't until the 19th century that an American crossed the Waterpocket Fold. Alan H. Thompson, a member of U.S. Army Major John Wesley Powell's expedition, completed this task in 1872. Mormons were next to settle in. Like the Fremont People before them, they lived in the Fremont River Valley, establishing settlements at Junction (later known as Fruita), Caineville, and Aldridge. Aldridge failed. Fruita prospered but was never home to more than 10 families. Caineville struggled to survive, but Mormon Bishop Ephraim Pectol operated a small convenience store that housed a private museum of Fremont artifacts.

Pectol noticed the area's finer qualities while scavenging through ruins seeking ancient relics to add to his personal museum. He and his brother-in-law, Wayne County High School Principal Joseph S. Hickman, began promoting the scenic beauty of what they called "Wayne Wonderland" in 1921. In 1933, Pectol was elected to the State Legislature, giving him a platform to pursue the park idea. Wasting no time, he contacted President Franklin D. Roosevelt, asking him to create Wayne Wonderland National Monument through executive order. For nearly a decade tourists trickled into the proposed park, largely thanks to lectures given by J.E. Broaddus, a Salt Lake City photographer hired by Pectol and Hickman. Images piqued federal interest, and soon survey parties arrived in south-central Utah. They didn't give it "wonderland" status, but on August 2, 1937, President Roosevelt created Capitol Reef National Monument and placed it under control of Zion National Park (page 410).

At the same time, Charles Kelley retired to the area and volunteered to serve as park custodian. In 1950, he was appointed the park's first superintendent. He became leery of the National Park Service's direction as they complied with demands made by the U.S. Atomic Energy Commission to open Capitol Reef to uranium mining, but little ore was excavated.

In 1962, construction of highway UT-24 was completed, drastically increasing tourism. Momentum was finally building to permanently protect the region as a national park; in 1971, President Richard Nixon signed a bill doing exactly that.

Capitol Dome

When to Go
Capitol Reef is most comfortable for hiking and other outdoor activities during spring and fall. Its only **visitor center** is open daily (except a few federal holidays) from 8am to 4:30pm, with hours extended to 6pm during the summer season (Memorial Day until Labor Day). **Ripple Rock Nature Center** is open during the summer season, with hours depending on available staff. **Gifford House Store and Museum** is open from 8am to 5pm, mid-March through October, with extended hours in summer. You can pick fruit from **Fruita Orchard** between June and October.

Transportation & Airports
Public transportation does not provide service to or around the park. The closest large commercial airport is Salt Lake City International (230 miles to the north).

Directions
The park area is extremely isolated and can only be accessed by one major road, UT-24, which conveniently intersects I-70 near Aurora (Exit 48). It then loops through the park intersecting with I-70 again just west of Green River, UT (Exit 149). To reach the park from I-15 traveling south from Salt Lake City, take Exit 188. Take US-50 S for 24 miles, and then turn right at UT-260/Main St. Continue for 4 miles before turning right at UT-24. Follow UT-24 south and east about 75 miles into the park.

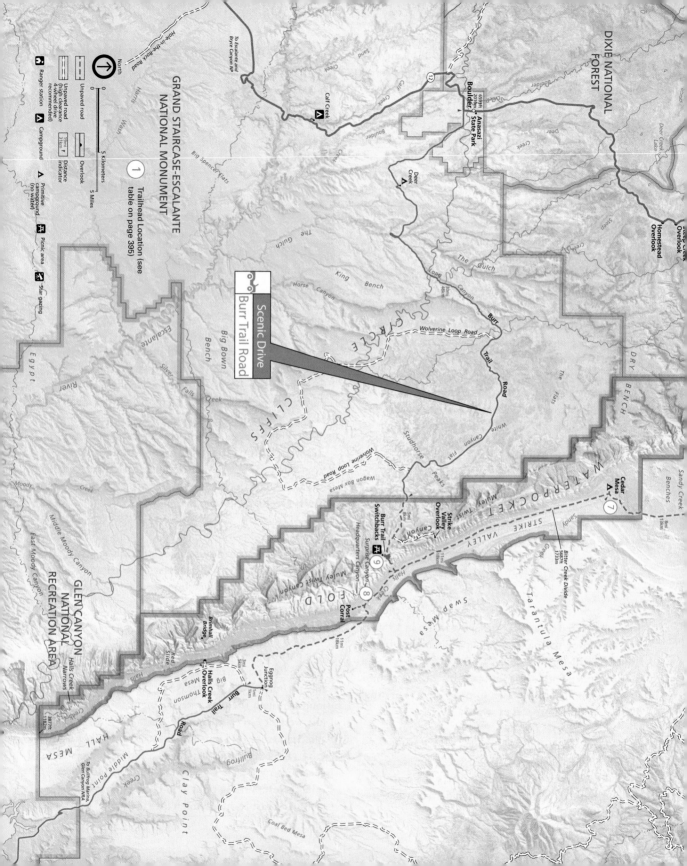

GRAND STAIRCASE-ESCALANTE
NATIONAL MONUMENT

Scenic Drive
Burr Trail Road

① Trailhead Location (see
table on page 395)

North

0   5 Kilometers
0   5 Miles

▤▤ Unpaved road
▤▤ Unpaved road (high clearance
     4-wheel drive recommended)

●——● Distance indicator 18mi 31km

▤ Overlook

🏠 Ranger station

▲ Campground

⊼ Picnic area

🏕 Primitive campground (no water)

✦ Star gazing

DIXIE NATIONAL FOREST

GLEN CANYON NATIONAL RECREATION AREA

WATERPOCKET FOLD

STRIKE VALLEY

CIRCLE CLIFFS

To Escalante and
Bryce Canyon NP

Hole-in-the-Rock Road

Harris Wash

Sand Creek

Calf Creek Creek

Big Spencer Flats

Escalante River

Egypt

Silver Falls Creek

Moody Creek

Middle Moody Canyon

East Moody Canyon

Halls Creek

HALL MESA

Middle Point Canyon

Big Thomson Mesa

Red Slide

Brimhall Bridge

Halls Creek Overlook

Burr Trail Road

Bullfrog

Clay Point

Coal Bed Mesa

To Bullfrog Marina,
Glen Canyon NRA

Eggnog Junction

Post Corral ⑧

Surprise Canyon ⑨

Burr Trail Switchbacks ⊼

Headquarters Canyon

Muley Twist Canyon

Wagon Box Mesa

Wolverine Loop Road

Strike Valley Overlook ▤

Muley Twist Canyon

Swap Mesa

Tarantula Mesa

Cedar Mesa ▲ ⑦

Bitter Creek Divide
5687ft 1733m

Sandy Creek

Sandy Creek Benches

8mi 13km

DRY BENCH

The Flats

White Canyon Flat

Studhorse Peaks

Burr Trail Road

Wolverine Loop Road

King Bench

Horse Canyon

Big Bown Bench

The Gulch

Long Canyon

Deer Creek ▲

Anasazi Boulder State Park

Boulder 6593ft 2010m

12

Deer Creek Lake

Homestead Overlook

Steep Creek Overlook

Boulder Creek

Deer Creek

5mi 8km

5mi 8km

11mi 18km

11mi 18km

1mi 1km

1mi 1km

3mi 5km

887ft 1182m

3877m

Driving

The 10-mile **Scenic Drive**, located south of the visitor center, is the park's most popular roadway. A free brochure is available at its entrance station where visitors must pay a $10 entrance fee per vehicle. Where Scenic Drive's pavement ends, **South Draw Road** begins. This high-clearance 4WD-only road follows the Waterpocket Fold before running alongside Pleasant Creek and exiting the park. **Capitol Gorge Road** also begins at the end of Scenic Drive. There's a large parking area near the mouth of the gorge where you can park and walk or bike, but the road is usually suitable for all motorists. Capitol Gorge Road ends at a more popular hiking trailhead.

A 4WD vehicle is not required for **Notom–Bullfrog and Burr Trail Roads**. Notom–Bullfrog Road traces the park's eastern boundary to Post Corral where there's an equestrian staging area. It exits the park and continues south to Glen Canyon National Recreation Area. Burr Trail Road provides an exhilarating experience thanks to switchbacks that climb some 800 feet in just a half-mile. It's also extremely bumpy within the park, but less so west of the park boundary. Washboard or not, the drive is pretty cool as it follows the waterpocket fold. In the north, **Cathedral Loop** offers the most scenic 4WD route, as it combines Hartnet and Caineville Wash Roads (high-clearance required, must cross the Fremont River).

Fruita

Fruita was originally a Mormon settlement established on the banks of the Fremont River. Compared to the rest of the surrounding desert, life at Fruita was good. Even so, no more than ten families occupied the settlement at any one time. Touring Historic Fruita District will lead you to an old barn, a restored schoolhouse, **Gifford Farmhouse** (open to the public during summer), a tool shed and blacksmith shop, and orchards containing almost 3,000 trees, including cherry, apple, apricot, peach, and pear. When fruit are in season you are welcome to pick and eat whatever you want free of charge while in the orchards. A small fee is charged for any fruit you take with you. Call (435) 425-3791 for information on blossom and harvest times. Fruita Campground is also set among stands of fruit-bearing trees.

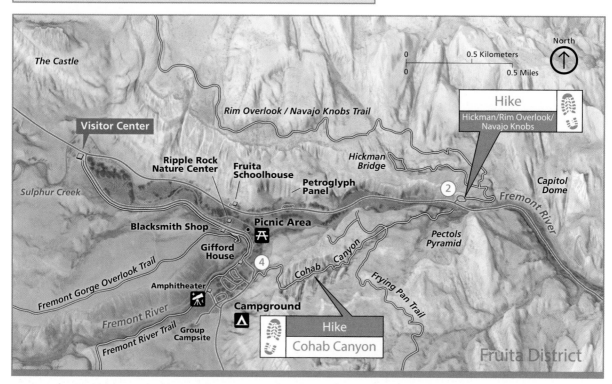

Camping

Capitol Reef's only developed campground is located at **Fruita**. All 71 sites are available on a first-come, first-served basis. Restrooms have flush toilets and sinks, but there are no showers. Hookups are not available for RVs, but a dump station is open during summer and a handful of sites can accommodate vehicles up to 52 feet in length. Rates are $20/night. The campground typically fills before afternoon from spring through fall.

Two no-fee primitive campgrounds are available. Cathedral Valley, located in the northwest corner, has six sites. Cedar Mesa, located on Notom–Bullfrog Road 35 miles south of UT-24, has five sites. Sites are available first-come, first-served all year. They have pit toilets, but no water. Always check road conditions before departing, because they are accessed via gravel roads.

Hiking

At Capitol Reef you'll find hikes similar in beauty and terrain to those at Zion National Park (page 416), but with much smaller crowds. The greatest concentration of trails is found along UT-24 and Scenic Drive. Three of the best can be combined to make a 5.8-mile loop; begin at **Cohab Canyon**, and connect to **Grand Wash via Frying Pan Trail**. This loop passes through a juniper-piñon forest and past a spur trail to **Cassidy Arch** as it traverses a narrow canyon back to UT-24. The downside of the loop is that it isn't exactly a loop. It's more like a 'C.' You exit Grand Wash 2.8 miles east of your starting point on UT-24. You'll have to plant a vehicle here, hitch a ride, hike along the road back to your car, or backtrack.

From Hickman Bridge Parking Area (UT-24), a small trail network leads to Hickman Bridge, Rim Overlook,

Capitol Reef Hiking Trails (Distances are roundtrip unless noted otherwise)

	Name	Location (# on map)	Length	Difficulty Rating & Notes
On UT-24	Goosenecks - ♿	Panorama Point (1)	0.2 mile	E – Outstanding views for a very short hike
	Sunset Point	Panorama Point (1)	0.8 mile	E – As the name implies, sunsets!
	Chimney Rock	UT-24 (1)	3.6 miles	M – Loop trail to mesa top
	Chimney Rock Canyon	UT-24 (1)	9.4 miles	S – Backpacking route (one-way)
	Hickman Bridge - ♿	Hickman Bridge Lot (2)	1.8 miles	M – Self-guiding trail to a natural bridge
	Rim Overlook - ♿	UT-24 (2)	4.6 miles	S – Great views of Fruita
	Navajo Knobs	UT-24 (2)	9.4 miles	S – Continues beyond Rim Overlook
	Grand Wash - ♿	UT-24 (3)	4.4 miles	E – Connects to Scenic Drive
	Cassidy Arch	UT-24 (3)	3.4 miles	S – Can also access from Grand Wash Road
	Frying Pan	UT-24 (3, 4)	5.8 miles	S – Connects Cohab Canyon with Grand Wash
Scenic Drive	Cohab Canyon - ♿	Fruita Campground (4)	3.4 miles	M – Pass through hidden canyon to overlooks
	Fremont River	Fruita Campground (4)	2.0 miles	M – Hike along river to a mesa top
	Fremont Gorge Overlook	Fruita Blacksmith Shop (4)	4.6 miles	S – 1,000-ft elevation gain to mesa top
	Old Wagon Trail	Scenic Drive (5)	3.8 miles	S – Loop west of Scenic Drive
	Capitol Gorge	Capitol Gorge Road (5)	2.0 miles	E – Short climb to waterpockets ("tanks")
	Golden Throne	Capitol Gorge Road (5)	4.0 miles	S – Short climb to viewpoint of throne
Other Areas	Burro Wash	Notom–Bullfrog Rd (6)	8.0 miles	M – Narrows
	Red Canyon	Cedar Mesa Camp (7)	3.5 miles	M – Leads into a large box canyon
	Surprise Canyon	Notom–Bullfrog Rd (8)	2.0 miles	M – Scrambling required but not difficult
	Lower Muley Twist Canyon	Burr Trail (9)	23.0 miles	S – Runs parallel to Waterpocket Fold
	Temple Rock	Off Hartnet Draw (10)	4.0 miles	M – Mostly unmarked with unreal views
	Lower Cathedral Valley - ♿	Off Hartnet Draw (11)	1.6 miles	M – Temple of the Sun and Temple of the Moon

Difficulty Ratings: E = Easy, M = Moderate, S = Strenuous

and Navajo Knobs. All three share the same trail at the start before diverging. The hike begins with a gradual climb. Shortly after you've reached the flat you'll come across the junction of Rim Overlook/Navajo Knobs and Hickman Bridge. **Hickman Bridge** is a very popular destination. It's a large natural sandstone arch or bridge that is worth a quick visit. If you're short on time and have to choose just one trail, continue on Rim Overlook/Navajo Knobs Trail. Spectacular panoramic views of Fruita and the surrounding desert region from **Rim Overlook** are strongly recommended and the favored destination (especially if you're coming from Arches National Park). From Rim Overlook the trail continues an additional 4.5 miles (roundtrip), running nearly parallel to UT-24 to **Navajo Knobs** where the views are even more incredible. At the trail's end you can see for miles, beyond Gooseneck Overlook through the Fremont River Valley and on to Miners Mountain. Completing an out-and-back of Cohab Canyon Trail (begins near Fruita Campground) to two scenic overlooks is another great choice for a somewhat strenuous trail with outstanding views of Fruita.

Some of the most memorable sites are located less than a mile from the main roadways. Short hikes like **Goosenecks, Sunset Point, and Petroglyphs Trails** are great if you're in a rush and just want to get out of the car and stretch your legs a bit. Exploring **Historic Fruita District** by foot is another excellent idea, especially when fruit is in season and you can treat yourself to a snack while walking through the orchard. Whether you're hiking in the busy Fruita area or the backcountry, all hikers should use caution and remember to carry plenty of water. Narrow canyons can flood quickly and should be evacuated at the first sign of thunderstorm. Additional hiking trails are listed in the table on the previous page.

Backpacking
Visitors can camp in the backcountry with a **free permit** (available at the visitor center). There are nice backpacking opportunities throughout the park's 100-mile length, but **Upper and Lower Muley Twist Canyon Trails** are two of the best destinations. They are located in the southern region near Burr Trail Switchbacks.

Biking
Biking is allowed, but only on designated roads. The 10-mile stretch of **Scenic Drive** south of the visitor center is the most popular section of roadway. It's narrow, without shoulders, and crowded with motorists between April and October. If you plan on pedaling Scenic Drive you must be alert at all times and proceed with caution. **Mountain bikers** can take on more strenuous routes like Cathedral Valley Loop, South Draw Road, or Burr Trail Road/Notom–Bullfrog Road.

Rock Climbing
Rock Climbing is gaining popularity. Permits are not required, but first-timers should join someone familiar with the area or purchase a dedicated climbing guidebook (available at the visitor center), because much of the rock is brittle sandstone.

Horseback Riding
Stock (horse, mule, and burro) are allowed in the park. However, no outfitters provide guided trail rides and you must trailer your own stock in. Recommended rides include South Draw, Old Wagon Trail, Halls Creek, and the South Desert.

Ranger Programs
Park personnel offer interpretive walks, talks, and evening programs from May through September. Program schedules are usually available online or at the visitor center. These programs provide insight to interesting aspects of the area that you can't experience by driving and hiking alone. Join a ranger program if possible.

For Kids
Children of all ages are invited to participate in Capitol Reef's **Junior Ranger Program**. Free activity booklets are available at the visitor center and nature center. Complete at least seven activities and your child will be rewarded with an official Junior Ranger Badge. Families are also welcome to check out a **Family Fun Pack** from the visitor center or nature center. These backpacks are filled with materials that aid in exploration of the park. Capitol Reef also offers a **Junior Geologist Program** for rock-lovers in your family or stop in at Ripple Creek Nature Center, where children can spin wool or pretend to milk a cow.

Flora & Fauna

Only a few perennial streams and rivers course through the arid region of Capitol Reef, but you can still find large mammals here. Mountain lions roam the mesa tops and have even been spotted in Fruita. Their main source of food is mule deer, which are quite common in Fruita's orchards. Bighorn sheep once flourished in this rocky terrain, but native sheep were hunted to extinction around the middle of the 1900s. Several reintroduction programs have infused a healthy population of desert bighorn sheep that are now seen on mesa tops and cliffsides. Most animals are small rodents, bats, and birds (200+ species). Plants have adapted to endure the harsh conditions, resulting in rare species, many of which are only found in this part of Utah. Barneby reed-mustard, Maguire's daisy, and Wright's fishhook cactus are a few rare and protected species.

Pets

Pets are allowed in developed areas like Fruita Campground, parking areas, picnic areas, and along roadways, as long as they are kept on a leash no more than six feet in length. Pets (except service animals) are not allowed in public buildings, in the backcountry, or on trails.

Accessibility

Capitol Reef protects a rugged landscape. The visitor center and Petroglyphs Trail (located just off UT-24) are the only fully-accessible destinations for individuals in wheelchairs. Five accessible campsites are available at Fruita Campground.

Weather

Capitol Reef spans an arid desert region. Summer days are hot, but evenings are comfortable. Winter lows fall below freezing, but average highs are around 40°F in January (the coldest month). Spring and fall bring average highs in the mid-60s to mid-70s°F. These seasons tend to be the most comfortable times of year. The region is typically dry, receiving an average of about 7 inches of precipitation each year.

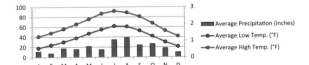

Scenic Drive

Vacation Planner

Capitol Reef often spells sweet relief to visitors of Utah's National Parks. Smaller crowds and similar red rock cliffs, narrow canyons, and natural arches make it one of the National Park System's best kept secrets.

Camping (page 395) is available in the park but dining and lodging are not. Nearby dining, grocery stores, lodging, festivals, and attractions are listed on pages 454–459. There are only 30 miles of paved roads, so a one-day trip is conceivable. The itinerary provided below outlines an ideal day in the park, but consider spending a few more on a **backpacking trip** (page 396) or driving more remote roads like **Burr Trail** (awesome but heavily wash-boarded) or **Cathedral Loop** (high-clearance 4WD/river crossing required).

Day 1: Whether entering the park from the east or west on UT-24, you'll be tempted to pull over and admire the stunning red rock formations. Fight the temptation and continue to the **visitor center** in Fruita. Check the schedule of ranger programs, making mental notes of the time and location for any programs of interest. While you're here have a look around **Fruita**. You'll find a little something for everyone. **Gifford Farmhouse** is particularly interesting. Don't forget to help yourself to fruit if it's picking season. Once you're finished at Fruita, head south on Scenic Drive, maybe even drive into **Capitol Gorge** (2.4 miles via Capitol Gorge Road) to hike to **Golden Throne Viewpoint** (strenuous) or take an easy stroll along the gorge's floor. Our favorite hikes end at overlooks of Fruita. Choose between **Cohab Canyon** (begins near Fruita Campground) or **Rim Overlook** (begins on UT-24). Regardless whether you do one of these more strenuous trails, drive east on UT-24, stopping at the **old schoolhouse** and **Petroglyphs Trail**. **Grand Wash** is another flat, easy hike you'll find along the way. Before the sun sets stop at **Goosenecks Overlook**, just west of Fruita on UT-24, to hike **Sunset Point Trail**.

Inspiration Point

Bryce Canyon

PO Box 640201
Bryce, UT 84764
Phone: (435) 834-5322
Website: nps.gov/brca

Established: February 25, 1928
June 8, 1923 (National Monument)
Size: 35,835 Acres
Annual Visitors: 1.7 Million
Peak Season: Summer
Hiking Trails: 50 Miles

Activities: Hiking, Backpacking,
Camping, Horseback Riding,
Stargazing, and Photography

Campgrounds: North and Sunset*
Fee: $20/night (tent), $30 (RV)
Backcountry Camping:
Permitted with a Backcountry Use
Permit ($5/person)
Lodging: Bryce Canyon Lodge
Rates: ($230–299/night)
Park Hours: All day, every day
Entrance Fee: $30/vehicle,
$15/individual (foot, bike, etc.)

*Reserve at recreation.gov or (877)
444-6777, May through September

In 1918, Stephen Mather, first director and sentimental father of the National Park Service, was guided to a seldom visited attraction in southwestern Utah. His tour guides required he close his eyes before arrival. Mather had just toured Zion National Park (page 410), but Zion's colorful canyons and expanses of unspoiled wildness could not prepare him for what he was about to see. He opened his eyes at Bryce Amphitheater, where a battalion of colorful rocky spires called hoodoos were waiting to greet him. Imagine having never seen a photograph of the eerie formations lining the eastern rim of Paunsaugunt Plateau. You arrive here, open your eyes, and in front of you is an indescribable masterpiece of nature. Even today, a time when everyone has seen everything on their computer or phone, this scene has the power to stop visitors dead in their tracks. These views are so divine and empowering they are inspirational to even the most casual sightseers. This is not just a place of inspiration. It's a place capable of stirring up religious sentiments. A place that invokes deep heartfelt patriotism. A place unlike all others.

To Ebenezer Bryce, it was simply "a hell of a place to lose a cow." In 1875, the Church of Jesus Christ of Latter-day Saints sent Bryce to settle the Paria Valley. He and his family chose to live right below what is known today as Bryce Amphitheater. Bryce built a home for his family, a canal for his crops and his cows, and a road to collect wood used to heat his home during the cool evenings and frigid winters. It became clear that Bryce and his family were sticking around, and soon locals began to call the area "Bryce Canyon." Not a true canyon, it's actually a horseshoe-shaped bowl or amphitheater formed by several creeks and streams rather than a single river and its tributaries. Life in and around Bryce Canyon was difficult. Herds of sheep and cattle quickly overgrazed the area's limited vegetation and the region was ravaged by cycles of drought and flooding. Settlers attempted to build a water diversion channel from the Sevier River to protect their crops, cattle, and homes from seasonal floods. The effort failed, and shortly after most settlers, including the Bryce family, left the area.

Capitulation in the face of nature has been a recurring theme in the history of southwest Utah. More than 8,000 years ago humans first visited the region, only to find it exceedingly difficult to survive for an extended period of time. Later, the Fremont Culture, hunter-gatherers who supplemented their diet with modest amounts of cultivated crops like corn and squash, lived in the area. By the mid-12th century, they also abandoned the region. Paiute Indians moved in, living much like the Fremont Culture, hunting and gathering. Paiute legends grew around the origin of the peculiar rock formations, or hoodoos. They called them "anka-ku-was-a-wits" or "red painted faces," and believed they were the Legend People turned to stone at the hands of the Coyote God.

Hoodoos may resemble beautifully colored humans sculpted from stone, but they are simply the result of thousands of years of continuous erosion. Minarets of soft sedimentary rock were left behind because they are topped by a piece of harder, less easily eroded stone. This caprock protects the column of sedimentary rock below from the erosive forces of wind, water, and ice. Several locations around the world display similar rocky spires, including nearby Cedar Breaks National Monument (page 457), but Bryce is different. It's more colorful, more abundant, and more mystical.

Bryce Canyon is a special place. A place woven into the legends of early inhabitants. A place where Ebenezer Bryce's cows got lost. A place that screamed "surprise" to Stephen Mather when he opened his eyes. A place that was almost completely inaccessible until the Union Pacific Railroad laid down track in the 1920s and the CCC built roads in the 1930s. Today, Bryce Canyon is a place accommodating to visitors, a place that will open your eyes to the natural beauty of the world around you. So close your eyes and open them once more at the rim of Bryce Canyon.

Navajo Loop switchbacks

When to Go
Bryce Canyon is open all year, 24 hours per day. Its visitor center is open every day except Thanksgiving, Christmas, and New Year's Days (see page 400 for operating hours). The park tries to keep one loop of North Campground open all year, but occasionally all sites close due to deep snow and freezing temperatures. Bryce Canyon Lodge, General Store, and Restaurant are open from April through October. Wildflowers bloom between April and August, peaking in June. The park is busiest from late spring to early fall when the weather is most pleasant. Bryce Canyon does not receive as many visitors as nearby Zion (page 410) or Grand Canyon (page 422), but it is the smallest of Utah's parks and can become congested, particularly in summer. To help reduce motorist traffic, the park provides free shuttle service from mid-April until late October.

Transportation & Airports
Public transportation does not service the park, but a free shuttle ferries visitors around Bryce Canyon Amphitheater (summer only). They also run a Rainbow Point Tour Shuttle (reservations required) that covers the entire park road from Ruby's Inn (outside the park) to Rainbow Point. The closest large commercial airports are Salt Lake City International (SLC), 274 miles to the north, and McCarran International (LAS) in Las Vegas, NV, 260 miles to the southwest. Car rental is available at each destination.

Directions

Bryce Canyon is located in southwestern Utah, about 75 miles northeast of Zion National Park (page 410).

From Zion National Park (86 miles): Heading east on UT-9 you will come to a T-intersection with US-89, turn left onto US-89 and continue north for 43 miles. Turn right at UT-12 East. Continue for 13 miles before turning right onto UT-63 S, which leads into the park. The visitor center is one mile beyond the park's boundary.

From Salt Lake City (270 miles): Heading south on I-15, take Exit 95 for UT-20 toward US-89. Turn left at UT-20 E and continue for 20 miles. Turn right at US-89 S. Drive 7 miles then turn left at UT-12 E. After 13 miles, turn right at UT-63 S, which leads into the park.

Visitor Center

The **visitor center** is located on UT-63 (the park's Scenic Road), 4.5 miles south of UT-12. It's open every day except Thanksgiving, Christmas, and New Year's Days. Hours are 8am to 6pm, but from May through

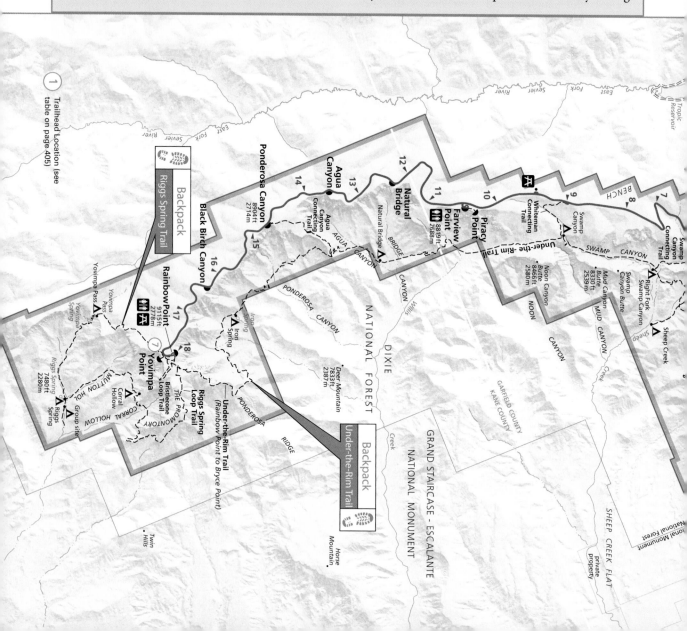

September hours are extended to 8pm, and from November through March hours are reduced to 4:30pm. At the visitor center you'll find exhibits, an information desk, bookstore, a short film, restrooms, and you can obtain backcountry permits. Bryce Canyon Shuttle stops at the visitor center.

Driving

The park's **Scenic Drive** is an 18-mile one-way paved road providing access to viewpoints and trailheads. All 14 viewpoints are on the east side of the road, so it is suggested that motorists proceed to **Rainbow Point** (the end) and stop at viewpoints as you head north on your return trip. Each viewpoint is unique, but overlooks found around **Bryce Amphitheater** present the most memorable panoramas. Expect it to take at least three hours to tour the main park road. If you don't drive the entire road, at least spend an hour or two enjoying the views between Bryce Point and Sunrise Point. During peak season you can drive to all the park's viewpoints, but consider leaving your car behind and taking the **shuttle** (page 404).

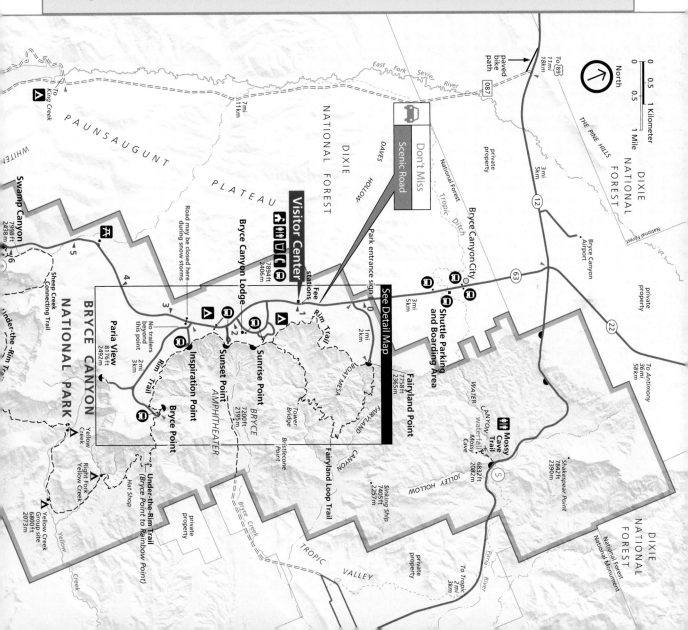

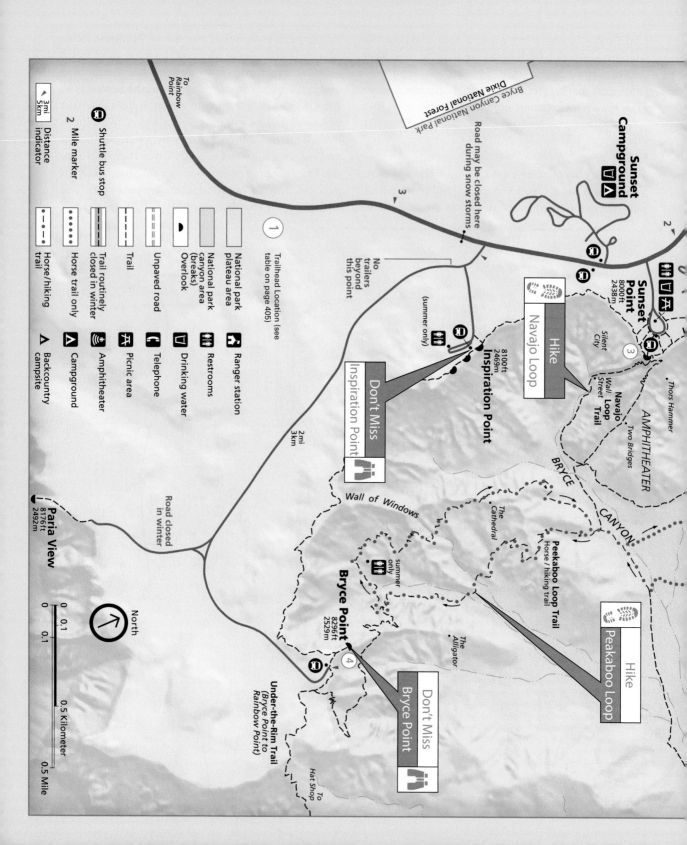

Bryce Canyon National Park

Dixie National Forest

Sunset Campground

To Rainbow Point

Road may be closed here during snow storms

No trailers beyond this point

Trailhead Location (see table on page 405)

National park plateau area

National park canyon area (breaks)

Overlook

Unpaved road

Trail

Trail routinely closed in winter

Horse trail only

Horse/hiking trail

Ranger station

Restrooms

Drinking water

Telephone

Picnic area

Amphitheater

Campground

Backcountry campsite

Shuttle bus stop

2 Mile marker

Distance indicator

3mi
5km

(summer only)

Sunset Point
8000ft
2438m

Hike
Navajo Loop

Silent City

Thors Hammer

Two Bridges

AMPHITHEATER

Wall Loop Street Trail

Navajo Loop

Inspiration Point
8100ft
2465m

Don't Miss
Inspiration Point

2mi
3km

Wall of Windows

The Cathedral

BRYCE

CANYON

Peekaboo Loop Trail
Horse / hiking trail

Hike
Peekaboo Loop

The Alligator

Road closed in winter

summer only

Bryce Point
8296ft
2529m

Don't Miss
Bryce Point

Paria View
8176ft
2492m

North

0   0.1   0.5 Kilometer
0   0.1   0.5 Mile

Under-the-Rim Trail
(Bryce Point to Rainbow Point)

To Hat Shop

Visitor Center

Overflow
Parking

Fee stations

**North
Campground**

RV dump station
(summer only)

**Bryce Canyon
Lodge**
Restaurant

Horse
Corral

High Plateaus
Institute

General store
Showers
Laundry
Food

**Sunrise
Point**
8017ft
2444m

Queens
Garden
Trail

Queen
Victoria

Horse Trail
(horses only)

BRYCE

Bryce Creek

To
Tropic

Rim

Trail

Fairyland

Loop

Trail

Chinese
Wall

CAMPBELL

Tower
Bridge

CANYON

BOAT
MESA

FAIRYLAND

Fairyland

Loop

Trail

FAIRYLAND CANYON

Fairyland Point
7758ft
2365m

Road closed
in winter

0

1mi
2km

Park
entrance
sign

63

2

1

Hiking Queen's Garden

Thor's Hammer
(near Sunset)

Park Shuttle

To conserve fuel and reduce traffic and pollution, the park furnishes a free shuttle between Ruby's Inn (outside the park) and Bryce Point from mid-April to late October. Buses depart every 10–20 minutes between 8am and 8pm (the last run varies depending on the time of year) at all of the most popular destinations around **Bryce Amphitheater**. If you aren't staying at Bryce Canyon Lodge or the park's campgrounds, it's highly recommended that you leave your vehicle outside the park and use the free shuttle. Park at the shuttle staging area located near Ruby's Inn.

The **Rainbow Point Tour** runs from Ruby's Inn to Rainbow Point, from May to September, twice daily (at 9am and 1:30pm). It covers 40 miles, lasting about 3.5 hours, as it makes eight stops at scenic viewpoints along the main park road. (Note that it does not stop at the park's most popular destinations around Bryce Amphitheater.) The tour service is free, but reservations are required (available up to 24 hours in advance). Reserve your spot by calling (435) 834-5290 or stopping in at the shuttle offices at Ruby's Inn, Ruby's Campground, or the Shuttle Parking Area. Dress for the weather and pack a lunch, snacks, and anything else you require.

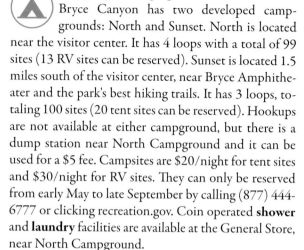

Camping & Lodging

Bryce Canyon has two developed campgrounds: North and Sunset. North is located near the visitor center. It has 4 loops with a total of 99 sites (13 RV sites can be reserved). Sunset is located 1.5 miles south of the visitor center, near Bryce Amphitheater and the park's best hiking trails. It has 3 loops, totaling 100 sites (20 tent sites can be reserved). Hookups are not available at either campground, but there is a dump station near North Campground and it can be used for a $5 fee. Campsites are $20/night for tent sites and $30/night for RV sites. They can only be reserved from early May to late September by calling (877) 444-6777 or clicking recreation.gov. Coin operated **shower** and **laundry** facilities are available at the General Store, near North Campground.

Bryce Canyon Lodge is located in between the two campgrounds. It's typically open from April to October, but a recent pilot program kept a few dozen motel-style rooms open for winter. Rooms cost anywhere from $230–299/night. There is a restaurant on-site. For reservations call (877) 386-4383 or click bryce-canyonforever.com. Please see page 455 for additional lodging facilities.

Hiking

At Bryce Canyon you don't have to stare at the balanced rocks, fluted walls, and colorful hoodoos from roadside overlooks; you are free to walk among them. A variety of trails lead into and around Bryce Amphitheater. Each trail has its merits, but a few are superior. These are some of the most outstanding trails in the entire National Park System.

Navajo Loop is tremendous, packing a whole lot of scenic bang for just 1.3 miles of hiking. The balanced rock called **Thor's Hammer** (near Sunset) and narrow passages of **Wall Street** are two of the trail's many highlights. (Note that the Wall Street portion of this loop closes in winter.) Extend the experience by combining it with one of the trails that merge at the canyon floor. Add **Queens Garden Trail** to Navajo Loop and make a 2.9-mile hike through this eroded paradise. If you don't mind hiking with horses, combine **Navajo and Peekaboo Loops**. This route leads beyond the destinations of typical Bryce Canyon day-hikers, but it merges with a path heavily trod by horses and their riders. It's dusty, steep at times, and somewhat difficult, but worth the effort and having to mingle with equines.

If you don't want to venture into the amphitheater, enjoy it from above by hiking the 5.5-mile (one-way) **Rim Trail**. It connects all of Bryce Amphitheater's viewpoints, and the free summer shuttle makes stops along the way. Soon you'll realize the views are just as beautiful from the trail as they are from the overlooks and you may decide to continue hiking along the rim.

The most popular hike beyond Bryce Amphitheater is **Fairyland Loop Trail**. It circles around two neighboring amphitheaters, connected by Rim Trail. Fairyland hikers are rewarded with a different sort of landscape as it passes through gently sloped badlands with denser tree cover. **Under-the-Rim Trail**, for its part, is not reserved for backpackers. It can be accessed

via connecting trails at Sheep Creek/Swamp Canyon, Whiteman, and Agua Canyon. The latter is the most scenic, but it's rarely used due to a very steep descent. The easiest connecting trail is Whiteman. At 2 miles, Sheep Creek is the longest connection to Under-the-Rim Trail. Swamp Canyon and Whiteman are just under 1 mile, and Agua Canyon is slightly less than 2 miles to the trail junction. Refer to the table below for a complete list of Bryce Canyon's hiking trails.

Backpacking

There are two backcountry trails with designated campsites for backpackers. The 22.9-mile (one-way) **Under-the-Rim Trail** runs parallel to Scenic Drive from Bryce Point to Rainbow Point. (It also intersects two popular Bryce Amphitheater hiking trails: Rim and Peekaboo Trails.) Begin at Bryce Point, checking out the Bryce Amphitheater viewpoint first if you haven't already, and head away from the amphitheater on Under-the-Rim Trail. Follow it south and

Bryce Canyon Hiking Trails (Distances are roundtrip unless noted otherwise)

	Name	Location (# on map)	Length	Difficulty Rating & Notes
Bryce Amphitheater	Rim	Fairyland to Bryce Point (1, 4)	5.5 miles	E – Connects amphitheater viewpoints (one-way)
	Tower Bridge	Sunrise Point (2)	3.0 miles	M – Follows Fairyland, spur trail to the bridge
	Queens Garden - 🐎	Sunrise Point (2)	2.0 miles	E – Easiest route into the canyon
	Navajo Loop - 🐎	Sunset Point (3)	1.3 miles	M – Wall Street section closed in winter
	Sunset to Sunrise	Sunset/Sunrise Points (2, 3)	1.0 mile	E – Paved portion of Rim Trail
	The 'Figure-8'	Sunset/Sunrise Points (2, 3)	6.4 miles	S – Queens Garden, Navajo, and Peekaboo
	Queens/Navajo Loop - 🐎	Sunset/Sunrise Points (2, 3)	2.9 miles	M – Extra 0.5-mile to connect Sunrise/Sunset • Check out Wall Street while you're down there!
	Navajo/Peekaboo Loop	Sunset Point (3)	4.9 miles	S – Make a smaller figure-8 than the entire Peekaboo Loop by starting/ending at Sunset Pt
	Bryce Amphitheater Traverse	Sunrise/Bryce Points (2, 4)	4.7 miles	S – Combine Peekaboo and Queens Garden and shuttle between viewpoints
	Peekaboo Loop - 🐎	Bryce Point (4)	5.5 miles	S – Southern amphitheater • Horse Trail
Other Areas	Fairyland Loop - 🐎	Fairyland/Sunset Points (1, 2)	8.0 miles	S – Reduce to 5.75 miles by using the shuttle
	Hat Shop	Bryce Point (4)	4.0 miles	S – First two miles of Under-the-Rim
	Under-the-Rim	Bryce to Rainbow Point (4, 6)	22.9 miles	S – Longest backpacking route (one-way)
	Mossy Cave - 🐎	Highway 12 (5)	0.8 mile	E – Short and easy walk to a small waterfall
	Sheep Creek/Swamp Canyon	Swamp Canyon (6)	4.0 miles	M – Not the easiest trail to follow, but it's away from the amphitheater crowds
	Bristlecone Loop	Rainbow Point (7)	1.0 mile	E – Stroll through ancient forest
	Riggs Spring Loop	Rainbow Point (7)	8.8 miles	S – 4 campsites along short backpacking route

Difficulty Ratings: E = Easy, M = Moderate, S = Strenuous

Sunrise Point

east to the first campsite, located just past Hat Shop. In all there are 8 backcountry campsites along Under-the-Rim Trail. Elevation ranges from 6,800 feet to 9,105 feet at Rainbow Point (highest elevation in park). The entire route can be completed easily enough in two days. **The Rainbow Point Tour Shuttle** (page 404) is ideal for Under-the-Rim backpackers, otherwise you'll have to stash a car at Rainbow Point or double your hiking distance by doing an out-and-back. If you plan on using the shuttle, know its pickup times and locations!

Riggs Spring Loop is the other backpacking route. It's an 8.8-mile circuit that begins and ends at Rainbow Point. Hikers pass through old forests before descending into the canyons east of Pink Cliffs. You return back to the plateau via Yovimpa Pass. There are four campsites along the trail. Camping is only allowed at these designated sites. Reliable water sources are available at all campsites except Swamp Canyon and Natural Bridge.

A **backcountry permit** is required for all overnight stays. They can be purchased at the visitor center during normal operating hours as long as you arrive at least one hour before closing. Permits are not available for reservation by mail or phone. However, they can be reserved up to 48 hours in advance, in person, at the visitor center. Permits cost $5/person (ages 16+). Open fires are not permitted in the backcountry. If you need to boil water bring a stove.

Horseback Riding

One of the easiest and most enjoyable ways to enter the amphitheater is to hop in the saddle and giddy-up into the canyon. Visitors are allowed to bring their own stock (horse or mule), but riders must depart at specific times and follow a predesignated route to avoid intermingling with concessioner-led trail rides. All private riders must be scheduled with the park at least 72 hours in advance, allowing a park ranger to meet your party for orientation and check-in. Overnight stock trips are not permitted. For everyone who didn't pack their horse, **Canyon Trail Rides** (435.679.8665, canyonrides.com) offers a 2-hour ride to the canyon floor ($65/person) and a half-day complete tour of the canyon on Peek-a-boo Loop Trail ($90/person). Trail rides are given from April through October. To check availability or join a tour, stop at the trail ride desk in the lobby of Bryce Canyon Lodge.

Stargazing

The combination of Bryce Canyon's remote location and thin desert air provide some of the darkest skies in the contiguous United States. To put things into perspective, a stargazer on a moonless night in a small town can see roughly 2,500 stars. On that same moonless night in Bryce Canyon more than 7,500 stars are visible without the help of a telescope. Stargazing is so exceptional here that the park offers an annual **Astronomy Festival**, typically held in early June. Check the park's online calendar for exact dates.

Bryce Point

Biking

Cyclists are allowed on all paved roads, but pedaling is not recommended as Scenic Drive is narrow and busy (especially in summer). However, a shared use path from Red Canyon to Bryce Canyon (continuing 6.2 miles into the park) opened in 2016. It's a great place to pedal. Bikes are available to rent just outside the park at Ruby's Inn (866.866.6616, rubysinn.com) for $10/hour, $25/half-day, and $40/day.

Winter Activities

Cross-country skiing and **snowshoeing** are popular activities in winter. Skiers are not permitted on trails below the rim, but snowshoers are. Contact the park to check snow conditions before you arrive.

Ranger Programs

Absolutely do not miss the chance to join at least one ranger program. Park rangers guide visitors on canyon hikes, rim walks, and the occasional **Full Moon Hike** (hiking boots required). Geology talks and evening programs are administered on a daily basis during the summer season. Evening programs take place in auditoriums at Bryce Canyon Lodge or the visitor center, and are sometimes held at North Campground's Amphitheater. All of these activities are very family-friendly, but discussion topics can be technical and difficult to understand for children. An alternative for families is the one-hour kid's interpretive program, which is available by reservation. To receive additional information, current schedules, or to make a reservation, call the visitor center at (435) 834-4747 or check the park's online calendar. Tickets are required for the Full Moon Hike due to limited capacity. They are distributed via lottery the day of the hike. You must register in person at the visitor center. Each member of your group must be present (with proper footwear) at the lottery. In winter, full moon hikes become full moon snowshoe adventures (snowpack permitting).

For Kids

Children are invited to participate in the park's **Junior Ranger Program**. To become a Junior Ranger, kids must attend a ranger program, complete an age-appropriate number of workbook activities, and pick up litter at an overlook parking lot or hiking trail. Activity booklets are available for free at the visitor center. Complete these tasks and return to the visitor center to be inducted as an official Junior Ranger and receive a free badge.

Flora & Fauna

Spires, pinnacles, and hoodoos steal the show, but if you look in the air and on the ground you'll spot a few animals and plants, too. Mule deer are the most common animal, but fox, bobcats, black bears, mountain lions, and Utah prairie dogs can also be found here. As a bonus, more than 170 species of birds either reside in or visit Bryce Canyon. Growing in the red rock's soil are at least 400 plant species, including a colorful array of wildflowers. In the harshest areas of the park only limber pine and Great Basin bristlecone pine exist. Some of these ancient trees are more than 1,300 years old.

Pets

Pets are only permitted in campgrounds, parking lots, and along paved roads and must be on a leash no more than six feet in length at all times. They are not allowed on unpaved trails, viewpoints, in public buildings, or on the summer shuttle. Pets may not be left unattended.

Accessibility

Bryce Canyon is one of the more wheelchair-friendly parks. Two campsites at Sunset Campground are reserved for wheelchair users. The summer shuttle is fully accessible. Rim Trail's first 0.5-mile is paved and level. Many of the ranger-guided activities and viewpoints are easily accessible to individuals with mobility impairments. The visitor center is fully accessible. Accessible restrooms can be found at the visitor center, Sunset Point, Bryce Canyon Lodge, and the General Store.

Weather

Summer at Bryce Canyon is pleasant, with average high temperatures from June to August in the high 70s to low 80s°F. Only a handful of days top out above 90°F. Clear skies and high elevation make for cool evenings. The average lows during this same period range from the high 30s to mid-40s°F. Winter isn't as comfortable. Variation in temperature is extreme. Any given day can be sunny and 50°F, or well below freezing.

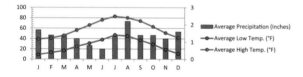

Vacation Planner

Bryce Amphitheater is the headliner, but the park isn't a one-trick pony. Many visitors arrive, look at the hoodoos, and continue on to Zion or Grand Canyon (do that too—you're in the middle of some of the country's best care-killing scenery, see the diagram below). (Others miss the amphitheater altogether, only driving up and down the main park road!) Plan to spend at least one full day. This allows enough time to hike a few trails or go **horseback riding** (page 406). **Camping and lodging** (page 404) are available in the park. Nearby dining, grocery stores, lodging, festivals, and attractions are listed on pages 454–459.

Day 1: First, if the **shuttle** is running, take it. It's convenient and gives your group's driver a break behind the wheel. Besides, who wants to spend vacation circling around parking lots? We like to stop at the visitor center to check the ranger program schedule, but it's understandable if you want to get right to **Bryce Amphitheater**. At a minimum you should make stops at **Bryce Point** and **Sunset Point** (also a great spot to see the sunrise). Better yet, hike **Rim Trail** to all Bryce Amphitheater's viewpoints. If you only have enough time to hike one trail, make it two by combining Navajo Loop and **Queens Garden Trail**. The trip down to the floor is pretty steep, but the entire circuit is still less than 3 miles long and by the time you reach the canyon rim you'll probably want to go right back down to take a closer look at **Wall Street** or the eerie hoodoos. Take the shuttle around the loop, and complete Scenic Drive in your own car or via a shuttle tour (page 404). If you choose to spend the night in the park, be sure to wake up early and catch the sun as it rises up over the amphitheater.

Inspiration Point

Looking down at Angel's Landing from Observation Point

Zion

Springdale, UT 84767
Phone: (435) 772-3256
Website: nps.gov/zion

Established: November 19, 1919
July 31, 1909 (National Monument)
Size: 146,598 Acres
Annual Visitors: 3.6 Million
Peak Season: April–September

Activities: Hiking, Backpacking,
Camping, Horseback Riding, Rock
Climbing, Kayaking, Stargazing,
Bird Watching, and Photography

Campgrounds: South & Watchman*
Fee: $20–30/night
Backcountry Camping: Permitted
with a Backcountry Use Permit (fee)
Lodging: Zion Lodge
Rates: $209+/night

Park Hours: All day, every day
Entrance Fee: $30/vehicle,
$15/individual (foot, bike, etc.)

*Reservations available from
late May through late October
(877.444.6777, recreation.gov)

The name Zion, Hebrew for "Jerusalem" (and "the Holy Sanctuary" in Arabic), was bestowed upon a sublime red rock canyon carved by the North Fork of the Virgin River. As they say, "If the shoe fits, wear it." This region of southwestern Utah has served as sanctuary for ancient cultures, Mormon settlers, government explorers, and today's solace-seeking tourists.

People have inhabited the Virgin River Valley for at least 8,000 years. Nomadic families camped, hunted, and collected plants and seeds. About 2,000 years ago they began cultivating crops, which led to construction of permanent villages called pueblos. The only remnants of these ancient cultures are baskets, rope nets, yucca fiber sandals, tools, and simple structures dating back to 500 AD. Tools used by the Fremont Culture and Virgin Anasazi include stone knives, drills, and stemmed dart points that were hurled with atlatls (a tool similar to today's dog ball throwers). Small pit-houses and granaries have been discovered at various archaeological sites within the park's canyons. Scientists speculate a combination of extended drought, catastrophic flooding, and depleted farmland forced these people to abandon their civilization around the turn of the 14th century. As the Fremont Culture and Virgin Anasazi left the region, Paiute and Ute Indians moved in. They migrated to the area on a seasonal basis, using its land for hunting and gathering, much like the original inhabitants. A few tribes cultivated fields of corn, sunflower, and squash, using the region as a sanctuary for hundreds of years.

It wasn't until the late 18th century that a pair of Franciscan missionaries became the first people of European descent to explore the region. Francisco Domínguez and Father Escalante led an eponymous expedition, which left Santa Fe in search of a route to Monterey, California. Before reaching the Sierra Nevada their journey was impeded by a shortage of rations and snowstorms. Forced to turn back, they headed south, passing nearby the site of present-day Kolob Canyons Visitor Center, and then crossing the Colorado River at Marble Canyon before returning to Santa Fe.

Mormon farmers settled the Virgin River region in 1847. A few years later, Parowan and Cedar City were established, and they named the area used as a pasture and lumber yard Kolob. According to Mormon scripture, Kolob is "the heavenly place nearest the residence of God." By 1858, new settlements were established along the South Virgin River. Expansion continued when Isaac Behunin became the first to settle on the ground floor of a canyon he named Zion, referring to a place mentioned in the Bible. The Behunins and two other families summered here. They grew corn, tobacco, and fruit trees, returning to nearby Springdale for winter.

In 1872, U.S. Army Major John Wesley Powell led an expedition through the region. He named the magnificent valley Mukuntuweap, the Paiute name for "canyon." His crew took photographs, helping satisfy the East Coast's curiosity about western wonders. The East took more interest after Frederick S. Dellenbaugh displayed his paintings of the colorful canyon at the St. Louis World Fair in 1904. Five years later, President William Howard Taft decided the region should be a public sanctuary, establishing Mukuntuweap National Monument.

The region—now preserved for everyone's enjoyment—was relatively inaccessible to the average man. But in 1917 a road was completed to the Grotto. Visitation increased, and so did confusion about the canyon's name. Locals disliked Mukuntuweap, and Horace Albright felt it needed to be more manageable. Congress and President Wilson agreed; land was added and it was redesignated Zion National Park. In 1923, a subsidiary of the Union Pacific Railroad purchased a small tent camp and replaced it with Zion Lodge. By 1930, construction crews completed Zion–Mount Carmel Highway, dramatically increasing access and visitation. Finally, Zion had become a sanctuary for everyone to enjoy.

When to Go

Zion is open all year, but visitation peaks in April through September. **Zion Canyon and Kolob Canyons Visitor Centers** are open every day except Christmas. **Zion Human History Museum** is open daily from mid-March through December. Watchman Campground is open all year. South Campground is open from March through November. Lava Point Campground is open from June through October. Zion Lodge is open all year (reduced rates in winter). Zion Canyon Scenic Drive is only accessible by the park's free shuttle system and guests of Zion Lodge from mid-March through October, and weekends in November. The road is plowed and open to motorists the rest of the year.

Transportation & Airports

Public transportation does not reach the park, but a free shuttle connects the neighboring town of Springdale with the park, and provides the only access to Zion Canyon from mid-March through October. The closest large commercial airports are McCarran International (LAS) in Las Vegas, NV, 170 miles to the southwest, and Salt Lake City International (SLC), 313 miles north of the park.

Directions

Zion National Park is in the very southwestern corner of Utah. Kolob Canyons is located in the park's northwest corner and reached by taking Exit 40 from I-15. Zion Canyon, the park's most popular area, is accessed via UT-9. Directions to Zion Canyon are provided below.

From Las Vegas (167 miles): Head east on I-15 through St. George, UT, all the way to Exit 16 for UT-9 toward Hurricane/Zion National Park. Take UT-9 east 32 miles to Zion Canyon Visitor Center.

From Salt Lake City (312 miles): Head south on I-15 to exit 27 for UT-17 for Toquerville/Hurricane. Turn left at UT-17 S/UT-228. After 6 miles, turn left onto UT-9, which leads into the park.

From Kanab/Grand Canyon (42/248 miles): Head north on US-89. Turn left at UT-9 W, which leads into the park. Visitors with large vehicles: please refer to page 412 for information regarding access to Zion–Mount Carmel Tunnel.

Regions

Zion is one continuous area, but three roads lead into the park's interior. **Zion Canyon** is by far the most popular region. You will find most facilities and trailheads along Zion Canyon Scenic Drive and Zion–Mount Carmel Highway (UT-9), which provide access to the canyon. Ultra-popular hikes through Zion Narrows and to Angel's Landing are located in this region. If you follow UT-9 west, beyond the south entrance, you will reach the small town of Virgin. Here, **Kolob Terrace Road** winds its way in-and-out of the park before terminating at Kolob Reservoir. Kolob Terrace Road provides access to Lava Point Primitive Campground and numerous trailheads, including the bottom-up (non-technical) and top-down (technical) trails to The Subway (permit required, even for a day-hike). In the park's northwest corner, far away from the crowds of Zion Canyon, is **Kolob Canyons**. This region has a visitor center, a scenic drive, and a few trailheads including the scenic hike to Kolob Arch.

Scenic Drives & Zion–Mt Carmel Highway

Zion–Mount Carmel Highway and Tunnel were built to provide a shorter route to Bryce Canyon (page 398). The tunnel is a feat of engineering nearly as magnificent as the surrounding geography, but it poses a significant problem to large vehicles wishing to access Zion Canyon. All vehicles 7'10" or wider, or 11'4" or taller (maximum of 13'1" tall) are too large to remain in a single lane through the tunnel and require an escort. They must pay a $15 fee (good for two trips through the tunnel within seven days of purchase) at the park entrance before driving to the tunnel. Oversized vehicles are only allowed to pass through during seasonal hours when it is manned by park rangers. Typical hours are from 8am–8pm in summer and 8am–7pm in spring and fall. It is a good idea to visit the park's website or call the visitor center for current hours of operation. **Cyclists and pedestrians are not allowed to use the tunnel.**

The 10-mile **Zion–Mount Carmel Highway** connects the park's East and South Entrances, but the highlight of a trip for many visitors is six-mile **Zion Canyon Scenic Drive**. In winter, visitors are allowed to drive this stretch of road all the way to the foot of Temple of Sinawava, which is also the mouth of the famous Zion Narrows. For the rest of the year, Zion Canyon Scenic Drive is only open to park shuttle buses and guests of Zion Lodge.

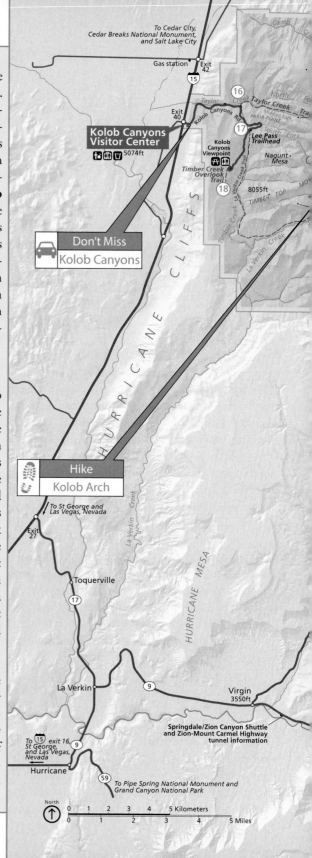

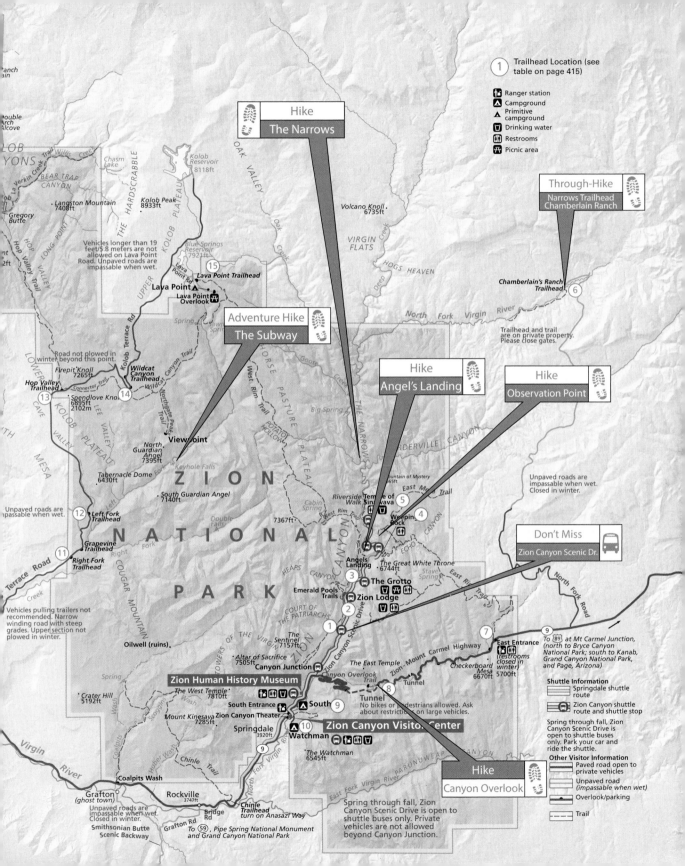

Trailhead Location (see table on page 415)

- Ranger station
- Campground
- Primitive campground
- Drinking water
- Restrooms
- Picnic area

Hike
The Narrows

Through-Hike
Narrows Trailhead
Chamberlain Ranch

Adventure Hike
The Subway

Hike
Angel's Landing

Hike
Observation Point

Don't Miss
Zion Canyon Scenic Dr.

Hike
Canyon Overlook

KOLOB CANYONS

Double Arch Alcove

Willis Creek Trail

La Verkin Creek Trail
BEAR TRAP CANYON

Gregory Butte

Langston Mountain 7408ft

THE HARDSCRABBLE

Chasm Lake

Kolob Peak 8933ft

Kolob Reservoir 8118ft

Blue Springs Reservoir 7921ft

Volcano Knoll 6735ft

OAK VALLEY

VIRGIN FLATS

HOGS HEAVEN

Chamberlain's Ranch Trailhead ⑥

North Fork Virgin River

Trailhead and trail are on private property. Please close gates.

Vehicles longer than 19 feet/5.8 meters are not allowed on Lava Point Road. Unpaved roads are impassable when wet.

Lava Point Rd
⑮ Lava Point Trailhead
Lava Point △
Lava Point Overlook

Kolob Terrace Rd

UPPER KOLOB PLATEAU

Road not plowed in winter beyond this point.

Firepit Knoll 7265ft

Hop Valley Trailhead ⑬

Spendlove Knoll 6895ft 2102m

Wildcat Canyon Trailhead ⑭

Connector Trail

Northgate Peaks Trail

Wildcat Canyon Trail

Hop Valley Trail

LOWER KOLOB PLATEAU

LEE VALLEY

Viewpoint

North Guardian Angel 7395ft

Tabernacle Dome 6430ft

South Guardian Angel 7140ft

Keyhole Falls

West Rim Trail

HORSE PASTURE PLATEAU

POTATO HOLLOW

Big Spring

Deep Creek

North Fork Virgin River

Goose Creek

Spring

CAVE VALLEY

KOLOB PLATEAU

Unpaved roads are impassable when wet.

⑫ Left Fork Trailhead

Grapevine Trailhead

⑪ Right Fork Trailhead

Terrace Road

Z I O N

7367ft

Double Falls

Cabin Spring

West Rim Trail

N A T I O N A L

Riverside Walk Temple of Sinawava ⑤

Weeping Rock ④

Mountain of Mystery 7265ft

East Mesa Trail

ORDERVILLE CANYON

ECHO CANYON

Unpaved roads are impassable when wet. Closed in winter.

Vehicles pulling trailers not recommended. Narrow winding road with steep grades. Upper section not plowed in winter.

Oilwell (ruins)

COUGAR MOUNTAIN

HEAPS CANYON

Angels Landing ③

The Grotto

Emerald Pools Trails

Zion Lodge ②

The Great White Throne 6744ft

Stave Spring

East Rim Trail

P A R K

COURT OF THE PATRIARCHS

①

The Sentinel 7157ft

TOWERS OF THE VIRGIN

Altar of Sacrifice 7505ft

Canyon Junction

Zion Human History Museum

The West Temple 7810ft

South Entrance

Mount Kinesava 7285ft Zion Canyon Theater

Springdale 3920ft

⑨

⑩ Watchman

The Watchman 6545ft

The East Temple

Canyon Overlook Trail

Zion-Mount Carmel Highway

Checkerboard Mesa 6670ft

⑦ East Entrance (restrooms closed in winter) 5700ft

⑨ To 89 at Mt Carmel Junction, (north to Bryce Canyon National Park; south to Kanab, Grand Canyon National Park, and Page, Arizona)

North Fork Road

Tunnel

⑧ Tunnel

No bikes or pedestrians allowed. Ask about restrictions on large vehicles.

Zion Canyon Visitor Center

Spring through fall, Zion Canyon Scenic Drive is open to shuttle buses only. Park your car and ride the shuttle.

Shuttle Information
Springdale shuttle route
Zion Canyon shuttle route and shuttle stop

Spring through fall, Zion Canyon Scenic Drive is open to shuttle buses only.

Other Visitor Information
Paved road open to private vehicles
Unpaved road (impassable when wet)
Overlook/parking
Trail

Virgin River

Coalpits Wash

Grafton (ghost town)

Rockville 3747ft

Grafton Rd

Bridge Rd

Chinle Trailhead turn on Anasazi Way

To 59, Pipe Spring National Monument and Grand Canyon National Park

Unpaved roads are impassable when wet. Closed in winter.

Smithsonian Butte Scenic Backway

Crater Hill 5192ft

Chinle Trail

Coalpits Wash

PARUNUWEAP CANYON

East Fork Virgin River

Spring through fall, Zion Canyon Scenic Drive is open to shuttle buses only. Private vehicles are not allowed beyond Canyon Junction.

Park Shuttle

The park provides **two free shuttle loops**. They operate from mid-March through October, and weekends in November. **Springdale Loop** completes laps from the south entrance/Zion Canyon Theater to Springdale. This loop is optional, but it's extremely convenient not only for anyone staying in Springdale, but for all visitors, because parking in the park is limited (and often full by 10am). From mid-March through October, you can only access Zion Canyon by shuttle, foot, or bicycle (unless you're staying at Zion Lodge). The **Zion Canyon Shuttle Loop** takes roughly 90 minutes, making seven stops between the visitor center and Temple of Sinawava. The vast majority of visitors explore Zion Canyon Scenic Drive (and its trails) via the free park shuttle. Sure, you lose a bit of freedom not having your own vehicle, but the trip is quite delightful. Bus drivers often point out wildlife or rock climbers spotted along the way.

Camping & Lodging

Zion has three drive-in campgrounds. **South and Watchman Campgrounds** are located along the Virgin River's shoreline near the south entrance and main visitor center. These campgrounds have running water and flush toilets. Watchman has 95 sites with electrical hookups for RVs. No sites have full hookups, but a dump station is available for campers. Watchman also has six group campsites that can accommodate 7 to 40 campers. They are tent-only sites, which cost $50–130, depending on group size. Watchman Campground accepts reservations for camping from early March through mid-November. You may reserve a campsite up to six months in advance at (877) 444-6777 or recreation.gov. **Lava Point** is a primitive campground located along Kolob Terrace Road, about one-hour from Zion Canyon Visitor Center (by car). Six free campsites are situated at 7,890 feet, where it's roughly 15°F cooler than other frontcountry campgrounds. Lava Point is typically open from June through October (weather dependent). Pit toilets are available, but water is not. Rapidly changing weather conditions can make Kolob Terrace Road impassable to 2WD vehicles, and visitors should check road conditions at the visitor center or park website prior to departure. All campgrounds often fill by late morning on weekends and holidays, and by noon on weekdays. **They fill almost every night from mid-March through November.** It's best to make reservations or arrive early if you plan on camping in the park. **Showers** are available at Zion Outfitter (435.772.5090, zionoutfitter.com) in Springdale, just a short walk from the main visitor center.

The only in-park lodging is provided by Xanterra Parks & Resorts at **Zion Lodge**, situated in the middle of Zion Canyon. Guests of the lodge are allowed to take their own vehicles down Zion Canyon Scenic Drive. The accommodations are basic, but how much time do you plan on spending in your room anyway? Red Rock Grill is on-site for breakfast, lunch, and dinner. Call (888) 297-2757 or click zionlodge.com to make reservations. See page 456 for nearby lodging and dining.

Zion Camping (Fees are per night)

Name	Location	Open	Fee	Sites	Notes
South	Near South Entrance	March–November	$20	117	No showers, no hookups, 4 group sites
Watchman*	Near South Entrance	All Year	$20 $30	87 95	87 tent-only sites (18 are walk-in) 95 sites have electrical hookups (no full)
Lava Point	Kolob Terrace Road	June–October	Free	6	Primitive, no water, pit toilets
*Reservations can be made up to 6 months in advance at (877) 444-6777 or recreation.gov for March–November					
Backcountry	A permit (fee) is required to camp at any of the 37 backcountry campsites. See page 418 for details.				

Zion Lodging (Fees are per night)

Name	Open	Fee	Notes
Zion Lodge (Zion Canyon Scenic Dr)	All Year	$209+	Only in-park lodging, fills early during peak season • Can drive to lodge • Make reservations at (888) 297-2757 or zionlodge.com

Bighorn sheep

Zion Hiking Trails (Distances are roundtrip unless noted otherwise)

	Name	Location (# on map)	Length	Difficulty Rating & Notes
Zion Canyon Scenic Drive	Sand Bench Loop	Court of the Patriarchs (1)	3.4 miles	M – Sandy trail used mainly for trail rides
	Emerald Pools	Zion Lodge (2)	1.2–2.5 mi	E/M – Hike to 1, 2, or 3 small pools
	Angel's Landing - 👍	The Grotto (3)	5.4 miles	S – Adventurous hike with excellent views
	Grotto	The Grotto (3)	1.0 mile	E – Connects Zion Lodge and The Grotto
	Kayenta	The Grotto (3)	2.0 miles	M – Connects Grotto with Middle Emerald
	Weeping Rock	Weeping Rock (4)	0.4 mile	E – Paved trail to a dripping wall
	Hidden Canyon	Weeping Rock (4)	2.4 miles	S – Follows a cliff ledge to a narrow canyon
	Observation Pt - 👍	Weeping Rock (4)	8.0 miles	S – Great! Look down on Angel's Landing
	Riverside Walk	Temple of Sinawava (5)	2.2 miles	E – Paved trail along the Virgin River
	The Narrows via Riverside Walk - 👍	Temple of Sinawava (5)	9.4 miles	S – Most scenic portion of the Narrows to Orderville Canyon •You will get wet
	The Narrows - 👍	Chamberlain's Ranch to Temple of Sinawava (6, 5)	16.0 miles	S – One-way, backpack (12 campsites) or day-hike (12+ hours), wading/swimming req'd
Zion–Mt Carmel Hwy	East Rim - 👍	Near East Entrance (7)	10.8 miles	S – East Entrance to Weeping Rock, one-way
	Canyon Overlook - 👍	East of the long tunnel (8)	1.0 mile	M – Short hike with excellent scenic value
	Pa'rus - 👍	South Camp (9)	3.5 miles	E – Paved trail to Canyon Junction
	Watchman - 👍	Watchman Camp (10)	3.3 miles	M – Short trail to a perch above the camp
	Archeology	Zion Canyon Visitor Center (10)	0.4 mile	E – Small prehistoric storage buildings
Kolob Terrace Rd	Right Fork	0.5-mile past Park Boundary (11)	11.8 miles	M – Follows creek to waterfalls
	Left Fork - 👍	Left Fork Trailhead (12)	9.0 miles	M – Non-technical (Bottom-up) to Subway
	Wildcat Canyon	Hop Valley Trailhead (13)	8.7 miles	M – One-way, connector to Lava Point Camp
	Northgate Peaks	Wildcat Canyon Trailhead (14)	4.4 miles	E – Lightly used flat trail to 7,200-ft peak
	Technical Subway	Wildcat Canyon Trailhead (14)	9.5 miles	S – One-way, requires rope, ends at Left Fork
	Wildcat Canyon	Lava Point (15)	11.6 miles	S – Scrambling over difficult terrain
	West Rim - 👍	Lava Point (15)	14.2 miles	S – One-way, ends at The Grotto
Kolob Canyons Rd	Taylor Creek - 👍	Taylor Creek Trailhead (16)	5.0 miles	M – Leads to Double Arch Alcove
	North Fork Taylor Cr	Taylor Creek Trailhead (16)	5.0 miles	M – Unmaintained spur from Taylor Creek
	Kolob Arch via La Verkin Creek - 👍	Lee Pass Trailhead (17)	14.0 miles	S –Trail can be made a long day hike or an overnight backpack trip
	Timber Creek	End of Kolob Terrace Rd (18)	1.0 mile	M – Short hike, follows ridge to an overlook

Difficulty Ratings: E = Easy, M = Moderate, S = Strenuous

Hidden Canyon Trail

Hiking

To truly appreciate the beauty of Zion, visitors must go for a hike. The park has a large network of well-maintained trails with trailheads conveniently located along Zion Canyon Scenic Drive (ZCSD), Zion–Mount Carmel Highway (ZMCH), Kolob Terrace Road (KTR), and Kolob Canyons Road (KCR). Whether you're looking for a casual leg-stretching stroll, or a boot-pounding multi-day backpacking adventure, you can find it here.

A few favorite short hikes are **Weeping Rock** (ZCSD), **Hidden Canyon** (ZCSD), **Canyon Overlook** (ZMCH), and **Taylor Creek** (KCR) **Trails**. Hidden Canyon Trail, located at Weeping Rock Shuttle Stop, is relatively short but quite strenuous and not for individuals with a fear of heights. Traversing an exposed cliff (aided by chains), makes it a good training route for Angel's Landing. Hiking the same trail but bypassing

its spur to Hidden Canyon will take you to **East Rim Trail**, which leads to **Observation Point**, the best vantage point in the entire park, where you can look down on Zion Canyon and Angel's Landing. Less strenuous favorites include **Watchman and Pa'rus Trails**. Both begin near the visitor center. Watchman involves only modest elevation gain, as it scales to a viewpoint on the flank of The Watchman, not its peak. Pa'rus Trail is flat and paved, following the Virgin River from South Campground to Canyon Junction. It's wheelchair accessible, and bikes and pets are allowed. An increasingly popular trail is the bottom-up (non-technical) route to **The Subway**. The trailhead is located on KTR, and all hikers, even day-hikers, require a **permit** (page 418). A complete table of Zion hiking trails is provided on the previous page. Meanwhile the park's two iconic trails, Angel's Landing and The Narrows, are discussed below.

Angel's Landing

One of the most memorable hikes in the entire National Park System is the 5.4-mile (roundtrip) adventure to Angel's Landing. Calling it an adventure sells it short. The last 0.5-mile is a hair-raising experience that takes you along a knife-edge ridgeline with 500-foot drops on either side. The journey begins at **Grotto Trailhead Parking Area**, located just beyond Zion Lodge. Once you've arrived at the trailhead, immediately cross the Virgin River via a short suspension bridge. On the opposite side of the river, ignore Kayenta Trail and head north, making a steady climb toward the mouth of Refrigerator Canyon. As you approach the mouth of the canyon you will loop back and ascend the canyon wall via 21 switchbacks known as "Walter's Wiggles." The ascent takes you to Scout's Lookout, which provides impressive views of Zion Canyon and a closer look at the landing. Do not follow the trail to the northwest, which leads into the backcountry and away from Angel's Landing via West Rim Trail. At Scout's Lookout you may begin to second guess your plans. The next 0.5-mile should never be attempted wearing improper footwear or in bad weather conditions. It is much more intimidating from a distance than up close, but there are no guardrails. Only a series of chains aid your passage along the backbone of Angel's Landing. Once you've made it to the promontory, have a seat, take a drink, and enjoy the view.

The Narrows

The Narrows is an iconic hike following the Virgin River as it winds its way through a 2,000-foot-deep canyon that is, as its name implies, narrow (20–30 ft). The water is cold, the rocks are slippery, and the sun rarely penetrates its depths, making the trek challenging and exhilarating. You will wade through knee-high water and take the occasional swim across deep holes. Visitors can explore the Narrows three ways: day-hike from Mount Sinawava, day-hike the entire length beginning at Chamberlain Ranch, or backpack overnight.

A **day-hike** into the canyon from **Mount Sinawava Shuttle Stop** via **Riverside Walk** is the simplest option. You are free to hike to **Orderville Canyon**, the most scenic and popular stretch, without a permit.

The alternatives eschew crowds, but require a **backcountry permit** (page 418). Completing the entire Narrows requires arranging a shuttle (page 458), since it's a one-way hike. The journey begins outside park boundaries at **Chamberlain Ranch**, accessed via North Fork Road, just outside the park's East Entrance. Ambitious hikers can day hike the entire 16-mile canyon in 10–14 hours. If you'd like to take your time and enjoy the scenery, spend a night at one of 12 backcountry campsites. Hiking the entire canyon provides hikers with the added bonus of solitude. You'll feel alone in the Narrows until reaching Orderville Canyon, where you'll meet day-hikers from Mount Sinawava.

The best time of year to hike the Narrows is late spring to early summer. Cool water of the Virgin River will be refreshing as you spend more than half your hike wading. Wear sturdy shoes and carry a walking stick. Be sure to check the weather before entering the Narrows, as flash flooding and hypothermia are constant dangers. See page 458 for **guide services and gear rental**.

Backpacking

Backpacking is allowed at designated sites along four popular trails. **Zion Narrows** (above) has 12 campsites, all located above the high-water line of the Virgin River and upriver from Big Spring. **West Rim Trail**, from the Grotto to Lava Point

The Narrows

Mount Moroni

Primitive Campground, is the most popular backpacking trail, with a total of nine designated campsites along the way. If you can arrange a shuttle, begin hiking at Lava Point Campground. From here, it will be a mostly downhill 14.2-mile trek that can be completed in two days without a problem. Kolob Canyons' only suitable backpacking route is **La Verkin/Kolob Arch Trail**, including its spur through the Hop Valley. There are also designated campsites in the park's southwest corner along **Coalpits Wash** and **Scoggins Wash**. In addition to the designated campsites, backpackers are allowed to camp in specified zones as long as they are one mile from roads, out of sight of trails, and 0.25-mile from springs. Spring and fall are the best seasons for backpacking trips. A **permit** (page 418) is required for all overnight stays in the backcountry.

Backcountry Permits

A backcountry permit is required for all overnight trips in the backcountry, Narrows thru-hikes, Narrows day-hikes beyond Orderville Canyon, all canyon trips requiring descending gear or ropes (including the Subway and Mystery Canyon), and all overnight trips in the backcountry. Zion Narrows and Subway permits can be obtained up to three months in advance via online lottery at zionpermits.nps.gov. If you don't secure permits through the online lottery, you can apply for Last Minute Drawing permits, seven to two days in advance. After the Last Minute Drawing, walk-in permits become available the day before your trip. (Walk-in permits for The Subway are unlikely.) There is a $5 non-refundable application fee for the online lottery. If you won the lottery, secured a reservation, or obtained a permit the day of your trip, you will have to pay an additional backcountry permit fee. Fees are based on group size: $15 for 1–2 people, $20 for 3–7 people and $25 for 8–12 people. Maximum group size is 12 people.

Camping in the Zion Wilderness requires a permit. Over half of all permits are available via an online reservation system up to three months in advance (starting on the fifth of each month). There is a $5 non-refundable fee for an online reservation, plus an additional permit fee (determined by the size of your group). If you intend to camp in more than one location, you will need to make a reservation for each location. All remaining permits can be obtained in person at park visitor centers the day before or the day of your trip.

Horseback Riding

Tourists can also experience the wonders of Zion on horseback. **Canyon Trail Rides** (435.679.8665, canyonrides.com) offers 1-hour ($45/person) and 3-hour ($90/person) trail rides from March through October. Guided rides begin at a corral by Emerald Pools Trailhead near Zion Lodge. Visitors are also allowed to trailer in stock. A stock camp is available at Hop Valley Site A, located on Hop Valley Trail. A **backcountry permit** (above) is required for overnight stays, but not for day use. Not all trails are approved for stock use, so check with the visitor center or online before you ride.

Biking

Biking is allowed on all of the park's roadways and **Pa'rus Trail**, which connects South Campground with Zion Canyon Scenic Drive. Bicycles are also a great way to explore **Zion Canyon Scenic Drive**, just be on the lookout for shuttle buses. A few bike outfitters are located next to the park in Springdale. Zion Cycles (435.772.0400, zioncycles.com) and Bike Zion (435.772.3303, bikingzion.com) offer **rentals and guided bicycle tours**. Zion Outfitter (435.772.5090, zionoutfitter.com) also offers rentals.

Paddling & Floating

Kayaking the Narrows is only recommended for advanced paddlers. A **backcountry permit** is required for all boat use in the park. With enough winter snowpack, Zion Outfitter (435.772.5090, zionoutfitter.com) and Zion Adventure Company (435.772.1001, zionadventures.com) offer **tubing trips** down the Virgin River.

Canyoneering & Rock Climbing

Technical canyoneering and rock climbing are popular activities (for experienced individuals only). Route descriptions are available at the Backcountry Desk. First-timers should buy a dedicated guidebook or hire a guide (page 458).

Stargazing

Visitors, especially those from large urban areas, should take a few moments to admire the stars. High elevation and remoteness make Zion an ideal location to admire the night sky.

Bird Watching

More than 290 species of birds visit or nest within the park. Watch cliff-faces for peregrine falcons and the lush vegetation along the Virgin River for Grace's warblers and Bullock's orioles.

Photography

Brightly colored rock layers, deep blue skies, vibrant green grasslands, and the occasional wildflower bloom make Zion one of the most photogenic parks. A tripod is essential for photographing the dimly lit Zion Narrows (page 417).

Visitor Centers

Zion has two visitor centers that are open every day of the year except Christmas. **Zion Canyon Visitor Center**, located near the park's south entrance on UT-9, is the primary destination for park information as well as the main hub for the **free shuttle service** (page 414). Standard operating hours are from 8am to 6pm, but are extended to 7:30pm during the busy summer season. A Backcountry Desk is located inside, where you can obtain backcountry information and permits. It's open from 7am to 7:30pm during summer and 8am to 4:30pm during winter. **Kolob Canyons Visitor Center** is a small facility with books and souvenirs for sale. It's staffed by a park ranger from 8am to 6pm during summer and 8am to 4:30pm during winter. **Zion Human History Museum** is located just north of Zion Canyon Visitor Center on Zion–Mount Carmel Highway. It features alternating art exhibits, a short introductory film, and book and gift stores. It's open daily, mid-March through November, from 9am to 7pm during summer (hours vary during the off-season).

Ranger Programs

From mid-March to November, park rangers administer a series of walks, talks, and interpretive programs. These activities explore the lives of resident plants and animals or discuss the difficulty of life in the desert. Walks range from a leisurely ramble along Riverside Walk to a strenuous hike up the Narrows. Evening discussions are held regularly at Watchman Campground's Amphitheater and Zion Lodge's Auditorium. A list of discussion topics is usually displayed on bulletin boards at the visitor centers, museum, and campgrounds. You can also find a current schedule of events online in the park's calendar. Many tours accept reservations up to three days in advance. To make a reservation, stop in at Zion Canyon Visitor Center. If you have the time and the opportunity to join a ranger-guided tour, don't think twice, just go.

For Kids

Zion offers guided and self-guided **Junior Ranger Programs** for children (ages 4 and older). To participate in the self-guided program, simply pick up a Junior Ranger activity booklet from either of the park's visitor centers or Zion Human History Museum. Complete the activities and return to a visitor center to be made an official Zion National Park Junior Ranger and receive an award. Guided programs are offered daily from Memorial Day weekend through late August. These family-oriented programs are free of charge. Participants are advised to bring water and wear close-toed shoes (i.e., no flip-flops or sandals). Canyon Overlook and Riverside Walk are two of the more popular family trails.

Flora & Fauna

Zion sits at the convergence of three geographic regions: the Colorado Plateau, Great Basin, and Mojave Desert. Geologic variance coupled with more than 4,000 feet of elevation change makes for an environment filled with incredible biodiversity. Zion is home to more than 78 species of mammals, 290 species of birds, 44 species of reptiles and amphibians, and 8 species of fish. Most notable are bighorn sheep, mule deer, mountain lions, peregrine falcons, and Mexican spotted owls. The park also supports more than 900 species of plants, ranging from cacti and desert succulents to riparian trees, shrubs, and wildflowers.

Pets

Pets are allowed in the park but are not permitted on the shuttle, in the backcountry, on trails, or in public buildings. These restrictions make travelling with a pet challenging. Pets are allowed in developed campgrounds, along park roads, in parking areas, and on Pa'rus Trail, but must be kept on a leash no more than six feet in length at all times. Doggy Dude Ranch (435.772.3105) is a nearby kennel where you can keep your pet while exploring the park.

Accessibility

Zion Canyon Visitor Center, Zion Human History Museum, and Kolob Canyons Visitor Center are fully accessible to individuals in wheelchairs. All shuttle buses (page 414) are accessible and equipped with a wheelchair lift. Zion Lodge has two accessible rooms, and there are a total of five accessible campsites at Watchman and South Campgrounds. Riverside Walk and Pa'rus Trail are paved and accessible to wheelchair users with assistance.

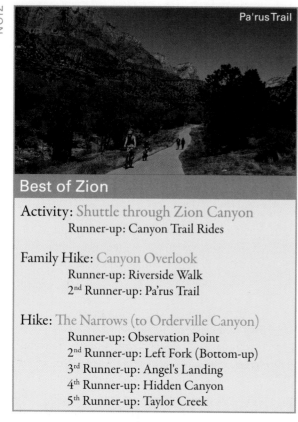
Pa'rus Trail

Best of Zion

Activity: Shuttle through Zion Canyon
    Runner-up: Canyon Trail Rides

Family Hike: Canyon Overlook
    Runner-up: Riverside Walk
    2nd Runner-up: Pa'rus Trail

Hike: The Narrows (to Orderville Canyon)
    Runner-up: Observation Point
    2nd Runner-up: Left Fork (Bottom-up)
    3rd Runner-up: Angel's Landing
    4th Runner-up: Hidden Canyon
    5th Runner-up: Taylor Creek

Weather

The weather is most comfortable between March and May, and September and November. These periods are marked by daytime highs in the low 60s to low 80s°F. Overnight temperatures drop into the 40s°F. Summer days are hot, with an average daily high of 100°F in July. It's not unheard of for the mercury to reach 110°F on the hottest days of the year. No matter how hot it gets during the day, summer nights remain comfortable with temperatures usually below 70°F. Winters are generally mild, but visitors arriving between November and March should be prepared for snowy conditions. January is the coldest month with an average daily high of 52°F and a daily low of 29°F. This region does not receive much precipitation, but short thunderstorms are common throughout the year.

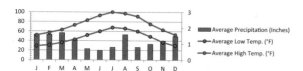

Vacation Planner

If you're visiting between mid-March and October, **Zion Canyon Scenic Drive** can only be accessed by the **free shuttle buses** (page 414) and guests of Zion Lodge. Alternatively, you can bike or walk to the canyon via Pa'rus Trail. Provided below is a three-day itinerary, allowing two days to explore the main canyon and one day at Kolob Canyons. **Kolob Terrace Road** leads to some of the park's more extraordinary hiking opportunities, but popular routes like **Left Fork Trail** to the Subway require advanced planning and a **backcountry permit** (page 418), so it is excluded. The park's **camping** and **lodging** facilities are referenced on page 414. Nearby dining, grocery stores, lodging, festivals, and attractions are listed on pages 454–459. If you plan on traveling to the park in an oversized vehicle or RV, be sure to check the size requirements for Zion Tunnel (page 412), because you may require an escort or not fit altogether.

Day 1: Entering Zion's East Entrance, make a quick stop just before **Zion Tunnel** to hike the 1-mile trail to **Canyon Overlook**. It's a great spot to view Zion Canyon before entering it. The short hike also gives you an opportunity to see the exterior of Zion Tunnel and the rock that was blown apart to build it in 1930. After the hike, return to your car and pass through the tunnel. On the other side is a set of switchbacks that makes for an easy descent to the canyon floor.

Continue along Zion–Mount Carmel Highway to **Zion Canyon Visitor Center** (if you enter at the South Entrance begin your trip here—parking is limited, so you may want to leave your vehicle in Springdale and use the free shuttle). Check the schedule of programs and pencil the interesting ones into your schedule. If members of your group are notorious for spending excessive amounts of time at gift stores, bookstores—any kind of store—leave them at the visitor center and go hike **Watchman Trail**.

Once you're back together and ready to go, head to the shuttle stop near the visitor center. Hop aboard a shuttle and ride until you reach **The Grotto**, where you'll hike to **Angel's Landing**. After cautiously making your way across this knife-edge ridgeline nothing about Zion will

View from Watchman Trail

be intimidating. It's strenuous, but feasible for those in average physical condition. Children are usually fearless of the precipitous drop-offs that mark the last 0.5-mile, so be sure to watch them closely. If you don't feel up to reaching the Landing, the view from **Scout's Lookout** is still worthwhile. Anyone fearful of heights might want to stay aboard the shuttle bus and exit at **Weeping Rock**, where you can hike to **Observation Point**. It's more strenuous than Angel's Landing, with a few exposed cliff-faces, but not nearly as intimidating. Observation Point may lack the thrills of Angel's Landing (and the crowds), but it ends at what we consider the best view in the park! Complete the hike, climb back aboard a shuttle and finish the circuit around Zion Canyon Loop. If you're spending the night in the park, check if there's an evening program at the lodge or campground.

Day 2: Take it easy in the morning. Maybe attend a **ranger program**, hike to **Canyon Overlook** (if you didn't yesterday), or walk along **Pa'rus Trail** into the canyon. In the afternoon, ride a shuttle bus back into the main canyon to hike the **Narrows**. Make sure you have sturdy hiking shoes on. If it's an abnormally cold day or there's a chance of thunderstorm, find an alternate activity. The Virgin River is perpetually cold and flash floods can occur with the slightest rainfall.

With cooperative weather take the shuttle to **Temple of Sinawava** and follow **Riverside Walk** to the canyon's mouth. Here you will often find hiking sticks left by previous hikers propped against the canyon walls; taking one is a good idea. Beyond Riverside Walk the river is your trail. There's no marked route. You simply choose your own way proceeding as fast or slow as you like. The entire trek is only 3.5 miles (one-way) to **Orderville Canyon**, but it's extremely slow going as you are constantly negotiating a slippery and rocky riverbottom, while weaving back and forth across the Virgin River. Many visitors hire a guide or rent equipment from one of the local outfitters (page 458). You'll want to rest your feet after the hike. Maybe stop at **Zion Human History Museum** to watch its 22-minute film.

Day 3: Drive to **Kolob Canyons**. The area's most exciting hike is another long one. If you feel like recording 14 more miles on your hiking boots, head for **Kolob Arch**. Otherwise drive the Scenic Road and hike 5 miles along **Taylor Creek Trail** to **Double Arch Alcove**. This trail proceeds along a gradual grade to views of a large alcove in a massive wall of red sandstone. A really great (and popular) activity nearby (but outside the park) is the short adventure hike to **Kanarra Falls** (page 458). It's a great little hike.

Mather Point (South Rim)

Grand Canyon

PO Box 129
Grand Canyon, AZ 86023
Phone: (928) 638-7888
Website: nps.gov/grca

Established: February 26, 1919
January 11, 1908 (Nat'l Monument)
Size: 1,217,403 Acres
Annual Visitors: 5.5 Million
Peak Season: May–September

Activities: Hiking, Backpacking, Camping, Mule Rides, River Trips, Air Tours, Biking, and Photography

Campgrounds: Mather ($18/night), Trailer Village ($41), Desert View ($12), and North Rim ($18–25)
Backcountry Camping: Permitted with a Backcountry Permit (fee)
South Rim Lodging: $93–513/night
North Rim Lodging: $130–190/night

South Rim Hours: All day, every day
North Rim Hours: All day, every day (closes Nov/Dec–mid-May)

Entrance Fee: $30/vehicle, $15/individual (foot, bike, etc.)

"There is of course no reason at all in trying to describe the Grand Canyon. Those who have not seen it will not believe any possible description. Those who have seen it know that it cannot be described..."

– J.B. Priestly (Harper's Magazine)

In Arizona's northwestern reaches, the Colorado River has carved the grandest of canyons. Measuring 277 miles long, up to 18 miles wide and more than one mile deep, the Grand Canyon is a gaping scar across the surface of the earth. Theodore Roosevelt declared it "the one great sight which every American should see." One man's thought became another man's goal. Stephen Mather, first director of the National Park Service, dedicated much of his time to obtaining the land and protecting it from commercial interests. Since the National Park Service became custodian of the Grand Canyon in 1919, it has sought to preserve and protect this iconic landscape of the American West for the enjoyment of people, present and future.

Before the National Park Service controlled the area, cattle grazed freely above the rim and miners filed claims for any location that might produce ore. One prospector in particular had a penchant for exploiting its resources. Ralph Henry Cameron—part-time prospector, full-time spinner of colorful yarns—claimed to have spent more than $500,000 "improving" the canyon's trails, blazing the first wagon path from Flagstaff to the South Rim, and opening the first successful mining operation within the canyon. Most of his mining claims were conveniently located at scenic points along the South Rim. At Cameron Trail, today's Bright Angel Trail, he constructed Cameron's Hotel and placed a gate across the trailhead. His brother manned the gate, collecting $1 per person for its use, the first of many swindles along Cameron Trail. He also held a claim at Indian Spring, the route's only source of clean water. Hot and dehydrated, hikers had no choice but to pay exorbitant prices at Cameron's watering hole.

It wasn't long until Cameron became a nuisance to the Santa Fe Railroad. Once the railway reached the South Rim, it wasted little time in constructing El Tovar Hotel. Cameron responded by filing claims all around the luxury abode. Claims were followed by lawsuits, and eventually he was bought out for $40,000. As tourism rose, Cameron watched money roll in, while neglecting the condition of his facilities. Outhouses were so appalling the Santa Fe Railroad offered to replace them free of charge. He declined the offer and filed a lawsuit on the grounds that they would have to illegally cross his claims to build the comfort stations. The court sided in favor of Cameron. When President Theodore Roosevelt created Grand Canyon National Monument, Cameron was instructed to abandon all claims not actively mined. He filed 55 more. It wasn't until 1919, more than a decade later, when Congress established the national park, that Cameron was forced to leave.

The State of Arizona always supported Cameron. He was tied to most of northern Arizona's jobs and locals saw him as a champion against the mighty railroad and wealthy Easterners. Showing their support, he was elected a member of the Senate in 1920, where he vehemently opposed the national park idea and made proposals for two hydroelectric dams and the development of a platinum mine in the canyon. In the end Congress tabled all dam projects and Cameron's crusade against the park finally ended when the public failed to reelect him after learning he used his position for personal gain. Today, the park is everyone's gain, protected for all mankind to see, just like President Roosevelt hoped.

Regions

Grand Canyon National Park consists of three well-defined regions: Colorado River/Canyon Floor, South Rim, and North Rim. The river and the immense canyon that it carved separate the rims. As a crow flies the rims are no more than 18 miles apart, but to reach one from the other by automobile requires a 210-mile, 4.5-hour drive. This causes most vacationers to visit one rim or the other.

The Colorado River/Canyon Floor (page 430): Adventurous visitors run more than 150 named rapids along 225 miles of the Colorado River between Lee's Ferry and Diamond Creek. You can also hike into the canyon, spend a night on the floor (camping or at Phantom Ranch), and then return to the rim the following day.

South Rim (page 435): 90% of the park's 5+ million guests only visit the South Rim. It's open all year and has myriad lodging, dining, and camping facilities, as well as an abundance of entertainment opportunities. The South Rim enjoys a slightly warmer and drier climate than the North Rim due to it being 1,000 feet lower in elevation. Several historic buildings, trailheads (like the popular Bright Angel and South Kaibab Trails), and numerous canyon viewpoints can be accessed via the region's free park shuttle system.

North Rim (page 441): The same great canyon views without the overwhelming crowds. It's also the best place to begin a rim-to-rim hike, since you'll spend more time going down (an extra 1,000 feet) than going back up. North Kaibab Trail provides access to the inner canyon, where it connects with South Kaibab and Bright Angel Trails. The North Rim has a wider variety of above-rim trails with some excellent backpacking routes.

Rim-to-Rim Shuttle

Transcanyon Shuttle (928.638.2820, trans-canyonshuttle.com) provides daily shuttle service between the North Rim and the South Rim, with an additional stop at Marble Canyon (Lee's Ferry). This service is ideal for rim-to-rim hikers not wanting to retrace their path back through the canyon or visitors who would rather not drive themselves. It costs $90/person (one-way). The commute between North and South Rims takes approximately 4.5 hours. One-way fare to Marble Canyon costs $80/person. Shuttle service is available between May 15 and October. Reservations are required.

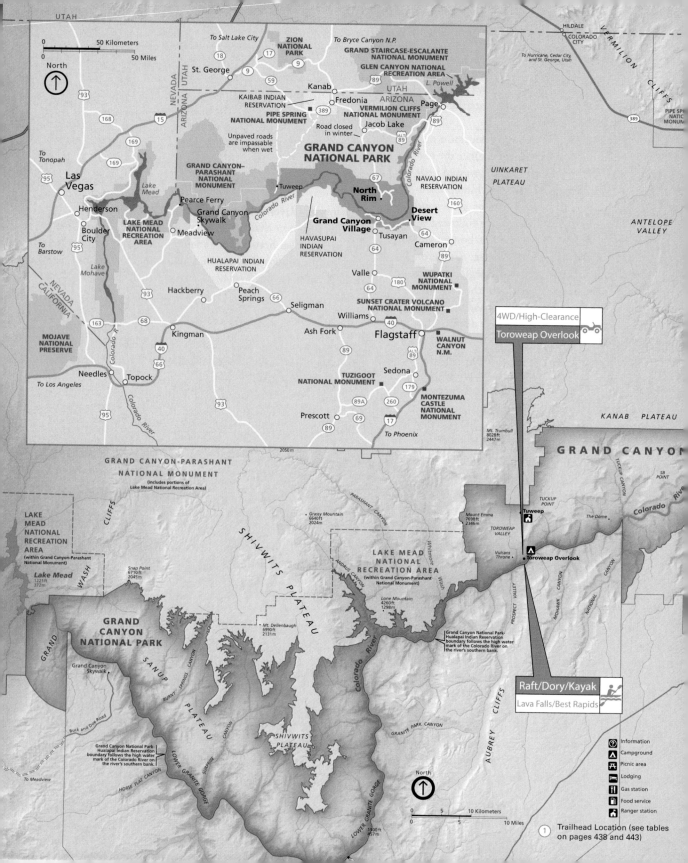

UTAH
ARIZONA

To Page, Arizona

To Bryce Canyon National Park,
Cedar Breaks National Monument,
and Zion National Park

KAIBAB INDIAN
RESERVATION

4750ft
1448m
FREDONIA

GLEN CANYON
NATIONAL
RECREATION AREA

Lake Powell
1700ft
128m
Glen Canyon
Dam

PAGE

89

To Kanab, Utah

PARIA PLATEAU

Grand Canyon National Park
boundary extends to the
mouth of the Paria River

3116ft
950m
Lees Ferry

MARBLE CANYON
Navajo Bridge

89

VERMILION
CLIFFS

ECHO CLIFFS

7921ft
2415m
JACOB LAKE
Camping is summer only

KAIBAB   NATIONAL

FOREST

HOUSE ROCK
VALLEY

89

ALT
89

SNAKE GULCH

JUMPUP CANYON

KAIBAB PLATEAU

LOOKOUT CANYON

67

Road to North Rim and all
services closed in winter.

Kaibab Lodge

De Motte
(US Forest Service)

6

KAIBAB PLATEAU

COCKS COMB

NAVAJO

NATION

RESERVATION

(Permit required for off-highway travel)

The Navajo Nation observes
daylight-saving time, the
rest of Arizona does not.

Grand Canyon National Park-
Navajo Nation Reservation boundary
follows the east rim of the canyon

KANAB CANYON

KANAB CREEK

GREAT THUMB MESA

Chikapanagi
Point

Great Thumb
6749ft
2057m

GRANITE NARROWS

Tapeats Creek

FOSSIL BAY

Swamp Point
7517ft
2292m

MUAV CANYON

Holy Grail
Temple

Point Imperial

11

NATIONAL   PARK

Mount
Sinyala

MIDDLE GRANITE GORGE

POWELL PLATEAU

Apache
Point

Mt. Huethawali
Point

Point Sublime
7459ft
2274m

North Rim Store area

7   8

10

North Rim
Visitor Center

9

8255ft
2516m

Bright Angel Point

WALHALLA
PLATEAU

Kwagunt Creek

12

Atoko
Point

Siegfried
Pyre

Cape Solitude
6144ft
1873m

Little Colorado River

PAINTED

DESERT

Supai
Fees required
Not accessible by road

Grand Canyon NP-
Havasupai Reservation
boundary 0.25 miles from rim

Hualapai
Hilltop
5189ft
1585m

HAVASUPAI
RESERVATION

HAVASU CANYON

AZTEC
AMPHITHEATER

Havasupai
Point
6635ft
2023m

GRANITE GORGE

CRYSTAL CREEK

Tower of Ra

Isis Temple

Zoroaster
Temple

Temple
Butte

Juno
Temple

13

Venus
Temple

Vishnu
Temple

Cape Royal

Swimming Hole
Havasu Falls

Diana
Temple

Tower of Ra

BRIGHT ANGEL CANYON

Bright Angel Creek

Phantom Ranch
2402ft
732m

14

Wotans
Throne

Comanche
Point

HAVASU CREEK

CATARACT CREEK

Hopi
Point

Hermits
Rest

GRAND CANYON VILLAGE

1

3

2

and other services

Grand Canyon
Visitor Center

7

6860ft
2091m

4

HORSESHOE
MESA

Cardenas
Butte

Desert View
Visitor Center

7438ft
2267m
Camping is summer only

Grandview
Point

5

Tusayan Museum
and Ruin

US Forest
Service

TUSAYAN

Grand
Canyon
Airport

Grand Canyon Railway

Ten-X (US Forest Service)
Camping is summer only

COCONINO   PLATEAU

64

KAIBAB   NATIONAL

FOREST

64

COCONINO
RIM

Red Butte
7324ft
2237m

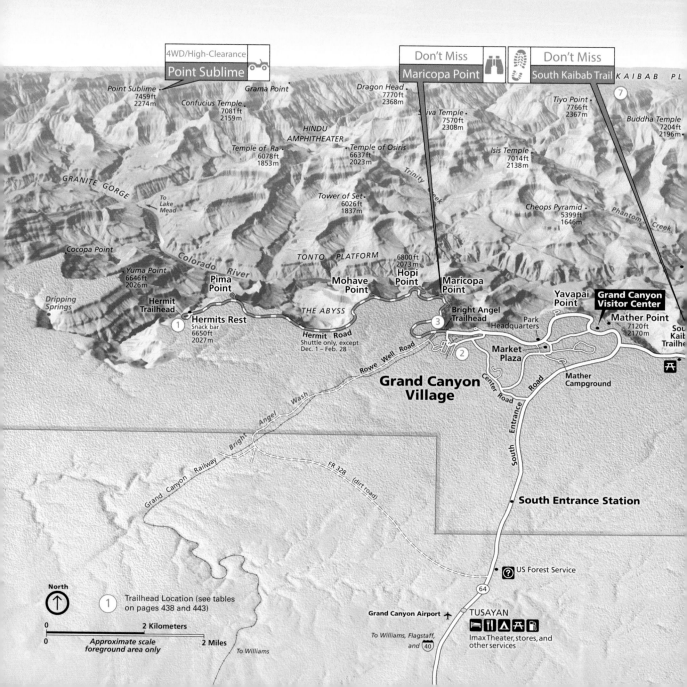

About the maps
These maps show a generalized overview only. Topography derives from 10-meter USGS Digital Elevation Models (DEMs) manipulated to show foreground areas in a more map-like manner than background areas. Vertical exaggeration is used. Graphical scales are shown on each map for general comparisons only; note that distant features are at much smaller scales than foreground areas.

4WD/High-Clearance
Point Sublime

Don't Miss
Maricopa Point

Don't Miss
South Kaibab Trail

KAIBAB PL

Point Sublime
7459ft
2274m

Grama Point

Dragon Head
7770ft
2368m

Tiyo Point
7766ft
2367m

7

Confucius Temple
7081ft
2159m

Shiva Temple
7570ft
2308m

Buddha Temple
7204ft
2196m

HINDU
AMPHITHEATER

Temple of Ra
6078ft
1853m

Temple of Osiris
6637ft
2023m

Isis Temple
7014ft
2138m

GRANITE GORGE

To Lake
Mead

Tower of Set
6026ft
1837m

Trinity Creek

Cheops Pyramid
5399ft
1646m

Phantom Creek

Cocopa Point

Colorado River

TONTO PLATFORM

6800ft
2073m

Yuma Point
6646ft
2026m

Pima Point

Mohave Point

Hopi Point

Maricopa Point

Yavapai Point

Grand Canyon Visitor Center

Dripping Springs

Hermit Trailhead

THE ABYSS

Bright Angel Trailhead

Park Headquarters

Mather Point
7120ft
2170m

Sou Kaib Trailhe

1 Hermits Rest
Snack bar
6650ft
2027m

Hermit Road
Shuttle only, except
Dec. 1 – Feb. 28

3

Market Plaza

Rowe Well Road

2

Grand Canyon Village

Center Road

Mather Campground

Bright Angel Wash

Grand Canyon Railway

Entrance Road

FR 328 (dirt road)

South Entrance Road

South Entrance Station

US Forest Service

North

↑

1 Trailhead Location (see tables on pages 438 and 443)

64

Grand Canyon Airport ✈

TUSAYAN
Imax Theater, stores, and other services

0 ———————— 2 Kilometers
0 ———————— 2 Miles
Approximate scale foreground area only

To Williams

To Williams, Flagstaff, and 40

Don't Miss
Lipan Point

⑪ *Point Imperial*
• 8803ft
  2683m

• *Vista Encantada*
  8480ft
  2585m

Chuar Butte
• 6394ft
  1949m

Cape Solitude
• 6144ft
  1873m

Little Colorado River

⑫

LLA PLATEAU

• *Cape Final*
  7916ft
  2413m

Temple Butte
• 5308ft
  1618m

From Lake Powell

PALISADES OF THE DESERT

⑬
• *Walhalla Overlook*
  7998ft
  2438m

Jupiter Temple
• 7081ft
  2158m

Espejo Butte •

④
reya Castle •
  7299ft
  2225m

Venus Temple •
  6257ft
  1907m

Apollo Temple •

shnu Temple •
  7829ft
  2386m

Comanche Point
• 7073ft
  2156m

Rama Shrine
• 6411ft
  1954m

TANNER CANYON

Sheba Temple

Solomon Temple
• 5670ft
  1545m

Colorado River

Cardenas Butte
• 6269ft
  1911m

Stores (campground and
gas station closed in winter)
• **Desert View**
🛈 ⛺ 🍴 ⛽ 🍴
  7438ft
  2267m

Navajo Point •

Lipan Point •
  7360ft
  2243m

🛈

East Entrance Station

Papago Point •

Pinal Point •

RED CANYON

Zuni Point •
  7278ft
  2219m

Desert View Drive

Tusayan Museum and Ruin
🛈

Don't Miss
Desert View Point

Moran Point •
  7160ft
  2182m

ado Butte
• 7108ft
  2167m

To Cameron →

64

GRAND CANYON NATIONAL PARK

KAIBAB NATIONAL FOREST

Buggeln
🏕

To Arizona Trail

▬▬ Restricted access road No private vehicles	▭▭ Paved road	🛈 Information	🛏 Lodging
		🏕 Picnic area	🍴 Food service
▬▬ Restricted access road Shuttle bus only, except Dec. 1 – Feb. 28 (accessibility pass available)	┅┅ Unpaved road High-clearance vehicles recommended	🚐 Trailer camping	⛽ Gas station
		⛺ Campground	➕ First aid
	─ ─ Trail	⛺ Backcountry campsite	🚻 Restrooms

Bright Angel Point (North Rim)

Grand Geology

While in the area you may hear or see the term "Grand Staircase." It is the stairway to many visitors' heaven, but this term simply refers to a sequence of sedimentary rock layers that form a massive "staircase" between Bryce Canyon and Grand Canyon. Each canyon's cliff edge acts as a giant step, displaying the earth's geologic history in its layers. As you move down the geologic column, each successive rock layer is older than the previous. The oldest exposed formation in Bryce Canyon is the youngest remaining layer at Zion Canyon. Likewise, the floor of Zion Canyon is Kaibab Formation, which is the same formation you stand on at the Grand Canyon's rim. (See page 408 for an illustration of the Grand Staircase.) As you stand at the South Rim staring into the depths of the grandest canyon of them all, you are witnessing some 2 billion years of geologic history.

The oldest exposed layers of rock are found at the bottom of the canyon's inner gorge. They are the Vishnu Basement Rocks, a collection of hard schist and granites formed by the heat and pressure of colliding tectonic plates. Moving up the geologic column, the next set of rocks is the Grand Canyon Supergroup. Its strata accumulated in basins formed as the land mass pulled apart. These layers of shale, limestone, and lava rock can be seen from a handful of locations, such as South Rim's Lipan Point. Grand Canyon Supergroup's rocks are often pinched off and absent from the canyon's exposed walls, creating a gap in the geologic record of more than one billion years between the Vishnu Basement Rocks and adjacent Tapeats Sandstone layer. Scientists believe this irregularity marks an extended period of erosion rather than deposition. Major John Wesley Powell recognized these disjointed rock layers during his expedition of the Grand Canyon in 1869 and named it the Great Unconformity. Beginning with Tapeats Sandstone numerous layers of sedimentary rock make up the set of Layered Paleozoic Rocks occupying the upper two-thirds of the canyon walls. These layers come from a variety of sources: limestone from ancient marine life, mudstone from river deposition, and sandstone from sand dunes.

All of these rock layers were formed near sea level. Some 20 million years ago, the uplift that created the Rocky Mountains also raised the Colorado Plateau, encompassing present-day northern Arizona, eastern Utah, northwestern New Mexico, and western Colorado. Gravity's perpetual force caused rivers to erode the landscape. Water wore away its path and carried with it sediment stripped from the earth. By five or six million years ago, the routes of the Colorado River and its tributaries were carved in stone, draining 90 percent of the plateau. So, why is the Grand Canyon so wide? First, the canyon is not carved at a constant rate. Lava dams formed and breached and Ice Ages came and went, both of which caused massive flows of water. Also, soft sedimentary rock erodes faster than hard rock. Today, the flow of the Colorado River is dramatically reduced by upstream dams, slowing the grinding away of layers of hard schist and granite at the canyon's floor. Meanwhile, the canyon walls are mostly soft sedimentary rock that erodes easily as rainwater and snowmelt drain into the canyon from the north and south rims. The North Rim receives more precipitation and therefore it's eroding faster than the South Rim.

Dory running Hance Rapid

The Colorado River

"It is not a show place, a beauty spot, but a revelation. The Colorado River made it; but you feel when you are there that God gave the Colorado River its instructions. The thing is Beethoven's Ninth Symphony in stone and magic light. I hear rumors of visitors who were disappointed. The same people will be disappointed at the Day of Judgment."

– J.B. Priestly (Harper's Magazine)

The Colorado River is sculptor of the Grand Canyon. Revealer of geologic history. Paradise to thrill-seekers. Ever so slowly these muddy waters of the Colorado dug the world's most magnificent ditch. Explorers crafted elaborate stories of impassable waterfalls, impossible portages, and inaccessible canyons. For decades it remained a blank spot on the map. Today, the map is filled in, and while Grand Canyon's beauty remains, its power is diminished by dams and irrigation.

The Colorado begins in Rocky Mountain National Park (page 326). From there it grows in size and majesty as it passes many of the United States' most treasured natural wonders. It forms the southern boundary of Arches National Park (page 370). In Canyonlands (page 378) it unites with the Green River and rumbles through Cataract Canyon. It floods a red rock labyrinth at Glen Canyon National Recreation Area. And this crescendo reaches its peak, the Grand Canyon, where it offers the greatest whitewater adventure in North America. The mighty Colorado, weakened by man, still churns down below the canyon's rims.

Why look into the canyon from above when you can meet its maker down below? Major John Wesley Powell must have shared that sentiment, as he famously set out on his namesake expedition in 1869. A most unlikely explorer, Powell lost an arm due to a Civil War injury. After the war, he worked as a geology professor, and a series of expeditions into the Rockies and around the Green and Colorado Rivers rekindled his thirst for adventure.

In 1869, he set out with nine men and four boats to explore the Colorado River. Their goal was to fill in the largest hole in the map of the United States. The journey began at Green River, Wyoming. When they arrived at the confluence of the Green and Grand Rivers (the official start of the Colorado) they had already lost one boat and a third of their supplies. Morale was low, but they had little choice but to press on. By the time they reached the Grand Canyon, Powell's men were coming apart at the seams. Starvation, summer heat, and constant pounding of rapid upon rapid had taken their toll. Three men opted to climb out of the canyon into an unknown landscape most likely inhabited by Native Americans. They were never seen again. Just two days later, Powell and his crew reached the mouth of the Virgin River, where they met a few Mormon fishermen.

River Adventures

More than a dozen experienced outfitters provide guided whitewater trips through the Grand Canyon. You can choose from upper-, lower-, and full-canyon adventures. Each trip includes exciting excursions to waterfalls, beaches, and side canyons. All meals, non-alcoholic drinks, and tents are included. The upper and lower halves typically begin or end at Phantom Ranch and require hiking into or out of the canyon. (A few tours substitute a helicopter ride for the hike.) Full canyon tours cover 225 miles from Lee's Ferry near Glen Canyon Dam to Diamond Creek in Hualapai Indian Reservation. You only get to run Lava Falls, the biggest rapid, on full- and lower-canyon tours. Several outfitters offer specialized trips focusing on subjects like geology or photography. All raft adventures generally run from mid-April through early November. Spring and fall are the best seasons to go. You'll avoid the summer heat and crowds, and summer trips often fully book up to a year in advance. Finally, you'll have to choose a watercraft. A wooden dory provides the wildest ride. Motorized J-Rigs smooth out the rapids and expedite the journey. Raft trips are also available, but not all trips allow passengers to paddle. If you want to have an oar in your hands look for "all-paddle" trips in the table on the opposite page.

Phantom Ranch Boat Beach

Colorado River Outfitters

River Outfitter	Dates/Length/Rates	Craft	Notes
Wilderness River Adventures riveradventures.com (800) 992-8022 • (928) 645-3296	April–October 3.5–16 Days $1,450–5,200	Dory J-Rig	Offers 4–8-day motorized J-Rig trips or 5.5–16-day oar boat trips (full canyon)
Arizona Raft Adventures azraft.com (800) 786-RAFT • (928) 526-8200	April–October 6–16 Days $2,085–4,230	Raft Dory J-Rig	Motorized, hybrid (one paddle raft, the rest ride), & all-paddle trips offered • Also offers 15-day kayak trip
Arizona River Runners raftarizona.com (800) 477-7238 • (602) 867-4866	April–October 3–13 Days $1,283–3,595	Dory J-Rig	Offers 3–8-day motorized J-Rig trips or 6–13-day oar-powered trips •Transportation not included in cost
Canyon Explorations/Expeditions canyonexplorations.com (800) 654-0723 • (928) 774-4559	April–October 6–17 Days $1,965–4,400	Raft J-Rig	Hybrid and all-paddle trips • Hard-shelled kayakers can join tours for an additional $200 •Transportation included in cost
Canyoneers canyoneers.com (800) 525-0924 • (928) 526-0924	April–September 3–14 Days $1,159–3,600	Raft Dory J-Rig	3–7-day motorized J-Rig trips or 6–14-day oar-powered trips •Transportation included in cost
Colorado River & Trail Expeditions crateinc.com (800) 253-7328 • (801) 261-1789	April–October 3–14 Days $1,480–3,450	Raft Dory J-Rig	Natural history, hiking trips, helicopter take outs or fly-ins are offered •Transportation included in cost
Colorado River Discovery raftthecanyon.com (888) 522-6644 • (928) 645-9175	March–November Half-day $92	J-Rig	This trip does not pass through the Grand Canyon • It begins at Glenn Canyon Dam • Scenery is still impressive
Grand Canyon Expeditions gcex.com (800) 544-2691 • (435) 644-2691	April–September 8–16 Days $2,750–4,399	Dory J-Rig	Specialized geology, photography, history, and ecology trips are offered •Transportation included in cost
Grand Canyon Whitewater grandcanyonwhitewater.com (800) 343-3121 • (928) 779-2979	April–October 4–13 Days $1,300–3,730	Raft J-Rig	Motorized J-Rig or oar-powered trips • Hike-out trips are offered •Transportation is optional
Hualapai River Runners grandcanyonwest.com (928) 769-2219	March–October 1 Day $188	J-Rig	Only single day trip in the Canyon, but there are additional fees (taxes, fuel surcharges, etc.)
Hatch River Expeditions hatchriverexpeditions.com (800) 856-8966 • (928) 526-4700	April–September 4–12 Days $1,326–3,988	Dory J-Rig	A smaller variety of motorized and oar-powered trips •They also offer kayak support (gear transport, etc.)
O.A.R.S. Grand Canyon oars.com (800) 346-6277 • (209) 736-4677	April–October 4–18 Days $2,379–5,561	Raft Dory	Wide variety of raft and dory trips with additional side-canyon hikes along the way • Transportation included
Outdoors Unlimited outdoorsunlimited.com (800) 637-7238 • (928) 526-4546	April–September 5–15 Days $1,820–4,120	Raft	Oar-powered and all-paddle trips of lower, upper, and full canyon •Transportation not included in cost
Tour West twriver.com (800) 453-9107 • (801) 225-0755	April–September 3–12 Days $1,475–3,850	Dory J-Rig	3-, 6-, and 8-night motorized J-Rig trips or 12-night oar-powered trip • Group and family discounts are available
Western River Expeditions westernriver.com (800) 453-7450 • (801) 942-6669	May–September 3–7 Days $1,299–2,999	J-Rig	3-, 4-, and 7-day motorized J-Rig trips • Transfers and transport, including helicopter (if required), included in cost

The Kolb Brothers

The Kolb Brothers

Beginning in 1904, Emery and Ellsworth Kolb ran a small photography studio at the South Rim, near Bright Angel Trailhead. Their main source of income came from taking photos of mule riders as they made their descent into the canyon. Emery often boasted that the two of them had "taken more pictures of men and mules than any other living man." And it was not an easy accomplishment. A clean water supply was needed to develop the pictures, but the closest reliable source was 4.5 miles and 3,000 feet below the rim. The Kolb brothers hiked this route countless times between 1904, when their studio was constructed, and 1932 when clean water became available on the rim. During this period, one brother took pictures of the mule riders descending into the canyon, and then raced down the trail to Indian Gardens, where the pictures were developed in a makeshift dark room. Once finished, he raced back to the rim, arriving just before the mule train returned from the bottom.

Adept oarsmen and explorers at heart, the Kolb brothers set out to retrace Major John Wesley Powell's journey from Green River, Wyoming through the Grand Canyon all the way to California. First to accomplish this feat since Powell in 1869, they even captured the epic adventure on film. Together, they penned a book and took the finished film on the East Coast lecture circuit. Emery started spending more time with his family and on personal adventures (like running the Black Canyon of the Gunnison • page 348), stressing the brothers' business relationship. Soon they decided to go their separate ways, and the only fair way to determine who would leave the canyon was to flip a coin. Emery won a best of three. He kept the studio and continued to show the film of their whitewater adventure until his death in 1976. Kolb Studio remains today. The restored building houses history and art exhibits.

Mule Rides

Modern mule riders aren't photographed by the energetic Kolb brothers, but they still descend into the mile-deep gorge from both of the canyon's rims. **Xanterra Parks & Resorts** (grandcanyonlodges.com) offers a one- or two-night mule trip down and back up Bright Angel Trail (**South Rim**), spending the night(s) at historic Phantom Ranch (see next page). A one night ride costs $961 for two people. Each additional person is $423. The two night ride costs $1,292 for two people. Each additional person costs $530. Fees include tax, breakfast, lunch, a steak dinner, and lodging. If you aren't interested in the steep descent or spending more than 10 hours in the saddle, there's a 3-hour trip ($135 per person) through Grand Canyon Village to Abyss Overlook.

South Rim mule trips are offered year-round. Riders must be at least 4'7" tall, weigh no more than 200 pounds, and speak fluent English (for the mules to understand commands). Everyone must check-in at Bright Angel Transportation Desk at least two hours prior to the scheduled departure time. **Overnight trips must be reserved and purchased in advance.** Reservations can be made up to 13 months in advance by calling Xanterra's reservations center at (888) 297-2757 or (303) 297-2757 (outside the U.S.). They fill early, so plan ahead.

On the **North Rim**, **Canyon Trail Rides** takes guests on 1-hour and half-day trips. One-hour rides cost $45 per person and follow the rim of the canyon along Ken Patrick Trail. Riders must be at least 7 years of age and weigh no more than 220 pounds. There are

Bright Angel Trail from Trail-
view Overlook (South Rim)

two choices for half-day trips. One stays above the rim following the 1-hour tour route and continuing around Uncle Jim Loop Trail. Alternatively, sure-footed mules lead riders into the canyon via North Kaibab Trail to Supai Tunnel, where you turn around and return to the rim. Both half-day tours cost $90 per person. Riders must be at least 10 years of age and weigh no more than 200 pounds. A shuttle bus to the trailhead leaves Grand Canyon Lodge a half-hour before trip departure. Trip departure times are typically 7:30 or 8:30 in the morning. North Rim mule rides are offered from mid-May through mid-October. Contact Canyon Trail Rides (435.679.8665, canyonrides.com) for reservations.

Phantom Ranch

One of the most unique experiences at the Grand Canyon is spending a night on the canyon's floor at Phantom Ranch. Located along Bright Angel Creek near the junction of North Kaibab, South Kaibab, and Bright Angel Trails, the only way to reach this secluded getaway is by foot, mule, or river. Designed by Mary Colter and constructed in 1922, the ranch's intent was, and still is, to provide food, lodging, and comfort to backcountry visitors.

Phantom Ranch offers men's and women's dormitories ($49/person) and 2–10 person cabins with shared showers. Hot meals and souvenirs are available for purchase. Meals cost anywhere from $20 for breakfast to $44 for a steak dinner. All meals must be reserved in advance and are served at a designated time. If you think you might be interested in souvenirs, be sure to leave space in your backpack for them. You don't have to carry your own gear; a duffel service is available for about $70 each way.

South Rim hikers are forced to make the difficult decision of which trail to take into and out of the canyon (South Kaibab in and Bright Angel out is recommended). Remember, South Kaibab Trail, although shorter, is extremely steep and strenuous with no clean water source available along the way. Pack plenty of water or take Bright Angel Trail.

Phantom Ranch is operated by Xanterra Parks & Resorts. Demand far exceeds capacity. Reservations are recommended and can be made up to 13 months in advance at (888) 297-2757. If you weren't able to secure reservations, consider inquiring about cancellations during your park visit.

South Kaibab Trail (South Rim)

Backpacking

The park is broken into four management zones. The **Corridor Zone** is recommended for hikers without previous experience at Grand Canyon. These popular trails are well-maintained and feature toilets, signs, and emergency phones. Ranger stations are also found along the way. Corridor trails include North and South Kaibab and Bright Angel Trails. All camping within the Corridor Zone must be done at designated campgrounds. Indian Garden (4.6 miles from the rim) and Bright Angel (9.6 miles) Campgrounds are located on Bright Angel Trail. Cottonwood Campground is located on North Kaibab Trail, 6.8 miles from the North Rim and 7.2 miles from Bright Angel Campground. There are no designated campsites along South Kaibab Trail.

Experienced Grand Canyon hikers may want to explore the park's **Threshold**, **Primitive**, and **Wild Zones**. Trails in these areas are either non-maintained or non-existent. Camping is available at designated sites or wherever you can find a flat space. Reliable water sources are often scarce or non-existent.

Backcountry Permits

All overnight camping trips outside the developed campgrounds require a backcountry permit. The park receives far more permit requests than it issues, so backcountry users, especially those hoping to visit during summer, should apply in advance. Applications are accepted no earlier than the first of the month four months prior to the proposed start of your trip. For example, if you're planning a trip for June, whether it starts on the 1st or the 30th, your application will be accepted beginning February 1. All fax and mail applications must be received at least three weeks in advance of the trip date; only in-person requests are accepted within 21 days of your proposed departure date. A permit request form can be found online. Permit requests may be submitted by fax (928.638.2125), through the mail, or in person at the North or South Rim Backcountry Information Center (BIC). The South Rim's BIC (928.638.7875) is open daily from 8am–noon and 1–5pm. The North Rim BIC holds the same operating hours, but it closes for winter from mid-October until mid-May.

The park responds to all permits via mail in the order they were received. Allow at least three weeks for a response. Successful applicants who have met the fee requirements will receive their permit at the time of response. Permit fees include a $10 non-refundable application fee plus $8 per person per night camped below the rim or $8 per group camped above the rim. These fees do not include the park entrance fee. Cancellations received three or more days prior to the start of your trip will receive a credit towards a future trip reserved within one year. In addition to the possibility of cancelled trips, the park holds a limited number of walk-up permits for corridor campgrounds (Indian Garden, Bright Angel, and Cottonwood). Walk-up permits are issued for a maximum of two nights. They are only issued in person and cannot be purchased earlier than one day prior to departure date.

South Rim – When to Go

Grand Canyon's South Rim is open all year. So are camping, lodging and dining facilities. Visitor Information Centers hold seasonal hours, but are usually open from 8am to 5pm with extended hours in summer. Visitation is high from March through October, peaking in summer when hotels are often booked a year in advance. Viewpoints are congested. Shuttle buses are full. (Popular activities like mule rides and river rafting also need to be booked well in advance.) The heat (particularly in the canyon) is unbearable. Try visiting during spring or fall when crowds are slightly thinner and the weather is more comfortable. Winter can also be an amazing time to visit. Lodging rates are reduced, and, if you're fortunate, you may see a beautiful white and red canyon thanks to a dusting of snow.

South Rim – Transportation & Airports

Amtrak (800.872.7245, amtrak.com) provides train service to Williams and Flagstaff, AZ. McCarran International (LAS) in Las Vegas, NV (270 miles away); Sky Harbor International (PHX) in Phoenix, AZ (225 miles); and Pulliam (FLG) in Flagstaff, AZ (82 miles) are the closest large commercial airports. Car rental is available at each destinations. A few airlines direct service to Grand Canyon Airport (866.235.9422, grandcanyonairlines.com). Car rental is not available, but there is shuttle and taxi service to the South Rim. Arizona Shuttle (877.226.8060, arizonashuttle.com) provides service between Flagstaff and Grand Canyon twice daily. Grand Canyon Shuttles (888.226.3105, grandcanyonshuttles.com) provides regular service between Flagstaff and the Grand Canyon, as well as rim-to-rim transfers. See page 437 for train excursions.

South Rim – Park Shuttle

A **free shuttle service** is available at the South Rim to help reduce traffic congestion and pollution. There are a total of four shuttle loops. Schedules do change, so it's best to refer to the South Rim Pocket Map you'll receive at the entrance. **Hermit's Rest Route** runs from March through November, stopping at viewpoints along Hermit Road. (Note that Rim Trail also provides access to Hermit Road viewpoints. So, if there's a long line at the bus stop near Bright Angel Trailhead, just walk down Rim Trail and enjoy the views.) **Tusayan Route** runs between Tusayan and Grand Canyon Visitor Center from early May until early October. **Village Route** runs all year and connects all Grand Canyon Village's lodging, restaurants, gift shops, and campgrounds. **Kaibab/Rim Route** runs year-round, and it takes riders to canyon viewpoints, South Kaibab Trailhead, and Yavapai Geology Museum. All shuttle buses run every 10–15 minutes during the day and about every 30 minutes the hour before sunrise and the hour after sunset. Buses are equipped with bike racks.

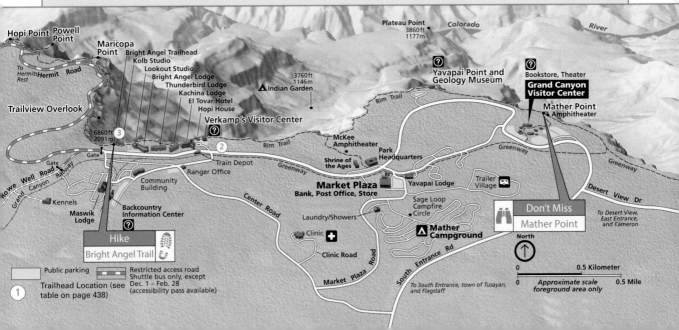

Desert View

South Rim – Directions

Whether you're arriving at the South Rim from the east or west, you'll most likely be taking I-40. Travelers passing through Flagstaff can also take US-180, which merges with AZ-64 and heads into the park.

From I-40: Heading east or west on I-40, take Exit 165 for AZ-64 toward Williams/Grand Canyon. Head north on AZ-64 for about 55 miles. You'll pass through Tusayan and into the park. Shortly thereafter, Grand Canyon Village will come into view on your left (west).

South Rim Camping & Lodging

Lodging accommodations range from **Bright Angel Lodge's** basic rooms with shared bathrooms to **El Tovar Hotel's** modern luxury suites. But these lodging facilities aren't about the accommodations; they're about the location. All lodges are located in Grand Canyon Village, and **Maswik** and **Yavapai** are the only ones not situated directly on the canyon's rim. Ideal location and convenience comes at a premium. Rooms on the rim with a private bath cost at least $207/night. Still, the demand is great. If you want to stay on the rim, you should make reservations well in advance, especially if you're traveling during summer. Reservations are accepted up to one year in advance. Campgrounds also tend to fill to capacity. There are **three developed campgrounds** at the South Rim. Reservations can be made up to six months in advance at Mather Campground and its neighbor, Trailer Village. Desert View Campground, located 25 miles east of the village on Desert View Road, has 50 sites available on a first-come, first-served basis. Please refer to page 454 for lodging and dining facilities outside the park.

South Rim Camping (Fees are per night)

Name	Location	Open	Fee	Notes
Mather*	Grand Canyon Village	All Year	$18 (peak) $15 (winter)	Laundry and showers available • No hookups, 30-ft max length
Trailer Village#	Grand Canyon Village	All Year	$41	Full hookups • No wood fires
Desert View -	25 miles east of Grand Canyon Village	mid-April–mid-Oct	$12	First-come, first-served, flush toilets, no hookups, 30-ft max length

*Campground reservations can be made at recreation.gov or (877) 444-6777
#Campground reservations can be made at visitgrandcanyon.com or (877) 404-4611

Backcountry	Permitted at designated sites or at-large areas • See page 434 for permit (fee) details

South Rim Lodging (Fees are per night)

Name	Open	Fee	Notes
Bright Angel Lodge*	All Year	$93–447	Basic rooms have shared bathroom and shower
El Tovar Hotel* -	All Year	$207–513	Premier lodging at the Grand Canyon • Exceptional views
Kachina Lodge*	All Year	$215–243	Identical to Thunderbird • Check-in at El Tovar
Thunderbird Lodge* -	All Year	$215–243	Check-in at Bright Angel Lodge
Maswik Lodge*	All Year	$93–205	Motel-style rooms, cabins available in summer
Yavapai Lodge#	All Year	$124–206	Largest lodge in the park • 198 rooms

All lodging facilities are located in Grand Canyon Village. Reservations are accepted up to one year in advance.
*Make advance reservations at (888) 297-2757 or grandcanyonlodges.com.
#Make advance reservations at (877) 404-4611 or visitgrandcanyon.com
Restaurants, market place, post office, clinic, bank, and pet kennel are available in the Village.

Nankoweap Granaries

Flightseeing

The Grand Canyon's size, depth, and remoteness are best understood when viewed from above. Airplane and helicopter pilots provide that unique perspective, but they must adhere to a few restrictions, including the fact more than 75% of park airspace is off-limits to help reduce noise pollution.

Several companies provide **helicopter** (slower and lower) and **airplane** (faster and higher) **tours** from Grand Canyon Airport in Tusayan. Grand Canyon Airlines (866.235.9422, grandcanyonairlines.com, $159/person for 40–45 minutes) and Papillon Grand Canyon Helicopters (888.635.7272, papillon.com, $139–149/person for 40–50 minutes) offer airplane tours. Maverick (800.541.4537, maverickhelicopter.com, $175–299/person for 40–50 minutes) and Pappilon ($139–289/person for 30–50 minutes) offer helicopter tours. All these companies offer a variety of package tours including additional land and water activities. Several offer trips departing Page, AZ and Las Vegas, NV. Visit their websites for a complete list of activities.

Biking

Bicycles are allowed on all roads open to vehicles. Roads are heavily-trafficked, and narrow with little to no shoulder, making it best to bike in the early morning before motorists come out to sightsee (or stick to Hermit's Rest Road). All South Rim shuttle buses are equipped with bike racks, allowing easy bike transportation from one area to another without having to pedal. **Bike rental and guided tours** are available at Bright Angel Bicycle (928.814.8704, bikegrandcanyon. com) in Grand Canyon Village. Guided tours provide an opportunity to learn more about the canyon as you pedal along Hermit's Rest Road. Tours (2–2.5 hours) cost $48/adult, $38/child under 17, and include bike rental, helmet, and roundtrip shuttle. Bike rental costs $12 for one hour, $30 for four hours, and $40 for a full day. Trailers and kid's rates are available. The bike shop is closed in winter.

Train Excursions

Santa Fe Railroad and the locomotive played a major role in the canyon's initial promotion, only to be run off the rim by the automobile. But over the past 50 years, increased tourism, congested roadways, and nostalgia have sparked resurgence in train passenger service to Grand Canyon.

Grand Canyon Railway (800.843.8724, 303.843.8724, thetrain.com) operates restored locomotives that travel from Williams, AZ directly to South Rim's Grand Canyon Village. The trip takes about 2 hours and is complete with strolling musicians, staged robberies, and shoot-outs. A roundtrip coach class ticket costs $79 for adults and $47 for children. First class seats cost $152/adult and $118/child. Observation Dome and Luxury Parlor Class cost $219 per adult, and children under the age of 15 are not permitted in these cars. Grand Canyon Railway is operated by Xanterra Parks & Resorts. A variety of rail and lodging packages are also available.

Yaki Point

South Rim Hiking

Many visitors are happy to revel in the Grand Canyon's glory from one of many well-placed viewpoints along the South Rim. Others want to immerse themselves in the canyon, hiking as far and deep as weather, attitude, and water supply allow. At the South Rim, there are three primary inner canyon hikes. **Bright Angel**, located at the west end of Grand Canyon Village near Bright Angel Lodge, is the most popular. While it's the favorite route for rim-to-rim hikers and backpackers, it also provides excellent day-hiking opportunities. Consider taking it 3 miles (roundtrip) to 1.5-Mile Resthouse or 6 miles (roundtrip) to 3-Mile Resthouse. Clean water and a restroom are available from May to October at each resthouse, and year-round a little farther down the trail at Indian Garden.

South Kaibab Trail, located near Yaki Point off Desert View Drive, is the most direct route to the canyon floor. It's steep and strenuous, but the views from the cliffside trail and open promontories are extraordinary. Day hikers can choose to hike to Ooh-Aah Point (1.8 miles roundtrip), Cedar Ridge (3 miles), or Skeleton Point (6 miles). Water is not available along South Kaibab Trail, so fill your bottle or hydration system before hopping aboard the shuttle bus to the trailhead. Plenty of hikers day-hike to the floor, but it isn't recommended.

For a more primitive inner canyon hiking experience, try Hermit or Grandview Trails. **Hermit Trail** is located at the west end of Hermit's Rest Road. **Grandview Trail** is located at Grandview Point on Desert View Drive. Both offer some of the finest canyon views in the park, but are unmaintained and without water. Grandview Trail is steep (and a little suspect) at the beginning before levelling out. Note that it doesn't reach the canyon floor.

Do not overestimate your physical fitness level. Expect hiking out of the canyon to take twice the time it took to hike in (watch the time and plan accordingly). **Hundreds of visitors are rescued from the canyon each year**, most suffering from heat exhaustion or dehydration. Carry plenty of water, allot ample time for your hike, use a bit of common sense, and you'll love the experience. If you're daunted by the inner canyon, **Rim Trail** from Grand Canyon Village to Hermit's Rest is for you. It is South Rim's only above-rim hiking trail, and it conveniently follows a shuttle route, so you can hop aboard a bus whenever it suits you.

Grand Canyon Field Institute offers educational hiking/backpacking classes. For details call (866) 471-4435 or click grandcanyon.org/fieldinstitute. Courses cost about $100 per day and discounts are available for Grand Canyon Association Members.

South Rim Hiking Trails (Distances are one-way)			
Name	Location (# on map)	Length	Difficulty Rating & Notes
Hermit	Hermit's Rest (1)	10.3 miles	S – Unmaintained trail to the Colorado River
Rim	Grand Canyon Village (2)	0–12.8 miles	E – Mostly level, follows the canyon's rim
Bright Angel - 🥾	Bright Angel Trailhead (3)	9.6 miles	S – Steep! South Rim's most popular hike
South Kaibab - 🥾	South Kaibab Trailhead (4)	7.3 miles	S – Shortest route to the canyon floor
Grandview - 🥾	Grandview Point/Trailhead (5)	3.2 miles	S – Starts steep, flattens out, 2,300-ft descent
Difficulty Ratings: E = Easy, M = Moderate, S = Strenuous			

Visitor Centers & Museums

Kolb Studio: The former home and business of the Kolb Brothers has been restored to house free art exhibits and a bookstore. The Studio is located in Grand Canyon Village's Historic District at Bright Angel Trailhead. (Open daily, 8am–6pm)

Verkamp's Visitor Center: Occupying one of the oldest buildings on the South Rim, Verkamp's Visitor Center now features displays telling the history of Grand Canyon Village. A bookstore and information desk are available. (Open daily, 8am–6pm)

Yavapai Geology Museum: Interested in geology, or just curious about the canyon? If so, stop at the park's Geology Museum located one mile east of Market Plaza. (Open daily, 8am–6pm)

Canyon View Information Plaza: Located near Mather Point, this is the best spot to begin your trip to the South Rim. The complex contains several outdoor exhibits, a visitor center, theater, and bookstore. Parking is limited, but the park's free shuttle system also provides transportation to Canyon View Information Plaza. (Open daily, 8am–6pm)

Tusayan Ruins and Museum: This free museum explores more than 10,000 years of cultural history. Ancient artifacts include projectile points, split-twig figurines, pottery, and a small Ancestral Puebloan ruins site. The museum is located three miles west of Desert View. (Open daily, 9am–5pm)

Desert View Visitor Center: Located at the eastern end of Desert View Drive, this small visitor center houses a collection of art inspired by the Grand Canyon. Find your own inspiration by viewing the Colorado River from Desert View Watchtower, originally designed by Mary Colter and built in 1932. A bookstore is also available. (Open daily, 9am–5pm)

All of the locations listed above are open every day of the year. Hours vary seasonally, but expect these facilities to be open during the listed hours of operation, with extended hours in summer.

Ranger Programs

A visit to any national park isn't complete without participating in at least one of the famous ranger programs. All programs are free and most are located in and around Grand Canyon Village. There are a few special events that take place at Desert View, Tusayan Museum, and Phantom Ranch. You'll find regularly scheduled walks and talks that explore the area's geology, history, and ecology. Check the current schedule of ranger-guided activities online or at a visitor center. All of these tours are highly recommended, and you're sure to come away with a new appreciation for one of the world's most remarkable natural wonders.

For Kids

Children have the opportunity to become official **Grand Canyon National Park Junior Rangers**. To become a member of this exclusive group, pick up a free activity booklet from any of the locations listed to the left and complete the activities required for your age group. Upon completion, bring the booklet back to a visitor center for review. If successful, children ages 4–7 will receive the Raven Award, children ages 8–10 receive the Coyote Award, and children 11 and up receive the Scorpion Award. There is a special prize for children ages 4–14 who complete the booklet's activities and make a trip to Phantom Ranch. The park also offers three family oriented summer programs: **Adventure Hike**, **Discovery Pack**, and **Junior Ranger Programs for Families**. Check out the park website or stop in at a visitor center for additional information.

Other Excursions

A trip to the **IMAX Theater** (page 458) or walking Skywalk (grandcanyonskywalk.com) is included in many families' vacation plans. **Skywalk** is expensive ($81 in total fees), inconvenient (accessed via a 10-mile dirt road), and unrecordable (cameras are not allowed). Save your time and money and check out some of South Rim's free hiking trails (page 438) and ranger programs instead.

On the other hand, visiting **Havasu Falls**, one of the United States' finest swimming holes, is worth the time, effort, and money. However, it's not easy to get to. Taking all paved roads from Grand Canyon Village, it's 195

Grandview Trail

Best of the South Rim

Overlook: Hopi Point
  Runner-up: Shoshone Point
  2nd Runner-up: Powell Point
  3rd Runner-up: Lipan Point

Hike: South Kaibab
  Runner-up: Bright Angel
  2nd Runner-up: Grandview

miles to the falls' trailhead. Leave South Rim via AZ-64/US-180, heading south. Head west on I-40 about 45 miles to Exit 121 toward AZ-66/Seligman/Peach Springs. Turn right at Interstate 40 Business Loop E. After about 1 mile, take another right onto AZ-66. Continue another 30 miles to a T-intersection. Turn right onto Hualapai Hilltop Highway. After 43 miles you will come to the trailhead to Havasu Canyon. From here, it's another 8 miles by foot, mule, or helicopter.

All visitors must have advance reservations at the campground or lodge. There's a $35/person entrance fee, plus a $17/person/night campground fee, and an additional $5/person environmental care fee. Tack on 10% tax and you are "free" to hike to the falls. Those who arrive without a reservation will be charged double. Note that a flood in 2008 drastically altered existing waterfalls and created new ones in the area. For more information click havasupaitribe.com.

South Rim – Vacation Planner

Grand Canyon's South Rim is one of the busiest areas in the entire collection of national parks. With an abundance of tourism comes a huge variety of commercial attractions and activities. You can take a **mule** into the canyon (page 432), spend two

weeks **rafting** the river (page 430), ride above it in a **helicopter** (page 437), or **camp in the park's backcountry** (page 434). All of these activities take considerable planning and preparation and are difficult to account for in this sample itinerary. Exclude these grand adventures, and a trip to the South Rim becomes fairly simple. Here's the best the canyon has to offer all in one action packed day. Nearby dining, grocery stores, lodging, festivals, and attractions are listed on pages 454–459.

Day 1: If you didn't already check a schedule of ranger programs, stop in at a visitor center to see what's happening. If you haven't been on a ranger program before, the Grand Canyon is a great place to do it. There's a ton of interesting geology and history going on in and on top of these heavily eroded rocks. The first viewpoint you should stop at is **Mather Point**, named after Stephen Mather, the first director of the National Park Service. For slightly less congested canyon viewing try **Yaki Point** or **Maricopa Point**, a short distance east and west, respectively of Canyon Village (shuttle rides required). Be sure to check out **Powell and Hopi Points** while at Maricopa Point, both extend into the canyon a short distance to rocky promontories. These viewpoints are accessed via **Hermit's Rest Shuttle Route** or consider hiking **Rim Trail**, which connects Hermit's Rest and Grand Canyon Village. Hermit's Rest Shuttle Transfer is located near Bright Angel Trailhead, while Rim Trail runs all the way from Yaki Point to Hermit's Rest. If you have enough time, **Lipan Point** and **Desert View** offer differing perspectives, with substantial views of the Colorado River. While the road to **Shoshone Point** (near Yaki Point) is gated, you can still walk down it!

To truly appreciate the canyon, hike into it via **Bright Angel or South Kaibab Trail.** (We prefer South Kaibab, but both are uniquely compelling.) The park's official line is to not day-hike beyond Cedar Ridge, but if you're in decent physical condition and carry ample water (know your body!), you should be able to make the trek to **Skeleton Point** and back (6 miles) without a problem. Allow at least one hour per mile, and time yourself as you descend. Expect it to take twice as long to climb out of the canyon as it took to get in.

North Rim – When to Go

The North Rim is open from mid-May until the first heavy snowfall in November. Facilities, including the lodge and campground, are open between mid-May and mid-October. During this time, the visitor center is open daily from 8am to 6pm. Summer is the busiest time of year, but only 10% of Grand Canyon's guests come here. Fall, when leaves change colors, is one of the most pleasant times to visit. The park road closes for winter, but that doesn't keep determined snowshoers and cross-country skiers out. A yurt is provided near North Kaibab Trailhead. It sleeps six, and is outfitted with chairs, table, and a wood-burning stove. A portable toilet is located nearby. The yurt can be reserved beginning the Monday after Thanksgiving until mid-April. Reservation and backcountry permit (page 434) are required.

North Rim – Transportation & Airports

Public transportation does not provide service to or around the North Rim, but there is a rim-to-rim shuttle service (page 423). The closest large commercial airports are McCarran International (LAS) in Las Vegas, NV, located 275 miles to the west, and Salt Lake City International (SLC), located 397 miles north of the park.

North Rim – Directions

Visitors can easily see from one rim to the other. The distance is usually no more than 10 miles. Hikers frequently descend into the canyon and emerge on the opposite rim after less than 25 miles on foot. But, by car it's a 210-mile, 4.5-hour trip: a long, but scenic journey. You can drive yourself or hop aboard the Transcanyon Shuttle (page 423). Directions are also provided below for those traveling north or south on I-15.

From South Rim (210 miles): Follow AZ-64/East Rim Drive out of the park. After 52 miles, you'll reach the small town of Cameron. Turn left onto US-89 N. Continue for another 58 miles, where you'll turn left at US-89 Alt N. After 55 miles, you'll reach a Y-intersection with AZ-67. Turn left onto AZ-67 and head south for 43 miles. Continue into the park.

From Las Vegas (256 miles): Heading east on I-15, take Exit 16 for UT-9 toward Hurricane/Zion National Park. Turn right onto UT-9 heading east. After about 10 miles, take a right onto S 100 E. Almost immediately take the first left onto UT-59. Follow UT-59 across the Utah–Arizona border where the road becomes AZ-389. After 54 miles on UT-59/AZ-389, you will reach Fredonia, turn right at US-89 Alt S. Continue south for 30 miles and then turn right at AZ-67, which leads to the North Rim.

From Salt Lake City (380 miles): Heading south on I-15, take Exit 95 for UT-20 toward US-89/Panguitch/Kanab. Turn left onto UT-20 E. Continue for 20 miles until the road terminates at US-89. Turn right onto US-89. Follow US-89 south for 76 miles to Kanab, UT. Here, US-89 follows Center St and S 100 E through the city. Do not follow US-89 to the east. Take US-89 Alt south and continue south for 36 miles to the Y-intersection with AZ-67. Turn right onto AZ-67 and continue for 43 miles into the park.

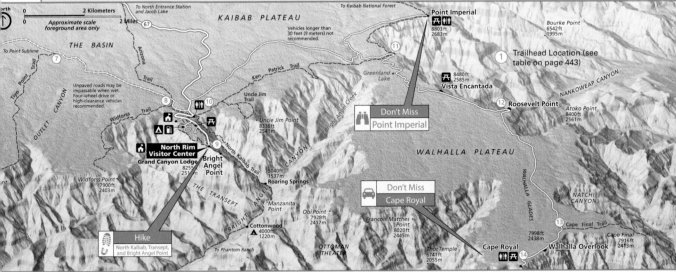

North Rim Camping & Lodging

It's easier to choose overnight accommodations on the North Rim. If you want to sleep in a bed, you'll have to stay at **Grand Canyon Lodge**. Perched atop Bright Angel Point, the lodge provides exceptional canyon views from a handful of cozy cabins (designed to sleep 3–4 guests) or basic motel rooms with one queen-sized bed. You'll find dining services to match your hunger and schedule. The Dining Room is a more formal setting where breakfast, lunch, and dinner are served. A dinner entrée averages about $20, and the view is generally more memorable than the food (note that the view is really, really good). Deli in the Pines offers quick meals. Coffee Saloon and Rough Rider Saloon offer beverages and snacks. Between June and September, the lodge holds daily **Grand Canyon Cookout Experiences**, providing outdoor dining with a hearty meal and entertainment. Tickets cost $35 for adults and $22 for children (6–15 years old). Reservations for the Grand Canyon Cookout Experience can be made from mid-May to late September by calling (928) 638-2611.

North Rim is the only campground. Standard sites cost $18/night or you can upgrade to a premium site (bordering Transept Canyon) for $25/night. All 90 campsites feature picnic tables and campfire rings. Coin-operated **showers** and **laundry** and a gas/service station are available near its entrance. Whether staying at the lodge or campground, it is recommended you reserve space early. Rooms and campsites are usually booked months in advance, especially during summer. See page 456 for nearby camping and lodging alternatives.

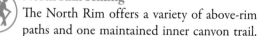

North Rim Hiking

The North Rim offers a variety of above-rim paths and one maintained inner canyon trail. **Ken Patrick, Uncle Jim, Widforss, and Transept Trails** begin at or near North Rim Visitor Center and stay above the canyon's rim. One short trail every visitor should hike is the 0.5-mile jaunt to Bright Angel Point. Bridle Trail is the only path that allows bikes and pets. Point Imperial, one of the best locations to watch the sunrise, is located a few miles drive from the visitor center. Head north on AZ-67 as if you were going to exit the park. After the large S-curve, turn right onto Fuller Canyon Road and continue east until it intersects Point Imperial Road. Turn left and drive to its end, where you'll find **Point Imperial Trail**. It's an easy 4-mile hike through forest burned more than a decade ago to the park's northern boundary. At the Fuller Road/Point Imperial Road intersection you can also turn right onto Cape Royal Road. The view from **Cape Royal** is fantastic (there's a backcountry campsite here, too). Four short and relatively easy trails are located nearby.

North Kaibab is the North Rim's only inner canyon trail. It's a good place to begin a rim-to-rim hike because you spare 1,000 feet of elevation gain, or to day-hike to Supai Tunnel (3.4 miles, roundtrip) or Roaring Springs (6.0 miles). North Kaibab is the most difficult and least visited of the park's three corridor trails. Potable water is available at the trailhead, Supai Tunnel, Roaring Springs, the Pumphouse Residence, Cottonwood Campground, and Bright Angel Campground. Still, carry plenty of water and expect your ascent to take twice as long as your descent.

North Rim Camping (Fees are per night)

Name	Location	Open	Fee	Notes
North Rim* - ⚬	AZ-67	mid-May–mid-October	$18–25	Showers and laundry available, dump station, no hookups • Canyon view sites more expensive
*Campground reservations can be made at recreation.gov or (877) 444-6777				
Backcountry	Permitted at designated sites or at-large areas • See page 434 for permit (fee) details			

North Rim Lodging (Fees are per night)

Name	Open	Fee	Notes
Grand Canyon Lodge - ⚬ (At the end of AZ-67)**	mid-May–mid-October	$130–190	Small, rustic cabins or motel-style rooms are available • North Rim's only lodging
**Lodging reservations can be made in advance at grandcanyonlodgenorth.com or (877) 386-4383			

Point Imperial

North Rim Hiking Trails (Distances are roundtrip unless noted otherwise)

Name	Location (# on map)	Length	Difficulty Rating & Notes
Thunder River	Forest Road 292/Monument Point/Bill Hall Trailhead (6)	15.2 miles	S – Backpacking Opportunities • Follows Tapeats Creek to Colorado River (steep)
Tiyo Point	Point Sublime Road (7)	12.5 miles	M – Above-rim out-and-back to Tiyo Point
Widforss	Point Sublime Road (8)	10.0 miles	M – Self-guiding through forest
Bright Angel Pt. - ♿	Near Visitor Center (9)	0.5 mile	E – Paved, self-guiding trail to viewpoint
Transept - ♿	Lodge & Campground (9, 10)	3.0 miles	E – Flat, connects camp and lodge
Bridle	Grand Canyon Lodge/North Kaibab (9)	2.4 miles	E – Connects lodge to North Kaibab
Ken Patrick	North Kaibab/Point Imperial (10, 11)	10.0 miles	M – Imperial Pt to North Kaibab (1-way)
Uncle Jim	Ken Patrick Trail (10)	5.0 miles	M – Loop overlooking canyon
North Kaibab - ♿	North Kaibab Trailhead on AZ-67 (10)	14.0 miles	S – Connects to Bright Angel (1-way)
Arizona	North Kaibab Trail (10)	10.0 miles	M – Spans from Utah to Mexico (1-way)
Point Imperial	Point Imperial Road (11)	4.0 miles	E – Fire-damaged forest to park border
Roosevelt Point	Cape Royal Road (12)	0.2 mile	E – Loop with excellent views
Cape Final	Cape Royal Road (13)	4.0 miles	E – Spectacular canyon overlook
Cliff Springs	Cape Royal Road (14)	1.0 mile	E – Puebloan granary and steep cliffs
Cape Royal - ♿	Cape Royal Road (14)	0.6 mile	E – Angel's Window and Colorado River

Difficulty Ratings: E = Easy, M = Moderate, S = Strenuous

Visitor Centers

North Rim Visitor Center, located next to Grand Canyon Lodge on Bright Angel Peninsula, offers park and regional information, restrooms, and a bookstore. It is open daily, mid-May to mid-October, from 8am–6pm. The visitor center is a great place to begin a trip to the North Rim. Park rangers are available to answer your questions, and interpretive exhibits help introduce you to the region.

Ranger Programs

Park rangers provide interpretive programs about the canyon and its environment between mid-May and mid-October. Most programs meet or take place at the Visitor Center or Grand Canyon Lodge. What's Rockin'? is a 30–40 minute talk about geology conducted at Grand Canyon Lodge's back porch. If you're busy hiking trails or admiring the panoramic views, you can always catch an evening program at North Rim Campground's amphitheater or Grand Canyon Lodge's auditorium.

For Kids

Children visiting the North Rim are invited to participate in the park's **Junior Ranger Program** (page 439). Free activity booklets are available at the visitor center.

North Rim – Vacation Planner

Receiving only 10% of all Grand Canyon visitors, a trip to the North Rim can be downright refreshing compared to the hubbub of South Rim. Hitting up the area's most popular attractions can easily be accomplished in a single day. Those interested in a backcountry adventure will require a longer visit, and a bit of preparation, **but the North Rim is without a doubt the superior location for backpackers.** In addition to a classic inner canyon route like North Kaibab Trail to Phantom Ranch (page 433) or Cottonwood Campground, there are a number of above-the-rim hiking trails (page 443) for backpackers to explore. All backcountry trips should be carefully planned with a good topographic map. Speak to a park ranger about water sources, permits, and trail conditions prior to departure.

Another great North Rim excursion is to drive (high-clearance required) the unpaved roads to **Toroweap Point,** the most dramatic overlook in the entire park. The trek is long and roads can be impassable if wet. Toroweap Point is accessed via a variety of routes on challenging roads from AZ-389. Camping at one of Toroweap's nine sites requires a permit and permitted campers must arrive before sunset. Come prepared, because there are no services and a tow from this area will cost upwards of $1,000. If interested, you should contact the park about road conditions and campsite availability. Toroweap is really cool and one of the best experiences you can have at the Grand Canyon, but a skilled driver is required.

For a more typical trip to the North Rim, here's a one-day sample itinerary. Also, remember that mule rides (page 432) are available on the North Rim. Nearby dining, grocery stores, lodging, festivals, and attractions are listed on pages 454–459.

Day 1: Stop at the visitor center and check what ranger programs are being offered (if you haven't checked online already). Try to plan around any activities that interest you. Once you've had your questions answered and curiosities satisfied, head outside and hike to **Bright Angel Point.** It's a short but rugged trail along a rocky ridgeline to outstanding views above Bright Angel Creek. **Transept Trail** is another excellent option. Return to your car and backtrack to Fuller Canyon Road. Stop at **Point Imperial,** and then head southeast on Cape Royal Road. **Wahalla Overlook** is worth a stop. **Wahalla Ruins,** a 1,000-year-old one-room structure, might be of interest to archeology buffs, but to the average person it looks like a pile of rubble. Skip it if you're short on time. Continue south on **Cape Royal** Road. From the road's end, hike 1 mile (roundtrip) to Cape Royal. This is a wonderful vantage point to watch the sunrise. If you want to get away from it all, this is the spot. Secure a backcountry permit for the campsite at Cape Final and you'll feel like you're alone in the park.

Flora & Fauna

Five of North America's seven life zones are represented at the Grand Canyon, and three of the continent's four deserts (Sonoran, Mojave, and Great Basin) converge at the canyon floor. These conditions create a diverse collection of wildlife. More than 355 species of birds, 89 mammal species, and 56 reptile and amphibian species reside in the park. Mule deer and bighorn sheep are the large mammals you're most likely to see. The largest and rarest bird in North America, the California condor, also lives here. The park offers special ranger programs that detail the reintroduction and current state of this endangered bird. Rocks are everywhere and among them is life. More than 1,737 species of vascular plants have been documented living within park boundaries. Such extreme diversity is due to the huge elevation change from rim to river and the amalgamation of ecosystems and deserts. The most prevalent plant community is desert scrub.

Pets

South Rim Visitors may walk their pets at all trails above the rim, Mather Campground, Desert View Campground, Trailer Village, and along all developed roadways and parking areas. The only location where pets are allowed at the North Rim is Bridle Trail, which connects Grand Canyon Lodge and North Kaibab Trail. Pets must be kept on a leash no more than six feet in length at all times and a kennel is available at Grand Canyon Village.

Accessibility

At the South Rim, accessibility permits are issued to individuals with mobility impairments so they can drive a private vehicle through areas closed to visitor traffic. Permits are free and can be obtained at most park facilities, including all entrance stations. To help reduce park congestion, these restricted areas are accessed via a free shuttle service (page 435). Only a few of the shuttles are accessible, but they can be requested with at least one day's notice by calling (928) 638-0591. Most South Rim facilities and viewpoints are accessible to wheelchair users, with the exception of Kolb Studios, Yaki Point, and South Kaibab Trailhead. Accessing locations like the Train Depot, the Community Building, and Park Headquarters requires assistance. All inner canyon trails are inaccessible. Free wheelchairs can be checked out for daily use from South Rim Visitor Center.

North Rim is more isolated and generally less accessible than the more popular South Rim. Grand Canyon Lodge, North Rim Visitor Center, and North Rim Campground are fully accessible. Bridle Trail and Point Imperial Overlook are also accessible to wheelchair users.

A few river outfitters (page 431) can accommodate wheelchair users. Contact them for details.

Weather

Temperatures at the Grand Canyon vary wildly, from day-to-day, rim-to-rim, and rim-to-floor. South Rim experiences comfortable summer highs, typically in the 80s°F. On average, temperature at the higher-elevation North Rim is 7°F cooler than the South Rim and 28°F cooler than the canyon floor. An arid climate and high elevation provide cool evenings. The South Rim's average summer lows are usually in the 50s°F, while the North Rim's drop into the 40s°F. Both rims are at high enough elevation to receive snow during winter, but winter is much more severe at the North Rim. In winter, average high temperatures drop into the 30s°F at the North Rim and 40s°F at the South Rim. It's also significantly wetter at the North Rim, receiving about 25 inches of precipitation each year compared to the South Rim's 15 inches. Seasonal patterns that typically occur in late summer and early winter contribute the majority of Grand Canyon precipitation. All visitors should come prepared for a variety of conditions. Dress in layers and carry a rain coat.

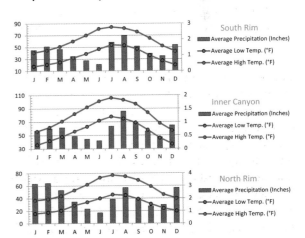

An ancient bristlecone pine and Wheeler Peak

Great Basin

100 Great Basin National Park
Baker, NV 89311
Phone: (775) 234-7331
Website: nps.gov/grba

Established: October 27, 1986
January 24, 1922 (Nat'l Monument)
Size: 77,180 Acres
Annual Visitors: 116,000
Peak Season: Summer
Hiking Trails: 65 Miles

Activities: Hiking, Backpacking,
Camping, Stargazing, Horseback
Riding, and Cave Tours ($8–10)

Campgrounds ($12/night):
Upper and Lower Lehman Creek,
Wheeler Peak, and Baker Creek
Free Primitive Camping along
Snake Creek and Strawberry Creek
Roads (high-clearance 4WD
required)
Backcountry Camping: Permitted

Park Hours: All day, every
day (except Wheeler Peak and
Lexington Arch Day-use Areas)
Entrance Fee: None

In east-central Nevada near the Utah border, a 13,000-foot mountain hides a brilliantly decorated cave. Both are protected by Great Basin National Park. The park itself is just a small portion of a much larger Great Basin region extending from the Sierra Nevada in California to the Wasatch Mountains in Utah. In between, mountains and valleys form dozens of smaller basins where rivers and streams are unable to drain into an ocean. All water flows inland, eventually collecting in shallow salt lakes, marshes, and mud flats where it evaporates. The region's aridity is well known, but beautiful and unique landscapes and life forms adapt and evolve to this harsh environment. Alpine lakes fed by snowmelt from the rocky slopes accent the high mountains, where groves of bristlecone pine have been defying the odds for thousands of years. Many of these twisted elders had already celebrated their 2,000th birthday by the time Christopher Columbus discovered America.

Americans would make an indelible mark on Great Basin. In 1855, Ezra Williams claimed to be the first white man to summit the tallest mountain in the central Great Basin, naming it Williams Peak. Shortly after, Lieutenant Colonel Edward Steptoe named the same mountain Jeff Davis Peak in honor of his superior, Secretary of War Jefferson Davis. When Jefferson Davis became President of the Confederate States of America, some cartographers began to regret the name. "Union Peak" was suggested as an alternative because a ridge united the mountain's twin summits, but it was an obvious jab at Jefferson Davis' secessionist leanings. Fortunately, map publication was postponed and in 1869 a military mapping expedition resulted in George Montague Wheeler climbing the mountain and naming its summit, definitively, "Wheeler Peak."

Eight years earlier, Absalom "Ab" Lehman moved to Snake Valley. Having experienced the highs and lows of mining in California and Australia, he decided to try his hand at ranching. By the time George Wheeler hiked to the top of Wheeler Peak, Lehman's ranch had 25–30 cows and an orchard. Prosperity and the loneliness of Ab's second wife, Olive Smith, prompted several family members to move into the area, and a community began to develop around Lehman Ranch. A butcher shop, blacksmith shop, carpenter shop, and milk house were established, and Absalom's orchard was regarded as the best in the region. Success allowed Ab to focus his attention on his ranch's latest addition, Lehman Caves. While exploring the cave, he reached a point where stalactites and stalagmites prevented entrance to its interior chamber. Ab returned to "develop" the "passages" with a little sweat and a sledgehammer. A path was cleared and the cave was open for tourism. After 1885, the cave received hundreds of visitors each year, nearly all of them guided by Ab.

The push to preserve the park came much later. In 1964, a graduate student searching for the world's oldest tree came to the grove of bristlecone pines at Wheeler Peak. After taking core samples, the researcher wanted to obtain a more accurate count by cutting down a tree. The Forest Service granted his request and he proceeded to fell a tree known today as Prometheus. Counting the rings proved his assumption correct. Prometheus was at least 4,862 years old; he had just cut down the oldest living single organism in the world. A cross-section of the tree resides in Great Basin Visitor Center, where you can count the rings for yourself. But all was not lost. The tragedy of Prometheus helped galvanize support for the creation of Great Basin National Park, and the young graduate student was one of the cause's leading advocates.

When to Go

Great Basin is open all year. Wheeler Peak Scenic Drive to Lehman Creek Campground is open all year, but the final 10 miles is generally closed from November to May, depending on the weather. Cave tours are offered at Lehman Caves Visitor Center year-round with the exception of New Year's Day, Thanksgiving, and Christmas. Great Basin Visitor Center is open from April until October (see page 452 for visitor center hours and locations). The park is busiest during holidays and summer weekends, when campgrounds can fill before noon, but crowds are rarely unmanageable.

Transportation & Airports

Public transportation does not provide service to or around the park. The closest large commercial airports are Salt Lake City International (SLC), located 238 miles to the northeast, and McCarran International (LAS) in Las Vegas, NV, located 307 miles south of the park. Car rental is available at each destination.

Directions

Great Basin is located at the center of one of the most remote regions of the continental United States.

From the West: You can arrive from the west via US-50 or US-6. These highways converge at Ely, where you continue south/east on US-50/US-93/US-6/Great Basin Blvd for more than 55 miles to NV-487. Turn right at NV-487 and travel 5 miles to Baker. At Baker, turn right onto Lehman Caves Road, which leads into the park.

From the North: I-80 picks up US-93 at Wells (Exit 352) and West Wendover, NV (Exit 410). Heading South on US-93 leads to Ely, NV (follow directions above from Ely).

From the East: From Delta, UT, head west on US-50/US-6 across the Utah–Nevada border to NV-487. Turn left onto NV-487 and continue for 5 miles to Baker. Turn right onto Lehman Caves Road, which leads into the park.

From the South: Heading north on US-93, turn right at US-50/US-6. Continue east for almost 30 miles to NV-487. Turn right onto NV-487 and after 5 miles turn right at Lehman Caves Road.

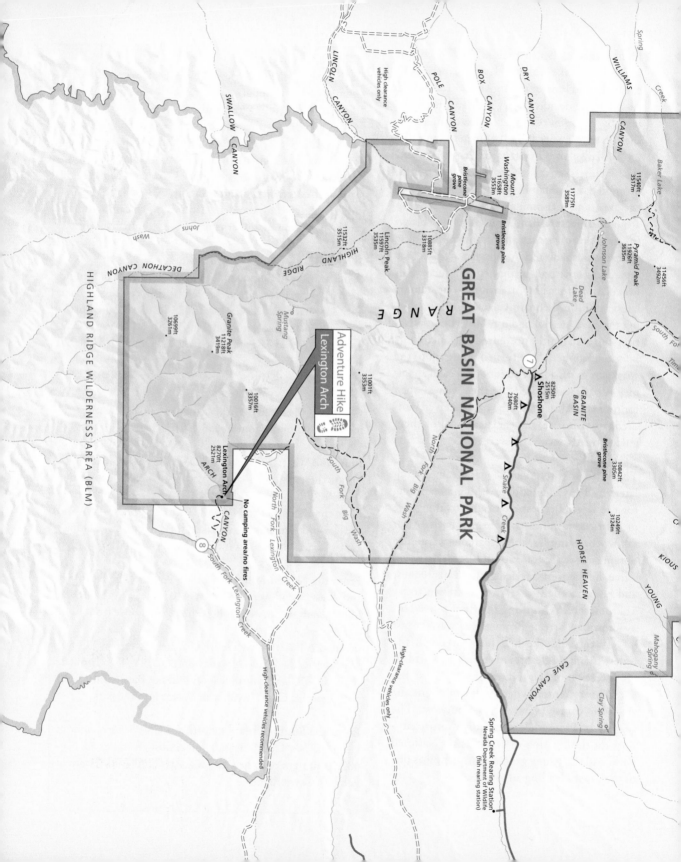

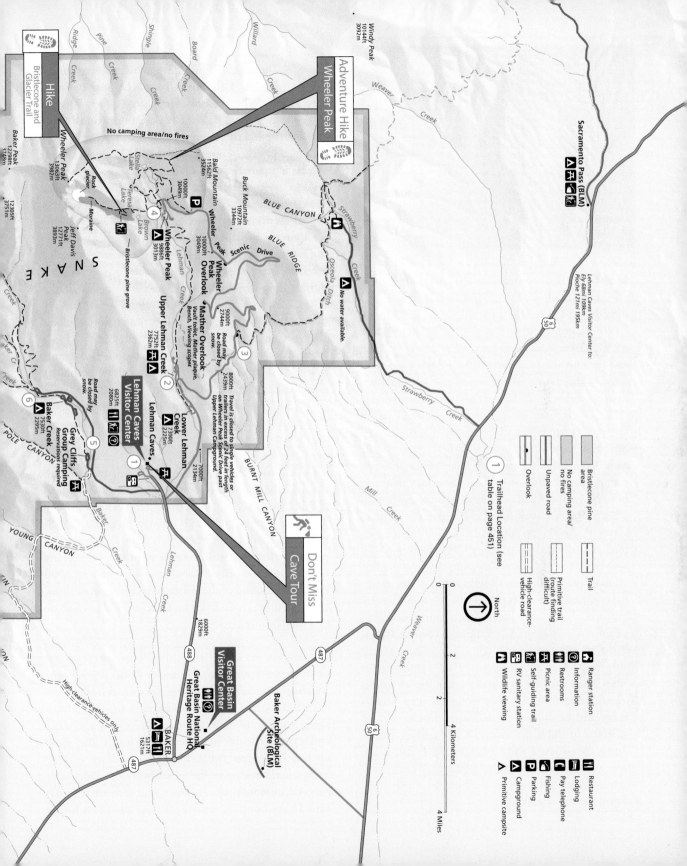

Parachute Shield
(Grand Palace Tour)

Driving

Most Great Basin visitors arrive via **NV-488/Lehman Caves Road**, which travels west from Baker, NV directly into the park and ultimately to Lehman Caves Visitor Center. The 12-mile **Wheeler Peak Scenic Drive**, which intersects Lehman Caves Road just beyond the park boundary, provides access to some of the most scenic viewpoints, climbing more than 3,000 feet to Wheeler Peak Campground. Vehicles longer than 24 feet are not allowed beyond Upper Lehman Creek Campground due to its steep (8% grade) and winding nature. Wheeler Peak Scenic Drive is open year-round to Upper Lehman Creek Campground, but usually closes beyond this point from November to May, depending on weather conditions. **Baker Creek Road** also intersects Lehman Caves Road. It's an unpaved but well-maintained road providing access to Baker Creek Campground and Grey Cliffs Group Camping Area, as well as some of the park's better backcountry hiking trails. Baker Creek Road is typically closed from December through April. Further south, running parallel to Lehman Caves Road, is the unpaved **Snake Creek Road**, which, not surprisingly, follows Snake Creek into the park. A high-clearance 4WD vehicle is recommended, but not required. A handful of primitive campsites are available along the way. **Strawberry** and **Lexington Arch Roads** should only be accessed by high-clearance 4WD vehicles. Snake Creek, Strawberry, and Lexington Arch Roads are open year-round, but may be impassable due to snow or mud. Always check with the park about road conditions before departing.

Camping

There are four developed campgrounds. **Lower Lehman Creek, Upper Lehman Creek, and Wheeler Peak** are located along Wheeler Peak Scenic Drive. **Baker Creek Campground** is located at the end of unpaved Baker Creek Road. Lower Lehman Creek is open year-round. Upper Lehman Creek is open from mid-April through September. Baker Creek is open from May to October. Wheeler Peak is open between June and October. The largest campground is Wheeler Peak (37 sites). It is not uncommon for campgrounds to fill, especially during summer weekends and holidays. Pit toilets are located at each campground, but water is only available during summer. (In winter, water is available at the visitor centers.) There are no hookups or showers. A dump station ($5 fee) is available near Lehman Caves Visitor Center during summer. All sites cost $12 per night. Non-group sites are available on a first-come, first-served basis. **Group camping** is available at Grey Cliffs on Baker Creek Road by reservation only (775.234.7331). Free primitive campsites are available along Snake Creek and Strawberry Creek Roads.

Hiking

Great Basin is a relatively small area, and all the maintained trails beginning along Wheeler Peak Scenic Drive can be completed in a day or two. The most interesting hike is **Bristlecone Trail**, a 2.8-mile (roundtrip) waltz through a forest of bristlecone pine trees, a few of which may have been growing long before the Phoenician Alphabet was created in 2,000 BC. From the end of the Bristlecone Trail you can continue 1.8 miles (roundtrip) on **Glacier Trail** to the base of Nevada's only glacier.

For views of the Great Basin, there's no better vantage point than the **summit of Wheeler Peak**. The 8.2-mile trail begins at Summit Parking Area on Wheeler Peak Scenic Drive and steadily climbs more than 3,000 feet across rocky mountain slopes. Be sure to pack water and a jacket for this heart-pounding romp. The climb up will make you sweat, but it cools down quickly once you're soaking in the views from the completely exposed mountaintop. Another visitor favorite is **Alpine Lakes Loop**. In just 2.7 miles of fairly easy hiking you visit two beautiful alpine lakes. Stella Lake is larger and more enchanting, but Teresa Lake is also nice and particularly pretty when snowpack remains on the surrounding slopes. They're great spots for a picnic!

Backpacking

There are more than 60 miles of hiking trails at Great Basin. Backpackers are not allowed to camp within 0.25-mile of developed areas (roads, buildings, campgrounds, etc.), within the Wheeler Peak or Lexington Arch Day Use Areas, or in bristlecone pine groves. You must set up camp a minimum of 100 feet away from all sources of water and at least 500 feet away from any obvious archeological site. Camping in the backcountry does not require a permit, but it is recommended you sign in at trailhead registers.

The park's best backpacking route is to take Baker Lake Trail, which begins at the end of Baker Creek Road, all the way to Baker Lake. From here you can follow an unmaintained trail to Johnson Lake and return to Baker Road via Timber Creek Trail or South Fork Baker Creek Trail. The entire loop is slightly more than 13 miles. Backpackers should always carry a good topographical map. For information on trail conditions and routes, stop in at a visitor center or call (775) 234-7331.

Cave Tours

Ever since Absalom Lehman discovered the cave in the 1880s, tourists have marveled at its intricate and fragile formations. The National Park Service continues the tradition by offering daily tours. The cave is only 0.25-mile deep and 2 miles long, making tours heavy on information and light on walking. **Lodge Room Tour** ($8, 60 minutes, 20 people) covers the first 0.2 miles of cave including Gothic Palace, Music Room, and Lodge Room. **Grand Palace Tour** ($10, 90 minutes, 20 people) travels 0.6 miles while visiting all the rooms of Lodge Room Tour as well as Inscription Room and Grand Palace, where you will see the famous **"Parachute Shield"** formation. Tickets are required and can be purchased in advance at (877) 444-6777 or recreation.gov. Tickets can also be purchased at Lehman Caves Visitor Center upon arrival. The cave is a constant 50°F with 90% humidity, so dress appropriately.

Great Basin Hiking Trails (Distances are roundtrip)

	Name	Location (# on map)	Length	Difficulty Rating & Notes
Wheeler Peak Scenic Dr	Mountain View	Rhodes Cabin (1)	0.3 mile	E – Trail guide available at visitor center
	Lehman Creek	Upper Lehman Creek Camp (2) Wheeler Peak Camp (4)	6.8 miles	M – Connects Upper Lehman Creek and Wheeler Peak Campgrounds
	Osceola Ditch	Wheeler Peak Scenic Drive (3)	0.3 mile	E – Old ditch built by gold miners
	Sky Islands Forest	Bristlecone Parking Area (4)	0.4 mile	E – Paved interpretive trail of alpine forest
	Alpine Lakes - ⚓	Bristlecone Parking Area (4)	2.7 miles	E – Scenic Stella and Teresa Lakes
	Bristlecone - ⚓	Bristlecone Parking Area (4)	2.8 miles	M – Walk among the world's oldest trees
	Glacier & Bristlecone	Bristlecone Parking Area (4)	4.6 miles	M – Nevada's only glacier
	Wheeler Peak - ⚓	Summit Trail Parking Area (4)	8.6 miles	S – Follows ridge, 2,900-feet elevation gain
Other Areas	Pole Canyon	Grey Cliffs Campground (5)	4.0 miles	E – Follows old mining road
	Baker Lake	Baker Creek Road (6)	12.0 miles	S – Leads to a beautiful alpine lake
	Baker Creek Loop	Baker Creek Road (6)	3.1 miles	M – Loop via South Fork Baker Creek Trail
	South Fork Baker Creek/Johnson Lake	Baker Creek Road (6)	11.2 miles	S – Doesn't reach Johnson Lake • Passes historic Johnson Lake Mine structures
	Baker/Johnson Lakes Loop	Baker Creek Road (6)	13.1 miles	S – Combines Baker Lake and Johnson Lake Trails • 3,000-feet elevation gain
	Johnson Lake	Snake Creek Road (7)	7.4 miles	S – Short, steep route to Johnson Lake
	Lexington Arch - ⚓	Outside park, south of Baker (8)	3.4 miles	M – Day-use area • Six-story limestone arch

Difficulty Ratings: E = Easy, M = Moderate, S = Strenuous

Spelunking

Lehman is one of more than 40 caves in the park. Eight are accessible with a **cave permit** (application form available online). Spelunkers must show adequate horizontal and vertical caving techniques to be issued a permit. It must be filled out and mailed to the park at least one week prior to your cave trip.

Stargazing

Clear skies, high altitude, and 200 miles of distance from cities' light provide the perfect atmosphere for gazing into the heavens. Park Rangers hold **astronomy programs** every Tuesday, Thursday, and Saturday evening between Memorial Day and Labor Day. The park also holds an annual Astronomy Festival. Additionally, "star parties" are held on various holidays. Telescopes are provided by the park to be shared among guests. Check the park's online calendar for an up-to-date schedule of events. If you'd like to view the stars on your own, Wheeler Peak Parking Area is a great place to camp out with a blanket and a set of binoculars.

Biking

Cyclists are only allowed on park roads. The ride up to Wheeler Peak is a relatively short workout with a fun descent back to Lehman Caves Visitor Center or Baker.

Fishing

Fishing is allowed in all creeks and lakes. A Nevada state fishing license is required (they are not available for purchase at the park).

Horseback Riding

Horses are allowed in the backcountry, but there are no nearby outfitters offering trail rides. You will have to provide your own horse(s) and follow park regulations regarding horseback riding in the backcountry. Horses are prohibited from Wheeler Peak Day Use Area trails, Osceola Ditch Trail, Lexington Arch Trail, and Baker to Johnson Lake Cutoff Trail.

Visitor Centers

Great Basin Visitor Center, located outside the park just north of Baker on the west side of NV-487, offers an information desk, exhibits, and a small theater playing an orientation film. It is open daily, May to September, from 8am to 5pm. **Lehman Caves Visitor Center** (775.234.7331) is located inside the park on NV-488/Lehman Caves Road. You can purchase cave tour tickets, browse exhibits, and view the orientation film here. It also houses a bookstore, cafe, and gift shop. Lehman Caves Visitor Center is open every day except New Year's Day, Thanksgiving, and Christmas, from 8am to 4:30pm.

Ranger Programs

In addition to Cave Tours (page 451) and Stargazing Programs, the park provides evening campfire programs, children's programs, and full-moon hikes between Memorial Day and Labor Day. For a current schedule of events, visit the park website, call the park at (775) 234-7331, or stop in at a visitor center.

For Kids

Children can become **Junior Rangers**. To receive an official certificate and badge, your child must attend one of the following programs: Lehman Caves Tour, Campground Evening Program, Night Sky Program, or a Ranger Talk. Children must also complete an age appropriate number of activities in the park's Junior Ranger booklet: three activities for kids 5 and under, five activities for children between the ages of 6 and 9, and seven activities for everyone else. Booklets are available free of charge at either visitor center.

Flora & Fauna

Great Basin is home to 73 species of mammals, 18 species of reptiles, 2 species of amphibians, and 8 species of fish. At least 238 species of birds reside in or visit the park, making it an excellent bird-watching destination. Mammals you're most likely to see include mule deer and squirrels, but fortunate visitors may spot a mountain lion, badger, or coyote. More than 800 species of plants, including 11 species of conifer trees, reside within park boundaries. Bristlecone pine are the elder statesmen of the bunch. At least one known tree, Prometheus, lived to the ripe old age of 4,862. Singleleaf piñon trees are fruit bearers, with pine nuts that can be gathered and eaten by visitors. You'll find them in areas between 6,000 and 9,000 feet elevation.

Pets

Pets are allowed in the park, but must be kept on a leash no more than six feet in length at all times. They are not allowed on trails, in the backcountry, in Lehman Caves, or at evening programs. Basically, pets are allowed wherever you can get with your car: along roads, in campgrounds, and in parking areas.

Accessibility

Both of the park's visitor centers are fully accessible to individuals with mobility impairments. Accessible campsites are available at Upper Lehman Creek, Wheeler Peak, and Baker Creek Campgrounds. Island Forest Trail is paved, but may require assistance for the second half, as the grade increases to about 8%. Cave tours are accessible with assistance. Wheelchair users can also enjoy evening programs at Upper Lehman Creek and Wheeler Peak Campgrounds.

Weather

With nearly 8,000 feet in elevation difference between Wheeler Peak (13,063 feet) and the valley floor, temperature varies greatly depending on where you are in the park as well as what season it is. Summer average high temperatures at Lehman Caves Visitor Center (6,825 feet) reach the low to mid-80s°F. Overnight summertime lows average in the 50s°F. Between December and February, the average highs are in the low 40s°F and average lows are right around 20°F. Even if it's 80°F at Lehman Cave Visitor Center, you should bring a jacket if you plan on hiking to Wheeler Peak or touring the cave. The temperature is usually 20 degrees cooler and it's often windy along the mountain's ridgeline. The cave is a constant 50°F all year. The region is arid, receiving about 20 inches of annual precipitation, but afternoon thunderstorms are common in summer and snow can fall in the high elevations any time of year. The majority of precipitation comes in the form of snow between November and March.

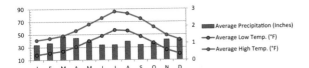

Wheeler Peak and Stella Lake

Vacation Planner

If you only want to catch the main attractions at Great Basin, a single day should suffice. Lehman Caves and the most popular hiking trails/viewpoints are all located in the same general area. With that said, Great Basin is a relief from bumper-to-bumper traffic and shoulder-to-shoulder hiking experienced at more popular parks of the West. So, you may want to pack a cooler and your tent and spend a few nights under the stars. Nearby dining, grocery stores, lodging, festivals, and attractions are listed on pages 454–459.

Day 1: Skip Great Basin Visitor Center (unless you want to see the cross-section of Prometheus, the 4,862-year-old tree). Stop at **Lehman Caves Visitor Center** to pick up or purchase cave tour tickets (page 451). Reservations are a good idea, but if your group is relatively small and you aren't traveling on a summer holiday weekend, you should be able to get tickets upon arrival. Plus, tours are offered several times a day during the summer. Fill in the blanks around your cave tour(s) by taking **Wheeler Peak Scenic Drive**, stopping at pull-outs of your choosing, to Summit Trail Parking Area. Hike the 8.2-mile **Wheeler Peak Trail** if you want a workout. Allow at least 4 hours for this mountain trek. **Bristlecone Trail** is one of our favorites, plus it can be combined with the loop to **Stella** and **Teresa Lakes**. This is a more leisurely stroll and a great alternative if some members of your group aren't interested in climbing a mountain. (Maybe pack a picnic and sit out at Stella Lake for a bit.) (Aggressive hikers with an early enough start can hike Wheeler Peak, Alpine Lakes Loop, and Bristlecone Trail in a day, but you'll be exhausted.) Cap the day off with an evening ranger program or stargazing from your campsite.

Dining

Arches/Canyonlands Area
Moab Brewery • (435) 259-6333
686 S Main St, Moab
themoabbrewery.com • Burgers: $8+

Moab Diner • (435) 259-4006
189 S Main St, Moab
moabdiner.com • Burgers: $7.5+

Milt's Stop & Eat • (435) 259-7424
356 Mill Creek Dr, Moab
miltsstopandeat.com • Burgers: $4.95+

Miguel's Baja Grill • (435) 259-6546
51 N Main St, Moab
miguelsbajagrill.com • Entrée: $11–26

Sunset Grill • (435) 259-7146
900 N US-191, Moab

Desert Bistro • (435) 259-0756
36 S 100 West, Moab
desertbistro.com • Entrée: $22–60

La Hacienda • (435) 355-0529
574 N Main St, Moab

Paradox Pizza • (435) 259-9999
702 S Main St, Moab
paradoxpizza.com • Pizza: $14.95+

Wake & Bake Cafe • (435) 259-2420
Ste 6, 59 S Main St, Moab • wakeandbakecafe.net

Peace Tree Juice Cafe • (435) 259-0101
20 S Main St, Moab
peacetreecafe.com • Breakfast: $8–12

Eklecticafe • (435) 259-6896
352 N Main St, Moab

Love Muffin Cafe • (435) 259-6833
139 N Main St, Moab • lovemuffincafe.com

K&A Chuckwagon • (435) 587-3468
496 N Main St, Monticello

Wagon Wheel Pizza • (435) 587-2766
164 S Main St, Monticello

Subway • (435) 587-2757
481 N Main St, Monticello

Peace Tree Juice Cafe • (435) 587-5063
516 N Main St, Monticello

Shake Shack • (435) 587-2966
364 N Main St, Monticello

Chow Hound • (435) 564-3563
30 E Main St, Green River

Ray's Tavern • (435) 564-3511
25 S Broadway, Green River • raystavern.com

Green River Coffee • (435) 564-3411
25 E Main St, Green River

Capitol Reef/Bryce Canyon Area
Rim Rock Restaurant • (435) 425-3398
2523 UT-24 E, Torrey • therimrock.net

Slacker's Burger Joint • (435) 425-3710
165 E Main St, Torrey

Chilizz • (435) 425-2600
155 E Main St, Torrey

Red Cliffs Restaurant • (435) 425-3797
156 E Main St, Torrey

Luna Mesa Oasis • (435) 456-9122
2000 E 925 N UT-24, Torrey

Subway • (435) 425-3302
675 E UT-24, Torrey

Cafe Diablo • (435) 425-3070
599 W Main St, Torrey

La Cueva • (435) 425-2000
875 N UT-24, Torrey

Castlerock Coffee & Candy • (435) 425-2100
875 E UT-24, Torrey • castlerockcoffee.com

Hell's Backbone Grill • (435) 335-7464
20 N UT-12, Boulder
hellsbackbonegrill.com • Entrée: $18–29

Sunglow Family Restaurant
91 E Main St, Bicknell • (435) 425-3701

Burr Trail Grill • (435) 335-7511
UT-12, Boulder

Blondie's Eatery • (435) 542-3255
30 N UT-95, Hanksville

Clarke's Restaurant • (435) 679-8383
141 N Main St, Tropic

Pizza Place • (435) 679-8888
21 N Main St, Tropic

Rubys Cowboy Buffet • (435) 834-8027
26 S Main St, Bryce Canyon City • rubysinn.com

Subway • (435) 834-5888
139 W UT-12, Bryce

Zion & Grand Canyon Area
Whiptail Grill • (435) 772-0283
445 Zion Park Blvd, Springdale, UT
whiptailgrillzion.com

Switchback Grille • (435) 772-3700
1149 Zion Park Blvd, Springdale, UT
switchbacktrading.com • Entrée: $38+

Flying Monkey • (435) 772-3333
961 Zion Park Blvd, Springdale, UT
pizzainzion.com

Cafe Oscars • (435) 772-3232
948 Zion Park Blvd, Springdale, UT
oscarscafe.com

Zion Pizza & Noodle Co • (435) 772-3815
868 Zion Park Blvd, Springdale, UT
zionpizzanoodle.com

Spotted Dog • (435) 772-0700
428 Zion Landing, Springdale, UT
flanigans.com

Cafe Soleil • (435) 772-0505
205 Zion Park Blvd, Springdale, UT
cafesoleilzionpark.com

Bit & Spur • (435) 772-3498
1212 Zion Park Blvd, Hurricane, UT
bitandspur.com • Entrée: $13–28

R P's Stage Stop • (928) 638-3115
400 AZ-64, Tusayan, AZ

Wendy's and McDonald's are available near the
Grand Canyon's South Entrance on AZ-64

Red Raven • (928) 635-4980
135 W Route 66, Williams, AZ
redravenrestaurant.com

Old Smokey's Restaurant • (928) 635-1915
624 W Route 66 (near 7th Ave), Williams, AZ

Pine Country • (928) 635-9718
107 N Grand Canyon Blvd, Williams, AZ
pinecountryrestaurant.com • Entrée: $8–25

Dara Thai Cafe • (623) 551-6676
3655 W Anthem Way, # B127, Anthem, AZ

Grand Canyon Coffee & Cafex • (928) 635-4907
137 Railroad Ave, Williams
grandcanyoncoffeeandcafe.com

Great Basin Area
Silver State Restaurant • (775) 289-8866
1204 Aultman St, Ely

Twin Wok Restaurant • (775) 289-3699
700 Park Ave, Ely

Evah's • (775) 289-4271
701 Avenue I, Ely

Margarita's • (775) 289-6296
945 N Mcgill Hwy, Ely

La Fiesta • (775) 289-4114
700 Avenue H, Ely

Grocery Stores
Arches/Canyonlands Area
City Market Food • (435) 259-5182
425 S Main St, Moab

Village Market • (435) 259-3111
702 S Main St, Moab

Dave's Corner Market • (435) 259-6999
401 Mill Creek Dr, Moab

Walmart • (435) 637-6712
UT-55, Price

Capitol Reef/Bryce Canyon Area
Chuck Wagon General Store
12 W Main St, Torrey • (435) 425-3335

Clarke's Country Market • (435) 679-8633
141 North Main St, Tropic

Ruby's General Store • (435) 834-5484
26 S Main St, Bryce Canyon City

Zion & Grand Canyon Area
Sol Foods • (435) 772-3100
95 Zion Park Blvd, Springdale, UT

Walmart Supercenter • (435) 635-6945
180 N 3400 W, Hurricane, UT

Farmers Market • (435) 635-0774
495 N State St, La Verkin, UT

Simpson's Market • (928) 679-2281
US-89 & AZ-64, Cameron, AZ

Great Basin Area
Ridley's Family Markets • (775) 289-3444
1689 Great Basin Blvd, Ely

Lodging
Arches/Canyonlands Area
Red Stone Inn • (435) 259-3500
535 S Main St, Moab
moabredstone.com • Rates: $114+/night

Big Horn Lodge • (435) 259-6171
550 S Main St, Moab
moabbighorn.com • Rates: $80+

River Canyon Lodge • (435) 259-8838
71 W 200 N, Moab
rivercanyonlodge.com • Rates: $109+

Apache Motel • (435) 259-5727
166 S 4th East St, Moab

Gonzo Inn • (435) 259-2515
100 W 200 S, Moab
gonzoinn.com • Rates: $174+

Aarchway Inn • (435) 259-2599
1551 US-191, Moab
aarchwayinn.com • Rates: $169+

Bowen Motel • (435) 259-7132
169 N Main St, Moab
bowenmotel.com • Rates: $124+

Kokopelli Lodge • (435) 259-7615
72 S 100 E, Moab
kokopellilodge.com • Rates: $98+

Adventure Inn • (435) 259-6122
512 N Main St, Moab • adventureinnmoab.com

Riverside Inn • (435) 259-8848
988 N Main St, Moab

Inca Inn • (866) 462-2466
570 N Main St, Moab
incainn.com • Rates: $60+

Red Cliffs Lodge • (866) 812-2002
Mile Post 14, UT-128, Moab
redcliffslodge.com • Rates: $239+

Sorrel River Ranch • (435) 259-4642
UT-128, Moab
sorrelriver.com • Rates: $429+

Desert Hills B&B • (435) 259-3568
1989 Desert Hills Dr, Moab • deserthillsbnb.com

Mayor's House B&B • (435) 259-3019
505 Rosetree Ln, Moab
mayorshouse.com • Rates: $130+

Cali-Cochitta B&B • (435) 259-4961
110 S 200 East St, Moab
moabdreaminn.com • Rates: $95+

Castle Valley Inn B&B • (435) 259-6012
424 E Amber Ln, Moab
castlevalleyinn.com • Rates: $115+

Sunflower Hill B&B • (435) 259-2974
185 N 300 E, Moab
sunflowerhill.com • Rates: $145+

Lazy Lizard Hostel • (435) 259-6057
1213 S US-191, Moab
lazylizardhostel.com • Dorm: $11

Archview Resort • (435) 259-7854
US-191 and UT-313, Moab
archviewresort.com • RV Sites: $59+

Canyonlands Campground • (435) 259-6848
555 S Main St, Moab
canyonlandsrv.com • RV Sites: $41+

Kane Springs Campground • (435) 259-8844
1705 Kane Creek Blvd, Moab
kanesprings.com

KOA • (435) 259-6682
3225 US-191, Moab

There are a dozen small BLM campgrounds located along Hwy 128, three each along Hwy 279, Hwy 313, and Kane Creek Road, one at Ken's Lake, another on Sand Flats Road, and two more on Canyon Rims Recreation Area Road.

Inn at the Canyons • (435) 587-2458
533 N Main St, Monticello
monticellocanyonlandsinn.com • Rates: $99+

Monticello Inn • (435) 587-2274
164 E Central St, Monticello
themonticelloinn.com

River Terrace • (435) 564-3401
1740 E Main St, Green River
river-terrace.com • Rates: $115+

Runnin' Iron Inn • (435) 587-2351
6780 N US-191, Monticello
canyonlandsbestkeptsecret.com • Rates: $79

Grist Mill Inn B&B • (435) 587-2597
64 S 300 E, Monticello
oldgristmillinn.com • Rates: $59+

Robbers Roost Motel • (435) 564-3452
325 W Main St, Green River
rrmotel.com • Rates: $42+

Shady Acres Campground • (435) 564-8290
690 E Main, Green River • shadyacresrv.com

AOK RV Park • (435) 564-8372
610 S Green River Blvd, Green River

Green River KOA • (435) 564-8195
235 S 1780 E, Green River

Capitol Reef/Bryce Canyon Area
Austin's Chuckwagon • (435) 425-3344
12 W Main St, Torrey
austinschuckwagonmotel.com • Rates: $91+

Broken Spur • (435) 425-3775
955 E UT-24, Torrey
brokenspurinn.com • Rates: $68+

Best Western Capitol Reef Resort
2600 E UT-24, Torrey • (435) 425-3761
capitolreefresort.com

Red Sands Hotel • (435) 425-3688
670 E UT-24, Torrey • redsandshotel.com • $89+

Boulder View Inn • (435) 425-3800
385 W Main St, Torrey
boulderviewinn.com • Rates: $40–75

Cowboy Homestead • (435) 425-3414
2280 S UT-12, Torrey
cowboyhomesteadcabins.com • Rates: $79–99

Torrey School House B&B • (435) 633-4643
150 N Center Street, Torrey
torreyschoolhouse.com • Rates: $125+

Sky Ridge B&B • (435) 425-3222
1092 E UT-24, Torrey
skyridgeinn.com • Rates: $109+

Thousand Lakes RV Park • (435) 425-3500
1110 W UT-24, Torrey
thousandlakesrvpark.com • Rates: $33.50+

Best Western Grand Hotel • (435) 834-5700
30 N 100 E, Bryce Canyon City
brycecanyongrand.com • $90+

Best Western Rubys Inn • (435) 834-5341
26 S Main St, Bryce Canyon City
rubysinn.com • Rates: $70+

Bryce Canyon Pines • (800) 892-7923
Milepost 10, UT-12, Bryce
brycecanyonmotel.com • Rates: $115+

Stone Canyon Inn • (435) 679-8611
1380 W Stone Canyon Ln, Tropic
stonecanyoninn.com • Rates: $125+

Bryce Canyon Inn • (435) 679-8502
21 N Main St, Tropic
brycecanyoninn.com • Rates: $72+

Bryce Country Cabins • (435) 679-8643
320 N Main St, Tropic
brycecountrycabins.com • Rates: $99+

Bryce Trails B&B • (435) 679-8700
1001 W Bryce Way, Tropic
brycetrails.com • Rates: $145+

Buffalo Sage B&B • (435) 679-8443
980 N UT-12, Tropic • buffalosage.com

Riverside Resort & RV Park • (800) 824-5651
594 N US-89, Hatch • riversideresort-utah.com

Grand Staircase Inn • (435) 679-8400
105 N Kodachrome Dr, Cannonville
grandstaircaseinn.com • Rates: $59+

Bryce Valley KOA • (435) 679-8988
215 Red Rock Dr, Cannonville

Zion & Grand Canyon Area
Driftwood Lodge • (435) 772-3262
1515 Zion Park Blvd, Springdale, UT
driftwoodlodge.net • Rates: $139+

Zion Pioneer Lodge • (435) 772-3233
838 Zion Park Blvd, Springdale, UT
zionpioneerlodge.com • Rates: $169+

Best Western Zion Park Inn • (435) 772-3200
1215 Zion Park Blvd, Springdale, UT

Desert Pearl Inn • (435) 772-8888
707 Zion Park Blvd, Springdale, UT
desertpearl.com • Rates: $229+

Cliffrose Lodge & Gardens • (888) 567-6027
281 Zion Park Blvd, Springdale, UT
cliffroselodge.com • Rates: $209+

Bumbleberry Inn • (435) 772-3224
97 Bumbleberry Ln, Springdale, UT
bumbleberry.com • Rates: $68+

Cable Mountain Lodge • (435) 772-3366
145 Zion Park Blvd, Springdale, UT

Canyon Ranch Motel • (435) 772-3357
668 Zion Park Blvd, Springdale, UT
canyonranchmotel.com • Rates: $109+

Majestic View Lodge • (435) 772-0665
2400 Zion Park Blvd, Springdale, UT
majesticviewlodge.com • Rates: $79+

Zion Ponderosa Ranch Resort • (800) 293-5444
Twin Knolls Rd, Mt Carmel, Utah, UT
zionponderosa.com • Rates: $172+

Red Rock Inn • (435) 772-3139
998 Zion Landing, Springdale, UT
redrockinn.com • Rates: $189+

Zion Canyon B&B • (435) 772-9466
101 Kokopelli Cir, Springdale, UT
zioncanyonbandb.com • Rates: $155+

Canyon Vista Lodge, B&B • (435) 772-3801
2175 Zion Park Blvd, Springdale, UT
canyonvistabandb.com • Rates: $155+

Harvest House B&B • (435) 772-3880
29 Canyon View Dr, Springdale, UT
harvesthouse.net • Rates: $130+

Under the Eaves • (435) 772-3457
980 Zion Park Blvd, Springdale, UT
undertheeaves.com • Rates: $115+

Novel House Inn • (800) 711-8400
73 Paradise Rd, Springdale • novelhouse.com

Flanigan's Villas • (435) 632-0798
425 Zion Park Blvd, Springdale, UT
flanigansvillas.com • Rates: $339-439

Amber Inn B&B • (435) 772-0289
244 W Main St, Rockville, UT
amber-inn.com • Rates: $115+

Desert Thistle • (435) 772-0251
37 W Main St, Rockville, UT
thedesertthistle.com • Rates: $145+

Best Western Squire Inn • (800) 622-6966
74 AZ-64, Grand Canyon, AZ

Canyon Plaza Resort • (928) 638-2673
406 Canyon Plaza Ln, Grand Canyon, AZ
grandcanyonplaza.com • Rates: $124+

Grand Canyon Hotel • (928) 635-1419
145 W Route 66, Williams, AZ
thegrandcanyonhotel.com • Rates: $45+

Red Feather Lodge • (928) 638-2414
106 AZ-64, Grand Canyon, AZ
redfeatherlodge.com • Rates: $125+

Holiday Inn Express • (928) 638-3000
226 AZ-64, Grand Canyon, AZ

The Lodge on Route 66 • (877) 563-4366
200 E Route 66, Williams, AZ
thelodgeonroute66.com • Rates: $99+

Canyon Country Inn • (928) 635-2349
442 W Route 66, Williams, AZ
thecanyoncountryinn.com • Rates: $76+

The Red Garter Inn • (800) 328-1484
137 W Railroad Ave, Williams, AZ
redgarter.com • Rates: $145+

Dumplin Patch B&B • (480) 652-6016
625 E Linger Ln, Williams, AZ
dumplinpatch.net • Rates: $185+

Canyon Motel & RV Park • (800) 482-3955
1900 E Rodeo Rd Route 66, Williams, AZ
thecanyonmotel.com • Rates: $75+

Kaibab Lodge • (928) 638-2389
18 miles north of North Rim • kaibablodge.com

Jacob Lake Inn • (928) 643-7232
45 miles north of North Rim, Jacob Lake, AZ
jacoblake.com • Rates: $85+

Lodging and dining are limited at the North Rim. See page 442 for in-park accommodations.

Great Basin Area
Hotel Nevada • (775) 289-6665
501 Aultman St, Ely
hotelnevada.com • Rates: $59–200

Prospector Hotel & Casino • (775) 289-8900
1501 Aultman St, Ely
prospectorhotel.us • Rates: $89+

Bristlecone Motel • (800) 497-7404
700 Avenue I, Ely
bristleconemotelelynv.com • Rates: $65+

Jail House Motel & Casino • (775) 289-3033
211 5th St, Ely • jailhousecasino.com

Four Sevens Motel • (775) 289-4747
500 High St, Ely

Many chain restaurants and hotels can be found in Moab, Richfield, Kanab, and Hurricane, UT; Page, and Williams, AZ; Ely, NV; and along I-70 and I-15.

Festivals
Sundance Film Festival • January
Park City, Salt Lake City, Ogden • sundance.org

Winter Birds Festival • January
St. George, UT • sgcity.org/birdfestival

Bryce Canyon Winter Festival • February
Bryce Canyon City, UT • (866) 866-6616

Skinny Tire Festival • March
Moab, UT • skinnytireevents.com

Dixie-Escalante Kite Festival • April
Sun River Golf Course • dixiepower.com

Moab Arts Festival • May
Moab, UT • moabartsfestival.org

Canyonlands PRCA Rodeo • June
Moab, UT • moabcanyonlandsrodeo.com

Utah Shakespeare Festival • June
Cedar City, UT • bard.org

Grand Canyon Music Festival • August
South Rim, AZ

Moab Music Festival • September
Moab, UT • moabmusicfest.org

Escalante Canyons Art Festival • September
Escalante, UT • escalantecanyonsartfestival.org

World of Speed • September
Bonneville Salt Flats, UT • saltflats.com

Red Rock Film Festival • November
Cedar City, UT • redrockfilmfestival.com

Moab Folk Festival • November
Moab, UT • moabfolkfestival.com

Dickens' Christmas Festival • December
St. George, UT • dickenschristmasfestival.com

Attractions
Arches/Canyonlands Area

Monument Valley
Famous sandstone buttes located near the Arizona–Utah border along US 163.

Castle Valley Ridge Trail
Advanced, 19 mile MTB loop, trailhead located on FR-110 (up Nuck Woodward Canyon from UT-31)

Corona Arch • 3 miles (roundtrip)
Trailhead is located on UT-279, 10 miles west of the UT-279/US-191 junction

Negro Bill Canyon • 4 miles (roundtrip)
Trailhead is located on UT-128, 3 miles east of UT-128/US-191 junction • Creek crossing is required (wear appropriate footwear)

Fisher Towers • 4.4 miles (roundtrip)
Trailhead located off a 2.2 mile dirt road accessed via UT-128, 21 miles east of the UT-128/US-191 junction

Dead Horse Point State Park
US-313, Moab • (435) 259-2614
stateparks.utah.gov • Day-use: $10/vehicle

Skydive Moab • (435) 259-5867
US-191 N, Moab • skydivemoab.com

Chile Pepper Bike Shop • (435) 259-4688
702 S Main St, Moab • chilebikes.com • *Rentals*

Rim Cyclery • (435) 259-5333
94 W 100 N, Moab • rimcyclery.com • *Rentals*

Moab Cyclery • (800) 559-1978
391 S Main St, Moab
moabcyclery.com • *Rentals & Tours*

Western Spirit Cycling • (435) 259-8732
478 Mill Creek Dr, Moab
westernspirit.com • *Tours (Road & MTB)*

Solfun Mtn Bike Tours • (435) 259-9861
solfun.com • Tours: $100+

Rim Mountain Bike Tours • (435) 259-5223
rimtours.com • Tours: $120+

Moab Adventure Center • (435) 259-7019
Climbing, rafting, hot air ballooning, and more
225 S Main St, Moab • moabadventurecenter.com

Moab Desert Adventures • (804) 814-3872
Guided rock climbing and canyoneering trips
415 N Main St, Moab • moabdesertadventures.com

Tag-A-Long Expeditions • (435) 259-8946
452 N Main St, Moab
tagalong.com • *Land & Water Adventures*

Coyote Land Tours • (435) 260-6056
731 Mulberry Ln, Moab
coyotelandtours.com • Tours: $59/adult

High Point Hummer & ATV • (435) 259-2972
281 N Main St, Moab
highpointhummer.com • *Rentals & Tours*

Canyonlands By Night • (435) 259-5261
1861 US-191, Moab • *Land, Air, and Water Tours*
canyonlandsbynight.com

Navtec Expeditions • (435) 259-7983
321 N Main St, Moab
navtec.com • *River & Jeep Tours*

Red River Adventures • (877) 259-4046
1140 S Main St, Moab
redriveradventures.com • *Multi-sport Tours*

Tex's Riverways • (435) 259-5101
691 N 500 W, Moab
texsriverways.com • *Rentals & Shuttles*

Museum of Moab • (435) 259-7985
118 E Center St, Moab
moabmuseum.org • Admission: $5

Castle Creek Winery • (435) 259-3332
Milepost 14, UT-128, Moab
castlecreekwinery.com

Slickrock Cinemas 3 • (435) 259-4441
580 Kane Creek Blvd, Moab

Gravel Pit Lanes • (435) 259-4748
1078 Mill Creek Dr, Moab

Hole N' the Rock • (435) 686-2250
11037 S US-191, Moab
theholeintherock.com • Admission: $6/adult

Goblin Valley State Park • (435) 275-4584
Goblin Valley Rd, Green River
stateparks.utah.gov • Day-use: $10/vehicle

John Wesley Powell River History Museum
1765 E Main, Green River • (435) 564-3427
johnwesleypowell.com • Admission: $6/adult

Green River State Park • (435) 564-3633
450 Green River Blvd, Green River
stateparks.utah.gov • Day-use: $5/vehicle

Colorado River & Trail Exp. • (435) 564-8170
1117 E 1000 N, Green River
crateinc.com • Rafting: $80+

Capitol Reef/Bryce Canyon Area
Hondoo Rivers & Trails • (435) 425-3519
90 E Main St, Torrey
hondoo.com • *Horseback & Vehicle Tours*

Backcountry Outfitters • (866) 747-3972
875 E UT-24, Torrey
ridethereef.com • *Multi-sport Adventures*

Anasazi State Park • (435) 335-7308
460 N UT-12, Boulder
stateparks.utah.gov • Fee: $5/person

Bicknell Theater • (435) 425-3123
11 E Main St, Bicknell

Grand Staircase Escalante NM
Loads of great hikes and formations, like Jacob Hamblin Arch (above)
669 S Hwy 89A, Kanab
ut.blm.gov/monument • (435) 679-8980

Escalante Canyon Outfitters • (888) 326-4453
ecohike.com • *Multi-day Hiking Tours*

Utah Canyons • (435) 826-4967
325 W Main St, Escalante
utahcanyons.com • *Hiking & Shuttle Service*

Kodachrome Basin State Park • (435) 679-8562
stateparks.utah.gov • Day-use: $8/vehicle

Escalante Petrified Forest • (435) 826-4466
710 N Reservoir, Escalante
stateparks.utah.gov • Day-use: $8/vehicle

Bryce Canyon ATV Adventures • (435) 834-5200
139 E UT-12, Bryce Canyon City
brycecanyonatvadventures.com • Rides: $45+

Moqui Cave • (435) 644-8525
4518 N US-89, Kanab • Admission: $5/adult

Frontier Movie Town • (435) 644-5337
297 W Center St, Kanab
littlehollywoodmuseum.org

Cedar Breaks NM • (435) 586-0787
2390 W UT-56, Suite 11, Cedar City
nps.gov/cebr • Entrance Fee: $5/person

Zion & Grand Canyon Area

Kanarra Creek/Falls
A short, relatively easy hike through a slot canyon to a series of waterfalls. You must cross the creek (dress appropriately). Ladder near waterfall may not be safe. There is a parking fee.
E 100 N St, Kanarraville, UT

Zion Adventure Company
Tons of tours, shuttle service for Zion Narrows, gear rental, courses, and tubing
36 Lion Blvd, Springdale • (435) 772-1001
zionadventures.com • Narrows Tour: $151+

Zion Outfitter • (435) 772-5090
Zion Narrows, bikes, tubing, rentals, guided trips, showers, and laundry
7 Zion Park Blvd, Springdale
zionoutfitter.com • Narrows Tour: $149+

Mild To Wild Rhino Tours • (435) 216-8298
145 Zion Park Blvd, Springdale
mildtowildrhinotours.com

Zion Rock & Mtn Guides • (435) 772-3303
Shuttle Service to Zion Narrows Trailhead (Chamberlain Ranch), Tours, & Rental
1458 Zion Park Blvd, Springdale
zionrockguides.com

Zion Cycles • (435) 772-0400
868 Zion Park Blvd, Springdale, UT 84767
zioncycles.com • Rentals ($15+/hr)

Southern Utah Adventure Center
Rentals (boat, jeep, ATV, etc.) and Tours
138 W State St, Hurricane • (435) 635-0907v
southernutahadventurecenter.com

Zion Canyon Theatre • (435) 772-2400
145 Zion Park Blvd, Springdale
zioncanyontheatre.com

The Wave • Coyote Buttes North
To prevent overuse, only 20 hikers are allowed to hike here each day. All permits ($7) must be purchased in advance. Ten permits can be obtained via an online lottery. Ten walk-in permits are available 24 hours in advance via lottery at Paria Contact Station (Kanab Field Office in winter). Successful applicants will be given detailed instructions & maps to reach the Wave. Additional information on the permit process is available at blm.gov.

Wire Pass • Coyote Buttes North
Don't forget to take a stroll down Wire Pass (1.7 miles, one-way) when visiting the Wave. It's the most scenic entry point to Buckskin Gulch. Wire Pass Trailhead is located 8.3 miles down House Rock Valley Road (washboard, dirt, inaccessible after rain). House Rock Valley Road is accessed from US-89 (between mile markers 25 and 26). A permit is required ($6).

Buckskin Gulch
One of the longest (13+ miles, one-way) and deepest slot canyons in the world is also one of the best hiking trails in the United States. Wire Pass is the most popular (and beautiful) access point. Buckskin Gulch continues into Paria Canyon. A permit is required ($6).

Paria Canyon
Paria Canyon can be accessed via Buckskin Gulch or from White House Trailhead (near Paria Contact Station). The trail follows the canyon and Paria River to Lee's Ferry Trailhead at the Colo-

rado River just southwest of Page, AZ and Lake Powell. A permit is required ($6).

These hikes are fantastic, but not without danger. Using a shuttle or two cars is a good idea (if not necessary). Pack plenty of water. Wear water shoes. Check the weather forecast (flash floods are a significant problem—in 2010 the area experienced multiple floods that removed high water campsites, added obstructions, and changed the river bed). Most importantly talk to a ranger at Kanab Field Office or Paria Contact Station.

Day-hike permits ($6) for Buckskin Gulch, Paria Canyon, and Wire Pass can be purchased at self-pay stations at each trailhead.

Kanab Field Office • (435) 644-1200
318 N 100 E, Kanab, UT
blm.gov/ut/st/en/fo/kanab.html

Paria Contact Station • (435) 644-4628
Located on US-89, about half-way between Kanab, UT and Page, AZ

Coral Pink Sand Dunes • (435) 648-2800
Accessed via US-89 north of Kanab, UT
stateparks.utah.gov • Day-use: $8/vehicle

Dinosaur Discovery Site • (435) 574-3466
2180 E Riverside Dr, St. George, UT
dinosite.org • Admission: $6/adult

St. George Temple • (435) 673-3533
250 E 400 S, St. George, UT

Tuacahn Ampitheatre • (435) 652-3200
1100 Tuacahn, Ivins, UT
tuacahn.org • Tickets: $27+

Snow Canyon State Park • (435) 628-2255
1002 Snow Canyon Dr, Ivins, UT
stateparks.utah.gov • Day-use: $6/vehicle

Sand Hollow State Park • (435) 680-0715
3351 S Sand Hollow Rd, Hurricane, UT
stateparks.utah.gov • Day-use: $10/vehicle

Quail Creek State Park • (435) 879-2378
472 N 5300 W, Hurricane, UT
stateparks.utah.gov • Day-use: $10/vehicle

Coral Cliffs Cinema 8 • (435) 635-1484
835 W State St, Hurricane, UT
coralcliffscinema8.com

Vermilion Cliffs NM • (435) 688-3200
Marble Canyon, AZ • blm.gov

Antelope Slot Canyon Tours by Chief Tsosi
55 S Lake Powell Blvd, Page,, AZ
antelopeslotcanyon.com • (928) 645-5594

Navajo Tours • (928) 698-3384
navajotours.com • Tours: $40–80/person

Glen Canyon NRA • (928) 608-6200
US-89, Page, AZ 86040 • nps.gov/glca

Antelope Canyon
The most-visited and most-photographed slot canyon in the American Southwest. A guide is required for both Upper and Lower Antelope Canyon.
navajonationparks.org

Grand Canyon Field Institute • (928) 638-2485
4 Tonto St, Grand Canyon, AZ
grandcanyon.org • *Day & multi-day classes*

Marvelous Marv's • (928) 707-0291
200 W Railroad Ave, Williams, AZ
marvelousmarv.com • Rates: $100/person

Pygmy Guides • (928) 707-0215
pygmyguides.com • *Overnight & Day Tours*

Ceiba Adventures • (928) 527-0171
Food/Shuttle Service & gear rental for river Trips
3051 N Fanning Dr, Flagstaff, AZ
ceibaadventures.com

Jeep Tours & Safaris • (800) 320-5337
106 AZ-64, Tusayan, AZ
grandcanyonjeeptours.com • Tours: $60+/adult

Canyon Dave Tours • (877) 845-3283
Williams, AZ • grand-canyon-tours-1.com

Fountain Outdoor Rec. • (928) 814-5038
875 E Ski Run, Williams, AZ
elkridgeski.com • *Snow Tubing & Skiing*

Bearizona Wildlife Park • (928) 635-2289
1500 E Route 66, Williams, AZ
bearizona.com • Rates: $20/adult

Grand Canyon Deer Farm • (928) 635-4073
6769 E Deer Farm Rd, Williams, AZ
deerfarm.com • Rates: $11.50/adult

Grand Canyon Brewery • (928) 635-2168
233 W Route 66, Williams, AZ
grandcanyonbrewery.com

Imax Theater • (928) 638-2468
AZ-64 & US-180, Grand Canyon, AZ
explorethecanyon.com • Tickets: $13.59/adult

Pipe Spring NM • (928) 643-7105
HC 65 Box 5, Fredonia, AZ
nps.gov/pisp • Entrance Fee: $7/person

Great Basin Area
Ward Charcoal Ovens State Hist. Park
Ely • (775) 289-1693
parks.nv.gov • Entrance Fee: $7/vehicle

NV Northern Railway Museum
Museum ($4/adult) & Train Excursions ($31+)
1100 Avenue A, East Ely
nnry.com • (775) 289-2085

Sunset Lanes • (775) 289-8811
1240 E Aultman St, # B, Ely

Las Vegas Area
Hoover Dam • (702) 494-2517
Located 30 miles southeast of Las Vegas on US-93
Parking: $10, Visitor Center Admission: $10,
Powerplant Tour: $15, Hoover Dam Tour: $30
(Tours include Visitor Center admission)
usbr.gov/lc/hooverdam

Red Rock Canyon Nat'l Conservation Area
1000 Scenic Dr, Las Vegas • (702) 515-5350
blm.gov • Day-use: $7/vehicle

Dig This • (702) 222-4344
3012 S Rancho Dr, Las Vegas
digthisvegas.com • Rates: $249/1.5 hrs

Bellagio Hotel • (888) 987-6667
3600 Las Vegas Blvd S, Las Vegas
bellagio.com • *Stop to see the famous fountains*

Vegas Indoor Skydiving • (702) 731-4768
200 Convention Center Dr, Las Vegas
vegasindoorskydiving.com • Rates: $75

Pinball Hall of Fame • (702) 597-2627
1610 E Tropicana Ave, Las Vegas
pinballmuseum.org • Free

The Atomic Testing Museum • (702) 794-5151
755 E Flamingo Rd, Las Vegas
nationalatomictestingmuseum.org • $22/adult

Exotics Racing • (702) 405-7223
6925 Speedway Blvd, Suite C105, Las Vegas
exoticsracing.com • $299/5 laps

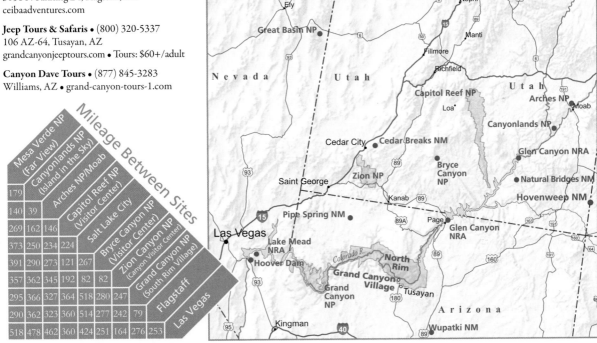

For more travel information, click www.utah.com, www.arizonaguide.com, and www.travelnevada.com

Mileage Between Sites

	Mesa Verde NP (Far View)	Canyonlands NP (Island in the Sky)	Arches NP/Moab	Capitol Reef NP (Visitor Center)	Salt Lake City	Bryce Canyon NP (Visitor Center)	Zion Canyon NP (Canyon Visitor Center)	Grand Canyon NP (South Rim Village)	Flagstaff	Las Vegas
	179									
	140	39								
	269	162	146							
	373	250	234	224						
	391	290	273	121	267					
	357	362	345	192	82	82				
	295	366	327	364	518	280	247			
	290	362	323	360	514	277	242	79		
	518	478	462	360	424	251	164	276	253	

Rock climber framed by a Joshua tree

Joshua Tree

74485 National Park Drive
Twentynine Palms, CA 92277
Phone: (760) 367-5500
Website: nps.gov/jotr

Established: October 31, 1994
August 10, 1936 (Nat'l Monument)
Size: 789,745 Acres
Annual Visitors: 2.0 Million
Peak Season: Spring & Fall

Activities: Hiking, Backpacking, Camping, Stargazing, Horseback Riding, Rock Climbing, and Biking

Campgrounds: Belle, Black Rock*, Cottonwood, Hidden Valley, Indian Cove*, Jumbo Rocks, Ryan, Sheep Pass, and White Tank
Fee: $15–20/night
Backcountry Camping: Permitted

Park Hours: All day, every day, except a few day-use areas
Entrance Fee: $20/vehicle, $10/individual (foot, bike, etc.)

*Reserve at recreation.gov or (877) 444-6777

The landscape of Joshua Tree National Park is as unique as the cast of characters who lived in and visited the region for the last 200 years. Forests of twisted Joshua trees and abstract rock piles mark a protected region where the Mojave and Colorado deserts converge in southeastern California. For at least 5,000 years, Native Americans, missionaries, miners, ranchers, and homesteaders have had their shake at life in this arid landscape. Life was difficult for all creatures: humans, animals, and plants. Only the gritty, resourceful, and adaptable survived in an inhospitable, seemingly lifeless wasteland.

Inhospitable? For most...probably. Lifeless wasteland? Certainly not. Hundreds of species found fascinating ways to beat the heat and conserve moisture. Red-spotted toads reside underground for most of their lives, only escaping the sandy soil after a soaking rain. Round-tailed ground squirrels sleep through the hottest part of summer and hibernate again in winter to avoid the cold. And of course there's the iconic Joshua tree, the largest species of yucca. Endemic to the southwestern United States, its primary habitat is the Mojave Desert between 1,300 and 5,900 feet elevation, thriving in open grasslands. To appreciate the Joshua tree forests you must first redefine the word "forest." Joshua trees are distributed sparsely across the desert so their roots can absorb sufficient water. For the first decade of its life a Joshua tree grows about three inches each year, an incredibly fast rate for a desert species. After its initial growth spurt, trees branch out more than up, slowing the growth rate to about an inch per year. Fortunately, they can live for hundreds of years, growing to more than 40 feet tall. The tree's name is owed to a group of Mormon settlers who crossed the Mojave Desert on their exodus west in the mid-19th century. As silhouettes, the trees appear human in form. Their extended limbs capped with spiky leaves evoked images of the Biblical Joshua with arms outstretched, leading his followers to the Promised Land.

Waves of miners, ranchers, and homesteaders came looking for their own promised land. Bill Keys was the most successful and colorful of the bunch. After a stint as sheriff, he settled into a life of mining and ranching in the desert of present-day Joshua Tree National Park, taking over the ranch of outlaw and cattle rustler Jim McHaney. Keys' spread gradually expanded and eventually became known as Desert Queen Ranch. He married, had children, murdered a man in a dispute over a mill, educated himself while in prison, and was later pardoned through the efforts of Erie Stanley Gardner, author of the Perry Mason novels.

John Samuelson was another colorful desert dweller. He carved political sayings into rocks that can still be found today about 1.5 miles from the turnout west of Quail Springs Picnic Area. Forced to leave his claim when his lack of citizenship came to light, he also murdered a man over a dispute, and spent time in California's State Hospital before escaping.

Minerva Hamilton Hoyt was a more refined patron of the desert. She grew up a southern belle on a Mississippi plantation before marrying a doctor and moving to Pasadena, where she spent much of her time organizing charitable and social events, gardening, and landscaping. Following the death of her husband and son, she turned her focus toward preserving the country's desert landscapes. She organized exhibitions of desert plants in New York, Boston, and London and founded the Desert Conservation League to gain support and publicity. Using her position on the California State Commission, she recommended large parks at Death Valley, Anza–Borrego Desert, and in the Joshua tree forests of the Little San Bernardino Mountains north of Palm Springs. Upon meeting President Franklin D. Roosevelt, she wasted no time expressing her opinions about the scenic and ecological value of these areas. Convinced—with the help of then Secretary of the Interior Harold Ickes—President Roosevelt created Joshua Tree National Monument in 1936, protecting the region from poachers and land developers while preserving it for future generations.

When to Go
Joshua Tree is open every day. Oasis (8:30am to 5pm), **Joshua Tree** (8am to 5pm), and **Cottonwood** (9am to 3pm) **Visitor Centers** are open all year. **Black Rock Nature Center** is open daily from October to May, 8am to 4pm, except on Fridays (noon to 8pm). Unlike most national parks, summer is the least popular time to visit, with daytime high temperatures exceeding 100°F. Temperatures gradually subside, and by fall the weather is pleasant. During winter, daytime highs reach into the 60s°F, but overnight lows are often below freezing. Spring is the best time to visit Joshua Tree. Temperatures are ideal in March and April. And depending on the amount of winter rain, you may have the opportunity to witness a spectacular array of wildflowers in bloom. Joshua Tree is often dry—after all it is a desert—receiving, on average, 4 inches of precipitation each year.

Transportation & Airports
Public transportation does not provide service to or around the park. The closest large commercial airport is Los Angeles International (LAX), 167 miles west of the park's South Entrance.

Directions
Joshua Tree is located in southeastern California, about 170 miles east of downtown Los Angeles. The park has three entrances, all easily accessed from I-10 and CA-62.

South Entrance: Heading east or west on I-10, take Exit 168 for Cottonwood Springs Road toward Mecca/Twentynine Palms. Turn right onto Cottonwood Springs Road into the park.

West and North Entrances: Heading east on I-10 from Los Angeles (150 miles away), take Exit 117 for CA-62/Twentynine Palms Hwy. Continue on CA-62 for almost 28 miles to Joshua Tree. Turn right at Park Blvd, which leads into the park. The North Entrance is reached by continuing on CA-62 past Park Blvd for another 17 miles to Utah Trail in Twentynine Palms. Turn right onto Utah Trail, which leads into the park.

Driving

Park Boulevard connects West and North Entrances. It also traverses the most popular areas of the park, including Hidden Valley, Ryan, and Jumbo Rock Campgrounds, and provides access to **Keys View Road**, Ryan Mountain Trail, and Skull Rock. In between the West and North Entrance Stations you'll find Indian Cove Road, which leads to a secluded campground popular among rock climbers. Farther west along the park's northern boundary is **Joshua Lane**, which leads to another remote campground: Black Rock Canyon. To cross the park from north to south you can take **Park Boulevard** from either the North or West Entrance to **Pinto Basin Road**, which continues south to **Cottonwood Springs Road**. There are several rugged dirt roads for 4WD vehicles. **Geology Tour Road** (18 miles) begins from

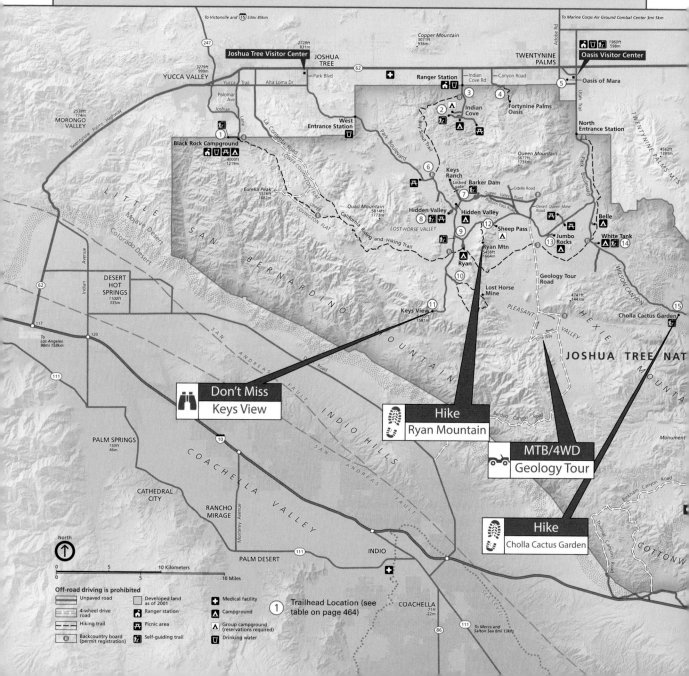

Park Boulevard between Sheep Pass and Jumbo Rocks. Brochures describing the fascinating landscapes at 16 designated stops are available at the beginning of the road. Most vehicles can make it 5.4 miles from pavement to Squaw Tank (Marker 9) under good conditions (no mud). Beyond this point 4WD is recommended. **Breedo Canyon, Black Eagle Mine, Covington Flat, Old Dale, Pinkham Canyon–Thermal Canyon, and**

Queen Valley Roads connect the park's remote regions for 4WD and mountain bike enthusiasts. You must stay on established roads (for your safety and to protect the environment). Off-road vehicles and all-terrain vehicles are not allowed in the park. Carry emergency supplies and inquire about road conditions before heading out on them. Bike racks are available at Queen Valley, so you can lock your bike and go hiking.

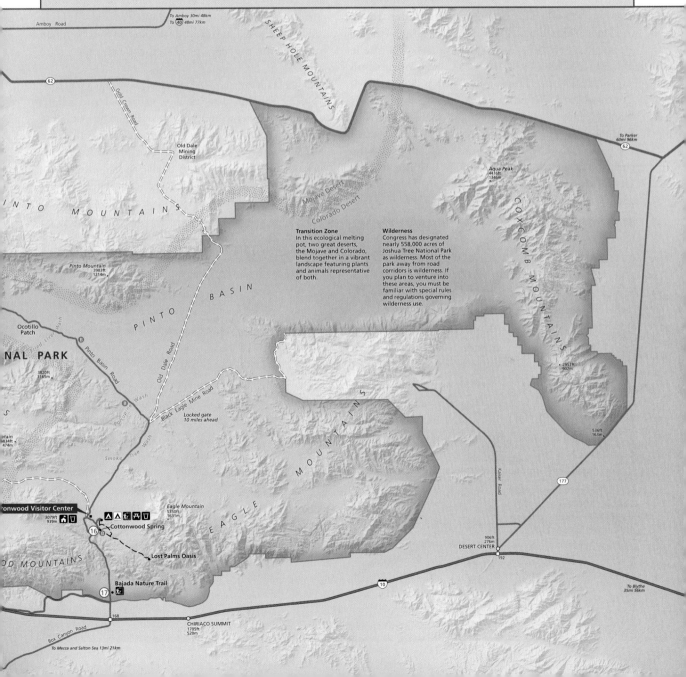

Camping

Joshua Tree National Park has nine designated campgrounds. **Black Rock** (100 sites) and **Indian Cove** (91) are the only campgrounds that accept reservations. Sites cost $20/night and can be reserved up to six months in advance from October through May at (877) 444-6777 or recreation.gov. All other campgrounds are first-come, first-served. From north to south on Park Boulevard and Pinto Basin Road are the following campgrounds: **Hidden Valley** (44 sites, $15/night), **Ryan** (31, $15), **Sheep Pass** (6 group sites, $35–50), **Jumbo Rocks** (124, $15), **Belle** (18, $15), **White Tank** (15, $15), and **Cottonwood** (62, $20). Water and flush toilets are available at Black Rock and Cottonwood. Water is also available at Oasis Visitor Center, Indian Cove Ranger Station, and West Entrance. There are no showers or hookups within the park, but you can find **showers** (fee) outside the park across the road from Joshua Tree Visitor Center. **Group sites** are available at Indian Cove, Sheep Pass, and Cottonwood (reservation required up to one year

in advance at 877.444.6777 or recreation.gov). There are fire rings, but you must bring your own wood. All campsites are typically occupied weekends from October through March. If you can't find a site, there is **free overflow camping** on Bureau of Land Management (BLM) land north of the park and Highway 62 at the intersection of Sunflower and Cascade Roads. It's a dry lakebed (occasionally it floods). You can also camp in the BLM's dispersed camping areas near the south entrance as long as you're at least 300 feet away from any roadway. You will not find restrooms or water at these locations, but they are a place to spend the night.

Hiking

You don't have to lug a heavy pack and gallons of water to enjoy the most beautiful vistas and rock formations this desert wilderness has to offer. The best way to discover the wonders of Joshua Tree is on foot, and it's easy thanks to twelve short, self-guiding nature trails. Or simply pull over (completely off the road) and walk among the Joshua trees.

Joshua Tree Hiking Trails (Distances are roundtrip)

	Name	Location (# on map)	Length	Difficulty Rating & Notes
Nature Trails (listed from NW to SW)	Hi-View	NW of Black Rock Camp (1)	1.3 miles	E – Loop, views of Mount San Gorgonio
	Indian Cove	West of Indian Cove Camp (2)	0.6 mile	E – Loop, explores history and ecology
	Oasis of Mara	Oasis Visitor Center (5)	0.5 mile	E – Accessible loop discusses oasis' history
	Barker Dam	Barker Dam Parking Area (7)	1.3 miles	E – Loop, visits early rancher's water tank
	Hidden Valley - ♿	Hidden Valley Picnic Area (8)	1.0 mile	E – Loop through a rock enclosed valley
	Cap Rock	Cap Rock Parking Area (9)	0.4 mile	E – Accessible loop, boulders and Joshua trees
	Keys View - ♿	Keys View Parking Area (11)	0.25 mile	E – Loop trail with the best views in the park
	Skull Rock	Jumbo Rocks Camp (13)	1.5 miles	E – Boulder piles and the renowned Skull Rock
	Arch Rock	White Tank Camp (14)	0.5 mile	M – Loop, explores park geology and an arch
	Cholla Cactus Garden	20 miles north of Cottonwood Visitor Center (15)	0.25 mile	E – Loop through dense field of Cholla Cactus • Don't get too close to the cacti, they hurt
	Cottonwood Spring	Cottonwood Spring Camp (16)	1.0 mile	E – Explores Colorado Desert ecosystem
	Bajada All-Access	Near south entrance (17)	0.25 mile	E – Loop explores plants of the Colorado Desert
Hiking Trails	Boy Scout	Indian Cove or Keys West (3, 6)	16.0 miles	S – Western edge of Wonderland of Rocks
	49 Palms Oasis	The end of Canyon Road (4)	3.0 miles	M – Desert oasis with stands of fan palms
	Lost Horse Mine - ♿	East of Keys View Rd (10)	4.0 miles	M – Visit a well-preserved defunct mining mill
	Ryan Mtn - ♿	Ryan Mtn Parking Area or Sheep Pass Camp (12)	3.0 miles	S – Best trail • Leads to 5,461-ft summit with 360° views of Eagle Mountains and Salton Sea
	Lost Palms Oasis	Cottonwood Spring Camp (16)	7.2 miles	M – Oasis, canyon, scrambling, and palm stands
	Mastodon Peak	Cottonwood Spring Camp (16)	3.0 miles	S – Summit provides views of Salton Sea

Difficulty Ratings: E = Easy, M = Moderate, S = Strenuous

Skull Rock, Barker Dam, and Keys View are the best of the bunch. **Skull Rock Trail** passes peculiar rock formations, including an eroded rock with the conical shape of a skull (located near the road). **Barker Dam** explores the difficulties of desert life. This short loop passes plenty of rocks for scrambling en route to an old cattle rancher's water tank. **Keys View** is a popular location due to outstanding panoramic views of Salton Sea, San Andreas Fault, and Mexico's Signal Mountain (on a clear day). A more arduous journey is the 3-mile (roundtrip) trek to **Ryan Mountain**, where views surpass those found at Keys. The 4-mile (roundtrip) **Lost Horse Mine/Mountain Trail** glimpses into Joshua Tree's era of mining, visiting the site of a ten-stamp mill where rock was crushed to extract its minerals. Hikers' most common problems are dehydration and getting lost, so carry plenty of water and pay attention to your route. Washes and animal paths can make route-finding difficult.

Backpacking

Tired of busy campgrounds? Looking for a night of the purest peace and quiet this side of the Sierra Nevada? Try backpacking in Joshua Tree's 585,000 acres of wilderness. If you plan on spending the night in the backcountry, be sure to **register** at one of 13 backcountry registration boards (marked with a Ⓑ on the map on pages 462–463). Failure to register can result in your vehicle being towed and/or cited. Backpackers must camp outside day-use areas, at least one mile from any road, and 500 feet from any trail. The main hurdle to backpacking at Joshua Tree is water. Park policy dictates that all water within the park boundary is reserved for wildlife. You will have to carry enough water for the duration of your trip. Excellent backpacking options include the 16-mile (roundtrip) **Boy Scout Trail**, which connects Indian Cove with Park Blvd just north of Hidden Valley, and 35 miles (one-way) of **California Riding and Hiking Trail** that passes through the park. The latter runs parallel to Park Boulevard, beginning at Black Rock Canyon and terminating near the park's North Entrance.

Rock Climbing

Joshua Tree is no longer just the winter retreat for Yosemite's rock climbers. It has become a **world class rock climbing destination** of its own, attracting thousands of climbers each year. With more than 400 climbing formations and 8,000 routes, there's something for everyone. If you are an experienced climber visiting the park for the first time you may want to pick up a comprehensive rock climbing guidebook (available at the visitor center). If you'd rather receive your information straight from the horse's mouth, there are always experienced climbers milling about the campgrounds and rock formations.

Beginners may want to join a **guide** for a rock climbing course. Joshua Tree Rock Climbing School (800.890.4745, joshuatreerockclimbing.com), Joshua Tree Guides (408.833.8308, joshuatreeguides.com), Vertical Adventures (800. 514.8785, verticaladventures.com), and Joshua Tree's Uprising Adventure Guides (888.CLIMB-ON, joshuatreeuprising.com) offer courses for climbers of all abilities. A full day rock climbing course costs about $175 per person. Private instruction is available at a variable rate dependent on group size.

Horseback Riding

Horseback riding is another excellent way to experience the park, with 253 miles of designated equestrian trails. Ryan and Black Campgrounds are the only designated camping areas allowing horses and stock. You can also camp in the backcountry with your stock, but a **free permit** is required. Call (760) 367-5545 to arrange a permit or to make reservations at Ryan Campground. Grazing is not permitted within the park. Water is usually the limiting factor when planning a trip, as horses are not permitted within 0.25-mile of any water source. You can put the planning into someone else's hands by taking a **guided trail ride** from Joshua Tree Ranch (760.902.7336, joshuatreeranch.com). Guided rides cost $35/hour or $45/hour for a private ride.

Biking

Biking is permitted on all park roads; unpaved and 4WD roads' limited traffic makes them ideal for mountain bikers. The park also hopes to develop 29 miles of trails for bike use but is awaiting approval by Congress. Check online or at a visitor center for the current status.

Juniper Flats

Headstone Rock (near Ryan Camp)

Queen Valley sunset

Stargazing

If you come from a busy metropolitan area like Los Angeles, there's nothing quite like a clear night sky. Bring a set of binoculars and tour the Milky Way on your own. You can also join one of the park's free Night Sky Programs, which are held about once a week between October and May. A current schedule can be found at the park website, campground bulletin boards, entrance stations, and visitor centers.

Ranger Programs

Guests of the park have the opportunity to **tour historic Keys Ranch** where Bill and Frances Keys thrived in the desert for nearly 60 years. The ranch is located at the end of a short spur road off Park Blvd just east of Hidden Valley (see the map on page 462). **Admission is restricted to guided walking tours.** They are offered from February until mid-May, 10am on Sundays; and 2pm on Wednesdays, Fridays, and Saturdays. Tours generally last 90 minutes and require that you walk a half-mile. Group size is limited to 25 people. Cost is

$10 per person (ages 12 and over), $5 for children (ages 6–11), and children under 6 are free. Reservations are required and can be made by calling (760) 367-5522 between 9am and 4:30pm any day of the week. You can also purchase tickets ahead of time at any of the park's visitor centers. **Tickets cannot be purchased at the ranch.**

Throughout the year, park rangers also offer a variety of walks, talks, star parties, and evening programs. Tours range from a simple 15-minute talk at Keys View to a 2.5-hour hike to Mastodon Peak. Check online for a current schedule of events. Schedules are also posted on campground bulletin boards, and at visitor centers and entrance stations.

The Desert Institute at Joshua Tree National Park (760.367.5525, joshuatree.org/desert-institute) provides educational programs. Reasonably priced courses in natural science, survival skills, arts, and more are offered regularly. Courses do not cater to children.

For Kids

Children are welcome to participate in the park's **Junior Ranger Program**. To get started, download the activity booklet from the park website or pick up a free hard copy from any visitor center or entrance station. Complete the activities to earn an official Joshua Tree National Park Junior Ranger badge.

Flora & Fauna

More than 800 species of plants, including the park's namesake, can be found at Joshua Tree National Park. It's a collection so diverse and unique that park supporters originally suggested the area be called "Desert Plants National Park." There's also exceptional animal diversity. More than 50 species of mammals and 250 species of birds have been documented. Animals are commonly seen near sources of water like fan palm oases, Barker Dam, or Smith Water Canyon.

When flowers are in bloom, Joshua Tree becomes a colorful paradise. Blooms vary from year-to-year with seasonal differences in rainfall and temperature. Flowers begin to bloom in the low elevations by February and may last until June in the higher elevations.

Pets

Pets are allowed in the park, but must be kept on a leash no more than six feet in length at all times. They are prohibited from all hiking trails and cannot be more than 100 feet from a road, picnic area, or campground.

Accessibility

All visitor centers are accessible to individuals in wheelchairs. Keys View and Bajada, Cap Rock, and Oasis of Mara Nature Trails are fully accessible. There's a designated wheelchair friendly campsite at Jumbo Rocks Campground.

Weather

Remember you're visiting a desert. Days are usually hot, dry, and clear (with the exception of smog from Los Angeles and the coast). Summers are hot, over 100°F during the day and usually not below 70°F through the night. Spring and fall bring perfect weather with highs around 85°F and lows averaging about 50°F.

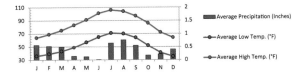

Vacation Planner

If you're planning an extended **backpacking** (page 465) or **rock climbing** (page 465) trip, go for it! The park is great for those activities, but this exercise focuses on a more typical visit. Provided below is a one-day itinerary to let you know where to go and what to see. **Camping** (page 464) is available in the park, but lodging is not. Nearby dining, grocery stores, lodging, festivals, and attractions are listed on pages 477–479.

Day 1: Arriving from the west, take CA-62 around the northern border to arrive at the park's **West Entrance** in Joshua Tree. Be sure to make a quick pit-stop at **Joshua Tree Visitor Center** before entering. Browse the exhibits, watch the introductory film (upon request), and remember to check the current schedule of ranger programs (if you haven't looked online already). Head into the park and stop at **Hidden Valley**. It's a great place for an introduction to the interesting rock formations. If you have enough time, drive over to **Barker's**

Highlining at Hemingway (Lost Horse)

Cholla Cactus Garden

Best of Joshua Tree

Attraction: Joshua Trees
Runner-up: Keys Ranch
2nd Runner-up: Cholla Cactus Garden

Activity: Joshua Tree Ranch Trail Ride
Runner-up: Rock Climbing

Hike: Ryan Mountain
Runner-up: Hidden Valley
2nd Runner-up: Keys View

Dam, which is also worth a visit. Head south past Cap Rock to **Keys View Road**. Drive to its end for one of the most stunning desert vistas in the park. On a clear day you can peer clear across southern California to Signal Mountain in Mexico. Make the return trip to Park Blvd. If you feel like a nice hike, pull into **Ryan Mountain Parking Area** to hike the 3-mile trail. Note that it's pretty strenuous, gaining more than 1,000-ft elevation, and the views are comparable to those at Keys. Continuing along Park Blvd you'll find plenty of opportunities to snap photos of intriguing Joshua trees. Stop at **Jumbo Rocks** to checkout some really cool rocks, including **Giant Marbles**. Return to Park Blvd and head south on **Pinto Basin Road**. Stop at **Cholla Cactus Garden** before exiting at South Entrance to I-10.

Inspiration Point (Anacapa)

Channel Islands

1901 Spinnaker Drive
Ventura, CA 93001
Phone: (805) 658-5730
Website: nps.gov/chis

Established: March 5, 1980
April 26, 1938 (Nat'l Monument)
Size: 249,354 Acres
Annual Visitors: 325,000
Peak Season: Summer

Activities: Hiking, Backpacking, Camping, Paddling, Swimming, Snorkeling, Sailing, and SCUBA

Each Island has a Campground*
Fee: $15/night (reservations req'd)

Backcountry Camping: Permitted at Del Norte Camp (Santa Cruz Island) and on Santa Rosa Island's beaches. Reservations are required.

The park is open every day, with regularly scheduled island trips
Entrance Fee: None

*Reserve at recreation.gov or (877) 444-6777

Off the coast of California, less than 100 miles from 18 million people living in the Greater Los Angeles Area, is a group of eight islands. Compared to their surroundings, the Channel Islands have been left undeveloped, even after continuous inhabitation for at least the last 8,000 years. Five of these islands—Santa Barbara, Anacapa, Santa Cruz, Santa Rosa, and San Miguel—comprise Channel Islands National Park. Rich history combined with incredibly diverse and often unique ecology make these volcanic islands stand alone in the National Park portfolio.

The park's geology is constantly changing thanks to relentless pounding of water on rock. However, the most startling change to the islands wasn't caused by water's erosive powers, but by its absence. More than 13,000 years ago, a blink of an eye in geologic terms, the four northern islands were one super-island. North America was in the middle of the last great Ice Age and water level was much lower than it is today. Climatic changes caused the glaciers to recede. As water levels rose the lowest valleys flooded, ultimately disconnecting the islands from one another.

Geologic changes also drastically altered the islands' ecology. Approximately 20,000 years ago, mammoths swam to the super-island, likely searching for vegetation whose scent was carried by the prevailing westward winds. As their population grew, resources became depleted. Natural selection favored smaller mammoths capable of surviving on less food. The woolly beasts lived on the islands for about 10,000 years before becoming extinct. Evidence of mammoths—once the most widely spread mammal—has been found on four continents: an engraving on a tusk found in a rock shelter in southwestern France, the preserved carcass of a baby male frozen in Siberia's permafrost, more than

100 mammoth remains at the bottom of a sinkhole in Hot Springs, SD, and a pygmy mammoth here on Santa Rosa Island. When these miniature remains were discovered in 1873, scientists believed elephants inhabited the islands. More than 100 years later, additional fossils helped conclude they were in fact pygmy mammoths, about one-tenth the size of a typical Columbian mammoth. They measured between 4.5- and 7-feet tall, weighing about one ton. A Colombian mammoth measured up to 14-feet tall, and weighed as much as ten tons. Human fossils have also been found on the Channel Islands. At Arlington Springs, on Santa Rosa Island, scientists discovered human remains dating back more than 13,000 years. This find has become known as Arlington Man, and it is among the oldest remains found in North America.

Humans have had a considerable effect on the islands. Early Chumash people relied on the sea for food and tools, traveling between the islands and mainland in canoes, called tomols, hollowed out from redwood trees that drifted down the coast. The Chumash were present when Juan Rodriguez Cabrillo reached San Miguel Island in 1542. Cabrillo and his fellow explorers introduced disease and overhunted sea life; by the 1820s the entire surviving island Chumash population had moved to the mainland.

Over the course of the next century, the island was home to Mexican prisoners, ambitious ranchers, and hermit fishermen. In 1864, the Civil War increased demand for wool and more than 24,000 sheep grazed the hills of Santa Cruz. During prohibition, Raymond "Frenchy" LeDreau watched over caches of liquor stored in Anacapa's caves. When Santa Cruz became part of the new National Monument, Frenchy was allowed to remain on the island as its caretaker. In 1956, at the age of 80, he was forced to leave after suffering severe injuries due to a fall. In 1969, more than 100,000 barrels of crude oil spilled into the Channel during the Santa Barbara oil spill, at the time the largest oil spill in United States waters. The National Park Service and Nature Conservancy have worked since to preserve this picturesque landscape and its unique ecosystem for the thousands of visitors that arrive each year.

When to Go
The park is open every day, but picking the best time to visit is not easy. It can be idyllic one day and awful the next. High winds and rough seas often prevent scheduled transportation services from reaching the islands. It's best not to plan a trip well in advance (unless you have a backup plan or you're spending several days in the area). Gray whales migrate through the coastal waters from late December through March. Blue and humpback whales come to feed between July and September. After a year of average rainfall, the wildflower bloom peaks around late winter/early spring. Type and abundance of wildflowers varies from island-to-island, so be sure to inquire at a visitor center if you're interested in flowers. Ocean conditions for SCUBA, snorkel, swimming, and kayaking are usually best from summer through fall.

Robert J. Lagomarsino Visitor Center (1901 Spinnaker Dr, Ventura • 805.658.5730) is open daily from 8:30am to 5pm. It is closed on Thanksgiving and Christmas. Exhibits, an introductory film, telescopes, and a bookstore are available. **Outdoors Santa Barbara Visitor Center** (113 Harbor Way, 4th Floor, Santa Barbara • 805.884.1475) provides information, exhibits, and excellent views of Santa Barbara. It is open daily from 10am to 5pm.

Airports
Los Angeles International (LAX) is located 70 miles southeast of park headquarters. Santa Barbara (SBA), Camarillo (CMA), and Oxnard (OXR) airports are closer and smaller alternatives.

Mainland Transportation
Amtrak (800.872.7245, amtrak.com), Metrolink (800.371.5465, metrolinktrains.com), Greyhound (800.231.2222, greyhound.com), Gold Coast Transit (805.487.4222, goldcoasttransit.org), Santa Barbara Metropolitan Transit District (805.963.3366, sbmtd.gov), and Ventura County Transportation Commission (805.642.1591, goventura.org) provide access to the park's mainland visitor centers but not its islands.

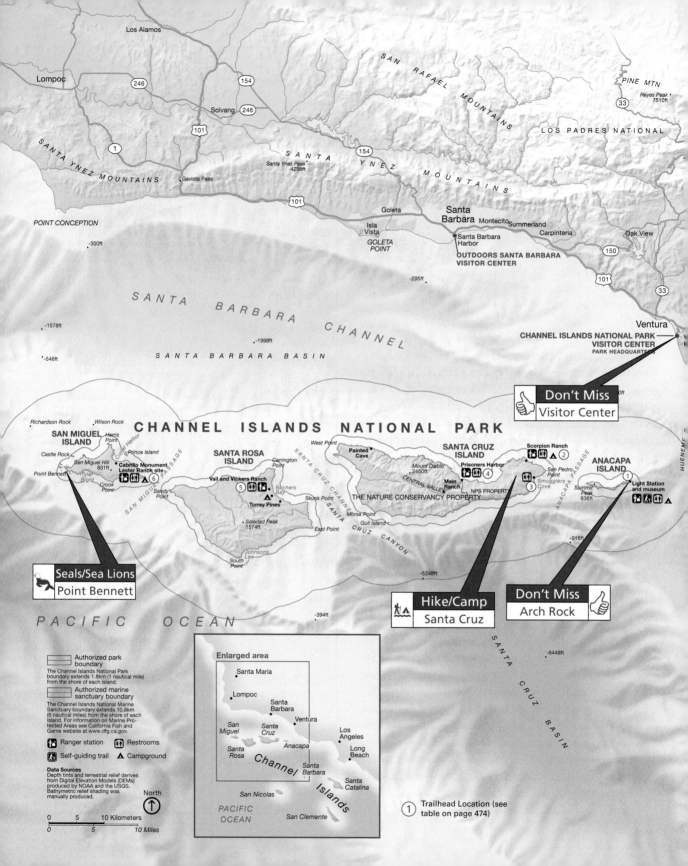

Los Alamos

Lompoc

246

154

Solvang 246

101

1

SANTA YNEZ MOUNTAINS

SAN RAFAEL MOUNTAINS

PINE MTN

Reyes Peak 7510ft

33

LOS PADRES NATIONAL

SANTA YNEZ Peak 4298ft

154

SANTA YNEZ MOUNTAINS

Gaviota Pass

POINT CONCEPTION

101

Goleta

Santa Barbara

Montecito Summerland

Carpinteria

Oak View

Isla Vista

GOLETA POINT

Santa Barbara Harbor

OUTDOORS SANTA BARBARA VISITOR CENTER

150

-300ft

-295ft

101

33

SANTA BARBARA CHANNEL

-1578ft

-1998ft

Ventura

CHANNEL ISLANDS NATIONAL PARK VISITOR CENTER
PARK HEADQUARTERS

SANTA BARBARA BASIN

-546ft

Don't Miss
Visitor Center

Richardson Rock

Wilson Rock

CHANNEL ISLANDS NATIONAL PARK

SAN MIGUEL ISLAND

Harris Point

Castle Rock

Cuyler Harbor

Prince Island

West Point

SANTA ROSA ISLAND

Carrington Point

Painted Cave

SANTA CRUZ ISLAND

Scorpion Ranch

ANACAPA ISLAND

Point Bennett

San Miguel Hill 831ft

Cabrillo Monument Lester Ranch site

6

Vail and Vickers Ranch

5

Bechers Bay

Mount Diablo 2450ft

CENTRAL VALLEY

Prisoners Harbor

4

Main Ranch

San Pedro Point

Smugglers Cove

3

Light Station and museum

1

Summit Peak 936ft

Tyler Bight

Crook Point

Sandy Point

Torrey Pines

Skunk Point

THE NATURE CONSERVANCY PROPERTY

NPS PROPERTY

Soledad Peak 1574ft

Morse Point

Gull Island

East Point

-918ft

Johnsons Lee

South Point

Seals/Sea Lions
Point Bennett

PACIFIC OCEAN

-394ft

-5248ft

Hike/Camp
Santa Cruz

Don't Miss
Arch Rock

SANTA CRUZ BASIN

-6448ft

Enlarged area

Santa Maria

Lompoc

Santa Barbara

Ventura

San Miguel

Santa Cruz

Anacapa

Los Angeles

Long Beach

Santa Rosa

Santa Barbara

Channel Islands

Santa Catalina

San Nicolas

PACIFIC OCEAN

San Clemente

North

0   5   10 Kilometers
0   5   10 Miles

1 Trailhead Location (see table on page 474)

Directions

Channel Islands is located in the Pacific Ocean, just off the coast of California. Island visitors arrive via transportation provided by Island Packers or Channel Islands Aviation, but most park guests also visit one of the mainland visitor centers located in Santa Barbara or Ventura. Driving directions to these facilities are provided below.

To Robert J. Lagomarsino Visitor Center (1901 Spinnaker Dr, Ventura)/Island Packers: Traveling south on US-101 toward Ventura, take Exit 68 toward Seward Ave. Turn left at Harbor Blvd. After two miles, turn right at Spinnaker Drive. Traveling north on US-101 toward Ventura, take exit 64 for Victoria Ave. Turn left at Victoria Ave. Take the second right onto Olivas Park Drive, which turns into Spinnaker Drive. Spinnaker Drive passes Island Packers (look for the sign) and terminates at the visitor center. Free parking is available at Island Packers and the beach parking lot.

Outdoors Santa Barbara Visitor Center (113 Harbor Way, 4th Floor, 90-minute free parking at harbor parking lot): Traveling south on US-101 toward Santa Barbara, take Exit 97 for Castillo St toward Harbor. Turn right at Castillo St, and then make another right at Shoreline Dr. Turn left at Harbor Way.

Traveling north, take US-101 Exit 96B for Garden St. Turn left at Garden St, and then make a right at Cabrillo Blvd. Continue onto Shoreline Drive, and then turn left at Harbor Way.

Island Transportation

Park concessioners provide boat and plane transportation to the islands. Once you reach an island, there is no transportation available; all areas must be accessed by foot, private boat, or kayak. **Island Packers** (805.642.1393, islandpackers. com) provides year-round transportation to the Channel Islands, and specialized whale watching and harbor tours. Ferries service Santa Cruz (Scorpion Anchorage and Prisoners Harbor) and Anacapa, year-round. Trips to the outer islands of Santa Barbara (April–October), San Miguel (May–October), and Santa Rosa (April–November) are seasonal. San Miguel reopened May 2016 after being closed due to concerns of possible unexploded ordnance. Santa Barbara Island was closed at time of publication due to storm damage, but it is only expected to last until 2017. Rates vary depending on where and how you visit. Roundtrip tickets for day-trippers to either Santa Cruz or Anacapa Island cost $59/adult and $41/child. Campers must pay a rate of $79/adult and $57/child. Adult roundtrip to San Miguel costs $105 (day-trip) and $147 (camper). Adult roundtrip to either Santa Rosa or Santa Barbara costs $82 (day-trip) and $114 (camper). Kayak transportation costs an additional $19 for all boats 13 feet or less and $28 for boats over 13 feet. Island Packers' Main Office is located at 1691 Spinnaker Drive, Suite 105B, just a short walk from Robert J. Lagomarsino Visitor Center.

Channel Islands Aviation (305 Durley Ave, 805.987.1301, flycia.com) provides year-round air transportation to Santa Rosa Island. This 25-minute flight departs Camarillo Airport, with deluxe and half-day trips starting at $1,100 plus tax (up to 8 passengers). They also offer transportation for campers, which costs $1,700 plus tax roundtrip (up to 7 passengers). Campsites are located a short distance from the airstrip and must be reserved prior to arrival (see page 473 for camping information).

Santa Cruz

The Islands

Some 13,000 years ago the four northern Channel Islands were united, forming one super-island. As glaciers from the last Ice Age receded, water levels began to rise and distinct islands formed. Today, Channel Islands National Park consists of five of the eight Channel Islands: San Miguel, Santa Rosa, Santa Cruz, Anacapa, and Santa Barbara. The official boundary extends one nautical mile beyond the islands' shorelines to protect marine environments, including giant kelp forests. These islands are some of the last undeveloped tracts of land in the Greater Los Angeles area. No services are available. You will have to pack everything you require, including food and water, and all trash must be packed out. The islands' primitive nature and limited transportation services (page 471) result in roughly 90% of park visitors never stepping foot on the islands. The other 10% find this an ideal environment to commune with nature. A short description of each island (listed from west to east) and its activities is provided below:

San Miguel Island (9,325 acres): If you are willing to endure the wind and the weather, San Miguel is a fantastic place for hiking and camping. A 16-mile trail leads across the island to **Point Bennett**, where more than 30,000 seals and sea lions have been seen during certain times of the year. These gatherings represent **one of the largest congregations of wildlife in the world**. Sea lions typically give birth around mid-June and the park provides ranger-guided walks to Point Bennett beginning in June.

Santa Rosa Island (53,000 acres): Santa Rosa is the second largest island in California. It's home to substantial archeological discoveries like the **pygmy mammoth** and **Arlington Man**. Today, very few visitors come to Santa Rosa. It's located 40 nautical miles from Robert J. Lagomarsino Visitor Center, and portions of the island are closed for several months to allow hunting of reintroduced elk and deer.

Santa Cruz Island (62,000 acres): Santa Cruz is the largest island in California and the only one not entirely owned by the National Park Service, with 76% controlled by the **Nature Conservancy**. Santa Cruz is the favorite destination for campers and hikers. A network of trails (and an old military road) connects popular destinations across the park's portion of the island. Beautiful beaches, clear water, and kelp forests make this a great island for swimming and snorkeling. Kayakers also frequent the island. Painted Cave, located on Nature Conservancy property in the northwest corner of the island, is a 0.25-mile long, 100-ft wide grotto with an entrance ceiling of 160 feet. The cave is particularly beautiful in spring when water falls over its entrance.

Anacapa Island (700 acres): Early Chumash people called it "Anyapakh," which translates to "mirage." Summer fog and afternoon heat tend to cloak or change the appearance of this volcanic island. Even more deceptive is the island itself. It's composed of three smaller islets descriptively named East, Middle, and West Anacapa. These islets are separated from one another and only reachable by boat.

Even though it's the second smallest of the park's islands, it's also the most visited due to close proximity to Ventura, CA, the port of departure for Island Packers' boats. Anacapa is just 12 miles from the mainland, and most visits consist of a walk around East Anacapa. A 1.5-mile trail leads to **Inspiration Point**, a small **campground**, and **Anacapa Island Light Station**. The trail also provides excellent views of the park's most notable feature, 40-foot high **Arch Rock**. It's one of many sea caves and natural bridges carved into the island's towering sea cliffs by the Pacific Ocean.

Anacapa is an excellent site to view wildlife, especially if you like seagulls. **It is home to the largest breeding colony of western gulls in the world.** Chicks hatch in May and June before flying away in July. **West Anacapa also boasts the largest breeding colony of endangered California brown pelicans.** Sea lions and harbor seals have been known to relax on the island's rocky shorelines. The area's nutrient rich water supports a diverse underwater ecosystem including forests of kelp. Divers, snorkelers, and kayakers all have the opportunity to see the massive seaweed.

Santa Barbara Island (639 acres): The smallest of the Channel Islands is a fair distance southeast of the others and 38 nautical miles from the mainland. This small variation in location results in a significant decrease in wind and rough water. Five miles of hiking trails span the entire island. It's a fantastic site for wildlife viewing, with **one of the world's largest colonies of Xantus's murrelets breeding here.** The park concessioner makes infrequent trips to Santa Barbara, which makes for overnight camping trips lasting a minimum of 3 days.

Camping
Channel Islands offers one designated campground on each island. All campgrounds are located at least a half-mile (usually uphill) from the boat landing area. Campers must bring their own water and carry all trash off the island. Campfires are not permitted. Pit toilets are available. Wind breaks are provided at Santa Rosa and Santa Cruz Island Campgrounds. Camping costs $15 per night per site and **reservations must be made in advance** by calling (877) 444-6777 or clicking recreation.gov.

Backcountry camping is available year-round on Santa Cruz and Santa Rosa Islands. Del Norte campsite, near Prisoners Harbor on Santa Cruz Island, is available for backcountry camping all year. It's a 3.5-mile hike from Prisoners Harbor and 12 miles from Scorpion Anchorage. **Reservations are required** ($15/night) and can be made at (877) 444-6777 or recreation.gov. Backpackers are also allowed to camp on Santa Rosa's beaches from mid-August until the end of December. Reservations for beach camping are free and must be made in advance by calling the park at (805) 658-5711.

Ferries (page 471) usually fill before campgrounds, so it is wise to book your transportation (if required) prior to your camping reservations.

Paddling
Sea kayaking is a common activity at the Channel Islands. Island Packers can **transport your boat** for $19–28, depending on its size. Visitors often choose to join one of the park's authorized outfitters to safely explore the islands while learning about its history from a knowledgeable guide. The Scorpion Beach area on East Santa Cruz Island is the most popular kayaking destination. Here you'll find plenty of sea caves and cliffs to paddle in and out of. Sand beaches and a campground are easily accessible. **San Miguel and Santa Rosa Islands** are exceptional destinations, but only the most highly experienced and conditioned sea kayakers should venture into these waters due to consistently extreme weather and sea conditions. It's not recommended, but you can paddle from the mainland to the islands. These paddlers should be particularly cautious. In addition to dicey weather and rough water, you must pass through a heavily trafficked shipping lane. Santa Barbara Adventure Company (877.884.9283, sbadventureco.com), Aquasports (800.773.2309, islandkayaking.com), Channel Islands Kayak Center (805.984.5995, cikayak.com), and Channel Island Outfitters (805.899.4925, channelislandso.com) are **authorized outfitters** who offer a multitude of kayak trips, including day-trips to Santa Cruz. Rates cost right around $150–200 per adult single kayak, which includes transportation to the island.

Sea lions (San Miguel)

Channel Islands Hiking Trails (Distances are roundtrip)

Name	Location (# on map)	Length	Difficulty Rating & Notes
Inspiration Point - ♿	Anacapa Island (1)	1.5 miles	E – East Anacapa Landing Cove to exceptional views
Lighthouse	Anacapa Island (1)	0.5 mile	E – Short stroll to lighthouse from landing
Historic Ranch	Scorpion Beach (2)	0.5 mile	E – Casual walk around historic Scorpion Ranch
Cavern Point	Scorpion Beach (2)	2.0 miles	M – Shoreline walk • Whale-watching opportunities
Potato Harbor	Scorpion Beach (2)	5.0 miles	M – Secluded Harbor • No beach access
Scorpion Canyon	Scorpion Beach (2)	4.5 miles	M – Loop through steep canyon walls
Smuggler's Cove - ♿	Scorpion Beach (2)	7.5 miles	S – Spur trails and beach along route
Montañon Ridge	Scorpion Beach (2)	8.0 miles	S – Off-trail • Map reading skills recommended
Smuggler's Canyon	Smuggler's Cove (3)	2.0 miles	M – Leads through native vegetation
Yellowbanks	Smuggler's Cove (3)	3.0 miles	M – Off-trail, along shoreline to overlook • No Beach
San Pedro Point	Smuggler's Cove (3)	4.0 miles	M – Go off-trail east of Smuggler's Cove
Prisoner's Harbor	Prisoner's Harbor (4)	0.5 mile	E – Short walk in and around Prisoner's Harbor
Pelican Bay	Prisoner's Harbor (4)	4.0 miles	M – Permit Required • Enters Nature Conservancy
Del Norte Camp	Prisoner's Harbor (4)	7.0 miles	S – Hike east to a backcountry camp
Navy Road–Del Norte	Prisoner's Harbor (4)	8.5 miles	S – Loop combines Navy Road and Del Norte Trail
Chinese Harbor	Prisoner's Harbor (4)	15.5 miles	S – Leads to only accessible beach on isthmus
China Pines	Prisoner's Harbor (4)	18.0 miles	S – Long trek to pine grove
Mantañon Ridge - ♿	Prisoner's Harbor (4)	21.0 miles	S – Off-trail • Map reading skills recommended
Water Canyon Beach - ♿	Santa Rosa (5)	3.0 miles	E – Access 2-mile-long white sand beach (near camp)
East Point	Santa Rosa (5)	16.0 miles	S – You'll pass torrey pines and unrestricted beaches
Torrey Pines	Santa Rosa (5)	5.0 miles	M – Fantastic views of torrey pines
Lobo Canyon	Santa Rosa (5)	9.0 miles	S – Amazing canyon sculpted by wind and water
Black Mountain	Santa Rosa (5)	8.0 miles	S – View other islands and mainland from here
Cuyler Beach	San Miguel (6)	2.0 miles	E – 1.75-mile-long white sand beach
Lester Ranch Site	San Miguel (6)	2.0 miles	M – Exceptional views and historic sites
Caliche Forest - ♿	San Miguel (6)	5.0 miles	S – Only allowed with a park ranger
Point Bennett - ♿	San Miguel (6)	16.0 miles	S – Only allowed with a park ranger
Lester Point - ♿	San Miguel (6)	5.0 miles	S – Only allowed with a park ranger
Arch Point	Santa Barbara (7)	1.0 mile	M – Wildflowers in late winter/spring
Sea Lion Rookery	Santa Barbara (7)	2.0 miles	M – Expansive views and (possibly) sea lions
Elephant Seal Cove	Santa Barbara (7)	2.5 miles	S – Maybe elephant seals, definitely steep cliffs
Webster Point	Santa Barbara (7)	3.0 miles	S – Continue beyond Elephant Seal Cove
Signal Peak	Santa Barbara (7)	2.5 miles	S – Highest point on the island

Difficulty Ratings: E = Easy, M = Moderate, S = Strenuous

Water Activities

Swimming, snorkeling, and SCUBA diving are popular pastimes best done on the islands of Santa Barbara, Anacapa, and Eastern Santa Cruz. These activities are allowed at San Miguel and Santa Rosa Islands, but should only be attempted by individuals who are properly trained, conditioned, and equipped. This recommendation is issued because of consistently strong winds and rough waters typical of these two islands. There are many fantastic swimming, snorkeling, and SCUBA diving locations around the other three islands. The water is clear with massive curtains of kelp. However, it's possible to see what's under the water without getting wet. **During summer, divers equipped with a video camera plunge into Landing Cove (East Anacapa).** High and dry, visitors can not only see the kelp forests, sea stars, and Garibaldi through the eye of the camera, but they can ask the divers questions using a voice communication system. Video monitors are located at Anacapa's dock and the mainland visitor center in Ventura. Truth Aquatics (805.962.1127, truthaquatics.com) offers multi-day, live-aboard excursions featuring diving, kayaking, and stand-up paddleboarding.

Dolphins and whales are often spotted swimming the waters surrounding the Channel Islands. Island Packers (805.642.1393, islandpackers.com) offers seasonal **whale watching and wildlife viewing boat trips**. Condor Express (888.779.4253, condorexpress.com) similar expeditions for $50–99 per adult. Private boaters are also welcome to explore the waters, but the Marine Mammal Protection Act stipulates boats must remain at least 100 yards away from whales (unless they approach you, then turn off your engine).

Private boaters have an easier time reaching the north shores of San Miguel and Santa Rosa, where you'll find the best surfing. Sail Channel Islands (805.750.7828, sailchannelislands.com) provides a **sailing school** and charter services (all-day, 4 passengers, $950).

Hiking & Backpacking

Anacapa, the park's most frequented island, has very limited hiking. A 1.5-mile trail leads to East Anacapa's **Inspiration Point**. You can extend this walk by adding the lighthouse, Pinnipied Point, and Cathedral Cove as destinations along the way. In all, it's a little more than two miles. Middle and West Anacapa are closed to hiking. **Santa Cruz is the number one destination for campers and hikers.** Trails and roads connect Scorpion Beach, Smugglers Cove, Prisoners Harbor, and many places in between. Unguided hiking is not allowed in Nature Conservancy property (marked by a fence line). The seldom visited trails on **San Miguel and Santa Rosa Islands are excellent too.** San Miguel's Caliche Forest and Bennett Point are particularly nice, but make sure you're prepared for windy weather. Caliche Forest, Bennett Point, and Lester Point Trails require accompaniment by a park ranger.

Camping (page 473) and **backpacking** are essentially synonymous at Channel Islands. All campgrounds are primitive without water and fire rings. Pit toilets are available. Del Norte Campground on Santa Cruz Island is the only designated backcountry campground. Backpackers visiting Santa Rosa Island are allowed to camp along the beaches between mid-August and the end of December. The closest beach is 10 miles from the boat/plane drop-off location.

Ranger Programs

Park rangers offer several free public programs at Robert J. Lagomarsino Visitor Center. Rangers and concessioner naturalists provide island hikes each day there's island transportation service (page 471). Evening programs are offered during summer at Scorpion Ranch Campground. Visit the park website or a visitor center for a current schedule of events.

For Kids

Children with their sea legs will enjoy a boat cruise to the islands. Whale watching and wildlife tours are favorites, but even the standard trip to the island has its thrills, and there's always a chance of seeing dolphins or whales. Children are invited to participate in the park's **Junior Ranger Program**. You can print an activity booklet at home from the park website or pick-up a free hard copy at the visitor center, on the island from park staff, or from the boat/plane concessioner offices. Complete the activities and receive an official Junior Ranger badge.

Flora & Fauna

The Channel Islands are relatively remote and home to a tempestuous climate. These factors make for an extraordinarily unique ecosystem. Even the individual islands are dramatically different thanks to variations in size and location. At least 145 endemic species of plants and animals reside within park boundaries. Most of these species have developed slight adaptations after centuries of life on a remote island. Island deer mouse is the only native terrestrial mammal common to all the Channel Islands. There are only two other endemic terrestrial mammals found here: spotted skunk and Channel Islands fox. Channel Islands fox is the smallest North American canid, only growing to about the size of your average house cat. Visitors' favorite animals tend to be those that swim in the ocean. Sea lions, seals, pacific gray whales, and Risso's dolphins are frequently seen patrolling the waters. The islands are also important breeding grounds for many species of bird. California brown pelicans, Xantu's murrelets, tufted puffins, western gulls, Cassin's auklets, and rhinoceros auklets all breed within park boundaries. The Island scrub jay is also unique to the islands. In 2006, bald eagles nested on the Channel Islands for the first time in more than 50 years.

Channel Islands' plant life is just as interesting and unique. Nearly 800 species of plants have been documented in the park, including 75 endemic plant species, 14 of which are listed as threatened or endangered. After nearly 150 years of ranching, the park has put forth great effort to aid in the recovery of these species.

Pets

To protect wildlife, pets are not allowed in the park.

Accessibility

Both visitor centers are fully accessible to individuals in wheelchairs. However, the islands themselves have extremely limited accessibility. Santa Rosa Island is accessible via air transportation (page 471).

Weather

Weather is moderated by the Pacific Ocean, keeping average high and low temperatures surprisingly consistent all year. Average highs only vary about 10°F from summer to winter. Another by-product of the Pacific Ocean is high humidity and fog. Humidity often reaches 100% at night and in the early morning. Annual rainfall is about 14 inches per year with 95% of that total occurring between November and April. Fog is most common in spring and summer, especially at San Miguel and Santa Rosa Islands. Wind is the one constant on the islands, blowing primarily from the north–northwest and tending to increase throughout the daylight hours. High velocity Santa Ana winds averaging 20–25 mph with gusts exceeding 100 mph can occur in any month, but are most common from September to December. Hikers, campers, and day-visitors should come prepared to deal with a variety of elements.

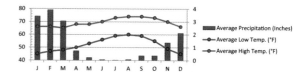

Vacation Planner

Unpredictable weather and water conditions, concessioner transportation dependence, and specialized activities make planning a trip to the Channel Islands a more structured project than most parks. If you'd like to make a spur of the moment trip, you'll be at the mercy of Island Packers' transportation schedule. More than likely, you will be able to visit Anacapa or Santa Cruz Island, but trips to Santa Rosa, Santa Barbara, and San Miguel are seasonal. **Day trips are easy.** Simply hop aboard the concessioner boat, and upon arrival they'll give you the option to explore at your leisure or to join a park ranger or concessioner naturalist on a walking tour. A few hours later, you pile back onto the boat to return to the mainland. **Overnight trips require reserving campsites and transportation.** Both fill occasionally. Regardless of which island(s) you visit and how many days you intend to spend, be sure to stop at the visitor center, pack plenty of sunscreen, plan on it being windy, and don't forget food and water (and to pack out your trash). Nearby dining, grocery stores, lodging, festivals, and attractions are listed on pages 477–479.

Dining

Joshua Tree Area
Palms Restaurant • (760) 361-2810
83131 Amboy Rd, Twentynine Palms

Palm Kabob House • (760) 367-2161
6341 Adobe Rd, Twentynine Palms

Rib Co • (760) 367-1663
72183 29 Palms Hwy, Twentynine Palms
theribco.com • Entrée: $13–32

Jackalope Ranch • (760) 342-1999
80400 CA-111, Indio • thejackaloperanch.com

Ciro's Ristorante And Pizzeria
81963 CA-111, Indio • (760) 347-6503

Pueblo Viejo Grill • (760) 342-5900
81931 CA-111, Indio • puebloviejogrill.com

El Mexicali Restaurant • (760) 347-1280
82720 Indio Blvd, Indio • elmexicalicafe.com

China Bistro • (760) 342-7288
45765 Towne St, Indio • chinabistroindio.com

Beer Hunter Sports Pub • (760) 564-7442
78483 CA-111, La Quinta • laquintabeerhunter.com

LG's Prime Steakhouse • (760) 771-9911
78525 CA-111, La Quinta
lgsprimesteakhouse.com • Entrée: $25–55

Okura Robata Grill & Sushi Bar • (760) 564-5820
78370 CA-111, #150, La Quinta
okurasushi.com • Entrée: $22–34

Rosati's • (760) 775-8900
79630 California 111, La Quinta
myrosatis.com • Pizza: $10+

Fisherman's Market & Grill • (760) 777-1601
78575 CA-111, # 100, La Quinta
fishermans.com • Sandwiches: $10+

Mimi's Café • (760) 775-4470
79765 CA-111, La Quinta • mimiscafe.com

La Quinta Baking • (760) 777-1699
78-395 CA-111, La Quinta • laquintabaking.com

Channel Islands Area
Anacapa Brewing Company • (805) 643-2337
472 E Main St, Ventura • anacapabrewing.com

Spasso Cucina Italiana • (805) 643-2777
1140 S Seaward Ave, Ventura
spassorestaurant.com • Entrée: $12–26

Meridians • (805) 676-1756
2417 Harbor Blvd, Ventura
meridianscafe.com • Pizza: $10+

I Love Sushi • (805) 639-4009
5722 Telephone Rd, Ventura • ilovesushiventura.com

Pete's Breakfast House • (805) 648-1130
2055 E Main St, Ventura

Café Nouveau • (805) 648-1422
1497 E Thompson Blvd, Ventura

Allison's Country Café • (805) 650-1766
3429 Telegraph Rd, Ventura
allisonscountrycafe.com

Sambos • (805) 965-3269
216 W Cabrillo Blvd, Santa Barbara
sambosrestaurant.com • Breakfast: $7+

Jane • (805) 962-1311
1311 State St, Santa Barbara • janerestaurantsb.com

Olio e Limone Ristorante • (805) 899-2699
11 W Victoria St, #17, Santa Barbara
olioelimone.com • Entrée: $18–39

Los Agaves Restaurant • (805) 564-2626
600 N Milpas St, Santa Barbara

The Palace Grill • (805) 963-5000
8 E Cota St, Santa Barbara • palacegrill.com

Brophy Brothers • (805) 966-4418
119 Harbor Way, Santa Barbara
brophybros.com • Entrée: $20–26

Brew House • (805) 884-4664
229 W Montecito St, Santa Barbara
sbbrewhouse.com • Entrée: $13–30

Super Cuca's Taqueria • (805) 966-3863
2030 Cliff Dr, Santa Barbara
cucasrestaurant.com • Burritos: $4+

Ming Dynasty • (805) 968-1308
290 Storke Rd, # G, Goleta
mingdynastysb.com • Entrée: $14–25

Habit Burger Grill • (805) 964-0366
5735 Hollister Ave, Goleta
habitburger.com • Burgers: $3+

South Coast Deli • (805) 967-8226
185 S Patterson Ave, Goleta
southcoastdeli.com • Sandwiches: $7+

Goodland Kitchen • (805) 845-4300
231 S Magnolia Ave, Goleta
goodlandkitchen.com • Sandwiches: $4.50+

Grocery Stores

Joshua Tree Area
Walmart Supercenter • (760) 564-3313
79295 CA-111, La Quinta

Costco • (760) 775-0370
79-795 CA-111, La Quinta

Channel Islands Area
Vons • (805) 650-2150
6040 Telegraph Rd, Ventura

Albertsons • (805) 647-0023
7800 Telegraph Rd, Ventura

Vons • (805) 648-0251
2764 E Thompson Blvd, Ventura

Walmart Supercenter • (805) 981-4884
2001 N Rose Ave, Oxnard

Whole Foods • (805) 837-6959
3761 State St, Santa Barbara

Costco • (805) 685-3199
7095 Market Place Dr, Goleta

Lodging

Joshua Tree Area
Harmony Motel • (760) 367-3351
71161 29 Palms Hwy, Twentynine Palms
harmonymotel.com • Rates: $75–95/night

Sunnyvale Suites • (760) 361-3939
73843 Sunnyvale Dr, Twentynine Palms
sunnyvalesuites.com • Rates: $83+

Roughley Manor B&B • (760) 367-3238
74744 Joe Davis Dr, Twentynine Palms
roughleymanor.com • Rates: $135–160

Fantasy Springs Casino • (760) 345-5000
84245 Indio Springs Pkwy, Indio
fantasyspringsresort.com • Rates: $99+

Indian Palms Vacation Club • (760) 342-1485
48-630 Monroe Ave, Indio
indianpalmsvacationclub.com • Rates: $109+

Date Tree Hotel • (760) 347-3421
81909 Indio Blvd, Indio
datetree.com • Rates: $91+

Shadow Hills RV Resort • (760) 360-4040
40655 Jefferson St, Indio
shadowhillsrvresort.com • Rates: $63

Indian Wells RV Resort • (760) 347-0895
47340 Jefferson St, Indio
indianwellsrvresort.com • Rates: $47/69

Miramonte Resort & Spa • (760) 341-2200
45000 Indian Wells Ln, Indian Wells
miramonteresort.com • Rates: $139+

Hyatt Resort & Spa • (760) 776-1234
44600 Indian Wells Ln, Indian Wells
indianwells.hyatt.com • Rates: $179+

Chateau at Lake La Quinta • (888) 226-4546
78-120 Caleo Bay, La Quinta
thechateaulakelaquinta.com • Rates: $139–489

Agua Caliente Casino • (866) 923-7244
32250 Bob Hope Dr, Rancho Mirage
hotwatercasino.com • Rates: $119–344

Channel Islands Area
Inn On the Beach • (805) 652-2000
1175 S Seaward Ave, Ventura
innonthebeachventura.com • Rates: $120–175

Crystal Lodge Motel • (805) 648-2272
1787 E Thompson Blvd, Ventura
crystallodgeventura.com • Rates: $55+

Viking Motel • (805) 643-3273
2107 E Thompson Blvd, Ventura
vikingmotelventura.com • Rates: $70

Victorian Rose B&B • (805) 641-1888
896 E Main St, Ventura
victorianroseventura.com • Rates: $99–179

Channel Islands Shores • (888) 476-9854
1311 Mandalay Beach Rd, Oxnard
channelislandshores.org • Rates: $135+

Casa Via Mar • (805) 984-6222
377 W Channel Islands Blvd, Port Hueneme
casaviamar.com • Rates: $109+

Santa Paula Inn • (805) 933-0011
111 N 8th St, Santa Paula
santapaulainn.com • Rates: $80+

Blue Iguana Inn • (805) 646-5277
11794 N Ventura Ave, Ojai
blueiguanainn.com • Rates: $129+

Casa Ojai Inn • (805) 646-8175
1302 E Ojai Ave, Ojai
ojaiinn.com • Rates: $116+

Secret Garden Inn • (805) 687-2300
1908 Bath St, Santa Barbara
secretgarden.com • Rates: $165+

Inn of the Spanish Garden • (805) 564-4700
915 Garden St, Santa Barbara
spanishgardeninn.com • Rates: $319+

Villa Rosa Inn • (805) 966-0851
15 Chapala St, Santa Barbara
villarosainnsb.com • Rates: $169+

Harbor House Inn • (805) 962-9745
104 Bath St, Santa Barbara
harborhouseinn.com • Rates: $199+

Lemon Tree Inn • (805) 687-6444
2819 State St, Santa Barbara • treeinns.com

Cheshire Cat Inn • (805) 569-1610
36 W Valerio St, Santa Barbara
cheshirecat.com • Rates: $229–449

*Many chain restaurants and hotels can be found
along Twentynine Palms Hwy, I-10 and US-101*

Festivals
Rose Parade • January
Pasadena • tournamentofroses.com

International Film Festival • January
Santa Barbara • sbiff.org

La Quinta Arts Festival • March
La Quinta • lqaf.com

Coachella Valley Music Festival • April
Indio • coachella.com

Stagecoach Festival • April
Indio • stagecoachfestival.com

Huck Finn Jubilee • June
Ontario • huckfinn.com

Life Oak Music Festival • June
Santa Barbara • liveoakfest.org

Ojai Music Festival • June
Ojai • ojaifestival.org

Aloha Beach Festival • September
Ventura • alohabeachfestival.us

Attractions
Joshua Tree Area
Salton Sea State Rec. Area • (760) 393-3052
100225 State Park Rd, North Shore • parks.ca.gov

Indian Canyons • (760) 323-6018
Hike through an oasis (tours available • $3)
38520 S Palm Canyon Dr, Palm Springs
indian-canyons.com • Admission: $9/adult

Slab City • near Niland
Winter home of snowbirds/squatters/campers

Desert Adventures • (760) 340-2345
74794 Lennon Pl, Palm Desert
red-jeep.com • Tours: $125–200

Adventure Hummer Tours • (760) 285-0876
74880 Country Club Dr, Palm Desert
adventurehummer.com • Tours: $149

Balloon Above The Desert • (760) 347-0410
36901 Cook St, Palm Desert
balloonabovethedesert.com • Rates: $225

Aerial Tramway • (760) 325-1449
1 Tramway Rd, Palm Springs
pstramway.com • Tickets: $24.95/adult

Integratron • (760) 364-3126
An all-wood, acoustically perfect sound chamber
2477 Belfield Blvd, Landers
integratron.com • Sound Bath: $26

Shields Date Garden • (760) 347-0996
80225 CA-111, Indio
shieldsdategarden.com

Gen. Patton Mem. Museum • (760) 227-3483
62510 Chiriaco Rd, Indio
generalpattonmuseum.com • Admission: $6/adult

Coachella Valley Hist. Mus. • (760) 342-6651
82616 Miles Ave, Indio • cvhm.org

Palm Springs Air Museum • (760) 778-6262
745 N Gene Autry Tr, Palm Springs
palmspringsairmuseum.org • $16/adult

Palm Springs Art Museum • (760) 322-4800
101 N Museum Dr, Palm Springs
psmuseum.org • Admission: Free

Smith's Ranch Drive-In • (760) 367-7713
4584 Adobe Rd, Twentynine Palms
29drive-in.com • Tickets: $5

Theatre 29 • (760) 361-4151 • theatre29.org
73637 Sullivan Rd, Twentynine Palms

McCallam Theatre • (760) 340-2787
73000 Fred Waring Dr, Palm Desert
mccallumtheatre.com

Augustine Casino • (760) 391-9500
84001 Ave 54, Coachella • augustinecasino.com

Channel Islands Area
Nojoqui Falls Park • (805) 688-4217
3250 Alisal Rd, Goleta • countyofsb.org

Refugio State Beach • (805) 968-1033
10 Refugio Beach Rd, Goleta
parks.ca.gov • Camp: $35/night

El Capitan State Beach • (805) 968-1033
El Capitan State Beach Rd, Goleta
parks.ca.gov • Camp: $35/night

Fairview Gardens
598 N Fairview Ave, Goleta
fairviewgardens.org • Self-guided Tour: Free

Cloud Climbers • (805) 646-3200
408 Foothill Rd, Santa Barbara
ccjeeps.com • Tours: $89–375

Island Packer Cruises • (805) 642-1393
Channel Islands concessioner, cruises and tours
1691 Spinnaker Dr, Ventura
islandpackers.com • Whale Watch: $37

Spectre Dive Boat • (805) 483-6612
1567 Spinnaker Dr, Ventura
spectreboat.com • Dives: $115–135

Lotusland • (805) 969-9990
Non-profit botanical garden on private estate
695 Ashley Rd, Santa Barbara
lotusland.org • Reservations Required

Sailing Center • (800) 962-2826
133 Harbor Way, Santa Barbara
sbsail.com • *Charters & Rentals*

Condor Express • (805) 882-0088
301 W Cabrillo Blvd, Santa Barbara
condorexpress.com • Whale Watch: $50

Captain Jack's Tours • (805) 564-1819
Fishing, glider, segway, ATV, trail rides, and more
933 Castillo St, Santa Barbara
captainjackstours.com • Whale Watch: $55

Sunset Kidd Whale Watching • (805) 962-8222
125 Harbor Way, #13, Santa Barbara
sunsetkidd.com • Whale Watch: $40

Land & Sea Tours • (805) 683-7600
99 W Cordillo Blvd, Santa Barbara
out2seesb.com • Tours: $30/adult

Wheel Fun Rentals • (805) 966-2282
22 State St, Santa Barbara
wheelfunrentalssb.com • *Bike Rental & Tours*

Maritime Museum • (805) 962-8404
113 Harbor Way, # 190, Santa Barbara
sbmm.org • Admission: $8/adult

South Coast Railroad Museum • (805) 964-3540
300 N Los Carneros Rd, Goleta • goletadepot.org

Botanic Garden • (805) 682-4726
1212 Mission Canyon Rd, Santa Barbara
sbbg.org • Admission: $10/adult

Museum of Art • (805) 963-4364
1130 State St, Santa Barbara, CA 93101
sbma.net • Admission: $10/adult

Zoological Gardens • (805) 962-5339
500 Ninos Dr, Santa Barbara
sbzoo.org • Admission: $17/adult

Mission Museum • (805) 682-4713
2201 Laguna St, Santa Barbara
santabarbaramission.org • Admission: $8/adult

Museum of Natural History • (805) 682-4711
2559 Puesta Del Sol, Santa Barbara
sbnature.org • Admission: $12/adult

Ty Warner Sea Center • (805) 962-2526
211 Stearns Wharf, Santa Barbara
sbnature.org • Admission: $8.50/adult

Oreana Winery • (805) 962-5857
205 Anacapa St, Santa Barbara
oreanawinery.com

Ventura Harbor Comedy Club
1559 Spinnaker Dr, Ventura • (805) 644-1500
venturaharborcomedyclub.com

Golf N' Stuff • (805) 644-7148
5555 Walker St, Ventura • golfnstuff.com

Lobero Theatre • (805) 963-0761
33 E Canon Perdido St, Santa Barbara
lobero.com

Rubicon Theatre Co. • (805) 667-2900
1006 E Main St, # 300, Ventura
rubicontheatre.org

Los Angeles Area

Getty Museum • (310) 440-7330
1200 Getty Center Dr, Los Angeles
getty.edu • Free

Griffith Park • (213) 473-0800
2800 E Observatory Ave, Los Angeles
griffithobservatory.org • Free

Hollywood Sign • (323) 258-4338
Restricted Access, Los Angeles
hollywoodsign.org

Natural History Museum • (213) 763-3466
900 Exposition Blvd, Los Angeles
nhm.org • Admission: $12/adult

Nethercutt Collection • (818) 364-6464
15200 Bledsoe St, San Fernando Valley
nethercuttcollection.org • Free

Free TV Show Tickets
Popular TV shows—Price is Right, Tonight Show, and Ellen Degeneres Show, just to name a few—offer free tickets to visitors. Most tickets must be reserved well in advance. More information can be found at tvtickets.com & tvtix.com.

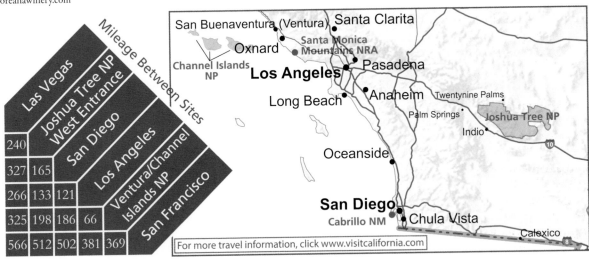

Mileage Between Sites				
Las Vegas				
240	Joshua Tree NP West Entrance			
327	165	San Diego		
266	133	121	Los Angeles	
325	198	186	66	Ventura/Channel Islands NP
566	512	502	381	369	San Francisco

For more travel information, click www.visitcalifornia.com

California condors and High Peaks

Pinnacles

5000 CA-146
Paicines, CA 95043
Phone: (831) 389-4485
Website: nps.gov/pinn

Established: January 10, 2013
January 16, 1908 (Nat'l Monument)
Size: 26,606 Acres
Annual Visitors: 200,000
Peak Season: Spring and fall

Activities: Camping, Hiking, Rock
Climbing, and Bird Watching

**Pinnacles Campground* (East
Entrance):** $23/night (standard)
or $36/night (w/ electric hookups)
No Backcountry Camping

Park Hours
East Entrance: All day, every day
West Entrance: 7:30am–4pm (PT)
(Note: No roads cross the park)

Entrance Fee: $10/vehicle,
$5/individual (foot, bike, etc.)

*Reserve at recreation.gov or (877)
444-6777

Pinnacles is the newest national park, established on January 10, 2013, but it's been long in the making. Today, Pinnacles is a natural haven for humans and wildlife alike amidst a rapidly urbanizing region.

The park's eponymous pinnacles, spires, crags, and cliffs were created through plate tectonics, earthquakes, and volcanic activity. Tens of millions of years ago, the Farallon Plate was subducting under—being pushed beneath—the North American Plate, a process that created California's coastal range and caused volcanic activity. Scientists believe a 15 mile-long, 8,000-foot-tall volcano—named Neenach—existed 195 miles southeast of the present-day park. This volcanic field split at the fault between the Farallon and North American plates, and as the latter moved north at 3–6 centimeters per year it took the volcanic rock with it, leaving the Neenach formation behind. Millions of years of movement and erosion by heat, frost, water, and wind revealed the pinnacles rock formations, originally poured from the earth at Neenach Volcano.

Humans began inhabiting this stark yet stunning landscape at least 2,000 years ago, when the Ohlone People came here seasonally to hunt and gather food. Spanish missionaries arrived in the 18th century, bringing with them new religion, education, and disease. Migrants seeking recreation in the form of picnicking, camping, and exploring, were the next to arrive in the late 1800s. Among them was Schuyler Hain, who followed his family from Michigan. He became the first postmaster of the Cook Post Office, located in Bear Valley. As John Muir was pushing for the preservation of Yosemite, Hain started to publicize Pinnacles and lead tours through the caves, and soon was considered the unofficial caretaker of the area. One of his guests was a Stanford professor, who spoke of the region's beauty to a California congressman, who in turn reached out to Gifford Pinchot, the first chief of the U.S. Forest Service.

By 1906, Pinnacles Forest Reserve was established. In 1908, Theodore Roosevelt made it a national monument.

The park was enlarged by Presidents Harding and Coolidge. The Civilian Conservation Corps (CCC) took up residence here in the 1930s, improving roads and trails, building the dam at Bear Gulch Reservoir, and even leading tours through the caves. The spirit of conservation continued, with 7,900 acres added under Bill Clinton's presidency. In 2003, Pinnacles was designated as a site for the nearly extinct California condor. On January 10, 2013, President Obama signed legislation making Pinnacles the newest national park and renaming Pinnacles Wilderness as Hain Wilderness in honor of the Michigan transplant affectionately known as "the father of Pinnacles."

Forged by violent volcanic eruptions. Shifted and buried by tectonic activity. Revealed and sculpted by millions of years of erosion. Explored, enjoyed, and preserved by humans. Today, you can walk among the High Peaks on trails created by the CCC. So come to the newest national park and explore caves that inspired Schuyler Hain to start a grassroots preservation movement.

Camping

Camping is limited to **Pinnacles Campground**, located on the park's east side. Here you'll find tent, RV (most with electrical hookups), and group sites. Many sites offer considerable privacy and shade thanks to large old-growth oak. Potable water is available throughout the campground. Coin-operated **showers** and a dump station are nearby, and there's a store stocked with all the camping essentials (beer included). And there's something extremely uncommon among national park campgrounds: a swimming pool. The pool is typically open from mid-April through September, weather permitting. Depending on the fire danger level, campfires may be prohibited. While it isn't popular, you are allowed to backpack in Hain Wilderness, which makes up 80% of the park.

The campground and camp store are operated by Elk Park Management. Tent and RV sites can be reserved up to 6 months in advance at recreation.gov or (877) 444-6777. The camp store (831.389.4538) is open from 3pm to 5pm, Sunday through Thursday; 2pm to 5pm on Fridays, and 10am until 4pm on Saturdays.

High Peaks Trail

When to Go

The East Entrance is open all day, every day. The park's West Entrance is open daily from 7:30am until 8pm (Pacific Time). The absolute best time to explore Pinnacles is spring (March through May), when wildflowers accent the red rocky spires. The duration and intensity of these annual blooms vary with rainfall and temperature, so check with the park before departing. Spring and fall weekends are particularly busy, so if you're not fond of crowds come on a weekday or in summer—if you can handle triple-digit heat (remember to pack plenty of water). In winter, a dusting of snow can create striking scenery, but caves can be flooded, negating a few of the park's more exciting attractions.

Free shuttles run between Pinnacles Visitor Center and the Bear Gulch Area (East Side) during the busiest spring weekends. **Pinnacles Visitor Center** (East Side, 831.389.4485) is open from 9:30am until 5pm, daily. **Bear Gulch Nature Center** (East Side, 831.389.4486 x235) is open weekends from 10am until 4pm (January through May). **West Pinnacles Visitor Center** (831.389.4427 x 4487) is open from 9am until 4:30pm on weekends, holidays and occasional weekdays (staff permitting).

Transportation & Airports

There is no public transportation to or around the park. Large airports are located in San Jose (SJC), San Francisco (SFO), Oakland (OAK), and Fresno (FAT), all within 150 miles of the park. Car rental is available at each destination.

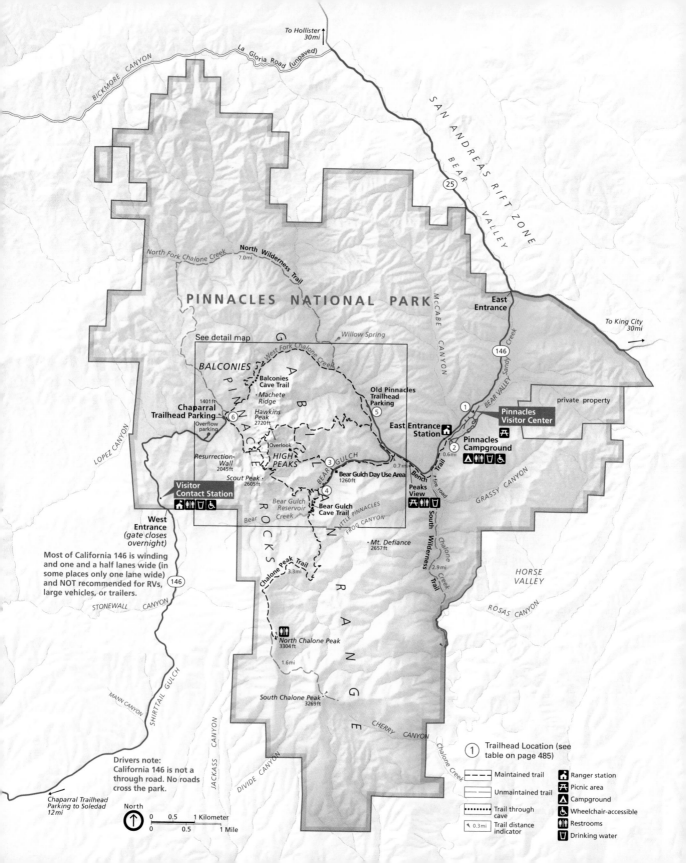

To Hollister
30mi

La Gloria Road (unpaved)

BICKMORE CANYON

SAN ANDREAS RIFT ZONE

BEAR VALLEY

25

East
Entrance

To King City
30mi

North Fork Chalone Creek

North Wilderness Trail
7.0mi

PINNACLES NATIONAL PARK

McCABE CANYON

Willow Spring

See detail map

West Fork Chalone Creek

146

BALCONIES

Balconies
Cave Trail

Machete
Ridge

Old Pinnacles
Trailhead
Parking
5

Pinnacles
Visitor Center

private property

1401ft

Chaparral
Trailhead Parking 6

Overflow
parking

Hawkins
Peak
2720ft

East Entrance
Station

1

Pinnacles
Campground

0.6mi

Resurrection
Wall
2045ft

Overlook

HIGH
PEAKS

Scout Peak
2605ft

3

BEAR GULCH

0.7 mi

Bench Trail

Fire road

Bear Gulch Day Use Area
1260ft

2

Visitor
Contact Station

4

Bear Gulch
Reservoir

Bear Gulch
Cave Trail

LITTLE PINNACLES

Peaks
View

South Wilderness Trail

GRASSY CANYON

West
Entrance
(gate closes
overnight)

Bear Gulch Creek

Bear

FROG CANYON

Mt. Defiance
2657ft

R

Chalone Creek

2.9 mi

HORSE
VALLEY

Most of California 146 is winding
and one and a half lanes wide (in
some places only one lane wide)
and NOT recommended for RVs,
large vehicles, or trailers.

LOPEZ CANYON

146

O

C

K

S

Chalone Peak Trail

3.3mi

A

N

G

E

ROSAS CANYON

STONEWALL   CANYON

North Chalone Peak
3304 ft

1.6mi

SHIRTTAIL GULCH

MANN CANYON

JACKASS CANYON

DIVIDE CANYON

South Chalone Peak
3269ft

CHERRY CANYON

Chalone Creek

Drivers note:
California 146 is not a
through road. No roads
cross the park.

Chaparral Trailhead
Parking to Soledad
12mi

North

0   0.5   1 Kilometer
0   0.5   1 Mile

1 Trailhead Location (see
   table on page 485)

- - - Maintained trail

____ Unmaintained trail

······ Trail through
        cave

↙0.3mi Trail distance
        indicator

🏠 Ranger station

🏕 Picnic area

⛺ Campground

♿ Wheelchair-accessible

🚻 Restrooms

🚰 Drinking water

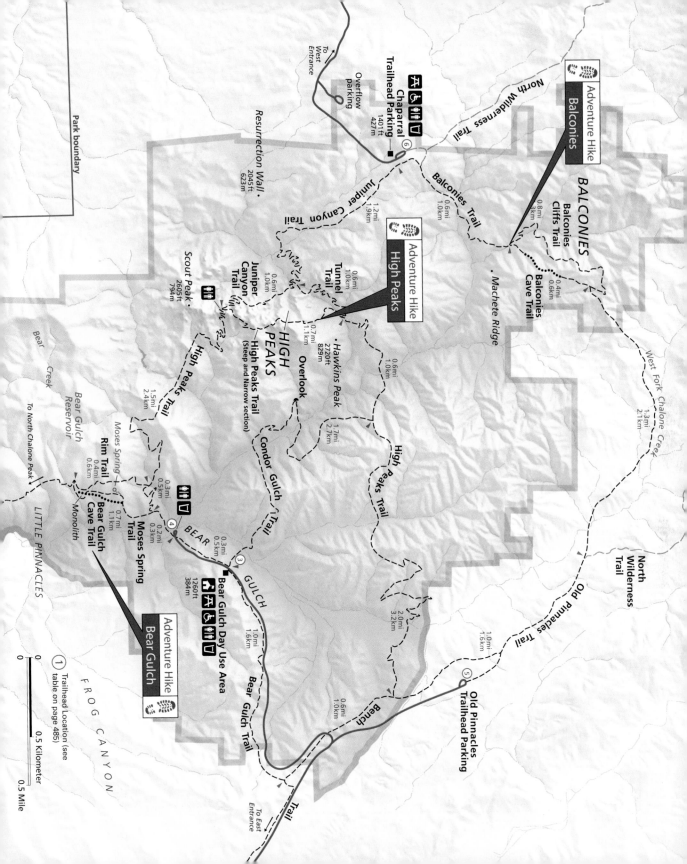

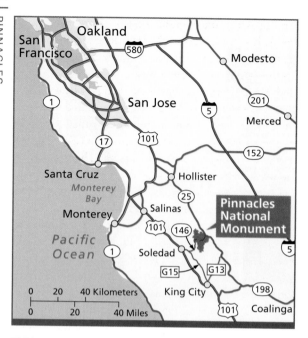

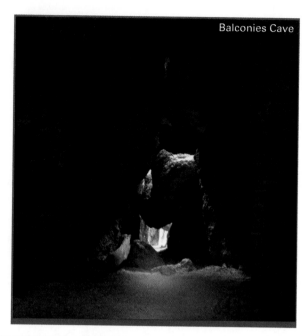

Balconies Cave

Directions

Pinnacles is surprisingly remote for being just 100 miles south of sprawling San Francisco. There are two distinct areas (East and West), not connected by a through road. It's about a 2.5-hour drive to either entrance from San Francisco and another hour to drive from the east entrance to the west entrance, driving around the park's southern boundary. When mapping your route, use coordinates for East Pinnacles Visitor Center (36.493545, -121.146646) and West Pinnacles Contact Station (36.4777000, -121.226136) or follow the directions below.

East Pinnacles Visitor Center

From the North: Take US-101 south to exit 353 for CA-25. Take CA-25 south, through Hollister, about 41 miles, and turn right onto CA-146 W, which leads into the park.

From the South: Take US-101 north to exit 281 for 1st Street toward King City. Turn right onto 1st Street. After 1.3 miles it veers right, becoming Lyons Street and then Bitterwater Road. Continue for roughly 15 miles to a T-intersection and turn left onto CA-25. Drive north for 14 miles and make a sharp left onto CA-146 W, which leads into the park.

West Pinnacles Visitor Contact Station

From the North: Take US-101 south to exit 302 for CA-146 toward Soledad. Continue onto CA-146 W and turn left onto Front Street after 0.25-mile. After less than 0.5-mile turn right onto East Street. Turn right onto CA-146 E/Metz Road after 0.3-mile. Drive for 2.7 miles, and then turn left onto CA-146 E, which leads into the park.

From the South: Take US-101 north to exit 281 for 1st Street toward King City. Turn right onto 1st Street. After 1.3 miles it veers right, becoming Lyons Street. Immediately after the bend, turn left onto Metz Road. Drive north on Metz Road for 17.2 miles, and then turn right onto CA-146 W. It is 7.1 miles to the visitor center and another 2.2 miles to the end of the road (Chaparral Trailhead Parking Area).

East Pinnacles to West Pinnacles (or west to east)

Remember: no roads cross the park. The shortest route from the east to the west entrance is to take CA-25 south. Turn onto Bitterwater Road and continue to King City. Turn right onto Metz Road, and then left onto CA-146 E.

Hiking

There are only 32 miles of hiking trails at Pinnacles. If you're ambitious you can hike all of them in a day and a half. But what the park lacks in quantity, it makes up for in quality; the NPS and the CCC (which constructed many of the trails) make those miles count. Unfortunately, not all of the best hikes are accessible to everyone.

Bench and Bear Gulch Trails, which visitors use to get from the East Visitor Center to Old Pinnacles Trailhead and Bear Gulch, are easy strolls, but their primary purpose is to connect longer loops and access popular east side trailheads when their parking areas fill (and the shuttle isn't running). However, there is a nice picnic spot between the parking areas at Bear Gulch and Condor Gulch. **Old Pinnacles Trail** leads into the heart of the park and is both pleasant and easy. Most hikes worth writing about lead through High Peaks or talus caves.

On the east side, we really like the **Condor Gulch–High Peaks Loop**, which passes through the steep and narrow section of High Peaks. You'll find that the nearly-vertical stairs and narrow ledges (with protective railings) that wind through peaks, pinnacles, and spires are also some of the best areas for raptor spotting. The loop simply connects High Peaks Trail (from Bear Gulch

Parking Area) and Condor Gulch Trail (from Condor Gulch Parking Area). Which direction you travel doesn't make much difference, but if you begin with Condor Gulch and your legs are fresh coming down High Peaks Trail, detour to **Rim Trail** and **Bear Gulch (Reservoir) Cave Trail**—another exceptional hike—to turn the normal 5.3-mile loop into 6.1 miles. (We also suggest walking over to Bear Gulch Reservoir.) Exploring the cave along the way requires a good light—preferably a headlamp—and ensuring that it's open to explore. The largest maternity colony of Townsend's big-eared bats between Mexico and San Francisco reside here, and the park does what it can to protect them. The lower half of the cave is open most of the year, but the entire passage is only open for a few weeks each year. Overall, this loop gains about 1,300 feet and takes roughly 3 hours. It is recommended for physically fit individuals who are not afraid of heights and tight spaces. The trail is well-marked, with an overlook one mile from Condor Gulch Trailhead and a restroom near Scout Peak (on High Peaks Trail). Hiking past Bear Gulch Reservoir to **North Chalone Peak**, the park's highest point, is another wonderful hike loaded with expansive views.

On the park's less popular west side, all trails begin at Chaparral Trailhead Parking Area. **Balconies Cliffs & Cave Loop** is 2.4 miles of fun and beautiful scenery.

Pinnacles Hiking Trails (Distances are roundtrip)

	Name	Location (# on map)	Length	Difficulty Rating & Notes
East	Visitor Center to Bear Gulch	Visitor Center (1)	4.6 miles	M – Walk to Bear Gulch when busy
	Visitor Center to Balconies	Visitor Center (1)	9.4 miles	M – Follows Bench and Old Pinnacles Trails
	South Wilderness	Campground (2)	6.5 miles	M – Follow Chalone Creek to park boundary
	Condor Gulch - ♿	Condor Gulch (3)	3.4 miles	S – Overlook at one mile, high peaks beyond
	Condor Gulch–High Peaks Loop - ♿	Condor Gulch (3)	5.3 miles	S – Great hike, steep sections, 1,300-ft gain
	Moses Spring–Rim Loop	Bear Gulch (4)	2.2 miles	M – Loop to Bear Gulch (Reservoir) Cave
	High Peaks–Bear Gulch Loop - ♿	Bear Gulch (4)	6.7 miles	S – Wildflowers in spring, 1,425-ft gain
	Chalone Peak - ♿	Bear Gulch (4)	9.0 miles	S – Highest point in the park, 2,040-ft gain
	Old Pinnacles	Old Pinnacles (5)	5.3 miles	M – Hike to Balconies from the east side
West	Balconies Cliffs & Cave Loop - ♿	Chaparral Trailhead (6)	2.4 miles	M – Scramble through a talus cave
	Juniper Canyon Loop - ♿	Chaparral Trailhead (6)	4.3 miles	S – High Peaks and Tunnel Trail, 1,215-ft gain
	North Wilderness Loop	Chaparral Trailhead (6)	9.3 miles	S – Unmaintained, follow the rock cairns
	High Peaks–Balconies Cave Loop	Chaparral Trailhead (6)	8.4 miles	S – Juniper Canyon-High Peaks-Old Pinnacles

Difficulty Ratings: E = Easy, M = Moderate, S = Strenuous

While this route only gains 300 feet, it's considered moderate because getting through the cave requires a flashlight and some scrambling (and possibly wading through water in winter). The trek begins by traveling 0.6-mile along **Balconies Trail**, where you'll encounter a junction (before the cave). Right leads to the cave, left leads to the cliffs. Most people find it easier hiking up the cave, so they start with the cave and return via **Balconies Cliffs** before returning via Balconies Trail to the parking area. The loop takes about 2 hours. (Note that you can also reach Balconies Cave & Cliffs via **Old Pinnacles Trail** from the east side of the park.) Old Pinnacles intersects Balconies Cave Trail at the cave's exit, 1.3 miles from Old Pinnacles Trailhead Parking Area. Another great trail on the west side is **Juniper Canyon Trail** up to High Peaks and Tunnel Trails. This loop, beginning and ending on Juniper Canyon Trail, climbs 1,215 feet over 4.3 miles and takes about 2 hours. You can also ascend Juniper Canyon Trail to Scout Peak and return to Chaparral Trailhead Parking Area via High Peaks, Old Pinnacles, and Balconies Trails for an 8.4-mile loop that climbs 1,540 feet. West side hikers must exit the park before 8pm, when the gate closes.

See the table on the previous page for a complete list of hiking opportunities. Don't hike without water. We did find a few confusing signposts. For instance, signs for Bear Gulch Cave still read "Reservoir Cave," and when looking to return to Condor Gulch from High Peaks, signs read "Bear Gulch Area."

A note about the caves: these are talus caves created by earthquakes and fault action. Cave purists might find them underwhelming as they're basically boulders lodged in deep narrow gorges, forming a ceiling and blocking out (most of) the sun. They're relatively short and can flood depending on conditions. They're home to bats, require a bit of dexterity and scrambling to pass through, and you will need a flashlight. It's possible to get by with a cell phone, but a headlamp is better.

Rock Climbing

Pinnacle's spires, crags, walls, and cliffs offer hundreds of routes for climbers of all ability levels. While this is a climbing hotspot, do not mistake its volcanic breccia rock with the towering granite monoliths found at nearby Yosemite (page 514). Breccia is comparatively weak, resulting in loose, flaky rocks. Longtime Pinnacles climbers are easily recognized as they tap all potential holds, listening for a response. A hollow sound means the rock may pull off the wall.

Loose rock is especially common on the park's west side at sites along Balconies Trail like the Citadel, Machete Ridge, and Elephant Rock, due to significantly less use (and longer routes). **Sticking to popular areas—Tourist Trap, Discovery Wall, and High Peaks—greatly reduces the likelihood of encountering loose rocks.** For an introduction to Pinnacles climbing, your best bet is Discovery Rock, the most popular destination, located on the park's east side, 20–30 minutes from Bear Gulch via Moses Spring Trail and a climber's access trail. Most of the climbing at Pinnacles is lead climbing, but there are a few good bouldering and top-rope climbing spots as well. Climbers come to Pinnacles year-round, with the season peaking in late January and remaining busy through May. Things pick back up again in September. No matter when you go, bring plenty of water.

Whether you are a beginner or experienced climber, please **respect the park**, its visitors, and its inhabitants. Dispose of your waste properly (there is a restroom near Scout Peak, along High Peaks Trail). Skip chalk altogether (the routes are already dusty) or use "chalk balls" to minimize chalk left on hand holds, which diminishes the rock's scenic beauty. Use the access trails. Climbing is not allowed on routes above established hiking trails. Respect route closures, which commonly occur between January and July in order to protect nesting raptor habitats. And don't forget to be safe. Wear a helmet. Tap your holds. Inspect the bolts. (Many of them are very old.) Use redundant anchor systems. And get comfortable with the rock. If you usually lead 5.10+, the park suggests you try one of the 5.6s or 5.7s for your first climb at Pinnacles. Whether you're climbing solo or with a small group, sign the climbing registers located at Moses Springs Trailhead (east side) and Balconies Trailhead (west side).

If you don't have access to a seasoned Pinnacles rock climber, check out pinnacles.org (Friends of Pinnacles) and mudncrud.com. They're two of the best resources for information on the park's 800+ climbing routes. Also, there are two climbing guidebooks. One by David Rubine, who established many of the classic routes in the park, and another by Brad Young, a longtime Pinnacles climber who serves on the Friends of Pinnacles board.

 Bird Watching

Pinnacles is home to more than 180 different types of birds, but one species, the **California condor**, captivates most birders. Weighing as much as 25 pounds and with a wingspan measuring up to 10 feet, it is the largest flying bird in North America. Its size is only surpassed by its scarcity: they are one of the rarest birds in the world. In the 1980s, California condors were pushed to the brink of extinction due to loss of habitat, poaching, and lead poisoning (contracted from carrion they feed on). In 1987, the last 22 remaining birds were captured and bred in captivity at San Diego Safari Park and Los Angeles Zoo as part of the California Condor Recovery Plan. To double reproduction rates, they fed each bird's first chick with hand puppets. The plan—although extremely expensive—has been a success. California condors were reintroduced at Pinnacles in 2003, and have now integrated into the Big Sur flock, numbering about 60 birds in total. California condors were also introduced in Utah and Arizona, where you'll find nesting condors at Zion (page 410) and Grand Canyon (page 422) national parks.

We were greeted by a dozen large birds our first time in the park while climbing up a High Peak's stone staircase. They soared above us, occasionally swooping down close enough to hear the whoosh of their wings slicing through the hot summer air. After sitting for quite some time, enjoying the spectacle, we hiked back down to Bear Gulch, thinking "Thank goodness they saved the California condor. That was a magical moment, feeling truly connected with these rare creatures." Turns out they were turkey vultures, not California condors.

It's a common mistake. With so many extremely large birds soaring high above such a relatively small area, you might think it would easy to spot them, but California condor sightings are uncommon. California condors and turkey vultures are in the same family and look remarkably similar from a distance. Up close, they're easy to distinguish if you know what to look for. First, there's a considerable size difference. Turkey vultures average just a 6-foot wingspan and weigh 2–4 pounds. When gliding above you, they can also be identified by their underwing markings. California condors have mottled white along the leading edges of their wings, while the rest, including their wingtips, is black. The back edges of turkey vulture wings are solid silver. California condors glide with their wings flat and without rocking back and forth. Turkey vultures hold their wings in a slight "V" and rock side to side in the wind. Condors have a bright orange head, while turkey vultures have bright red heads. Still unsure? The surefire way to know you've spotted a California condor is to see a numbered wing tag. All condors are tagged and equipped with radio transmitters to help monitor their activity.

Your best bet to see these massive scavengers is to explore High Peaks, Chalone Peak Trail, and the ridge southeast of the campground in the morning and evening. Our not-so-scientific approach to raptor-watching is to look for rock formations with an abundance of bird droppings. That's where raptors like to roost. Bring your binoculars and you might be fortunate enough to see a condor soaring in the thermal updrafts. Enjoy their presence while you can as they fly up to 55 mph and as high as 15,000 feet up. They can cruise to Big Sur—about 40 miles—in about an hour. Should you see one, please share your condor sighting with a park ranger.

Ranger Programs

Free ranger programs are fun activities for all ages. Pinnacles typically offers weekend programs on the east side from mid-January through May. We highly recommend all ranger programs, so it's a good idea to check with a park ranger or one of the Activity Boards outside the East Visitor Center, Bear Gulch Nature Center, or the West Contact Station.

For Kids

Be sure to bring a few flashlights along because your children are going to want to explore the talus caves (page 485). There's one on each side of the park: Balconies Cave on the west, Bear Gulch (or Reservoir) Cave on the east. Both are cool, but you'll have to do some scrambling and squeezing (particularly at Balconies).

Turkey vulture

California condor

Deer near West Entrance

Best of Pinnacles

Hike: High Peaks–Condor Gulch Loop
Runner-up: Bear Gulch Cave/High Peaks
2nd Runner-up: Balconies Cave & Cliffs
3rd Runner-up: Juniper Canyon Loop

Flora & Fauna

Much of the life found at Pinnacles has adapted to survive in this seemingly inhospitable environment. Chaparral dominates the landscape, canvassing 82% of the park's area. Some of these shrubby species have even adapted to wildfires, which are common here, evolving seeds that lie dormant for years until fire stimulates them to sprout. Pinnacles comes alive from March through May, when over 80% of the park's plants—including more than 100 species of flowers—are in bloom. The one plant you definitely want to avoid is poison oak, which is common along most hiking trails. It's the chameleon of the plant world, growing as a shrub, vine, or small tree. Its leaves can be red, green, and any color in between. The best way to identify poison oak is that its leaves are arranged in groups of three.

You might not expect it, but Pinnacles supports a lot of animal life: nearly 200 species of birds; dozens of mammals, reptiles, butterflies, and dragonflies; a handful of amphibians; thousands of invertebrates; and about 400 species of bees. Those bees represent the world's greatest known diversity per unit area. Over 260 different species of bees have been spotted along Old Pinnacles Trail alone. The most common mammals include black-tailed deer, bobcat, gray fox, raccoon (don't leave your trash or cooler out), rabbits, squirrels, chipmunks, and bats, including Townsend's big-eared bats, which are protected in Bear Gulch (Reservoir) Cave. All visitors, but especially rock climbers, must be cautious of rattlesnakes, which commonly hole-up under rocks and in crevasses.

Pets

Pets must be kept on a leash no more than six feet in length at all times. They are only allowed in picnic areas, parking lots, and on paved roads. They are prohibited from all trails and you must not leave them unattended, even in the campground.

Accessibility

Both visitor centers and their restrooms are fully accessible. Trails are another story. They're steep, often with narrow stairs carved into rock. A small portion of Bench Trail is accessible to wheelchair users with assistance.

Weather

Being just 40 miles from the ocean (as the condor flies), you'd expect Pinnacles to have a climate moderated by the Pacific, but the intervening Santa Lucia Mountains subdue the ocean's influence, creating many summer days when it can be 60°F along the Pacific and 100°F in the park. Similarly, in winter, it can be below freezing at Pinnacles and temperate along the coast. Weather-wise, spring and fall are the most pleasant seasons.

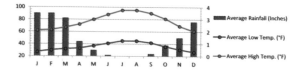

Vacation Planner

Pinnacles is small and there aren't too many universally appealing activities. If you're a **rock climber** (page 486), find an experienced Pinnacles climber or a good climbing guidebook and scale some rocks. If you crave adventure and excitement and are in good physical condition, spend a day or two **exploring High Peaks** and the park's two talus caves. Those of you looking for a nice leisurely stroll should walk along **Old Pinnacles Trail**, from the east side or the west side (via Balconies Trail), which is particularly wonderful in late winter or spring when it's bursting with colorful wildflowers and buzzing with busy bees. If you're passing through the area, it's worth stopping to enjoy the compelling scenery and wildlife, the park's pinnacles illuminated in the early morning light, and maybe even a California condor (page 488) soaring above this rocky retreat. On the east side, you can get a pretty good view of High Peaks and any birds circling them at Peaks View, located just off the main park road, between the entrance station and the turn off for Bear Gulch.

Our primary recommendation is to begin at the park's east side. Skip the west side unless you want to explore Balconies Caves and Cliffs and Juniper Canyon from a closer trailhead, but those trails are accessible from the west side as well. Save yourself the 1-hour drive to the west entrance from the east entrance (remember there is no through road!) and hike to Balconies via Old Pinnacles Trail on the east side, which is stunning in spring, and return via the much more strenuous Juniper Canyon and Tunnel Trails. **Our favorite loop hike is Condor Gulch—High Peaks.** If you want to make a day of it, extend the journey to North Chalone Peak and through Bear Gulch (Reservoir) Cave, a trek totaling 12.7 miles. You won't regret those extra miles one bit, unless you start late and don't have enough time. Watch for California condors along the way.

If you visit the west side, stop at the visitor station, watch the park video, spend a little time with a park ranger, and continue to the end of the road, Chaparral Trailhead Parking Area. This is the access point for Balconies and Juniper Canyon Trails. Balconies goes off to the left from the trailhead registry, Juniper Canyon goes off to the right, up and into High Peaks. Both routes are great. Balconies Trail, if you skip the cave and cliffs portion, is easy and still breathtaking, walking past Machete Ridge and the Citadel, two massive rock monoliths.

Mesquite Flat Sand Dunes

Death Valley

PO Box 579
Death Valley, CA 92328
Phone: (760) 786-3200
Website: nps.gov/deva

Established: October 31, 1994
February 11, 1933 (Nat'l Monument)
Size: 3.4 Million Acres
Annual Visitors: 1.1 Million
Peak Season: November–April

Activities: Hiking, Backpacking, Camping, Backcountry Roads, Biking, Tours, and Bird Watching

Campgrounds: 5 Fee ($12–18/night) and 4 Free Campgrounds
Lodging: Furnace Creek, Stovepipe Wells, and Panamint Springs
Rates: $79–500/night
Backcountry Camping: Permitted

Park Hours: All day, every day
Except Day-use Areas: Cottonwood Canyon, Titus Canyon, Aguereberry Point, Skidoo, Wildrose, Racetrack, West Side, and Mosaic Canyon Roads
Entrance Fee: $20/vehicle, $10/individual (foot, bike, etc.)

In 1917, Death Valley experienced 52 days—43 consecutive—with temperatures over 120°F. In 1929, not a single drop of measurable rain was recorded. During a 40 month period from 1931 through 1934, only 0.64 inches of rain fell. It's the hottest and driest national park in the United States. Not exactly a ringing endorsement for tourism. But Death Valley's superlatives extended far beyond historical weather data. At more than three million acres, it's also the largest national park in the contiguous U.S. Badwater is the lowest place in North America. And it's otherworldly. The first rays of light dance off the mudstone of Zabriskie Point. Only the afternoon sun penetrates the narrow depths of Titus Canyon. Signs of a volcanic past are visible at Ubehebe Crater. And Rocks move of their own accord across the flat expanse of Racetrack Playa.

People have visited Death Valley for nearly 10,000 years. Little is known of the earliest inhabitants, but it's likely they made seasonal migrations to the valley, collecting piñon nuts and mesquite beans. Not until 1849 did the first non-Native American step foot in the region, completely by accident. More than 100 wagons wandered into the valley after getting lost on what they believed to be a shortcut off the Old Spanish Trail. Roaming the desert for nearly two months, their oxen became weak and their wagons battered. By the time they approached present-day Stovepipe Wells, it was clear they would not be able to pass the mountains with a full complement of oxen and wagons; they made jerky of the former and burned the latter, and then set out on foot to cross Emigrant Pass, leaving the "Death Valley" behind. Only one man died during the ordeal, but the name stuck thanks to *Death Valley in '49*, a book written by a member of the group, William Lewis Manly. His book became an important chapter in California's pioneer history and brought newfound publicity to this inhospitable region.

Before it became a park, mining was the primary activity in the valley. Boom towns (now ghost towns) sprang up around local bonanzas of gold, but the most profitable ore was borax, used to make soap and industrial components. Today, it's an essential component in various glassware. Harmony Borax Works was the engine that opened up the valley, building hundreds of miles of roads as they raked borax from the valley floor. Forty men could produce three tons each day. Next, it was hauled out of the valley 10 tons at a time by twenty-mule teams, the original semi-trailers; a single caravan stretched 180 feet. During six years of production, they hauled more than 20 million pounds of borax out of Death Valley. Stephen Mather, first director of the National Park Service, made his fortune with 20 Mule Team Borax. Success allowed him to pursue the preservation of natural wonders like Death Valley.

Walter Scott, also known as Death Valley Scotty, was a less industrious Death Valley resident. After working for Harmony Borax and the Buffalo Bill Wild West Show, he convinced wealthy easterners to invest in his highly productive gold mine. Unfortunately, Scotty didn't have a gold mine. He took the money and went on legendary spending sprees. With no returning profits, investors began pulling their funding until only Albert Mussey Johnson, an insurance magnate from Chicago, remained. He sent thousands of dollars to Scotty only to hear of an assortment of calamities that always "prevented" shipments of gold. Johnson decided to visit Death Valley to check out the operation. But even as he realized he had been swindled, he fell in love with Death Valley and began a long-lasting friendship with Death Valley Scotty. Johnson funded construction of a vacation home (Scotty's Castle) and Scotty's real home (Lower Vine Ranch). To Scotty and Albert Johnson, Death Valley was a magical place filled with character and wonder they described with their own superlatives, not the inhospitable wasteland others made it out to be. *The Death Valley Chuck-Walla*, an old mining newspaper, may have said it best when they wrote: "Would you enjoy a trip to hell? You might enjoy a trip to Death Valley, now! It has all the advantages of hell without the inconveniences." Once again, not a ringing endorsement, but it is Death Valley after all.

When to Go
The park is open all year, but you may want to avoid summer when temps consistently rise above 100°F. Ranger programs are offered between November and April. **Furnace Creek Visitor Center** is open daily from 8am to 5pm. Scotty's **Castle Visitor Center** is open daily from 8:30am to 5:30pm with shorter summer hours (9am–4:30pm). With the right combination of well-spaced winter rainfall, sunlight, and lack of drying winds, the valley can fill with a sea of gold, purple, pink, and white wildflowers. Wildflowers typically bloom from late February (low elevations) until mid-July (high elevations). Every year is different, but 2016 was an exceptional bloom. Sometimes only a few plants bloom in the desert, but the presence of life in such a desolate place is a beautiful thing to behold.

Transportation & Airports
Public transportation does not provide service to or around the park. The closest large commercial airport is McCarran International (LAS) in Las Vegas, NV (136 miles to the east), where car rental is available. There is a small public airfield at Furnace Creek, where private planes can land and refuel.

Directions
Death Valley is a massive remote region of eastern California, located along the California–Nevada border. The park can be entered from the west via CA-190 and CA-178 or from the east via CA-190, CA-178, NV-374, or NV-267.

From Los Angeles (235 miles): Heading east on I-15, take Exit 245 onto Baker Blvd. Turn left at CA-127/Death Valley Road. Travel north about 58 miles, and then turn left at CA-178, which leads into the park. (Note that the southern end of CA-178/Badwater Road was closed due to flood damage at time of publication. You may have to continue north on CA-127 to enter at Death Valley Junction via CA-190.)

From Las Vegas (87 miles): Head west on US-95 for about 85 miles to Amargosa Valley, and then turn left onto NV-373. Continue south for 21 miles, and then turn right onto CA-190, which leads into the park.

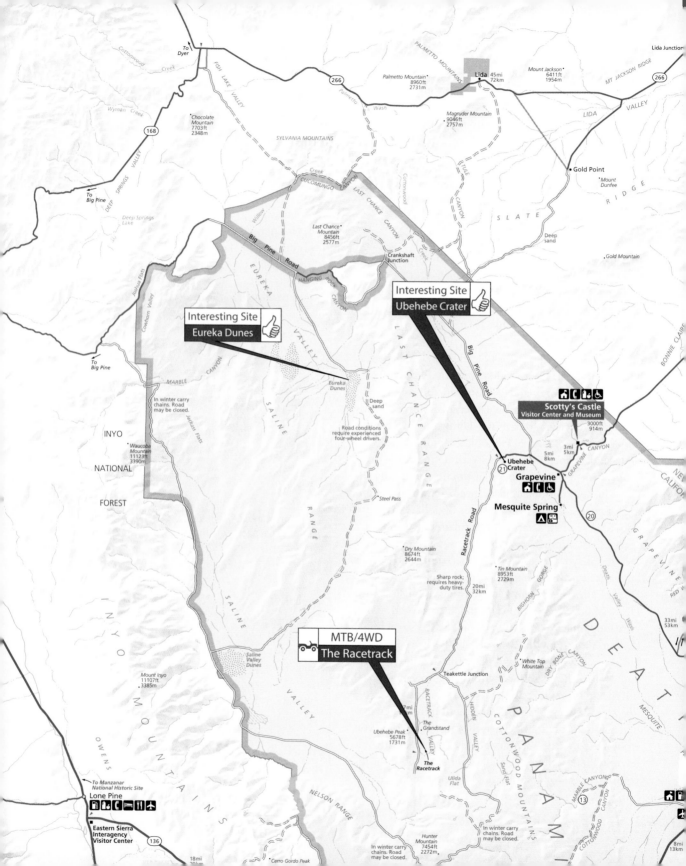

Interesting Site
Eureka Dunes 👍

Interesting Site
Ubehebe Crater 👍

MTB/4WD
The Racetrack

Scotty's Castle
Visitor Center and Museum
3000ft
914m

Ubehebe
Crater
21
Grapevine
Mesquite Spring
5mi
8km
3mi
5km
20

Lida 45mi
72km

To
Dyer

Palmetto Mountain
8960ft
2731m

Mount Jackson
6411ft
1954m

Lida Junction
266

Chocolate
Mountain
7703ft
2348m

Magruder Mountain
9046ft
2757m

Gold Point

Mount
Dunfee

Gold Mountain

SYLVANIA MOUNTAINS

PALMETTO MOUNTAINS

MT JACKSON RIDGE

LIDA VALLEY

SLATE RIDGE

266

168

To
Big Pine

DEEP SPRINGS VALLEY

Deep Springs
Lake

Wynan Creek

Cottonwood Creek

FISH LAKE VALLEY

CULCOMUNGO CANYON

LAST CHANCE CANYON

Creek

Last Chance
Mountain
8456ft
2577m

Crankshaft
Junction

Big Pine Road

HANGING ROCK CANYON

Deep
sand

Deep sand

BONNIE CLARE

NEW CALIFORNIA

Interesting Site
Eureka Dunes 👍

EUREKA VALLEY

Joshua Flats

Cowhorn Valley

MARBLE CANYON

In winter carry
chains. Road
may be closed.

Eureka
Dunes

Deep
sand

Road conditions
require experienced
four-wheel drivers.

LAST CHANCE RANGE

Big Pine Road

To
Big Pine

INYO

NATIONAL

FOREST

Waucoba
Mountain
11123ft
3390m

Jackass Flats

SALINE RANGE

Steel Pass

Racetrack Road

Dry Mountain
8674ft
2644m

Tin Mountain
8953ft
2729m

Sharp rock;
requires heavy-
duty tires.

20mi
32km

BIGHORN GORGE

DEATH VALLEY

RED WALL

33mi
53km

INYO MOUNTAINS

Saline
Valley
Dunes

SALINE VALLEY

Mount Inyo
11107ft
3385m

MTB/4WD
The Racetrack

7mi
km

Ubehebe Peak
5678ft
1731m

Teakettle Junction

RACETRACK

The
Grandstand

HIDDEN VALLEY

The
Racetrack

White Top
Mountain

DRY BONE CANYON

COTTONWOOD MOUNTAINS

PANAMINT

MESQUITE

Sand Flat

MARBLE CANYON

13

To Manzanar
National Historic Site

Lone Pine

Eastern Sierra
Interagency
Visitor Center

136

OWENS MOUNTAINS

NELSON RANGE

Hunter
Mountain
7454ft
2272m

Ulida
Flat

In winter carry
chains. Road
may be closed.

In winter carry
chains. Road
may be closed.

18mi
30km

Cerro Gordo Peak

8mi
13km

COTTONWOOD CANYON

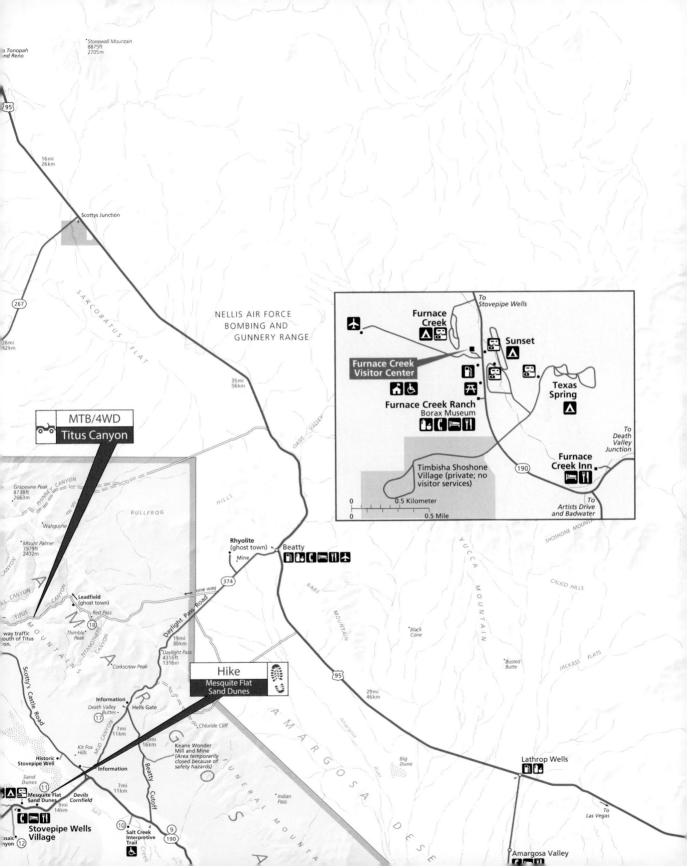

95

16mi
26km

·Stonewall Mountain
8875ft
2705m

o Tonopah
nd Reno

Scottys Junction

267

26mi
42km

NELLIS AIR FORCE
BOMBING AND
GUNNERY RANGE

35mi
56km

SARCOBATUS FLAT

OASIS VALLEY

Furnace Creek map inset

To
Stovepipe Wells

**Furnace
Creek**

Sunset

**Furnace Creek
Visitor Center**

**Texas
Spring**

Furnace Creek Ranch
Borax Museum

To
Death
Valley
Junction

Timbisha Shoshone
Village (private; no
visitor services)

190

**Furnace
Creek Inn**

0   0.5 Kilometer

0   0.5 Mile

To
Artists Drive
and Badwater

Grapevine Peak
8738ft
2663m

PHINNEY CANYON

BULLFROG   HILLS

·Wahguyhe

·Mount Palmer
7979ft
2432m

MTB/4WD
Titus Canyon

Leadfield
(ghost town)

18

Red Pass

Thimble
Peak

TITANOTHERE CANYON

·Corkscrew Peak

one way traffic
outh of Titus
on.

Scotty's Castle Road

PANAMINT MOUNTAINS

AMARGOSA

Rhyolite
(ghost town)

Mine

Beatty

374

Daylight Pass Road

one way

19mi
30km

Daylight Pass
4316ft
1316m

BARE MOUNTAIN

YUCCA MOUNTAIN

CALICO HILLS

·Black
Cone

JACKASS FLATS

·Busted
Butte

SHOSHONE MOUNTAIN

Information

Death Valley
Buttes

17

Hells Gate

7mi
11km

Chloride Cliff

·0mi
16km

Keane Wonder
Mill and Mine
(Area temporarily
closed because of
safety hazards)

95

29mi
46km

Hike
Mesquite Flat
Sand Dunes

Kit Fox
Hills

Information

7mi
11km

Historic
Stovepipe Well

Sand
Dunes

11

**Mesquite Flat
Sand Dunes**

Devils
Cornfield

9mi
14km

10

Salt Creek
Interpretive
Trail

9

190

MUD CANYON

Beatty Cutoff

Salt Creek

FUNERAL MOUNTAINS

AMARGOSA DESERT

AMARGOSA RIVER

Amargosa
River

·Indian
Pass

Big
Dune

Lathrop Wells

To
Las Vegas

osaic
nyon

12

**Stovepipe Wells
Village**

Amargosa Valley

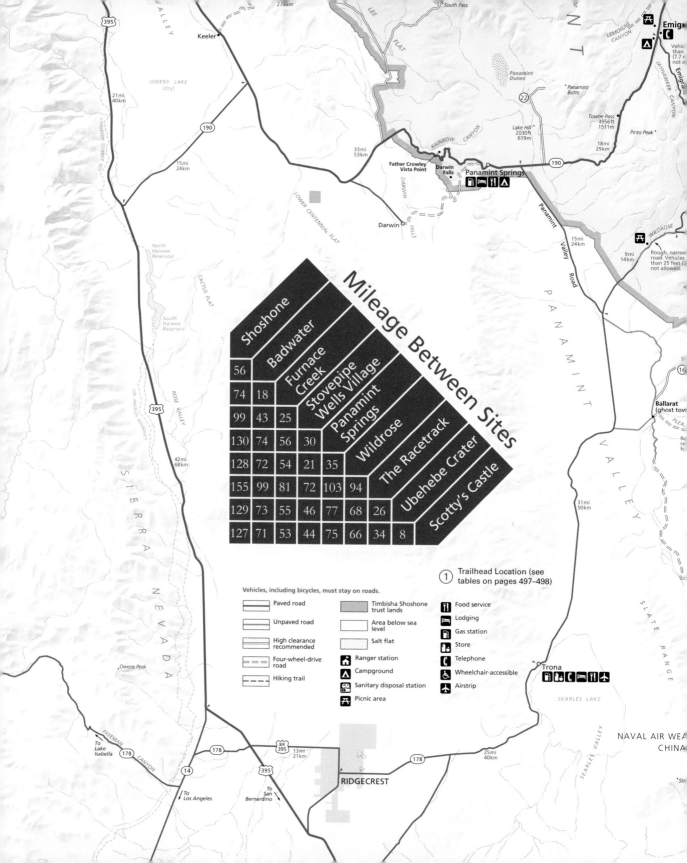

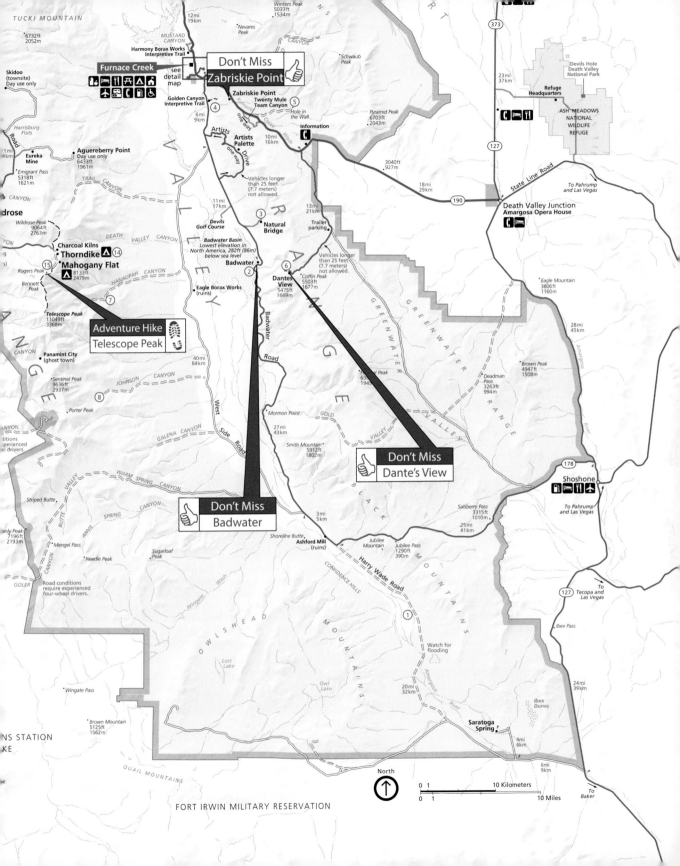

Regions

Two roads cross the center of the park diagonally making a large 'X'. The southeast leg includes Furnace Creek and Badwater. The southwest leg consists of Stovepipe Wells near the center of the 'X' and Panamint Springs along the park's western boundary. The northwest leg follows Death Valley up to Scotty's Castle.

Furnace Creek: The park's most popular region offers a wide variety of natural landscapes, scenic vistas, hiking trails, and visitor accommodations. Harmony Borax Works, Golden Canyon, Devil's Golf Course, and Natural Bridge provide hiking opportunities through otherworldly terrain. Artist's Drive and Twenty Mule Team Canyon allow motorists to drive past a few of Death Valley's more remote wonders. Zabriskie Point is a popular perch to watch the sunrise. Dante's View serves up the valley's most breathtaking vista. Badwater is the lowest point in North America. Visitor Center, camping, lodging, food, gas, wi-fi, and postal service are available.

Stovepipe Wells: Mesquite Flat Sand Dunes crease and curl just north of CA-190. Mosaic Canyon, Salt Creek, and Titus Canyon are waiting to be explored. Lodging, camping, and gas are available.

Panamint Springs: Darwin Falls, Father Crowley Vista, Lee Flat Joshua Trees, Wildrose Charcoal Kilns, and Aguereberry Point are the main attractions at your disposal. Lodging, camping, dining, bar, showers, RV hookups, and gas are available.

Scotty's Castle: A lavish "castle" built by a desert rat for his wealthy financier from Chicago, a 300-year-old volcanic crater, 700-feet-tall sand dunes, and an eerie mesa where rocks move on their own accord highlight this region. Racetrack Playa is one of the creepiest and most befuddling sights in all the national parks (high-clearance 4WD vehicle or mountain bike required). (At time of publication Scotty's Castle was closed due to flood damage. Be sure to check status before visiting.)

Death Valley Camping (Fees are per night)

Name	Location	Open	Fee	Sites	Notes
Furnace Creek*	North of Visitor Center	All Year	$18	136	W, F, DS
Sunset	Furnace Creek (CA-190)	October–April	$12	270	W, F, DS
Texas Spring	West of Sunset	October–April	$14	92	W, F, DS
Stovepipe Wells	Stovepipe Wells Village	October–April	$12	190	W, F, DS
Mesquite Spring - ♿	Scotty's Castle Road	All Year	$12	30	W, F, DS
Emigrant (tent only)	Near Stovepipe Wells	All Year	Free	10	W, F
Wildrose	Emigrant Canyon Road	All Year	Free	23	W, P
Thorndike	Emigrant Canyon Road	March–November	Free	6	P
Mahogany Flat	Emigrant Canyon Road	March–November	Free	10	P

W = Water, F = Flush Toilets, P = Pit Toilets, DS = Dump Station
RV hookups are available at Stovepipe Wells RV Park, Panamint Springs Resort, and a few sites at Furnace Creek
*Reservations can be made up to six months in advance by calling (877) 444-6777 or clicking recreation.gov

Backcountry Camping	Permitted in the backcountry as long as you camp at least one mile from any developed area, paved road, or day-use area. Free voluntary permits recommended.
Group Camping	Two group sites are available at Furnace Creek (40 people, 10 vehicle capacity)

Death Valley Lodging (Fees are per night)

Name	Open	Fee	Notes
Stovepipe Wells Village (760) 786-2387	All Year	$132–210	Centrally located with pool and wi-fi • Full hookup RV sites for $33/night • deathvalleyhotels.com
Furnace Creek Inn (800) 236-7916 - ♿	October–Mother's Day	$349–500	Fine dining, swimming pool, tennis courts, massage therapy, and an oasis garden • furnacecreekresort.com
Furnace Creek Ranch (800) 236-7916	All Year	$159–289	Features 224 guest units, 2 restaurants, saloon, swimming pool, golf course • furnacecreekresort.com
Panamint Springs Resort (775) 482-7680	All Year	$79–169	10–15°F cooler than valley lodging • Full hookup RV sites for $35/night • panamintsprings.com

Camping & Lodging

Death Valley has **nine designated frontcountry campgrounds**. All campsites, except those at Furnace Creek, are available on a first-come, first-served basis. Furnace Creek, Sunset, and Texas Spring Campgrounds are located on CA-190 near Furnace Creek Visitor Center. Showers are not available, but you can **shower** at Furnace Creek Ranch's pool building for a nominal fee.

Stovepipe Wells has a National Park Service-run campground and a concessioner-run RV Park. A **pool** and **showers** are available to all campers for a nominal fee. Farther west on CA-190 is **Emigrant Campground**, the only free campground with flush toilets and water, but there are just ten, tent-only sites. Continuing south on Emigrant Canyon Road leads up the Panamint Range. Located along the last five miles of road are three campgrounds: Wildrose, Thorndike, and Mahogany Flat. These are **excellent locations if you want to escape the heat** of the valley floor, as temperatures are typically 10°F cooler at Wildrose and 20°F cooler at Mahogany Flat. If you're interested in climbing Telescope Peak, spend the night at Thorndike or Mahogany Flat. Extreme weather conditions close these campgrounds from December through April. **Lodging** is available at Furnace Creek, Stovepipe Wells, and Panamint Springs (see the table on the opposite page).

Hiking

Death Valley is a desert hiker's paradise. Colorful canyons, arid flats bookended by steep sloping mountains, a volcanic crater, and rolling dunes are dispersed across the largest national park in the contiguous United Sates. All of these sights are best explored on foot. So lace up your hiking shoes and hit the trails.

A few trails should not be skipped. **Dante's Ridge Trail** provides the best views of Death Valley. It's located at the end of a 13-mile (one-way) paved road that intersects CA-190 near the park's East Entrance. About halfway down the road to Dante's View is a trailer parking area. Vehicles longer than 25 feet are not allowed beyond this point. The road gets extremely steep (15% grade) near its end. From the viewpoint parking area you can head north or south along Dante's Ridge, which follows the crest of the Black Mountains. Heading north, it is a half-mile to the first summit and another 3.5 miles up and down along a trail-less route to Mount Perry. To the south, just beyond Dante's View, is a short rocky trail descending to a promontory with panoramic views of Badwater Basin and the Panamint Range. Elevation

Death Valley Hiking Trails (Distances are roundtrip)

	Name	Location (# on map)	Length	Difficulty Rating & Notes
Furnace Creek	Badwater Salt Flat	Badwater (2)	1–10 miles	E – No trail, hot, occasionally muddy
	Natural Bridge Canyon	Natural Bridge (3)	1–2 miles	E – 0.5-mile to bridge, 1 mile to canyon's end
	Golden Canyon - ♨	Golden Canyon (4)	2.0 miles	E – Interpretive Trail through colorful canyon
	Gower Gulch Loop	Golden Canyon (4)	4.3 miles	M – Follow Golden Canyon to marker 4, and then follow gulch to complete loop
	Dante's Ridge - ♨	Dante's View (6)	8.0 miles	M – 1 mile to first summit, 8 miles to Mt Perry
	Salt Creek	Salt Creek (10)	0.5 mile	E – Interpretive Trail, may see rare pupfish
Stovepipe Wells	Mesquite Flat Sand Dunes - ♨	Sand Dunes (11)	2.0 miles	M – No trail, about 2 miles to highest dune
	Mosaic Canyon	Mosaic Canyon (12)	1–4 miles	M – Scrambling required, Day-use area
	Wildrose Peak	Charcoal Kilns (14)	8.4 miles	S – Great views, 2,200-ft elevation gain
	Telescope Peak	Mahogany Flat (15)	14.0 miles	S – Even better views, 3,000-ft elevation gain
	Death Valley Buttes	Hell's Gate (17)	2.4 miles	S – No trail, Narrow and exposed ridges
	Darwin Falls	Darwin Falls (17)	2.0 miles	M – Hike to a year-round waterfall
Scotty's Castle	Titus Canyon - ♨	Titus Canyon Mouth (19)	3.0 miles	E – Extremely beautiful canyon, Day-use area
	Fall Canyon	Titus Canyon Mouth (19)	6.0 miles	S – No trail, spectacular canyon
	Little Hebe Crater	Ubehebe Crater (21)	1.0 mile	M – Follows west rim of bizarre crater, can make extremely difficult hike into crater

Difficulty Ratings: E = Easy, M = Moderate, S = Strenuous

gain from Badwater to Telescope Peak (highest point in the park) is more than 13,000 feet. On clear days, the highest and lowest points in the Lower 48 states—Mount Whitney (14,505 feet above sea level) and Badwater (282 feet below sea level)—are visible.

Badwater Salt Flat is another good place for a short hike. It's quite peculiar to look up into the Amargosa Mountains and see a "Sea Level" sign a few hundred feet above the ground you stand on. From Badwater Parking Area on Badwater Road, you're free to walk beyond the boardwalk. There isn't a maintained trail, but trampled ground makes it clear that most visitors only walk a few hundred feet away from the boardwalk. You should also hike **Titus Canyon Narrows Trail**. High-clearance vehicles can enter Titus Canyon Road from Daylight Pass Road just beyond the park's eastern boundary. Daylight Pass Road is one-way until it reaches the mouth of the canyon near Scotty's Castle Road, where all other vehicles can enter via a short, two-way unpaved road. **Little Hebe Crater, Golden Canyon, and Mesquite Flat Sand Dunes Trails** are nice options, too. A more complete list of Death Valley hiking trails is provided on the previous page.

Backpacking

Backpacking in Death Valley is not an easy task. Very few established trails exist. Reliable water sources are hard to find. Weather conditions can be, well, deadly. But those who explore the backcountry are rewarded with complete solitude and private displays of scenic splendor found nowhere else in the world.

Telescope Peak is the only maintained backpacking trail. It's a great summer trek, with temperatures some 25°F cooler at the summit than the valley floor, but snow often covers its upper reaches into June. Winter hiking requires crampons and an ice axe and should only be attempted by experienced hikers. The rest of the trails listed below follow washes, canyons, or old mining roads. One-night backpackers should try hiking **Surprise Canyon** to Panamint City (ghost town). The canyon is located on the park's western boundary, off of CA-178 near Ballarat (ghost town). Ballarat is worth a visit by itself. It's suggested you obtain a **free voluntary backcountry permit** at Furnace Creek Visitor Center or Stovepipe Wells Ranger Station. Carry water, compass, and map, and pack out your trash.

Death Valley Backpacking Trails (Distances are roundtrip)

	Name	Location (# on map)	Length	Notes
Furnace Creek	Olwshead Mountains	6.6 miles south on Harry Wade Rd (1)	16.0 miles	Return via Granite Canyon for loop, side canyons, high-clearance required
	Hole-in-the-Wall	On 4WD Road, opposite Twenty Mule Team Canyon (5)	2–10 miles	No trail, side canyons, scrambling, high-clearance 4WD required
	Hanaupah Canyon	5 miles west on Hanaupah Canyon Rd, off West Side Rd (7)	6.0 miles	Accessed via a high-clearance 4WD road, old mining area and spring
	Hungry Bill's Ranch	End of Johnson Canyon Rd (8)	14.0 miles	Informal path, historic ranch, orchard
	Indian Pass	6.5 miles north of Visitor Center (9)	16.0 miles	Gravel wash, mountain pass, canyon
Stovepipe Wells	Cottonwood–Marble Canyon Loop	8–10 miles northwest on Cottonwood Canyon Road (13)	26–30 miles	Loop, no trail, high-clearance 4WD required, take map and compass
	Telescope Peak	Mahogany Flat Camp (15)	14.0 miles	Maintained trail, wonderful views
	Surprise Canyon	Outside the park, north of Ballarat (16)	10.0 miles	Ghost town, high-clearance 4WD
	Panamint Dunes	End of dirt road, beyond CA-190 and Panamint Valley Rd Intersection (22)	6.0 miles	No trail, fighter jet training area, high-clearance required
Scotty's Castle	Titanothere Canyon	Titus Canyon Road, near Red Pass (18)	9.0 miles	No trail, high-clearance
	Fall Canyon	Mouth of Titus Canyon (19)	6–12 miles	Camp beyond first dry fall (3 miles)
	Bighorn Gorge	On Scotty's Castle Rd, 3.9 miles south of Grapevine Ranger Station (20)	20.0 miles	Out-and-back, no trail, requires some scrambling
All Backpacking Trails Are Strenuous				

Backcountry Roads

Death Valley, the largest national park outside of Alaska, has more miles of roads than any other park (roughly 1,000 miles of paved and unpaved roadways). Backcountry roads unlock some of the most fascinating remote locations in the U.S. to visitors with high-clearance 4WD vehicles. Before racing into the backcountry, make sure you are prepared. Pack basic tools, like a shovel, extra food, and water. Equip your vehicle with "off-road" tires. Carry at least one spare tire (two is better), a can of fix-a-flat or tire plug kit, a 12-volt air compressor, and a car jack and lug-wrench. Last but not least, top-off your gas tank before entering the backcountry. These simple precautions could save your life or at least prevent a considerable amount of grief. Should you break down, it is usually better to stay with your vehicle and wait for another traveler. Leave the car's hood up and mark the road with a large X visible to aircraft. Traveling in a group of two or more 4WD vehicles can minimize the risks of exploring Death Valley's backcountry roads. If you come across a stranded vehicle, please stop to lend a hand. Next time, it could be you in need of help.

After making the proper preparations, choose your backcountry destination. **Titus Canyon and Racetrack Valley are the most popular attractions.** Titus Canyon Road is 26.8 miles (high-clearance required) and it begins at Daylight Pass Road (NV-374), 2.7 miles east of the park boundary, eventually winding its way through the Grapevine Mountains, past a ghost town and petroglyphs, and through a spectacular canyon. Racetrack Valley Road spans 28 miles from Ubehebe Crater Road to the Racetrack. Do not walk on the Racetrack when wet and never drive on it. Lippincott, North and South Eureka Valley, and Echo Canyon Roads are also excellent options. A brochure and map of all backcountry roads is available at visitor and information centers. Do not drive off designated roads.

Biking

Bicycles are allowed on all of the park's paved and unpaved roads. **Road cyclists** can cruise along Badwater Road or climb to Dante's View (the last ascent is a 15% grade). **Mountain bikers** like to explore Titus Canyon Road. Bike rental is available adjacent to

Badwater Basin

the General Store at Furnace Creek Ranch. Twenty-four speed mountain bikes cost $15/hour, $34/half-day, and $49/day. Call (760) 786-3371 for reservations.

The Racetrack

The Racetrack is a dry lakebed located in the northwestern corner of the park and home to an unexplained phenomenon: moving rocks known as sailing stones. It's difficult to explain where they're going and how they're getting there. No one has actually seen the rocks move, but proof of movement lies in the trails left behind these heavy boulders. Some rocks have traveled more than 1,500 feet. It could be an elaborate prank, but scientists believe a combination of rain and wind allows the rocks to "move" on this extremely flat and dry lakebed. Rain reduces the friction between hard rock and the earth's surface. Winds of 50 mph or more are capable of pushing the boulders across this slippery substrate. Ironically, in a place called "Death Valley," the rocks of the Racetrack come to life and move about the valley.

It's one of those sights you have to see for yourself to believe. Access it via **Racetrack Road** (high-clearance recommended), which begins at Ubehebe Crater at the very north end of Scotty's Castle Road. The road is rough washboard, so be prepared for a flat tire, and expect the 26-mile (one-way) trip on Racetrack Road to take about 2 hours each way. Don't move or take the rocks!

Scotty's Castle

Walter Scott, known as Death Valley Scotty, was a desert rat who duped wealthy easterners into investing in his "gold mine." Scotty took the money and went on infamous spending sprees, never producing an ounce of ore. All but one investor pulled their funding. Albert M. Johnson, an insurance magnate, became friends with Scotty and funded construction of what is now known as Scotty's Castle. Today, the house is a museum with regularly scheduled **Living History Tours** offered 365 days a year. Tours cost $15/adult, $7.50/senior, and $7.50/child. Call (760) 786-2392 for current hours. Advance tickets may be purchased at recreation.org or by calling (877) 444-6777. Tours of Lower Vine Ranch (Scotty's home • $20/adult), and an Underground Tour ($15/adult) are available daily, between November and April. Note that Scotty's Castle was closed due to flood damage at time of publication. Be sure to check its status before making the long drive up to this corner of the park.

Horseback Riding

Furnace Creek Stables, located at Furnace Creek Ranch (760.614.1018, furnacecreek-stables.net), offers **guided trail, carriage, and wagon rides**. Two-hour guided trail rides ($70/rider) provide a taste of the desert as you travel into the foothills of the Funeral Mountains. More experienced riders who want freedom to gallop can take a private ride for $70/hour. Carriage rides cost $30 per adult and $15 per child (ages 5–12). Hay wagon rides ($20/person) are also available.

Ranger Programs

Whether you've decided to pass through Death Valley on your way to Las Vegas or you're on a family vacation, do not exit the park without joining at least one ranger program. The park offers guided ranger programs from November to April. All of them are free except tours of Scotty's Castle and Scotty's home (Lower Vine Ranch), and the Underground Tour. Call (760) 786-2392 for information and reservations on these for fee tours. Almost all of the free programs are offered near Furnace Creek or Stovepipe Wells. They explore a variety of interests: photography, geology, natural history, and ecology. Mesquite Dunes, Zabriskie Point, Golden Canyon, Harmony Borax Works, Badwater, and Dante's View are all sites of ranger talks or walks. These locations are made even more memorable by the colorful stories, history, and anecdotes provided by knowledgeable park rangers. During peak-season many programs

are offered daily. You can pick up a current schedule of events at any visitor or information center or refer to the calendar of events found at the park's website.

For Kids

Most kids prefer desserts to deserts, but this desert is a pretty cool treat. Children should like exploring the lowest spot in North America or looking down at Death Valley from Dante's View. They are the park's special guests and are invited to participate in its **Junior Ranger Program**. Junior Ranger Booklets are available, free of charge, at any visitor center. Complete an age-appropriate number of activities, do something to help the park, and attend a ranger program for an official Death Valley National Park Junior Ranger badge.

Flora & Fauna

More than 1,400 species of plants and animals have been found living in Death Valley. The most obvious animals are the park's birds. Hundreds of species of migratory birds stop at the desert oases or mountains. Saratoga Spring, Furnace Creek Ranch, Scotty's Castle, Wildrose, and the High Panamints are popular birding areas. The park's famed wildflower eruption is not a regular occurrence, so check the park website for wildflower updates. They do an exceptional job of providing timely updates as to where the best (accessible) flower hotspots are.

Pets

Pets are permitted in Death Valley, but owners must adhere to several regulations. Pets must be kept on a leash no more than six feet in length at all times. They are not allowed on trails, in the backcountry, or in public buildings (with the exception of service animals). They must not be left unattended at any time. Owners must clean up after their pets and make sure they do not make unreasonable amounts of noise. Basically, you can take your pet anywhere your car can go: campgrounds, parking areas, and roadways.

Accessibility

Visitor centers, contact stations, and museums are fully accessible to individuals in wheelchairs. Accessible campsites are available at Furnace Creek, Stovepipe Wells, Mesquite Spring, and Emigrant Campgrounds. The first floor of Scotty's Castle Tour is accessible.

Weather

Death Valley is renowned for its remarkably hot and dry climate. Average annual rainfall is less than two inches. The driest stretch on record is a 40-month period from 1931 to 1934 when just 0.64 inches of rain was recorded. An entire year can pass without any measurable precipitation. The high mountain ranges lining the valley cause hot air to recirculate rather than dissipate. The area's low elevation is also responsible for it being the hottest spot in North America. Day time highs in July average 115°F. Hot and dry with clear skies make the park extremely pleasant from late fall to early spring.

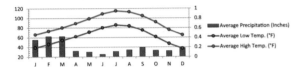

Vacation Planner

Death Valley is huge. More than 1,000 miles of paved and dirt roads stretch across 3.4 million acres of mostly undeveloped desert. It's possible to blast through the park in a day, but spending the night allows visitors to **hike more trails** (page 497), **ride a horse** (page 500), **tour Scotty's Castle** (page 499), **drive to the Racetrack** (page 499), and catch a Death Valley sunrise as the first rays of light illuminate colorful badlands and jagged peaks found at **Zabriskie Point** (CA-190 near Furnace Creek). For a more proper introduction, plan on spending at least three days. Unless you really like to drive, you'll want to spend your nights at an in-park **campground** or **lodging** facility (page 497). Nearby dining, grocery stores, lodging, festivals, and attractions are listed on pages 535–537.

Day 1: Assuming you enter the park on CA-178/Badwater Road at Shoshone, CA (if it's open, it was closed due to flood damage when we went to print), begin your trip by following Badwater Road north along the eastern side of Death Valley. If you're arriving in late winter or spring, you may see beautiful fields of **wildflowers**. The five-mile stretch of road between Jubilee Pass and Ashford Mill is a particularly good spot for wildflowers early in the season. Continuing north, the next stop to stretch your legs is **Badwater**, the lowest spot in North America. Most visitors wander about the boardwalk, but you can venture further out into the valley if you're interested in an extended flat hike. Return to your car and hop back onto Badwater Road. Skip Natural Bridge, but take the short detour along **Artist's Drive**. This 9-mile, one-way loop passes through colorful volcanic and sedimentary hills before returning to Badwater Road. The next stop is **Golden Canyon**, one of the park's best short hikes and the last stop before reaching **Furnace Creek**. If you have enough spare time (about 2 hours) before dark, take CA-190 toward the park's eastern boundary where you'll find the road to **Dante's View**, one of the best spots to see the sunset.

Day 2: Follow the best sunset with the best sunrise. Retrace your route to Dante's View but stop short at **Zabriskie Point**. The first rays of sunlight creep over the Amargosa Range illuminating the colorful bands of rock and Zabriskie Point. Travelers in high-clearance vehicles should exit the park on Daylight Pass Road/NV-374 and take **Titus Canyon Road** back into the park. Hike **Titus Canyon Trail**. All other visitors can reach the trail via Scotty's Castle Road. After the hike, drive north to **Ubehebe Crater**. If you aren't driving a high-clearance 4WD vehicle or don't have interest in Scotty's Castle, this is a good leg to skip. Those prepared for backcountry roads should drive to the **Racetrack** (page 499). Allow at least 4 hours to make the roundtrip journey from Ubehebe Crater. (**Eureka Dunes** is another worthwhile excursion in this area, if you have a high-clearance vehicle. These dunes, some of the tallest in North America, are known for "singing sand" heard as it avalanches down the steep dune faces. Note that it's only heard when the sand is dry.)

Day 3: Unless you made it to Eureka Dunes yesterday, check out **Mesquite Flat Sand Dunes** in the morning. There isn't a trail, but following the ridgelines is pretty easy. After playing in the dunes, spend the day in the pool (fee) at Stovepipe Wells. (If you're looking for a real workout, consider driving to the **Telescope Peak** trailhead at dawn. Weather permitting, complete the 14 arduous miles to the park's highest peak. The trail is usually snow free by June. If snow-covered, it should not be attempted without proper experience and equipment. It's also one of the better summer backpacking destinations.)

Ranger talk at General Sherman

Sequoia & Kings Canyon

47050 Generals Highway
Three Rivers, CA 93271
Phone: (559) 565-3341
Website: nps.gov/seki

Established:
September 25, 1890 (Sequoia)
October 1, 1890 (General Grant)
March 4, 1940 (Kings Canyon)
Size: 865,257 Acres
Annual Visitors: 1.6 Million
Peak Season: Summer

Activities: Hiking, Backpacking,
Camping, Stargazing, Horseback
Riding, Rock Climbing, and Biking

Campgrounds*: 14 Campgrounds
Fee: $12–22/night
Backcountry Camping: Permitted
Lodging: 4 Lodges ($129+/night)

Park Hours: All day, every day
Entrance Fee: $30/vehicle
$15/individual (foot, bike, etc.)

*Reservations available at Lodgepole
and Dorst Campgrounds by using
recreation.gov or (877) 444-6777

Sequoia and Kings Canyon National Parks reside in a contiguous region of the southern Sierra Nevada. Each park has its own boundary and entrance, but they share the same backbone, the Sierra Nevada Mountains. Since 1943 the parks have been administered jointly by the National Park Service. John Muir, one of the first American naturalists, was an early advocate of preserving and protecting regions of exceptional natural beauty. While wandering the High Sierra he formed a kinship with the trees, the rocks, and the mountains, and few areas were more important to Muir than the groves of giant sequoia and mountains of the High Sierra (including Mount Whitney, the highest peak in the lower 48 states). He spent much of his life writing, speaking, and petitioning on their behalf.

"Most of the Sierra trees die of disease, fungi, etc., but nothing hurts the Big Tree. Barring accidents, it seems to be immortal." – John Muir

Muir was just about right. The wood and bark of the park's namesake is infused with chemicals that provide resistance to insects and fungi. Its bark—soft, fibrous, and in excess of two feet thick—is a poor conductor of heat, making the giant sequoia highly resistant to fire damage. They rarely die of old age, either. Many sequoias are more than 2,000 years old. Ironically, extreme size is its greatest threat. Most die by toppling over under their immensity. Relative to their massive size and height, the roots are shallow and without a taproot. Wet soil, strong winds, and shallow roots are a recipe for a toppled sequoia.

"God has cared for these trees, saved them from drought, disease, avalanches, and a thousand tempests and floods. But he cannot save them from fools." – John Muir

Fools found their way to the sequoia groves of the Sierra Nevada and did what they could to topple these mighty trees. In 1888, Walter Fry sought work as a logger (even though sequoias were a relatively poor wood that splintered easily). Somewhere between felling a sequoia (which took a five-man team five days to complete) and counting its 3,266 rings, he had a change of heart. At the same time conservationists were collecting signatures to protect the forest; the third signature was none other than Walter Fry, who decided to put down his axe and channel his efforts toward protecting the trees from the men he had worked alongside. Protection was achieved in 1890 thanks to establishment of a national park. Fry was hired as a road foreman in 1901 and four years later he became a park ranger. Over the next three decades, he became the first civilian superintendent (originally the park fell under army supervision) and the first nature guide, who continued to lead guests on guided walks until his retirement in 1930 at the age of 71.

"When I entered this sublime wilderness the day was nearly done, the trees with rosy, glowing countenances seemed to be hushed and thoughtful, as if waiting in conscious religious dependence on the sun, and one naturally walked softly awestricken among them." – John Muir

John Muir didn't have to cut down a sequoia tree to understand its significance. The privilege of being able to walk among them was enough. Muir's communion wasn't just with the trees, it was with nature itself. He led energetic hikes into the High Sierra and forged a trail along the steep east face of Mount Whitney. Today, the 211-mile trail from Yosemite National Park to Mount Whitney bears his name. He dreamed of an expanded park, reaching far into King's Canyon, but it wasn't until 1940 that Kings Canyon National Park was established. Harold Ickes, Secretary of the Interior, wanted to make a park that was impenetrable to automobiles. Kings Canyon was ideal. Today, a single road leads into the canyon and terminates abruptly at Roads End. No road within either park crosses the Sierra Nevada. Mount Whitney, the tallest point in the lower 48, cannot be seen from any roadway. The park is left mostly undeveloped, allowing visitors to walk softly awestricken among its natural beauty, much like John Muir did when he first came to the Sierra Nevada.

Bear near Mineral King

When to Go
Sequoia and Kings Canyon National Parks are open all year. The parks are busiest on summer weekends. Some campgrounds and lodging facilities close for winter, but you can almost always find a place to spend the night any time of year. If you can't find a campsite in the park, campgrounds are also available at adjacent Sequoia National Forest and Monument. During winter, roads to Cedar Grove and Mineral King close. Generals Highway is open year-round, but closes during heavy snowstorms. From December to April, visitors can cross-country ski around Giant Forest, but most visitors arrive between spring and fall.

Transportation & Airports
Sequoia Shuttle (877.287.4453, sequoiashuttle.com) provides transportation between Visalia and Giant Forest Museum. Roundtrip fare is $15 and includes the park entrance fee. Reservations are required. During summer the park operates a free shuttle service with three routes through the park's most popular sections between Dorst Campground and Crescent Meadow. The closest large commercial airport is Fresno Yosemite International (FAT) in Fresno, CA, located 83 miles from Sequoia's Ash Mountain Entrance. Car rental is available at the airport.

Directions
The parks are located in eastern California's Sierra Nevada. Ash Mountain Entrance is 34 miles from downtown Visalia. It is reached by CA-198, which turns into Generals Highway inside the park. Generals Highway connects the two parks. It is 80 miles from Ash Mountain Entrance to the end of Kings Canyon Scenic Byway. Kings Canyon Visitor Center is 53 miles east of Fresno via CA-180.

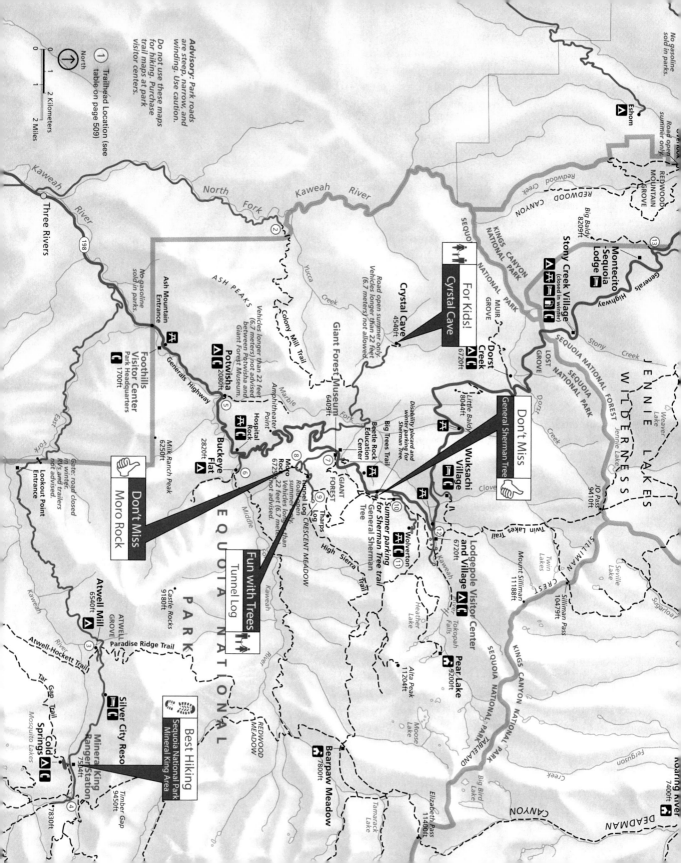

Advisory: Park roads are steep, narrow, and winding. Use caution.

Do not use these maps for hiking. Purchase trail maps at park visitor centers.

① Trailhead Location (see table on page 509)

North

0   1   2 Kilometers
0   1   2 Miles

Three Rivers

Kaweah River
North Fork Kaweah River

No gasoline sold in parks.
Road open summer only.

REDWOOD MOUNTAIN GROVE

Eshom

KINGS CANYON NATIONAL PARK

Big Baldy 8209ft

Stony Creek Village

Montecito Sequoia Lodge

REDWOOD CANYON

Redwood Creek

Generals Highway

JENNIE LAKES WILDERNESS

Weaver Lake
Jennie Lake

JO Pass 9410ft

SEQUOIA NATIONAL FOREST

LOST GROVE

Stony Creek

Dorst Creek

Crystal Cave 4540ft

For Kids!
Crystal Cave 6720ft

Road open summer only. Vehicles longer than 22 feet (6.7 meters) not allowed.

ASH PEAKS

Ash Mountain Entrance

Foothills Visitor Center
Park Headquarters 1700ft

Milk Ranch Peak 6250ft

Potwisha 2080ft

Yucca Creek

Colony Mill Trail

Giant Forest Museum 6409ft

Vehicles longer than 22 feet (6.7 meters) not advised (between Potwisha and Giant Forest Museum).

Marble Fork

Amphitheater Point

Hospital Rock

Buckeye Flat 2820ft

Little Baldy 8044ft

Disability placard and winter parking for Sherman Tree.

Big Trees Trail
Beetle Rock Education Center

Wuksachi Village

General Sherman Tree

Don't Miss

Summer parking for Sherman Tree trail
General Sherman Tree

Lodgepole Visitor Center and Village 6720ft

Clover Creek

Twin Lakes Trail

SEQUOIA NATIONAL FOREST

Mount Silliman 11188ft

SILLIMAN CREST

Twin Lakes

Seville Lake

Silliman Pass 10479ft

Sugarloaf

KINGS CANYON NATIONAL PARK / TABLELAND

GIANT FOREST

Tunnel Log
CRESCENT MEADOW

Moro Rock
Moro summit only. Vehicles longer than 22 feet (6.7 meters) not advised.

Don't Miss
Moro Rock

Fun with Trees
Tunnel Log

⑧ ⑦ ⑨
Congress Trail Loops
High Sierra Trail

Wolverton

Heather Lake

Tokopah Falls

Pear Lake 9200ft

Alta Peak 11204ft

Moose Lake

SEQUOIA NATIONAL PARK

Castle Rocks 9180ft

Middle Fork Kaweah River

Atwell Mill 6540ft

ATWELL GROVE
Paradise Ridge Trail

Atwell-Hockett Trail

Tar Gap Trail

Mosquito Lakes

Silver City Reso
Cold Springs 7450ft

Mineral King Ranger Station 7830ft

Best Hiking
Sequoia National Park
Mineral King Area

Timber Gap 9450ft

REDWOOD MEADOW

Bearpaw Meadow 7800ft

Elizabeth Pass 11400ft

Tamarack Lake

Big Bird Lake

Ferguson Creek

Roaring River 7400ft

DEADMAN CANYON

KINGS CANYON NATIONAL PARK

No gasoline sold in parks.

Gate: road closed in winter. RVs and trailers not advised.

Lookout Point Entrance

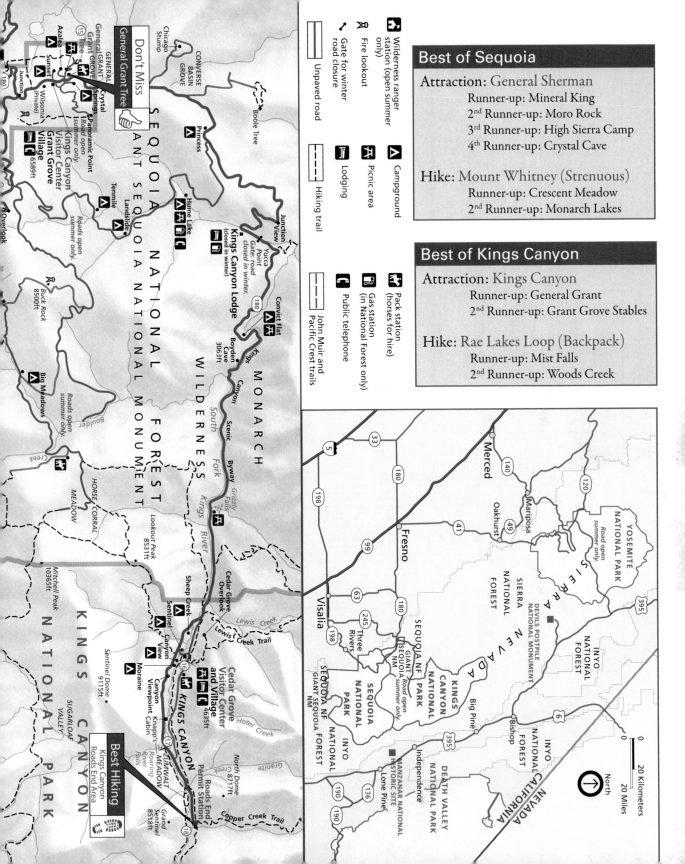

Best of Sequoia

Attraction: General Sherman
  Runner-up: Mineral King
  2nd Runner-up: Moro Rock
  3rd Runner-up: High Sierra Camp
  4th Runner-up: Crystal Cave

Hike: Mount Whitney (Strenuous)
  Runner-up: Crescent Meadow
  2nd Runner-up: Monarch Lakes

Best of Kings Canyon

Attraction: Kings Canyon
  Runner-up: General Grant
  2nd Runner-up: Grant Grove Stables

Hike: Rae Lakes Loop (Backpack)
  Runner-up: Mist Falls
  2nd Runner-up: Woods Creek

Wilderness ranger station (open summer only)

Fire lookout

Gate for winter road closure

Unpaved road

Hiking trail

Lodging

Picnic area

Campground

Pack station (horses for hire)

Gas station (in National Forest only)

Public telephone

John Muir and Pacific Crest trails

Don't Miss
General Grant Tree

Best Hiking
Kings Canyon
Roads End Area

North

Trailhead Location (see table on page 509)

0 5 Kilometers
0 5 Miles

To Fresno
216
198
To Visalia
To Lemoncove
245
General's Highway
Dry Creek Road
Badger
245
180
Pinehurst
Kings Canyon Scenic Byway

15 Kings Canyon Visitor Center Grant Grove Village
Big Stump Entrance
Grant Tree
Big Stump
No gasoline sold in parks.

14 REDWOOD MOUNTAIN GROVE
13 Montecito-Sequoia Lodge
Stony Creek Village (closed in winter)

LAKE KAWEAH

Three Rivers

Advisory: Park roads are steep, narrow, and winding. Use caution.

Crystal Cave
Road open summer only. Vehicles longer than 22 feet (6.7 meters) not advised between Potwisha and Giant Forest Museum.

No gasoline sold in parks.

Foothills Visitor Center Park Headquarters
Ash Mountain Entrance

5 Potwisha
General's Highway
6 Buckeye Flat
Moro Rock 8
7 GIANT FOREST Giant Forest Museum
9 General Sherman Tree
10 Wolverton
11
12 Lodgepole Visitor Center
Wuksachi Village
Dorst Creek
GIANT FOREST GROVE
MURO GROVE

SEQUOIA NATIONAL PARK
KINGS CANYON NATIONAL PARK

Denision Mountain 8650ft
South Fork
1 South Fork 3620ft
GARFIELD GROVE
DILLONWOOD GROVE
Homers Nose
Kaweah

Lookout Point Entrance
Gate: road closed in RVs and trailers not advised.

Silver City Resort
ATWELL MILL GROVE
Atwell Mill
3
Mineral King Ranger Station
4
Cold Springs
Hockett Meadows 8459ft
Quinn Peak 10167ft
Eagle Lake
White Chief Lake
Mosquito Lakes
Blossom Lakes
Sheep Mountain 10051ft
Farewell Gap 10587ft

SEQUOIA NATIONAL FOREST
GIANT SEQUOIA NATIONAL MONUMENT

Pear Lake 9200ft
Bearpaw Meadow 7800ft
Roaring River 7400ft
16 Visitor Center and Village

Franklin Lakes
Sawtooth Pass 11700ft
Franklin Pass 11800ft
Little Five Lakes 10476ft
Black Rock Pass 11600ft
Mount Stewart 12205ft
Triple Divide Peak 12634ft
Kaweah Gap 10700ft
Black Kaweah 13765ft
KAWEAH BASIN
GREAT WESTERN DIVIDE
KINGS-KERN DIVIDE
Mount Brewer 13570ft
Avalanche Pass 10040ft
SPHINX CREST
Sphinx 10040ft

Backpack Rae Lakes Loop

Centennial Peak 13255ft
Table Mountain 13630ft
Mount Genevra 13055ft
Forester Pass 13100ft
University Peak 13632ft
Mount Bradley 13289ft
Center Peak 12700ft
Shepherd Pass 12050ft

Kern Canyon 6450ft
Backpack High Sierra Trail
GREAT WESTERN DIVIDE
Coyote Pass 10101ft
Coyote Pass 10650ft
Coyote Peaks 10892ft
SIERRA NATIONAL FOREST

Florence Peak 12432ft
Shotgun Pass
Rattlesnake
Moraine Lake
CHAGOOPA PLATEAU
PLATEAU
Big Arroyo Canyon
High Sierra Trail
Mount Kaweah 13802ft
KERN CANYON
Kern River
Mount Guyot 12300ft
803ft
Junction Meadow
Kern Point 12789ft
Mount Tyndall 14018ft
Tyndall Creek 10827ft
Mount Williamson 14375ft
Junction Pass 13888ft
Mount Barnard 13990ft

GOLDEN TROUT WILDERNESS
INYO NATIONAL FOREST
BOREAL PLATEAU
Tower Rock 8469ft
Golden Trout Creek
Natural bridge
Funston Lake
Rock Creek 9602ft
Kern River 10950ft
Siberian Pass 11200ft
Siberian Outpost
Cottonwood Pass 11147ft
New Army Pass
Cottonwood Lakes
Sky Blue Lake 836ft

Backpack Crabtree 10720ft
Mount Hitchcock 13184ft
Crabtree Lakes
Backpack Mount Whitney
John Muir Trail
Pacific Crest Trail
Guitar Lake
Mount Whitney 14491ft 14,505ft in U.S.!
Mount Whitney Portal
To Lone Pine 18
Whitney Zones: special permits are required year-round for day hikes to the summit and for all overnight trips. Inquire where permits are issued.
Mount Langley 14026ft
BIGHORN PLATEAU
Shepherd Peak 12050ft
Mount Russell 14088ft

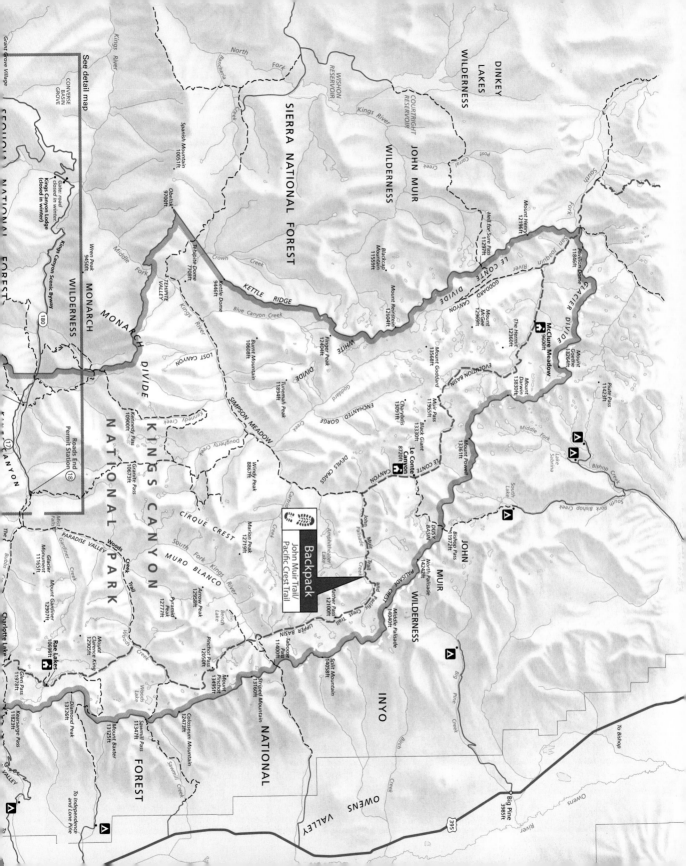

Camping & Lodging

There are 14 campgrounds, 4 lodges, and 2 backcountry tent-cabin camps within the two parks. Dorst and Lodgepole are the only campgrounds that accept reservations (summer only) up to six months in advance for standard sites and a year in advance for group sites. Campgrounds often fill in summer, especially on weekends and holidays. You must use

the food-storage containers. There are no RV hookups in the parks. Two High Sierra Camps offer a hybrid camping/lodging experience. They offer the tranquility of the backcountry with all the creature comforts of a modern lodge. The catch is you must hike-in, but Sequoia High Sierra Camp has a 1-mile hike option. The table below provides a more comprehensive look at the parks' camping and lodging facilities.

Sequoia & Kings Canyon Camping (Fees are per night)

Name	Location	Open	Fee	Sites	Notes
Potwisha	4 miles from entrance	All Year	$22	42	F, DS, RV
Buckeye Flat	Middle Fork Kaweah	mid-March–Sept	$22	28	F
South Fork	South Fork Drive	late June–early Oct	$12	10	P
Atwell Mill	Mineral King Road	late May–Oct	$12	21	P
Cold Springs	Mineral King Road	late May–Oct	$12	40	P
Lodgepole*	Giant Forest	mid-April–Nov	$22	214	F, RV
Dorst*	10 miles from Giant Forest	mid-June–early Sept	$22	210	F, DS (summer), RV
Azalea	Kings Canyon Entrance	All Year	$18	110	F, DS (summer), RV
Crystal Springs	Kings Canyon Entrance	late May–early Sept	$18	50	F, RV
Sunset	Kings Canyon Entrance	late May–early Sept	$18	157	F, RV
Sentinel	Cedar Grove	late April–Nov	$18	82	F, RV
Sheep Creek	Cedar Grove	late May–late Sept	$18	111	F, RV
Canyon View	Cedar Grove	late May–late Sept	$35–60	16	F, RV
Moraine	Cedar Grove	late May–late Sept	$18	120	F, RV

F = Flush Toilets, P = Pit Toilets, DS = Dump Station, RV = RVs & Trailers are allowed
*Summer reservations can be made up to six months in advance by calling (877) 444-6777 or clicking recreation.gov

Backcountry	Allowed with a wilderness permit. Permits are free (and self-issued) from late September to late May, and $10 (+$5/person) for the remainder of the year. Reservations are allowed. Quotas are enforced.
Group	Available at Dorst, Sunset, and Canyon View (group only) Campgrounds. Fees range from $35–70/night. Sites must be reserved in advance. All group sites may be reserved at recreation.gov or (877) 444-6777.

Sequoia & Kings Canyon Lodging (Fees are per night)

Name	Open	Fee	Notes
Wuksachi Village (888) 252-5757	All Year	$129–385	Located in Giant Forest of Sequoia National Park, features restaurant and lounge • visitsequoia.com
John Muir Lodge (877) 436-9615	All Year	$80–310	Located in Grant Grove Village, 36 rustic, well-appointed, recently updated rooms • visitsequoia.com
Grant Grove Village (877) 436-9615	All Year Cabins (May–Nov)	$80–310	Located in Grant Grove Village • Cozy cabins near Grant Grove, new restaurant under construction • visitsequoia.com
Cedar Grove Lodge (877) 436-9615	early May–late Oct	$140–172	Deep in the heart of Kings Canyon (Cedar Grove Village) overlooking Kings River • visitsequoia.com
Sequoia Camp (866) 654-2877	mid-June–mid-Sept	$250	Unique backcountry lodging • 1- or 12-mile trail options to camp • ($150 per child per night) • sequoiahighsierracamp.com
Bearpaw Camp (866) 807-3598	mid-June–mid-Sept	$385	Tent cabins, 11.5 miles on High Sierra Trail • Meals, bedding included • Hot showers and flush toilets • visitsequoia.com

See page 535 for additional camping and lodging facilities in Sequoia National Forest/Monument and surrounding areas

Sequoia & Kings Canyon Hiking Trails (Distances are roundtrip)

	Name	Location (# on map)	Length	Difficulty Rating & Notes
Sequoia	Lady Bug	South Fork Campground (1)	6.0 miles	M – 1.75 miles to camp, 3 miles sequoia grove
	Garfield Grove	South Fork Campground (1)	10.0 miles	S – Ends at a remote sequoia grove
	North Fork	North Fork Rec. Area (2)	8.4 miles	M – Get trailhead location from visitor center
	Padadise Peak	Atwell Mill Campground (3)	9.6 miles	S – Large sequoias, fantastic views, not popular
	Monarch Lakes - ♿	End of Mineral King Rd (4)	8.4 miles	M – Wonderful views of the southern Sierra
	Crystal Lake	End of Mineral King Rd (4)	9.8 miles	S – Branch from Monarch Lakes Trail (steep)
	Timber Gap	End of Mineral King Rd (4)	4.0 miles	M – Follows old mining route along Monarch Creek
	Franklin Lakes - ♿	End of Mineral King Rd (4)	10.8 miles	M – Popular first leg for multi-day trips
	White Chief	End of Mineral King Rd (4)	5.8 miles	M – Steep but scenic mining trail
	Eagle Lake - ♿	End of Mineral King Rd (4)	6.8 miles	M – Fairly steep but popular trail to majestic lake
	Mosquito Lakes	End of Mineral King Rd (4)	7.2 miles	M – Three small lakes in the High Sierra
	Marble Falls	Potwisha Campground (5)	7.8 miles	M – Marble Fork–Kaweah River/Deep Canyon
	Middle Fork	Off dirt road, before Buckeye Flat Campground (5)	5.5 miles	M – Views of Moro Rock and Castle Rocks, popular in spring, creek crossings required
	Paradise Creek	Buckeye Flat Camp (6)	1.5 miles	E – Popular swimming holes
	Big Trees - ♿	Giant Forest Museum (7)	1.3 miles	E – Paved loop with benches and interpretive signs
	Moro Rock - ♿	Crescent Meadow Rd (8)	0.5 mile	M – Almost 400 steps to granite dome/great views
	Crescent Meadow	Crescent Meadow Rd (9)	3.2 miles	E – Leads to Tharp's Log and Chimney Tree
	High Sierra	Crescent Meadow Rd (9)	49.0 miles	S – 11.4 miles to High Sierra Camp, backpacker trail
	Gen. Sherman - ♿	General Sherman Tree (10)	1.0 miles	M – Handicap parking available on Generals Hwy
	Congress	General Sherman Tree (10)	2.0 miles	E – Paved loop accessed from Gen. Sherman Trail
	Alta Peak	Wolverton Picnic Area (11)	13.8 miles	S – Vews of Mount Whitney from Alta Peak
	Tokopah Falls	Lodgepole Camp (12)	3.4 miles	E – Walk along Marble Fork of the Kaweah River
	Mt Whitney - ♿	Whitney Portal (18)	22.0 miles	S – East side of park • Shortest route to the summit
Kings Canyon	Big Baldy Ridge	8 mi. S on Generals Hwy (13)	4.0 miles	E – Provides views down into Redwood Canyon
	Buena Vista Peak	Dirt road off Generals Hwy, 6 miles SE of Grant Grove (14)	2.0 miles	E – Easiest summit hike, where visitors obtain decent views of the canyon and mountains
	Redwood Canyon	Dirt road off Generals Hwy, 6 miles SE of Grant Grove (14)	16.0 miles	E–S – Network of trails through one of the largest of all Sequoia groves • Road closed in winter
	General Grant - ♿	Grant Tree Parking Area (15)	0.7 mile	E – Short loop to the Nation's Christmas Tree
	North Grove Loop	Grant Tree Parking Area (15)	1.5 miles	E – High granite walls and lush meadows
	Zumwalt Meadow	Cedar Grove Village (16)	1.5 miles	E – Popular loop/Burnt in 2015 fire
	Hotel/Lewis Creek	Cedar Grove Village (16)	8.0 miles	M – Loop includes Cedar Grove Overlook
	Roaring River Falls	3 miles east of village (17)	0.3 mile	E – Short roadside hike to powerfull waterfall
	Mist Falls - ♿	Roads End (18)	8.0 miles	M – Relatively flat trail, large waterfall
	Rae Lakes Loop - ♿	Roads End (18)	46.0 miles	S – Popular backcountry hike
	Woods Creek	Roads End (18)	28.0 miles	S – Follows Mist Falls to Paradise Valley and PCT
Both	John Muir	Backcountry	211 miles	One-way • Connects Yosemite and Mt Whitney
	Pacific Crest (PCT)	Mexico–British Columbia	2,663 mi	One-way • Follows Sierra Nevada and Cascades

Difficulty Ratings: E = Easy, M = Moderate, S = Strenuous

Marble Fork
(Kaweah River)

Hiking

With more than 800 miles of hiking trails, it's difficult to choose what to see and where to hike. In Sequoia, the short hike up nearly 400 stairs to the top of **Moro Rock** provides spectacular views (when there isn't smog). The one activity every visitor must do is stand next to a giant sequoia. **General Sherman** is the tree to visit in Sequoia National Park. At Kings Canyon, say hello to **General Grant**, a tree President Coolidge called the "Nation's Christmas Tree" and President Dwight D. Eisenhower declared a "National Shrine," the only living object to receive this distinction. Respectively, they are the first and second largest trees in the world. For classic High Sierra trails, go to **Mineral King** in Sequoia or **Roads End** at Kings Canyon. Note that the road to Mineral King is long, narrow, and winding. Check out the hiking table on the previous page for additional trails.

Backpacking

Backpacking in the Sierra Nevada is an indescribable experience. This setting inspired John Muir to dedicate much of his life to the conservation of the United States' irreplaceable natural wonders. Largely thanks to Muir, Sequoia and Kings Canyon National Parks' backcountry is left as it was when he hiked these trails. Nowadays, more people have become appreciative of nature's beauty, and the backcountry is so popular a **wilderness permit quota system** is in place during summer (May–September). Permits cost $10 plus $5 per person and can be reserved in advance by completing the application form available at the park website. Not interested in reserving permits? One-quarter of all permits are available on a first-come, first-served basis. Fees still apply. Walk-up and reserved permits must be picked up at the issuing station closest to your trailhead, no earlier than the afternoon before you depart. From late September to late May visitors can obtain a free wilderness permit from self-issue stations located at Lodgepole Visitor Center, Foothills Visitor Center, Roads End Permit Station, and Mineral King Ranger Station. Food must be stored in a portable bear-resistant canister or metal food storage locker.

John Muir and **Pacific Crest** are legendary long-distance trails that pass through the parks. If you'd like to sample the best of the Sierra Nevada, try Sequoia's 49-mile High Sierra Trail or Kings Canyon's 46-mile Rae Lakes Loop. **Rae Lakes Loop** is regarded as the best backpacking trail in the entire High Sierra. If you're looking for a shorter, more comfortable trek, take **High Sierra Trail** 12 miles to **High Sierra Camp** (866.654.2877, sequoia-highsierracamp.com), where you can reserve tent cabins for $250 per person per night, and $150 per child per night. If you aren't interested in a strenuous hike, there is a 1-mile trail option. Breakfast, lunch, and dinner are included. **Bearpaw High Sierra Camp** (866.807.3598, visitsequoia.com) offers a similar pampered backpacking experience for $385 per person per night. Reaching Bearpaw requires an 11.5-mile (one-way) hike along High Sierra Trail, beginning at Crescent Meadow Parking Area. A wilderness permit (free to Bearpaw guests and available at Lodgepole Visitor Center) is required to park at Crescent Meadow.

Caves

There are more than 265 known caves within the park and at least one new cave is discovered each year. Since 2003, at least 17 caves have been found. At 17 miles in length, Liburn is the longest cave in California. **Crystal Cave** is the only one available for tours. It's located 15 miles from the Sequoia National Park entrance at CA-198, and 3 miles south of General Sherman. Tours are given daily from mid-May through November. They cost $16/adult and $8/child. **Discovery Tours** are offered during summer for $18/person. **Wild Cave and Junior Cave tours** are also offered. Tickets can only be purchased at Giant Forest Museum from mid-October through November. From March through mid-October, tickets can be purchased online at recreation.gov or by calling (877) 444-6777. It's recommended you purchase tickets at least 30 days in advance, but tickets are occasionally available during your visit at Foothills or Lodgepole Visitor Centers. You must have tickets before arriving at the cave. Wear a jacket; the cave is 50°F year-round.

Rock Climbing

Rock found at Sequoia and Kings Canyon National Parks is similar to Yosemite in terms of quality and quantity. The main difference is that you have to pack up your gear and hike (usually a full-day) to the best climbing locations. In Kings Canyon, Bubbs Creek Trail (part of Rae Lakes Loop) is a good place to find multi-pitch climbing routes. Moro Rock (Sequoia) is the most easily accessible feature for climbing. There are also excellent options along High Sierra Trail. Climbing in remote regions is not recommended for inexperienced climbers. Sierra Mountain Guides (708.648.1122, sierramtnguides.com) offers a variety of **introductory courses and custom trips** throughout the eastern Sierra.

Horseback Riding

Horse enthusiasts aren't excluded from the fun. Those looking to explore the Sierra Nevada on horseback have **three outfitters** to choose from. Grant Grove Stables (559.335.9292, summer • 559.779.7247, winter, visitsequoia.com) offers 1- and 2-hour guided trips to General Grant Tree, through North Grove, Lion Meadow, and Dead Giant Meadow. Cedar Grove Stables (559.565.3464, visitsequoia.com) has a wider range of services. You can enjoy anything from an hour-long trail ride to multi-day pack trips in Kings Canyon's backcountry. Backcountry trips include Monarch Divide and Rae Lakes Loop. Horse Corral Packers (559.565.3404, summer • 559.564.6429, winter, hcpacker.com) is located east of Big Meadows Campground in Sequoia National Forest. They offer half-day, full-day, and extended pack trips. Horseback rides are generally offered from late spring to fall. Reservations are recommended (and required for pack trips). Rates are about $40/rider for 1 hour and $70/rider for 2 hours. Multi-day backcountry trips cost about $200 per rider per day.

Winter Activities

Winter is a wonderful time of year to visit the parks. The lower foothills remain snow free year-round, but you can usually find snow for cross-country skiing and snowshoeing in the higher elevations.

Pear Lake Ski Hut (Sequoia) is open from mid-December through April. Located just north of Pear Lake at 9,200-feet elevation, it can be reached via a steep six-

Tharp's Log

mile trail from Wolverton Meadow. The hut sleeps 10, costs $38–42 per person per night, and reservations are required. **Sequoia Parks Conservancy** (559.565.3759, exploresequoiakingscanyon.com) has additional information on the reservation process. Ski rental is available at Wuksachi Lodge and Grant Grove Market.

The park offers **ranger-guided snowshoe walks** on Saturdays and holidays (weather permitting). Snowshoes are provided (free). These two-hour treks usually begin at Giant Forest Museum (559.565.4480) and Grant Grove (559.565.4307). Group size is limited, so reserve your place by calling or stopping at any visitor center. Sequoia Parks Conservancy (559.565.3759, exploresequoiakingscanyon.com) also offers naturalist-guided snowshoe treks and stargazing opportunities in winter. Snowshoe trips may be difficult for small children. Two miles north of General Sherman Tree is an open area with **two sledding hills** where children of all ages are welcome to race down the hills and play in the snow.

Flora & Fauna

When it comes to biodiversity, there's much more than big trees. The tallest mountain and one of the deepest canyons in the contiguous United States, 265 known caves, and everything in between provide a variety of ecosystems, supporting some 1,200 species of plants and 260 vertebrate species. There's a chance you may see a bear lumbering about a sequoia grove or a bighorn sheep scaling the rocky ledges of the backcountry, but you're more likely to spot mule deer or squirrels. The parks also provide habitat for more than 200 species of birds. Golden eagle, peregrine falcon, and blue grouse have all been spotted here. One of the best places to begin a birding expedition is Giant Forest.

Giant sequoias tend to steal the show for anyone's first visit to the park. Stand next to one of these towering giants and you can finally grasp their impressive size. Try to hug one (it will take more than one of you). Walk, drive, and peer through sequoias that have been hollowed out. Whatever you do, you'll be sure to come away inspired. **Giant Forest** (Sequoia) and **Grant Grove** (Kings Canyon) are the two most popular sequoia groves, but there are 75 total groves, containing more than 15,000 trees, within park boundaries along the western slope of the Sierra Nevada. Sequoias reside in the middle elevations (5–7,000 feet) with a mix of evergreens. Giant Forest is home to five of the ten largest trees in the world, including General Sherman, the world's largest tree. Grant Grove is home to General Grant, the world's second largest tree. Lower elevations are home to chaparral vegetation, and high elevations are mostly rocky and barren with the exception of the occasional foxtail and whitebark pine.

Ranger Programs
In addition to cave tours and snowshoe treks, the park offers a variety of free ranger-led activities. These programs usually begin at Giant Forest, Grant Grove, and the Foothills. A current listing of programs can be found on bulletin boards located at each visitor center or check the park's online calendar before visiting. In Sequoia, you'll find **Foothills Visitor Center** (559.565.4212), **Giant Forest Museum** (559.565.4480), **Beetle Rock Family Nature Center** (559.565.4480), **Lodgepole Visitor Center** (559.565.4436), and **Mineral King Ranger Station** (559.565.3768). In Kings Canyon you'll find **Kings Canyon Visitor Center** (559.565.4307) and **Cedar Grove Visitor Center** (559.565.3793). Hours are seasonal so please call to see when they're open.

For Kids
Almost all ranger programs are great activities for the whole family. The scenery, stories, and sweet hats topping each ranger's head can inspire children to want to join them. The **Junior Ranger Program** allows children of all ages to participate in some ranger fun while at the park. Pick up a free Junior Ranger Activity Booklet at a visitor center. Complete an age appropriate number of activities and return to a visitor center to become a Junior Ranger and receive an award.

Pets
Pets are allowed in the park, but must be kept on a leash no more than six feet in length at all times. They are not permitted on park trails or in the backcountry. Pets may not enter public buildings (except service animals), but are allowed along roadways, in parking areas, and in frontcountry campgrounds.

Accessibility
Accessible restrooms are available at each campground and visitor center, as well as Giant Forest Museum. General Sherman Tree and Big Trees trails are accessible to individuals in wheelchairs. Beetle Rock, Crescent Meadows, Tharp's Log, Grant Tree, Zumwalt Meadows, Muir Rock, and Roaring River Falls trails are all manageable, but they may require assistance to navigate due to a fairly steep grade.

Weather
Temperature and weather conditions change drastically depending on your elevation, which ranges from 1,500 to 14,494 feet within the park. A visitor might enter at Three Rivers (1,700 feet) wearing shorts and a t-shirt, while a hiker climbing to the summit of Mount Whitney (14,494 feet) is covered from head to toe in winter apparel. That's an extreme scenario; most areas are pleasant. The middle elevations (~4,0000–7,000 feet) feature comfortable summer temperatures with average highs in the 70s°F. Weather is rarely excessively hot, with the hottest days only sneaking into the lower 90s°F. Overnight temperatures can fall below freezing, but the average low in summer is in the low 50s°F. Expect the temperature to be 10–15°F warmer in the foothills than it is in the middle elevations.

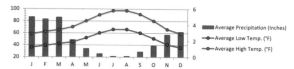

Vacation Planner

Sequoia and Kings Canyon National Parks have a lot to offer. Together, they're easily one of the best backpacking (page 510) destinations in the United States. **Backpackers** will want to head to **Mineral King** (Sequoia) or **Roads End** (Kings Canyon). A more comfortable backpacking adventure can be had at two **High Sierra Camps** (page 508). This excursion wines and dines you with three full meals made by an executive chef. If that doesn't sound good enough, you'll also have the luxury of sleeping in a tent cabin. Backpacking is popular in the High Sierra, but it's not what most visitors have in mind when making a trip here. **Park lodging and camping facilities** are listed on page 508. Facilities fill up in summer. Avoid paying the premium for convenience and location within the park by staying in Visalia or other gateway communities. Nearby dining, grocery stores, lodging, festivals, and attractions are listed on pages 535–537.

Provided below is a sample three-day itinerary beginning in Sequoia and ending in Kings Canyon. Stop at a **visitor center** when it's convenient. Browse the exhibits, watch a short introductory film, and squeeze a few ranger programs into the schedule below. **Mineral King** is great (and highly recommended), but the long and winding road is a bit nerve-racking. Traveling to Mineral King requires at least a full day, but overnight is better. It has been omitted from the following itinerary because it isn't for everyone (but do it if you seek great hiking!). If touring **Crystal Cave** (page 510) is on your list of things to do, remember tickets for tours can be purchased in advance at recreation.gov or (877) 444-6777 (book early, especially for weekends and holidays). **Note that vehicles longer than 22 feet are not advised to travel between Potwisha Campground and Giant Forest Museum. Additionally, vehicles longer than 24 feet are not advised to travel between Foothills Visitor Center and Potwisha Campground.**

Day 1: Enter Sequoia's **Ash Mountain Entrance** via CA-198/Generals Highway. Moro Rock will appear to the north as you climb to around 6,000 feet in elevation. Take Crescent Meadows Road to **Moro Rock**. It's a great place to get an outstanding view of the Sierra Nevada and valley below. Hopefully smog will not impede your views of this canyon carved by the Middle

Tunnel Log near Crescent Meadow)

Fork of the Kaweah River. If you'd like to leave the driving to the park, during summer you can pick up a **free shuttle** at Moro Rock. Hop aboard and stop at **Giant Forest Museum** and **General Sherman Tree**. Otherwise, make the same stops in your car and don't forget to drive through **Tunnel Log** (great spot for a photo), which is a short hike/drive northeast of Moro Rock. **Crescent Meadows** is another exceptional short hike, where bear sightings are quite common.

Day 2: Today you'll make your way over to **Grant Grove Village** and **Kings Canyon**. If you'd like to do a little more hiking, **Little Baldy, Big Baldy and Redwood Canyon Trails** are excellent choices located between Lodgepole Visitor Center and Grant Village. At Grant Village, turn right at the visitor center and continue to Panoramic Point, where you'll find a short hike to some of the best views near the roadway. Return to Grant Village to have a look at the Nation's Christmas Tree, **General Grant**. Where you spend your second night depends on when you're traveling and how much time you have. It's another 30 miles from Grant Village to Cedar Grove where additional overnight accommodations are found.

Day 3: Saving the best for last, spend your final day hiking into the High Sierra from **Kings Canyon's Roads End Permit Station**. Copper **Creek, Mist Falls, Bubbs Creek Trails** are all exceptional hikes. The only thing better than hiking one of these for a day, is hiking them for 2, 3, 4, or more days.

If you choose to begin your vacation at Kings Canyon, ending it by hiking at **Mineral King** (Sequoia) provides a similar climactic conclusion.

The view from on top Sentinel Dome

Yosemite

PO Box 577
Yosemite National Park, CA 95389
Phone: (209) 372-0200
Website: nps.gov/yose

Established: October 1, 1890
June 30, 1864 (State Park)
Size: 761,268 Acres
Annual Visitors: 4.1 Million
Peak Season: May–September
Hiking Trails: 800+ Miles

Activities: Hiking, Backpacking, Camping, Rock Climbing, Rafting, Horseback Riding, and Biking

13 Drive-In Campgrounds*
Fee: $12–26/night
Backcountry Camping: Permitted with a Backcountry Use Permit
Lodging: $98–800/night

Park Hours: All day, every day, except Hetch Hetchy (Day-Use)
Entrance Fee: $30/vehicle, $15/individual (foot, bike, etc.)

*Reserve at recreation.gov or (877) 444-6777

"I have seen persons of emotional temperament stand with tearful eyes, spellbound and dumb with awe, as they got their first view of the Valley from Inspiration Point, overwhelmed in the sudden presence of the unspeakable, stupendous grandeur."

– Galen Clark

Times have changed, but the scenery remains the same. The first sight of the valley still possesses the power to leave guests weak in the knees and with a tear in their eye. These very sites were the catalyst fueling the conservation movement. The smooth granite peaks inspired a man, by his own admission an "unknown nobody," to become one of America's great naturalist writers, thinkers, speakers, and the unofficial "father of the National Parks." Giant sequoias encouraged one of the country's greatest presidents to protect similar exhaustible resources and landscapes. Beautiful vistas motivated a photographer to capture their essence, their "unspeakable, stupendous grandeur," allowing the world to experience the spellbinding awe felt when a visitor first views the valley from Glacier Point or Tunnel View.

The first non-Native visitors to this majestic valley didn't come for respite or rejuvenation. In 1851, the Mariposa Battalion was called to the Sierra Nevada to settle a skirmish between Native Americans and local '49ers hoping to dispossess their land. These soldiers found the Natives, whom they believed to be the Yosemite Tribe, in a valley about one mile wide and eight miles long. Upon arrival, the battalion didn't stop to stare in bewilderment or give thanks to a greater power capable of creating such a spectacle; instead they prepared to burn it down, thus starving the Natives. Eventually the feud was settled and it was learned that the natives were known as Ahwahneechee; Yosemite was actually their name for the Mariposa Battalion.

"If no man ever feels his utter insignificance at any time, it is when looking upon such a scene of appalling grandeur."

– James Mason Hutchings

James Mason Hutchings and Galen Clark shared similar sentiments when it came to Yosemite Valley. In 1855, Natives led Hutchings into the valley. He quickly became enamored with the scenery and wasted no time moving in. In his opinion, the region had "value" as a tourist attraction, so he immediately began promoting it as such. From 1855–1864, the valley was visited by just 653 tourists. Insufficient infrastructure resulted in trips from San Francisco to Yosemite Valley that took 4–5 days (on foot, horseback, and carriage).

Galen Clark's wife died young, so he too moved to California seeking his fortune. In 1853, Clark contracted a severe lung infection. Doctors gave him six months to live. "I went to the mountains to take my chances of dying or growing better, which I thought were about even (Galen Clark, 1856)." Shortly after his arrival he discovered Mariposa Grove, and from that point on much of his time was spent writing friends and Congress requesting passage of legislation to protect the area. He gained the support of John Conness, a Senator from California. In 1864, in the midst of the Civil War, President Abraham Lincoln signed a bill preserving Yosemite Valley and Mariposa Grove under state control. Clark happily became guardian of the Yosemite Grant, including the grove of trees that inspired him. As guardian he was expected to protect the park from overeager tourists, maintain roads and bridges, and deal with residents and businesses residing here. All this needed to be done on a meager $500 annual budget.

One business in the valley was Hutchings House Hotel. James Mason Hutchings became Galen Clark's biggest pest. He refused to abide by the $1/year government lease. Essentially squatting on public land, he expanded his operations and built a sawmill.

Hutchings hired a wandering shepherd by the name of John Muir to run his sawmill. Born in Scotland, raised in Wisconsin, Muir skedaddled to Canada to avoid the Civil War and returned to work as an industrial engineer

When to Go

Yosemite is open all day, every day, with the exception of Hetch Hetchy Entrance Station (open during daylight hours). Yosemite Valley and Wawona are accessible by car year-round. Tioga, Glacier Point, and Mariposa Grove Roads close for winter (usually beginning in November) and do not reopen until late May. Glacier Point/Badger Pass Road to Badger Pass Ski Area is plowed from mid-December through early April. In winter, tire chains are often required to drive park roads. You must carry chains with you and know how to use them. Mariposa Grove is closed until spring 2017 for a restoration project.

Spring is the best time of year to see waterfalls. Most wildflowers bloom in June. In fall, crowds thin and leaves of the few stands of maple, oak, and dogwood trees begin to change. Overcrowding is a significant problem, especially at Yosemite Valley in summer. Park roads, shuttles, and popular trails become extremely congested during this time. You will want to reserve accommodations well in advance or arrive early to obtain a first-come, first-served campsite.

Transportation & Airports

Amtrak (800.872.7245, amtrak.com) provides a combination of train and bus service directly to Yosemite Valley. Greyhound (800.231.2222, greyhound.com) provides bus service to Merced, where you can board a Yosemite Area Regional Transportation System (YARTS) (877.989.2787, yarts.com) bus to Yosemite Valley. YARTS also provides service from communities along CA-140 between Merced and Yosemite (Mariposa, Midpines, and El Portal). Service is available east of Yosemite via CA-120 from Lee Vining, June Lake, and Mammoth Lakes during summer.

Fresno–Yosemite International (FAT), Merced (MCE), and Modesto City–County (MOD) Airports are all within a 2.5-hour drive of Yosemite Valley. San Francisco International (SFO), Oakland International, San José International (SJC), Sacramento International (SMF), and Reno/Tahoe International (RNO) Airports are within 5 driving hours of Yosemite Valley.

Yosemite Falls

Free Shuttle Service
The park operates a fleet of free and accessible shuttle buses. Not only do they decrease traffic congestion and pollution, they can decrease visitor frustration by taking the steering wheel out of your hands. Park shuttles are best utilized in Yosemite Valley.

Valley Shuttle Route operates all year, looping around Upper Pines Campground, Curry Village (Half Dome Lodge), Ahwahnee (Yosemite Hotel), Yosemite Village, and Yosemite (Valley) Lodge. **Express and El Capitán Shuttles** only operate in summer. The short Express Route is direct transit between the large visitor parking area at the northeast end of the valley and Yosemite Village. **El Capitán Shuttle** completes a one-way loop between El Capitán Bridge and Valley Visitor Center. Each of these shuttles runs daily every 10–20 minutes depending on the time of day. **Valley Shuttle** operates from 7am–10pm and El Capitán and Express Shuttles operate from 9am–6pm.

in Indiana. The sharp mind that had allowed memorization of the Bible's New Testament and most of the Old Testament by age 11 was on display in an industrial environment. His inventiveness and intellect helped improve many machines and processes, making life easier for the laborers at a plant manufacturing carriage parts. When a work accident nearly left him blind, Muir chose to be true to himself. He had always wanted to study plants and explore the wilderness. He set out on a 1,000-mile walk from Indiana to Florida, where he planned to board a ship to South America. Unfortunately, he contracted malaria before he could set sail across the Caribbean. While recuperating in Florida, he read about Yosemite and the Sierra Nevada. Nursed back to health, Muir booked passage to California instead. He arrived in 1868. After a brief stint as a shepherd, Muir moved into Yosemite Valley to run Hutchings' sawmill, where he built a cabin near the base of Yosemite Falls for $3, what he considered to be "the handsomest building in the valley."

As Muir was settling into his new life, Hutchings was being evicted. In 1875, Galen Clark allowed him to store his furniture in a vacant building. Hutchings moved in more than his furniture, he set up his entire operation: Wells Fargo Office, telegraph, post office, everything. Once again, he was running a hotel. This was the final straw. Hutchings, banished from Yosemite, moved to San Francisco where he started a tourist agency and wrote two best-selling books including *In the Heart of the Sierras*.

Meanwhile, Muir had become a bit of a Yosemite celebrity. All of the park's guests wanted exposure to his brand of enthusiasm and passion for the ecology and geology of the High Sierra. In 1871, Ralph Waldo Emerson, the author whose work Muir had read many a night from the light of a campfire, arrived at Yosemite. After just one day in Muir's company, Emerson offered Muir a teaching position at Harvard. Even though he had spent much of the past three years unemployed, Muir declined the offer to remain in what he called "the grandest of all the special temples of Nature I was ever permitted to enter...the sanctum sanctorum of the Sierra."

By 1889, Yosemite Valley was officially a tourist trap. A cliff-side hotel was constructed at Glacier Point. Raging fires were hurled over the cliff's edge to create a waterfall of fire. Tunnels were carved into trees. Muir had seen too much, so he set out to make Yosemite a national park. Witnessing how the establishment of Yellowstone National Park increased passenger traffic for Northern Pacific Railroad, the Southern Pacific placed their support behind the endeavor. In 1890, Sequoia, General Grant, and Yosemite became National Parks.

James Mason Hutchings, now 82, wanted to make one last trip into Yosemite Valley. His wish was granted, but a tragic horse carriage accident resulted in Hutching's death. In what can be seen as a peculiar twist of fate in a seemingly tragic accident, the funeral service was held in the Big Tree Room, formally known as Hutchings House: the old hotel he was evicted from and the one place he loved more than any other.

In 1903, John Muir and President Theodore Roosevelt camped beneath the stars at Glacier Point. President Roosevelt stated "it was like lying in a great solemn cathedral, far vaster and more beautiful than any built by the hands of man." It wouldn't be long until the hands of man wanted to dramatically change Yosemite. San Francisco required water to support its ballooning population. Dam proposals were focused on a tract of land within park boundaries known as Hetch Hetchy Valley. Muir found Hetch Hetchy even more appealing than the more popular Yosemite Valley. He passionately opposed the dam proposal and for years legislation was held up in a political quagmire. In 1913, Woodrow Wilson finally signed a bill approving the dam. One year later, an exhausted Muir died at the age of 76. John Muir arrived in Yosemite, "the sanctum sanctorum of the Sierra," as an "unknown nobody." He left as president and founder of the Sierra Club, renowned writer and naturalist, and catalyst in the creation of Yosemite, Sequoia, Mount Rainier, and Grand Canyon National Parks. He is the father of the National Parks.

In 1916, a shy 14-year-old boy, sick and in bed, decided to read James Mason Hutchings' *In the Heart of the Sierras*. Intrigued, he convinced his parents to vacation at Yosemite. What he saw left an indelible mark. Years later, the young man worked as caretaker at the Sierra Club's LeConte Memorial Lodge in Yosemite Valley, where he spent time as a photographer for Sierra Club outings and classical pianist for lodge guests, wowing them with striking imagery and wistful music. This man is Ansel Adams, one of the greatest photographers, a man who had a special affinity for Yosemite. A visit to Yosemite can become a life-changing experience. Its unspeakable grandeur is so overwhelming you may find yourself inspired like James Mason Hutchings, Galen Clark, John Muir, President Roosevelt, and Ansel Adams were before you.

Lembert Dome

Directions

Yosemite National Park is located in east-central California's Sierra Nevada. There are a total of five park entrances. Hetch Hetchy Entrance, leading to O'Shaughnessy Dam and Hetch Hetchy Backpackers Camp, is only open during daylight hours. It does not connect to Yosemite Valley and is far less crowded. Big Oak Flat and Arch Rock Entrance enter the park from the west. South Entrance enters from the south via Oakhurst. On the eastern side you'll find Tioga Pass Entrance Station. Due to high elevation (9,945 feet) the entrance and Tioga Road usually close from November until April (depending on the weather).

To Hetch Hetchy: From CA-120, on the park's western side, turn left onto Evergreen Road just before you reach Big Oak Flat Entrance Station. Continue on Evergreen Road for about 7 miles, and then turn right at Hetch Hetchy Road, which leads to the reservoir and camp.

To Big Oak Flat Entrance: From San Francisco/Oakland, take I-580 E and continue onto I-205 E. Merge onto I-5 N. After less than a mile on I-5, take Exit 461 to CA-120. Follow CA-120 to Big Oak Flat Entrance.

To Arch Rock Entrance: From CA-99, take CA-140 E/Yosemite Pkwy at Merced, which leads into the park.

To South Entrance: From Fresno, take CA-41 N through Oakhurst into the park.

To Tioga Pass Entrance: From US-395/US-6, take US-395 north from Bishop. After about 64 miles, turn left onto CA-120/Tioga Road. It is 12 miles to the entrance.

Driving

Hetch Hetchy Road enters from the west and dead ends at **O'Shaughnessy Dam**, roughly tracing the Tuolumne River. Hetch Hetchy is a particularly good location to avoid crowds, and lower elevation makes it ideal for late winter/early spring visits when the high country is cold and covered in snow.

Big Oak Flat Road enters from the west via CA-120. After the entrance station you immediately pass **Hodgdon Meadow Campground** and then **Tuolumne Grove**. Gas is available at its intersection with **Tioga Road**. A little farther south, **El Portal Road** follows the Merced River into the park, where it eventually merges with **Big Oak Flat Road** just before entering **Yosemite Valley**.

Wawona Road enters from the south, passing **Mariposa Grove** and **Glacier Point Road**. Campgrounds, dining, gas, and trail rides are available near Wawona. Glacier Point Road provides access to some of the best views of **Half Dome** at **Glacier Point** (and Washburn Point), but it closes in winter (beyond Badger Pass Ski Area). Wawona Road continues north to **Tunnel View**, one of the most photographed vistas in the world, and finally into **Yosemite Valley**.

Tioga Road is the only route that crosses the Sierra Nevada within the park. Gas is available at **Tuolumne Meadows**. Dining is available at Tuolumne Meadows and White Wolf. Five designated campgrounds are available along the way (and High Sierra Camps are in the backcountry). Tioga Road closes seasonally.

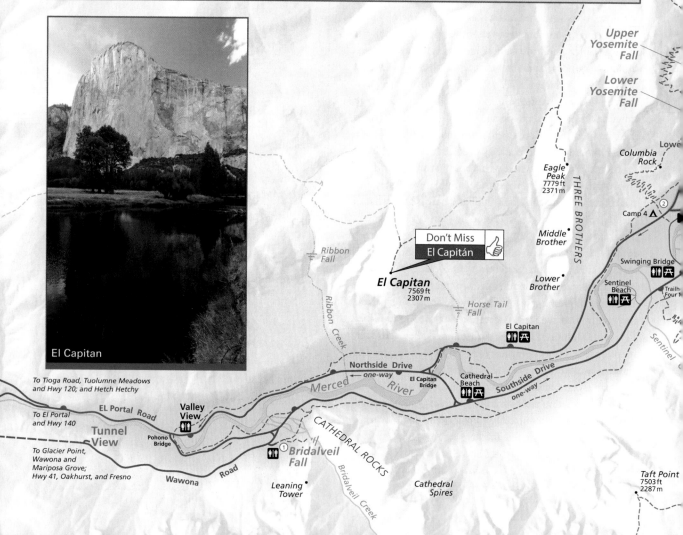

El Capitan

Don't Miss
El Capitán

Upper Yosemite Fall

Lower Yosemite Fall

Columbia Rock

Lowe

Eagle Peak
7779 ft
2371 m

THREE BROTHERS

Camp 4

Ribbon Fall

Middle Brother

Swinging Bridge

El Capitan
7569 ft
2307 m

Lower Brother

Sentinel Beach

Trailh
Four M

Horse Tail Fall

El Capitan

Sentinel

Ribbon Creek

Northside Drive
← one-way

El Capitan Bridge

Cathedral Beach

Southside Drive
one-way

Merced River

To Tioga Road, Tuolumne Meadows and Hwy 120; and Hetch Hetchy

EL PORTAL Road

Valley View

To El Portal and Hwy 140

Tunnel View

Pohono Bridge

To Glacier Point, Wawona and Mariposa Grove; Hwy 41, Oakhurst, and Fresno

Wawona Road

Bridalveil Fall

CATHEDRAL ROCKS

Bridalveil Creek

Leaning Tower

Cathedral Spires

Taft Point
7503 ft
2287 m

Regions

Tuolumne Meadows/White Wolf/Crane Flat (summer only): These areas located along Tioga Road offer amazing vistas of Yosemite's high country. Opportunities for peaceful solitude abound on wilderness hiking trails and backpacking trips. Merced and Tuolumne Grove are two of the park's three sequoia groves.

Hetch Hetchy (all year, daylight hours only): Today's source of power and water for San Francisco was a miniature replica of Yosemite Valley before being dammed.

Yosemite Valley: Waterfalls, precipitous granite cliffs, and plenty of tourists are found here. More than 90% of the park's guests visit Yosemite Valley, which comprises less than 1% of the total park land. Upon your first sight of the valley it becomes crystal clear why this cathedral of nature is their primary destination.

Glacier Point: This overlook provides views of Yosemite Valley, Half Dome, and Yosemite's high country. It's a one-hour drive from Yosemite Valley or Wawona, and can also be reached by foot from the valley via Panorama or Four Mile Trail. Excellent hiking trails and viewpoints are found along the way. Do not skip Glacier Point!

Wawona & Mariposa Grove: Mariposa Grove and Wawona are located near the park's South Entrance. Mariposa is the most popular sequoia grove in the park. Note that Mariposa Grove is closed until spring 2017 for a restoration project.

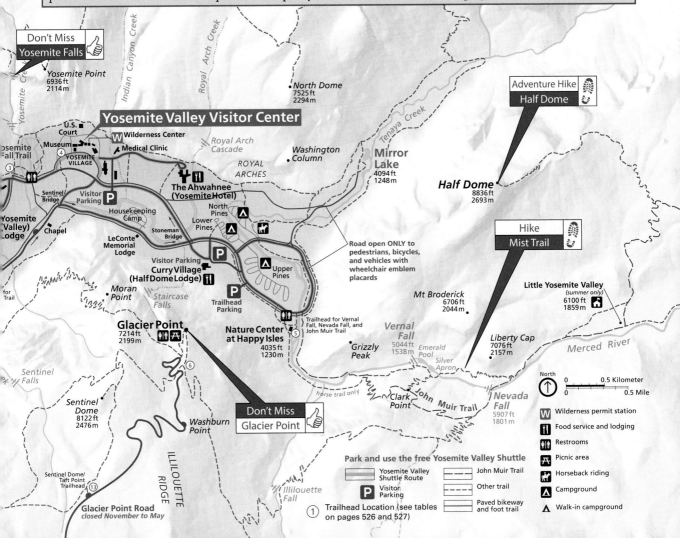

STANISLAUS NATIONAL FOREST

EMIGRANT WILDERNESS

Emigrant Lake

Maxwell Lake

Dorothy Lake Pass

Dorothy Lake

Bond Pass

Tower Peak

Cherry Creek

Pacific Crest Trail

Mary Lake

Twin Lakes

Huckleberry Lake

Backpack
Pacific Crest Trail

Tilden Lake

STUBBLEFIELD CANYON

Haystack Peak

Schofield Peak

Styx Pass

Richardson Peak
9877 ft
3010 m

Otter Lake
(staffed intermittently)

Wilma Lake

KERRICK CANYON

Many Island Lake

Kibbie Lake

Kendrick Creek

JACK MAIN CANYON

TILTILL MOUNTAIN

Piute Mountain
10541 ft
3213 m

Piute Creek

Smedberg Lake

Benson Lake

(staffed intermittently)

Laurel Lake

Eleanor Creek

Frog Creek

LAKE ELEANOR

Lake Vernon

Mount Gibson

Rancheria Creek

PLEASANT VALLEY

Table Lake

RODGERS CANYON

Rodgers Lake

Pettit Pea
10788
3288

Vo
Pe

Lake Eleanor
(summer only)

(staffed intermittently)

MIGUEL MEADOW

Tueeulala Falls

Wapama Falls

HETCH HETCHY RESERVOIR

No swimming or boating

Tiltill Creek

Tiltill Falls

Rancheria Falls

TILTILL VALLEY

RANCHERIA MOUNTAIN

PATE VALLEY

GRAND CANYON OF THE

O'Shaughnessy Dam

28

Hetch Hetchy Backpackers Camp
(wilderness permit required)

Quieter Side
Hetch Hetchy

Smith Peak
7751 ft
2363 m

Harden Lake

Morrison Creek

YOSEMITE WILDERNESS

Hetchy Road

POOPENAUT VALLEY

Hetch Creek

River

Ten Lakes

Hetch Hetchy Entrance
(open limited hours)

27

W

Tuolumne River

Mather

Birch Lake

Middle

Tuolumne

YOSEMITE NATIONAL PAR

White Wolf

16

Lukens Lake

Grant Lakes

Tuolumne Peak
1084 ft
3306 m

Evergreen Road

Bald Mountain
7261 ft
2213 m

Don't Miss
Drive Tioga Rd

Tioga Road

Siesta Lake

17

18

Mount Hoffmann
10850 ft
3307 m

May Lake

Ma

ASPEN VALLEY

Yosemite Creek

20

To Manteca

120

Information Station
Big Oak Flat Entrance
W

South Fork Tuolumne River

Facilities along Tioga Road available summer only

Yosemite Creek

19

Porcupine Flat

Hodgdon Meadow

Tioga Road closed November to May

Olms
Point

Mount

TENAYA

Greater Yosemite Area

North

0 10 20 Kilometers
0 10 20 Miles

STANISLAUS NATIONAL FOREST

YOSEMITE NATIONAL PARK
Road open summer only

Groveland
120

El Portal
49   140
Midpines
Mariposa
Oakhurst
Merced

99   41

Fresno

33
180

5   198
Visalia

Yosemite Valley to San Francisco
195 miles
314 kilometers

Yosemite Valley to Los Angeles
313 miles/504 kilometers

Yosemite Valley to Lake Tahoe and Reno
218 miles / 351 kilometers

Mono Basin Scenic Area Visitor Center
Lee Vining
395

Mammoth Lakes

DEVILS POSTPILE NATIONAL MONUMENT

Fish Camp

SIERRA NEVADA

INYO NATIONAL FOREST

6

Bishop

Big Pine

SIERRA NATIONAL FOREST

KINGS CANYON NATIONAL PARK

SEQUOIA NF
GIANT SEQUOIA NM

SEQUOIA NATIONAL PARK

Three Rivers

SEQUOIA NF GIANT SEQUOIA NM

395

Independence
MANZANAR NATIONAL HISTORIC SITE
Eastern Sierra Interagency Visitor Center

Lone Pine
136

NEVADA
CALIFORNIA

INYO NATIONAL FOREST

DEATH VALLEY NATIONAL PARK

190

Buckeye Pass
927 ft
7 m

Barney Lake

TWIN LAKES

Peeler Lake

Crown Lake

Slide Mountain

HOOVER WILDERNESS

SAWTOOTH RIDGE

Matterhorn Peak

Burro Pass

Whorl Mountain

Virginia Peak

Virginia Pass

Summit Lake

Green Lake

HUMBOLDT NATIONAL FOREST

SPILLER CREEK

CANYON

MATTERHORN CANYON

Virginia Lake

Benson Pass

Return

McCabe Creek

Upper McCabe Lake

McCabe Lakes

VIRGINIA CANYON

North Peak

Roosevelt Lake

Mount Conness
12590 ft
3837 m

HARVEY MONROE HALL RESEARCH NATURAL AREA

White Mountain

Saddlebag Lake

Gardisky Lake

Tioga Peak
11526 ft
3513 m

INYO NATIONAL FOREST

Lundy Lake

To Carson City, Nev.

395

MONO LAKE

Mono Basin Scenic Area Visitor Center

Lee Vining

Highway 120 closed in winter

120

To Mammoth Lakes

Ellery Lake

High Sierra Camps
Backcountry Comfort

Ragged Peak

Granite Lakes

Gaylor Peak

Gaylor Lakes

Tioga Lake

Tioga Pass Entrance
9945 ft
3031 m

Tioga Road closed November to May west of this point

Mount Dana
13057 ft
3979 m

PACIFIC CREST TRAIL

COLD CANYON

Glen Aulin

TUOLUMNE RIVER

Wheel Falls

Tuolumne River

Pothole Dome

Delaney

21

Dog Lake

Lembert Dome

22   23

TUOLUMNE

24   W

MEADOWS

26

25

DANA MEADOWS

Dana Fork

Facilities along Tioga Road available summer only

Mount Gibbs
12764 ft
3890 m

Mono Pass
10604 ft
3232 m

Parker Pass

Tuolumne Meadows Visitor Center

Fairview Dome

Medlicott Dome

Cathedral Peak
10940 ft
3335 m

John Muir Trail

Tresidder Peak

Cathedral Lakes

Budd Creek

Unicorn Peak

Echo Peaks

Mammoth Peak
12117 ft
3693 m

Elizabeth Lake

Johnson Peak

Lyell Fork

KUNA CREST

Koip Peak
12962 ft
3950 m

Tenaya Lake

Sunrise Lakes

Sunrise

ECHO CREEK

Nelson Lake

Vogelsang

CATHEDRAL RANGE

Rafferty Creek

Potter Point

Evelyn Lake

LYELL CANYON

KOIP CREST

Vogelsang

Ireland Lake

Amelia Earhart Peak

Pacific

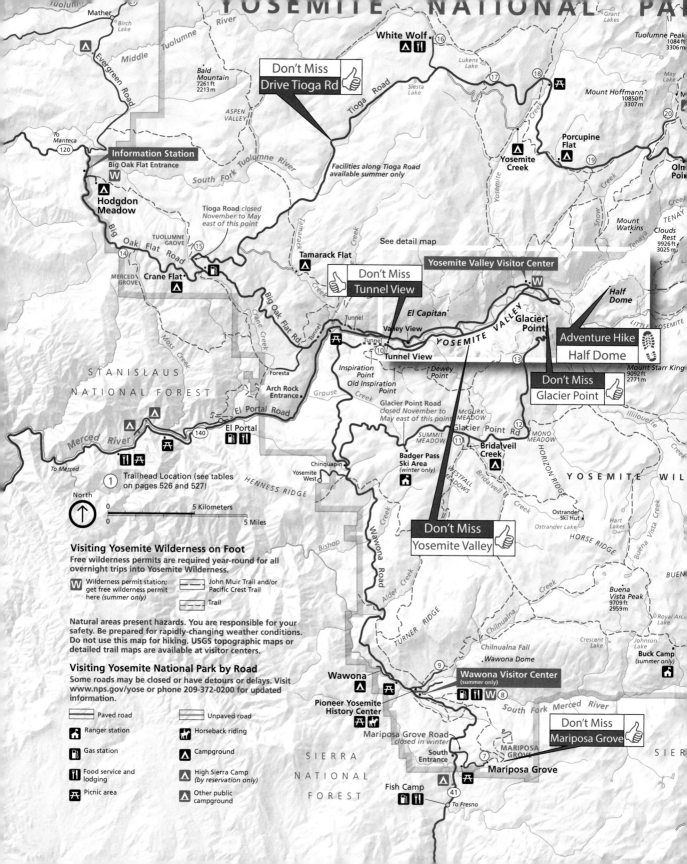

Mather

Birch Lake

Middle

Tuolumne River

Grant Lakes

White Wolf 🏕 🍴 16

Tuolumne Peak 10841 ft 3306 m

Evergreen Road

Bald Mountain 7261 ft 2213 m

ASPEN VALLEY

Tioga Road

Lukens Lake

Siesta Lake

17

18 🏕

Mount Hoffmann 10850 ft 3307 m

May Lake

M

20

Don't Miss
Drive Tioga Rd 👍

To Manteca
120

Information Station
Big Oak Flat Entrance
W

🏕 Hodgdon Meadow

South Fork Tuolumne River

Tioga Road closed November to May east of this point

Facilities along Tioga Road available summer only

Yosemite Creek 🏕 🍴

Porcupine Flat 🏕

19

Olm Poin

Big Oak Flat Road

TUOLUMNE GROVE 15

14

MERCED GROVE

🏕 Crane Flat

Tamarack Creek

Tamarack Flat 🏕

See detail map

Yosemite Creek

Snow Creek

Mount Watkins

Clouds Rest 9926 ft 3025 m

TENAY

LITTLE YOSEMITE

Crane Creek

Moss Creek

STANISLAUS

NATIONAL FOREST

Tunnel

Tunnel

🏕

Don't Miss
👍 **Tunnel View**

El Capitan

Valley View

Tunnel

Tunnel

10

Tunnel View

Inspiration Point

Old Inspiration Point

Dewey Point

YOSEMITE VALLEY

Yosemite Valley Visitor Center
W

13

Glacier Point

Half Dome

Adventure Hike
Half Dome 👣

Mount Starr King 9092 ft 2771 m

Illilouette

YOSEMITE WIL

Foresta

Arch Rock Entrance

El Portal Road

Grouse Creek

Glacier Point Road closed November to May east of this point

McGURK MEADOW

Don't Miss
Glacier Point 👍

Merced River

140 El Portal
🍴

🏕

To Merced
🍴 🏕

Chinquapin

Yosemite West

🏕 Trailhead Location (see tables on pages 526 and 527)

HENNESS RIDGE

SUMMIT MEADOW

11

Badger Pass Ski Area (winter only)

Glacier Point Rd

Bridalveil Creek 🏕

MONO MEADOW

12

HORIZON RIDGE

Y O S E M I T E   W I L

Ostrander Ski Hut

Ostrander Lake

HORSE RIDGE

Buena Vista Creek

BUEN

North
↑

0   5 Kilometers
0   5 Miles

Bishop Creek

Buena Vista Peak 9709 ft 2959 m

Royal Arc Lake

Don't Miss
👍 **Yosemite Valley**

Visiting Yosemite Wilderness on Foot
Free wilderness permits are required year-round for all overnight trips into Yosemite Wilderness.

W Wilderness permit station; get free wilderness permit here (summer only)

John Muir Trail and/or Pacific Crest Trail

Trail

Wawona Road

Alder Creek

Chilnualna Creek

TURNER RIDGE

Chilnualna Fall

Wawona Dome

Crescent Lake

Hart Lakes

Johnson Lake

Buck Camp (summer only) 🏕

Natural areas present hazards. You are responsible for your safety. Be prepared for rapidly-changing weather conditions. Do not use this map for hiking. USGS topographic maps or detailed trail maps are available at visitor centers.

Visiting Yosemite National Park by Road
Some roads may be closed or have detours or delays. Visit www.nps.gov/yose or phone 209-372-0200 for updated information.

Paved road

Unpaved road

🏠 Ranger station

🐎 Horseback riding

⛽ Gas station

🏕 Campground

🍴 Food service and lodging

🏠 High Sierra Camp (by reservation only)

🏕 Picnic area

🏕 Other public campground

Wawona 🏕

🏕 Pioneer Yosemite History Center

🏕 🐎

9

Wawona Visitor Center (summer only)
🍴 🍴 W 8

South Fork Merced River

MARIPOSA GROVE

7

Don't Miss
Mariposa Grove 👍

SIER

Mariposa Grove Road closed in winter

SIERRA

NATIONAL

FOREST

South Entrance

Mariposa Grove

🏕 🍴

Fish Camp ⛽ 🍴

41

To Fresno

Pothole
Dome
TUOLUMNE 22
Lembert Dome
DANA Fork 3979 m
21
23

Fairview
Dome
Medlicott
Dome
Cathedral
Peak
10940 ft
3335 m

TUOLUMNE MEADOWS
Facilities along Tioga Road
available summer only

Mount Gibbs
12764 ft
3890 m

Tuolumne Meadows
Visitor Center

W 24

Mammoth
Peak
12117 ft
3693 m

Mono Pass
10604 ft
3232 m

Cathedral
Lakes
Budd
Lake
Elizabeth Lake
Unicorn Peak

Parker
Pass

Tresidder
Peak
Echo
Peaks
Johnson
Peak

CATHEDRAL

Koip Peak
12962 ft
3950 m

Tenaya
Lake

Sunrise
Lakes

Nelson
Lake
Vogelsang

Rafferty Creek

Evelyn
Lake

RANGE

Potter
Point

Sunrise

Vogelsang
Lake

Ireland
Lake

Amelia
Earhart
Peak

Donohue Peak
12023 ft
3665 m

Emeric
Lake

Vogelsang
Peak

Bernice
Lake

Waugh
Lake

Babcock Lake

Fletcher Creek

Lewis Creek

Merced Lake

Mount
Maclure

Donohue
Pass

Merced Lake
(staffed intermittently)

Mount Florence
12561 ft
3829 m

Mount Lyell
13114 ft
3997 m

Bunnell
Point

Washburn
Lake

Lyell Fork

Banner Peak
12936 m

Mount Clark
11522 ft
3512 m

Lyell Fork

Mount Ansel Adams
11760 ft
3584 m

Three Brothers/Merced River

Foerster Peak
12057 ft
3675 m

Gray Peak

CLARK

Triple Peak Fork

Long Mountain
11502 ft
3506 m

RANGE

Red Peak
11699 ft
3566 m

Isberg
Peak

RNESS

Ottoway Lakes

Isberg
Pass

Merced Peak
11726 ft
3574 m

Post Peak Pass

Triple
Divide
Peak

Post
Peak

ANSEL
WILD

Upper Merced Pass
Lake

Merced Pass
Lake

Merced Pass

STA CREST

Moraine
Mountain

Fernandez
Pass

Breeze
Lake

Gale Peak
10693 ft
3259 m

Chain Lakes

Sing Peak
10552 ft
3216 m

Chiquito Pass

A NATIONAL FOREST

Camping

Four campgrounds are located in Yosemite Valley. **Upper, Lower, and North Pines,** located at the valley's eastern edge, require advance reservations (book early, especially for summer). Camp 4 is the only first-come, first-served campground in Yosemite Valley. This walk-in, tent-only campground is located southwest of Yosemite (Valley) Lodge north of the Merced River. In summer, long lines form early for the next available campsite. If your heart is set on camping in Yosemite Valley, it's a good idea to make a reservation at one of the "Pines" campgrounds. Reservations can be made up to five months in advance at (877) 444-6777 or recreation.gov. Summer months are usually booked nearly as soon as they become available. **Showers** (fee) are available at **Curry Village (Half Dome Lodge)** and **Housekeeping Camp** in Yosemite Valley.

Several camping options are available outside of Yosemite Valley. **Wawona and Bridalveil Creek Campgrounds** are south of the valley. Wawona is a really nice place for visitors entering from the south/Oakhurst to spend their first night. You can explore Mariposa Grove, set up camp, and get an early start on the drive into Yosemite Valley the following day. Wawona requires reservations (877.444.6777, recreation.gov) during peak season. Bridalveil Creek is first-come, first-served.

Seven **seasonal campgrounds** are available north of Yosemite Valley. Tuolumne Meadows is the largest in the park and it's the last designated campground (1.5 hours from Yosemite Valley) you'll encounter driving east on Tioga Road. Advance reservations (877.444.6777, recreation.gov) are available for half its sites.

Lodging

If you hope to reserve a room at any of Yosemite's seven lodges during the busy summer season, book your room early, otherwise plan on visiting during the off-season when rooms are easier to come by and are often sold at discounted rates (a welcome relief, because lodging is pricey). It's important to note that due to a change in park concessionaire and a bit of trademark law, several of the park's iconic hotels have

Yosemite Camping (Fees are per night)

Name	Location	Open	Fee	Sites	Notes
Upper Pines*	Yosemite Valley	All Year	$26	238	F, RR (mid-Feb–Nov)
Lower Pines* - 🏕	Yosemite Valley	late March–Oct	$26	60	F, RR
North Pines*	Yosemite Valley	early April–mid-Nov	$26	81	F, RR
Camp 4	Yosemite Valley	All Year	$6/person	35	Walk-in sites • F, NRV, FCFS
Wawona*	Wawona Road	All Year	$26	93	Horse sites available • F, RR (mid-April–mid-Oct)
Bridalveil Creek	Glacier Point Road	July–mid-Sept	$18	110	F, FCFS
Hodgdon Meadow *	Big Oak Flat Road	All Year	$26	105	F, RR (mid-April–mid-Oct)
Crane Flat*	Big Oak Flat Road	mid-July–mid-Oct	$26	166	F, RR
Tamarack Flat - 🏕	Tioga Road	July–mid-Oct	$12	52	P, NRV, FCFS
White Wolf - 🏕	Tioga Road	July–mid-Oct	$18	74	F, FCFS
Yosemite Creek	Tioga Road	July–mid-Oct	$12	75	P, FCFS
Porcupine Flat	Tioga Road	June–mid-Oct	$12	52	P, FCFS
Tuolumne Meadows	Tioga Road	mid-July–late Sept	$26	304	F, RR (50%), FCFS (50%)

F = Flush Toilets, P = Pit Toilets, NRV = No RV Sites, FCFS = 1st-Come, 1st-Served, RR = Reservation Required
*Reservations can be made up to five months in advance at recreation.gov or (877) 444-6777
Shower and laundry facilities are available year-round in Yosemite Valley • Dump stations are available at Yosemite Valley (all year), Wawona (summer), and Tuolumne Meadows (summer) • Firewood collection is not permitted

Backcountry	Permitted with a wilderness permit. Daily quotas are enforced due to trail popularity. 60% of each trailhead's permits are available via reservation. The remaining 40% of permits are available on a first-come, first-served basis beginning one day before your intended departure. See page 528 for details.
Group	Group campsites are available year-round at Wawona Camp, and in summer at the following campgrounds: Hodgdon Meadow, Bridalveil Creek, and Tuolumne Meadows. Reservations required.

been forced to change names. We've included both (new names in parentheses), hoping this is temporary.

In **Yosemite Valley**, visitors have four choices for lodging: The Ahwahnee (Yosemite Hotel), Yosemite (Valley) Lodge, Curry Village (Half Dome Lodge), and Housekeeping Camp. **The Ahwahnee (Yosemite Hotel) is often regarded as the finest lodge in America.** Comfort, beauty, and premium location have their price: $400+/night for a standard room. Yosemite (Valley) Lodge provides more reasonable accommodations at 245–265/night. It offers large family rooms with one king bed, two single beds, and a sofa sleeper (queen). **Curry Village (Half Dome Lodge) and Housekeeping Camp are "budget" options**, with both units checking in at about $100/night. Curry Village (Half Dome Lodge) has small rustic cabins, motel-style rooms, and canvas tent cabins. Tent cabins are affordable, but the canvas is thin, providing little protection from noisy neighbors. Housekeeping Camp is simple living. Each of the 266 units has a bunk bed, a double bed, table, chairs, mirror, lights, and outlets. A curtained wall separates the living space from a covered patio. Bear-proof food storage containers are provided.

Located near the park's southern boundary is **Wawona Hotel (Big Trees Lodge)**. Wah-wo-nah means "Big Tree," and that's what you'll find near this Victorian-style hotel. Rooms come with or without a private bath. Golf, swimming, tennis, fishing, stable rides, and ranger-led walks are available nearby. Rooms here are much easier to reserve than those found in the valley.

Alternatively, **White Wolf and Tuolumne Meadows are great High Sierra lodging options** located off Tioga Road. Canvas tent cabins, sprinkled about the Sierra Nevada, are open from mid-June until mid-September. Illuminated by candlelight, they do not have electricity. Shared **showers** and restrooms are available. White Wolf also offers a few wooden cabins with propane heating, private baths, and limited electricity.

All lodges and hotels are operated by Yosemite Hospitality. For reservations and additional information call (888) 413-8869 or click travelyosemite.com.

Finally, there are **five High Sierra Camps** in the backcountry. These comfortable camping accommodations give hikers the opportunity to enjoy the peace and quiet of the backcountry with the comforts of a bed, hot shower, and hearty home-style meals. Not having to carry a tent, sleeping bag, and food is an added bonus. A night's stay at any one of the High Sierra Camps includes a filling dinner and breakfast. Camps are located at: Merced Lake, Vogelsang, Glen Aulin, May Lake, and Sunrise Camp (see the map on pages 520–523). **May Lake is the easiest to reach**, just 1.2 miles from May Lake Parking Area (1.75 miles north of Tioga Road). Located 14 miles from Tuolumne Meadows, **Merced Lake is the most remote camp**. All of the camps are most easily accessed from hiking trails beginning along Tioga Road. High Sierra Camp reservations are made through a lottery system. Applications are accepted in September and October for the next calendar year. Lottery details can be found at travelyosemite.com.

Yosemite Lodging (Fees are per night)			
Name	Open	Fee	Location & Notes
The Ahwahnee (Yosemite Hotel) - ♨	All Year	$250–800	Yosemite Valley • Elegant Four-Diamond hotel in a perfect location • Views of Yosemite Falls & Half Dome
Yosemite (Valley) Lodge	All Year	$180–245	Yosemite Valley • Close to Yosemite Falls • Family favorite thanks to family rooms with bunk beds
Curry Village (Half Dome Lodge)	All Year	$114–278	Yosemite Valley • Cabins, motel rooms, and tents • Half Dome and Glacier Point views
Housekeeping Camp	All Year	$99	Yosemite Valley • 266 units accommodate six guests each
Wawona Hotel (Big Trees Lodge)	All Year	$136–201	Wawona • Victorian accommodations, some shared baths • Golf, tennis, and horseback riding nearby
Tuolumne Meadows	mid-June–mid-Sept	$115	Tioga Road • A collection of private candlelit tent cabins
White Wolf Lodge	mid-June–mid-Sept	$108	Tioga Road • Smaller complex of 24 canvas tent cabins
High Sierra Camps - ♨	mid-June–mid-Sept	$151	Tioga Road • Comfortable camping with lodging and meals
All in-park lodging facilities are operated by Yosemite Hospitality (travelyosemite.com, 888.413.8869)			

Hiking

More than 800 miles of hiking trails crisscross Yosemite National Park. Well-trod paths lead through lush meadows, meander along rivers to thunderous waterfalls, and climb to the crown of bald granite domes. Hiking in Yosemite is highly dependent on when you arrive. Spring is fantastic. Snowpack in the High Sierra is melting and rivers begin to swell and pour over granite cliffs, some plummeting with such force you can feel the earth shaking beneath your feet. However, it's not all fun and waterfalls. Mosquitoes can be a bit of a pain and High Sierra trails are often

inaccessible without proper equipment. Each year is different, but you can expect mosquitoes to be worst during the three weeks after the snow melts. Muddy trails and treacherous creek crossings are also likely.

Summer is the busiest season. Trails are crowded, but most are open by this time. Still, just because Tioga Road is open doesn't mean you should assume all its trails are accessible. Depending on the amount of winter snowfall, some in the highest elevations may not be passable until well into July. Check the park website, or ask a ranger about conditions if you think you might

Yosemite Hiking Trails (Distances are roundtrip)

	Name	Location (# on map)	Length	Difficulty Rating & Notes
Yosemite Valley	Bridalveil Fall -	Bridalveil Fall Parking Area (1)	0.5 mile	E – Paved trail to the base of Bridalveil Falls
	Mirror Lake	Camp 4/Shuttle Stop #7 (2)	5.0 miles	E/M – 2 miles to lake and back or 5-mile loop
	Valley Floor Loop	Camp 4/Shuttle Stop #7 (2)	13.0 miles	E – Follows original trails and wagon roads
	Upper Yosemite -	Camp 4/Shuttle Stop #7 (2)	7.2 miles	S – Top of North America's tallest waterfall
	Four Mile	Camp 4/Shuttle Stop #7 (2)	9.6 miles	S – Hike from Sentinel Rock to Glacier Point
	Lower Yosemite -	Shuttle Stop #6 (3)	1.0 mile	E – Paved trail, Yosemite Falls views
	Cook's Meadow	Shuttle Stop #5 or #9 (4)	1.0 mile	E – Loop, Half Dome views (sunset location)
	Vernal & Nevada Falls -	Happy Isles/Shuttle Stop #16 (5)	1.6–8.0 miles	M/S – Popular •Take Mist (600 granite steps) or John Muir Trail or loop (recommended)
	Half Dome - (Permit Required, see page 527)	Happy Isles/Shuttle Stop #16 (5)	14.0 miles 16.4 miles 15.2 miles	Via Mist Trail (shortest but steepest) Via John Muir Trail (longest, most gradual) Mist up, John Muir down (compromise)
	Panorama-	Happy Isles/Shuttle Stop #16 (5)	8.5 miles	S – One-way, long way to Glacier Point
Wawona	Grizzly Giant -	Mariposa Grove (7)	1.6 miles	E – Big trees!
	Wawona Point	Mariposa Grove (7)	6.0 miles	M – Pass both sequoia loops to vista
	Outer Loop	Mariposa Grove (7)	6.9 miles	M – Loops around Mariposa Grove
	Wawona Meadow	Big Trees Lodge/Pioneer Store (8)	3.5 miles	E – Loop follows a fire road around meadow
	Swinging Bridge	Big Trees Lodge/Pioneer Store (8)	4.8 miles	E – Self-guiding loop via old dirt road
	Wawona to Mariposa	Big Trees Lodge/Pioneer Store (8)	12.0 miles	S – Follows horse ride route
	Alder Creek	Chilnualna Falls Road (9)	12.0 miles	S – Begin at Alder Creek Trailhead
	Chilnualna Falls	Chilnualna Falls Road (9)	8.2 miles	S – Begin at Chilnualna Falls Trailhead
	Inspiration Point	Wawona Tunnel Overlook (10)	2.6 miles	S – A little tricky to find clear valley views
Glacier Point Rd	McGurk Meadow	Glacier Point Road (11)	1.6 miles	E – Meadow and cabin of John McGurk
	Ostrander Lake -	Glacier Point Road (11)	11.4 miles	S – Beautiful backcountry lake
	Mono Meadow	Glacier Point Road (12)	3.0 miles	M – Wet through summer, log crossings
	Taft Point -	Glacier Point Road (13)	12.0 miles	M – Views of Yosemite Valley and El Capitan
	Sentinel Dome -	Glacier Point Road (13)	12.0 miles	M – Scramble up granite dome

Panorama and Four Mile connect Yosemite Valley and Glacier Point. Combine them for a strenuous 13.1-mile loop.

Difficulty Ratings: E = Easy, M = Moderate, S = Strenuous

encounter a snow-packed trail. Try hiking in September if you'd like pleasant temperatures, smaller crowds, and access to the entire network of trails. Unfortunately, it's likely many of the waterfalls (including Yosemite Falls) will be bone dry or just a trickle. Hiking in winter without snowshoes or skis is limited to trails in Hetch Hetchy and Yosemite Valleys.

Yosemite Valley hikes are easily accessed via the free shuttle (page 516). Mist Trail has earned the title of most popular trail in the park. The scenery is magnificent as you hike to the top of Vernal Falls (continue to Nevada Falls, or ambitious hikers with a permit follow the trail all the way to the top of Half Dome). This trek begins at Happy Isles (Shuttle Stop #16) at the far eastern end of Yosemite Valley. Depending on water volume, Yosemite and Bridalveil Falls are worth a quick look. **Wawona** has a decent selection of trails beginning near the hotel and

Mariposa Grove, including two loops around Mariposa Grove (busy in summer). Most trailheads in **Tuolumne Meadows/Crane Flats/White Wolf areas** are well-marked and accessed via Tioga Road. **Hetch Hetchy** has some nice paths and it's an excellent place to shake the crowds of Yosemite Valley. You really can't go wrong with any trail at Yosemite, but some of our favorites are marked with thumbs up in the provided hiking tables.

Half Dome

Half Dome is one of Yosemite's iconic landscapes, so renowned its image resides on the California state quarter alongside images of John Muir and the California condor. This famous granite dome is situated at the east end of Yosemite Valley, where it rises some 4,800 feet above the valley floor. Up until the 1870s, Half Dome was declared "perfectly inaccessible." Seeking to access the inaccessible, George Anderson

Yosemite Hiking Trails (Distances are roundtrip)

	Name	Location (# on map)	Length	Difficulty Rating & Notes
Crane Flat/White Wolf	Merced Grove	Merced Grove Parking Area (14)	3.0 miles	E – Small and secluded sequoia grove
	Tuolumne Grove	Tuolumne Grove/Crane Flat (15)	2.5 miles	E – Nature Trail through grove of sequoias
	Harden Lake	White Wolf Lodge (16)	5.8 miles	M – Can loop to Grand Canyon of the Tuolumne
	Lukens Lake	Lukens Lake Trailhead (17)	1.6 miles	E – Or hike 4.6 miles from White Wolf Lodge
	North Dome	Porcupine Creek Trailhead (18)	10.4 miles	S – Fantastic views of Half Dome
	Ten Lakes - ♨	Ten Lakes Trailhead (19)	12.6 miles	S – Cross Yosemite Creek to beautiful lakes
	May Lake	May Lake Parking Area (20)	2.4 miles	E – Views of Half Dome along the way
Tuolumne Meadows	Glen Aulin - ♨	Soda Springs (21)	11.0 miles	M – Glen Aulin = "Beautiful Valley"
	Tuolumne Meadows	Lembert Dome/Dog Lake (22, 23)	1.5 miles	E – Hike to Soda Springs and Parsons Lodge
	Lyell Canyon	Lembert Dome/Dog Lake (22, 23)	8.0 miles	E – Creek crossings, follows John Muir Trail
	Dog Lake/Lembert Dome - ♨	Lembert Dome/Dog Lake (22, 23)	2.8 miles	M – Begins with a steep grade, but flattens (4 miles to hike both)
	Elizabeth Lake	Tuolumne Meadows Camp (24)	4.8 miles	M – Climb to a glacially carved lake
	Vogelsang Area	John Muir Trailhead (24)	13.8 miles	S – John Muir Tr to Vogelsang Camp and Lake
	Cathedral Lakes - ♨	Cathedral Lakes Trailhead (24)	7.0 miles	M – One of the most popular trails in the area
	Mono Pass - ♨	Mono Pass Trailhead (25)	8.0 miles	M – Views of Mono Lake from the pass
	Gaylor Lakes - ♨	Tioga Pass Entrance (26)	2.0 miles	M – Wonderful high country views
Hetch Hetchy	Lookout Point	Hetch Hetchy Entrance (27)	2.0 miles	M – Viewpoint overlooking Hetch Hetchy
	Smith Peak	Hetch Hetchy Entrance (27)	13.4 miles	M/S – Great Hetch Hetchy views
	Poopenaut Valley	Hetch Hetchy Entrance (27)	3.0 miles	S – Drops down to the Tuolumne River
	Wapama Falls - ♨	O'Shaughnessy Dam (28)	5.0 miles	M – Waterfalls and wildflowers in spring
	Rancheria Falls	O'Shaughnessy Dam (28)	13.4 miles	M – Continues past Wapama Falls

Difficulty Ratings: E = Easy, M = Moderate, S = Strenuous

Half Dome

backpack trips. Day hikes cost between $20 and $75 and visit many of the most spectacular and popular locations. They are only offered between Memorial Day and Labor Day. Trips can be reserved at (888) 413-8869 or travelyosemite.com. You can also hire a private hiking guide. Guided custom backpacking or High Sierra Camp trips are offered between June and September. Rates are variable and usually include permits, meals, tents, stove, and water filters. Call Yosemite Mountaineering School at (209) 372-8344 for reservations and information. To book a guided High Sierra Camp trip, you still have to win their reservation lottery (page 525).

Backpacking & Permits
Nearly 95% of Yosemite is designated wilderness, and more than 750 miles of trails traverse this undeveloped region. To plan a Yosemite backpacking trip, you should start with a good topographical map. If it's your first time, you will want to hike in one of the popular backcountry areas like Ten Lakes (White Wolf) or Cathedral Rocks (Tuolumne Meadows).

Once you've selected your route, the next obstacle is getting a permit. **Wilderness permits are required for all overnight trips.** Day-hikers do not require one. You can apply for a permit up to 24 weeks in advance and they cost $5 per confirmed reservation plus $5 per person. Permits for some of the more popular trailheads fill the same day they become available. (Over 97% of all John Muir Trail through-hike permit applications are denied due to high demand.) Of each trailhead's daily quota, 60% can be reserved ahead of time while the remaining 40% is available first-come, first-served no earlier than 11am the day before your hike begins. **Permits can be obtained** at Yosemite Valley Wilderness Center, Tuolumne Meadows Wilderness Center, Big Oak Flat Information Station, Wawona Visitor Center at Hill's Studio, Hetch Hetchy Entrance Station, and Badger Pass Ranger Station. From November through April, permits are available on a self-registration basis (when permit stations are closed). Information regarding wilderness permits and the reservation process can be found at the park website. You can fax, phone, or mail in your permit requests, but all faxed reservation requests will be handled first.

constructed his own route to its summit by drilling and placing iron eyebolts into the smooth granite surface, completing the first successful ascent in 1875.

Today, the dome is accessed by more than a dozen rock climbing routes and a hiking path along its rounded east face. Hikers are aided by metal cables strung between steel polls. Without these cables the final 700-foot ascent would be impossible. They are removed during winter and are usually installed before Memorial Day weekend (May) and taken down around Columbus Day (October). The hike to Half Dome should be taken seriously. Three separate routes reach its eastern face. They range from 14–16.4 miles (roundtrip). The trek gains nearly 4,800 feet in elevation. Be sure to wear shoes with good grip. Many people wear gloves for the cable section to prevent blisters. There's usually a big pile of used gloves near the start of the cables, but don't rely on it. **All hikers expecting to scale Half Dome require a permit.** Permits, good for up to four hikers, cost $8/person and are only available at (877) 444-6777 or recreation.gov. Enjoy the trip; this is one of the best hikes in the world.

Guided Hikes
Rugged terrain, intimidating wildlife, and a plethora of trails often leave visitors bewildered when it comes to selecting their hiking adventure. To make things simple Yosemite Hospitality provides an array of guided and unguided day and multi-day

Cathedral Peaks

Horseback Riding

Yosemite Hospitality (travelyosemite.com) runs **three stables** within the park. Yosemite Valley Stable (209.372.8348) is the only outfitter that leads guided trips in Yosemite Valley. Tuolumne (209.372.8427) and Big Trees (209.375.6502) Stables offer guided rides through the high country and big tree forests, respectively. Rates are the same for all three locations. Two-hour rides ($65/rider) and half-day rides ($88.50) are available. All riders must be at least 7 years old and 44 inches tall. The maximum rider weight is 225 lbs. Big Trees and Tuolumne Stables are seasonal. Yosemite Valley Stables is open all year. Reservations are recommended.

Custom pack and saddle trips are also offered. There is a minimum of 3 animals per trip. The stable simply provides transportation and/or guide. You are responsible for wilderness permits, food, water, and any other supplies. An additional transportation fee is added if your itinerary begins at a trailhead not serviced by one of the stables. If you'd like them to plan your trip for you, they offer 4- and 6-day saddle trips. For High Sierra Camp pack trips, you'll have to win the High Sierra Camp reservation lottery. After receiving your confirmation, you'll be able to apply for a pack trip. Call (801) 559-4909 or click travelyosemite.com for more information.

Rafting

Rafts are available for rent at Curry Village (Half Dome Lodge) Recreation Center (Yosemite Valley). Each raft holds four adults and costs $31/person. Trips begin at Curry Village (Half Dome Lodge) and end 3 miles later at Sentinel Beach Picnic Area. Rafting season changes from year-to-year, but the Merced River is usually runnable from late May until the end of July. For additional information call Curry Village (Half Dome Lodge) Recreation Center at (209) 372-4386. Visitors are welcome to bring their own floatables. All river users should help protect the resource by entering and exiting the river on sandy beaches. Beyond Yosemite Valley, rafting is also permitted on the South Fork of the Merced River near Wawona.

Bus Tours

Yosemite Hospitality (888.413.8869, travelosemite.com) operates guided bus tours. They're a great, hassle-free way to explore the most popular areas of the park and a professional guide joins you every step of the way. Valley Floor Tour ($25/adult, $13/child) is a 2-hour drive through Yosemite Valley. It's offered all year, and on days leading up to the full moon a moonlight edition is available. Glacier Point Tour ($41/$23) is a 4-hour trip that takes visitors from the valley floor to Glacier Point.

Rock climbing near Tenaya Lake

Visit travelyosemite.com for more detailed information. Reservations can be made by calling (209) 372-4386 and are recommended (especially in summer). Same day reservations are available (space permitting).

Rock Climbing

Thousands of visitors come to Yosemite National Park for one thing and one thing only: rock climbing. This is Mecca for climbers all around the world. Advanced climbers enjoy the challenges of multi-day ascents of **Half Dome** or 3,000-foot **El Capitán (El Cap)**, but there's a little something here for people of all abilities. Experienced climbers new to Yosemite should head to Camp 4 to mingle among Yosemite's rock climbing communities or pick up a more climbing-centric guidebook from one of the park's bookstores. Beginners can find plenty of good places for scrambling. Much of the high country is covered with granite boulders and Bridalveil Falls Trail has a nice collection of boulders to enjoy.

You can also join one of Yosemite Mountaineering School's (209.372.8344, travelyosemite.com) **climbing lessons or guided climbs**. Lessons are held as long as there are at least three participants. Their basic "Go Climb a Rock" course costs $148/person. Crack Climbing and Anchoring classes are for novices at a cost of $154/person. They offer advanced courses as well. Guided climbs range from 6 hours ($293+/person) to a 6-day El Cap climb ($4,466/person).

Biking

Cyclists are free to enjoy the 12-mile **Yosemite Valley Loop**. This paved path is a fantastic alternative to driving congested park roads or riding packed shuttle buses. Cyclists are permitted on all park roads, but it's not recommended unless you plan on pedaling during the off-season or early morning. Bikes are prohibited on all hiking trails. **Bike rental** is available at Yosemite (Valley) Lodge and Curry Village (Half Dome Lodge) Bike Stands. They are typically open from early spring to late fall. Rental rates are $12/hour and $34/day. Strollers and trailers are available for an additional fee.

Winter Activities

Snow rarely sticks in Yosemite Valley, but the higher elevations are often buried in the fluffy white stuff. Winter's cold and snow-capped mountains add a little more diversity to park activities. **Cross-country skiing**, **snowshoeing**, **skiing**, **tubing**, and **ice-skating** are popular. Marked trails are available at Badger Pass, along Glacier Point Road, in Mariposa Grove of Giant Sequoias, and around the Crane Flat area. **Free ranger-guided snowshoe walks** are also offered. You can usually find a current schedule of ranger programs at the park website or a visitor center.

Badger Pass (209.372.8430) is the oldest **downhill skiing** area in California. It has 5 lifts, and runs range from easy to difficult with an 800-ft elevation drop. Lift tickets cost $48.50/adult and $25/child for a full day. Badger Pass also offers **snow-tubing** ($17/person, per 2-hour session). Rentals, lessons, and multi-day cross-country tour packages are also available. Badger Pass is usually open from mid-December through April (conditions permitting). A daily snow report can be found at travelyosemite.com.

Visitors have been **ice skating** in Yosemite Valley since the 1930s. The Ice Rink at Curry Village (Half Dome Lodge) (209.372.8319) is nestled below the foot of majestic Half Dome and Glacier Point, right in the heart of Yosemite Valley. It is open from mid-November until early March. A 2.5-hour session costs $11/adult, $10/child, and $4.50 for skate rentals. For more information on winter activities visit travelyosemite.com.

Vernal Falls

Photography

Many introductions to Yosemite are made through the lens of **Ansel Adams**, who became interested in this granite wonderland at the age of 14 after reading James Mason Hutchings' *In the Heart of the Sierras*. Yosemite helped drive Adams to become the pre-eminent landscape photographer of the American West. Today, thousands of photographers attempt to recapture many of his famous images. Tunnel View (Wawona Road) and Glacier Point provide two of the most photographed vistas in the world. Then there's the February phenomenon known as the **"Natural Firefall."** There are no guarantees you'll see a "firefall," but with the right amount of water and light Horsetail Falls ignites as if it's caught on fire. Interested photographers should stop at El Capitán Picnic Area on Northside Drive in February. **Yosemite Valley's Ansel Adams Gallery** (209.372.4413, anseladams.com) helps preserve the life, the work, and the vision of one of America's greatest photographers and conservationists. They give free camera walks and guided photography classes for $95.

Ranger Programs

Park rangers lead interpretive programs in every region of the park, from Mariposa Grove to Tuolumne Meadows (when accessible). There is, quite literally, something for everyone. Photo walks, art workshops, twilight strolls, junior ranger programs, watercolor classes, and much more are at your disposal. And the best feature is that almost all of these National Park Service programs are free. If you're looking to get the most out of a visit to Yosemite, you'll want to visit the park's website prior to your arrival and check the calendar for an up-to-date schedule of events. After a little preparatory work, you can plan your arrival, lodging, and dining around a collection of ranger programs. Many park programs are designed with families in mind.

For Kids

With so many kid-friendly activities, easy hiking trails, and awe-inspiring vistas, Yosemite is an exceptional family getaway. Children can also become **Junior Rangers** (ages 7–13) or Little Cubs (ages 3–6) while visiting. To do so, you must first purchase a Junior Ranger ($3.50) or Little Cub ($3) Booklet. They are available at Yosemite Valley Visitor Center, Nature Center at Happy Isles (May–Sept), Wawona and Tuolumne Meadows Visitor Centers (June–Sept), and Big Oak Flat Information Station (May–Sept). Complete the booklet, pick-up trash, and attend a guided program to become a member and receive an award.

Flora & Fauna

More than 400 mammals reside here. Most commonly seen are mule deer and black bear. Grizzly bears do not reside here. Marmots are often seen in the rocky high country, even on top of Half Dome. Vegetation changes dramatically from Yosemite Valley to the high country. Dense forests and meadows cover the valleys and foothills, while the alpine zone is treeless and rocky.

Information Centers

Valley Visitor Center (9am–5pm): Located just west of the main post office (shuttle stops #5 and #9), this visitor center is the main hub for information, maps, and books. Exhibits focusing on the park's geology and a 30-minute orientation film are available.

Yosemite Museum (9am–5pm): Located next to Valley Visitor Center, the museum displays exhibits from Yosemite's past as well as a digital slide show of historic visitors and hotels.

Ansel Adams Gallery (9am–6pm, 209.372.4413, anseladams.com): Located next to Valley Visitor Center, the gallery displays work of Ansel Adams as well as that of other photographers and artists.

Valley Wilderness Center (8am–5pm): Adjacent to the post office, the wilderness center is here to help plan backcountry trips, obtain wilderness permits, and rent bear canisters.

Yosemite Art & Education Center (Yosemite Valley, 9am–4:30pm): Located south of the Village Store, the Arts & Education Center provides a selection of original art and art supplies, and offers regularly scheduled art workshops.

Nature Center at Happy Isles (Yosemite Valley, 9:30–5pm): Located near shuttle stop #16, the nature center offers natural history exhibits and a bookstore specifically designed for children and their families.

Wawona Visitor Center at Hill's Studio (8:30am–5pm, 209.375.9531): Wilderness permits, bear canister rentals, trail information, and books and maps are available here.

Pioneer Yosemite History Center (Wawona): This time-period open-air museum brings guests back to the days of log cabins and horse-drawn carriages. It's open 24/7.

Tuolumne Meadows Visitor Center (9am–6pm, 209.372.0263): Trail information, books, and maps are available.

Tuolumne Meadows Wilderness Center (8am–5pm): Maps, wilderness permits, bear canister rental, and guidebooks are available.

Yosemite Conservancy: The Yosemite Conservancy (800.469.7275, yosemiteconservancy.org) is a non-profit organization that helps protect the park and educate its visitors via geology, photography, and painting workshops (among many other ecologically conscious programs). Course schedules and rates are available at the conservancy's website.

Pets

Pets must be kept on a leash no more than six feet in length at all times. They are only allowed in developed areas, on fully paved trails and roads (unless marked otherwise), and in campgrounds (except walk-in campgrounds and group sites).

Accessibility

Yosemite Valley Visitor Center, Ansel Adams Gallery, Nature Center at Happy Isles, Tuolumne Meadows Visitor Center, and Mariposa Grove Museum are all fully accessible to wheelchair users. Several trails are fully accessible with assistance, including the eastern part of Yosemite Falls Loop, most of Valley Loop Trail, and Glacier Point Vista. Many ranger-guided programs are fully accessible. All park shuttle buses are accessible to wheelchair users. The Ahwahnee (Yosemite Hotel), Yosemite (Valley) Lodge, and Curry Village (Half Dome Lodge) have rooms or cabins accessible to individuals in wheelchairs. Accessible campsites are available at Lower Pines, Upper Pines, North Pines, Crane Flat, Wawona, Tuolumne Meadows, Yosemite Creek, Tamarack Flat, White Wolf, and Porcupine Flat Campgrounds. All food-service facilities are accessible except The Loft, Tuolumne Meadows Lodge, and Wawona Hotel's (Big Trees Lodge's) dining room.

Weather

Yosemite Valley is hot and dry in summer. The average high temperature for July and August is 90°F. Overnight lows dip into the mid-50s°F. Summer averages less than 2 inches of precipitation each year, but thunderstorms are a serious concern. You do not want to be caught on a massive, exposed slab of granite like Half Dome when an afternoon thunderstorm rolls in. During the winter, average highs are around 50°F in Yosemite Valley with lows slightly below freezing. Most precipitation falls between November and March. In the higher elevations snow can fall any month of the year. Regardless of when you hike, be sure to pack warm clothes and dress in layers if you're heading into the High Sierra.

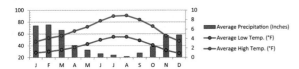

Vacation Planner

Most of Yosemite's **main attractions** (El Capitán, Half Dome, Yosemite Falls, Vernal Falls) are in a relatively small area (Yosemite Valley), but it's a disservice to yourself and your family to race into the valley, check-off these sites, and zoom away to the next destination. A park ranger said it best when a visitor hastily asked the question: "I've only got an hour to see Yosemite. If you had an hour to see Yosemite, what would you do?" The ranger pointed to a rock and replied bluntly, "Well, I'd go right over there, I'd sit down and I'd cry." Don't make this mistake. The only tears shed should be those of joy as you view the granite magnificence of Yosemite. Allow at least three days to explore the main park regions (excluding **Hetch Hetchy**, approximately a 2-hour drive from Yosemite Valley). All of the guided activities: **horseback riding** (page 529), **bus tours** (page 529), **rock climbing** (page 530), and **ranger programs** (page 531) are highly recommended and should be done based on your specific interests as time and budget allow. Reserve your accommodations in advance, because they fill up early. All **camping** and **lodging** facilities are listed on pages 524–525. Nearby dining, grocery stores, lodging, festivals, and attractions are listed on pages 535–537. The itinerary provided below begins at South Entrance, but it can easily be adjusted for visitors entering from the east or west. Remember that Tioga Road is only open in summer.

Day 1: Arrive early at the park's **South Entrance**. Begin by driving to **Mariposa Grove** (closed until spring 2017), located just 5 miles from the South Entrance. At least hike the grove's lower loop, which includes **Grizzly**

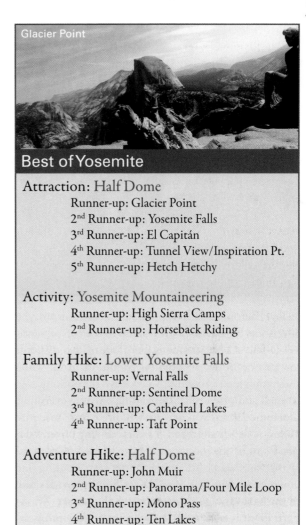

Glacier Point

Best of Yosemite

Attraction: Half Dome
   Runner-up: Glacier Point
   2nd Runner-up: Yosemite Falls
   3rd Runner-up: El Capitán
   4th Runner-up: Tunnel View/Inspiration Pt.
   5th Runner-up: Hetch Hetchy

Activity: Yosemite Mountaineering
   Runner-up: High Sierra Camps
   2nd Runner-up: Horseback Riding

Family Hike: Lower Yosemite Falls
   Runner-up: Vernal Falls
   2nd Runner-up: Sentinel Dome
   3rd Runner-up: Cathedral Lakes
   4th Runner-up: Taft Point

Adventure Hike: Half Dome
   Runner-up: John Muir
   2nd Runner-up: Panorama/Four Mile Loop
   3rd Runner-up: Mono Pass
   4th Runner-up: Ten Lakes

Giant and **California Tunnel Tree**. Allow a solid hour to explore the Giant Sequoia Grove. Return to Wawona Road and head north. Take a right onto Glacier Point Road. Drive to its conclusion at Glacier Point. Allow at least 2.5 hours to reach **Glacier Point** (from the South Entrance). From here, look across the valley and the Merced River to **Half Dome** or stare 3,000 feet below you into the bustling and immensely beautiful valley. Hikers should walk to **Sentinel Dome** or **Taft Point** (2.2-miles each, roundtrip) or do both (about a 6-mile loop). Both are great and they begin at Sentinel Dome/Taft Point Trailhead (6 miles east of Bridalveil Campground turnoff). From the trailhead, heading left takes you to Taft Point and The Fissures. Right leads to Sentinel Dome. Both lead to more extraordinary views of the

Yosemite Valley from Tunnel View

valley. Each hike takes approximately an hour, maybe 3–4 hours for the loop. (The climb to the top of Sentinel Dome is a bit strenuous, but nothing too difficult for anyone in decent physical condition. And, while these trails aren't Yosemite Valley busy, the parking area is small and often full.) Depending on your overnight accommodations you may have to drive into Yosemite Valley, which is another 1.5 hours (driving) from Glacier Point. If the room or campsite where you plan on laying your head is still up in the air, start hunting one down immediately. If not, **Glacier Point provides one of the best vantage points to watch the sunset** (Washburn Point is cool, too!). Sit atop the granite promontory and enjoy the show.

Day 2: Wake up early to beat the Yosemite Valley crowds. Begin your day by hiking **Mist and Lower Yosemite Falls trails**. These are two of the busiest trails in the park. If you don't get there early, it will feel more like a weekend at the mall than a day spent in a natural wonderland. Daytime is the right time to join an interpretive program. If none interest you, think about taking an extended hike. You could stretch your trek to Mist Falls all the way to the top of **Half Dome** (strenuous, permit required, start at dawn, wear shoes with good grip, pack gloves and plenty of water). Hiking to **Upper Yosemite Falls** (strenuous) is another great way to avoid the commotion. Before leaving the valley, be sure to stop in at **Valley Visitor Center** and browse its

modern exhibits. **Yosemite Valley sunsets?** Anywhere you can see Half Dome is a good place to be. Stoneman Meadow (across the street from Curry/Half Dome Village) and Sentinel Bridge are two good choices.

Day 3: Once again, wake-up early to avoid joining the parade of cars that tend to circle the valley's floor like a pack of sharks. Expect the 17-mile drive from the east end of Yosemite Valley to Tioga Road to take about 30 minutes. If you skipped Mariposa Grove in a hurry to reach the valley, catch a glimpse of a few Giant Sequoias at **Merced Grove**. The trailhead is located on Big Oak Flat Road. It's a 1.5-mile (one-way) moderate hike down to the grove. **Tuolumne Grove** is another option. Its trailhead is located on Tioga Road, where a steep 1-mile hike leads to it. These forests are smaller, but the sequoias remain impressive. It's at least a 1-hour drive from Tuolumne Grove to Tioga Pass Entrance Station on the park's eastern boundary. Break up the drive by stopping at **Olmsted Point** for exceptional views. Spend the rest of the day exploring the trails of the High Sierra. **Gaylor Lakes Trail**, beginning at Tioga Pass Entrance Station, is a perfect choice. If you'd like a longer journey, hike to **Mono Pass**. Its trailhead is a short distance west of Tioga Pass Entrance Station. A really great (and popular) moderate hike in the area is **Cathedral Lakes Trail**. Or you can train for a Half Dome ascent at **Lembert Dome**. But really, any mile you spend on foot in this magical place is a mile you won't soon forget. Enjoy!

Dining

Pinnacles Area

La Plaza Bakery • (831) 678-1452
901 Front St, Soledad • laplazabakery.com

La Fuente • (831) 678-3130
101 Oak St, Soledad

Palma's Restaurant • (831) 678-1480
331 Gabilan Dr, Soledad

Cheezer's Gourmet Pizza • (831) 678-8000
235 West St, Soledad • californiagourmetpizza.com

Death Valley Area

Happy Burro Chili & Beer • (775) 553-9099
100 W Main St, Beatty, NV

Sequoia/Kings Canyon Area

Anne Lang's Emporium • (559) 561-4937
41651 CA-198, Three Rivers

Sierra Subs & Salad • (559) 561-4810
41717 Sierra Dr, Three Rivers
sierrasubsandsalads.com • Sandwiches: $6+

VIP Pizza • (559) 592-5170
180 E Pine St, Exeter

Seasons Restaurant • (760) 876-8927
206 S Main St, Lone Pine

Alabama Hills Café • (760) 876-4675
111 W Post, Lone Pine

Yosemite Area

Cocina Michoacana • (209) 962-6651
18730 Main St, Groveland

Buckmeadows • (209) 962-5181
7647 CA-120, Groveland
buckmeadowsrestaurant.com • Entrée: $14–23

Dori's Tea Cottage • (209) 962-5300
18744 Main St, Groveland • doristeacottage.com

Narrow Gauge • (559) 683-7720
48571 CA-41, Fish Camp
narrowgaugeinn.com • Entrée: $15–39

Savoury's Restaurant • (209) 966-7677
5034 CA-140, Mariposa
savouryrestaurant.com • Entrée: $17–31

Happy Burger Diner • (209) 966-2719
5120 CA-140, Mariposa
happyburgerdiner.com • Burgers: $8+

Sugar Pine Café • (209) 742-7793
5038 CA-140, Mariposa
sugarpinecafe.com • Sandwiches: $7+

Hitching Post • (559) 683-7917
42592 CA-49, Ahwahnee

Erna's Elderberry House • (559) 683-6800
48688 Victoria Ln, Oakhurst
chateausureau.com • Entrée: $78–125

Crab Cakes Restaurant • (559) 641-7667
49271 Golden Oak Loop, Oakhurst
crabcakesrestaurant.com • Entrée: $15–36

Alice's Cookhouse BBQ • (559) 642-4900
40713 CA-41, Oakhurst

Sugar Pine Take & Bake Pizza • (559) 642-4642
40487 CA-41, Oakhurst

Judy's Donuts • (559) 683-2095
40444 CA-41, # A, Oakhurst

Lakefront Restaurant • (760) 934-2442
163 Twin Lakes Rd, Mammoth Lakes
lakefrontmammoth.com • Entrée: $25–46

Skadi • (760) 914-0962
94 Berner St, Mammoth Lakes
skadirestaurant.com • Entrée: $28–38

Rafters Restaurant • (760) 934-9431
202 Old Mammoth Rd, Mammoth Lakes
raftersmammoth.com

Burgers Restaurant • (760) 934-6622
6118 Minaret Rd, Mammoth Lakes
burgersrestaurant.com

Stellar Brew & Deli • (760) 924-3559
3280 Main St, Mammoth Lakes
stellarbrewnaturalcafe.com

Giovanni's Pizzeria • (760) 934-7563
437 Old Mammoth Rd, Mammoth Lakes
giovannismammoth.com • Pizza: $12–34

The Stove • (760) 934-2821
644 Old Mammoth Rd, Mammoth Lakes

Schat's Bakery • (760) 934-6055
3305 Main St, Mammoth Lakes

Good Life Café • (760) 934-1734
126 Old Mammoth Rd, Mammoth Lakes
mammothgoodlifecafe.com • Breakfast: $6+

Whoa Nellie Deli • (760) 647-1088
22 Vista Point Rd, Lee Vining
whoanelliedeli.com

Mono Cone • (760) 647-6606
51508 US-395, Lee Vining

Tiger Bar & Café • (760) 648-7551
2620 CA-158, June Lake

Grocery Stores

Pinnacles Area

Foodsco • (831) 678-1937
2443 H Dela Rosa Sr St, Soledad

Safeway • (831) 385-7820
530 Canal St, King City

Death Valley Area

Ruby's Store • (775) 372-1118
1578 S NV-373, Amargosa Valley, NV

Pioneer Point Market • (760) 372-4804
84508 Trona Rd, Trona, CA

Albertsons • (775) 751-0160
200 S NV-160, Pahrump, NV

Walmart Supercenter • (775) 537-1400
300 S NV-160, Pahrump, NV

Sequoia/Kings Canyon Area

Walmart • (559) 636-2302
1819 E Noble Ave, Visalia

Yosemite Area

Mar-Val Food Store • (209) 962-7452
19000 Main St, Groveland

Vons • (559) 642-4250
40044 CA-49, Oakhurst

Raley's Supermarket • (559) 683-8300
40041 CA-49, Oakhurst

Lodging

Pinnacles Area

Inn at the Pinnacles • (831) 678-2400
32025 Stonewall Canyon Rd, Soledad
innatthepinnacles.com • Rates: $235–275/night

Keefer's Inn • (831) 678-2400
615 Canal St, King City
keefersinn.com • Rates: $79

Death Valley Area

El Portal Motel • (775) 553-2912
420 Main St, Beatty, NV
elportalmotel.com • Rates: $68

Atomic Inn • (775) 553-2250
350 S 1st St, Beatty, NV • theatomicinn.com

Amargosa Opera House/Hotel • (760) 852-4441
608 Death Valley Junction, CA
amargosa-opera-house.com • Rates: $70–80

Longstreet Inn & Casino • (775) 372-1777
4400 S NV-373, Amargosa Valley, NV
longstreetcasino.com • Rates: $75–160

Death Valley Inn • (775) 553-9400
651 US-95 S, Beatty, NV
deathvalleyinnmotel.com • Rates: $77

Beatty RV Park • (775) 553-2732
Mile Marker 63 US-95 N, Beatty, NV
beattyrvpark.com • Rates: $15–25

Sequoia/Kings Canyon Area

Dow Villa Motel • (760) 876-5521
310 S Main St, Lone Pine
dowvillamotel.com • Rates: $115–173

Whitney Portal Hostel • (760) 876-0030
238 S Main, Lone Pine • whitneyportalstore.com

Boulder Creek RV Resort • (760) 876-4243
2550 S NV-395, Lone Pine
bouldercreekrvresort.com • Rates: $43

🛏Buckeye Tree Lodge • (559) 561-5900
46000 Sierra Dr, Three Rivers
buckeyetree.com • Rates: $110–229

🛏Rio Sierra Riverhouse • (559) 561-4720
41997 Sierra Dr, Three Rivers • rio-sierra.com

Gateway Lodge • (559) 561-4133
45978 Sierra Dr, Three Rivers
gateway-sequoia.com • Rates: $109–199

🛏Sequoia Motel • (559) 561-4453
43000 Sierra Dr, Three Rivers
sequoiamotel.com • Rates: $105–185

Log House Lodge B&B • (559) 561-3017
42182 Mynatt Dr, Three Rivers
loghouselodge.com • Rates: $225–385

🛏River Jewel Suites • (559) 799-8201
43325 C Sierra Dr, Three Rivers
theriverjewel.com • Rates: $185–225

🛏Bellevue Guesthouse Hotel • (559) 561-6405
45317 Mineral King Rd, Three Rivers

🛏Sequoia River Dance • (559) 561-4411
40534 Cherokee Oaks Dr, Three Rivers
sequoiariverdance.com • Rates: $100–150

There are 10 additional campgrounds in Sequoia NF/Giant Sequoia NM.

Yosemite Area
🛏Yosemites Scenic Wonders • (888) 967-3648
7403 Yosemite Pkwy • scenicwonders.com

🛏Redwoods In Yosemite • (877) 753-8566
8038 Chilnualna Falls Rd, Yosemite NP
redwoodsinyosemite.com

Yosemite Blue Butterfly Inn • (209) 379-2100
11132 CA-140, El Portal
yosemitebluebutterflyinn.com • Rates: $200+

🛏Evergreen Lodge • (209) 379-2606
33160 Evergreen Rd, Groveland
evergreenlodge.com • Rates: $120–1,175

🛏Hotel Charlotte • (209) 962-6455
18736 Main St, Groveland
hotelcharlotte.com • Rates: $99–175

Blackberry Inn B&B • (209) 962-4663
7567 Hamilton Station Loop, Groveland
blackberry-inn.com • Rates: $195–275

Tenaya Lodge • (888) 514-2167
1122 CA-41, Fish Camp
tenayalodge.com • Rates: $155–355

🛏Yosemite Big Creek Inn B&B
1221 CA-41, Fish Camp • (559) 641-2828
yosemiteinn.com • Rates: $159–229

Narrow Gauge Inn • (559) 683-7720
48571 CA-41, Fish Camp
narrowgaugeinn.com • Rates: $79–248

🛏River Rock Inn • (209) 259-6803
4993 7th St, Mariposa
riverrockncafe.com • Rates: $84–199

Highland House B&B • (209) 966-3341
3125 Wild Dove Ln, Mariposa
highlandhouseinn.com • Rates: $130–165

🛏Poppy Hill B&B • (209) 742-6273
5218 Crystal Aire Dr, Mariposa
poppyhill.com • Rates: $150

🛏Homestead Cottage • (559) 683-0495
41110 Road 600, Ahwahnee
homesteadcottages.com • Rates: $135–379

Sierra Mtn Lodge B&B • (559) 683-7673
45046 Fort Nip Tr, Ahwahnee
sierramountainlodge.com • Rates: $115–195

🛏The Forks Resort • (559) 642-3737
39150 Road 222, Bass Lake
theforksresort.com • Rates: $165–295

Hounds Tooth Inn • (559) 642-6600
42071 CA-41, Oakhurst
houndstoothinn.com • Rates: $119+

🛏Yosemite Gateway Inn • (559) 683-2378
40530 CA-41, Oakhurst • yosemitegatewayinn.com

Chateau du Sureau • (559) 683-6800
48688 Victoria Ln, Oakhurst
chateausureau.com • Rates: $385–645

High Sierra RV Park • (559) 683-7662
40389 CA-41, Oakhurst
highsierrarv.com • Rates: $28–52

🛏Mammoth Mtn Inn • (800) 626-6684
10400 Minaret Rd, Mammoth Lakes

Tamarack Lodge & Resort • (760) 934-2442
163 Twin Lakes Rd, Mammoth Lakes

🛏Juniper Springs Resort • (800) 626-6684
4000 Meridian Blvd, Mammoth Lakes
mammothmountain.com for 3 listed above

Double Eagle Resort & Spa • (760) 648-7004
5587 CA-158, June Lake
doubleeagle.com • Rates: $189+

Fern Creek Lodge • (760) 648-7722
4628 CA-158, June Lake
ferncreeklodge.com • Rates: $125–400

🛏June Lake Villager Motel • (760) 648-7712
2640 CA-158, June Lake
junelakevillager.com • Rates: $79–269

Reverse Creek Lodge • (760) 648-7535
4479 CA-158, June Lake
reversecreeklodge.com • Rates: $85–380

🛏Gull Lake Lodge • (760) 648-7516
132 Bruce St, June Lake
gulllakelodge.com • Rates: $85–189

June Lake RV & Lodge • (760) 648-7967
155 Crawford, June Lake
junelakervpark.com

Many chain restaurants and hotels can be found in Soledad, Pahrump (NV), Visalia, and Oakhurst.

Festivals
Asian American Film Festival • March
San Francisco • caamedia.org

Harmony Sweepstakes A Capella Festival
March • S.F. • harmony-sweepstakes.com

Cherry Blossom Festival • April
San Francisco • sfcherryblossom.org

Mariposa Butterfly Festival • April
Mariposa • mariposabutterflyfestival.net

Napa ARTwalk • May
Napa • NapaARTwalk.org

Strawberry Music Festival • May/August
Camp Mather • strawberrymusic.com

High Sierra Music Festival • June
Quincy • highsierramusic.com

Gilroy Garlic Festival • July
Gilroy • gilroygarlicfestival.com

Sierra Storytelling Festival • July
North Columbia • sierrastorytellingfestival.org

Festival Of Beers & Bluesapalooza • August
mammothbluesbrewsfest.com • Mammoth Lakes

Sonoma Wine Country Weekend • September
sonomawinecountryweekend.com

Hardly Strictly Bluegrass • September
San Francisco • hardlystrictlybluegrass.com

Attractions
Pinnacles Area
Smith & Hook Winery • (831) 678-2132
37700 Foothill Rd, Soledad • smithandhook.com

Hahn Family Wines • (831) 678-4555
37700 Foothill Rd, Soledad • hahnwines.com

Death Valley Area
🛏Goldwell Open Air Museum
NV-374, Beatty, NV • (702) 870-9946
goldwellmuseum.org • Free

Pahrump Valley Winery • (775) 751-0333
3810 Winery Rd, # 1, Pahrump, NV
pahrumpwinery.com • Tours: Free

Farrabee's Jeep Rentals • (760) 786-9872
CA-190, Furnace Creek • farabeejeeps.com

Barker Ranch • Death Valley
Near Ballarat (ghost town), infamous last hide-out of Charles Manson and his "family" (burned down in 2009). Accessed via Goler Canyon Road (high-clearance 4WD recommended).

Sequoia/Kings Canyon Area

Three Rivers Hist. Museum • (559) 561-2707
42268 Sierra Dr, Three Rivers • 3rmuseum.org

Boyden Cavern • (866) 762-2837
74101 E Kings Canyon Rd, Grant Grove
caverntours.com • Zip Lines & Cave Tours

Regal Cinemas • (559) 741-7294
120 S Bridge St, Visalia • regmovies.com

Project Survival Cat Haven • (559) 338-3216
38257 E Kings Canyon Rd, Dunlap
cathaven.com • Admission: $12/adult

Lone Pine Film Hist. Museum • (760) 876-9909
701 S Main St, Lone Pine
lonepinefilmhistorymuseum.org • $5/adult

Alabama Hills Natural Arch
Also known as the Mobius Arch. A short loop accesses this popular destination from Whitney Portal Road on the east side of the Sierra Nevada. Definitely worth a stop if you're passing through or headed this way to hike up to Mount Whitney.

Yosemite Area

Sugar Pine Railroad • (559) 683-7273
56001 CA-41, Fish Camp
ymsprr.com • Tickets: $18–55/adult

Arta River Trips • (800) 323-2782
24000 Casa Loma Rd, Groveland
arta.org • Rafting: $269+

Yosemite Trails Pack Station • (559) 683-7611
7910 Jackson Rd, Fish Camp
yosemitetrails.com • Trail Rides: $50+

Yosemite Ziplines & Adventure Ranch
4808 CA-140, Mariposa
yosemiteziptours.com • (209) 742-4844

Devil's Postpile Nat'l Mon. • (760) 934-2289
Devils Postpile Access Road, Mammoth Lakes
nps.gov/depo • Access Shuttle: $7/adult

June Mtn Ski Area • (760) 648-7733
3819 CA-158, June Lake
junemountain.com • Lift Ticket: $89/adult

Mariposa Museum • (209) 966-2924
5119 Jessie St, Mariposa
mariposamuseum.org • Admission: $5/adult

CA Mining Museum • (209) 742-7625
5005 Fairgrounds Rd, Mariposa

Met Cinema • (559) 683-1234
40015 CA-49, # 1, Oakhurst
movieheroes.com

Black Tie Ski Rentals • (866) 838-3754
12219 Business Park Dr, Truckee
blacktieskis.com

Mammoth Mtn Bike Park • (760) 934-0745
10001 Minaret Rd, Mammoth Lakes
mammothmountain.com

San Francisco Area

MacKerricher State Park • (707) 937-5804
Cool park famous for its Glass Beach
24100 MacKerricher Park Road, Fort Bragg

Alcatraz Island • (415) 561-4900 • nps.gov/alca
alcatrazcruises.com • Tours: $31–38

Muir Woods National Monument
Mill Valley • (415) 388-2595
nps.gov/muwo • Entrance Fee: $10/adult

Golden Gate Nat'l Recreation Area
Fort Mason, Building 201, San Francisco
nps.gov/goga • (415) 561-4700 • Free

Exploratorium • (415) 528-4444
3601 Lyon St, San Francisco
exploratorium.edu • Admission: $29/adult

Cable Car Museum • (415) 474-1887
1201 Mason St, San Francisco
cablecarmuseum.org • Free

Beach Blanket Babylon • (415) 421-4222
678 Beach Blanket Babylon Blvd, San Francisco
beachblanketbabylon.com • Tickets: $30+

Asian Art Museum • (415) 581-3500
200 Larkin St, San Francisco
asianart.org • Admission: $20/adult

Musée Mécanique • (415) 346-2000
Pier 45 Shed A, San Francisco
museemecaniquesf.com • Free

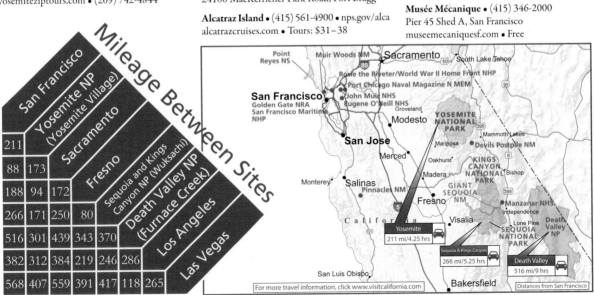

Mileage Between Sites

	San Francisco	Yosemite NP (Yosemite Village)	Sacramento	Fresno	Sequoia and Kings Canyon NP (Wuksachi)	Death Valley NP (Furnace Creek)	Los Angeles
Yosemite NP (Yosemite Village)	211						
Sacramento	88	173					
Fresno	188	94	172				
Sequoia and Kings Canyon NP (Wuksachi)	266	171	250	80			
Death Valley NP (Furnace Creek)	516	301	439	343	370		
Los Angeles	382	312	384	219	246	286	
Las Vegas	568	407	559	391	417	118	265

For more travel information, click www.visitcalifornia.com

Yosemite 211 mi/4.25 hrs
Sequoia & Kings Canyon 266 mi/5.25 hrs
Death Valley 516 mi/9 hrs
Distances from San Francisco

Bumpass Hell

Lassen Volcanic

PO Box 100, Mineral, CA 96063
Phone: (530) 595-4480
Website: nps.gov/lavo

Established: August 9, 1916
May 1907 (Nat'l Monument)
Size: 106,000 Acres
Annual Visitors: 468,000
Peak Season: Summer

Hiking Trails: 150 Miles
Activities: Hiking, Horseback
Riding, Boating, Biking, and Fishing

Campgrounds: Butte Lake*, Volcano
Adventure Camp, Juniper Lake,
Manzanita Lake*, Summit Lake (2)*,
Southwest Walk-in, and Warner Valley
Fee: $12–24/night
Backcountry Camping: Permitted
Lodging: Drakesbad Ranch
Rates: $199–219/person/night

Park Hours: All day, every day
Entrance Fee: $20/vehicle,
$10/individual (foot, bike, etc.)

*Reserve at recreation.gov or (877)
444-6777

The Cascade Range stretches from Canada into northeastern California. Among these mountains is 10,457-foot Lassen Peak, the largest plug dome volcano in the world and the southernmost non-extinct volcano in the Cascade Range. Lassen Peak stands above its surroundings, serving as the centerpiece of Lassen Volcanic National Park. Beyond the prominent peak is a collection of deep blue alpine lakes, dense conifer forests, stinking fumaroles, belching mudpots, roiling hot springs, and boisterous streams. It's a place where features that are so obviously of this earth blend with those that are altogether otherworldly. Perhaps a greater mystery than how these landscapes were united is how today they go by relatively unnoticed.

Native Americans first took notice of the mountain and its surrounding landscapes, visiting seasonally to hunt and gather food. Lassen Peak served as a meeting site for four American Indian groups: Atsugewi, Yana, Yahi, and Maidu. Thanks were given for the food the region provided, but Natives eyed Lassen Peak with great suspicion. They knew it was filled with fire and water and believed there would come a day when it would blow apart, causing considerable damage to the region and potentially its people.

During the mid-19th century, California was flooded with gold-seeking 49ers. While trekking across the Cascades to fertile soils of the Sacramento Valley, they used the mighty peak as a landmark to assure their course was correct. One of the guides who led hopeful prospectors on this journey was Peter Lassen, a Danish blacksmith who settled in northern California in the 1830s. Together with William Nobles, they blazed the first two pioneer trails. Portions of Lassen and Nobles Emigrant Trail are still visible and used today.

As the gold rush subsided, Lassen Peak and its surroundings returned to a life of anonymity. But the United States was growing and forests were being cut at an astonishing rate. No tree was sacred to the lumberjacks. Neither the coastal redwoods nor the Sierra Nevada's giant sequoias were safe from the loggers' axe and saw. If these trees were in danger, so too were the pine and fir of the southern Cascades. With its forests in peril, a conservationist president took notice of this volcanic region. President Theodore Roosevelt preserved vast tracts of land for the enjoyment of the American people, including two regions in the southern Cascades: Cinder Cone National Monument and Lassen Peak National Monument. This designation spared the trees and opened the region to an era of tourism.

But few Americans took notice. In May of 1915, as if to make people aware of its presence once more, the volcano woke up with a series of minor eruptions. These events created a new crater, released lava and ash, and razed several homes. Incandescent blocks of lava could be seen rolling down the flanks of Lassen Peak from 20 miles away. No one was killed by the eruptions, but people began to observe its fury. Scientists took interest in the park's volcanoes. Washington also was aware of these events, and in 1916, largely thanks to volcanic activity, the two monuments were combined and expanded to create Lassen Volcanic National Park. The eruptions stopped in 1921. Once again the region was forgotten.

Perhaps some things are best left forgotten. Roads are rarely congested. Campgrounds seldom fill. If you're looking for a California getaway where volcanic past meets picturesque present, a place filled with wildlife not automobiles, a place where the mud boils and the earth steams, Lassen National Park is for you. Let this serve as your reminder that there's a national park in northern California filled with natural beauty, rich history, and most importantly, peace and quiet from the busy everyday lifestyle that tends to make a person forget a few things.

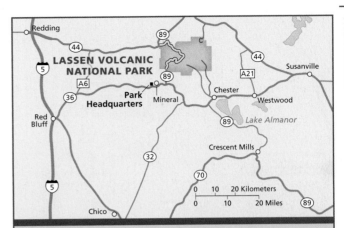

When to Go

Lassen Volcanic National Park is open 24 hours a day, every day of the year, but the park's main road is usually closed or restricted due to snow coverage from fall through late spring. Many facilities are also seasonal. Manzanita Lake Camper Store, Loomis Museum, and all campgrounds (except Southwest Walk-In) close for winter. **Kohm Yah-mah-nee Visitor Center** is open all year. Summer and fall are the best times to visit.

Transportation & Airports

Public transportation does not provide service to or around the park. The closest major airports are Sacramento International (SMF), located 172 miles south of the park's Southwest Entrance, and Reno/Tahoe International (RNO), 151 miles to the southeast.

Directions

There are a total of five entrances to Lassen Volcanic National Park. Southwest and Northwest, both on CA-89, are the two primary entry points. Warner Valley, Juniper Lake, and Butte Lake entrances are accessible via unpaved roads from the south, southeast, and northeast, respectively.

Southwest Entrance from Sacramento (158 miles): Take I-5 north to Exit 649 for Antelope Blvd/CA-36. Follow signs for Lassen National Park, taking CA-36 E approximately 45 miles before turning north onto CA-89 into the park.

Northwest Entrance from Oregon (150 miles): Traveling south on I-5, take Exit 736 onto CA-89 S toward Mc-Cloud/Lassen National Park. CA-89 leads directly to the Northwest Entrance.

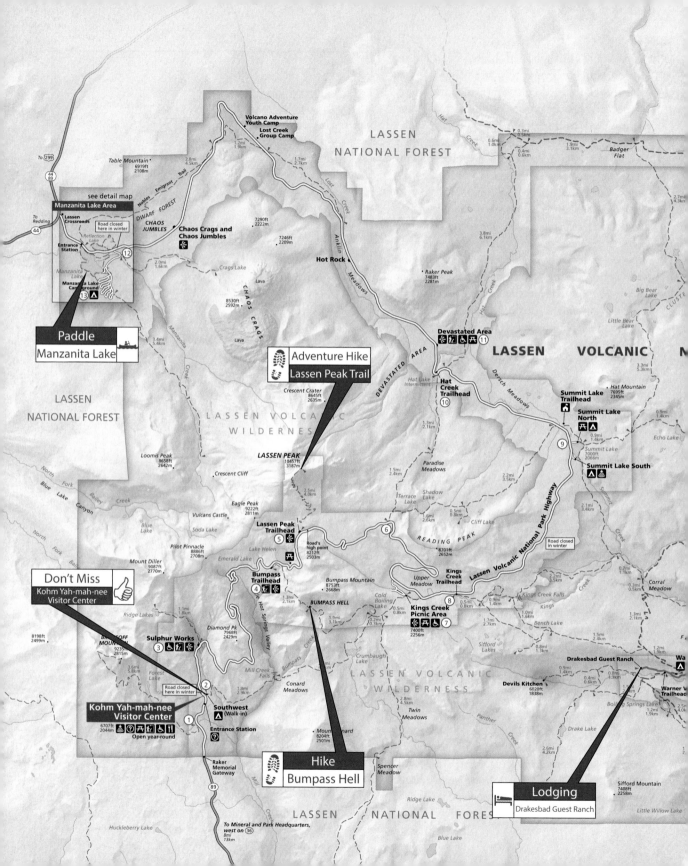

Paddle
Manzanita Lake

Adventure Hike
Lassen Peak Trail

Don't Miss
Kohm Yah-mah-nee Visitor Center

Kohm Yah-mah-nee Visitor Center
6707ft
2044m
Open year-round

Hike
Bumpass Hell

Lodging
Drakesbad Guest Ranch

LASSEN NATIONAL FOREST

LASSEN VOLCANIC WILDERNESS

LASSEN VOLCANIC

LASSEN VOLCANIC WILDERNESS

LASSEN NATIONAL FOREST

To 299

To Redding

44

44
89

Table Mountain
6919ft
2108m

see detail map
Manzanita Lake Area
Lassen Crossroads
Road closed here in winter
Entrance Station
Reflection Lake

Manzanita Lake

Manzanita Lake Campground

Volcano Adventure Youth Camp
Lost Creek Group Camp

Chaos Crags and Chaos Jumbles

CHAOS JUMBLES

DWARF FOREST

CHAOS CRAGS

7290ft
2222m

7246ft
2209m

8530ft
2592m

Lava

Lava

Hot Rock

Raker Peak
7483ft
2281m

Devastated Area

Hat Creek Trailhead

Summit Lake Trailhead

Summit Lake North
7695ft
2345m

Summit Lake South
Summit Lake
7000ft
2066m

Echo Lake

Big Bear Lake

Little Bear Lake

Badger Flat

Crescent Crater
8645ft
2635m

LASSEN PEAK
10457ft
3187m

Road's high point
8212ft
2503m

Crescent Cliff

Eagle Peak
9222ft
2811m

Vulcans Castle

Soda Lake

Pilot Pinnacle
8886ft
2708m

Lake Helen

Emerald Lake

Loomis Peak
8658ft
2642m

Mount Diller
9087ft
2770m

Lassen Peak Trailhead

Bumpass Trailhead

Bumpass Mountain
8753ft
2668m

BUMPASS HELL

Cold Boiling Lake

Kings Creek Trailhead

Kings Creek Picnic Area
7400ft
2256m

Upper Meadow

READING PEAK
8701ft
2652m

Kings Creek Falls

Corral Meadow

Paradise Meadows

Shadow Lake

Terrace Lake

Cliff Lake

Road closed in winter

8198ft
2499m

BROKEOFF MOUNTAIN
9235ft
2815m

Sulphur Works

Ridge Lakes

Diamond Pk
7968ft
2429m

Mill Creek Falls

Forest Lake

Conard Meadows

Southwest (Walk-in)

Entrance Station

Raker Memorial Gateway

89

Drakesbad Guest Ranch

Devils Kitchen
6020ft
1838m

Warner Valley Trailhead

Twin Meadows

Spencer Meadow

Mount Conard
8204ft
2501m

Crumbaugh Lake

Sifford Lakes

Bench Lake

Drake Lake

Boiling Springs Lake

Panther Creek

Sifford Mountain
7408ft
2258m

Little Willow Lake

Ridge Lake

Blue Lake

Huckleberry Lake

To Mineral and Park Headquarters, west on 36
8mi
13km

North Fork Blue Canyon

North Fork Bailey Creek

Blue Lake

Bailey Creek

Crags Lake

Manzanita Creek

Lost Creek

Anklin Meadows

Hat Creek

Dersch Meadows

Hat Lake Intermittent

Lassen Volcanic National Park Highway

DEVASTATED AREA

Hot Springs Valley

Bumpass Creek

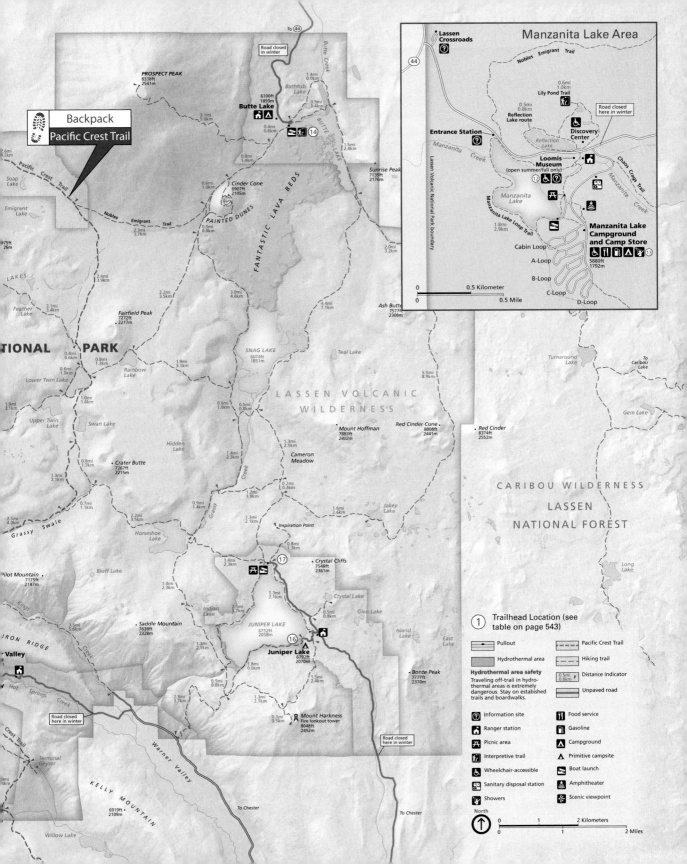

King's Creek

Black bear cub

Driving

The 29-mile **Main Park Road** winds and climbs its way across the park, passing the vast majority of facilities and attractions. Only short sections of the road at Northwest and Southwest Entrances are open all year. The remainder is closed beginning in late fall (with the first significant snowfall) until late spring or early summer.

Butte Lake, Warner Valley, and Juniper Lake Roads are unpaved roads leading to remote regions. All three are open seasonally (weather dependent). Butte Lake and Warner Valley Roads are at lower elevation and therefore open earlier and remain open later than Juniper Lake Road and the Main Park Road. You can find current road conditions at the park website.

Visitor Centers

Kohm Yah-mah-nee Visitor Center (530.595.4480), located at Southwest Entrance, is your one-stop shop for park information, books, maps, and exhibits. It houses an auditorium where visitors can view a short introductory film. The visitor center is open every day of the year, except for Thanksgiving and Christmas Day, from 9am–5pm. Hours are 9am–5pm for the rest of the year. **Loomis Museum** (530.595.6140), near Manzanita Lake, is open daily, 9am–5pm, from late May through October. It features exhibits, videos, and publications.

Camping

There are eight designated campgrounds. Along Main Park Road from Northwest to Southwest Entrance Stations are **Manzanita Lake** (179 sites, $18/night), **Volcano Adventure Camp**, **Summit Lake North** (46, $22), **Summit Lake South** (48, $20), and **Southwest Walk-in** (20, $16). **Volcano Adventure Camp** is designed for youth groups, featuring tent cabins, cooking pavilion, shared amphitheater, and **showers**. Southwest is the only year-round campground, but it is not conducive to RVs (all campsites are a short walk from Southwest Entrance Parking Area). RV sites are available at Butte Lake, Manzanita Lake, Summit Lake (North and South), and Warner Valley. **Warner Valley** (18, $16), **Juniper Lake** (18, $12), and **Butte Lake** (101, $20) Campgrounds are accessed via rough and remote gravel roads. Coin-operated **showers** and **laundry**, and a dump station (fee) are only available near Manzanita Lake. Flush toilets are available at Butte Lake, Manzanita Lake, and Summit Lake North. Sites at Manzanita Lake, Summit Lake (North and South), and Butte Lake can be reserved up to six months in advance by calling (877) 444-6777 or clicking recreation.gov.

Group sites are available at Manzanita Lake (5, $70), Butte Lake (6, $60), Lost Creek (8, $60, near Volcano Adventure Camp), and Juniper Lake (2, $30). Group sites must be reserved in advance. All campgrounds (other than Southwest) open sometime between May and July and close between September and October. Open and close dates are weather dependent.

Hiking

You can see alpine lakes and peer up at Lassen Peak from your driver's seat, but it's impossible to appreciate them with your hands on a steering wheel. Visitors determined to explore the park to the fullest must hit the trails. Two of the most popular ones are **Lassen Peak** and **Bumpass Hell**, both located along Main Park Road. If you can arrange a shuttle, or plant a bicycle, it's possible to hike to Southwest Campground from Bumpass Hell by combining it with Cold Boiling Lake and Mill Creek Falls Trails. Together they offer a wide variety of scenery, including mudpots, hot springs, fumaroles, a boiling lake, and a waterfall. Bumpass Hell looks, feels, and smells like a miniature Yellowstone.

Other popular trails along Main Park Road include Brokeoff Mountain, Devastation, and Manzanita Lake. The best locations for peaceful hiking lie beyond Main Park Road at Warner Valley, Juniper Lake, and Butte Lake. These locations provide plenty of solitude as you walk among a pristine wilderness filled with conifer forests and perfectly clear alpine lakes. (Note that these area's gravel access roads are long and rough.) **Cinder Cone Trail** in the Butte Lake area is a really nice moderate hike to the top of the cinder cone that created Fantastic Lava Beds and Painted Dunes. But, if you have to choose one of these more remote areas, go with Juniper Lake. It has a dense network of trails, allowing hikers to assemble looped routes of varying distances.

Backpacking

More than 150 miles of trails, including 18 miles of the Pacific Crest Trail provides ample backpacking opportunities. All overnight trips in the backcountry require a **free wilderness permit**, available in person during operating hours at Loomis Museum, Kohm Yah-mah-nee Visitor Center, and by self-registration at Summit Lake, Juniper Lake, Butte Lake, and Warner Valley Ranger Stations. Permits are also available via e-mail (application form and contact info at park website). Backpackers must use a bear-resistant food canister (or hang your food) and camp at least 300 feet from other groups, 100 feet from streams and lakes, and at least 0.5 mile from any developed area.

Lassen Volcanic Hiking Trails (Distances are roundtrip)

	Name	Location (# on map)	Length	Difficulty Rating & Notes
Southwest Entrance	Brokeoff Mountain	0.25 mile south of SW Entrance (1)	7.0 miles	S – Steep trail to summit, excellent views
	Mill Creek Falls - ♿	Southwest Parking Area (2)	3.8 miles	M – Hike through forest to falls overlook
	Ridge Lakes	Sulphur Works Parking Area (3)	2.0 miles	S –Up a ridge, through a ravine to alpine lakes
	Bumpass Hell - ♿	Bumpass Hell Parking Area (4)	3.0 miles	M – Boardwalk through a hydrothermal area
	Lassen Peak - ♿	Lassen Peak Parking Area (5)	5.0 miles	S – Hike up mountain slope of loose rock
	Terrace, Shadow and Cliff Lakes	21 miles from NW Entrance (6)	4.0 miles	M – Great trail to view Lassen Peak
	Cold Boiling Lake	Kings Creek Picnic Area (7)	2.6 miles	E – Pass through forest to a bubbling lake
	Kings Creek Falls - ♿	Kings Creek Falls Trailhead (8)	3.0 miles	M – Meadows, forest, flowers, and falls
Northwest Entrance	Echo Lake	Summit Lake Ranger Station (9)	4.4 miles	M – Forest, lake, and views of Lassen Peak
	Paradise Meadow	Hat Lake Parking Area (10)	2.8 miles	M – Footbridges to talus cliff lined meadow
	Devastated Area	Devastated Parking Area (11)	0.25 mile	E – Interpretive trail discusses past eruptions
	Lily Pond	Across from Loomis Museum (12)	0.5 mile	E – Nature trail with interpretive brochures
	Manzanita Creek	Manzanita Lake (13)	7.0 miles	M – Switchbacks lead to meadow along creek
	Manzanita Lake - ♿	Manzanita Lake (13)	1.8 miles	E – Flat trail around lake, birding area
	Chaos Crags and Crags Lake	Manzanita Lake (13)	4.2 miles	M – Lake is often dry in summer
Butte Lake	Cinder Cone - ♿	Butte Lake Parking Area (14)	4.0 miles	S – Pass lava beds and painted dunes
	Prospect Peak	Spur from Cinder Cone (15)	6.6 miles	S – Forested trail to rim of shield volcano
Warner Valley	Devil's Kitchen	Warner Valley Rd (15)	4.4 miles	M – Mudpots, steam vents, and fumaroles
	Boiling Springs Lake	Warner Valley Rd (15)	3.0 miles	E – Mudpots, wildflowers, and 125°F lake
	Terminal Geyser	Warner Valley Rd (15)	5.8 miles	M – Not a geyser, a fumarole and steam
Juniper Lake	Mount Harkness	Juniper Lake Campground (16)	3.8 miles	S – Fire lookout provides wonderful views
	Crystal Lake	Juniper Lake Campground (16)	0.8 mile	E – Short trail to small tarn in rocky basin
	Inspiration Point - ♿	Juniper Lake Picnic Area (17)	1.4 miles	M – Views of the park's prominent peaks
	Horseshoe Lake	Juniper Lake Picnic Area (17)	2.8 miles	E – Gentle trail to a good fishing hole

Difficulty Ratings: E = Easy, M = Moderate, S = Strenuous

Horseback Riding

The park does not offer guided horse rides or pack trips, but visitors are welcome to bring their own stock. Horses, llamas, burros, and mules are allowed on all designated trails with the exception of Manzanita Lake Trail, Lassen Peak Trail, and portions of Cinder Cone, Reflection Lake, and Bumpass Hell Trails, and any paths within Devil's Kitchen and Sulphur Works thermal areas. A **free wilderness permit** must be obtained prior to trail use.

Fishing

Fishing is not a particularly popular activity, but many of the park's waters are known for their rainbow and brown trout. Manzanita Lake is the most frequented fishing hole. You must practice catch and release and use single-hook, barbless, artificial lures. A California fishing license is required for all anglers 16 and older.

Boating

Boat launches are available for non-motorized watercraft at Manzanita, Butte, and Juniper Lakes. Paddlers must also use these designated launch areas. You can **rent** kayaks ($16/hr), canoes ($25), SUPs ($15), and catarafts ($30) at Manzanita Lake Camper Store (lassenrecreation.com). All equipment is available on a first-come, first-served basis. Rentals are available from 9am until 30 minutes before sunset.

Bird Watching

Bird watching is another popular past-time. Manzanita Lake and Cluster Lakes loops are popular among birders. No matter where you travel, you're likely to spot a few of the 83 species of birds nesting within the park. Favorites include osprey, bald eagle, bufflehead, peregrine falcon, California spotted owl, and red-breasted sapsucker. Lassen Volcanic National Park is one of the few areas where bufflehead breed in northern California.

Winter Activities

In winter, Main Park Road may be closed but the fun doesn't stop where the road is not plowed. Southwest Parking Area is a great place to begin a **snowshoe trek**, **cross-country ski adventure**, or a **family sledding excursion**. Several sledding hills and miles of ski trails are available nearby Kohm Yah-mah-nee Visitor Center. Over at the Northwest Entrance, cross-country skiers and snowshoers can embark upon a 7-mile trail along Manzanita Creek (begins at Loomis Ranger Station) or the 7-mile Nobles Emigrant Trail (begins across from Loomis Parking Area).

Ranger Programs

Lassen Volcanic offers free ranger-led activities during summer and winter. Summer programs run from mid-June to mid-August. They consist of a variety of walks, talks, and evening activities. For "Starry Nights," a ranger points out stars, planets, and galaxies visible in the brilliant night sky. There are bird-watching hikes, junior ranger programs, and a slew of educational talks, discussing the park's unique ecology, geology, and history. During winter you can join park rangers on a 1–2-mile snowshoe adventure. These walks are held on Saturdays and Sundays beginning after Christmas Day and ending in March. Snowshoes are provided free of charge, but a $1 donation is requested for their use. To view a complete and current schedule of events at the park, check bulletin boards at park facilities or view the park's online calendar before visiting.

For Kids

The park offers ranger-led **Junior Ranger Programs** for kids. Junior Ranger Activity Booklets are available at Loomis Museum or Kohm Yah-mah-nee Visitor Center (or download it from the park website). Complete the activities and share your booklet with a park ranger at Loomis Museum or Kohm Yah-mah-nee Visitor Center to be sworn in as a Junior Ranger and receive a patch.

Flora & Fauna

Elevation ranging from 5,000 to nearly 10,500 feet creates an environment full of ecological diversity. More than 700 species of flowering plants reside in the park. Communities vary from dense conifer forests of the lower elevations to barren alpine mountaintops where trees are unable to survive. During the summer months meadows burst with color. Trails like Paradise Meadows and Kings Creek Falls guide hikers directly through beautiful foliage. More than 300 species of vertebrates, including 57 species of mammals, call the park home. Most famous are the black bears from whom you must lock your food away (use the bear lockers provided at the campgrounds). Bobcat, mountain lion, and Sierra Nevada and red fox live here, but are seldom seen. Animals you're most likely to see are the rodents (chipmunks, squirrels, and possibly skunks) and birds.

Pets

Pets are allowed in the park, but must be kept on a leash no more than six feet in length at all times. They are only allowed on established roadways, campgrounds, picnic areas, and other developed areas. Pets (with the exception of service animals) are not allowed in public buildings.

Accessibility

Loomis Museum and Kohm Yah-mah-nee Visitor Center are accessible to wheelchair users. Devastated Trail is accessible, as are most restrooms. A wheelchair-accessible site is available at Manzanita Lake, Summit Lake, and Butte Lake Campgrounds.

Weather

There's more than 4,000 feet of elevation difference between Manzanita Lake and Lassen Peak. Such a dramatic change creates wild variations in temperature, wind, and weather. Expect temperatures to decrease about 4°F per 1,000 feet of increased elevation. Winters are cold and snowy in the high elevations; one year Lake Helen received some 40 feet of accumulated snow. At Manzanita Lake the average high temperature from December through February is 50°F, with lows falling into the teens. During summer average highs reach the mid-80s°F, with overnight lows dropping into the low 40s°F. All campgrounds are above 5,600 feet so expect cool nights. Come prepared for wind, rain, and chilly evenings, and always dress in layers.

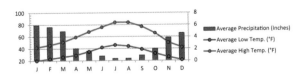

Vacation Planner

Most visits to Lassen Volcanic National Park begin and end on Main Park Road (CA-89). As far as overnight accommodations are concerned, you'll only find **campgrounds** (page 542) between Southwest and

Lassen Peak from Upper Meadow

Northwest Entrances. Tucked away in Warner Valley is the park's only lodge, **Drakesbad Guest Ranch** (866.999.0914, drakesbad.com). Accommodations are simple (most without electricity), and rates range from $199–219 per person per night (meals are included). Nearby dining, grocery stores, lodging, festivals, and attractions are listed on pages 562–565. The roads to Warner Valley, Juniper Lake, and Butte Lake are long and rough, but the peacefulness found at their conclusion is often worth the journey. With that said, most visitors only travel along Main Park Road. Expect the 29-mile (one-way) drive to take one hour without stopping. Here's a one-day itinerary to help guide you along Main Park Road (beginning at the SW Entrance).

Day 1: Introduce yourself to the park at **Kohm Yah-mah-nee Visitor Center**. Watch the introductory film, browse through the exhibits and bookstore, and check the day's schedule of ranger-guided activities. Adjust your schedule in order to squeeze in any programs of interest. Return to your car and begin touring Main Park Road. After a few miles you'll reach two of the premier destinations: **Bumpass Hell and Lassen Peak**. Hike their respective trails. At a leisurely pace it takes 2 hours to complete Bumpass Hell Trail and 4 hours to hike to the summit of Lassen Peak and back (it's all uphill!). If you're sufficiently worn out from the hikes, complete the drive all the way to the NW Entrance and **Manzanita Lake**. Here you can sit down, set up camp, or continue on to your next vacation destination. Hiking **Crags Lake, Kings Creek Falls, or Manzanita Lake Trails** are easier alternatives if you aren't up for the thigh-burner to the top of Lassen Peak.

Boy Scout Tree Trail

Redwood

1111 Second Street
Crescent City, CA 95531
Phone: (707) 465-7335
Website: nps.gov/redw

Established: January 1, 1968
Size: 133,000 Acres
Annual Visitors: 527,000
Peak Season: Summer

Activities: Hiking, Backpacking, Camping, Horseback Riding, Biking, Paddling, and Fishing

Campgrounds ($35/night): Mill Creek* (Seasonal), Jedediah Smith*, Elk Prairie*, and Gold Bluffs Beach
Backcountry Camping: Permitted at designated sites with a free permit (however, there is a $5 fee at Gold Bluffs Beach, site #23)
Lodging: None

Park Hours: All day, every day
Entrance Fee: None (National Park)
$8 Day-use Fee (State Parks)

*Reserve at reserveamerica.com or (800) 444-7275

Redwood trees once grew all over the Northern Hemisphere. They have lived on the California coast for the last 20 million years, providing a link to the Age of Dinosaurs. As recently as 1850, more than two million acres of old-growth covered this coastline where fog supplies up to one-third of their annual water. Today, Redwood National and State Parks protect less than 39,000 acres of old-growth forest, representing 45% of all remaining coastal redwoods. They are some of the oldest trees in the world, many of which have been growing here for more than 2,000 years. If they could speak they'd tell stories of times long before Christopher Columbus discovered America. These are the tallest trees in the world. Some appear to scratch the sky, towering more than 370 feet into the air; at 379 feet, Hyperion is the tallest of them all. Credit bark more than 12 inches thick infused with tannin, providing protection from disease, insects, and fire. Roots, no deeper than 10–13 feet but up to 80 feet long, support these monsters to become more than 22 feet in diameter at their base and to weigh up to 500 tons. Until prospectors and loggers arrived on the scene, the only threat to the mighty redwood was itself. They simply grew too big and too tall for their shallow roots, planted in wet soil, to support themselves against the winds off the Pacific Ocean.

By the 1850s strong winds weren't the only threat these majestic giants faced. Jedediah Smith, trapper and explorer, was the first non-Native to reach California's northern coast by land in 1828. More than two decades later gold was found along the Trinity River. In 1850, settlers established the boom town of Eureka and miners steadily displaced Native Americans who had lived there for the past 3,000 years, longer than the oldest trees of the redwood forests. The Yurok, Tolowa, Karok, Chilula, and Wiyot Indian tribes all resided in the region. They used fallen redwoods for boats, houses, and small villages. Deer, elk, fish, nuts, berries, and seeds provided more than enough food to sustain tribes as large as 55 villages and 2,500 people. After two minor gold booms went bust, gold-seeking settlers, who had forced the Natives out, now had to seek something else, a new way to earn wages.

Gold fever became redwood fever, and more settlers were drawn to the area to exploit a seemingly endless supply of colossal trees. Harvested trees helped boost the rapid development of West Coast cities like San Francisco. In 1918, conservationists, appalled by the swaths of clear-cut coastal lands, formed the Save-the-Redwoods League. They drummed up support, which ultimately led to establishment of Prairie Creek, Del Norte Coast, and Jedediah Smith Redwoods State Parks. At the same time US-101, which would provide unprecedented access to untouched stands of coastal redwoods, was under construction. Conservationists spent the next four decades requesting the creation of Redwood National Park. Demand for lumber during WWII delayed the park's creation, but finally, in the 1960s, the Save-the-Redwoods League, Sierra Club, and National Geographic Society made one last push for a national park. It was signed into law by President Lyndon B. Johnson in 1968. At the time more than 90% of old-growth forests had been logged.

Some of the trees have been saved. Native Americans still live among nature's sacred giants, even though treaties establishing reservations for the displaced Natives were never ratified. They perform traditional ceremonies, hunt and fish, and speak their native language. Guests are left awestruck by the soaring timber, sharing the same spiritual connection between nature and man. Hollywood has helped create a more tangible connection between man, nature, and the Age of Dinosaurs. Redwood Forest served as backdrop for Steven Spielberg's *The Lost World: Jurassic Park*. Another Spielberg flick, *Star Wars: Return of the Jedi*—a movie set "a long time ago, in a galaxy far, far away"—was also filmed here. Let's hope Redwood National Park goes back to the future, looking more like it did in 1850 than 1950.

Tall Trees Trail

When to Go
Redwood National Park is open all day, every day. Summer is busy and often foggy. Winter is rainy. Spring and fall are marked by visiting migratory birds. No matter when you visit, anticipate temperatures ranging between 40°F and 60°F along the coast. This fairly constant temperature is moderated by the Pacific Ocean. Smaller crowds, reduced chances of fog and rain, and a wide variety of visiting bird species make spring and fall ideal times to visit the Redwood Forest. It's also a great time to cruise US-101/Redwood Highway and CA-1/Pacific Coast Highway.

All Visitor and Information Centers are open spring to fall, with typical hours from 9am to 5pm. **Jedediah Smith Visitor Center** (707.458.3496) is open from 12pm to 8pm in summer. **Crescent City Information Center** (707.465.7335, 1111 2nd St) and **Thomas H. Kuchel Visitor Center** (707.465.7765) are the only visitor facilities that stay open year-round, except New Year's Day, Thanksgiving, and Christmas. In winter, hours are shortened to 9am to 4pm. **Hiouchi Information Center** (707.458.3294) is located 9 miles northeast of Crescent City on US-199. **Prairie Creek Visitor Center** (707.488.2171) is located 6 miles north of Orick on Newton B. Drury Scenic Pkwy.

Transportation & Airports
Public transportation does not provide service to or around the park. The closest large commercial airports are Portland International (PDX), 340 miles north of the park, and San Francisco International (SFO), 330 miles to the south. Small regional airports are located nearby at Crescent City and McKinleyville, CA; and Medford, OR.

Directions

Redwood National Park is oriented along US-101, one of the most scenic highways in the United States. The park does not have a formal entrance. Directions to US-101:

From the South: US-101 crosses the opening of San Francisco Bay, via the Golden Gate Bridge, and then runs parallel to California's Coast all the way to Redwood National Park.

From the North: Follow US-101 along the Oregon/California Coast (fantastic). You can also take I-5 South to Exit 58, where you'll merge onto CA-99 S toward US-100/Grants Pass. After 3 miles, turn right at US-199 S/Redwood Highway. Continue for 88 miles to the park.

Northern Region

Jedediah Smith Redwoods State Park: The northernmost unit of the park is home to Hiouchi Information Center (summer only), camping, fishing, and

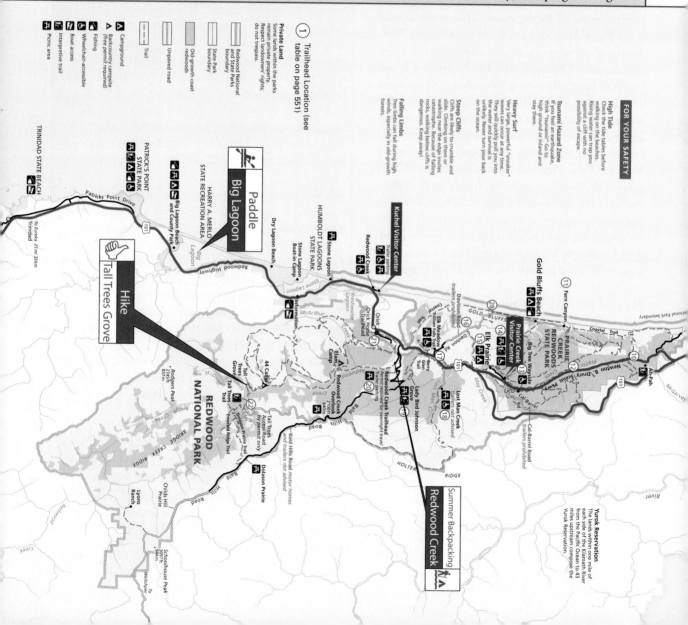

Howland Hill Road (unpaved), which leads to many of the area's hiking trailheads.

Del Norte Coast Redwoods State Park: A large undeveloped region home to camping (summer only) and plenty of hiking.

Southern Region
Redwood National Park: This is the most disjointed of all the National Parks. There are plots of park land in both the northern and southern halves, but most of the area consists of a large tract south of Prairie Creek where you'll find two of the most popular areas: Lady Bird Johnson Grove and Tall Trees Grove (permit required). These sites are accessed by Bald Hills Road.

Prairie Creek Redwoods State Park: Newton B. Drury Scenic Parkway enters this scenic area from US-101. You'll find information and exhibits at Prairie Creek Visitor Center. Camping is available at Elk Prairie Campground. An abundance of hiking trails fan out from Newton B. Drury Scenic Parkway.

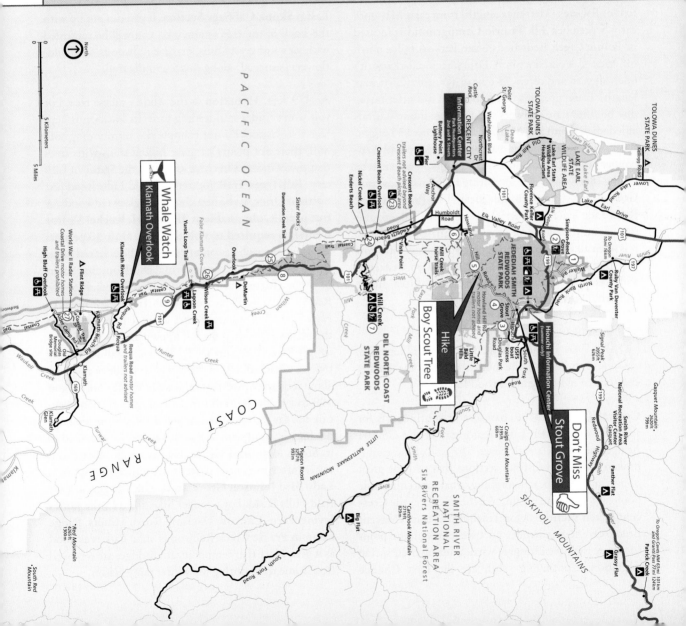

Camping

There are no developed campgrounds in Redwood National Park, but three state parks (jointly administered with the national park) furnish four developed campgrounds. **Jedediah Smith Campground** is in an old-growth redwood grove on the banks of the Smith River. It is located on US-199, 10 miles east of Crescent City. You can hike, fish, and swim right at the campground. It's open all year, and offers 86 tent or RV sites (36-ft max length). **Mill Creek Campground** is located in Del Norte Coast Redwoods State Park, 7 miles south of Crescent City on US-101. It offers 145 tent or RV sites (31-ft max length) from early May until early September. **Elk Prairie Campground** is located in Prairie Creek Redwoods State Park, 6 miles north of Orick, CA on Newton B. Drury Scenic Parkway. It's open all year, and offers 75 tent or RV sites (27-ft max length). Campgrounds listed above do not offer hookups, but they have **showers** and there are dump stations at Jedediah Smith and Mill Creek. Sites cost $35/night. Reservations (recommended between May and September) can be made up to six months in advance by calling (800) 444-7275 or visiting reserveamerica.com. **Gold Bluffs Campground**, located in Prairie Creek Redwoods State Park on Davison Road, has 26 sites that are only available on a first-come, first-served basis. It is open all year. **Solar showers** are provided. Sites cost $35/night. Campgrounds fill, especially on weekends and holidays, but there are more than a dozen public and private campgrounds located nearby.

Hiking

There are more than 200 miles of hiking trails. The best of the bunch explore the Pacific coastline or old-growth redwood forests.

Coastal Trail traces the coast almost continuously for some 35 miles. There's one major gap at the US-101 Bridge over the Klamath River. The rest of the trail is broken into seven distinct sections that provide great opportunities for beach-combing, whale-watching, tide pool-exploring, and birding. Farthest north is the **Crescent Beach Section**. Before reaching the trail, Crescent Beach Overlook provides an excellent vantage point to survey the ocean for gray whales during their spring migration. Continuing south are the **Last Chance and Demartin Sections**. Longer and more strenuous, they provide greater solitude. Backcountry campsites are available along these portions. Further south you'll find the 5.5-mile **Klamath Section** and Klamath River Overlook (another excellent perch to peer across the Pacific). The 4.5-mile **Flint Ridge Section** provides a unique combination of old-growth redwood forests and ocean vistas. (Most redwoods grow at least a mile or two away from shore as salty water inhibits growth.) **Gold Bluffs** (4.8 miles)—where hikers pass through a 30-foot high wall of ferns at Fern Canyon, and can spend the night at Ossagon Camp—is the next stretch. Last is **Skunk Cabbage Section**. If you can put up with the smell of the trail's namesake, you will be rewarded with views of grassy hills, massive redwoods, and wildflowers (seasonal) along this 5.25-mile trail.

At 379 feet, **Hyperion** is the world's tallest tree, but you won't find a trail leading to it. Its location is kept secret so visitors do not trample the surrounding soil. Still, there are plenty of great hiking trails with trees that tower more than twice as high as the Statue of Liberty. **Tall Trees Trail**, located off Bald Hills Road just north of Orick, is the best choice for giant redwoods. **A free permit, obtainable at Thomas H. Kuchel Visitor Center, is required to visit the area.** Only 50 permits are given out each day on a first-come, first-served basis. If you're unable to secure a permit, check out Boy Scout or Stout (Memorial) Grove Trails in Jedediah Smith Redwoods State Park. **Boy Scout Trail** is 2.8 miles to Fern Falls. The waterfall isn't all that impressive, but the massive double redwood known as Boy Scout Tree is. Just make sure you see it. The spur trail to the big tree isn't marked. It's on the right-hand side of the trail, about a quarter-mile from the waterfall. It's only about 100 feet from the trail (up a small hill), so don't venture too far into the forest if you don't see a really huge double redwood with a "Boy Scout Tree" sign nailed to it. **Stout Memorial Grove Trail** is much shorter and easier (after the initial descent). Another alternative is **Lady Bird Johnson Grove Trail**, which begins just off Bald Hills Road. For a longer hike, the 12-mile **James Irvine/Fern Canyon/Davison Road/Miners Ridge Loop** in Prairie Creek Redwoods State Park is as good as it gets. Note that temporary footbridges are removed from some trails during the winter rainy season.

Redwood Hiking Trails (Distances are roundtrip, except Coastal Trails)

	Name	Location (# on map)	Length	Difficulty Rating & Notes
Jedediah Smith	Leifer–Ellsworth Loop	Off Walker Road (1)	2.6 miles	E – Follows an old plank road
	Simpson–Reed	US-199 (North Side) (2)	1.0 mile	E – 1,000-year-old redwoods
	Little Bald Hills	Howland Hill Road (3)	6.6–9.6 mi	S – Backpack • Bikes/horses allowed
	Stout Grove - 🐾	Howland Hill Road (4)	1.0 mile	E – Steep descent to great grove
	Boy Scout Tree - 🐾	Howland Hill Road (5)	5.6 miles	M – Fern Falls/giant redwood (via spur)
	Mill Creek	Howland Hill Road (6)	7.2 miles	M – Access for fishing or photos
Del Norte	Trestle Loop	Mill Creek Camp (7)	1.0 mile	M – Old railroad trestles, berries
	Damnation Creek	Milepost 16 on US-101 (8)	4.4 miles	S – Ancient redwoods and coast
	Yurok Loop	Lagoon Creek Picnic Area (9)	1.0 mile	E – Family-friendly/False Klamath Cove
Prairie Creek	Ossagon	Newton B. Drury Scenic Pkwy (10)	3.6 miles	M – Old rough road • Bikes allowed
	Fern Canyon Loop	Fern Canyon Parking Area (11)	0.7 mile	E – Ferns and cliffs, floods in winter
	Rhododendron - 🐾	Newton B. Drury Scenic Pkwy (12)	12.6 mile	M – Loop w/ Brown Creek & South Fork
	Circle	Big Tree Wayside Parking Area (13)	0.6 mile	E – Easiest access to the Big Tree
	Cathedral Trees	Big Tree Wayside Parking Area (13)	2.8 miles	M – Great big tree family hike
	Prairie Creek	Prairie Creek Visitor Center (14)	8.0 miles	M – Spur to Corkscrew Tree
	James Irvine - 🐾	Prairie Creek Visitor Center (14)	8.4 miles	M – Ends at Fern Canyon, loop options
	Miner's Ridge - 🐾	Prairie Creek Visitor Center (14)	8.2 miles	M – Loop with James Irvine
	Revelation	Prairie Creek Visitor Center (14)	0.6 mile	E – Designed for visually impaired
	Elk Prairie Loop	Elk Prairie Campground (15)	2.8 miles	M – Roosevelt elk sightings likely
	Streelow Creek	Davison Road (16)	5.6 miles	M – Second-growth • Bikes allowed
	Davison	Elk Meadow Day Use Area (17)	6.0 miles	M – Old logging road • Bikes allowed
Redwood NP	Trillium Falls	Elk Meadow Day Use Area (17)	2.5 miles	M – Loop to 10-ft cascade
	Lost Man Creek	Lost Man Creek Picnic Area (18)	20.0 miles	S – Big trees and ferns • Bikes allowed
	Lady Bird Johnson Grove - 🐾	Bald Hills Road (19)	2.0 miles	E – Self-guiding loop • Very popular, site where park was dedicated
	Redwood Creek	Bald Hills Road (20)	16.0–28.0 mi	M/S – All uphill to Dolason Prairie
	MacArthur Creek Loop	Orick Rodeo Grounds (21)	14.0 miles	M – Backpacker/horse-friendly
	Elam Loop/Horse Camp	Orick Rodeo Grounds (21)	20.0 miles	M – Backpacker/horse-friendly
	44 Loop/Horse Camp	Orick Rodeo Grounds (21)	32.0 miles	M – Backpacker/horse-friendly
	Tall Trees - 🐾	Bald Hills Road (22)	3.5 miles	M – World's tallest trees • Permit Req'd
	Dolason Prairie	Bald Hills Road (22)	11.8 miles	M – Open space, panoramic views
Coastal (One-way)	Crescent Beach - 🐾	Crescent Beach Picnic Area (23)	3.5 miles	E – Beachcombing, Roosevelt elk
	Last Chance	Enderts Beach Road (24)	6.0 miles	S – Steep • Bikes allowed
	Demartin	Mile Marker 15.6 of US-101 (25)	6.0 miles	M – Backcountry campsites
	Klamath - 🐾	Wilson Creek Picnic Area (26)	5.5 miles	S – Overlook, beach, tidepools
	Flint Ridge	Coastal Drive (27)	4.5 miles	M – Backcountry campsites
	Gold Bluffs	Davison Road (11)	4.8 miles	M – Steep then flat, camp access
	Skunk Cabbage	Davison Road (28)	5.3 miles	M – Wide variety of plants and trees

Difficulty Ratings: E = Easy, M = Moderate, S = Strenuous

Backpacking

Backcountry camping is only allowed at designated sites and along Redwood Creek gravel bars. There are four free sites: Nickel Creek, DeMartin, and Flint Ridge, located along the Coastal Trail; and Little Bald Hills, located on Little Bald Hills Trail. Little Bald Hills, Nickel Creek, and DeMartin are north of the Klamath River. Permits are required. They can be obtained at any visitor or information center (except Prairie Creek). Five sites are located south of the Klamath River. Site #23 at Gold Bluffs Beach Campground (considered a backcountry site) requires a permit and $5 fee (payable at campground). Elam Creek and 44 Camp are located on Orick Horse Trail. Backcountry sites are also dispersed along Redwood Creek Trail. Elam Creek, 44 Camp, and Redwood Creek sites are free, but a permit must be obtained from Kuchel Visitor Center prior to departure. All sites feature picnic tables, fire pits, food storage lockers, and toilets. Proper food storage is required. Bear-resistant food canisters are available at Kuchel Visitor Center.

Biking

Long distance **road cyclists** love the challenge and the scenery associated with pedaling along the Pacific Coast, including the section of US-101 that travels through Redwood National Park. For **mountain bikers**, Little Bald Hills, Coastal (Last Chance and Gold Bluffs sections), Ossagon, Davison, and Lost Man Creek Trails permit bicycle use. See the hiking table on the previous page for trail location and mileage. Redwood Rides (707.951.6559, redwoodrides.com) offers **guided bike (and paddling) tours**, as well as **mountain bike (and kayak) rentals**. It costs $50/day for a Trek 3500.

Horseback Riding

Many of the park's trails are open to horses. If you'd like to explore the majestic redwoods on a **guided ride or overnight pack trip** contact one of these outfitters: Redwood Trail Rides (707.498.4837, redwoodhorserides.com, $65/90 min), Redwood Creek Buckarettes (707.499.2943, redwoodcreek-buckarettes.com, $90/2 hrs), and Crescent Trail Rides (707.951.5407, crescenttrailrides.com, $90/2 hrs). Rides must be reserved in advance.

Paddling

Paddling is a great way to explore the coast, coves, and rivers. **Big Lagoon**, just south of the park, is popular among paddlers. **Rentals** are available during summer from Kayak Zak's (707.498.1130, kayakzak.com); they bring a rental trailer to the lagoon beginning at 10am on weekends and noon on weekdays. Single kayak rates are $25/hr, $30/half-day, and $40/full-day. They also offer guided trips and sea kayaking courses. Migratory bird and whale watching trips ($75, 2–3 hours) are available during spring and fall. It's a good idea to call before stopping in to make sure they have rentals available. Redwood Rides (707.951.6559, redwoodrides.com) offers half-day (2–3 hrs) kayak trips for $75/adult and full-day (5–6 hours + lunch) trips for $110/adult. They also lead rafting excursions of the Smith River, bike tours of the park, and multi-sport adventures (5–7 hrs, $140/adult). Inflatable kayak rentals are available for $50/day.

Ranger Programs

Ranger programs at Redwood National Park are available from mid-May to mid-September. Time, location, and topics of current programs can be found at visitor center or campground bulletin boards. Campfire programs are offered regularly at Jedediah Smith, Mill Creek, and Elk Prairie Campgrounds. Listen to the stories of a park ranger while sitting near a crackling fire or let a ranger guide you through the park on a Tide Pool or Nature Walk.

For Kids

Children have the opportunity to become a **Redwood National Park Junior Ranger**. Pick up an activity booklet from one of the park's five visitor centers or download it from the park website to participate. Activities are designed for children (ages 7–12), but visitors of any age are welcome. Complete an age appropriate number of activities, collect a bag of litter, attend a ranger program or hike a trail, write down a park rule, and understand and sign the Junior Ranger Pledge to earn a badge.

Flora & Fauna

The main draw is the coastal redwoods, the world's tallest trees soaring more than 300 feet above their massive bases, but there's much more to the region's lush ecosystem. The park protects a variety of threatened species: brown pelican, tidewater goby, bald eagle, Chinook salmon, northern spotted owl, and Steller sea lion. Large mammals such as bear and Roosevelt elk are commonly seen. Not surprisingly, Elk Prairie and Elk Valley are two of the best places to spot their namesake grazing. They cross the roads, use the trails, and appear to be domesticated, but don't mistake their docile nature as an invitation to pose in a photograph with them. All of the animals are wild and should be treated with respect. Do not feed, provoke, or approach any native wildlife.

Pets

Pets are allowed in the park, but must be kept on a leash no more than six feet in length at all times. They are prohibited from all hiking trails. Pets can essentially go anywhere your car can, like along roads, parking areas, picnic areas, campgrounds, and Crescent and Gold Bluffs beaches.

Accessibility

All of the park's visitor centers are accessible to individuals with mobility impairments. Many of the park's campgrounds, picnic areas, beaches, and overlooks are also accessible. Please refer to the maps on pages 548–549 that designate all wheelchair-accessible sites.

Weather

Thunderstorms and fog are difficult to predict, but the temperature is not. Average high temperatures range from the mid-50s to mid-60s°F all year. Average lows range from the low to high 40s°F. This consistency is due to the park's location along the Pacific Coast. The farther you travel from the coast, the greater the seasonal temperature difference becomes. On average the park receives 70 inches of rain each year, most of which falls between October and April.

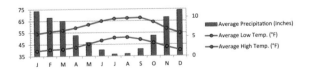

Vacation Planner

If you're traveling along the northern coast of California, a stop at Redwood National Park is a must. Even if you just hop out at **Klamath River Overlook** to smell the salty air and drive to **Lady Bird Johnson Grove**

Elk in casino parking spot at Elk Valley

to walk among 2,000-year-old trees, it's worth it. But, there are plenty of trails and activities to keep you entertained for an extended stay. Provided below is an itinerary for one spectacular day here. **Campgrounds** (page 550) are the only overnight accommodations in the park. Nearby dining, grocery stores, lodging, festivals, and attractions are listed on pages 562–565.

Day 1: Entering from the south via US-101, stop at **Kuchel Visitor Center to see if you can get a permit to access Tall Trees Trailhead.** Continue north past Orick and turn right onto Bald Hills Road. Head to **Tall Trees Grove** if you got a permit, otherwise hike **Lady Bird Johnson Grove.** Return to US-101 and drive to Newton B. Drury Scenic Pkwy. If you like to hike, stop at Prairie Creek Visitor Center for the 12-mile **James Irvine/Miners Ridge Loop.** Otherwise continue north, stopping at **Ah-Pah Trail** and **Klamath River Overlook.** Time permitting, stop at Jedediah Smith to hike **Stout Memorial Grove** or, if you have a few hours and plenty of energy, hike to **Boy Scout Tree** (a massive double redwood). The only problem here is that Boy Scout Tree isn't directly on the path and last time we hiked it, there wasn't a sign at the spur trail. The short spur is on the right, up a small but somewhat steep hill, less than a quarter-mile from the somewhat underwhelming conclusion at Fern Falls. You should notice it, as there are quite a few "social trails" in the area, made by people unsure where to go, but if you miss it, hike to the falls, turn around and look for the spur trail (and giant tree) now on your left-hand side. Even if you don't hike to Boy Scout Tree or visit Stout Grove, the drive out here is fantastic!

Crater Lake

Wizard Island (obscured by smoke from 2015 fire) from Discovery Point

PO Box 7
Crater Lake, ORx 97604
Phone: (541) 594-3000
Website: nps.gov/crla

Established: May 22, 1902
Size: 183,224 Acres
Annual Visitors: 614,000
Peak Season: Summer

Activities: Hiking, Backpacking, Camping, Boat Tours, Swimming, Fishing, Biking, and Snowshoeing

Campgrounds: Mazama (213 sites) and Lost Creek (16, tent-only)
Fee: $10–32.50/night
Lodging: Crater Lake Lodge, Cabins at Mazama Village
Rates: $152–318
Reservations: craterlakelodges.com or (888) 774-2728
Backcountry Camping: Permitted with a free Backcountry Use Permit

Park Hours: All day, every day
Entrance Fee: $15/vehicle, $10/individual (foot, bike, etc.)

Nearly 8,000 years ago a cataclysmic eruption of Mount Mazama caused the mountain to shatter and collapse into itself, forming a massive five-mile wide caldera rimmed by cliffs almost 4,000 feet high. Sealed by molten rock, the caldera gradually filled with water from melted snow and rain. The lake's water level has finally settled, seepage and evaporation balance the incoming flow. After 750 years, roughly five trillion gallons of almost perfectly pure water filled the caldera, creating one of the most impressive natural settings in the world. Crater Lake is so deep (up to 1,943 feet deep, 1,148 feet deep on average) and so pure that the true blueness of water becomes obviously, almost indescribably, apparent. Today, soaring cliffs line a lake whose brilliant deep blue hue leaves guests, past and present, spellbound.

Makalak Indians have their own legend about the creation of Crater Lake. Llao, Chief of the Below World, sometimes came up from the earth to stand atop Mount Mazama. On one of his visits, Llao fell in love with the Makalak chief's beautiful daughter. Llao promised her eternal life if she would return with him to his home below the mountain. She refused. Enraged, Llao began pummeling the village with balls of fire. Skell, Chief of the Above World, witnessed Llao's rage from the top of Mount Shasta. He took pity on the helpless villagers and chose to wage war with Llao. The two chiefs hurled fiery hot boulders at one another from their respective mountains. The earth trembled in the wake of their violence. As villagers fled to the waters of Klamath Lake, two holy men remained behind. Their plan was to jump into the fiery pit hidden within Llao's mountain as a sacrifice to the Chief of the Below. Moved by their bravery, Skell ambushed Llao, driving him back into Mount Mazama, where the fight raged on through the night. The following morning Mount Mazama was gone. In its place was a gaping hole that filled with water from torrents of rain, which fell after the epic battle.

Makalak Indians may well have witnessed the formation of Crater Lake. Evidence of permanent ancient settlement has not been found, but the area was used for seasonal hunting and gathering, vision-quests, and prayer for at least 10,000 years. Mount Mazama erupted about 7,700 years ago. The event produced more than 100 times as much ash as Mount St. Helens' eruption in 1980, scattered as far south as central Nevada, as far east as Yellowstone National Park, and as far north as British Columbia. After its eruption, Indians were definitely aware of the lake filling the caldera of Mount Mazama. They believed it took great power and strength to look at the saturated blue waters. Even today, Klamath Indians (descendants of the Makalak) refuse to look at the lake for religious reasons.

John Wesley Hillman, the first white man to glimpse Crater Lake, had no such religious proclivities. After returning from a successful gold mining trip in California, Hillman funded a small gold mining expedition into Oregon's southern Cascades. On June 12, 1853, the group reached present day Discovery Point where a lake of incomprehensible majesty was on display. They named it Deep Blue Lake, returned to civilization to restock supplies, and continued on their quest for gold. William Gladstone Steel visited the area in 1885. It was still used by local Indians for hunting, gathering, and religious purposes, but Steel spent the next 17 years campaigning for the creation of Crater Lake National Park (the name preferred by locals over the likes of Blue Lake, Lake Majesty, and the original, Deep Blue Lake). Steel named other features: Wizard Island, Llao Rock, and Skell Head. On May 22, 1902, Steel's efforts came to fruition when President Roosevelt signed legislation creating Crater Lake, the 6th oldest national park. Steel's focus shifted to making the area a spectacle, catering to wealthy tourists. It was a difficult task considering the rim receives more than 40 feet of snow annually. Erection of Crater Lake Lodge was constantly over-budget and behind schedule. In 1915 the lodge finally opened to popular fanfare, but it remained in a relatively constant state of construction. Three years later, Rim Drive was completed and the park was officially open for business.

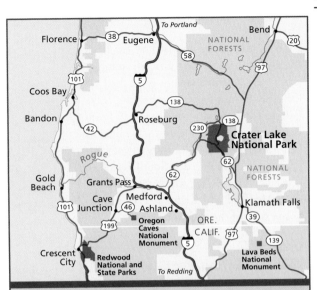

When to Go
The park is always open, but a few roads and facilities close during winter. **Steel Visitor Center** is open every day except Christmas. **Rim Visitor Center** closes from October to May. All dining, lodging, and camping facilities are seasonal, except Rim Village Café and Gifts, which is open all year. Rim Drive and the North Entrance are closed from mid-October until July (weather dependent). Most tourists arrive immediately after the snow melts and the roads open in July and August. During this time, Crater Lake Lodge is booked well in advance and campgrounds fill by noon. The same great views are available in September and October with smaller crowds. Or visit in winter. The road to Rim Village remains plowed. You're also free to camp along the rim at this time (with a permit).

Transportation & Airports
Public transportation does not provide service to or around the park. Crater Lake Trolley (541.882.1896, craterlaketrolley.net) provides 2-hour, ranger-guided tours along Rim Drive during the summer months. Tickets cost $27/adult, $24/senior, and $17/child (5–13). They can be reserved over the phone or online. Pick up or purchase tickets at the ticket booth near the Community House at Rim Village. The closest airports are Klamath Falls (LMT) and Rogue Valley–Medford (MFR). Portland International Airport (PDX) is about 244 miles to the north.

Directions

Crater Lake can be accessed by car from the south (all year) and the north (summer only). The North Entrance is reached via OR-138. From I-5 (west of the park), take Exit 124 at Roseburg to OR-138 E. From Bend, take US-97 S about 75 miles to OR-138. After 15 miles turn left at Crater Lake North Hwy. The South Entrance is reached via OR-62, which travels north from Medford and Klamath Falls on opposite sides of the park.

Visitor Centers

Steel Visitor Center is located at Park Headquarters, south of Crater Lake. It's open daily from 9am–5pm during summer and from 10am–4pm during winter (closed Christmas). Inside you'll find exhibits and a short film. **Rim Visitor Center**, located in Rim Village, is open daily from 9:30am–5pm (June–September). Backcountry permits are available at both facilities.

Driving

Rim Drive is one of the most scenic roadways in all the national parks. The narrow road winds its way around Crater Lake over the course of 33 miles. It's typically open from July to late October, but open and close dates vary from year-to-year depending on snowfall. The route can be traversed in under an hour, but plan on spending at least two, because there are more than two dozen overlooks and picnic areas along the way.

The Old Man

Old Man of the Lake is a 30-ft-tall tree stump, which has been floating about Crater Lake for more than a century. It is roughly 2 feet in diameter and stands 4 feet above the water. Old man is buoyant enough to support a person's weight. **Tour boats** (page 559) may pass the stump.

Camping & Lodging

Mazama Campground, located just past the South Entrance, is operated by Xanterra Parks & Resorts (888.774.2728, craterlakelodges.com). It's open from June through late September. More than 200 sites can be reserved in advance. Tent sites cost $23/night and RV sites cost $31/night ($32.50/night with electric hookups). Coin-operated **showers** and **laundry** facilities are available. The nearby camper store sells groceries, firewood, and gasoline. **Lost Creek Campground** offers 16 tent-only campsites located on the spur road to Pinnacles Overlook. These secluded sites are usually open from July through mid-October and are available on a first-come, first-served basis via self-registration for $10/night. Running water and flush toilets are available. Campgrounds typically fill up in July and August around noon.

Crater Lake Lodge and the Cabins at Mazama Village are also operated by Xanterra Parks & Resorts (888.774.2728, craterlakelodges.com). **Crater Lake Lodge** is part of Rim Village, and it overlooks Crater Lake. There are 71 rustic rooms with incomparable views available from mid-May through mid-October.

Rates range from $179–318/night and they book up to a year in advance (particularly for summer). **Cabins at Mazama Village**, located near the South Entrance, offers 40 basic rooms at $152/night. A restaurant is available at both locations.

Hiking

Only 90 miles of maintained hiking trails penetrate the park's wilderness and explore the lake's rim. This place is buried in snow much of the year and Crater Lake is so magnificent and spellbinding it monopolizes most visitors' time, but you should take a few hours to explore the area on foot. A relatively small trail network makes choosing one very manageable. For unsurpassed views of Crater Lake, hike to **Garfield Peak** or **Mount Scott**. Both lead high into the Cascades where you can peer down into the lake's pure blue depths. For more easily accessible vantage points, try **Discovery Point or Watchman Peak Trails**. To reach the shore of Crater Lake, you'll have to hike 2.2-mile **Cleetwood Cove Trail**. The park closed it for improvements in 2016, but it's no less steep than it was before. Still, if you want to go swimming or join a boat tour, you'll have to make the moderately strenuous trip.

Crater Lake Hiking Trails (Distances are roundtrip)

Name	Location (# on map)	Length	Difficulty Rating & Notes
Union Peak	Hwy 62, PCT TH (1)	11.0 miles	S – Interesting geology and ecology, no lake views
Annie Creek Canyon	Mazama Campground (2)	1.7 miles	M – Self-guided loop • Wildflowers July to mid-August
Godfrey Glen	Munson Valley Rd (3)	1.0 mile	E – Self-guided loop • Canyon views, old forest
Castle Crest Wildflower	Park Headquarters (4)	0.4 mile	E – Self-guided loop • Wildflowers July to mid-August
Lady of the Woods	Steel Info. Center (4)	0.3 mile	E – Self-guided loop • Explores architecture and nature
Discovery Point - 🥾	Rim Village (5)	2.2 miles	E – Follows Crater Rim, stunning views
Garfield Peak	Crater Lake Lodge (6)	3.4 miles	S – Highly rewarding wildflowers and lake views
Watchman Peak - 🥾	Watchman Overlook (7)	1.6 miles	M – Outstanding sunsets and views of Wizard Island
Cleetwood Cove	Rim Drive (8)	2.2 miles	S – Steep • Only access point to Crater Lake
Mount Scott - 🥾	Rim Drive (9)	5.0 miles	S – Highest point in the park • Wonderful lake views
Pinnacles	Pinnacles Spur Rd (10)	1.0 mile	E – View volcanic spires • Bikes allowed
Sun Notch Viewpoint	Rim Drive (11)	0.5 mile	M – Uphill walk to views of Phantom Ship
Crater Peak	Rim Drive (12)	6.4 miles	M – Meadow, forest, volcano summit, no lake views
Fumarole Bay	Wizard Island (13)	1.8 miles	E – Rocky trail around Wizard Island's shoreline
Wizard Summit - 🥾	Wizard Island (13)	2.0 miles	M – Rocky trail to 90-ft deep crater atop Wizard Island
Boundary Springs	Hwy 230 Milepost 19 (14)	5.0 miles	M – Unmaintained trail to Rogue River headwaters

Difficulty Ratings: E = Easy, M = Moderate, S = Strenuous

Sunset from Watchman Peak

Backpacking

Comfortable cabins or developed camp-grounds aren't for everyone. Some visitors seek solitude and solace. For them, Crater Lake offers more than 100,000 acres of wilderness. All overnight backcountry users must obtain a **free backcountry permit** and follow a few simple regulations. Permits are available at both visitor centers and Park Headquarters Ranger Station. Pacific Crest Trail (PCT) thru-hikers do not require a permit, but should sign the trail registry upon entering the park. Backpackers must camp at least one mile from roads and facilities, out of sight of other campers and visitors, more than 100 feet away from any water source, and not within view of the lake. **Winter backcountry camping** adheres to the same rules, except you are free to camp at the lake's rim. Overnight parking is available for backpackers year-round at Rim Village and Park Headquarters.

Guided Tours

Xanterra Parks & Resorts (888.774.2728, craterlakelodges.com) offers **guided boat tours** of Crater Lake from late June through August (subject to weather). Standard Tours (105 minute) circle the lake while a ranger discusses its cultural and natural history, cost $40/adult, $27/child, and depart every hour from 9:30am–3:45pm. Wizard Island Tours (3-hour/6-hour) drop guests off at Wizard Island, cost $57/adult, $36/child), and depart at 9:45am and 12:45pm. Wizard Island Tour allows plenty of time to explore the island, fish, or do whatever else you can think of (provided it's socially acceptable and reasonably safe). Both tours require hiking 1.1-mile (one-way) Cleetwood Trail to the lake's shore. It's steep and strenuous, but short. Tours can be reserved online or by phone (888.774.2728). Tickets (subject to availability) can also be purchased at Cleetwood Cove ticketing kiosk. The kiosk opens at 8am and all guests must check-in here prior to departure.

You can let **Crater Lake Trolley** (541.882.1896, craterlaketrolley.net) handle the driving with their 2-hour ranger-guided tour of 33-mile Rim Drive. Tours are only offered during summer. Tickets cost $27/adult, $24/senior, and $17/child (5–13) and can be reserved over the phone or online. Pick up or purchase tickets at the ticket booth near the Community House at Rim Village. Trolleys help alleviate traffic congestion and reduce pollution thanks to modern engines that run on compressed natural gas.

Biking

Cyclists are allowed on all paved roads and on unpaved Grayback Drive. The 33-mile Rim Drive is the most popular bicycling destination. Bikers must be acutely aware of motorists, because the road twists, turns, climbs, and descends its way around the rim of Crater Lake. Strong winds are common, which make for not-so enjoyable biking. To avoid traffic and winds, try pedaling early in the morning.

Wizard Island

Fishing
Fish didn't inhabit the lake until 1888 when William Gladstone Steel stocked it with 6 species. Today, only rainbow trout and kokanee salmon thrive in the deep blue waters. Fishing licenses are not required and there are no catch limits. Anglers must use artificial lures and flies only. Cleetwood Cove Trail (page 558) is the only route to the lake's shoreline. Fishermen are also welcome to cast their lines from Wizard Island (accessed via boat tour).

Swimming
Swimming in the lake is not for everyone, but it's allowed at Cleetwood Cove and Wizard Island. Sure, it's fun to say you swam in Crater Lake, but to stay in the 55°F water for an extended amount of time is not the most enjoyable way to spend your trip.

Winter Activities
Winter can be a remarkable time to visit Crater Lake, but Rim Village is the only car-accessible location (weather permitting) where the lake is visible. Park Rangers offer **free snowshoe walks** every Saturday and Sunday at 1pm from late November through the end of April. Tours last two hours and snowshoes are provided. No experience is necessary. Call (541) 594-3100 to make reservations. **Cross-country skiing** is gaining popularity as well. Many visitors set out to complete the 33-mile trek around the rim. Marked but ungroomed trails are available at Mazama and Rim Village for skiers of all ability levels. North Entrance Road is open and groomed for **snowmobiles** up to the rim of Crater Lake. Snowmobiles are not allowed on Rim Drive. **Backcountry camping** (page 559) is allowed.

Ranger Programs
In addition to trolley and boat tours (page 559) and snowshoe treks, park rangers offer regularly scheduled talks, walks, and evening programs from early June to early September. All of these tours are free of charge. Current schedules of events are available at all visitor centers and online.

For Kids
Children of all ages are invited to participate in **Crater Lake's Junior Ranger Program**. Pick up a free activity booklet from either visitor center. Explore the park, completing activities as you go, return the book to a park ranger at one of the visitor centers, and your child will receive a Junior Ranger badge. An alternative option is to go to Rim Visitor Center between 1:30–4:30pm (late June–early September). At this time your child can join a ranger-led activity (geared for ages 6–12) to earn a Junior Ranger patch.

Flora & Fauna
Crater Lake is home to 680 species of plants, 74 species of mammals, 26 species of reptiles and amphibians, and 158 species of birds. Threatened or endangered species include lynx, northern spotted owl, bull trout, and tailed frog. Elk, deer, and bear are often seen at dawn or dusk feeding in meadows. Hairy woodpeckers, bald eagles, and the American kestrel are frequently spotted during summer.

Pets
Pets are allowed in the park, but must be kept on a leash no more than six feet in length at all times. They are essentially allowed anywhere a car can go, including roadsides, parking areas, picnic areas, and developed campgrounds. Pets are not allowed in the backcountry, on trails, or in public buildings (except service animals).

Accessibility

Many of the park's facilities and trails are accessible to individuals with mobility impairments. The store, campground, and restaurant at Mazama Village are accessible, as is Godfrey Glen Trail and the upper section of Annie Creek Canyon Trail. Facilities at Park Headquarters and Rim Village are fully accessible. Trolley tours (page 559) also accommodate wheelchair users.

Weather

It's important to consider the weather when planning a trip to Crater Lake. Most years the rim is buried beneath several feet of snow from October until June. Hwy 62 and the access road to Rim Village are plowed during winter, but Rim Drive is closed. Average daytime highs reach into the upper 60s°F during summer. In the evenings temperatures cool off quickly, often falling below freezing. Summer is typically dry and sunny, but visitors should come prepared for afternoon thunderstorms and high winds. The first major snowfall usually occurs by mid-October. Crater Lake is magnificent when the rim is covered in snow; the only real problem is there's just so much of it. In an average winter more than 500 inches of snow falls, making Crater Lake one of the snowiest regions of the Pacific Northwest. Winter temperatures are much less variable than the summer. Average highs are right around freezing and average lows are about 20°F.

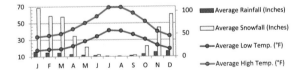

Vacation Planner

Crater Lake is one of our all-time favorite places. It isn't big. With a 33-mile road around the rim of the crater and just 90 miles of trails, you can do a lot in one day (compared to larger parks like Yellowstone and Death Valley). But what it has is spectacular. **Camping** and **lodging** (page 558) are available in the park, but campsites generally fill by noon in July and August, and lodging can be booked well in advance. Nearby dining, grocery stores, lodging, festivals, and attractions are listed on pages 562–565

Wizard Island in winter

Best of Crater Lake

Attraction: Crater Lake
  Runner-up: Rim Drive
  2nd Runner-up: Wizard Island
Hike: Watchman Peak
  Runner-up: Mount Scott

Day 1: Arriving at the **South Entrance**, stop at **Steel Information Center** before continuing up to Rim Drive. If you enter from the north, drive directly to Rim Drive. There's nothing that can really prepare you for your first sight of Crater Lake. Just have your camera close by, your first reflex will be to grab it and start snapping pictures, paparazzi-style. Stop and capture the moment, then continue on to Rim Visitor Center. Ask your questions, watch the short video, and pick up a brochure and newspaper if you didn't upon entry. Drive all 33 miles of Rim Drive (at least 2 hours without hiking). You'll find the views of Crater Lake are better from the west (closer to Wizard Island). It's a good practice to save the best for last, but in this case circle the lake clockwise, because it's easier to turn right into the overlook parking areas. **Discovery Point** and **Watchman Overlook** (via Watchman Trail) are recommended stops. If you want to see the water from up close, hike down to its shore via **Cleetwood Trail**. Continuing around the lake, **Cloudcap Overlook** is worth a stop. Take the nearby trail to the top of **Mount Scott**. Well-conditioned hikers can complete the trek in less than 2 hours. If you're short on time, skip Pinnacles and Sun Notch. For an alternative to the Mount Scott hike, return to Rim Village and hike to **Garfield Peak**. It's a great place to absorb a few last impressions of such indescribable beauty.

Dining

Lassen Volcanic Area

Red Onion Grill • (530) 258-1800
303 Peninsula Dr, Lake Almanor
redoniongrill.com • Entrée: $23–26

Kopper Kettle Café • (530) 258-2698
243 Main St, Chester

Coffee Station • (530) 258-4112
192 Main St, Chester

Ranch House • (530) 258-4226
669 Main St, Chester

Luciano's Cucina di Pasta • (530) 596-4133
449 Peninsula Dr, Lake Almanor

J J's Café • (530) 335-7225
13385 CA-89, Old Station

Tantardino's • (530) 596-3902
401 Ponderosa Circle, Westwood

Art's Outpost • (530) 335-2835
37392 CA-299 E, Burney

The Rex Club • (530) 335-4184
37143 CA-299 E, Burney
burneysrexclub.com • Entrée: $11–30

Dragon Palace • (530) 335-3288
37345 CA-299 E, Burney

Pacific Coast Area

Brick & Fire • (707) 268-8959
1630 F St, Eureka • brickandfirebistro.com

Sea Grill • (707) 443-7187
316 E St, Eureka

Restaurant 301 • (800) 404-1390
301 L St, Eureka
carterhouse.com • Entrée: $22–29

Cookhouse Samoa • (707) 442-1659
908 Vance Ave, Samoa • samoacookhouse.net

A A Bar & Grill • (707) 443-1632
929 4th St, Eureka

Lost Coast Brewery & Café • (707) 445-4480
617 4th St, Eureka • lostcoast.com • Entrée: $11–18

Chalet House of Omelettes
1935 5th St, Eureka • (707) 442-0333

Pachanga Mexicana • (707) 442-2587
1802 5th St, Eureka

Café Nooner • (707) 443-4663
409 Opera Alley, Eureka

Bless My Soul Café • (707) 443-1090
29 Fifth St, Eureka
blessmysoulcafe.com • Entrée: $14–24

Old Town Coffee & Chocolates
211 F St, Eureka • (707) 445-8600
oldtowncoffeeeureka.com

Café Brio • (707) 822-5922
791 G St, Arcata • briobaking.com

Kebab Café • (707) 826-2121
5000 Valley West Blvd, # 19, Arcata

Wildflower Café & Bakery • (707) 822-0360
1604 G St, Arcata
wildflowercafebakery.com • Entrée: $7–11

Los Bagels Co • losbagels.com
1061 I St, Arcata • (707) 822-3150
1 Harpst Street, Arcata • (707) 826-5308
403 2nd Street, Eureka • (707) 442-8525

Abruzzi • (707) 826-2377
780 7th St, Arcata
abruzziarcata.com • Entrée: $16–37

Tomo Japanese Restaurant • (707) 822-1414
708 9th St, Arcata
tomoarcata.com • Entrée: $18–24

Big Blue Café • (707) 826-7578
846 G St, Arcata

Toni's 24 Hour Restaurant • (707) 822-0091
1901 Heindon Rd, Arcata

Japhy's Soup & Noodles • (707) 826-2594
1563 G St, Arcata • japhys.com • Soups: $5.50–8

Folie Douce • (707) 822-1042
1551 G St, Arcata
foliedoucearcata.com • Entrée: $28–37

Live From New York Pizza • (707) 822-6199
670 9th St, # 102, Arcata

Renata's Creperie • (707) 825-8783
1030 G St, Arcata

Good Harvest Café • (707) 465-6028
575 US-101, Crescent City

Chart Room Restaurant • (707) 464-5993
130 Anchor Way, Crescent City

Wing Wah Restaurant • (707) 465-3935
383 M St, Crescent City

Perlita's Authentic Mexican • (707) 465-6770
297 US-101 S, Crescent City

Fisherman's Restaurant • (707) 465-3474
700 US-101 S, Crescent City

Hiouchi Café • (707) 458-3445
2095 US-199, Crescent City

CC Diner & Ice Cream • (707) 465-5858
1319 Northcrest Dr, Crescent City

Crater Lake/Southwest Oregon

Art Alley Grille • (541) 469-0800
515 Chetco Ave, Brookings

Mattie's Pancake & Omelette • (541) 469-7211
15975 US-101 S, Brookings

Pancho's Restaurante • (541) 469-6531
1136 Chetco Ave, Brookings

Kitanishi Café • (541) 469-7864
632 Hemlock St, Brookings

Beckie's Café • (541) 560-3563
56484 OR-62, Prospect • unioncreekoregon.com

Gorge Restaurant • (541) 560-3774
2651 Mill Creek Dr, Prospect

Trophy Room & Café • (541) 560-3641
311 Mill Creek Dr, Prospect

Prospect Pizza • (541) 560-4000
51 Mill Creek Dr, Prospect

Butte Falls Café • (541) 865-7707
443 Broad St, Butte Falls

Pho Hong • (541) 850-9441
3620 Washburn Way, Klamath Falls

Thai Orchid Café • (541) 273-0707
900 Main St, # D, Klamath Falls

Nibbley's Café • (541) 883-2314
2424 Washburn Way, Klamath Falls
nibbleys.com • Entrée: $13–25

Roosters Steak & Chop House
205 Main St, Klamath Falls • (541) 850-8414

Hidalgos Mexican Restaurant
430 Main St, Klamath Falls • (541) 850-8317

Casey's Restaurant • (541) 882-9676
4706 S 6th St, Klamath Falls

Grocery Stores

Lassen Volcanic Area

Holiday Quality Foods • (530) 258-2122
271 Main St, Chester

Mineral Grocery
18968 Husky Way, Mineral

Safeway • (530) 335-3212
37264 Main St, Burney

Walmart • (530) 251-2000
2900 Main St, Susanville

Pacific Coast Area

Safeway • (707) 465-3353
475 M St, Crescent City

Grocery Outlet • (707) 464-3131
1124 3rd St, Crescent City

Fred Meyer • (541) 469-1610
325 5th St, Brookings

Walmart • (707) 464-1198
900 E Washington Blvd, Crescent City

Crater Lake/Southwest Oregon

Walmart Supercenter • (541) 885-6890
3600 Washburn Way, Klamath Falls

Safeway • (541) 273-5502
211 N Eighth St, Klamath Falls

Fred Meyer • (541) 884-1086
2655 Shasta Way, Klamath Falls

Safeway • (541) 608-3680
1003 Medford Shopping Centre, Medford

Safeway • (541) 774-4340
3169 Crater Lake Hwy, Medford

Walmart • (541) 227-5396
3615 Crater Lake Hwy, Medford

Fred Meyer • (541) 857-4650
1301 Center Dr, Medford

Lodging

Lassen Volcanic Area
Drakesbad Guest Ranch • (866) 999-0914
Chester Warner Valley Rd, Chester
drakesbad.com • *In-Park Lodging*
Rates: $199–219/person/night

Antlers Motel • (530) 258-2722
268 Main St, Chester
antlersmotel.com • Rates: $80

Cedar Lodge • (530) 258-2904
1487 County Rd 324, Chester
cedarlodgefun.com • Rates: $59–75

Bidwell House • (530) 258-3338
1 Main St, Chester
bidwellhouse.com • Rates: $80–285

Cinnamon Teal Inn • (530) 258-3993
227 Feather River Dr, Chester
cinnamontealinn.net • Rates: $140–270

Rim Rock Ranch • (530) 335-7114
13275 CA-89, Old Station
rimrockcabins.com • Rates: $95–135

Hat Creek Resort & RV Park • (530) 335-7121
12533 CA-44/89, Old Station
hatcreekresortrv.com • Rates: $54–209

Burney Motel • (530) 335-4500
37448 Main St, Burney
theburneymotel.com • Rates: $140+

Green Gables Motel • (530) 335-2264
37371 CA-299 E, Burney
greengablesmotel.com • $99+

Shasta Pines Motel & Suites • (530) 335-2201
37386 CA-299 E, Burney
shastapinesmotel.com • Rates: $62–89

McCloud Hotel • (530) 964-2822
408 Main St, McCloud
mccloudhotel.com • Rates: $135–199

McCloud Mercantile Hotel • (530) 964-2330
241 Main St, McCloud
mccloudmercantile.com • Rates: $129–250

McCloud River Inn • (530) 964-2130
325 Lawndale Court, McCloud
riverinn.com • Rates: $99–199

Sleepy Hollow Lodge • (530) 335-2285
36898 CA-299 E, Burney

Pacific Coast Area
Town House Motel • (707) 443-4536
933 4th St, Eureka
eurekatownhousemotel.com

Bayview Motel • (707) 442-1673
2844 Fairfield St, Eureka
bayviewmotel.com • Rates: $108–201

Carter House Inns • (707) 444-8062
301 L St, Eureka
carterhouse.com • Rates: $189–595

Eureka Inn • (707) 497-6093
518 7th St, Eureka
eurekainn.com • Rates: $120+

Eagle House Victorian Inn • (707) 444-3344
139 2nd St, Eureka
eaglehouseinn.com • Rates: $115–225

Abigail's Elegant Victorian Mansion
1406 C St, Eureka • (707) 444-3144
eureka-california.com • Rates: $135–145

Rose Court Cottage • (707) 822-0935
814 13th St, Arcata
rosecourtcottage.com • Rates: $149+

Lady Anne Victorian Inn • (707) 822-2797
902 14th St, Arcata
ladyanneinn.com • Rates: $115–200

Lighthouse Inn • (877) 464-3993
681 US-101 S, Crescent City
lighthouseinncrescentcity.com • Rates: $89–145

Hiouchi Motel • (707) 458-3041
2097 US-199, Crescent City

Curly Redwood Lodge • (707) 464-2137
701 US-101 S, Crescent City
curlyredwoodlodge.com • Rates: $71–105

Crescent Beach Motel • (707) 464-5436
1455 US-101 S, Crescent City
crescentbeachmotel.com • Rates: $85–124

Anna Wulf House B&B • (707) 951-0683
622 J St, Crescent City
annawulfhouse.com • Rates: $100–150

Crater Lake/Southwest Oregon
Ocean Suites Motel • (541) 469-4004
16045 Lower Harbor Rd, Brookings
oceansuitesmotel.com • Rates: $89–109

Wild Rivers Motorlodge • (541) 469-5361
437 Chetco Ave, Brookings
wildriversmotorlodge.com • Rates: $79–106

South Coast Inn • (541) 469-5557
516 Redwood St, Brookings
southcoastinn.com

The Chetco River Inn • (707) 496-9509
21202 High Prairie Rd, Brookings
thechetcoriverinn.com • Rates: $140–550

Out'n'About Treehouse Treesort
Take the kids or relive your youth by spending a night in the trees • horseback rides, tree climbing, rafting, camping, hiking, and zip-lining available
300 Page Creek Rd, Cave Junction
treehouses.com • (541) 592-2208 • Rates: $130–310

The Wilson Cottages • (541) 381-2209
57997 OR-62, Fort Klamath
thewilsoncottages.com • Rates: $75–110

Aspen Inn • (541) 381-2321
52250 OR-62, Fort Klamath • theaspeninn.com

Crater Lake B&B • (866) 517-9560
52395 Weed Rd, Fort Klamath
craterlakebandb.com

Jo's Motel/Campground • (541) 381-2234
RV hookups available ($25/2 guests)
52851 OR-62, Fort Klamath
josmotel.com • Rates: $90–150

Cimarron Inn • (541) 882-4601
3060 S 6th St, Klamath Falls
cimarroninnklamathfalls.com • Rates: $75–129

Running Y Resort • (541) 850-5500
5500 Running Y Rd, Klamath Falls
runningy.com • Rates: $107–189

Lake of the Woods Resort • (541) 949-8300
950 Harriman Route, Klamath Falls
lakeofthewoodsresort.com • $270–630 (2 nights)

Crystal Wood Lodge • (541) 381-2322
38625 Westside Rd, Klamath Falls • $95–150
craterlakelodgingatcrystalwoodlodge.com

Many chain restaurants and hotels can be found nearby in Chico, Eureka, Arcata, and Crescent City, CA; and Brookings, Medford, Ashland, Klamath Falls, OR; as well as along I-5.

Festivals
Winter Wings Festival • February
Klamath Falls, OR • winterwingsfest.org

Shakespeare Festival • February–July
Ashland • osfashland.org

Redwood Coast Jazz Festival • March
Eureka, CA • rcmfest.org

Independent Film Festival • April
Ashland • ashlandfilm.org

Apple Jam Music Festival • May
Williams, OR • applejam.webs.com

Britt Festival Grounds • Summer Concerts
Jacksonville, OR • brittfest.org\

Jazz Festival • October
Medford, OR • somusicfest.org

Attractions
Lassen Volcanic Area
Lassen National Forest • (530) 336-5521
43225 CA-299 E, Fall River Mills

☝**Subway Cave Lava Tubes**
*Located 0.25 mile north of the junction of CA-44
and CA-89 across from Cave Campground*
Lassen National Forest, Old Station, CA 96071

McArthur-Burney Falls Memorial State Park
Burney • (530) 335-2777 • parks.ca.gov

Westwood Museum • (530) 256-2233
311 Ash St, Westwood

Mt Burney Theatre • (530) 335-2605
37022 CA-299 E, Burney
mtburneytheatre.com • Tickets: $8.50/adult

Sierra Theatre • (530) 257-7469
819 Main St, Susanville • Tickets: $8/adult
sierratheatreanduptowncinemas.com

National Yo-Yo Museum
320 Broadway, Chico • nationalyoyo.org

Lava Beds National Monument
Tulelake • (530) 667-8113
nps.gov/labe • Entrance Fee: $15/vehicle

Castle Crags State Park • (530) 235-2684
Sacramento Canyon • parks.ca.gov

Gold Nugget Museum • (530) 872-8722
502 Pearson Rd, Paradise • goldnuggetmuseum.com

Olive Pit • (530) 824-4667
A unique stop with olive tasting bar and deli
2156 Solano St, Corning • olivepit.com

Plumas National Forest • (530) 284-7126
128 Hot Springs Rd, Greenville

Kelly Griggs House Museum • (530) 527-1129
311 Washington St, Red Bluff

Sierra Nevada Brewery • (530) 899-4776
1075 E 20th St, Chico
sierranevada.com • Free Tours

Pacific Coast Area
☝**North Coast Adv. Centers** • (800) 808-2856
*Canopy Tours, Ropes Courses, Training & Cer-
tificates, and Outdoor Programs*
1065 K St, Suite C, Arcata

Arcata Community Forest • Arcata

Sequoia Park Zoo • (707) 441-4263
3414 W St, Eureka
sequoiaparkzoo.net • Admission: $5/adult

Blue Ox Mill Works & Hist. • (707) 444-3437
1 X St, Eureka
blueoxmill.com • Admission: $10/adult

Clarke Hist. Museum • (707) 443-1947
240 E St, Eureka • clarkemuseum.org

Fort Humboldt State Hist. Park • (707) 445-6547
3431 Fort Ave, Eureka • parks.ca.gov

The Spa at Personal Choice • (707) 445-2041
130 G St, Eureka • thespaatpersonalchoice.com

Carson Mansion
143 M St, Eureka • ingomar.org

☝**Humboldt Redwoods State Parks**
17119 Ave of the Giants, Weott
humboldtredwoods.org • (707) 946-2263
Entrance Fee: $8/vehicle • Camping: $35/night

One Log House Espresso • (707) 247-3717
705 US-101, Garberville • oneloghouse.com

Confusion Hill Gravity House
75001 US-101 N, Piercy • (707) 925-6456
confusionhill.com • Admission: $5/adult

Del Norte County Museum • (707) 464-3922
577 H St, Crescent City
delnortehistory.org • Free

Ocean World • (707) 464-4900
304 US-101 S, Crescent City
oceanworldonline.com • Tours: $12.95/adult

Tolowa Dunes State Park • (707) 465-7335
1375 Elk Valley Rd, Crescent City
parks.ca.gov

Battery Point Lighthouse • (707) 464-3089
577 H St, Crescent City

Crescent City Cinemas • (707) 570-8438
375 M St, Crescent City

Humboldt Lagoon State Park
Trinidad • (707) 677-3570

Golden Bear Fishing Charters • (707) 951-0119
Citizens Dock Rd, D Dock, Crescent City

Castle Rock National Wildlife Refuge
Crescent City

Trees of Mystery • (707) 482-2251
15500 US-101 N, Klamath
treesofmystery.net • Admission: $15/adult

Lucky 7 Casino • (707) 487-7777
350 N Indian Rd, Smith River • lucky7casino.com

Elk Valley Casino • (707) 464-1020
2500 Howland Hill Rd, Crescent City
elkvalleycasino.com

Lighthouse Repertory Theatre
PO Box 171, Crescent City • (707) 465-3740
lighthouserepertorytheatre.org

Klamath River Jet Boat Tours • (707) 482-7775
17635 US-101 South, Klamath
jetboattours.com • Tours: $45/adult

FunBus Tours • (707) 482-1030
1661 W Klamath Beach Rd, Klamath
funbustours.com

Crater Lake/Southwest Oregon
Samuel H Boardman State Park
US-101, Brookings • oregonstateparks.org

Redwood Cinema • (541) 412-7575
621 Chetco Ave, Brookings
redwood-cinema.com • Tickets: $8.50/adult

☝**Harris Beach State Park** • (800) 452-5687
1655 US-101 N, Brookings
oregonstateparks.org • Camping: $20–30/night

☝**Great Cats World Park** • (541) 592-2957
27919 Redwood Hwy, Cave Junction
greatcatsworldpark.com • Admission: $14/adult

Oregon Caves Nat'l Mon. • (541) 592-2100
19000 Caves Hwy, Cave Junction
nps.gov/orca • Cave Tours: $10/adult

Collier Logging Museum • (541) 783-2471
46000 US-97 N, Chiloquin
collierloggingmuseum.org

Kla-Mo-Ya Casino • (541) 783-7529
34333 US-97 N, Chiloquin
klamoyacasino.com

Klamath Marsh NWR • (541) 783-3380
13750 Silver Lake Rd, Chiloquin
fws.gov/refuge/klamath_marsh

Pelican Cinemas • (541) 884-5000
2626 Biehn St, Klamath Falls • catheatres.com

Ross Ragland Theater • (541) 884-0651
218 N 7th St, Klamath Falls • rrtheater.org

Movies 6 • (541) 826-7308 • cinemark.com
7501 Crater Lake Hwy, White City

Varsity Theatre • (541) 488-0619
166 E Main St, Ashland • catheatres.com

Craterian Ginger Rogers Theater
23 S Central Ave, Medford
craterian.org • (541) 779-3000

(Rogue River) Rafting, hiking, and fishing outfitters, rental and shuttle services

Rogue Wilderness Adventures
Rogue River: $95 (full-day), $79 (half-day)
wildrogue.com • (541) 479-9554

Rogue River Outfitters • (888) 767-3144
3 day/2 night Rogue River rafting trips
nwriveroutfitters.com

Noah's River Adventures • (541) 201-0912
Upper Klamath Whitewater: $169 (full-day)
noahsrafting.com

Orange Torpedo Rogue River Rafting Trips
Widest selection of rivers and trips
Rogue River: $95 (full-day), $84 (half-day)
orangetorpedo.com • (541) 479-5061

Kokopelli River Guides • (541) 201-7694
Rafting McKenzie ($75–95), Deschutes ($105–555), and North Umpqua ($125–379) Rivers
kokopelliriverguides.com

Momentum River Expeditions • (541) 488-2525
Rogue River (Class II-III): $89 (half-day), Upper Klamath (Class IV+): $169 (full-day)
momentumriverexpeditions.com

Ouzel Outfitters • (800) 788-7238
Rogue River: $95 (full-day), $79 (half-day)
oregonrafting.com

Echo River Trips • (800) 652-3246
Best selection of multi-day rafting trips with unique tours like "Yoga and Rafting," "Brews and Views," and "Bluegrass on Whitewater"
echotrips.com

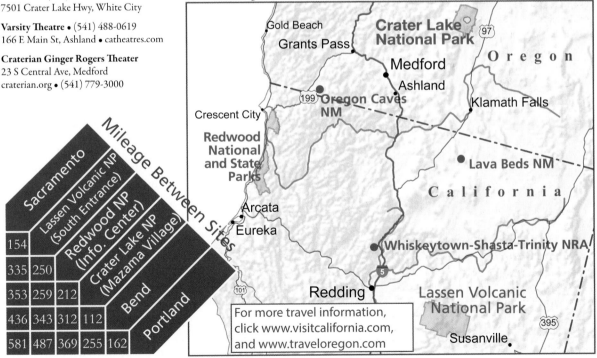

Mileage Between Sites					
Sacramento					
154	Lassen Volcanic NP (South Entrance)				
335	250	Redwood NP (Info. Center)			
353	259	212	Crater Lake NP (Mazama Village)		
436	343	312	112	Bend	
581	487	369	255	162	Portland

For more travel information, click www.visitcalifornia.com, and www.traveloregon.com

View from Sunrise Nature Trail

Mount Rainier

55210 238th Avenue East
Ashford, WA 98304
Phone: (360) 569-2211
Website: nps.gov/mora

Established: March 2, 1899
Size: 235,625 Acres
Annual Visitors: 1.2 Million
Peak Season: Summer

Activities: Hiking, Backpacking,
Camping, Mountain Climbing,
Horseback Riding, Biking, Fishing,
Snowshoeing, and Skiing

Campgrounds: Cougar Rock*,
Ohanapecosh*, White River, Ipsut
Creek (free), Mowich Lake (free)
Fee: $20/night
Backcountry Camping: Permitted
with a Backcountry Use Permit

Park Hours: All day, every day
Entrance Fee: $25/vehicle,
$10/individual (foot, bike, etc.)

*Reserve at recreation.gov or (877)
444-6777

Mount Rainier, the 14,410-foot volcano, towers above its surroundings and greets visitors from all directions more than 100 miles before entering the park boundary. Cowlitz, Nisqually, Puyallup, and Yakima tribes called the mountain Tahoma or "the Big Mountain where the waters begin." Much more than water begins here. Natives began vision-quests at this location. Today's guests' search for respite begins and ends at majestic Mount Rainier. Nearly 1.5 million visitors admire these mountain views each year, and some 10,000 climbers attempt to trek to its summit, where they are able to look down on 26 glaciers covering its upper reaches and to the Pacific Northwest beyond.

The snow-capped mountain's dramatic presence caught the attention of several groups and soon commercial interests and conservationists were mired in a contentious debate over the best way to utilize the area. Intending to settle the dispute, federal government officials created the Pacific Forest Reserve in 1893, encompassing the mountain. Gifford Pinchot, head of the United States Forest Service, believed in "conservation through use," treating the nation's forests like a crop to be maintained and used. John Muir, a beloved naturalist who had successfully advocated for preservation of Yosemite Valley, formed a kinship with Mount Rainier in 1888 when he joined a group that completed the mountain's 5th recorded ascent. He wrote in a letter to his wife that he had absolutely no intention of climbing the mountain, but when five others showed interest in the idea he couldn't help but tag along. Muir vehemently opposed the "conservation through use" idea. Not a single tree would fall at the hands of an ax or river be impeded by a dam if he had his way. Preservation, plain and simple, was his goal. These sublime works of nature were beyond the scope of anything man could ever make in terms of beauty and grandeur. They needed to be preserved and protected for the enjoyment of all, not looted and plundered for the benefit of private interests. Support from influential bodies with concerns of their own helped galvanize the conservationist movement. The National Geographic Society wished to study volcanism and glaciology in the area. The Northern Pacific Railroad was on board because a park could draw more passenger service on their trains—a tried and tested method already yielding substantial benefits for Northern Pacific and Southern Pacific Railroads with the creation of Yellowstone (page 218) and Yosemite (page 514) National Parks, respectively. The Sierra Club and commercial leaders in Tacoma and Seattle joined the cause, supporting what would become a long and arduous battle. Over the course of five years of bitter debate and six attempts, a bill was finally passed with two provisions: the government needed assurances that no park land was suitable for farming or mining and that no government appropriations were required for its management and procurement. The provisions were met, and on March 2, 1899 Mount Rainier became the fifth national park and first to be created from a national forest.

Park establishment and construction of a road to Paradise in 1911 ushered in a new era of tourism. President William Howard Taft's touring car was the first vehicle to christen the road in very unique fashion: muddy conditions resulted in his car being pulled through the upper portion by a team of mules. Six years later the National Park Service was established and trails, facilities, roads, and campgrounds were developed in earnest, enhancing the overall visitor experience. Mountain climbers could experience summiting Rainier much like John Muir did, and now thousands of climbers make the trek each year. Today's visitors realize what Muir and Native Americans knew: Mount Rainier is more than a pleasure ground; it's a sacred place in need of preservation and protection.

When to Go

Mount Rainier National Park is open all year. Visitation peaks in July and August when the weather is best, most trails are free of snowpack, and wildflowers are in full bloom. Traffic can create considerable frustration during summer months and winter weekends. Traveling midweek or delaying your vacation until September or early October is a good way to avoid the crowds.

Longmire Museum (360.569.6575) is open all year, 9am–5pm. **Jackson Visitor Center** (360.569.6571), located in Paradise, is open, May–mid-October, 10am–6pm; and mid-October–May (weekends only), 10am–5pm. **Ohanapecosh Visitor Center** (360.569.6581) is open late May–October, 9am–5pm. Sunrise Visitor Center (360.569.2425) is open July–early September, 10am–6pm. **Longmire** (360.569.6650) and **White River** (360.569.6670) **Wilderness Information Centers** (WIC) are open late May–mid-October, 7:30am–5pm. **Paradise Climbing WIC** (Guide House) (360.569.6641) is open mid-May–September, 7am–12pm and 12:30pm–4:30pm. **Carbon River Ranger Station** (360.829.9639) is open intermittently. Call (360) 569-2211 for park road and facility status. Operating hours are extended in summer and shortened in winter.

Transportation & Airports

The free **Paradise Shuttle** (page 570) ferries visitors between Longmire and Paradise on weekends, mid-June–early September. (Note that the shuttle did not run in 2015–2016 due to lack of funding.) The closest large airports are Seattle–Tacoma International (SEA) and Portland International (PDX).

Directions

The park's eastern half is not accessible during winter. Carbon River and Nisqually Entrances on the west side are open all year. However, unexpected road closures can occur at any time. Always check the park's website for current road status prior to your trip. Directions to Paradise, the most popular region, are provided below.

Nisqually Entrance (Longmire/Paradise):

From Seattle (104 miles), take I-5 S to WA-512 E (Exit 127) to WA-7 S. Take WA-7 to WA-706, which leads into the park.

From Portland (155 miles), take I-5 N to US-12 E (Exit 68). Take US-12 to WA-7 N. Turn right at WA-706, which leads into the park.

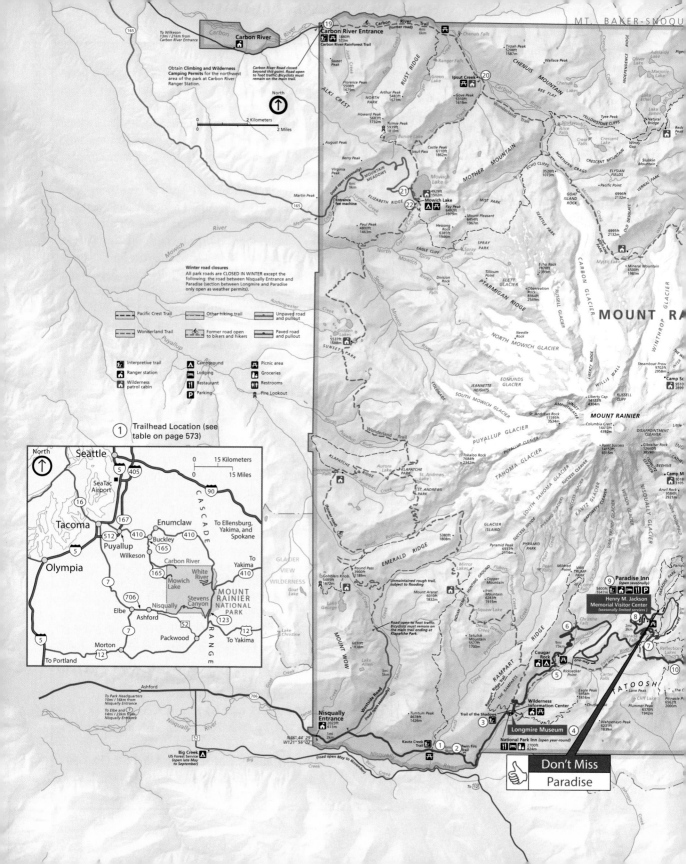

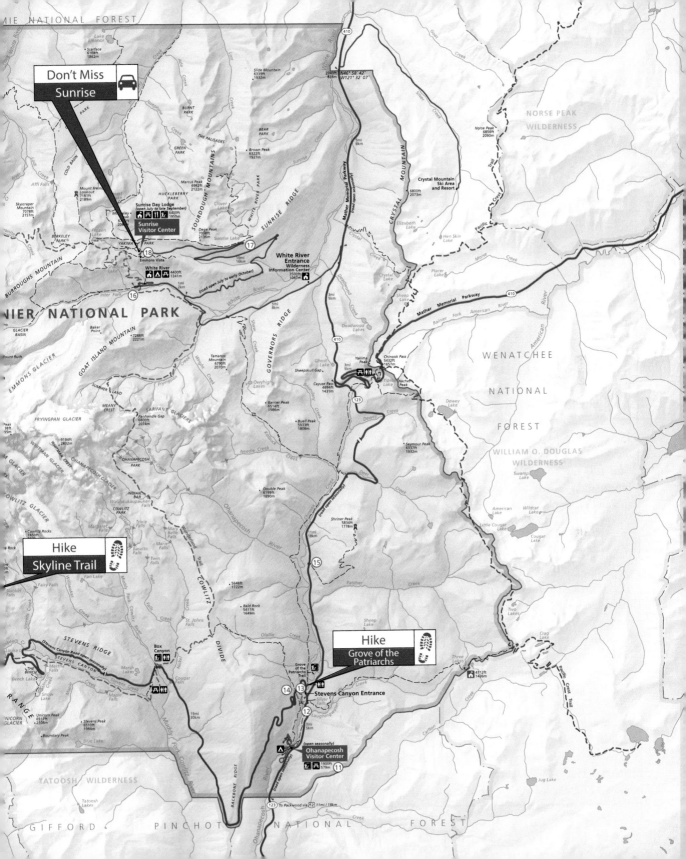

Don't Miss
Sunrise

Hike
Skyline Trail

Hike
Grove of the Patriarchs

MIE NATIONAL FOREST

NORSE PEAK
WILDERNESS

2749m N46° 58' 42"
838m W121° 32' 07"

Norse Peak
6858ft
2090m

Crystal Mountain
Ski Area
and Resort
6800ft
2073m

Hen Skin
Lake

Elizabeth
Lake

Placer
Lake

Crystal
Lake

Sheep
Lake

Mather Memorial Parkway

WENATCHEE

NATIONAL

FOREST

WILLIAM O. DOUGLAS
WILDERNESS

Swamp
Lake

American
Lake

Wildcat
Lake

Little Cougar
Lake

Cougar
Lake

Two
Lakes

Crag
Lake

Three
Lakes

4312ft
1426m

Sunrise Day Lodge
(open July to late September)
6400ft
1950m

Sunrise
Visitor Center

White River Park

Huckleberry
Park

Sourdough Mountains

Sunrise Ridge

White River
Entrance
Wilderness
Information Center
3500ft
1067m

White River
4400ft
1341m

Emmons Vista

Dege Peak
7006ft
2136m

Sunrise Lakes

Governors Ridge

Mather Memorial Parkway

Ghost
Lake

Sheepskull Gap

Owyhigh
Lakes

Deadwood
Lakes

Yakima
Peak

Chinook Pass
5432ft
1657m

Cayuse Pass
4694ft
1431m

Dewey
Lake

Nachez
Peak

Seymour Peak
6337ft
1932m

Barrier Peak
6514ft
1986m

Buell Peak
5933ft
1808m

RANIER NATIONAL PARK

GOAT ISLAND MOUNTAIN

Baker
Point
7288ft
2221m

Tamanos
Mountain
6790ft
2070m

Wyeth Creek

Panhandle Gap
6800ft
2074m

Double Peak
6199ft
1890m

Shriner Peak
5834ft
1778m

(road open seasonally)

Ohanapecosh Park

INDIAN
BAR

Wauhaukaupauken
Falls

Cowlitz Divide

Ohanapecosh River

Chinook Creek

Panther Creek

Sheep Creek

Olallie Creek

Stevens Ridge

Box
Canyon

Grove of the
Patriarchs Trail

Stevens Canyon Entrance

Silver
Falls

Three
Lakes

Grove of the
Patriarchs

Ohanapecosh Visitor Center
1900ft
579m

To Packwood via 11mi / 18km

TATOOSH WILDERNESS

GIFFORD   PINCHOT   NATIONAL   FOREST

Edith Creek
Skyline Trail

Best of Mount Rainier

Region: Paradise
   Runner-up: Sunrise

Hike: Skyline Loop
   Runner-up: Burrough Mountain
   2nd Runner-up: Comet Falls

Regions
Mount Rainier National Park is essentially broken into five road accessible regions.

Longmire (All Year) is located in the SW corner of the park, 7 miles east of Nisqually Entrance. Here you'll find **Longmire Museum**, **National Park Inn**, Trail of the Shadows (popular), and access to the 93-mile Wonderland Trail that circles the mountain. There's a Wilderness Information Center where you can plan a backcountry trip and pick up a permit. Cougar Rock Campground is about 2 miles beyond Longmire.

Paradise (All Year), the most popular destination, is located 12 miles east of Longmire. It receives almost 70% of all visitors. The region's wildflowers, glaciers, and dramatic mountain vistas provide some of the best scenery the Pacific Northwest has to offer. **Henry M. Jackson Memorial Visitor Center** provides the perfect venue to begin a trip to Mount Rainier with its exhibits and introductory film. Accommodations are available at **Paradise Inn. Guide House** is your spot for planning overnight hikes and climbs. Even though Paradise receives an average of 680 inches of snow per year, it is also the premier winter destination. Some sources have called it "the snowiest place on earth." Individuals familiar with the winter of '71–'72 wouldn't argue with them; that year 1,122 inches of snow were recorded here.

Ohanapecosh (June–October) is located 42 miles east of Nisqually Entrance and 3 miles north of the park boundary on WA-123. Here you'll find dense old-growth forests of Douglas fir, western red cedar, and western hemlock. Camping and a visitor center are available.

Sunrise and White River (June/July–October) are located 60 miles NE of Nisqually Entrance. Sunrise is the highest point in the park that can be reached by vehicle and the second most popular destination. Excellent trails, spectacular wildflowers, White River Campground, **Sunrise Visitor Center**, and **Sunrise Day Lodge** are all at your disposal at the foot of mighty Rainier.

Carbon River and Mowich Lake (All Year) are in the park's northwest corner. Cars can travel as far as **Carbon River Ranger Station**. Unpaved and heavily washboarded Mowich Lake Road (mid-July–mid-October) leads to Mowich Lake Campground (walk-in sites) and a few exceptional trailheads.

Park Shuttle
Paradise Shuttle didn't run in 2015–'16 due to lack of funding, but they're looking to bring it back. The Upper Paradise lot is intended for short-term parking and it usually fills before noon on weekends. The Lower Paradise lot is intended for long-term parking. The shuttle provides free transportation between Longmire and Paradise, reducing congestion and pollution. Stops are also made at Cougar Rock Campground, Narada Falls (when traveling to Paradise), and Comet Falls (when traveling from Paradise). Shuttles stop at each scheduled location every 45 minutes on Fridays and every 15–25 minutes on Saturdays and Sundays from mid-June through early September (weekends only!). Service begins at Longmire at 10am, and the last bus leaves Paradise at 7pm.

Additional free shuttle service between Ashford (outside the park, entrance fee still applies) and Longmire is available Saturdays and Sundays. Buses depart every 25 minutes beginning at 9:15am until 10:30am, and then every 75 minutes beginning at 11:30am. The last shuttle leaves Ashford at 4:30pm, with the final bus leaving Longmire by 7:50pm.

Camping

Choosing where to camp boils down to deciding which section(s) of the park you want to visit. The most popular developed campground is **Cougar Rock** at Longmire/Paradise. **Ohanapecosh**, the largest campground, is located in the park's southeast corner. Sites at these two locations can be reserved up to six months in advance by calling (877) 444-6777 or clicking recreation.gov. Reservations are a good idea, especially from late June through early September, and weekends and holidays. **White River Campground**, in the Sunrise/White River Region, is an excellent alternative. All 112 sites are available on a first-come, first-served basis. The campground fills quite frequently, but usually not until noon. A more isolated experience is available at **Mowich Lake Campground** in the park's northwest corner. It offers a more primitive experience with walk-in, tent-only sites, located at the end of (rough and unpaved) Mowich Lake Road. Hookups and hot water are not available at any campground. Coin-operated **showers** are available at Jackson Visitor Center in Paradise.

Lodging

Don't want to rough it? No problem. **National Park Inn** and **Paradise Inn** are located at Longmire and Paradise, respectively. The locations are unbeatable and rates are reasonable (all things considered). A single room at either facility with very basic accommodations and a shared bath will set you back about $120/night. A two-room unit with private bath costs right around $250/night. **National Park Inn** is the only year-round lodging facility in the park. A general store is located on-site with essential goods like food and camping supplies, and cross-country skis and snowshoes are available for rent in winter. Each inn has a dining room open from 7am–8pm. Paradise Inn Dining Room closes temporarily between breakfast and lunch and lunch and dinner. Both inns are operated by **Mount Rainier Guest Services**. For reservations or additional information please call (360) 569-2275 or click mtrainierguestservices.com. If you'd like to sacrifice location in favor of cost or are looking for more luxurious lodging facilities, check outside the park. A list of nearby accommodations is provided on page 600.

Mount Rainier Camping (Fees are per night)

Name	Location (# on map)	Open	Fee	Sites	Notes
Cougar Rock*	Between Longmire & Paradise (5)	late May–mid-October	$20	173	W, F, DS
Ohanapecosh*	Near Ohanapecosh VC (11)	late May–mid-October	$20	188	W, F, DS
White River - ♿	White River (16)	late June–early October	$20	112	W, F
Mowich Lake	Mowich Lake (22)	July–early October	Free	10	Walk-in sites, no potable water • P

W = Water, F = Flush Toilets, P = Pit Toilets, DS = Dump Station • RV hookups are not available at any campground
*Reservations can be made up to six months in advance by calling (877) 444-6777 or clicking recreation.gov
Reservations are strongly recommended from late June through early September (especially for weekend travel)

Backcountry	Backcountry camping requires a free wilderness permit. Permits are available at Longmire Wilderness Information Center (WIC), Jackson Visitor Center, White River WIC, and Carbon River Ranger Station
Group	Group sites are available at Cougar Rock ($60/night), Ohanapecosh ($60), and Mowich Lake (free). Reservations (877.444.6777, recreation.gov) are required (available up to one year in advance).

Mount Rainier Lodging (Fees are per night)

Name	Open	Fee	Notes
National Park Inn	All Year	$121–253	Basic accommodations, rooms have shared or private baths
Paradise Inn	late May–early October	$119–274	Rooms with shared or private baths in historic building

Contact Mount Rainier Guest Services (855.755.2275, mtrainierguestservices.com) for information and reservations

Hiking

There are more than 260 miles of maintained hiking trails. All five regions of the park have trails that explore pristine lakes, peaceful meadows, old-growth forests, and, of course, many offer exceptional views of Mount Rainier. **But the best views are available at Paradise.** When Martha Longmire first set eyes on the area's wildflower meadows and spectacular mountain vistas she exclaimed, "Oh, what a paradise!" Most visitors agree. And no trip to Paradise is complete without hitting the trails. At the very least hike the first 0.5-mile of **Skyline Trail to Myrtle Falls.** Unfortunately, most visitors have the same agenda, making it extremely busy, especially after 10am. It's a good idea to get an early start; if you begin by 7am you can complete the entire 5.5-mile circuit just as the crowd pours in.

Skyline Loop continues beyond Myrtle Falls to Sluiskin Falls, where you have the option to take the 0.75-mile Paradise Glacier Spur Trail. Eventually you'll hit Panorama Point (restrooms available), and then begin the return trip via High Skyline Trail. Here you'll have outstanding views of Nisqually Glacier, which moves down the mountain's slope 6–12 inches each day in summer. Skyline Loop is considered strenuous (1,700-ft elevation gain), but you'll be busy taking in a smorgasbord of scenic beauty along the way.

In Longmire you should hike to **Comet Falls.** The trailhead's small parking area, located near Christine Falls, fills early in summer, and there's no alternative parking nearby. This 300-ft falls earned its name because it resembles the tail of a comet. Note that you'll come to a "Comet Falls 200 feet" sign. It refers to your first view of the impressive waterfall. (To make things confusing, if you missed the Comet Falls viewpoint, you may mistake Bloucher Falls, located just upstream from the spur trail and log bridge to Comet Falls, as your final destination.) You can take a short obvious spur trail, crossing Van Trump Creek and hiking up and over a small ridge to the base of Comet Falls. The main trail continues (steeply) to **Van Trump Park** (commonly snow-packed well into summer), offering tremendous views. This hike is quite steep and often inaccessible due to snow or avalanche conditions. The short hike to nearby **Christine Falls** is worth visiting, too.

Ohanapecosh offers a change of pace with **Grove of the Patriarchs Trail.** This relatively flat trail featuring massive trees more than 300 feet tall and 1,000 years old is a great family hike.

If you're looking for a more rugged adventure, try **Glacier Basin Trail**, which begins at White River Campground (Loop D). The trail follows the White River to Glacier Basin Camp and Inter Glacier. **Burroughs Mountain Trail**, beginning at Sunrise and looping around Shadow Lake, is another exceptional choice.

Be aware that many of these trails are inaccessible due to snow and mud until June or July. It is always a good idea to check trail conditions at a visitor center or the park website before you arrive. Hikers should carry plenty of water, wear sunscreen, and stay on marked trails. Pets and bicycles are not permitted on any trails.

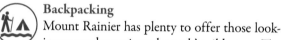

Backpacking

Mount Rainier has plenty to offer those looking to get deeper into the park's wilderness. The Pacific Crest Trail skirts the eastern boundary and **Wonderland Trail** spends 93 miles circling around Mount Rainier. These are the two most notable long-distance hiking trails in the park, but you'll find designated campsites throughout the backcountry. Begin planning your backcountry trip with a good topographical map.

Backpackers must obtain a **wilderness camping permit** (required for all overnight stays in the backcountry). Starting in 2016, Mount Rainier no longer accepts reservations for wilderness camping or climbing permits. (Climbers require a Climbing Pass and Wilderness Permit to camp.) First-come, first-served permits can be obtained no earlier than one day before your departure date. In summer, permits are available at the following facilities: Longmire Wilderness Information Center, Jackson Visitor Center at Paradise, White River Wilderness Information Center, and Carbon River Ranger Station. In winter, permits are only available at Longmire Museum (every day) and Jackson Visitor Center (weekends only). Plan on arriving at least one hour before the facility closes. In winter, you can also self-register at Carbon River Ranger Station, Ohanapecosh Ranger Station, and at the Highway 410 entrance arch (north entrance).

Mount Rainier Hiking Trails (Distances are roundtrip)

	Name	Location (# on map)	Length	Difficulty Rating & Notes
Longmire	Kautz Creek	3 mi west of Longmire (1)	2.0 miles	M – Self-guided, continues to Indian Henrys
	Trail of the Shadows	Longmire Museum (2)	0.7 mile	E – Self-guiding loop explores area's history
	Rampart Ridge	Trail of Shadows (3)	4.6 miles	M – Steep forested loop, stunning vistas
	Eagle Peak Saddle	Longmire (4)	7.2 miles	S – Steep trail through old-growth forest
	Carter/Madcap Falls	Cougar Rock Campground (5)	2.0 miles	M – Madcap Falls is just beyond Carter Falls
	Comet Falls - 👟	4.4 mi east of Longmire (6)	3.8 miles	S – Steep, a short spur leads to Comet Falls
	Christine Falls	4.5 mi east of Longmire (6)	0.5 mile	E – 100-ft descent from road to view of falls
Paradise	The Lakes Loop - 👟	Reflection Lakes (7)	5.0 miles	M – Intersects road and Skyline Trail
	Bench and Snow Lk	1.5 mi east of Reflection Lakes (7)	2.5 miles	M – Rolling hills, lakes, views, wildflowers
	Nisqually Vista	Lower Parking Lot (8)	1.2 miles	E – Stroller-friendly self-guiding loop
	Deadhorse Creek	Lower Parking Lot (8)	2.5 miles	M – Can loop with Glacier Vista and Skyline
	Myrtle Falls	Upper Parking Lot (9)	1.0 mile	E – Stroller/Wheelchair (with assistance)
	Panorama Point	Upper Parking Lot (9)	4.0 miles	S – Via Skyline Trail and Golden Gate Trail
	Skyline Loop - 👟	Upper Parking Lot (9)	5.5 miles	S – Best hike, Snowpack until summer
	Pinnacle Peak	SE of Paradise (10)	2.5 miles	S – South of Paradise to peak and glacier
Ohanapecosh	Hot Springs	Visitor Center (11)	0.5 mile	E – Self-guiding loop, access at campground
	Silver Falls	Three access points (see notes)	0.6–3.0 mi	M – Access via Route 123, Ohanapecosh Campground, or Stevens Canyon Road
	Laughingwater Crk	Route 123 (12)	12.0 miles	S – Long day hike, 2,700-ft elevation gain
	Grove of the Patriarchs	Stevens Canyon Entrance (13)	1.3 miles	E – Self-guided, old (1,000+ years) and tall (300-ft) trees
	Cowlitz Divide - 👟	Stevens Canyon Rd (14)	8.5 miles	S – Leads to Ollalie Creek and Wonderland Trail
	Shriner Park	Route 123 (15)	8.4 miles	S – Traverses old burn area, minimal cover
Sunrise	Emmons Moraine	White River Campground (16)	3.0 miles	M – Follows Glacier Basin Trail for 1 mile
	Glacier Basin - 👟	White River Campground (16)	6.5 miles	S – Flood damage (scrambling required)
	Upper Pallisades Lk	Sunrise Point (17)	7.0 miles	S – No views of Mount Rainier, alpine lakes
	Silver Forest	South of the Parking Lot (18)	2.0 miles	E – Leads to Emmons Vista Overlook
	Sunrise Nature	North of the Parking Lot (18)	1.5 miles	M – Views of Rainier over Sunrise Day Lodge
	Sourdough Ridge	North of the Parking Lot (18)	3.0 miles	M – Loop via Wonderland Trail
	Sunrise Rim	South of the Parking Lot (18)	5.2 miles	S – Leads to Shadow Lake/Glacier Overlook
	Burroughs Mtn - 👟	North of the Parking Lot (18)	4.7 miles	S – Leads to Sourdough Ridge/Frozen Lake
	Freemont Lookout	North of the Parking Lot (18)	5.6 miles	S – Follow Sourdough Ridge Tr to Fremont Tr
	Berkeley Park	North of the Parking Lot (18)	7.0 miles	S – Follow Sourdough Ridge to Northern Loop
Carbon/Mowich	Rain Forest Loop	Carbon River Ranger Station (19)	0.3 mile	E – Self-guiding loop through rain forest
	Green Lake	Carbon River Ranger Station (19)	10.8 miles	M – A short spur trail leads to Ranger Falls
	Chenuis Falls	Carbon River Ranger Station (19)	7.4 miles	M – Mostly along Carbon River Road
	Lake James & Windy Gap	Ipsut Creek (20)	22.0 miles	S – Follows Wonderland Tr to Northern Loop
	Tolmie Peak	Mowich Lake Rd (21)	6.5 miles	M – Cross Ipsut Pass to Eunice Lake
	Spray Park - 👟	Mowich Lake Campground (22)	6.0 miles	M – Short spur to Spray Falls (300-ft cascade)

Wonderland Trail - 👟 • 93.0 miles • Circles Mount Rainier • Accessible from Longmire Wilderness Info. Center, Mowich Lake and Ipsut Creek Campgrounds, Sunrise, Fryingpan Creek Trailhead and Box Canyon

Difficulty Ratings: E = Easy, M = Moderate, S = Strenuous

Tipsoo Lake

Spray Falls

Mountaineering

Each year approximately 10,000 visitors attempt to climb 14,410-foot Mount Rainier. About 25% of them successfully reach the summit of the most heavily glaciated peak in the contiguous United States. Not only is Mount Rainier the ultimate in American mountaineering (excluding Denali), it also serves as training ground for professional and amateur climbers. Physical preparation, specialized equipment, and finely tuned skills are required to ascend more than 9,000 feet over a distance of (at least) eight miles. **All climbers who intend on traveling above 10,000 feet or on a glacier must register and pay a fee.** Registration is available at Paradise Ranger Station, White River WIC, and Longmire WIC. The fee is $46/person (25 and older), and $32/person (24 and younger). Passes are valid for one year from the date of purchase. You can also climb with an **experienced guide.** Rainier Mountaineering, Inc. (360.569.2227, rmiguides.com), Alpine Ascents International (206.378.1927, AlpineAscents.com), American Alpine Institute (360.671.1505, alpineinstitute.com), and Mount Rainier Alpine Guides (360.569.2889, mountainguides.com) offer a variety of routes and trips. Standard 3–4 day Muir Climbs cost about $1,400 (meals & permit included, gear rental costs extra).

Biking

There are no designated biking trails within the park and bikes are not allowed on hiking trails, but all park roads are open to cyclists. Be careful, as roads are steep, narrow, and winding with unpaved shoulders. Bike rental is not available in the park. If you want to pedal in the Paradise/Longmire region between June and August, leave as early in the morning as possible to beat the traffic. Most roads are congested with motorists, but there is one exception: **Carbon River Road.** Somewhat hidden in the park's northwest corner, this 5-mile unpaved road is closed to motorists due to recent flood damage. It is shared with hikers. Running parallel to Carbon River Road, slightly to the south, is Mowich Lake Road. This 5-mile unpaved road leads to beautiful subalpine meadows. These aren't particularly great mountain bike destinations, but it's your only option in the park. More **extreme pedalers** should check out RAMROD (Ride Around Mount Rainier One Day, redmondcyclingclub.org). Every July cyclists test themselves against a 154-mile course with 10,000 feet of elevation gain.

Winter Activities

Abundant snow turns Paradise into a winter wonderland. **Sledding** is allowed in the snow play area located north of Paradise's upper parking lot. **Cross-country skis** ($18.75/day) and **snowshoes** ($14.50/day) are available for **rent** at National Park Inn. **Snowmobiles** are permitted in a few designated areas. Contact the park for snow conditions, avalanche danger, and the weather forecast before you arrive.

Ranger Programs

Ranger-led interpretive programs are an integral component of the national park experience. Free walks, talks, and campfire programs are offered daily during summer. In winter, you can join a ranger on a **snowshoe walk** ($5 donation suggested). A current schedule of events is available online or in the park's free newspaper, *The Tahoma News*. Do not miss out on a ranger program during your visit to Mount Rainier.

For Kids

Mount Rainier is one of the most family-friendly national parks. In summer, children enjoy walking along creeks and viewing wildflowers. Sledding, snowshoeing, and snowball fights are all fun-filled activities during winter. Any time of year, children are invited to participate in the park's **Junior Ranger Program**. Activity booklets can be picked up from any of the visitor centers. Complete an age appropriate number of activities and return to a visitor center to have your work checked by a park ranger. If successful your child will be sworn in as a Junior Ranger and receive an official Mount Rainier Junior Ranger badge.

Flora & Fauna

Mount Rainier National Park is home to more than 800 species of vascular plants, including at least 100 species of wildflowers. Wildflower season peaks from mid-July through August. Douglas, western red cedar, and western hemlock comprise most of the park's forests. Large mammals include elk, deer, black bear, and mountain lions.

Pets

Pets are allowed in the park, but must be kept on a leash no more than six feet in length at all times. Visitors with pets are extremely limited to where they can travel as they are only allowed along roadways and in parking areas and developed campgrounds. They are not permitted in public buildings (except service animals), at ranger programs, in the backcountry, or on hiking trails.

Accessibility

Jackson Visitor Center (Paradise) is fully accessible to wheelchair users. Ohanapecosh and Sunrise Visitor Centers and Longmire Museum are accessible, but

Comet Falls

passages are narrow and may require assistance. Accessible rooms are available at Paradise Inn and National Park Inn. Accessible campsites are available at Cougar Rock and Ohanapecosh Campgrounds. Kautz Creek Trail, Trail of Shadows, and Paradise's Lower Meadow Trail are accessible with assistance.

Weather

Mountain weather is unpredictable. The best you can do is to have a contingency plan for all possible conditions. One of the most disappointing aspects of the park is that its 14,410-ft mountain is often hidden behind a blanket of clouds. July and August are typically the clearest, driest, and warmest months of the year. At Paradise (5,400 ft elevation), summer average highs are in the low 60s°F with lows in the mid-40s°F. The area's proximity to the Pacific Ocean helps moderate seasonal changes in temperature. Winter highs average in the mid-30s°F with lows in the low 20s°F. Expect Longmire (2,762 ft) to be a few degrees warmer than Paradise and Ohanapecosh (1,950 ft) to be a few degrees warmer than Longmire.

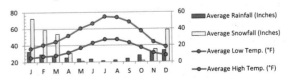

View from First Burroughs

Vacation Planner

When and where are the two main questions you must answer before taking a trip to Mount Rainier National Park. The answer to these questions will vary depending on your tolerance of massive crowds and need for solitude. **Most visitors only visit Paradise.** It's beautiful, but the crowds and cars deprive the area of a bit of its natural majesty. Additionally, most guests come to the park between July and August. So, if you're planning a trip to Paradise in the middle of July, expect plenty of company. **You may want to pencil in a side-trip to a more secluded area** like Ohanapecosh, Mowich Lake, or Carbon River to shake the crowds for a day or two. For a weekend at Longmire/Paradise consider taking the free shuttle (if it's running) rather than driving your own car into the park. A well-rounded trip includes visits to Longmire, Paradise, and Sunrise. **Camping** (page 571) is available in each region. **Lodging** (page 571) is only available at Longmire and Paradise. Nearby dining, grocery stores, lodging, festivals, and attractions are listed on pages 600–603. Provided below is a 2-day itinerary that visits the park's most popular regions.

Day 1: Begin your trip at **Nisqually Entrance** (southwest corner of the park). After one mile you'll come to Westside Road. This unpaved route provides access to trailheads for Gobblers Knob (12.8 miles) and Emerald Ridge (17.2 miles) trails, much more secluded and uncongested areas compared to Paradise. If you need to escape the crowds for a bit, head back to this location, but for now continue on the main park road. History buffs should make a quick stop (1–2 hours) at **Longmire Museum**; otherwise continue past Cougar Rock Campground to **Comet Falls Trailhead**. Hike the steep and somewhat strenuous 3.8-mile trail to its 300-ft falls. Allow 3–4 hours so you have ample time

to enjoy the views. (Make sure you read the details on page 572, so you don't mistake Bloucher Falls—also impressive—for Comet!) If you have the energy, continue (steeply up) to Van Trump Park, otherwise return to your car and drive to Paradise. En route, you'll pass **Narada Falls**. It's worth the short hike. (Note: If you want to see something, don't stop in the road; ogling motorists are good for causing accidents, and that's a sure-fire way to ruin a day in Paradise.) At Paradise, stop at **Jackson Visitor Center** to watch a short video. Check the schedule of ranger programs and squeeze the interesting ones into your itinerary. Next, stretch your legs on **Skyline Trail**. Begin in a counterclockwise direction toward Myrtle Falls. If the meadows, mountain vistas, and flowing waterways inspire you to go further, continue around the loop another 5 miles past Panorama Point, along Nisqually Glacier, and right back down to Paradise. The trail to **Snow and Bench Lakes** is a good alternative.

Day 2: Start the day by driving east to **Stevens Canyon Road Entrance** (45 minutes from Paradise, 65 minutes from Longmire). Big tree aficionados should have a look around **Grove of the Patriarchs**, located near the entrance station. Otherwise turn left on WA-123 and drive to **White River/Sunrise** (about 75 minutes). (Heading over to **Tipsoo Lake**, located on Mather Memorial Highway near the park's western boundary, is a worthwhile photo-op.) After more than two hours driving, you're probably ready to pound the paths. How about getting a closer look at Mount Rainier? To do so, take **Burrough Mountain Trail** from **Sunrise**. You can make a loop, following Burrough Mountain Trail past Frozen Lake to Burrough Mountain (we recommend continuing uphill on the out-and-back to 2nd Burrough Mountain) and returning via **Sunrise Rim Trail** past Glacier Overlook and Shadow Lake. This hike is considered strenuous, and it is mostly uphill to Burrough Mountain, but you can make it easier by simply doing out-and-backs to Frozen Lake or Shadow Lake. There are also plenty of day-hikes leading into the nearby mountains. One of the best is the trail to Berkeley Park, which leads to the base of Skyscraper Mountain on the north side of Mount Rainier. Once you've worn yourself out, return home knowing you've had the opportunity to spend a little time in Paradise.

Christine Falls

Sunset at Shi Shi Beach

Olympic

600 East Park Avenue
Port Angeles, WA 98362
Phone: (360) 565-3130
Website: nps.gov/olym

Established: June 29, 1938
March 2, 1909 (National
Monument)
Size: 922,561 Acres
Annual Visitors: 3.2 Million
Peak Season: Summer

Activities: Hiking, Backpacking,
Camping, Fishing, Rafting, Biking,
Beachcombing, and Swimming

Campgrounds: 16 Campgrounds*
Fee: $15–22/night
Backcountry Camping: Permitted
Lodging: 4 Locations
Rates: $72–370/night

Park Hours: All day, every day
Entrance Fee: $20/vehicle,
$7/individual (foot, bike, etc.)

*Reservations only available at
Kalaloch, Lake Crescent, and Sol
Duc Campgrounds

Mount Olympus (7,980 feet), the park's centerpiece, was named by English explorer Captain John Meares in 1788 when he saw the mighty summit from a distance. He deemed it a worthy home of the Greek gods. Mount Olympus may have been named in the 18th century, but the Olympic Peninsula remained a blank spot on maps for another 100 years. Today, the mountainous region of western Washington State has been explored, but the landscape has not changed. Its temperate rain forests, steep cliffs, and high ridgelines remain relatively inaccessible. No roads enter the heart of the park where the Olympic Mountain Range is shaped by 13 rivers. Add 73 miles of wild Pacific coastline and Olympic National Park offers an unsurpassed diversity of relatively undisturbed ecosystems.

Juan de Fuca spotted the Olympic Peninsula in 1592. Captain Meares, Charles William Barkley, and George Vancouver explored the region nearly two centuries later, but Native Americans had lived here for more than 12,000 years. Ancestors of eight distinct tribes survived the decimation brought on by European diseases; the Hoh People still live along the Hoh River, and the Quileute People live at La Push on the Pacific Coast. Americans did not explore the Olympic Range until the late 19th century. In 1885, Lieutenant Joseph P. O'Neil led an expedition into the mountains. Their journey began at Port Angeles, a small village at the time, and took one month to reach Hurricane Ridge. Today, 17-mile Hurricane Ridge Road follows roughly the same path O'Neil took, but allows visitors to reach the ridge with its scenic views of Mount Olympus in less than half an hour.

Lumber interests seeking untapped old-growth forests to harvest spent decades making the Olympic Peninsula more accessible. Lumbermen couldn't have asked for a better location to cut trees than this lush environment. Forests of the Pacific Northwest produce three times the biomass of tropical rain forests. Lumber was being hauled out of the Olympic Peninsula as the general public gained interest in the outdoors, largely thanks to adoption of the automobile. These opposing sides helped fuel a controversial national park movement. President Theodore Roosevelt settled the dispute by establishing Olympic National Monument in 1909 to protect the calving grounds of the area's Roosevelt elk herds. But logging continued, and by the 1920s logging interests faced a swell of public dissent. In 1938, the monument was reestablished as a national park. A new title, but the same results. Largely due to increased demand caused by WWII, illegal logging continued long after the park was established.

Visitors no longer find fresh swaths of clear-cut. About 366,000 acres of old-growth are left unharmed, the largest of its kind in the Pacific Northwest. These impressive stands are nourished by ample rain. Mount Olympus receives as much as 220 inches of annual precipitation (half snow). Forks, located near Hoh Rainforest, receives more rain than any city in the contiguous U.S., about 120 inches annually. Lush and lively, the Olympic Peninsula provides refuge and nourishment for hundreds of species of plants and animals, including several species found nowhere else in the world: Olympic marmot, Olympic torrent salamander, Olympic mudminnow, Olympic grasshopper, Flett's violet, and Piper's bellflower just to name a few. President Roosevelt's goal to preserve elk habitat worked. The park's population is the largest unmanaged herd of Roosevelt elk. Not only does the park preserve an impressive collection of coastline, mountains, and rivers along with its incredible plant and animal life, but it also created a reservation for people. A refuge used to escape the doldrums of everyday life by immersing one's self in nature.

Mountain goats
(Klahhane Ridge)

When to Go
Olympic National Park is open all day, every day. However, many of the park's roads, visitor centers, campgrounds, and lodging facilities close for winter. Very few tourists come to the park during the harsh Olympic Peninsula winters, but Hurricane Ridge is open for cross-country skiing on weekends and holidays. Most visitors arrive during the dry season (June–September). At this time sunny skies are common, but so are mosquitoes and black flies.

Transportation & Airports
Ferry and bus service is available to the Olympic Peninsula, but not within the park. See page 581 for ferry and bus details. The closest large commercial airport is Seattle–Tacoma International (SEA). From Seattle, visitors can fly to William R. Fairchild International Airport (CLM) in Port Angeles.

Directions
Olympic is not the most convenient park for motorists. No road crosses the Olympic Mountain Range, but 12 separate roads penetrate the main park boundary encircling Mount Olympus. In addition, a sliver of Pacific coastline has three separate regions with their own access point. No matter where you're headed you'll be traveling on US-101. Park Headquarters is located in Port Angeles, where most trips begin. Several different routes can be utilized between Port Angeles and Seattle. Motorists can use the Washington State Ferry System (page 581) or drive south around Puget Sound via Tacoma or Olympia.

Port Angeles via Tacoma (~140 miles): Heading south on I-5, take Exit 132 to merge onto WA-16 W toward Bremerton. Cross the Tacoma Narrows Bridge (eastbound toll: $6). Just before Bremerton, WA-16 becomes WA-3. At Hood Canal Bridge WA-3 becomes WA-104. After about 15 miles, take the ramp to US-101 N. Continue north to Port Angeles.

Port Angeles via Olympia (~180 miles): Head south on I-5 from Seattle. After about 60 miles, take Exit 104 to merge onto US-101 N. Continue north for about 118 miles to Port Angeles.

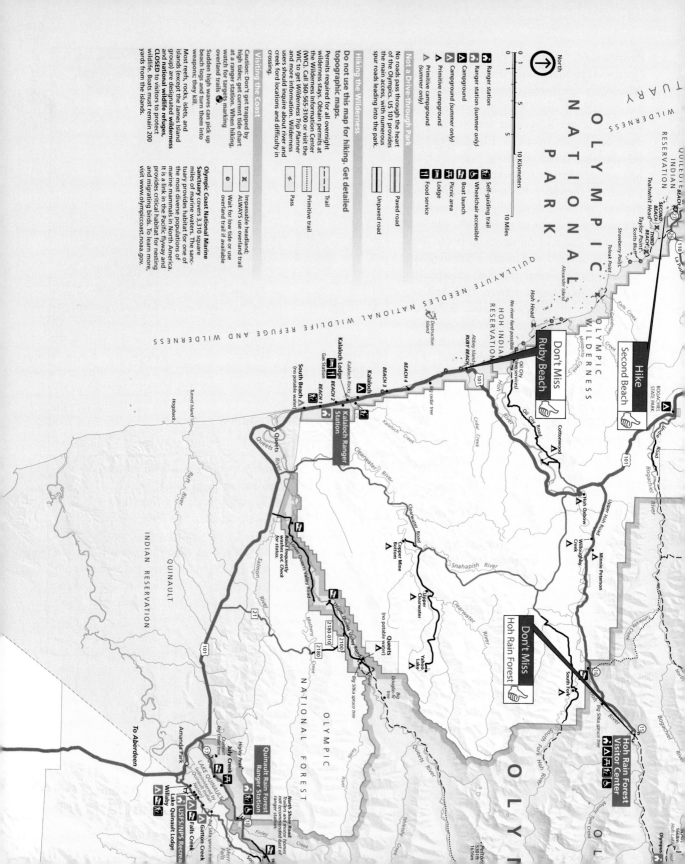

OLYMPIC NATIONAL PARK

North

0 — 10 Kilometers
0 — 10 Miles

Legend:
- Ranger station
- Ranger station (summer only)
- Campground
- Campground (summer only)
- Primitive campground
- Primitive campground (summer only)

- Self-guiding trail
- Wheelchair accessible
- Lodge
- Picnic area
- Food service
- Boat launch

- Paved road
- Unpaved road
- Trail
- Primitive trail
- Pass

- ✕ Impassable headland; ALWAYS use overland trail
- ● Wait for low tide or use overland trail if available

Not a Drive-through Park
No roads go through the heart of the Olympics. US 101 provides the main access, with numerous spur roads leading into the park.

Hiking the Wilderness
Do not use this map for hiking. Get detailed topographic maps.

Permits required for all overnight wilderness stays. Obtain permits at the Wilderness Information Center (WIC). Call 360-565-3100 or visit the WIC to get Wilderness Trip Planner and more information. Wilderness users should inquire about river and creek ford locations and difficulty in crossing.

Visiting the Coast
Caution: Don't get trapped by high tides; get current tide chart at a ranger station. When hiking, watch for targets marking overland trails ●.

Sudden high waves can pick up beach logs and turn them into weapons; they kill.

Most reefs, rocks, islets, and islands (except the James Island group) are designated wilderness and national wildlife refuges. CLOSED to visitors to protect wildlife. Boats must remain 200 yards from the islands.

Olympic Coast National Marine Sanctuary covers 3,310 square miles of marine waters. The sanctuary provides habitat for one of the most diverse populations of marine mammals in North America. It is a link in the Pacific flyway and provides critical habitat for nesting and migrating birds. To learn more, visit www.olympiccoast.noaa.gov.

Map labels:

OLYMPIC WILDERNESS · QUILLAYUTE NEEDLES NATIONAL WILDLIFE REFUGE AND WILDERNESS · HOH INDIAN RESERVATION · QUINAULT INDIAN RESERVATION · OLYMPIC NATIONAL FOREST

Hike — Second Beach · Don't Miss — Ruby Beach · Don't Miss — Hoh Rain Forest

Quileute Beach, Teahwhit Head, Taylor Point, Strawberry Point, Scotts Bluff, Toleak Point, Goodman Creek, Alexander Island, Hoh Head, No river ford possible, Oil City (no services), Abbey Island, Destruction Island, RUBY BEACH, Cottonwood, BEACH 4, BEACH 3, Kalaloch Rocks, Kalaloch, Kalaloch Lodge, Gas Station, BEACH 2, BEACH 1, South Beach (no potable water), Kalaloch Ranger Station, Big cedar tree, Kalaloch Creek, Clearwater Creek, Hoh Oxbow, Willoughby Creek, Minnie Peterson, Cedar Creek, Copper Mine Bottom, Upper Clearwater, Snahapish River, Clearwater Road, Clearwater, Queets (no potable water), Yahoo Lake, Big Sitka spruce tree, Douglas-fir tree, Matheny Creek, Upper Queets Valley Road, Road frequently washes out. Check for status, Salmon River, Raft River, Queets River, Tunnel Island, Hogsback, 2180, 2180-010, 2100, 21, 101, Amanda Park, July Creek, Higley Peak, LAKE QUINAULT, Quinault Rain Forest Ranger Station, Gatton Creek, Falls Creek, Willaby, Lake Quinault Lodge, USFS/NPS Recreation, Merriman Falls, Finley Creek, Big Sitka spruce tree, North Shore Road, Big cedar tree

Hoh Rain Forest Visitor Center · South Fork · Hoh River · South Fork Hoh River · Upper Hoh Road · Mount Tom Creek · Pelton Peak 1616m, Mount Olympus, 101, 110, La Push, Bogachiel State Park, Bogachiel River, Calawah River

To Aberdeen

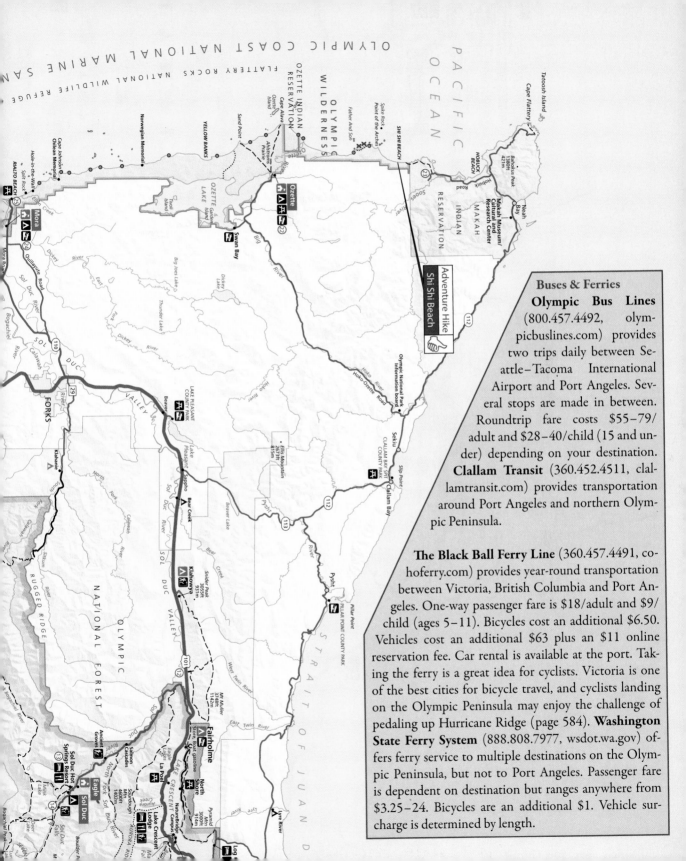

Buses & Ferries

Olympic Bus Lines (800.457.4492, olympicbuslines.com) provides two trips daily between Seattle–Tacoma International Airport and Port Angeles. Several stops are made in between. Roundtrip fare costs $55–79/adult and $28–40/child (15 and under) depending on your destination. **Clallam Transit** (360.452.4511, clallamtransit.com) provides transportation around Port Angeles and northern Olympic Peninsula.

The Black Ball Ferry Line (360.457.4491, cohoferry.com) provides year-round transportation between Victoria, British Columbia and Port Angeles. One-way passenger fare is $18/adult and $9/child (ages 5–11). Bicycles cost an additional $6.50. Vehicles cost an additional $63 plus an $11 online reservation fee. Car rental is available at the port. Taking the ferry is a great idea for cyclists. Victoria is one of the best cities for bicycle travel, and cyclists landing on the Olympic Peninsula may enjoy the challenge of pedaling up Hurricane Ridge (page 584). **Washington State Ferry System** (888.808.7977, wsdot.wa.gov) offers ferry service to multiple destinations on the Olympic Peninsula, but not to Port Angeles. Passenger fare is dependent on destination but ranges anywhere from $3.25–24. Bicycles are an additional $1. Vehicle surcharge is determined by length.

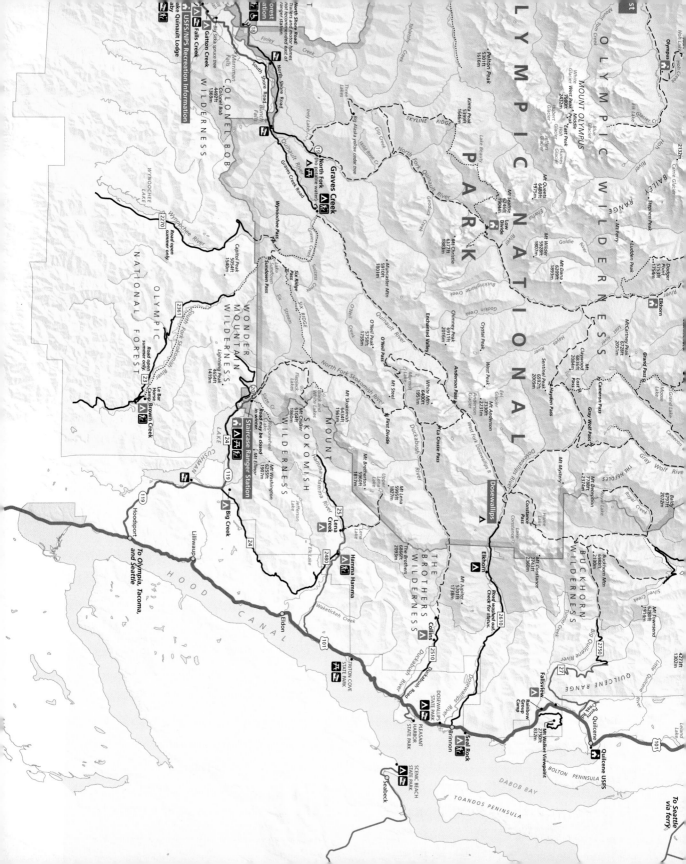

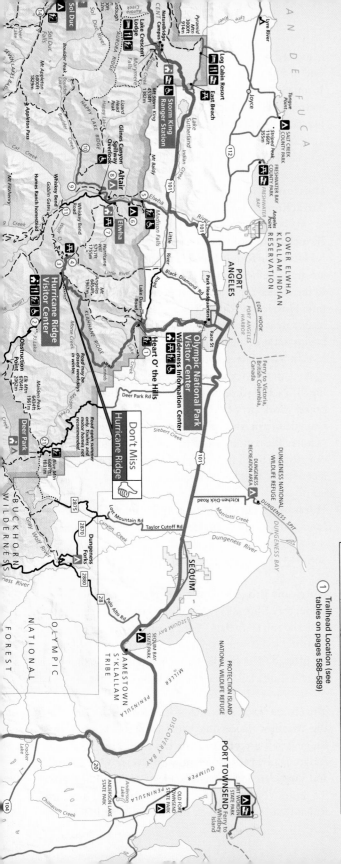

Best of Olympic

Mainland Region: Hurricane Ridge
Runner-up: Hoh Rain Forest

Coastal Region: Mora
Runner Up: Ozette

Regions

Olympic National Park consists of more than a dozen vehicle accessible regions, but it isn't a drive-thru park. Almost every distinct region is accessed from a spur road off US-101, which circles the Olympic Range. A few of the more popular regions include: the mountain vistas of Hurricane Ridge, the hot springs and waterfalls of Sol Duc, the temperate rain forest of Hoh Rain Forest, and the tide pools and coastline of Ozette. Each area is unique in its own way, and for this reason **Olympic National Park is examined region by region.**

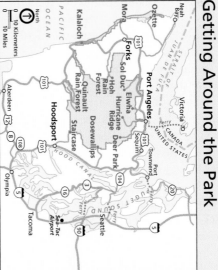

Getting Around the Park

① Trailhead Location (see tables on pages 588–589)

Park Headquarters

Attractions: Visitor Center, Wilderness Info. Center (WIC) • Backcountry Permits, Hiking

Park Headquarters (360.565.3130) is located just south of Port Angeles on Mount Angeles Road. The visitor center has a variety of exhibits, including a hands-on "Discovery Room" for kids and a 25-minute introductory film. It's open daily in summer from 8:30am until 5pm, and from 9am until 4pm in winter, but it closes for Thanksgiving and Christmas. If you want to get straight to exploring the outdoors **Living Forest and Peabody Creek Trails** are two short forested walks that begin at the visitor center. Living Forest Loop is wheelchair accessible (with assistance).

Stop in at the **Wilderness Information Center** (360.565.3100), located inside the visitor center, for **backcountry permits** and current trail conditions. A permit is required for all overnight stays in the backcountry. Park Headquarters is an ideal place for an introduction to the Olympic Peninsula before continuing south along Hurricane Ridge Road to Heart O' the Hills and Hurricane Ridge.

Heart O' the Hills

Attractions: Ranger/Entrance Station, Camping, Hiking

Heart O' the Hills is located just 5 miles south of Port Angeles and Park HQ. The **campground** has 102 sites available on a first-come, first-served basis for $20/night. It's open all year, but may be walk-in only depending on the amount of snow. Interpretive programs are held at the campground from late June through September. Potable water and flush toilets are available. There are no hookups. All sites accommodate 21-ft RVs. Some suit 35-ft RVs. Showers are not available, but the Sequim KOA (80 O'Brien Road, Port Angeles) allows visitors to use their **showers** for a nominal fee (just ask at their office).

Heart O' the Forest Trail begins in Loop E of the campground. It's an easy 4.0-mile (roundtrip) hike through old-growth forest. For a much more strenuous trek, hikers can loop Lake Angeles and Heather Park Trails (seasonal, check trail conditions). The trailhead

is located near the campground entrance on the west side of Hurricane Ridge Road. The loop covers nearly 13 miles and passes Lake Angeles. The top of the loop intersects Klahhane Ridge/Heather Park/Switchback Junction where extremely ambitious hikers can continue hiking parallel to Hurricane Ridge Road another 3+ miles to Hurricane Ridge Visitor Center.

Hurricane Ridge

Attractions: Visitor Center, Driving, Biking, Hiking

If you have to choose one area of the park to visit, make it Hurricane Ridge. Some of the most spectacular vistas are available here as you peer across river-carved valleys to the glacier-capped peak of **Mount Olympus**. The 17-mile **Hurricane Ridge Road** is an attraction in and of itself. Great for motorists, and a challenge for cyclists, it begins in Port Angeles. An avid biker can climb from sea level to 5,242 feet in about 20 miles. Rest your legs while soaking in the views from Hurricane Ridge before making the exciting descent back to sea level (make sure your brakes work properly, because you'll need them). The main deterrent for exploring Hurricane Ridge is Mother Nature. The region earned its name thanks to winds that can gust up to 75 miles per hour, and as much as 30–35 feet of snow falls here annually.

Hurricane Ridge Road is open 24 hours a day between June and October. The rest of the year it is primarily open on weekends (weather permitting). Call (360) 565-3131 for up-to-date road and weather conditions.

Hurricane Ridge Visitor Center offers exhibits, an introductory film, and restrooms. It's open all year. Hours typically run from 9am–6pm in summer and 9am–4pm in winter (when the road is open). Interpretive programs are offered from late June to September. Snowshoe and ski rental are available at the gift shop in winter.

This is an excellent area for **hiking**. Cirque Rim, Big Meadow (accessible with assistance), and High Ridge Trails are one mile or less roundtrip. Klahhane Ridge Trail heads down toward Heart O' the Hills and intersects Lake Angeles/Heather Park Loop after 3.8 miles (one-way). At the very end of Hurricane Ridge Road you can pick up Hurricane Hill Trail. It's a partially accessible (the first 0.25-mile is paved) 3.2-mile (roundtrip) initially-flat path (that gets steep) with stunning panoramic views. Most visitors do a quick out-and-back along Hurricane Hill Trail, but it continues to Elwha Valley if you're looking for a backcountry route or long (one-way) day hike (arrange a shuttle).

Elwha
Attractions: Camping, Rafting, Fishing, Hiking

The three-year dam removal process was completed in 2014, restoring the Elwha River to its original state, wild and free. Once again water and salmon travel unimpeded through Elwha Valley, the largest watershed in Olympic National Park, greatly improving the quality of fishing and rafting. The park's only **rafting concessioner** is Olympic Raft and Kayak (888.452.1443, raftandkayak.com). Elwha River trips (Class II+) cost $60/adult and $50/child (ages 5–11).

Elwha Campground has 40 campsites (first-come, first-served) for $20/night. They are available all year (pit toilets and no water in winter). Altair Campground has 30 sites available from late May to mid-October for $20/night.

Elwha is also one of the better **hiking** areas. Near the park boundary you'll find a paved 0.2-mile trail (accessible) to Madison Falls (60 ft). Geyser Valley Loop Trail (6 miles, roundtrip) begins at the end of Whiskey Bend Road. Cascade Rock Trail (4.2 miles, roundtrip) is a good hike beginning at Elwha Campground.

Lake Crescent
Attractions: Lake Crescent Lodge and Log Cabin Resort, Boating, Camping, Hiking, Swimming

This area is difficult to miss. US-101 skirts the lake's southern shoreline for about 10 miles. From east to west you'll pass several short spur roads: **East Beach Road** to Log Cabin Resort and East Beach, **Lake Crescent Road** to Storm King and Lake Crescent Lodge, and **Camp David Jr. Road** to Fairholme Campground.

Lake Crescent Lodge closes for winter (October–April), but **Roosevelt Cabins** remain open on

View from the former site of Elwha River Dam

winter weekends. Rates range from $189–291 per night. **Log Cabin Resort** has everything from A-Frame Chalets ($190/night) to RV sites with full hookups ($60/night). It is open from late May to mid-September. While the campground provides an exceptional setting, there's little-to-no privacy. Reservations for both lodges and the campground can be made at (888) 896-3818 or olympicnationalparks.com.

You can also **camp** at Fairholme. The campground has 88 sites available on a first-come, first-served basis for $20/night. It is open from May through fall. Canoe, kayak, and motorboat rentals are available at Fairholme General Store (360.928.3020).

Swimming is popular at Fairholme, East Beach, and Devil's Punch Bowl.

A handful of **hiking trails** are available in the area. The 4.2-mile trek to **Mount Storm King** is one of our favorite hikes, but it's a bit tricky due to a few steep ascents aided by ropes. Access the trail near Lake Crescent Lodge. From here you head south across US-101, turn right on Marymere Falls Trail (the easier, more popular alternative), then left onto Mount Storm King Trail, climbing 2,000 feet to the site where Indian legend states the mountain spirit hurled a gigantic boulder down at two quarrelling tribes. The boulder struck the river, damming it up, creating Lake Crescent. Don't attempt Mount Storm King when the trail is muddy. On the lake's north shore, hikers can take **Pyramid Peak Trail** (7 miles, roundtrip) to an old WWII spotting tower with exceptional views of the lake.

Sol Duc

Attractions: Sol Duc Hot Springs Resort, Camping, Fishing, Hiking, Backpacking

Sol Duc Road, just west of Fairholme and Lake Crescent, is open all year (weather permitting). It leads to the area's resorts, campground, and trailheads.

Sol Duc Hot Springs Resort (888.896.3818, olympicnationalparks.com) offers RV sites with full hookups ($43/night), basic cabins ($173), kitchen-cabins ($248), and a River Suite ($375). Pool admission is included with all overnight accommodations except RV sites. The resort is open from late March to mid-Fall. It also operates three mineral hot spring soaking pools and one freshwater pool from late March to late October. A soak will cost you $13.50/adult and $10/child (4–12). Massages are available for $55 (30 minutes), $75 (60), and $100 (90).

Sol Duc Campground has 82 sites available on a first-come, first-served basis for $20/night. Sites are available all year (pit toilets and no water in winter). Reservations at Sol Duc Campground should be available in 2017, as Sol Duc Resort has taken over its operation.

Sol Duc is a good location for **backpacking**. The Seven Lakes Basin Area, south of Sol Duc Road, offers an excellent loop trail with views of Mount Olympus. Bear canisters, topographic maps, and backcountry permits are available at Sol Duc Ranger Station. One of the park's most popular walks is the 1.6-mile **Sol Duc Falls Trail**, which leads to a picturesque three-legged falls.

Hoh Rain Forest

Attractions: Visitor Center, Camping, Rafting, Hiking

Hoh Rain Forest should not be skipped. It's located on the west side of the Olympics where winters are mild and wet. The area receives 140–170 inches of annual precipitation, which help make it one of the most spectacular examples of temperate rain forest in the world.

Hoh Rain Forest Visitor Center offers information, exhibits, a bookstore, and maps. It's open daily from 9am–5pm during summer and from 10am–4pm on weekends during winter (except Christmas and Thanksgiving). **Hoh Campground** has 88 sites available on a first-come, first-served basis for $20/night. Potable water is available year-round. There are no hookups, and RVs must be less than 21 feet.

Olympic Raft and Kayak (888.452.1443, raftandkayak.com) offers whitewater rafting trips on the Hoh River (Class I–II). These summer-only excursions cost $60/adult and $50/child (ages 5–11). It's mostly a float trip, but things get a little "splashy" near the take-out.

Several **hiking trails** begin at Hoh Rain Forest Visitor Center and penetrate deep into the forest's depths. **Hall of Mosses Trail** (0.8 mile) and **Spruce Nature Trail** (1.2 miles) are wonderful self-guiding options that explain the area's ecology. Hoh Rain Forest is also the gateway to **Mount Olympus**. The 17.4-mile (one-way) **Hoh River Trail** leads to Glacier Meadows, which provides excellent views of Mount Olympus and Blue Glacier (do not attempt to climb to its summit without proper equipment and experience, permit required). Whether you're in the campground, rafting the river, or hiking the trails, you'll have an excellent chance of spotting Roosevelt elk. Olympic is home to the largest unmanaged herd, and about 400 reside in the Hoh area.

Queets

Queets is located in the park's southwest corner. This lightly visited region, accessed via an 11-mile unpaved road, is the perfect destination for some peace and solitude. The **campground** offers 20 primitive sites on a first-come, first-served basis for $15/night. It is open year-round. RVs are not recommended. **Two boat launches** are available to explore the water, and **Sam's River Loop** (2.8 miles) and **Queets River Trail** (15.8 miles, one-way) let you explore the land.

Quinault

Attractions: Lake Quinault Lodge, Camping, Hiking

Quinault is located along the park's southern boundary, just north of US-101 before it heads south along the Pacific Coast. **Lake Quinault Lodge** (888.896.3818, olympicnationalparks.com) is open year-round. Rooms range from basic hotel accommodations ($179/night) to luxury suites ($352/night). Reduced rates are available during winter. **Massage** rates are $75 (60 minutes) and $100 (90). Pool, sauna, and a game room are also on-site.

Camping is available at **Graves Creek** (30 sites, $20/night, no water in winter) and **North Fork** (9, $15, no water in winter). During summer, extra camping space is available nearby in Olympic National Forest.

Quinault is one of the best locations to hear newborn elk in spring or bulls bugling in fall. The region is also known for its record setting trees. Several champion or former champion trees can be found along the area's **hiking trails**. Two of the largest are easily accessible. A massive western red cedar is found at the end of 0.4-mile **Quinault Big Cedar Trail**. The trailhead is located on North Shore Road on the northwest side of Lake Quinault, 2 miles north of US-101. The other is **Big Sitka Spruce**, which is actually located in Olympic National Forest. It stands at the northeastern edge of Lake Quinault and can be accessed via a short spur road from South Shore Road. Several trails venture deep into the backcountry from the end of North Fork Road and Graves Creek Road. **Backpackers** can pick up bear canisters, backcountry permits, and topographic maps from the USFS/NPS Information Station on South Shore Road. It's open daily in summer, and weekends only for the remainder of the year.

Staircase

Staircase is located in the park's southeast corner. Staircase Road may be gated in winter. Call (360) 565-3131 for status. Backcountry permits, bear canisters, and maps are available at the **ranger station** (open intermittently when staffing allows). The **campground** has 49 campsites available on a first-come, first-served basis for $20/night. During winter, sites may be walk-in only and water is not available. The majority of hiking trails follow the North Fork Skokomish River.

Deer Park

Deer Park Road runs south from US-101 between Port Angeles and Sequim. At the park boundary pavement gives way to gravel and the road twists, turns, and climbs nearly 6,000 feet to Deer Park on the east side of the Olympics. The road is narrow, steep, not suitable for

Bobcat in Hoh Rainforest

RVs or trailers, and only open in summer. A **ranger station** is staffed intermittently during summer and fall. A total of 14 tent-only **campsites** are available on a first-come, first served basis from mid-June through mid-fall for $15/night. Water is not available.

Deer Park resides in the rain shadow of the Olympic Mountain Range, receiving only 18 inches of rain annually. It is especially phenomenal compared to Mount Olympus, located just 20 miles west of Deer Park, which receives up to 220 inches of precipitation (half snow) each year. Another 10 miles to the west is Hoh Rain Forest and Forks, which receives the most rain in the contiguous U.S., roughly 120 inches annually, an incredible contrast considering the two areas are only 100 miles apart (by car, even closer as the crow flies).

There are some nice trails at Deer Park. **Experienced hikers** with good map-reading and route-finding skills can make a loop by hiking from Deer Park to Obstruction Point (7.4 miles, one-way) then heading south to Grand and Moose Lakes (~3 miles). From here, continue along a primitive trail across Grand Pass (~1 mile) and follow Cameron Creek Trail (~3 miles) to Three Forks Trail (2.1 miles) back to Deer Park.

Flora & Fauna

You may see Roosevelt elk, black bear, mountain goats, beavers, or marmots. The park is also home to about 300 species of birds. Among them are bald eagles, osprey, and northern pygmy owl. Over 1,450 types of vascular plants grow on the Olympic Peninsula. Most famous are the giant Sitka spruce, western hemlock, Douglas fir, and western red cedar of Queets, Quinault, and Hoh Rain Forest.

Olympic Mainland Hiking Trails (Distances are roundtrip)

	Name	Location (# on map)	Length	Difficulty Rating & Notes
Heart O' Hills/Hurricane Ridge	Heart O' the Forest	Campground Loop E (1)	4.0 miles	E – Trek through pristine old-growth forest
	Heather Park	Near Camp Entrance (1)	12.4 miles	S – Climbs 4,150 ft, 4 miles to meadow
	Lake Angeles	Near Camp Entrance (1)	12.6 miles	S – Loop w/ Heather Park, Lake Angeles at 3.4 mi
	Big Meadows Trails	Near Visitor Center (2)	2.0 miles	E – Cirque Rim, Big Meadows, and High Ridge Trails
	Klahhane Ridge - 🐾	Near Visitor Center (2)	5.6 miles	S – Switchbacks, connects to Heart O' the Hills
	Wolf Creek	Near Picnic Area A (3)	16.0 miles	M – Descends almost 4,000 ft to Whiskey Bend
	Hurricane Hill - 🐾	End of Hurricane Hill Rd (4)	3.2 miles	M – First 0.25-mile is paved, panoramic views
	Little River	Hurricane Hill Trail (4)	16.0 miles	S – Descends 4,000+ feet to Little River Road
	Hurricane Hill/Elwha	Hurricane Hill Trail (4)	11.6 miles	S – Descends 5,250 feet to Whiskey Bend Road
Elwha	Madison Falls	Near Park Boundary (5)	0.2 mile	E – Wheelchair-accessible, 60-ft waterfall
	Cascade Rock	Elwha Campground (6)	4.2 miles	M – Hike through forest to valley views
	Griff Creek	Elwha Ranger Station (7)	5.6 miles	M – Forested trail to wide open viewpoint
	West Lake Mills	Glines Canyon Dam (8)	3.8 miles	E – Flat trail along the west shore of Lake Mills
	West Elwha	Altair Campground (8)	6.4 miles	E – Flat trail along the west bank of Elwha River
	Happy Lake Ridge	Near Observation Pt (9)	19.0 miles	M – Steep climb (4,100-ft gain) to ridge and lake
	Appleton Pass	Olympic Hot Springs Rd (10)	15.4 miles	S – Hot springs, Boulder Lake, can start at Sol Duc
	Humes Ranch	Whiskey Bend Rd (11)	6.5 miles	M – Loop, can shorten via intersecting trails
	Upper Lake Mills	Whiskey Bend Rd (11)	1.0 mile	M – Short but steep, inaccessible due to flooding
Sol Duc	Ancient Groves	Near Park Boundary (12)	0.6 mile	E – Self-guiding loop through old-growth forest
	Lover's Lane	Sol Duc Campground (13)	5.8 miles	M – Loop connects Sol Duc Resort and Falls
	Mink Lake	Sol Duc Campground (13)	5.2 miles	M – Climb through dense forest to small lake
	Sol Duc Falls - 🐾	Sol Duc Falls Trailhead (14)	1.6 miles	E – Popular hike to a three-pronged falls
	Deer Lake	Sol Duc Falls Trailhead (14)	15.2 miles	M – Trail junction just before Sol Duc Falls
Hoh	Hall of Mosses - 🐾	Visitor Center (15)	0.8 mile	E – Loop through old-growth rain forest
	Spruce Nature	Visitor Center (15)	1.2 miles	E – Skirts Hoh River (elk potential) for a bit
	Hoh River	Visitor Center (15)	34.8 miles	S – Ends at Glacier Meadows (Mt Olympus views)
	S Snider–Jackson	Near Entrance Station (16)	10.0 miles	M– Primitive trail to Bogachiel River (must ford)
Quinalt	Quinault Big Cedar	North Shore Road (17)	0.4 mile	E – Short and flat walk to huge cedar tree
	Maple Glade	Near Ranger Station (18)	0.5 mile	E – Short loop through big leaf maple grove
	Kestner Homestead	Ranger Station (18)	1.3 miles	E – Self-guiding loop about homesteading life
	Irely Lake	Near North Fork Camp (19)	2.2 miles	E – Short and relatively flat hike to shallow lake
Staircase	Wagonwheel Lake	Ranger Station (20)	5.8 miles	S – Very steep, gains more than 1,000 feet per mile
	Shady Lane	Campground (20)	1.8 mile	E – Leads to Four Stream Rd and Lake Cushman
	Flapjack Lakes	Campground (20)	15.0 miles	S – Spur trail to Black and White Lakes
	N Fork Skokomish	Campground (20)	15.1 miles	S – Intersects Duckabush River Trail
Deer Park	Rain Shadow	Blue Mtn Parking Area (21)	0.5 mile	E – Self-guiding loop to the top of Blue Mountain
	Obstruction Point	Ranger Station (21)	14.8 miles	M – Highest trail in park, Mount Olympus views
	Three Forks	Campground (21)	8.6 miles	S – Connects with Gray Wolf River Trail

Difficulty Ratings: E = Easy, M = Moderate, S = Strenuous

Ozette

Ozette is located on the northwestern coast of the Olympic Peninsula. It can be reached by taking WA-113/WA-112 north from US-101 to Hoko–Ozette Road, which eventually runs along the northern shoreline of Ozette Lake and to the coastline. Ozette is one of the more remote regions, at least an hour away from the next closest destination. The **campground** is open all year. All 15 sites are available on a first-come, first-served basis for $20/night. Running water is not available, and there are only pit-toilets.

Cape Alava (6.6 miles) and **Sand Point** (5.6 miles) are two **hiking trails** that have become quite popular thanks to the addition of boardwalks and stairs. You can connect both trails by a 3.1-mile stretch of sand and rock beach for a 9.2-mile loop. If you're looking for a more remote gem, look no further than **Shi Shi Beach**. It's located at the very northern corner of the Ozette area and is accessed via a short hiking trail beginning at the end of Hobuck Road in the Makah Indian Reservation. (**Parking requires a Makah Recreation Pass**, which can be purchased in Neah Bay at Makah Marina, The Museum at the Makah Culture and Research Center, Washburn's General Store, Makah Mini Mart, Makah Tribal Center, or Hobuck Beach Resort.) Reaching the beach requires a short but steep final descent (aided by a rope). You can also reach Shi Shi Beach from Ozette, following the coast for 15 miles. Backpackers can camp along the Ozette Coast (at Shi Shi Beach and beyond). Due to popularity, reservations are required from May through September. Contact the Wilderness Information Center in Port Angeles at (360) 565-3100 to make reservations. Animal-resistant food containers are required for storing food because of raccoons, not black bears. Make sure you have everything you need for your trip. The only close place to restock or purchase last minute supplies is a small store just outside the park boundary. It carries bare essentials and rents food storage buckets. **All hikers exploring the coast should carry (and know how to use) a tide table.** Several areas are only passable at low tides, and getting trapped is a possibility.

Mora & La Push

WA-110 runs west from US-101, just north of Forks (of Twilight book fame). **Mora Campground**, located along the Quillayute River, is open all year. There are 94 sites, all first-come, first-served, with access to running water for $20/night. Hookups are not available, but a dump station (fee) is. Some sites can accommodate RVs up to 35 feet in length. Short **hikes** to **Second Beach** (1.4 mile), **Third Beach** (2.8 miles), and **Rialto Beach** (3.0 miles) provide opportunities to explore the rocky shore that is pounded by waves and covered with giant drift logs. All three of these trails are really great.

Olympic Coast Hiking Trails (Distances are roundtrip unless noted otherwise)

	Name	Location (# on map)	Length	Difficulty Rating & Notes
Ozette	Cape Alava	Ranger Station (22)	6.6 miles	E – Boardwalk through forest and prairie to beach
	Sandpoint	Ranger Station (22)	5.6 miles	E – Mostly boardwalk to sandy beach
	Ozette Loop - ♿	Ranger Station (22)	9.2 miles	E – Beach connects Cape Alava and Sandpoint Trails
	Shi Shi Beach - ♿	Hobuck Road (23)	4.0 miles	M – Steep descent to beach, Makah Rec. Pass required
Mora	James Pond	Ranger Station (24)	0.3 mile	E – Flat loop through forest to small pond
	Slough	Ranger Station (24)	1.8 miles	E – Hike through forest to the Quillayute River
	Rialto Beach - ♿	End of Mora Road (25)	3.0 miles	E – Long driftwood-covered beach near parking area
	N Coast Wilderness	End of Mora Road (25)	20.6 miles	E/M – Continue north beyond Rialto Beach (1-way)
La Push	Second Beach - ♿	La Push Road (26)	1.4 miles	E – Short trail, you'll have to crawl over some driftwood
	Third Beach - 👍	La Push Road (27)	2.8 miles	E – Short trail with somewhat steep descent to beach
	S Coast Wilderness	La Push Road	17.1 miles	E/M – Permit required for backcountry camping (1-way)

Kalaloch features 1-mile Kalaloch Nature Trail, which passes through coastal forest • Seven separate trails lead from US-101 to the ocean • Ruby Beach and Beach Trail #4 have wheelchair-accessible viewpoints and restrooms

Difficulty Ratings: E = Easy, M = Moderate, S = Strenuous

Kalaloch Beach

Kalaloch

Kalaloch, Olympic's southernmost stretch of Pacific Coast land, is easily accessed via US-101, which runs directly through the region. **Kalaloch Lodge** (866.662.9928, thekalalochlodge.com) is open all year. During peak season, rooms cost anywhere from $235/night for a basic motel style room to $370/night for a suite. Just north of the lodge is a **campground** that features 170 campsites available year-round for $22/night. Sites can be reserved from mid-June through early September by calling (877) 444-6777 or clicking recreation.gov. A dump station (fee) is available on-site.

Easy access and abundant overnight accommodations make Kalaloch one of the most popular regions of Olympic National Park. **Beachcombers** can rejoice as there are seven short trails leading to the waterfront. **It's also a great location to watch for whales during their spring migration (March–May).** Still, we prefer nearby Ruby Beach and La Push/Mora for beaches.

Flora & Fauna

Lucky guests may spot seals, sea lions, puffins, or sea otters while exploring the coastline. Look for gray whales between March and May during their annual migration north to summer feeding grounds. In all, 29 species of marine mammals have been documented in the park's waters. Beach gives way to dense coniferous forests where you may see bald eagles perched atop a towering western red cedar.

Ranger Programs

Ranger-led programs are available throughout the summer at Park Headquarters, Heart O' the Hills, Hurricane Ridge, Lake Crescent, Sol Duc, Staircase (weekends only), Hoh Rain Forest, Quinault, Mora, and Kalaloch. Activities include walks, talks, and campfire programs. Check the current issue of the park publication, *The Bugler* (available online, and at visitor centers and entrance stations), for an up-to-date schedule of events. It is highly recommended that you try to incorporate at least one ranger-led activity into your plans.

For Kids

Children are invited to participate in the park's **Junior Ranger Program**. First, pick up a free activity booklet at any visitor center. After completing the activities return to a visitor center to show your work to a park ranger. Successful participants will become an official Olympic National Park Junior Ranger and receive a badge for the effort.

Pets

Pets are allowed in the park, but must be kept on a leash no more than six feet in length at all times. They are permitted only in park campgrounds, picnic areas, and parking lots. Pets are not allowed on trails or beaches, except the following: Rialto Beach, all Kalaloch Beaches, and Peabody Creek Trail.

Accessibility

Accessibility is mentioned in each respective region.

Weather

Extreme differences in elevation and rainfall make generalizing weather here exceptionally difficult. Elevation varies from sea level to 7,980 feet at Mount Olympus. Average annual rainfall varies from 18 to 220 inches depending on where you are. There are distinct dry and wet seasons. Dry season is the most popular time to visit and typically lasts from June through September. Only a few weekend cross-country skiing diehards venture to Hurricane Ridge during winter.

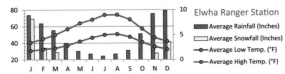

Elwha Ranger Station
■ Average Rainfall (Inches)
□ Average Snowfall (Inches)
—●— Average Low Temp. (°F)
—●— Average High Temp. (°F)

Vacation Planner

When planning a trip to Olympic National Park you have to determine overnight accommodations, regions to visit, and how much driving you want to do. **Lodges** are available at Lake Crescent, Sol Duc, Quinault, and Kalaloch. Nearby dining, grocery stores, lodging, festivals, and attractions are listed on pages 600–603.

There are 16 campgrounds and more than 900 sites to choose from, but they do fill during summer. You can play it safe by reserving a site at Lake Crescent (page 585), Sol Duc (page 586), or Kalaloch (page 590). All other campgrounds are first-come, first-served. Stop and set up camp before you begin exploring a region (especially on summer weekends).

If you want to see several regions without moving your tent or camper, you may want to set up base camp at Kalaloch or Fairholme on Lake Crescent. Quinault, Queets, and Hoh Rain Forest are relatively close to Kalaloch. Hurricane Ridge, Elwha, and Sol Duc are all within a reasonable drive from Lake Crescent. Fairholme is also a good location to make the trip to Ozette (see driving distances chart).

If you're planning on driving the entire Olympic Peninsula Loop on US-101, make sure you stop at Hurricane Ridge, Hoh Rain Forest, Ruby Beach at Kalaloch, and Quinault. Shi Shi Beach at Ozette and the Mora Beaches (Second, Third, and Rialto) are really nice, too, with Second Beach being our favorite.

Family hiking in Sol Duc

Elwha Trail/Hurricane Hill

Elwha	Fairholme	Heart O'The Hills	Hoh Rain Forest	Hurricane Ridge	Kalaloch	Lake Crescent	Mora/La Push	Port Angeles	Seattle (by ferry)	Sol Duc	Staircase	Quinault
23												
18	31											
79	57	96										
30	43	12	108									
81	59	100	40	112								
16	7	26	65	38	67							
60	36	75	47	87	49	44						
11	26	5	91	17	95	21	70					
85	100	77	156	89	160	93	137	72				
39	16	45	72	57	72	16	49	40	114			
111	126	105	191	117	195	121	170	100	110	140		
123	102	133	75	146	33	108	84	128	362	132	126	

Easy Pass

North Cascades

810 State Route 20
Sedro–Woolley, WA 98284
Phone: (360) 854-7200
Website: nps.gov/noca

Established: October 2, 1968
Size: 684,000 Acres
Annual Visitors: 20,000
Peak Season: Summer

Activities: Hiking, Backpacking,
Whitewater Rafting, Boating,
Rock Climbing, Biking, Horseback
Riding, and Cross-Country Skiing

Campgrounds: Goodell Creek,
Newhalem Creek*, George Lake,
Colonial Creek, and Hozomeen
Fee: Free–16/night
Backcountry Camping: Permitted
with a free Backcountry Use Permit

Park Hours: All day, every day
Entrance Fee: None
National Forest Day Pass: $5/day

*Reserve at recreation.gov or (877)
444-6777

The North Cascades are brimming with old-growth forests, hundreds of glaciers, and pure alpine lakes. They are a hiker's paradise as unique in landscape as in name: North Cascades National Park Service Complex. The only one of its kind, this complex unites three park units: North Cascades National Park (North and South Units), Ross Lake National Recreation Area (NRA), and Lake Chelan NRA. The mountains, named for an abundance of waterfalls, form an imposing natural barrier, preventing all but the most determined visitors from entering their depths. Many people have tried their luck at making a living among these mountains, but few succeeded. Today, that task is much easier thanks to considerable infrastructure and a healthy, but not overwhelming, tourism industry. North Cascades Scenic Highway pierces the Cascades, crossing them from east to west as the roadway runs the entire length of Ross Lake NRA. Travel further from the beaten path—into river-carved valleys, on top of rocky ridgelines, far away from the scenic byway—and you'll begin to see the landscape as its earliest inhabitants saw it, wild and free.

Native Americans lived in these mountains for thousands of years. Their lives were tied to the surroundings. Two major tribes lived in the region, one on each side of the Cascades. People of the Columbia River Basin lived to the east. People of the Pacific Northwest/Puget Lowlands lived to the west. They traded between each other, blazing trails across Stehekin (meaning "the way through"), and Cascade and Twisp Passes. They often followed high ridgelines to avoid navigating dense vegetation common in the lower elevations. Natives lived in harmony with the land; many Americans did their best to exploit it.

Several American expeditions traversed the North Cascades, mapping and documenting what they witnessed. Fur trappers came and went. Hundreds of miners hoping to strike it rich arrived in the late 1870s. They panned for gold along the banks of the Skagit River, but found very little. The rush ended by 1880. Trees were felled and floated along the Skagit River and Lake Chelan, but inadequate transportation and infrastructure spared the forests. The most significant alterations to the landscape came in the form of three dams along the Skagit River, but for the most part this rugged land remains wild and free.

Camping

The park runs five drive-in campgrounds. From west to east, **Goodell Creek** (Milepost 112, 19 sites, $16/night), **Newhalem Creek** (120, 111, $16), **George Lake** (126, 6, free), and **Colonial Creek** (130, 142, $16) Campgrounds are all located along North Cascades Highway (WA-20). **Hozomeen Campground** (75 sites, free), located in the park's northeast corner, is accessed via Skagit Road from Canada. Reservations are only accepted at Newhalem Creek Campground. They can be reserved for $16/night by calling (877) 444-6777 or clicking recreation.gov. All other campsites are available on a first-come, first-served basis.

Group sites are available at Upper and Lower Goodell Creek ($25/night or $34/night with reservation) and Newhalem Creek ($32 or $41). These sites may be reserved by calling (877) 444-6777 or clicking recreation.gov.

There are more than 100 designated campsites for backpackers and boaters in the backcountry. Beyond park boundaries there are more than a dozen developed campgrounds in national forest, state park, and county park land.

When to Go
The park is open all year, but winter weather impacts when most visitors arrive. Roads and facilities are generally open between late May and late October. Visitation is rarely excessive, but most guests arrive during July and August when the weather is usually pleasant and almost all trails are free of snow.

Transportation & Airports
Amtrak (1.800.872.7245, amtrak.com) and Greyhound (800.231.2222, greyhound.com) provide transportation along the I-5 corridor, but do not travel directly to the park. **Lady of the Lake** ($35.75–40.50 roundtrip, 888.682.4584, ladyofthelake.com) provides ferry service between Chelan and Stehekin. It operates daily from mid-March through early fall. The closest major airport is Seattle–Tacoma International (SEA), 130 miles southwest of North Cascades Visitor Center.

Directions
North Cascades National Park Service Complex is not easy to access by vehicle. The South Unit is only accessed via unpaved Cascade River Road. No roads penetrate the North Unit or Lake Chelan National Recreation Area. Most visitors enter the complex via WA-20 (North Cascades Scenic Highway), which crosses the Cascades and Ross Lake National Recreation Area (NRA).

Ross Lake NRA via Seattle (~140 miles): Heading north on I-5, take Exit 230 for WA-20 toward Burlington/Anacortes/Skagit Airport. Turn right at WA-20, and follow it about 60 miles to the park.

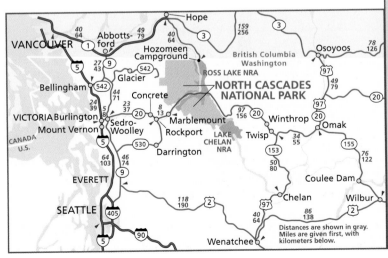

Regions

One of the most unique features about this park is that it's a **National Park Service Complex** consisting of three distinct units: North Cascades National Park (North and South Units) and Ross Lake and Lake Chelan National Recreation Areas (NRA). The National Recreation Areas have more lenient preservation and protection regulations, allowing local interests like hydroelectric facilities, resorts, and hunting to continue with limited federal intervention. Stephen Mather Wilderness unites the units as it encompasses roughly 94% of the entire complex.

North Cascades National Park is the least accessible portion. It is broken into north and south units by Ross Lake NRA, which straddles North Cascades Highway and Ross Lake, bisecting the complex. The North Unit is only accessible by foot. **Cascade River Road** provides vehicle access to the South Unit and is the only vehicle access point into the park. The 23-mile dirt and gravel roadway is typically open from summer through fall. It's rough, but also one of the most gorgeous drives in the entire collection of parks. Along the way you'll pass two National Forest campgrounds before crossing the park boundary. Eventually the road terminates at Cascade Pass Trailhead. Cascade Pass and the spur

trail to Sahale Mountain are two of the best hikes you'll find. Still, most visitors choose to hike into the north or south unit beginning at one of several trailheads located along WA-20 in Ross Lake NRA.

Ross Lake NRA serves as the centerpiece of the complex. Easy access via **North Cascades Scenic Hwy/ WA-20** and the majority of campgrounds, trailheads, and visitor facilities makes Ross Lake NRA the park's most popular region. The area protects stretches of the Skagit River, Diablo Lake, and 24-mile-long Ross Lake. Skagit River provides recreation all summer. Diablo and Ross Lakes provide paddlers with the opportunity for some unique multi-day backcountry trips or casual day-trips. Regularly scheduled boat tours are available on Ross Lake. But its only boat launch is accessed via a dirt and gravel road from Canada. **North Cascades Visitor Center**, located off WA-20 near Newhalem, is where you'll want to begin your trip. It's open daily, spring through fall, and on weekends in winter.

Lake Chelan NRA is located deep in the complex's southern reaches. It wraps around the north end of 55-mile-long Lake Chelan, the nation's third-deepest lake (1,486 ft). Visitors must hike, fly, or boat into this picturesque setting fit for a postcard. Even the ferry

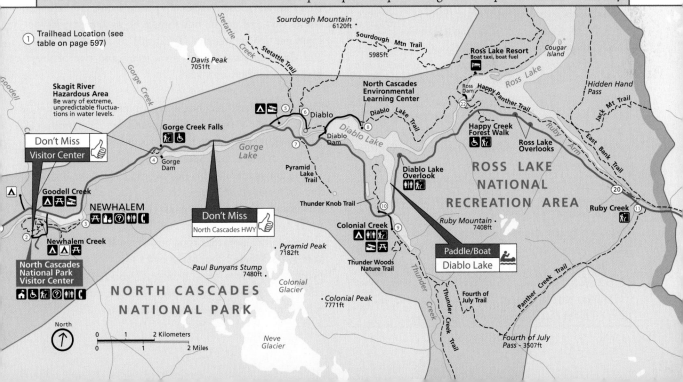

Sahale Glacier Trail

trip is great for viewing wildlife, waterfalls, and the shores of the glacially carved lake. The sights don't stop once you've reached **Stehekin**. You can explore historic Buckner Orchard or marvel at 312-foot Rainbow Falls. Stehekin cannot be reached by car, but there is a road; a shuttle ($7/adult, $4/child, $7/bike) transports visitors through the valley.

Visitor Centers
North Cascades Visitor Center (206.386.4495 ext. 11), located on North Cascades Highway (NCH) near Milepost 120, is open daily, May through late September, and weekends in October from 9am–5pm. It's closed November through April. **Park and Forest Information Center** (360.854.7200), located on NCH in Sedro–Wooley, is open daily, late May through September and weekdays only for the rest of the year, from 8am–4:30pm. **Wilderness Information Center** (360.854.7245), located on NCH near Marblemount (Milepost 105.3), is open daily from early May through mid-October, 8am–4:30pm (weekdays), 7am–6pm (weekends), with extended hours in summer. It's closed from mid-October through April. **Golden West Visitor Center** (360.854.7365 ext. 14), located near the passenger ferry landing in Stehekin, is open daily from mid-May through early October, 8:30am–5pm. It's closed from early October through mid-May.

Hiking

North Cascades Highway is nice, but to share a more intimate experience with the Cascades leave the car behind and set out on foot. Nearly 400 miles of hiking trails allow guests to explore the stunning beauty of the park's river-carved valleys and glacier-capped peaks. Most trailheads are located along North Cascades Highway and in Stehekin (Lake Chelan NRA), but the true day-hiker's paradise is **Cascade River Road** (closed seasonally). After mile 10, it becomes dirt and gravel, but should be passable by low-clearance 2WD vehicles. The trails to **Hidden Lake** and **Cascade Pass** are this area's gems and two of the best hikes in the Cascades.

Desolation Peak may not look impressive from a distance, but the views from its summit are tremendous. This peak is where Jack Kerouac found solitude working as a fire-watcher. Spellbinding scenery and isolation inspired some of his best work: *Desolation Angels* and *Dharma Bums*. To reach Desolation Peak, follow **East Bank Trail** from WA-20 (Milepost 138) for 16 miles to the junction for Desolation Peak. You can also reach this point via tour boat from **Ross Lake Resort** (206.386.4437, rosslakeresort.com) or your own private boat. From the junction it's another 6.8 miles climbing 4,400 feet to the peak. See the table on the following page for a more complete list of trails.

North Cascades Hiking Trails (Distances are roundtrip unless noted otherwise)

Section	Name	Location (# on map)	Length	Difficulty Rating & Notes
North Cascades Scenic Hwy (WA-20)	Thornton Lake	Thornton Lake Road (1)	10.4 miles	M – Steep climb to classic cirque lakes
North Cascades Scenic Hwy (WA-20)	Sterling Munro	North Cascades Visitor Center (2)	330 feet	E – Views of the Picket Range
North Cascades Scenic Hwy (WA-20)	River Loop	North Cascades Visitor Center (2)	1.8 miles	E – Forested hike to river and camp
North Cascades Scenic Hwy (WA-20)	To Know a Tree	New Halem Campground (3)	0.5 mile	E – Self-guiding, explores ecology
North Cascades Scenic Hwy (WA-20)	Rock Shelter	New Halem Campground (3)	0.3 mile	E – Visits 1,400-year-old hunting camp
North Cascades Scenic Hwy (WA-20)	Trail of the Cedars	River Loop/Linking Trails (3)	0.3 mile	E – Links Main Street and River Loop
North Cascades Scenic Hwy (WA-20)	Ladder Creek Falls	Gorge Powerhouse (4)	0.4 mile	E – Pretty cool "downtown" waterfall
North Cascades Scenic Hwy (WA-20)	Stetattle Creek	Near Diablo (5)	6.0 miles	M – Rock scrambling required
North Cascades Scenic Hwy (WA-20)	Sourdough Mtn	Near Diablo (6)	11.1 miles	S – 5.2 miles to lookout (1-way)
North Cascades Scenic Hwy (WA-20)	Pyramid Lake	WA-20 Milepost 126.8 (7)	4.2 miles	M – Small deep lake made by landslide
North Cascades Scenic Hwy (WA-20)	Diablo Lake - 👍	North of Diablo Lake (6)	7.6 miles	M – Lower elevation trail, glacier views
North Cascades Scenic Hwy (WA-20)	Thunder Creek - 👍	Colonial Creek Campground (9)	27.6 miles	E/S – Leads to Stehekin Valley
North Cascades Scenic Hwy (WA-20)	Thunder Knob	Colonial Creek Campground (10)	3.6 miles	M – Kid-friendly, Diablo Lake views
North Cascades Scenic Hwy (WA-20)	East Bank - 👍	WA-20 Milepost 138 (11)	31.0 miles	E – To Hozomeen (1-way), spurs to Little Jack and Desolation Peaks
North Cascades Scenic Hwy (WA-20)	Panther Creek	WA-20 Milepost 138 (11)	13.0 miles	M – 4th of July Pass, melts out early
North Cascades Scenic Hwy (WA-20)	Easy Pass/ Fisher Creek - 👍	WA-20 Milepost 151 (US Forest Pass required to park) (12)	7.0 miles 14.8 miles	S – One of the best trails, but difficult S – Thunder Creek Trail junction (1-way)
North Cascades Scenic Hwy (WA-20)	Rainy Lake - 👍	Rainy Pass on WA-20 (13)	1.0 mile	E – Excellent! Not in park, waterfalls
North Cascades Scenic Hwy (WA-20)	Maple Pass - 👍	Rainy Pass on WA-20 (13)	7.5 miles	M – Loop to easier pass than Easy Pass
North Cascades Scenic Hwy (WA-20)	Bridge Creek (PCT)	WA-20 Milepost 159 (14)	12.8 miles	E – PCT to Bridge Creek Camp (1-way)
Cascade RR	Monogram Lake	Travel 7 miles south on Cascade River Road from Marblemount (15)	10.0 miles	S – Climb 4,040 ft via switchbacks, and meander through subalpine meadows
Cascade RR	Hidden Lake - 👍	End of Sibley Creek Rd (16)	9.0 miles	M – 2,900-ft gain, popular day-hike
Cascade RR	Cascade Pass - 👍	End of Cascade River Rd (17)	7.4 miles 11.8 miles	M – Great views from the pass S – Or continue to Sahale Glacier
Stehekin (Lake Chelan)	Agnes Gorge	High Bridge (18)	5.0 miles	E – Wildflowers early and mid-summer
Stehekin (Lake Chelan)	Coon Lake	High Bridge/Bullion Camp (18)	2.6–3.8 mi	M – Birding and mountain views
Stehekin (Lake Chelan)	Old Wagon (PCT)	High Bridge (18)	Varies	E – Pacific Crest Trail • Connects valleys
Stehekin (Lake Chelan)	Goode Ridge	Old Wagon Trail (18)	10.0 miles	S – Views of Stehekin River drainage
Stehekin (Lake Chelan)	McGregor Mtn	Via Old Wagon Trail (18)	15.4 miles	S – Switchbacks to mountain summit
Stehekin (Lake Chelan)	Buckner Orchard	Near Rainbow Falls (19)	Varies	E – Self-guiding, pick apples in fall
Stehekin (Lake Chelan)	Rainbow Creek	Stehekin Valley Road (20)	19.4 miles	M – To McAlester Pass/Trail
Stehekin (Lake Chelan)	Rainbow Loop - 👍	Stehekin Valley Road (20)	8.8 miles	M – Loop via Stehekin Valley Road
Stehekin (Lake Chelan)	Purple Creek - 👍	Golden West Visitor Center (21)	16.2 miles	S – To Juanita Lake, loop options
Backpack Loops	Beaver Loop	Ross Dam Trail, Milepost 134 (22)	34.2 miles	Big and Little Beaver • Water taxi req'd
Backpack Loops	Rainbow and McAlester Pass	WA-20/Stehekin (14/20)	31.5 miles	M – Bridge Creek, McAlester Lake, Rainbow Creek and Lake Trail
Backpack Loops	Copper Ridge/ Chilliwack River - 👍	Hannegan Road in Mount Baker Wilderness (23)	33.5 miles	S – Sites along Copper Ridge fill quickly • Ice axe required until July
Backpack Loops	Devil's Dome	East Bank or Canyon Creek Trail-head on WA-20 (11)	40.4 miles	S – Through Okanogan National Forest, finishes on East Bank Trail (Lake Diablo)

Difficulty Ratings: E = Easy, M = Moderate, S = Strenuous

Backpacking

Wilderness camping is only allowed at designated sites along trail corridors. All overnight stays in the backcountry require a **free backcountry permit**. Permits are issued in person up to one day prior to your intended date of departure at the **Wilderness Information Center** (WIC, 360.854.7245) in Marblemount. It is located just off WA-20 on the park's west side. In summer it's open from 7am to 8pm on Friday and Saturday and 7am to 6pm from Sunday to Thursday. It's typically closed from mid-fall to early May. If you do not pass through Marblemount, you can obtain a permit at the ranger station closest to your destination. Permits are limited and popular areas like Cascade Pass, Ross Lake, Copper Ridge, and Thorton and Monogram Lakes can fill quickly. Backpacking trips should be planned in advance using a good topographic map. A few suggested loop trips are provided in the table on the previous page.

Stehekin Outfitters (509.682.7741, stehekinoutfitters.com), located in Stehekin, offers 5-day hiking trips ($495/person) and horseback rides ($60, 2.5 hours).

Biking

Bikes are only allowed on park roads. Road cyclists have one option: **North Cascades Highway**. Traffic is manageable, but the elevation gain is sure to make your thighs burn. Bicycling is also a great way to explore **Stehekin Valley Road**. Bicycles can be brought aboard Chelan Lake Ferry ($13.50/one-way, $24/roundtrip) or you can **rent** one from Discovery Bikes (stehekindiscoverybikes.com). Rentals cost $5 (hour), $25 (8am–5pm), and $30 (24 hours).

Fishing

Stehekin Fishing Adventures (stehekinfishing-adventures.com) offers guided fishing trips on Lake Chelan and around Stehekin. Rates are $195–215/person (half-day) and $340–360/person (full-day).

Other Activities

Opportunities for mountaineering, rock climbing, kayaking, canoeing, rafting, snowshoeing, and cross-country skiing are also available at North Cascades. Refer to page 602 for a list of the park's approved outfitters. **North Cascades Institute** (360.854.2599, ncascades.org) offers a wealth of courses and experiences throughout northwest Washington. Many programs take place right in the heart of North Cascades National Park at North Cascades Environmental Learning Center on the north shoreline of Diablo Lake. Programs include bird-watching expeditions, photography classes, mountain hikes, and educational discussions. Cost is anywhere from $50 to $395 per day. Meals and lodging are often included at the Learning Center campus.

Ranger Programs

Rangers offer guided boat tours (fee) on Lake Chelan and Ross Lake, bus tours (fee) of Stehekin Valley Road, and a variety of free walks, talks, and evening programs in summer. Current schedules are available at the park website or at any visitor information center.

For Kids

Children are welcome to participate in the **Junior Ranger Program**. Four booklets are available at the park's information centers. They are also available online at the park website. Complete the activities in the booklet appropriate for your age and head to a visitor center to receive a Junior Ranger badge, patch, and certificate.

Flora & Fauna

North Cascades is home to more than 1,600 species of vascular plants and at least 500 species of animals. Wildflower meadows burst with color; some bloom as early as February and others as late as September. Trees, including western red cedar, Sitka spruce, Douglas fir, and western hemlock, dominate all but the highest elevations. You're most likely to spot black-tailed deer, Douglas squirrel, or playful pika, but you may encounter black bears, mountain goats, or wolves while exploring the park.

Pets

Bringing your pet severely limits what you can do here. In the national park pets are only allowed on a leash on the Pacific Crest Trail and within 50 feet of roads. They must be kept on a leash at all times in Ross Lake or Lake Chelan NRAs.

Accessibility

North Cascades Visitor Center, Sedro–Woolley Information Station, and the Wilderness Information Office are fully accessible to wheelchair users. Golden West Visitor Center is accessible with assistance. Rock Shelter is the only accessible hiking trail.

Weather

Mountain weather is downright baffling. Snow can fall any day of the year in the North Cascades. WA-20 can close and be buried in snow between November and February. Then there are outliers like the winter of 1976–'77 when North Cascades Highway/WA-20 remained open all year. The western slopes receive, on average, 76 more inches of rain and 407 more inches of snowfall than their eastern counterparts that reside in the mountain's rain shadow. You're never guaranteed beautiful weather in the Cascades, but the best bet is to travel between mid-June and late September.

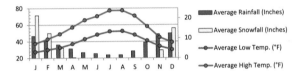

Vacation Planner

Most visitors drive through the park via **North Cascades Highway** or take a **ferry ride to Stehekin** (page 593). **Campgrounds** (page 593) are rarely full. **Lodging** facilities are also available in Stehekin and Ross Lake NRA. We combined them with the nearby dining, grocery stores, lodging, festivals, and attractions listed on pages 600–603. Provided below is a sample one-day itinerary for each destination. Cascade Pass (accessed via Cascade River Road from Marblemount) is one of the best attractions, but it's been omitted because many visitors are uncomfortable or unwilling to traverse the gravel road leading into this region (but you really should—it's incredible!).

North Cascades Highway: Beeline for the **Visitor Center** (Milepost 120), where you can ask a ranger questions, check a schedule of the day's ranger programs, watch an introductory film, browse exhibits, and use the restrooms. If you'd like to stretch your legs, **Sterling Munro and River Loop Trails** are available. However,

Diablo Lake Overlook

there are better hikes ahead. Stop at **Gorge Creek Falls and Overlook** for a couple short interpretive trails. Continuing east, stop at **Diablo Lake Overlook**. Next, stop at **East Bank Trailhead** (Milepost 138). To the north, East Bank Trail is great for families. It's flat and easy, following the shoreline of Ross Lake. To the southwest is Panther Creek Trail. It is more rigorous (and more beautiful). Hike 6.5 miles (one-way) to 4th of July Pass. Alternatively, you can continue along North Cascades Highway outside the park to **Rainy Pass**. The 7.5-mile Maple Pass Loop found nearby is challenging and stunning. (Just down the road, the 2.2-mile trail to **Blue Lake** is an easier alternative. It's also really great!)

Stehekin: This remote community of 80 or so year-round residents is completely disconnected from society. No roads lead in or out of the quiet mountain retreat. That's one of the biggest draws, not to mention the fact that you're surrounded by glaciated mountains, tumbling waterfalls, and pristine water. From **Stehekin Landing**, begin by stopping in at **Golden West Visitor Center** where you can view exhibits of the area's natural and cultural history. When it comes to exploring the region you have three choices: hike, bike, or shuttle. To get right after the hiking, head into the mountains to Juanita Lake via **Purple Creek Trail**. Energetic hikers can combine Purple Creek Trail with Boulder Creek Trail, which loops back to Stehekin Valley Road at Rainbow Falls. In fall, stroll over to Buckner Orchard to pick an apple or two. (**If you're only here for a day-trip, your best bet is to join a shuttle tour.**)

Dining

Mount Rainier Area

Wild Berry Restaurant • (360) 569-2277
37718 WA-706 E, Ashford
rainierwildberry.com

Highlander Steak House • (360) 569-2953
30319 WA-706 E, Ashford

Butter Butte Coffee Co • (360) 494-5600
105 Main St E, #791, Packwood

Cruisers Pizza • (360) 494-5400
13028 US-12, Packwood

Blue Spruce Diner • (360) 494-5605
13019 US-12, Packwood

Sushi Town • (253) 987-7632
20649 WA-410, Bonney Lake

Wally's White River Drive-in
282 WA-410 North, Buckley • (360) 829-0871

Olympic Peninsula

Alder Wood Bistro • (360) 683-4321
139 West Alder St, Sequim
alderwoodbistro.com • Entrée: $17–26

Dockside Grill • (360) 683-7510
2577 W Sequim Bay Rd, Sequim
docksidegrill-sequim.com

Dynasty Chinese Restaurant • (360) 683-6511
990 E Washington St, Sequim

Hi-Way 101 Diner & Pizza • (360) 683-3388
392 W Washington St, Sequim

Oak Table Café • (360) 683-2179
292 W Bell St, Sequim
oaktablecafe.com • Breakfast: $9+

Sunshine Café • (360) 683-4282
145 W Washington St, Sequim

Café Garden • (360) 457-4611
1506 E 1st St, Port Angeles
cafegardenpa.com • Entrée: $18–32

Michael's Seafood & Steakhouse
117-B E 1st St, Port Angeles • (360) 417-6929
michaelsdining.com • Entrée: $15–49

Toga's • (360) 452-1952
122 W Lauridsen Blvd, Port Angeles

Sabai Thai • (360) 452-4505
903 W 8th St, Port Angeles
sabaithaipa.com

First Street Haven • (360) 457-0352
107 E 1st St, Port Angeles

Gordy's Pizza & Pasta • (360) 328-7977
1123 E 1st St, Port Angeles
gordyspizza.com • Pizza: $3.50–32

Taqueria Santanna • (360) 374-3339
80 Calawah Way, Forks

Forks Coffee Shop • (360) 374-6769
241 S Forks Ave, Forks

Pacific Pizza • (360) 374-2626
870 S Forks Ave, Forks

Hard Rain Café • (360) 374-9288
5763 Upper Hoh Rd, Forks
hardraincafe.com

Banana Leaf Thai Bistro • (360) 379-6993
609 Washington St, Port Townsend

Lanza's Ristorante • (360) 379-1900
1020 Lawrence St, Port Townsend

Hanazono Asian Noodle • (360) 385-7622
225 Taylor St, Port Townsend

Waterfront Pizza • (360) 385-6629
951 Water St, Port Townsend

Blue Moose Café • (360) 385-7339
311-B Haines Pl, Port Townsend

Sweet Laurette Café • (360) 385-4886
1029 Lawrence St, Port Townsend
sweetlaurette.com

North Cascades Area

Buffalo Run • (360) 873-2103
60084 WA-20, Marblemount
buffaloruninn.com

Marblemount Diner • (360) 873-4503
60147 WA-20, Marblemount

Annie's Pizza Station • (360) 853-7227
44568 WA-20, Concrete

Cascade Burgers • (360) 853-7580
45292 WA-20, Concrete

Milano's Restaurant & Deli • (360) 599-2863
9990 Mt Baker Hwy, Glacier

Chair 9 Pizza & Bar • (360) 599-2511
10459 Mt Baker Hwy, Glacier
chair9.com • Pizza: $17–23

Blue Mountain Grill • (360) 595-2200
974 Valley Highway, Acme
bluemountaingrill.com • Entrée: $10–22

Grocery Stores

Mount Rainier Area

Safeway • (360) 825-5023
152 Roosevelt Ave East, Enumclaw

Fred Meyer • (253) 891-7300
20901 WA-410, Bonney Lake

Walmart Supercenter • (253) 826-9144
19205 WA-410 E, Bonney Lake

Albertsons-Sav-on • (253) 826-2401
20025 WA-410 E, Bonney Lakes

Rose's IGA • (360) 829-0810
29393 WA-410 E, Buckley

Olympic Peninsula

Safeway • (360) 457-0788
110 E 3rd St, Port Angeles

Albertsons • (360) 452-2307
114 E Lauridsen Blvd, Port Angeles

Safeway • (360) 457-1461
2709 E US-101, Port Angeles

Safeway • (360) 681-8767
680 W Washington St, Sequim

Walmart • (360) 452-1244
3411 E Kolonels Way, Port Angeles

Costco • (360) 406-2023
955 W Washington St, Sequim

Walmart • (360) 683-9346
1110 W Washington St, Sequim

North Cascades Area

Walmart • (360) 428-7000
2301 Freeway Dr, Mount Vernon

Costco • (360) 757-5703
1725 S Burlington Blvd, Burlington

Lodging

Mount Rainier Area

Deep Forest Cabins • (360) 569-2054
33823 WA-706 E, Ashford
deepforestcabins.com • Rates: $125–350/night

Jasmer's • (360) 569-2682
30005 WA-706 E, Ashford
jasmers.com • Rates: $135–350

Wellspring Spa • (360) 569-2514
54922 Kernahan Rd E, Ashford
wellspringspa.com • Rates: $95–575

Nisqually Lodge • (360) 569-8804
31609 WA-706, Ashford
whitepasstravel.com • Rates: $110+

Copper Creek Inn & Restaurant
35707 WA-706 E, Ashford • (360) 569-2799
coppercreekinn.com • Rates: $89+

Mountain Meadows B&B • (360) 569-2788
28912 WA-706 East, Ashford
mountainmeadows-inn.com • Rates: $120

Crest Trail Lodge • (360) 494-4944
12729 US-12, Packwood
whitepasstravel.com • Rates: $109+

Hotel Packwood • (360) 494-5431
104 Main St, Packwood
packwoodwa.com • Rates: $29–49

Mountain View Lodge • (360) 494-5555
13163 US-12, Packwood
mtvlodge.com • Rates: $45–150

Olympic Peninsula

Sequim Bay Lodge • (360) 683-0691
268522 US-101, Sequim
sequimbaylodge.com • Rates: $74+

Dungeness Bay Cottages • (360) 683-3013
140 Marine Dr, Sequim
dungenessbaycottages.com • Rates: $160–225

Dungeness Barn House B&B
42 Marine Dr, Sequim • (360) 582-1663
dungenessbarnhouse.com • Rates: $145–230

Red Caboose Getaway • (360) 683-7350
24 Old Coyote Way, Sequim
redcaboosegetaway.com • Rates: $175+

Sequim West Inn & RV Park • (800) 528-4527
740 W Washington St, Sequim
sequimwestinn.com • Rates: $59–199

Port Angeles Inn • (360) 452-9285
111 E 2nd St, Port Angeles
portangelesinn.com • Rates: $99+

All View Motel • (360) 457-7779
214 E Lauridsen Blvd, Port Angeles
allviewmotel.com • Rates: $69–109

Olympic Lodge • (800) 600-2993
140 S Del Guzzi Dr, Port Angeles
olympiclodge.com • Rates: $149–179

Colette's B&B • (360) 457-9197
339 Finn Hall Rd, Port Angeles
colettes.com • Rates: $195–375

Inn At Rooster Hill • (360) 452-4933
112 Reservoir Rd, Port Angeles
roosterhillshortstay.com • Rates: $109–179

Eden by the Sea • (360) 452-6021
1027 Finn Hall Rd, Port Angeles
edenbythesea.net • Rates: $150–215

George Washington Inn • (360) 452-5207
939 Finn Hall Rd, Port Angeles
georgewashingtoninn.com • Rates: $225–330

Pacific Inn Motel • (360) 374-9400
352 S Forks Ave, Forks
pacificinnmotel.com • Rates: $104+

Forks Motel • (360) 374-6243
351 S Forks Ave, Forks
forksmotel.com • Rates: $69+

Quillayute River Resort • (360) 374-7447
473 Mora Rd, Forks
qriverresort.com • Rates: $125–195

Miller Tree Inn B&B • (800) 943-6563
654 E Division St, Forks
millertreeinn.com • Rates: $115–250

Palace Hotel • (360) 385-0773
1004 Water St, Port Townsend
palacehotelpt.com • Rates: $89–159

Thornton House B&B • (360) 385-6670
1132 Garfield St, Port Townsend
thorntonhousept.com • Rates: $155–165

Inn At Mccurdy House • (360) 379-4824
405 Taylor St, Port Townsend
innatmccurdyhouse.com • Rates: $120–175

Blue Gull Inn B&B • (360) 379-3241
1310 Clay St, Port Townsend
bluegullinn.com • Rates: $110–140

Huber's Inn • (360) 385-3904
1421 Landes St, Port Townsend
hubersinn.com • Rates: $135–210

North Cascades Area

Buffalo Run Inn • (360) 873-2103
60117 WA-20, Marblemount
buffaloruninn.com • Rates: $54–124

Totem Trail Motel • (360) 873-4535
57627 WA-20, Rockport
totemtrail.com • Rates: $50+

Ross Lake Resort • (206) 386-4437
Water taxi service, boat/kayak rentals and portage
530 Diablo St, Rockport
rosslakeresort.com • Rates: $185–370

Ovenell's Heritage Inn • (360) 853-8494
46276 Concrete Sauk Valley Rd, Concrete
ovenells-inn.com • Rates: $145–250

Wintercreek B&B • (360) 599-2526
9253 Cornell Creek Rd, Glacier
wintercreekbandb.com

Stehekin

Silver Bay Lodging • (509) 670-0693
silverbayinn.com • Rates: $225–425

Stehekin Log Cabin • (509) 682-7742
stehekinpastry.com • Rates: $200–220

Rustic Retreat • (509) 682-2288
stehekinvalley.com

Stehekin Valley Ranch • (509) 682-4677
stehekinvalleyranch.com • Rates: $100–135

Many chain restaurants and hotels can be found nearby in Seattle, Tacoma, Sequim, Port Angeles, and along I-5.

Festivals

Tulip Festival • April
Skagit Valley • tulipfestival.org

Puyallup Fair • April
Puyallup • thefair.com

Apple Blossom Festival • April/May
Wenatchee • appleblossom.org

Northwest Folklife Festival • May
Seattle • nwfolklife.org

Sasquatch! Music Festival • May
George • sasquatchfestival.com

Independent Film Festival • May
Ashford • rainierfilmfest.com

Seafair • Summer
Seattle • seafair.com

Festival of Music • July
Bellingham • bellinghamfestival.org

Raspberry Festival • July
Lynden • lynden.org

International Kite Festival • August
Voted "Best Kite Festival in the World"
Long Beach • kitefestival.com

Bumbershoot • September
Seattle • bumbershoot.com

Rainier Mountain Festival • September
Ashford • RainierFestival.com

Decibel Festival • September
Seattle • dbfestival.com

Crab & Seafood Festival • October
Port Angeles • crabfestival.org

Juan De Fuca Festival • May
Port Angeles • jffa.org

Attractions
Mount Rainier Area

Mt St Helens Nat'l Volcanic Mon.
3029 Spirit Lake Hwy, Castle Rock
fs.usda.gov • (360) 274-0962 • Fee: $5

NW Trek Wildlife Park • (360) 832-6117
11610 Trek Dr E, Eatonville
nwtrek.org • Admission: $21.95/adult

Pioneer Farm Museum • (360) 832-6300
7716 Ohop Valley Rd E, Eatonville
pioneerfarmmuseum.org • Tours: $9/adult

John Day Fossil Beds Nat'l Mon.
32651 OR-19, Kimberly, OR
nps.gov/joda • (541) 987-2333 • Free

<u>Olympic Peninsula</u>
Olympic Raft & Kayak • (360) 452-1443
Kayaking, Rafting, and Rentals Available
123 Lake Aldwell Rd, Port Angeles
raftandkayak.com

Adventures Through Kayaking • (360) 417-3015
Kayaking, Mountain Biking, and Rafting
2358 US-101 W, Port Angeles
atkayaking.com

Feiro Marine Life Center • (360) 417-6254
315 N Lincoln St, Port Angeles
feiromarinelifecenter.org • Admission: $4/adult

Fine Art Center • (360) 457-3532
1203 E Lauridsen Blvd, Port Angeles
pafac.org • Free

Harbinger Winery • (360) 452-4262
2358 US-101 West, Port Angeles
harbingerwinery.com

Salt Creek Rec. Area • (360) 928-3441
3506 Camp Hayden Rd, Port Angeles

Olympic Cellars Winery • (360) 452-0160
255410 US-101, Port Angeles
olympiccellars.com

Renaissance • (360) 565-1199
401 E Front St, Port Angeles
renaissance-pa.com • Massage: $75 (1 hr)

Olympic Game Farm • (360) 683-4295
1423 Ward Rd, Sequim
olygamefarm.com • Admission: $14/adult

Purple Haze Organic Lavender Farm
180 Bell Bottom Rd, Sequim
purplehazelavender.com • (360) 683-1714

Dungeness NWR • Agnew-Carlsborg, WA

Forks Timber Museum • (360) 374-9663
1421 S Forks Ave, Forks

Wheel-In-Motor Movie Drive In
210 Theatre Rd, Port Townsend • (360) 385-0859

Puget Sound Express • (360) 385-5288
Whale Watch (Orca • $95/adult, Gray • $64)
227 Jackson St, Port Townsend
pugetsoundexpress.com

Port Townsend Brewing Co
330 10th St, Port Townsend
porttownsendbrewing.com • (360) 385-9967

Fort Worden State Park • (360) 344-4431
200 Battery Way, Port Townsend

Chetzemoka Park • (360) 379-3951
900 Jackson St, Port Townsend

Kelly Art Deco Light Museum • (360) 379-9030
2000 W Sims Way, Port Townsend

Jefferson County Historical • (360) 385-1003
540 Water St, Port Townsend
jchsmuseum.org • Admission: $6/adult

<u>North Cascades Area</u>
Pearrygin Lake State Park • (509) 996-2370
561 Bear Creek Rd, Winthrop

North Cascade Heli-Skiing • (509) 996-3272
31 Early Winters Dr, Mazama
heli-ski.com • Tours: $500+

Shafer Museum • (509) 996-2712
285 Castle Rd, Winthrop
shafermuseum.com

Lost River Winery • (509) 429-8122
26 WA-20, Winthrop
lostriverwinery.com • Tasting: Free

Howard Miller Steelhead Park • (360) 853-8808
52804 Rockport Park Rd, Rockport

Rasar State Park • (360) 826-3942
38730 Cape Horn Rd, Concrete
parks.wa.gov

Rockport State Park • (360) 853-8461
51905 WA-20, Rockport

Lake Chelan State Park • (509) 687-3710
7544 S Lakeshore Rd, Chelan

Mt Baker-Snoqualmie NF • (425) 783-6000
You'll find some excellent hiking trails along Mount Baker Scenic Byway, like the one above to Lake Ann (with Mount Shuksan, located in North Cascades National Park's North Unit) looming in the background.

Mt Baker • (360) 734-6771
1420 Iowa St, Bellingham
mtbaker.us • Lift Ticket: $53+

Chelan Seaplanes • (509) 682-5555
1328 W Wodin Ave, Chelan
chelanseaplanes.com • Tours: $249.98+

<u>Rafting Outfitters</u>
Alpine Adventures • (360) 863-6505
207 Croft Ave W, Gold Bar
alpineadventures.com • Rafting: $74+

Blue Sky Outfitters • (800) 228-7238
3400 Harbor Ave SW, Seattle
blueskyoutfitters.com • Rafting: $82+

N Cascades River Exp. • (360) 435-9548
31207 Bumgarner Rd, Arlington
riverexpeditions.com • Rafting: $70

Orion River Expeditions • (509) 548-1401
12681 Wilson St, Leavenworth
orionexp.com • Rafting: $70+

Pacific NW Float Trips • (360) 719-5808
20200 Cook Rd, Burlington
pacificnwfloattrips.com • Rafting: $77

Wildwater River Tours • (509) 470-8558
5706 US-97, Pashastin
wildwater-river.com • Rafting: $69

<u>Mountaineering/Hiking Guides</u>
Alpine Ascents International
alpineascents.com • (206) 378-1927

Alpine Endeavors
alpineendeavors.com • (877) 486-5769

American Alpine Institute
alpineinstitute.com • (360) 671-1505

American Mountain Guides
amga.com • (303) 271-0984

Cascade Adventure Guides
cascadeadventureguides.com • (425) 322-4675

Deli Llama Wilderness Adventures
delillama.com • (360) 757-4212

International Mountain Guides
mountainguides.com • (360) 569-2609

KAF Adventures
kafadventures.com • (206) 713-2149

North Cascades Mountain Guides
ncmountainguides.com • (509) 996-3194

Northwest Mountain School
mountainschool.com • (509) 548-5823

Peregrine Expeditions
peregrineexpeditions.com • (360) 393-8098

Pro Guiding Service
proguiding.com • (425) 888-6397

Rainier Mountaineering
rmiguides.com • (360) 569-2227

Beyond the Parks

👍**Snoqualmie Falls**
Famous waterfall, known from Twin Peaks
6501 Railroad Ave SE, Snoqualmie
snoqualmiefalls.com

👍**Kerry Park** • (206) 684-4075
211 W Highland Dr, Seattle

Discovery Park • (206) 386-4236
3801 Discovery Parkway, Seattle

Alki Beach Park • (206) 684-4075
1702 Alki Ave SW, Seattle

Pike Place Market • (206) 682-7453
85 Pike St, Seattle

Space Needle • (206) 905-2100
400 Broad St, Seattle
spaceneedle.com • Admission: $22/adult

Pacific Science Center • (206) 443-2001
200 Second Ave N, Seattle
pacificsciencecenter.org • Admission: $20/adult

Seattle Aquarium • (206) 386-4300
1483 Alaskan Way, Pier 59, Seattle
seattleaquarium.org • Admission: $22.95/adult

👍**Klondike Gold Rush Park** • (206) 220-4240
319 2nd Ave S, Seattle
nps.gov/klse • Free

The Museum of Flight • (206) 764-5700
9404 E Marginal Way S, Seattle
museumofflight.org • Admission: $20/adult

Seattle Art Museum • (206) 654-3000
1300 1st Ave, Seattle
seattleartmuseum.org • Admission: $20/adult

Olympic Sculpture Park • (206) 654-3100
2901 Western Ave, Seattle
seattleartmuseum.org • Free

Woodland Park Zoo • (206) 548-2500
5500 Pinney Ave N, Seattle
zoo.org • Admission: $13.75/adult

Washington Park Arboretum • (206) 543-8800
2300 Arboretum Dr E, Seattle

Seattle Wine Tours • (206) 444-9463
4660 E Marginal Way S, Seattle
seattlewinetours.com

Moss Bay Center • (206) 682-2031
1001 Fairview Ave N, Seattle
mossbay.co • Kayak Tours: $50/adult

Unexpected Productions Improv
1428 Post Alley, Seattle • (206) 587-2414
unexpectedproductions.org

Seattle Seaplanes • (206) 329-9638
1325 Fairview Ave E, Seattle
seattleseaplanes.com • Tours: $97.50+

San Juan Safaris • (800) 450-6858
2 Spring St Landing, Friday Harbor
sanjuansafaris.com • Kayak Tours: $89

👍**San Juan Excursions** • (360) 298-7755
2 Spring St, Friday Harbor
watchwhales.com • Whale Watch: $99

Island Adventures • (800) 465-4604
1801 Commercial Ave, Anacortes
island-adventures.com • Whale Watch: $69+

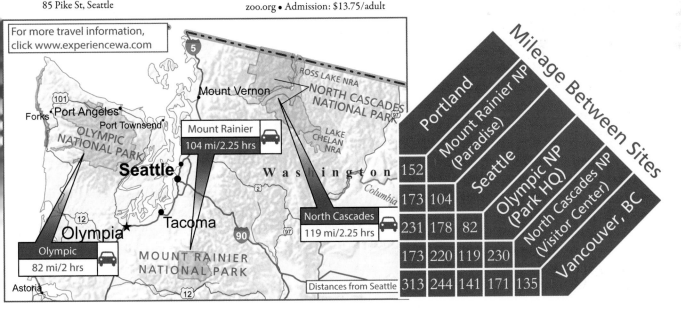

For more travel information, click www.experiencewa.com

Mount Rainier
104 mi/2.25 hrs

North Cascades
119 mi/2.25 hrs

Olympic
82 mi/2 hrs

Distances from Seattle

Mileage Between Sites

	Portland	Mount Rainier NP (Paradise)	Seattle	Olympic NP (Park HQ)	North Cascades NP (Visitor Center)	Vancouver, BC
	152					
	173	104				
	231	178	82			
	173	220	119	230		
	313	244	141	171	135	

A harbor seal pup

Glacier Bay

PO Box 140
Gustavus, AK 99826
Phone: (907) 697-2230
Website: nps.gov/glba

Established: December 2, 1980
February 25, 1925 (National
Monument)
Size: 3,283,000 Acres
Annual Visitors: 550,000
Peak Season: Summer (Peaks from
mid-July to mid-August)

Activities: Boat Tours (fee),
Hiking, Backpacking, Camping,
Kayaking, Boating, Flightseeing,
Fishing, and Wildlife Viewing

Campground: Bartlett Cove*
Fee: None
Backcountry Camping: Permitted*
Lodging: Glacier Bay Lodge
Rates: $199–224/night

Park Hours: All day, every day
Entrance Fee: None

*Campers must obtain a free permit
and attend an orientation program

Glacier Bay National Park, located in southeastern Alaska just 60 miles west of the state capital of Juneau (by boat or plane, there are no roads), is an incredible world of ice, mountains, and sea. More than one quarter of the park is ice, permanent but retreating at a frightening rate. When Joseph Whidbey sailed to the mouth of Glacier Bay in 1794 it was choked with ice more than 4,000 feet thick and up to 20 miles wide. The immense glacier stretched back to its source, more than 100 miles away in the St. Elias Mountain Range. By 1879, John Muir found that ice had already retreated 48 miles into the bay. In 1916, Grand Pacific Glacier had withdrawn all the way to the head of Tarr Inlet, roughly 65 miles from the mouth of Glacier Bay. This phenomenon has been one of the fastest glacial retreats on record, exposing new land and providing opportunities for scientists to study glaciation, plant succession, and animal dynamics. And hundreds of thousands of guests come to witness giant icebergs as they break away from tidewater glaciers in explosive fashion—also known as calving—from the deck of a cruise ship or tour boat.

Glacier Bay protects 50 named glaciers (including nine tidewater glaciers that terminate in the sea). Climatic changes caused most glaciers in the eastern and southwestern regions, like McBride, Muir, Reid, and Riggs Glaciers to retreat. Muir Glacier, with a 2-mile calving face, was once the most impressive, but it completely receded in the 1990s. On the bay's western shoreline, Johns Hopkins, Lamplugh, and Margerie Glaciers are stable or advancing and thickening. Today, most visitors stop and wait aboard a tour boat or cruise ship at the latter two, hoping ice will break from the glacier's face.

"To the lovers of pure wilderness Alaska is one of the most wonderful countries in the world...it seems as if surely we must at length reach the very paradise of the poets, the abode of the blessed."

– John Muir

John Muir, beloved naturalist and writer, became deeply interested in glaciers after years of hiking Yosemite Valley (which he proposed was carved by glaciers, not shaped by earthquakes). In 1879, Muir was first in a long line of scientists to visit Glacier Bay. He studied the recession of glaciers while enriching his spirit in the wilderness he loved so dearly. Muir visited again in 1899 as a member of the Harriman Alaska Expedition, organized by railroad tycoon Edward Harriman. His group of scientists, photographers, artists, and writers formed a who's who list of their respective fields. In September of that year, a massive earthquake shook Glacier Bay. Severed icebergs made the bay completely inaccessible to vessels for more than a decade, causing steamships to remove this destination from their itineraries. Visitation, exploration, and scientific research halted temporarily, but the area's beauty never diminished.

In 1925, President Calvin Coolidge established Glacier Bay National Monument. The area was preserved for its "tidewater glaciers in a magnificent setting, developing forests, scientific opportunities, historic interest, and accessibility." Commercial interests kept their eyes on the bay as well. In 1936, President Franklin D. Roosevelt reopened the area to mining. Ore was extracted from the mountains of Glacier Bay sporadically, and today there's still a claim on a significant nickel-copper bed that lies directly beneath Brady Glacier. In 1939, land was added to the national monument, doubling its size and making it the largest unit of the National Park System at the time. During WWII, the nearby city of Gustavus served as a strategic military location where a supply terminal was built. On a 600 acre tract of land, 800 buildings, 3 large docks, and an airstrip were constructed by 1943. After just a few months of use they were given to civilian control. Today, a short road linking Bartlett Cove and the airfield at Gustavus greatly increases park accessibility, allowing amateur scientists and lovers of nature to explore Glacier Bay on their own.

When to Go

Glacier Bay National Park is open all year, but you'd hardly know it come winter time. The visitor center (907.697.2661), located on the second floor of Glacier Bay Lodge, is open daily from late May to early September. Exhibits are open 24-hours and the information desk and bookstore are staffed from 11am to 9pm. The **Visitor Information Center for Boaters and Campers**, located at the head of the public-use dock in Bartlett Cove, is open daily, May to September. Hours are typically from 8am to 5pm. Extended hours from 7am to 9pm are available between June and August. **Glacier Bay National Preserve Office** (907.784.3295), located in Yakutat, provides rafting info. The Visitor Information Station, located at the head of the public-use dock in Bartlett Cove, is your go-to-location for information about camping and boating. It's open from May to September. Services in winter are extremely limited. Most visitors arrive via cruise ships from late May through mid-September. **Humpback whales** are seen during this entire period, but sightings increase in mid-June and peak around July and August. Regardless when you travel, be sure to dress in layers and pack rain gear.

Transportation & Airports

Glacier Bay National Park can only be reached by plane or boat. Within the park there is a 10-mile road that connects Gustavus and its airfield to the park headquarters at Bartlett Cove. It is possible to bring your vehicle via the Alaska Marine Highway Ferry System (page 607), but that's not recommended. Taxis run between Gustavus and Bartlett Cove upon request, and buses run a limited schedule. Cruise ships (page 611), tour vessels (page 611), and private boats all enter the bay. Private boaters entering Glacier Bay anytime between June and August must obtain a free permit (page 611) prior to their arrival. Permits are limited. The application form is available at the park website.

Air travel is the easiest method of arrival. Alaska Airlines (800.252.7522, alaskaair.com) provides daily service from Juneau to Gustavus (~30 minutes, ~$100) during the busy summer season. Other small

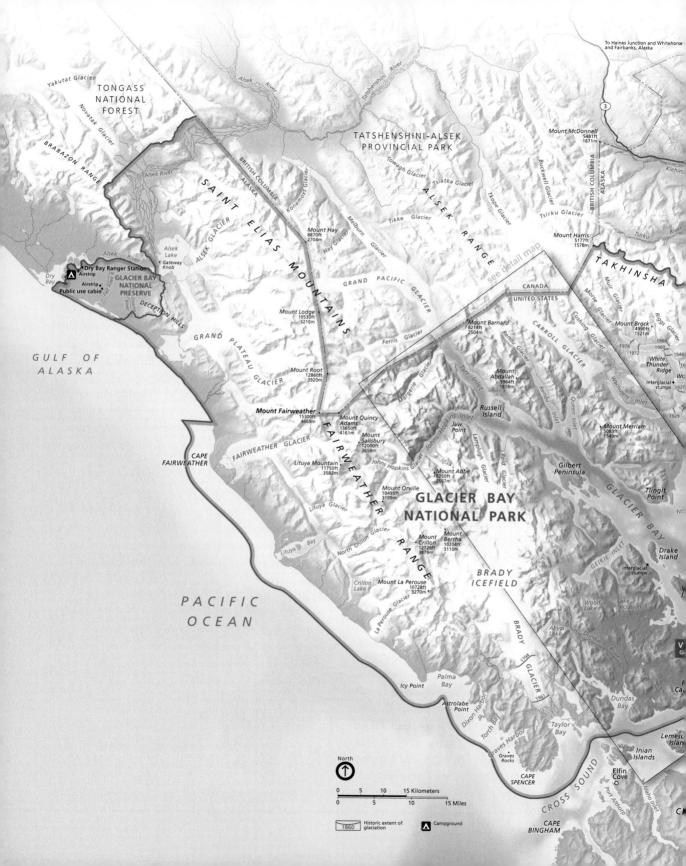

TONGASS
NATIONAL
FOREST

To Haines Junction and Whitehorse
and Fairbanks, Alaska

Yakutat Glacier

Alsek   River

Tatshenshini   River

TATSHENSHINI-ALSEK
PROVINCIAL PARK

Novatak Glacier

BRABAZON   RANGE

Alsek River

Konamoxt Glacier

Alsek Glacier

SAINT

ELIAS

Towagh Glacier

Tsiatka Glacier

ALSEK   RANGE

Tkope Glacier

Tikke   Glacier

Mount McDonnell
5481ft
1671m

3

BRITISH COLUMBIA
ALASKA

Buckwell Glacier

Tsirku Glacier

TAKHINSHA

Mount Harris
5177ft
1578m

BRITISH COLUMBIA
ALASKA

Tsirku   River

Klehin

Dry Bay Ranger Station
Airstrip

Alsek   River

Dry
Bay

Airstrip
Public use cabin

GLACIER BAY
NATIONAL
PRESERVE

DECEPTION HILLS

Alsek
Lake

Gateway
Knob

Deception River

Mount Hay
8870ft
2704m

Hay Glacier

Melburn   Glacier

MOUNTAINS

GRAND   PACIFIC   GLACIER

see detail map

CANADA
UNITED STATES

Moose Glacier

Muir   Glacier

CARROLL   GLACIER

Rendu Glacier

Cushing Glacier

Mount Brock
4990ft
1521m

1976

1972

1966

1960

Riggs Glacier

1948

GULF   OF
ALASKA

GRAND   PLATEAU   GLACIER

Mount Lodge
10530ft
3210m

Ferris   Glacier

Mount Barnard
8214ft
2504m

Mount
Abdallah
5964ft
1818m

Rendu   Inlet

Queen   Inlet

Washbagel   Inlet

White
Thunder
Ridge

Interglacial
stumps

1929

Wo

Mount Merriam
5083ft
1549m

Mount Root
12860ft
3920m

Margerie   Glacier

Tarr   Inlet

Russell
Island

Mount Fairweather
15300ft
4669m

Mount Quincy
Adams
13650ft
4161m

FAIRWEATHER   GLACIER

FAIRWEATHER

Mount
Salisbury
12000ft
3658m

Johns Hopkins Glacier

Johns   Hopkins   Inlet

Jaw
Point

Lamplugh   Glacier

Reid   Glacier

Gilbert
Peninsula

GLACIER   BAY

Tlingit
Point

CAPE
FAIRWEATHER

Lituya Mountain
11750ft
3582m

Mount Abbe
8750ft
2667m

GLACIER BAY
NATIONAL PARK

RANGE

Mount Orville
10495ft
3199m

Lituya   Glacier

Drake
Island

North Crillon Glacier

Mount
Crillon
12726ft
3879m

Mount
Bertha
10204ft
3110m

GEIKIE   INLET

Interglacial
stumps

V
G

Lituya   Bay

BRADY
ICEFIELD

PACIFIC
OCEAN

Crillon
Lake

Mount La Perouse
10728ft
3270m

La Perouse Glacier

BRADY   GLACIER

Wood
Lake

Lake
Seclusion

Abyss
Lake

Dundas   River

Dundas Bay

Lemesu
Island

Icy Point

Palma Bay

1794

1961

Taylor
Bay

Inian
Islands

Astrolabe
Point

Dixon Harbor

Torch Bay

Graves Harbor

Graves
Rocks

CAPE
SPENCER

CROSS   SOUND

Elfin
Cove

Port Althorp

Idaho Inlet

H
Ca

C

CAPE
BINGHAM

North

0   5   10   15 Kilometers

0   5   10   15 Miles

1860   Historic extent of
glaciation

Campground

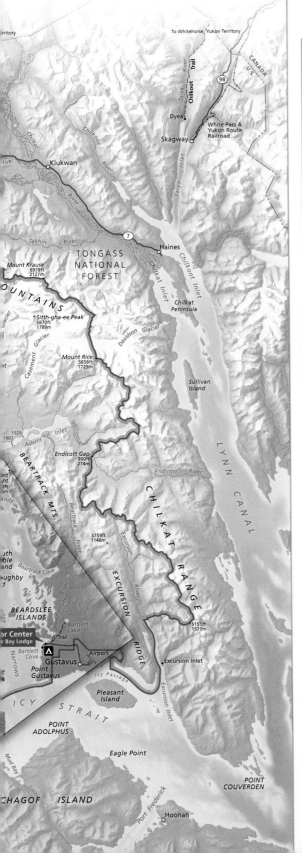

Blue ice

air taxis and charters provide year-round service to Gustavus. They include Alaska Seaplanes (907.789.3331, flyalaskaseaplanes.com), Fjord Flying Service (877.460.2377, fjordflying.com), and Wings of Alaska (907.789.0790).

Alaska Marine Highway System

Gustavus is accessible via the **Alaska Marine Highway System** (800.642.0066, dot.state.ak.us/amhs). During summer, ferries make twice weekly trips from Juneau to Gustavus, 10 miles north of Bartlett Cove. This is an excellent method of arrival for individuals transporting kayaks, bikes, or a vehicle (bringing your vehicle isn't recommended). The following are base fares from Juneau: $35/Passenger (P), $13/Bike (B), $20/Kayak (K), and $61/vehicle (V). Roadways do not run directly to Juneau, either. To reach Juneau by car you'll have to board another Alaska Marine Highway System ferry from Bellingham, Washington ($359/P, $59/B, $89/K, $431/V) or Prince Rupert, British Columbia ($156/P, $32/B, $46/K, $332/V). Children under 6 travel free. Fare for children ages 6–11 is about half the adult fare. Vehicle rates do not include the driver and are for vehicles up to 15 feet in length.

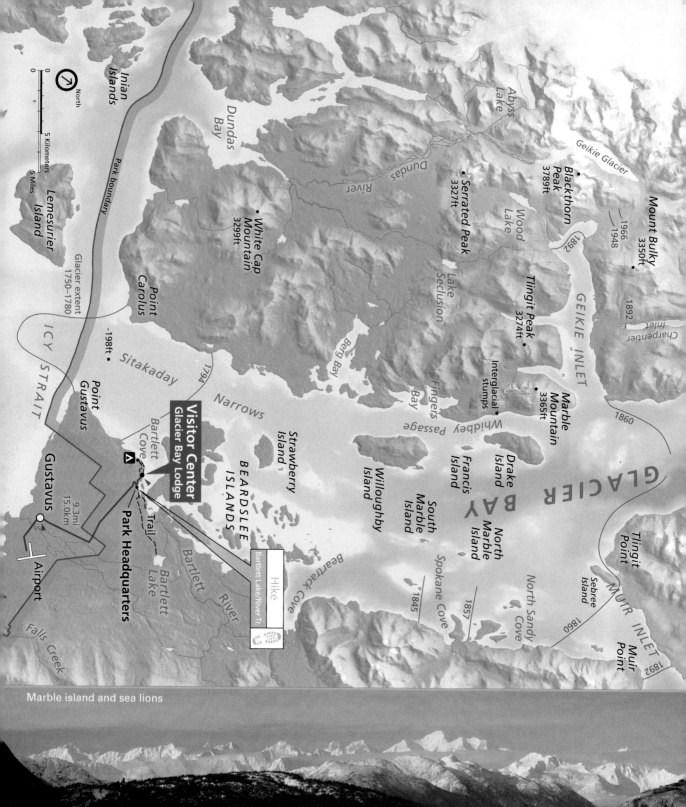

North

0
5 Kilometers

5 Miles

Park boundary

Glacier extent
1750–1780

Inian
Islands

Lemesurier
Island

Dundas
Bay

Dundas
River

White Cap
Mountain
3299ft

Serrated Peak
3327ft

Blackthorn
Peak
3789ft

Mount Bulky
3350ft

Geikie Glacier

1966
1948

Abyss
Lake

Wood
Lake

1892

GEIKIE INLET

Lake
Seclusion

Tlingit Peak
3274ft

Marble
Mountain
3365ft

Charpentier
Inlet

1892

1860

Point
Carolus

-198ft

Sitakaday

1794

Narrows

Berg
Bay

Berg Bay

Fingers
Bay

Interglacial
stumps

Whidbey Passage

ICY STRAIT

Point
Gustavus

Bartlett
Cove

Visitor Center
Glacier Bay Lodge

Park Headquarters

Gustavus

Airport

9.3mi
15.0km

Falls Creek

Bartlett
River

Bartlett
Lake

Trail

BEARDSLEE
ISLANDS

Strawberry
Island

Willoughby
Island

Francis
Island

Drake
Island

South
Marble
Island

North
Marble
Island

Spokane Cove

1845

1857

North Sandy
Cove

GLACIER BAY

MUIR INLET

Tlingit
Point

Sebree
Island

Muir
Point

1860

0981

1892

Beartrack Cove

Hike

Bartlett Lake/River Trl.

Marble island and sea lions

July Fourth
Mountain
500ft

BRADY
ICEFIELD

Aurora Glacier

Hugh Miller Glacier

Johns
Hopkins
Glacier

1929 1966

Hoonah Glacier

Gilman Glacier

Mount
Cooper
6780ft

Johns Hopkins

Johns Hopkins Glacier

Topeka Glacier

Margerie
Glacier

Park boundary

1912

Lamplugh Glacier

Jaw
Point

1941

Reid Glacier

Inlet

1907

1925

1892

18

1892

Russell
Island

1907

Tarr Inlet

1966

Skidmore
Bay

Gilbert
Peninsula

1892

1892

1892

Composite
Island

Active Glaciers

Margerie/
Johns Hopkins

1879

1892

Mount
Abdallah
5964ft

Grand Pacific Glacier

Hugh Miller Inlet

Blue Mouse
Cove

•1416ft

Rendu   Inlet

Rendu Glacier

1892
1966

Tidal Inlet

Gloomy Knob
1331ft

Queen Inlet

Paddle

Muir Inlet

Mount
Merriam
5083ft

1892
1966
1916
1966

Sentinel Peak
4355ft

CARROLL

GLACIER

UNITED STATES

CANADA

Gable
Mountain
4780ft

Cushing Glacier

Wachusett Inlet

1966

1949

Grand Pacific and
Margerie Glacier

Black bear

Kayaking the bay

Puffin

Camping & Lodging

Glacier Bay National Park has one primitive campground at **Bartlett Cove**. It's a free walk-in, tent-only camp, located 0.25-mile south of Bartlett Cove dock. It is open all year and features a bear-proof food cache, fire pit with firewood, and warming shelter near the shore. Group camping is available for groups of 12 or more. To use the campground you must first obtain a **free permit** and participate in a 30-minute orientation program. **Showers** are available at Glacier Bay Lodge during summer.

Glacier Bay Lodge (888.229.8687, visitglacierbay.com) is the only hotel in the park. All rooms can accommodate up to four guests and have a private bath and/or shower. Fairweather Dining Room serves breakfast, lunch, and dinner. Rooms cost $219/night (forest view) and $249/night (ocean view). The lodge is open from mid-May through early September.

Paddling

Looking to get up close and personal to whales, wildlife, and glaciers? If so, put a paddle in your hands, a boat in the water, and begin exploring the wonders of Glacier Bay.

Muir Inlet is a great place to paddle because it's off-limits to motorized boats in summer. Paddlers can bring their own boats via the Alaska Marine Highway System (page 607), but rental and guide services are available. Glacier Bay Sea Kayaks (907.697.2257, glacierbayseakayaks.com) provides rentals ($45/day, single, $60/day, double) and half-day ($95/person) and full-day ($150) guided tours. Glacier Bay Lodge's tour boat provides drop-offs at designated backcountry sites in summer. **A free wilderness permit and camping orientation (at Bartlett Cove) are required for all overnight stays in the backcountry.**

Spirit Walker Expeditions (800.529.2537, seakayakalaska.com), Mountain Travel Sobek (888.831.7526, mtsobek.com), and Alaska on the Home Shore (800.287.7063, homeshore.com) offer **multi-day expeditions**.

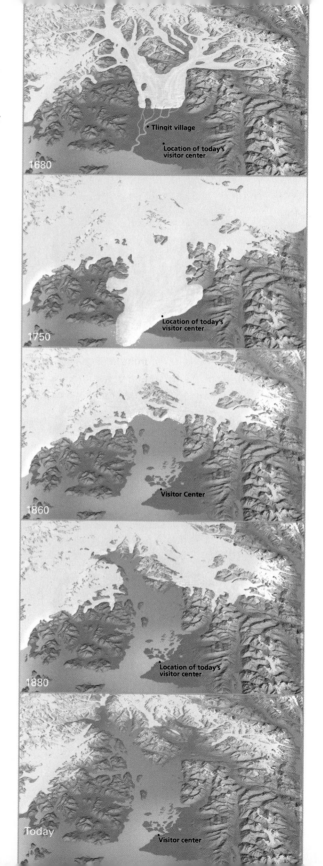

Boat Tours & Cruises

Commercial boat tours and cruises are the easiest and in many respects, the best way to explore the inlets and coves of Glacier Bay. Visitors spending the night in Bartlett Cove or Gustavus can embark on a full-day tour of the bay. Others come and go aboard massive luxury liners or specialized expedition cruise ships. Bring rain gear, binoculars, and warm layers of clothing no matter what time of year you plan on touring the bay.

Glacier Bay Lodge (888.229.8687, visitglacierbay.com) provides daily tours of Glacier Bay from Bartlett Cove during summer. The voyage is highlighted by stunning views of tidewater glaciers, snow-capped mountains, and abundant wildlife. A park ranger narrates the trip, discussing the area's history while pointing out whales, Steller sea lions, coastal bears, seals, and eagles. At one glacier, you will wait up to 30 minutes for a giant mass of snow and ice to break free, plummeting to the icy water and crashing with a thunderous boom. You board the boat at 7am, departure is at 7:30am, and you'll return around 3:30pm. The full-day cruise costs $205/adult and $102.50/child (ages 3–12). Lunch and a beverage are included. One-way service for campers and kayakers is available for $115/adult and $57.50/child (ages 3–12).

The most popular way to visit Glacier Bay is aboard one of the **luxury cruise liners** that ply these waters from late May to mid-September. Carnival Cruise Line (800.764.7419, carnival.com), Holland America Line (877.932.4259, hollandamerica.com), Norwegian Cruise Lines (866.234.7350, ncl.com), and Princess Cruises (800.774.6237, princess.com) offer 4–22 night trips that pit-stop at Glacier Bay. Cruises depart from various locations along the Pacific Coast including Vancouver, Seattle, and San Francisco. The base rate is around $100 per night per person. A park ranger typically boards the cruise ship upon entering Glacier Bay.

Natural born explorers should consider Un-Cruise Adventures (888.862.8881, un-cruise.com) or Linblad Special Expeditions (800.397.3348, expeditions.com). These companies provide a different, more intimate, cruising experience. Groups are smaller, guides are knowledgeable experts and easily accessible, and all side

trips are planned and included in the tour price. These tours cost about $700 per night per person.

Private Boating

Private boaters wanting to enter Glacier Bay from the beginning of June until the end of August must obtain a **free permit**, available up to 60 days in advance. The application form is available at the park website. To confirm or see if permits are available, call the Visitor Information Station "KWM20 Bartlett

Cove" on marine band 16 or phone (907) 697-2627. Permits must be confirmed at least 48 hours before your scheduled entry date or your permit will be cancelled. You must also stop at the Bartlett Cove Information Station at the end of the public-use dock for a brief boater orientation.

Whitewater Rafting

Whitewater rafting is possible on the **Alsek River** and its major tributary, the **Tatshenshini River**. Both are large volume, swift glacial rivers that breach the coastal range passing through Tatshenshini–Alsek Provincial Park in Canada and Glacier Bay National Preserve in Alaska. A typical trip begins on the Tatshenshini at Shawshe (Dalton Post). This is the last road-accessible put-in off Haines Highway in Canada. From here it's 140 miles of continuous Class III–IV (at high water) rapids to Dry Bay, Alaska. The trip usually takes six days. A permit is required for all private trips. To get on the waiting list, send your name, address, home and work telephone numbers, e-mail address, and payment of $25 to cover administrative charges to: National Park Service, Yakutat Ranger Station, River Permits, PO Box 137, Yakutat, AK 99869.

Several **outfitters** provide 10+ day expeditions along the Alsek–Tatshenshini. Chilkat Guides (907.766.2491, RaftAlaska.com), Colorado River & Trail Expeditions (801.261.1789, crateinc.com), James Henry River Journeys (800.786.1830, riverjourneys.com), Mountain Travel–Sobek (888.831.7526, mtsobek.com), Nahanni River Adventures (800.297.3180, nahanni.com); Rivers, Oceans, and Mountains (R.O.A.M) (888.639.1114, iroamtheworld.com); Tatshenshini Expediting (867.633.2742, tatshenshiniyukon.com), and Wilderness River Outfitter (800.252.6581, wildernessriver.com) offer trips for all experience levels that begin around $3,500 per person.

Hiking

There are only four maintained trails totaling less than 10 miles. **Forest Loop Trail** (1 mile) begins at Glacier Bay Lodge and passes through a temperate rain forest. During summer, park rangers lead guided walks along this trail every afternoon. The 4-mile (roundtrip) **Bartlett River Trail** heads north from the road to Gustavus along an intertidal lagoon through spruce-hemlock forest before ending at Bartlett River estuary, an excellent place to spot wildlife such as ducks, geese, moose, bear, and river otter. In late summer you might come across hungry harbor seals feeding on salmon as they run up the river. The 8-mile (roundtrip) **Bartlett Lake Trail** diverges from Bartlett River Trail at a signpost located about 0.25-mile into the hike and then climbs to Bartlett Lake following a relatively unmaintained trail (pay attention). **Tlingit Trail** (1 mile) strolls along the stretch of shoreline in front of the lodge. Ask a park ranger for a free tide table before hiking.

Backpacking

With no maintained trails in the park's wilderness backpackers are left to their own devices when negotiating the unforgiving terrain of Glacier Bay's mountains and shorelines. Alpine meadows, rocky coasts, and deglaciated areas provide a wealth of hiking opportunity where you may not encounter another human for days at a time. One thing you're sure to stumble upon is alder. This successional plant grows in abundance along beaches, stream edges, avalanche chutes, and mountain slopes. Hiking is much more tedious than paddling largely due to alder's presence, which is notorious for slowing down and aggravating hikers. Wherever you plan on going, it is imperative that backpackers are well-prepared and have planned their trip thoroughly prior to heading into the backcountry. Areas of the park are often closed to campers due to animal activity. Always ask a park ranger for closure updates before you depart. **A free permit and orientation program (Bartlett Cove) are required for overnight camping in the backcountry.** This is also an opportunity to check out a bear-resistant food container (BRFC). Food and scented items must be stored in your BRFC. If you'd like to let someone else take care of logistics, Alaska Mountain Guides (800.766.3396, alaskamountainguides.com) offers **guided hiking, climbing, and paddling tours**.

Flightseeing

Leave the cruise ships behind and enjoy the spectacular scenery of Glacier Bay with a unique aerial view. Float or wheel planes are available. **Flightseeing**

providers are listed below with contact information and departure location: Fjord Flying (907.723.2471, fjordflying.com, Gustavus/Juneau), Alaska Seaplanes (907.697.2375, flyalaskaseaplanes.com, Gustavus/Juneau), Seaport Airlines (907.789.0790, seaportair.com, Gustavus/Juneau), Harris Air (907.966.3050, harrisair.com, Sitka), Drake Air (907.314.0675, flydrake.com, Haines), Mountain Flying Service (907.766.3007, mountainflyingservice.com, Haines), Ward Air (800.478.9150, wardair.com, Juneau), Yakutat Coastal Airlines (907.784.3831, flyyca.com, Yakutat), and Gulf Air (800.925.2828, gulfairak.com, Yakutat).

Fishing

Anglers come to Glacier Bay in search of halibut and salmon. Fishermen 16 years and older require a valid Alaska State Fishing License, which can be purchased at Glacier Bay Lodge during summer. Please refer to page 657 for a list of fishing charters and guides who can help plan your trip or take you on a fishing adventure.

Ranger Programs

From Memorial Day weekend to Labor Day weekend, park rangers invite guests of Bartlett Cove to join them on a morning walk, a guided walk of Forest Loop, a ranger talk, and an evening program. A park film is also shown daily at the visitor center.

For Kids

An abundance of ice, water, mountains, and wildlife make Glacier Bay an intriguing place for children, but it's often difficult finding ways to engage them in their environment. The **Junior Ranger Program** is designed to do exactly that. Your child can become the next Junior Ranger one of two ways (depending on your mode of transportation). If you come by plane or private boat, you must stop by the visitor center on the second floor of Glacier Bay Lodge. Here you can obtain an activity booklet. Once completed, return the booklet to a park ranger to be inducted into this special club and earn a Junior Ranger badge. Most cruise ships have a children's center where they offer a Junior Ranger Program that can be completed over the course of the cruise. Park rangers aboard tour vessels can also point you in the right direction to become a Junior Ranger.

Flora & Fauna

Life in and around Glacier Bay is constantly changing. As glaciers continue to recede a succession of plant life appears in its path. Lichens, moss, fireweed, cottonwood, and willows all grow where glaciers used to exist. Western hemlock and Sitka spruce make up the temperate rain forests. Moose immigrated to the park, and were first spotted in 1966. Other large mammals include orca, humpback whales, black and brown bears, wolves, mountain goats, harbor seals, Steller sea lions, and porpoises.

Pets

Pets are only allowed at Bartlett Cove Public Use Dock, on the beach between the dock and the National Park Service Dock, within 100 feet of Bartlett Cove Developed Area's park roads and parking areas, and on a vessel in open water. Pets must be on a leash or physically restrained at all times. They are prohibited from all trails, beaches (except already mentioned), and backcountry.

Accessibility

Glacier Bay Lodge has wheelchair-accessible rooms upon request. Forest Trail is accessible. Contact specific tour operators for accessibility.

Weather

Pack your rain gear! Bartlett Cove receives about 70 inches of precipitation each year. On average, 228 days of the year experience some form of precipitation. April, May, and June are usually the driest months. Most visitors arrive between late May and mid-September. September and October tend to be the wettest months. Temperature is greatly influenced by the Pacific Ocean. Summers are typically cool and moist, while winters are mild and cool. During the summer you can expect highs between 50 and 60°F near sea level. As elevation increases it becomes cooler and windier.

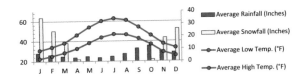

Wrangell–St. Elias

Mount Drum fall sunrise

PO Box 439
Copper Center, AK 99573
Phone: (907) 822-5234
Website: nps.gov/wrst

Established: December 2, 1980
November 16, 1978 (National
Monument)
Size: 13.2 Million Acres
Annual Visitors: 80,000
Peak Season: Summer

Activities: Hiking, Backpacking,
Rafting, Kayaking, Air Tours, ATV
Riding, Mountain Biking, Fishing,
Hunting, and Mountaineering

Campgrounds: None*
See page 660 for alternative
camping and lodging facilities
Backcountry Camping: Permitted
(backcountry permit not required)

Park Hours: All day, every day
Entrance Fee: None

*Camping is allowed at pullouts
along McCarthy and Nabesna Roads
(no water; first-come, first-served)

"The region is superlative in its scenic beauty and measures up fully and beyond the requirements for its establishment as a National Monument and later as a National Park. It is my personal view that from the standpoint of scenic beauty, it is the finest region in Alaska. I have traveled through Switzerland extensively, have flown over the Andes, and am familiar with the Valley of Mexico and with other parts of Alaska. It is my unqualified view that this is the finest scenery that I have ever been privileged to see."

– Ernest Gruening
Director of U.S. Territories/Governor of Alaska/U.S. Senator

Wrangell–St. Elias National Park lies in the southeastern corner of Alaska, a few hundred miles south of the Arctic Circle. It's far from the northernmost point in Alaska, but these jagged mountains—including 9 of the 16 highest peaks on United States' soil—harbor more than 60% of Alaska's glacial ice. Scientists estimate that 150 glaciers fill the valleys and ravines between mountain ridgelines. One of them, Malaspina, is larger than Rhode Island. Not only are the glaciers big, the park itself is monstrous, easily the largest in the United States. It's nearly four times the size of Death Valley, the largest national park in the contiguous United States.

Such a vast expanse of eye-catching mountains should not go unnoticed or unexplored for thousands of years, but this is the case of Wrangell–St. Elias. Mount St. Elias, the second highest mountain in the United States (at 18,008 feet), was unnamed until the feast day of St. Elias in 1741 when Vitus Bering spotted it while exploring the Alaskan coast. Mount Wrangell was named for Baron Ferdinand Petrovich von Wrangell, a Russian naval officer, arctic explorer, government administrator, and main opponent to selling Alaska to the United States. Despite his protest in 1867 Alaska was sold for $0.03 per acre, and the rest, as they say, is history. Eyak and Tlingit people lived in villages along the coast for thousands of years and in middle Copper Basin for at least the last 1,000 years, but Americans didn't penetrate the western Wrangell Mountains until 1885. Scientific expeditions occurred, but not until the gold rush in 1899 did the region receive any significant attention. More than one billion pounds of ore were hauled out of Kennecott mines during 27 years of operation. The mining boom went bust and tourism gradually took hold. Thanks to rapid increase in visitation at Denali National Park and being one of only three road-accessible Alaskan National Parks, Wrangell–St. Elias has continued to show a steady increase in tourism.

Camping & Lodging

There are **no developed campgrounds** at Wrangell–St. Elias National Park, but visitors are allowed to camp at pullouts along McCarthy and Nabesna Roads. These pullouts are perfect for small to medium RVs, camper trailers, pick-up campers, or tents. All sites are primitive and available on a first-come, first-served basis. You'll find pullouts at Mileposts 6.1, 16.6, 21.8, 27.8, and 35.3 along Nabesna Road and Mileposts 0, 17.3, 29, and 55.2 along McCarthy Road.

If you're looking for a true wilderness experience, consider spending a night at one of fourteen **backcountry cabins**. Most cabins are available on a first-come, first-served basis, but Viking Lodge Cabin on Nabesna Road and Esker Stream Cabin near Yakutat accept reservations. Most cabins are extremely remote, requiring significant trip planning or access by air-taxi. All of them have a woodstove and bunks. Sleeping and dining gear are not provided. Leave the cabin fully stocked with firewood and at least as clean as it was when you arrived.

Lodging is available at Devil's Mountain Lodge (707.400.6848, devilsmountainlodge.com, $110/person or $150/couple), located at the end of Nabesna Road. Refer to page 660 for additional lodging like Ultima Thule's (ultimathulelodge.com) fly-in luxury lodge.

When to Go

Most visitors arrive at Wrangell–St. Elias National Park between early June and mid-September, but the park never closes. Services are extremely limited beyond these dates and only the hardiest of visitors who possess extremely proficient winter survival skills visit during the off-season. Early September offers fewer mosquitoes and pleasant temperatures.

Main Visitor Center • (907) 822-7250
Mile 106.8 Richardson Highway, Copper Center
Features: Exhibits, Film, Ranger Programs, Bookstore
Open: mid-May to mid-September, daily, 9am–6pm; September to late October and April to mid-May, Mon–Fri, 9am–4pm (as staffing permits); November to March, closed

Ahtna Cultural Center • (907) 822-3535
Next to Main Visitor Center
Features: Exhibits
Open: Year-round, hours vary

Kennecott Visitor Center • (907) 554-1105
Historic Kennecott Mill Town
Features: Exhibits, Ranger Programs, Backcountry Planning
Open: Memorial Day to Labor Day, daily, 9:30am–6:30pm

Slana Ranger Station • (907) 822-7401
Mile 0.5 Nabesna Road
Features: Exhibits, Ranger Programs, Bookstore
Open: Memorial Day to September, daily, 8am–5pm

Chitina Ranger Station • (907) 823-2205
Mile 33 Edgerton Highway
Features: Exhibits and Trip Planning
Open: Memorial Day to Labor Day, Thur–Mon, 10am–4:30pm

McCarthy Road Information Station
Mile 59 McCarthy Road
Features: Day-Parking and Trip Planning
Open: Self-service during summer (staffed occasionally)

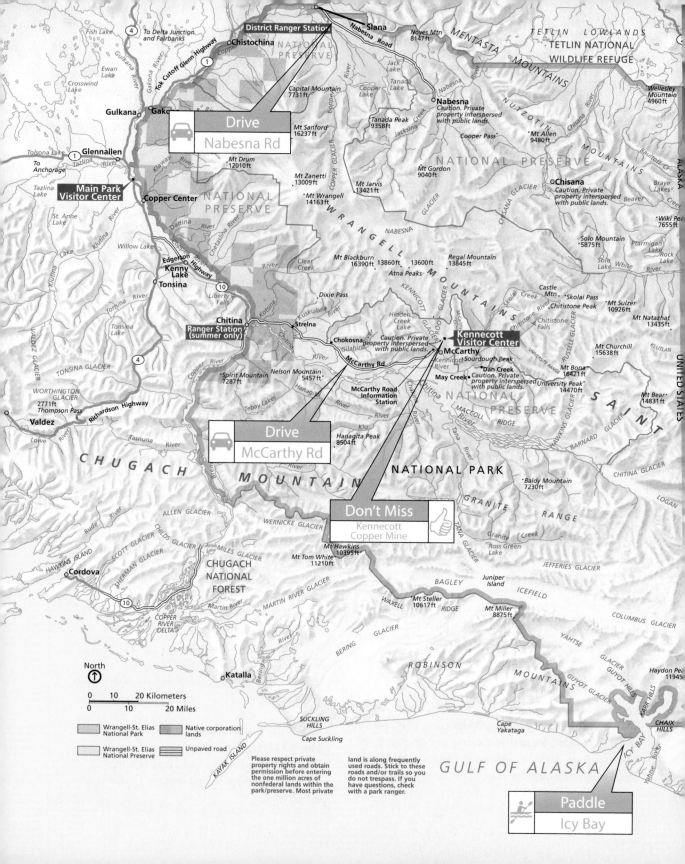

To Delta Junction and Fairbanks
Fish Lake

④

Tok Cutoff Glenn Highway

Gulkana River

Chistochina

District Ranger Station

Slana

Nabesna Road

Noyes Mtn 8147ft

MENTASTA

TETLIN LOWLANDS

TETLIN NATIONAL WILDLIFE REFUGE

Crosswind Lake

Ewan Lake

Gulkana

Gakona

①

Capital Mountain 7731ft

Jack Lake

Tanada Lake

Nabesna Road

Copper Lake

Nabesna
Caution. Private property interspersed with public lands.

Wellesley Mountain 4960ft

MOUNTAINS

NUTZOTIN

Chisana River

Braye Lakes

ALASKA

Drive
Nabesna Rd

Mt Sanford 16237ft

Tanada Peak 9358ft

Mt Allen 9480ft

Mt Wrangell 14163ft

Cooper Pass

NATIONAL PRESERVE

Chisana
Caution. Private property interspersed with public lands.

Wiki Pea 7655ft

Glennallen

①

To Anchorage

Tazlina River

Main Park Visitor Center

Tolsona Lake

Klawasi River

Mt Drum 12010ft

Mt Zanetti 13009ft

Mt Jarvis 13421ft

Mt Gordon 9040ft

Ptarmigan Lake

Rock Lake

St. Anne Lake

Copper Center

NATIONAL PRESERVE

Dadina River

Chetaslina River

NABESNA

Solo Mountain 5875ft

Solo White Lake

Willow Lake

Klutina River

Klutina Lake

Kenny Lake

Edgerton Highway

Tonsina

⑩

Liberty Falls

Dixie Pass

Clear Creek

River

Kuskulana River

Mt Blackburn 16390ft

13860ft

13600ft

Regal Mountain 13845ft

Castle Mtn.

Skolai Pass

Chitistone Peak

Mt Sulzer 10926ft

Mt Natazhat 13435ft

WRANGELL

Atna Peaks

GLACIER

Skolai Creek

Chitistone River

Chitistone Falls

Tonsina River

Tonsina Lake

④

Chitina
Ranger Station (summer only)

Strelna

Chokosna

Gilahina

Kotsina River

Hidden Creek Lake

Caution. Private property interspersed with public lands.

Kennecott Visitor Center

McCarthy

RUSSELL GLACIER

UNIVERSITY RANGE

Mt Churchill 15638ft

KLUTLAN

⑩

Spirit Mountain 7287ft

Nelson Mountain 5457ft

McCarthy Rd

Kennicott River

May Creek

Sourdough Peak

Dan Creek
Caution. Private property interspersed with public lands.

Mt Bona 16421ft

University Peak 14470ft

Mt Bear 14831ft

UNITED STATES

VALDEZ GLACIER

TONSINA GLACIER

MOUNTAINS

Copper River

Tebay Lakes

Hanagita River

Klu River

McCarthy Road Information Station

CHITINA

NATIONAL PRESERVE

MACCOLL RIDGE

Tana River

SAINT

WORTHINGTON GLACIER 2771ft

Thompson Pass

Richardson Highway

Drive
McCarthy Rd

Hanagita Peak 8504ft

RUSSELL

Barnard GLACIER

CHITINA GLACIER

Valdez

Lowe River

Tasnuna River

CHUGACH

MOUNTAIN

NATIONAL PARK

Baldy Mountain 7230ft

GRANITE

Granite Creek

Ross Green Lake

LOGAN

Bremner River

ALLEN GLACIER

Don't Miss
Kennecott Copper Mine

MOUNTAINS

Mt Hawkins 10395ft

TANA GLACIER

RANGE

WERNICKE GLACIER

Rude River

Childs GLACIER

SCOTT GLACIER

Miles GLACIER

CHUGACH NATIONAL FOREST

Mt Tom White 11210ft

JEFFERIES GLACIER

Cordova

⑩

COPPER RIVER DELTA

SHERMAN GLACIER

Martin River GLACIER

MARTIN RIVER GLACIER

Martin River

BAGLEY

Juniper Island

ICEFIELD

COLUMBUS GLACIER

Hawkins Island

Mt Steller 10617ft

WAXELL RIDGE

Mt Miller 8875ft

GUYOT GLACIER

Haydon Pea 11945ft

North
⬆

0 10 20 Kilometers
0 10 20 Miles

BERING GLACIER

ROBINSON

MOUNTAINS

GUYOT HILLS

KARR HILLS

CHAIX HILLS

Katalla

Bering River

SUCKLING HILLS

Cape Yakataga

ICY BAY

Yahtse River

Wrangell–St. Elias National Park

Native corporation lands

Wrangell–St. Elias National Preserve

Unpaved road

KAYAK ISLAND

Cape Suckling

Please respect private property rights and obtain permission before entering the one million acres of nonfederal lands within the park/preserve. Most private

land is along frequently used roads. Stick to these roads and/or trails so you do not trespass. If you have questions, check with a park ranger.

GULF OF ALASKA

Paddle
Icy Bay

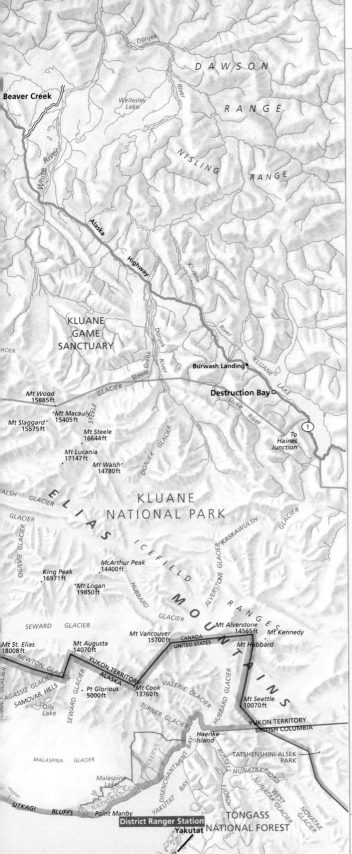

Transportation & Airports

Alaska Direct Bus Line (800.770.6652, alaska-directbusline.com) and Soaring Eagle Transit (907.822.4545, gulkanacouncil.org) can get you around Alaska's interior. Traveling from Anchorage to Fairbanks costs about $195 per person. Kennicott Shuttle (907.822.5292, kennicottshuttle.com) or Wrangell–St. Elias Tours (888.478.5258, alaskayukontravel.com) or Wrangell Mountain Air (800.478.1160, wrangellmountainair.com) will shuttle you into the park. There are many more air taxi services that make stops or drop-offs at a variety of airstrips throughout the park. See page 656 for a complete list of air taxi service providers.

Directions

Wrangell–St. Elias National Park is one of three national parks in Alaska accessible by road. Two rough gravel roads penetrate the park's interior. McCarthy Road begins at Chitina, where it enters the park and continues 60 miles into its heart at Kennecott. Nabesna Road enters the northern border at Slana and continues for 42 miles to Nabesna, an old mining town. Directions provided below begin at Glennallen, AK, which is about 170 miles east of Anchorage along AK-1.

McCarthy Road: From Glennallen head south for 31 miles on AK-4 toward Valdez. Continuing south you'll pass through Copper Center, where the main park visitor center, theater, and exhibit building are located, before turning left at Edgerton Highway/AK-10. Continue east for nearly 34 miles to Chitina, where McCarthy Road enters the park.

Nabesna Road: From Glennallen, head north on AK-1/AK-4. Continue for almost 73 miles. Turn right at Nabesna Road, which passes through Slana and into the park.

Driving

McCarthy Road follows the path of an old railway constructed in 1909 to support the booming mining industry at Kennecott Mill. It's a dusty, winding, washboard gravel road, but during summer most

Skookum Volcano

Mount Blackburn and Willow Lake

passenger vehicles are capable of making the trip. The primitive journey from Chitina to Kennecott is 60 miles and takes about 2 hours (one-way). In between, you'll find plenty of grade-A scenery that is sure to leave you breathless.

In 1934, **Nabesna Road** was built to simplify ore transportation to the coast. More than 75 years later very little has changed. It's a rough, twisting, 42-mile gravel road with unparalleled scenic value. It is typically accessible to all passenger vehicles, but at times creek crossings beyond Mile 29 can be problematic.

Both roads provide exceptional wildlife viewing opportunities. Do not travel without a full-size spare and an adequate jack. No fuel or services are available along these roads and cell phone service is extremely limited.

Hiking & Backpacking

There are five short maintained trails near **Copper Center. Boreal Forest Trail** (0.5-mile loop) begins at the Main Visitor Center. A self-guiding brochure helps introduce visitors to the area. In Glennallen you'll find **Aspen Interpretive Trail** (1.0 mile, roundtrip). The trailhead is located on Co-op Road just off AK-1. **Tonsina River Trail** (2.0 miles) begins just beyond mile marker 12 of AK-10/Edgerton Highway. It leads to a perch overlooking Tonsina River. **Liberty Falls Trail** (2.5 miles) begins just before mile marker 25 of AK-10. **O'Brien to Haley Creek Trail** (10.0 miles) begins on O'Brien Creek Road near Chitina.

Three maintained trails begin from Nabesna Road: Caribou Creek (6.0 miles, near mile 19), Skookum Volcano (5.0 miles, near mile 37), and Rambler Mine (1.5 miles, near mile 42). They provide spectacular views of rugged terrain. Near Kennecott/McCarthy Road you can hike these trails: Crystalline Hills (2.5 miles, mile 36), Root Glacier (3.0 miles, Kennecott Visitor Center), Donoho Basin (14 miles roundtrip to Donoho Summit, multi-day, follows Root Glacier Trail), or Jumbo Mine (10 miles, Root Glacier Trailhead). Most **backpackers** prefer to hike above the tree line where vegetation and mosquitoes are more manageable. Many day-hikes and multi-day trips require river crossings. Use proper judgment when selecting an area to cross. Hypothermia is a threat, even in summer. Adequate planning is required for a successful trip. Be sure you have the right gear, a good topographic map, and are comfortable camping in bear-country. Proper food storage is required. Bear-resistant food containers are available at any visitor center. Permits are not required for backcountry trips, but completing a backcountry itinerary (available at any park office) is encouraged. You should also leave your itinerary with a friend or family member. If you do not return on schedule, rangers will not administer a search party until a formal request is made by a friend or family member. Many hikers choose to hire a local guide to help ensure a safe and enjoyable trip. Guides also lead visitors on mountain climbing expeditions. With 9 of the 16 highest peaks on U.S. soil within park boundaries, Wrangell–St. Elias is a popular destination among mountain climbers. See page 657 for a list of outfitters authorized to guide trips in the park.

Flightseeing

To truly grasp the size of Wrangell–St. Elias National Park you should fly above it, peering across massive sheets of ice and jagged mountain ranges. A slew of local **air taxi businesses** (page 656) provide flightseeing tours or backcountry drop-offs and pick-ups to otherwise unreachable regions.

Rafting & Floating

Float trips, wild whitewater, and everything in between can be found at Wrangell–St. Elias. Plan your own rafting adventure or join an **authorized outfitter** (page 657). **Guide companies** (page 657) also lead guests on sea kayaking trips around Icy Bay. It is relatively "new" water; the bay was formed when four massive tidewater glaciers retreated beginning in 1900. Paddlers are usually dropped off at Kageet Point or Point Riou by air-taxi. Sea kayaking is a great way to spot marine and terrestrial wildlife.

ATVs & Mountain Biking

ATVs are allowed in some areas. All recreational users require a permit (available at Slana Ranger Station or Park Headquarters). McCarthy and Nabesna Roads provide excellent locations for mountain bikers.

Fishing

Lake trout, Dolly Varden, grayling, cutthroat and rainbow trout, sculpin, and whitefish are found in small lakes and streams. Sockeye, coho, and king salmon can be caught in the Copper River and its tributaries. An Alaska fishing license is required for all anglers 16 or older.

Ranger Programs

In summer, Park Rangers provide talks, walks, and evening programs at the Main Visitor Center and Kennecott Mill Town. Check out the park website or stop at a visitor center for a current schedule of activities.

For Kids

Children are invited to learn about the park and its valuable resources by participating in the **Junior Ranger Program**. Visit the park's website, print an activity booklet and complete it (either in the park or at home).

Logan Glacier

Once it's finished, mail it to the park and a ranger will review your answers. For the effort, you'll be rewarded with a Wrangell–St. Elias Junior Ranger badge.

Flora & Fauna

Wrangell–St. Elias National Park features a variety of plants and animals. More than half of all Alaskan flora can be found in the Wrangells. Quaking aspen are the most prevalent tree, but paper birch and black and white spruce are also common. In all, more than 800 species of vascular plants color the landscape and provide nutrition for the park's residents. Animals include moose, bear (black and grizzly), lynx, caribou, mountain goats, wolves, bison, and the largest concentration of Dall sheep in North America.

Pets

Pets are allowed in the park, but remember that dogs (and even dog food) may attract bear or moose.

Accessibility

The Main Visitor Center is accessible to wheelchair users, as are the historic mill, recreation hall, visitor center, and Blackburn School at Kennecott. An accessible backcountry cabin is available at Peavine.

Weather

Winters are long and cold (highs of 5–7°F). Summers are short, warm, and dry. June and July are the warmest months. Highs might sneak into the 80s°F on some days. Leaves typically begin to change by mid-August and the first significant snowfall arrives about a month later.

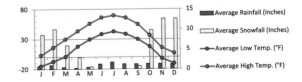

Denali Park Road

Denali

PO Box 9
Denali Park, AK 99755
Phone: (907) 683-9532
Website: nps.gov/dena

Established: February 26, 1917
Size: 6.1 Million Acres
Annual Visitors: 560,000
Peak Season: Summer

Activities: Bus/Shuttle Tours, Hiking, Backpacking, Biking, Mountaineering, Flightseeing, Fishing, and Whitewater Rafting

Campgrounds ($12–28/night): Riley Creek*, Savage River*, Sanctuary River, Teklanika River*, Igloo Creek, and Wonder Lake*
Backcountry Camping: Permitted
Lodging: See page 660

Park Hours: All day, every day
Entrance Fee: $10/individual (16 and older), Youth under 15 are free

*Reserve at reservedenali.com or (866) 761-6629

Denali, at 20,320 feet, is the tallest mountain in North America. It serves as the centerpiece and main attraction of Denali National Park. So tall and massive is this magnificent mountain that it creates its own weather, often in the form of clouds, which shroud its glory. When the clouds lift, Denali commands attention; from base to summit it is more prominent than Mount Everest, which rises 12,000 feet from its base on the Tibetan Plateau. Denali's base is at roughly 2,000-ft elevation, giving it a prominence of some 18,000 feet. Appropriately, the Koyukon Athabaskan people call the peak Denali or "The High One." It wasn't until 1869 that a failed businessman turned prospector named the mountain "McKinley" in honor of the presidential candidate who supported the gold standard. The name stuck just like its superlatives. It wasn't until 1980 when the park expanded and became known as Denali. North America's tallest peak was still known as McKinley until August 2015, when President Obama restored its native Alaskan name, Denali. This park and its majestic mountain, located in Alaska's interior, provide refuge for wildlife, respite for backpackers, and the ultimate challenge for mountain climbers.

People supposedly climb mountains because they're there, but the race to summit Denali was all about bragging rights. Frederick Cook, president of the Explorer's Club, claimed he reached the summit in 1903. And he returned with a picture to prove it. Another group retraced his route, duplicating the photo at a lower peak. In 1910 a group of prospectors boasted they were going to plant an American flag at the summit. It took them from January through April to reach the mountain's base and establish a camp. In May, two members wearing nothing but overalls and unlined parkas made a push for the summit with a thermos of hot chocolate and a bag of doughnuts. Amazingly, they backed up their words. The American flag was firmly planted at 19,470 feet, atop Denali's North Peak (850 feet lower than its South Peak). Three years later a group led by Alaska's Episcopal archdeacon, Hudson Stuck, climbed to the top of South Peak. The trek was so grueling and air so thin that Stuck blacked out several times during ascent.

Just as the race to the summit was heating up, Charles Sheldon, a close friend of President Theodore Roosevelt, was wintering in a cabin on the Toklat River. While camped out in what was thought to be the last tract of unexploited American wilderness, he witnessed the slaughter of animals brought on by the rush of gold miners in 1903. He recorded his observations in a journal and later wrote *The Wilderness of Denali*. In his journal he described the idea of a park that would allow visitors to see Alaska as he saw it while living along the Toklat River. He spent years advocating a national park and hand delivered his proposal to Washington, D.C. On February 26, 1917, President Woodrow Wilson signed a bill creating Mount McKinley National Park, but it failed to include McKinley's summit in the preserved lands. Sheldon received additional disappointment when he learned the mountain and new park would not be returned to its original name, Denali. In 2015, the mighty mountain became Denali again.

The area's distinctive wildlife and landscapes are protected from commercial interests, but the National Park Service can't shelter the environment from all threats. Changes in climate affect the environment in subtle ways. As you increase elevation there's a distinct tree line where average temperatures are too cold for trees to grow. As the climate warms, the tree line conspicuously rises. With continually increasing visitation, park staff must find new ways to manage and maintain the delicate habitat without ruining the experience. Limiting the 92-mile Denali Park Road to bus tours and enforcing backcountry permit quotas help maintain the pristine wilderness that Koyukon Athabascans, Charles Sheldon, and all past park visitors have enjoyed. With the work of the park rangers and conservation-minded patrons like yourself, Denali will remain an example of the Last Frontier.

Sled dog demonstration

When to Go

Denali National Park is open all year, but Denali Park Road is first plowed beginning sometime in March (weather dependent), and is usually accessible to private vehicles by mid-April. Bus service shuttles visitors along the road, beginning in late May and running until mid-September. Most visitors arrive between mid-June and mid-August. The park usually turns green by the end of May and wildflowers begin to bloom in early June. Mosquitoes are most active in early summer. Chances of seeing the Northern Lights increase in fall as the days grow shorter.

Transportation & Airports

Several private bus and van companies provide transportation to the park in summer. Refer to page 656 for a list of businesses. The **Alaska Railroad** (800.321.6518, alaskarailroad.com) connects Fairbanks and Anchorage, passing directly through the main park entrance. Car rental is available at each destination. One-way fare during peak season from Anchorage to Denali is $165/passenger and $72/passenger from Fairbanks to Denali. Ted Stevens Anchorage International (ANC) and Fairbanks International (FAI) are the easiest destinations to fly into. Once you've reached the park you can explore Denali Park Road aboard a public shuttle or tour bus (page 623), on foot (page 625), or by bicycle (page 627).

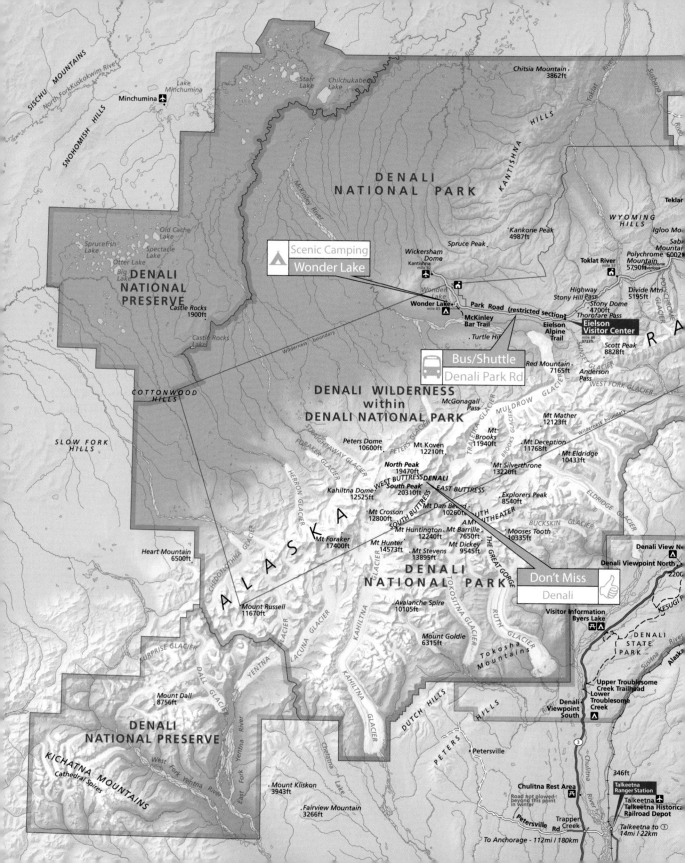

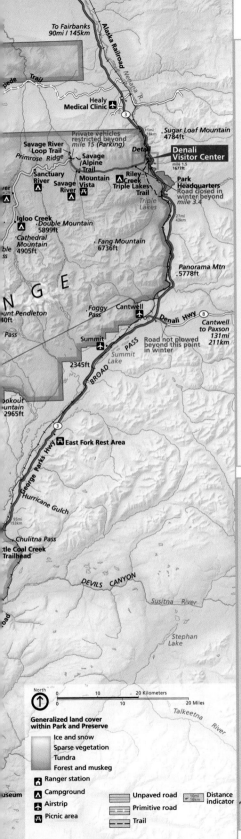

Directions

The 92-mile (one-way) Denali Park Road provides the only motor vehicle access to the park. Its first 15 miles are open to vehicles in summer. A "road lottery" is held for four days in fall. Lottery winners can purchase a single, day-long permit that allows them to drive as much of Denali Park Road as conditions permit. Denali Park Road is 238 miles north of Anchorage and 121 miles south of Fairbanks.

From Anchorage (238 miles): Take AK-1/N/E 5th Ave north about 34 miles, where you continue onto Interstate A-4 W. Take AK-3 N/George Parks Way. After 201 miles, turn left at Denali Park Road, which leads into the park.

From Fairbanks (121 miles): Take AK-3 S/George Parks Highway 117 miles, and then turn right at Denali Park Road, which leads into the park.

Denali Park Road & Shuttle/Bus Tours

The 92-mile **Denali Park Road** provides the only vehicular access into the heart of the park. For all but four days, private vehicles are only allowed to travel to Savage River (Mile 15). Beyond this, traffic is restricted to shuttle buses and tour buses. **Shuttle buses** are less expensive and give passengers the freedom of being dropped off and picked up anywhere along the road (simply flag it down). They also make stops for wildlife viewing, restroom breaks, and beautiful scenery, including dramatic vistas of Denali (clouds permitting). If you want to hike, picnic, or just sit and admire mighty Denali, shuttle bus is the way to go. The shuttles' only downside is they are not narrated. They

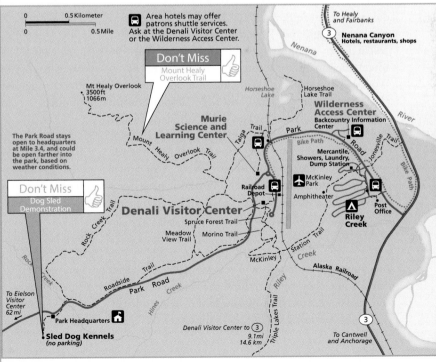

Denali and Reflection Pond

stop at four scheduled destinations. There are specially designed **camper shuttles for backpackers** in which the rear seats are removed for packs and bikes. They stop at each campground. Roundtrip rates are as follows: Toklat River (6.5 hours roundtrip, Mile 53, $26.50/adult), Eielson Visitor Center (8 hours, Mile 66, $34), Wonder Lake (11 hours, Mile 85, $46.75), Kantishna (13 hours, Mile 92, $50), and the Camper Shuttle ($35, campers and backpackers only). Children 15 and under ride free. Car seat laws apply for young children. Shuttles typically run from late May through mid-September (weather permitting). Every September, once the shuttles have stopped running, the park hosts an event called **"Road Lottery."** During these four days, lottery winners can purchase a single-day permit ($25) to drive the park road.

Bus tours are narrated by a trained naturalist (and driver), but they do not allow the freedom to exit and board wherever you please. Tours begin and end at various locations around the park entrance. There are four bus tours: Denali Natural History Tour (4.5 hours, to Mile 17, $77.25/adult, $33.75/child 14 and under), Tundra Wilderness Tour (8 hours, Mile 53, $130.25/$60.25), Kantishna Experience Tour (11 hours, Mile 92, $194/$92), and Windows Into Wilderness Tour (5–6 hours, Mile 30, $87.75/$39). A $10 per person 16 and older entrance fee is included in the tour price.

Shuttle bus and bus tour tickets can be reserved in advance at (866) 761-6629 or reservedenali.com. Reservations are highly recommended. If you plan on getting shuttle bus tickets upon arrival, you may have to wait a day or two before they are available.

Three free courtesy buses help visitors navigate the park entrance area while reducing parking requirements and traffic congestion. Bus stops are located at Wilderness Access Center and Denali Visitor Center. Shuttles serve Savage River Campground, Riley Creek Campground, and the Sled Dog Demonstration Area.

Lodging

The park doesn't operate lodging facilities, but a few can be found on privately owned land within park boundaries. Additional overnight accommodations are available outside the park at Healy (11 miles north of the park entrance) and Cantwell (30 miles to the south). For a list of lodging and camping facilities in and near the park please refer to page 660.

Camping

There are six developed campgrounds, all located along Denali Park Road. Only two, Savage River and Wonder Lake, provide views of Denali. Since Riley Creek and Savage River Campgrounds are located within the first 15 miles of Denali Park Road, they are easily accessed via personal vehicles. You can also drive your vehicle/RV to Teklanika (Mile 29) if you spend a minimum of three nights there, but your vehicle must stay at the campsite for the duration of your stay. A better way to visit Teklanika is to take the Camper Bus (page 623) and purchase a Tek Pass, which allows campers to use the park shuttle buses at will (if space allows, but not beyond Teklanika) during the course of your stay. Denali's most wondrous campground is the one located farthest from the park entrance: **Wonder Lake** (Mile 85). It is a tent-only campground accessed via the Camper Bus. Just 26 miles from Denali, the behemoth of a mountain reflects upon the mirror-like water of Wonder Lake on clear days. This location is a wilderness lover's paradise, but there are a few drawbacks: cloudy skies often obscure Denali, and you're camping near water, a breeding ground for mosquitoes that can be incredibly fierce from mid-June until late August. A large food-storage building provides picnic tables where you can avoid the rain and bugs.

Hiking & Backpacking

Relative to its size there are very few hiking trails at Denali. Most exploration is done off-trail, but there are a handful of maintained trails near the park entrance. Most are practical, connecting visitor facilities. **McKinley Station Trail** spans 1.6 miles between the Visitor Center and Riley Creek Campground. **The Bike Path** runs 1.7 miles from the Visitor Center to the Wilderness Access Center and ends at the Park Entrance. **Roadside** (1.8 miles, one-way) and **Rock Creek** (2.4 miles, one-way) **Trails** connect the Visitor Center with Park Headquarters and the Sled Dog Kennels. Meadow View Trail is a 0.3-mile trail that connects Roadside and Rock Creek Trails. A few trails actually show off the area's impressive scenery. **Spruce Forest Trail** (0.2 miles, one-way) begins at Denali Visitor Center and explores a forested area where seasonal wildflowers and berries can be found.

Denali Camping (Fees are per night)

Name	Location	Open	Fee	Sites	Notes
Riley Creek*	Mile .4	All Year	$14/22/28	147	RVs up to 40 ft • W (summer), F, DS (free)
Savage River*	Mile 13	May–Sept	$22/28	33	Denali views (clear days), RVs up to 40 ft • W, F
Sanctuary River**	Mile 23	May–Sept	$12***	7	Tent-only, access via Camper Bus • P
Teklanika River*	Mile 29	May–Sept	$22***	53	Vehicle/RV accessible with 3-night stay • W, P
Igloo**	Mile 35	May–Sept	$12***	7	Tent-only, access via Camper Bus • P
Wonder Lake* - ♿	Mile 85	June–Sept	$16***	28	Denali views (clear days), tent-only • W, F

W = Water, F = Flush Toilets, P = Pit Toilets, DS = Dump Station; RV hookups are not available at any campground
Campground permits can be picked up at the Wilderness Access Center (WAC) or at Riley Creek Mercantile
Open and close dates subject to weather; Multiple fees apply to tent/RVs < 30 ft in length and RVs 30–40 ft in length
*Reservations can be made beginning in December by calling (866) 761-6629 or clicking reservedenali.com
**Reservations are only available in person, no more than 2 days in advance at the WAC or Riley Creek Mercantile
***Prices do not include a one-time, non-refundable reservation fee of $6
Showers (fee), laundry (fee), wi-fi (free), and a camper convenience store are available at Riley Creek Mercantile

Backcountry	All overnight stays in the backcountry require a free wilderness permit. Permits are only available at the Backcountry Information Center. They must be obtained in person and no more than 24 hours in advance of the first day of your trip.
Group	Two sites available at Savage Creek ($45/night) • Reserve at (866) 761-6629 or reservedenali.com

A pika

The 3.2-mile roundtrip hike to **Horseshoe Lake** provides wildlife viewing opportunities, along with views of Oxbow Lake and the Nenana River. If you don't have enough time to explore the park's interior aboard one of the shuttle or tour buses (page 623), you should hike the 5.4-mile (roundtrip) **Mount Healy Overlook Trail**. It is the most strenuous (and popular) hike in the area. Although, not ideal for a casual family hike, it shouldn't be a problem for the average day-hiker. You hike for a short distance along an exposed ridgeline where wind and weather are always unpredictable (pack a waterproof windbreaker). Mount Healy Overlook, Horseshoe Lake, and Rock Creek Trails are accessed via the 0.9-mile **Taiga Trail**, which begins at the Visitor Center. Also from Denali Visitor Center, you can begin the 9.5-mile **Triple Lakes Trail**. It loosely follows Riley Creek from McKinley Village to Hines Creek Bridge. To view Denali, try stopping at **Mountain Vista Trailhead** (Mile 13), where you'll find a short loop trail (0.7 miles).

With proper preparation **backpacking** in Denali's wilderness can be one of the park's most rewarding adventures. You must craft your own itinerary, obtain a **backcountry permit** (not required for day-hikes), and practice proper backcountry hiking/camping techniques. Be conservative when estimating your daily mileage. There are no trails, terrain is challenging, and it's likely you'll have to make several river crossings. Backcountry campers must set-up camp at least 0.5-mile away from and out of sight

of the park road. Camp on durable surfaces where others have not camped before you. Fires are not permitted in the backcountry, so pack your camp stove. Water should be filtered, treated with iodine tablets, or boiled for one minute. Bear-resistant food containers are issued free of charge with each backcountry permit. Backpackers can park their vehicle(s) at Riley Creek Camp's overflow parking area free of charge.

Backcountry Permits
A backcountry permit is required for all overnight stays in the wilderness areas. Permits must be obtained in person at the Backcountry Information Center. In order to obtain a permit you must first plan your itinerary. Be prepared with several alternatives, because many wilderness areas reach their quota during the busy summer months. If your itinerary is available, each member of your group must watch a safety video and speak to a park ranger. It is your responsibility to know unit boundaries and wildlife closure areas. Delineate these boundaries on your map, and adjust your camping/hiking plans accordingly. Finally, obtain a Camper Bus ticket (page 623) that will drop you off at your desired starting location along Denali Park Road.

Mountaineering
Denali is one of the premier mountaineering destinations in the world. Each year climbers from all over the globe test their climbing and wilderness survival skills against the 20,320-foot peak. If you plan on climbing Denali or Mt Foraker (17,400 feet), you must register with the park at least 60 days prior to your intended start date and pay a $365 per climber fee. (If you cancel prior to January 15 of the year in which the climb is scheduled, you will receive a $265 refund. Refunds will not be made for cancellations after January 15.) Registration is available online at pay. gov. All climbers must check-in, pay the entrance fee, and check-out at Talkeetna Ranger Station. Less than 1,000 climbers summit Denali each year, with a success rate right around 50%. Climbing Denali requires much training, preparation, and experience. AK Mountaineering School (907.733.1016, climbalaska. org), Alpine Ascents International (206.378.1927, alpineascents.com), American Alpine Institute

(360.671.1505, alpineinstitute.com), Mountain Trip International (866.886.8747, mountaintrip.com), N.O.L.S. (907.745.4047, nols.edu), and Rainier Mountaineering (888.892.5462, rmiguides.com) are authorized to lead intrepid individuals on summit attempts. Should you choose to use an unauthorized guide, your trip may be cancelled at any time. Please contact the Talkeetna Ranger Station for any climbing and mountaineering related questions. They can be contacted by phone (907.733.2231), fax (907.733.1465), or mail (Talkeetna Ranger Station, PO Box 588, Talkeetna, AK 99676).

Whitewater Rafting

Private outfitters near the park entrance provide exhilarating whitewater adventures through the 10-mile Nenana River Canyon or float trips along its more placid stretches. Denali Raft Adventures (888.683.2234, denaliraft.com), Denali Outdoor Center (888.303.1925, denalioutdoorcenter.com), and Nenana Raft Adventures (800.789.7238, alaskaraft.com) offer 2–4 hour trips ranging from $89 to $187 per person. You can also head out on a multi-day expedition of the Talkeetna River from here.

Biking

Pedaling a **mountain bike** along the 92-mile Denali Park Road is a fantastic way to see the sights and get a bit (or an awful lot) of exercise along the way. The first 15 miles from the Park Entrance to Savage River are paved. The rest is narrow, graded gravel road without shoulders. Cyclists can shorten their trip by driving to Savage River or loading your bicycle onto the **Savage River Shuttle** or **Camper Buses**. **Bike space can be reserved at the Wilderness Access Center.** Note that you must have a campground reservation or backcountry permit to reserve bike space. Cyclists are allowed on park roads, parking areas, campground loops, and the designated campground Bike Trail between Nenana River and Denali Visitor Center. Bicycles are not permitted on any park trails or in the backcountry. If it's inconvenient to bring your own bike, **rentals** are available at Denali Outdoor Center (888.303.1925, denalioutdoorcenter.com). Rates are $8/hour, $25/half-day, $40/day, and $35/day (>1 day). They also offer 2–2.5 hour bicycle tours for $57/person.

Flightseeing

Flightseeing gives visitors the opportunity to see Denali at eye level as you soar high above climbers attempting the much more laborious journey to its summit. From the air you gain a new appreciation for the park's immensity and its mountain. Flightseeing also provides the unique opportunity to land on a glacier where you can partake in a summertime snowball fight or make a snow angel. Fly Denali (907.683.2359, flydenali.com), Sheldon Air Service (800.478.2321, sheldonairservice.com), K2 Aviation (800.764.2291, flyk2.com), and Talkeetna Air Taxi (800.533.2219, talkeetnaair.com) are authorized park concessioners for flightseeing trips. They offer a variety of routes and itineraries, ranging in price from $210–524/person. All trips are weather dependent. Unauthorized private companies also provide flightseeing tours, but they are not allowed to land in the park. See page 656 for a complete list.

Fishing

Denali is not renowned for its fishing like other Alaskan parks, but fishermen enjoy dipping their line in Wonder Lake or one of the park's many streams. A state fishing license is not required, but you should inquire about catch limits and regulations that may be enforced.

Winter Activities

Just because the temperature drops below 32°F doesn't mean activities in the park come to a freezing halt. Winter visitors will find **Murie Science & Learning Center** open year-round, and from here you can head into the park on cross-country skis, snowshoes, dog sleds, or snowmobiles. **Camping** is available in the backcountry and at Riley Creek Campground. Spending a night in the park gives visitors an outstanding chance of seeing the **Aurora Borealis**. This phenomenon occurs all year, but there's only enough darkness to see it between fall and spring. Remember that services are extremely limited. You'll have to head to Healy, 11 miles to the north, for the nearest service stations with essentials like food and gas.

Ranger Programs

During summer, park rangers lead guests on walks, talks, demonstrations, and evening programs. These activities occur daily at both Denali and Eielson Visitor Centers. **Discovery Hikes** are a great way to explore the heart of the park with an experienced and engaging park ranger. "Disco" hikes are limited to 11 people, and you're only able to sign up in person, 1–2 days in advance at Denali Visitor Center. Park Rangers turn away unprepared hikers, so be sure to bring warm layers of clothing, adequate food and water, Discovery Hike Bus Ticket ($35), and be prepared to be in the park for 11 hours (~5 hours of hiking).

You can also catch a **Sled Dog Demonstration** at the Sled Dog Kennels. These unique experiences are offered daily at 10am, 2pm, and 4pm during summer. There is no parking in the area, so arrive via shuttle bus from the WAC or on foot. Program and shuttle are free of charge.

Evening programs are held at Riley Creek, Savage River, Teklanika River, and Wonder Lake Campgrounds. Hikes and Theater Programs are available from Denali Visitor Center. Check out a current schedule of activities in the park's publication, *Alpenglow* (available online or at a visitor center).

Visitor Facilities

Denali Visitor Center • Mile 1.5 • (907) 683-9275
Features: Exhibits, film, ranger programs, bookstore
Open: mid-May–mid-September, daily, 8am–6pm

Murie Science & Learning Center • Mile 1.4 • (907) 683-6432 • murieslc.org
Features: Exhibits, classes, field seminars w/ AK Geographic Institute
Open: All year, daily, 9am–4:30pm (except major holidays)

Wilderness Access Center (WAC) • Mile 0.75
Features: Bus tickets, campground reservations, bookstore, film
Open: mid-May–mid-September, daily, 5am–7pm

Backcountry Information Center • Mile 0.75 • (907) 683-9590
Features: Backcountry information and permits, bear-resistant food containers, maps
Open: mid-May–mid-September, Daily, 9am–6pm

Riley Creek Mercantile • Mile 0.4
Features: Campground check-in, bus tickets, groceries, firewood, **showers** and laundry
Open: Summer, daily, 7am–11pm (reduced hours in May and September)

Toklat Ranger Station • Mile 53 Denali Park Road
Features: Bookstore, park information
Open: mid-May–mid-September, daily, 9am–7pm

Eielson Visitor Center • Mile 65.9 Denali Park Road
Features: Park information, exhibits, ranger walks
Open: early June–mid-September, daily, 9am–7pm

Talkeetna Ranger Station • Downtown Talkeetna (140 miles south of the park entrance) • (907) 733-2231
Features: Mountaineering and park information, climbing film, interpretive programs, bookstore
Open: mid-May–mid-September, daily, 8am–5:30pm

For Kids

There's plenty of fun to be had for children and families, but one of the best ways to introduce kids to the unique history and geography is the park's **Junior Ranger Program**. To get started, pick up a free Junior Ranger Activity Booklet at Denali Visitor Center, Toklat Contact Station, Murie Science & Learning Center, or Talkeetna Ranger Station. Complete the activities in any order you choose, and then show your work to a park ranger. For a job well done you'll receive an official Denali National Park Junior Ranger certificate and badge.

Flora & Fauna

More than 650 species of flowering plants, 39 species of mammals, 167 species of birds, 10 species of fish, and one lonely species of amphibian live at Denali National Park. You are a visitor in their land, so protect it and respect it. The park is so far north that very few species of trees can survive, but black and white spruce, quaking aspen, paper birch, and balsam poplar populate the lower elevations. Some descriptions of the park's wildlife may lead you to believe you're embarking upon an Alaskan safari. It's not quite like that, but you'll have a good chance of spotting a few of the big five: moose, grizzly bears, caribou, Dall's sheep, and wolves.

Pets

Pets are allowed in the park, but must be kept on a leash no more than six feet in length at all times. They may be walked on the Park Road, in parking lots, or on campground roads. They are not permitted on trails, buses, or in the backcountry.

Accessibility

Denali Visitor Center, Wilderness Access Center, Murie Science & Learning Center, Eielson Visitor Center, Toklat Rest Area, and the Sled Dog Kennels are wheelchair accessible. The Bike Path, McKinley Station Trail, and Spruce Forest Trail are wheelchair accessible (with assistance). Savage River and Riley Creek Loop Shuttles are accessible. At least one of the Sled Dog Demonstration Shuttles is accessible. Many, but not all, Denali Park Road shuttle and tour buses are accessible. If visitors have special needs, you may apply for a road travel permit. Please contact the park (907.683.2294).

Weather

Warm weather from late May through early September attracts 90% of the park's visitors, but don't go expecting clear skies and temperatures in the 70s°F. Denali is so massive it creates its own weather system. Clouds hide the prominent peak for about half the year. You have a better chance of viewing Denali early or later in the day, but for the best chance of seeing the massive mountain, spend a night or two camping in the park. Temperatures are just as unpredictable, ranging from 33°F to 75°F during summer. Winters are downright nasty. On warm days the temperature might top out at 20°F, but it's not uncommon for the mercury to dip below -40°F. Extreme cold usually begins in late October and lasts through March. Don't forget a raincoat for your visit. June through August is the wettest period of the year, but precipitation is also difficult to predict. The table provided below gives you a general idea of what to expect.

Wonder Lake

Stony Overlook

Vacation Planner

The best advice a person can get when visiting Denali National Park is to **spend more than one day in the park**. Too many visitors come and go without ever catching a glimpse of her majesty, Denali, when she peeks out from behind a mask of clouds. It also requires an awful lot of time to properly explore the park. Most activities, like joining a park ranger on a **Discovery Hike** (page 627) or riding the **Tour Bus** (page 623) to Kantishna, are full-day commitments. Not to mention, you may want to **whitewater raft** (page 627), **pedal Denali Park Road** (page 623), or go **flightseeing** (page 627). Take your time, soak in the splendor, and admire the unspoiled wild beauty at a leisurely pace (as long as you aren't being attacked by a swarm of angry mosquitoes). Nearby dining, grocery stores, lodging, festivals, and attractions are listed on pages 656–663.

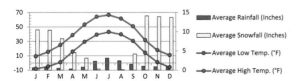

Harding Icefield sunrise

Kenai Fjords

PO Box 1727
Seward, Alaska 99664
Phone: (907) 422-0535 (summer)
(907) 422-0500 (winter)
Website: nps.gov/kefj

Established: December 2, 1980
Size: 699,983 Acres
Annual Visitors: 300,000
Peak Season: Summer

Activities: Boat Tours, Hiking,
Backpacking, Mountaineering,
Flightseeing, Paddling, Fishing,
Snowshoeing, Snowmobiling, and
Cross-Country Skiing

Campground: Exit Glacier (12 free
sites, first-come, first-served)
Backcountry Camping: Permitted
Backcountry Cabins: Coast
Cabins* (2, $75/night, summer
only); Exit Glacier Cabin** (1, $50/
night, winter only)
*Reserve at recreation.gov
**Reserve at (907) 422-0500

Park Hours: All day, every day
Entrance Fee: None

Kenai Fjords, located in south-central Alaska near the town of Seward, is the smallest of Alaska's national parks. Of course, small by Alaskan standards is large anywhere else. It's roughly the size of Grand Teton (page 206) and Rocky Mountain (page 326) National Parks put together. Along the coast, towering peaks rise abruptly from the sea. Glaciers that slowly carved the fjords are now receding along the ravines and valleys between mountain ridges. Tracing each glacier back to its origin inevitably leads to Harding Icefield. Named for President Warren G. Harding, the mile-high mass of ice covers more than 300 square miles, roughly the size of Crater Lake National Park (page 554) by itself. If you include some 40 glaciers that fan out from the icefield, it measures over 1,100 square miles. It accumulates as much as 400 inches of snow annually, and it is the largest of four icefields remaining in the United States. Exit Glacier Road leads to, you guessed it, Exit Glacier. It's the most accessible interior glacier. From the Nature Center, visitors can hike a short trail to the glacier's base or make a more arduous journey to the top of Harding Icefield. During winter, visitors arrive at Exit Glacier by skis, dogsleds, snowshoes, and snowmobiles.

From the first Russian navigators who explored the Kenai coast in search of harbors for whalers, to today's visitors seeking nothing more than seclusion and grand natural beauty, everyone takes with them memories of the same dramatic landscape. Portraits of narrow, gradually deepening fjords bracketed by precipitous cliffs rising above the glaciers and icefield are burnt into their collective subconscious. Sea and land are home to Steller sea lions, puffins, Dall's porpoises, black and brown bears, mountain goats, and humpback and orca whales. Tens of thousands of seabirds migrate to the coastline in summer. Kenai Fjords National Park might be small by Alaskan standards, but it's big in scenery, untamed wilderness, and wildlife, and it possesses infinite opportunities to inspire awe in adventurers. Traits that epitomize the Alaskan National Park.

Camping

There is a 12-site, walk-in, tent-only **campground** at **Exit Glacier**. Sites are available free of charge on a first-come, first-served basis. The camp features central food storage and a cooking and dining shelter. Water and pit-toilets are available.

Backcountry Cabins: Aialik and **Holgate** are rustic cabins located on the Kenai Fjords coast. They are available for public use from late May through mid-September. The cabins are accessible via float plane, water taxi, private vessel, or charter boat. Kayakers should be dropped off by boat due to extremely strong currents around Cape Aialik. All visitors must make their own transportation arrangements. Coastal cabins are equipped with heating stove (propane provided), pit toilet, table and chairs, and wooden bunks. You are responsible for bedding and sleeping pads, cook stove and utensils, drinking water or filter/iodine tablets, and toilet paper, in addition to whatever food, clothing, gear, and emergency supplies you might need. The cabins do not have electricity and sleep up to 4 people. Cost is $75/night and reservations are required. Reservations can be made through recreation.gov. Demand for the cabins is high so stays are limited to three nights per group per season. Reservations must be cancelled at least 10 days in advance to receive a refund or credit.

Willow Cabin is available for public use after Exit Glacier Road closes due to snow, usually from November through March. The cabin can be reached by snowmobile, cross-country skis, snowshoes, or dogsled. It is located approximately 7 miles down Exit Glacier Road from Box Canyon Gate (1.5 miles off AK-9/Seward Highway). This rustic cabin has propane heat, propane stove, oven, refrigerator, lights, and basic cooking utensils. There is no running water. It sleeps four and costs $50/night. Stays are limited to three nights and must be reserved in advance in person at the Park Headquarters or by calling (907) 422-0500.

When to Go

Kenai Fjords is open all year, but services and accessibility are extremely limited during winter. Exit Glacier Road is typically closed from fall through spring due to snow. The park's coastal backcountry is inaccessible from late fall through early spring because of rough seas. **Kenai Fjords Visitor Center**, located at Seward's boat harbor, is open daily from early May to mid-September. Hours typically run from 9am–5pm, and are extended to 7pm between Memorial Day and Labor Day. **Exit Glacier Nature Center** is open daily from Memorial Day to Labor Day, 9am–8pm. Most tourists arrive during summer, but flightseeing excursions (page 634) and fishing charters (page 634) can be arranged year-round (weather permitting). Guests also enjoy cross-country skiing, snowshoeing, or snowmobiling along Exit Glacier Road after it closes to cars in fall.

Transportation & Airports

Seward Bus Lines provides year-round transportation between Anchorage and Seward. The trip takes 3 hours (one-way) and costs $39.95/adult (one-way). Call (888) 420-7788 or visit sewardbuslines.net for additional information. A number of seasonal motor coach companies also provide transportation between Seward and Denali/Anchorage.

Alaska Railroad (800.321.6518, alaskarailroad.com) serves Seward (port of call for many cruise lines) from May to September.

Ted Stevens Anchorage International (ANC) is the closest major airport.

Directions

Kenai Fjords National Park is located in south-central Alaska, just west of Seward and 132 miles south of Anchorage. Exit Glacier is the only portion of the park accessible by road.

Exit Glacier: From Anchorage, head south on AK-9/Seward Highway. Continue on AK-9 for 122 miles. Turn right at Exit Glacier Road (seasonal) and follow it into the park.

KENAI
NATIONAL
WILDLIFE
REFUGE

KENAI FJORDS
NATIONAL
PARK

HARDING

CEFIELD

MOUNTAINS

KENAI

KACHEMAK
BAY STATE PARK

KENAI NATIONAL
WILDLIFE REFUGE

KACHEMAK BAY
STATE PARK

KACHEMAK BAY
STATE WILDERNESS PARK

KACHEMAK BAY
STATE PARK

Kachemak Bay

Public Use Cabin
Aialik

Paddle
Aialik Bay

Public Use Cabin
Holgate

Aialik Bay Ranger Station
Holgate
Public Use Cabin

Exit Glacier
Nature Center

Willow Public
Use Cabin (winter only)

USFS Cabin

Resurrection River Trail

AIALIK PENINSULA

Aialik Bay

PYE ISLANDS
ALASKA MARITIME
NATIONAL WILDLIFE REFUGE

Nuka
Bay

Ragged
Island

CHISW

Seal Rock

Lone Rock

Harbor Island

Chat
Island

Aligo
Point

Granite
Island

Granite
Cape

Matushka
Island

Three Hole Point

Elevation / feature labels

Twin Lakes
4443ft 1355m
5005ft 1526m
5720ft 1744m
5355ft 1633m
6197ft 1889m
5912ft 1802m
3768ft 1149m
5641ft 1720m
5269ft 1606m
5288ft 1612m
5873ft 1791m
6450ft 1996m (Highest point in park)
4430ft 1351m
6340ft 1933m
-876ft -267m
4734ft 1443m
1900
-726ft -221m
1615ft 492m
-834ft -254m
-972ft -296m
1942
-750ft -229m
4540ft 1384m
Storm Mountain 3793ft 1156m
Iceworm Peak 5800ft 1767m
1926
1905
Cloudy Mountain 1810ft 552m
Black Mountain 2028ft 618m
-762ft -232m
-1032ft -315m
-203ft -62m
5155ft 1572m
Phoenix Pe

Map warning
Do not use this map for
navigation or backpacking.
Use nautical charts and tide
tables for navigation.
Topographic maps and
area information are
available at the visitor
center.

Native Corporation land
Private lands owned by
Port Graham Corporation,
labeled Native Corpora-
tion, may be accessed only
on public easements or
with special use permits
issued by the village. Check
with the park for detailed
maps of boundaries and
easement locations before
venturing into the fjords.

North

0   5 Kilometers
0   5 Miles

Unpaved road
Trail
Historic extent of
glaciation
Campground
Landing/camping
beach

Generalized land cover
Ice and snow
Barren
Low vegetation
Cottonwood, alder, willow
Spruce, hemlock

Hiking & Backpacking

Hiking is somewhat limited. All maintained trails are in or nearby Exit Glacier. The 8.2-mile (roundtrip) **Harding Icefield Trail** is as good as it gets. You'll pass through forests and meadows before climbing above tree line to outstanding views of the massive icefield (the largest icefield entirely in the United States). It is a strenuous trek. You gain about 1,000 feet of elevation each mile and may have to scramble over rocks. Before departing, inquire about trail conditions, pack plenty of water, and be prepared to hike in bear country. The best way to enjoy the trail is with a ranger. On Saturdays in July and August, a park ranger leads guided hikes of Harding Ice Field Trail. Hikers depart Exit Glacier Nature Center at 9am.

A small network of shorter and easier trails originates at the Nature Center. From here you can hike to **Exit Creek's shoreline** (easy) or to the toe of **Exit Glacier** (moderate). The backcountry is trailless wilderness where hiking is not recommended due to dense vegetation and rugged terrain. **Backpackers** can camp along Harding Icefield Trail as long as you set up camp at least an eighth of a mile from the trail. If you're determined to explore the backcountry or Harding Icefield, we recommend hiring a **private outfitter**. See page 657 for a list of park-approved operations.

Bear Glacier icebergs

Harbor seals

Steller sea lion

Boat Tours & Cruises

In summer visitors can join **boat tours** that explore the coves and bays of Kenai Fjords. Major Marine Tours (800.764.7300, majormarine.com) and Kenai Fjords Tours (877.777.4051, kenaifjords.com) offer similar tour menus, with offerings ranging from $74 to $214 (3.5 to 9 hours). All tours focus on wildlife and tidewater glaciers—things this area has in abundance. You'll have a good chance of seeing Steller sea lions, sea otters, Dall's porpoises, orca whales, gray whales, humpback whales, and bald eagles. Each company offers specials and overnight packages. Lodging for Major Marine Tours is at Seward's Holiday Inn Express. Kenai Fjords Tours uses their privately owned lodging: Kenai Fjords Wilderness Lodge. It consists of eight beachfront cabins on Resurrection Bay's Fox Island, providing a peaceful setting where meals (included in package price) are prepared by the island's private chef.

Royal Caribbean (866.562.7625, royalcaribbean.com), Celebrity X Cruises (855.995.4654, celebritycruises.com), Holland America Line (877.932.4259, hollandamerica.com), Princess Cruises (800.774.6237, princesstours.com), and Norwegian Cruise Lines (866.234.7350, ncl.com) offer **cruises** that port at Whittier or Seward. From here, operators generally offer an optional cruise along the shores of Kenai Fjords. By this time, it's likely that you've been through Glacier Bay National Park and Wrangell–St. Elias National Park's Icy Strait, so maybe you've seen enough tidewater glaciers and marine life. If not, the tours of Kenai Fjords are just as memorable.

Paddling

Kayakers are welcome to explore the seemingly endless supply of bays and coves. Inexperienced paddlers should travel with a **guide** (page 657). Most kayakers are dropped off by boat or plane at Aialik Bay, Northwestern Lagoon, or Nuka Bay. Day trips paddling Resurrection Bay from Seward are safe, but you should not attempt to round Aialik Cape because of extremely treacherous waters.

Flightseeing

Like all of Alaska's National Parks, flightseeing is a safe and enjoyable way to view some of the world's most exceptional scenery. A list of providers is available on page 656.

Fishing

If you'd like to try your hand at fishing (fresh or saltwater), you'll need an Alaska State fishing license for all fishermen over the age of 16. Before dipping your lines, visit adfg.alaska.gov for a list of up-to-date fishing regulations. Or put your fishing fortunes in the hands of a guide by joining one of several year-round **fishing charters** (page 657).

Ranger Programs

Programs are held regularly between Memorial Day and Labor Day. For a current schedule of all walks and interpretive talks visit the park website or stop in at Exit Glacier Nature Center.

For Kids

Kenai Fjords has a few offerings designed specifically for kids. **Art for Parks Backpack Program** allows families to check out a backpack filled with art supplies. Packs are checked out free of charge and your artwork might be featured on the park website. Children are also invited to take part in the **Junior Ranger Program**. Download and print an activity booklet from the park website. Complete the activities appropriate for your age and show your work to a ranger or mail the booklet back to the park. Once your work is checked you'll receive an official Junior Ranger certificate and badge.

Flora & Fauna

Most land is bare or covered in ice and snow. The coastline supports vegetation and is covered with Sitka spruce and salmonberry. Sedges and grasses are the only plants capable of living in the park's Arctic–Alpine environments. In between the coast and the mountaintops you'll find alder, willow, and mature stands of spruce and hemlock trees.

Animals abound on land and in the sea. Black and brown bears, moose, mountain goats, and marmots live off the land. Whales, seals, sea lions, and sea otters patrol the seas.

Pets

Pets must be kept on a leash no more than six feet in length at all times. They are only allowed on Exit Glacier Road and in the parking lot. The only exceptions are dogs used for mushing or skijoring on Harding Icefield or in Exit Glacier when the road is closed.

Accessibility

Seward Information Center and Exit Glacier Nature Center are accessible to individuals in wheelchairs. The first one-third mile of Glacier Trail is also accessible. Boat and flightseeing tours may be accessible; contact individual providers for details.

Weather

Visitors should come prepared for all sorts of weather. Mittens, hat, and a warm/waterproof windbreaker are essential gear for a boat tour. Even when the temperature is comfortable, the wind on the open water can make for a chilly afternoon. Summer highs range

Humpback whale

Sea otter

Harbor seal

from the mid-40s to low 70s°F. Winter temperatures range from the low 30s to -20s°F. Rainy/snowy weather is common. The Exit Glacier area averages about 200 inches of snowfall each year.

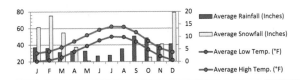

Sedge Meadow bear viewing

Lake Clark

95 Sterling Highway, Suite 2
Homer, AK 99603
Phone: (907) 781-2117
Website: nps.gov/lacl

Established: December 2, 1980
December 1, 1978 (National
Monument)
Size: 4 Million Acres
Annual Visitors: 18,000
Peak Season: Summer

Activities: Hiking, Backpacking,
Camping, Rafting, Canoeing,
Kayaking, Flightseeing, Fishing,
Boating, and Hunting

Campgrounds: None
Backcountry Camping: Permitted
(Backcountry Permit not required,
but leave a copy of your itinerary
at the field headquarters in Port
Alsworth)

Park Hours: All day, every day
Entrance Fee: None

See page 656 for a complete list of
local businesses and guide services

Lake Clark provides a sample of all Alaska's parks. In this relatively small area of the Alaskan Peninsula (southwest of Anchorage) there are a variety of geographical features not found together in any of Alaska's other national parks. Three mountain ranges meet: the Alaska Range from the north, the Aleutian Range from the south, and the Chigmit Mountains in between. There are two active volcanoes: Iliamna and Redoubt, the latter erupting twice since 1966. Temperate hemlock-spruce rainforest covers the coast. Plateaus of arctic tundra are interrupted by turquoise lakes. Lake Clark is "the essence of Alaska." The very thing some people are searching for.

Richard Louis Proenneke was a man who understood the essence of Alaska, and he found it along the shores of Twin Lakes. Born in Iowa, he worked as a farmhand before enlisting in the Navy the day after Pearl Harbor was bombed. He was discharged for medical reasons in 1945. Four years later he made his first trip to Alaska, where he lived and worked intermittently for years, but not until 1962 did he visit the Twin Lakes area. By this time, demand for furs was waning and tourism was waxing. The indelible memories of his first journey drew him back in 1967 when he began working on a cabin. The modest abode was completed in 1968, built from the ground up using only hand tools, many of which he fashioned himself. He lived in this exquisite piece of craftsmanship from 1968 to 1998, when he was 82 years old. Throughout 30 years of life on the shores of Twin Lakes he created homemade furniture, filled journals with weather and wildlife observations, and set the standard for wilderness ethics: "Twin Lakes and the wildlife therein should not suffer for his presence." Today, like-minded individuals can admire Proenneke's foresight and vision by reading edited volumes of his journals: *One Man's Wilderness* and *More Readings from One Man's Wilderness*, or by watching the documentary film, *Alone in the Wilderness*. Better yet, come to Lake

Clark National Park and see Proenneke's cabin for your-self. (Note: Dick Proenneke's cabin is locked from late September until late May.)

Camping

There are no designated campgrounds. A back-country permit is not required for hiking or camping, but it's a good idea to discuss your plans with a park ranger, especially if you aren't hiring a guide service (page 657). Bear-resistant food containers are available, free of charge, at the park visitor center in Port Alsworth. Tulchina Adventures (907.781.3033, tulchinaadventures.com) offers camping and cabin rental in Port Alsworth. Camping costs $50 per night for 2 people, but includes tent platform, firewood, water, and solar shower.

Hiking & Backpacking

Two trails begin near the Port Alsworth Visitor Center. **Beaver Pond Loop** and **Falls and Lake Trail** are 1.7-mile legs that run parallel to one another and intersect **Tanalian Mountain Trail**. At the intersection, a left (north) leads to Tanalian Mountain after 2.4 miles. A right (south) leads to Tanalian Falls and Kontrashibuna Lake after 1.1 miles. A short (unmarked) spur trail descends from the boardwalk to the base of the falls.

Camping is allowed around Kontrashibuna Lake as long as you set up camp at least 100 feet from the water and out of sight and sound of other users. From Tanalian Falls Trail you will find short spur trails at the signed junctions for Beaver Pond Loop and Tanalian Mountain. Venturing any deeper into the park requires careful planning and route selection. Hiking is easiest above the tree line. The northwestern parts (Telaquana Lake, Turquoise Lake) offer the least challenging routes. **Telaquana Trail** (unmaintained) is an historic Dena'ina Athabascan route that connects Telaquana Lake to Kijik Village on Lake Clark. Originally blazed by the native Inland Dena'ina, and later by trappers, miners, and homesteaders, today it is primarily used by adventurous backpackers. Alder, river crossings, and inclement weather will slow down your travel. Expect your hiking rate to be about one mile per hour. A well-planned itinerary, good map, compass, warm layers of clothing, rain gear, knife, water, and snacks are

Kontrashibuna Lake

Telaquana Lake

When to Go

Lake Clark National Park is open all year, but the majority of guests visit between June and September. **Port Alsworth Field Headquarters** (907.781.2218) and **Homer Field Office** (907.781.2117) are open Mon–Fri from 8am–5pm. Before entering the park, plan on stopping at one of these facilities, especially if you intend on hiking or backpacking without an authorized guide.

Transportation & Airports

Roads do not reach Lake Clark National Park. The region is primarily accessed by air taxi service (page 656). Depending on your destination, you may arrive via float plane or wheeled plane. Commercial flights between Ted Stevens Anchorage International Airport (ANC) and Iliamna (30 miles outside the park boundary) are available.

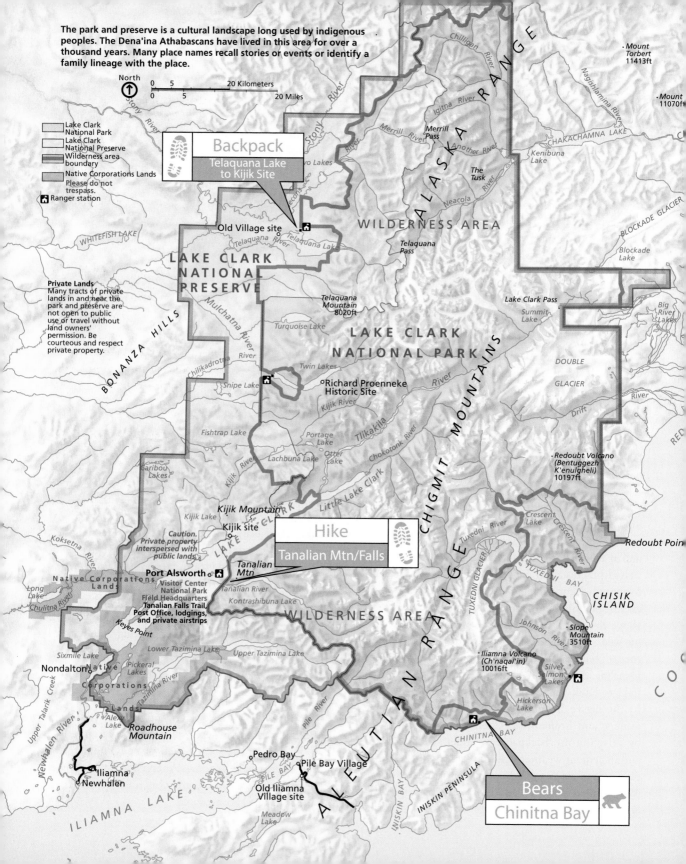

The park and preserve is a cultural landscape long used by indigenous peoples. The Dena'ina Athabascans have lived in this area for over a thousand years. Many place names recall stories or events or identify a family lineage with the place.

North

0   5   20 Kilometers
0   5   20 Miles

Lake Clark National Park
Lake Clark National Preserve
Wilderness area boundary
Native Corporations Lands
Please do not trespass.
Ranger station

Backpack
Telaquana Lake to Kijik Site

Old Village site

WILDERNESS AREA

ALASKA RANGE

Mount Torbert 11413ft

Mount 11070ft

CHAKACHAMNA LAKE

Merrill Pass

The Tusk

Kenibuna Lake

Neacola River

Another River

Igitna River

Merrill River

Chilligan River

Stony River

Telaquana Lake

WHITEFISH LAKE

LAKE CLARK NATIONAL PRESERVE

Telaquana River

Telaquana Pass

BLOCKADE GLACIER

Blockade Lake

Private Lands
Many tracts of private lands in and near the park and preserve are not open to public use or travel without land owners' permission. Be courteous and respect private property.

BONANZA HILLS

Mulchatna River

Chilikadrotna River

Telaquana Mountain 8020ft

Turquoise Lake

Twin Lakes

Snipe Lake

Richard Proenneke Historic Site

Kijik River

LAKE CLARK NATIONAL PARK

Lake Clark Pass

Summit Lake

Big River Lakes

DOUBLE GLACIER

Drift River

Fishtrap Lake

Caribou Lakes

Kijik River

Portage Lake

Lachbuna Lake

Otter Lake

Tlikakila

Chokotonk River

Little Lake Clark

CHIGMIT MOUNTAINS

Redoubt Volcano (Bentuggezh K'enulgheli) 10197ft

Crescent Lake

Crescent River

Redoubt Point

RED

Koksetna River

Kijik Mountain

Kijik Lake

Kijik site

Caution. Private property interspersed with public lands.

Hike
Tanalian Mtn/Falls

LAKE CLARK

Tanalian Mtn

Port Alsworth
Visitor Center
National Park
Field Headquarters
Tanalian Falls Trail, Post Office, lodgings, and private airstrips

Tanalian River

Kontrashibuna Lake

WILDERNESS AREA

Tuxedni River

TUXEDNI GLACIER

AEUTIAN RANGE

Iliamna Volcano (Ch'naqal'in) 10016ft

Hickerson Lake

TUXEDNI BAY

CHISIK ISLAND

Slope Mountain 3510ft

Silver Salmon Lakes

Johnson River

Native Corporations Lands

Long Lake

Chulitna River

Keyes Point

Lower Tazimina Lake

Upper Tazimina Lake

Sixmile Lake

Pickerel Lakes

Nondalton

Native Corporations Lands

Upper Talarik Creek

Newhalen River

Roadhouse Mountain

Alexy Lake

Iliamna
Newhalen

ILIAMNA LAKE

Pedro Bay

Pile Bay Village

Old Iliamna Village site

Meadow Lake

PILE BAY

INISKIN BAY

INISKIN PENINSULA

CHINITNA BAY

Bears
Chinitna Bay

CO

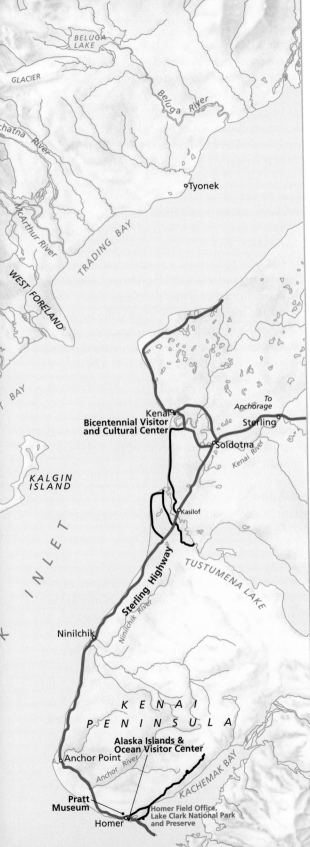

imperative for hiking in Lake Clark's backcountry (even on day hikes). If you plan on hiking without a guide, be sure to contact a ranger in Port Alsworth (907.781.2218) before departing. Bear-resistant food containers (BRFC) are required for travel in many areas. BRFCs are available, free of charge, at the park visitor center in Port Alsworth. A properly prepared hiker/backpacker will find a trip into Lake Clark's wilderness to be nourishment for the soul. Anyone unprepared for this unforgiving environment is likely to have an unrewarding and potentially fatal experience. **Experienced guide services** (page 657) are available.

Boat Tours

Visitors have the opportunity to take a boat tour of 42-mile-long Lake Clark or the craggy shorelines of Cook Inlet. If you're short on time, it's the ideal way to see the beautiful unadulterated landscapes that ring these picturesque settings. See page 658 for a list of commercial operators that provide guests with boating trips and charters. Fishing guides are often more than happy to include a tour of the waters and landscapes with a fishing expedition.

Paddling

Rafting, canoeing, and kayaking opportunities abound. Muchatna, Chilikadrotna, and Tlikakila are three National Wild Rivers offering fast moving water with occasional whitewater. Popular trip lengths vary from 70 to 230 miles. June through September is the best time to paddle. If you plan on rafting on your own, discuss your itinerary with a park ranger. **Outfitters** (page 657) are available to guide you on an epic journey through the pristine wilderness of Lake Clark.

Flightseeing

An **air taxi** (page 656) is required to reach Port Alsworth, but they can also be used to access otherwise unreachable regions of the park, supplying visitors with a bird's eye view of glacier-clad volcanoes, deep blue lakes, and endless expanses of open tundra.

Hunting

Big game hunters with proper licenses and permits are allowed to hunt and trap in **Lake Clark National Preserve**. Hunting is not permitted within National Park boundaries. Licenses and permits can be purchased in Anchorage. Hunters must follow all state regulations. Big game transporters are listed on page 657.

Playful grizzly

Paddling Lake Clark

Kontrashibuna Lake from Tanalian Mtn

Fishing

Saying that Lake Clark National Park is a good place to fish is like saying Lambeau Field is a good place to watch a football game. Lake Clark is home to some of the finest fishing grounds in the National Park System. The scenery isn't too shabby, either. Mountain lakes contain arctic grayling, Dolly Varden, several species of salmon, lake trout, and northern pike. All fishermen 16 and older require an Alaska State fishing license and must comply with State of Alaska fishing regulations. You can join a **sport fishing guide** (page 657) on a stock fishing trip, or they'll help you customize the fishing trip of your dreams based on ability, experience, time, and budget.

Ranger Programs & For Kids

Park rangers do not provide regularly scheduled walks and talks, but lectures and special programs are offered intermittently at Port Alsworth Visitor Center, Islands and Ocean Visitor Center, and Pratt Museum. For more information, contact Port Alsworth Visitor Center or Homer Field Office (907.781.2117). The park does not offer any specific children's programs.

Flora & Fauna

Lake Clark's terrain varies from irregular coastlines to snow-clad volcanoes, forest to tundra to grassland, and glaciers of slow-moving ice to streams of fast-moving water. Diversity in terrain and ecosystem leads to top-rate wildlife viewing and bird watching. Caribou reside in the hills around Turquoise, Twin, and Snipe Lakes. Moose live below the tree line. Dall sheep scale the steep slopes of the Chigmit Mountains. Brown bears are found in all habitats, but are most common along the coast, particularly the Chinitna Bay Area. Throw in 125 species of birds and you won't want to forget your binoculars.

Pets

Leashed pets are allowed in the park, but for your safety, your pet's safety, and the health of the ecosystem, it is suggested you leave them at home.

Accessibility

Air charters may be able to transport wheelchair users, but no facilities or trails are accessible.

Weather

You never really know what sort of weather to expect while visiting Alaska, but at Lake Clark National Park there are two distinct climates. The coast is wet (40–80 inches of annual rainfall) with more moderate temperatures. The interior is drier (17–26 inches of annual rainfall) with more extreme temperature differences (-40°F in winter). Snow can fall any day of the year, but it's most common from September to early June. Lake Clark begins to freeze in November and thaw in April.

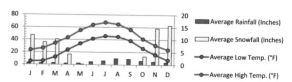

Average Rainfall (Inches)
Average Snowfall (Inches)
Average Low Temp. (°F)
Average High Temp. (°F)

Brooks Falls

Katmai

PO Box 7
King Salmon, AK 99613
Phone: (907) 246-3305
Website: nps.gov/katm

Established: December 2, 1980
September 24, 1918 (National
Monument)
Size: 4.7 Million Acres
Annual Visitors: 38,000
Peak Season: Summer

Activities: Bear Viewing, Hiking,
Camping, Backpacking, Fishing,
Flightseeing, and Paddling

Campgrounds: Brooks Camp*
Fee: $12 per person per night
Backcountry Camping: Permitted
Lodging: Brooks Lodge,
Grosvenor Lodge, and Kulik Lodge
(800.544.0551, katmailand.com)

Park Hours: All day, every day
Entrance Fee: None

*Reservations are required and
are available at recreation.gov or
877.444.6777

Originally created to protect features of the Novarupta Volcano eruption in 1912, Katmai is now one of the premier wildlife viewing destinations among all United States National Parks. Bristol Bay is home to
the world's largest run of Sockeye salmon. When they spawn in July, a
small fraction make their way up the Naknek drainage to Brooks Camp.
Sounds simple, but it's an incredibly treacherous journey. Along the
way, they must pass a gauntlet of brown bears, sometimes numbering
as many as one hundred. Each one is searching for dinner, and salmon
is the main course. The best seats at the all-you-can-eat buffet are near
Brooks Falls where salmon back-up as they jump up the falls. It's dinner
(for the bears) and a show (for you), and the show is spectacular. Specta-
tors flock to two viewpoints where they can safely admire the feeding
frenzy.

To many visitors, bear terminology is a bit confusing. What's the difference between brown, grizzly, or Kodiak bears? They're actually the same
species; they just come from different places. Kodiak bears reside on
Kodiak Island, southeast of Katmai across Shelikof Strait. Browns refer
to any bear living near the coast and grizzlies live in the interior. So, if a
Kodiak bear moved to the Katmai coast it would become a brown, and
if it traveled another 100 miles inland it would then be called a grizzly. Unfortunately bears do not carry birth certificates to prove their
place of origin. However, habitat causes dramatic differences in their
appearance. Kodiaks are much larger than grizzlies. Thanks to a steady
diet of spawning salmon and very little competition for food, Kodiaks
can weigh up to 1,500 pounds. Food for the inland grizzly is often less
abundant; forced to scavenge, some full-grown grizzlies weigh as little
as 350 pounds. At birth the differences are superficial. Kodiaks, browns,
and grizzlies are all born as one pound baby cubs.

Brown bears of the Brooks River may be the headliner at Katmai, but the eruption of Novarupta and resulting Valley of Ten Thousand Smokes is an unforgettable encore. Novarupta Volcano erupted June 6–9, 1912. It was the single largest volcanic eruption of the 20th century. The explosion was heard over 140 miles away. Nearby mountains were covered in ash up to 700 feet deep. Even Seattle, 1500 miles away, was dusted with ash from Novarupta. The sky over Kodiak Island was darkened for three days. Years later, Robert Griggs, a botanist on a National Geographic Expedition, recounted his visit to the devastated area: "The whole valley as far as the eye could see was full of hundreds, no thousands—literally tens of thousands—of smokes curling up from its fissured floor." The smoke stopped, but the name stuck. Valley of Ten Thousand Smokes is a curiosity left behind to be explored by inquisitive backpackers. There remain 15 active volcanoes in the park, and Alaska is by far the most volcanically active region of the Ring of Fire (an area in the basin of the Pacific Ocean where large numbers of earthquakes and volcanic eruptions occur). But volcanoes aren't the only hazard the park faces. More than 1,055 tons of oiled debris was removed from shorelines following the Exxon Valdez oil spill in 1989. In some areas oil is still seen today.

Islands in the sky
Brooks Camp

Camping

Brooks Camp Campground (60-person capacity), located on the shores of Naknek Lake, is the only developed campground. Its scenic location and second-to-none wildlife viewing opportunities make this one of the best campgrounds in North America. Due to its unique setting in the midst of an extremely active bear habitat, campers must store all food and scented items in the food cache, cook in one of three shared cooking shelters, and wash dishes at the water spigot near the food storage cache. Campfires are allowed in three designated fire rings near each cooking shelter, but you may not cook over an open fire. Vault toilets are available. To help protect campers from the locals (bears), the campground is enclosed within an electric fence. The fence is not a physical bear barrier, but it deters most of them from entering. The campground is open from the beginning of June until mid-September. It costs $12 per person per night and sites must be reserved prior to arrival. Reservations can be

When to Go

Katmai National Park is open all year, but concessioner services are only offered from June through mid-September. Bear watching at Brooks Camp is best during July and September. Bears can be found in other areas like Hallo Bay, Geographic Harbor, Swikshak Lagoon, and Moraine/Funnel Creek during June and August.

Transportation & Airports

Katmai National Park is located on the Alaska Peninsula. Park Headquarters is in King Salmon, about 290 miles southwest of Anchorage as the crow flies. Brooks Camp, the main visitor destination, is 30 miles east of King Salmon. Neither area is accessible by car. Visitors can reach these remote destinations by plane or boat. Ted Stevens Anchorage International Airport (ANC) offers regularly scheduled commercial flights to King Salmon (AKN), which is the starting point for most Katmai adventures. Brooks Camp can also be accessed via boat from the villages of King Salmon or Naknek. See page 656 for a list of private businesses that provide transportation services to and around the park.

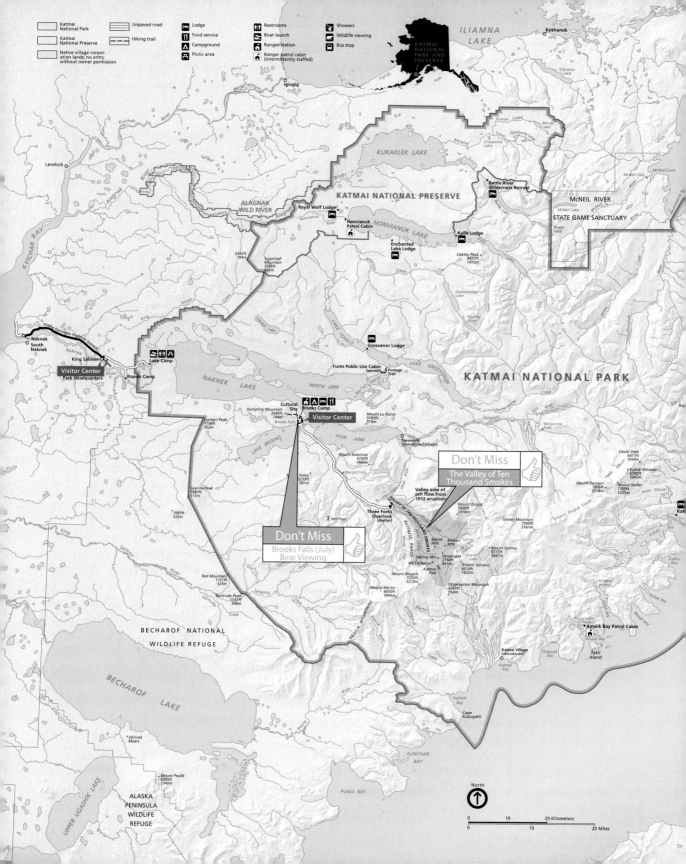

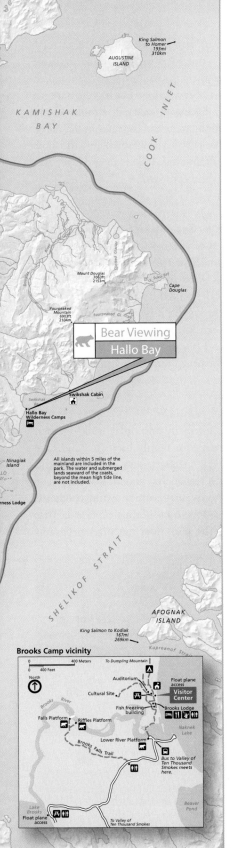

Brooks Camp vicinity

made by calling (877) 444-6777 or clicking recreation.gov. Be aware that reservations during peak bear viewing time can fill within hours of becoming available. During July, campsites can be reserved for a maximum of seven nights. The best time to visit Brooks Camp is July and September when bear viewing is prime.

Lodging

Lodging within Katmai National Park is provided by Katmailand (800.544.0551, katmailand.com). They offer **three lodges**: Kulik Lodge, Grosvenor Lodge, and Brooks Lodge. **Kulik Lodge** is the ideal destination for fly fishermen. Its cabins are situated along the shores of the Kulik River. Three nights costs $3,175 per person. **Grosvenor Lodge** consists of three guest cabins with heat and electricity. Three nights costs $3,050 per person. Pricing includes roundtrip air transportation from Anchorage, lodging, meals, boat and guide services, fishing license, rods and waders, and complimentary cocktails. **Brooks Lodge** consists of 16 modern rooms that can accommodate 2–4 persons. It's located in the heart of the park, just a short distance from Brooks Falls of salmon-fishing brown bears' fame. Three night packages based on double occupancy cost $1,836 per person and include roundtrip air transportation from Anchorage, meals, and a half-day guided Brooks River fishing orientation.

Bear Viewing

Katmai National Park and Preserve is home to as many as 2,200 brown bears. At times up to one hundred may be fishing for salmon along the Brooks River. This density and activity make Katmai one of the premier bear viewing destinations in the world. There are several good areas to watch. **Brooks Camp** is the most visited area of the park, and bear viewing is best during July and September. Three strategically located platforms provide safe viewing opportunities. **Lower River Platform** is located a short walk from the visitor center. An additional 0.9-mile (one-way) hike takes bear watchers to **Falls and Riffles Platforms**. A limited number of guests are allowed on each platform at a time. In July, bear can be seen at Brooks Falls as they fish for sockeye salmon swimming up river to spawn. In September the bears return to the Brooks River to feed on dead/dying salmon, but are usually found down river from the falls. Very few bear are seen along the Brooks River during June and August, but they are active at this time in other areas. **Outfitters** who provide bear-viewing tours are listed on page 657.

Hiking & Backpacking

There are a handful of maintained hiking trails in the Brooks Camp area. The most popular is **Brooks Falls Trail**. It's an easy 1.2-mile hike leading from the visitor center to Brooks Falls, where Falls and Riffles Platforms are located. **Cultural Site Trail** (0.1 mile) is an easy self-guiding stroll through prehistoric camps and a reconstructed native dwelling. It begins at Brooks Camp Visitor Center. In summer, every day at 2pm park rangers lead guests on a 1-hour-long interpretive walk of the area. Lake Brooks Road begins at Lower Platform. This 1-mile path leads to the head of Brooks River and a large, glacially carved lake that is a good location to see salmon during spawning season (August and September), and bear occasionally fish here. **Dumpling Mountain Trail** begins at Brooks Camp Campground and climbs 800 feet over 1.5 miles to an overlook with outstanding views. You can continue another 2.5 miles to the summit of Dumpling Mountain (2,440 ft).

Katmai's other must-see attraction is **Valley of Ten Thousand Smokes**. Ambitious hikers can make the 23-mile (one-way) hike along Valley of Ten Thousand Smokes Road, which begins at Lower Platform, or you can sign up for a **bus tour** provided by Katmailand (800.544.0551, katmailand.com). The bus driver is your tour guide and will lead a fairly strenuous hike into the valley from Overlook Cabin (where the bus stops). The tour costs $96 (w/ lunch) or $88 (w/o), but those hoping to explore the region on their own can purchase a one-way ticket for $51. Valley of Ten Thousand Smokes is the site of the largest volcanic eruption of the 20th century, and it's a fantastic destination for **backpackers**. About 12 miles from the road are **Baked Mountain Huts**. Originally built for research, these plywood bunkhouses now provide refuge for visitors. The 12-mile trek requires two river crossings which can be particularly dangerous. High volume of volcanic ash makes it nearly impossible to judge the depth. Always check river depth with a hiking pole or walking stick before each step. Bear-resistant food containers are required (available at King Salmon and Brooks Camp Visitor Centers). A backcountry permit is not required, but it is encouraged that you leave your hiking itinerary at Brooks Camp Visitor Center. Drinking water can be scarce in the valley. Water is only available early in the season before the snow melts at Baked Mountain Huts. Hikers should carry rain gear and a good map and compass.

Paddling

The 80-mile **Savonoski Loop** follows the North Arm of Naknek Lake, where paddlers portage to Lake Grosvenor and continue on the Savonoski River to Iliuk Arm and back to Brooks Camp. Along the way you can spend the night at historic Fure's Cabin. It costs $45 per night. Reservations are required and can be made at recreation.gov.

See page 656 for fishing, hunting, and flightseeing providers.

Ranger Programs & For Kids

Children and bears normally don't play well together. But if all members of your family listen to (and take seriously) a brief "Bear Etiquette" training course and safety talk, there's no reason you should not enjoy the park in harmony with its furry, salmon-eating residents. A trip to Katmai is a once-in-a-lifetime experience that you'll never forget. The park does not offer programs

Bears: Where They Are and What They Are Eating

Location	Eating	June	July	August	September
Brooks Camp	Salmon	Few	Many	Few	Many
Hallo Bay	Vegetation & Clams	Many	Some	Some	Some
Geographic Harbor	Salmon	Few	Few	Many	Some
Swikshak Lagoon	Vegetation	Many	Few	Few	Few
Moraine/Funnel Creek	Salmon	Few	Some	Some	Few

🐾 = Few Bears, 🐾🐾 = Some Bears, 🐾🐾🐾 = Many Bears

specifically for children, but park rangers at Brooks Camp provide regularly scheduled cultural walks, hikes to Dumpling Mountain, talks, evening slide shows, and narrated bus tours ($96) to the Valley of Ten Thousand Smokes from early June through mid-September.

Fauna

Visitors come from around the world to see the bears of Katmai National Park, but they aren't the only animal roaming around this remote wilderness. Moose, caribou, red fox, wolf, lynx, wolverine, river otter, marten, porcupine, and other species live within the park's vast wilderness. Along the coast you may spot sea lions, sea otters, and beluga, killer and gray whales.

Pets

Leave them at home. Pets aren't banned entirely, but they are not allowed within 1.5 miles of Brooks Camp Developed Area.

Accessibility

Most public buildings in Brooks Camp and all bear viewing platforms are accessible to individuals in wheelchairs, but the narrow dirt paths that connect facilities are often muddy, slippery, and difficult to navigate without assistance. Trails to Brooks Falls and Riffles are accessible. Close encounters with bears occur with some frequency, and there is a strong possibility visitors may need to leave the trail quickly and enter the woods to allow bears to pass. Air taxis may be accessible; contact the specific provider for details.

Weather

Visitors should come prepared for all types of weather. You might experience rain, sun, wind, or snow (unlikely in summer) during your stay, or even in a single day. Summer temperatures range from high 30s to low 80s°F. Winter is cold. Temps range from -40 to 40°F.

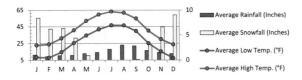

Legend:
- Average Rainfall (Inches)
- Average Snowfall (Inches)
- Average Low Temp. (°F)
- Average High Temp. (°F)

Valley of 10,000 Smokes

Hallo Bay

Mount Martin

Underwater bear

Hiking the Last Frontier

Gates of the Arctic

PO Box 30
Bettles, AK 99726
Phone: (907) 692-5494
Website: nps.gov/gaar

Established: December 2, 1980
December 1, 1978 (National Monument)
Size: 8.5 Million Acres
Annual Visitors: 11,000
Peak Season: Summer

Activities: Hiking, Backpacking, Camping, Paddling, Fishing, Flightseeing, and Wildlife Viewing

Campgrounds: None
Backcountry Camping: Permitted*
Lodging: Lake Wilderness Lodge and Wilderness Cabins (877.479.6354, gofarnorth.com)

Park Hours: All day, every day
Entrance Fee: None

*Backcountry Permit not required, but leave a copy of your itinerary with a ranger prior to departure

Gates of the Arctic, about the size of Switzerland, is the 2nd largest national park in the United States. The entire park resides north of the Arctic Circle, but it was still christened "Gates of the Arctic" by Bob Marshall while exploring the North Fork of the Koyukuk River. When he reached Frigid Crags and Boreal Mountain, one peak on each side of the river, he felt as though he had passed through the Arctic's stony gates. For explorers and outdoorsmen, the park is the gateway to a vast expanse of unspoiled wilderness and adventure. Rivers flow freely. Wildlife is undiminished. It represents nature at its purest, unscathed by roads, trails, and facilities. It's a land covered in snow and shrouded in darkness for most of the year. A land many people declare uninhabitable. A land that challenges outdoorsmen as they immerse themselves in nature. Wild, uninhibited, primitive nature.

Some 1,500 residents prove that this unforgiving landscape is in fact inhabitable. They reside in ten small communities within the park's "resident subsistence zone," where they still live lives similar to their ancestors who arrived more than 10,000 years ago from present-day eastern Siberia. Caribou, moose, and sheep provide sustenance. Caribou are of particular importance, used for food, shelter, clothing, and transportation. The animal's skin is fashioned into tents, parkas, pants, boots, socks, mittens, snowshoes, and sleds. Tendons are used to make nets to catch ptarmigan and fish. While exploring the park interior visitors may encounter relics of a caribou-dependent life. Remains of caribou skin tents are scattered throughout the wilderness. Iñuksuit, or "stone people," are found along migratory routes; Nunamiut Eskimos used these stone effigies to drive caribou to locations where their hunters were waiting.

Throughout the years, gold miners, military officers, explorers, and government scientists came and went. Meanwhile, descendants of the original Inupiaq and Athabascan people continue to reside in the central region of the Brooks Mountain Range that crosses the park. A land filled with glacial cirques, six Wild and Scenic Rivers, and an undisturbed wilderness waiting to challenge the most seasoned backcountry explorers and winter survivalists. Indeed, Gates of the Arctic is the last American Frontier.

Hiking & Backpacking

Anyone traveling to Gates of the Arctic National Park has to have a thorough agenda planned well in advance. **There are no developed campgrounds or designated campsites.** Rather than camping on fragile Arctic tundra, **backpackers** should search for durable surfaces like gravel bars, which have the added benefit of fewer mosquitoes. Just be sure to choose a location well above the water line since water levels can rise at any time. If you must camp on a vegetated site, choose a location with hardier plants like grasses and sedges rather than lichens and moss. You should make every effort to return your campsite to a natural appearance before leaving. Cooking should be done using a gas or propane stove. While open fires are allowed, wood and other burnable material is often scarce. Cook and eat all food at least 100 yards away from your camp. All food and scented items should be stored in a bear-resistant food container (BRFC). Visitor centers and ranger stations will loan BRFCs to visitors, free of charge, on a first-come, first-served basis. It is a good idea to call ahead to check availability.

Just as there are no designated backcountry campsites, there are no established hiking trails. Planning is essential to a safe and satisfying trip. Expect to move at a slower pace than usual. Vegetation can be dense, ground can be moist and boggy, and frequent river crossings will slow your travel. Going slowly isn't necessarily a bad thing. It affords time to savor this wild and rugged mountain wilderness. For easier travel, hike above the tree line or hire a guide (page 659).

When to Go

Gates of the Arctic National Park is open all year. Summer is the best time to visit, but it's not perfect. Swarms of gnats and mosquitoes emerge once the snow melts (typically June–July). Like all Alaskan National Parks, weather can be extreme, and visitors must be prepared for all conditions. Snow can fall any day of the year. Precipitation usually peaks in August. Hikers often rejoice when the sun comes out and the mercury rises, but heat causes rivers to swell, often making them impassable. Visitors should have flexible plans and extra food in case your pick-up flight is delayed, or you need to wait out a storm or reroute your itinerary. Regardless of when you visit, all guests should be well versed in wilderness survival and self-rescue techniques.

Transportation & Airports

No roads enter the park, but Dalton Highway (AK-11) comes within 5 miles of its eastern boundary. Economically minded hikers can begin on foot from Dalton Highway (river crossing required). Most visitors enter and exit the park via air taxi. Flights are available from Bettles (no road access), Coldfoot, and Anaktuvuk Pass (no road access), which can be reached by plane from Fairbanks International Airport (FAI). A list of air taxis authorized to land within the park is available on page 656.

Paddling

Rivers make for swifter travel. Many of the park's Wild and Scenic rivers can be navigated for hundreds of miles. Most are relatively easy floats, but the water is always cold and can be fast, especially when water levels peak in May and June or after particularly hot days or heavy rains. See page 659 for a list of **outfitters**.

Flightseeing

Easier yet, you can go on a flightseeing tour. **Air taxis** (page 656) fly above the park or land on lakes and backcountry airstrips, transporting visitors deep into otherwise inaccessible wilderness.

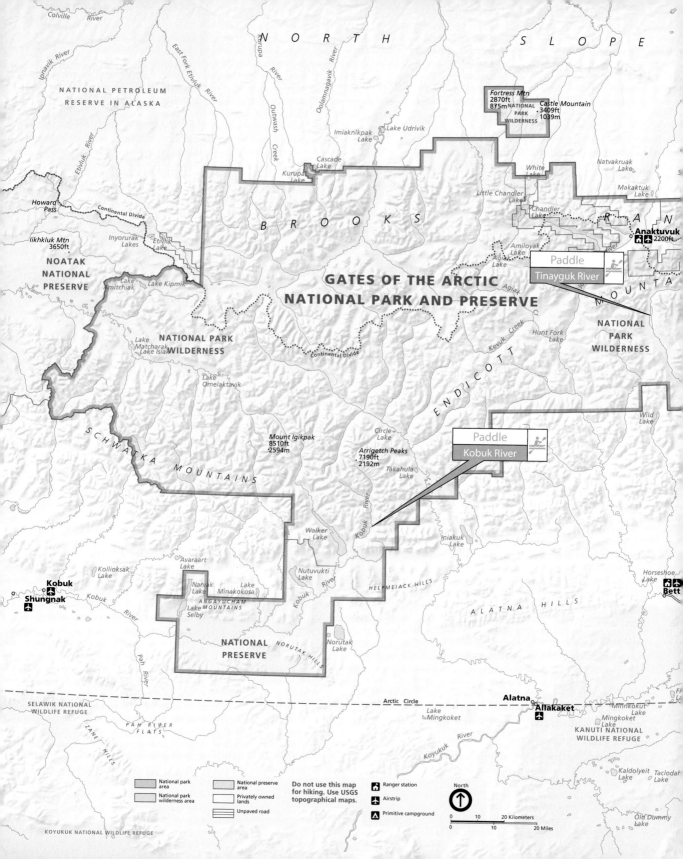

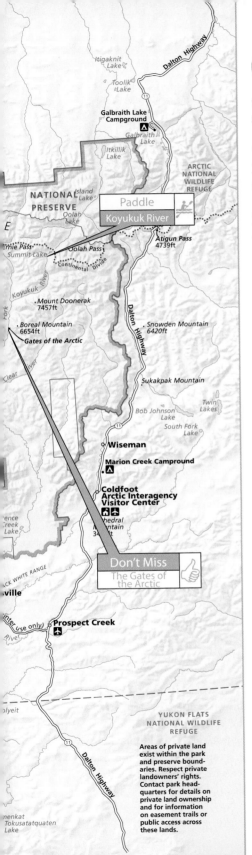

Wildlife Viewing

Gates of the Arctic is ideal for self-sufficient bird watchers and wildlife enthusiasts. Grizzlies, wolves, fox, caribou, and migratory birds gorge on food that becomes abundant during the short summer season.

Visitor Facilities

It is a good idea to leave your travel itinerary with a park ranger at one of the following facilities. Call to confirm hours of operation.

Fairbanks Administrative Center • (907) 457-5752
4175 Geist Road, Fairbanks, AK 99709 • Open: All Year, Mon–Fri, 8am–4:30pm

Bettles Visitor Center • (907) 692-5495; PO Box 26030; Bettles Field, AK 99726; Open: mid-June–September, Daily, 8am–5pm; October–mid-June, Mon–Fri, 1pm–5pm

Arctic Interagency Visitor Center • (907) 678-5209 • Dalton Highway, Coldfoot • Open: Memorial Day–Labor Day, Daily, 10am–10pm

Anaktuvuk Pass Ranger Station • (907) 661-3520 • Call for Hours

Ranger Programs & For Kids

The park does not offer regularly scheduled ranger or children's programs.

Pets

Pets are not allowed at Gates of the Arctic National Park.

Accessibility

Gates of the Arctic is one of the last tracts of untamed wilderness in the world. Terrain is unforgiving and difficult to navigate. Air taxis may be able to transport wheelchair users into the park (call specific air taxi operators to verify), but there are no accessible park facilities or maintained trails.

Weather

Visitors should come prepared for all types of weather. The park's interior is relatively dry. The wettest months are June, August, and September. Summers are short, but the days are long (in summer the sun does not set for 30 straight days).

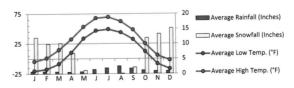

Kobuk Valley

Baird Mountains

PO Box 1029
Kotzebue, AK 99752
Phone: (907) 442-3890
Website: nps.gov/kova

Established: December 2, 1980
Size: 1.7 Million Acres
Annual Visitors: 17,000
Peak Season: Summer

Activities: Backpacking, Hiking,
Paddling, Camping, Flightseeing,
Wildlife Viewing, and Photography

Campgrounds: None
Backcountry Camping:
Permitted*
Lodging: None
Refer to page 660 for lodging
outside the park

Park Hours: All day, every day
Entrance Fee: None

*Backcountry Permit not required,
but leave a copy of your itinerary
with a ranger prior to departure

Kobuk Valley National Park protects an arctic wilderness roughly the size of Delaware. It is a land so desolate and remote that it can only be reached by foot, plane, boat, dogsled, or snowmobile. Unimaginable to modern people, natives have lived here for 10,000 years. Locals continue to follow in their ancestors' footsteps by hunting caribou at Onion Portage during the animal's southward migration in fall. The Western Arctic caribou herd is nearly half a million strong. Twice annually, they migrate across the park's southern reaches between summer calving grounds north of the Baird Mountains and winter breeding grounds south of the Waring Mountains. Along their journey, they leave tracks across Great Kobuk Sand Dunes, the largest active dune field in arctic North America. Today, it covers 23.5 square miles, but scientists believe the sand—ground down by glaciers of the last Ice Age—once covered an area more than ten times its present size. The landscape is constantly changing as wind and water reshape the dunes; some rise 200 feet above the tundra.

North of the Kobuk (Inupiaq for "Big") River are the Baird Mountains. Mount Angayukaqaraq (4,760 feet) is the park's highest peak. A modest mountain compared to Denali, but it presents an intimidating barrier for intrepid travelers. Lower in elevation, much of the tundra is soggy even though the park receives, on average, just 20 inches of snow and rain each year. Permafrost, many feet below the surface, prevents water from draining before everything freezes for the long, frigid winter. Life is forced to adapt or perish. The wood frog has found an interesting way to survive. In fall, it burrows beneath leaves and soil, where its body temperature drops below freezing. In spring, it thaws out only to hop about the valley and enjoy summer with a handful of humans seeking the ultimate adventure and solitude.

Activities

Visitors must possess a fairly unique set of skills. Self-sufficiency is paramount. Survival and self-rescue skills are, quite literally, a matter of life and death no matter what time of year you travel. This is not your typical drive-thru family vacation. You won't find visitors parking their cars to snap a picture of a grizzly bear lumbering across the tundra. There are no roads. No trails. No facilities. It's a vast expanse of relatively unexplored, completely wild wilderness. You are the guest of the grizzly, the caribou, and the gray wolf. It is not the sort of place for inexperienced paddlers or backpackers. If you get lost, you won't eventually "pop-out" at a fast-food joint, gas station, or even a road. The only thing that will be there to greet you is more wilderness. If you want to call for help, you better be carrying a satellite phone, because your cell phone won't work. Paddlers and hikers are completely alone out there. It's just you and Mother Nature, exactly what Kobuk Valley's visitors seek.

Unless you're flying over the park—viewing its rivers and mountains from above—trips into Kobuk Valley are usually extended expeditions. Guests create their own itineraries, possibly with the help of a **guide** (page 659) or park ranger (907.442.3890). Most trips begin with an air taxi ride to your starting point. **Air taxis** are available from nearby towns of Kotzebue and Bettles. See page 656 for a list of authorized operators. Before your trip, it's a very good idea to stop at **Northwest Arctic Heritage Center** in Kotzebue to drop off a copy of your trip itinerary and borrow a bear-resistant food container if you don't have one. The easiest **hiking** is along the ridgelines of the Baird Mountains. Ridgelines are exposed to chilling winds, but travel is free of swampy soil and impenetrable vegetation. **Paddlers** can float the 350-mile **Kobuk River**. This may be the best way to experience the park. The river is wide (up to 1,500 feet) but shallow as it crosses the park's southern half from east to west. The 80-mile trip from Ambler to Kiana can be made in about a week. This journey provides plenty of opportunities to explore on foot, too. In late August/September you can stop to watch **caribou** as they swim across the Kobuk River at Onion Portage, near the park's eastern boundary. Further down river you can hike along Kavet Creek to **Great Kobuk Sand Dunes**. And paddling allows you to leave your gear behind while exploring these sites.

When to Go

The park is open all year, but only the hardiest adventurers (if any) enter the park during winter when the days are incredibly short, if the sun rises at all. All visitors should have extensive backcountry experience and advanced self-sufficiency skills. Summer is the time to visit. The season is short (June–September), but the days are long (the sun doesn't set for more than a month around the Summer Solstice). Mosquitoes and gnats hatch in late May/early June. Daytime highs peak in July. August is often wet. The **caribou migration**, between winter breeding grounds south of the Waring Mountains and summer calving grounds north of the Baird Mountains, begins in September. Summer high temperatures average a comfortable 54°F, but visitors must come prepared for all types of weather. Snow and freezing temperatures may occur at any time, and temperatures exceeding 90°F have been recorded in certain regions of the park in July.

Visitor Facilities

The park's headquarters and office, located at **Northwest Arctic Heritage Center** in Kotzebue, is open June to September, Mon–Fri (8:30am–6:30pm) and Saturday (10:30am–6:30pm). From October to May, it is open Mon–Fri (8am–12pm and 1–5pm). **Ranger stations** at Onion Portage and Kallarichuk are staffed intermittently.

Transportation & Airports

No roads enter Kobuk Valley. Air taxis (page 656) provide access to remote villages, lakes, and landing strips inside the park. Kotzebue and Bettles are the primary launch points for air taxi trips, but they aren't accessible by road either. Commercial airlines from Ted Stevens Anchorage International Airport (ANC) provide service to Kotzebue. Fairbanks International Airport (FAI) provides service to Bettles.

In summer, it is possible to access the park via motorized/non-motorized watercraft, or by foot. In winter, the park can be accessed via snowmobile or dogsled. Entering the park by foot is not recommended for anyone but the most skilled outdoorsmen.

ARCTIC OCEAN
CHUKCHI SEA

NATIONAL PETROLEUM RESERV

National preserve
National park or
national monument

⌂ Ranger station

North

0   20 Kilometers
0   20 Miles

**Map warning: Do not
use this map for hiking
or river running. Write to
the superintendent
for information about
U.S.G.S. topographic
maps.**

DE LONG MTNS

INACCESSIBLE RIDGE

BROOKS RANG

Black Mountain
5020 ft

Mount
Bastille
4480 ft

Amphitheatre
Mountain
3528 ft

IGGIRUK
MOUNTAINS

Desperation
Lake

Aniralik
Lake

Fer
La

Iyikrok Mountain
2195 ft

Red Dog Mine

Red Dog Mine

Deadlock
Mountain
2995 ft

IMIKNEYAK
MOUNTAINS

KINGASIVIK
MOUNTAINS

POKTOVIK
MOUNTAINS

NOATAK NATIONAL PRESERVE

Okoklik
Lake

Anigaaq (seasonal)

Lake Narvakrak

ISACHELUICH
MOUNTAINS

Lake
Kangilipak

Kikmiksot Mountain
2285 ft

Kelly River
(seasonal)

MAIYUMERAK
MOUNTAINS

Tututalak
Mountain
4474 ft

Kanaktok Mountain
3320 ft

Mount
Angayukaqsraq
4760 ft

MULGRAVE HILLS

Red
Dog
Mine
Port Site

Imik
Lagoon

CAPE

Noatak

B A I R D

M T N S

Kotlik
Lagoon

KRUSENSTERN

NATIONAL

NAGLATUK
HILL

MONUMENT

IGICHUK

HILLS

KOBUK VALLEY
NATIONAL PARK

KALLARICHUK HILLS

AKIAK MOUNTAINS

Cape
Krusenstern

Krusenstern
Lagoon

Mount Noak
2010 ft

KIANA

Anigaaq
(seasonal)

Aukulak
Lagoon

HILLS

Kallarichuk
(seasonal)

GREAT KOBUK
SAND DUNES

On

Sheshalik Spit

LITTLE KOBUK
SAND DUNES

Kiana

ARCTIC OCEAN
CHUKCHI SEA

Kotzebue
Park Headquarters and
Information Center

BALDWIN
PENINSULA

HOTHAM INLET (KOBUK LAKE)

Noorvik

HOCKLEY HILLS

WARING

MOUNTAINS

👍 Don't Miss
Kobuk Sand Dunes

🦌 Caribou Crossing
September

SELAWIK NATIONAL WILDLIFE REFU

KOBUK
RIVER
DELTA

Arctic   Circle

For a detailed map of Bering
Land Bridge National Preserve,
please refer to its official map
and guide.

Selawik

Field Station
(seasonal)

BERING LAND BRIDGE

SELAWIK LAKE

INLAND
LAKE

NATIONAL PRESERVE

KOTZEBUE SOUND

ESCHSCHOLTZ BAY

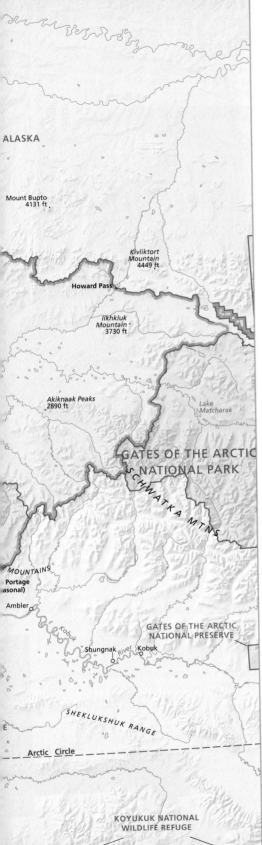

ALASKA

Mount Bupto
4131 ft

Kivliktort
Mountain
4449 ft

Howard Pass

Iikhkluk
Mountain
3730 ft

Akiknaak Peaks
2890 ft

Lake
Matcharak

GATES OF THE ARCTIC
NATIONAL PARK

SCHWATKA MTNS

MOUNTAINS
Portage
asonal)

Ambler

GATES OF THE ARCTIC
NATIONAL PRESERVE

Kobuk

Shungnak   River   Kobuk

SHEKLUKSHUK RANGE

Arctic   Circle

KOYUKUK NATIONAL
WILDLIFE REFUGE

Ranger Programs

The park does not offer any regularly scheduled ranger-led activities, but rangers are available to provide assistance over the phone or in person at Northwest Arctic Heritage Center in Kotzebue. This site also holds community activities throughout the year. Topics include natural and cultural history, local research, local crafts and children's activities. Call (907) 442-3890 before your arrival for a current schedule of events and programs.

For Kids

Kobuk Valley isn't a very kid-friendly park, but children are invited to complete the **Western Arctic Parklands Junior Ranger book** (available online) to earn a badge, saber toothed cat patch, and a water bottle.

Flora & Fauna

The Kobuk River is the lifeblood of an otherwise inhospitable region. North of this ribbon of scenic waterway rise the Baird Mountains. Each year some 490,000 caribou, the largest herd in Alaska, cross the Kobuk River as they migrate from their summer calving grounds north of the Baird Mountains to their breeding grounds south of the Waring Mountains. Caribou are vitally important to the people of Northern Alaska. Nearly 1,500 locals reside in ten small communities within the park's "resident subsistence zone." These residents still hunt caribou at Onion Portage, just like their ancestors did for hundreds of years. Seeing the migrating herd of caribou can be a more rewarding experience than watching grizzlies fish at Brooks Falls of Katmai National Park (page 642) or gray whales swimming in Glacier Bay (page 604).

Caribou aren't the only show in the valley. It is estimated that there are 32 mammals, 23 fish, 119 birds, and 1 amphibian that live in or visit the park. Other popular mammals include grizzly bear, wolf, black bear, mink, lynx, fox, wolverine, moose, and Dall's sheep.

South of the Kobuk River are the Great Kobuk Sand Dunes and the northernmost reaches of boreal forest. Caribou leave tracks across the 23.5-mile^2 dune field during their biannual migration (north in the spring, south in the fall). Little Kobuk and Hunt River dunes also reside south of the Kobuk River. Much of the southern reaches are covered in sand created by the grinding action of ancient glaciers. Sand was then sculpted by wind and water, and eventually stabilized by vegetation. In all more than 400 species of plants grow in the park, remarkable diversity for an area with such a harsh climate.

Pets

Kobuk Valley National Park is a remote wilderness area with extremely active wildlife. For the safety of your pets, yourself, and the delicate ecosystem pets are not allowed within the park.

Salmon River drainage

Art in the park

Accessibility

There are no visitor facilities or designated trails inside park boundaries. This is an extremely wild and undeveloped region that should not be accessed by anyone other than people with significant backcountry experience and skill. Individuals in wheelchairs may be able to tour the park by plane or boat. Please contact specific transportation providers for details.

Weather

Visitors must come prepared for all types of weather. Snow, wind, rain, and clouds can occur any time of year. Average summer temperatures in the mid-60s°F sounds pleasant, but they may reach into the mid-80s°F one day in July only to fall below freezing the next. Average January lows are -8°F, but lows can fall below -40°F. Due to extreme day-to-day temperature variance, average temps are not always a good guideline. One thing you can be sure of is that there will be long summer days. The sun never sets between June 3 and July 9. In winter, twilight lasts for hours each day, but the sun is only above the horizon for 1.5 hours on December 21. The northern lights (aurora borealis) are active year-round, but it is best seen on dark winter nights.

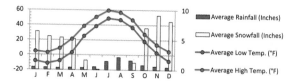

National Park Abbreviations

Glacier Bay: GLBA, Wrangell–St Elias: WRST, Denali: DENA, Kenai Fjords: KEFJ, Lake Clark: LACL, Katmai: KATM, Gates of the Arctic: GAAR, Kobuk Valley: KOVA

Ground Transportation

Alaska Railroad • (800) 544-0552 • alaskarailroad.com • DENA, KEFJ

Denali Overland Transportation • (907) 773-2384 • denalioverland. com • DENA

Talkeetna Taxi • (907) 355-8294 • talkeetnataxi.com • DENA

Bud's Rent-A-Car • (907) 697-2403 • GLBA

TLC Taxi • (907) 697-2239 • glacierbaytravel.com/tlctaxi.htm • GLBA

PJS Taxi • (907) 224-5555 • pjstaxi.com • KEFJ

Air Taxis/Flightseeing

Alaska Seaplane Service • (907) 789-3331 • akseaplanes.com • GLBA

Fly Drake • (907) 314-0675 • GLBA, WRST • *Flightseeing ($250+), River/Ski/Climb Support* • flydrake.com

Fjord Flying Service • (877) 460-2377 • fjordflying.com • GLBA

Mountain Flying Service • (907) 766-3007 • *Flightseeing ($159+), Flightskiing, and Cruises* • glacierbayflightseeing.com • GLBA, WRST

Sky Trekking Alaska • (907) 315-6098 • *Multi-Day Flightseeing, Iditarod Trail Treks, Wildlife Viewing, and Fishing Trips* • skytrekkingalaska. com • GLBA, LACL, DENA, KEFJ

Ward Air • (907) 789-9150 • *Flightseeing, Wildlife Viewing, and Fishing Trips* • wardair.com • GLBA

Yakutat Coastal Airlines • (907) 784-3831 • *Flightseeing, Fishing, Kayaking & Rafting* • flyyca.com • GLBA, WRST

40-Mile Air • (907) 883-5191• *Flightseeing, Fishing, Wildlife Viewing, Hunting, Rafting, and Hiking Trips* • fortymileair.com • WRST, GAAR

Copper Valley Air Service • (907) 822-4200 • *Flightseeing, Fishing, Wildlife Viewing, Hunting, Rafting, and Hiking Trips* • copperval-leyairservice.com • WRST

Lee's Air Taxi • (907) 822-3574 • leesairtaxi.com • WRST

McCarthy Air • (907) 554-4440 • *Flightseeing, and Backcountry/River Transport* • mccarthyair.com • WRST

Meekin's Air Service • (907) 745-1626 • *Flightseeing, Hunting, and Air Support* • meekinsairservice.com • WRST

Ultima Thule Air Taxi Service • (907) 854-4500 • farfargnargnar.com • WRST

Wrangell Mountain Air • (800) 478-1160 • *Flightseeing Tours ($110+) & Backcountry Trips* • wrangellmountainair.com • WRST

Fly Denali • (907) 683-2359 • *Flightseeing ($524+) & Expedition Support* • flydenali.com • DENA

K-2 Aviation • (907) 733-2291 • *Flightseeing ($220+) & Expedition Support* • flyk2.com • DENA

Talkeetna Air Taxi • (907) 733-2218 • *Flightseeing ($210+), #1 choice for climbing & expedition support* • talkeetnaair.com • DENA

Trail Ridge Air • (907)248-0838 • *Flightseeing ($150+), Bear Viewing, Rafting, Fishing, & Hunting* • trailridgeair.com • DENA, KEFJ, LACL

Alaska Air Taxi • (907) 243-3944
Flightseeing, Bear Viewing, Fishing, and Hunting
alaskaairtaxi.com • DENA, KEFJ, LACL, KATM

Rust's Flying Service • (800) 544-2299
Flightseeing ($100+), Bear Viewing, and More
flyrusts.com • DENA, KEFJ, LACL, KATM

Talon Air Service • (907)262-8899
Flightseeing, Bear Viewing, Fishing, and Hunting
talonair.com • KEFJ, LACL

Alaska West Air • (907) 776-5147
Flightseeing, Bear Viewing, Fishing, and Hunting
alaskawestair.com • KEFJ, LACL, KATM

High Adventure Air • (907) 262-5237
highadventureair.com • KEFJ, LACL, KATM

Homer Air • (907) 235-8591
homerair.com • KEFJ, LACL, KATM

Northwind Aviation • (907) 235-7482
Flightseeing and Backcountry Support
northwindak.com • KEFJ, LACL, KATM

Stellar Air Service • (907) 299-0284
Flightseeing ($99+), Bear Viewing, and More
stellarairservice.com • KEFJ, LACL, KATM

Lake Clark Air • (888) 440-2281
lakeclarkair.com • LACL

Natron Air • (907) 262-8440
natronair.com • LACL

Andrew Airways • (907) 487-2566
andrewairways.com • LACL, KATM

Smokey Bay Air • (888) 482-1511
Volcano & Bear Tours, and Backcountry Support
smokeybayair.com • LACL

Sunlight Aviation • (907) 301-6993
sunlightaviation.com • LACL, KATM

Bald Mountain Air Service • (907) 235-7969
Brown Bear Photo Safaris ($675)
baldmountainair.com • KATM

Branch River Air Service • (907) 246-3437
branchriverair.com • KATM

Emerald Air Service • (907) 235-9600
Brown Bear Photo Safaris ($675)
emeraldairservice.com • KATM

Harvey Flying Service • (907) 487-2621
harveyflyingservice.com • KATM

Sea Hawk Air • (907) 486-8282
seahawkair.com • KATM

Katmai Air • (907) 243-5448
katmailand.com • KATM

K-Bay Air • (877) 221-5029
Brown Bear Photo Safaris ($695)
kbayair.com • KATM

Brooks Range Aviation • (800) 692-5443
brooksrange.com • GAAR, KOVA

Coyote Air • (907) 678-5995
flycoyote.com • GAAR, KOVA

Wright Air Service • (907) 474-0502
wrightairservice.com • GAAR, KOVA

Adventure Outfitters
Alsek/Tatshenshini River Trips
The Alsek River flows from the Yukon into Northern British Columbia, where it is joined by the Tatshenshini River. It reaches the Pacific Ocean at Dry Bay. Both rivers are suitable for beginners.

Chilkat Guides • (907) 766 2491
RaftAlaska.com • GLBA

James Henry River Journeys • (800) 786-1830
riverjourneys.com • GLBA

Mountain Travel-Sobek • (888) 831-7526
mtsobek.com • GLBA, WRST, DENA

Nahanni River Adventures • (800) 297-6927
nahanni.com • GLBA

Tatshenshini Expediting • (867) 633-2742
tatshenshiniyukon.com • GLBA

Wilderness River Outfitter • (800) 252-6581
wildernessriver.com • GLBA

Beyond the Alsek
Sundog Expeditions • (208) 877-7104
sundogexpeditions.com

River Wrangellers • (907) 822-3967
riverwrangellers.com • WRST

Hunting & Fishing Guides/Lodges
Fishing excursions often consist of trolling for salmon, jigging for halibut, or floating one of the many Wild & Scenic Alaskan Rivers. While fishing, it's likely you'll be treated to a world class whale (salt water) and wildlife show.

Alaska Glacier Guides • (907) 321-2180
Boat Tours, Hunting & Fishing Expeditions
glacierguidesinc.com • GLBA

Alaskan Angler's Inn • (866) 510-2800
alaskananglersinn.com • GLBA

Doc Warner's Alaska Fishing • (801) 298-8060
docwarners.com • GLBA

Elfin Cove Sport Fishing Lodge • (801) 922-3474
elfincoveresort.com • GLBA

Glacier Bay Sportfishing • (907) 697-3038
glacierbaysportfishing.com • GLBA

Inner Harbor Lodge • (888) 828-1970
eaglecharters.com • GLBA

Wild Alaska Glacier Bay Adventure & Fishing
glacier-bay.com • (907) 697-2704 • GLBA

Ultima Thule Lodge • (907) 854-4500
A remote paradise accessible only by bush plane...discover an outpost designed for adventure, enhanced by comfort, 100 miles from the nearest road
ultimathulelodge.com • WRST

Alaska River Adventures • (907) 595-2000
alaskariveradventures.com • KEFJ

Alaska Wildland Adventures • (800) 334-8730
alaskawildland.com • KEFJ

Alaskan Wilderness Outfitting • (907) 424-5552
alaskawilderness.com • KEFJ

Deep Creek Fishing Club • (800) 770-7373
alaskafishinglodge.com • KEFJ

Great Alaska Fish Camp • (866) 411-2327
greatalaska.com • KEFJ

All Alaska Outdoor • (907) 953-0186
allalaska.com • Kenai Peninsula

Alaska's River Wild Lodge • (907) 781-2304
lakeclark.com • LACL

Cavner And Julian • (970) 300-3336
cavnerandjulian.com • LACL

The Farm Lodge • (888) 440-2281
lakeclarkair.com • LACL

Island Lodge • (206) 317-1242 (Skype)
islandlodge.com • LACL

Lake Country Lodge • (907) 781-2245
lakecountrylodge.com • LACL

Angry Eagle Lodge • (907) 850-4153
angryeagle.com • LACL

Rainbow King Lodge • (800) 458-6539
rainbowking.com • LACL

Rainbow River Lodge • (503) 720-5063
rainbowriverlodge.com • LACL

Redoubt Mtn Lodge • (907) 733-3034
redoubtlodge.com • LACL

Silver Salmon Creek Lodge • (888) 872-5666
silversalmoncreek.com • LACL

Stoney River Lodge • (907) 526-5211
stoneyriverlodge.com • LACL

Within The Wild • (907) 274-2710
withinthewild.com • LACL

Women's Flyfishing
womensflyfishing.net • LACL

Alaska's Fishing Unlimited • (907) 781-2220
alaskalodge.com • LACL, KATM

Alaska Fly Anglers • (907) 252-2868
alaskaflyanglers.com • LACL, KATM

Alaska's Valhalla Lodge • (907) 243-6096
valhallalodge.com • LACL, KATM

Bristol Bay Sportfishing • (907) 571-6524
bristol-bay.com • LACL, KATM

Alagnak Lodge • (800) 877-9903
alagnaklodge.com • KATM

Frontier River Guides • (877) 818-2278
frontierriverguides.com • KATM

Salmon Grove • (907) 822-5822
groveklutina.com • KATM

Kvichak Lodge • (907) 230-6370
kvichaklodge.com • KATM

Naknek River Camp • (907) 246-2894
naknekrivercamp.com • KATM

Deneki Outdoors • (800) 344-3628
deneki.com • KATM

Tikchik Narrows Lodge • (907) 243-8450
tikchiklodge.com • KATM

Tracy Vrem's Blue Mtn Lodge • (907) 439-2419
bluemountainlodge.com • KATM

Whale Watch/Boat Tours

In spring gray whales migrate through Alaskan waters on their way to summer feeding grounds in the Bering and Chukchi seas (Arctic waters). Humpback whales are commonly seen between April and October. Orcas reside in these waters year-round. One of the best places to whale watch is Southeast Alaska's Inside Passage. The following whale tours explore this area, but riding on the Alaska Marine Highway is a good alternative.

Whale watch tours are permitted to enter Glacier Bay. Whales are encountered here, but from 0.5-mile away (minimum). Tours also stop at humpback whale feeding grounds at Point Adolphus,

where boats can approach to within 100 yards. Rain gear and binoculars are essential whale watching gear.

First Out, Last In Adventures • (877) 881-2854
firstoutlastin.com • GLBA

Pacific Catalyst II • (800) 378-1708
pacificcatalyst.com • GLBA

Sea Wolf Adventures • (907) 957-1438
seawolf-adventures.net • GLBA

S.E. Alaska Outdoor Adventures • (907) 747-8800
seadventures.com • GLBA

Sound Sailing • (907) 887-9446
soundsailing.com • GLBA

Taz Whale Watching • (907) 321-2302
Whale Watching, Charter, and Kayak Drop-offs
taz.gustavus.com • GLBA

Woodwind Adventures • (907) 697-2282
sailglacierbay.homestead.com • GLBA

Boat Charters/Taxis

Charters provide whatever you want: fishing, kayak transport, whale/wildlife viewing and photography.

Alaska on the Home Shore • (360) 592-2375
Multi-Day Sea Kayak Tours/Charter Ship
homeshore.com • GLBA

Alaska Yacht Charters • (206) 780-0822
alaskansong.com • GLBA

Black Rock Charters • (800) 998-2384
blackrockcharters.com • GLBA

Eagle Charters • (888) 828-1970
eaglecharters.com • GLBA

Gull Cove Alaska • (907) 789-0944
gullcove.com • GLBA

Hobbit Hole Guesthouse & Charters
(907) 723-8514 • alaska-hobbithole.com • GLBA

Taylor Charters • (801) 647-3401
taylorchartersfishing.com • GLBA

Alaska Fjord Charters • (907) 362-7763
alaskafjordcharters.com • KEFJ

Saltwater Safari Company • (907) 224-5232
saltwatersafari.com • KEFJ

Seward Water Taxi • (907) 362-4101
sewardwatertaxi.com • KEFJ

Cruise Ships & Tour Vessels

Cruise lines offer land excursions to Denali & Kenai Fjords National Parks (and other destinations).

Carnival Cruise Line • (800) 764-7419
carnival.com • GLBA, WRST, KEFJ

Celebrity X Cruises • (855) 995-4654
celebritycruises.com • GLBA, WRST, KEFJ

Holland America Line • (877) 932-4259
hollandamerica.com • GLBA, WRST, KEFJ

Norwegian Cruise Lines • (866)-234-7350
ncl.com • GLBA, WRST, KEFJ

Princess Cruises • (800) 774-6237
princesstours.com • GLBA, WRST, KEFJ

Un-Cruise Adventures • (206) 284-0300
un-cruise.com • GLBA, WRST

Lindblad Special Expeditions • (800) 397-3348
expeditions.com • GLBA, WRST

Mountaineering Outfitters

St Elias Alpine Guides • (907) 554-4445
steliasguides.com • WRST

American Alpine Institute • (360) 671-1505
aai.cc • WRST, DENA

Alaska Mountaineering School • (907) 733-1016
climbalaska.org • DENA

Alpine Ascents International • (206) 378-1927
alpineascents.com • DENA

Mountain Trip International • (970) 369-1153
mountaintrip.com • DENA

Rainier Mountaineering • (888) 892-5462
rmiguides.com • DENA

Multi-sport Outfitters

Glacier Bay Sea Kayaks • (907) 697-2257
Kayak Rentals, Trip Planning, and Day Trips
glacierbayseakayaks.com • GLBA

Packer Expeditions • (907) 983-3005
Kayak, Hike, Rail, and Heli Trips, Rental Available
packerexpeditions.com • GLBA

Spirit Walker Expeditions • (800) 529-2537
seakayakalaska.com • GLBA

Allen Marine Tours • (907) 789-0081
allenmarinetours.com • GLBA

Alaska Mountain Guides & Climbing School
Best variety of adventures (day and multi-day)
(800) 766-3396 • alaskamountainguides.com • GLBA, WRST, DENA

Exposure Alaska • (907) 351-7587
exposurealaska.com • GLBA, WRST, DENA

Sierra Club Outings • (415) 977-5522
sierraclub.org/outings • GLBA, WRST, DENA, LACL, GAAR

Jody Young Adventure Travel
jodyyoung.com • Women-centric Tours

The World Outdoors • (800) 488-8483
theworldoutdoors.com • GLBA, DENA, KEFJ

Off The Beaten Path • (800) 445-2995
offthebeatenpath.com • GLBA, KEFJ

Natural Habitat Adventures • (800) 543-8917
nathab.com • GLBA, KEFJ, KATM

International Wilderness Leadership School
Provides high-quality guide training, outdoor leadership training, wilderness education, and technical instruction
iwls.com • (907) 799-3366 • GLBA, WRST

Copper Oar • (800) 523-4453
Raft, Kayak, Hike, and Wildlife Trips
copperoar.com • WRST

Kennicott Wilderness Guides • (800) 664-4537
kennicottguides.com • WRST

Pangaea Adventures • (800) 660-9637
alaskasummer.com • WRST

Sun Valley Trekking • (208) 788-1966
svtrek.com • WRST

Trek Alaska • (907) 554-1088
trekalaska.com • WRST

Wrangell Outfitters • (724) 427-5350
wrangelloutfitters.com • WRST

NOLS • (800) 710-6657
nols.edu • WRST, DENA

Get Up And Go! Tours • (888) 868-4147
getupandgotours.com • WRST, DENA, KEFJ

Alaska Alpine Adventures • (907) 351-4193
Hike/Backpack, Kayak, and Ski Adventure Vacations
alaskaalpineadventures.com • WRST, DENA, KEFJ, LACL, KATM, GAAR

Alaska Outdoors • (800) 320-2494
travelalaskaoutdoors.com • WRST, DENA, KEFJ

Adventures Cross Country • (415) 332-5075
adventurescrosscountry.com • DENA

Backcountry Safaris • (907) 222-1632
backcountrysafaris.com • DENA, KEFJ

Lazer's Guide Service • (907) 250-1120
lazertours.com • DENA, KEFJ

Trek America • (800) 873-5872
trekamerica.com • DENA, KEFJ

Nichols Expeditions • (800) 648-8488
nicholexpeditions.com • DENA, KEFJ

Premier Alaska Tours • (907) 279-0001
premieralaskatours.com • DENA, KEFJ

Alaska Wilderness Guides • (907) 345-4470
Hiking, Rafting, Skiing, and Snowmobiling
akwild.com • DENA, KATM

Adventure 60 North • (907) 224-2600
adventure60.com • KEFJ

Kayak Adventure Worldwide • (907) 224-3960
kayakak.com • KEFJ

Liquid Adventures • (907) 224-9225
liquid-adventures.com • KEFJ

Miller's Landing • (907) 224-5739
millerslandingak.com • KEFJ

Sunny Cove Sea Kayaking • (907) 224-4426
sunnycove.com • KEFJ

Exit Glacier Guides • (907) 224-5569
exitglacierguides.com • KEFJ

AK Saltwater Lodge and Tours • (907) 224-5271
alaskasaltwaterlodge.com • KEFJ

Allen's Alaska Adventure
allensalaskaadventures.com • KEFJ

Austin-Lehman Adventures • (800) 575-1540
austinlehman.com • KEFJ

Backroads • (800) 462-2848
backroads.com • KEFJ

Arctic Wild • (888) 577-8203
Raft, Canoe, and Backpack Trips
arcticwild.com • KATM, GAAR

Country Walkers • (800) 234-6900
countrywalkers.com • KEFJ

Freshwater Adventures • (907) 842-5060
freshwateradventure.com • LACL

Lifetime Adventures • (907) 746-4644
lifetimeadventures.net • KATM

Wilderness Alaska • (907) 345-3567
wildernessalaska.com • GAAR

Iniakuk Lake Wilderness Lodge • (877) 479-6354
gofarnorth.com • GAAR

Box Arctic Treks • (907) 455-6502
arctictreksadventures.com • GAAR, KOVA

Kobuk River Lodge • (907) 445-2166
kobukriverlodge.com • KOVA

Bear Viewing Outfitters
*Most fishing, multi-sport, and air taxis outfitters
near LACL & KATM offer bear viewing tours.*

AK Adventures • (907) 235-1805
goseebears.com • KATM

Alaska Bear Quest • (269) 362-7757
alaskabearquest.com • KATM

Coastal Outfitters • (907) 747-8759
alaskahunting.com • KATM

Grizzly Skins of Alaska • (907) 942-7625
grizzlyskinsofalaska.com • KATM

Hallo Bay Wilderness Camps • (907) 235-2237
hallobay.com • KATM

Homer Flyout Adventures • (800) 219-1592
homerflyoutadventures.com • KATM

Toft Photo Safaris & Gallery • (760) 788-6003
toftphoto.com • KATM

Out In Alaska • (907) 339-0101
outinalaska.com • GLBA, WRST, DENA, KEFJ

Rental Equipment

Alaska Mountaineering & Hiking • (907) 272-1811
2633 Spenard Rd, Anchorage
alaskamountaineering.com

AMS Mountain Shop • (907) 733-1016
F Street, Talkeetna • climbalaska.org

REI • (907) 272-4565 • rei.com
1200 W Northern Lights, Anchorage

Dining

Tracy's King Crab Shack • (907) 723-1811
406 S Franklin St, Juneau • kingcrabshack.com

Southeast Waffle Co • (907) 789-2030
11806 Glacier Hwy, Juneau

Paradise Café • (907) 586-2253
9351 Glacier Highway, Suite 10, Juneau

Marx Bros. Café • (907) 278-2133
627 W 3rd Ave, Anchorage • marxcafe.com

Moose's Tooth Pub & Pizzeria
3300 Old Seward Hwy, Anchorage
moosestooth.net • (907) 258-2537

Glacier Brewhouse • (907) 274-2739
737 W 5th Ave, #110, Anchorage
glacierbrewhouse.com

Simon & Seafort's Saloon • (907) 274-3502
420 L St, Anchorage • simonandseaforts.com

Falafel King • (907) 258-4328
930 Gambell St, Anchorage

Sacks Cafe and Restaurant • (907) 274-4022
328 G St, Anchorage • sackscafe.com

Smoke Shack • (907) 224-7427
411 Port Ave, Seward

Salmon Bake • (907) 224-2204
31832 Herman Leirer Rd, Seward
sewardalaskacabins.com

Le Barn Appétit • (907) 224-8706
11786 Old Exit Glacier Rd, Seward
lebarnappetit.net

Lemon Grass Thai Cuisine • (907) 456-2200
388 Old Chena Pump Rd, # K, Fairbanks
lemongrassalaska.com

Lavelle's Bistro • (907) 450-0555
575 1st Ave, Fairbanks • lavellesbistro.com

Aloha BBQ Grill • (907) 479-7770
402 5th Ave, Fairbanks

Grocery Stores

Walmart Supercenter • (907) 789-5000
6525 Glacier Hwy, Juneau

Breeze-In Grocery • (907) 789-7878
3370 Douglas Hwy, Juneau

Safeway • (907) 339-2870
1725 Abbott Rd, Anchorage

New Sagaya City Market • (907) 274-6173
900 W 13th Ave, Anchorage
newsagaya.com

Pak N Save • (907) 297-0221
3101 Penland Pky, Anchorage

Fred Meyer • (907) 267-6700
2000 W Dimond Blvd, Anchorage

Costco • (907) 269-9500
4125 Debarr Rd, Anchorage

Walmart Supercenter • (907) 344-5300
8900 Old Seward Hwy, Anchorage
3101 A St, Anchorage
7405 Debarr Rd, Anchorage

Sam's Club • (907) 276-2996
8801 Old Seward Hwy, Anchorage
1074 Muldoon Road, Anchorage

Pudgy's Meat & Groceries • (907) 235-3997
Mile 2.4 East End Rd, Homer

Safeway • (907) 224-6900
1907 Seward Hwy, Seward

Safeway • (907) 456-8501 • Fairbanks
30 College Rd, 3627 Airport Way, 3678 College Rd

Fred Meyer • (907) 474-1400
3755 Airport Way, Fairbanks

Sam's Club • (907) 451-4800
48 College Rd, Fairbanks

Walmart Supercenter • (907) 451-9900
537 Johansen Expy, Fairbanks

Lodging

Aimee's Guest House • (907) 697-2330
gustavus.com/guesthouse • GLBA

Tanaku Lodge • (800) 482-6258
tanakulodge.com • GLBA

Annie Mae Lodge • (844) 807-0702
anniemae.com • GLBA

Beartrack Inn • (888) 697-2284
beartrackinn.com • GLBA

Blue Heron B&B • (907) 697-2293
blueheronbnb.net • GLBA

Eagle's Nest Lodge • (801) 376-6513
glacierbayfishing.com • GLBA

Alsek River Lodge • (907) 784-3451
alsekriverlodge.com • GLBA

Glacier Bay Country Inn • (480) 725-1494
glacierbayalaska.com • GLBA

Glacier Bay Lodge • (888) 229-8687
visitglacierbay.com • GLBA

Gustavus Inn • (800) 649-5220
gustavusinn.com • GLBA

Johnny's East River Lodge
johnnyseastriverlodge.com • GLBA

Yakutat Lodge • (907) 784-3232
yakutatlodge.com • GLBA

Kennicott Glacier Lodge • (800) 582 5128
kennicottlodge.com • WRST

McCarthy Lodge • (907) 554-4402
mccarthylodge.com • WRST

Tonsina River Lodge • (907) 822-3000
tonsinariverlodge.com • WRST

Gilpatrick's Hotel • (907) 823-2244
hotelchitina.com • WRST

Wellwood Center B&B • (907) 822-3418
wellwoodcenter.com • WRST

P J's Golden Spruce Cabins • (907) 822-5556
goldensprucecabins.com • WRST

Glacier View Campground • (907) 441-5737
glacierviewcampground.com • WRST

Kennicott River Lodge & Hostel • (907) 554-4441
kennicottriverlodge.com • WRST

Log Cabin Wilderness Lodge • (907) 883-3124
logcabinwildernesslodge.com • WRST

Chistochina B&B • (907) 822-3989
chistochinabedandbreakfast.com • WRST

Tanada Lake Lodge • (970) 260-7770
tanadalakelodge.com • WRST

Camp Denali • (907) 683-2290
campdenali.com • DENA

Hotel Seward • (907) 224-8001
hotelsewardalaska.com • KEFJ

Murphy's Alaskan Inn • (907) 224-8090
murphysmotel.com • KEFJ

Van Gilder Hotel • (907) 224-3079
vangilderhotel.com • KEFJ

Harborview Inn • (907) 224-3217
sewardhotel.com • KEFJ

Angels Rest on Resurrection Bay
angelsrest.com • KEFJ

Beach House • (907) 362-2727
beachhousealaska.com • KEFJ

Breeze Inn Motel • (907) 224-5237
breezeinn.com • KEFJ

Moby Dick Hostel • (907) 224-7072
mobydickhostel.com • KEFJ

Marina Motel • (907) 224-5518
sewardmotel.com • KEFJ

Seward Military Resort • (907) 224-5559
sewardresort.com • KEFJ

Brass Lantern B&B • (907) 224-3419
brasslanternbandb.com • KEFJ

Sea Treasure's Inn • (907) 224-7667
innalaska.com • KEFJ

Serenity By the Sea Cabins • (608) 632-9113
serenitybytheseacabins.com • KEFJ

Lost Lake Trailhead Lodging • (907) 224-9262
lostlaketrailheadlodge.com • KEFJ

Adams Street B&B • (907) 224-8879
adamsstreetseward.com • KEFJ

Alaska Creekside Cabins • (907) 224-1996
welovealaska.com • KEFJ

Steller B&B • (907) 224-7294
stellerbandb.com • KEFJ

Orca Island Cabins • (907) 362-9014
orcaislandcabins.com • KEFJ

Camelot Cottages • (800) 739-3039
camelotcottages.com • KEFJ

Stoney Creek Inn B&B • (907) 224-3940
stoneycreekinn.net • KEFJ

Sourdough Sunrise B&B • (907) 224-3600
sourdoughsunrise.com • KEFJ

Sunshine House B&B • (907) 394-2013
asunshinehouse.net • KEFJ

Box Canyon Cabins • (907) 224-5046
boxcanyoncabin.com • KEFJ

Moose Creek Cabins • (907) 235-6406
moosecreekcabins3.com - KEFJ

Arctic Paradise B&B • (907) 491-1253
arcticparadise.com • KEFJ

Crane's Rest B&B • (907) 226-3276
cranesrest.com • KEFJ

Alaska Homestead Lodge • (907) 398-1960
alaskawildlife.com • LACL

Bear Mountain Lodge • (907) 252-1450
akbearmountainlodge.com • KATM

Alaska Fishing Lodge • (907) 512-0810
alaska-adventures.net • KATM

Kulik Lodge • (907) 243-5448
katmailand.com • KATM

Kachemak Bay Wilderness Lodge • (907) 235-8910
alaskaswildernesslodge.com • Haines

Crystal Creek Lodge • (907) 246-3153
crystalcreeklodge.com • LACL, KATM

Fox Bay Lodge • (661) 706-3930
foxbaylodge.com • LACL, KATM

Mission Creek Lodge • (800) 819-0750
missionlodge.com • KATM

Bettles Lodge • (907) 692-5111
bettleslodge.com • GAAR, KOVA

There are more than 200 public-use cabins ($25–75/night) scattered throughout the Alaskan wilderness. Nearly all of them are only accessible by trail, boat, or bush plane, and must be reserved in advance. For information and reservations contact the National Recreation Reservation Service at (877) 444-6777 or recreation.gov.

Most road-accessible restaurants, lodging facilities, and grocery stores are in Seward, Anchorage, and Fairbanks. Lodging and dining possibilities are also abundant along the southeastern coast in port cities like Ketchikan, Juneau, Skagway, and Gustavus.

Attractions

Totem Bight Park • (907) 247-8574
9883 N Tongass Hwy, Ketchikan

Panhandle Motorcycle Adventures
515 Water St, Ketchikan
panhandlemoto.com • (907) 247-2031

Alaska Canopy Adventures
116 Wood Road, Ketchikan
alaskarainforest.com • (907) 225-5503

Misty Fjords Nat'l Mon. • (907) 225-2148
3031 Tongass Ave, Ketchikan

Great Alaskan Lumber Jack Show
420 Spruce Mill Way, Ketchikan
alaskanlumberjackshow.com • (907) 225-9050

Alaska Raptor Center • (907) 747-8662
1000 Raptor Way, Sitka • alaskaraptor.org

Alaska State Museum • (907) 465-2901
395 Whittier St, Juneau • museums.state.ak.us

Alaskan Brewing Co. • (907) 780-5866
5429 Shaune Dr, Juneau • alaskanbeer.com

Alaska Canopy Adventures • (907) 523-2920
76 Egan Dr, Ste 100, Juneau • alaskacanopy.com

Mendenhall Glacier • Juneau

Mt Roberts Tramway • (888) 461-8726
490 S Franklin St, Juneau • goldbelttours.com

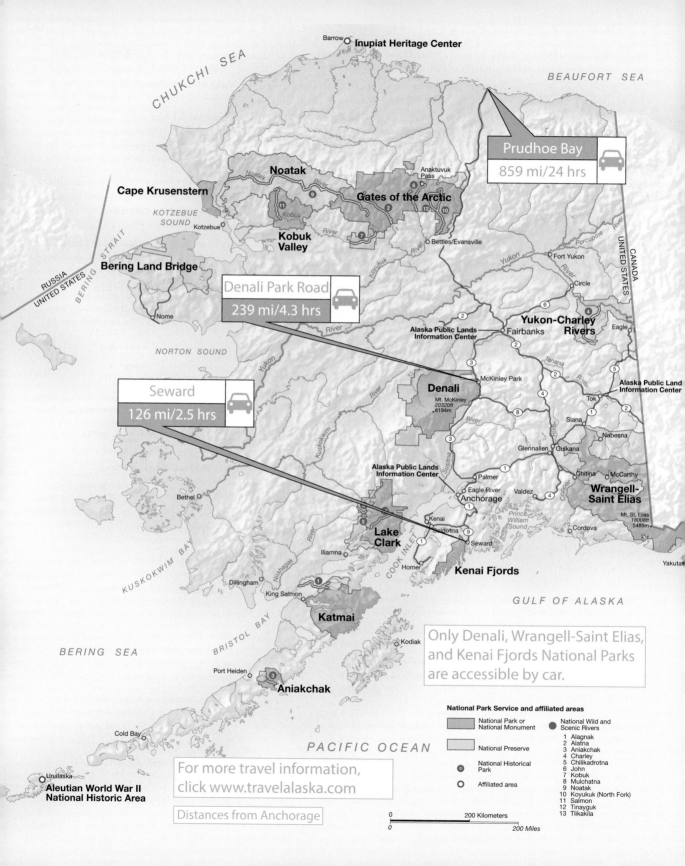

CHUKCHI SEA

BEAUFORT SEA

Barrow **Inupiat Heritage Center**

Noatak

Cape Krusenstern

Anaktuvuk Pass

Gates of the Arctic

KOTZEBUE SOUND

Kotzebue

Kobuk Valley

Bettles/Evansville

Bering Land Bridge

RUSSIA
UNITED STATES

BERING STRAIT

Nome

NORTON SOUND

Fort Yukon

Circle

Yukon River

Porcupine River

UNITED STATES
CANADA

Prudhoe Bay 🚗
859 mi/24 hrs

Yukon-Charley Rivers

Eagle

Denali Park Road 🚗
239 mi/4.3 hrs

Alaska Public Lands Information Center

Fairbanks

Tanana River

Alaska Public Land Information Center

Seward 🚗
126 mi/2.5 hrs

Denali
Mt. McKinley 20320ft 6194m

McKinley Park

Tok

Slana

Nabesna

Bethel

Glennallen Gulkana

Chitina McCarthy

Wrangell-Saint Elias

Alaska Public Lands Information Center

Palmer

Eagle River
Anchorage

Valdez

Prince William Sound

Cordova

Mt. St. Elias 18008ft 5489m

Kenai

Soldotna

Lake Clark

Iliamna

Homer

Seward

Kenai Fjords

Yakutat

KUSKOKWIM BAY

Dillingham

King Salmon

Nushagak River

COOK INLET

GULF OF ALASKA

Port Heiden

Katmai

Kodiak

Only Denali, Wrangell-Saint Elias, and Kenai Fjords National Parks are accessible by car.

BERING SEA

BRISTOL BAY

Aniakchak

Cold Bay

PACIFIC OCEAN

Unalaska

Aleutian World War II National Historic Area

For more travel information, click www.travelalaska.com

Distances from Anchorage

National Park Service and affiliated areas

National Park or National Monument

National Preserve

National Historical Park

Affiliated area

National Wild and Scenic Rivers
1 Alagnak
2 Alatna
3 Aniakchak
4 Charley
5 Chilikadrotna
6 John
7 Kobuk
8 Mulchatna
9 Noatak
10 Koyukuk (North Fork)
11 Salmon
12 Tinayguk
13 Tlikakila

0   200 Kilometers
0   200 Miles

Mileage Between Sites

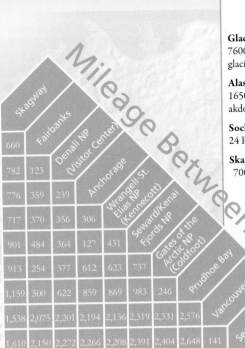

	Skagway	Fairbanks	Denali NP (Visitor Center)	Anchorage	Wrangell-St. Elias NP (Kennecott)	Seward/Kenai Fjords NP	Gates of the Arctic NP (Coldfoot)	Prudhoe Bay	Vancouver, BC
Fairbanks	660								
Denali NP (Visitor Center)	782	123							
Anchorage	776	359	239						
Wrangell-St. Elias NP (Kennecott)	717	370	356	306					
Seward/Kenai Fjords NP	901	484	364	127	431				
Gates of the Arctic NP (Coldfoot)	913	254	377	612	623	737			
Prudhoe Bay	1,159	500	622	859	869	983	246		
Vancouver, BC	1,538	2,075	2,201	2,194	2,136	2,319	2,331	2,576	
Seattle	1,610	2,150	2,272	2,266	2,208	2,391	2,404	2,648	141

Klondike Gold Rush
Skagway
Haines
Glacier Bay
Gustavus
Juneau
Hoonah
Sitka
Sitka
Petersburg
Wrangell
Ketchikan
CANADA
UNITED STATES
Alaska Public Lands Information Center
Dixon Entrance

Glacier Gardens Rainforest
7600 Glacier Hwy, Juneau
glaciergardens.com • (907) 790-3377

Alaska Icefield Expeditions
1650 Maplesden Way, Juneau
akdogtour.com • (907) 983-2886

Sockeye Cycle • (907) 766-2869
24 Portage Dr, Haines • cyclealaska.com

Skagway Museum • (907) 983-2420
700 Spring St, Skagway • skagway.org

Klondike Gold Rush Nat'l Hist. Park
Skagway • (907) 983-9200
nps.gov/klgo

Icy Strait Point
Home of the "World's Largest Zip Line Ride." They also offer wildlife (including bear) searches, whale watches, ATV expeditions, a nature tram, bird-watching tours, and jeep rentals. Discounts are available for combined tours.
108 Cannery Rd, Hoonah
icystraitpoint.com • (907) 789-8600

Anchorage Yoga • (907) 562-9642
701 W 36th Ave, Anchorage • anchorageyoga.com

Fourth Avenue Trolley Tours
546 W 4th Ave, Anchorage • (907) 276-5603

Imaginarium • (907) 929-9200
625 C St, Anchorage • anchoragemuseum.org

Anchorage Museum • (907) 929-9200
625 C St, Anchorage • anchoragemuseum.org

Alaska Native Heritage Center
8800 Heritage Center Dr, Anchorage
alaskanative.net • (907) 330-8000

Salmon Berry Tours • (907) 278-3572
515 W 4th Ave, Anchorage
salmonberrytours.com

Midnight Sun Brewing Co. • (907) 344-1179
8111 Dimond Hook Dr, Anchorage
midnightsunbrewing.com

Chugach State Park • (907) 345-5014
Anchorage

Denali State Park • (907) 745-3975
Trapper Creek • dnr.alaska.gov

Alaska SeaLife Center • (888) 378-2525
alaskasealife.org • KEFJ

Bardy's Trail Rides • (907) 224-7863
Lot 16 Resurrection Bay Rd, Seward
sewardhorses.com

Ididaride Sled Dog Tours • (907) 224-8607
ididaride.com • KEFJ

Trails End Horse Adventures
53435 E End Rd, Homer • (907) 235-6393

Alaska Islands & Ocean Visitor Center
95 Sterling Hwy, Homer
islandsandocean.org • (907) 235-6961

Center for Alaskan Coastal Studies
708 Smoky Bay Way, Homer
akcoastalstudies.org • (907) 235-6667

Pratt Museum • (907) 235-8635
3779 Bartlett St, Homer • prattmuseum.org

Kodiak Island Brewing Co.
117 Lower Mill Bay Rd, Kodiak
kodiakbrewery.com • (907) 486-2537

Fountainhead Antique Auto Museum
212 Wedgewood Dr, Fairbanks
fountainheadmuseum.com • (907) 450-2100

Running Reindeer Ranch • (907) 455-4998
Goldstream Rd, Fairbanks • runningreindeer.com

Morris Thompson Cultural & Visitors Center
101 Dunkel St, Fairbanks • (907) 459-3700
morristhompsoncenter.org

Large Animal Research Station
2220 Yankovich Rd, Fairbanks
lars.uaf.edu • (907) 474-5724

Northern Lights (Aurora Borealis)
The northern lights are best from Fairbanks in winter, but September and March are good times to visit thanks to clear skies, generally mild weather, and frequent displays.

Salomon Beach

U.S. Virgin Islands

1300 Cruz Bay Creek
St. John, VI 00830
Phone: (340) 776-6201 ext. 238
Website: nps.gov/viis

Established: August 2, 1956
Size: 14,689 Acres
Annual Visitors: 438,000
Peak Season: December–April

Activities: Sunbathing, Snorkeling,
SUP, SCUBA, Bird Watching,
Fishing, Sailing, Paddling,
Windsurfing, and Hiking

Best Beaches: Trunk Bay, Salomon
Beach, Maho Bay, and Denis Bay

Campground: Cinnamon Bay
Bare Campsite: $37/night
Tent Campsite: $93/night
Cottages: $126–163/night
Backcountry Camping: Prohibited
Lodging: Caneel Bay Resort
Rates: $450+/night

Entrance Fee: None
Overnight Anchoring: $26/night
Trunk Bay Day Pass: $5/person

Virgin Islands National Park is a tropical paradise of sandy white beaches and lush tropical forests wrapped in brilliant turquoise waters. Whether you're perched above a secluded bay or watching gentle waves roll onto a pristine beach, the views here are fit for a postcard. Stray away from the leisurely comforts of the bays and beaches, and you can learn of the area's not-so-perfect past. A past at odds with such an idyllic environment.

It's believed that humans have inhabited the Virgin Islands since 1,000 BC. Like many primitive people, they progressed from a nomadic village lifestyle to a complex religious culture with ceremonial sites for worshipping the spirits of the cassava (their main crop) and the sea. Europeans arrived in 1493, when Christopher Columbus, on his second voyage to the West Indies, spotted more than 100 emerald isles. He named them after Saint Ursula's legendary 11,000 virgins. Europeans began to colonize the islands, creating a melting pot of cultures where pre-Columbians perished from disease and harsh labor conditions.

Spain, France, Holland, England, Denmark, and the United States have all controlled various Virgin Islands at different times. St. John, the centerpiece of Virgin Islands National Park, was owned by Denmark prior to the United States. At this time, sugarcane, which thrived in the tropical climate, was the primary cash crop, and more than 90 percent of the island's native vegetation was stripped away in favor of farming. For nearly two centuries Danes produced huge quantities of sugar, rum, and molasses, which were shipped back to Europe. Such impressive production was a boon to the plantation owners, but the burden was placed squarely on the shoulders of enslaved Africans and their descendants. More than 80 plantations were constructed on St. John alone. Decades of growth left an island where slaves outnumbered the plantation owners by a rate of five to one. In 1848, a slave revolt led by General Buddhoe resulted in the release of Danish slaves in Frederikstad, St. Croix. Emancipation, low sugar prices, and nutrient-depleted soil marked the end of the "sugar is king" era of the Virgin Islands.

In 1917, construction of the Panama Canal and rise of German naval strength spurred the United States to purchase St. Croix, St. Thomas, St. John, and about 50 smaller islands from Denmark for $25 million. The islands served a role in military strategy, but they gained notoriety as a vacation destination. St. John's heavenly beaches have served as sun-bathing ground for millions of tourists. The sight of Little Maho Bay was enough to make Ethel McCully jump out of her boat and swim to shore. Once the eccentric American arrived, she never left; throwing caution to the wind, she lived her life in a setting most people only dream about. With six donkeys and two laborers she built a home, and then sat down to pen a book about the experience.

Ethel wasn't the only person smitten by the island's allure. Developers began purchasing land and building extravagant resorts and hotels. Laurance Rockefeller, philanthropist, conservationist and son of John D. Rockefeller, Jr., also took notice of the island's unique beauty and its rapid development. In 1956, he purchased 5,000 acres, half of St. John Island, for $1.75 million. He ended up donating this tract of land to the United States for use as a national park. Today, Rockefeller's personal estate in Caneel Bay serves as the park's only resort.

Tourism is currently king, but ruins of plantations, factories, and mills serve as reminders of the islands' past. You can learn all about the history and process of sugar production at Catherineberg and Annaberg Sugar Mill Ruins. Still, the park's main attractions are its warm and crystal clear water, ideal subtropical climate, and powdery beaches. It's a setting that many of the park's nearly 500,000 annual visitors can only dream about, but maybe you'll be the next person so enthralled with its beauty that you refuse to leave paradise, much like Ethel McCully.

Drunk Bay

When to Go
The park is open all year, but most travelers visit between December and mid-April. **Cruz Bay Visitor Center** is open daily from 8am to 4:30pm. Trunk Bay's bathhouse, snack bar, and souvenir shop are open until 4pm. Life guards are on duty daily at Trunk Bay Beach. Cinnamon Bay Campground closes to unregistered guests at 10pm.

Transportation
Due to its remote location in the Caribbean, Virgin Islands National Park must be reached by plane or boat. The park consists of half of the Island of St. John plus a few other isolated smaller islands. Its visitor center is located near the dock at Cruz Bay on St. John.

Cyril E. King Airport (STT) in Charlotte Amalie, St. Thomas serves as gateway to the U.S. Virgin Islands. From here you can reach Cruz Bay by ferry from two different docks. To reach the downtown Charlotte Amalie ferry dock you will need to take a short taxi ride ($7 for one person, $6 each for more than one traveler). The ferry takes about 40 minutes and costs $13 each way. Ferry service from Charlotte Amalie to Cruz Bay departs three times per day. You can also take a taxi or bus from Charlotte Amalie to Red Hook. A taxi ride ($13 for one person, $9 each if there is more than one traveler) provides a decent tour of St. Thomas Island. Ferries depart Red Hook for Cruz Bay every hour between 6am and midnight. The ferry takes about 20 minutes and costs $7 each way. Contact Varlack Ventures (340.776.6412, varlack-ventures.com) for additional information on ferry services. Visitors can also find private water-taxis and car ferries. Car rental is available near the dock at Cruz Bay ($75–120/day, $450–720/week). Remember to drive on the left-hand side of the road. Private taxi service can be arranged by calling Island Taxi Service (340.774.4077) or Christopher Taxi Service (340.690.1581).

Public transportation is available on St. John. VITRAN buses travel between Cruz Bay and Saltpond Bay, leaving the dock at 20 minutes after the hour from 6am until 7:25pm.

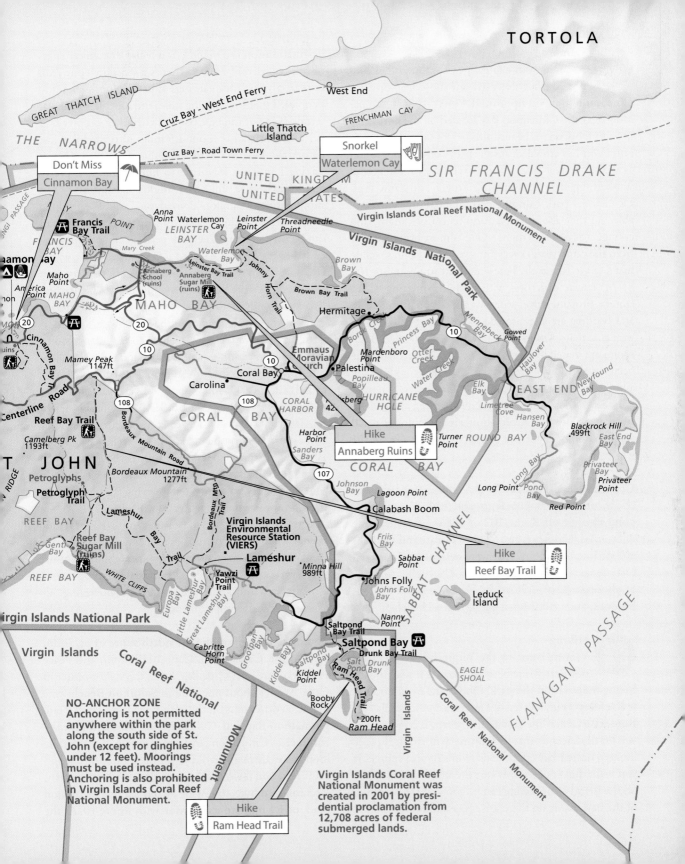

TORTOLA

GREAT THATCH ISLAND

Cruz Bay - West End Ferry

West End

FRENCHMAN CAY

Little Thatch Island

THE NARROWS

Cruz Bay - Road Town Ferry

SIR FRANCIS DRAKE CHANNEL

Don't Miss
Cinnamon Bay

Snorkel
Waterlemon Cay

UNITED KINGDOM
UNITED STATES

Virgin Islands Coral Reef National Monument

Francis Bay Trail

Anna Point

Waterlemon Cay

Leinster Point

Threadneedle Point

Virgin Islands National Park

Cinnamon Bay

LEINSTER BAY

Mary Creek

Waterlemon Bay

Brown Bay

Francis Point

Maho Point

Annaberg School (ruins)

Leinster Bay Trail

Johnny Horn Trail

Brown Bay Trail

Menneback Bay

Gowed Point

America Point

MAHO BAY

Annaberg Sugar Mill (ruins)

Hermitage

Princess Bay

10

Water Creek

Otter Creek

Haulover Bay

20

Cinnamon Bay Trail

Mamey Peak 1147ft

20

10

Emmaus Moravian Church

Coral Bay

Mardenboro Point

Palestina

Popilleau Bay

HURRICANE HOLE

Elk Bay

Limetree Cove

EAST END

Newfound Bay

Centerline Road

Carolina

108

CORAL BAY

CORAL HARBOR

42

Ramsberg

ROUND BAY

Hansen Bay

Blackrock Hill 499ft

East End Bay

Reef Bay Trail

108

Bordeaux Mountain Road

Harbor Point

Sanders Bay

Hike
Annaberg Ruins

Turner Point

CORAL BAY

Long Point

Long Bay

Pond Bay

Privateer Bay

Privateer Point

Camelberg Pk 1193ft

ST. JOHN

Petroglyphs

Bordeaux Mountain 1277ft

107

Johnson Bay

Lagoon Point

Red Point

Petroglyph Trail

Lameshur Bay

Bordeaux Mtn Trail

Calabash Boom

REEF BAY

Reef Bay Sugar Mill (ruins)

Virgin Islands Environmental Resource Station (VIERS)

Lameshur

Trail

Minna Hill 989ft

Friis Bay

Sabbat Point

Hike
Reef Bay Trail

Genti Bay

WHITE CLIFFS

Yawzi Point Trail

Johns Folly

Johns Folly Bay

Leduck Island

REEF BAY

Europa Bay

Little Lameshur Bay

Great Lameshur Bay

Nanny Point

SABBAT CHANNEL

Virgin Islands National Park

Virgin Islands

Coral Reef National

Cabritte Horn Point

Grootpan Bay

Kiddel Bay

Saltpond Bay Trail

Saltpond Bay

Drunk Bay Trail

Saltpond Bay

Drunk Bay

EAGLE SHOAL

FLANAGAN PASSAGE

Kiddel Point

Ram Head Trail

Booby Rock

200ft
Ram Head

Virgin Islands

Coral Reef National Monument

NO-ANCHOR ZONE
Anchoring is not permitted anywhere within the park along the south side of St. John (except for dinghies under 12 feet). Moorings must be used instead. Anchoring is also prohibited in Virgin Islands Coral Reef National Monument.

Virgin Islands Coral Reef National Monument was created in 2001 by presidential proclamation from 12,708 acres of federal submerged lands.

Hike
Ram Head Trail

Camping

As far as National Park campgrounds are concerned, they don't get any more tropical than **Cinnamon Bay Campground** (340.776.6330, cinnamonbay.com). Cinnamon Bay, located on the north side of Saint John, isn't as beautiful as neighboring Trunk Bay, but it's far less crowded. It's the park's only campground as well as a great place for snorkeling, swimming, and sun-bathing. Bare campsites ($37/night), similar to typical national park camping accommodations, are available, but they also offer platform tents ($93/night) and cottages ($126–163/night). Guests must bring (or rent from the camp store) everything required (tent, sleeping mat, etc.) to stay at the bare sites. Platform tents are 10'-by-14' canvas structures with mosquito netting. Cots, lantern, propane stove, water container, cooking utensils, and bedding are also provided. Cottages are 15'-by-15' with electricity, 4 twin beds, and an outside terrace. Bathrooms are shared by all guests. Rates are based on double occupancy. Additional guests cost $10 each for a bare site and $20 each for platform tents and cottages. A restaurant, beach shop, watersports activity center, and general store are on location. Reservations are available and you'll want to book early if you plan on traveling around the winter holidays.

Concordia Eco-Resort (800.392.9004, concordiaecoresort.com), offers Eco-Tents and studios near Saltpond Bay just off Route 107 on the southeastern side of St. John. Eco-Tents and Studios feature full kitchens and private bathrooms that were designed using green techniques. Eco-Tents cost $135–230/night and Eco-Studios cost $210–295/night. Rates are based on double occupancy. Additional guests cost $25 each.

Hiking

Visitors come to the Virgin Islands to enjoy powdery white beaches, but you'll also find 20 hiking trails within the park. One of the most popular is **Reef Bay Trail**, located 4.9 miles east of Cruz Bay on Route 10/Centerline Road. This steep, 2.2-mile (one-way) trail descends through a variety of tropical plant life to a decent bay (pack your swimsuit and snorkel if you want, but it's certainly not the most beautiful bay on the island—snorkeling can be good on the west side of the bay, but again there are easier and better snorkel

destinations on the island). You'll also encounter ruins of four sugar mill estates. There's a 0.3-mile **spur trail** to petroglyphs (rock carvings of pre-Columbian Taino people), a small swimming hole, and an ephemeral waterfall. (One of the best parts of the hike, so don't skip it.) The spur trail is about 1.5 miles into the hike, just before the junction with Lameshur Bay Trail. (Note: Taking Lameshur Bay Trail to Europa Bay is a pretty good alternative hike-and-snorkel adventure.) You should notice a sign for "Petroglyph Trail." Wear hiking boots (or at least don't wear flip-flops), because the trail can be very slippery. The park periodically offers **ranger-led hikes** of Reef Bay and L'Esperance Trails, where you hike down to Reef Bay and boat back to Cruz Bay. (L'Esperance Trail also begins on Route 10/Centerline Road and ends at Reef Bay.) For reservations and inquiries, stop by the Friends of the Park Store, located in Cruz Bay Visitor Center. The hike costs $40/person to cover transportation expenses (boat and taxi rides). Located on the south shore of St. John is **Bordeaux Mountain Trail**. It's a 1.2-mile (one-way) path leading to the highest point in the park, Bordeaux Mountain (1,300 ft). The trail connects Bordeaux Mountain Road with Lameshur Bay. Southeast of Lameshur Bay off Route 107 near Saltpond Bay you'll find three short trails. **Ram Head Trail** is the best of the bunch. It's a 1.0-mile (one-way) walk to a rock outcropping 200 feet above the Caribbean. The views are awe-inspiring. The other two trails are Saltpond Bay and Drunk Bay. **Drunk Bay Trail** offers opportunities to see wading birds (and plenty of visitor-created coral artwork) while **Saltpond Bay Trail** leads to Salt Pond Beach, where you'll find a picnic area and good swimming and snorkeling, although the seafloor is a bit rough.

There are 12 trails along the north shore of St. John. Lind Point, Caneel Hill, Caneel Hill Spur, and Peace Hill Trails are near Cruz Bay. From the visitor center in Cruz Bay, it's about one mile to **Salomon Beach** (one of our favorite spots on the island) via Lind Point Trail. **Cinnamon Bay Self-Guiding Trail** is located near the entrance to Cinnamon Bay Campground. This 0.5-mile loop passes through an old sugar mill estate and a tropical forest. You'll also find Cinnamon Bay Trail nearby. It's a forested hike, following an old Danish plantation road for 1.1 miles to its junction with Route 10. At the west end of Mary Creek Road is **Francis Bay Trail**. This 0.5-mile (one-way) trail is a favorite of snorkelers, swimmers, and birdwatchers. Just south of Mary Point are **Annaberg School Ruins** and a bit further east are Annaberg Sugar Mill Ruins, where you'll find a self-guiding tour that helps explain the Danes' sugar industry during the 18th and 19th centuries.

Paddling & Sailing

It's unlikely that you'll be bringing your own kayak or sailboat to the Virgin Islands, but that's alright because Cinnamon Bay Campground (340.776.6330) **rents** kayaks ($20–37/hour), small sailboats ($70/hour), SUP ($35/hour), and windsurfers ($75/hour). Before heading out on the water with your rental, you will be given a brief tutorial. Beginner sailors or windsurfers can sign up for a 2-hour lesson ($200). There are few locations better than the Virgin Islands to introduce yourself to these sports.

Snorkeling

More than one-third of the park is underwater and several reefs can be reached directly from the park's beaches. There's even a **snorkel trail at Trunk Bay** where underwater plaques describe the marine life as you swim by it (although much of the coral has been ruined by overuse). Nearly the entire St. John's shoreline is a snorkeler's playground. If you enjoy seeing colorful fish and feisty sea life, you'll want to have snorkel gear with you every day you're on the island. Several locations rent gear, including **Cinnamon Bay Campground's Water Activities Center**. Rental costs about $8/day or $40/week. Trunk Bay, Cinnamon Bay, Hawksnest Beach, Saltpond Bay, Francis Bay, and Maho Bay are some of the best locations to hop in the water for a little underwater exploration. **Waterlemon Cay** offers a unique snorkeling experience where visitors must complete a short 10–20 minute hike from Annaberg Sugar Mill Ruins Parking Area to the edge of Waterlemon Bay. From here, Waterlemon Cay is just to the northeast across the bay. Swim out to the small emerald island, but be sure to circle it in a counter-clockwise fashion; swimming in this direction will be much easier thanks to the water's current. Snorkeling this fairly-long stretch provides excellent opportunities to see turtles, starfish, stingrays, sharks, and barracudas.

Strong swimmers might also consider snorkeling from Francis Bay across Fungi Passage, and around **Whistling Cay**. If you'd like to snorkel with an experienced guide, several **outfitters** provide guided trips (page 672) or the park offers **ranger-led trips** for $5. Stop by or call Cruz Bay Visitor Center (340.776.6201, ext. 238) for a current schedule of ranger-led snorkel tours.

SCUBA Diving

The U.S. Virgin Islands wealth of water and reefs make it a great place to SCUBA dive. Within the park you can receive **SCUBA lessons** at Cinnamon Bay Campground (340.776.6330). Courses are offered for beginners and certified divers. Diving arrangements can be made at the activities desk. **Buck Island Reef National Monument** (nps.gov/buis), just north of Saint Croix Island, is a popular SCUBA diving destination close to the park. Numerous outfitters provide SCUBA lessons and charters for divers of all experience levels. They offer beginner courses, certification courses, night dives, wreck dives, and multi-dive discounts. Cruz Bay Watersports (340.776.6234, cruzbaywatersports.com, Dives: $90–160, Certificate: $450), Low Key Watersports (800.835.7718, divelowkey.com, $95–195, $475), and Patagon Dive Center (340. 776.6111 ext. 7290, patagondivecenter.com, $85–185, $450) offer dives and diving certification.

Fishing

Refer to page 672 for **outfitters** on St. John and the surrounding islands. Most charters provide four- and eight-hour excursions. Fishing is allowed in park waters with the exception of Trunk Bay and other swim areas. A fishing license is not required if you fish from the shore. The Virgin Islands may be best known for world record blue marlins pulled from its waters, but you'll also find bonito, tuna, wahoo, sailfish, and skipjack. Fishing is good year-round, but you're likely to have the most success between May and October.

Bird Watching

Approximately 144 species of birds have been documented within the park. This includes both resident and migratory species. Not only is winter the best time for tourists, it's the birds' favorite season as well. Brown pelicans, brown boobies, magnificent

Hummingbird (Saltpond Bay)

frigatebirds, and royal terns are commonly seen near the shoreline. Mangrove cuckoos, zenaida cloves, Antilliean-crested hummingbirds, gray kingbirds, pearly-eyed thrashers, and bananaquits are commonly seen in the park's dry forests. Serious birders can find a bird checklist at the park website or visitor center. It includes information regarding breeding status, habitat, abundance, and best season to spot each species.

Ranger Programs

The park offers a handful of ranger-led activities. On weekdays, rangers lead guests on a free tour of Cinnamon Bay Estate ruins, one of the first plantations on the island. You can explore the sea with a park ranger on a **snorkel trip** ($5/person). The **ranger-led Reef Bay Hike** (or L'Esperance Hike) offered by Friends of Virgin Islands National Park (friendsvinp.org) is a 3.1-mile trek through the history of St. John Island. Bring along a lunch and your swimsuit for this tour. It costs $40/person, but transportation to and from the trailhead is provided. A taxi will take you to the trailhead, while a boat brings you back to Cruz Bay Visitor Center (no uphill hiking required!). Several other hikes, early morning bird watch tours are also offered. For a current schedule, meeting locations, and to make reservations stop in at the visitor center or check out the park's online calendar of events.

For Kids

Virgin Islands National Park offers a **Junior Ranger Program** for children. Workbooks can be picked up at the park's visitor center. When completed, return to the visitor center to receive a certificate and badge.

An abundance of snorkeling, swimming, beaches, and short hiking trails make the Virgin Islands one of the most kid-friendly national parks in the United States, but you'll be tempted to leave the children at home for this one, because it's also one of the most romantic parks.

Flora & Fauna

More than 90% of St. John's native vegetation was destroyed in favor of cash crops like cotton and sugarcane and to graze livestock. It wasn't until the 1950s—when Laurance Rockefeller donated more than half of St. John Island to the National Park Service—that natural reforestation began. From underwater seagrass to mangrove shorelines, moist forests to dry cactus scrubland, the landscapes of the U.S. Virgin Islands are once again changing and adapting in a more natural manner.

Very little is natural about the islands' mammals. Bats are the only natives. Goats, donkeys, and mongoose were all introduced by humans. Dolphins are frequently seen in the winter months, and sea turtles are commonly spotted by snorkelers and SCUBA divers. In fact, Trunk Bay got its name from Danes who believed the leatherback turtle resembled a great leather traveling trunk. You'll also find a multitude of coral and mosquitoes can be troublesome.

Accessibility

Wheelchair-accessible campsites are available at Cinnamon Bay Camp. The visitor center and picnic areas at Trunk Bay and Hawksnest are accessible. Most trails are steep, slippery, and relatively inaccessible.

Pets

Pets are not allowed on beaches, in campgrounds, or in picnic areas. They are permitted on trails, but must be on a leash no more than six feet in length at all times.

Weather

Virgin Islands National Park is a tropical paradise. All year-long high temperatures are in the mid-80s°F with lows in the 70s°F. While the weather is always out-of-this-world, most visitors arrive between December and April. The summer months from June through August are hottest. Hurricane season spans from June until November, which also happen to be the wettest months of the year. Water temperature is about 83°F in summer and 79°F in winter.

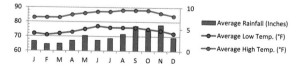

Vacation Planner

When we went to print, **Zika virus** was present in the U.S. Virgin Islands. Be sure to pack mosquito repellent and/or wear long sleeves, pants, and socks. While the symptoms of Zika virus are mild, infection during pregnancy can cause serious birth defects.

Most visitors will want to create a budget for a trip like this, because things are a bit more expensive in paradise. **Camping** (page 668) is available and **Caneel Bay Resort** is a part of the park, but there are plenty of other options nearby. See pages 672–673 for a list of the area's best restaurants, lodging facilities, and attractions.

If you **rented a car**, chances are they'll pick you up at the Cruz Bay dock. (Note that your phone may not work in the Virgin Islands or you may be charged international rates.) **Taxis** are also available near the dock. Taxi fare from Cruz Bay to Cinnamon Bay should cost about $9 for one person or $7 per person for more than one. (You can also hire a taxi for a 2-hour island tour for about $30/person—a good choice if you are short on time or don't want to rent a car.) If you're staying at Caneel Bay, they'll pick you up from the dock. With an abundance of resort and campground activities at most facilities there's no real need to rent a car. However, for the trip detailed below, you'll want a vehicle. If you don't plan on bringing your own snorkel gear, rent some in Cruz Bay. Lastly, if you're traveling all the way to the Virgin Islands you may as well stay a few days. Here's a three day template to help plan your vacation.

Day 1: In all likelihood your first day will be spent reaching St. Thomas and then St. John (page 665), stopping at **Cruz Bay Visitor Center**, and getting situated on the island. Spend the evening exploring your lodging's property. If you have the time for it, we suggest going directly to **Trunk Bay** or hiking from Cruz Bay Visitor Center to **Salomon Beach** via Lind Point Trail.

Day 2: Today you'll follow **Route 20/North Shore Road**. Stop at **Cinnamon Bay** (if you aren't already staying there) and hike the self-guiding trail. Return to Route 20. Shortly after Maho Bay, the road becomes one-way and leads directly to **Annaberg School and Sugar Mill ruins**. Explore the ruins all you want, but

Trunk Bay

you're really here to snorkel **Waterlemon Cay** from Leinster Beach. This is Saint Johns' best snorkeling spot. The western shore of Waterlemon Cay is particularly good. Plan on spending a half- to full-day here, as it's roughly a 15-minute walk to the beach and 200-yard swim to the cay. Stronger swimmers might want to consider snorkeling from Francis Bay (start at the north end of the beach) across Fungi Passage, and around **Whistling Key**. It's a pretty long swim and you'll have to be aware of potential boat traffic at Fungi Passage. Francis Bay is also a great place to watch the sunset.

Day 3: Start your day off right by visiting **Trunk Bay**, the park's most enchanting beach. (If you already spent a few hours at Trunk Bay when you arrived, consider making the hike to **Salomon or Honeymoon Beach** via Lind Point Trail. Both are great, but we prefer Salomon.) It gets busy, so arrive early. Next it's back in the car and along Route 20/North Shore Road to Route 10/Centerline Road. Take Route 10 to Route 107, which skirts the southeastern shoreline. Eventually you'll come to Johns Folly and Saltpond Bay. **Hikers** should head to **Ram Head Trail**. **Snorkelers** will want to dip into **Saltpond Bay**. Time permitting, head east on Route 10 to hike **Reef Bay Trail** (allow 2–5 hours depending on amount of beach and snorkel time you require). Note that the trail is all downhill to the beach. If you'd rather not hike back up it, you'll either have to get lucky and arrive when Friends of the Park (friendsvinp.org) are offering a guided hike ($40/person) or plan your vacation around their schedule. Maybe cap off the trip with a meal and sunset at Asolare (340.779.4747, asolarestjohn.com).

Dining

St. John Island

La Tapa • (340) 693-7755 • Cruz Bay
latapastjohn.com • Entrée: $34–44

Beach Bar • (370) 777-4220 • Cruz Bay
beachbarstjohn.com • Entrée: $12–15

Sun Dog Café • (340) 693-8340
Mongoose Junction, Cruz Bay
sundogcafe.com • Entrée: $14.50–22

The Tap Room • (340) 715-7775
Mongoose Junction, Cruz Bay • stjohnbrewers.com

Morgan's Mango • (340) 693-8141 • Cruz Bay

Banana Deck • (340) 693-5055 • Cruz Bay
thebananadeck.com • Entrée: $24–35

Waterfront Bistro • (340) 777-7755 • Cruz Bay
thewaterfrontbistro.com • Entrée: $31–39

Rhumb Lines • (340) 776-0303 • Cruz Bay
rhumblinesstjohn.com • Entrée: $23–39

Miss Lucy's • (34) 693-5244
Friis Bay, Cruz Bay

Jake's • (340) 777-7115 • Cruz Bay

Margarita Phil's • (340) 693-8400 • Cruz Bay

Da Livio • (340) 779-8900 • Cruz Bay
dalivio.it • Entrée: $13–26

Sogo's • (340) 779-4404 • Cruz Bay

Vie's Snack Shack • (340) 693-5033
E End Rd/Rt 10, Cruz Bay

Wharfside Café
Wharfside Village, Cruz Bay

Café Roma • (340) 776-6524 • Cruz Bay
stjohn-caferoma.com • Entrée: $18–31

Sam & Jack's Deli • (340) 714-3354 • Cruz Bay
stjohndeli.com • Sandwiches: $10+

Woody's • (340) 779-4625
woodysseafood.com

ZoZo's Ristorante • (340) 693-9200
Caneel Bay Resort, Salomon Bay Rd
zozos.net • Entrée: $42–48

Le Château de Bordeaux • (340) 776-6611
5 miles east of Cruz Bay

Skinny Legs Bar & Grill
skinnylegsvi.com • Coral Bay

Sweet Plantains • (340) 777-4653
16119 Little Plantation, Coral Bay
sweetplantains-stjohn.com

Aqua Bistro Restaurant • (340) 776-5336
aquabistro.com • Coral Bay

Island Blues • (340) 776-6800 • Coral Bay

Shipwreck Landing • Route 107, Coral Bay
shipwrecklandingstjohn.com

The Tourist Trap • (340) 774-0912
Route 107, Salt Pond
wedontneednostinkingwebsite.com

Asolare • (340) 779-4747 • 6A Caneel Hill
asolarestjohn.com • Entrée: $24–45

Castaway Tavern • (340) 777-3361
Castawaystjohn.com • Entrée: $9–25

St. Thomas Island

Pie Whole • (340) 642-5074
24A Honduras, Frenchtown
piewholepizza.com • Pizza: $9

Fatty's Bar, Grill, & Games • (340) 777-4275
Red Hook Rd • fattysbarandgrill.com

Lattitude 18 • (340) 777-4552
Vessup Ln, Red Hook

Sunset Grill • (340) 779-2262
6280 Estate Nazareth, Nazareth Bay
sunsetgrillvi.com

Amalia Café • (340) 714-7373
24 Palm Passage St, Charlotte Amalie
amaliacafe.com

Big Kahuna Rum Shack • (340) 775-9289
Waterfront St, Charlotte Amalie
bigkahunausvi.com • Sandwiches: $11+

Jen's Island Café & Deli • (340) 777-4611
43-46 Norre Gade, Charlotte Amalie
jensdeli.com

The Old Stone Farmhouse • (340) 777-6277
Mahogany Run • oldstonefarmhouse.com

Thirteen • (340) 774-6800
13A Estate Dorothea

Hook Line and Sinker • (340) 776-9708
Frenchtown
hooklineandsinkervi.com • Entrée: $14–28

Groceries

St. John Island

Lily's Gourmet Market • (340) 777-3335
Harolds Way, Coral Bay

Pine Peace Grocery • Route 104, Cruz Bay

Starfish Market • (340) 779-4949
Route 104, Cruz Bay • starfishmarket.com

St. Thomas Island

Red Hook Food Center • (340) 777-8806
Route 32, Red Hook

Lodging

St. John Island

Caneel Bay, A Rosewood Resort
N Shore Rd, 830 • (340) 776-6111
caneelbay.com • Rates: $450+/night

Hillcrest Guest House • (340) 776-6774
#157 Estate Enighed, Cruz Bay

The Westin St John Resort & Villas
Cruz Bay • (340) 693-8000
westinresortstjohn.com • Rates: $448+

Caneel Bay Hotel • (340) 776-6111 • Cruz Bay

The Inn at Tamarind Court
Cruz Bay • (800) 221-1637
innattamarindcourt.com • Rates: $148–240

Gallows Point Resort • (800) 323-7229
gallowspointresort.com • Rates: $295–695

St John Inn • (340) 693-8688
277 Enighed, Cruz Bay
stjohninn.com • Rates: $180–290

Coconut Coast Villas • (800) 858-7989
268 Enighed, Turner Bay, Cruz Bay
coconutcoast.com • Rates: $179–579

St. Thomas Island

Ritz-Carlton St Thomas Residence Club
6900 Great Bay • (340) 775-3333 • Rates: $669+
ritzcarlton.com

Wyndham Sugar Bay Resort & Spa
6500 Estate Smith Bay • (340) 777-7100
sugarbayresortandspa.com

Bolongo Bay Beach Resort • (340) 775-1800
7150 Bolongo, Charlotte Amalie
bolongobay.com • Rates: $250–440

Festivals

8 Tuff Miles Race • February
St John • 8tuffmiles.com

St John Blues Festival • March
St John • stjohnbluesblowout.com

Paradise Jam • November - St Croix, St John,
St Thomas • paradisejam.com

Attractions

St. John Island

Kekoa Sailing Expeditions
Lumberyard Complex, Cruz Bay
blacksailsvi.com • (340) 244-7245

St John Yacht Charters • (340) 998-9898
stjohnyachtcharters.com

Calypso • (340) 777-7245
calypsovi.com

Palm Tree Charters • (340) 642-8522
palmtreecharters.com

Fly Girl • (340) 626-8181
Snorkeling, Sailing, Charters, and More
sailsafaris.net/flygirl/

Lion In Dá Sun • (340) 626-4783
lionindasun.com

St John Spice • (877) 693-7046
stjohnspice.com

Sadie Sea • (340) 514-0778
sadiesea.com

VI Snuba Excursions • (340) 693-8063
visnuba.com • Trunk Bay

Hidden Reef Eco-Tours • (877) 529-2575
Route 10, Coral Bay
hiddenreefecotours.com • Tours: $65–115

Cruz Bay Watersports • (888) 853-9241
Diving, Sailing, Snorkeling, & Wave Runners
Also located in St. Thomas (340.775.3333)
cruzbaywatersports.com • Cruz Bay

St. Thomas Island
Virgin Island Ecotours • (877) 845-2925
Kayak, Hike, and Snorkel Adventures
viecotours.com

Daysail High Pockets Adventure
6292 Est. Nazareth, #100 St
sailhighpockets.com • (340) 690-0587

Morningstar Charters
morningstarcharter.com • (340) 626-8743

Big Blue Excursions • (340) 201-3045
6501 Red Hook Plaza Ste 201
bigblue-usvi.com

Simplicity Charters
6501 Red Hook Plaza, Ste 201
simplicitycharters.com

Captain Max • (340) 690-0200
6501 Red Hook Plaza, Ste 201
sailwithcaptainmax.com

St Thomas Diving Club • (340) 776-2381
7147 Bolongo Bay • stthomasdivingclub.com

Red Hook Dive Center • (340) 777-3483
6100 Red Hook Quarters, E1-1
redhookdivecenter.com • Dives: $90–125

Yacht Nightwind • (340) 775-7017
Sapphire Beach Marina Slip S33
stjohndaysail.com

SunSea Charters • (340) 626-6785
Dock D, Red Hook

Blue Island Divers • (340) 774-2001
Crown Bay Marina
blueislanddivers.com

St. Croix Island

Buck Island Reef National Monument
2100 Church St, #100, Christiansted, VI
nps.gov/buis • (340) 773-1460

Ultimate Bluewater Adventures
stcroixscuba.com • (340) 773-5994

Geckos Island Adventures • (340) 713-8820
69 Queen St, Frederiksted
geckosislandadventures.com

Salt River Bay NHP & Ecological Preserve
2100 Church St, #100, Christiansted
nps.gov/sari • (340) 773-1460

Paul & Jill's Equestrian Stables
Frederiksted • (340) 772-2880
paulandjills.com • Trail Rides: $99

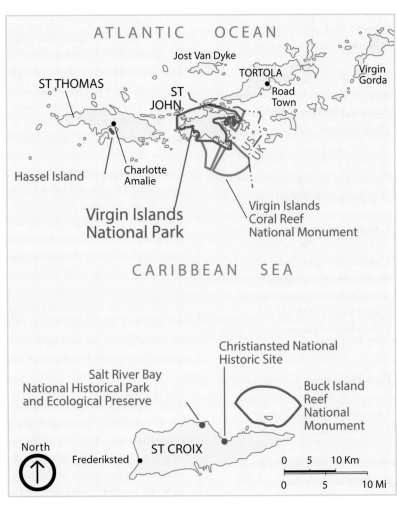

A honeycreeper at Hosmer Grove

Haleakala

PO Box 369; Makawao, HI 96768
Phone: (808) 572-4400
Website: nps.gov/hale

Established: August 1, 1916
Size: 30,183 Acres
Annual Visitors: 1.2 Million
Peak Season: mid-Dec–mid-April

Activities: Hiking, Biking, Horseback Riding, Swimming, Bird Watching, and Stargazing

Campgrounds (Free): Kīpahulu and Hosmer Grove Campgrounds
Cabins: 3 Backcountry Cabins*
Backcountry Camping: Permitted at designated sites and cabins*
Cabin Fee: $75/night
Cabin Reservations: recreation.gov or (877) 444-6777

Park Hours: All day, every day (may close for severe weather)
Entrance Fee: $25/vehicle, $12/individual (foot, bike, etc.)

*Permit required for backcountry camping and cabins

A sea of clouds floats below you. Burnt red rocky slopes lie in front of you. Haleakalā Summit is the sort of scene that makes a person feel like you've woken up in another world. A world where myths seem like reality, rather than a story as colorful as the crater itself. Haleakalā National Park consists of two distinct regions. Haleakalā summit, nearly two miles above sea level, is a seemingly lifeless landscape that should require a space shuttle and lunar rover to reach. And Lower Kīpahulu—a lush rainforest brimming with life, forests of bamboo, and waterfalls that stir sacred pools—provides yin to the summit's yang.

Clouds often surround Haleakalā like a barrier between worlds. On one side is civilization and everything else you find familiar. On the other side is the sun and brilliant blue sky as you're transported to the heavens above. The experience of walking through the clouds may have inspired ancient Hawaiians to name the volcano Haleakalā or "house of the sun." Legend has it that Māui, the Hawaiian demigod who had raised the Hawaiian Islands with a homemade fishhook and line, knew where the sun resided. Māui overheard his mother complain that the days were too short, and that there wasn't enough time for her kapa (bark cloth) to dry. He climbed Haleakalā to lasso the sun with his sister's hair. Caught, the sun pled for its life and agreed the days would be longer in summer and shorter in winter. In a paradise like this, who wouldn't want longer days?

Haleakalā Summit, at 10,023 feet above sea level, is the island's highest peak. From here, sure-footed visitors can descend 2,600 feet into the crater. Geologically speaking, it is a dormant volcano that hasn't erupted for more than 400 years. It's not a crater either, but two valleys joined together when the ridgeline between them eroded away. Pīpīwai Spring, at the very southeast corner of the park, is continuously wearing away the land as water tumbles some 400 feet over Waimoku Falls and on into ʻOheʻo

Gulch. This area is Kīpahulu. A location where you can spend the long summer days bathing in its idyllic, nay, sacred swimming pools, hiking Pīpīwai Trail, or just enjoying the sights along Hāna Highway (one of the most scenic—and stressful—drives in the world). The only visitors who want the sun to set are those who wish to gaze at the night sky or arrive at the summit with blankets and coffee early enough to see the sun's glorious return above Haleakalā, its home. Those who do will find that the night is often as spectacular as the day.

As the sun rises up over Haleakalā there are few places in the world that appear so lifeless yet so beautiful. Volcanic islands, like Hawai'i, begin as barren masses of molten rock. It takes hundreds of thousands of years for species to arrive by wind, water, or wings. Prior to civilization, a species arrived every 10,000 to 100,000 years, in part because the destination was the most isolated significant island chain in the world. This remote setting is exactly what makes the species that have survived and evolved here all the more unique.

Haleakalā silversword, a relative of the sunflower that reaches maturity after seven years, is found nowhere else in the world. It blooms, sending forth a stalk three to eight feet tall containing several hundred tiny sunflowers, then it dies. Silversword was once so abundant the crater floor looked as if it was covered with glistening snow. Vandalism and grazing by cattle and goats nearly led to its extinction.

More endangered species live in Haleakalā than any other national park in the United States, and the park's unique ecosystems make for one of the world's most interesting and studied living laboratories. Scientists hope to preserve the biology found here, so areas like upper Kīpahulu Valley and Waikamoi are closed to tourism or accessible only when guided by a ranger or naturalist. Invasive species and destructive tourism are constant threats. Today, aided by over a million annual visitors, about 20 alien species arrive on the islands each year. We must find a way to strike a balance between nature and tourism so that this one park—two worlds, part moon and part jungle—can be preserved for future generations.

When to Go

The park is open all year. It closes occasionally for severe weather conditions. Visitation is steady year-round, but there is a noticeable spike from mid-December through mid-April. We feel the best time to visit Maui is between December and May, when humpback whales migrate to these waters. **Park Headquarters Visitor Center** (VC) is open daily from 8am until 3:45pm. **Haleakalā VC** is open daily from sunrise until 3pm. **Kīpahulu VC** is open daily from 9am until 4:30pm. All facilities close on Christmas and New Year's Day.

Transportation & Airports

The park is located on the Island of Māui. Most visitors arrive via commercial airline from the U.S. mainland or another Hawaiian Island. Māui's primary airport is Kahului Airport (OGG). Public transportation does not service the park. Car rental is available at the airport.

Directions

The two regions of the park, Haleakalā Summit and Kīpahulu Valley, are not directly connected by roads. In fact, from the airport they are in the exact opposite directions from one another.

To Haleakalā Summit (37 miles): Exit the airport on HI-37. Turn left onto HI-377. After about 6 miles, turn left at Crater Road (HI-378/Haleakalā Highway). After 1.5 miles, turn right to stay on Crater Road. Continue on Crater Road for approximately 20 miles to the summit of Haleakalā. The road to the summit is extremely steep. You leave near sea level in Kahului and arrive at the 10,023-ft summit after less than 40 miles.

To Kīpahulu (60 miles from airport/80 miles from Haleakalā Summit): Exit the airport on HI-36 (Hāna Highway). Continue to follow Hāna Highway, one of the most scenic roadways in the United States, to Kīpahulu Visitor Center. This region of the park can also be reached via HI-37 and HI-31 from the summit (about 60 miles), but you must traverse a narrow, rough, unpaved (generally passable) section of road that is a little more than 3 miles in length. Inquire at your rental car office about traveling this stretch of road. Many agreements become void if you explore unpaved roadways.

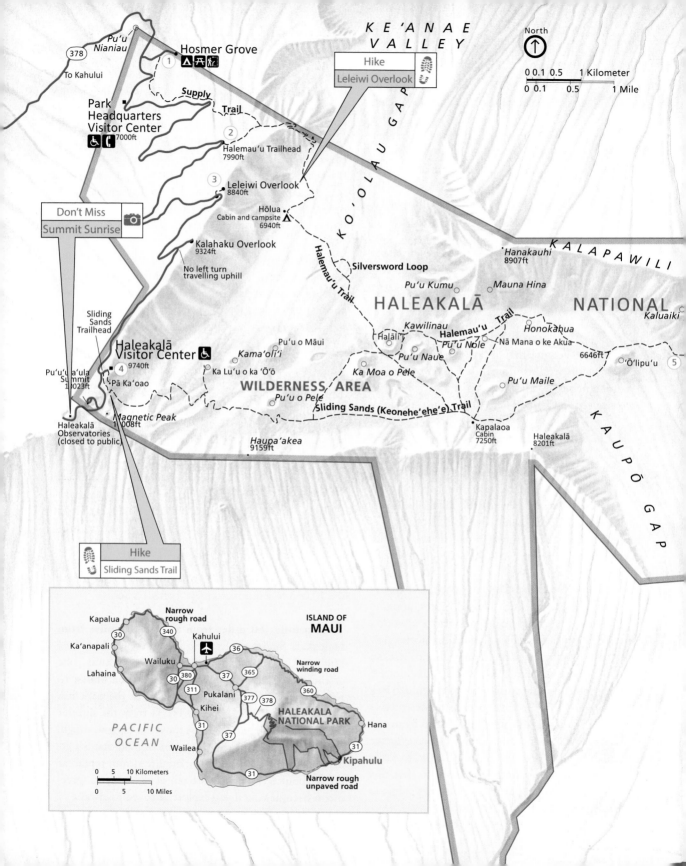

North

0 0.1 0.5   1 Kilometer
0 0.1   0.5   1 Mile

378
Pu'u
Nianiau
To Kahului

Hosmer Grove
1

Supply

Park
Headquarters
Visitor Center
7000ft

Trail

2

Halemau'u Trailhead
7990ft

3

Leleiwi Overlook
8840ft

Hōlua
Cabin and campsite
6940ft

Kalahaku Overlook
9324ft

No left turn
travelling uphill

Don't Miss
Summit Sunrise

Sliding
Sands
Trailhead

Haleakalā
Visitor Center
9740ft

Pu'u 'ula'ula
Summit
1,023ft

4

Pā Ka'oao

Magnetic Peak
1,008ft

Haleakalā
Observatories
(closed to public)

Kama'oli'i

Ka Lu'u o ka 'Ō'ō

Pu'u o Māui

WILDERNESS AREA

Pu'u o Pele

Haupa'akea
9159ft

Silversword Loop

Pu'u Kumu

HALEAKALĀ

Halemau'u Trail

Kawilinau

Halāli'i

Pu'u Naue

Ka Moa o Pele

Sliding Sands (Keonehe'ehe'e) Trail

Kapalaoa
Cabin
7250ft

Haleakalā
8201ft

KE'ANAE
VALLEY

Hike
Leleiwi Overlook

KO'OLAU GAP

KALAPAWILI

Hanakauhi
8907ft

Mauna Hina

Kaluaiki

NATIONAL

Honokahua

Pu'u Nole

Nā Mana o ke Akūa

6646ft

'Ō'lipu'u

5

Pu'u Maile

Halemau'u Trail

KAUPŌ GAP

Hike
Sliding Sands Trail

ISLAND OF
MAUI

Kapalua
Narrow
rough road
340

30
Ka'anapali

Lahaina

Wailuku
30
380

311

Kihei

Wailea

31

37

365

377 378

PACIFIC
OCEAN

Kahului
36

37

360

Pukalani

HALEAKALA
NATIONAL PARK

Hana

Kipahulu

31

Narrow
winding road

Narrow rough
unpaved road

0   5   10 Kilometers
0   5   10 Miles

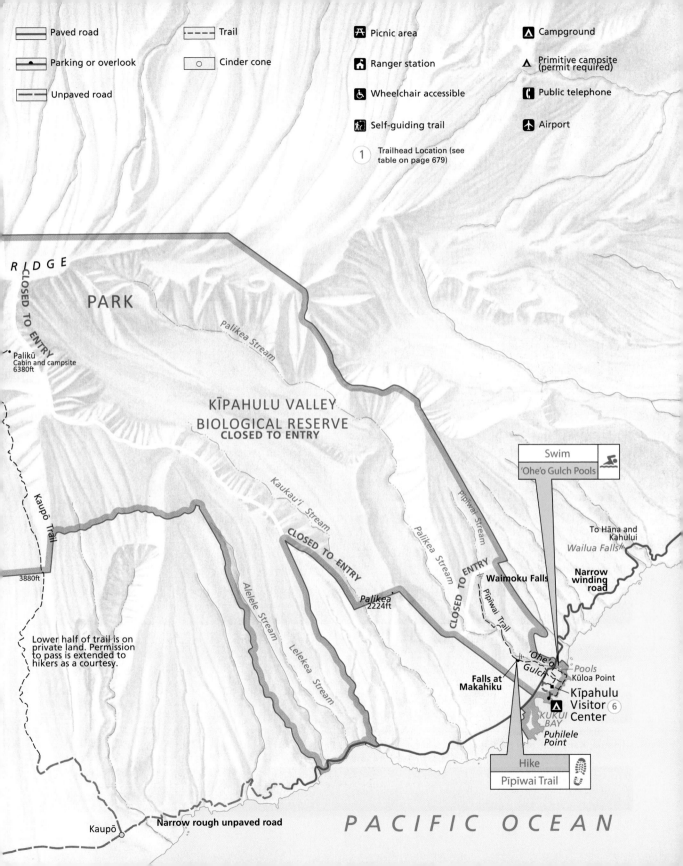

Legend

Paved road	Trail	⚷ Picnic area	⚑ Campground
Parking or overlook	⊙ Cinder cone	⌂ Ranger station	⚑ Primitive campsite (permit required)
Unpaved road		♿ Wheelchair accessible	☎ Public telephone
		🚶 Self-guiding trail	✈ Airport
		① Trailhead Location (see table on page 679)	

R I D G E

CLOSED TO ENTRY

PARK

• Palikū
Cabin and campsite
6380ft

Palikea Stream

KĪPAHULU VALLEY
BIOLOGICAL RESERVE
CLOSED TO ENTRY

Kaupō Trail

3880ft

Kaukau'i Stream

CLOSED TO ENTRY

Palikea
2224ft

Alelele Stream

Lelekea Stream

Lower half of trail is on
private land. Permission
to pass is extended to
hikers as a courtesy.

Palikea Stream

Pipiwai Stream

CLOSED TO ENTRY

Waimoku Falls

Pipiwai Trail

Swim
'Ohe'o Gulch Pools 🏊

To Hāna and
Kahului
Wailua Falls

**Narrow
winding
road**

**Falls at
Makahiku**

'Ohe'o
Gulch

Pools
Kūloa Point

**Kīpahulu
Visitor ⑥
Center**

*KUKUI
BAY*

*Puhilele
Point*

Hike
Pīpīwai Trail 👣

Kaupō ⊙

Narrow rough unpaved road

PACIFIC OCEAN

Camping

The park offers **two frontcountry camp-grounds**. **Hosmer Grove** is located near Haleakalā Summit, where it's windy and cold, often near freezing at night. **Kīpahulu Campground** is located south of the visitor center, a short walk from 'Ohe'o Gulch. Both campgrounds are free of charge and available on a first-come, first-served basis. You are allowed to camp 3 nights per month in each campground.

Backpackers can camp at Hōlua or Palikū camps, which are located in the park's wilderness area and are only accessibly by trails. Space is available on a first-come, first serve basis. A **free permit**, available at Headquarters Visitor Center between 8am and 3pm up to one day in advance, is required. Additionally, there are three, trail-accessible **wilderness cabins**. Hōlua is the closest cabin to a trailhead at 3.7 miles via Halemau'u Trail. Palikū is the farthest at 9.3 miles via Sliding Sands Trail. Each cabin features 12 bunks, non-potable water (filter or treat before drinking), a wood-burning stove, cookware, and dishes. These are simple cabins without electricity. Cabins can be reserved up to 180 days in advance at recreation.gov or (877) 444-6777 for $75 per cabin per night. Cancel at least three weeks in advance and you will receive a full refund, less a $10 per night service fee.

We know hotels and resorts are expensive and packing all your gear can be a hassle, but please don't buy camping gear at Walmart and leave it on the island. Hostels and Airbnb are good, cost-effective alternatives.

Hiking

Most visitors drive up to the summit, have a look around, maybe watch the sunrise, and then go on their merry way. Don't follow the path of the average tourist. The park boasts more than 30 miles of hiking trails in the summit area and another 10 miles or so around Kīpahulu. Do you enjoy hiking? Want to explore the crater? Are you trying to escape the crowds? If you answered "yes" to any of these questions, hike **Halemau'u** or **Sliding Sand Trails** into the valley below Haleakalā Summit. Sliding Sands is more strenuous, beginning at a higher elevation. Both trails offer short spurs to cinder cones and silverswords. They also provide access to the park's backcountry campsites and cabins sprinkled throughout the wilderness. Before departing on either of these journeys, be sure to honestly assess your physical abilities and amount of free time. The trails are challenging, and it will take slightly longer to make the return trip uphill to the summit.

You can also hike a few short and relatively flat trails in the summit area. **Hosmer's Grove Nature Trail** is a self-guided hike through a forest of native tree species planted by Ralph Hosmer while experimenting with what plant species would grow best. The hike from **Leleiwi Overlook** is a short walk packed with amazing panoramic vistas. In addition, park rangers provide guided tours of **Waikamoi Preserve** (reservation required) that focus on bird watching (page 680).

Pīpīwai Trail at Kīpahulu is one of the best, if not the best hiking trail on the island of Māui. It's an uphill

Haleakala Camping (Fees are per night)

Name	Location	Fee	Notes
Kipahulu	Kipahulu Area	Free	100 camper limit, pit toilets, no water
Hosmer Grove	Summit Area	Free	50 camper limit, restrooms and water
Holua (backcountry)	Sliding Sands (7.4 mi) or Halemau'u (3.7 mi) Trails	Free	Pit toilets, non-potable water
Paliku (backcountry)	Sliding Sands (9.3 mi) and Halemau'u (10.4 mi) Trails	Free	Pit toilets, non-potable water
Backcountry Cabins (Holua, Kapalaoa, and Paliku)	Holua: Halemau'u Trail (3.7 mi) Kapalaoa and Paliku: Sliding Sands Trail (5.5 mi and 9.3 mi)	$75	Bunks, cook & dinnerware, and stove

All Campsites are open all year and available on a first-come, first-served basis • Cabins can be reserved up to 180 days in advance at (877) 444-6777 or recreation.gov • Camping is limited to a maximum of 3 nights per 30 day period • Permits are required for all backcountry campsites and cabins (available at Headquarters Visitor Center)

climb, but your effort will be rewarded with 400 feet of **Waimoku Falls**. Due to the small selection of hiking trails and popularity of **'Ohe'o Gulch**, it is often crowded, so get an early start if possible.

Horseback Riding

If you don't feel like hiking into the crater, how about hoofing it on the back of a horse? It's unlikely you brought your own, but Charley's (808.264.5885, mauihikes.com) offers trail rides ($150/3 hours) and pack trips ($700/person, 2 nights) into Haleakalā Crater. Reserve pack trips at least three months in advance for the best chance of securing a backcountry cabin (page 678).

Biking

Oddly enough, biking is a popular activity in the summit area. Recent rule changes prohibit bikes from descending Crater Road from the summit (and within the park boundary), but guests can still join a descent beginning just outside the park entrance at 6,700 feet. Aloha Bicycle Tours (808.870.7409, mauibike.com, $70–100), Cruiser Phil's Volcano Riders (808.893.2332, cruiserphil.com), Haleakalā Bike Co (808.575.9575, bikemaui.com, $75–135), Māui Downhill Bicycle Tours (808.871.2155, mauidownhill.com, $149–189), Māui Sunriders Bike Co (808.579.8970, mauibikeride.com, $59.95–94.95), and Mountain Riders (800.706.7700, mountainriders.com, $67.50–120) offer **bicycle tours**. It's fun to cruise downhill, but for your time and dollar, opt for other activities like stargazing, horseback riding, or go on a whale watch. You can rent a bicycle from a number of locations around the island, but Krank Cycles (808.572.2299, krankmaui.com) and Crater Cycles (808.893.2020, cratercycleshawaii.com) offer road and mountain bikes.

Stargazing

Haleakalā is such a great spot for viewing what exists beyond earth's atmosphere the government built an observatory at its summit. This lair is reserved for scientists and professional stargazers, but everyone has access to the stars shining brightly on clear Hawaiian nights. There is very little artificial light to dim the sky, allowing you to see more stars than you ever knew existed. Note that it's extremely cold (40°F), by Hawaiian standards, at the summit and often windy. Stargazers may be leery of the return drive down the mountain's slope, but there will be very little traffic to deal with and the usually distracting scenery will be hidden under cover of darkness. Still, the best option is to camp at Hosmer's Grove, where you can see the stars at night and the sun as it rises in the morning.

Swimming

Swimming is a popular pastime at Kīpahulu Valley. Most visitors bathe or swim in the waterfall pools of **'Ohe'o Gulch** known as the **seven sacred pools**. Arrive early, because the gulch can get busy. (It's also best to drive Hāna Highway early in the morning; there are only a few parking spots at each viewpoint

Haleakala Hiking Trails (Distances are roundtrip unless noted otherwise)

	Name	Location (# on map)	Length	Difficulty Rating & Notes
Summit	Hosmer Grove	Hosmer Grove Camp (1)	0.5 mile	E – Self-guiding nature trail
	Halemau'u	8,000 Foot Parking Area (3.5 miles above Park HQ) (2)	11.7 miles	S – Hike into the valley to view cinder cones and Haleakala silverswords (1-way)
	Leleiwi Overlook	Leleiwi Parking Area (3)	0.3 mile	E – Uncrowded spot with excellent photo-ops
	Sliding Sands (Keonehe'ehe'e) - ♿	Haleakala Visitor Center Parking Area (4)	11.2 miles	S – Steep descent into valley • Leads to cinder cones, backcountry camps and cabins (1-way)
	Kaupo	Junction with Sliding Sands near Paliku Camp (5)	8.6 miles	S – Unmaintained trail across private property to Kaupo on the coast (1-way)
Kipahulu	Kuloa Point	Kipahulu Ranger Station (6)	0.5 mile	M – A bluff overlooking 'Ohe'o Gulch
	Pipiwai - ♿	North end of the visitor center (6)	4.0 miles	M – Hike through bamboo forest to 400-foot Waimoku Falls

Difficulty Ratings: E = Easy, M = Moderate, S = Strenuous

Waimoku Falls (Pipiwai Trail)

or attraction. A good time to start is 6am.) More secluded swimming holes are found further upstream. Note that these pools are a part of the park and you will have to pay the entrance fee.

Bird Watching

A large collection of rare birds, including many found nowhere else in the world, makes Haleakalā National Park a popular destination among bird watchers. Hawaiian petrel (or ʻuaʻu) and Hawaiian goose (or nēnē, also the state bird of Hawaiʻi) nest at the summit. One of the most popular avian attractions is the park's unique family of honeycreepers. Several species have evolved from one common ancestor, and over thousands of years they have become strikingly different due to variations in their individual habitats. Waikamoi Cloud Forest at Hosmer's Grove is one of the best places to see birds. Guests can only view this area on a 3.5-hour special hike led by the nature conservancy or park staff. Tours are typically offered Mondays and Thursdays. Reservations are required and can be made up to one week in advance by calling (808) 572-4400. Show up at least 15 minutes early and be prepared with layered clothing, rain gear, water, and sturdy shoes.

Ranger Programs

Ranger-led activities are held regularly at Hosmer Grove and the summit area. The Waikamoi Cloud Forest Hike is one of the most regularly offered tours available here, but stargazing programs, hikes, and talks are also held periodically. For activity details and a current schedule of events stop in at one of the visitor centers, call (808) 572-4400, or check the online calendar of events.

For Kids

Children find Haleakalā's otherworldly moonscapes and pristine swimming holes more than agreeable. Kids of all ages may participate in the **Junior Ranger Program**. Stop at a visitor center to pick-up a free activity booklet (also available at the park website). Complete the booklet and return to a visitor center for a badge. Kids will also find the park ranger's interpretive programs engaging and educational.

Flora & Fauna

There are approximately 370 species of native plants living at Haleakalā National Park. Of these, about 90% are found only on the Hawaiian Islands. **Haleakalā silversword**, found at and around the summit and nowhere else in the world, is the most famous.

The Hawaiian Islands are home to just two native mammal species: monk seal and hoary bat. No land amphibians or reptiles are native to the park. Some of the most sought after animals are found in the ocean. Whales, turtles, dolphins, and seabirds are occasionally seen offshore from Kūloa Point near Kīpahulu.

Pets

Pets are permitted, but must be kept on a leash no more than six feet in length at all times. They are only allowed in parking lots, campgrounds, and along paved roads and paths. Visitors are not allowed to take pets on hiking trails or leave them unattended.

Accessibility

The park's visitor centers are wheelchair accessible. Haleakalā's summit building is accessible with assistance via a steep ramp. Wheelchair-accessible campsites are available. Trails are unpaved and difficult for wheelchairs or individuals requiring assistance.

Weather

Haleakalā National Park's two distinct locations have completely contrasting climates. Haleakalā summit is cool and dry while Kīpahulu is wet and hot (see graphs below). Visitors can expect a 30°F temperature difference from sea level to Haleakalā summit at 10,023 feet, where high winds and intense solar radiation are common. Snowstorms can even occur in the higher elevations. Kīpahulu enjoys the tropical climate Hawai'i vacationers have come to expect, with year-round warm temperatures and a wet winter. Pack clothes for all conditions, especially if you plan on going to the summit. Check the weather forecast prior to leaving, because conditions change rapidly with little warning.

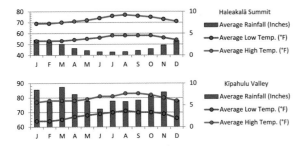

Vacation Planner

Select your own lodging and dining arrangements from pages 682–683 (nearby festivals, grocery stores, and attractions are also included). **Camping** (page 678) is recommended (especially at the summit) for an economical and truly unforgettable high-altitude adventure. Hitch-hiking is fairly common and safe, but visitors hoping to explore both regions of the park in an efficient manner should rent a car. Visit the summit area first, as a day of strenuous hiking can make soaking in **'Ohe'o Gulch** even more enjoyable. It also provides proper motivation to wake up for the sunrise (5:30–6:30am), which allows you to get an early start on driving **Hāna Highway**. (Note that sunrise at Haleakalā Summit is extremely popular. Parking lots fill, and if you're late on the scene you may find yourself tip-toeing to look at the sun over someone's shoulder. Still, it's worth doing once. Also, we prefer watching the sunrise from the visitor center, rather than the summit. To avoid the crowds, consider dressing warm, packing a headlamp, and completing the short hike to Leleiwi Overlook.) But you can't go wrong. A first night at

Haleakala summit

Kīpahulu (or more likely Hāna) allows for a morning swim at 'Ohe'o Gulch before the crowds arrive.

Day 1: Begin by heading to the **Haleakalā summit** area. You won't find any food or fuel in the park, so make sure you top off your gas tank (and stomachs) before entering. Packing warm clothes is another good idea. En route to the summit, stop at **Hosmer's Grove**. Campers should secure a first-come, first-served site, and the short self-guiding nature trail is a nice leg-stretcher. Return to Crater Road and make your next stop **Leleiwi Overlook**. Hike the 0.25-mile trail for a glimpse of Hōlua Cabin and Camp on Halemau'u Trail below. Return the way you came and continue up the mountain to the 10,023-ft summit. You'll find a **visitor center** and **Sliding Sands Trailhead** slightly below the summit. Both are worth checking out, but Sliding Sands is pretty strenuous and all uphill coming out of the valley. If you don't plan on camping at the summit and missed sunrise, consider sticking around for sunset. It's not nearly as popular as sunrise, but can be equally breathtaking (with the help of some clouds).

Day 2: The ideal itinerary has you catching the sunrise from Haleakalā before returning to sea level to drive **Hāna Highway**. (Note that you may want to include a day just to explore Hāna Highway. It's spectacular.) This scenic drive turns into an unpaved road near the park's Kīpahulu Valley. Fortunately you're stopping at **'Ohe'o Gulch** (still on pavement), where you'll hike **Pīpīwai Trail** to Waimoku Falls. If you can't reach the 400-foot-tall falls (sometimes closed due to mud), swimming in the sacred pools of 'Ohe'o Gulch is a very satisfactory substitute before returning to Hāna Highway.

Dining

Serpico's Restaurant • (808) 572-8498
7 Aewa Pl, Pukalani
serpicosmaui.com • Pizza: $16+

Pizza Fresh • (808) 572-2000
1043 Makawao Ave, Makawao

Polli's Mexican Restaurant • (808) 572-7808
1202 Makawao Ave, Makawao
pollismexicanrestaurant.com • Entrée: $15–24

Stopwatch Sportsbar & Grill • (808) 572-1380
1127 Makawao Ave, Makawao

Makawao Garden Café • (808) 573-9065
3669 Baldwin Ave, # 1101, Makawao

Kula Bistro • (808) 871-8466
4566 Lower Kula Rd, Kula • Breakfast: $9+

Capische? • (808) 879-2224
555 Kaukahi St, Wailea
capische.com • Entrée: $38+

Sansei Seafood & Sushi Bar • (808) 879-0004
1881 S Kihei Rd, # Kt116, Kihei
sanseihawaii.com

Matteo's Osteria • (808) 891-8466
100 Wailea Ike Dr, Kihei
matteosmaui.com • Pizza: $12–20

Coconut's Fish Café • (808) 875-9979
1279 S Kihei Rd, Kihei
coconutsfishcafe.com • Entrée: $12+

Market Fresh Bistro • (808) 572-4877
3620 Baldwin Ave, # 102A, Makawao

808 Deli • (808) 879-1111
2511 S Kihei Rd, Kihei
808deli.net • Sandwiches: $7.50+

Kihei Caffe • (808) 879-2230
1945 S Kihei Rd, Kihei
kiheicaffe.com • Breakfast: $6–15

Ruth's Chris Steak House • (808) 874-8880
3750 Wailea Alanui, Wailea • ruthschris.com

Paia Fish Market • (808) 579-8030
100 Baldwin Ave, Paia
paiafishmarket.com • Fish: $13+

Flatbread Company • (808) 579-8989
89 Hāna Hwy, Paia • flatbreadcompany.com

Paia Gelato Co • (808) 579-9201
115 Hāna Hwy, # D, Paia • paiagelato.com

Gazebo Restaurant • (808) 669-5621
5315 Lower Honoapiilani Rd, Lāhainā

Ono Gelato Co • (808) 495-0203
815 Front St, Lāhainā • onogelatocompany.com

Sunrise Café • (808) 661-8558
693 Front St, # A, Lāhainā

Penne Pasta Café • (808) 661-6633
180 Dickenson St, # 113, Lāhainā
pennepastacafe.com

Ululani's Hawaiian Shave Ice
819 Front St, Lāhainā • (808) 877-3700
ululanisshaveice.com • $4–9

Groceries

Safeway • (808) 891-9120
277 Pi'ikea Ave, Kihei

Costco • (808) 877-5241
540 Haleakalā Hwy, Kahului

Lodging

Kula Lodge & Restaurant • (808) 878-1535
15200 Haleakalā Hwy, Kula • kulalodge.com

Eva Villa B&B • (808) 874-6407
815 Kumulani Dr, Kihei • mauibnb.com

Māui Coast Hotel • (808) 874-6284
2259 S Kihei Rd, Kihei
mauicoasthotel.com • Rates: $195+

Māui Kamaole • (808) 879-5445
2777 S Kihei Rd, Kihei
mauikamaole.com • Rates: $191+

Wailea Beach Villas • (808) 891-4500
3800 Wailea Alanui Dr, Kihei
waileabeachvillasresort.com • Rates: $700+

Dreams Come True on Māui B&B
3259 Akala Dr, Kihei • (808) 879-7099
mauibednbreakfast.com • Rates: $115–199

Hale Huanani B&B • (877) 433-1768
808 Kupulau Dr, Kihei
halehuananibandb.com • Rates: $85–95

Pineapple Inn Māui • (808) 298-4403
3170 Akala Dr, Kihei
pineappleinnmaui.com • Rates: $159–255

Aloha Rainbow Cottage • (808) 573-8555
1879 Olinda Rd, Makawao • alohacottage.com

Hale Hookipa Inn B&B • (877) 572-6698
32 Pakani Place, Makawao
maui-bed-and-breakfast.com • Rates: $125–175

Hale Hoomana Spa Retreat • (808) 573-8256
1550 Piiholo Rd, Makawao
hoomanaspamaui.com • Rates: $119–129

Banyan Tree House • (808) 572-9021
3265 Baldwin Ave, Makawao
bed-breakfast-maui.com • Rates: $175–220

Fairmont Kea Lani • (808) 875-4100
4100 Wailea Alanui Dr, Wailea-Makena
fairmont.com • Rates: $391+

Hotel Wailea • (866) 970-4167
555 Kaukahi St, Wailea
hotelwailea.com • Rates: $479+

Four Seasons Māui • (808) 874-8000
3900 Wailea Alanui, Wailea
fourseasons.com • Rates: $500+

Huelo Point Lookout • (800) 871-8645
222 Door of Faith, Huelo
maui-vacationrentals.com • Rates: $250–405

Māui Ocean Breezes • (808) 283-8526
240 N. Holokai Rd, Haiku
mauivacationhideaway.com • Rates: $165–235

Old Wailuku Inn • (808) 244-5897
2199 Kahookele St, Wailuku
mauiinn.com • Rates: $330+ (2 nights)

Paia Inn Hotel • (808) 579-6000
93 Hāna Hwy, Paia • paiainn.com • Rates: $199+

Travaasa Hāna • (808) 359-2401
5031 Hāna Hwy, Hāna
travaasa.com • Rates: $400+

Hāna Kai-Māui Resort • (808) 346-2772
4865 Uakea Rd, Hāna • hanakaimaui.com

Honua Kai Resort and Spa • (855) 718-5789
130 Kai Malina Pkwy, Lāhainā
honuakai.com • Rates: $334+

Wai Ola Vacation Paradise • (800) 492-4652
1565 Kuuipo St, Lāhainā
waiola.com • Rates: $179–280

The Guest House • (800) 621-8942
1620 Ainakea Rd, Lāhainā
mauiguesthouse.com • Rates: $169–189

Aston MaHāna • (844) 331-7037
110 Kaanapali Shores Pl, Lāhainā
themahana.com • Rates: $221+

Attractions

Paragon Sailing Charters • (808) 244-2087
675 Wharf St, Lahaina • sailmaui.com

Skyline Eco Adventures • (808) 419-3179
2580 Keaa Dr, Lahaina
zipline.com • Zipline: $150

Pacific Whale Foundation • (808) 249-8977
300 Maalaea Boat Harbor Rd, Wailuku
pacificwhale.org • Whale Watch: $29+

Aqua Adventure • (808) 573-2104
Slip 51 Maalaea Harbor, Wailuku
mauisnorkelsnuba.com • Rates: $110+

Māui Hiking Safaris • (808) 573-0168
26 Makani Rd, Makawao
mauihikingsafaris.com • Tours: $75–200

Piiholo Ranch Zipline • (800) 374-7050
Piiholo Rd, Makawao
piiholozipline.com • Zipline: $99

Māui Spa Retreat • (808) 573-8002
Olinda Rd, Makawao

Blue Water Rafting • (808) 879-7238
1280 S Kihei Rd, Ste 225, Kihei
bluewaterrafting.com • Tour: $39 (1.5 hr)

Kai Kanani Sailing Charters • (808) 879-7218
Charter, Sail, Snorkel, and Whale Watch
5400 Makena Alanui, Kihei
kaikanani.com

Makena State Park • (808) 984-8109
hawaiistateparks.org • Kīhei • Free

Māui Classic Charters • (800) 736-5740
Maalaea Harbor Slip 80, Wailuku
mauiclassiccharters.com • Snorkel: $44–95+

Māui Dive Shop • (800) 542-3483
1455 S Kihei Rd, Kihei
mauidiveshop.com • *Snorkel & Diving*

Dive & Sea Māui • (808) 874-1952
432 Kupulau Dr, Kihei
diveandseamaui.com • Snorkel: $95

Shaka Divers • (808) 250-1234
24 Hakoi Pl, Kihei
shakadivers.com • Snorkel & Diving

Snorkel Bob's • (800) 262-7725
2411 S Kihei Rd, # A2, Kihei • snorkelbob.com

Molokini
A popular destination for SCUBA diving and snorkeling, this partially submerged volcanic crater is located between the islands of Māui and Kahoʻolawe

Māui Kayaks • (808) 874-4000
505 Front St, Lahaina
mauikayaks.com • Kayak: $69 (2 hr)

Kelii's Kayak Tours • (808) 874-7652
215 S Kihei Rd, #420, Kihei
keliiskayak.com • Tour: $69 (2.5 hrs)

Māui Eco Tours • (808) 891-2223 • Kihei
mauiecotours.com • Tours: $74

Māui Beach Boys • (808) 283-7114 • Kihei
mauibeachboys.com • Surfing: $70

Garden of Eden Arboretum • (808) 572-9899
10600 Hāna Hwy, Haiku
mauigardenofeden.com • Admission: $15/adult

Māui Ocean Center • (808) 270-7000
192 Maalaea Boat Harbor Rd, Wailuku
mauioceancenter.com • Admission: $28/adult

Air Māui Helicopter Tours • (808) 877-7005
Hangar 110, 1 Kahului Airport Rd, Kahului
airmaui.com • Tours: $188+

Blue Hawaiian Helicopters • (808) 871-8844
Kahului Heliport, 2 Lelepio Pl, Kahului
bluehawaiian.com • Tours: $152–509

Hike Māui • (808) 879-5270
hikemaui.com • Tours: $85–199

Valley Isle Excursions • (808) 661-8687
tourmaui.com

Zack Howard Surf Lessons • (808) 214-7766
513 Kuanana St, Paia
zackhowardsurf.com • Group Lesson: $90

Kaʻeleku Caverns • (808) 248-7308
205 Ulaino Rd, Hāna
mauicave.com • Admission: $12/adult

ʻĪao Valley State Mon. • (808) 587-0300
hawaiistateparks.org • $5/vehicle

Skyview Soaring • (808) 248-7070
Hāna Airport
skyviewsoaring.com • Rates: $160 (0.5 hr)

Ocean Project • (808) 667-6706
843 Wainee, #551, Lāhainā

Shoreline Snuba • (808) 281-3483
6 Kai Ala Dr, Lāhainā
shorelinesnuba.com • Tours: $59+

Warren & Annabelle's Magic Show
900 Front St, Lāhainā • (808) 667-6244
warrenandannabelles.com • Tickets: $64

Lāhainā Stables • (808) 667-2222
Punakea Loop, Lāhainā
mauihorse.com • Trail Rides: $129–151

Banyan Tree Park • (808) 661-4685
Front St, Lahaina

Māui Zipline Company • (808) 633-2464
1670 Honoapiilani Hwy, Wailuku
mauizipline.com • Zipline: $110

Waiʻanapanapa State Park • (808) 661-8687
70 Waiʻanapanapa Rd, Hāna
hawaiistateparks.org • Free

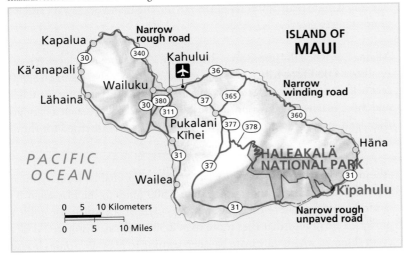

Kapalua
Narrow rough road
ISLAND OF MAUI
Kā'anapali
30
340
Kahului
Lāhainā
30
36
Wailuku
Narrow winding road
30
380
365
37
311
360
Pukalani
377 378
Kīhei
Hāna
31
HALEAKALĀ NATIONAL PARK
37
Wailea
31
Kīpahulu
Narrow rough unpaved road
31

PACIFIC OCEAN

0 5 10 Kilometers
0 5 10 Miles

Hawai'i Volcanoes

Halema'uma'u Crater from Jaggar Museum

PO Box 52
Hawai'i National Park, HI 96718
Phone: (808) 985-6000
Website: nps.gov/havo

Established: August 1, 1916
Size: 323,431 Acres
Annual Visitors: 1.8 Million
Peak Season: All Year
#1 Tourist Attraction in Hawai'i
International Biosphere
World Heritage Site

Activities: Hiking, Biking, Caving,
Lava Watching, and Bird Watching

Campgrounds: Nāmakanipaio ($15/
night) and Kulanaokuaiki (free)
Camping Fee: Free
Cabins: 10 at Nāmakanipaio
Cabin Rates: $80/night
Lodging: Volcano House Hotel
Rates: $285–385/night
Backcountry Camping: Permitted
with a free permit

Park Hours: All day, every day,
except Kahuku Unit (9am–3pm)
Entrance Fee: $15/vehicle,
$8/individual (foot, bike, etc.)

Hawai'i Volcanoes National Park is fire and water, rock and sand, rain forest and desert, desolation and beauty, creation and destruction. Such contradictions have the power to leave visitors speechless. Short of words. Lost in thought. The mind flooded with questions. Where does the lava come from? When will the eruption stop? How did plant and animal life reach the island? Was there ever a huge eruption? Musings range from genesis to apocalypse. Hawai'i Volcanoes is a world where creation never looked so destructive.

To native Hawaiians, Kīlauea Volcano is a holy place. They consider it the "body" of Pele, the volcano goddess of ancient Hawaiian legends. Today, Kīlauea is the center of the park and the world's most active volcano. The Pu'u 'Ō'ō Cone has been erupting continuously since 1983. Pele roils at Halema'uma'u Crater, where a lava lake lights up the night sky. A sky admired by visitors from Jaggar Museum and Volcano House. Past lava flow has added more than 550 acres of land to the Big Island of Hawai'i and it's continuing to grow.

Mauna Loa is equally impressive. Rising 13,679 feet above sea level, it towers above 4,000-foot Kīlauea. When measured from its base, some 18,000 feet below the water's surface, Mauna Loa is earth's largest mountain, taller and more massive than Mount Everest. It's hard to believe such a gargantuan land mass could go unnoticed, undisturbed, and unsettled for thousands of years.

About 1,500 years ago, Polynesian pioneers, probably from Samoa, steered double-hulled canoes more than 2,500 miles to the Hawaiian Islands. Scientists believe they followed the path of the koleo (or golden plover), a small bird that flies more than 2,500 miles non-stop to Alaska every summer, where they mate before returning to Hawai'i. Some choose to continue another 2,500 miles to Samoa. It's plausible that early Samoans, curious as to where these birds were going, hopped in their canoes, following their feathered friends only to learn the closest significant land was more than one-tenth of the way around the globe (Insert punch line: "and man were their arms tired.") Luckily, they were prepared for settlement. Pigs, dogs, chickens, taro, sweet potato, and seeds of coconut, sugar cane, banana, and other edible and medicinal plants accompanied them on their voyage. Very little is known beyond the arrival of Hawai'i's original culture. It is widely believed they were assimilated, killed, or forced into exile by a second wave of colonists, this time from Tahiti.

Tahitian colonists brought with them practices of human sacrifice and a distinct class structure. Professionals, commoners, and slaves were ruled by chiefs. Settlements with new leadership began to be established across all the Hawaiian Islands. War was common between rival tribes. Canoes were used for fishing rather than exploring. Samoa and Tahiti were long forgotten. Hawai'i was now their home.

It was a home without room for Western explorers like Captain James Cook, who stumbled upon the Hawaiian Islands in January 1778 while on his way to Alaska. He returned three more times, and on his third visit he sailed into Kealakekua Bay of the Big Island, where he and his crew were greeted by villagers, many of whom believed Cook was Lono, the god of fertility (land). Cook and his crew left the island, but returned shortly after departing to make repairs to a broken mast. This time they were greeted with hostility. Natives stole a small rowboat and Captain Cook attempted to hold the tribe's king hostage (a common practice) in exchange for their boat. The attempt failed; Natives struck Captain Cook on his head, stabbing him to death before he could flee.

By the 1840s, visitors were once again a welcome sight on the Big Island. Tourism had become the island's leading industry, and just as it is today, Hawai'i Volcanoes was the most popular attraction. In 1916, a national park was created to protect this spectacular area from grazing cattle, over-development, and ultimately, its destruction. And now visitors like you are free to conjure questions about this land filled with contradictions.

Holei Sea Arch at sunset

When to Go
The park is open all year. Visitation is steady with peaks during winter and major holidays. Weather is also fairly consistent throughout the year, but it varies greatly depending on your location in the park. It's warm and breezy by the coast, comfortable and wet at Kīlauea (4,000 ft), and temperatures frequently dip below freezing at the summit of Mauna Loa (13,677 ft). To make the weather even more interesting, temperatures can exceed 100°F near sites of volcanic activity. Pack for all conditions if you intend on exploring all the park's ecosystems.

Kīlauea Visitor Center is open daily from 9am to 5pm. **Jaggar Museum** is open daily from 10am to 8pm. The Kahuku section of the park, south of Hilo between mile markers 70 and 71, is open Saturdays and Sundays from 9am to 3pm, but closed weekdays and federal holidays.

Transportation & Airports
Hawai'i Volcanoes National Park is on the island of Hawai'i (also known as the Big Island). Hilo International (ITO) and Kona International at Keahole (KOA) are the major airports. Direct flights from the continental U.S. to Kona and Hilo are available. Car rental is available at both airports. Rental rates are reasonable (Compact: $25/day, Jeep: $70/day), but be mindful of additional fees and restrictions (like permission to drive Mauna Kea Road).

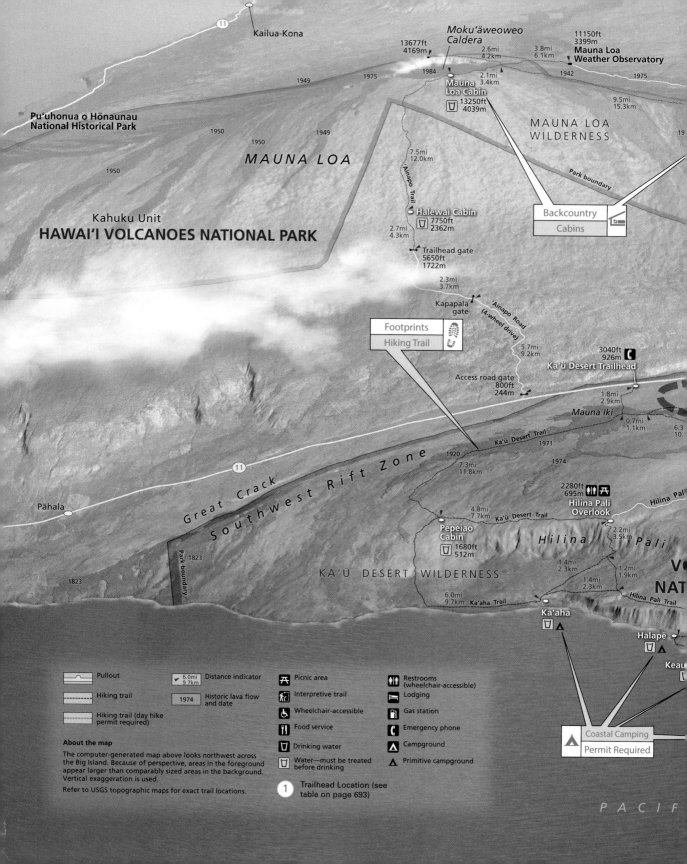

11
Kailua-Kona

Moku'āweoweo Caldera

13677ft
4169m

11150ft
3399m
Mauna Loa Weather Observatory

2.6mi
4.2km

3.8mi
6.1km

1949   1975   1984

Pu'uhonua o Hōnaunau
National Historical Park

1950   1949

Mauna Loa Cabin
2.1mi
3.4km

13250ft
4039m

1942   1975   19

MAUNA LOA WILDERNESS

9.5mi
15.3km

1950   1950   7.5mi
12.0km

Āinapo Trail

Park boundary

MAUNA LOA

Kahuku Unit
HAWAI'I VOLCANOES NATIONAL PARK

Halewai Cabin
7750ft
2362m

2.7mi
4.3km

Backcountry
Cabins

Trailhead gate
5650ft
1722m

2.3mi
3.7km

Kapapala gate

'Āinapo Road
(4-wheel drive)

Footprints
Hiking Trail

5.7mi
9.2km

3040ft
926m
Ka'ū Desert Trailhead

Access road gate
800ft
244m

1.8mi
2.9km

Mauna Iki

0.7mi
1.1km

6.3
10.

Ka'ū Desert Trail   1971

1920   7.3mi
11.8km

1974

Pāhala

Great Crack

Southwest Rift Zone

4.8mi
7.7km   Ka'ū Desert Trail

2280ft
695m
Hilina Pali Overlook

Hilina Pali

Hilina Pal

Pepeiao Cabin

1680ft
512m

2.2mi
3.5km

Park boundary   1823

1.4mi
2.3km

1.2mi
1.9km

V O
N A T

1823

KA'Ū DESERT WILDERNESS

6.0mi
9.7km   Ka'aha Trail

1.4mi
2.3km

Hilina Pali Trail

Ka'aha

Halapē

Keau

Coastal Camping
Permit Required

Legend

Pullout		Picnic area		Restrooms (wheelchair-accessible)
Hiking trail		Interpretive trail		Lodging
Hiking trail (day hike permit required)		Wheelchair-accessible		Gas station
6.0mi 9.7km Distance indicator		Food service		Emergency phone
1974 Historic lava flow and date		Drinking water		Campground
		Water—must be treated before drinking		Primitive campground

About the map
The computer-generated map above looks northwest across the Big Island. Because of perspective, areas in the foreground appear larger than comparably sized areas in the background. Vertical exaggeration is used.

Refer to USGS topographic maps for exact trail locations.

1 Trailhead Location (see table on page 693)

P A C I F

Mauna Kea
Visitor Center
9,300ft
2835m

200

6632ft
2022m

1843

12.2mi
19.6km

Mauna Loa Observatory Road

1855

1899

10035ft
3059m
Puʻuʻulaʻula
Red Hill Cabin

1855

Island of Hawaiʻi

KOHALA

270

Kawaihae   Honokaʻa

Puʻukoholā Heiau
National Historic Site

Waimea   19

MAUNA KEA

190

Kaloko-
Honokōhau
National
Historical Park

19

HUALĀLAI   200

Hilo

Kailua-
Kona

1881

130

200

1880

7.5mi
12.1km

Mauna Loa Trail

1942

Puʻuhonua o
Hōnaunau
National
Historical Park

MAUNA LOA

Keaʻau

11

130

Adventure Hike
Mauna Loa Trail

6662ft
2031m
Mauna Loa
Lookout

Kīlauea Visitor Center

Volcano
Village

HAWAIʻI
VOLCANOES
NATIONAL PARK

Pāhoa

1

11mi
17.7km

Pāhala

North

40 Km
40 Miles

Nāʻālehu

11

VIEW

1942

Mauna Loa
Road
(paved, one lane)

Kīpukapuaulu

2

3980ft
1213m

Kīlauea Visitor Center

ʻŌlaʻa Forest
HAWAIʻI VOLCANOES
NATIONAL PARK
ʻŌLAʻA WILDERNESS

Active Vent
Puʻu ʻŌʻō

Nāmakanipaio

Volcano
House

Jaggar
Museum

Crater Rim Drive

Volcano
Village

Wright
Road

11

Glenwood

6.1mi
9.8km

Kaʻū Desert Trail

AREA CLOSED
(see detail map)

1974

KĪLAUEA
(see detail map)

1974

Thurston
Lava Tube (Nāhuku)

Escape Road

Puʻu ʻŌʻō

Mauna Iki Trail

4.0mi
6.4km

1969

Puʻu
Huluhulu

Kulanaokuaiki

Pauahi Crater

3

Mauna
Ulu
3,200ft
975m

Nāpau Trail

5.0mi
8.0km

EAST RIFT
WILDERNESS

1969

2600ft
792m
Nāpau

E a s t   R i f

HAWAIʻI
VOLCANOES
NAL PARK

5mi
8km

Hiking trail (seasonally closed)

Chain of Craters Road

1.4mi
2.3km

36mi / 58km
roundtrip

Makaopuhi
Crater

2.0mi
3.2km

Nāpau
Crater

1983-2010s

0mi
8km

1.1mi
1.8km

1969-1974

1.2mi
1.9km

Kupai
Lava S

1.3mi
2.1km

Keauhou Trail

3.6mi
5.8km

1.2mi
1.9km

Mau Loa o
Mauna Ulu
2680ft
817m

1969

Naulu Trail

2.0mi
3.2km

Kalapana Trail (unmaintained)

Potential
Lava Viewing

1.6mi
2.6km

Kealakomo
2000ft
610m

*Eruption activity and
the course of lava flows
are constantly changing.
Check with park staff
for current conditions.*

2.0mi
3.2km

H ō l e i

1972

P a l i

Park boundary

ʻĀpua Point

Puna Coast Trail

1973

1972

1983-2010s

*Road closed
by lava flow.*

6.6mi
10.6km

1971

Puʻu Loa
Petroglyphs

0.7mi
1.1km

4

Puʻu Loa
Petroglyphs Trail

Hōlei
Sea Arch

C   O C E A N

1 Trailhead Location (see table on page 693)

1.2mi
2.0km

Kīpukapuaulu

Highway 11 to
Mauna Loa Lookout
11.4mi/18.3km

Don't Miss
Crater Rim Drive

Park boundary

Pi'i Mauna Dr

Tree Molds

Mauna Loa Road

1.5mi
2.4km

Kīlauea
Military Camp

Steam

0.6m
1.0kr

Nāmakanipaio
Campground

Jaggar Museum

4078ft
1243m

Crater Rim Drive

Crater Rim Trail

Steaming

1.2mi
1.9km

11

Kīlauea Overlook

Lava flows before 1924

To Kailua-Kona
95mi/154km

0.5mi
0.8km

Hawaiian Volcano Observatory
(not open to the public)

1.4mi
2.7km

Uwēkahuna

KĪLAUEA CALDE

AREA CLOSED
Check with rangers for latest

Ka'ū Desert
Trail

1982 lava

Halema'uma'u Trail

1982 lava

0.4mi
0.6km

1971 lava

Halema'uma'u
Crater

Halema'uma'u
Overlook

Kea

Southwest Rift

0.2mi
0.3km

Hazardous volcanic fumes
3640ft
1110m

1974 lava

1971 lava

0.5mi
0.km

Southwest
Rift Zone

Lava flows
before 1924

Halema'uma'u Trail

1982 lava

KA'Ū
DESERT

Holoholoakōlea

1.4mi
2.7km

1971 lava

2.3mi
3.7km

Crater Rim Trail 11.6mi/18.7km loop

Lava!!
Halema'uma'u Crater

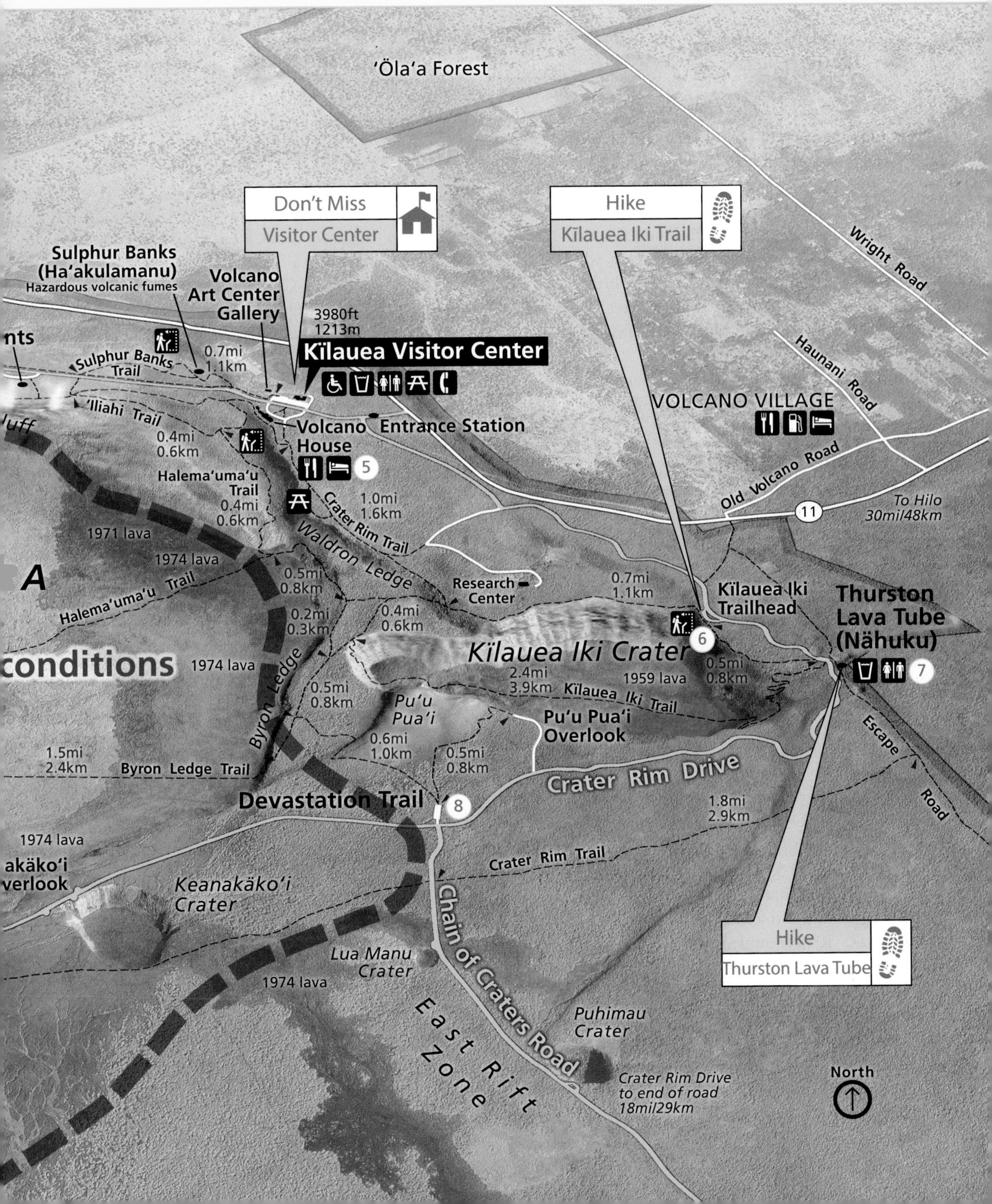

'Öla'a Forest

Don't Miss
Visitor Center

Hike
Kīlauea Iki Trail

Wright Road

**Sulphur Banks
(Ha'akulamanu)**
Hazardous volcanic fumes

**Volcano
Art Center
Gallery**

nts

Sulphur Banks
Trail

0.7mi
1.1km

'Iliahi Trail

luff

3980ft
1213m

Kīlauea Visitor Center

Haunani Road

VOLCANO VILLAGE

Volcano
House

Entrance Station

0.4mi
0.6km

5

Old Volcano Road

11

To Hilo
30mi/48km

Halema'uma'u
Trail
0.4mi
0.6km

Crater Rim Trail

1.0mi
1.6km

1971 lava

Waldron Ledge

A

1974 lava

0.5mi
0.8km

Research
Center

0.7mi
1.1km

**Kīlauea Iki
Trailhead**

**Thurston
Lava Tube
(Nāhuku)**

Halema'uma'u Trail

0.2mi
0.3km

0.4mi
0.6km

conditions

1974 lava

Byron Ledge

0.5mi
0.8km

Kīlauea Iki Crater

2.4mi
3.9km   Kīlauea Iki Trail

6

0.5mi
0.8km

1959 lava

7

Pu'u
Pua'i

0.6mi
1.0km

**Pu'u Pua'i
Overlook**

0.5mi
0.8km

Escape Road

1.5mi
2.4km

Byron Ledge Trail

Devastation Trail

8

Crater Rim Drive

1.8mi
2.9km

1974 lava

akāko'i
verlook

**Keanakāko'i
Crater**

Crater Rim Trail

Chain of Craters Road

Hike
Thurston Lava Tube

Lua Manu
Crater

1974 lava

East Rift Zone

**Puhimau
Crater**

Crater Rim Drive
to end of road
18mi/29km

North

Directions

Kona is farther from the park, but the drive is more interesting as you'll pass beautiful beaches and the southernmost point of the United States, cleverly named South Point. From Hilo it is a relatively short drive through villages and forest. The lesser known Kahuku Unit is discussed below.

From Kona (~111 miles): From Keahole Airport Road take HI-19 south for about 7 miles, where it turns into HI-11. Continue on HI-11 for a little more than 93 miles, and then turn right at HI-11/Crater Rim Road. Follow Crater Rim Road to the visitor center.

From Hilo (~30 miles): Take Airport Road to HI-11 and head south for about 27 miles. Turn left at Crater Rim Road to the park.

Driving

Hawai'i Volcanoes is essentially a drive-in volcano. The 11-mile **Crater Rim Drive** circles Kīlauea Crater. At the time of publication Crater Rim Drive was closed between Jaggar Museum and Chain of Craters Road due to volcanic activity/elevated levels of sulfur dioxide gas. The loop provides access to many of the park's main attractions: Kīlauea Visitor Center, Volcano House, Jaggar Museum, Halema'uma'u Overlook (closed), Thurston Lava Tube, and Kīlauea Iki Trail. Another popular drive, **Chain of Craters Road**, is accessed via Crater Rim Drive. After 19 miles, it dead-ends abruptly where recent lava flow covers the road. It also provides access to Hilina Pali Road and several popular hiking trails like the self-guided Mauna Ulu and Pu'u Loa Petroglyphs Trails. **Mauna Loa Road** is a one-lane, paved road ending at Mauna Loa Lookout.

Kahuku Unit

Located 40 miles west of the main park entrance, this unknown region offers everything from volcanic craters to grassy ranchlands. The unit is 116,000 acres of mostly undeveloped land. The 6-mile gravel road is accessible to all vehicles up to Upper Palm Trailhead, beyond that a high-clearance 4WD vehicle is recommended. The draw here is hiking. A handful of trails explore area's ecology and volcanic features. Ranger-guided hikes are offered regularly (check the park website for a current schedule of events). Note that the unit is only open from 9am until 3pm, Saturdays and Sundays.

Camping & Lodging

Two drive-in campgrounds are available. **Nāmakanipaio Campground**, located on State Highway 11 just a few miles west of Kīlauea Entrance, costs $15/night. It features shared restrooms, water, picnic tables, and grills. Pack for cool evenings. Temperatures here can drop into the 30s°F at night and rain is common. **Kulanaokuaiki Campground**, about 5 miles west on Hilina Pali Road, features 8 campsites with vault toilets and picnic tables, but no water. Camping here is free. Temperatures can drop into the 40s°F at night and rain is less common. Sites at both campgrounds are available on a first-come, first-served basis. Campgrounds occasionally fill, but there's an overflow walk-in camping area at Nāmakanipaio.

Backcountry camping is allowed with a free permit, available in person no more than one day in advance from the Backcountry Office (808.985.6178). To get to the Backcountry Office, take an immediate left after the Entrance Station, and then an immediate right. Park in the parking area on your left and walk to the nearby building. That's it. Along Mauna Loa Trail you'll find two **backcountry cabins**. Mauna Loa Cabin is near the summit and Puʻuʻulaʻula Red Hill Cabin is at 10,000-ft elevation. Both have several bunk beds and are shared on a first-come, first-served basis. (Note that if you plan on hiking to the summit of Mauna Loa from Mauna Loa Observatory Road—a shorter route— spending the night at Mauna Loa Cabin, you still need a permit, but you can reserve one over the phone by calling the Backcountry Office.) There are also designated **backcountry campsites** along the Pacific Coast at ʻApua, Halape and Kaʻaha, and in land at Nāpau and Pepeiao (cabin). Halape is our favorite spot among the backcountry sites, but it takes some work getting there.

Thurston Lava Tube

If you'd rather leave your camping gear at home, **Nāmakanipaio also features 10 rustic, one-room cabins**, each with one full bed and a bunk bed for $80/ night. Cabins have electricity and a communal shower/ restroom is nearby. Another option is to pay for **camping gear rental and set-up**. For $40, plus $15/night campsite fee, a tent for two (with a foam mattress, hotel linens, cooler, lantern, and two chairs) will be yours. They even take it down. Guests can check-in at 3pm and must check-out by noon. Contact Volcano House (808.756.9625, hawaiivolcanohouse.com) for cabin and tent rental details and reservations. For a more luxurious stay spend the night at recently-renovated **Volcano House Hotel**. Nightly rates range from $285– 385, and a few rooms have views of Halemaʻumaʻu Crater, allowing you to watch the volcano's glow right from your bedroom. Even if you don't spend the night, we recommend checking out the hotel. Maybe have a meal at The Rim (reservations at 808.756.9625) or a drink at Uncle George's Lounge, or skip them and have a look at the views across the caldera. It's a pretty incredible setting. You'll also find a couple shops and a communal fireplace (in case you didn't dress for Hawaii at 4,000+ feet). To make hotel reservations, call (866) 536-7972 or click hawaiivolcanohouse.com.

Hawaii Volcanoes Camping (Fees are per night)

Name	Location	Fee	Notes
Namakanipaio	Off Hwy 11, near Kilauea	$15	16 sites, restroom (no showers), water, pavillion
Kulanaokuaiki	5 miles down Hilina Pali Road	Free	8 sites, no water, pit toilets
	All campsites are open all year and available on a first-come, first-served basis. Camping is limited to a maximum of 7 days per month and cannot exceed 30 days per year. Camping equipment rental and setup is available at Namakanipaio for $40 per night. Contact Volcano House (808.756.9625, hawaiivolcanohouse.com) for reservations.		
Backcountry	Permitted with a free permit, available no more than one day in advance at the backcountry office (at the Visitor Emergency Operations Center) from 8am to 4pm. Contact the office at (808) 985-6178.		

Volcano Etiquette

➤ Obey park rangers and posted signs. Park rangers do not close sections of the park to keep the best scenery to themselves. They do it for your safety. Please obey them.

➤ Pack water and sunscreen. The sun affects more visitors than any other danger, and visitors often become sun burnt or dehydrated without noticing due to the cool ocean breeze.

➤ Volcanic smog can cause closures around Kīlauea Caldera. It is dangerous, especially to individuals with respiratory problems and children.

➤ Be especially careful on shoreline cliffs. New lava land is prone to cracking and you'd rather not go with it when it falls.

Lava Viewing

Even though the volcano has been erupting almost continuously at **Pu'u 'Ō'ō** in the East Rift Zone since 1983, there are no guarantees visitors will see surface flows. Lava is often flowing in inaccessible locations or being deposited directly into the ocean via underground lava tubes. **The best way to learn if and where you can see lava is to stop at Kīlauea Visitor Center, give them a call (808.985.6000), or visit the USGS website (volcanoes.usgs.gov/hvo/activity/kilaueastatus.php).** Our point is that things change here more than any other national park in the United States. Back in 2012, lava was pouring into the ocean from Pu'u 'Ō'ō, about seven miles from the end of Chain of Craters Road and boat tours frequented this site. At the same time, Halema'uma'u Crater became active, causing most of Crater Rim Drive to close, but also treating guests to a pretty unique phenomena: the lava lake regularly illuminates the night's sky (best seen from Jaggar Museum or Volcano House)! In 2015, the lava lake at Halema'uma'u was still going strong, but Pu'u 'Ō'ō's lava began to flow into Pahoa-town. That flow has ended, and as this was written, lava was flowing back into the Pu'u 'Ō'ō lava field (within the park, 7 miles from the end of Chain of Craters Road). We're saying we don't know where lava will be flowing when you visit. **Most likely, your best bet is to view the**

Halema'uma'u lava lake show after dark from Jaggar Museum or Volcano House (but you can see the glow from miles away). One thing we do know is that this is a relatively safe active volcano (due to the lava's composition), so you shouldn't be scared of Pele.

When we went to print, the trail to Pu'u 'Ō'ō Vent was closed by the park superintendent. (Visitors are allowed as far as the backcountry campsite at Nāpau.) However, it is possible to **hike to view Pu'u 'Ō'ō from outside the park** via Kahaualea Trail. It's accessed from South Glenwood Road between mile markers 19 and 20 on HI-11, about 20 miles from Hilo. Follow South Glenwood Road, which becomes Captain's Drive/Ala Kapena and continue to its end, 3.5 miles from the highway. Do not leave valuables in your car. This hike is a little more than 5 miles (one-way) through thick rain forest to the 500-ft cone built during the current eruption. Kahaualea Trail begins on state land, but it was under a closure order by the park at time of publication. Please obey all park closures and advisories. For a list of current closures and advisories visit the park website.

Hiking

Hawai'i Volcanoes National Park is without a doubt the best destination for hiking in the state of Hawai'i. More than 150 miles of trails crisscross the black sand shores, arid deserts, lush rain forests, and delicate volcanic surfaces. Expect a few trail closures when hiking in an area with volcanic activity. Trails often close suddenly due to fumes, lava flows, and poor trail conditions. Closures are made for your safety, so please heed these warnings. For a current list of closures and advisories please visit the park website.

The best and most popular hike in the Kīlauea/Crater Loop Drive area is the 4-mile **Kīlauea Iki Trail**. Kīlauea means "spewing," and the hike leads you on an up-close-and-personal look at the volcanic geology of Kīlauea's last "spew." Its trailhead is located at Kīlauea Iki Overlook. Walking counter-clockwise you will pass through rain forest before Pu'u Pua'i cinder cone, the main vent of an eruption on November 14, 1959, comes into view. Lava gushed out of the vent, shooting arcs as high as 1,900 feet. That's a personal record for Pele, the goddess of fire. Next you'll pass through a forest destroyed by the eruption, which is followed by another view of Pu'u Pua'i. Hike past a few large boulders and through another forest before descending into the caldera. Here you'll notice cones, fractures, and the "bathtub ring" that marks the high lava mark of a 2,000°F lake of molten rock that once filled the caldera. The lake didn't cool completely until the mid-1990s. Today you can walk across its solid surface. Before exiting the crater and returning to the overlook, look back and imagine a lake of spouting and spitting lava, waves of thick molten rock oozing at your feet. You'll exit near **Thurston Lava Tube**. Time permitting, take a short walk through the tube. It was created when the outer layer of lava cooled, acting as insulation to the inner lava as it continued to flow down the slope to the ocean. **Devastation Trail**, and **Byron Ledge** are pretty decent, too.

Pu'u Loa Petroglyphs Trail is located near the end of Chain of Craters Road at Milepost 16.5. There are more

than 23,000 cryptic symbols scrawled onto lava rocks in this region of the park. The trail is a 2-mile boardwalk that traverses old lava flows to one of Hawai'i's most extensive petroglyph fields. Please stay on the boardwalk to protect the fragile environment and its artifacts.

At first sight these images could pass as the handiwork of a 14-year-old vandal, but with a bit of explanation their meaning becomes clearer. For example, you may see petroglyphs consisting of a dot with concentric circles around it. The dot signifies a man, and each circle represents a member of his traveling party that made the journey around the island with him. Anthropologist Martha Beckwith visited Pu'u Loa in 1914 and argued that holes in the lava's surface were created to deposit umbilical cords at birth. She believes that the cord was placed in the hole and a rock was set on top of it. If the cord was gone in the morning it ensured a long life. So, no one really knows.

Hawaii Volcanoes Hiking Trails (Distances are roundtrip)

Name	Location (# on map)	Length	Difficulty Rating & Notes
Mauna Loa - ♿	Mauna Loa Lookout (1)	38.2 miles	S – 9.4 more miles to true summit (13,679 ft)
Kipukapuaulu	Mauna Loa Road (2)	1.2 miles	E – Loop trail through island forest (kipuka)
Mauna Ulu	Chain of Craters Road (3)	2.5 miles	E – Lava fields, fissures, and flows
Pu'u Huluhulu	Mauna Ulu Trailhead (3)	18.6 miles	S – Old lava flows, lava trees, and kipuka
Napau	Mauna Ulu Trailhead (3)	14.0 miles	S – Recent lava flows and rain forest
Pu'u Loa Petroglyphs	Chain of Craters Road (4)	1.5 miles	E – Boardwalk trail across old lava flows where ancient petroglyphs were drawn
Earthquake	South of Volcano House (5)	1.0 mile	E – A section of Old Crater Rim Drive
Halema'uma'u	Behind Volcano House (5)	1.8 miles	M – Significant portion closed due to gas
'Iliahi	West of Volcano House (5)	1.5 miles	M – Hike past steam vents and rain forest
Kilauea Iki - ♿	Kilauea Iki Overlook (6)	4.0 miles	M – Loop trail (proceed counter-clockwise)
Thurston Lava Tube - ♿	Crater Rim Drive (7)	0.5 mile	E – Cave-like feature equipped with lights formed by a massive flow of lava, pretty gradual grade
Devastation	Crater Rim Drive (8)	1.0 mile	E – View effects of 1959 eruption
Crater Rim	Accessible from several locations along Crater Rim Drive	11.6 miles	M – Closed from Jaggar Museum south to the junction with Chain of Craters Rd
Pu'u o Lokuana Cinder Cone	Kahuku Road (9)	0.4 mile	M – Short but steep climb to the top of a cinder cone, stay back from the edge
Pu'u o Lokuana	Kahuku Road (10)	2.0 miles	E – Historic ranch, tree molds and lava flows
Palm	Kahuku Road (11)	2.6 miles	M – Connect the loop via Kahuku Road, big views
Glover	Kahuku Road (12)	3.0 miles	M – Loop through rain forest, pit crater
Kona	Kahuku Road (13)	4.7 miles	M – Loop through ranching era relics

Difficulty Ratings: E = Easy, M = Moderate, S = Strenuous

Fossilized footprints are found along **Ka'ū Desert Trail**. They were created in 1790 after a massive eruption of Kīlauea. Years of erosion have taken their toll, but the outlines of ancient feet can still be seen today. The trail is accessed via Ka'ū Desert Trailhead, adjacent to Highway 11 near Mile Marker 38. It can also be reached via Ka'ū Desert Trail from Crater Rim Drive. The prints are fragile, so please remain on the path.

Legend holds that a retreating army was passing by Kīlauea Volcano in 1782. The volcano was angry that day. To appease the goddess Pele, they chose to stay near the volcano's rim offering sacrifices for several days. Upon leaving the summit, the army split into three companies. The first company had not gone far when Kīlauea exploded, emitting ash and gas. Unable to escape, everyone in the second company died, except a lone pig. Members of the third company survived, but they encountered the remains of the second party lying dead, face first in the ashes. Ash provided an excellent medium for fossilization of the warriors' footprints. It's impossible to know exactly whose footsteps have been preserved along Ka'ū Desert Trail, but there most certainly was an eruption in 1790. Reports state that anywhere from 80 to over 5,000 individuals were killed by it. What's the truth? We'll never know, but feel free to hike it and imagine that day's events for yourself.

Backpacking

More than half the park is designated wilderness, providing ample opportunity for solitude and volcanic exploration. Take proper precautions before heading into the backcountry. Pack the essentials: water, first aid kit, stove, map, flashlight and batteries, rain gear, toilet paper, and food (pack out what you pack in). You must camp at designated sites, so plan your route in advance. **A free permit is required.** It can be obtained at the Backcountry Office (page 691) no more than a day before departure. Permits are issued on a first-come, first-served basis (day-hikers do not require a permit). Campers are allowed a maximum stay of three consecutive nights per site, and just 16 people/night are allowed in each backcountry location. All sites have pit toilets. Do not dispose of trash in toilets. Backpackers must check out upon completion at Kīlauea Visitor Center. There are three main backpacking areas.

Mauna Loa: The 19.1-mile (one-way) **Mauna Loa Trail** to Mauna Loa Cabin begins at the end of Mauna Loa Road. **(It's an additional 9.4 miles out-and-back to the true summit from the cabin.)** Rock piles, commonly called cairns, mark the trail. From the trailhead it is 7.5 miles to **Pu'u'ula'ula Red Hill Cabin**. It has 8 bunks with mattresses. Rest here, because it's another 11.6 miles to **Mauna Loa Cabin**. It has 12 bunks. Both cabins have water catchments (the only reliable source of water along the trail). Check on water levels when registering, and treat all water before drinking. Plan on spending a night at each cabin to acclimatize. Mauna Loa's summit is 13,679 feet, so altitude sickness can be a problem. Extreme weather conditions can also occur at any time of year. Eruptions are possible, but unlikely. Campfires are not permitted due to the prevalence of flammable grasses and brush. (You can also hike to Mauna Loa Summit from Mauna Loa Observatory Road on the mountain's north flank. Aggressive hikers can make it a day-hike, but you'll probably want to spend a night acclimatizing by sleeping in your car at the trailhead or at Mauna Kea State Recreation Area. A permit is required if you plan on spending the night at Mauna Loa Cabin. Fortunately you do not have to drive all the way to the Backcountry Office to get one. You can call (808) 985-6178 to request a permit and receive trail/water updates the day of your hike.)

East Rift Zone: The trail to **Pu'u 'Ō'ō vent** is closed by the park superintendent, but backpackers can still hike Nāpau or Nāulu Trails and camp at Nāpau Crater. This campsite does not have shelter or water. Due to extreme instability, these trails can close at any time.

Coastal Areas: From Pu'u Loa Petroglyphs Parking Area backpackers can take **Puna Coast Trail** to one of three backcountry camps. **Ka'aha, Halapē, and Keauhou campsites** have three-walled shelters, but tents are advised due to bugs. These sites and **Pepeiao Cabin** (farther west along Ka'aha Trail) have water catchments. Water must be treated before drinking. **'Āpua Point** has no shelter and no water. You can make a semi-loop by hiking in via **Keauhou Trail** (follow the cairns carefully) and out via Puna Coast Trail, but you'll need to arrange a shuttle or hitch back up the hill to Keauhou trailhead on Chain of Craters Road. Hiking

The well-worn path across Kilauea Iki Trail

across open lava field is pretty brutal, especially after noon when the lava has had a chance to absorb the sun's heat. There's very little shade, and while the terrain is more-or-less level from point A to point B, you're constantly going up and down on these gnarly lava folds. With that said, a little oasis, like Halapē, in the barren lava field is all the more refreshing.

Biking

Biking in Hawai'i Volcanoes National Park can be an extremely rewarding experience. It can also be unbelievably frustrating if the roads are packed with tour buses and rental cars, so it's best to pedal early in the morning before the masses arrive. **Crater Rim Drive** (may be closed from Jaggar Museum to Chain of Craters Road) is an excellent 11-mile loop. While pedaling this paved road you'll pass through lush forest and barren desert as you circle Kīlauea Caldera. Climbers can go from Kīlauea to the Coastal Plains and back up the 18-mile (one-way) **Chain of Craters Road. Mauna Loa Road** (3,700-ft climb) offers another excellent challenge. It ascends nearly 3,000 feet in 13.5 miles before terminating at Mauna Loa Trailhead, where you can continue (by foot—you'll need backpacking gear and a permit) to the mountain's summit (13,000+ feet) or turn around and enjoy the rapid descent back to where you started (Namakanipaio Campground is a good choice). **Hilina Pali Road** (off Chain of Craters Road) is 9 miles long and open to cyclists. **Escape Road** (a dirt escape route in case of eruption) runs mostly parallel to Chain of Craters Road and can be accessed from Thurston Lava Tube or Highway 11. There's also a 5-mile (one-way) dirt hiking trail between Chain of Craters Road and Hilina Pali that allows cyclists. **If you're really looking for a challenge**, consider renting a mountain bike and pedaling from Hilo (sea level) to the Summit of Mauna Kea (13,796 feet). You'll have to rent a bicycle in Kona or Hilo.

Ranger Programs

A current schedule of ranger programs can be found at the park website or on the ranger activity bulletin board at Kīlauea Visitor Center. Visitors can expect rangers to give a 20-minute talk on "How It All Began" outside the visitor center every day. Attending a ranger program is one of the best uses of your time in the park.

For Kids

If a miniature papier-mâché volcano with a vinegar-baking soda eruption draws "ooohs" and "ahhhs" from you children (like they're viewing 4th of July fireworks) imagine what they'll think about seeing a real volcano with a river of molten rock? Here you can (probably) see lava, hike through a lava tube, and view a collection of ancient Hawaiian artifacts. If that's not enough entertainment, children (ages 7–12) can take part in the park's **Junior Ranger Program**. A free activity booklet (available online or at the visitor center) helps families learn more about the park, and kids earn a badge for completing its activities. They also have an Adventure Book for the entire family that explores all the National Park Service units on the island, as well as a Junior Ranger Handbook for children 6 and under.

Nene (Chain of Craters Road)

Flora & Fauna

Hawai'i, the world's most isolated island group, is a fascinating biological laboratory. After hundreds of thousands of years of volcanic activity the Hawaiian Islands finally broke the surface of the Pacific Ocean, creating a new and unique habitat for life. Life faced one major obstacle. The islands were more than 2,000 miles from the nearest significant land mass.

Plant life would have to be carried there by wind, water, or birds. Eventually several species of plants and animals made the seemingly impossible journey. After millions of years of evolution and adaptation, a unique world was created where more than 90% of the species of flora and fauna are only found on these islands.

The park is home to many fascinating creatures: happy-face spiders, carnivorous caterpillars, picture wing flies, and honeycreepers. It's also refuge to a variety of endangered species: hawksbill turtles, nēnē, dark-rumped petrel, and hoary bat. Hawksbill turtles use some of the park's beaches as nesting areas, and backpackers should not camp in areas posted as turtle nesting habitat. This is also a great area for bird watching. Sea birds can be seen from the end of Chain of Craters Road. Kipukapualu Loop is another exceptional birding location; this 100-acre island of vegetation contains the richest concentrations of native plants and bird life in Hawai'i.

Nēnēs (Hawaiian geese, descendent of Canadian geese) nest in the park. Motorists should always drive cautiously, as nēnēs have a tendency to get in the way.

Pets

In general it's not a good idea to bring your pets to Hawai'i. They are permitted in the park, but must be kept on a leash no more than six feet in length at all times. Pets are permitted in developed areas including paved roadways, parking areas, and Nāmakanipaio Campground, but are prohibited in all undeveloped areas, Hilina Pali Road, and Kulanaokuaiki Campground. Do not leave your pets unattended in a vehicle.

Accessibility

Many facilities are wheelchair accessible. These include Kīlauea Visitor Center, Jaggar Museum, Volcano House Hotel, and Volcano Art Center. Both the visitor center and Jaggar Museum have wheelchairs available for use. Namkanipaio and Kulanaokuaiki Campgrounds have accessible campsites and restrooms. Only a few trails are fully accessible, including Waldron Ledge (Earthquake Trail), Devastation Trail, and Pauahi Crater, Muliwai a Pele, and Kealakomo Overlooks.

Weather

Weather on the Big Island is unpredictable. Visitors should come prepared for rain, wind, sun, and maybe even a little snow if you plan on trekking around the summit of Mauna Loa. A good example of the weather's unpredictability is to compare rainfall measurements at Kīlauea Visitor Center. In March of 2006, rainfall measured 34 inches. In March of 2008 it was 4.5 inches. In December of 2007 more than 40 inches of rain fell. December 2005, 1.6 inches. With stats like this it's difficult to make generalizations, but if you had to pick the driest months (on average) choose somewhere between May and October (see graph below).

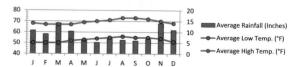

Puʻu ʻOʻo Vent

Vacation Planner

Most people spend too little time at Hawaiʻi Volcanoes National Park. They drive in, look at the crater, complete the 11-mile **Crater Rim Drive** (when open), drive down **Chain of Craters Road**, and then it's a race to the exit. Yes, there are an awful lot of amazing attractions in Hawaiʻi, but few are as fascinating as Hawaiʻi Volcanoes. **Plan to spend a full day at the park.** If you don't want to rent a car, consider joining Roberts Hawaii (800.831.5541, robertshawaii.com) on a **coach tour**, stopping at the visitor center, Thurston Lava Tube, and Jaggar Museum. **Volcano House Hotel** (808.756.9625, hawaiivolcanohouse.com) offers in-park dining, lodging, and drinks. **Campers** (page 691) should secure a site upon arrival. Even though these campgrounds aren't extremely popular, they fill pretty frequently and all sites are first-come, first-served. You won't find a gas station in the park, so fill up on the way. Some of the best dining, grocery stores, lodging, festivals, and attractions outside the park are listed on pages 698–699.

Day 1: We know. We know. You would like to see lava, right? Check out what we have to say about that on page 692. Even if you checked the USGS website, called the park, and saw cool nighttime photos of Halemaʻumaʻu Crater the night before, it's still a good idea to stop in at the visitor center after entering the park to see what's going on. You'll get the scoop on current volcanic activity, area closures, and ranger-led activities. You can also watch a short film, browse exhibits, and shop at the gift shop (for those who really like shopping, two more gift shops are found at Volcano House, a short walk across the road from the visitor center). If half of Crater Rim Drive is still closed (like it was when we went to press), take the drive clockwise from the visitor center to **Kīlauea Iki Trailhead**. If you only have time for one hike, this is the one (add in **Thuston Lava Tube** because it's along the way). Next, explore the trails and overlooks along **Chain of Craters Road**. **Mauna Ulu** and **Petroglyphs Trails** are good choices. Also stop at the end of Chain of Craters Road to look at **Hōlei Sea Arch**. If you're still in the park after the sun sets (and rangers said Halemaʻumaʻu was still active), drive to **Jaggar Museum** to see the park's night light, a giant lava lake roiling within the home of Pele.

Note: If there's an accessible surface flow, we recommend having a look, even if that means hiking 14 miles across uneven lava fields to see it (we've done that knee-jarring hike too many times!). An easier way is to look down on the lava from a helicopter in the sky. Helicopter pilots even fly right over Puʻu ʻŌʻō! Blue Hawaiian (800.786.2583, bluehawaiian.com) and Safari (safarihelicopters.com) offer helicopter tours departing from Hilo.

Dining

Volcano's Lava Rock Café • (808) 328-2612
19-3972 Old Volcano Hwy, Volcano

Thai Thai Restaurant • (808) 967-7969
19-4084 Old Volcano Rd, Volcano

Eagles Lighthouse Café • (808) 985-8587
19-4005 Haunani Rd, Volcano

Kaleo's Bar & Grill • (808) 965-5600
15-2969 Pahoa Village Rd, Pahoa

Coffee Shack • (808) 328-9555
83-5799 Mamalahoa Hwy, Hōnaunau
coffeeshack.com • Breakfast: $11+

Mi's Italian Bistro • (808) 323-3880
81-6372 Mamalahoa Hwy, Kealakekua
misitalianbistro.com • Entrée: $14–35

Patz Pies • (808) 323-8100
82-6127 Mamalahoa Hwy, Captain Cook

Holuakoa Café • (808) 322-2233
76-5901 Mamalahoa Hwy, Holualoa

Annie's Island Fresh Burgers • (808) 324-6000
79-7460 Mamalahoa Hwy, #105, Kealakekua
anniesislandfreshburgers.com • Burgers: $14+

Da Poke Shack • (808) 329-7653
76-6246 Alii Dr, Kailua
dapokeshack.com

Jackie Rey's Ohana Grill • (808) 327-0209
75-5995 Kuakini Hwy, Kailua-Kona
jackiereys.com • Entrée: $18–38

Blue Dragon Coastal Cuisine and Musiquarium
61-3616 Kawaihae Rd, Waimea • (808) 882-7771
bluedragonrestaurant.com • Entrée: $19–34

Hawaiian Style Café • (808) 885-4295
65-1290 Kawaihae Rd, Waimea

Akasushi Bar • (808) 887-2320
65-1158 Mamalahoa Hwy, Waimea

Hilo Bay Café • (808) 935-4939
123 Lihiwai St, Hilo
hilobaycafe.com • Entrée: $17–35

Roy's • (808) 886-4321
69-250 Waikoloa Beach Dr, # E1, Waikoloa
royshawaii.com

Groceries

Safeway • (808) 959-3502
381 Makaala St, Hilo

Safeway • (808) 329-2207
75-1027 Henry St, Kailua Kona

Walmart • (808) 334-0466
75-1015 Henry St, Kailua Kona

Costco • (808) 331-4800
73-5600 Maiau St, Kailua

Lodging

Volcano Teapot Cottage • (808) 967-7112
19-4041 Kīlauea Rd, Volcano
volcanoteapot.com • Rates: $195/night

Kīlauea Lodge & Restaurant
19-3948 Old Volcano Rd, Volcano
kilauealodge.com • (808) 967-7366

Volcano Inn • (808) 967-7773
19-3820 Old Volcano Rd, Volcano
volcanoinnhawaii.com • Rates: $79+

Volcano Rainforest Retreat • (808) 985-8696
11-3832 12th St, Volcano
volcanoretreat.com • Rates: $195–350

Volcano Village Lodge • (808) 985-9500
19-4183 Road E, Volcano
volcanovillagelodge.com • Rates: $199–375

My Island B&B • (808) 967-7110
19-3896 Old Volcano Rd, Volcano
myislandinnhawaii.com • Rates: $94–129

Volcano Mist Cottage • (808) 895-8359
11-3932 Ninth St, Volcano
volcanomistcottage.com • Rates: $295–395

Volcano Forest Inn • (808) 985-9026
19-4034 Old Volcano Rd, Volcano
volcanoforestinn.com • Rates: $160–200

Holo Holo In • (808) 967-7950
19-4036 Kalani Honua Rd, Volcano
volcanohostel.com • Dorm: $30

Country Goose B&B • (808) 967-7759
11-3870 Ruby Ave, Pahoa
country-goose.com • Rates: $105–115

The Bali Cottage • (808) 965-2361
12-7198 Kapoho Kalapana Rd, Pahoa
thebalicottage.com • Rates: $139

Luana Inn • (808) 328-2612
82-5856 Napoopoo Rd, Captain Cook
luanainn.com • Rates: $169–209

Manago Hotel • (808) 323-2642
82-6151 Mamalahoa Hwy, Captain Cook
managohotel.com • Rates: $38–83

Keauhou Kona Surf & Racquet Club
78-6800 Alii Dr, Kailua-Kona • (808) 329-6488
konacondo.net • Rates: $125–225

Kona Tiki Hotel • (808) 329-1425
75-5968 Alii Dr, Kailua-Kona
konatikihotel.com • Rates: $89–179

Mauna Kea Beach Hotel • (808) 882-7222
62-100 Mauna Kea Beach Dr, Waimea
princeresortshawaii.com • Rates: $344+

Waipio Rim B&B • (808) 775-1727
48-5561 Honokaa-Waipio Rd, Honokaa
waipiorim.com • Rates: $220

Attractions

Volcano Bike Tours • (808) 934-9199
bikevolcano.com • Rates: $110+

Green Sand (Papakōlea) Beach/South Point
Green Sand (Papakōlea) Beach is about a 5-mile (roundtrip) hike from the end of South Point Road. South Point—not quite the southernmost tip of the island—is a popular cliff-jumping destination. (Don't jump unless you're a strong swimmer and the conditions are favorable.)

Pu'uhonua o Honaunau Nat'l Hist. Park
Nearby Two Step is one of the best snorkeling spots around. The park is cool, too!
Hwy-160, Honaunau • (808) 328-2288

Captain Cook Mon./Kealakekua Bay
Really great (somewhat remote) snorkeling location. It requires hiking or boating in.

Kona Boy's • (808) 328-1234
Rent a kayak or take a tour of Kealakekua Bay
79-7539 Hawaii Belt Rd, Kealakekua
konaboys.com • Kayak Tour: $119–169

Dolphin Discoveries • (808) 322-8000
Whale Watching and Dolphin/Snorkel Cruises
dolphindiscoveries.com

Body Glove Cruises • (800) 551-8911
Whale Watching, Dolphin, and Sunset Cruises
bodyglovehawaii.com

Jack's Diving Locker • (808) 329-7585
Go on the Manta Night Snorkel/Dive
jacksdivinglocker.com • Dives: $135+

Kona Honu Divers • (808) 324-4668
konahonudivers.com • Dives: $119+

Kamanu Sail & Snorkel • (808) 329-2021
74-381 Kealakehe Pkwy, # L, Kailua
kamanu.com • Snorkel: $99+

Ocean Eco Tours • (808) 324-7873
oceanecotours.com

SeaQuest • (808) 329-7328 • Keauhou
seaquesthawaii.com • Snorkel Tours: $88+

Coral Reef Snorkel Adventures • (808) 987-1584
coralreefsnorkeladventures.com • Rates: $105+

Kona Mike's Surf Adventures • (808) 334-0033
konasurfadventures.com • Lessons: $99+

Surf Lessons Hawaii • (808) 324-0442
surflessonshawaii.com • Lessons: $75+

Kona Surf Company • (808) 217-5329
konasurfschool.com • Lessons: $99+

Kekaha Kai State Park • (808) 882-6206
Makalawena Beach (hiking required) is widely regarded as the island's most enchanting beach. The main access road (high-clearance required) is located north of Kona International Airport.

Hapuna Beach State Park
South Kohala • $5/vehicle

Mauna Kea
Mauna Kea—the highest point in the state of Hawai'i—is one of the best sites in the world for astronomical observation, evident by the 13 observation facilities located at its summit (13,796 ft). You can drive (4WD required), hike (extremely strenuous), or bike (also strenuous) to the summit.

Hawaii Forest and Trail • (808) 331-8505
Hiking, Birding, and Zip-Lining Tours, and a great way to get to the top of Mauna Kea
73-5593 A Olawalu St, Kailua
hawaii-forest.com • Tours: $89+

Mauna Kea Summit Adventures
74-5606 Pawai Pl, Kailua-Kona
maunakea.com • (808) 322-2366 • Tours: $192

Kahua Ranch • (808) 882-4646
Trail Rides, ATV Tours, and Ranch BBQ Dinner
Kohala Mountain Rd, Waimea
kahuaranch.com

Rainbow Falls
Beautiful waterfall located in downtown Hilo.

Pe'e Pe'e Falls/Boiling Pots
This setting is incredible, especially considering it's located in Hilo, but it can be dangerous. Reaching the falls requires swimming/hiking, a journey that isn't for everyone.

Paniolo Adventures • (808) 889-5354
Great ride across the Kohala Mountains (north)
panioloadventures.com • Trail Rides: $89–175

'Akaka Falls State Park
0.4-mile path to a majestic 442-ft waterfall
'Akaka Falls Rd, Off Hwy 19, Honomu
hawaiistateparks.org • (808) 974-6200
Admission: $5/vehicle

Skyline Eco Adventures • (888) 864-6947
Best zipline on the island
281710 Honomu Rd, Honomu
zipline.com/bigisland • Zipline: $160–300

Unauma Falls and Zipline • (808) 930-9477
Zipline or just look at the stunning falls (fee)
31-313 Old Mamalahoa Hwy, Hakalau
umaumaexperience.com • Zipline: $189–239

Kohala Zipline • (888) 864-6947
55-515 Hawi Rd, Hawi
kohalazipline.com • Zipline: $169–249

Zip Isle Zip Line Adventure • (808) 963-5427
31-240 Old Mamalahoa Hwy, Hakalau
zipisle.com • Zip Line: $167

Waipio Valley
A sacred valley, towering waterfalls, a black sand beach, and the trailhead to Waimanu Valley (above, best backpack destination on the island). The access road is steep and narrow, requiring a 4WD vehicle. You can walk down to the valley. Hiking to Hi'ilawe Falls crosses private property.

Waipi'O-Ride the Rim • (808) 775-1450
48-5416 Kukuihaele Rd, Honokaa
ridetherim.com • ATV Tour: $159+

Waipio Ridge Stables • (808) 775-1007
48-5416 Kukuihaele Rd, Honoka'a
waipioridgestables.com • Rides: $90 (2.5 hrs)

Na'alapa Stables • (808) 775-0419
Another way to explore Waipio Valley is on a horse. They'll drive you down to their ranch.
Old Hwy 240, Waipi'o Valley, Honoka'a
naalapastables.com • Rides: $94 (2.5 hrs)

Greenwell Farms • (808) 323-2862
81-6581 Mamalahoa Hwy, Kealakekua
greenwellfarms.com • Free Tours

Hawaii Tropical Botanical Garden
27-717 Old Mamalahoa Hwy, Papaikou
htbg.com • (808) 964-5233

Hula Daddy Kona Coffee • (808) 327-9744
74-4944 Mamalahoa Hwy, Holualoa
huladaddy.com • Free Tours

Ocean rider - Seahorse Farm • (808) 329-6840
73-4388 Ilikai Pl, Kailua-Kona
seahorse.com • Admission: $42/adult

Kona Brewing Company • (808) 329-2739
75-5612 Pawai Pl, Kailua-Kona
konabrewingco.com • Tours: $5

Mountain Thunder Coffee Plantation
73-1944 Hao St, Kailua-Kona • (808) 325-2136
mountainthunder.com • Free Tours

Lyman Museum • (808) 935-5021
276 Haili St, Hilo
lymanmuseum.org • Admission: $8/adult

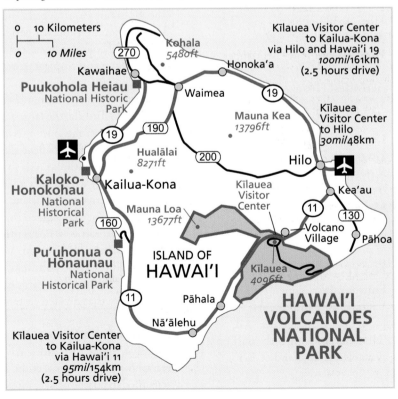

Pago Pago Harbor

American Samoa

Superintendent
National Park of American Samoa
Pago Pago, AS 96799
Phone: (684) 633-7082
Website: nps.gov/npsa

Established: September 3, 1993
Size: 10,550 Acres
Annual Visitors: 14,000
Peak Season: June–September

Activities: Hiking, Snorkeling,
SCUBA Diving

Campgrounds: None
Homestay Program
Rates: Determined by the host
(typically between $50–150/night)
Lodging: Available on all islands
except Olosega*
Rates: $40–200/night

Park Hours: Open all year
Entrance Fee: None
Visitation Requirements: Passport

*Homestay lodging is the only type
available on the island of Ta'ū

American Samoa is one of the least visited and developed national parks the United States has to offer. Culturally and geographically, it's one of the most unique. Park land spans four separate islands located deep in the South Pacific on the only United States territory south of the equator. It's a park that isn't built for motorists. Like the Hawaiian Islands, American Samoa was built by volcanoes. What's different is that most of the region is free of man-made improvements. The climate is tropical. The mountains are rugged. The land is covered with dense rain forest. The beaches are postcard-perfect. The waters are home to some of the oldest coral colonies in existence. In short, it's a small park overflowing with cultural and tropical treasures.

American Samoa is extremely isolated. Even in today's global world, traveling to Tutuila, the largest and most populous island, can be a challenge. However, the journey is much easier today than it was for the first Samoans. Historians believe that some 3,000 years ago a few adventurous souls left Southeast Asia in boats with absolutely no idea where the ocean currents would take them. After covering 5,000 miles of open water they arrived at an island oasis. A land they embraced and made their home. They continued to worship the same gods and upheld their Polynesian traditions. For centuries, the early Samoans were left undisturbed by the outside world. Whalers, pirates, missionaries, and European explorers came and went. But in the 1870s their world was torn apart from the inside. An argument between kings started a contentious civil dispute that divided eastern and western halves of Samoa.

Years later, Great Britain, Germany, and the United States were offered exclusive rights to build a naval base in Tutuila's Pago Pago Bay in return for military protection. Each nation ignored the offer, but they remained to pursue private interests. German interests involved invading a Samoan village, an act resulting in destruction of American property. American response was swift; two warships were sent to Pago Pago Harbor. Before either side fired, a typhoon swept through the area, wrecking three German warships and both American vessels. Time settled their differences and the United States began to formally occupy Samoa in 1900.

Samoans were forced to make many difficult decisions upon American occupation. Most importantly was the choice to be Samoan or American? Many Samoans still weave mats, paint bark of the mulberry tree, and decorate their bodies with traditional tattoos. Samoan women still dance the siva and the sasa. Men do the fa'ataupati, a slap dance performed without music. The 'ava ceremony is a highly ritualistic ceremonial drink with specific gestures and phrases. It is considered a great honor if a visitor is asked to share 'ava (do not decline). Samoans also continue the ritual of Fa'aaloaloga. It's the process of exchanging gifts at formal events. Most people are bilingual, speaking both Samoan and English.

That said, the American influence on Samoa is clear. Schools, a hospital, roads, sewage treatment facilities, and canneries were built in the 1960s. Many of these structures proved far too costly to maintain, and have since fallen into a state of disrepair. (But you'll find popular fast food restaurants in Pago Pago.) However, not all local politicians were interested in mimicking the rest of the United States. Laws were passed to curb exploitation and development. For example, non-Samoans cannot own land and foreign companies must partner with a Samoan before starting any venture on the islands. These laws, and the islands' remote location, have helped prevent coastlines from being littered with ostentatious resorts. Roads don't weave past every scenic vista. Visitors aren't piling into the park by the busload. There isn't any bumper-to-bumper traffic to deal with like a summer weekend in Yosemite Valley. In American Samoa you'll find nothing but seclusion and peace in a laid-back environment. The park may be small in stature, but it's rich in culture, and with only a few thousand outsiders visiting each year, it may feel like your own tropical paradise.

When to Go
In an entire year National Park of American Samoa receives roughly the same amount of visitors Grand Canyon sees on a slow winter day. So overcrowding isn't a problem. Don't plan on being shoulder-to-shoulder with fellow hikers trekking to 'Alava Peak or having to wake up at the crack of dawn to secure a sliver of prime beach realty. Weather is what you have to worry about. Tropical storms are most common during the rainy season (October–April), but visitors are treated to year-round warmth and rain (June–September is slightly drier than the rest of the year). The **visitor center**, located in Pago Pago across from Pago Way Service Station, is open on weekdays, 8am until 4:30pm. It's closed on weekends and federal holidays. When we went to print, **dengue fever** and **Zika virus** were present in American Samoa. Be sure to pack mosquito repellent and/or wear long sleeves, pants, and socks. While the symptoms of Zika virus are mild, infection during pregnancy can cause serious birth defects.

Transportation & Airports
American Samoa is an unincorporated territory of the United States located in the South Pacific Ocean. The island chain is some 2,500 miles southwest of Hawai'i. Most trips begin and end at Tafuna International Airport (PPG) in Pago Pago on the island of Tutuila. Currently two flights per week arrive in Pago Pago from Honolulu, HI. The International Airport at Upolo, (Western) Samoa receives weekly flights from Australia, Fiji, and New Zealand.

Car rental is available at or near the airport (about $120/day), but there is only one main road on the island of Tutuila. 'Aiga or "family" buses provide transportation around the island. Buses originate and terminate at Fagatogo market and fares are anywhere from $1–$2.50. Buses do not run on Sundays. Taxis, available at the airport or market, are a more expensive alternative. Inter-Island Vacations (684.699.7100) provides flights to the park's locations on Ofu and Ta'ū Islands. There are no set schedules to these remote islands, so contact the provider for more information.

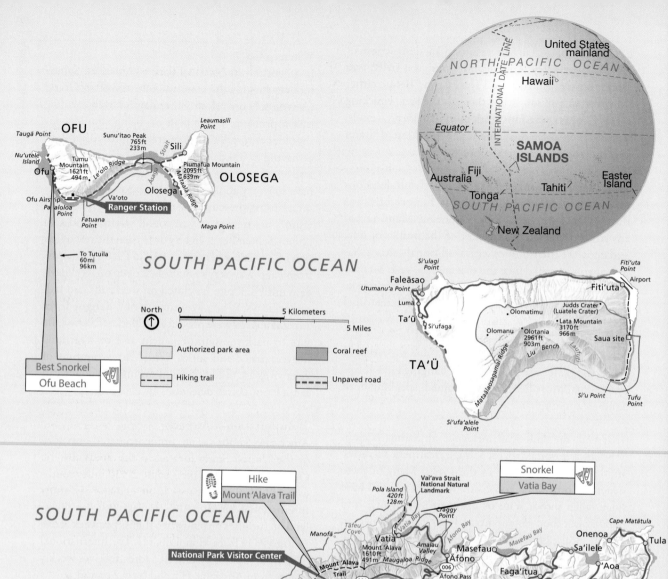

OFU

Taugā Point

Nu'utele Island

Ofu

Ofu Airstrip
Paloloa Point

Fatuana Point

Le'olo Ridge

Tumu Mountain 1621ft 494m

Sunu'itao Peak 765ft 233m

Asaga Strait

Sili

Va'oto

Ranger Station

Olosega

Piumafua Mountain 2095ft 639m

Maugaālā Ridge

Leaumasili Point

OLOSEGA

Maga Point

→ To Tutuila 60mi 96km

SOUTH PACIFIC OCEAN

North ↑

0 — 5 Kilometers
0 — 5 Miles

Authorized park area

Hiking trail

Coral reef

Unpaved road

Best Snorkel
Ofu Beach 🐾

SAMOA ISLANDS (globe)

NORTH PACIFIC OCEAN
United States mainland
Hawaii
INTERNATIONAL DATE LINE
Equator
SAMOA ISLANDS
Fiji
Australia
Tahiti
Easter Island
Tonga
SOUTH PACIFIC OCEAN
New Zealand

Si'ulagi Point

Faleāsao

Utumanu'a Point

Luma

Ta'ū

Si'ufaga

Olomatimu

Olomanu

Fiti'uta Point

Airport

Fiti'uta

Judds Crater (Luatele Crater)

Lata Mountain 3170ft 966m

Saua site

Olotania 2961ft 903m

Mataalaosagamaī Ridge

Liu Bench

Laufuti

Si'u Point

Tufu Point

TA'Ū

Si'ufa'alele Point

SOUTH PACIFIC OCEAN

Hike
Mount 'Alava Trail 👣

Snorkel
Vatia Bay 🐾

Pola Island 420ft 128m

Vai'ava Strait National Natural Landmark

Craggy Point

Tāfeu Cove

Manofā

Vatia

Vatia Bay

Afono Bay

Masefau Bay

Cape Matātula

Onenoa

Tula

Mount 'Alava 1610ft 491m

Amalau Valley

Maugaloa Ridge

Sa'ilele

Masefau

Āfono

'Aoa

National Park Visitor Center

Mount 'Alava Trail

Pago Pago

(005)

(001)

Fono Building

Fagatogo

Executive Office Building

Utulei

Fagasā (bay)

Fagasā Pass

Fagasā

Hospital

Faga'alu

Afono Pass

(006)

Aūa

Rainmaker Mountain National Natural Landmark

North Pioa Mountain 1718ft 523m

Faga'itua

Faga'itua (bay)

Ālega

Āmouli

Au'asi

'Aunu'u

'Aunu'u Island National Natural Landmark

'AUNU'U ISLAND

Māloatā Bay

Fagamalo

Massacre Bay

Matafao Peak National Natural Landmark

Matafao Peak 2142ft 653m

Fatumafuti

Fatu Rock (Flower Pot Rock)

Breakers Point

TĀEMĀ BANK

NĀFANUA BANK

Poloa

'Āmanave

Cape Taputapu National Natural Landmark

A'oloaufou 1340ft 408m

American Samoa Community College

Tāfuna

Pala Lagoon

Nu'uuli

Coconut Point

Pago Pago International Airport

→ To Manu'a Islands 60mi 96km

Leone

Pava'ia'i

(001)

Star Mound site

Golf Course

Fūtiga

'Ili'ili

Fogāgogo

Vaitogi

Turtle and Shark Legend site

Vailoatai

Le'ala Shoreline National Natural Landmark

Fogama'a Crater National Natural Landmark

Fagatele Bay National Marine Sanctuary

Larsen Bay

Steps Point

North ↑

0 — 5 Kilometers
0 — 5 Miles

Authorized park area

Coral reef

Hiking trail

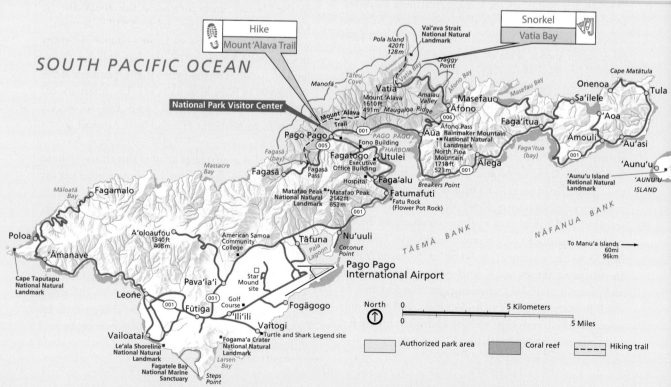

Regions

Tutuila: Roughly 2,500 acres of land and 1,200 acres of water on the north end of Tutuila are leased by the National Park Service. This is the only section of park that is accessible by car. **'Alava Trail** is located here.

Ofu and Olesega: Home of the best reefs and snorkeling in the park, and the most beautiful beach in American Samoa: **Ofu Beach**.

Ta'ū: The park protects 5,400 acres of land, including **Lata Mountain**, American Samoa's highest peak, and another 1,000 acres of water.

Homestay Program

American Samoa's Homestay Program allows visitors to become more closely acquainted with Samoan people and culture. Participants live in the home of local residents associated with the park. This living situation has its advantages. You may be invited to make crafts, weave a mat, fish the Samoan way (with poles and nets), or collect giant clams and spear octopus. It is an incredibly unique opportunity where visitors are not only welcomed into a local home, but into their lives. If you're looking for a truly authentic Samoan experience that you'll never forget, the Homestay Program is for you. All fees, including accommodations and cultural activities, are set by the local host. The park encourages you to contact hosts directly. A list of current hosts is available at the park website. We've provided a list of local customs you should be aware of and follow when you visit. Put in a little effort and you'll earn the local's respect.

Samoan Etiquette

Samoa is an American territory, but many Samoans remain loyal to their traditions and culture. As a visitor, respect and follow local customs.

- Always ask villagers or the village mayor for permission to walk in the village, take photographs, or use the beach.
- Take your shoes off before entering a traditional home or fale. Cross your legs while sitting on the floor.
- Sunday is a day of rest. Even activities like swimming are sometimes not permitted.
- Every evening around dusk villagers observe a special time of prayer called Sa. If you are in a village during this time, stop and wait quietly until Sa ends.
- It is considered an honor to share a drink called 'ava. 'Ava is a local drink made from the root of the pepper plant.
- Do not eat or drink while walking through a village.
- Do not begin eating until prayer has finished and the head of the house begins eating.
- It is impolite to reject food.
- Only stay with one host family in a village to prevent embarrassing your hosts.
- Samoans of all ages swim in shorts and shirts. Avoid short shorts, bathing suits, and bikinis unless you wear a T-shirt over it. In villages, wear long shorts, pants, skirts, or sarongs.
- Like at home, excuse yourself when crossing someone's path. Lower your head and say excuse me ("tulou").
- Women and men holding hands is acceptable, but other public displays of affection are frowned upon.
- Time on the island goes a bit slower and plans change frequently. To avoid frustration, simply go with the flow.

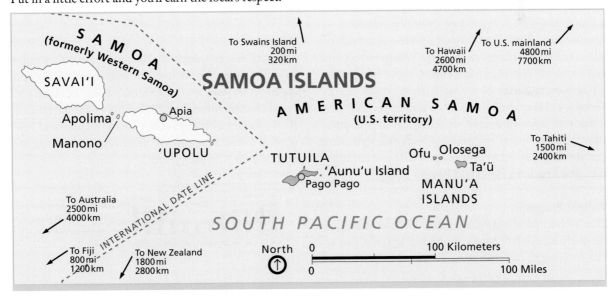

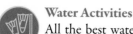

Water Activities

All the best water activities are found on the island of Ofu, where you'll find the park's true gem: **Ofu Beach**. The best **snorkeling** of all the islands is here too, but be sure to bring your own gear because you won't find any outfitters nearby. People in general are hard to come by. More than 95% of American Samoa's population lives on the island of Tutuila. In fact, it's often difficult for tourists to reach Ofu; an interisland flight (page 701) is required to reach this secluded tropical paradise. Vatia Bay on Tutuila is a worthy alternative for those that cannot make the trip to Ofu. The tiny village of Vatia is situated at the bay's edge where guests can enjoy the water and impressive views of the uninhabited island of Pola. You can also find good snorkeling and swimming locations beyond park boundaries on Tutuila, like Airport Beach near Pago Pago International Airport. Swimming in Pago Pago Harbor isn't recommended due to heavy pollution.

Pago Pago Marine Charters (684.699.9234, pagopago-marinecharters.com) offers **fishing and SCUBA charters**, as well as coastline tours. Dive Adventures (diveadventures.com), based out of Australia, offers an American Samoa **SCUBA diving trip**.

Hiking

Most of the park is completely inaccessible, but there is a 7.2-mile (roundtrip) trail on the island of Tutuila that leads to the summit of 1,610-ft **Mount 'Alava**. The trailhead is located at Fagasā Pass, a short drive west of Pago Pago. From the summit, hikers can view Pago Pago Harbor and the surrounding islands. The trail continues to **Vatia Village** where you can swim or snorkel in Vatia Bay. A short hiking trail along **Sauma Ridge** begins at Alamau Valley Scenic Overlook. Here you'll find a lower and upper trail. The lower trail leads to unique archeological sites and the upper trail connects to Mount 'Alava's ridgeline. You can also find easy hikes to historic WWII gun emplacements at **Breaker's Point** and **Blunt's Point**.

Ranger Programs

Due to limited visitation the park does not offer any regularly scheduled ranger programs. If you'd like to talk to a ranger, call (684) 633-7082.

For Kids

National Park of American Samoa isn't the ideal family vacation destination, but its beaches and shorelines are wonderful locations for children to play and explore. The **Homestay Program** (page 703) can be an immensely rewarding experience, where children can gain first-hand knowledge about a culture very different from their own.

Flora & Fauna

The Samoan Islands are dominated by dense rain forests. More than 400 native flowering plant species are found here. All of the islands' flowering plants rely on flying foxes, or fruit bats, for pollination. Likewise, fruit bats rely on plants' nectar or fruit for sustenance. Bats are the only mammal native to the islands. You can also find several species of reptiles including skinks, geckos, and an extremely small population of Pacific boas that reside on the island of Ta'ū. Beneath the sea are nearly 900 species of fish and more than 200 species of coral.

Pets

You aren't really thinking about bringing your dog all the way to American Samoa, are you? It is understood that pets are a part of your family, but it is still highly recommended that you leave them at home.

Accessibility

The Park is relatively new and undeveloped. Most of the land is steep, rugged, and inaccessible to individuals in wheelchairs.

Weather

The park enjoys a tropical climate. Temperatures range from the high 70s to low 90s°F year-round. Rain is common all year. Even the driest regions of American Samoa receive more than 100 inches of annual rainfall. Rain subsides a bit (on average) between June and September. Tropical storms are more common during the rainy season (October–April).

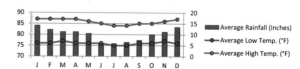

Ofu Lagoon

Vacation Planner

Proper planning is essential for a trip to National Park of American Samoa. Flights are considered international even though it's a United States territory. **All visitors are required to have a valid passport.** Flights to Pago Pago are expensive, but food and lodging are priced more reasonably. Car rental is available at Pago Pago International Airport, but the park isn't the most motorist-friendly place in the world. It's mostly rugged peaks, impenetrable jungle, and clear water. Regions of Ofu-Olosega and Ta'ū can only be reached by plane.

These islands are even more remote than Tutuila. Once you arrive the main mode of transportation is foot. However, local motorists often stop to offer a ride when they pass a visitor on the road. No matter which island(s) you visit, you will have the opportunity to live with a Samoan family thanks to the **Homestay Program** (page 703). Since the park is undeveloped and distributed over three separate islands, visitors should create their own individual itineraries based on personal interests, budget, and time.

Dining
Sadie Thompson Inn • Pago Pago

Sadie's By The Sea • (684) 633-5981
Main Road, Pago Pago • sadieshotels.com

Goat Island Café • Sadie's By The Sea

Famous II Seafood Restaurant • Pago Pago

Mom's Place • Tafuna • (684) 699-1987

Sook's Sushi Restaurant
Pago Pago • (684) 633-5525

Tradewinds • (684) 699-1000
Ottoville Rd, Pago Pago • tradewinds.as

Tessarea Vaitogi Inn
Vaitogi, Pago Pago • (684) 699-7793

DDW (Don't Drink the Water)
Utulei Beach, Pago Pago

McDonalds • Pago Pago

Tisa's Barefoot Bar • (684) 622-7447
Pago Pago • tisasbarefootbar.com

Groceries
Super K Supermarket • Pago Pago

Cost U Less • (684) 699-5975 • Pago Pago

KS Mart • Ilili Road, Pago Pago

Lodging
Sliding Rock Lodge • Vailoatai

Sadie's By The Sea • (684) 633-5981
Main Road, Pago Pago • sadieshotels.com

Sadie Thompson Inn • (684) 633-5981
Pago Pago • sadieshotels.com

Tradewinds • (684) 699-1000
Ottoville Road, Pago Pago • tradewinds.as

Tisa's Barefoot Bar • (684) 622-7447
Pago Pago • tisasbarefootbar.com

Scanlan Motel
Pago Pago • (684) 633-4451

Vaoto Lodge
Ofu Island • vaotolodge.com • Rates: $80–120

S & T Asaga Inn • (684) 655-7791
Ofu Island • asagainn.com • Rates: $90

Attractions
Tradewinds • (684) 699-1000
Tradewinds offers day tours around the island
Ottoville Road, Pago Pago
tradewinds.as

Fagatele Bay National Marine Sanctuary
On the island of Tutuila, this coral reef ecosystem is nestled within an eroded volcanic crater—the hike to the beach is quite rigorous
fagatelebay.noaa.gov • (684) 633-6500

Jean P. Haydon Museum
The old U.S. Naval Station Tutila Commissary turned into a museum

Maugaoalii Government House
Arrange tours by calling (684) 633-4116

Samoa Fiafia Night Show
Traditional show features authentic Samoan food, Samoan Siva, and Fireknife Dance.

Wind Canyon (Theodore Roosevelt)

Photo Credits

Michael J. Oswald: Cover, Intro Pages, 1, 2, 5, 6, 8, 11, 17, 25, 27, 28, 37, 38, 44, 45, 45, 45, 48, 50, 51, 52, 53, 58, 59, 62, 65, 66, 67, 70, 76, 77, 79, 86, 87, 90, 93, 94, 95, 95, 98, 99, 105, 110, 111, 112, 119, 137, 138, 140, 140, 142, 143, 154, 155, 158, 161, 164, 165, 174, 178, 179, 182, 186, 187, 189, 191, 192, 192, 193, 194, 200, 201, 201, 201, 202, 206, 207, 207, 211, 218, 223, 236, 240, 241, 246, 247, 252, 255, 25, 260, 263, 270, 273, 273, 273, 276, 278, 281, 283, 285, 286, 287, 305, 308, 311, 311, 314, 318, 319, 326, 327, 333, 333, 335, 348, 353, 354, 356, 362, 363, 363, 363, 371, 374, 374, 378, 379, 384, 385, 388, 388, 388, 389, 391, 397, 398, 399, 404, 404, 406, 407, 409, 410, 416, 417, 420, 421, 422, 433, 436, 440, 446, 450, 453, 481, 484, 488, 488, 502, 503, 510, 511, 513, 514, 517, 518, 528, 530, 533, 542, 546, 547, 553, 554, 559, 566, 574, 577, 578, 585, 592, 596, 599, 664, 665, 670, 671, 674, 680, 681, 684, 685, 691, 695, 696, 697, 698, 699, 706, 707, 708, 709, 710

National Park Service: Jim Peaco (4, 232, 233, 243), 16, Jacob W. Frank (26, 258, 266, 370, 376, 377, 620, 629), Kaitlin Thoresen (31, 634, 635), 116, 117, Ted Schantz (122), 124, G. Gardner (130), Brian Call (134), 136, 138, S. Cotrell (141), Steve Dimse (166), Neal Herbert (237), (Doug Smith (244), Tim Rains (253, 261, 269, 624), Buehler (288), Jackson (292), Appler (292), Bieri (295), 298, 303, 304, 305, 308, Patrick Meyers (340, 346, 347, 367), Art Hutchinson (345), Kris Illenberger (345), Joseph Tumidalsky (347), 415, Marc Neidig (417), Michael Quinn (429, 431, 434, 443), Kristen M. Caldon (430), Mark Lellouch (437), 438, Hannah Schwalbe (460, 466), Brad Sutton (466, 466, 467), Daniel Elsbrook (467), Gavin Emmons (480), 490, 499, 538, 542, 545, 579, 587, 590 (D. Archuleta), 591 (C. Bubar), 604, 607, 608, 609, Bryan Petrtyl (614, 618, 619), 618, 621, 626, 629, 630, Jim Pfeiffenberger (634, 635, 640, 658), Poppy Benson (636), 637, J. Mills (637), 640, C. Carson (641), 643, M. Fitz (647), Wendy Artz (647), 648, 652, 656, 658, 659, 700, Peter Craig (705)

Shutterstock: 7, 9, 10, 15, 21 (Andy Lidstone), 22, 24, 32, 33, 57 (Christopher Penler), 69, 97 (Amy Nichole Harris), 115 (Fotoluminate, LLC), 152, 153, 176, 177, 205, 244, 245, 268, 269, 277, 296, 299, 300, 302, 312, 322, 323 (turtix), 324, 325, 367, 368, 369, 390, 457, 458, 459, 468, 472, 474, 478, 479, 488, 489 (Elgad), 523, 529, 560, 561, 570, 575, 576, 640, 642, 658

iStock: 12, 13, 14, 18, 19, 20, 516, 531, 534, 537, 564, 565, 601, 602, 603, 656, 657, 659, 660, 661, 672, 673, 682, 683

Other: Northern Arizona University, Cline Library (432)

Index

The index was eliminated. Partly to save eight pages, partly because the book is well organized with all key words in bold. Still, if you'd like to search through this book, e-mail your receipt to mike@stoneroadpress.com and I'll send you a search-friendly pdf version.

We Hope You Enjoyed
Your National Parks

and Your Guide to
the National Parks